Rock 'n' Road

Help Us Keep This Guide Up to Date

Every effort has been made by the authors and editors to make this guide as accurate and useful as possible. However, many things can change after a guide is published—trails are rerouted, regulations change, techniques evolve, facilities come under new management, etc.

We would love to hear from you concerning your experiences with this guide and how you feel it could be improved and kept up to date. While we may not be able to respond to all comments and suggestions, we'll take them to heart and we'll also make certain to share them with the authors. Please send your comments and suggestions to the following address:

The Globe Pequot Press
Reader Response/Editorial Department
P.O. Box 480
Guilford, CT 06437

Or you may e-mail us at:

editorial@GlobePequot.com

Thanks for your input, and happy travels!

Rock 'n' Road

An Atlas of North American Rock Climbing Areas

Second Edition

Tim Toula

FALCON®

GUILFORD, CONNECTICUT
HELENA, MONTANA
AN IMPRINT OF THE GLOBE PEQUOT PRESS

Falcon and FalconGuide are registered trademarks of The Globe Pequot Press.

Text design by Amanda Smith/Osprey Design
Maps created by Equator Graphics © The Globe Pequot Press

Library of Congress Cataloging-in-Publication Data

Toula, Tim.
     Rock 'n' road: rock climbing areas of North America /
          Tim Toula. —2nd ed.
               p. cm.
     Includes bibliographical references and index.
     ISBN 0-7627-2306-8
     1. Rock climbing—North America—Guidebooks. 2. North America—Guidebooks. I.
Title: Rock 'n' road. II. Title.

GV199.44.N654 T68 2002
796.52'23—dc21

Manufactured in the United States of America   2002019653
Second Edition/Second Printing

To any spirited soul who has ever dreamed of climbing a rock . . .
and standing on the summit.

"Begin at the beginning," the king said gravely, "and go till you come to the end; then stop."

—*Lewis Carroll, Alice's Adventure in Wonderland*

And along the way . . . kick some butt.

—*Tim Toula*

Contents

Preface

Dear friends of the rock and road,

More than twenty years ago, I sat in the dimly lit depths of the Northern Arizona University Library flipping through the dusty, brittle pages of a meager stack of climbing magazines. At the time, I was looking for climbing areas to visit on the East Coast. It was with some difficulty that I began to gather a traveling syllabus to guide me to unknown crags. "Why doesn't somebody put a book of all the areas together so I don't have to do this?" I pondered. How do you arrest the waves of climbers in an ocean of rock? Well, somehow, more than twenty years later, through the course between the power of positive driving and the power of positive typing, this atlas came into being. (Now I realize why nobody ever undertook such a project.)

Today, rock climbing has grown and changed so dramatically from the date at which the seed was sown. In just ten years, it is impossible to keep abreast of all climbing knowledge. There are so many climbers involved in developing new areas and routes, it is simply impossible to record them all. This, then, is an attempt at a climbing-area record book . . . a look at where the climbing's been done and what's to come.

It is my sincerest hope that this book will assist climbers in their travels and further their love of a great sport. Moreover, I hope this atlas will unite all climbers, awaken us to the incredible resource we possess, and compel us to use it wisely.

Climbing is a multifaceted sport consisting of bouldering, cragging, rockaneering, big walls, and artificial walls. This guide tries to shed light on them all. For no matter which branch you choose, the one binding cord that ties it all together is man and woman in an upward direction.

The focus of this book is to identify climbing areas and help rock climbers access them. As an extra, there is information in a variety of flavors for the rock climber, alpinist, and hiker. *Rock 'n' Road* is not intended as a guidebook as much as an atlas. For the real details support the individual area guidebook authors listed under each area.

This volume looks at all forms of rock climbing in North America via capsule summaries for each included area. In effect, there are a lot of nutshells in this book. Most of the information favors crags and bouldering areas. It takes a cursory look at the climbing within the confines of the mountain ranges in the lower forty-eight states, Alaska, Canada, and Mexico. These are better looked at in person or with the help of regional mountain guides. Still, the more popularly climbed mountain ranges are included.

Just exactly how much climbing is there in this guide? If you add up all the areas in this book, it would take a fast climber, upon visiting one area per day and then driving to another the next day, a total of six years or more to see them all. That leaves little time to savor any area.

When people ask if I have personally visited every area in this book, I've been tempted to say yes. While I have visited quite a few, I've relied on other climbers who have graciously provided information. To them, I am indebted, raise a goblet, and shout, "Cheers!"

Finally, the more I climb, the more I realize that climbing is more than just bolts on a section of rock. It is not so much about reaching a number with a goal attached and not so much about rock, but people. The upward challenge is accompanied with ridiculous, insane laughter; boldness; daring; calm; persistence; patience; pain; and is like a birth. Each visit to a new area is like a little piece of enlightenment. In short, it is the heightening of the experience of being alive. Hopefully, you will find this as well.

The endless highway—it draws one near and it hurls one headlong into new paths, closer to others who share the secrets of travel. It renews one's energy and rejuvenates a waning psyche. It ignites a spirit that comes from meeting new people and talking to new climbers, seeing new rock and grasping new stone, learning new lessons and reliving old ones, and seizing new adventures with others in a heartfelt passion.

In this little episode called *Rock 'n' Road*, may you gather these moments and sustain them. They are yours to keep and relive. Most of all, may your next adventure be greater than the last.

I can't give you just one reason to go climbing in North America, so here are more than 2,000 of them.

Hope to see you on the rock. Until then, assume the sensational, suggest the insane, expect the unexpected, and ascend to new heights.

—Tim Toula

Acknowledgments

While there are those crag fauns who certainly could do a more informative job, somehow this peri undertook this penance. I'd like to thank these folks for their saving graces.

Johnny Superstar, otherwise known as the Verm, otherwise known as John Sherman, otherwise known as one hell of a boulderer for organizing a load of information, providing right-brain comments, and giving me just enough of a hard time to make me want to finish.

George Meyers, who said he'd send a couple of pinstriped members of a certain, nontaxable business organization to my front door to break my fingers if I didn't finish. What a kidder that George is! (Knock, knock . . .)

Thanks also to a load of other charitable rock climbers, including: Gary Brocarde, Mike Lawson, and Carl Tobin (Alaska); Tom Addison, Mark Cole, Kurt Merchant, and Betty Ratchford (Alabama); Billy Biswanger, Don Newton, Rick Oliver, and John Shireman (Arkansas); Scott Baxter, Rand Black, Jon Bernhard, Tony Cosby, Chris Dunn, Jim Gaun, Bill Hatcher, Ira Hickman, Chuck Hill, Dave Insley, John Middendorf, Glen Rink, Pernell Tomasi, and Jim Waugh (Arizona); Gray Alexander, John Christie, Tom Kelley, Tom Herbert, Harrison Hood, Dave Houchin, Neil Kaptain, Richard Leversee, Peter Mayfield, Roy McClenahan, Terry Parrish, Heidi Pesterfield, and Frank Saab (California); Jeff Achey, K.C. Baum, Bobbi Bensman, Bob Bernholz, Michael Chessler, Ken Duncan, Charlie Fowler, George Gardiner, Don Goodhew, Bob Horan, Craig Luebben, Greg Johnson, Chris Jones, Randy Joseph, Andy Petefish, Gary Sapp, Doug Scott, Pete Steres, University of Colorado librarians, Mark Wilford, Beth Wald, and Kathy Zaiser (Colorado); Tim Maloney, Jeff Sargeant, and Chris Tacy (Connecticut); Jeff Gruenberg and Janean Thorne (Florida); Phil Fisher and Chris Watford (Georgia); Matt Laggis (Idaho); Robert Mitchell and Jim Moers (Indiana); Alan Carrier, Dave Moore, Jim Thurmond, and Eric Ulner (Illinois); Bill Leo and Chris O'Halloran (Kansas); Jack Dickey, Will Hobbs, and Emmanuel LaCoste (Kentucky); Bob, Jocalyn, and Kyle Van Belle, and Alan Rubin (Massachusetts); Andy Peter Beal (Maine); Eric Rice (Michigan); Bill Bancroft, Mike Dahlberg, Doug Dokken, Chris Hendricks, and Mark Strege (Minnesota); Mike Jenner, Jim Karpowicz, Ginger Porter, and Michael Stites (Missouri); Bill Dockins (Montana); Joe Benson, Sue Decker, Nancy Feagin, Porter Jarrard, and Woody Keen (North Carolina); John Mallery and Eric Mushial (New Hampshire); Tom Andrews, Jim Balzer, Mike Freeman, and Mike Siacca (New York); Jean Detaillade, Dave Jacobsen, Bob Murray, Bryan Pletta, Lee Sheftel, and John Whitney (New Mexico); Mike Tupper and Amy Whisler (Nevada); Tony Berlier (Ohio); Duane Raleigh and Tony Wilson (Oklahoma); Eric Horst, Eric Janoscrat, and Richard Thompson (Pennsylvania); Francois Lafond, Stephane Lapierre, Paul Laterriere, Sylvain Malchelosse, Jean Claude Maurice, Alex Soucy, and Michel Tremblay (Quebec); Judy Barnes, Chris Oates, and Shaun Parent (Ontario); Kevin Lawlor and Metalhead (Oregon); Sean Cobourn (South Carolina); Mark Jacobs and Paul Piana (South Dakota); Alex Catlin, James Crump, Dave Dyess, JP Gamertsfelder, John Gogas, Don Hardin, Gail McClanahan, Mike O'Leary, Carol Sperl, Jacob Valdez, and Martin Ziebell (Texas); Arno Ilgner, Mark Ilgner, Rob Robinson, Rob Turan, and Eddie Whittemore (Tennessee); Erik Bjornstadt, James and Franzizka Garrett, Lisa Gnade, Bob Milton, Steve Petro, Allen Sandersen, and Brad Santell (Utah); Kenny Parker (Virginia); Andy Holt (Vermont); John Petroske, Alex Van Steen, and Marty Vidak (Washington); Rich Bechler, Mickey's Bigmouth, David Groth, and Brad Werntz (Wisconsin); Tom Cecil and John Govi (West Virginia); Steve Bechtel, Scott Blunk, Greg Collins, Richard Collins, Kirt Cozzens, Ken Driese, Don Hoover, Sam Lightner, NOLS staff and library, Richard Pampe, Bob Scarpelli, Erik Sawyer, Todd Skinner, and Julia Wilmerding (Wyoming). Thanks also to all those listed in the reference sections, and extra special thanks to: Chockstone Press; *Climbing* magazine; *Rock & Ice* magazine; DeLorme Mapping Company; Michael Chessler Books; John Burbidge; Scott Goldsmith, Big Country Chiropractic Clinic, for keeping me "in line" and in health; the Lander Social Committee for keeping me in good spirits; the Double Diamond and the boys at the Bellstand at Copper Mountain for keeping me on the steep and narrow. Pete and Queta, Hueco Tanks Country Store, for putting a "wild fire" (salsa) in my spirit and stomach to keep me firin'; Johnny Carson, David Letterman, Arsenio Hall, and Jay Leno for helping me make it through the nights; Prince Abruzzi, the master author of guidebooks; Mike Chessler for showing me the beauty in guidebooks; the Egyptians for turning papyrus into paper and Aldus Manutius for cranking up the printing press; and lastly, for that special gal in my heart.

As any climber who has been crankin' around the country for a while knows, we are all really links in a big chain. John Muir once said, "When we try to pick out anything by itself, we find it hitched to everything else in the universe." With this thought in mind, I'd like to thank every climber in North America. In some way, you have made this book and my life better, and hopefully every other climber's life a bit better as well.

Introduction

How to Use This Book

This book describes climbing areas in North America and their resources. States and areas are listed in alphabetical order, and each section includes a map with numbered climbing areas, an introduction, and a list of the climbing areas with corresponding map numbers and individual characteristics.

The descriptions for individual climbing areas contain the following information:

Identification Number

Climbing area identification numbers correspond with those on the maps. Maps are usually numbered in a northwest to southeast direction.

Name of Area

The common area name is listed, and also, often listed in parentheses next to the name, if appropriate, is either a prominent formation/climb in that area, another local name, the mountain range/geographical province containing the climbing area, or abbreviations used to indicate a cluster or geographical grouping of areas in a large contiguous area. If the area was closed at press time, this is mentioned as well.

Thus:

1 Fisher Towers (The Titan)

Occasionally, the most outstanding climb or feature (e.g., The Titan) is listed in parentheses alongside the area name (e.g., Fisher Towers). In this example, The Titan is the most famous spire of the Fisher Towers. Names in parentheses are usually explained in the general description for each climb.

2 Paradise Forks (aka The Forks)

An alternative name (e.g., The Forks) is something listed in parentheses after the area name (e.g., Paradise Forks). In this example, The Forks is a common local name for Paradise Forks.

3 Granite Point (on Pend Oreille Lake)

A geographical province (e.g., Pend Oreille Lake) is occasionally listed in parentheses alongside the area name (e.g., Granite Point). In this example, Granite Point is found on Pend Oreille Lake.

4 16 LT☆ (Lake Tahoe Areas) Overview & Donner Summit
    17 LT—Split Rock

In this example, LT indicates an abbreviation for the geographical area in parentheses (in this case, it's the Lake Tahoe area in California). The asterisk indicates that it is the beginning of a cluster of areas found in the Lake Tahoe area, and subsequent areas will follow with the LT abbreviation. "Overview" simply means that a general overall description may be given for the entire vicinity, and one can expect specific areas to follow. It also implies that more climbing may still be discovered in this general region in addition to the specific areas listed below it. "Donner Summit" is a specific area added with the overview and is described separately in the same directions and general climb descriptions sections as "Overview."

"LT—Split Rock" indicates that Split Rock is a specific climbing area described in the Lake Tahoe region.

Stars

What creates a quality climbing experience? For some, it's a total wilderness setting with big walls, virgin rock, natural beauty, and solitude. Others do fine on crags with a squad of D9s building a new freeway below, many well-defined routes, a competitive atmosphere, climbing queues, and blasting stereo boom boxes. While the appeal of an area is subjective, *Rock 'n' Road* uses the following criteria for star ratings (which appear directly after the name of an area):

For boulders and cragging areas, these are quality of climbing, quality of rock, and accessibility. Most climbers want to rock climb and not hike or bushwhack. Therefore, the easier the access, the higher the rating. The motto here is We climb first, we walk second.

For more remote areas (e.g., alpine), only the quality of climbing and quality of rock are considered, since most climbers are going to these regions for the experience and scenery as well as the climbing. Logistical concerns (e.g. hiking) are not an important quality factor.

Thus, a five-star-rating would have great climbs, beautiful rock, and easy accessibility. Admittedly, this is a highly subjective rating scale. A fanatical boulderer might rate the Black Canyon of Gunnison, Colorado, one-star, whereas a multipitch rockaneer might rate it five stars. Conversely, a multipitch rockaneer might rate Horsetooth Reservoir, Colorado, one star whereas the disciplined boulderer would surely rate it five stars. Needs vary. Hence, the scale tries to rate each area for what it is: a bouldering, cragging, or big wall area, based on a continental view.

Thus, the following rating system is used here:

★★★★★ Excellent. A must-stop, internationally famous area.

★★★★ Very, very good; high quality at affordable prices. Regionally famous.

★★★ Good; most people would enjoy it and consider it a good stop. Locally famous.

★★ So-so; only stop if you happen to be there. Locally infamous.

★ Might do in a pinch, but you'd do well to keep driving. For locals only.

● A black hole; i.e., an area so bad it sucks stars away from others.

Why even include a black hole? Every area has value. In some cases, areas of poor or dubious rock quality are included. Hopefully, this will answer a motoring rock climber's frequently asked question, "I wonder if that rock is any good?"

New to this edition is a simpler format of the area's description, "Classics" climbs, references, and directions:

Area Descriptions

Under the name of the area there is a description of the area. This includes any specific information about the climbing and/or the locale that may enhance a visiting climber's stay. Information such as climbing type, rock type, rock height, grades, camping notes, and land ownership is included here. The descriptions also include notes on historical development and local ethics, scenic attractions, and restaurants, as well as hazards such as poison oak, rattlers, etc. Regrettably, time and space do not allow more information on the colorful history and important climbers of many areas.

Climbing Type

The type of climbing that exists in the area. These are divided into the following categories:

Alpine. High-altitude or mountainous conditions.
Bouldering. Areas with short boulder problems or optional topropes, approximately 25'.
Crag. Definite lead climbs (or very long topropes) up to 750' in height.
Pinnacle. A freestanding spire.
Sport Crag. An area with rappel-bolted climbs.
Wall. For this book, a wall is distinguished from a crag at 750' and implies multipitch techniques and bivy potential.

Grades

The predominant grade level of routes found in the area.
  Mixed. All levels.
  Beginner. 5.8 or less.
  Intermediate. 5.9–5.10.
  Expert. 5.11–5.13.
  World-class. 5.14 and up.

Height

The maximum height of the rock; provided in feet for the United States and in meters for Canada and Mexico. This indicates the potential height of climbs, even though the actual length of the routes may be far shorter. The letter p stands for pitch and serves to describe the length of the routes when the actual height is not known. For example 1p means "one pitch."

Rock Type

The geological rock classification.

Season

The most comfortable season to climb in the area (e.g., dry rock conditions, stable weather, few insects, low-water river crossings, etc.).

Camping

Recommended or known campsites are mentioned in the area description as either pay, free, or not existing at the climbing area. This is always subject to change. Please do not trespass.

Ownership

The owners of the land, private or government. For federal government–owned land, the following abbreviations have been used: BIA (Bureau of Indian Affairs), BLM (Bureau of Land Management), NPS (National Park Service), USFS (United States Forest Service), NWR (National Wildlife Refuge). Dual or multiple ownerships are denoted with a slash (/). Phone numbers are provided for contacting government agencies.

Classics

These are the must-do, mega-classic climbs of the area that any visiting climber would enjoy. When possible, a route from at least one of each grade was selected as a representative of an area; i.e., beginner (<5.8), intermediate (5.9–5.10), and expert (5.11–5.14). The 5 and the decimal have been left out in most cases for brevity; e.g., the route Hogsnout 5.8 is written simply as Hogsnout 8.

Reference

This category includes the informational resources used in researching this book and is the source of more in-depth knowledge for the climber wanting detailed topos, history, etc. The references are broken down into four groups (in order of appearance):

1) Personal interviews as well as the author's knowledge (not noted).

2) Climbing magazines, referenced with the following abbreviations: A (*Ascent*), AAJ (*American Alpine Journal*),

C (*Climbing*), OB (*Off Belay*), R (*Rock & Ice*), S (*Summit*), and SC (*Sport Climbing* formerly *Sport Climbing Connection*). Other publications are randomly mentioned.

3) Climbing-related books that might have useful photos.

4) Guidebooks. The guidebook author's last name and/or the title was used. A reference in the listed guidebook could be anything from an exquisite topo to confusing directions to the area. New to this edition, on-line guides have also been mentioned so that readers can conduct a search for them. Most contain fine information about the specific areas.

Directions

Directions start from the nearest town on a map. For really small towns, a larger nearby town is noted. Also under directions is the cliff aspect, which is the general direction in which the area or cliff faces: north, east, south, or west.

Land-Use Thoughts for the Traveling Rock Climber

As a youngster, you may have heard the expression, There are two sides to every story. This is applicable to climbers' use of the land resource. On one hand, there are those who don't care if the earth gets trashed. The earth is doomed anyway, so why waste time picking up trash? On the other hand are those who are environmentally conscious, who think littering is unspeakable. While the two sides of this argument may never be reconciled, keep in mind another expression: There is no right or wrong, there are only consequences.

Another way to look at this is perhaps the earth is our mother. If you love your mother and think that she's been nice to you and deserves some love in return, you could show that you love her back. So, here are suggestions for some Mother's Day gifts:

- Keep areas clean. Offer to take out the trash for your mom. Pick up your trash and just one other piece of trash from each area you visit.

- Protect rock art. You wouldn't destroy your mom's art collection, would you? Or spray paint Bucky loves Sue on her dining room wall?

- Use a "zero-impact" ethic in your climbing area. Maybe your mom's guests don't like seeing colored slings and bolt hangers, chips and dents all over the walls of her house.

- Carry toilet paper out with you in a Ziploc bag. Don't you think your mom would be mad if she found T.P. under the rocks in her garden? While we're at it, how about "unloadin' your truck" a good ways from the cliff?

- Ask other guests in your mom's house whom you've witnessed littering to please pick up their trash.

- Keep climbing areas open. Do you think your mom would like it if she found you locking the doors on her guests?

The bottom line is, there are several reasons why you don't want to trash an area:

- Because you may get handed a ticket.
- Because it detracts from the visual enjoyment of others.
- Because you'll get an earful of grief.
- Because you love your mom.

Dangers for the Traveling Climber

The following survey is a quick glance at lurking dangers that could turn your climbing trip in North America into a quick trip to the hospital. *Beware!*

Animals

- Ants. Occasionally they will bite, but they are more of a belay nuisance.

- Bees. Anaphylactic shock is a real concern, since death can come swiftly to the susceptible. An Epi-pen is a wise choice for your first-aid kit. Ask your doctor for one. Killer bees are now found as far north as southern Arizona.

- Wasps. They're mellow in areas like Devil's Lake, Wisconsin, and Shawangunks, New York, but they will come at you like a lunging swordsman in areas like Oak Creek Canyon, Arizona.

- Scorpions. Prevalent in the Southwest and Mexico. Found under and on rock. The sting is sensational.

- Snakes. Rattlesnakes are found in many cragging areas except alpine areas. Copperheads are found on the East Coast and in the Midwest.

- Ticks. Can be carriers of Rocky Mountain Spotted Fever, a real concern from March to July in the Rocky Mountain states. The Black Canyon of the Gunnison, Colorado, is perhaps the most famous tick and poison-ivy factory among rock climbers. More than one climber has counted more than two dozen of these bloodsuckers on their bodies at one time. Checking yourself and your partner can save you from a hideous illness. Ticks also carry Lyme disease, an eastern counterpart of the western Rocky Mountain Spotted Fever. Again, check your clothes and body thoroughly during tick season.

- Mosquitoes and black flies. Clouds of mosquitoes can prompt any gutless climber onto an X-rated pitch during their peak season of July in the Wind River Mountains of Wyoming. During the spring (May–June) in the Northeast, black flies are the plague of the crag.

- Bears. Appear in various areas. They're not a concern of the crag so much as of the campsite. In Yosemite NP, more than one bear has been known to rip into a car to fetch a visible cooler.

- Giardia. A waterborne parasite that can turn your gastrointestinal tract into a real hurt box and make you forget the price of your climbing rope.

- Varmints (mice, rats, raccoons, etc.). Well-known for chewing into food, ropes, and gear.

- Climbing parasites. Identified by unwashed hair, unmatched and unlaundered clothing, and their wandering eyes at your pot of stew.

- California and Boston drivers.

- Drunken rednecks on Friday and Saturday nights. A can of Skoal and a National Rifle Association cap may help you blend in.

- Hunters. Some of these harmless curmudgeons couldn't hit the side of a barn, but somehow during the months of October through December they become awful darn good shots at human targets. Wearing a bright orange vest or hat is a good idea if you happen to find yourself in a hunting area, which is most areas.

- Border guards. Border crossings keep getting more and more complicated, so keep your birth certificate, visa, or passport handy. To avoid unnecessary delays, check ahead on car insurance before entering Mexico. Talk to your local travel agent. Also, expect to have your car searched entering or exiting Canada or Mexico.

Plants

- Poison ivy. Ubiquitous. Learning to identify this one plant can save you a lot of grief and itching before the onset of a rash. Poison ivy is often mentioned in the general descriptions of the climbs when especially bad. Poison oak is more frequent on the West Coast. Poison ivy affects your rope and dogs as well.

- Cactus, agave, lechugilla. These plants can stick you for more than a crooked auto mechanic and are found mainly in the Southwest. (Crooked auto mechanics can be found anywhere.)

Camping Notes

The following is a brief look at camping in the United States. The ownership of the land determines how and where you camp. Regardless of the notes presented here, please contact the appropriate land-managing agency for current information. Compared to the western United States, the amount of public land in the eastern United States is scarce. Thus, it's often harder to find camping on public lands. But private campgrounds are often closer together.

Public (Government Land-Managing Agencies)

- State park. Usually very good facilities. Expect fees and

tight supervision by rangers.

- State wildlife area. Regulations vary from state to state. Check locally.

The following are run by federal agencies. Most have a fourteen-day limit on camping.

- BLM (Bureau of Land Management). Pay for developed sites; free on undeveloped land, of which the BLM has a lot. Perhaps the least restrictive of federal agencies.

- NPS (National Park Service). Pay campgrounds are standard unless you go into the backcountry. Permit systems. Tightly controlled by rangers.

- USFS (United States Forest Service). Pay for developed sites; free in undeveloped sites. Fourteen-day time limit.

- BIA (Bureau of Indian Affairs). Campgrounds and regulations vary for each given reservation.

- NWR (National Wildlife Refuge). Varies with refuge.

Most of the public agencies listed here have Web sites full of current information.

Private

Private campgrounds are usually run by a mom-and-pop or by a chain, like KOA (Kampgrounds of America). Thus, they are usually cleaned and maintained more attentively than government ones but also cost more. They have everything from hot showers to horseshoes.

Trespassing

Some climbing areas in this directory lie on private land. These areas were included as a historical and informational source. It does not give anyone the right to trespass.

While we have tried to acquire the most up-to-date information, we have not personally visited every area described herein. Your use of this book indicates two things: your assumption that it will contain errors as land ownership and access change through the passage of time, and your acknowledgment of your sole responsibility for your safety.

Land ownership is constantly changing. Please make it your responsibility to find out who owns the land you wish to ascend.

On private land, please ask permission *first,* or do not climb there. It is your responsibility as a climber and a civilian, and to the world climbing community. This book frequently indicates areas known to be closed to climbing. Please take heed. While some of these closures may in the future revert to open climbing areas, more than likely they will not.

Alabama

Life is either a daring adventure or nothing. —Helen Keller, born in Tuscumbia

Country music is just one of the state's gifts to Alabama climbers. The other is rock (not the Rolling Stones). Chances are you will become a fan of the state upon your first visit to Fort Payne, in the northeast sector of Alabama. Better dubbed Fort Sandstone, the surrounding countryside protects a wealth of climbing potential within a one-hour radius of town.

Sandstone crags abound. And if steep, overhanging sandstone routes are your pleasure, be prepared to "hang" a spell. Sand Rock and Little River Canyon are just a couple of the finer areas along the southern extension of the Appalachian Mountains. Don't stop there. From Birmingham to Florence, good rock climbing awaits in other parts of the state.

1 I-59 Cliffs

Exploratory area of 200′ sandstone cliffs. Be certain to stay on public lands . . . or buy a cliffline lot. Trenton. Public/private land.

Directions: From Trenton, Georgia, this long line of sandstone cliffs is visible south along I-59 into Alabama. Several points east from the interstate access Thunder Canyon.

2 Desoto State Park (closed) ✫✫

Varied overhanging cragging and bouldering near a scenic waterfall on 100′ sandstone bluffs. Explorer Desoto traveled through Alabama (meaning "thicket clearers," derived from the Choctaw language) in 1519 and 1528 in search of gold. Pay campground at park; reservations, (800) ALA-PARK; state park, (256) 845–0051.

Ref: Guidebooks: Detterline's *A Climber's Guide to the Mid-South,* Hall's *Southern Rock: A Climber's Guide.*

Directions: From Ft. Payne scuttle up Hwy. 35 E. Turn north on Desoto State Park Rd. (follow signs). Look for bouldering along Visitor Center Trail (old fixed pin) and cragging at Waterfall Bluffs.

3 Monte Sano State Park ✫✫✫

Limited, but the focus here is the great workout pump on an angling 30′ sandstone bouldering wall. A toprope may be desired. More overhanging boulders and crags exist, notably the extensive rock bands that lie on adjacent canyon hillsides (uncertain of out of park boundaries). Monte Sano also has a 120′ deep natural well that experienced climbers can rappel into and toprope out. Huntsville is home of the Redstone Arsenal where the Patriot Missile is manufactured. Pay camping. State park, (256) 534–3757.

Directions: East Huntsville. Drive east on Bankhead Pkwy. (follow signs) to parking at Monte Sano State Park picnic area. Hike south toward the valley approximately 100 yd. to the chalked overhang.

4 Buck's Pocket State Park ✫✫✫

These 80′ sandstone crags feature overhanging face climbs with one hundred routes in the 1990s. Potential for steep sandstone routes. All climbers must obtain permits at the ranger station. No bolting! This is a totally traditional/toprope area. Bouldering potential is great in winter; summer is really bad due to poison ivy/spiders. Pay camping. State park, (256) 659–2000.

Directions: From Grove Oak it's just north of town. Follow park signs to Buck's Pocket State Park.

5 Painted Bluff (closed) ✫✫✫

A 1990s sport crag for 200′ limestone experts on natural face edges with routes from 5.10–5.13. Nearby Guntersville Lake is known for its huge largemouth bass catches, as are other Alabama lakes. Alabama ranks in the top three states in the United States for having the greatest variety of freshwater fish—more than 200 species. Private land.

Directions: South of Huntsville.

6 Yellow Bluff (closed) ✫✫✫✫

In the late 1980s, this 80′ sandstone sport crag was the ark of face-climbing science. Bomber sandstone and excellent face edges gave way to forty routes. Extreme face routes, like Rainbow Warrior, were developed by Jessie Guthrie and others. Access sensitive. Private landowner has wavered on use of bolts. Yellow Bluff may be closed. If it isn't, toprope the routes.

Classics: Astral Projection 5.12a, Lab Rat 5.12+, Rainbow Warrior 5.13a, Groovin' 5.13b.

Ref: C [103, 102].

Directions: South of Huntsville. Ask locally first.

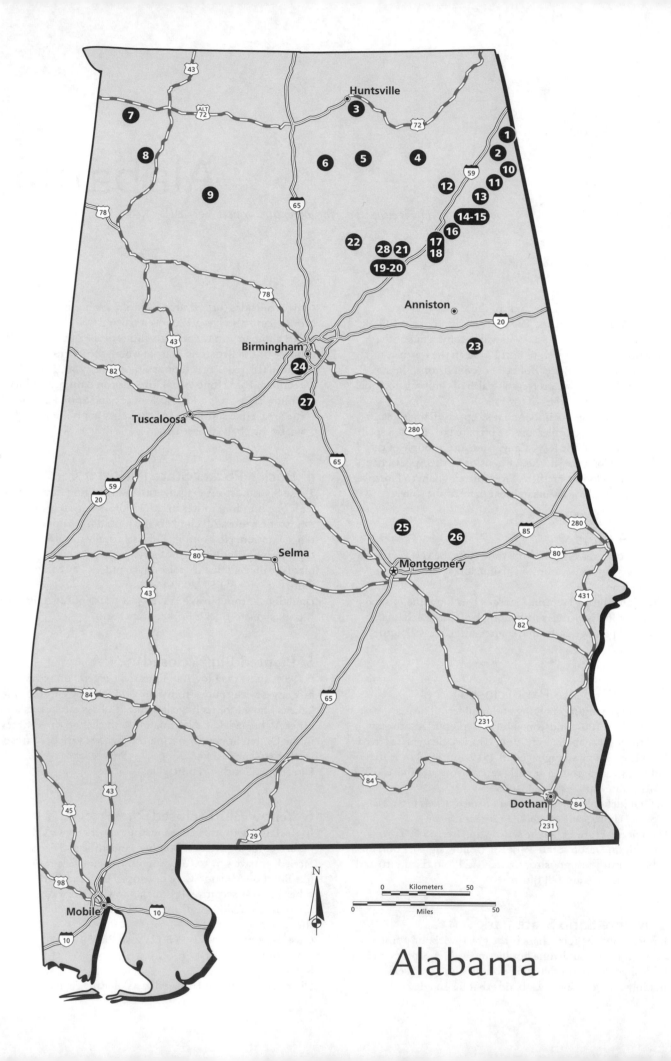

Alabama

7 Red Rocks ✮✮

A 60′ sandstone crag with overhanging face. Private land. Near Florence.

8 Rockwood Crags ✮✮

A 100′ sandstone crag. Private land. Near Rockwood.

9 Sipsey River (in Bankhead National Forest) ✮✮

The Sipsey Wilderness Area contains gorges; cool, moist canyons; and virgin timber. This area features a rock-rimmed box canyon with sheer vertical walls rising 100′ or more. Interesting honeycomb rock of uncertain rock quality. Exploratory area. USFS–Bankhead NF, (205) 489–5111.
Ref: C 68; Guidebook: Detterline's *A Climber's Guide to the Mid-South.*
Directions: From Forkville follow Hwy. 195 S. Turn left at USFS sign for 4 mi. Go past Sipsey River. Turn left at dirt road for 6 mi. Hike trail. The Sipsey River Cliffs are at the junction of the Bee Branch with the Sipsey River.

10 Jamestown Crags (closed) ✮✮✮

Before being closed to climbing, these classic 100′ sandstone crags offered fifty routes. Bouldering, too. Found in 1978 by Chick Holtkamp and developed by Gottlieb, Zschiesche, Chislet, Robinson, and Smith. Closed in 1993 but may be reopened. The White Seam 5.12a is a classic for its grade. Camping at Little River Canyon. Private land.
Classics: Crimson Corner 8, Glitter Girls 9, Autumn Sonata 9+, The Gift 10, Dust Bowl Blues 10b/c, Dirty White Boy 10, Rainbow Bridge 11, Spiritus 11, Salamander Eulogy 11, White Seam 12a, White Lightning 12, Bone Roof 12+.
Ref: C [137(4/93)-72, 105(12/87)-58, 101, 97, 94, 75(12/82), 72, 68]; Guidebook: Hall's *Southern Rock: A Climber's Guide.*
Directions: At Jamestown. East of Fort Payne.

11 Little River Canyon National Preserve ✮✮✮✮

The Grand Canyon of Alabama and Alabama sport climbing. This stately canyon possesses mi. of sandstone cliffs and class VI white water. Since the time Henry Barber climbed here, Little River has now become the sport-climbing focus of southeastern sport climbers. Protected winter climbing at Lizard Wall and others. Con Cave is the radical cave of the canyon. Other 80′ sandstone sport crags feature overhanging face on 400+ routes mainly harder than 5.11. Bring stick clip. Deepest gorge east of the Mississippi and the only one in the nation to form and flow on top of a mountain. The musical group Alabama originated right down the road from Fort Payne. Camp at Desoto State Park (see above) or Little River Campground on Hwy. 35 west of Little River. Take car-theft precautions. NPS, (256) 845–9605.
Classics: Perma Torque 12b, many classics.
Ref: C 174-111; Guidebook: Detterline's *A Climber's Guide to the Mid-South.*

Climbers at Little River Canyon.

TIM TOULA

Directions: From Fort Payne head east on Hwy. 35 for approximately 8 mi. Turn right on Little River Canyon Rd. Various parking areas yield access to cliffs below rim.

12 Griffin Falls ✮✮✮

This beautiful 100′ sandstone crag offers more than two dozen traditional and sport routes of high-caliber southern sandstone. Developed since the 1980s by a mix of climbers. No camping. Private land.
Classics: Knife Crack 9+, Romano's Crack 10, Grace Under Pressure 10+, Power Windows 11b, Smashing Pumpkins 11b, Black Sabbath 11, Lost Humanoids 11+, Steeplechase 12b, Whimsical Promise 12, High Horse 13a.
Ref: C [106, 99]; Guidebooks: Watford's *Dixie Cragger's Atlas,* Robinson and Watford's *Deep South Climber's Companion.*
Directions: From I–59 (exit 205) glide west on Hwy. 68 for approximately 3 mi. Rock cliffs visible on left side of road. Turn left on dirt road. Shortly, park on right after small wooden bridge. Hike up to waterfall (Griffin Falls Cliffs). Note: Private landowner requests leaving CLIMBING sign in car and no more than five cars in parking pullout at one time.

13 Yellow Creek Falls (closed) ✩✩✩✩

Today's climbing weather forecast: big pump and scattered sweat. This overhanging pump palace has marvelously steep routes. These 150′ sandstone crags and bouldering problems yield fifty crack and face routes on either side of a scenic waterfall. Camping on railroad bed. You should see yellow when you realize this great area is closed to climbing. Private land.

Classics: Feats Don't Fail Me Now 7, Land of Cotton 9, Supreme Crack 10, Genetic Drift 10, Sultans of Swing 11, Locomotive Breath 11a, Quest for Fire 11c/d, Grand Dragon 12, Stimulator 12c, Man Eater 12c; Bouldering: More than thirty B5.12 (creekbed boulder).

Ref: C [134, 106, 105, 102, 99, 96, 94, 75(12/82)], R 45; Guidebooks: Robinson's *Yellow Creek Plus,* Harlin's *East Coast.*

Directions: East of Collinsville.

14 Sand Rock (aka Cherokee Rock Village) ✩✩✩✩

Swell labyrinths of 80′ sandstone bouldering and 150 face routes. Bouldering problems like Chinese Water Torture B5.12 are more deceptive than a wolf in sheep's clothing. The home of the amazing Champagne Jam roof crack 5.12+. Popular with sport climbers in the 1990s and into the twenty-first century. This is a theft area, so stash valuables. Camping in parking lot. Government park.

Hidetaka Suzuki popping the cork on Champagne Jam, Sand Rock.

Classics: Pinnacle Std Rt 6, Pin Chimney 8, Comfortably Numb 9+, Wall of Horns 9+, They Call Me Cruiser 10, Misty 10, Geraldine 11b, Dreamscape 11+, Bocephus 11d, Steel Sky 12a, Champagne Jam 12, Whammy 12b, Mud Puppy 13a, Firepit Roof B5.12, Chinese Water Torture B5.12a.

Ref: C [199-80, 174-108, 134, 108, 105, 94, 75(12/82), 68], R [100-91, 65-87]; Sherman's *Stone Crusade;* Guidebooks: Watford's *Dixie Cragger's Atlas,* Robinson and Watford's *Deep South Climber's Companion,* Harlin's *Climber's Guide to North America (East).*

Directions: From Collinsville rock approximately 6 mi. east on Hwy. 68. Turn 1½ mi. south on Hwy. 36. Go east onto CR 70 (at first fence on left) for 3 mi. (bearing right at fork) on dirt road to top of ridge past radio towers and to Sand Rock formations at parking cul-de-sac.

15 Sand Valley ✩✩✩

There are 80′ sandstone crags here. Extension of Sand Rock. Mountain-biking run. Private land.

Classics: Boardwalk 10, Whimsical Promise 12.

Ref: P. Jarrard; C 99.

Directions: From Sand Rock (see number 14), head south on dirt road 3 mi. along ridge to Sand Valley.

16 High Rocks (closed) ✩✩✩

Fun, classic, and difficult sandstone (gritstone) boulder problems; 35′ sandstone boulders and short walls. More than 25 routes. Private land.

Directions: North of Gadsden.

17 Noccalula Falls (closed) ✩✩✩

During runoff season, an amazing 90′ waterfall drops down to sandstone walls and base bouldering. Named for a forlorn Native American maid who did the first and last BASE jump without a chute here after realizing she would never be with her true love. Private park.

Directions: In Gadsden.

18 Seven Room Rock ✩✩✩✩

An exquisite, compact bouldering and toprope area. Marblelike, white sandstone rock lends itself to classic 45′ face edge routes. Moss on north faces. Heavy graffiti in 1994. No camping. Private land.

Classics: Dynamite Roof B5.12+, Plumbline Arête 5.12-, Pork Chop Roof 5.12+, Sherman's March V7.

Ref: Sherman, Jarrard.

Directions: From Gadsden take Noccalula Falls Rd. Turn south on Scenic Hwy. Park when rock slab on right comes into view. Hike up and over to other side of slab for Seven Room Rock.

19 Peter's Point (closed) ✩✩✩
A 100' sandstone crag with difficult routes. Private land.
Classics: French Benefits 5.11+, The Ultimatum 5.12, Hot Tamale 5.12TR.
Ref: C 99.
Directions: Near Steele.

20 Blount Mountain ✩✩
A 100' sandstone crag. Private land.
Directions: South of Gadsden, near Gallant.

21 Palisades Park ✩✩✩
Sandstone cliff bands yield a nice variety of ninety, one-pitch trad routes for mainly the beginning or intermediate climber, with small sums of bouldering desperates below the cliff on the Solitude Boulder. The Fireside Wall (main crag) is 50' high. No bolting allowed. Open 8:00 A.M.–9:00 P.M. summer, 8:00 A.M.–5:00 P.M. winter. City park.
Ref: J. Sherman, Toula; C 143; Guidebooks: Watford's *Dixie Cragger's Atlas,* Robinson and Watford's *Deep South Climber's Companion.*
Directions: From Oneonta go north on Hwy. 231 for 1 mi. following brown park signs. Once inside Palisades Park, it's a short saunter from car to rock bands and boulders.

22 Steele (aka Chandler Mountain) (closed) ✩✩✩✩
Wildly steep, orange 250' sandstone crags offer excellent-quality cragging. The Alabama crag of the 1980s. More than fifty routes ranging to 5.13 routes. Unfortunately, a history of access problems. First-ascent route contributors include Robinson, Cole, Gruenberg, and Smith. Private land.
Classics: Oak Tree Dir 7, Wisdom 7, Graham's Crack 8, Cop Out 9, Pinch It 9, Olympia 10, Cloak and Dagger 10, Man Overboard 11, Hot Steele Direct 11, Tech Noir 12a, Jet Stream 12-, Challenger 12, Carnivore 12, Chandler's Roof 12, Meathooks and Memories 13a.
Ref: C [199-80, 164-30, 106, 105(12/87)-58, 102, 99, 96, 68]; Guidebooks: Detterline's *A Climber's Guide to the Mid-South,* Hall's *Southern Rocks: A Climber's Guide.*
Directions: West of Steele.

23 Cheaha Mountain State Park ✩✩
At 2,407', the highest point in Alabama offers 150' sandstone crags and bouldering on featured face climbing. Nearby Talladega is home of the Talladega Superspeedway and home of the International Motorsports Hall of Fame and Museum. Talladega sits atop the largest known white-marble deposits in the world, which are 35 mi. long and 1/2 mi. wide. Don't miss the world's largest office chair in Anniston. Pay camping. State park, (256) 488–5111.
Ref: J. Sherman; C 68; Guidebooks: Watford's *Dixie Cragger's Atlas,* Hall's *Southern Rock: A Climber's Guide.*

Alabama Road Thoughts
After several climbing trips to southern sandstone, I concluded that taking a trip there was as wise as handing a bottle of nitro to an epileptic.

First of all, the routes are tough! No, brutal . . . I mean downright core-pumping. The steepness is unrelenting. These southern boys and girls are strong. But if the climbing is crazy, the culture can be more so.

A checkout clerk in Fort Payne confirmed this theory one afternoon. Noticing us perusing the newspaper rental section while in line, he ventured,

"Yew mohwen hair?" shaking his head with a look that made *Mississippi Burning* seem like a Disneyland ride.

(My first thought was, "No, I'm not a barber.")

"Well we were think" . . .

"Wooduntt rekomaind et, main, wood nott rekomaind et!"

"Why not?"

"Plase is wayh tew volcanek, main!"

I knew enough about sandstone to recognize he wasn't talking about geology.

Directions: From Lineville head approximately 15 mi. north of Lineville on Hwy. 49 (park signs). Check out these three areas in Cheaha Mountain State Park: Bald Rock Trail Bouldering, Rock Garden Lake Trail, and Pulpit Rock Trail.

24 Shades Crest (partially closed) ✩✩✩
This is an old sandstone block bouldering garden, probably first visited by bouldering legend John Gill. The 35' sandstone boulders offer varied face climbs. Areas are now on their way to becoming housing developments and shopping malls. Ask locals for more details. Birmingham is well known as a city of medical research and is the home of the 65' Vulcan, the world's largest cast-iron man. Private land.
Ref: C 68; Access Fund Notes Vol. 11; Ament's Master of Rock; Guidebooks: Watford's *Dixie Cragger's Atlas,* Robinson and Watford's *Deep South Climber's Companion,* Detterline's *A Climber's Guide to the Mid-South,* Hall's *Southern Rock: A Climber's Guide.*
Directions: South Birmingham. I-65, exit 205 (Alford Ave. exit). Bump west up Shades Crest Rd. Three Shades Crest areas can be found beginning approximately 1 mi. after Park Ave. (on left): Emmys (closed) is before firetower on left. Fire Tower Area (closed) is at firetower on left. Dee Tennessee Area (closed). Shortly (approximately 1/2 mi.) thereafter look on right over side of hill for boulders. A fourth area, Lover's Leap Area (damn near closed due to shopping mall), is farther down CR 97.

25 Coosa Slabs ✪✪

An 80′ metamorphic mica-schist beginner's slab. Two bolts for Rat Job 5.6 and a dihedral named Just Like a Bull 5.6. Private land.
Ref: P. Trice.
Directions: From Montgomery go north on Hwy. 231. Turn west toward Jordan Dam. East of the dam, a road cuts 1 mi. southwest to rocks below the dam. Coosa Slabs are just below the dam at Lake Jordan.

26 Tallassee Rocks (parking and trail closed) ✪✪

A once-popular Auburn practice area of 30′ sandstone boulders with classic 5.7 crack and 30′ overhangs. Rampant graffiti. Civil War armory nearby. Private land.
Ref: P. Trice.
Directions: In Tallassee, below Thurlow Dam on east bank.

27 Weatherly Subdivision

Sandstone crag. No camping. Private land.
Ref: D. Wilkins.
Directions: Near Alabaster. No known reasonable access.

28 Horse Pens 40 ✪✪✪

Excellent bouldering area near Steele. Site of Mortal Kombat climbing competition held November 2000. Civil War and Bluegrass Music Festivals. Full accommodations. Private land, (800) 421-8564.
Ref: www.horsepens40.com.
Directions: From I-59 (Oneonta exit 166), go north on Hwy. 231. Turn right on CR 35N. Turn right on CR 42. Turn right to Horse Pens 40.

Alaska

It's not the high cost of living. . . it's the cost of living high. —Maverick road map

Alaska is more famous for its mountaineering than its rock climbing. With fifty distinct mountain ranges and seventeen of the twenty highest peaks in the United States, it is the mountaineer's quintessential resource. Mt. McKinley, Mt. St. Elias, and Mt. Blackburn are just a few of the big-name peaks that stoke a mountain climber's passion.

Nevertheless, Alaskan weather can turn nasty in the high country, leaving the would-be Denali summiteer with little option but to climb elsewhere or drink heavily. Fortunately, Alaskan climbers have developed a number of crags near Anchorage like Archangel Valley and Seward Highway. Granite Tors, outside of Fairbanks, is another recommended cragging stop.

Beyond the scope of this collection, but worthy of mention, are the many mountaineering goals, which are primarily rock climbs, found in areas such as Kichatna Spires, Devil's Paw, and The Tusk.

Alaska! This big land summons all who dream big.

1 Arrigetch Peaks (in the Brooks Range) ★★★★

These are 3,000′ granite mountain walls/cirques. Large expanse of rock-walled towers, spires, and cirques in a wild, super-remote range of northern Alaska, 100 mi. north of the Arctic Circle. Formations in the Arrigetch Peaks include Shot Tower, Badile, Wichmann Tower, Tasmania, Disneyland, Camel, The Albatross, and Elephant's Tooth. Please see map in AAJ 1970-70. A short summer season from June to August, but continuous days of sunlight make long climbs possible. Copious and large mosquitoes. NPS—Gates of the Arctic National Park.
Classics: Mt. Igikpak (8570′), Tupik Tower.
Ref: AAJ ['98, '97, '79-176, 72-46, 70 to 68, 65-315], S 6/69; Marshall's *Arctic Wilderness, Brooks Range: The Ultimate Mountains.*
Directions: West of Wiseman. In the west-central portion of the Brooks Range. Access by bush plane.

2 Seward Peninsula

Nome. Granite Mountain (2,844′) lies north of Koyuk (northeast of Nome).

3 Grapefruit Rocks ★★★

Popular 120′ limestone sport crag. One hundred routes. Copious rock-climbing possibilities. Many newly bolted routes at Lower Grapefruit; some bolted routes at Upper Grapefruit. Nearly every route is accessible to a toprope. Current routes range from 5.5–5.13a. There are a large number of 5.9–5.10d and possibly a few 5.11s. Free camping. Peregrine falcon nesting. Federal land.
Classics: Barney Rubble 5.9+ (lower section of Lower Grapefruit, 65′). Hole in the Wall 5.9 (Upper Grapefruit, 75′, good trad or toprope). I Am a Climbing God 5.11c-d (lower section of Lower Grapefruit, 50′, eight bolts).
Ref: D. Haas, K. Tobin.
Directions: Northeast of Fairbanks. Drive north of Fairbanks on the Elliot Hwy. 2, following the Alaska Pipeline for about forty-five minutes to one hour. Grapefruit Rock has two distinct areas: Upper and Lower Grapefruit. Heading north, Upper is on the right, on the small mountain. The Lower follows a trail at a parking area on the highway about ten minutes past the parking lot for the Wickersham Dome Ski Loop. Less than 1-mi. hike to either of the crags; however, Lower Grapefruit has a close crag and one about ¹/₂ mi. farther down the trail.

4 Angel Rocks ★★★

Well-developed, 60′ granite crag sport cracks in the wooded and hilly Tanana uplands. State land.
Classics: Teenage Wasteland, Pump Master.
Ref: K. Tobin.
Directions: Fairbanks. Northeast of town, at Mile 49 Chena Hot Springs Rd. Angel Rocks is visible from the road. Twenty-minute hike.

5 Granite Tors ★★★

Described as being "a Joshua Tree at tundra line." Could this land of 200′ granite spires and boulders be the best climbing in Fairbanks? State land.
Directions: From Fairbanks go about 40 mi. northeast up Chena Hot Springs Rd. in the Yukon Tanana Uplands. Two trails provide access to the Granite Tors Rock via a 4 ¹/₂-mi. hike.

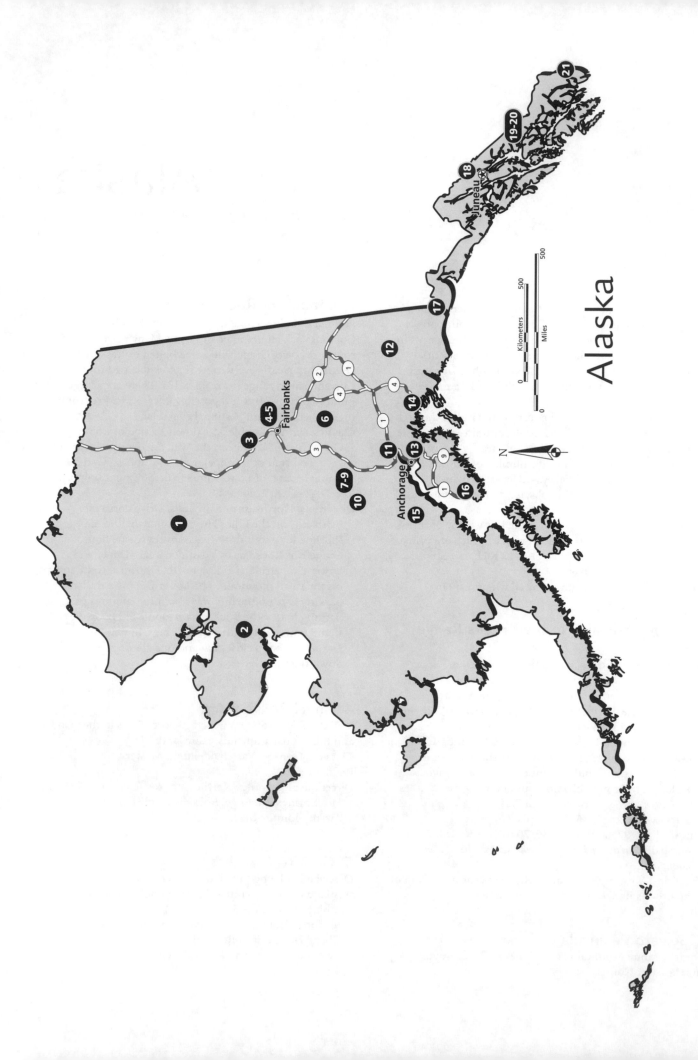

Alaska

6 Hayes Range (Mt. Hayes) ☆☆☆☆

Alpine granite mountain range. A remote, glaciated range of the great Alaska Range with peaks nearing 14,000'. Mt. Hayes (13,832') is the highest mountain in the range, while Mt. Deborah is the most famous in climbing circles. Mountaineering ascents (ice/snow) are best made in May, with June through August standard. April is usually good. Federal land.

Classics: Mt. Hayes, Mt. Deborah.

Ref: AAJ ['97, '96, '89-137, 77-114, 76 to 74, 69 to 65], C [178-102, 177-30, 145, 111, 94,88], R 88-79, M 96, S 6/75; Jones's *Climbing in North America, Deborah,* and Roberts's *Mountain of My Fear;* Guidebook: Kelsey's *Climber's and Hiker's Guide to the World's Mountains.*

Directions: This range lies southwest to southeast of Delta. The standard approach for Mt. Hayes is via a dot on the map called Denali, then hiking up the Susitna Glacier. This expedition can be done on foot or with assistance from a plane.

7 Denali National Park (Mt. McKinley, 20,320') ☆☆☆☆☆

The continent's greatest alpine walls and mountaineering summits. Famed peaks include Mt. McKinley, Mt. Huntington, and Moose's Tooth. Various approaches. Mt. McKinley, the highest point in North America at 20,320', was first ascended in 1913. Though not a rock climb, it's included here for its sheer size, allure, and reputation as the goal of every North American mountaineer. Other classic mixed ice, snow, and rock routes in the Alaska Range: Mt. Hunter, Mt. Huntington, and Moose's Tooth (first ascent 1964). Consult with NPS rangers for permits (907-733-2231), which must be made six months in advance and cost $150 per person. Little Switzerland area is primo for shorter multipitched alpine rock climbs.

Classics: Mt. McKinley (West Buttress), Cassin Ridge, Mt. Huntington (west face), Harvard Rt., Moose's Tooth (west ridge), Mt. Hunter (west ridge).

Ref: AAJ ['98>89, 87>84, 82>74, 72, 70 to 65], C [198-36, 196-90, 179-82/118, 170-22, 167-31, 166-98, 157-78, 151-120, 150-86, 149-46, 143, 133, 130(2/92)-60, 129, 128, 127, 119, 112, 110, 105, 88, 80-28, 96, 94, 75 to 72, 69 to 66, 64, 60, 57, 52, 50(10/78), 56, 49, (1/73) 2, 10/72, many base camps], M [85, 43], R [99-37, 97-40, 94-22, 89-88, 88-82, 85-60, 81-18, 79-82, 58, 40], S [1/89, 7/87, 1/86, 11/80, 2/77, 10/76, 11/69, 10/68, 4/68, 3/68, 1/68, 9/67, 9/65, 8/61]; Balch's *Mt. McKinley;* Browne's *The Conquest of Mt. McKinley;* Jones's *Climbing in North America, Denali Diary,* and *Alaska Alpine Journal;* Waterman's *Surviving Denali; Heroic Climbs;* Guidebooks: Secor's *Denali Climbing Guide,* Coombs's *Denali's West Buttress: A Climber's Guide,* Beckey's *Mt. McKinley: Icy Crown of North America,* Waterman's *High Alaska,* Washburn's *Tourist Guide to Mt. McKinley,* Randall's *McKinley Climber's Handbook,* Roper and Steck's *Fifty Classic Climbs of North America,* Alaska Alpine Club's *Mt. McKinley Climber's Guide,* Hoeman's *Alaska Mountain Guide.*

Directions: From Anchorage Denali National Park is two hours north on Hwy. 3. For Mt. McKinley, fly from Talkeetna to Kahiltna Glacier (for West Buttress Route of Mt. McKinley) or from the north at Wonder Lake, involving approximately twenty-five sporty crossings of the McKinley River to McGonagall Pass, Muldrow Glacier, Karsten Ridge, and finally the South Summit of Mt. McKinley.

8 Denali National Park–Ruth Gorge (Alaska Range)

South of Mt. McKinley, this granitic alpine wall area in the Ruth Gorge has peaks that include Mt. Barrille, Mt. Dickey, Mt. Bradley, and Mt. Johnson.

Ref: AAJ '95, C 98, 181-64, 178-102, 177-30/86.

Directions: South of McKinley on the Ruth Glacier. Requires air travel.

9 Denali National Park–Little Switzerland ☆☆☆☆

Striking granite spires, such as The Trolls and The Throne off Pika Glacier. NPS. Talkeetna Ranger Station, (907) 733-2231.

Classics: Royal Jester 10b 7 pitches, south face of Middle Troll.

Ref: J. Bernhard; C 196-92.

Directions: Airplane access or long trudge in from Petersville. Northeast of Talkeetna off the Kahiltna Glacier in Denali National Park.

10 Denali National Park–Kichatna Mountains (aka Cathedral Spires, 8,985') ☆☆☆☆☆

Glaciated 2,000' granite alpine walls and spires with grade VIs. The Kichatna Mountains (aka Cathedral Spires) comprise 8 square mi. in the southwest Alaska Range and are recognized as one of the finest group of mountains in North America, offering elegant lines arising from elephantine glaciers. Difficult climbing and severe weather. The Trinity Spire V (10p) 10 A1, the largest spire of the Flattop Cirque, reportedly (*Climbing* 64) has one of the best rock climbs in Alaska. Successful ascents require "blitzkrieg" alpine tactics. NPS land.

Classics: Kichatna Spire (west, south, and east faces). Mt. Jeffers (west face), Gurney Peak, Grendel Peak, Middle Triple Peak: East Buttress VI 9 A3, Riesenstein, The Citadel, Trinity Spire.

Ref: A 4(5/70)-2, AAJ ['98, '97, '95>93, 88-69, 85-179, 83-80, 82 to 80, 79-169, 77-106, 76-304, 75-123, 67, 66], C [181-30, 172-21, 166-20, 152-42, 128-18, 127, 126, 88, 75, 65, 64, 57(11/79)-10, 48], M 69-24, S [3/84, 4/75, 6/68, 10/66]; Guidebook: Roper and Steck's *Fifty Classic Climbs of North America.*

Directions: From Talkeetna it is 85 mi. due west to the Kichatna Mountains. Access via round-trip chartered air service.

East Face of Kichatna Spire.

JAMES GARRETT

11 Archangel Valley (Talkeetna Mountains) ✫✫✫

Be sure to visit this valley's 300' granite crags and boulders. Vast potential of granite walls on alpine peaks rising above flowered valleys. New route log at Alaska Mountaineering and Hiking in Anchorage. NPS land.

Classics: Zulu Wall: Zulu Warrior 10a; The Diamond: Toto 7; Aurora Slab: Aurora Slabiaulus 8, The Monolith Chickenhead 4, Local Motion 5; Snowbird Slab: Thin As Ice 10; The Inferno: Escape from the Lemming Ranch 10b; Nugget Boulder (35'): Banana Show 11a toprope.

Ref: C [110, 105, 110-10]; Guidebooks: Sieling's *The Scar: South Central Alaska Rock Climbing*, Pollard and Whitelaw's *First Steps: A Climber's Guide to the Archangel Valley*.

Directions: From Palmer (60 mi. north of Anchorage), head north on Hatcher Pass Rd. (aka Fish Hook Rd.). Turn right (north) on Archangel Rd. into Archangel Valley of the Talkeetna Mountains. Many areas include: Broken Dick (⁷/10 mi. up from Little Susitna Bridge on the right on Hatcher Pass Rd.) Archangel Valley Rd. webfoot formation (3 ⁸/10 mi. up Archangel Rd. from junction with Hatcher Pass Rd. across from mining cabins; excellent

walls of sound granite with eastern exposure), which contains Zulu Wall and The Diamond Wall (quickest access from road and lowest walls on webfoot), Whitespot and Catch the Wave (both accessed by mossy ramps up and left of the Diamond), and The Monolith, a nice granite crag above Fern Mine buildings and parking; Reed Valley–Snowbird Slab and Cornerstone, a 160' clean granite slab (park at Reed Valley Parking Lot, then go 1½ mi. up the jeep trail to a cabin; cross the creek, then take the trail toward Reed Lakes; slab is 100 yd. after crossing creek), The Inferno, and Nugget Boulder.

12 Wrangell Mountains National Park (Mt. Blackburn, 16,390') ✫✫✫

For alpinists, a remote glaciated range with peaks of 16,000' with granite walls. Mt. Blackburn is the highest, most famous mountain in the range, though the most visible is Mt. Sanford. Best months are May or September with June through August standard. NPS land.

Classics: Mt. Blackburn, University Peak.

Ref: AAJ ['97>94,'87-160], C [155-124, 105, 64], R [88-85, 61], S 7/69; Guidebook: Kelsey's *Climber's and Hiker's Guide to the World's Mountains*.

Directions: The Wrangell Mountains lie east of Glennallen Junction. Mt. Blackburn is usually accessed via Strelna. Other areas require use of airplane assists.

13 Seward Highway Areas ✫✫

Sedimentary bouldering and 80' sport climbing on road cuts with ugly, loose, fractured rock known locally as the "Chugach Crud." Mostly face-climbing routes with a few multipitch routes from 5.8–5.12. Rock must be treated with extreme caution and is not for climbers used to polished granite or splitter cracks. Beware of all trad placements and back up protection when possible. Great views of the inlet.

Classics: King Dome: Road Warrior 5.8, I Love Bea (two pitch trad, 5.8), Kingdom Reformed 9, Pivot Point 5.10a, Twinkle Toes 5.10c, Sky Pilot 5.10b, Suffering Simians 5.10b, Wild Kingdom 10b, Code Red 5.10c, Kingdome Reality 5.11+; Grunge Wall: If Then 11b, The Ram 12b.

Ref: C [119-30,110, 90]; Guidebooks: Sieling's *The Scar: South Central Alaska Rock Climbing*, Denkewalter and Whitelaw's *Thin White Line: A Climber's Guide*.

Directions: From Anchorage it's just 1 mi. south of town. Areas start 1 ²/10 mi. south of the Potters Marsh Weigh Station and proceed as follows: King Dome (approximately 1 ²/10 mi.), Grunge Wall (1 ⁴/10 mi.), Crack In The Woods (2 ¹/10 mi.) Pivot Point (2 ³/10 mi.), McHugh Boulders (2 ⁷/10 mi.), Boy Scout Rock (2 ⁷/10 mi.), Resolution Bluff (3 ⁶/10 mi.), Roadside Acracktion (3 ⁶/10 mi.), 5.5 crack (4 ³/10 mi.), Sunshine Ridge (4 ⁷/10 mi.), Sky Pilot (5 ⁷/10 mi.), Main Street 7 ½ mi.), Gorilla Rock (8 mi.), and Mosquito Ledge (32 ½ mi.). Also, another popular area, 36 mi. south of Seward, lies Middle Glacier Canyon, which is 4 mi. down the Portage Glacier Rd. Park at the viewing area and walk south.

14 Valdez Areas ✩✩✩✩✩

Valdez. Famed ice-climbing area of Alaska.

15 Lake Clark National Park (The Tusk, 5,780') ✩✩✩

Alpine granite formations. The Tusk is a 2,500' decomposing granite pinnacle and just one of many outstanding alpine summits in this glaciated area near Merrill Pass in the Chigmit Mountains, a virgin range in Alaska. Tusk-Speer/Bellamy Route IV 5.8 of 1986 is the classic. NPS land.

Ref: AAJ ['96-179, '87-91,'72-108], C 98(10/86)-5, S 8/77.

Directions: From Anchorage it's 125 mi. west in Lake Clark National Park.

16 Anchor Point Boulder ✩✩✩

One big, 20' granite boulder. This is one of the few bits of climbable rock in the Homer area. It's only one boulder, but it's a good one with twelve routes. The big plus is Mexican food and beer within a mile.

Classics: The Nose 5.10 (scary), The Traverse 5.10, The Cave Problem.

Ref: R. Meiners.

Directions: From Anchor Point drive south to Homer. At ½ mi. from Anchor Point, you cross the Anchor River. From the river it is approximately ⅛ mi. to a pullout on the left. Park here. Walk north approximately 200 yd. Boulder is visible from top of hill. Rubber boots are recommended for approach.

17 Wrangell–St. Elias National Park—St. Elias Mountains (Mt. St. Elias, 18,008') ✩✩✩✩✩

Alpine mountaineering. Mt. St. Elias lies on the border of Alaska and the Yukon. Most big-name peaks in this range (e.g., Mt. Logan, at 19,524') sit inside the Yukon territories (see Yukon and Northwest Territories chapter) and are big game trophies for mountaineers. NPS land, (907) 784–3295 (mountaineering information).

Classics: Mt. St. Elias's Hummingbird Ridge.

Ref: AAJ ['98-78, '93, 91-111, '86-178], C [165(12/96)-94, 105], R 8(5/85), S 2/75; For culture and history see H.R.H. Prince Luisi Amedeo's *The Ascent of Mt. St. Elias 1900*; Guidebooks: Roper and Steck's *Fifty Classic Climbs of North America,* Kelsey's *Climber's and Hiker's Guide to the World's Mountains.*

Directions: From Yakutat fly onto Malispina Glacier for approach to Mt. St. Elias.

18 Juneau Icefields (Devil's Paw and Mendenhall Towers) ✩✩✩✩

The Juneau Icefields comprise 1,500 sq. mi., feeding thirty-nine glaciers located in the Coast Mountains north and east of Alaska's state capital. There are 2,000' granite alpine walls and spires here. Devil's Paw, a little more than 8,400', is the highest summit of the area and a major rock spire on the border of Alaska and British Columbia. The Mendenhall Towers (6,910') also offers fine rock climbing with multipitch climbs on granite spires next to Mendenhall Glacier. One more thing: The annual snowfall exceeds 100'.

Ref: AAJ [98, 97, 96, 95, 94, 75-123, 70, 67], C [75,10/72]; Guidebooks: Kelsey's *Climber's and Hiker's Guide to the World's Mountains,* Delorme's *Alaska Atlas and Gazetteer.*

Directions: From Juneau, Devil's Paw and Mendenhall Towers lie north to northeast of town.

19 Burkett's Needle ✩✩✩✩

Alpine fifteen-pitched granite needle with a Kor/Davis Route done in August 1964. Foweraker, Cauthorn, and Collum completed the South Pillar Route in May 1995.

Classics: South Buttress V 5.10+ A3+.

Ref: AAJ '96-181(topo), C 168-62/106, R 99-32.

Directions: Outside of Petersburg. Fly into Baird Glacier.

20 Devil's Thumb (also listed in British Columbia chapter) ✩✩✩✩

Majestic alpine granite pinnacle.

Classics: Devil's Thumb's East Ridge IV 5.6.

Ref: *Alaska Sportsman* 9/49, AAJ [97, 96, '94 '92-80, 78, 74-34, 72-112, 47-269], C [168-106, 139, 128,118, 64, 58, 50(10/78)-8], M 59(1/78)-32, R 2(5/84), S [3/73, 5/72]; Jones's *Climbing in North America;* Guidebook: Roper and Steck's *Fifty Classic Climbs of North America.*

Directions: Devil's Thumb is usually accessed by helicopter or plane from Petersburg.

21 Misty Fjords National Monument (Punchbowl Wall) ✩✩✩✩

Granite walls/slabs on the Punchbowl Wall comprise the climbing in this incredible Alaskan region. The scenic 3,000' K-F-H Route done in 1994 starts just left of center of the whole wall at the water's edge and follows a steep bushwhack up the water channel to a tent ledge at 800'. Then there is much 5.4–5.7 climbing, with a 1,500–2,000' rock staircase (4' wide) of fourth-class simul-climbing with amazing views of the fjords. Twenty-three double-rope rappels. Very wet. NPS land.

Classics: Kruis–Fitch–Highleyman Route III 7.

Ref: S. Kruis 2/98.

Directions: Outside. of Ketchikan. Access by floatplane.

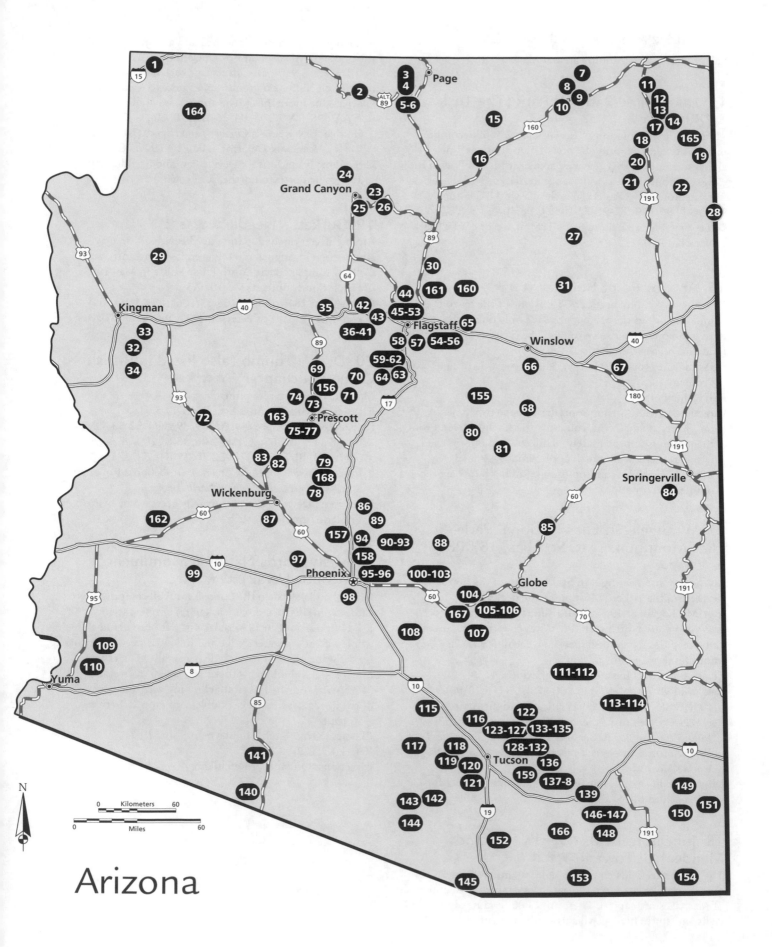

Arizona

Arizona

If winning isn't the only thing why doesn't anyone go for the bronze? —Bud Dry billboard

Arizona. It's where people go to retire, right? Not if you're a climber. The geology, a combination of basin and range territory in the south and the Colorado Plateau up north, yields more exposed rock than in any other state. Add an arid to semiarid climate, and the only thing growing on the cliffs is the number of routes and climbers.

Tucson is the southern hub of Arizona climbing and a popular stopping point between the winter destination areas, Hueco Tanks and Joshua Tree. Mt. Lemmon rises 6,000′ above Tucson's sprawl to an elevation of 9,157′. Crags line the dangerous winding highway all the way to the top. Sixty mi. east of Tucson are the Dragoon Mountains, where the famous Apache chief, Cochise, hid out amid the nest of granite spires and boulders. Fifty mi. west of Tucson is Arizona's sole grade VI big wall, Baboquivari Peak.

Many more areas dwell far from the beaten path. So, draw a circle around the southeast corner of Arizona and start climbing. As longtime Tucsonites know, the multitude of backcountry granite spires and domes will keep one well-laden with enough climbs for an adventurous career.

Phoenix is the hot spot of Arizona climbing, in the literal sense. Queen Creek and The Superstitions are two of the warmest areas in the nation. The coolest climbing, both literally and figuratively, surrounds Flagstaff. Perched on the Colorado Plateau, Flagstaff teems with numerous short basalt, sandstone, and limestone areas. If you're a crack climber, Paradise Forks is aptly named. Slightly southwest, Prescott showcases the intimidating bastion of Granite Mountain. Moving north, the Grand Canyon offers backcountry climbers an adventure/epic playground.

Last, and least due only to its illicit nature, is the climbing in the northeast corner of the state, Navajoland. Sandstone spires don't get any more impressive, attested to by the numerous movies and advertisements filmed in and around Monument Valley.

Retire in Arizona? Don't count on it.

1 Virgin River Gorge ✫✫✫✫
The sport climbing gorge of I–15. This enormous canyon's wild geology offers 180′ grueling limestone sport climbs featuring one of the United State's hardest, Necessary Evil 5.14c. Approximately sixty routes, mostly above 5.11, are on various walls, including Sun Wall, Sun Cave, Paradigm Wall, Mentor Wall, Planet Earth Wall, Grassy Ledges Wall, Warm Up Wall, and Blasphemy Wall. Randy Leavitt's Planet Earth 5.14a and Boone Speed's F-Dude are just a couple of the many testpieces. Sport climbs require 55 m ropes as well as ear plugs for road noise. Camping at Virgin River Recreation Area (fee), a few miles east on nearby Blackrock Rd. Late autumn through early spring. BLM, (435) 688–3200.

Classics: The Paradigm 12a, Acid Test 12a, Velvet Underground 12c, Heroine 12d, Dark Boy 13b, Fall of Man 12d/13a, Dude 13c, Homo Sapien 13d, Necessary Evil 14c.

Ref: C [195-23, 194-32, 183-20, 177-58, 168-25], C [167-26, 162-47, 160-46, 131(4/92), 127], R [94-86, 90-24, 79-16, 74-24, 73-21, 44], SC [9/92, 6/91]; online guide www.thedeadpoint.com/guides/vrg.html; Guidebooks: McCray's *Welcome to Las Vegas Limestone*, Green's *Rock Climbing Arizona*, Goss's *Rock Climbs of Southwest Utah*, McQuade's *Vegas Rocks: Rock Climbs*, Goss's *Too Much Rock, Not Enough Life.*

Directions: From St. George, Utah, pop approximately 20 mi. south on I–15 to Virgin River Gorge. Best parking at strip south of bridge. Hike east 300 yd. Beware: Citations issued for pull-off parking.

2 Jacob Lake Boulders ✫✫
These 30′ limestone/sandstone, south-facing boulders and shelves lend to sharp challenges on this part of the Kaibab Plateau. Fun exploration. USFS–Kaibab NF, (520) 635–8200.

Ref: C. Dunn.

Directions: East of Jacob Lake, visible from road.

3 Toothrock (in the Vermilion Cliffs) ✫✫✫
This remarkably huge, isolated 2,000′ sandstone monolith of twenty varied pitches gets lost in the immensity of the Vermilion Cliffs. This is a big wall undertaking, so come prepared for loose rock with a helmet on your head and expect a big wall bivy. Summit elevation is 6,158′. Lowrey Spring is potable but mineralized. Toothrock was first ascended by Spencer McIntyre and George Bain via the

Lost Love Route in 1977 and is still today a proud notch in the belt for any climber ascending the remote heights. While Toothrock is sought for its summit experience, the rugged surrounding cliffs also offer untold climbing adventures. BLM, (602) 417–9200.

Classics: Lost Love Route V 5.9 A3, Keith/Insley Aid Route (Matter In Motion V 5.9 A3+), East Buttress (Gagner/McDonald Route) 11p 5.10 A2.

Ref: G. Bain, G. Rink; AAJ '94-147; Guidebook: Bjornstad's *Desert Rock.*

Directions: From Marble Canyon head north approximately 2 mi. down Lee's Ferry Rd. to Cathedral Wash. Toothrock is approximately 2 ½ mi. to the west, separate from but appearing subtly as one with the massive cliffs. Hike halfway up the wash exiting on left up a talus slope, just before the dry falls. Dirt road leads to Lowrey Spring (base of rock). Three difficult aid routes start on south side.

4 Lee's Ferry Boulders ✰

Thirty-foot-high mushroom summits on friable, high-risk rock. The Shinarump sandstone may provide a "skin-a-rump" experience. Glean a new sensation from the pump of sketchiness. Lee's Ferry is the departure point for Grand Canyon river trips. BLM, (602) 417–9200.

Directions: Just west of bridge over Marble Canyon, turn right and stem north on Lee's Ferry Rd. Bizarre bouldering forms are obvious on left. Toothrock is farther north up road. From junction of Hwy. 89A and Lee's Ferry Rd., more sandstone bouldering blocks lie farther west on Hwy. 89A toward House Rock and are visible along road.

5 Jackass Canyon ✰✰✰

Tight, "roadrunner-cartoon-style" canyon with sandstone boulders and walls leads down to Colorado River. Potential wild leads. Trout fishing, too. BLM, (602) 417–9200.

Ref: I. Hickman, J. Gaun, and J. Symans.

Directions: From Page head south on Hwy. 89. Turn north onto Hwy. 89A, heading toward Marble Canyon Bridge. A few miles south of bridge look for silver water tank 100 yd. off to west of pavement. Head west, following dirt roads a few miles to drainage entrance (usually cars parked). Steep scrambling (enough to stop anyone's Parkinje fibers) in Jackass Canyon continues for an hour to boulders through drainage and near river. (Recommend obtaining topo map in Flagstaff or Page.)

6 Echo Cliffs ✰✰✰

Mostly unexplored area of jumbled bouldering blocks and cliffs—good problems. Scenic views of the incipience of the Grand Canyon and the Vermilion Cliffs. Matt Penrod and Kyran Keisling, and others from Page, have put up another eight to ten routes at the Echo Cliffs. Most of the routes are right near "the cut." BLM, (602) 417–9200.

Directions: From Page head south on Hwy. 89 to obvious road cleft overlooking the beautiful incipience of the Grand Canyon to the west. Echo Cliffs and boulders start at Antelope Pass (large roadcut) above Bitter Springs. (Bitter Springs is at the junction of Hwy. 89 and Hwy. 89A.)

7 Monument Valley Navajo Tribal Park (closed) ✰✰✰✰✰

The world's most visually inspiring chessboard of 500′ sandstone pieces. Classic formations include Mitchell Butte, Gray Whiskers, Mitchell Mesa, West Mitten, East Mitten, Merrick Butte, Elephant Butte, Three Sisters, Camel Butte, Totem Pole, the Yei-bi-chei, Rooster Rock, and The Thumb. Illegal and off-limits to all rock climbers (except big-dollar movie and advertising expeditions). As this is a historical reference work as much as a practical road guide to climbing, Navajo Reservation climbs are included here. Climbing is still illegal for all rock climbers on reservation lands. The yearning for soft sandstone spires can easily be fulfilled in other parts of Arizona, Utah, New Mexico, and Colorado legally. BIA.

Directions: From Kayenta go north on Hwy. 163 to the Utah border. Head east into Monument Valley Navajo Tribal Park.

Ref: A (5/70), AAJ ['97, '96-159, '94-148, '76-453, 72-130, 68-154, 67], C [189-112, 181-88, 157-106, 91], OB 55(2/81), R [89-48, 79-56], S [6/76, 3/68]; Kar's *Beyond the Vertical*, Jones's *Climbing in North America*; Guidebook: Bjornstad's *Desert Rock.*

8 Agathla–Owl Rock–Half Dome ✰✰✰

Agathla means "piles of wool" in Navajo, "El Capitan of the Desert" in climbing, and 1,500′ volcanic neck in geologic terms. Owl Rock is a 350′ sandstone spire. Half Dome is a 400′ circular sandstone butte. A helmet and loose-rock savvy are a must on Agathla's not-to-be trusted volcanics. First ascents of Agathla's West Face: Herb Conn, R. Garner, and L. Pedrick in May 1949. First ascents of Owl Rock by F. Beckey and H. T. Carter in 1966 and Half Dome by G. Rink and T. Toula in 1990. From a photographer's standpoint this is perhaps the world's most inspiring landscape. BIA.

Classics: Agathla: West Face IV 7, Owl Rock; Half Dome: Southeast Corner III 5.12a.

Ref: A (5/70) Guidebook: Bjornstad's *Desert Rock.*

Directions: From Kayenta go 7 ½ mi. north on Hwy. 163. Agathla is the stunning 1,500′ volcanic neck on the east side of the road. Owl Rock is perched directly to the west. Half Dome is the rounded dome a few miles southwest of Owl Rock.

9 Church Rock and Miscellaneous Volcanic Necks ✰

Sizeable 500′, miscellaneous volcanic necks that are crumbly, crumbly to the core, like mini-Agathlans. Chaistla Butte was first climbed by Gary Ziegler and Bob Doane. BIA.

Ref: Guidebook: Bjornstad's *Desert Rock.*

Directions: From Kayenta it is a few miles north/northeast of town, accessible either north along Hwy. 163 (Chaistla

Butte is before mm 400) or east along Hwy. 160 (Church Rock is past mm 400).

10 Kayenta Boulders ✪✪
Roadside Dakota sandstone blocks on Highway 160. BIA.
Directions: From Kayenta trend south on Hwy. 160 to Tsegi Canyon. The Kayenta Boulders are Dakota sandstone blocks that present themselves at various times on the east side of the road.

11 Standing Rock ✪✪
Obvious, super-soft 400′ Wingate sandstone spire/blob. The south face hand crack (5.8) is the route to the top. BIA.
Classics: South Face I 8.
Ref: C 83(4/83)-34; Guidebook: Bjornstad's *Desert Rock.*
Directions: From Rock Point go 1 mi. north to Standing Rock, on the east side of Hwy. 191 at mm 497. Turn at dirt road on the north side of formation and park.

12 The Whale's Tail and The Whale (aka Dancing Rocks) ✪✪
One-of-a-last-kind, whale-shaped, soft 500′ sandstone twin spires. From south of the formation on Hwy. 191, these look like a whale's head with the tip of the tail coming out of the water. One must have liver for these two. Don't forget: It's 80 mi. to the nearest liquor store. BIA.
Classics: The Whale Northeast IV 10 A1 6p and The Whale's Tail SE Arête III. 10a C1.
Ref: C [88, 83(5/83)-34]; Guidebook: Bjornstad's *Desert Rock.*
Directions: From Rock Point go 2 mi. south on Hwy. 191 to mm 490. The Whale (600′) and The Whale's Tail (550′) are both on the east side of road.

13 Smith Spire and Rock Point Spire ✪
Loose 400′ sandstone spires, both with aid routes. Smith Spire resembles a light bulb from the side and is north of Lukachukai Wash. Rock Point Spire is shaped like a pyramid and is south of Lukachukai Wash, near mm 488. The first ascent was made by Todd Gordon et al. in 1983. Be prepared for the loose! BIA.
Classics: Smith Spire: West Face I 8 A4; Rock Point Spire II 9 A3.
Ref: C 83(4/83)-34; Guidebook: Bjornstad's *Desert Rock.*
Directions: From Rock Point go south on Hwy. 191 past The Whale (at 2 mi.) continuing until Smith Spire is visible as semiattached to the mesa to the east of the road. Rock Point Spire is the next thin spire against the mesa.

14 Los Gigantes Buttes ✪✪
Giant 400′ sandstone buttes. Loose rock. 5.10 aid routes. Gigantic beauties holding super-soft sandstone curves in a backdrop of the Lukachukai Mountains. BIA.
Classics: Los Gigantes Butte III 5.10 A3 East Face.
Ref: C [88, 83(5/83)-34]; Guidebook: Bjornstad's *Desert Rock.*
Directions: From Round Rock, near Round Rock Trading Post, follow dirt roads north/northeast to the southeast side of Los Gigantes Buttes for about 9 mi. Los Gigantes Butte III has a double top and is located north of Buttes I and II.

15 Portal to Paradise Pinnacle (aka The Poodle) ✪✪
The route on this slender, white 70′ sandstone spire is I 5.7 A2. First done by S. Baxter, L. Dexter, and J. Whitfield in 1967 on the south side of the tower. Pictured in *Standing Up Country* by C. Gregory Crampton. This 60′ pointy got its name from the inscription at its base, PORTAL TO PARADISE (aka The Poodle or The Monolith). BIA.
Ref: S. Baxter; AAJ '71-370, R 66-56; Guidebook: Bjornstad's *Desert Rock.*
Directions: From Red Lake go north on Hwy. 160 for a few mi. Turn north on Hwy. 16 for 3 7/10 mi., then turn left onto Navajo Route 6270 (dirt road) for approximately 5 6/10 mi. Turn left again on Navajo Route 6260 (dirt road) for 1 7/10 mi. Turn right onto dirt tracks, pass a windmill at 7/10 mi., and a hogan at 2 mi. Ask permission to go on through the horse corrals and the south side of White Mesa, a few mi. northeast of White Mesa Arch. (Approximate directions.) The Portal to Paradise Pinnacle is barely visible as a slender needle on the south skyline of White Mesa. Locate this and use your nose to sniff it out. Approach during the day.

16 Elephant's Feet (closed) ✪✪
Twinned, 70′ white sandstone spires. Aid climbs. BIA.
Ref: AAJ '88-142, C 111.
Directions: From Red Lake the Elephant's Feet I 5.9 A2 are just northeast on Hwy. 160, about a mile on the left. Psst . . . stealth isn't just a rubber found on 5.10 climbing shoes.

17 Chinle Spire, Round Rock Butte, and The Pope ✪✪✪
Wonderfully soft 400′ sandstone spires. BIA.
Classics: Chinle Spire III 5.9 A4 and The Pope III 5.10 A3+.
Ref: C [99, 83(4/83)-34]; Guidebook: Bjornstad's *Desert Rock.*
Directions: From Round Rock, at the junction of Hwy. 191 and Hwy. 12, go north on Hwy. 191 for approximately 3 mi. (north of Round Rock and Little Round Rock) at mm 482.4. Turn southwest onto a dirt road with a gate that may be locked. This private road branches to the north/northwest side of Round Rock Butte (the slender shaft of Chinle Spire is obvious here). The Pope is south of Chinle Spire a short distance and is clearly visible. Chinle Spire and The Pope have wonderfully soft sandstone. Round Rock Butte is fourth class. Illegal.

18 Many Farms Pinnacle ☆☆

A 200' sandstone pinnacle. Campground at Many Farms. BIA.

Ref: C [83(4/83)-34] Guidebook: Bjornstad's *Desert Rock*.

Directions: From Many Farms, Many Farms Pinnacle is 3 mi. north, adjacent to Hwy. 191.

19 Tsaile Peak

Large, dark, volcanic peak (mound) to the east of Canyon De Chelly. BIA.

Ref: C 83(5/83)-34.

Directions: From the town of Tsaile, Tsaile Peak is approximately 2 mi. east.

20 Window Rock III Crag/Pratilus Spire ☆☆

Sandstone features. Dr. Shredmore, a renowned rad mountain biker, reports Route 59 from Chinle to Kayenta is the preferable road for drinking and driving . . . mountain bikes. Black Mesa to the southwest rises 1,500', while slickrock beckons on the other side of the highway. BIA.

Ref: C [88, 83(5/83)-34]; Guidebook: Bjornstad's *Desert Rock*.

Directions: North of Chinle. At Many Farms (junction of Hwy. 191 and Hwy. 59), go south on Hwy. 191 toward Chinle for 1 2/10 mi. Turn west (right) onto Navajo Route 18, trending left at 3 1/2, 3 8/10, and 4 mi. until you arrive at the parking area at 7 4/10 mi. Vehicles not good in soft sand (i.e., two-wheel drive) may park earlier. Window Rock III arch is 1/4 mi. on the left (south), and Window Rock III crag is a little farther west.

21 Dead Horse Crag and Elephant Butte ☆☆☆

A 200' sandstone locomotive-shaped crag with classic 5.8–5.10 hand cracks. BIA.

Ref: C [88, 83(5/83)-34]; Guidebook: Bjornstad's *Desert Rock*.

Directions: West of Chinle. At Many Farms (junction of Hwy. 191 and Hwy. 59), go south on Hwy. 191 toward Chinle for 1 2/10 mi. Turn west (right) onto Navajo Route 18, trending left at 3 1/2, 3 8/10, and 4 mi. until you arrive at the parking area at 7 4/10 mi. Vehicles not good in soft sand (i.e., two-wheel drive) may park earlier. Window Rock III arch is 1/4 mi. on left (south), and Window Rock III crag is a little farther west.

22 Spider Rock (in Canyon De Chelly) (closed) ☆☆☆☆☆

Spiritual 800' sandstone spire in a magical canyon. Spider Rock is a full day's climb of chimneys and offwidths. First ascent in 1956 by Californians Jerry Gallwas, Don Wilson, and Mark Powell. As Navajo legend has it, the Spider Woman hoards the bones of her victims on top. Read Chuck Pratt's classic article, "View from Deadhorse Point"

(*Ascent*, May 1970). Also, a climb ascends Arachnid Mesa. Unfortunately, Spider Rock is closed to climbing, as is all climbing on reservation lands. Navajo guides must accompany hikers just to legally enter this classic, Southwestern canyon. Expect bigger busts than Dolly Parton's. But, both are American classics. BIA.

Classics: Spider Rock IV 5.10+, Arachnid Mesa IV 5.10 A4.

Ref: A (5/70), AAJ '84, C [88, 83(4/83)-5/34], S 6/71; Jones's *Climbing in North America*; Guidebook: Bjornstad's *Desert Rock*.

Directions: From Chinle saunter east to Canyon De Chelly (park signs). Go to Spider Rock overlook (signs) and dwell on the spirit of rock climbing. Access down into the canyon and Spider Rock is via the Bat Trail. A National Park Service guide must accompany visitors.

23 Grand Canyon (of the Colorado River) ☆☆☆☆

Larger than life itself. Exotic riverside rock encompassing climbing on obsidian, sandstone and granite on the ubiquitous walls, crags, and boulders of the inner Grand Canyon. For starters: The Kwagunt III 5.9 is one of the more technically named summits, with a 3,000' approach climbed in 1979 by Peter Gibb. Or, the Grapevine Buttress V (10p) 5.10 A4, done in 1972 by Bego Gerhart. Finally, The Monument III 5.10, near Granite Rapids, is a unique 3-pitch desert spire with just one 165' rappel. Climbers on a Colorado River trip will be enticed to utilize a rope, harness, and shoes . . . if they had just brought them along. NPS, (520) 638-7875; 1:00–5:00 P.M. Monday–Friday.

Ref: G. Rink, J. Middendorf, J. Olson, J. Symans, R. Turan; M 77, R 72-58; S [6/73, 12/69, 12/68, 3/68, 3/66, 9/65, 6/64]; Guidebooks: Butchart's *Grand Canyon Treks*, Annerino's *Hiking the Grand Canyon*, Steck's *Hiking Grand Canyon Loops*.

Directions: Grand Canyon Village. Requires rafting/boating the Colorado River through the Grand Canyon. Many potential bouldering/cragging opportunities, e.g., Soap Creek Canyon. River permits (since 1995 there has been a ten-year waiting list) needed for private parties (602–638–7843).

24 Grand Canyon National Park Temples ☆☆☆

Climbing as timeless as the Canyon itself. The main allure of Grand Canyon climbing is the Indiana Jones aerobic-adventure session to be garnered from ascents of the 150 varied sandstone temples up to 1,000' (Zoroaster, Mt. Hayden) on small mesas, summits, and pinnacles away from the canyon rim. Temple names were derived from Eastern religions. Credit for many of the ascents is given to steel-calved Harvey J. Butchart. See Annerino's *Hiking the Grand Canyon* for a list of climbs and climbers. Routes vary from nontechnical, exposed summits to roped, technical routes. Count on at least a couple grueling approach days if attempting a distant backcountry summit. Try the Web site below for extensive beta. Backcountry permit required for overnight camping; $10.00 per permit and $5.00 per person per night. Bring water. NPS, (520) 638-7875; 1:00–5:00 P.M. Monday–Friday.

Classics: Mt. Hayden: Pegasus 10+; Zoroaster Temple: SW Face 9+, Angel's Gate, Brahma Temple, Commanche Point Pinnacle (Lost Arrow Spire of the Grand Canyon), and many others.

Ref: G. Bain; M 77, R [72-58, 21(44)], S 10/83; Annerino's *Adventuring in Arizona*, Adkison's *Hiking Grand Canyon National Park*, www.arizonas-vertical-web.com/Grand Canyon.htm; Guidebooks: Green's *Rock Climbing Arizona*, Butchart's *Grand Canyon Treks*, Annerino's *Hiking the Grand Canyon*, Steck's *Hiking Grand Canyon Loops*.

Directions: From Grand Canyon Village get a permit and information from the NPS backcountry office on the South Rim. Prepare to hike your butt off on various park trails to various isolated temples such as Zoroaster, Mt. Hayden, et al.

25 Grand Canyon National Park (Bright Angel Trailhead/Twins Overlook) ✯✯✯

The Grand Canyon offers unlimited short limestone rim-rock routes. Two places to start are just west of the Bright Angel Trailhead (developed with anchors—see Green's guide), and Twins Overlook is a popular 40' limestone climbing area for the local rangers. Fifty routes. Some bolts. Fantastic views. The stay for an average visitor to this geologic wonder of the world is about one hour; the bouldering/toproping here should keep you longer than that. Please consult with NPS rangers for climbing information and guides. NPS, (520) 638-7875.

Ref: M 56, Guidebooks: Green's *Rock Climbing Arizona*, Toula's *A Cheap Way to Fly: Free Climbing Guide to Northern Arizona*, NPS guide.

Directions: From Grand Canyon Village float east along the rim to Twins Overlook. Practice area below road.

26 Cameron Boulders (Little Colorado River Gorge Area) ✯✯✯

Excellent, difficult boulder problems on 20' sandstone blocks and short-walled arroyos. The sublime Little Colorado River Gorge, a favorite among itinerant tightrope walkers, is a click of a shutter to the north. USFS—Kaibab NF, (520) 635-8200.

Ref: D. Cilley, B. Hatcher.

Directions: Cameron to Desert View. From Cameron go west approximately 20 mi. on Hwy. 64, climbing the grade to Grand Canyon Village. The Cameron Boulders consist of at least three bouldering bands that are visible from mm 283 to 275. A couple bands are distant left of the road, requiring about ten-minute approaches. There's also another area on the right in the junipers via a dirt road.

27 Keams Canyon ●

Short walls and blocks of soft sandstone hardly justify a stop. The three Hopi mesas to the west are an interesting rest-day visit containing Oraibi, the oldest continuously inhabited settlement in the United States. Authentic pottery, kachina dolls, and weavings. This is sacred land to the Hopi—no photography is allowed. BIA.

Directions: At Keams Canyon along Hwy. 264; rocks and boulders are obvious.

28 Angel Wing (closed) ✯✯

See New Mexico number 74.

29 Hackberry Dome ✯✯✯

An off-the-beaten-track quality granite dome with multi-pitched routes. Hackberry Dome is a white apron with the left side sloping off. Many routes done by the Syndicato Granitica and Prescott College with more to do. Rock quality varies from Joshua Tree quartz monzonite to Yosemite granite. Many other domes. If you're traveling through Seligman and want a shake and a chuckle, stop in at Delgadillo's Snow Cap. BLM, (602) 417-9200.

Classics: Super Blue (layback flake).

Ref: S. Baxter, L. Coats.

Directions: From Hackberry head west on Hwy. 66 for approximately 6 mi., then turn northwest on a good dirt road (possibly called Antares Rd.) to the granite dome. Hackberry Dome can be seen from the dirt road off in the distance as one drives in. Park at base of slope. Long hike up slope.

30 Citadel Sink (in Wupatki National Monument) (closed) ✯✯

A climbing curio amid the windswept volcanic cinder cones. This 50' basalt sinkhole with limestone below lends company to the Anasazi ruins of Wupatki. Minimal climbing has been done here due to the long arm of the NPS law; i.e., it's illegal. Mostly roped climbs (trasher rope recommended) with very little bouldering. Fractured rock requires "sound" judgment. NPS, (520) 333-4301.

Ref: J. Gaun.

Directions: From Flagstaff go 12 mi. north on Hwy. 89. Turn east on Wupatki, New Mexico, turnoff (CR 395), going approximately 4 mi. to Citadel Ruin. Park. Hike five to ten minutes west to visible basalt rim.

31 Hopi Buttes ✯

An airy landscape of volcanic buttes, 300' pinnacles (6,500' summits), and friable boulders split between the Navajo and Hopi Reservations; perfumed dung heaps from a true rock-climbing perspective. Mostly fourth-class ascents although walls of grainy, chossy rock injected with volcanic bombs could challenge the aid-climbing adventurer. Picturesque boulders with holds that'll snap back at you faster than a surly climbing partner. BIA.

Directions: From Winslow hop north on Hwy. 87 to the small village of Dilkon. Most of the Hopi Buttes formations are visible along Hwy. 87 and include the named buttes of (south to north): Chimney Butte, Castle Butte, Elephant Butte, Round Top, Montezuma's Chair, Bad Medicine Butte, Nipple Butte, and Egloffstein Butte.

32 Walnut Creek Wall ✮✮✮

Large, dark, granite dome with multipitched routes. Alluring adventures. Rattlesnakes. BLM, (520) 692-4400.

Ref: R 21 (insert); Guidebook: Toula's *A Cheap Way to Fly: Free Climbing Guide to Northern Arizona.*

Directions: From Kingman go 12 mi. west and south on I-40 to exit 37 (Griffith Rd.). Take the dirt road east over the railroad tracks near town, then continue 8 mi. over foothills to Walnut Creek Wall. It's a forty-minute approach up the drainage south of the road.

33 Hualapai Mountain Park ✮✮✮

Plenitude of 300′ granite, pegmatitic rock formations in a rugged, high-elevation (8,400′) desert environment. The

Climbers on Liquid Sky, 5.11, Paradise Forks.

DAVID NATIONS

Hualapai (or "Pine Tree Folk") is an Indian tribe that was moved from this land to a nearby reservation in the 1870s. Pay camping/cabins. Mohave County Parks, (520) 757-0915.

Ref: Guidebook: Martin's *Arizona Mountains: Hiking and Climbing Guide.*

Directions: From Kingman jump east on I-40 to exit 51. Follow Stockton Hill Rd. south (signs) for 14 mi. to Hualapai Mountain Park. Rock scattered about park in dense chaparral.

34 Hualapai Wall ✮✮✮

The 600′ gneissic Hualapai Wall boasts positive incut holds. There are two subsidiary towers, Lost Angel of the Desert (slender) and Eagle's Nest (large and square). Teeming with Mojave rattlesnakes. BLM, (520) 692-4400.

Classics: All Eagles' Nest routes.

Ref: R 21 (insert); Guidebook: Toula's *A Cheap Way to Fly: Free Climbing Guide to Northern Arizona.*

Directions: From Kingman jump 25 mi. west and south on I-40 to Alamo Rd. (exit 25) at Yucca. Go east on Alamo Rd., then south past golf ball house. Hualapai Wall is visible high up in the distant eastern hills. Continue east on Boriana Mine Rd. (Mohave CR 15), a paved road passing Apache Rd. in 1 ½ mi. from I-40 and hitting rough dirt road at 2 ⁶/10 mi. from I-40. Reach old mine (locked gate may force early parking). It's a one-and-a-half hour hiking approach to Hualapai Wall.

35 Johnson Crater (aka Ashfork Bouldering) ✮✮✮

Sinkhole lined with short, 25′ basalt challenges. USFS-Kaibab NF, (520) 635-8200.

Ref: Aitchison and Grubbs's *The Hiker's Guide to Arizona.*

Directions: From Williams descend west from town on I-40 for approximately 15 mi. Exit at Welch Interchange. Go north on FR 6 for 2 mi. Johnson Crater is on the left. A little farther up the road, Johnson Canyon is on the right. (You may want to check here, too.)

36 Bill Williams Monument (aka Finger Rock or Chimney Rock) ✮✮✮

This 100′ volcanic pinnacle lies on the serene southwest flank of Bill Williams Mountain. Bill Williams Monument (aka Finger Rock or Chimney Rock) saw its first ascent in 1956 by Powell, Gallwas, and Wilson. This landmark is visible on the western flank of Bill Williams Mountain when traveling east on I-40 from Ash Fork. Good North Face Route 5.9 by Gary Sapp et al. Rappel off north side, one rope. Three routes total. USFS-Kaibab NF, (520) 635-8200.

Ref: AAJ '71-371, R 21(9/87)-32; Guidebooks: Martin's *Arizona Mountains: Hiking and Climbing Guide,* Toula's *A Cheap Way to Fly: Free Climbing Guide to Northern Arizona.*

Directions: From Williams bounce 4 mi. south of town (follow ski-area signs). Turn right up road FS 111 toward the lookout on Bill Williams Mountain. After numerous switchbacks, find a CHIMNEY ROCK sign on the left. Park. From the sign hike the trail to the west side of the mountain. Bill Williams Monument is the obvious pinnacle on the south-facing slope, 1/2 mi. distant to the northwest. Numerous other rock formations exist in the area.

37 The Balls (on Bill Williams Mountain) ★★★

Mountainside bouldering on 18' dacite B1–B2 Bob Murray fingertip specialist toprope problems. Bring 3/8" hanger and wrench, extension slings, and steel tendons. Nine classic 20' toprope or hiball routes. USFS–Kaibab NF, (520) 635–8200.

Ref: Guidebooks: Murray's *Flagstaff Bouldering Guide*, Toula's *A Cheap Way to Fly: Free Climbing Guide to Northern Arizona*.

Directions: From Williams bounce 4 mi. south of town (follow ski-area signs). Turn right up road FS 111 toward the lookout on Bill Williams Mountain. Continue a few switchbacks up until a rock dike (pay attention here!) meets the road on left. Now backtrack 100 yd. down the road. The Balls are located below the road, partially obscured by trees. (Much farther up the road, via many switchbacks, is Bill Williams Monument, Number 36).

38 Paradise Forks ★★★★

For any crack climber worth a jam, this is a must-visit. One of the best condensed 5.10–5.12 crack climbing areas in the United States. Classic traditional crack and arête cragging on smooth, clean 120' basalt flows. Had Henry Barber stopped here before going to Yosemite Valley, he might never have hit California. Climbable year-round, if roads allow access. One hundred and twenty-five 5.8–5.13 routes. At 7,000', the Flagstaff area features fine diversified bouldering and cragging in the world's largest ponderosa pine forest. Free camping on National Forest lands away from parking area. September–May. USFS–Kaibab NF, (520) 635–8200.

Classics: Black Rose 8, Yogi Cracks 8/9, Heart of Darkness 9+, Waterslip Down 10a, East of Eden 10, Jolly Roger 10, Sine Language 10+, Prow Crack 11a, Liquid Sky 11, Paradise Lost 11d, Sail Away 12-, Americans At Arapiles 12, The Equalizer 13a.

Ref: C [186-64, 178-113, 105, 102,100, 99], R 21(9/87)-32; Guidebooks: Toula's *A Cheap Way to Fly: Free Climbing Guide to Northern Arizona*, Bloom's *Paradise Forks*, Lawson's *A Climber's Guide to the Paradise Forks*.

Directions: From Flagstaff parade approximately 25 mi. west on I–40. Head south at Garland Prairie exit (a few mi. east of the town of Williams) for 1 3/10 mi. Turn left after tracks onto FS 141 for 4 7/10 mi. Turn right on FS 109 for 3 3/10 mi. Just before white-railed bridge, turn left into USFS cul-de-sac (sans portapotties). Park. Hike a few minutes east to canyon rim and the climbs below in Paradise Forks. Rappel in. Welcome to paradise!

39 Sycamore Point ★★★

Long, remote rim of 50' basalt columns above scenic Sycamore Canyon Wilderness. More than fifty routes. Many unnamed routes done by D. Cilley, J. Mattson, T. Toula, et al. in the 1980s. Panoramic views and camping in situ. USFS–Kaibab NF, (520) 635–8200.

Ref: Guidebook: Toula's *A Cheap Way to Fly: Free Climbing Guide to Northern Arizona*.

Directions: From Flagstaff go approximately 25 mi. west on I–40. Head south at Garland Prairie exit for 1 3/10 mi. Turn left after tracks onto FS 141 for 4 7/10 mi. Turn right on FS 109 (passing Paradise Forks turnoff at 3 1/2 mi.). Turn left at White Horse Lake, following signs to Sycamore Point on FS 12 to overview. Park at cul-de-sac. Hike along rim to the west (that's right as you look into the canyon) to better quality, longer (40') basalt columns.

40 Boy Scout Canyon ★★

Columnar, 80' basalt flows similar to the Oak Creek Overlook. Obtain permission from the Boy Scout Camp before climbing here. USFS–Kaibab NF, (520) 635–8200.

Ref: I. Hickman; Guidebook: Toula's *A Cheap Way to Fly: Free Climbing Guide to Northern Arizona*.

Directions: From Flagstaff (approximately an hour drive), follow I–40 W. Turn south on Parks Rd. exit, number 178. Take FS 141 south. Turn south on FS 527 to Boy Scout Camp. Signs present. Boy Scout Canyon is south of the Boy Scout Camp. Ask for permission there.

41 Volunteer Canyon ★★★

Startling side canyon of the Sycamore Canyon Wilderness Area. More than 12 routes that are mostly 5.8–5.10. Tralfamidore 5.9+, on an 180' long basalt flow, is one of the longest climbs near Flagstaff. Other nice climbs are Beautiful Day 5.8 and the brilliant yellow-lichened Canary Crack 5.10. Ice climbing sometimes. Also, Volunteer Spire, at a junction with Sycamore Canyon, offers a backcountry five-pitch 300' 5.10 route on an isolated limestone finger. Rough roads; when wet they have sticky "Krazy glue" mud. USFS–Kaibab NF, (520) 635–8200.

Ref: A. Newman; Guidebook: Toula's *A Cheap Way to Fly: Free Climbing Guide to Northern Arizona*.

Directions: From Flagstaff follow I–40 W. Turn south on Parks Rd. exit, number 178. Take FS 141 south. Turn south on FS 527 to Boy Scout Camp. Continue on FS 527 until the canyon (sign) appears on right.

42 The Horseshoe ★★

This 40' horseshoe of short basalt walls is valued for nice bouldering, short toproping, and a Forest Service petroglyph area. USFS–Kaibab NF, (520) 635–8200.

Ref: Mangum's *Flagstaff Hikes*; Guidebook: Toula's *A Cheap Way to Fly: Free Climbing Guide to Northern Arizona*.

Directions: From Parks go west of town to the "snowplay area." Then go north on USFS roads to The Horseshoe of basalt.

43 Parks Wall ✫✫✫

Fun bouldering and short 25' topropes up to B1 on sunny, south-facing bouldering wall. Old Granitico Syndicato climbing party site. More than 20 routes to B1+. USFS–Kaibab NF, (520) 635–8200.

Classics: Petroglyph Corner 8, Webster's Low Traverse, The Eraser B1.

Ref: C 62; Guidebooks: Toula's *A Cheap Way to Fly: Free Climbing Guide to Northern Arizona,* Murray's *Flagstaff Bouldering Guide.*

Directions: From Flagstaff zip west for fifteen minutes on I–40. At Parks Rd. exit, number 178, turn south over I–40. Turn left (east) paralleling the railroad tracks (and I–40) on north side of the tracks for 6/10 mi. on dirt service road. Park. Hike south across tracks, over fence, and into pines for 100 yd. With a nose for basalt, sniff out a small southeast-facing outcrop known as the Parks Wall.

44 Southwest Face of San Francisco Peaks ✫✫✫

Visible (especially with binoculars) on southwest shoulder of San Francisco Peaks, a 100' volcanic row offering out-of-the-way cranking. Early routes put up by Tim Coats and others. USFS–Coconino NF, (520) 527–3600.

Ref: T. Coats; Guidebook: Toula's *A Cheap Way to Fly: Free Climbing Guide to Northern Arizona.*

Directions: Get a USFS road and topo map.

45 Museum of Northern Arizona (closed) ✫✫✫

Classic bouldering in the midrange grades on 20' vertical basalt walls. Beloved by beginner and intermediate climbers. Now off-limits to climbers. More than 20 routes from B5.6–5.12. Private land.

Classics: Jug or Not B5.9, B5.9 finger crack, Gunks Roof B1-.

Ref: Guidebook: Toula's *A Cheap Way to Fly: Free Climbing Guide to Northern Arizona.*

Directions: Northwest Flagstaff. Just 5 mi. north of downtown on Hwy. 180. Park at Museum of Northern Arizona on the left. (Gates close at 5:00 P.M.). Hike west behind the museum to short basalt walls in drainage.

46 West Elden ✫✫✫

Venerable Flagstaff bouldering purlieu with short 40' leads and beginners' teaching area. More than one hundred 5.5–5.13 climbing challenges. Cooler in the summer than most other Flagstaff areas. USFS–Coconino NF, (520) 527–3600.

Classics: Five Easy Pieces 5, Deception Cracks 7-10a, Baby's Butt 10, Twilight Zone Crack 10+, Orangutan B1-, Impossible Boulder Problem B1, Murray Overhang B2+.

Ref: Guidebooks: Murray's *Flagstaff Bouldering Guide,* Toula's *A Cheap Way to Fly: Free Climbing Guide to Northern Arizona.*

Directions: From Flagstaff jump 5 mi. north on Hwy. 180. Just north of the Museum of Northern Arizona, take the first right on Schulz Pass Rd. After 6/10 mi. bear right on dirt road, past houses, to gate (locked in winter) and West Elden Rocks on right at 2 2/10 mi.

47 Gloria's Rocks ✫✫✫

Difficult dacite fingertip-cranking on boulders and short 30' topropes under the big ponderosa pines. These are among Flagstaff's toughest tip problems. There are a number of Bob Murray testpieces (B2s like Tombstone and Flyswatter) that may make you want to quit climbing and go bowling. Fifty routes. USFS–Coconino NF, (520) 527–3600.

Classics: Heart Cave Boulder: East face B1+, Tombstone B1+, Bill's Boulder B1-2, AC Bulge B1.

Ref: Guidebooks: Murray's *Flagstaff Bouldering Guide,* Toula's *A Cheap Way to Fly: Free Climbing Guide to Northern Arizona.*

Directions: East Flagstaff. From city hospital on Beaver St., go east on Cedar Ave. Turn left on West St., then make a quick left on Paradise Lane. Park at end of road. Hike through gate north/northeast on trails, then on the gas line road. Total of ten minutes to the base of Mt. Elden (just past gas line road) and Gloria's Rocks. The cave with the heart painting is Heart Cave.

48 Middle Elden Canyon ✫✫

A small bouldering and dacite cragging area with a few classic B1s and toprope/leads on the south face of Mt. Elden. The Radio Forest Fire of 1977 still shows its effect on the landscape. USFS–Coconino NF, (520) 527–3600.

Classics: B5.9 hand crack and B1s put up by John Mattson in the 1980s.

Ref: Guidebook: Toula's *A Cheap Way to Fly: Free Climbing Guide to Northern Arizona.*

Directions: North Flagstaff. Travel north on Fourth St. to Trinity Heights church at base of Mt. Elden. Park. Hike northeast to the obvious cleft splitting Mt. Elden in two halves as seen from town. This is Middle Elden Canyon.

49 Mt. Elden Bird Sanctuary ✫✫✫

Sunny, warm bouldering area offers pleasant winter bouldering on rather rough rock. Forty routes to B5.12. Short toprope or heavy spotters might allay sweaty palms. Good mountain-bike ride to the west on gas line road. Bring the binoculars for birding. USFS–Coconino NF, (520) 527–3600.

Classics: King Kongerer B5.10, Gill Memorial B1, Laughing Clown B1.

Ref: Guidebook: Toula's *A Cheap Way to Fly: Free Climbing Guide to Northern Arizona.*

Directions: East Flagstaff. (Just across from [west of] Flagstaff Mall.) From Hwy. 89 turn west on Cummings St. Turn west on east El Paso St. Park at White Gas Line outside the Mt. Elden Bird Sanctuary. Obvious 20' rock band on first tier has highest concentration of problems.

50 Secret Canyon ★★★

Flagstaff's longest approach to any of its crags offers nice climbing on 60' traditional and sport routes on Mt. Elden dacite. Fifty routes to 5.12 in a complex of landscapes. Expansive views of eastern Arizona. USFS-Coconino NF, (520) 527-3600.

Classics: Wild-Eyed Southern Boys 9, Importance of Being Earnest in Minnesota 10, Blue Desire 11a, Sun King 11+, Black Prince of Arkansas 12a, Mama Don't Take My Kodachrome Away 12, The Thing 13a TR.

Ref: Guidebooks: Bloom's *Big Fat Funky Booty: Secret Canyon,* Toula's *A Cheap Way to Fly: Free Climbing Guide for Northern Arizona.*

Directions: East of Flagstaff on Mt. Elden. Park at slot west of junction of Snowflake and Glacier Dr. (just north of 6,289' Snowflake). Hike: thirty minutes and go through the wooden post; then go north along the fence and up dirt roads, aiming for the largest, most obvious rock band downsloping to the north. En route, pass a brown hut at a plowed meadow. Continue through the meadow to the end. Find the trail (with a cairn) that takes you into the Chockstone Amphitheatre. Secret Canyon is the large diagonal band of dacite on the east side of Mt. Elden.

51 Elysian Buttress ★★★

Classic multipitched 5.7 adventure route that lies on the largest, middle, red dacite buttress on the northeast flank of Mt. Elden. The integrity of the rock has suffered since it was burned by the 1977 Radio Forest Fire. Other routes done in area. USFS-Coconino NF, (520) 527-3600.

Ref: R 21(9/87)-32; Guidebook: Toula's *A Cheap Way to Fly: Free Climbing Guide to Northern Arizona.*

Directions: From Flagstaff take Hwy. 89N out of town past last businesses on left. Turn west when you come to Forest Service Rd. for Little Elden Springs on left. Hike west to the base of Elysian Buttress (the largest buttress). Look for a large cairn at the base of first pitch.

52 Buffalo Park ★★★

Classic small bouldering area—the perfect Pupu Platter of more than thirty basalt problems. Check out John Mattson's Willful Unconsciousness B2 or Bob Murray's Block Roof B1. Popular running and mountain-biking course in park (just past statue of buffalo). City of Flagstaff Park.

Classics: Centerpiece 5.10, Prow 5.11, Community Services B1, Double Dip B1, Block Roof B1+, Willful Unconsciousness B2.

Ref: Guidebooks: *Buffalo Park Bouldering Guide,* Toula's *A Cheap Way to Fly: Free Climbing Guide to Northern Arizona,* Murray's *Flagstaff Bouldering Guide.*

Directions: In Flagstaff. Go east of hospital on Cedar St. to Buffalo Park. Go left at signs. Park at green water tank just past U.S. Geologic Center. Hike east along fenceline ¼ mi. until standing atop 20' walls that can be seen on the right. Bouldering below.

53 Switzer Canyon Boulders ★★

An hour's worth of backyard bouldering for the beginner through advanced intermediate on 20' basalt formations. 5.6–B1. Private land.

Classics: Centerpiece Boulder B5.10+.

Ref: Guidebook: Toula's *A Cheap Way to Fly: Free Climbing Guide to Northern Arizona.*

Directions: Flagstaff. Follow Switzer Canyon to Turquiose Rd. to 1/10 mi. east on East Ponderosa Dr. Switzer Canyon Boulders are on the north side of the road behind the chalet houses.

54 Le Petit Verdon (aka The Pit)/Arm Pit ★★★

Flagstaff's most heavily traveled 80' limestone sport crag. Pocketed sport routes and a few manufactured drilled routes have led to the nickname "the Wash of the Bosch." While it's dubbed "The Pit," it has ninety-six enjoyable and challenging routes to 5.13. Bouldering and sport climbing at the Arm Pit, too. Very climbable on sunny winter days. Free camping at Le Petit Verdon in summer (gate closed in winter). USFS-Coconino NF, (520) 527-3600.

Classics: Popeye Meets the Burrito Master 9+ (lower half), English Landscape 10, Mr. Slate 10b, True Value 11a, Avalon 11b, Fast Eddy 11, The Viper 11d, L'Aerial Vermin 12a, Purple Shark 12a, Body Language 12, Joker 12+, Total Recall 13c; Arm Pit: Pleasant Dreams 8, Popeye 11-.

Ref: SC 3/92; Guidebooks: Green's *Rock Climbing Arizona,* Miller's *Climbing Guide to the Pit,* McMullen's *Topo to the Pit,* Toula's *A Cheap Way to Fly: Free Climbing Guide to Northern Arizona,* Symans's *A Topo Guide to the Pit,* Seuss's *The Arm Pit.*

Directions: From Flagstaff go south on Hwy. 89A. Just past Wal-Mart, turn left on Lake Mary Rd. for 5 7/10 mi. Turn left on first gated dirt road past cattle guard. (Gate closed in winter.) Park at dead-end parking lot. Hike trail (northeast of talus field) to The Pit. The Arm Pit is a smaller beginner area to the southeast and is basically part of the same hillside of rock.

55 Lake Mary Basalt (North and South) ★★★

Canyon rows of 30' east-facing basalt walls split by a small section of vegetated canyon. Twenty routes to 5.12. Especially good for the 5.7–5.9 climber with a few bolted leads. USFS-Coconino NF, (520) 527-3600.

Classics: Catharsis 9, Guinevere 12a, bouldering wall at north end.

Ref: Guidebook: Toula's *A Cheap Way to Fly: Free Climbing Guide to Northern Arizona.*

Directions: From Flagstaff go south on Hwy. 89A. Just past Wal-Mart, turn left on Lake Mary Rd. for 5 7/10 mi. For North Area: Turn left on first dirt road past cattle guard into USFS area. (Parking is same as for The Pit.) Hike east into canyon ¼ mi. south of the trail leading into The Pit. For South Area: Continue on Lake Mary Rd. past the country store and before Lower Lake Mary Picnic Area to a pullout on the right. Park and walk across road to the east. Hop over the guardrail into the drainage where the basalt walls pick up on the left.

56 Booze Pig Area and Long Ryder's Wall (aka Lower Lake Mary) ★★★

Overhanging 15' limestone bouldering walls and cave. The right side of the limestone cave offers the classic problem, Booze Pig V6, and twelve other routes at the pine tree. This area and Priest Draw represent just a couple of an infinite amount of possible bouldering opportunities the adventurous boulderer can seek out on the Kaibab Limestone capped area of the Coconino NF. Free camping at Le Petit Verdon in summer or in other areas of the national forest. USFS–Coconino NF, (520) 527–3600.

Ref: Guidebook: Toula's *A Cheap Way to Fly: Free Climbing Guide to Northern Arizona.*

Directions: From Flagstaff go south on Hwy. 89A. Just past Wal-Mart, turn left on Lake Mary Rd. for approximately 8 mi. to Lower Lake Mary. Go past the country store and park at the first pullout on the right by a plaque (mm 337). Cross road. Hike up and left to a short-in-length pink limestone band (Long Ryder's Wall) and then farther left to a wall with a big roof (Booze Pig).

57 Priest Draw Rocks (aka Holiday Boulders) ★★★★

To Robert Drysdale, a good friend to many Flagstaff climbers. Robert, an enthusiastic climber on and off the rocks, lost his life in a bizarre bouldering accident while on a climb here in an area he developed (a gold plaque now marks the spot). Refreshing 30' limestone bouldering walls and boulders feature naturally smooth pockets, varied and unique bouldering roofs and traverses. USFS–Coconino NF, (520) 527–3600.

Classics: Triangle Boulder, Salt Boulders, Killer Inside Me Wall, MOAB (Mother of All Boulder Problems) V5; Pottery Wall: Street Fighter Traverse V7, Anorexic Nerve Dance V7, Carnivore V8, and more than one hundred routes to V10.

Ref: Sherman's *Stone Crusade;* Guidebook: Toula's *A Cheap Way to Fly: Free Climbing Guide to Northern Arizona.*

Directions: From Flagstaff go south on Hwy. 89A. Just past Wal-Mart, turn left on Lake Mary Rd. for 6 1/10 mi. Turn right at first dirt road past cattle guard (and before mm 338), FS 132, for 3 1/10 mi. south on main dirt road. Then turn right onto smaller dirt road (FS 235) when rocks become visible. Priest Draw Rocks start on the right side of the wash past a brown A-frame house. There are several areas, starting with the obvious Triangle Boulder on the right.

58 Oak Creek Overlook (aka The Overlook) ★★★

Since the 1960s, a favorite 80' basalt cliffband for beginning and intermediate crack climbers on the north fringe of Oak Creek Canyon. Tends to be a sunny reflector oven, thereby making winter days quite pleasant. Navajo jewelry stands. Bellicose wasps. Watch out for tourist projectiles. The area under the overlook cages has been closed to climbers by the USFS. The reasoning: Tourists are endangered by leaning over the edge to watch rock climbers. Year-round climbing on one hundred 5.6–5.12 routes. USFS–Coconino NF, (520) 527–3600.

Classics: Bearly Crack 5, Angel's Delight 7, Morning's Mourning 8, Isaiah 9, The Trinities 10, Finger Licking Good 11-, Don't Fade Away 11d, Cakewalk 12-, Jungleland 12-.

Ref: C [139, 107, 102], R [101-39, 21(9/87)-32]; Guidebooks: Green's *Rock Climbing Arizona,* Toula's *A Cheap Way to Fly: Free Climbing Guide to Northern Arizona.*

Directions: From Flagstaff (approximately 15 minutes), shoot 13 mi. south on Hwy. 89A. Park at Oak Creek Canyon Overlook. One-minute approach to top of cliff. Descents are on either end of cliff, or rappel in off a tree.

59 Oak Creek Canyon (Coconino Walls/Grasshopper Point) ★★★

A warm diversity of climbing: from scary, soft-sandstone multipitch walls and spires to basalt crags to sandstone topropes. More than forty routes to 5.12. A sandstone route like Lucky Goes to the Creamery will have you shakin' like a sick dog. The Oak Creek Waterfall is a springtime spectacle with good to excellent basalt. Grasshopper Point presents 30' fun topropes and is known locally for its cliff jumping, parties, and tanning-bed activities. This spectacular canyon still has much to offer; seek and ye shall find. Pay camping in canyon. USFS–Coconino NF, (520) 527–3600.

Classics: Dresdoom 9, Book of Friends 10, Ultimate Dihedral 10+, Ultimate Finger Crack 11c, Grasshopper Point, Dick's Bowling Ball, B1s at Slide Rock State Park, Anvil Rock Boulders.

Ref: AAJ ['98-200, 97-151], R 21(9/87)-32; Guidebooks: Toula's *A Better Way to Die: Rock Climber's Guide to Sedona and Oak Creek Canyon,* Toula's *A Cheap Way to Die: Climber's Guide to Sedona and Oak Creek Canyon.*

Directions: From Flagstaff soar 13 mi. south on Hwy. 89A to the north rim of Oak Creek Canyon. Hwy. 89A escorts climbers down to Sedona. Parking points: Grim Reaper–Pine Flat campground, mm 386.7; Dresdoom/Book of Friends, west of Troutdale Ranch/Cave Springs campground, mm 384.4; Coke Wall, west of Don Hoel's Cabin, at mm 383.6; Slide Rock State Park Bouldering, mm 381.7. Waterfall area (basalt cliffs high to the east; sandstone routes up north Wilson Trail): Park at Encinoso Picnic Area, mm 379.4; Grasshopper Point, mm 376.7; Submarine Rock (first formation northwest of Midgley Bridge), mm 376.1; Anvil Rock bouldering, east of mm 375, across stream.

60 Grasshopper Point ★★

Known locally for its cliff jumping, streamside parties, and tanning scene. Some good stone presents short and fun bouldering with intense 30' sandstone topropes. USFS-Coconino NF, (520) 527-3600.

Ref: Guidebooks: Toula's *A Better Way to Die: Rock Climber's Guide to Sedona and Oak Creek Canyon,* Toula's *A Cheap Way to Fly: Free Climbing Guide to Northern Arizona.*

Directions: From Sedona (at the junction of Hwy. 179 and Hwy. 89A), hop north on Hwy. 89A for approximately 2 ½ mi. to the road leading down to a creek and at the GRASSHOPPER POINT sign. Rock in the inner gorge has been climbed on.

61 Oak Creek Waterfall ★★★

Obvious, 100' basalt columns on east side of canyon. A seasonally spectacular waterfall in wet spring. Fifty-five steep, quality routes in the 5.10–5.12 range on either side of the falls. Early routes done by J. Gault, T. Toula, S. Bartlett, and S. Mish. Many new hard routes developed by Darren Singer, T. Maloney, and J. Keith. Watch for snakes! USFS-Coconino NF, (520) 527-3600.

Classics: Tube Chocks and Socks 8, No Feelings 10, Double Clutching 11-, Yucca Valley Pants 11-, Spite and Malice 11-, Susie and Ishmael Do the Nasty 12b arête.

Ref: Guidebooks: Toula's *A Better Way to Die: Rock Climber's Guide to Sedona and Oak Creek Canyon,* Singer Topo, Toula's *A Cheap Way to Fly: Free Climbing Guide to Northern Arizona.*

Directions: From Flagstaff drop down Hwy. 89A south into Oak Creek Canyon. Park at Encinoso picnic ground. Hike back on the road east for 100 yd. to hairpin turn and cross creek. Boulder-hop thirty minutes up a steep drainage to the base of Oak Creek Waterfall and the basalt cliffs.

62 East Pocket ★★★

Ethereal views of Oak Creek Canyon backcountry highlight this panoramic 80' basalt crag. Fine basalt cragging, with some loose rock, scorpions, and rattlers. Want a stimulating, getaway experience? It's in the pocket. More than eighteen routes to 5.11+. USFS-Coconino NF, (520) 527-3600.

Classics: Fat Lady Sings 8, Alley of Aeolus 9+, Syscrusher 10, The Pod 11, Finger Socket Pocket 11, Pocket Change 11+.

Ref: Guidebook: Toula's *A Cheap Way to Fly: Free Climbing Guide to Northern Arizona.*

Directions: From Flagstaff, after going 2 mi. west on Old Hwy. 66, turn left on Woody Mountain Rd. (FS 231). Drive one hour to East Pocket Fire Tower (via USFS signs). Park near gate. Just before the gate, a small, south-trending, four-wheel-drive road allows the ardent climber to hike or drive south (stay right at Y) approximately twenty minutes to the rimrock at East Pocket. Coconino NF map is useful.

63 Schnebly Hill Road Overlook ★★★

Breathtaking views of the Sedona Red Rock country from this small, fun 60' beginner's basalt crag. Twelve routes to 5.10. Cream Corner 5.8+ is surely that. This panorama was used in many films. USFS-Coconino NF, (520) 527-3600.

Classics: Hand Job 6, Schnebly Schlip 7, Cream Corner 8+, Court of the Crimson King 10.

Ref: Guidebook: Toula's *A Cheap Way to Fly: Free Climbing Guide to Northern Arizona.*

Directions: From Sedona trend 6 6/10 mi. up Schnebly Hill Rd. to Schnebly Hill Overlook. Park. Hike north ¼ mi. to small basalt crag.

64 Sedona Red Rock Spires ★★★★

Northern Arizona's wine cellar of vintage adventure climbing on soft rock spires and 700' walls. More than 130 5.5–5.13 routes. Like the beauty of danger? Go boldly with offwidth protection and a bold partner for the leads you don't want to do. A splendid red-rock setting that deserves National Park status. Nearly every red-rock spire/formation visible from the road has seen an ascent. Bob Kamps, T.M. Herbert, and Dave Rearick first ascended the famed climber's golf tee of the Mace in 1959. Sedona supports a host of Southwest artists and is known for its earth-energy centers called vortices and its New Age ambience. Get metaphysical, dude! Pay camping. Private land/USFS-Coconino NF, (520) 527-3600.

Classics: Fourth Class: Capitol Butte, Chimney Rock I 6, Oak Creek Spire II 6-10, Queen Victoria II 7, Streaker Spire II 8, Screaming Besingi I 8, Epitaph 9+ (First 3p); Summit Block Spire: Dr. Rubo's Wild Ride III 9+; Coffee Pot Rock: Original Route III 9 and South Face 11+, The Mace II 9+, Peter's Ladder III 10+, Princess Spire I 10+, Earth Angel Spire IV 10, Technicolor Corner 4p 5.10+, Tomahawk Tower I 10d, The Mushroom IV 10 A2, Aladdin's Lamp 11a; Courthouse Butte: A Day in Court 11+, The Watchtower 12, Shangrila 12+, Red Planet 13.

Ref: AAJ ['78-532, 77-186, '76-453], *Arizona Climber* #10, C [186-64, 177-20, 105, 103, 48(1978)], R [21(9/87)-32, 66-57]; Grubbs's *Hiking Northern Arizona: Sedona Hikes and Mountain Bike Rides;* Guidebooks: Green's *Rock Climbing Arizona,* Toula's *A Better Way to Die: Rock Climber's Guide to Sedona and Oak Creek Canyon,* Toula's *A Cheap Way to Fly: Free Climbing Guide to Northern Arizona.*

Directions: Sedona area. Approaches for popular areas/climbs (clockwise): 1) Submarine Rock, Princess, Acropolis: Park at Midgley Bridge and hike northwest. 2) Pointed Dome to Flying Buttress: Up Schnebly Hill Rd. on left. 3) Marg's Draw (Slingshot et al.): east from USFS trailhead on Sombart Ln. 4) Church Spires: east from end of Chapel Hill Rd. 5) Bell Rock and Courthouse Butte: Bell Rock parking on Hwy. 179. 6) Oak Creek Spire: End of Jacks Canyon Rd. to the north. 7) Cathedral Spires (Mace): Back-O-Beyond Rd. parking lot, to the south. 8) Mushroom and Earth Angel: north end of Jordan Rd. Hike north one hour. 9) Coffee Pot Rock et al.: Rim Shadows Dr. to north. 10) Chimney Rock: Skyview Way. 11) West Sedona Areas: Via Dry Creek Rd. To really get lost, see the guidebook *A Better Way to Die: Rock Climber's Guide to Sedona and Oak Creek Canyon.*

65 Canyon Diablo ✯✯✯

Long, sinuous, and bizarre canyon of 40' topropes and boulder problems. At least twelve routes. Hangdog Piñata Roof Crack 5.13a toprope is a very difficult and classic roof crack first toproped by T. Toula. Railroad trestle is site of a few bungee bridge jumps. Private land/BLM, (602) 417-9200.

Classics: Ira's Traverse B1, 200' long Power Alley Traverse, Ira Shrugged 5.12b toprope, 5.12 roof, Hangdog Piñata Roof Crack 12+/13a.

Ref: I. Hickman, D. Cilley; Guidebook: Toula's *A Cheap Way to Fly: Free Climbing Guide to Northern Arizona*.

Directions: From Flagstaff travel approximately 30 mi. east on I-40 to the Two Guns exit, number 230. Go left (north) off freeway (over overpass) until pavement ends. Canyon Diablo lies just to the west. From here begin mileage. Bear left on dirt road for 2 1/10 mi. to parking for Ira's Traverse/5.12 Roof Area located via the biggest side drainage west of the road. Continue to water tank (requires left turn) at 2 9/10 mi. before railroad tracks. Park at tank. Hike southwest to rim, then south past corroding scrap metal heaps until descents become feasible into canyon. Hangdog Piñata Roof Crack and Sherman's Power Alley Traverse are located here.

66 Winslow Wall (aka East Clear Creek) ✯✯✯

This long, varnished sandstone chasm, with classic 200' crack lines, will have you giggling like a hyena. More than twenty 5.10-5.12 routes. Fishing and swimming, too. Private land/BLM, (602) 417-9200.

Ref: R 21 (insert); Guidebooks: Toula's *A Cheap Way to Fly: Free Climbing Guide to Northern Arizona*.

Classics: American Beauty 10+, Hanging Judge 11+/12a.

Directions: From Winslow drive south on Hwy. 87. In a few mi., turn east on Hwy. 99 to McHood Park Reservoir. Go 1 mi. after passing reservoir. Turn right immediately after cattle guard and barbed-wire fence. Parallel fence on faint road, bearing left at fork near end of road. Park before driving over cliff. Descent gully, 1/4 mi. south of parking along rim, allows access to Winslow Wall.

67 Petrified Forest National Park ✯

Sandstone slump-block bouldering area. Check out the Petrified Wood Bridges and fossil logs (Agate Bridge). NPS, (520) 524-6228.

Directions: From Holbrook go east for approximately 25 mi. on I-40 to Petrified Forest National Park, exit 311. At approximately 12 mi., boulders lie just 100 yd. west of road below parking area. Check out the Petrified Wood Bridges and fossil logs (Agate Bridge) at mile #18.4 and 20.8 (Crystal Forest Parking Area).

68 Chevelon Canyon ✯✯✯

Varnished 150' sandstone walls present climbers with crack- and face-climbing challenges. Limestone bands also present. This is a long canyon with lots to explore. Please leave Indian artwork for all to enjoy. Private land/state land.

Ref: Guidebook: Aitchison and Grubbs's *The Hiker's Guide to Arizona*.

Directions: From Winslow go south on Hwy. 99, then southeast on FR 504 to Chevelon Crossing/Chevelon Canyon. The canyon gets steep north of Chevelon Crossing. Other access points to the south via USFS roads. A Coconino NF or topo map is helpful.

69 Sullivan Canyon (aka Sullies) and Verde River Gorge ✯✯✯

Short but excellent lead/toprope problems in expanding basalt canyon. More than one hundred excellent routes from 5.9-5.12. The Upper Sullies Area was developed in the 1970s by Lovejoy and Goff and Prescott College students. The rock tends to be glassy by the dam, but there are still "some of the finest fissures that ever coalesced from the primal flows," according to the venerable and legendary Arizona sandbagger Rusty Baillie, who developed Lower Sullies along with other Prescott climbers. Please stay off the private land beyond the gas pipeline on the south side of canyon. State land/private land.

Classics: Twin Cracks 5.8, Basalt and Battery 5.9, Apple Pie 5.10a, Finger Licking Good 5.10c, Gemstone 5.11a, Bohemian 5.11c.

Ref: R 57(11/93); Guidebooks: J. Gross's *Verde Basalt*, Murray and Baillie's *The Promised Land: Sullivan's Canyon*.

Directions: From Prescott go north on Hwy. 89 to the airport, then another 13 2/10 mi. north on Hwy. 89. Turn right (historical marker at Del Rio Springs) to southeast side of pond. Rocks line Sullivan Canyon below dam (Upper Sullies) and extend eastward 1 mi. before basalt Lower Sullies (Suntrap Cliffs below and Timmies Crag above) in lower canyon turns to rotten limestone. For drive-up access to Lower Sullies, go north from the dam to Sweet Valley Rd. Turn right for 1 1/10 mi. Turn right again for 1 mi. Turn right for 4/10 mi. to parking. Hike southwest to Timmies Gully and the Lower Sullies (44 routes). This area is just southeast of the hamlet of Paulden and 6 mi. north of Chino Valley.

70 Verde River Crags (near Clarkdale) ✯✯

Various 60' basalt routes along the Verde River and just south of the mouth of Sycamore Canyon Wilderness. About twenty-five routes, mostly 60'. Beware: Dangerously loose rubble on tops. At less than 4,000' in elevation, this is a nice winter spot for chilled Flagstaff climbers. Government land.

Classics: Communism Wall 5.8-5.11.

Ref: D. Bloom.

Directions: From old town Cottonwood follow Hwy. 260 west to Tuzigoot National Monument sign. Cross small bridge over Verde River. Go left (private ranch sign) for 6 1/2 mi. to cattle guard and barbed-wire fence. Turn left and go 1/2 mi. to dead end. Follow your nose to the rimrock overlooking Verde River. Verde River Crags below. The best routes on the river are 1/4 mi. north of the hike-in.

71 Mingus Mountain ⭐⭐

Supposedly good limestone cragging. Sport crag. Camping.
Prescott NF, (520) 771-4700.
Ref: J. Waugh.
Directions: From Jerome the rock is on Mingus Mountain
along Hwy. 89A south of town and the mountain pass.

72 Hwy. 93 Boulders ⭐⭐

Heaps of 35' granite pegmatite bouldering outcrops
abound in this remote desert environment. Climbers
should come ready to explore. State land/BLM, (602)
417-9200.
Ref: J. Waugh.
Directions: From Wickieup go south on Hwy. 93 to the little outpost of Nothing (pop. four). Here, between mm
149 and 151, the highest concentration of Hwy. 93
Boulders can be found adjacent to the road. Beware: Hwy.
93 has more fatalities than any other Arizona highway.

73 Granite Dells (partially closed) ⭐⭐⭐

Granite wonderland of 200' coarse granite walls and spires
in three distinct areas containing more than 115 routes
from mainly 5.9 to 5.12. Private land—access problems.
Popular training area for Prescott College students.
Spring/fall. City of Prescott/private land.
Classics: Chute 10d, Thank God 11c, Non Dairy Screamer,
Steal Your Face 12a, many others.
Ref: C (7/72); R [81-86, 57(11/93)]; Guidebooks: Green's
Rock Climbing Arizona, Dennison and Malfatto's *A
Climber's Guide to the Granite Dells of Prescott, Arizona,*
Mezra's *The Dells,* Baillie's *Rockclimbing Routes in Granite
Dells.*
Directions: North of Prescott. From Prescott toddle east on
Gurley St. (Hwy. 69) to the junction with Hwy. 89. Go
north on Hwy. 89 for approximately 5-6 mi. As you head
north, the main Granite Dells area, High Rappel Dells, is
the rampart to the east of the road and is directly above
and before the junction with Hwy. 89A. Westside Dells
Area (in private housing) lies west of Hwy. 89, while the
Watson Lake Dells lies south of High Rappel Area via east
turn on Willow Lake Rd. Climbing is on the north shores
of the lake. Pay camping there, too.

74 Granite Mountain and Lizard Head ⭐⭐⭐⭐

At 7,000', Granite Mountain's magnificent west-facing,
500' buttress offers outstanding granite cragging. With its
intimidating exposures, "The Mountain" regularly elicits a
trembling visceral response from greenhorns. Stiff, true ratings on clean white granite faces and cracks. Plan to climb
for the day. Peregrine nesting closures February–July (check
first). Day-use fees. Fifty to one hundred 5.5-5.13 routes.
Lizard Head Pinnacle (200') offers poor-weather alternatives. Pay camping. Raptor restrictions February 1–July 16.
Best time to visit is September–October. USFS–Prescott NF,
(520) 771-4700.

Tiptoeing out the Great Roof's Candyland Exit, Granite Mountain.

TIM TOULA

Classics: Granite Moutain: Debut 6, Classic 7 (with high
exposure exit), Magnolia Thunderpussy 8, Chue Hoi 9,
Candyland 10-, Thin Slice 10, Delphinia Lightning Ass
11-, The Sorcerer 11, Help Me Mr. Wizard 11+, Guioco
Piano 5.11+, Twin Cracks 12-, The Good, The Bad . . .
12b, Improbability Drive 12, A Bridge . . . 13a; Lizard
Head: Northwest Ridge 4, West Ridge 6, Why Oh Why? 9.
Ref: C [186-64, 167-44, 117, 111, 108, 105, 97, 95, 63, 49,
(7/72)], M 118, R [57(11/93), 24]; Annerino's *Adventuring
in Arizona;* Guidebooks: Green's *Rock Climbing Arizona,*
Black's *Granite Mountain Topo,* Harlin's *Rocky Mountain,*
Waugh's *A Topo Guide to Granite Mountain,* Lovejoy's
*Granite Mountain: Rockclimbing Routes in Granite Basin:
"Lizard Head."*
Directions: From Prescott set a course northwest on Iron
Springs Rd. In a few mi. from town, turn right on Rd.
#374 (signs) to the end of Granite Basin campground.
Park on right past boat ramp. Granite Moutain: Hike one
hour on trail 261 to Blair Pass and then turn right up
switchbacks on summit trail. A way's up the main trail,
find a climber's trail by a small rock outcropping to a
500' main wall. Lizard Head Pinnacle: En route to
Granite Mountain, fifteen minutes up trail 261, turn left
at a tree pointing south and hike cairns through boulders
up to 200' Lizard Head Pinnacle. Stay on trails or se
habla "heinous bushwhacking"?

75 Flora Street (aka Sears Boulders) (closed) ☆☆☆

A real rose. Fun problems on clean, 25' granite boulders. More than twenty routes. Enjoy the Golf Ball Boulder or Cilley's Traverse B5.12. Private land—closed to climbing.

Directions: In Prescott, behind the Sears store. Best approached by parking at end of Flora Street. Hike west through trees to scattered boulders. Good boulders can be difficult to find without the help of locals.

76 Thumb Butte ☆☆☆

One thumb up! A 250' basalt plug rising above the city of Prescott. Fine, clean crack and face climbing offering sound to shrieking protection as well as bolted face possibilities. More than one hundred routes for sport climbs from 5.2–5.12. First rock climbs established as early as 1967 by the Syndicato Granitica. Raptor restrictions February–July. Prescott NF, (520) 445-7253.

Classics: Sunshine Slab 6, Hotdog In A Bun 7, Yellow Edge 8, Pickle Relish 9, Thunder Roof 10, White Death 11c, Acrobatic Flying 12a.

Ref: R 57(11/93), C (7/72); Guidebooks: Baillie's *Thumb Butte Climbing Guide,* Rugeley's *Thumb Butte: A Climber's Guide.*

Directions: From Prescott prance west of town on Gurley St. turning onto Thumb Butte Rd. for several miles to Thumb Butte campground. Hike up to Thumb Butte via USFS trails.

77 Groom Creek Boulders (aka Senator Highway) ☆☆☆

Quality, dispersed, steel-gray 20' granite bouldering that is never very far from your car. Hundreds of boulder problems are scattered in this bouldered pineland. Private land/Prescott NF, (520) 771-4700.

Classics: The Wave 10, Martha's Mantel 10, Nail Up Rock Hand Crack 10, many V0 problems, Curt Shannon Problem V7.

Ref: J. Erdman; R 57(11/93) Guidebooks: Cramer's *Prescott Bouldering Guide,* Karabin's *Groom Creek Topo Sheet,* Lauradunn's *Prescott Bouldering.*

Directions: From Prescott head south on Senator Hwy. (FR 52) past the village of Groom Creek. In a few miles, granite Groom Creek Boulders appear on the left. Problems scattered throughout forest. Best parking: Turn left past Groom Creek onto Camp Wamatochick Rd. Park on right at first road on right. Hike east on Spruce Mountain Loop Trail to scattered boulders.

78 Castle Rock (4,800') ☆☆☆

A remote little quartzite crag with eighty-degree face climbing on incut edges. Nice! First routes developed by Bruce Grubbs and Larry Beau in the early 1970s. USFS–Prescott NF, (520) 771-4700.

Classics: While's Bloodbath 6, Last Will and Testament 6.

Ref: Guidebooks: Opland's *Phoenix Rock,* Waugh's *A Climber's Guide to Central Arizona Crags.*

Directions: From Phoenix drive approximately 50 mi. north on I–17 to Bumblebee exit. Haul ass on 28 mi. of dirt road to Crown King. From Crown King go south 1 mi. and turn west on Senator Rd. Go 1 more mile and turn left onto Fort Misery Rd. going south for 5 mi. until the road passes to the right of Castle Rock.

79 Bloody Basin ☆☆☆

Developed by Jim Guano and Black in the early 1990s. Quality granite desert buttresses. Prescott NF, (520) 771-4700.

Ref: J. Gaun.

Directions: North of Black Canyon City. From Black Canyon City go north on I–17 and go west at Bloody Basin (exit 259) until Bloody Basin granite is reached (approximately 24 mi.).

80 Blue Ridge Reservoir ☆☆☆

These 35' basalt cliffs are at the campground near Blue Ridge Reservoir. Coconino NF, (520) 527-3600.

Ref: D. Grimwood.

Directions: North of Payson. Good climbing may be found by exploring roads near Blue Ridge Reservoir.

81 Woods Canyon Lake (on the Payson Rimrock) ☆☆

Good climbing may be found on short, 30' sandstone rock bands. Coconino NF, (520) 527-3600.

Directions: Have fun exploring roads to Mogollon rimrock south of Woods Canyon Lake.

82 Yarnell Boulders ☆☆

Massive boulder piles and small 60' granite crags are scattered around town, but there are few climbing-route possibilities. Private/government land.

Directions: In and around Yarnell. Or, go 1 mi. west on Hwy. 89 to park on the left-hand side. Park at Charles Small (sign) pulloff.

83 Yarnell Wall ☆☆☆

Couple-hundred-foot granite outcrop with good rock overall. Twelve routes. Routes done by Los Banditos in 1979. Government land.

Classics: LB's Panhead 5, Languish 9, The Sultan 10.

Ref: G. Rink; Guidebooks: Opland's *Phoenix Rock,* Kerry's *Backcountry Climbing in Southern Arizona,* Waugh's *A Climber's Guide to Central Arizona Crags.*

Directions: Just west of Yarnell, follow Hwy. 89 west toward Congress. Where highway goes from divided back to two lanes, park (before sanitary landfill). A "Carhardts-recommended" bushwhack and thrash gets one to the base of Yarnell Wall to north of Hwy. 89. Or, access by four-wheel-drive roads from top of cliff.

84 Hall Creek ✩✩

Basalt crags. Apache-Sitgreaves NF, (520) 333-4301.
Directions: From Springerville emigrate west on Hwy. 260. Then go south on Hwy. 373 to Hall Creek, north of Greer.

85 Salt River Canyon Area (Seneca Falls) ✩✩✩

Before 1994, The Cienega Wall at Seneca Falls (approximately 5 mi. south of bridge on Hwy. 60 at Salt River Canyon, then west of highway) was reportedly loose and dangerous, though impressive and somewhat climbable. Now 250′ diabase sport bolted by Jim Steagall, Dave Sobocan, and Deirdre Burton of Salt River Rafters in cooperation with San Carlos Indian Reservation. Thirty routes to 5.12. All routes, up to 165′ in length, protected by bolts. Bring at least twenty-five draws and two 165′ ropes. Poison ivy! Check before going about climbing opening. BIA.
Classics: Sacred Passage 10d, War Cry 10d, Victorio 11a, Crown Dance 11b, Warpath 12a.
Ref: G. Rink; *Arizona Climber* #10; C 163-119; R [74-93, 71, 70-92, 67-52, 66-17]; Guidebook: Steagall's *Seneca Falls Sport Climbing Guide*.
Directions: From Globe go north on Hwy. 60 for 35 mi. toward Salt River Canyon Area until you arrive at mm 287.6 and Seneca Lake Trading Post. Pick up a permit at the trading post. Then proceed 1 1/2 mi. to Seneca Falls and sport climbing. Approach to rock is about the length of an egg timer. Rappel in with two 165′ ropes.

86 Jacuzzi Spires (aka New River Area) ✩✩✩

A 150′ volcanic crag with ten trad and sport routes up to 5.12 in a remote, desert setting. Tonto NF, (602) 595-3300.
Classics: Redtail Diner 10/12-, 5.12 face.
Ref: Desert Mountain Sports, *Arizona Rock Climbing Areas Map*; Guidebook: Opland's *Phoenix Rock*.
Directions: New River (north of Phoenix). From Phoenix go north on I-17 to the Table Mesa exit (approximately thirty minutes). Head east for 1 mi. to USFS gate. (A private residence is to the right.) Go through gate on FR 41 (high clearance necessary to negotiate washes and rocky road) for approximately 3 mi. passing rock quarry. Then, continue on foot on FR 1484 (four-wheel-drive road) to gray knob (landmark) along river. At end of road, hike trail along river channel for approximately 1 mi. to south-facing Jacuzzi Spires on left. (Can't see spires until a bit up the trail.)

87 Vulture Peak (3,658′) ✩✩

A dominant 600′ volcanic face of the Vulture Mountains. One of the first ascents was made October 1967 by Phoenix legends Bill Sewrey and Larry Treiber on East Face IV 5.5 A4 6p. Beautiful western Arizona desert environment. BLM, (602) 417-9200.
Ref: B. Sewrey, AAJ '69-398; Guidebooks: Opland's *Phoenix Rock*, Waugh's *A Climber's Guide to Central Arizona Crags*.
Directions: Southwest of Wickenburg. From Wickenburg, Vulture Peak is visible approximately 8 mi. southwest of town. From the junction of Hwy. 60 and Hwy. 93, fly west on Hwy. 60 a short distance to Vulture Mine Rd. Turn right on Vulture Mine Rd. for 3 7/10 mi. Turn left on dirt road for 1 3/10 mi. to a junction with a four-wheel-drive road on right. Turn right on four-wheel road to base of Vulture Peak's East Face. Other rock is on the west side of Vulture Mountain.

88 Four Peaks Area (aka Brushy Basin) ✩✩✩

A gigantic array of desert granite boulders and short cliffs dispersed below the dominant skyline of Four Peaks's 7,000′ summits. Besides many rock-climbing routes on the abundant formations in the valleys, mountaineering ascents of Four Peaks have been made (e.g., Lady Bug Route II 5.4 in 1969 and the North Ridge of Four Peaks by Chuck and Bob Graf and Bruce Grubbs). Tonto NF, (602) 595-3300.
Ref: Arizona Highways 2/87, Guidebooks: Opland's *Phoenix Rock*, Kurtz's *Arizona Rock Climbing Areas Map*, Waugh's *A Climber's Guide to Central Arizona Crags*.
Directions: East of Phoenix. From Mesa make a beeline northeast on Hwy. 87 (Beeline Hwy.) to mm 202–204. Multitudes of granite boulders. More boulders farther north on Hwy. 87 between mm 207–217. For Four Peaks ascent turn left onto FR 143 (sign) for approximately 16 mi., passing Cline Cabin. Turn right and follow FR 648 south for 2 mi. to its end at Lone Pine Saddle. Hike up trail (fenceline north along steep ridge) 2 mi. to upper saddle, just north of Four Peaks.

89 Carefree Rockpile (closed) ✩✩✩

Expensive 150′ granitic rockpiles now amongst the front yards of high-dollar resort homes at 34505 North Scottsdale Yards Rd. at El Pedregal Resort. Now off limits to climbing. In the 1970s these granitic clusters and walls were an often-frequented climbing area for many Phoenix valley climbers. Unfortunately for climbers, they have been strangled by a commercial boa constrictor known as El Pedregal since the early 1980s. At one time more than seventy routes put up by Phoenix climbers Treiber, Waugh, Sewrey, Smith, Hollister, Taber, Parker, and others. Named formations of Carefree Rockpile once included School Area, Carefree Wedge, Crooked Book Boulder, Dork Wall, Disappointment Slab, Flesh Ripper Boulder, Rasputin Boulder, and the largest formation, the 150′ East Wall. Private land.
Ref: C 108; Guidebooks: Waugh's *A Climber's Guide to Central Arizona Crags*, Treiber and Grubbs's *Topo Guide to Carefree Rocks/Camelback Mountain*.
Directions: In Carefree.

90 Pinnacle Peak (closed) ✩✩✩

This is strict traditionalist's crag of Phoenix and one of long historical standing. Foreboding (aka sandbag) 200′ granitic leads await as well as some scattered bouldering. On a hot day, the rock can get slipperier than Catalonian olive oil. Pinnacle Peak is now a granite golf tee amid the outlying privately owned desert greens. More than one hundred routes of all grades. Climbing developers included Ficker, Sands, Hill, Parker, Mish, Noebels, Smith, Johnson, Waugh, and Daughertys. City of Scottsdale Park.

Classics: South Crack 3, Birthday Party 7, Hangovers 9; Wedge: Redemption 9, Double Digit Dilemma 10b, Fear of Flying 10c, Never Never Land 11a, Powder Puff Direct 11a, Beegee 11a, Sidewinder 11a, Lesson in Discipline 11c, Scar Wars 12a, Lost Nuts 12b.

Ref: R 72-30; Guidebooks: Green's *Rock Climbing Arizona,* Opland's *Phoenix Rock,* Waugh's *Phoenix Rock: A Guide to Central Arizona Crags,* Waugh's *A Climber's Guide to Central Arizona Crags.*

Directions: From Scottsdale go north on Scottsdale Rd. Turn east (right) on Pinnacle Peak Rd. for three bends. To the north is the obvious Pinnacle Peak; on the right (to the east) is Troon Mountain (Windy Walks). Park at lot west of restaurant (Pinnacle Peak Patio). Hike west up to Pinnacle Peak's three (north, east, and west) rock summits. Other formations around peak include The Wedge, AMC Boulder, Loafer's Choice Boulder, Y-Crack, Cactus Flower Boulder, Lower East Wall, Satan's Slab, and Knob Wall.

91 Little Granite Mountain ✩✩

More than twenty small crystalline 170′ granite domes located north of the McDowell Mtns. The Moguls Wall (east face) hosts (approximately seventeen) beginning/intermediate climbs. Low desert—bring water. City of Scottsdale land.

Classics: Dueling Hammers 6, Blow Fly's Last Ride 10.

Ref: C [111, 109, 107, 103, 102]; "Touch the Edge"; Guidebooks: Green's *Rock Climbing Arizona,* Opland's *Phoenix Rock,* Waugh's *Phoenix Rock: A Guide to Central Arizona Crags.*

Directions: From Scottsdale go north on Scottsdale Rd. Turn east (right) on Pinnacle Peak Rd. for three bends. To the north is the obvious Pinnacle Peak. From Pinnacle Peak take Jomax Rd. to Rio Verde Dr. (2 3/10 mi.). Follow Rio Verde Dr. east past Reata Pass to 136th St. north to power lines. Head west toward Little Granite Mountain for Southern Half. For Moguls Wall continue north on 136th St. to two gates; travel west to Shotgun parking area.

92 Troon Mountain (aka Windy Walks) (closed) ✩✩✩

At least one hundred routes, climbing above the desert greens of golf courses, are scattered on different levels and locations on a massive mountain of 150′ granite crags and boulders. Rhythm and Blues 5.10 crack at the very top of the mountain has a classic ambience. Touchy access situation. Private/City of Scottsdale land.

Classics: Acme Acres 9, Pussy Foot 10, Only The Strong Survive 11-, Ray's Face Area.

Ref: C 109; Guidebooks: Opland's *Phoenix Rock,* Waugh's *Phoenix Rock: A Guide to Central Arizona Crags,* Waugh's *A Climber's Guide to Central Arizona Crags.*

Directions: From Scottsdale go north on Scottsdale Rd. Turn east (right) on Pinnacle Peak Rd. for three bends. To the north is the obvious Pinnacle Peak. From Pinnacle Peak, go ½ mi. off Jomax Rd. (west of 118th St.) on dirt roads to the north/northeast side of the mountain. Rough hiking. Troon Mountain is situated between Pinnacle Peak and Tom's Thumb. Climbing areas on the west side include Ray's Face Area, Tranquility Spire, Rhythm and Blues Area, and Summit Boulder Area. Other areas on the mountain are the Southeast Rockpile, East Pinnacles, Tapered Wall, April Fool's Wall, and The Nose.

93 McDowell Mountains (Tom's Thumb) ✩✩✩

Many nice one- to two-pitch climbs on scattered 200′ granite domes such as Renaissance Direct 5.7 on Gardener's Wall or Treiber's Deception on Tom's Thumb. There are 110 routes. Bouldering, too. As of 1995, the access has been determined with Scottsdale City Council and private land developers. The 200′ Library Wall offers mostly loose rock with scattered sections of optimism. Routes put up since the 1970s by Bruce Grubbs, Larry Treiber, et al. Private/City of Scottsdale land.

Classics: Sven Slab: Nit Nat 9; Gardener's Wall: Renaissance Direct 7; Tom's Thumb: Treiber's Deception 7, Succubus 10a, Hard Drivin' 11a, Deep Freeze 11-, Pretty Girls Make Graves.

Ref: C [111, 100, 99], R 69-30; Guidebooks: Green's *Rock Climbing Arizona,* Opland's *Phoenix Rock: A Guide to Central Arizona Crags,* Waugh's *Phoenix Rock,* Waugh's *A Climber's Guide to Central Arizona Crags.*

Directions: From Pinnacle Peak (north of Scottsdale) take Jomax Rd. to Rio Verde Dr. (3 3/10 mi.). Turn 3 3/10 mi. south on 128th St. Head south on dirt roads to four main features. Tom's Thumb is on top of ridge; other formations in the McDowell Mountains include (below and left of Tom's Thumb) Gardener's Wall, Sven Slabs, and Morrell's Wall. For The Library Wall: From Phoenix drive east on Shea Blvd. toward Beeline Hwy. (Hwy. 87). As the road approaches the southern McDowells, The Library Wall becomes visible at the south end of a ridge south of the road. The paved road curves around the north end of this ridge, then curves left. At this point, turn right onto a very rough dirt road that ends at a point southwest of wall.

94 Beardsley Rock Pile ✩✩

Beardsley sports thin edge cranks on gritty rock with twenty lead routes and ninety boulder problems. Problems like

Pencil Thin B2 are not for lard asses. Early Phoenix Bouldering Contest guides have described the problems. Nearby housing developments encroaching. Skillful driving and a good road map will get one to the Phoenix climbing areas. These are among the warmest climbing areas in the state during the winter months. BLM, (623) 580–5500.

Classics: Pencil Thin Boulder (center V6, right/left V4); Wiley Thompson Boulder: Whale's Back V0, Gunfighter V3, Bill's Problem V6.

Ref: C 96; Guidebooks: Opland's *Phoenix Rock*, Karabin's *Beardsley Boulder Pile* topo.

Directions: North Phoenix. From I-17 go 6 9/10 mi. east on Beardsley Rd. Go 1/2 mi. north on Cave Creek Rd., then go west on Lone Cactus to north side of mountain. Beardsley Rock Pile is the small bouldering area on the north side of the slope, a step from your car door.

95 Camelback Mountain (Camel's Head) ☆☆

A distinct landmark in the city of Phoenix. If you like climbing rubble ("breccia"), you'll like this heap. Actually, there are some redeeming climbs of historical and aesthetic value situated here amid the desert palo verde trees. The Praying Monk is an especially poignant figurehead and climb. More than seventy routes and much bouldering since the 1940s. Developed by a legion of Phoenix climbers including: Forrest, Sewrey, Treiber, Garber, Waugh, and Hollister, beginning as far back as the 1940s with a group of mountaineers called The Kachinas. Some fine bouldering problems. Raptor restrictions March–May. Gates open 6:00 A.M. to sunset; please check. City of Phoenix Park, (602) 261–8318.

Classics: Praying Monk; East Face 4, Line of Fire 7; Forrest Roof 9 A1, possibly sport climbs.

Ref: Guidebooks: Green's *Rock Climbing Arizona*, Opland's *Phoenix Rock*, Karabin and Hynes's *Camelback Mountain Climbing Guide*, Waugh's *Phoenix Rock: A Guide to Central Arizona Crags*, Waugh's *A Climber's Guide to Central Arizona Crags*, Treiber and Grubbs's *Topo Guide to Carefree Rocks/Camelback Mountain*.

Directions: In Phoenix. From the intersection of Tatum Blvd. and McDonald Rd., go east on McDonald Rd. and turn right into Echo Canyon parking lot. Climbing is an obvious short hike to the south. Two summits of Camelback Mountain are Camel's Hump (highest at 2,704') and Camel's Head, the lower summit. Named climbing areas include Chipmunk Boulder, Praying Monk, Headwall, Gargoyle Wall, Camel's Neck, Camel's Hump, August Canyon, Boulder Canyon, Bobbie's Rock, Camel's Ear, and the Bolus. Bolus (see the next write-up) bouldering area a longer hike to the southwest. Gates open 6:00 A.M. to sunset; please check.

96 The Bolus (at Camelback Mountain) (closed) ☆☆☆

A boulderer's dessert in a desert megalopolis. This long-standing and well-loved Phoenix breccia bouldering and 60'

cragging area was one of the early sites of the acclaimed Phoenix Bouldering Contest. Many problems now surrounded by houses. Now closed; tickets issued by police. Private land.

Classics: Long Wall Traverse, Garburator, Iron Cross, many others.

Ref: C [108, 91]; Guidebooks: Karabin's Topo Guide Series, Opland's *Phoenix Rock*, Phoenix Bouldering Contest topo sheet, Waugh's *Phoenix Rock: A Guide to Central Arizona Crags*, street map to Phoenix climbing areas, Waugh's *A Climber's Guide to Central Arizona Crags*.

Directions: In Phoenix. From the intersection of Tatum Blvd. and McDonald Rd., go east on McDonald Rd. and turn right into Echo Canyon parking lot (open from 6:00 A.M. to sundown). From Echo Canyon parking lot (south of McDonald, just east of Tatum), walk southwest around Camelback Mountain to Bolus. Alternate access: Take Camelback Rd. to Camelback Mountain. Just east of 44th St., turn north off Camelback Rd. via residential road.

97 White Tank Mountain Regional Park ☆☆

Desert climbing on good to loose rock and route finding on twenty-five routes. Water-polished granite rock is more solid in gully with a couple nice bolted routes to 5.9. There are 350' multipitched beginner routes by Bob Blair. Minimal $3.00 park entrance fee. Open 6:00 A.M.–8:00 P.M. weekdays, until 10:00 P.M. on weekends. Maricopa County Park, (623) 935–2505.

Classics: Leaping Lizards 4, Massacre 7, Exit Stage Left 9.

Ref: Guidebooks: Opland's *Phoenix Rock*, Waugh's *Phoenix Rock: A Guide to Central Arizona Crags*, Waugh's *A Climber's Guide to Central Arizona Crags*.

Directions: West of Phoenix. From Grand Ave. go west on Olive Ave. to White Tanks Regional Park. Park at Waterfall Canyon Trail. Hike up gully approximately 1 mi. to War Wall, Waterfall Area (nice solid leads and topropes), Triangle Boulder (short bouldering or topropes), and Fall Factor Wall (multipitched). One can also access White Tanks by exiting I-10 at exit 124 and going north on Cotton Ln./Seventy-first Ave. to a right on Olive Ave. and continuing into park. Minimal park entrance fee.

98 South Mountain Park (Teddy Bear Wall) ☆☆

Scattered rock piles greet the climber on the park's north slopes. Teddy Bear Wall is a two-minute walk from the parking lot at a picnic area. It is a short 40' toprope wall of fractured volcanics, with about twelve routes from 5.6–5.10. City of Phoenix Park, (602) 261–8318.

Ref: G. Opland.

Directions: South Phoenix. Take Central Ave. south to South Mountain Park. Proceed to the central picnic area.

99 Eagletail Mountains (Eagletail Peak) ✯✯

An area of 600′ mountaineering routes on low desert peaks with rock-climbable summits (e.g., Eagletail Peak, where first known ascent party was C. Beal, B. Grubbs, and L. Treiber in 1977). Courthouse Rock is a superb classic beginner's 5.6 adventure summit. Six other routes. Rock is mainly desert junkoid, allowing climbing when coated with a dark, brown patina. BLM, (602) 417-9200.

Ref: *Arizona Highways* 2/87; Guidebooks: Opland's *Phoenix Rock*, Annerino's *Adventuring in Arizona*, Kurtz's *Arizona Rock Climbing Areas Map*, Waugh's *A Climber's Guide to Central Arizona Crags*.

Directions: West of Tonopah. From Phoenix hightail it for one and one-third hours west on I-10. Take exit 81. Go south briefly a few hundred yd. to Buckeye Salome Rd., then go right on Harquahala Valley Rd. for 5 $^8/_{10}$ mi. to a west turn onto Courthouse Rd. (Courthouse Rock is visible at the foot of the Eagletails while approaching.) At 7 $^7/_{10}$ mi., pass road on left. Go for 2 $^7/_{10}$ mi. farther to road on left for base of Courthouse Rock. Or, continue $^6/_{10}$ mi. farther down the road, turning left for 3 $^4/_{10}$ mi. to dead-end campsite. For Eagletail Peak follow Harquahala Valley Rd. to a right turn on Elliot to trailhead. Hike for 3 mi. via Sheep Trail to V-Notch to Eagletail Saddle onto Eagletail Peak.

100 Superstition Mountains (North) ✯✯✯

The Superstition Mountains, aka "The Supes," are characterized by scenic saguaro hills. The Northern section has lighter climbing use than other Superstition trailheads and 350′ volcanic pinnacles and walls. Low elevation makes for warm winter climbing. USFS-Tonto NF, (602) 610-3300.

Classics: The Hand 7; Hobgoblin Rink: Kudo Route 7, Grandfather Hobgoblin 9, Crying Dinosaur.

Ref: C [138, 126, 117, 114, 113, 111, 109 to 106, 102, 100, 99], S [11/85, 12/66]; Guidebooks: Green's *Rock Climbing Arizona*, Waugh's *Phoenix Rock: A Guide to Central Arizona Crags*.

Directions: From Apache Junction truck northeast on Hwy. 88 to just past Lost Dutchman State Park. Turn right on FR 78 to First Water Trailhead. Hike to numerous formations of the Superstition Mountains. A Superstition Trailhead synopsis: There are five popular trailheads for the Superstition Mountains, reached by going east from Apache Junction: FR 78 to First Water Trailhead (just described); Lost Dutchman State Park; northeast on Hwy. 88 for approximately 3-5 mi. to Miner's Camp Rd.; Hwy. 60 southeast to King's Ranch Rd.; and Peralta Rd.

101 Superstition Mountains (West)— Northwest Pinnacles et al. ✯✯✯

A 300′ volcanic hobnob of spires and other formations high in the beautiful saguaro desert. Rock tends to be fractured peanut brittle. Forty wild routes like The Hand 5.8 provide the adrenaline and killer views of Four Peaks. USFS-Tonto NF, (602) 610-3300.

Ref: Guidebooks: Green's *Rock Climbing Arizona*, Opland's *Superstition Select: Climber's Guide to Multipitch Routes of the Superstition Mountains*, Waugh's *Phoenix Rock: A Guide to Central Arizona Crags*.

Directions: From Apache Junction stroll approximately 3 mi. northwest on Hwy. 88 to a right-hand turn on Miner's Creek Rd. for trails (4 $^4/_{10}$ mi. hike from Miner's Camp Restaurant trailhead) leading to Los Banditos Towers, Hobgoblin Spires, North Buttress, Forrest Spires, and The Flatiron; or to Lost Dutchman State Park for trails leading to Northwest Pinnacles.

102 Superstition Mountains (South) ✯✯✯

Multipitched 600′ volcanic routes in a spectacular desert environment featuring Vertigo Spire 5.7, Carney Springs Wall 5.7, and The Acropolis 5.11-. USFS-Tonto NF, (602) 610-3300.

Ref: Guidebooks: Green's *Rock Climbing Arizona*, Opland's *Superstition Select: Climber's Guide to Multipitch Routes of the Superstition Mountains*, Waugh's *Phoenix Rock: A Guide to Central Arizona Crags*.

Directions: From Apache Junction go 7 $^1/_{10}$ mi. west on Hwy. 60/89 to Kings Ranch Rd. Turn north on dirt road to Superstition Mountains Trailhead for the Mirage and Vertigo Spire. Be careful where you park (tow-away zones).

103 Superstition Mountains (East) ✯✯✯

Many, many volcanic rock formations throughout the scenic saguaro-studded desert hills. Among these is the stunning and famed 600′ Weaver's Needle, home to the Lost Dutchman Gold Mine. Plentitude of more than 300 volcanic, pocket-pulling sport climbs in areas like Zonerland and Labyrinth. USFS-Tonto NF, (602) 610-3300.

Classics: Weaver's Needle: West Chim 5.0; Bark Canyon Wall: Glory Road III 7, Long Lead III 8, Stoke It Gently 10a; Wild Horse Wall: The Bronc 8, Mustang Sally 9, Zonerland, Land of Nod, Labyrinth Sport Routes, Pinyon Camp.

Ref: *Arizona Highways* 2/87, Annerino's *Adventuring in Arizona*; Guidebooks: Green's *Rock Climbing Arizona*, Opland's *Superstition Select: Climber's Guide to Multipitch Routes of the Superstition Mountains*, Percival's *Supes Climbs: Supplement Climbing Guide to the Superstition Mountains*, Waugh's *Phoenix Rock: A Guide to Central Arizona Crags*.

Directions: From Apache Junction go 8 $^6/_{10}$ mi. east on Hwy. 60/89 to Peralta Rd. Turn north on Peralta Rd. (dirt road) to a left on Carney Springs Rd. for The Acropolis and Carney Springs Wall or Peralta Campground and trailhead. Peralta Trailhead takes one via various trails to Nosepicker Pinnacles, Weaver's Needle, the Fortress, Wild Horse Wall, Miner's Needle, and many other wild formations.

104 Queen Creek ✯✯✯✯

Scenic volcanic pinnacles offering good crack and face routes. Sport climbs up to 5.13. Hynes and Karabin's *Queen*

Creek Canyon guidebook lists more than 650 climbing routes and 1,200 boulder problems and is creatively displayed with 200 photographs and 300 illustrations and maps. October–April. Camping at Oak Flats. USFS–Tonto NF, (602) 610-3300.

Classics: Apache Leap: Kinder Words 9, Smash It Up 11a, Toyekoyah 11a; Eurodog Valley: Speed Clip Pantie 10c, The Last Gentleman 12a/b, Love in the Ruins 11c/d, The Second Coming 13a. Bouldering Areas—Euro Dog Valley: Hook Wall, Lost Boys Wall; Oak Flat West: Shark Wall, Guppie Wall; Oak Flat East: Piranha Wall, Vector Arena.

Ref: C [158-50, 153-59, 152, 117, 113, 109], R 65-93, SC (6/91); Guidebooks: Green's *Rock Climbing Arizona*, Karabin's *Rock Jock's Guide to Queen Creek Canyon, Superior, Arizona*, Waugh's *Phoenix Rock: A Guide to Central Arizona Crags*, Hynes and Karabin's *Queen Creek Canyon*, Karabin's *A Sport Climber's Guide to Atlantis (Queen Creek Canyon)*, Waugh's *A Climber's Guide to Central Arizona Crags*, Karabin's *Euro Dog Valley*, Karabin's *Mine Area*.

Directions: From Superior go approximately 4 mi. east on Hwy. 60 to Queen Creek area. From the bridge the big palisades back to the south is called Musicland. Little England Wall and Triumvirates and a sport-climbing area known as Atlantis are just past the tunnel on the right below the road at first pullout. At second pullout, find Queen's Sceptre Pinnacle below and right across stream. The Pond Area is to the north of the road at the third pullout. Other climbs are obvious from blacktop. Top of the World Boulders is at the summit on Hwy. 60. Formations just 1 mi. past the tunnel include Sunday School Wall (to the north) and Diamond Buttress, Wounded Knee Wall, and South Side Wall (to the south). (Oak Flats Campground/Devils Canyon are farther east on Magma Mine Rd.) Climbing at highway level is frowned upon by highway patrol for safety reasons.

105 Oak Flats Campground ✯✯✯

Site of the nationally acclaimed Phoenix Bouldering Contest. Nice winter playground offering more than 400 bouldering/toprope problems on 40' volcanic rock, e.g., Piranha Wall. Violent on the tips. Camping on-site. USFS–Tonto NF, (602) 610-3300.

Ref: C [187-34, 169-92,126, 114]; Guidebooks: Phoenix Bouldering Contest topos, Karabin's Topo Series.

Directions: From Superior go east on Hwy. 60. Turn right (sign) on Magma Mine Rd., following it into Oak Flats Campgound. The actual climbing lies out of the campground via four-wheel-drive roads—ask at Desert Mountain Sports. Euro Dog Valley is a sport-climbing area that lies farther down Magma Mine Rd.

106 Devils Canyon (Upper and Lower) (4,100') ✯✯✯

Popular sport-climbing canyon in an attractive, desert canyon setting. Upper Canyon has at least sixty routes on volcanic pinnacles. The wildly scenic Lower Canyon also has more than sixty routes, featuring the picturesque Totem Pole Spire 5.10d and Eyes of the World 5.11. USFS–Tonto NF, (602) 610-3300.

Classics: Upper: Ferocious Flo 9, Deviled Hands 11b, Speak of the Devil 11c, Spice 13a; Lower: Ready Set Arête 8, Centerpiece 9, Sublime Line 10, Adios Larry 10b, Proto Pipe 11.

Ref: Guidebooks: Karabin's *Upper Devils Canyon* (topo map), Karabin's *Lower Devils Canyon Topo Sheet*.

Directions: From Superior go east on Hwy. 60. After passing mm 230, turn right (sign) on Magma Mine Rd. Pass a cattle guard and turn left (before Oak Flats Campground) on road number 469 to trailhead. Hike east (a short stroll past power lines running north to south) to Upper Devils Canyon. Many little cliffs with at least three different parking areas. Lower Devils Canyon is accessed south of Oak Flats Campground past cattle guard (Euro Dog Valley sport climbs on right) to hairpin. Turn left at fenced dirt road before pullout on left. Go south on an extremely rocky and jolting four-wheel-drive road that'll rip the tread right off a rim, then east past a ranch on the right for a total of 3 ½ mi. to a dead-end pullout/ camping area. Hike east into Lower Devils Canyon, where the Totem Pole can be viewed. Ask locals for further directions and about where you can get new tires.

107 Picket Post Mountains ✯

The volcanic Picket Post Mountains lie above (south) of Boyce-Thompson Arboretum. The visible spire below the main mesa (the thick pinnacle on the slope behind the arboretum), The Picket Post 5.6X, was first climbed in 1965 by Bill Forrest and Gary Garbert. There looks to be climbing potential in this desert mountain range, but reports are that rock tends to be fried.

Ref: G. Rink; Guidebooks: Opland's *Phoenix Rock*, Kurtz's *Arizona Rock Climbing Areas Map*, Waugh's *A Climber's Guide to Central Arizona Crags*.

Directions: From Superior, southwest of the junction of Hwy. 177 and Hwy. 60, the Picket Post Mountains lie above Boyce-Thompson Arboretum. Park at arboretum. The Picket Post, a thick, visible pinnacle on the slope behind the arboretum, has been climbed.

108 San Tan Mountains Regional Park ✯✯

Loose desert rock (got helmet?) makes for consistently interesting climbing. The volcanic, 200', east-facing Owl's Head, with a couple dozen beginner's routes, like Left Hand Edge 5.7, is the rock of most note. Good in winter. Maricopa Country Parks and Rec. (602) 506-2930.

Ref: Guidebooks: Waugh's *Phoenix Rock: A Guide to Central Arizona Crags*, Waugh's *A Climber's Guide to Central Arizona Crags*.

Directions: From Olberg, at obscure gas station, go 3 mi. left (east) on dirt road. Climbing in the Santan Mountains is found on Owl's Head (most climbing), Monkey Wall, and Obituary Wall.

109 KOFA Mountains (Palm Canyon) ★★★

Austere mountainous volcanic stone of varying quality amid desert bighorn sheepland. The idea of climbing here is described best by Karl Karlstrom in his account of the first ascent of the definitive climb of the range, Summit Peak, in *On the Wings of Icarus*. "This monolith is a tribute to true desert climbing . . . a staunch representative of the spirit of the desert where desolation, beauty, eternity, and change all seem to merge into an indefinite force which, to the desert climber, becomes an irresistible attraction." Highest peaks all done by Flagstaff legend, Scott Baxter. Remote areas, extremely rotten rock, hiking, and technical ascents. USGS topo maps a must. Native palm trees in Palm Canyon. Open year-round. KOFA National Wildlife Refuge, (520) 783-7861.

Classics: Summit Peak IV 8 A3.

Ref: S. Baxter; *Arizona Highways* 2/87, C 10/72; Guidebooks: Aitchison and Grubbs's *The Hiker's Guide to Arizona*, Annerino's *Adventuring in Arizona*, Kurtz's *Arizona Rock Climbing Areas Map*.

Directions: From Quartzite hotfoot it south on Hwy. 95 into the canyons of the KOFA (King of Arizona) Mountains. Roads lead east from Hwy. 95 south of mm 90 (Valve Two Rd.) and north of mm 85 (Palm Canyon Rd.) and mm 55 (Castle Dome Mine Rd.). Four highest peaks in the KOFAs are Signal (4,877'), Summit, Squaw (4,416'), and Bartolomo. USGS topo maps a must.

110 Castle Dome Mountains (The Brothers and Sisters) ★★

Wild, rugged volcanic desert mountain land. Castle Dome (3,788'), east of the road, is a classic. There's 5.6 knife-edge scrambling on this statuesque monolith. KOFA National Wildlife Refuge, (520) 783-7861.

Ref: AAJ '75-132.

Directions: From Yuma pop northeast of town on Hwy. 95. Follow the Castle Dome Rd. #75 to its end. Castle Dome (3,788') is east of the road.

111 Santa Teresa Mountains ★★★

Remote Shangri-la of pristine 400' granite domes and spires. In the incipient stage of development since 1991. Tricky hiking approaches with rough, vegetated hiking. Bears. USFS-Coronado NF, (520) 428-4150.

Ref: R 59; Guidebooks: Martin's *Arizona Mountains: Hiking and Climbing Guide*, Kerry's *Backcountry Climbing in Southern Arizona*.

Directions: From Klondyke go 1 mi. northwest past post office to FS 94. Turn right on FS 94 (left at fork at 1 mi.) 7 mi. to Poncho Tank in the Santa Theresa Mountains. Hike along discontinuous ridges east of road. Domes visible from top of ridge. Roads bad when wet, high-clearance vehicle recommended. Can also be approached via Holdout Basin Trail at end of FS 94. Tricky hiking approaches.

112 Klondyke Wall (in Santa Teresa Mountains) ★★★

The Klondyke Wall is a remote, high-quality 800' granite formation. Strike It Rich is probably the best wall at Klondyke. The Santa Teresa Mountains conceal a Fort Knox of granite domes. Coronado NF, (520) 428-4150.

Classics: Falling for Gold 11, Mother Lode 11, Strike It Rich Wall.

Ref: R 53(1/93)-70; Guidebook: Kerry's *Backcountry Climbing in Southern Arizona*.

Directions: From Safford (located on Hwy. 70) strike west on Hwy. 70 until signs for town of Klondyke direct you southwest on dirt roads. After 15-18 mi., turn right on side road marked 678. Take 678 1 mi. to big corral. Hike 2 mi. (ninety minutes) cross-country to Klondyke Wall. Between Safford and Thatcher, turn left off Hwy. 70 onto Black Rock Rd. until it ends at an enormous bowl and a new world of granite marked as Pinnacle Ridge on topos.

113 Mt. Graham Area (in Pinaleno Mountains)—Dutch Henry Canyon ★★★

Remote areas of exploratory multipitch gneiss/granite backcountry area. Minimal climbing has been done. Loaded with granite; topos recommended. Coronado NF, (520) 428-4150.

Ref: R 53(1/93)-70; Guidebook: Kerry's *Backcountry Climbing in Southern Arizona*.

Directions: From Wilcox go 12 mi. east on I-10 to the Safford exit. Take Hwy. 666 north for 3 mi. past junction with Hwy. 266. Turn left at USFS sign, follow road past P Ranch to fork. Go right up short, steep hill and continue bearing right en route to a windmill at the mountain's base. Trailhead is across the creek from the windmill. Three-mile hike to main rock faces in Dutch Henry Canyon: Honkey Pinnacle on right, Lions Head on left.

114 Mt. Graham Area (Faraway Faces and Hell's Hole) ★★★

Remote areas and exploratory granite backcountry areas with 500' routes. This area is loaded with granite; topos recommended. Beware of bears. In the Pinaleno Mountains. Coronado NF, (520) 428-4150.

Classics: Faraway Faces: Blind Pigs Eat Rocks 10; Hell's Hole: Angels on Horseback 9+, My Urine Melts Rock Like Acid 9.

Ref: R 53(1/93)-71; Guidebook: Kerry's *Backcountry Climbing in Southern Arizona*.

Directions: West of Safford. From Wilcox go 12 mi. east on I-10 to the Safford exit. Go north up Hwy. 666 to 3 mi. past Hwy. 266; follow this 12-15 mi. to Ladybug Saddle in the Mt. Graham Area. Approach Faraway Faces via Ladybug Trail, 3 mi. (until wall is visible). To get to Hell's Hole, continue toward end of the Swift Trail (main road) and (½ mi. past Chesney Meadow) turn right on dirt road. Go ½ mi. to campsite and start of 2-mi. (two-hour) approach. Hell's Hole lies just northwest of Grand View Peak on topo.

115 Picacho Peak State Park ☆☆

Many-faceted walls adorn this obvious landmark rising 1,500' above valley floor, visible from I-10. Rumors of sport climbing on the 200' volcanics. Possibly good rock. Nice 2 2/10 mi. hike to the summit via Hunter Trail. Civil War reenactments in the state park in March. Pay camping. State park, (520) 466-3183.
Ref: J. Waugh; Guidebook: Annerino's *Adventuring in Arizona*.
Directions: Just west of Picacho, Picacho Peak is the obvious landmark visible from I-10. Take exit 219 and drive west into state park.

116 Tortolitas Boulder ☆☆

One good expert 20' granite bouldering traverse problem. Tucson is the home of University of Arizona, some of the best Mexican food this side of the border, and Mt. Lemmon Highway, a climber's wonderland. Land may be privately owned.
Ref: J. Sherman.
Directions: North of Tucson. From Tucson go west on I-10 to exit 236 (Marana). Go east and northeast on dirt roads approximately 8 mi. into Cottonwood Canyon (right at fork at 1 mi. (see USGS maps). Tortolitas Boulder is a single boulder that is ½ mi. southeast (right) of road, ½–1 mi. before ranch.

117 Silver Bell Boulders (closed) ☆☆☆

Tucson's best low-elevation, expert bouldering. Volcanic 15' fingery overhangs; Bob Murray et al. testpieces. Closed to climbing by landowner. Private land.
Directions: West of Tucson. From Tucson go north on I-10 to Rillito exit (number 242). Head west to Silver Bell Boulders on Avra Valley Rd. to Silver Bell.

118 Red Boulder ☆☆☆

An excellent 20' granite boulder with more than a dozen problems for the specialist. Toprope bolt at top. It's hard to find and isn't visible until within 100 yd. Hike along base of slope. Land may be government owned.
Ref: C 154-101; Guidebook: Murray's *Bouldering Beyond Campbell*.
Directions: Northwest Tucson. From Tucson take Ina Rd. west from I-10. After 3 mi. turn left onto Wade Rd. Drive through Contzen Pass and park near 35 mph speed limit sign. The Red Boulder is 1 mi. away at the base of the slopes below the cliffs to the northwest. Not visible until at slopes. (Hard to find without a local who's been there.)

119 Saguaro National Park (West) ☆☆

These 15' white granite boulders have problems visible on the hillside to the east and more boulders (toprope slab) ½ mi. up Hugh Norris Trail. Entrance fee. Open dawn until dusk. No camping. NPS, (520) 733-5153.
Ref: Guidebook: Murray's *Bouldering Beyond Campbell*.
Directions: West of Tucson. From Tucson take Speedway west through Gates Pass to T-junction. Go right, past Desert Museum, then right into Saguaro National Park. After a few miles, turn right onto the Bajada Loop. Follow this 1 mi. to Hugh Norris Trailhead.

120 Gates Pass ☆☆

A 20' granite boulder with six routes at bottom of west side of pass. Keep eyes peeled—partially hidden in cactus. City park/NPS.
Classics: Broken Rubber Boulder, Son of Broken Rubber Boulder.
Directions: West of Tucson. From Tucson go west of town on Speedway, which turns into Gates Pass Rd. Go 1–2 mi. west past summit; boulders to south of road at base of grade. Also some boulders east of summit, approximately 1 mi. north of road (five-minute hike).

121 The Beehive ☆☆

A mixture of 200' volcanic rock formations and knobs. Little used by Tucson climbers. Rock may be brittle. Private/government land.
Ref: Guidebook: Kurtz's *Arizona Rock Climbing Areas Map*.
Directions: Southwest of Tucson. North of Bilby Rd. Various rock outcrops of The Beehive must be accessed through several housing tracts.

122 Santa Catalina Mountains ☆☆☆☆☆

An incredible range of 1,000' granite domes, cliffs, and bouldering in the desert within one hour of Tucson are a rock-climber's dream. USFS-Coronado NF, (520) 749-8700.
Classics: Climbing areas are found on Mt. Lemmon Hwy. and Pusch Ridge.
Ref: C [117, 111, 95], R 53(1/93); Guidebooks: Green's *Rock Climbing Arizona*, Kerry's *Backcountry Climbing in Southern Arizona*, Steiger's *Climber's Guide to Sabino Canyon and Mt. Lemmon Highway*, Fazio-Rhicard's *Squeezing the Lemmon: A Rock Climber's Guide to the Mt. Lemmon Highway*, Fazio-Rhicard's *A Supplement to Climber's Guide to Sabino Canyon and Mt. Lemmon Highway*.
Directions: From Tucson the Santa Catalina Mountains are the mountain range to the northeast. Many access points and areas described here (see write-ups 123–136 and 159); Mt. Lemmon Hwy. most used.

123 Leviathan Dome, Wilderness Dome, and Solitude Pinnacle ☆☆☆☆

On the north side of Pusch Ridge lie these amazing, 1,000' gneissic backcountry rock domes, though they are seldom climbed due to long approaches. Leviathan Dome's North Face 5.10c is the classic completed by Gary Hervert and Brett Oxberry in June 1974; it was freed completely by Dave Baker and Fig in 1977. Other big domes nearby. USFS-Coronado NF, (520) 749-8700.
Classics: Leviathan Dome: User Friendly 6p 9, Over the Rainbow 7p 12; Wilderness Dome: Rivendell 6p 10; at least five other long routes.

One of the finer granite showpieces of southern Arizona, Leviathan Dome.

TIM TOULA

Ref: R 53; Guidebooks: Green's *Rock Climbing Arizona*, Kerry's *Backcountry Climbing in Southern Arizona*.

Directions: North of Tucson. From Tucson go north on Oracle Rd. (Hwy. 89) to Catalina State Park (entrance fee). Park at end of road in park. Two- to four-hour hike starting at the "birding loop" of Sutherland Trail, then going left at BIRDING LOOP sign 7/10 mi. to "stairs" onto a dirt road, which turns into a horse trail to the mouth of Alamo Canyon (main canyon leading down from Leviathan Dome). (Avoid going into the brushy canyon bottom early on.) Follow streambed straight uphill to toe of Leviathan Dome. Wilderness Dome is another thirty minutes around and up the left side of Leviathan Dome. Solitude Pinnacle is to the west and on equal level with Leviathan Dome.

124 Golder Dome ✩✩✩

Santa Catalina Mountains. A thirty-minute bushwhack up a ridge with big granite slabs gets one to 400' Golder Dome. The Grunt 5.9 was one of the first climbs here, in 1977. Bring double ropes for rappel. State land/USFS–Coronado NF, (520) 749-8700.

Classics: Sunnyside Up 6, Dam Bureaucrats 8+, The Grunt 9/10, Buzzworm's Backyard 12a.

Ref: C [109, 108], R 53(1/93)-66; Guidebook: Kerry's *Backcountry Climbing in Southern Arizona*.

Directions: North of Tucson. From Tucson sail north on Hwy. 89 for approximately 10 mi. Just before Catalina, turn right on Golder Ranch Rd. Continue on dirt and take a right on FR 643. Either park at Sutherland Wash or four-wheel another 1 4/10 mi. to trail (sign) from Catalina State Park.

125 Table Mountain (6,265') ✩✩✩

Airy bastion of north Tucson on the north side of Pusch Ridge. Scenic and airy seven-pitch routes on gneissic rock wall. Cherry Jam 8+ is one classic. One can backcountry camp at base of Table Mountain. USFS–Coronado NF, (520) 749-8700.

Ref: Guidebook: Kerry's *Backcountry Climbing in Southern Arizona*.

Directions: North of Tucson. From Tucson go north on Oracle Rd. (Hwy. 89) to La Reserve subdivision (1 mi. south of Catalina State Park). Turn right at stables and factory parking at the start of the horse trail. The two and a half hour rough hike (aka "heinapproach") is the price to pay for the pleasure of the climbing and gives a backcountry feel to this Tucson landmark.

126 Pusch Peak ✩✩✩

Stunning ridge of four pitched, gneissic rock routes. Topo at Summit Hut. USFS–Coronado NF, (520) 749-8700.

Classics: Pusch Push 10d.

Ref: Guidebook: Kerry's *Backcountry Climbing in Southern Arizona*.

Directions: North of Tucson. From Tucson push north on Oracle Rd. (Hwy. 89). Go right on Loma Linda for 1/4 mi. to cul-de-sac. Park. One-hour hike to Pusch Peak.

127 Frying Pan Boulder ✩✩✩

The 20' gneissic Frying Pan Boulder is visible on hillside from national forest access parking lot below Pusch Peak. Hike twenty minutes up the trail, then bushwhack left to rocks. Topropes. Bring 3/8" hanger and 9/16" wrench for anchor bolt on top. USFS–Coronado NF, (520) 749-8700.

Ref: Guidebook: Murray's *Bouldering Beyond Campbell*.

Directions: North of Tucson. From Tucson go north on Oracle Rd. (Hwy. 89) to an unmarked right turn a few yards before mm 78 (road to Pusch Ridge Estates). Drive a short distance to national forest access parking. Frying Pan Boulder is visible on hillside from parking lot. Hike twenty minutes up the trail, then bushwhack left to rocks.

128 Campbell Cliff (closed) ✩✩✩

A well-loved Tucson play area. Thin 30' granite vertical bouldering and toprope routes near posh housing development on north side of town. Closest natural rock climbing to town. Unfortunately, now closed to climbers. Private land.

Classics: Bamboo Shoots B1, Chimi Express B2.

Ref: C 62(8/80)-38.

Directions: In Tucson, shoot north to end of Campbell Rd. A ten-minute hike north on trail between fences of plush estates. This trail may be gone now that Campbell Cliff is closed.

129 Finger Rock Canyon ✩✩✩

Rock-lined granite-gneissic canyon. Named formations include Death Wall, Prominent Point, Finger Rock, and

Finger Rock Guard. Good boulder 1 mi. up the trail on right side of trail. Poor rock for leading down low in canyon. USFS–Coronado NF, (520) 749-8700.

Classics: 5.7 route on Finger Rock.

Ref: Guidebook: Kerry's *Backcountry Climbing in Southern Arizona*, Murray's *Bouldering Beyond Campbell*.

Directions: North Tucson. From Tucson go to the north end of Alvernon Way. Hike up steep trail to Finger Rock Canyon.

130 SC–Esperero Spires ☆☆

These are 450′ gneiss pinnacles. Darker rock is usually more sound. Backcountry camping, water available in winter. USFS–Coronado NF, (520) 749-8700.

Classics: Ziggurat 5.9.

Ref: R 53(1/93)-68; Guidebook: Kerry's *Backcountry Climbing in Southern Arizona*.

Directions: Northeast of Tucson. Take Sabino Canyon Rd. north from Tanque Verde Rd. From Sabino Canyon approach on Esperero Trail. Two-hour hike to Esperero Spires.

131 Sabino Canyon ☆☆

Tall 600′ walls of loose, putrescent, layered gneiss in a 4-mi.-long canyon. Shuttle bus with fee or bike in free. Nearest camping on Mt. Lemmon (Molino Basin). Udall Center has showers (small fee). USFS–Coronado NF, (520) 749-8700.

Classics: Kor Wall: Kor Route 8; Acropolis: Sissyphus 11; new sport routes.

Ref: Guidebooks: Kerry's *Backcountry Climbing in Southern Arizona*. Steiger's *Climber's Guide to Sabino Canyon and Mt. Lemmon Highway*, Fazio-Rhicard's *Squeezing the Lemmon: A Rock Climber's Guide to the Mt. Lemmon Highway*, Fazio-Rhicard's *A Supplement to Climber's Guide to Sabino Canyon and Mt. Lemmon Highway*, Jimmerson and Smolinsky's *Southern Arizona Climber's Guide*.

Directions: Northeast of Tucson. Short drive from Tucson city limits. Take Sabino Canyon Rd. north from Tanque Verde Rd. Park at Sabino Canyon Visitor Center. Buy shuttle ticket. Formations on the way into the canyon include The Acropolis (forty-five-minute hike), Mission Control Area, Crocodile Rock, Whipple Wall (loose), and Fruitstand. The Acropolis's 500′ red cliff is up the canyon to the right.

132 Lower Bear Canyon ☆☆☆

A 450′ winter gneiss crag. USFS–Coronado NF, (520) 749-8700.

Ref: Guidebooks: Fazio-Rhicard's *Squeezing the Lemmon: A Rock Climber's Guide to the Mt. Lemmon Highway*, Kerry's *Backcountry Climbing in Southern Arizona*.

Directions: Tucson; southeast and parallel to Sabino Canyon. Park north of Snyder Rd. Short trail leads to Bear Canyon Trail. Three-mi. approach to Lower Bear Canyon.

133 Mt. Lemmon Highway ☆☆☆☆☆

Pythonic ridges of gneiss crags and boulders. Mt. Lemmon makes Tucson a magnet for winter climbers. Rock quality seemingly improves as one gains elevation though good routes are abundant. Windy Point (6800′), Mt. Lemmon Summit (9157′). The highly acclaimed Beaver Wall has fanned the flames of traditional/sport-climbing controversies. Camping scattered along highway (or Molino Campground during winter). Raptor restrictions March 15–June 30. Caution: Dangerous winding highway. USFS–Coronado NF, (520) 749-8700.

Classics: So many classics, so little time: Hairpin Turn: Rosie 10+; Jailhouse Rock: Sentenced . . . 12; Pumphouse: Forged . . . 12-; Hawk's Bill Spire: Pitfalls . . . 10, Children of the Revolution 12+; Cornerstone: Raising Arizona 10-, Hearthstone- 9+; Chimney Rock: Fiutt 8, Mistaken Identity 9, Crow's Nest 10-, Centerpiece 10-, Jungle Gym 10+, Today . . . 12; Pharoah: Cripple Creek 10-, T. T. Avenger 12-; Lost Hawk Pinnacle: Chihuahua Power 9; Windy Point East–Punch and Judy Towers: Birthday Girl 10, Lizard Marmalade Dir 10+, Raindance 11+, Power Hungry 11+, Wild Thing 13; Honeymooner's Wall, New Wave Wall: Tsunami 12, New Wave 12, Goosed but Smilin' 11-, Windy Point West–Beaver Wall: Right Tissue 12, Rooting . . . 11+, Climb w/a View 13-, Hebe 13+, Air Monsters 12-, Slippery . . . 7, Pucker Up 13-, Nang 10-; Neptune: Rapture . . . 10, Agent Orange 10+, Ma'adim 12, Naranja 11, Catch the Wave 12+; Poseidon: Heat Wave 12; Rappel Rock: Black Quacker 7, The Corner 8+, Chiboni 10a, Voodoo Child 11b.

Ref: C [179-21/115, 166(2/97)-49, 153-131, 144, 130, 125, 117, 114, 109 to 105, 103, 102, 101(4/87)-44, 100, 99, 97, 95, 91],R [53(1/93) 51, 35(1/89)]; Guidebooks: Green's *Rock Climbing Arizona*, Kerry's *Backcountry Climbing in Southern Arizona*, Karabin's *Mt. Lemmon (East Windy Point)* Topo Map, Fazio-Rhicard's *Squeezing the Lemmon: A Rock Climber's Guide to the Mt. Lemmon Highway*; Ayers's *An Anarchist's Guide to Climbing Routes on the Mid-Mountain, Mt. Lemmon*; Fazio-Rhicard's *A Supplement to Climber's Guide to Sabino Canyon and Mt. Lemmon Highway*, Steiger's *Climber's Guide to Sabino Canyon and Mt. Lemmon Highway*, Murray's *Bouldering Beyond Campbell*, Baker's *Tucson Area Climber's Guide*.

Directions: Northeast of Tucson, take Tanque Verde Rd. to Mt. Lemmon Hwy. (signs). Numerous cliffs along Mt. Lemmon Hwy. See Steiger's or Fazio-Rhicard's guidebooks. Cragging areas from south to north include Bear Canyon, Windy Point Overlook 14 3/10 mi. from beginning of Catalina Hwy. Windy Ridge, and, at the very top at 9,000′, Reef of Rocks, Rappel Rock, Ravens, and The Fortress (summer areas). Bouldering: see Molino Canyon, Weeping Wall between mm 9 and 10. Park on left before 5,400′ ELEV. sign. It's 200 yd. above the sign. Barefoot Wall is just past mm 10 and just above road, blocked by trees. Windy Point is on obvious plateau. Matterhorn Boulder (and Amphitheatre Boulder, best hard boulder in Tucson arena?) is past mm 16. Park just past FUELWOOD sign on right. Go uphill 100 yd. Rose Canyon is on the first dirt road on left past Rose Canyon entrance. It's on the right down the road. Amphitheater Boulder is at the end of Rose Canyon Rd. Also, Rappel Rock and Back of Ravens areas.

134 Molino Basin (New Wave Wall) ✸✸✸

Tall walls of loose, layered 600′ gneiss close to town and low in elevation. This is a good bet for winter camping. Best rock on Choo-Choo Rock formation. USFS–Coronado NF, (520) 749-8700.

Classics: Weathertop Mesa: It 11; Lost Wall: Unhinged 11-.

Ref: Guidebooks: Kerry's *Backcountry Climbing in Southern Arizona*, Fazio-Rhicard's *Squeezing the Lemmon: A Rock Climber's Guide to the Mt. Lemmon Highway*, Fazio-Rhicard's *A Supplement to Climber's Guide to Sabino Canyon and Mt. Lemmon Highway*, Steiger's *Climber's Guide to Sabino Canyon and Mt. Lemmon Highway*, Murray's *Bouldering Beyond Campbell*.

Directions: Northeast of Tucson. Take Mt. Lemmon Hwy. just up to Molino Basin Campground. Most climbing in Weathertop Mesa/Choo Choo Rock area south of campground. Other areas to northeast of campground include Stonewall and Lost Wall. Painted Boulder is past mm 4 at first pulloff past roadcut rock with hole through it near top on right. Directly below road. More boulders upstream.

135 Spencer Fins ✸✸✸

A cluster of a dozen pinnacles visible from Tucson below Mt. Bigelow Observatory. Try the classic Eclipse 10d A0. USFS–Coronado NF, (520) 749-8700.

Ref: Guidebook: Kerry's *Backcountry Climbing in Southern Arizona*.

Directions: From Tucson get on Catalina Hwy. Start hiking at mm 22 on Catalina Hwy. Spencer Fins are five rock fins in Santa Catalinas below Mt. Bigelow Observatory. A two-hour approach from Box Camp Trail, then cross-country.

136 Tanque Verde Canyon (aka The Sandbox) ✸✸✸

Tucson's finest collection of 25′ gneissic bouldering problems. Polished boulders. Best area is called The Sandbox. More than twenty routes. There may be car thieves. USFS–Coronado NF, (520) 749-8700.

Ref: Guidebook: Murray's *Bouldering Beyond Campbell*.

Directions: East of Tucson. From Tucson take Tanque Verde Rd. east about 1 ½ mi. after the road turns to dirt, park at turnout for Tanque Verde Falls. Hike down to the wash. Noteworthy large block ¼ mi. downstream and white wall across from it. But the best area is called The Sandbox (at tall white boulder), upstream from large block and around prominent bend.

137 Rincon Mountains ✸✸✸

A wonderland of 500′ granite rock that has seen very little development. In a granite-domed mountain range east of Tucson. USFS–Coronado NF, (520) 749-8700.

Ref: Guidebook: Kerry's *Backcountry Climbing in Southern Arizona*.

Directions: East of Tucson. From Tucson (visible from town), go to Redington Pass to Italian Trap Rd., then go up dirt road. Hike one and a half hours into the Rincon Mountains.

138 Valley of the Moon ✸✸✸

These are 500′ granite cliffs in the Rincon Mountains. USFS–Coronado NF, (520) 749-8700.

Classics: Dark Side of the Moon 5.9+.

Ref: R 53(1/93)-69; Guidebook: Kerry's *Backcountry Climbing in Southern Arizona*.

Directions: East of Tucson. From Tucson drive east on I-10. Take the Mescal Rd./J-Six Ranch exit. Go north 11 8/10 mi. to a small pullout on the left (can't see cliffs). Hike west one hour into drainage to Valley of the Moon cliff.

139 Texas Canyon ✸✸

These 300′ granite formations are reminiscent of Joshua Tree, but they're minimally developed. Could make for interesting exploratory bouldering sessions. For a sure bet, there's better climbing nearby at Cochise Stronghold. Private/state land.

Classics: The Thing 5.10.

Ref: Guidebook: Kerry's *Backcountry Climbing in Southern Arizona*.

Directions: East of Benson. From Benson travel along I-10 just north of Texas Canyon rest area (mm 320–321). Or follow innumerable billboards to The Thing, a few miles east of the rocks.

140 Organ Pipe National Monument ✸✸

Boulder problems scattered along Ajo Moutain Dr. as well as large formations on park loop drive. Check climbing guide in ranger's office. November–April. Primitive free camping at Alamo Campground; pay at Twin Peaks Campground. NPS, (520) 387-6849.

Ref: B. Murray.

Directions: From Gila Bend drive 75–80 mi. south on Hwy. 85 to Organ Pipe National Monument.

141 Montezuma's Head (3,601′) (Ajo Mountains) ✸✸✸

Located in north Organ Pipe National Monument, this 400′ volcanic multipitched desert adventure summit looks like the safety cap of a large propane cylinder. Sketchy rock quality reminiscent of dried Montezuma's Revenge. Montezuma's Revenge 5.7 (north face) makes for a fine day's outing from the road. NPS, (520) 387-6849.

Ref: Guidebook: Kerry's *Backcountry Climbing in Southern Arizona*.

Directions: From Why head south on Hwy. 85 a short distance. Park at mm 62. Montezuma's Head is visible on the left. A one-hour cross-country hike through incredible organ pipe cactus stands takes one to base. Then, one-hour scrambling to north column where ropework starts.

142 Mendoza Canyon (aka Coyote Domes Wilderness Area) ★★★★

A beautiful wilderness area of large, 1,000' granitic domes. Wily Javelina, six-pitch 5.9, is the classic. Good winter area. Expect some questionable rock quality and long runouts. Register at Fish and Game sign-in. October–April. State/BLM land, (602) 417–9200.

Classics: Elephant Dome: Elephant's Trunk II 7, Elephantiasis 6p 10d, B Cubed 6p 10; Table Dome: Wily Javelina 6p 9.

Ref: R 53(1/93)-69; Guidebook: Kerry's *Backcountry Climbing in Southern Arizona*.

Directions: One and a half hours west of Tucson; southwest of Robles Junction. From Tucson go west on Hwy. 86 (Ajo Way) approximately 15 mi. to Robles Junction. Turn left on Hwy. 286 for 8 mi. to King Anvil Ranch (not Kings Ranch). Turn right through ranch yard. Go west through wash, then right at bigger of two small dirt roads past water tank. Follow this road to Mendoza Canyon's mouth. Two-mi. hike if gate is locked. Brushy canyon approaches—some climber's cairns. A Pulaski may be handy for trails. Domes face mainly east.

143 Kitt Peak Areas (Aquagomy Wall, 10-4 Wall, and Forbidden City) ★★★

Lofty desert views inspire climbing on 300' granite walls and boulders. Be aware of gate closure times. Climbers need to be punctilious in respect to landowners, the Tohono O'odham Indians. Site of world's largest solar telescope. The visitors center is open 9:00 A.M.–3:45 P.M. Tours: 10:00 A.M., 11:30 A.M., 1:30 P.M., $2.00 donation. BIA/private land.

Classics: Splashdown 8, Cosmic Streaker 9.

Ref: Guidebook: Kerry's *Backcountry Climbing in Southern Arizona*.

Directions: One and a half hours west of Tucson. From Tucson foot it west 50–60 mi. on Hwy. 86. Turn south on Hwy. 386 (Kitt Peak Rd.). Aquagomy Wall is between mm 5 and 6. One mile farther is 10-4 Wall. Forbidden City is at top, down and right of the solar telescope. Big slabs to south of road. Forbidden City is on top near trespass areas (fine) but has spectacular rock.

144 Baboquivari Peak ★★★★

Spectacular 1,000' desert monarch. The first ascent of this 7,734' monolith was in 1898. The first technical ascent was in 1957 on the scenic, SE Arête Route 5.6 (still classic today). Thirty mi. long and 5–10 mi. wide, Baboquivari's east face overhangs for 500' of its 1,000' porphyritic felsite east face. Seven long routes exist—see Kerry's guidebook for detailed route descriptions. In Pima, Baboquivari means "water on the mountain." A year-round spring on Lion's Ledge (east face) is a reliable source of water. The peak is the dwelling place of I'itoi, a Tohono O'odham Indian deity. BIA/federal/state land.

Classics: Forbes Rt. fourth-class with rope for rap; East Face: Don's Crack 5.9, Spring Route VI 5.9 A4, Northeast Face: Waugh Rt 11+; South Face: Time Lost IV 5.9, Cradle of Stone A4.

Ref: AAJ ['69-397, 67], *Arizona Highways* 2/87, C 48, R [53(1/93)-71, 30(3/89)-16], S 11/68; Guidebooks: Martin's *Arizona Mountains: Hiking and Climbing Guide*, Annerino's *Adventuring in Arizona*, Green's *Rock Climbing Arizona*, Kerry's *Backcountry Climbing in Southern Arizona*.

Directions: Two hours southwest of Tucson. Two approaches: 1) For the east side (rougher roads and used most), go west from Tucson on Hwy. 86. Turn south on Hwy. 286 at Robles Junction to mm 16. At first dirt road past mm 16, turn west onto dirt roads for 2 7/10 mi. to first road at right fork in road. Veer right. Continue on to gate at 8 mi. Park. Hike (ninety minutes) past ranch houses/corral up Thomas Canyon (steep trail) to north saddle; bushwhack south under east face to Lion's Ledge. Lion's Ledge is start of east face routes. 2) For the west side approach (longer), go west on Hwy. 86 to Sells, then south from Sells on pavement 10 mi. to a sign marking the turnoff to Baboquivari Campground (small fee; water) for 12 mi. on dirt road. Hike on trail, bushwhacking east to south slope of Baboquivari Peak. Campsites in the north saddle.

145 Pena Blanca ★★

Twenty-five foot expert volcanic bouldering and topropes. USFS-Coronado NF, (520) 281–2296.

Directions: West of Nogales. From Nogales take Hwy. 289 west past lake after road turns to dirt. Pena Blanca has a couple areas of rock to north of road. Also, reddish rock on hilltop above road is hard to find.

146 Cochise Stronghold (East) ★★★★★

A classic compilation of beautiful 500' granite domes. Ample routes to 5.12. Rockfellow Group consists of the following named domes: End Pinnacle, Chay desa Tsay, Rockfellow Dome, Bastion Towers, Hawk Pinnacle, and Lost Tower. These domes are wind magnets; i.e., wind in the campground could mean tornadoes up top. Approaches vary from minutes to the boulders to hours to the upper domes. Fine bouldering circuit in the campground, along nature trail, and along trail to west Stronghold. Arizona Beanfest site. Cochise Stronghold is named after the Chiricahuan Apache chief who raided settlers in the area and would then return laden with booty to the rocky fortress. Raptor restrictions February 15–June 30. Mid-September–November/April. Pay camping with water. USFS-Coronado NF, (520) 364–3468.

Classics: Beeline 5.9; Cochise Dome: What's My Line 5.6A0; Rockfellow Domes: Wasteland 8, Days of Future Passed 8AO/10, Forest Lawn 9, Nightstalker 9, Abracadaver 10+, Cap'm Pissgums III 10+; Murray Canyon: Mangas Coloradas 11a; Campground: Dominatrix w/o Mercy 12-, north face of Firepit Rock V7.

Ref: C [182-43, 181-56, 106, 90], R [75-87, 47], S [7/88, 9/86]; Guidebooks: Green's *Rock Climbing Arizona*, Kerry's

Backcountry Climbing in Southern Arizona, Davidson's *A Bouldering Thing: Caveat Emptor (East Cochise Stronghold)*.

Directions: South of Wilcox. From Wilcox take I-10 west. Exit south on Hwy. 666 for approximately 28 mi. Turn west at Sunsites onto Ironwood Rd. to east Cochise Stronghold, following signs. First east-facing domes seen on drive in (to west of road before reaching campground) include North to South, Entrance Dome, Wasteland, and Out-of-Towner's Dome. These are reached by turning right after a cattle guard, then continuing to a parking/camping zone. Drainages to west lead the way in. For Rockfellow Dome et al., park at campground. Various short excellent climbs/boulders near campground. Stronghold Dome is closest to campground, approximately thirty minutes. To get to the high domes, hike prudently up gully approximately one hour to the major high domes of Rockfellow Group/Cochise Dome.

147 Cochise Stronghold (West) ★★★★

Cochise West, "The other side of the Stronghold," features tons of 500' rock domes and slightly more moderate approaches (one to two hours) than the east Stronghold. In the past it's been less crowded than the East Stronghold. Access to many granite domes, including Westworld Dome, Squaretop, Cochise, Rockfellow Group, The Hands, The Tombstone, and Warpath Domes. Beanfest Site II. Fall/spring. Undeveloped campsites. Raptor restrictions February 15–June 30. USFS-Coronado NF, (520) 364–3468.

Ref: AAJ '74-149, R 99-152; Guidebooks: Green's *Rock Climbing Arizona*, Kerry's *Backcountry Climbing in Southern Arizona*, Off White's *A Beanfester's Guide to the West Stronghold*.

Classics: Whale Dome: Moby Dick 7+, Warpath 9+; L. Squaretop: Cragaholics Dream 10+; Westworld Dome: Warpaint 10c; Tombstone: Stiletto 11d.

Directions: Northeast of Tombstone. From Benson flock south on Hwy. 80 to just a few mi. before Tombstone. Turn left (northeast) on Middlemarch Rd. (just after mm 315) and continue to sign for west Stronghold (where you turn left on FS 687). Note: The old access route via St. David across from the monastery now requires a special code to enter.

148 Cochise Stronghold (Southwest—Sheepshead) ★★★★

Runout and difficult route finding in a granite spectacle of 1,000' domes. These west-facing formations include Big, Little, and Middle Sister Domes; Mallethead; Sheepshead; Carnivore Pinnacle; and Watchtower. Watchtower is most southerly dome in the Stronghold—drive to top. Isle of You sport-climbing area near camp. Raptor restrictions February 15–June 30. Noteworthy climbs Fall/spring. Undeveloped camping. USFS-Coronado NF, (520) 364–3468.

Classics: Sheepshead: Absinthe of Malice III 5.9+, Crazyfinger 10c, Too Steep for Sheep 11c, Sheep Thrills 5.11; Watchtower: Mr. Stay Puft 10a.

Ref: R 59; Guidebooks: Green's *Rock Climbing Arizona*, Kerry's *Backcountry Climbing in Southern Arizona*, Ayers's *Beanfest Fall 88 Southwest Stronghold*.

Directions: Northeast of Tombstone. From Benson flock south on Hwy. 80 to just a few mi. before Tombstone. Turn left (northeast) on Middlemarch Rd. (just after mm 315) and continue to sign for west Stronghold (where you turn left on FS 687) then take the first right. Go to windmill and park at fence. Hike thirty minutes across meadow to domes of Southwest Cochise Stronghold and the stunning 1,000' granite dome known as Sheepshead. For Isle of You sport-climbing area, go farther north on FS 687 for 2 mi. Just past cattle guard, take right leading shortly to primitive cul-de-sac camping and Trad and Rad Rock behind it, adorned with excellent bolted routes.

149 Chiricahua National Monument ★★★

The premiere area, Rhyolite Canyon, is known as the land of 1,000 spires. Usually, at least one side of a 165' spire has quality rock, setting the stage for wild face climbing. Many spires have been ascended (as early as 1959 with Bob Kamps and others) before the climbing ban in the national monument was enacted. The 137' high and 3' diameter "Totem Pole" is one of many in the spire collection. Pay camping. NPS, (520) 824–3560.

Ref: S 7/64; Guidebooks: Aitchison and Grubbs's *The Hiker's Guide to Arizona*, Kerry's *Backcountry Climbing in Southern Arizona*.

Directions: Southeast of Wilcox. From Wilcox travel approximately 25 mi. southeast on Hwy. 186 to Chiricahua National Monument headquarters. Rhyolite Canyon starts at park headquarters.

150 Turkey Creek ★★★

Granite wonderland of face cragging. Fee campground. USFS-Coronado NF, (520) 364–3468.

Ref: Guidebook: Kerry's *Backcountry Climbing in Southern Arizona*.

Directions: Southeast of Wilcox. From Wilcox travel approximately 25 mi. southeast on Hwy. 186, passing south of Chiricahua National Monument on Hwy. 181. In several mi., when Hwy. 181 turns right (west), turn east onto Turkey Creek Rd. toward mountains to rock.

151 Silver Peak (aka Portal Cliffs) ★★

Potential volcanic cliffs on the east side of Chiricahua Mountains. Cave Creek Canyon bouldering and toproping. Fee camping. USFS-Coronado NF, (520) 364–3468.

Ref: J. Gamertsfelder; Guidebook: Kerry's *Backcountry Climbing in Southern Arizona*.

Directions: From Portal go southwest past ranger station to Silver Peak. Cathedral Rock is on left. Beyond, rock lies on north side of entrance to Cave Creek Canyon and again farther west.

152 Elephant Head ✯✯✯

Large, singular 1,000′ gneiss dome located on west side of the Santa Rita Mountains. South side looks like Joshua Tree walls stacked on top of each other. Steep north side. No known routes on north face. West Gully 5.6 route is more mountaineering than rock climbing; i.e., loose, wandering route. From top, descend to saddle between head and ridge, then down and right into gully back to start. High-clearance vehicles recommended. USFS-Coronado NF, (520) 281-2296.

Ref: C. Dunn; Guidebook: Kerry's *Backcountry Climbing in Southern Arizona.*

Directions: South of Tucson. From Tucson drive south on I-19. Elephant Head's huge 1,000′ wall (north face) can be seen on left. Wander on dirt roads to West Buttress like so: Take Canoa Rd. exit (number 56), going 3 mi. south on East Frontage Rd. to Elephant Head Rd. and turn left, following road (named Canoa/Hawk) until it becomes dirt. At Y, take left fork at Texas gate. At ⁴/10 mi., go right at crossroad down into wash (poor road). After two more gates, slabs at west gully are evident. For a hike to the top, drive via the Amado exit from I-19 on various dirt roads (get a map for more information).

153 Carr Canyon Falls (in Huachaca Mountains) ✯✯

One- and two-pitch granite 5.10 crag climbs near waterfall area. Longest Day 5.10 is one of the better routes. Lichenous and slippery at top, where unwary tourists often take the big death plunge. USFS-Coronado NF, (520) 378-0311.

Ref: Guidebook: Kerry's *Backcountry Climbing in Southern Arizona.*

Directions: South of Sierra Vista. From Tucson motor east on I-10 to Sierra Vista exit. Take Hwy. 92 south past Sierra Vista. Green sign for Carr Canyon Falls directs you to turn on dirt road 2 mi. to second or third large hairpin turn at top of cliff. Descend gully on east side of cliff to base of routes.

154 College Peaks (North and South) ✯✯

Potential granite crags on North (6,240′) and South College Peaks (6,391′). State land.

Ref: J. Gamertsfelder.

Directions: From Douglas go northeast on Hwy. 80 for approximately 7 mi. College Peaks cliffs to south of highway.

155 Jack's Canyon (Moenkopi Wall) ✯✯✯✯

Overhanging limestone sport climbs put up by Deirdre Burton, Jim Steagall, Melissa Tucker, Steve Tucker, and Dave Sobocan in 1995. More than 200 routes to 5.13 in a beautiful canyon draw sport climbers from all over. Bring supplies. Spring/autumn. Free camping in situ. USFS-Coconino NF, (520) 527-3600.

Classics: Casino Cliffs: Mickey Goes to Vegas 9, One-Armed Bandit 10a, Sports Book 10b, Queen of Jacks 10b, Poker Face 11b, High Roller 12b, Hold or Fold 12c; Main Wall: Genesis 10d, Sacrificial Lizard 11b, Swiss Arête 12a, Under Attack 12a, Sweet Dreams 12c, Hooke on Pockets 12d/13a, Unpopular Mechanics 13a.

Ref: C 186-64, R 73-52; Guidebooks: Green's *Rock Climbing Arizona,* Steagal and Burton's *Jack's Canyon Sport Climbing.*

Directions: South of Winslow. From Winslow go south on Hwy. 87 for 30 mi. At mm 313.7, turn right (northwest) for 1 ²/10 mi. (At ¹/10 mi. stay right, ³/10 mi. stay left, at ½ mi. stay right, then follow 1 ²/10 mi. to camp and departure spot for canyon.) From end of road (camping) hike northwest to canyon rim.

156 The Promised Land ✯✯✯

Nice 50′ cragging on crisp, sound quartzite edges. Thirty routes. Government/private land.

Ref: T. Roberts; *Arizona Climber #10;* Guidebook: Murray and Baillie's *The Promised Land: Lower Sullies.*

Directions: Chino Valley (north of Prescott). From Prescott go north on Hwy. 89 for 20 mi. to Chino Valley. Turn east onto Perkinsville Rd. for 3 ³/4 mi. Then go north on dirt roads (don't drive here when wet) for 5 ⁶/10 mi. (Pass green gate at ⁴/10 mi., bearing left at 2 ¹/10 mi., 2 ⁷/10 mi., 3 ¹/10 mi.; pass FR 638 on right). At 3 ⁶/10 mi. pass white gate. At 5 ⁶/10 mi. turn left and park at dead-end. Short hike to The Promised Land, which is broken into the following areas: Solomon, Valerie's Book, and Star Trek. Best to go with someone who's been there before.

157 Ice Castles ✯✯

Granitic rock piles offer sport and traditional climbs. State land.

Classics: Ice Castles 7, Desert Jewel 11b.

Ref: Guidebook: Karabin's *Ice Castles Topo Sheet.*

Directions: North Phoenix. From Phoenix take I–17 north to the Carefree Hwy. exit. Go west for 4 mi. Just past cattle guard, turn left (south) for 2 mi. down bumpy dirt road to Ice Castles. Also accessed from south via Happy Valley Rd. to north on Fifty-first St.

158 Lookout Mountain (Dead Dobie Wall) ✮

Small wall of twenty crumbling 75′ basalt sport climbs done in 1993 by Karabin, Pinessa, Johnson, and Bastek. Try Speed Freak 5.11. City of Phoenix Park.

Ref: C 96; Guidebooks: Green's *Rock Climbing Arizona*, Karabin's *Lookout Mountain Topo Sheet*.

Directions: North Phoenix. From I–17 take Bell Rd. east to Sixteenth St. Head south on Sixteenth to dead-end at base of Lookout Mountain. Hike trail 308 west briefly, then south up to a second switchback, then go up climber's trail south to Dead Dobie Wall.

159 La Milagrosa Canyon ✮✮✮

Gneiss winter sport crag. More than one hundred sport routes. The new hot spot for Tucsonites in 1993–94. USFS–Coronado NF, (520) 749–8700.

Ref: E. Roache, J. Littlefield.

Directions: East Tucson. Ask locals about current access through private land.

160 Grand Falls ✮✮✮

Unique 200′ sandstone rock-climbing setting at the chocolate waterfalls of Grand Falls. Good hueco and thin-edge bouldering. Avoid spring run-off or your climbing career will be washed up. There are 25′ expert crack and face routes. BIA.

Classics: Hayduke Lives 5.11 (175′), Chocolate Milkshake 5.10 (65′), Hershey's Disaster 5.10 (90′), Little Colorado Crack 5.11 (35′), Big Colorado Crack 5.12 (75′).

Directions: Northeast of Flagstaff. From Flagstaff head north to Camp Townsend–Winona Rd. Turn right and head 14 mi. Turn left on Luepp Rd. Go 12 mi. and turn left at Navajo Reservation line. Follow signs to Grand Falls. Numerous side trails lead down to rock.

161 North O'Leary Peak ✮✮✮

Large basalt cliffs are easily visible from top. Most excellent 120′ basalt crack climbing up to 5.12. Beautiful scenery, sixty secluded climbs. USFS–Coconino NF, (520) 749–8700.

Classics: O'Leary's Oracle (horseshoe-shaped crack) 5.8+ (35′), Sudden Death Crack 5.12- (75′), It Takes Two (parallel cracks) 5.10 (70′).

Directions: North of Flagstaff. From Flagstaff head north on Hwy. 89. Turn onto Sunset Crater Rd. Turn left on dirt road immediately before park boundary; drive 3 mi. to summit. Park and walk 250 yd. down north slope to large outcrop of cliffs (toward Wupatki National Monument). Large basalt cliffs are easily visible from top.

162 Indian Springs ✮✮✮

In the desert north of Salome. Winter rock land of 300′ granite formations. One hundred routes established in 1998. BLM, (602) 417–9200.

Ref: D. Sullivan.

Directions: From Salome go north on Center St. In 3 blocks, turn left on Hall St. for ½ mi. to a dirt road that goes through farm fields. Turn right (north) for about 1 mi. to irrigation devices and top of obvious farm fields. Turn left for 6 ½ mi. (four-wheel drive is helpful). For starters, two prominent domes sport two good bolted 5.10 routes.

163 Skull Valley

Granite climbing formations. West of Prescott off Iron Springs Rd.

Ref: Guidebook: Baillie's *Skull Valley Topo Sheet*.

164 Dutchman Draw (Phalanx of Will) ✮✮✮✮

In the middle of nowhere out in the Arizona strip country, sits this pulpited stronghold like the Leaning Tower of Pisa. Bolted limestone routes up to 160′ with challenges up to 5.14 reside on all sides of this tilted pinnacle. One traditional crack, the 5.6 Ingrown Thumb Crack, is unlike the rest of the more than fifteen difficult routes on this tower. Bring supplies. Autumn–spring. Camp at will. BLM, (435) 688–3200.

Classics: Ingrown Thumb Crack 6, Nickel Bag of Funk 11c, Fossil of Man 13c, Fossil Eyes 14a.

Ref: R 86; Guidebook: Goss's *Rock Climbs of Southwest Utah*

Directions: Involved approach; four-wheel drive recommended. From St. George, Utah, go south on River Rd., crossing Virgin River. Immediately after crossing river, turn left onto 1450 South. Follow this road through various curves (passing horse corral) for 5 ½ mi., at which point it turns to graded gravel road. In 3 more miles, yield left. One mile farther after passing a stock chute, turn right. Go 1 more mile onto BLM road Number 1035. Enter Arizona for 4 more miles to Dutchman Draw. A four-wheel drive can go up into Draw to within ½ mile Other-wise, hike roughly 1 ½ mile into wash and go left at fork to the Phalanx.

165 Chuska Mountains

These aesthetic pinnacles were first ascended by the omnipresent soft-rock spire entrepreneurs Cameron Burns and Luke Laeser on Tombstone with help from Curtis and Marty Bennally and John Butler on Downs Tower. BIA.

Classics: Tombstone IV 6 A2+, Down Tower III 7 A2.

Ref: AAJ 94-62.

Directions: These pinnacles are located at the north end of the Chuska Mountains.

166 The Dry

Limestone sport climbing one hour southeast of Tucson features the classic The Renaissance 13-. USFS–Coronado NF, (520) 378-0311.

Ref: Guidebook: Green's *Rock Climbing Arizona.*

Directions: From Tucson drive east on I–10 to exit 302. Go south on Hwy. 90 for 12 ½ mi. Then go west into the Whetstone Mountains to a T-intersection. Turn right. Go left at first possible chance, heading up Dry Canyon. On ridge to right is limestone band accessed by first right turn. Four-wheel drive is useful here.

167 Dromedary Peak

Fun sport and crack routes (5.9–5.11) on this desert hump were put up by Marty Karabin in 1994. BLM, (623) 580-5500.

Ref: Guidebooks: Green's *Rock Climbing Arizona,* Karabin's *Dromedary Peak Rock Climbing Guide.*

Directions: From Florence Junction go 5 mi. west on Hwy. 60. Near mm 217, turn south on dirt road (rough) to as close as your vehicle will get you. Follow trails steeply to base of climbs. Popular Ivory Tower wall faces south.

168 King Dome

Granite-domes climbing—on rock equal to Yosemite—east of Crown King. Many fun 5.10 face routes. USFS–Prescott NF, (520) 771-4700.

Ref: Guidebook: Green's *Rock Climbing Arizona.*

Directions: Just east of Crown King, on FR 259 at mm 26. King Dome and Dungeon are to the north. Roadside Wall is back west on the north side of the road.

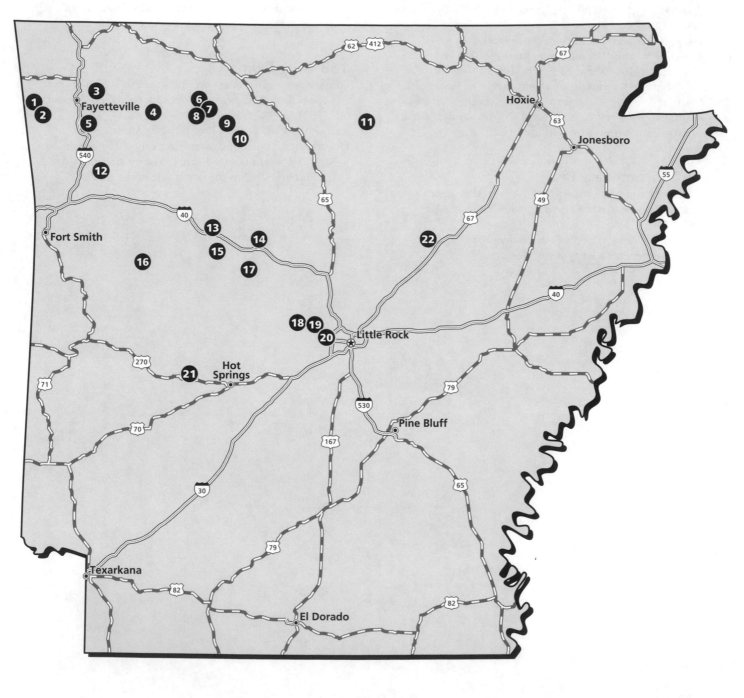

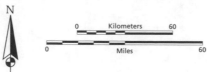

N

Kilometers
0   60

Miles
0   60

Arkansas

Arkansas

I picked a winner at Booger Hollow. —A Todd Skinner T-shirt concept

The Razorback State abounds with rustic beauty, rock climbing, and friendly rock climbers. It is the birthplace of Sam Walton, founder of Wal-Mart stores and once the richest man in America. It is also the birthplace of some of the Midwest's richest climbing.

The west and northwestern regions are the state's major rock holding pens. For years, Pinnacle Mountain has long been the feeding trough of Little Rock climbers.

Tops on the scenic list, Magazine Mountain, Arkansas's highest point, gives climbers fine sandstone cragging with metamorphic views. But don't save the best for last! In the back hollers of the Arkansas Ozarks, along the Buffalo River, are the prize hogs. Traditional climbing has taken a stronghold in places like Sam's Throne and Red Rock Point, both parochial, sandstone cliffs of venerable stature. If you're lucky, you may be able to attend the annual Climber's Rendezvous and experience Arkansas hospitality. If you're hungry, you can be a razorback at the Tippecanoe Cafe in Ponca. And if you're rooting for new rock, new routes you may find.

1 Wedington Cliff ★★★
A vertical 60′ sandstone cliffband with a few classic face lines and a giant roof crack, Out and Beyond 5.10 A1, among the persimmon trees lining the base. Fifty routes to 5.12. Also features a short bouldering wall. Ask permission from landowner. Private land.
Directions: West of Fayetteville.

2 Lake Lincoln ★★★
Forty-foot sandstone cliffs and overgrown boulders on Lake Lincoln. Fifty-five routes with good 5.9s and 5.10s up to 5.13. Guidebooks available in Fayetteville at the Pack Rat and Uncle Sam's. City land.
Classics: Quest for the Sticky Stuff 5.9+, Hung in the Fence 5.10+, Beer and Petzls 5.10+, 13 Crack 5.12.
Ref: Guidebook: Robertson's *A Climber's Guide to Lake Lincoln.*
Directions: From Lincoln it's a short drive (a little more than 3 mi.) on farm roads north of town on CR 669 to cliffs. Turn right at first bridge onto fisherman access road and parking. Cliffs are on the lake with both south and north exposures.

3 Goshen (closed) ★★★
Nice 60′ face cragging in northwest Arkansas on this small sandstone wall. Twenty-five routes. This area was closed in 1996 by the private landowners—do not trespass!
Directions: West of Goshen, near Fayetteville.

4 Highway 74 Rest Area ★★★
Incredibly grueling approach . . . not. This 35′ sandstone bouldering or terse toprope swings up pocketed overhangs. Twelve hard routes. Strenuous climbs for a place that's supposed to be a rest area. Boulders to left of fence are on private land—stay off these. State land.
Directions: From Huntsville drive south on Hwy. 23, then turn left (east) on Hwy. 74 for a few miles to roadside rest area (after curve) on right.

5 West Fork (closed) ★★
These 35′ white limestone walls offer some nice short leads, boulder problems, and traverses. The bizarre quarry underneath the cliffs is a great place for a natural indoor rock gym. Closed as the owner built a house at the cliff in 1998. Private land.
Classics: Pendulum 5.9, Bitchin' Wall 5.10.
Directions: South of Fayetteville at West Fork.

6 Compton Bluffs ★★★
Eighty-foot sandstone crags. Private land. Near Compton.

7 Steele Creek (on the Buffalo River) (aka Big River Bluffs) ★★★
The mini-Verdon of Arkansas. These scenic 200′ limestone bluffs lie along the Buffalo River. Camping on-site. NPS, (870) 446–5373.
Ref: J. Karpowicz; Guidebook: Detterline's *A Climber's Guide to the Mid-South.*
Directions: From Ponca steal just east on Hwy. 74. Turn left at NPS sign for Steele Creek. Gaze covetously on obvious limestone cliffs along Buffalo River.

Checking the hollers for rock, White Rock Mountain.

TIM TOULA

Kermit's Demise, The Toad Not Taken.
Ref: D. Justice; R 41(1/91)-50.
Directions: This prominent bluff is visible west of Mt. Judea. Go west on Hwy. 374 to top of grade. Turn right on private dirt road to dead-end. Hike east, dropping down to Red Rock Point cliffline.

10 Sam's Throne ☆☆☆☆

Well-loved Arkansas area features an extensive 80′ sandstone bluffline of puce crags. More than one hundred routes. Strong traditional ethic-minimal bolts. Bouldering, too. Site of the often-wild Climber's Rendezvous. This plug of rock was named after Sam Davis, 1820s farmer, buffalo hunter, and preacher who would shout at the top of his lungs every morning at the cliff how he would live to be 1,000 years old. Even today the locals are as colorful as the trees in the fall. Some are so colorful they steal your goods out of your car . . . beware! Camping at top of cliff. USFS–Ozark National Forest, (501) 968–2354.
Classics: Poison Ivy 7, Blind in Both Eyes 10c, Edge of Flight 10a, Wendy Armbuster 10c, Instant Karma 10c, Face of Fear 10d, Dry County 11, Arkansas Reality 12.
Ref: J. Karpowicz; C 160, R 41(1/91)-50; Guidebooks: Floyd's *A Climber's Guide to the Midwest Metamorphic Forms*, Frisbee's *Sam's Throne: Classic Rock Climbs*, Frisbee's *The Natural: Climber's Guide to Sam's Throne*.
Directions: From Lurton wind 10 mi. north on Hwy. 123 (1 mi. past the overlook). Park on left. Hike west ½ mi. to main cliff. Also accessible from a dot on the map called Mt. Judea. From Mt. Judea wind slowly south on Hwy. 123. From where road turns to gravel on 123, the odometer reading for Sam's Throne climbing areas goes: Mt. Perversion (abundance of bouldering) 2 ½ mi.; Northern Exposure (well-shaded bluffs), 4 mi.; Sam's Throne, Main Bluff (most developed and site of classic Windy Armbuster 5.10c), East and West Main Bluff, Outback (nasty, overhanging, sick cracks), and main free camping areas at 4 3/10 mi.; Hero Maker 4 8/10 mi.; Lookout Point (difficult adventure routes on the area's biggest walls—90′), 5 4/10 mi., Valley of the Blind, 5 6/10 mi., Deliverance 6 mi.; and Cave Creek, 7 ½ mi.

11 Blanchard Springs Caverns (closed?) ☆☆

Impressive 100′ sandstone face with fifteen routes. May be closed to climbing. Pay camping. USFS–Ozark-St. Francis NF, (870) 269–2211.
Ref: Guidebook: Detterline's *A Climber's Guide to the Mid-South*.
Directions: From Mountain View go north on Hwy. 9 to Hwy. 14W. From Hwy. 14 follow park signs into Blanchard Springs Caverns. Bluff at Shelter Cave near amphitheater.

12 White Rock Mountain (2,320′) ☆☆☆

This 60′ sandstone cliff harbors a grand tradition of drunks taking headers from the clifftop. Could they have

8 Busby Hollow (closed) ☆☆☆

Refreshing variety of routes on 80′ sandstone crag and boulders. More than twenty routes. Private land.
Classics: Triple Threat 8+, Red Neck Girl 9, King of Pain 9, Orange Face 5.11s, Flying Frog Arête 5.12, Stay Hungry Roof 12c.
Ref: J. Karpowicz; R 41(1/91)-50.
Directions: East of Ponca. Near Steele.

9 Red Rock Point ☆☆☆

Scenic, 180′ sandstone crag hovering over a more scenic valley. Forty routes. Access sensitive; local climbers have built rapport with private landowner. Private land; you *must* ask permission to go out there. The owners of the land live at the bottom of the hill on Hwy. 374. Take a mountain bike or be ready for a small hike because they *will not* allow vehicles up there. As continued access here hinges on good rapport with the landowner, behave like kings and queens. Camp at Sam's Throne (Number 10) campsites.
Classics: Krackatoa (Crack of the Ozarks) 5.8+, Critters 5.9, Batso's Revenge 5.10b, Just Passing Through 5.11,

been pushed? Be considerate and limit the level of noise, and no one should bother you. Beautiful panoramic views. Areas are marked where climbing is prohibited. Respect marked areas! NPS land.

Ref: B. Bisswanger.

Directions: From Fayetteville go southeast on Hwy. 16. Turn south on Hwy. 23 to town of Cass. From Cass follow CR 1003 west to White Rock Mountain (signs). Bluffs just minutes from car.

13 Forty Acre Rock ★★★

Possibly the best pure overhanging 20′ sandstone bouldering blocks in Arkansas. Private land.

Directions: From Russellville drive south of I-40 exit. Take first right, heading west and paralleling I-40 and over lake bridge. In 3-4 mi., turn north and cross back (north) over I-40 overpass. Take first right after overpass and park at power line. Walk 200 yd. Forty Acre rocks are on left.

14 Crow Hill Bluffs ★★

The 60′ sandstone crags of I-40. These obscure climbing grounds are popular with Arkansas rock climbers and graffiti enthusiasts. Private land.

Directions: From Russellville travel 10 mi. east on I-40 as the crow flies to the Atkins exit. Bluffs visible from I-40 (especially when trees are leafless) to north. Trend north from I-40, turning left at old building (in approximately 1 mi). Wind uphill to Crow Hill Bluffs.

15 Dardanelle Rock ★★

Though small, this prominent 100′ sandstone rock juts out of the side of a small mountain and offers interesting climbing opportunities. Expansive views from the top overlooking the scenic Dardanelle Lock and Dam. Long history of events. Named after an Indian, Dardanelle, who tossed himself into the waters below when his love did not show up (he should have gone to Alabama number 17 and met Noccalula). Corp of Engineers.

Directions: From Russellville tread south past I-40 just outside of town to the burg of Dardanelle. Dardanelle Rock is high bluff visible from road along river.

16 Magazine Mountain State Park ★★★

An entertaining one-pitch, 90′ sandstone cliff band with panoramic vistas from the highest point in Arkansas (2,753′). Enjoyable climbing on more than sixty routes, especially for the 5.10 level. Camping at park. State park, (501) 963-8502.

Classics: Radical Changes 5.9, Eurodog 5.10a, Velvet Elvis 5.10b, Where Beagles Dare 5.11a.

Ref: C 158, R 41(1/91)-50; Guidebooks: Allen's *Mt. Magazine: A Rock Climber's Guide,* Bearden's *Rock Climber's Guide to Mt. Magazine.*

Directions: From Paris drive 20 mi. south on Hwy. 309.

Follow LODGE signs to top of mountain. Magazine Mountain State Park at road's end. From summit parking lot hike south to cliff below.

17 Petit Jean State Park ★★★

Hard 50′ sandstone sport routes on overhangs. Bouldering, too. Pay camping at park. State Park, (501) 727-5441.

Directions: From Morrilton (exit 108 off I-40), go south on Hwy. 9 for 9 mi. Turn west on Hwy. 154 for 12 mi. Follow Petit Jean State Park signs.

18 West Pinnacle Mountain Bouldering ★★

Small but good 25′ sandstone bouldering area. May be private land.

Classics: St. Vitas' Dance 9, Local Legend 11.

Ref: Guidebook: Detterline's *A Climber's Guide to the Mid-South.*

Directions: From Little Rock drive 10 mi. west on Hwy. 10. Turn north on Hwy. 300 to just past Pinnacle Mountain park entrance. Take first left to dead end. Hike west to West Pinnacle Mountain Bouldering Wall.

19 Pinnacle Mountain State Park ★★★

The prominent landmarks west of Little Rock offer 60′ cragging and bouldering on sandstone faces on different levels of the northeast side of the hill. Enjoy airy views of Arkansas from Pinnacle Mountain's summit. Camping available at Maumelle Park, 2 mi. east on Pinnacle Valley Rd. State park, (501) 868-5806.

Classics: Moovin' and Groovin' 8, Crotalus Horridus 10.

Ref: C [107, 68]; Guidebook: Detterline's *A Climber's Guide to the Mid-South.*

Directions: From Little Rock (exit 9 off I-430), go 7 mi.

west on Hwy. 10. Turn north on Hwy. 300 for about 2 mi. Turn right on Pinnacle Valley Rd. Park at Pinnacle Mountain's east Summit Trail lot. (Follow park signs.) Hike up trail ten minutes amongst rocks (visible from parking area).

20 Chenal ✩✩✩

Good 40′ granite sport crag. Ten routes. Nice views. Possibly private land.

Classics: Agent Orange 8, Smokin and Chokin 8, Lumberjack 10.

Ref: J. Honey.

Directions: West of Little Rock. Take I–630 west to Chenal Pkwy. Take Chenal Pkwy. and turn left past the Kroger Store onto Kanis Rd. Take Kanis and drive straight onto Denny Rd. Take Denny Rd. and turn right onto Gordon Rd. Continue past yellow gate. Cliffs are visible to the right fairly soon thereafter. Park near power lines and it's a short but steep hike to the crags.

21 Crystal Mountain

West of Hot Springs and south of Mt. Ida.

22 Riverside Park

Shale cliffs offer bouldering and toproping on climbs like Critically Acclaimed 5.10. No camping. City park.

Classics: Slippy's Trip, Curious George, Glad That Cows Don't Fly, Critically Acclaimed 10.

Ref: D. Fosbinder 5/98.

Directions: From downtown Searcy follow Main St. north for 2 mi. Turn right on Johnston Rd. for 1 mi. to Riverside Park. Park by red caboose. Follow trail past pavilion into woods to 30′ high main bouldering area and the 70′ high Critically Acclaimed.

California

"At either end of the social spectrum there lies a leisure class." —Eric Beck, Yosemite leisure-class climber

To say California has good climbing is like saying Death Valley is sunny. The state is blessed with climbing in every conceivable shape and form. The rock and weather go together like fine wine and good cheese. After a quick perusal of the multitude of areas it is understandable why Californian climbers were delayed in reaching other American crags.

What is the first word uttered when talking California rock climbing? Yosemite, a Mecca for world-touring rock climbers and nonclimbers alike. It is the origin of big-wall climbing. It is abundant in multipitched free-climbing adventures and superb granite cragging and bouldering. The Valley has been and continues to be a must-stop for all climbers.

As for the rest of the state, starting south from Mexico, the San Diego area could best be described as granite boulders undergoing mitosis. The plethora of short, quality climbs and ocean sunsets is a present to anyone visiting areas such as Mt. Woodson, Deerhorn Valley, or Santee.

Joshua Tree National Monument, with more than 3,500 routes and heaps of granitic boulders, remains the top winter rock-climbing destination of Los Angeleans and Europeans. Nearby Suicide and Tahquitz, currently less publicized, still offer climbers a scenic, forested cragging experience.

Continuing north, a two-hour drive from megalopolitan Los Angeles will bring the bouldering/cragging breed to more than thirty uniquely satisfying areas such as Black Mountain, Mt. Rubidoux, Horse Flats, Purple Stones, and the venerable Stoney Point, not to mention budding artificial bridge climbing walls.

The Sierra Nevada Range is the "Mother Lode" of California climbing. While miners in the 1800s found their gold in "them thar hills," climbers in the twenty-first century will find their gold in the form of granite. The Needles, Kings Canyon, Buttermilks, Yosemite, Tuolumne Meadows, and the Tahoe area form a list of heavy hitters the likes of which no state can compare (not even North Dakota—just kidding). Backcountry rock in the Sierra Range is a lifetime's worth of claim staking.

No tour of California would be complete without sampling the fine areas (and wines) of the San Francisco area. While sitting on the dock of the Bay, climbers would do well to include the Pinnacles, Mazzones, Indian Rocks, Glen Canyon, and Mickey's Beach on their taste list. Last but not least, more northern areas like Castle Crags State Park will surprise the unknowing climber.

A visit to the Golden Gate State will point out to any climber why "Californny" is the place you ought to be.

1 Patrick's Point State Park ✮✮✮

Freestanding 50′ sandstone pinnacles have classic crack routes north of Wedding Rock and Robin's Slab, south of Wedding Rock. Ceremonial Rock also has lots of routes. Beautiful bouldering. Topropes off fence. Dramatic shoreline with Zen sea stacks, seals, sea lions, and migrating whales. Check with rangers for info. Camping information for California state parks call (800) 444–PARK. State park, (707) 677–3570.

Ref: Romonchuk; R 89-64; Guidebook: LaFarge's *Climber's Guide for Moonstone and Luffenholtz Beach.*

Directions: From Arcata drive approximately 16 mi. north on Hwy. 101, following park signs to coast in Patrick's Point State Park.

2 Luffenholtz ✮✮✮

Small amounts of 25′ sandstone bouldering by the seashore. Not as much climbing as Moonstone, but who cares? This coastline is bouldering for the soul! State land.

Ref: Romonchuk; R 89-64; Guidebook: LaFarge's *Climber's Guide for Moonstone and Luffenholtz Beach.*

Directions: From Arcata blast 10 mi. north on Hwy. 101. Turn left at Westhaven exit. Take first right past Hwy. 101 to first right. Luffenholtz Rocks are by the beach.

3 Moonstone ✮✮✮

Fun sandstone bouldering and topropes by the seashore. State land.

Classics: Flattop Boulder, South Boulder, Karen Rock.

Ref: Romonchuk; Guidebook: LaFarge's *Climber's Guide for Moonstone and Luffenholtz Beach.*

Directions: From Arcata launch 10 mi. north on Hwy. 101. Turn left at Westhaven exit. Take first left past Hwy. 101 to first right. Moonstone Rocks are by the beach. Areas include South Boulder, North End Boulders, and Karen Rock (60′ face). Also bouldering at Houda Point, ½ mi. north on Scenic Drive.

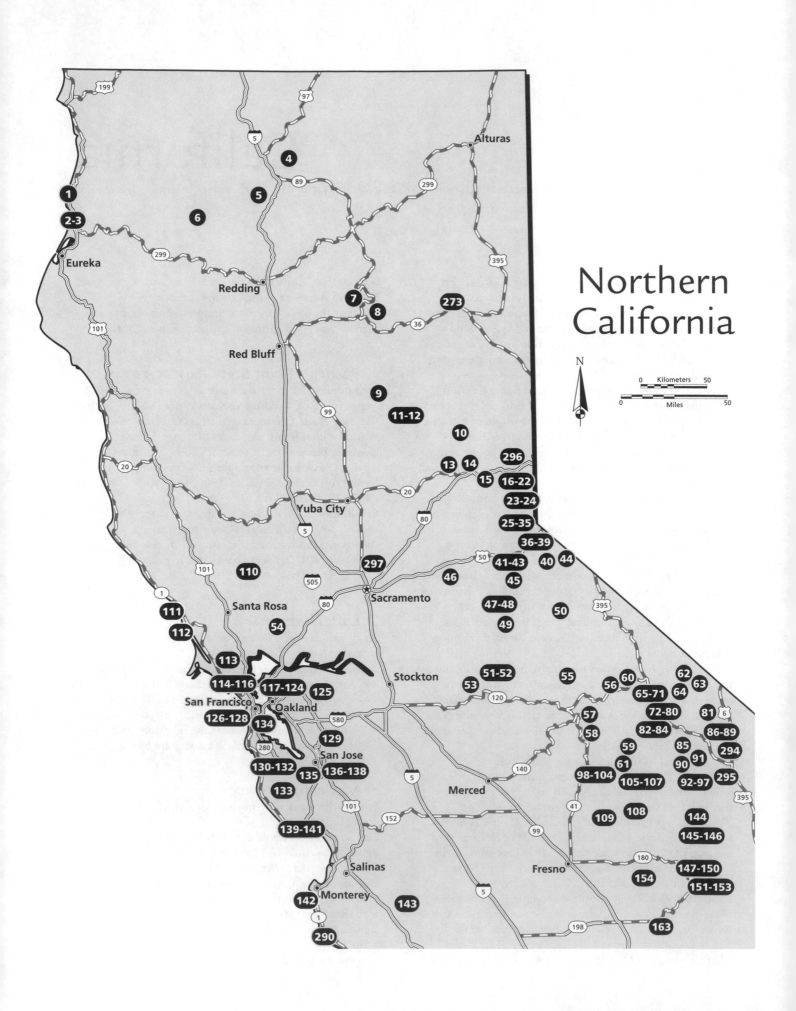

Northern California

199

97

5

Alturas

4

89

299

1

5

2-3

6

Eureka

299

395

Redding

7

273

8

36

Red Bluff

9

101

11-12

10

99

13 14 296

15 16-22

20

23-24

Yuba City

25-35

80

5

36-39

50

41-43 40 44

110

45

297

46

505

47-48

Santa Rosa

80

49

50

395

54

Sacramento

111

112

51-52 55

56 60 62 63

113

53

65-71 64

Stockton

120

72-80 81 6

114-116 117-124 125

57 82-84 86-89

San Francisco Oakland

580

58 85 294

126-128 134

59 90 91 295

129

280

61 92-97

130-132 135 136-138

98-104 105-107

San Jose

140

133

5

139-141

109 108 144

152

145-146

Merced

101

99

180

Salinas

147-150

Fresno 154

151-153

142 Monterey

1

143

5

198 163

290

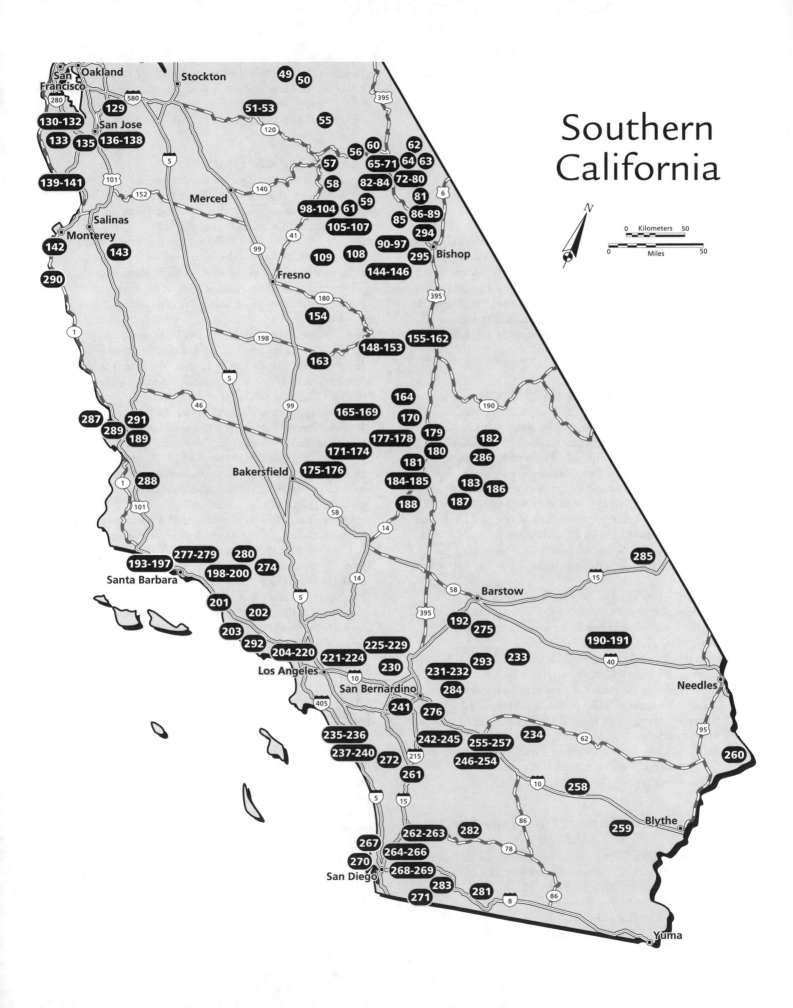

Southern
California

N

0 ____ Kilometers ____ 50
0 ____ Miles ____ 50

4 Mt. Shasta National Park ✮✮✮

Mt. Shasta is northern California's premier volcano, attracting mountaineers, skiers, and snow sloggers to its 14,162' summit. Avalanche Gully (South Side) sees three-quarters of summit bids, although seventeen established routes exist. The Hotlum Glacier is most challenging of Shasta's Glaciers. Whitney Glacier is the largest glacier in California. Last eruption: May 30, 1914. Entrance and climbing fees. Pay camping. NPS, (530) 595-4444.

Classics: Avalanche Gulch, Hotlum Glacier, and Casual Ridge.

Ref: C 107, R 78-144, S 5/71; Guidebooks: Lewis's *Climbing Mt. Shasta* (online guide), Smoot's *Summit Guide to Cascade Volcanoes*, Selters and Zanger's *The Mt. Shasta Book: A Guide to Hiking, Climbing, Skiing, and Exploring*, Mt. Shasta Climber's Review, Selters's *Mt. Shasta Book*, Porcella and Burns's *California's Fourteeners: A Hiking and Climbing Guide*.

Directions: From Mt. Shasta go east on Everitt Memorial Hwy. Or, several other access points circle Mt. Shasta National Park.

5 Castle Crags State Park ✮✮✮✮

A treasury of 500' granite cliffs, parapets, and spires exist in the Castle Crags Wilderness. Castle Dome, with its 1,200' east face, attracts the spotlight. Mt. Hubris and Battle Mountain enter in prominently. Views of Mt. Shasta. Mineral springs. Pacific Crest Trail floats through the area. Day-use fee allows one to enter park and shower. Camping in state park (fee; 530-235-2684) or on Shasta-Trinity NF.

Classics: Castle Dome: West Ridge 6p 8; South Face: Good Book 9/10a, East Face 6p 10+; Mt. Hubris: Cosmic Wall 6p 6, Six Toe Crack 3p 8; Luden's Overhang: Premeditated Leisure 8+, Guides Holiday 10a, Hit or Miss Rock.

Ref: AAJ '77-184, C 166(2/97)-58, R 19-36, S 1/73; Guidebooks: Davis's *Castle Crags: California Classic Rock Climbs*, Bald's *Castle Crags Wilderness*, Selters's *Mt. Shasta Book*.

Directions: From Redding go 70 mi. north on I-5. The park is off I-5 at Castella (south of Dunsmuir). Follow signs to Castle Crags State Park. Go past park headquarters to Vista Point Parking. Hike on Castle Dome Trail to Castle Dome. To reach other formations to south and west end of crags, branch west on FR 25. North End and Railroad Park areas are reached by going 3 mi. north of Castella on I-5 to Railroad Park exit. Then trend west on FR 39N43. Wilderness maps available from USFS.

6 Stonehouse Pinnacle (in Trinity Alps) ✮✮✮

Backcountry 1,000' climbing on abundant granite that may be almost as good as Yosemite. Permits required. USFS-Shasta-Trinity NF, (530) 623-2121.

Classics: Stonehouse Pinnacle.

Ref: AAJ '70-124, R 94-122.

Directions: From Weaverville rock west on Hwy. 299 to Junction City. Then cut north up Canyon Creek Rd. to trailhead for Canyon Creek Lakes. Stonehouse Pinnacle is in the Trinity Alps on the prominent formation just left of Lower Canyon Creek Lake approximately 7 mi. in.

7 Lassen National Park ✮✮✮

Crags, volcanic hot springs, fumaroles, and a 10,457' volcanic plug dome (Lassen Peak). Eagle Peak cliffband is a sun magnet, which is great when it's cold. Bellybutton is biggest formation in park. A 165' volcanic crag with lots of cracks and more than one hundred climbs, mostly from 5.9-5.11. Power drills prohibited; users have been cited. First known climbing in the 1970s. Lassen last steamed in 1850. Hwy. 89 closed in winter due to snow. Free camping is available outside park in Lassen NF. Pay in NPS, (530) 595-4444.

Classics: Eagle Peak: Rick's Boulder 9, Stegosaurus 10b, Peon U 10+, Chips north Salsa 11a, Social Pressure 11-, Arms Control 11c, Eruption 12a; Bellybutton: Mejto 9, Trinity Cracks 10a/11a, Pyroclastic Pump 11a, Busload of Faith 11c, Viva Gorby 11+.

Ref: Guidebooks: Bald's *Rock Climbing Guide to Lassen Volcanic National Park*, Neff's *Lassen County Climbs*.

Directions: From Redding (approximately one hour), explode for 47 mi. east on Hwy. 44 to Mt. Lassen National Park.) Three different areas to rock climb in park can be approached from Summit Parking Lot and include: 1) Eagle Peak (south side, good bouldering below terrace): Hike west from lot. 2) Bellybutton: Hike summit trail north, cutting west at second switchback. 3) Crescent Cliff (200', short, broken): north of Eagle Peak, drop down Manzanita Creek or hike approximately 3 mi. up Manzanita Creek Trail from lake. 4) Raker Peak (outcrops/boulders away from summit): Along Hwy. 89 just north of devastated area. 5) Terrace/Cliff Lakes: toprope wall and big boulder ½ mi. up Terrace Lake Trail from Hwy. 89. Going farther, Cliff Lake has thin finger cracks.

8 Warner Valley (The Loading Zone) ✮✮✮

This 70' volcanic crag is a warmer alternative to higher-elevation climbs in Lassen NP. USFS-Lassen NF, (530) 257-6952.

Classics: Scatmando 10a, Lady Fantasy 10a, The Loading Zone 11b.

Ref: Guidebook: Bald's *Rock Climbing Guide to Lassen Volcanic National Park*.

Directions: Near Chester. After approximately 3 mi., leave Hwy. 36 going north 6 ½ mi. on road to Drakesbad. Just north of Warner Creek Campground, Climb and Die Cliff sits on left. Slightly farther up and just past bridge on right sits The Loading Zone. This area is south of Lassen National Park boundary.

9 Grizzly Dome and Arch Rock Tunnel
★★★

Multipitched routes on 400′ granite domes and crags. More information at Mountain Sports in Chico. USFS–Plumas NF, (530) 283–2050.

Ref: Guidebook: Stahl's *Feather River Rock: A Trenchant Guide*.

Directions: From Oroville trend north approximately 30 mi. on Hwy. 70 above Pulga between Arch Rock and Elephant Butte Tunnel. Grizzly Dome up on right at Elephant Butte Tunnel. Arch Rock at tunnels.

10 Sierra Buttes and Lakes Basin ★★★

Scattered backcountry granite cragging areas. Brightly colored pinnacles and spires. Young America Buttress 5.10 is a classic, 600′, plumb line crack climb in the area. Summer. USFS–Tahoe NF, (530) 265–4531.

Classics: Bat Attack Corner 9, Young American Buttress, Jambo 9.

Ref: AAJ 83, C 95-7.

Directions: For Sierra Buttes: Just north of Sierra City on Sierra Buttes Rd. or north on Hwy. 49, then west on Sardine Lake Rd. For Lakes Basin: Just south of Johnsville above Grass Lake or Gold Lake Forest Hwy. south of Graeagle.

11 Bald Rock Dome ★★★

Four-hundred-foot granite dome with up to four pitch routes. Bald Rock Picnic Area has many granite boulders with a variety of cracks. Spectacular views of the Feather River Canyon. USFS–Plumas NF, (530) 283–2050.

Classics: Nose Route 7, Bit of Honey 10, Paradox 11.

Ref: S [9/81, 10/67]; Guidebook: *Bald Rock Dome*.

Directions: From Oroville drive 15 mi. northeast on Oroville Quincy Hwy. 162. Turn right onto Bald Rock Rd. following it to area. Good bouldering at Bald Rock Picnic Area. Bald Rock Dome lies north of Lake Oroville and west of Feather Falls. Big Bald Rock and Little Bald Rock (to north) lie farther west.

12 Bald Rock Canyon ★★★

Massive 2,000′ granitic slab dome. First ascent team was Nelson and Rears in 1960. A mountaineer's climb with slabs and intermittent fourth class. USFS–Plumas NF, (530) 283–2050.

Classics: Nose Route 7.

Ref: S 10/67.

Directions: From Oroville slide north to Bald Rock Canyon of middle fork of Feather River.

13 Emerald Gorge (aka The Emeralds)
★★★

Rad sport-climbing area. Steep, pocketed 80′ metamorphic sport crags above the flowing south fork of the Yuba River on sedimentary/igneous rock blend. Emerald swimming pools just south of bridge. Camping along river; watch for rises in water level, especially in spring. Please pay attention to Pacific Gas and Electric signs. Autumn. Private/government land.

Classics: Benches: Shadows on the Earth 11a, Steel Monkey 12a; Gorge: Pimp the Hoe 12d, Bustin' Rhymes 13a, Still Life 13a/b.

Ref: C [143, 126(6/91)-66, 123], SC [3/91, 12/92]; Guidebooks: Carville's *Rock Climbing Lake Tahoe*, Thornburg's *Quickdraw Guide to Northern California Sport Climbing Areas*, Carville's *Climber's Guide to Tahoe Rock*.

Directions: From Nevada City go east on Hwy. 20 (5 mi. before I–80). Turn left on Bowman Lake Rd. for approximately 2 mi. Turn right before bridge on dirt road to two areas: Steel Monkey Wall on right or Emerald Gorge at end of road. Hike through boulders 200 yd. Gorge visible on right.

14 Indian Springs ★★★

Small, fun granite slab climbing area for intermediate climbers. Seldom visited. Camping just a little farther down road. USFS–Tahoe NF, (530) 265–4531.

Classics: Lower Wall: Out of the Blue 10, Zephyr 10c.

Ref: C 126(6/91)-66, SC [3/91, 12/92]; Guidebooks: Carville's *Rock Climbing Lake Tahoe*, Thornburg's *Quickdraw Guide to Northern California Sport Climbing Areas*, Carville's *Climber's Guide to Tahoe Rock*.

Directions: From Truckee jump west on I–80 to Eagle Lakes exit. Go north a couple minutes. Park below left edge of slabs. Lower Wall Slab is reached via trail first, then Mid and Upper Wall Slabs above. This area is east of The Emeralds and west of Rainbow.

15 Rainbow Crag and Big Bend ★★★

Quiet 100′ granite cul-de-sac with fine climbing 5.10 and harder. Bouldering, too. Camping at east end of town, off Hampshire Rock Rd. USFS–Tahoe NF, (530) 265–4531.

Classics: Aja 10d (crack), Dark Special 10a (face).

Ref: C 105, Guidebooks: Carville's *Rock Climbing Lake Tahoe*, Carville's *Climber's Guide to Tahoe Rock*, Jenkewitz-Meytras's *Tahoe Rock Climbing*.

Directions: From Truckee crank approximately 15 mi. west down I–80. Exit I–80 via Big Bend. Turn onto Hampshire Rock Rd. going to a roadside parking area just east of South Yuba River. Obvious granite cliffs of Rainbow Crag and Big Bend are reached by a ten-minute hike on trail behind storage garage across street from Big Bend Ranger Station. Be watchful to stay on public land.

16 LT★ (Lake Tahoe Areas) Overview and Donner Summit ★★★★

Donner Summit sports many high-quality crags and routes, with clean cracks and knobby faces. Features the desperate and highly touted Steep Climb Named Desire 13d. Bouldering traverses atop Donner Peak (above Snowshed). Many fine bouldering areas abundant in white granite faces; the clean-cut edges draw boulderers with problems like

White Line V8. Swimming and camping/ showers at
Donner Lake or free camping on National Forest land.
Bouldering at southwest corner of Donner Lake on hillside
above Conifer Street—please don't trespass. Supplies in
Truckee. Private/USFS–Tahoe NF, (530) 265-4531.

Classics: Black Wall: One Hand Clapping 9, New
  Fascination 10d; Roadcut: Goldfinger 11d, Penguin Lust
  12c, Transmogrifier 12d; Space Wall: Neanderthal Dudes
  11d; Snowshed Walls: Ariel 11b, Brainchild 12b,
  Cannibals 13a, Pump Lust 13c, Green Phantom 10a, Star
  Walls: Ice Pirates 11, Star Walls Crack 13a, Ice Pirates 11;
  School Rock: Short Subject 11TR; Goldilocks 10+, Steep
  Climb 13d.

Ref: C [163-120, 143, 124, 118(2/90) 32-4, 105, 104, 93]; R
  [69-84, 38-40], SC 12/92, S 3/75; Rock and Ice on-line;
  Guidebooks: Carville's *Rock Climbing Lake Tahoe*,
  Sutton's *Select Rock Climbs of Tahoe*, Carville's *Climber's
  Guide to Tahoe Rock*, Jenkewitz-Meytras's *Tahoe Rock
  Climbing*, Harlin's *West*, Thornburg's *Quickdraw Guide to
  Northern California Sport Climbing Areas*, G. Dexter et al.'s
  Climber's Guide to Lake Tahoe Region, Sumner's *Climber's
  Guide to Lake Tahoe Region*, Beck's *Climber's Guide to Lake
  Tahoe and Donner Summit*, Drake's *Donner Summit*,
  Jones's *Rock Climbing Guide to Donner Summit*.

Directions: From Soda Springs drive 4 mi. east on Old Hwy.
  40 to Donner Pass Rd. From the top of summit just past
  Alpine Skills Institute, crags appear in order: Goldilocks
  Wall is south of summit (7,042'), School Rock is 150 yd.
  east of pass to north closest to pullout; Grouse Slabs is
  ten-minute walk north on Pacific Crest Trail from summit proper. At bridge and north of road is Green
  Phantom Rocks. Snowshed Wall is most prominent crag
  on south side of road just past overlook. Peanut Gallery,
  Roadcut (bumper belays), is on north side of road just
  past scenic overlook. Finally, Black Wall is largest crag
  north of road.

17 LT–Split Rock ☆☆☆

A 20' granite bouldering area with twenty problems to V6.
Try the "bear hugs." USFS–Tahoe NF, (530) 265-4531.

Ref: Guidebooks: Carville's *Rock Climbing Lake Tahoe*,
  Carville's *Climber's Guide to Tahoe Rock*, Jenkewitz-
  Meytras's *Tahoe Rock Climbing*.

Directions: From Truckee take I-80 west to Donner Lake
  exit (at west edge of town). Turn south, crossing Donner
  Pass Rd. Drive by gas stations to end of pavement
  (approximately 1 mi.). Park. Hike west 1/4 mi. past small
  reservoir on left and a campground on right. The boulders are approximately 50 yd. west of the reservoir. Split
  Rock is southeast from the east end of Donner Lake.

18 Truckee River Basalt Area ☆☆☆

Fine-grained 250' basalt crags can be found in several areas
in this river gorge. Autumn. USFS–Tahoe NF, (530)
265-4531.

Ref: SC 12/92; Guidebooks: Carville's *Rock Climbing Lake
  Tahoe*, Carville's *Climber's Guide to Tahoe Rock*.

Directions: From Truckee go south on Hwy. 89 on east side
  of highway. Wade river and hike up talus to crags.
  Alternative (nonwading) approach: Go west on south River
  Dr. (east end of Truckee off Hwy. 267) just past bridge.
  Continue past pavement until road ends. Follow river to
  talus and hike up. Truckee River Basalts extend from
  Tahoe City north past the town of Truckee. Two areas
  (covered separately in this guide) are of interest to sport
  climbers: Big Chief (on east side of Truckee River, a few
  miles south of Truckee) and The Amphitheater (across
  from entrance of Alpine Meadow Ski Resort on east-facing
  hillside above Hwy. 89).

19 Truckee Boulder ☆☆☆

Twenty-foot granite crack bouldering. May be private land.

Ref: Guidebook: Carville's *Climber's Guide to Tahoe Rock*.

Directions: From the junction of I-80 and Hwy. 89, truck 5
  mi. to shopping center on right (west side of road,
  between railroad bridge and Deer Field Rd.). Truckee
  Boulder is behind shopping center.

20 The Columns ☆☆

A 25' basalt crag with toprope cracks in the range from
5.8-5.11. Autumn. USFS–Tahoe NF, (530) 265-4531.

Ref: Guidebook: Carville's *Climber's Guide to Tahoe Rock*.

Directions: From Truckee go south on Hwy. 89 to Cabin
  Creek Rd. Park north of Cabin Creek Rd. at south end of
  campground. The Columns are hidden in trees a few
  hundred feet up slope to west.

21 Big Chief ☆☆☆

This 250' basalt sport crag with the prominent red wall
offers steep, solid rock—the best in Truckee Canyon.
Excellent moderate sport climbs and cave with more difficult sport challenges. Autumn. USFS–Tahoe NF, (530)
265-4531.

Classics: War Path 9, Just Another Day Hike 9, Festus 10a,
  Pain Killer 10d, Flying High Again 11c, Raindance 12a,
  The Scalper 12a, Totally Chawsome 12b, All Guns
  Blazing 13a.

Ref: SC 12/92; Guidebooks: Carville's *Rock Climbing Lake
  Tahoe*, Carville's *Climber's Guide to Tahoe Rock*.

Directions: From Truckee go 1 mi. southeast on Hwy. 267.
  Turn south onto Ponderosa Palisades Rd. Follow to top
  of hill and turn right on Silver Fir, then left on Thelin.
  Take right branch past gate onto good dirt road. Follow
  this road 5 2/10 mi., then turn right on bumpy dirt road
  6/10 mi. to end. Hike west fifteen minutes on faint trail
  through manzanita to notch. Descend and contour left
  along west face of Big Chief.

22 Speedboat (aka Brockway) ☆☆

The 30' granite bouldering here was first developed in the
1960s. Tahoe trivia: Lake Tahoe is 27 mi. long and 15 mi.
wide. The well-traveled climber/boulderer Dick Cilley asks

if this "[bleeping] area" even exists, as his attempts to find it have been futile. He suggests the volcanic bouldering along the Old Country Rd. may be time better spent. USFS–Tahoe NF, (530) 265–4531.

Ref: Guidebooks: Carville's *Rock Climbing Lake Tahoe*, Carville's *Climber's Guide to Tahoe Rock*, Jenkewitz-Meytras's *Tahoe Rock Climbing*, Dexter et al.'s *Climber's Guide to Lake Tahoe Region*, Beck's *Climber's Guide to Lake Tahoe and Donner Summit*.

Directions: North shore of Lake Tahoe, just ¼ mi. west of state line. From California/Nevada border proceed west on Hwy. 28 to Speedboat Ave. Park at end. Speedboat Boulders scattered for several blocks on both sides of street. Best boulders off first road to right. Residential area—please respect landowners.

23 The Amphitheater ✩✩✩

This popular 100' southwest-facing basalt sport-climbing area sports nuts and bolts face routes. Autumn. USFS–Tahoe NF, (530) 265–4531.

Classics: As You Like It 10d, Poor Man's Pump 11b, Mental Slavery 12a.

Ref: SC 12/92; Guidebooks: Carville's *Rock Climbing Lake Tahoe*, Carville's *Climber's Guide to Tahoe Rock*.

Directions: From Tahoe City zip 4 mi. north on Hwy. 89. Rock lies across Hwy. 89 from Alpine Meadows entrance on east-facing hillside above Hwy. 89. Park near Alpine Meadows entrance, then walk north ¼ mi. along Hwy. 89 to base of wall. Or, turn right at first dirt road past Alpine Meadows. Park. Hike straight up talus to the obvious Amphitheater.

24 Twin Crags ✩✩✩

Good variety of crack climbing on excellent southwest-facing basalt columns. Rappel anchors. Beware loose blocks on top. Autumn. USFS–Tahoe NF, (530) 265–4531.

Classics: A Fine Line 10b, Wild Bull Rodeo 11a, Throne of Gold 11d, Jamolator 12c.

Ref: R 38; Guidebooks: Carville's *Rock Climbing Lake Tahoe*, Carville's *Climber's Guide to Tahoe Rock*.

Directions: From Tahoe City go 1 mi. west above north side of Hwy. 89. Park north of Twin Crag Summer Home Tract. Hike talus left of Twin Crags.

25 Crag Peak ✩✩

Least-climbed mountain in Tahoe Basin. This 400' granite crag is best in late summer. Camping below face. USFS–Eldorado NF, (530) 622–5061.

Classics: Poopout Pinnacle 7, Ivory Book 9.

Ref: Guidebooks: Carville's *Rock Climbing Lake Tahoe*, Carville's *Climber's Guide to Tahoe Rock*, Jenkewitz-Meytras's *Tahoe Rock Climbing*, Dexter et al.'s *Climber's Guide to Lake Tahoe Region*, Beck's *Climber's Guide to Lake Tahoe and Donner Summit*.

Directions: From South Lake Tahoe snag Hwy. 89 north to Meeks Creek by Meeks Bay. Hike 8 mi. on Tahoe Trail to base of Crag Peak in Upper Meeks Canyon. Faces northeast.

26 D. L. Bliss State Park ✩✩✩

Find your bliss in this 25' granite bouldering area adjacent to Emerald Bay State Park on the California shore of Lake Tahoe. Don't miss The Brain Boulder at second pullout and the exquisite Ladder Boulder, two minutes on the road from the pay campground in the trees. Its deceptively slabby face on one side protects its jewels on the other. One mi. to swimming at Bliss State Park (916–525–7277).

Ref: Guidebooks: Carville's *Rock Climbing Lake Tahoe*, Carville's *Climber's Guide to Tahoe Rock*, Jenkewitz-Meytras's *Tahoe Rock Climbing*, Dexter et al.'s *Climber's Guide to Lake Tahoe Region*, Beck's *Climber's Guide to Lake Tahoe and Donner Summit*.

Directions: From South Lake Tahoe trot north on Hwy. 89 to D. L. Bliss State Park. The vast majority of boulders are poor for bouldering. The best of the good boulders are ½ mi. south of park entrance, below Hwy. 89 and 1 mi. north of park entrance around Balanced Rock. Rocks are ¼–½ mi. north of park at first turnout on right. Then walk northeast ten minutes toward boulders or walk due east, across gully, fifteen to twenty minutes to boulders. Also, small toprope cliffs at Rubicon Point.

27 Emerald Bay ✩✩✩

Climbing adjacent to D. L. Bliss State Park on 50' granite boulders with incredible scenic beauty. Camp at Bliss State Park. USFS–Eldorado NF, (530) 622–5061.

Ref: Guidebooks: Carville's *Rock Climbing Lake Tahoe*, Carville's *Climber's Guide to Tahoe Rock*, Jenkewitz-Meytras's *Tahoe Rock Climbing*, Dexter et al.'s *Climber's Guide to Lake Tahoe Region*, Beck's *Climber's Guide to Lake Tahoe and Donner Summit*.

Directions: From South Lake Tahoe go north on Hwy. 89 to Emerald Bay to Eagle Falls. Go north of creek below road.

28 ECC✩–Eagle Creek Canyon Area ✩✩

Wilderness canyon with established routes and exploration. Emerald Point is the dominant feature in Eagle Creek Canyon and is a hodgepodge of 200' granite ledges, lattices, and ridges with a lot of rock therein. The Plectrum is the most spectacular of the many summit pinnacles. USFS–Eldorado NF, (530) 622–5061.

Classics: Off the Wall 10-, Seams to Me 10c, Space Walk 11+, Der Fuhrer 11d.

Ref: Guidebooks: Carville's *Rock Climbing Lake Tahoe*, Carville's *Climber's Guide to Tahoe Rock*, Jenkewitz-Meytras's *Tahoe Rock Climbing*, Dexter et al.'s *Climber's Guide to Lake Tahoe Region*, Beck's *Climber's Guide to Lake Tahoe and Donner Summit*.

Directions: At Emerald Bay. Go to west shore on Hwy. 89. Park at trailhead for Eagle Creek Canyon.

29 ECC–Bay Area Cliffs ✪✪

Small, east-facing, quick access, 70′ granite cracks toprope crag. Summer. USFS-Eldorado NF, (530) 622–5061.

Classics: Routes up to 5.11+.

Ref: Guidebooks: Carville's *Rock Climbing Lake Tahoe*, Carville's *Climber's Guide to Tahoe Rock*, Jenkewitz-Meytras's *Tahoe Rock Climbing*, Dexter et al.'s *Climber's Guide to Lake Tahoe Region*, Beck's *Climber's Guide to Lake Tahoe and Donner Summit*.

Directions: At Emerald Bay. Follow west shore on Hwy. 89. Park at trailhead for Eagle Creek Canyon. Hike 50 yd. up Hwy. 89 and down 150 yd. toward bay for Bay Area Cliffs.

30 ECC–Eagle Lake Buttress ✪✪

Mountain 450′ granite tower. Sweeping panoramic views. Summer. USFS-Eldorado NF, (530) 622–5061.

Classics: East Ridge Route 7, A Line 9, Orange Sunshine 9, Monkey Business 10a.

Ref: C 66, Guidebooks: Carville's *Rock Climbing Lake Tahoe*, Carville's *Climber's Guide to Tahoe Rock*, Jenkewitz-Meytras's *Tahoe Rock Climbing*, Dexter et al.'s *Climber's Guide to Lake Tahoe Region*, Beck's *Climber's Guide to Lake Tahoe and Donner Summit*.

Directions: At Emerald Bay. Follow west shore on Hwy. 89. Park at trailhead for Eagle Creek Canyon. Hike Eagle Lake Trail to Eagle Lake. West of lake, follow obvious drainage to ridge crest, then hike ¼ mi. north to base of Eagle Lake Buttress.

31 ECC–Eagle Lake Cliffs ✪✪

Highly scenic, summertime backcountry lake crag offers 200′ of granite at 7,200′. USFS-Eldorado NF, (530) 622–5061.

Classics: Space Truckin' 5.10b, Off the Wall 10, Space Walk 11d.

Ref: C [95, 43]; Guidebooks: Carville's *Rock Climbing Lake Tahoe*, Carville's *Climber's Guide to Tahoe Rock*, Jenkewitz-Meytras's *Tahoe Rock Climbing*, Dexter et al.'s *Climber's Guide to Lake Tahoe Region*, Beck's *Climber's Guide to Lake Tahoe and Donner Summit*.

Directions: At Emerald Bay. Follow west shore on Hwy. 89. Park at trailhead for Eagle Creek Canyon. Hike 2 mi. west on trail (signs) to Eagle Lake Cliffs.

32 ECC–Maggie's Peak ✪

Some fine 800′ granite routes; ice climbing. Summit ridge of pinnacles offers best technical climbs. Long approach. Summer. USFS-Eldorado NF, (530) 622–5061.

Ref: Guidebooks: Carville's *Rock Climbing Lake Tahoe*, Carville's *Climber's Guide to Tahoe Rock*, Jenkewitz-Meytras's *Tahoe Rock Climbing*, Dexter et al.'s *Climber's Guide to Lake Tahoe Region*, Beck's *Climber's Guide to Lake Tahoe and Donner Summit*.

Directions: At Emerald Bay. Follow west shore on Hwy. 89. Park at trailhead for Eagle Creek Canyon. Hike Eagle Lake Trail for ¼ mi. to Velma Lake Trail. Maggie's Peak Cliff visible on left.

33 Ninety-Foot Wall ✪✪✪

Popular 70′ granite weekend workout crag. Bolted 70′ topropes or can be lead clean. Most popular area in Eagle Creek Canyon. Dries off quickly in spring. USFS-Eldorado NF, (530) 622–5061.

Classics: Holdless Horror 6, Strontium 90 8, Fallout 9, Lost in Space 11a.

Ref: C 66; Guidebooks: Carville's *Rock Climbing Lake Tahoe*, Carville's *Climber's Guide to Tahoe Rock*, Jenkewitz-Meytras's *Tahoe Rock Climbing*, Dexter et al.'s *Climber's Guide to Lake Tahoe Region*, Beck's *Climber's Guide to Lake Tahoe and Donner Summit*.

Directions: At Emerald Bay. Follow west shore on Hwy. 89. Park at trailhead for Eagle Creek Canyon. Hike up trail to bridge and follow creek upstream and right to the not-so-90′ Ninety-Foot Wall.

34 ECC–Smoke Rock and Mayhem Cove ✪✪✪

Smoke Rock's 50′ granite crag sports topropes up to 5.11. Mayhem Cove, though it appears like trash, has excellent overhanging face and crack and tests a crag person's route-finding skills. Another small cliff with a long roof one-third of the way up, God Wall, can be found below upper Eagle Creek Canyon parking. USFS-Eldorado NF, (530) 622–5061.

Classics: Mayhem Cove: Main Attraction 12d, Guillotine Direct 11a, Diamond in the Ruff 10a, Huntin' Gators 12b.

Ref: R 38; Guidebooks: Carville's *Rock Climbing Lake Tahoe*, Carville's *Climber's Guide to Tahoe Rock*, Jenkewitz-Meytras's *Tahoe Rock Climbing*.

Directions: At Emerald Bay. Follow west shore on Hwy. 89. Park at trailhead for Eagle Creek Canyon. For Smoke Rock: Visible through trees from lower Eagle Creek Canyon parking. For Mayhem Cove: From top of Smoke Rock, follow faint trail to blocky, broken crag.

35 ECC–The Stomach ✪✪

This 100′ granite crag has good intermediate routes but is unpopular due to hike. USFS-Eldorado NF, (530) 622–5061.

Classics: Mostly 5.9.

Ref: C 95; Guidebooks: Carville's *Rock Climbing Lake Tahoe*, Carville's *Climber's Guide to Tahoe Rock*, Jenkewitz-Meytras's *Tahoe Rock Climbing*, Dexter et al.'s *Climber's Guide to Lake Tahoe Region*, Beck's *Climber's Guide to Lake Tahoe and Donner Summit*.

Directions: At Emerald Bay. Follow west shore on Hwy. 89. Park at trailhead for Eagle Creek Canyon. Hike up trail to bridge and follow creek upstream to the Ninety-Foot Wall. From Ninety-Foot Wall bushwhack up and east to The Stomach. Faces east.

36 Space Domes and Space Invaders ✮✮✮

Small granite formations for experts. USFS–Eldorado NF, (530) 622–5061.

Classics: Space Invaders: America's Most Wanted 11d, Space Invaders 12a, Skyshark 12c, Double Dragon 12d; Space Domes: Meteor 12a.

Ref: R 38.

Directions: West of South Lake Tahoe. From junction of Hwy. 50 and Sawmill Rd., go approximately 2 mi. on Sawmill Rd. to Echo View Estates. Turn right on Echo View Estates, then right on Mountain Canary. Boulders at end of Mountain Canary. Space Domes and Space Invaders on left and right respectively in gully to east behind Pie Shop Crag.

37 Pie Shop (South Face of West Twin Peaks) ✮✮✮

Accessible and popular orange, knobby-faced crag. Bouldering at Echo View Estates (top of road) and Sawmill Rd. (1 mi. from Hwy. 50). Due to the southern exposure here, these 230′ granite crags are often accessible and pleasant during winter months. Concentrated number of routes. Fine bouldering, too. USFS–Eldorado NF, (530) 622–5061.

Classics: Short Cake 6, Crepes Corner 6, Humble Pie 7, The Archer 8, Hand Masseuse 8, BT Express 9, True Grip 10b, Dudley Doright 10, Cake Walk 11b, Natural High 11c, Bear Claw 12a, Jet Set 12b, Double Dragon 12d.

Ref: C [114, 109, 95, 66]; Guidebooks: Carville's *Rock Climbing Lake Tahoe*, Carville's *Climber's Guide to Tahoe Rock*, Jenkewitz-Meytras's *Tahoe Rock Climbing*, Dexter et al.'s *Climber's Guide to Lake Tahoe Region*, Beck's *Climber's Guide to Lake Tahoe and Donner Summit*.

Directions: At South Lake Tahoe, go past airport 1 mi., then ¼ mi. up Sawmill Rd. Park. A profusion of boulders lie up on the hill. Hike up past houses northwest toward eastern summit of Twin Peaks. When below it, go left to gully. Pie Shop is on the western peak of Twin Peaks. Descend northwest.

38 Indian Rock ✮✮

The 800′ dual-ledged cliff of excellent granite is the largest escarpment in Tahoe Basin. Much potential. Lengthy approach. Summer. USFS–Eldorado NF, (530) 622–5061.

Classics: Doologoga Dihedral 7.

Ref: C [105, 95]; Guidebooks: Carville's *Rock Climbing Lake Tahoe*, Carville's *Climber's Guide to Tahoe Rock*, Jenkewitz-Meytras's *Tahoe Rock Climbing*, Dexter et al.'s *Climber's Guide to Lake Tahoe Region*, Beck's *Climber's Guide to Lake Tahoe and Donner Summit*.

Directions: From South Lake Tahoe go 3 mi. northwest on Hwy. 89. Turn left on Fallen Leaf Lake Rd. to Lily Lake. Hike one hour to Triangle Lakes Trail to base of Indian Rock. Descent to southwest.

39 Echo Lakes ✮✮✮

This series of 100′ granite outcrops supplies Tahoe climbers with lithic challenges on excellent rock . . . excellent rock . . . excellent rock. . . . Flagpole Peak (8363′) is 1 mi. from lodge with good climbs, e.g., The Ramp 5.8/ Jam Session 5.10. At one time this was home to Warren Harding's Downward Bound School. USFS–Eldorado NF, (530) 622–5061.

Classics: Slip n' Slide 7, Summer Breeze 8, Leapin' Lizards 9, Rawl Will 9, Pitchfork 8-10a, Jam Session 10a, Gold Finger 10b, If I Had a Hammer 11b, Freon 11c, Good Day to Die 12-, Hip Hop Hipe 12, Aesop 12c, Metallica 12d.

Ref: C 109, R 38; Guidebooks: Carville's *Rock Climbing Lake Tahoe*, Carville's *Climber's Guide to Tahoe Rock*, Jenkewitz-Meytras's *Tahoe Rock Climbing*, Dexter et al.'s *Climber's Guide to Lake Tahoe Region*, Beck's *Climber's Guide to Lake Tahoe and Donner Summit*.

Directions: From South Lake Tahoe go south on Hwy. 50 to 2 mi. past Echo Summit on right. Spread along north shore of Lower and Upper Echo Lakes. Formations from east to west: Echo Edge, Bat Wall, Corkscrew Area, Mid Dome, Fly Girl Buttress, Flag Pole Peak, Blind Man's Bluff, 5.12 Wall, 5.13 Wall, Climax Wall, Billy Land, Old Peculiar, and Goldfinger.

40 Luther Rock and The Shire ✮

This is a little-used 200′ granite cliff at 6,800′. Poor rock, but good intermediate lines exist. USFS–Eldorado NF, (530) 622–5061.

Classics: Pearl Pillar 10.

Ref: Guidebooks: Carville's *Rock Climbing Lake Tahoe*, Carville's *Climber's Guide to Tahoe Rock*, Jenkewitz-Meytras's *Tahoe Rock Climbing*, Dexter et al.'s *Climber's Guide to Lake Tahoe Region*, Beck's *Climber's Guide to Lake Tahoe and Donner Summit*.

Directions: From South Lake Tahoe go south on Hwy. 89 to 3 mi. southeast of Meyers. Look for large black cliff (Luther Rock). Approach from higher of two vista points. Follow creek up hill to right side of cliff. The Shire is on ridge up and right of Luther.

41 Lover's Leap ✮✮✮✮

A very popular Tahoe crag and a permanent fix for marital problems, Lover's Leap is known for its granite horizontal dikes that form ledges/shelves (natural ladders on steep ground). Obvious features are The Line, a 300′ crack on the Center Wall, and Traveler's Buttress on the Main Wall. Features a wide selection of 5.6–5.10 multipitch free climbs with excellent natural protection. Bouldering below cliff. Raptor restriction from March to June (530-644-2324). USFS–Eldorado NF, (530) 622–5061.

Classics: Craven Image 7, Corrugation Corner 7, The Groove 8, Surrealistic Pillar 7-10a, Anesthesia 8, The Line 9, Scimitar 9, Fantasia 9, Traveler Buttress 9, Showtime 10a, Roofer Madness 10c, Boothill 11-, God of Thunder 11/12a, Stony God 11d, Fight the Power 12a, Silly Willy Crack 12c, Stone Cold Crazy 12c.

Ref: AAJ '84, C [178-90, 143, 109, 95, 66], R 94-106, S 1/64; Guidebooks: Carville's *Rock Climbing Lake Tahoe,* Carville's *Climber's Guide to Tahoe Rock,* Jenkewitz-Meytras's *Tahoe Rock Climbing,* Harlin's *West,* Grow's *Lover's Leap,* Drake's *A Climber's Guide to Lover's Leap,* Steck and Roper's *Fifty Classic Climbs,* Dexter et al.'s *Climber's Guide to Lake Tahoe Region,* Beck's *Climber's Guide to Lake Tahoe and Donner Summit.*

Directions: From South Lake Tahoe motor 18 mi. southwest on Hwy. 50. Across road from Strawberry Lodge and American River to campground. Hike ten minutes to Lover's Leap. Easy approach. Descend to east. Four main sections: East Wall, Main Wall, Lower Buttress, and Hogsback.

42 Phantom Spires ✩✩✩

A phalanx of small (mostly one-pitch) granite pinnacles amid a burnt forest setting contains one to three routes on each formation: Armadillo, Holiday Rock, Phantom Wall, Lower Spire, Middle Spire, Club Tower, Bucks Pile, Lizard Head, Upper Spire, Flathead, and Lost John. Excellent rock. Knobs and good cracks. Bring water, high-clearance vehicle. Camping in area. Climbable year-round, but hot in summer. USFS–Eldorado NF, (530) 622–5061.

Classics: Tyro's Test Piece 5, Over Easy 7, Jacks Corner 9, Crispy Critters 10a, Candyland 10c, Steppin' Stone 11a, Lounge Lizard, Sizzler 11b, North Face of Lizard Head 11+, Dewlap 11d, The Siren 11d.

Ref: C 143, R 38; Guidebooks: Carville's *Rock Climbing Lake Tahoe,* Carville's *Climber's Guide to Tahoe Rock,* Jenkewitz-Meytras's *Tahoe Rock Climbing.*

Directions: From Kyburz go 4 9/10 mi. east on Hwy. 50. Turn north on Wright's Lake Rd. for 1 mi., then go left on logging road to spires. Obvious hikes to formations of Phantom Spires. Middle parking area is best launching spot for most areas.

43 Sugarloaf and Sugarbun ✩✩✩✩

Enjoyable face climbing on secure granite knobs in a relaxed atmosphere. Excellent routes up to four pitches. Totes the reputation for having Grand Illusion crack, the first 5.13 in North America done in 1979 by Tony Yaniro. Boulders offer toprope problems. Year-round climbing, though not a summer area. Camping at Phantom Spires east up Hwy. 50. Kyburz Lodge meals are popular. USFS–Eldorado NF, (530) 622–5061.

Classics: Sugarloaf: Harding's Chimney 7, Scheister 7, Pony Express 9, Farky 9, TM's Deviation 9, Fingerlock 10b, Bolee Gold 10, Blue Velvet 10c, Pan Dulce 10d, Fracture 10+, Taurus 11b, Face With No Name 12a, Ghost in the Machine 12a, Captain Fingers 12c, Grand Illusion 13; Sugar Bun: Fingerlock 10b, Make That Move . . . 10d.

Ref: C [143, 95, 66, 8(7/71)]; Guidebooks: Carville's *Rock Climbing Lake Tahoe,* Carville's *Climber's Guide to Tahoe Rock,* Jenkewitz-Meytras's *Tahoe Rock Climbing,* Dexter et al.'s *Climber's Guide to Lake Tahoe Region.*

Directions: At Kyburz. Park on Hwy. 50 southeast of

Silverfork School. Sugarloaf is visible from school. Hike thirty minutes on uphill trail right of school past Sugarbun (in two minutes from road) and other boulderable formations. Parking problems (i.e., cars towed); safest bet is pullout near Pacific Bell. Please stay off school/private property.

44 Woodford's Canyon ✩✩✩

Where Tom Herbert got his start. Some established 160' granite routes and exploratory area. Single well-developed cube boulder to north of highway. Farther up highway are developed crags on left (south) side of highway. Autumn. USFS–Eldorado NF, (530) 622–5061.

Ref: Guidebooks: Carville's *Rock Climbing Lake Tahoe,* Carville's *Climber's Guide to Tahoe Rock,* Jenkewitz-Meytras's *Tahoe Rock Climbing,* Dexter et al.'s *Climber's Guide to Lake Tahoe Region.*

Directions: From the junction of Hwy. 89 and Hwy. 88 in Woodfords, drive 1-2 mi. east on Hwy. 88 to Woodford's Canyon.

45 Kirkwood Lake ✩✩

Two developed 70' granite sport crags west of campground loop. USFS–Eldorado NF, (530) 622–5061.

Classics: Emergency Vehicle 10d, Idle Love 12a.

Ref: Guidebooks: Thornburg's *Quickdraw Guide to Northern California Sport Climbing Areas.*

Directions: From Kit Carson go west on Hwy. 88 to Kirkwood Lake Campground. Park at campground. Hike west on trail to rock.

46 Consumnes Gorge ✩✩✩

Excellent 100' granite crag with remarkable holds. Short practice jam cracks and friction slabs. Autumn–spring.

Classics: Testpiece 7, Unconquerable Crack 8, Dinkum 8, The Struggler 9.

Ref: AAJ '79, S 10/71; Guidebooks: Cottrell's *Rock Climbs of Consumnes River Gorge,* Roper's *Climber's Guide to the High Sierra.*

Directions: From Placerville go south on Hwy. 49 to Diamond Springs. Turn east to Somerset going to Bucks Bar. Cross Consumnes River. On banks of north fork of Consumnes River are two areas of the Consumnes Gorge: The Traditional Area and The Main Slabs.

47 Hammer Dome ✩✩✩

The 400' twin sister of Calaveras Dome. Enjoyable, sunny granite doming. At least a dozen routes up to six pitches. Camping at White Azalea Campground, 1/4 mi. away. USFS–Stanislaus NF, (530) 622–5061.

Classics: Wings and Stings 7, Gemini Cracks 8, Red Eye Express 10a, Sea of Holes 10, Set the Controls . . . 11.

Ref: C 5/2000-108; Guidebook: Harlin's *West.*

Directions: From Pioneer go 26 mi. east to west side of Salt Springs Reservoir. Hammer Dome is on left before reservoir. Calaveras Dome sits to the south across road. Faces south.

48 Calaveras Dome ★★★★

Clean 500' Sierra granite dome with routes up to eight pitches in length. Long climbing season due to 4,000' elevation. Camping at White Azalea Campground. Free campsites at Mokelumna. Private land/USFS–Stanislaus NF, (530) 622-5061.

Classics: Blockhead 9, Wall of the Worlds IV 10c, Vaya Con Pollos 11, Tsunami 11c, Rastaman Vibrations 12-.

Ref: C 194-98; Guidebooks: Cottrell's *Rock Climbs of Calaveras,* Harlin's *West.*

Directions: From Pioneer drive 26 mi. east to west side of Salt Springs Reservoir. On right before reservoir water sits Calaveras Dome. Alternate access from Ellis Rd. off Hwy. 88. Hammer Dome is south-facing rock across river. East access road sometimes closed by snow.

49 Ramsey Cliff ★★★

Numerous slabs and 300' granite crags. USFS–Stanislaus NF, (530) 622-5061.

Classics: Foster Farm 7, Keystone 9, Born to Party 10.

Ref: C 100(2/87).

Directions: Near Ebbets Pass. From Dorrington creep 5 mi. east on Hwy. 4. Turn right on FS road (before Cottage Springs picnic area) 2 mi. to summit. Hike east to Ramsey Cliff.

50 Dardanelle Rest Area ★★

Topropes and 40' granite micro leads in rest area. Viewpoint of middle fork of Stanislaus River. USFS–Stanislaus NF, (530) 622-5061.

Ref: J. Sherman.

Directions: From Dardanelle shoot out 3 mi. west on Hwy. 108 to Dardanelle Rest Area on north side of highway.

51 Columbia ★★★

Hydraulically mined, 35' polished limestone spires and otherworldly topropes. The weather can be good all year, although summer can be hot. Good for a rest day from Jailhouse or the Grotto. Marvel at the abundant poison oak—be careful of landings. Autumn. County land.

Classics: Limestone Express 5.6, Mondo Bondo 5.10+, Mushroom Boulder Traverse 5.11, Triple Cracks 5.11+.

Ref: J. Sherman; M. Cresci 2/97.

Directions: In Columbia, at Columbia Junior College on the nature trail. From the parking area at the student housing, follow the road around the campus. When you reach the Toyon building, head down the Nature Trail; this will land you in the Arboretum.

52 Table Mountain (Sonora) (closed?) ★★★

Great cranking on fractured basalt holds on several good walls, e.g., The Grotto. Watch for loose holds, snakes, poison oak. Spring/autumn. Camping thirty minutes south at Lake Don Pedro at Moccasin Point Hwy. 120. Bureau of Reclamation.

Classics: Rawhide 10+, Geronimo 11b, Cave 12a.

Ref: C 149-48, R 65-83; Guidebook: Hiskes's *A Climber's Guide to Table Mountain.*

Directions: From Jamestown (just south of Sonora), go south on Hwy. 108, turn northwest on Rawhide Rd. to left turn on Shell Rd. to pavement's end at a gate. Drive 1 ½ mi. farther, closing gates, and park. Short hike to rock.

53 Jailhouse Rock (near Sonora) ★★★

A powerhouse of pump on 200' overhanging granite, super-featured sport crag. 5.12s and 5.13s. Access-sensitive private land.

Classics: Whipping Boy 12b, Alcatraz 13c, Lockdown 13c.

Ref: T. Herbert.

Directions: At Tullock Reservoir. Jailhouse Rock is approximately 12 mi. west of Sonora, north of Hwy. 120.

54 Napa Bouldering

This bouldering area offers the Noreltny Traverse V7.

Ref: R 84-94.

Directions: Near Napa.

55 Yosemite National Park–Hetch Hetchy Reservoir ★★★★

The Grand Canyon of the Tuolumne River (a half-scale Yosemite Valley) dammed and flooded by the city of San Francisco. Hetch Hetchy Dome 1,800' walls are one of the focal points for rock climbers. While rock in Yosemite National Park is ubiquitous (that means everywhere, dudes), four areas have been selected for this guide: Hetch Hetchy Valley, Yosemite Valley, Tuolumne Meadows, and Wawona Dome. Raptor restrictions: Hetch Hetchy, February–July. NPS, (209) 372-0200.

Classics: Hetch Hetchy Dome, Kolana Rock, Wapama Rock.

Ref: Ascent, AAJ ['72-178, 71, 70-65], C [143 to 47], M 79, R [67-54, 60], S [3/90, 5/87, 5/85, 1/85, 7/84, 5/81, 8/78, 4/78, 8/77, 12/75, 10/75, 4/74, 3/73, 10/72, 5/71, 12/70, 7/70, 1/70, 11/69, 5/69, 3/69, 1/69, 9/68, 11/67, 9/66, 5/65, 4/64, 1/62]; Meyer's *Vertical World of Yosemite, Yosemite Climber, Climbing in N.A.*; Guidebooks: Reid's *Yosemite Climbs,* Harlin's *West,* Nicol's *Rock Climbs in Yosemite,* Roper's *Climber's Guide to Yosemite Valley.*

Directions: From Hwy. 120 at west entrance to Yosemite National Park, take Tioga Pass Rd. northwest to Carl Inn. Then go north on Evergreen Rd. to Mather. From Mather, follow road northeast to Hetch Hetchy Reservoir/Dome. (Hetch Hetchy lies north of Yosemite Valley.)

56 Yosemite National Park–Tuolumne Meadows ☆☆☆☆☆

Superb, sensational, spectacular! Glistening granite domes in the Yosemite high country at 8,000′. Well known for airy, seriously runout knob pulling, and the summer getaway from the Valley. Fantastic bouldering. The Bachar-Yerian Route 5.11b on Medlicott Dome was considered the height of first-ascent purity for its era. To the east in the high country along the Sierra Divide, the 5.10c Harding Route on the southwest face of Mt. Conness is considered a classic. Many beautiful bouldering areas in Tuolumne include the classic "Gunks" bouldering. Best months: June, July, and August. Tuolumne Campground, open from June to October, requires reservations (800) 436–7275. Tenaya and Tuolumne are walk-in campgrounds. NPS, (209) 372–0200.

Classics: Stately Pleasure: Great White Book 6, South Crack 8; Fairview: North Face III 9, Lucky Streaks 10b, Piece de Resistance 11c, Heart of Stone 12-; Morning Thunder 9; Pywiack: Dike Route 9 R, Phobos 9, Needle Spoon 10b, Clash of the Titans 13a; Polly Dome Phobos 9; Pennyroyal Arches: The Vision 10a; North Whizz: Handbook 11a; Harlequin: By Hook or By Crook 11b; Mariuolumne: Oz 10d, Blues Riff 11c, Gold Finger 12a, Electric Africa 12b, Love Supreme 13a; Lamb Dome: On the Lamb 9; Lembert Dome: Northwest Books 6/9; Cathedral Peak 6/8, Third Pillar of Dana 5.9, Cathedral Peak 5.6.

Ref: *Ascent*, AAJ ['85-192, 85-195, 84 to 82, 77-176, 76-447, 74-66, 69]; C [194-70, 191-84, 190-117, 187-104, 159(3/96)-70, 157-32, 152-124, 127(8/91)-60, 124, 118, 114, 111, 109, 105 to 102, 100 to 98, 95 93, 90, 88, 75(12/82), 73, 71], M 60(3/78)-28, R [73-84, 46(11/91)-43, 32(7/89)], S 3/85; Sherman's *Stone Crusade*; Guidebooks: Floyd's *Tuolumne Topropes*, Falkenstein and Reid's *Rock Climbs of Tuolumne Meadows*, Schneider's *Tuolumne Sport Climbs*, Nelson's *A Guide to Yosemite Domes*, Steck and Roper's *Fifty Classic Climbs*, Harlin's *West*.

Directions: Tuolumne Meadows is in Yosemite National Park. Heading east from Tenaya Lake on Hwy. 120 many domes abound. The largest include Stately Pleasure Dome (north side of Hwy. 120), Harlequin Dome (north), Pywiack Dome (south), Polly Dome (north), Medlicott Dome (south), Mariuolumne Dome (south), Daff Dome (north), Fairview Dome (south), and Lembert Dome (north). NPS map or guidebook recommended. The best bouldering can be found at The Gunks Boulders, ¹⁄₁₀ mi. east of Pothole parking at crest of road south of Hwy. 120; The Knobs, just north of Pywiack on west side of Hwy. 120; and Tenaya Boulders, across from Tenaya Dome parking; and bouldering at base of Puppy Dome, at base of Do or Fly.

Testing rock integrity atop Half Dome, Yosemite National Park.

TIM TOULA

57 Yosemite National Park–Yosemite Valley (aka The Valley) ☆☆☆☆☆

An American institution and world-renowned rock-climbing Mecca. With granitic climbing of every type, grade, and spectrum, The Valley is famed for its infinite cracks, traditional clean climbing, and big walls (e.g., El Capitan at 3,300′, the largest continuous granite monolith in the United States, and Half Dome's 2,200′ striking splendor). Noteworthy as the "light bulb" of big-wall technique, initiated in 1958 by Harding, Merry, and Whitmore with the first ascent of the Nose followed by Pratt, Robbins, and Frost in 1962 with the Salathé Wall, then followed by Bridwell, Long, and Westbay's Nose-in-a-Day ascent in the 1970s. Amazing first free ascents of big walls: e.g., Skinner/Piana, The Salathé; Lynn Hill, The Nose; and the Huber brothers' achievements. Incredible one-day solo speed ascents of El Cap and Half Dome by Potter and Florine. Free soloing instituted by John Bachar and amplified by Croft's solo of Astroman. World-class bouldering grounds since the first ascent of Midnight Lightning by Ron Kauk . . . and another book of great climbing achievers and achievements. Spectacular waterfalls: Yosemite Falls (at 2,425′, third highest in the world), Bridalveil, and Vernal. Famed Ahwahnee Hotel brunches. Degnan's Deli renowned for its coffee statesmen. Raptor restrictions. Best from mid-March to mid-May and mid-September to mid-November. Camping by reservations . . . entertainment by the summer crowds. Note: Seven-day limit for camping in the Valley May 1 to September 15. Sunnyside Walk-in Campground (Camp 4) is open all year on a first-come, first-served basis. NPS, (209) 372–0200.

Classics: Bishop's Terrace 8, Nutcracker 8, Reed's Direct 9,

Royal Arches Route 9, Separate Reality 11d, Crimson
Cringe 12-, Tales of Power 12b, Phoenix 13, Magic Line
14b; Cookie Cliff: Outer Limits 10b, Butterballs 11c;
Rostrum: North Face 11c; Middle Cathedral Rock:
Central Pillar of Frenzy 9; Washington's Column:
Astroman IV 11c; El Capitan: East Buttress IV 10a,
Moratorium II 11b, The Nose V 13+ or 8C2, Salathé Wall
VI 13b or 9C2 or Freebird VI 12d, Zodiac VI 7A2+;
Glacier Point Apron: Mr. Natural 10d; Half Dome: Snake
Dike 7, Autobahn IV 11+, Reg. Northwest Face 12, Dir.
Northwest Face 13d; Midnight Lightning B2, The
Dominator V13.

Ref: AAJ ['98>95, '91, 89>76, 74, 71], C [197-104, 196-18,
195-97, 192-81, 191-16, 190-22/78, 189-21/80, 188-27/42,
187-68, 186-76, 185-26, 183-78, 182-24/84, 181-25/113,
179-79, 178-114, 177-29/124, 176-44/98, 174-18, 173-20,
172-18/23/90, 170-19/98, 169, 168-80, 167-26, 166-22,
165(12/96)-22/24/114, 164-122, 163-24, 162-86, 161-106,
159(3/96)-74, 158-123, 157-94, 156-40/120, 154-70, 153-
90/135, 152-114, 150-63/159, 144, 141-54, 140, 126-47,
118-78, 105 to 99, 98-48, 97, 96, 94, 70-22, 66], M [106,
102, 93, 91, 70, 69, 66, 31, 8], R [98-28, 95-22, 93-22/112,
91-66/98 (wall topos), 90-20/54, 89, 87, 85-16/36, 79-
56/94, 78, 77, 76, 75-17/64, 69, 67, 65, 58, 57, 46-13, 24-
14, 19, (5/73), 8, 7, 5], S [5/87, 5/85, 5/73, 5/72, 10/71,
4/71]; Piana's *Big Walls,* Sherman's *Stone Crusade,*
Benington's *Heroic Climbs,* Kor's *Beyond the Vertical;*
Guidebooks: McNamara's *Yosemite Big Walls Supertopos,*
Reid's *Rock Climbing Yosemite's Select Climbs,* Reid's *Selected
Bouldering: Yosemite Valley,* Wadman's *El Capitan Climbing
Poster Guide,* Falkenstein's *Yosemite Valley Sport Climbs,*
Reid's *Yosemite Climbs: Big Walls,* Reid's *Yosemite Climbs: Free
Climbs,* Reid's *Camp 4 Bouldering Guide,* Black's *El Cap Route
Map,* Meyer and Reid's *Yosemite Climbs,* Roper's *Climber's
Guide to Yosemite Valley,* Harlin's *West,* Morris's *A Climber's
Guide to Glacier Point Apron,* Steck and Roper's *Fifty Classic
Climbs,* Meyer's *Yosemite Climbs,* Nicol et. al.'s *Rock Climbs
in Yosemite,* Harmon's *Climbing Routes on Yosemite's Walls.*

Directions: Areas lie in and around Yosemite Village in
Yosemite Valley. Many cliffs: Arch Rock, Cookie Cliff,
Elephant Rock, Rostrum, Pat and Jack, Cathedral Rocks,
Manure Pile Buttress. And many walls: Leaning Tower, El
Capitan, Sentinel Rock, Glacier Point Apron, Washing-
ton's Column, Half Dome, Mt. Watkins, and Quarter
Dome. Most popular bouldering at Camp 4 Boulders,
though a good circuit exists around the other areas of
valley floor, e.g., Base of Sentinel Rock Boulders.

58 Yosemite National Park–Wawona Dome ☆☆☆

Big granite dome and several small crags overlooked only
because of its proximity to the Valley. In Iowa, they'd be
jumpin' for the first lead. Clothing-optional swimming
holes. NPS, (209) 372–0200.

Ref: AAJ '128, C [111, 101]; Guidebooks: Spencer's *Southern
Yosemite Rock Climbs,* Spencer's *Wawona Rock.*

Directions: From Yosemite Valley go 25 mi. south on Hwy.
41 to Wawona Village. Wawona Dome is east/northeast

The Nose at El Capitan, Yosemite National Park.

TIM TOULA

of the village. Take Chilnualna Rd. east from Wawona
Village to abandoned logging road that leads to base of
dome.

59 Sierra Range ☆☆☆☆

Possibly the greatest rock climbing range in the Lower 48.
Several lifetimes of adventurous rock climbing can be had
on the Sierra Range's granite alpine walls made known by
legendary Sierra travelers and summiteers John Muir,
Norman Clyde, and Clarence King. The 1,700' east face of
Keeler Needle (14,300') and Mt. Conness (12,590') are just
two of the many fine, big wall climbs. Other outstanding
formations include Bear Creek Spire (a crest pinnacle), Mt.
Whitney (the kingpin of the Sierras), Clyde Minaret (alpine
pinnacles), Matthes Crest (your basic lobate cockscomb),
The Incredible Hulk (fine wall), and Tehipite Dome (a granite monster). A vast history of guidebooks for the Sierras
abound (see below). The Secor or Roper guidebooks will
help one to find climbs on a plethora of formations. Long
approaches with big rewards, that is, a Midas's wealth of
high-quality rock climbing on granite walls, domes, and
spires. Backcountry camping; wilderness permits may be
required. Treat water for giardia. Protect food from bears
and other vermin. Good topo maps a must. USFS–Sierra,
(559) 784–1500; Stanislaus, (209) 532–3671, Sequoia NF,
(559) 784–1500; Yosemite/Sequoia/King's Canyon National
Parks (see separate listings).

Classics: Northern Yosemite—Incredible Hulk; Red Dihedral IV 10, Mt. Conness: West Ridge 5.6, Southwest 5.10c; Tuolumne Domes—Fairview Dome: North Face III 9; Southern Yosemite: Cathedral Pk Southeast Face II 4; Ritter Range: Banner Pk III 8, Mt. Ritter VI 9, Clyde Minaret Southeast Face IV 8; Mono Recesses: Seven Gables V 9, Fresno Dome, The Balls, East Fuller Butte; Evolution: Mt. Goode North Butt. III 9; The Palisades—Temple Crag: Moon Goddess Arête III 9; Mt. Sill: Swiss Arête II 4; Kings River Region (Tehipite Dome, Obelisk); Kearsage Pass Area: Center Pk III 7; Charlotte Dome: South Face III 7; Great Western Divide: Eagle Scout Pk II 8, Lippincott Mountain III 10; Mt. Whitney Area: Mt. Williamson IV 7, Mt. Muir III 9, Mt. Russell III 10, Mt. Chamberlin V 10 A2; Keeler Needle: Harding Rt IV 10.

Ref: AAJ ['98>95, '93, 91-125/166, 90-176, 89-145, 88-134, 86-155, 85-191, 83 to 79, 77-173, 76-443, 75-125, 74, 72, 70], C [178-62, 169-122, 160-108, 149-53/114, 133, 132, 111, 110, 105, 88, 67, 66, 10/72], M 111, OB 21(6/75), R [94-28, 93-68, 92-50, 74-44, 73-66, 65-20, 61, 16(9/86)-48], S [9/88, 7/87, 7/85, 9/82, 11/80, 6/77, 4/72, 5/71, 10/70, 11/69, 4/69, 1/69, 12/68]; Jones's *Climbing in North America*, *History of Sierra Nevada*, Winnett's *Sierra South 100 Backcountry Trips*; Guidebooks: Steck and Roper's *Fifty Classic Climbs*, Spencer's *Southern Yosemite Rock Climbs*, Moser, Vernon, and Hickey's *Sequoia/Kings Canyon: Southern Sierra Rock Climbing*, Moynier and Fiddler's *Sierra Classics: 100 Best Climbs in the High Sierra*, Porcella and Burns's *Sierra Classics: Best Routes in Sierra Backcountry*, Moser and Vernon's *Domelands*, Secor's *The High Sierra*, Bard's *Shooting Star Guides (Whitney, Matterhorn, Cathedral, Swiss Arête)*, Hellweg and McDonald's *Mt. Whitney Guide*, Bartlett and Allen's *Sierra East Side*, Vernon's *Courtright Reservoir*, Peer's *A Climbing Guide to the Bastille Buttress*, Joe and Leversee's *Stonemasher Guide to Kern River Canyon and Environs (Needles)*, E. C. Joe's *Stonemasher Guide to the Kern Slabs*, Roper's *Timberline Country: The Sierra High Route*, Roper's *Climber's Guide to the High Sierra*, Voge et al.'s *Mountaineering Guide to the High Sierra*, Voge's *Climber's Guide to the High Sierra*, Voge and Brower's *Climber's Guide to the High Sierra: The Palisades*, Brower's *A Climber's Guide to the High Sierra*, Hedden and Brower's *A Climber's Guide to the High Sierra: The Evolution Region*, Mendenhall's *A Climber's Guide to the High Sierra: The Whitney Region*, Starr's *A Climber's Guide to the High Sierra: The Ritter Range*, Leonard's *A Climber's Guide to the High Sierra: The Sawtooth Ridge*.

Directions: There are no roads crossing the High Sierra Range between Tioga Pass on the north and Sherman Pass to the south. Regions in the Sierra Range, as broken down by Roper's *High Sierra Climbing Guide*, include: Northern Yosemite (Kettle Peak, Matterhorn Peak, Mt. Conness, Hetch Hetchy Dome, etc.), Tuolumne Domes (Fairview, et al., see Tuolumne listing), Southern Yosemite (Mt. Dana, Mt. Lyell, Cathedral Range, Clark Range), Ritter Range (Mt. Ritter, The Minarets, etc.), Mono Recesses (Mt. Abbott Group, Mt. Humphreys), Evolution Region (Mt. Goddard, Mt. Goode, Devil's Crags), Palisades (Mt. Sill, Temple Crag), Kings River Region (Tehipite Dome, Obelisk, Gorge of Despair

Turrets, south Fork), Kearsage Pass (Charlotte Dome), Great Western Divide (The Watchtower, Castle Rock Spire, Moro Rock, Angel Wings), and Mt. Whitney Area (Mt. Whitney, Keeler Needle). A starter sampler is Mt. Conness, reached 2 mi. east of Tioga Pass. Turn left onto Saddlebag Lakes Rd. In 1 ½ mi. turn left up blocked road. Go past Carnegie Institute. Up creek. Pass large rock cliff on left via notch to east shoulder. Drop down gully to southwest shoulder.

60 Lee Vining Canyon ✫✫✫

Summer rock, winter ice. Alpine 500′ granite cliffs, spires, and sport crags. USFS. The two cliffs sport routes like Master Cylinder 5.12b. Camping above and below. Tioga Pass Resort (store, cafe) is a frequent hang for Tuolumne locals. USFS–Inyo NF, (760) 873-2400.

Classics: Master Cylinder 12b.

Ref: C [173-52, 151-97], R 32(7/89)-58.

Directions: Along Hwy. 120 between Lee Vining and Tioga Pass. Lee Vining Canyon's most popular crags are toward the top of the grade at 9,000′, ½ mi. below the Ellery Lake dam. Private Property Cliff is 3 ³/10 mi. below Tioga Pass on right-side turnout. Ten-minute hike down talus to not-visible cliff. Also, Transpire Wall is 4 ³/10 mi. below the pass on left above talus slope.

61 The Balls ✫✫✫

A group of about eight small granite domes with beautiful granite on the south faces. Intermediate routes. Bowler Campground at east end of Balls. USFS–Sierra NF, (559) 297-0706.

Ref: AAJ ['80, 77-176], C 111; Guidebooks: Spencer's *Southern Yosemite Rock Climbs*, Roper's *Climber's Guide to the High Sierras*.

Directions: A few mi. below the southern Yosemite National Park boundary. From Bass Lake (north shore) go north on Beasore Rd. 26 mi. (last 6 mi. are dirt). The Balls are north of road. No gas services available past Bass Lake.

62 Granite Basin (Sagehen Summit Area) ✫✫✫

Granite Basin is a high desert, 300′ granite dome with decomposing granite, so look for better varnished rock. The Sierra East Side is characterized by world-class bouldering to alpine walls. Year-round climbing. Mt. Whitney, Buttermilks, Owens River Gorge, and Deadman's Summit. The scenery that photographer Ansel Adams made famous. USFS–Inyo NF, (760) 873-2400.

Classics: Kinda Now 6, Gay 4 Wheeler's Club 8, Hair Raiser Buttress 9, Along the Watchtower 10-.

Ref: Guidebook: Bartlett and Allen's *Sierra East Side*.

Directions: From June Lake Junction drive north on Hwy. 395 to Hwy. 120 and go northeast/east on Hwy. 120. Go left on dirt road 3 ⁷/10 mi. east of Sagehen Summit to dirt road to Granite Basin domes.

63 North Canyon (Sagehen Summit Area) ✪✪✪

North Canyon has an 80' volcanic crag. Government land.
Classics: American Hero 11c, The Shredder 12b.
Ref: Guidebook: Bartlett and Allen's *Sierra East Side.*
Directions: From June Lake Junction drive north on Hwy. 395 to Hwy. 120 and go northeast on Hwy. 120. Turn right on 1S15 for 1 ½ mi. Park. Hike north for 100' to North Canyon.

64 Dexter Canyon (Sagehen Summit Area) ✪✪✪

Several areas offer nice 5.10 routes on 100' volcanic multi-pitched routes in this northeast/southwest-running canyon on the north side of the Glass Mountains. USFS–Inyo NF, (760) 873–2400/private land.
Classics: A Dollar Short 10b, Vapor Lock 10d, Bowling for Keeps 11a.
Ref: S 3/73; Guidebook: Bartlett and Allen's *Sierra East Side.*
Directions: From June Lake Junction take Hwy. 395 north to east on Hwy. 120. Turn right on Sagehen Meadows Rd. 1N02. Follow signs to Johnny Meadow to rim. Park. Hike up Dexter Canyon to descent. Other approaches possible.

65 Aeolian Buttes ✪✪✪

High 30' bouldering on soft, rhyolite rock. Glacially polished faces with pockets, much loose rock, and soft landings. USFS–Inyo NF, (760) 873–2400.
Classics: Know When to Say When, Childeater.
Ref: C 120; Guidebook: Bartlett and Allen's *Sierra East Side.*
Directions: From June Lake Junction go approximately 2 ½ mi. north on Hwy. 395. Turn right (northeast) on West Portal Rd., go ½ mi. left (north) on less-used dirt road to Aeolian Buttes. Boulders are 150' to east. Pit Bull ¼ mi. farther north on road at T junction.

66 Roadside Attractions and Bachar Boulders ✪✪✪

Small areas of good 20' rhyolite bouldering. USFS–Inyo NF, (760) 873–2400.
Ref: Guidebooks: Lewis's *Mammoth Area Rock Climbs,* Bartlett and Allen's *Sierra East Side.*
Directions: From June Lake Junction, Roadside Attractions and Bachar Boulders are approximately 1 and 2 mi. north on Hwy. 395 to east and west of Hwy. 395, respectively.

67 Chinquapin Area ✪✪✪

Bouldering area. USFS–Inyo NF, (760) 873–2400.
Ref: Guidebooks: Lewis's *Mammoth Area Rock Climbs,* Bartlett and Allen's *Sierra East Side.*
Directions: From June Lake Junction go west on June Lake Loop to right at OH RIDGE sign for 6/10 mi. Go right on pole line road 1 mi., then left for 4/10 mi. Chinquapin Area is on right.

68 June Lake Village Areas ✪✪

Scenic granite bouldering and topropes in the pines. Private land/possibly USFS–Inyo NF.
Classics: Three Pops 10b, Fire 11d, Cling or Spring 12.
Ref: R 30(3/89)-64; Guidebooks: Lewis's *Mammoth Area Rock Climbs,* Bartlett and Allen's *Sierra East Side,* Harlin's *West.*
Directions: Near June Lake Village. From June Lake Junction go west on June Lake Loop to right at fire station. Park. Hike to lake. Or, at Hideaway Meadows Rd.

69 Lion's Den ✪✪✪

Small 45' rhyolite bouldering area. USFS–Inyo NF, (760) 873–2400.
Classics: Bulldog 11c, Block and Tackle 11d, Schneider Arête 12a.
Ref: Guidebooks: Lewis's *Mammoth Area Rock Climbs,* Bartlett and Allen's *Sierra East Side.*
Directions: From June Lake Junction trend south on Hwy. 395 for 2 2/10 mi. Turn east on dirt road for ½ mi. Go left 7/10 mi. Lion's Den is on left.

70 Deadman's Summit ✪✪✪

Renowned East Side bouldering. Pocketed faces, cracks, tall problems. Good overhanging rhyolite pocket pulling. Most concentrated number of problems of all Hwy. 395 areas. Free camping. USFS–Inyo NF, (760) 873–2400.
Classics: Classic Thin Crack Problem B1.
Ref: C [151-97, 93], R 30(3/89)-64; Sherman's *Stone Crusade;* Guidebooks: Lewis's *Mammoth Area Rock Climbs,* Bartlett and Allen's *Sierra East Side.*
Directions: From Lee Vining go 14 ½ mi. south on Hwy. 395 to top of hill. Deadman's Summit is to west.

71 Triple Cracks

Small East Side volcanic bouldering area. USFS–Inyo NF, (760) 873–2400.
Ref: Guidebooks: Lewis's *Mammoth Area Rock Climbs,* Bartlett and Allen's *Sierra East Side.*
Directions: From Mammoth Lakes (junction of Hwy. 203 and Hwy. 395) go 9 8/10 mi. north on Hwy. 395. Turn right on unmarked road for ½ mi. Triple Cracks are on right.

72 Indiana Summit Natural Area ✪✪✪

A king's supply of boulders and 70' volcanic crags scrambled in a maze of Forest Service roads (good USFS map a must). Watch for soft shoulders, where cars can get stuck. USFS–Inyo NF, (760) 873–2400.
Classics: At The Stumps: EZ Money 6, Spearhead Arête 8, Curly Shuffle 11a.
Ref: Guidebooks: Lewis's *Mammoth Area Rock Climbs,* Bartlett and Allen's *Sierra East Side.*
Directions: From Mammoth Lakes, Indiana Summit Natural Area is just north on Hwy. 395 to June Lake. Area between Owens River Rd. and Bald Mountain Rd. east of Hwy. 395. See guidebook and maps for this complex area.

73 SE–IS–Trifle Tower ✩✩✩

Bolted microleads and rhyolite topropes in 5.11 to 5.12 range. USFS-Inyo NF, (760) 873-2400.

Classics: Left 5.11+, Right 12a.

Ref: R 30(3/89)-64; Guidebooks: Lewis's *Mammoth Area Rock Climbs,* Bartlett and Allen's *Sierra East Side.*

Directions: From Mammoth Lakes take Hwy. 395 north and go right on Bald Mountain Rd. (1S05) 1 $^8/_{10}$ mi. to right on 2S42 (may be marked) for 1 mi. Go left $^2/_{10}$ mi. on rough road. Trifle Tower topropes above road end.

74 SE–IS–The Fault Line ✩✩✩

Small East Side rhyolite 25' bouldering area. USFS-Inyo NF, (760) 873-2400.

Classics: Schneider's Roof 11+ crack.

Ref: Guidebooks: Lewis's *Mammoth Area Rock Climbs,* Bartlett and Allen's *Sierra East Side.*

Directions: From Mammoth Lakes take Hwy. 395 north to right on Bald Mountain Road (1S05) 1 $^8/_{10}$ mi. Then go right on 2S42 for 1 $^8/_{10}$ mi. Go left for $^2/_{10}$ mi. on pumiced rough road. Then left for $^1/_{10}$ mi. to The Fault Line.

75 SE–IS–Rick's Rocks ✩✩✩

Forested 30' rhyolite boulders, pleasant setting. Nice intermediate-level problems. USFS-Inyo NF, (760) 873-2400.

Ref: C 120; Guidebooks: Lewis's *Mammoth Area Rock Climbs,* Bartlett and Allen's *Sierra East Side.*

Directions: From Mammoth Lakes take Hwy. 395 north and go right on Owens River Rd. Then go left on S204 for 3 $^1/_2$ mi. to junction with 2S42. Park on right and hike down a gully east of road to Rick's Rocks.

76 SE–IS–The Swiss Cheese Boulder ✩✩✩

Pumping 50' overhang with big rhyolite pockets. A 1 $^1/_2$ mi. wandering hike before Bald Mountain Lookout. USFS-Inyo NF, (760) 873-2400.

Ref: Guidebooks: Lewis's *Mammoth Area Rock Climbs,* Bartlett and Allen's *Sierra East Side.*

Directions: From Mammoth Lakes take Hwy. 395 north and go right on Bald Mountain Rd. (1S05) for 10 mi. Go right past LOCKED GATE 600 YARDS sign. Turn right at sign onto most-used road (the left of the two possibilities) $^2/_{10}$ mi. to road closure. Hike $^3/_{10}$ mi. downhill to old parking area. Hike south down left-hand gully $^3/_{10}$ mi. to The Swiss Cheese Boulder.

77 SE–IS–The Tall Boys and Temple of Doom ✩✩✩

Small East Side 40' rhyolite bouldering area. USFS-Inyo NF, (760) 873-2400.

Ref: Guidebooks: Lewis's *Mammoth Area Rock Climbs,* Bartlett and Allen's *Sierra East Side.*

Directions: From Mammoth Lakes start on Hwy. 395 north and go right on Owens River Rd. At Big Springs Campground, take left on S204 for 4 $^1/_{10}$ mi. Go right on 2S09 $^1/_2$ mi. to INDIANA SUMMIT NAT. AREA sign. Temple of Doom area is straight ahead at dead-end, then hike southeast through woods. Tall Boys Boulders: Take a sharp left at sign for approximately $^1/_2$ mi. to small parking area NATURAL AREA sign, then 300' north on faint road. Pull right off road. Hike east through trees 200 yd. bypassing small rocks to 40' steep topropes and boulders.

78 SE–IS–Clark Canyon ✩✩✩

Sport routes, topropes, and bouldering on volcanic welded tuff. Unique and enjoyable. USFS-Inyo NF, (760) 873-2400.

Classics: Jihad 11b, King Spud 11c, Dirty Dancing 12a, Maltese Falcon 12b.

Ref: C 151-97, R 59; Guidebooks: Lewis's *Mammoth Area Rock Climbs,* Lewis and Moynier's *Mammoth Area Sport Climbs,* Bartlett and Allen's *Sierra East Side.*

Directions: From Mammoth Lakes take Hwy. 395 north and go right on Owens River Rd. Go left on S204 2 $^2/_{10}$ mi. Turn right on Alpers Canyon Rd. for 1 $^6/_{10}$ mi. Go right on 1S47 for $^1/_{10}$ mi. through gate for another 1 $^8/_{10}$ mi. to topropes in Clark Canyon.

79 SE–IS–The Stumps ✩✩✩

Fifty-foot volcanic bolted leads and bouldering. USFS-Inyo NF, (760) 873-2400.

Classics: 12a overhanging face.

Ref: Guidebooks: Lewis's *Mammoth Area Rock Climbs,* Bartlett and Allen's *Sierra East Side.*

Directions: From Mammoth Lakes take Hwy. 395 north and go right on Owens River Rd. Go left on S204 and go left on S203. Then go right on S208 to The Stumps.

80 SE–IS–Alpers Canyon ✩✩

Volcanic crag. USFS-Inyo NF, (760) 873-2400.

Classics: Mind Dart 10d.

Ref: Guidebooks: Lewis's *Mammoth Area Rock Climbs,* Bartlett and Allen's *Sierra East Side.*

Directions: From Mammoth Lakes take Hwy. 395 north and go right on Owens River Rd. Then go left on S204 for 2 $^2/_{10}$ mi. Go right on Alpers Canyon Rd. Take second left in $^9/_{10}$ mi. Continue for $^6/_{10}$ mi., which leads to Mind Dart (10d) in Alpers Canyon. Topropes farther up canyon to left.

81 SE–Benton Crags ✩✩

Wonderland of rock allows for climbing almost year-round in a high desert granite setting. Popular, readily accessible formations include Locals Only Rock, Psycho Killer Rock, Junk Food Rock, and Crocodile Rock; up to 100' granite crags. USFS-Inyo NF, (760) 873-2400.

Classics: Get Lost 7, Surfin' Safari 9, Psycho Killer 10a, Challenger 10c.

Ref: Guidebook: Bartlett and Allen's *Sierra East Side.*

Directions: From Benton go west on Hwy. 120 to Benton Crossing Rd., then go 6 mi. southwest on Benton

Crossing Rd. Go ½ mi. east on 3S50 then 1 2/10 mi. left on dirt roads to rock of Benton Crags and camping.

82 SE–Devil's Postpile National Monument ☆☆☆

Summertime 160' volcanic crack crag. Check with NPS before climbing. Gateway and trailhead for backcountry Sierra climbs in the Minarets. For Mammoth Ranger Station backcountry permits, call (760) 924–5500.
Classics: Wishbone Cracks 10-11, Clyde Minaret.
Ref: R 93-72; Guidebook: Bartlett and Allen's *Sierra East Side*.
Directions: From Mammoth Lakes check with Devil's Postpile National Monument Visitor Center at east end of Mammoth. Mandatory shuttle system during summer peak season.

83 SE–Rainbow Wall ☆☆☆

Volcanic crag. USFS.
Classics: Wishbone Cracks 10b/11a, Somewhere Over The Rainbow 12-.
Ref: Guidebook: Bartlett and Allen's *Sierra East Side*.
Directions: Approach from Devil's Postpile National Monument. Take Rainbow Falls Trail south to Fish Creek Trail. Go south on Fish Creek Trail 1 ½ mi. to Rainbow Wall on left side of trail. Road to Devil's Postpile National Monument closed 7:00 A.M.–5:00 P.M. in peak summer months, must take shuttle bus (fee).

84 SE–Mammoth Lakes Basin ☆☆☆

Several types of climbing south of Mammoth Lakes on this summertime 400' granite crag. USFS–Inyo NF, (760) 873–2400.
Classics: Horseshoe Lake Boulder, Crystal Crag; Dike Wall: Lake George.
Ref: C 151-97, Guidebooks: Moynier and Lewis's *Mammoth Area Sport Climbs*, Bartlett and Allen's *Sierra East Side*.
Directions: From Mammoth Lakes go south of town on Lake Mary Rd. Two parking areas for Mammoth Lakes Basin: At Lake George (Dike Wall: Go left to right around lake past cabins, taking fifteen-minute trail up to not-visible crag, Crystal Crag, Mammoth Crest, and TJ Lake) and at end of Lake Mary Road's end (Horseshoe Lake parking area) for Secret Stash and Horseshoe Lake Boulder.

85 SE–Rock Creek ☆☆☆

Hillsides of 300' granite formations. Iris Slab is a good beginner's area/teaching slab. The Gong Show Area has many fine routes, up to three pitches. Fine boulder in Big Meadow Campground. Bear Creek Spire (13,713') is farther south up canyon in the magnificent Sierra backcountry. Free camping. Backcountry permits at USFS–Inyo NF, (760) 873–2500.
Classics: Easy Street 7, Sideshow 9+, He She 10b, Roots in the Sky 10c, The Magnus 10c, Skidrow Wilson 10d, Moving Over Stone 10d, Gong Show roof crack 11+,

Holiday in Cambodia 11+, Anything Goes 11d, Never Say Never 12a, Man Overboard 12a.
Ref: C [151-97, 99, 52], R 59; Guidebooks: Moynier and Lewis's *Bishop Area Rock Climbs*, Vogel's *Bishop and Mammoth Areas*, Artz's *Iris Slab Mini Guide*, Moynier's *Sierra Classics 100 Best Climbs in the High Sierra*, Bartlett and Allen's *Sierra East Side*.
Directions: From Bishop go 25 mi. north on Hwy. 395 to Tom's Place. Go south of town on Rock Creek Rd. All Rock Creek climbing areas are on west side of road. From Rock Creek Rd. Tinytown is at 3 8/10 mi., Iris Slab is at 4 1/10 mi., Sugar Mountain is at 4 4/10 mi., Gong Show Area (park outside campground) is at 4 6/10 mi., and Hone-Yak and Skidrow Wilsom are at 5 ½ mi.

86 SE–Owens River Gorge ☆☆☆☆

The Smith Rocks of California. Traditional and 200' sport routes with vertical pockets in a pleasant high desert climate on layered ash flows. Canyon buttresses of cleaved arêtes, cracks, roofs, and overhanging face sport many great routes. Mostly vertical climbs. Anchors on all climbs. Property of Los Angeles Dept. of Water and Power. Free camping at Horton Campground. City land.
Classics: Crowd Pleaser 8, Heart of the Sun 9, Gorgeous 10a, Show Us Your Tits 10b, Light Within 10c, Love Stinks 10d, The Towering Inferno 5p 11a, Santana 11c, Klingon 12, Enterprise 12b, Circo Gringo 12b, Excelsior 12d, Roadkill 13a, Shocker 13c.
Ref: C [179-16, 168-120, 151-97, 129, 126(6/91)-20, 122-4, 120(20-2)]; R [92-46, 69-42, 53(1/93)-51, 34], SC 12/91; Guidebooks: Lewis's *Owens River Gorge Rock Climbs*, Vogel's *Bishop and Mammoth Areas*, *California Classic Rock Climbs*, Moynier and Lewis's *Bishop Area Rock Climbs*, Vogel's *Southern California Select*, Bartlett and Allen's *Sierra East Side*.
Directions: From Bishop shoot approximately 10 mi. north on Hwy. 395. Turn right on Gorge Rd. exit for ½ mi. Turn left at T 3 2/10 mi. Turn right at T, ¼ mi. to south entrance gate of Owens River Gorge. Two other access points (Central, North) farther up Gorge Parallel Rd. Caution advised when entering gorge: Climbers may be below, so watch rock fall!

87 SE–The Pink Cliffs ☆☆

One-hundred-foot volcanic crag. Winter climbing area on mild days; steaming in summer. Government land.
Ref: Guidebooks: Bartlett and Allen's *Sierra East Side*.
Directions: From Bishop go 1 ½ mi. north on Hwy. 6. Go left on Five Bridges Rd. Turn right approximately 7 mi. on Casa Diablo Rd. past cliffs on left. Go left 1 ½ mi. back to The Pink Cliffs on dirt road.

88 SE–Fish Slough ☆☆

Twenty-foot volcanic bouldering. Autumn–spring. Camping at Pleasant Valley. Private land/BLM, (916) 978–4400.

Ref: J. Sherman.

Directions: From Bishop follow North Main (Hwy. 6) out of town. Continue straight (north) as Hwy. 6 turns east. Drive 2 mi. to intersection (road bends west at cement plant, turns into Five Bridges Rd.). Turn right (north) and drive 2 mi. to Fish Slough's short cliff bands on west side of road and separate boulders to east of road.

89 SE–Chalk Bluffs ✮✮

This 50′ volcanic crag with bouldering is among the best of the Bishop volcanic tuff areas. Nice winter climbing area. Soft volcanic rock. Fishing, too. Autumn–spring. City/BLM, (916) 978–4400.

Classics: Catalog Cracks 9, Birdie Cracks 11.

Ref: C 182-58; Guidebook: Bartlett and Allen's *Sierra East Side.*

Directions: From Bishop drive 7 mi. north on Hwy. 395. Go north on Pleasant Valley Rd. Turn right on Chalk Bluff Rd. (1 ³/10 mi. east to Birdie/2 mi. east to Catalog Cracks). Hike ³/4 mi. due east to petroglyphs from top of bluffs.

90 SE–Wheeler Crest ✮✮

A throng of 1,000′ granitic towers and faces of Wheeler Crest include Hardy Wall, Rabbit Ears, Neptune Tower, Tower of Babel, and Big and Little Grey Pinnacles. Consult with climbers locally. Alan Bartlett calls it "The best climbing in the U.S.A." USFS–Inyo NF, (760) 873–2400.

Classics: Chicken Delight 6-8, Smokestack 9, Violet Green 9+.

Ref: AAJ ['84, 82, 80, 79, 72-119]; Guidebooks: Bartlett and Allen's *Sierra East Side,* Roper's *Climber's Guide to the High Sierra.*

Directions: From Bishop go 9 mi. north on Hwy. 395 and turn left on Pine Creek Rd. Turn right on Round Valley Rd. to Sphinx Station or Station Rd. Various parking. One- to three-hour rugged approaches up six different gullies.

91 SE–Scheelite (Pine Creek Canyon) ✮✮✮

This canyon features one- to four-pitch beautiful granite routes close to the road. Long history of routes with development from the 1960s by Smoke Blanchard, The Armadillo mountain guides, Chuck Pratt, Tom Herbert, Louie Anderson, et al. April–October. Camping across from parking. Private/USFS–Inyo NF, (760) 873–2400.

Classics: Pratt's Crack 9, Sheila 10-, Joint Effort 10d, Footloose 11b, Eclipsed 11d, Atomic Gecko 12-, Ecstasy 13a.

Ref: C 151-97, R [92-52; 66-85]; Guidebook: Bartlett and Allen's *Sierra East Side.*

Directions: From Bishop drive approximately 9 mi. north on Hwy. 395. Turn left on Pine Creek Rd. for 7 mi. to three parking pullouts on right for Scheelite: at telephone lines crossing road (Rattler Area), ¼ mi. farther (PSOM Pinnacle), or ½ mi. farther before mining storage

area. Park. Follow right-most road to reach Pratt's Crack/Ecstasy Arête in the Dihedrals Area and box canyon, which face north, or left up to Cyanide Cliffs.

92 SE–Buttermilks (aka Peabody Boulders) ✮✮✮

Top five on the most wanted list of bouldering areas in the United States. Renowned for bold overhanging face problems 40′ off the ground and stunning scenery under and behind one's feet. This scenic tub of granite boulders keeps the climber's energy centers churning. Topropes or sporty solos on the largest boulders. Bouldering began here in the 1940s with the earliest Buttermilker Smoke Blanchard, continued through the 1960s with Doug Robinson, followed by Yosemite locals, right up to the present with Chris Sharma's Mandala, now one of the most impressive boulder problems. Bolts chopped. Bishop amenities: Schat's Bakery, Taqueria Las Palmas, Western Thai, Keough Hot Springs (7 mi. south of town), and Wilson's East Side for local information and resoles. Autumn/spring. USFS–Inyo NF, (760) 873–2400.

Classics: Peabody Boulders, Cave Boulder-Buttermilker, Mandala V 12.

Ref: C [188-36, 185-102, 182-58, 174-84, 173-110, 151-97, 120, 75(12/82), 73(6/82)], R [101-18/81, 92-39, 74-74, 11(11/85)]; Sherman's *Stone Crusade;* Guidebooks: Moynier and Lewis's *Bishop Area Rock Climbs,* Vogel's *Bishop and Mammoth Areas, California Classic Rock Climbs,* Bartlett and Allen's *Sierra East Side,* Harlin's *West.*

Directions: From Bishop go 7 ⁷/10 mi. west on Hwy. 168. Go right on Buttermilk Rd. for 3 ⁴/10 mi. Park and run to the obviously large Peabody Boulders. Other bouldering that exists in the area includes Lydia Boulders, Backside Boulders, Dale's Camp, Bardini Boulders, and Sherman Acres. Ask locally.

93 SE–Little Egypt ✮✮✮

Best hard cracks in Bishop on 200′ of granite. First outcrop of rock is the best. Bring tape! Also, crags are north facing and unbearable in the cold. USFS–Inyo NF, (760) 873–2400.

Classics: Classic Crack 9, King Tut's Tomb 10a, Cannibal 11c, For Those About to Rock 11d, Expresso 12a.

Ref: C 182-58; Guidebook: Bartlett and Allen's *Sierra East Side.*

Directions: From Bishop go 10 ⁷/10 mi. west on Hwy. 168. Go left on unmarked paved road to power station. Park. Hike across dam ½ mi. to left. Stay low on trail to ridge crest and Little Egypt crag.

94 SE–Bridge Crags ✮✮✮

Sixty-foot granite outcrops on hillside. USFS–Inyo NF, (760) 873–2400.

Classics: The Shyster 7, Flaked Out 9.

Ref: Guidebook: Bartlett and Allen's *Sierra East Side.*

Directions: From Bishop hop west on Hwy. 168 to 5 mi. south on South Lake Rd. Go past footbridge. Park.

Bridge Crags on east side of road near Tyee Lakes trail-head.

95 SE–Cardinal Pinnacle ✩✩✩
The finest granite crag (400′) in Bishop. USFS–Inyo NF, (760) 873-2400.
Classics: Red Bush 9, Cucumbers III 10a, Red Line 11d.
Ref: C 132; Guidebook: Bartlett and Allen's *Sierra East Side*.
Directions: From Bishop go 20 mi. west on Hwy. 168. Go 2 mi. south on Lake Sabrina turnoff past Aspendell. Park. Hike uphill forty-five minutes on southeast side of road to Cardinal Pinnacle. This area is before Lake Sabrina.

96 SE–Wild Rose Buttress ✩✩✩
Small east-facing 200′ granite outcrop. USFS–Inyo NF, (760) 873-2400.
Classics: Bobcrack 10a, Bob-bob-a-ramp 10a, Wild Rose 11a, To Shadows on the Earth 11a, Artichoke Crack 11b.
Ref: Guidebook: Bartlett and Allen's *Sierra East Side*.
Directions: From Bishop go 20 mi. west on Hwy. 168. Go 6 mi. south on South Lake Rd. just past Parcher's Camp. Park on right. Hike past homes to Wild Rose Buttress on west side of road.

97 SE–Billy's Pillar ✩✩
Good Sierra summer 350′ granite crack crag. USFS–Inyo NF, (760) 873-2400.
Classics: Billy's Pillar 8.
Ref: Guidebook: Bartlett and Allen's *Sierra East Side*.
Directions: From Bishop go 20 mi. west on Hwy. 168. Turn left to South Lake. Park. Hike over dam to west and up one hour to Billy's Pillar, northwest of South Lake.

98 Fresno Dome (7,540′) (aka Wamello Dome) ✩✩✩
Classic five-pitch Sierra granite dome. USFS–Inyo NF, (760) 873-2400.
Ref: AAJ ['79-190, 77-445, 72-119], C 111; Guidebooks: Spencer's *Wawona Rock*, Robbins's *Guide to the Hinterlands (Tollhouse Rock, et al.)*, Roper's *Climber's Guide to the High Sierra*.
Directions: From Oakhurst go 4 mi. north on Hwy. 41 to Skyranch Rd. (6S10). Travel 12 mi. on Skyranch Rd. to T junction (road coming in from right; Willow Creek Wall is 1 mi. down this road, to the north). Continue 2 mi. north and east on Skyranch Rd. to Fresno Dome.

99 SP–✩ Shuteye Pass Area Overview ✩✩✩✩
Scenic and secluded ridge of 500′ granite domes with mainly slab climbing. Eight-pitch routes. Summer. USFS–Sierra NF, (559) 297-0706.
Classics: Queen's Throne, Eagle Domes, A Fistful of Dog Hairs 12+/13a.
Ref: AAJ ['84-116, 80], C 119-40, R 38-48; Guidebook: Spencer's *Southern Yosemite Rock Climbs*.
Directions: From Bass Lake take Beasore Meadows Rd. for 10 mi. to Central Camp Rd. for 5 ¼ mi. Then go 4 mi. up fire lookout road to Little Shuteye Pass.

100 SP–Catnap Rock and Maelstrom Dome ✩✩✩
Small 80′ granitic domes. Summer. USFS–Sierra NF, (559) 297-0706.
Classics: Cat's Meow 8, Cat O' Nine Tails 10+, A Tail of Two Kitties 11, Pussy Galore 12c.
Ref: C 119-40; R 38-49.
Directions: From Bass Lake take Beasore Meadows Rd. for 10 mi. Go to Central Camp Rd. for 5 ¼ mi. Go 4 mi. up fire lookout road to Catnap Rock and Maelstrom Dome.

101 SP–Chiquito Dome ✩✩✩
Four-hundred-foot granitic dome slab climbing. USFS–Sierra NF, (559) 297-0706.
Classics: Elegant Inclinations 10+, Kopa 11a.
Ref: AAJ ['84-116, 83, 81, 79-194], C [119-40, 68], R 38(7/90).
Directions: From North Fork travel 39 mi. on Minarets/Mammoth Pool Rd. to Chiquito Dome. Camp at Soda Springs Campground.

102 SP–Dreamscape and Gavilan Cliffs ✩✩✩
A smaller 100′ dome. USFS–Sierra NF, (559) 297-0706.
Classics: Sleepwalker 8, Fish Lips, 10c Contrails 10c, Prince of Darkness 10d.
Ref: C119-40, R [38,49].
Directions: Above Queen's Throne. See 104.

103 SP–Eagle Domes ✩✩✩✩
Beautiful granite domes. Summer. USFS–Sierra NF, (559) 297-0706.
Classics: Triple Dihedral 5 pitch 8, Great Depression 9.
Ref: C 119-40, right 38(7/90)-28.
Directions: From Bass Lake take Beasore Meadows Rd. for 10 mi. Take Central Camp Rd. for 5 ¼ mi. Go 4 mi. up fire lookout road to Little Shuteye Pass and Eagle Domes.

104 SP–Queen's Throne ✩✩✩
Granite dome invites summertime slab climbing. USFS–Sierra NF, (559) 297-0706.
Classics: Scepter 6, Thieves in the Night 7, The Risin' of the Moon 10, Snake Eyes 12+.
Ref: AAJ '84-116, C 119-40, R 38(7/90)-28.
Directions: This area is ½ mi. before Little Shuteye Pass. Trend west down cattle road to Queen's Throne.

105 Mammoth Pool Area ☆☆☆☆

Multipitch domes and vast amounts of granite along spectacular San Joaquin River canyon. Balloon Dome is a conspicuous landmark. Many USFS campgrounds. Road along reservoir to Mammoth Pool Dome closed May 1–June 16 for deer migration. USFS–Sierra NF, (559) 297-0706.

Ref: AAJ ['79-189, 72], C 111, R 38(7/90)-insert; Guidebooks: Spencer's *Southern Yosemite Rock Climbs*, Roper's *Guide to the Hinterlands (Tollhouse Rock, et al.)*.

Directions: From North Fork go 40 mi. on FS 4S00 to Mammoth Pool Reservoir. Formations include Balloon Dome (6,841'), Chiquito Dome, Fuller Buttes, Jackass Rock, Squaw Dome, Disappearing Dome, and Mammoth Pool Dome.

106 Kerkhoff Dome ☆☆☆

This granite dome at 6,000' has close to fifty routes. Good year-round climbing. USFS–Sierra NF, (559) 297-0706.

Classics: Away 9, Centerfold 10a, The Wizard 11a, Dream Stream 11d, Aid routes.

Ref: AAJ '79-190, R 30; Guidebook: Moser, Vernon, and Hickey's *Sequoia/Kings Canyon: Southern Sierra Rock Climbing*.

Directions: From Fresno go east on Hwy. 168 for approximately 55 mi. Turn north on road to Big Creek. Kerkhoff Dome is east of the town of Big Creek. Park by penstocks and hike up the railroad trestle to routes. Sunset Point is a buttress across the valley.

107 Dogma Dome ☆☆☆

Multipitched granite crag. USFS–Sierra NF, (559) 297-0706.

Ref: R 30; Guidebooks: Vernon's *Sequoia–Kings Canyon Courtright Climber's Guide*, Spencer's *Southern Yosemite Rock Climbs*.

Directions: From Fresno take Hwy. 168 east approximately 50 mi. to Shaver Lake. Dogma Dome is north of Hwy. 168 and north of the lake.

108 Courtright Reservoir ☆☆☆☆

Tuolumne-like five-pitch granite routes in High Sierra setting. Trapper and Power Dome's unique horizontal pockets require good nutcraft/tricams to protect. Pay camping at Courtright Reservoir. See guidebooks for detailed layouts of domes. USFS–Sierra NF, (559) 297-0706.

Classics: Penstemon Dome: Rope-a-Dope 8, Song of the Earth 10; Power Dome: A Little Nukey 9, Welcome to Courtright 5p 10-, Helms Deep 10c, Straw Dogs 10+, Powerline 11, Tiger by the Tail 11; Trapper Dome: Most routes; Spring Dome: Joy Spring 10.

Ref: AAJ [84, 79, 78], C [105, 103], R [30(3/89)-39, 19-73, 14(5/86); Guidebooks: Moser, Vernon, and Hickey's *Sequoia/Kings Canyon: Southern Sierra Rock Climbing*, Vernon's *Sequoia–Kings Canyon Courtright Climber's Guide*, Vernon's *Courtright Reservoir*.

Directions: From Fresno cruise northwest on Hwy. 168 to Shaver Lake. Go 40 mi. east on Dinkey Creek Rd. (turns into McKinley Grove Rd.). Turn left (north) on Courtright Rd. (before Wishon Village). Many domes surrounding Courtright Reservoir include: south–north (counterclockwise): Power Dome, Punk Rock, Penstemon Dome, Dusy Dome, Voyager Rock, Maxon Rock, Locke Rock, Leopold Dome, Dogtooth Peak, Trapper Dome, and Spring Dome.

109 Tollhouse Rock ☆☆☆

Fresno locals' year-round crag. This 45' andesite crag carries one hundred routes and variations. Home of the Annual Tollhouse Face-off featuring contests and festivities. Autumn–spring. BIA.

Classics: Tollhouse Rock: Left Lane 7, Headwall 9, United Express 10-; Cap Rock: The Palmist 12d; Tollhouse Traverse: three pitch with 60-meter rope, four pitches with 50-meter rope. Newly rebolted on first pitch, and third belay; (5.5) Elephant Walk: four pitch climb, first pitch 130' crack. Next three pitches are all bolted (5.7), Motherlode 5.14a.

Ref: C 155-49; Guidebooks: Moser, Vernon, and Hickey's *Sequoia/Kings Canyon: Southern Sierra Rock Climbing*, Vernon's *Sequoia–Kings Canyon Courtright Climber's Guide*, The Unknown Climber's *A Climber's Guide to Tollhouse Rock and Vicinity*, Haymond's *Climber's Guide to Tollhouse Rock and Vicinity*, Robbins's *Guide to the Hinterlands*, Fresno Big Wall Society's *Climber's Guide to Tollhouse Rock*.

Directions: East of Fresno. Go southwest of the town of Pine Ridge on Hwy. 168. Turn south on Tollhouse Rd. Tollhouse Rock is the obvious dome to left (northeast) of road above town of Tollhouse. Most common access is via dirt road north (back side) of dome. Cap Rock is the exfoliating top of Tollhouse Rock and offers hard free climbs. Squarenail is another small granite dome southwest of Pine Ridge on the downhill side of Hwy. 168 (four-lane section). Park in pullout before roadcut.

110 SF☆ (San Francisco Areas)–Mt. St. Helena State Park ●

One-hundred-foot volcanic crags and bouldering in Mt. St. Helena. Questionable rock quality. San Francisco offers climbers a plentitude of short crags and bouldering areas. Some of the most popular areas in San Francisco include Indian Rock and Mickey's Beach. Some recommended eats: Bean There (coffee), Café Raj. Much buildering, too. No camping. State park, (707) 942-4575.

Ref: Guidebooks: Thornburg's *Bay Area Rock*, Jensen's *Bouldering, Buildering, and Climbing in the San Francisco Bay Area* (third ed.), Phelan's *Of Rocks, Fog, and Poison Oak: Pseudo Climbing Guide to Bay Area*, Craig's *Day Climber's Guide to the Santa Clara Valley*.

Directions: From Calistoga go north on Hwy. 29 to Robert L. Stevenson State Park. Rocks are on trail to Mt. St. Helena.

111 SF–Goat Rock State Park ☆☆

These 45′ metamorphic rocks offer bouldering and short cragging in this scenic state park.
Ref: C (10/85); Guidebooks: Jensen's *Bouldering, Buildering, and Climbing in the San Francisco Bay Area* (third ed.), Nickerson's *Goat Rock.*
Directions: From Jenner go west on coast on Hwy. 1 to Goat Rock State Park, turning right at sign for Goat Rock State Beach. Park at second pullout on left. Hike past gate downhill to boulders. Overlooks Pacific coast.

112 SF–Dillon Beach ●

Fifty-foot sandstone pinnacles. Autumn–spring. Government land.
Ref: Guidebook: Jensen's *Bouldering, Buildering, and Climbing in the San Francisco Bay Area* (third ed.).
Directions: From Tomales go 2 1/2 mi. west on Dillon Beach Rd. Dillon Beach Pinnacles are by roadside.

113 SF–Big Rock ☆

Five 40′ paint-covered routes occupy this crag. Autumn/spring. May be private land.
Ref: Guidebook: Jensen's *Bouldering, Buildering, and Climbing in the San Francisco Bay Area* (third ed.).
Directions: Marin County. Blast approximately 5 mi. west of Hwy. 101 on Lucas Valley Rd. Big Rock is roadside.

114 SF–Mickey's and Stinson Beach State Park ☆☆☆

Beware the tides and march to the gorgeous 50′ slippery greenstone boulder climbing along the coast of the Pacific Ocean. Now transposed into sport routes. Once famed for Mickey's Beach Crack 5.12b, the area experienced a "blockbuster" storm that cracked the right half off in 1992, dropping Plate-O-Shrimp 13c, Flounder 13a, and Scorpio 12b into the sea as well. Poison oak along trail—put your clothes back on before the hike out. Mickey's Beach (nude) is "clothing frowned upon," so, men, be careful what you thread through your Gri Gri. By the way, who is the most popular guy at the nudist colony? The guy who can carry a cup of coffee in each hand and a dozen donuts. Autumn. State park, (415) 868-0942.
Classics: California Beach Crack 12b, Sex Porpoises 12c, Dream of White Porsches 13b, Flounder 13, Surf Safari 14a.
Ref: C [176-127, 164-85, 153-44, 141, 138, 113(4/89)-18, 104], R [71-21, 54, 49, 12], S [3/86, 7/86]; Guidebooks: Thornburg's *Bay Area Rock,* Thornburg's *Quickdraw Guide to Northern California Sport Climbing Areas,* Jensen's *Bouldering, Buildering, and Climbing in the San Francisco Bay Area* (third ed.), Harlin's *West,* North Face's *Stinson Beach Area.*
Directions: From San Francisco take Hwy. 101 across Golden Gate Bridge. Go north on Hwy. 1 to Stinson Beach. Park at Stinson Beach. Hike south along beach past much bouldering, or park 1 mi. south on Hwy. 1 at a big pullout and hike down trail to Mickey's.

115 SF–Mt. Tamalpais State Park ☆☆☆

Good 40′ volcanic beginner's area and good views. Autumn. State park, (415) 388-2070.
Classics: Roof 10+.
Ref: C 108, S 9/65; Guidebook: Jensen's *Bouldering, Buildering, and Climbing in the San Francisco Bay Area* (third ed.).
Directions: From San Francisco follow Hwy. 101N to Hwy. 1. Follow signs to Mt. Tamalpais State Park. Go to east Peak. Park. Cliffs are on trail to top of East Peak.

116 SF–Split Rock and Turtle Rock ☆☆☆

Solid 25′ schist bouldering in Ring Mountain Nature Preserve. Glorious views of the San Francisco Bay. Autumn. Private land.
Classics: Turtle Rock Traverse, Split Rock Chimney.
Ref: C 164-85; Guidebooks: Thornburg's *Bay Area Rock,* Jensen's *Bouldering, Buildering, and Climbing in the San Francisco Bay Area* (third ed.).
Directions: From San Rafael go south on Hwy. 101 to east on Paradise Dr. for 3 mi. Turn right on Taylor, following it to a dead-end. Hike 1/4 mi. on dirt road. Split Rock is across small valley to the left and small boulders are on right. Turtle Rock is farther on road over ridge and to the right.

117 SF–B☆ (Berkeley Rocks)–Indian Rock and Mortar Rock ☆☆☆

Berkeley's famed bouldering area. Since 1930, a 35′ rhyolite training ground of generations of top climbers. Countless variations and pundits: Be prepared to be told you're "off-route." Traverse wall in park across street. Mortar Rock has the hard stuff. Several small areas. No camping. City park.
Classics: No Hands Slab 2, Beginner's Crack 4, Flake Traverse 10, Watercourse 10-B2, The Bubble B1, Nat's Traverse B2, New Wave V9, The Kraken V10, Don't Worry Be Snappy V11.
Ref: C [188-34, 164-85, 69(11/81)]; Jones's *Climbing in North America, Sherman's Stone Crusade;* Guidebooks: Thornburg's *Bay Area Rock,* Jensen's *Bouldering, Buildering, and Climbing in the San Francisco Bay Area* (third ed.), Leonard's *A Climber's Guide to Local Rock Climbing: Indian Rock 1939.*
Directions: In Berkeley, take Marin Ave. east from I-80 to Marin Circle at base of steep hill. Go north from traffic circle onto Arlington, then instantly branch right onto Indian Rock Rd. Two blocks to rocks on left of road. Go 1 1/2 blocks more uphill to Mortar Rock.

118 Cragmont ☆☆

Soft volcanic 40′ practice crag and bouldering. City park.
Ref: S 5/64; Guidebook: Jensen's *Bouldering, Buildering, and Climbing in the San Francisco Bay Area* (third ed.).
Directions: In Berkeley, near junction of Marin Ave. and Euclid. Go south on Euclid 1 block, then left (southeast) on Regal Rd. for 1 1/2 blocks to park on right. Crag along

southeast margin of park. Gomer's Pile Boulder 20 yd. north of shelter.

119 SF–B–Remillard Park (aka Pinnacle Rock) ✩✩

A 35' volcanic practice rock used for toproping since 1925. Don't spend too long in the Piss Chimney. No camping. City park.

Ref: Guidebook: Jensen's *Bouldering, Buildering, and Climbing in the San Francisco Bay Area* (third ed.).

Directions: In Berkeley, from the junction of Marin Ave. and Keeler, turn south on Keeler. Take first left at Poppy, then go 1 block to Remillard Park.

120 Grizzly Peak Boulders ✩

Handful of 15' problems visible from road. Poison oak. Government park.

Classics: Scott's Super Traverse B2.

Ref: Jensen's *Bouldering, Buildering, and Climbing in the San Francisco Bay Area* (third ed.).

Directions: From junction of Centennial and Grizzly Peak Blvd., go 4/10 mi. south on Grizzly Peak Blvd. Rocks 10–50 yd. left (north) of road.

121 SF–B–Skull Rock (aka Grizzly Caves) ●

Choss pile of 35' volcanic rock and party spot with great views of the glow of San Francisco Bay at night. Glass, bees, and abysmally loose rock. No camping. Government park.

Ref: S 11/64; Guidebook: Jensen's *Bouldering, Buildering, and Climbing in the San Francisco Bay Area* (third ed.).

Directions: From junction of Centennial and Grizzly Peak Blvd. go 1 3/10 mi. south on Grizzly Peak Blvd. Grizzly Caves are 40 yd. downhill west of road.

122 SF–B–Great Stone Face ✩

Berkeley crag. Potential for a handful of hard 15' rhyolite boulder problems. City park.

Ref: J. Sherman.

Directions: In Berkeley, from Marin Circle, go north on Arlington Ave. 2 long blocks, then left on Yosemite 3 blocks to Great Stone Face on left.

123 SF–University of California (Berkeley) ✩✩✩

Illegal buildering on most buildings. Night raids. Get local tour guide. State land.

Ref: J. Sherman.

Directions: Various areas at University of California–Berkeley include Agnes Fay Morgan Hall, Worster Liebacks, Optometry Building, Stadium Cracks, Lawrence Hall of Science, and Hildebrand.

124 SF–Golden Gate Wall Area ✩✩

Good 30' cracks under overpasses. Seven difficult toprope cracks and 200' traverse. State land.

Classics: Golden Gate Cracks 10-, Playground Cracks 12-.

Ref: C 106; Guidebook: Jensen's *Bouldering, Buildering, and Climbing in the San Francisco Bay Area* (third ed.).

Directions: South Berkeley. Three areas of Golden Gate Wall: At junction of 13 and 24-13 south ramp, at Broadway and Golden Gate Ave., and at overpass and park wall.

125 SF–Mt. Diablo State Park (Boy Scout Rocks) ✩✩

One of the better toproping areas in San Francisco. Soft sandstone—90' routes change as holds break, i.e., better to go elsewhere after a rain. Bouldering at Boy Scout Park (harder rock). *No bolting!* Fossil displays. Great views of California from atop Mt. Diablo (3,849'). Entrance and camping fees. State park, (925) 837-2525.

Classics: West Crack 7, Amazing Face 10c, left Diagonal 10a, Bolt Route 10b/12a.

Ref: C 164-64; Guidebooks: Thornburg's *Bay Area Rock*, Jensen's *Bouldering, Buildering, and Climbing in the San Francisco Bay Area* (third ed.), Ciminera's *Mr. Bobo's Guide*, Harlin's *West*.

Directions: From Walnut Creek go east on I–680 to signs for Mt. Diablo State Park. Rock is 1/4 mi. below Rock City parking area. Boy Scout Rocks is another area in park.

126 SF–Sea Stacks (Turtle Rock, Cigar, Cigarette, Thumb) ✩✩✩

Unique conglomerate, cream-colored sea stacks.

Ref: S 7/86.

Directions: San Francisco. Formations at Land's End along coast in Pacific Ocean. Turtle Rock, Cigar, Cigarette, and Thumb are all within a few mi. of one another. Turtle Rock is most prominent and easily accessible. May be reachable by foot.

127 SF–Ocean Beach ✩

Beachfront 15' buildering wall. Also may be rock at cliff house. Autumn. City land.

Ref: Guidebook: Jensen's *Bouldering, Buildering, and Climbing in the San Francisco Bay Area* (third ed.).

Directions: San Francisco. At Ocean Beach near junction of Fulton and Great Highway.

128 SF–Mt. Davidson Cross ✩

Mt. Davidson Cross is a San Francisco landmark. Bolt ladder that Clint Eastwood looks up at while being cold-cocked in the movie *Dirty Harry*. Illegal: See the movie, forget the climb. Possibly city land.

Ref: *Dirty Harry* movie; Guidebook: Jensen's *Bouldering, Buildering, and Climbing in the San Francisco Bay Area* (third ed.).

129 SF–Indian Joe Caves ☆

Basalt block piles form caves between blocks. Thirty-five-foot topropes. Highest face is known as the Little Eiger (40′). Dusty. Poison oak. Autumn. Government park.
Classics: Little Eiger, 5.12 topropes.
Ref: J. Sherman; Guidebook: Jensen's *Bouldering, Buildering, and Climbing in the San Francisco Bay Area* (third ed.).
Directions: East Bay. Follow I–680 to south on Calaveras Rd. Go left on Geary Rd. Park to Sunol Regional Park office. Hike approximately 1 mi. north up Indian Joe Creek Trail to Indian Joe Caves.

130 Peninsula Rocks ☆

A day's worth of 35′ sandstone backyard boulders.
Ref: Guidebook: Jensen's *Bouldering, Buildering, and Climbing in the San Francisco Bay Area* (third ed.).
Directions: South Bay. Off Farm Hill Rd.

131 SF–Woodside Road Rock ☆

Toprope 45′ sandstone boulder. Autumn. Private land.
Ref: Guidebook: Jensen's *Bouldering, Buildering, and Climbing in the San Francisco Bay Area* (third ed.).
Directions: San Francisco. Follow Hwy. 280 to ⅛ mi. east on Woodside Rd. Woodside Road Rock is found by going back on Hwy. 280 south and turning right on, you guessed it, Woodside Rd. On left.

132 SF–Stanford University Campus ☆☆☆

Collegiate buildering at Stanford. Private land.
Ref: C [108, 97, 58]; Guidebooks: Jensen's *Bouldering, Buildering, and Climbing in the San Francisco Bay Area* (third ed.), Stanford Alpine Club's *Mountaineering, Freedom of the Quad.*
Directions: At Stanford University Campus, Art and Chemistry buildings. Famed college buildering on Art Gallery and Chemistry buildings. Chalk use not allowed. Restrictions enforced.

133 Castle Rock State Park ☆☆☆

A most popular South Bay area. Sandstone boulders scattered throughout a forest of giant trees. Sport climbing in Stevens Canyon and Castle Rock Falls. Scattered formations with honeycomb holds on roofs. Morris's 2000 guide describes all the complexities of these areas in fine detail. Check with park department for bolting policy and guidelines. Linked to Big Basin Redwoods State Park by Skyline-to-Sea Trail. Scenic waterfalls. Lock your car well to ward off sticky-fingered opportunists. State park, (408) 867-2952.
Classics: Farewell to Arms 10a, Megablast 10c, Aeronautical Engineer 11b.
Ref: C [164-85, 112(2/89)-106, 106], R [81-32, 80-28]; Guidebooks: Morris's *Rock Climber's Guide to Skyline Boulevard*, Thornburg's *Bay Area Rock,* Caunt and Morris's *A Sport Climber's Guide to the Castle Rock Area.*

Directions: From San Jose trek southwest on Skyline Blvd. Follow state park signs. Take Ridge Trail west to Castle Rock. Various areas: 1) Bates Boulder between main area and parking. 2) For Castle Rock Falls, Billy Goat Rock, Goat Rock: Hike west from main parking along creek. 3) Hash Rock is about 300 yd. south of main parking on east side of Skyline Rd. 4) Summit Rock is 1 mi. north of main parking and east of Skyline Rd. 5) Outside the park, don't miss the climbing treasures found north on Hwy. 35 (Skyline Blvd.)/Aquarian Valley/Eagle Peak.

134 SF–Glen Canyon Park ☆☆☆

Popular San Francisco 20′ bouldering area climbed since the 1930s. Intermediate-level problems. Cherty, okay rock. Don't wear Lycra unless you want to titillate the locals. City park.
Classics: Gunks Revisited.
Ref: C 164-85; Guidebooks: Thornburg's *Bay Area Rock,* Jensen's *Bouldering, Buildering, and Climbing in the San Francisco Bay Area* (third ed.).
Directions: In San Francisco, follow Hwy. 280 to San Jose exit. Take Bosworth west to Glen Canyon Park. Ten-minute walk in canyon to rock.

135 SF–Lexington Rock ☆

Small 45′ sandstone crag. Rotten rocks on the other side of the creek.
Ref: Guidebook: Jensen's *Bouldering, Buildering, and Climbing in the San Francisco Bay Area* (third ed.).
Directions: Los Gatos. At Hwy. 17 and Los Gatos Blvd. Park. Hike south 1 mi. along west side of Los Gatos Creek. Lexington Rocks are between the trail and the creek.

136 SF–Mazzones ☆☆☆☆

One of the most fruitful of the Bay bouldering areas. Approximately twenty to thirty acres of good sandstone bouldering with about 200 problems. Sandstone becomes soft when wet, i.e., refrain from climbing then. Autumn-spring. Private land. Access sensitive, possibly becoming a subdivision or perhaps an open space park.
Classics: Tall Man, The Dihedrals, Two Arrows.
Ref: C 106, R 77-28; Guidebook: Jensen's *Bouldering, Buildering, and Climbing in the San Francisco Bay Area* (third ed.).
Directions: South San Jose. At Almaden Expwy. and Redmond, slip north on Almaden and soon turn right on Winfield then right on Cross Springs and right on Crossview. Park at the southwest end of Crossview. Hike in east on dirt road under power lines to Mazzones.

137 SF–Almaden Dam ☆

Thin face and friction climbs on a 35′ dam wall. Good intermediate and expert problems. Autumn-spring. Private land.

Ref: Guidebook: Jensen's *Bouldering, Buildering, and Climbing in the San Francisco Bay Area* (third ed.).
Directions: South San Jose; 2 mi. south of New Almaden on Almaden Expwy. Parking on the Almaden Dam is illegal, though possible.

138 SF–Guadalupe Rocks ✩

Short routes on 40′ metamorphic boulders. Good beginner and intermediate routes. Private/government land.
Ref: Guidebook: Jensen's *Bouldering, Buildering, and Climbing in the San Francisco Bay Area* (third ed.).
Directions: South Santa Clara Valley. Take Camden Ave. to Hicks Rd. to Guadalupe Reservoir Dam. Guadalupe Rocks include three areas: West Dam, Upper Reservoir, and Hicks Rd.

139 Garden of Eden ✩

Small granite outcroppings lend themselves to bouldering and cragging. Autumn/winter. State land.
Classics: The Penis 10d, 5.12 toprope.
Ref: Guidebooks: Morris's *Rock Climber's Guide to Skyline Boulevard*, Jensen's *Bouldering, Buildering, and Climbing in the San Francisco Bay Area* (third ed.).
Directions: Between Santa Cruz and Felton. From Felton blast 2 ½ mi. south on Hwy. 9. Park at pullout on San Lorenzo River side. Hike down to river, staying right. At railroad tracks, go left for 1,000′, then go down to river to the Garden of Eden. Cross river 100 yd. east of big rock.

140 Panther Beach ✩

Low-tide, soft sandstone bouldering. Autumn.
Ref: Guidebook: Jensen's *Bouldering, Buildering, and Climbing in the San Francisco Bay Area* (third ed.).
Directions: Panther Beach is 6 ½ mi. north of the northern-most stoplight in Santa Cruz.

141 University of California–Santa Cruz ✩✩

Hard 50′ limestone toprope cracks on overhanging limestone quarry. Illegal. Autumn. State land.
Ref: Guidebook: Jensen's *Bouldering, Buildering, and Climbing in the San Francisco Bay Area* (third ed.).
Directions: At UC–Santa Cruz. Park at bookstore. Follow signs to quarry. Off Hager St.

142 Granite Creek ✩✩

Thirty-foot granite toprope cliffs and boulders along coast south of Carmel. Poor landings. Go at low tide. Pay camping. Autumn.
Ref: Guidebook: Jensen's *Bouldering, Buildering, and Climbing in the San Francisco Bay Area* (third ed.).
Directions: From Carmel take Hwy. 1S to 6 mi. south of Point Lobos State Reservoir. Go 300′ south of Granite Creek Bridge on beach.

143 Pinnacles National Monument ✩✩✩

Rappel, bolt-protected, breakable knob climbing on 200′ breccia volcanic spires, domes, and walls. Long history of ascents. Suspect welded rock. Or, as one nonlocal described it, "You know what your poop looks like after eating corn-on-the-cob and a Payday Bar? It looks like the Pinnacles National Monument." Main pay camping on east side at Pinnacles Campground. Fun spire bagging. North Chalone Peak (3,304′). Area closures due to raptor nesting February–June. Autumn–spring. NPS, (831) 389–4485.
Classics: East: 1st Sister 4, Monolith Direct 6, Reg Route 8 2p, The Ordeal 8, Heat Seeking Moisture Missile 10d, Post Orgasmic Depression 11a, Hot Lava Lucy 13a; West: Shake and Bake 10a, Machete Direct 11+.
Ref: AAJ ['88-134, 86-156, 83, 80, 79-193, 77-184], C [174-84, 167-62, 142, 139-110, 106, 101, 88, 59, 52], OB 35(10/77), R [101-120, 71-144, 39(9/90)-41], S [11/87, 8/76, 10/74, 5/69]; Guidebooks: Rubine's *Climber's Guide to Pinnacles National Monument*, Gagner's *A Rock Climber's Guide to Pinnacles National Monument*, Thornburg's *Quickdraw Guide to Northern California Sport Climbing Areas*, Harlin's *West*, Johnson and Cordone's *Pinnacles Guide*, Richards's *Pinnacles National Monument Topographical Maps*, Roper's *Climber's Guide to Pinnacles National Monument*, Hammack's *A Climber's Guide to Local Rock Climbing: Pinnacles National Monument*, Leonard's *A Climber's Guide to Local Rock Climbing: Pinnacles National Monument*, Brower's *A Rock Climber's Guide to Local Rock Climbing: Pinnacles National Monument*.
Directions: Pinnacles National Monument can be approached from the east or the west. For east side approach (most crags): From Hollister go south on Hwy. 25 to east side (follow signs to park headquarters). Hike south on Moses Spring Trail to Discovery Wall, Monolith, Five Sisters, Hatchet, Frog, and Hand. For west side approach: From Soledad go east, following signs to ranger station. Hike north on Balconies Trail to Machete Ridge on right, Balconies on left.

144 KC✩–(Kings Canyon National Park) Kings Canyon National Park ✩✩✩✩✩

Majestic High Sierra climbing exemplified in the beauty of the 1,000′ south face of Charlotte Dome, first ascended in 1970 by Jones, Rowell, and Beckey. Incredible amounts and heights of granite walls. Summer. Pay. NPS, (559) 565-3341.
Classics: Charlotte Dome: Regular Rt (South Face) III 7, Neutron Dance (10p) 10d; Bubbs Creek Wall (2,000′): Crystal Bonzai VI 10 A3, The Citadel; Grand Sentinel: North Face V+ 9 A3, Nowhere to Run 11a, Scarlet Slipstream 11, Obelisk, Kettle Dome, Tehipite Dome.
Ref: AAJ ['98, '94, '91-168, 87-174, 84, 83, 81, 80, 77-179, 71], C [176-24, 103, 94, 93], R 28(11/88), S [5/86, 6/78]; Guidebooks: Moser, Vernon, and Hickey's *Sequoia/Kings Canyon*, Vernon's *Sequoia–Kings Canyon Courtright Climber's Guide*, Steck and Roper's *Fifty Classic Climbs*, Roper's *Climber's Guide to the High Sierra*.
Directions: From Fresno strike a course west on Hwy. 180

to Kings Canyon National Park. Long approaches. Consult climbing guides for this area.

145 KC–Tehipite Dome ★★★★★

This immense, 3,600′, south-facing backcountry monolith is the largest dome in the Sierras. Fred Beckey and Herb Swedlen cranked the southwest face in 1963. Summer. NPS, (559) 565–3341.

Classics: Time Warp IV 9, Wilderness Serenity 10b, Southwest Face VI 9 A4, In the Nick of Time VI 5.10 A3+ 21 pitches (with 60 m ropes).

Ref: AAJ ['98-171, '71], C 82(2/84)-4, S [11/63, 9/63]; Guidebooks: Moser, Vernon, and Hickey's *Sequoia/Kings Canyon,* Vernon's *Sequoia–Kings Canyon Courtright Climber's Guide,* Roper's *Climber's Guide to the High Sierra.*

Directions: Kings Canyon. Tehipite Valley. Tehipite Dome is approached from the north via USFS dirt roads.

146 KC–Obelisk ★★★

Remote, spectacular 400′ granite backcountry dome with much potential. Summer. NPS, (559) 565–3341.

Classics: West Arête 5, Southeast Face 6, Original Route 7, Flake Rt 9, Hands of Fate 10.

Ref: AAJ ['98-194, '72-120], C 4(11/70), R 30(54); Guidebooks: Vernon's *Sequoia–Kings Canyon Courtright Climber's Guide,* Roper's *Climber's Guide to the High Sierra.*

Directions: From Fresno cruise northwest on Hwy. 168 to Shaver Lake. Go east on Dinkey Creek Rd. to southeast of Wishon Reservoir. Approach trailheads start from Wishon Reservoir. All-day approach from trailheads on east side of Wishon Reservoir into Geraldine Lakes via Randheria Creek/Statum Meadows trail or Spanish Lake Jeep Trail to Spanish Lake. From Spanish Lake go over Spanish Pass and descend to lower Geraldine Lake. From the sound end of Geraldine Lake, ascend gully to near top, then contour left toward forest (water and camp-sites). Easy walk via subalpine meadows to Obelisk (spring at base of west arête).

147 Seq★–(Sequoia National Park) Overview

In two words: California majesty. Some of California's best granite and with fewer crowds. Angel Wings (10,252′) is the largest, most stupendous wall in the park at approximately 1,800′. Castle Rock Spire is a most impressive Sierra pinnacle. A spectacular landscape with vast amounts of granite. Free camping outside park on USFS land. NPS entry fee. Route information at the Lodgepole visitors center. Beware: Rattlers, poison oak, bears, bubonic plaque (from fleas on squirrels), Lyme disease (ticks), giardia, and guidebook writers warning you about such things. Go there, it's worth the visit. Spring–autumn. For free backcountry permits at least three weeks ahead, call (209) 565–3708. NPS, (559) 565–3341.

Tehipite Dome, Kings Canyon National Park.

DAVE HOUCHIN

Classics: Moro Rock: South Face 7, South Crack 9, Levity's End 10, One Thin Line 10, Piece de Resistance 10a A1; Castle Rocks: Reg Rt 11a; Chimney Rock: Dry Run 5, Pop-a-Top 7, Crystal 8, Beckey Rt 10b, Ask Mr. Lizard, Good and Plenty 11a, Angel Wings, Mono Dome; The Fin: IV 5.9, Castle Rock Spire.

Ref: AAJ ['97-143, '86-151/173, 82, 78-527, 76-447, '72-70], C [106, 94, 92, 88, 72, 66, 65], R 28(11/88)-insert, S [5/70, 9/69, 6/78]; Guidebooks: Moser, Vernon, and Hickey's *Sequoia/Kings Canyon,* Vernon's *Sequoia–Kings Canyon Courtright Climber's Guide,* Roper's *Climber's Guide to the High Sierra.*

Directions: From Visalia go west on Hwy. 198 to Sequoia National Park entrance. Tokopah Valley offers close-to-the-road climbing: Chimney Rock (short routes) is 3 mi. from Generals Hwy. Store near Stony Creek Lodge, Watch Tower dominates valley, the Baldies just off Generals Hwy., and Moro Rock is a popular rock-climber and tourist attraction. Backcountry areas: Castle Rocks (The Fin, Castle Rock Spire) is very popular. Angel's Wings and Hamilton Dome are spectacular hunks; the price is a 16-mi. trek. Others include Moose and Big Bird Lakes Cirques, Deadman or Cloud Canyon.

148 Seq–Chimney Rock ✪✪✪✪

Six major granite formations (up to 700') and more than fifty routes. Chimney Rock (7,711'). Free camping at end of road. Spring–autumn. NPS, (559) 565-3341.

Classics: Dry Run 5, Pop-A-Top 7, Crystal 8, Plenty Good 11; Chimney Spire: Reg Rt (Beckey Rt) 10b.

Ref: R 28(11/88); Guidebooks: Moser, Vernon, and Hickey's *Sequoia/Kings Canyon*, Vernon's *Sequoia–Kings Canyon Courtright Climber's Guide*.

Directions: From Hwy. 180 go north of Sequoia National Park entrance, then turn south on USFS Rd. 14S29 for Chimney Rock.

149 Seq–Little Baldy ✪✪✪

High-quality four- to five-pitch granite slab routes. Spring–autumn. Pay camping in NPS campground, (559) 565-3341.

Classics: Welcome to Little Baldy 10-.

Ref: R 28(11/88); Guidebooks: Moser, Vernon, and Hickey's *Sequoia/Kings Canyon*, Vernon's *Sequoia–Kings Canyon Courtright Climber's Guide*, Roper's *Climber's Guide to the High Sierra*.

Directions: Inside Sequoia National Park near north entrance on Hwy. 180 east side of Generals Hwy., approximately 5 mi. north of Lodgepole Campground. Approach from first turnout south of Little Baldy parking area. Hike five minutes.

150 Seq–Tokopah Valley (The Watchtower) ✪✪✪

Two granite grade V wall routes, ice climbing in winter. Autumn. Pay camping in NPS, (559) 565-3341.

Classics: Moonage Daydream WI4, Watchtower.

Ref: C (1/73)-20, R 28(11/88), S 7/85; Guidebooks: Moser, Vernon, and Hickey's *Sequoia/Kings Canyon*, Moser, Vernon, and Hickey's *Kings Canyon: Southern Sierra Rock Climbing*, Vernon's *Sequoia–Kings Canyon Courtright Climber's Guide*, Roper's *Climber's Guide to the High Sierra*.

Directions: In Sequoia National Park, along Generals Hwy. Park at Lodgepole Trailhead. Hike up trail toward Tokopah Falls. The Watchtower is the main feature here.

151 Seq–Moro Rock ✪✪✪✪

Prominent, monolithic 1,000' granite dome of high quality. This dome has more than forty routes. Several aid lines on big east face. Approaches from two-minute walks to rappel-ins and bushwhacks. Descend via stairs. Route details at Lodgepole Visitor Center. Tourists trundling and trashing provide added hazards. Spring–autumn. Pay camping at NPS campground (559-565-3341).

Classics: South Cracks 9, Aerial Boundaries 10, Levity's End 10, Pressure Sensitive 11, Moro Oro 9 A3.

Ref: AAJ ['91-168, '89-150,'86-155], C 110, R 28(11/88); Guidebooks: Moser, Vernon, and Hickey's *Sequoia/Kings Canyon*, Vernon's *Sequoia–Kings Canyon Courtright Climber's Guide*, Roper's *Climber's Guide to the High Sierra*.

Directions: Moro Rock is on Generals Hwy. 180/198 in Sequoia National Park. See ranger station in Lodgepole for climbing information.

152 Seq–Castle Rocks and The Fin ✪✪✪✪

Drama and aesthetics congeal on these remote 1,000' granite domes and spires. Backcountry camping. Treat water for giardia. NPS, (559) 565-3341.

Classics: Aspire 9, Silver Lining 10- R.

Ref: AAJ '86-173, R 28(11/88); Guidebooks: Moser, Vernon, and Hickey's *Sequoia/Kings Canyon*, Vernon's *Sequoia–Kings Canyon Courtright Climber's Guide*, Roper's *Climber's Guide to the High Sierra*.

Directions: In Sequoia National Park. From Buckeye Flat Campground take Paradise Creek Trail to Castle Rocks Trail for Castle Rocks and The Fin.

153 Seq–Hospital Rock ✪✪✪

Pick a line, any line on this beginner-intermediate crag. Countless variations. Routes 5.9 or less. Autumn–spring. Pay camping at NPS campground (559-565-3341).

Ref: R 28(11/88); Guidebooks: Vernon's *Sequoia–Kings Canyon Courtright Climber's Guide*, Roper's *Climber's Guide to the High Sierra*.

Directions: In Sequoia National Park, on Generals Hwy. Park ⁴/10 mi. above the Hospital Rock Indian Display parking lot. Walk straight up steep hill to Hospital Rock.

154 Land of the 100' Giants ✪✪✪

A 300' expert's basalt sport crag. Thirty-foot boulders. Spring/autumn. Private ranch land.

Directions: Orosi area. Ask locals about Land of the 100' Giants.

155 SE–Lone Pine Campground Boulders ✪✪

Thirty-five-foot granite boulders in campground and across stream. Spring/autumn. Pay camping. USFS-Inyo NF, (760) 873-2400.

Ref: J. Sherman.

Directions: At Whitney Portal, approximately 7 mi. west of town of Lone Pine, sit the Lone Pine Campground Boulders.

156 SE–Whitney Portal ✪✪✪✪

One-thousand-foot granite routes up to grade V in length. Climbable year-round. Consult local guides. Trail for Mt. Whitney starts at road end. Campgrounds at road end (limited) at Lone Pine Campground 5 mi. from road end, or 10 mi. east of road end in Alabama Hills. Spring–autumn. Campground on USFS-Inyo NF, (760) 873-2400.

Classics: Bastille Buttress, Nimbus 10c, Venus 11d.

Ref: AAJ ['85-191, 79-185, 77-180, 72, 68], C [92,

88,4(11/70)]; Guidebooks: Moynier and Lewis's *Bishop Area Rock Climbs,* Vernon's *Sequoia–Kings Canyon Courtright Climber's Guide,* Moser, Vernon, and Hickey's *Sequoia/Kings Canyon,* Bartlett and Allen's *Sierra East Side,* Roper's *Climber's Guide to the High Sierra.*

Directions: From Lone Pine, Whitney Portal is approximately 12 mi. west on Whitney Portal Rd. Most approaches to buttresses made from last 1 ½ mi. of road's end. Many buttresses and crags with up to ten pitch routes on several formations: The Whale, Tango Tower, Premier Buttress, Whitney Portal Buttress, and Candlelight Buttress start the list.

157 SE–Mt. Whitney ✫✫✫✫✫

At 14,491' the sublime highest point in California overlooks the deepest valley in the United States, Owens Valley. Incredible 2,000' alpine granite walls. The massive East Buttress route is a sought-after trophy on any alpineer's list. Advanced fee permit reservations required; call (619) 876-6200. Summer/autumn. Pay camping. USFS–Inyo NF, (760) 873-2400.

Classics: Mt. Whitney: East Face III 6, East Face V5.11a; Keeler Needle: 10+, Crimson Wall V5.12-; Langille Peak 3,000' northeast wall.

Ref: AAJ ['93, 92-130, '89-145, '88-146, 83], C [160-108, 92, 10/72], R 68-66/74, S [3/82, 8/76, 1/79, 5/72]; Guidebooks: Baker-Salony's *How to Climb Mt. Whitney in One Day,* Wheelock and Benti's *Climbing Mt. Whitney,* Suttle's *California County Summits,* Hellweg's *Mt. Whitney Guide for Climbers and Hikers,* Vernon's *Sequoia– Kings Canyon Courtright Climbers Guide,* Secor's *The High Sierra, Shooting Star Guides: Whitney East Face and East Buttress,* Hellweg and McDonald's *Mt. Whitney Guide,* Porcella and Burns's and Steck and Roper's *Fifty Classic Climbs,* Wheelock and Condon's *Climbing Mt. Whitney,* Roper's *Climber's Guide to the High Sierra.*

Directions: From Lone Pine on Hwy. 395, shoot west up to Whitney Portal. Whitney Trail is main hiking trail. Multihour approaches to Mt. Whitney areas.

158 SE–Alabama Hills ✫✫

A multitude of 50' granite rock. Most rock is friable. North faces offer best chances for good stone. Bolted boulders. Popular filming location for Hollywood westerns. Spring/autumn. Free camping. Possibly BLM land.

Classics: Sweet Home Arizona 8, Blockade Runner 10c.

Ref: Guidebook: Bartlett and Allen's *Sierra East Side.*

Directions: From Lone Pine, Alabama Hills is 5 mi. west on Whitney Portal. Turn left on Horseshoe Meadows Rd. for ¾ mi. Go left to parking for Gunga Din area. Tuttle Creek is just up the road.

159 SE–Tuttle Creek ✫✫✫✫

Excellent long granite cracks on good stone. Super Sierra scenery. BLM campground at Tuttle Creek. Spring–

autumn. USFS–Inyo NF, (760) 873-2400.

Classics: Shark's Tooth: Beckey 5.7, Mt. Corcoran, Keyhole Wall.

Ref: AAJ ['94-140, '84, 77-179, R 33(9/89), C [94, 92], S 10/83; Guidebooks: Peer's *A Climber's Guide to the Bastille Buttress,* Roper's *Climber's Guide to the High Sierra.*

Directions: From Lone Pine go west on Whitney Portal Rd., left (south) on Horseshoe Meadows Rd., and right (west) on Granite View Rd. to parking at end. Granite formations in John Muir Wilderness include Stonehouse Buttress, Keyhole Wall, Blank Wall, Obelisk, Shark's Tooth, Mt. Corcoran, Red Baron Tower, Lone Pine Peak, Mt. Russell, Mt. Langley, and Bastille Buttress.

160 SE–Putterman's Rock ✫✫✫✫

Good potential 300' granite crack cragging. Spring-autumn. Good free camping. USFS–Inyo NF, (760) 873-2400.

Ref: Guidebook: Moser and Vernon's *Domelands.*

Directions: From Lone Pine putt 15 8/10 mi. from the junction of Whitney Portal Rd. and Horseshoe Meadow Rd. Putterman's Rock is on the way to Cottonwood Lakes trailhead, across road from parking.

161 SE–Horseshoe Launch (Walt's Point) ✫✫✫✫

Good potential granite cragging. Good camping. Internationally famous hang glider's launch spot. Spring-autumn. USFS–Inyo NF, (760) 873-2400.

Ref: Guidebook: Moser and Vernon's *Domelands.*

Directions: From Lone Pine go 12 mi. from junction of Horseshoe Meadows Rd. and Lubken Canyon Rd. at 9,000'. From Horseshoe Launch continue on road for 2 mi. of virgin crags.

162 SE–Cottonwood Creek ✫✫✫✫

Good potential granite cragging. Spring-autumn. Free camping. USFS–Inyo NF, (760) 873-2400.

Ref: Guidebook: Moser and Vernon's *Domelands.*

Directions: From Lone Pine go south of town on Hwy. 395 and go up Cottonwood Rd. and Cottonwood Creek drainage.

163 Rocky Hill ✫✫✫

Good group of 40' boulders. Ask locals about other areas to avoid loose rock runaround. Car-theft area. Winter-spring. May be government land.

Ref: R 28.

Directions: From Visalia take Hwy. 198 east to first large hill to right of road near Exeter. Turn right off highway, then left on Rocky Hill Rd. Go over saddle and park where road levels out. Three-minute hike west of parking. Access may be poor.

164 Granite Knob/Jackass Peak ☆☆☆

Part of the mixed faces of quality granite contain a couple dozen 5.8–5.11 routes on these northern Domelands crags. Summer. USFS-Inyo NF, (760) 873-2400.

Classics: Granite Knob: Vain and Abell 8, Blood Baby 9/10b, Moonshine 10c, Bust a Move 11c, Surface Tension 11d; Jackass Peak: Donkey Kong 7, Smart Ass 10 (south face), Living on Burro-ed Time 11b.

Ref: SC 3/92-25; Guidebooks: Mayr and Sweeney's *Southern California Sport Climbing*, Mayr's *Sport Climbing Guide to Southern California*, Moser and Vernon's *Domelands*.

Directions: Granite Knob: From Kennedy Meadows go west on Sherman Pass Rd. to Black Rock Station and turn right (north) for 3 mi. Turn right again at Powell Meadow sign (21S36). Stay on main road for approximately 5 mi. Park at large turnout (fire pit) on right after road turns to dirt. Granite Knob ten minutes north of road. Jackass Peak: Continue past Granite Knob on 21S36 to its end. Hike east approximately 1 mi. to Jackass Peak.

165 Hermit Spire ☆☆☆☆

Spire-topped, 500′ granitic dome with climbing similar to the Needles just to the south. Many good routes, up to 4 pitches. Numerous short cliffs and boulders on west side. Spring–autumn. USFS-Sequoia NF, (559) 784-1500.

Classics: Horseshoe Traverse 8, South Face 8, Falcon 9, Rising Spirits 10+, Land Down Under 10d, The Schmatta Kid 11d, American Kennel Club 12-.

Ref: AAJ 1970s; Guidebook: Moser, Vernon, and Paul's *Needles: Southern Sierra Rock Climbing*.

Directions: From Springville go east on Hwy. 190 to Camp Nelson. Farther east on Hwy. 190, turn left on 21S50 for 4 6/10 mi. Turn right on road to Lewis Camp for 2 1/2 mi. After pack station, turn right on 20S53A for 7/10 mi. (high-clearance vehicle recommended). Park here. Hike east to ridge crest and on to Hermit Spire.

166 Sky Garden Wall/Powerhouse Wall ☆☆☆

Both areas are hefty chunks of roadside granite. Silver Sword, a seven-pitch route, ascends Sky Garden's center face. Powerhouse Wall is 500′. Spring–autumn. Free/pay camping. USFS-Sequoia NF, (559) 784-1500.

Classics: Sky Garden: Thriller 10d, Silver Sword IV 11a.

Ref: C 72; Guidebook: Moser, Vernon, and Paul's *Needles: Southern Sierra Rock Climbing*.

Directions: From Springville plow 6 mi. east on Hwy. 190.

Sky Garden Wall is large face on left side of road between Powerhouse and campground. Powerhouse Wall is on right, 1/2 mi. south of Powerhouse on Hwy. 190.

167 Trilogy (aka McIntire Rock) ☆☆☆

Nice summer 250′ granite crag for the intermediate climber with about twenty one- and two-pitch routes. Spring–autumn. Free camping. USFS-Sequoia NF, (559) 784-1500.

Classics: Skyline Arête 8, Dogwood Arête 9, Can't Get Enough 10, Slot Machine 11a.

Ref: Guidebook: Moser, Vernon, and Paul's *Needles: Southern Sierra Rock Climbing*.

Directions: From Springville go east on Hwy. 190 to Camp Nelson (visible from here). Farther east on Hwy. 190, turn left on 21S50 for 1 2/10 mi., then left onto 20S81 for 1 7/10 mi. Turn right at Jordan Peak lookout sign onto 31E24 for 1/2 mi. Hike west 1 mi. through cool, old-growth forest to top of rock. Hike west to base of Trilogy.

168 The Needles ☆☆☆☆☆

One of California's finest crack climbing and scenic areas in an incredible series of 900′ granite domes with climbs of eight pitches. Any climber shown a picture of the colorful yellow-green, lichened-covered granite will instantly recognize it as The Needles. The popular Sorcerer sports vertical climbs on arêtes, cracks, and newer sport face. Dome Rock offers zero approach slabbing. At 7,000′, varying weather conditions exist (though usually cool). Camp at road's end. USFS-Sequoia NF, (559) 784-1500.

Classics: Magician: Black Magic 7; Charlatan: Spooky 9, Fancy Free 10; Voodoo: Summer Sojourn 7, White Punks . . . 8, Super Nova 12a, Dark Side 12c, Millennium Falcon 13b; Sorcerer: Airy Interlude 10a, Thin Ice 10b, Wailing Banshees 11-, Atlantis 11+, Sirocco 12a, Davey Jones' Locker 12b; Fire Wall: Spontaneous Combustion 12+, Pyromania 13a; Wizard: Yellow Brick Rd. 9, Shiver . . . 12c; Sorcerer's Apprentice: Love Potion #9 10, Piranha 12c; Witch N: Igor . . . 9, Spook Book 10+; Warlock: South Face 9.

Ref: AAJ ['87-176, 80, 78, 77-176, 76-448, 72-123, 71-354], C [181-110, 138(6/93), 114, 98, 94, 92, 82(2/84)-34, C [198-68, 50(10/78)], R [95-42, 91-93, 87-152, 85-96, 69-86, 22], S [12/76, 2/74]; Glowacz et al.'s *Rocks Around The World*; Guidebooks: Moser, Vernon, and Paul's *Needles: Southern Sierra Rock Climbing*, Harlin's *West*, Joe and Leversee's *Stonemasher Guide to Kern River Canyon and Environs (Needles)*, Leversee's *Dome Rock Climber's Guide*, Paul's *Climber's Guide to the Needles*, Roper's *Climber's Guide to the High Sierra*.

Directions: From Springville go east on Hwy. 190 past Camp Nelson, and then beyond turn left (after Quaking Aspen campground, and just before Ponderosa Lodge/store) at "Needles Lookout" to parking at end. Hike approximately 2 1/2 mi. (one hour) southeast to fire lookout. Then head northeast downhill to slabs (approximately fifteen minutes). After traversing slabs, trail markers diagonal down to climbs on the following Needles formations: Magician, Djin, Charlatan, Sorcerer, Wizard, Witch, Necromancer, and Warlock. For Voodoo/Demon Domes: Hike east from Lower Kern River Rd. Just north of creek, take climber's trail to Voodoo. For Demon park ¼ mi. past Needlerock Creek. Hike thirty minutes through forest on steep ground. (Also approached from Kernville via Hwy. 190.)

169 Dome Rock ✷✷✷
A 400' granite dome southwest of The Needles. Friction face climbing with knobs and chickenheads for the purist of face routes. The first pitches are usually steepest and hence cruxy. Latter pitches tend to be runout. Spring–autumn. Free/pay camping. USFS–Sequoia NF, (559) 784–1500.
Classics: The Tree Route 6, More Raisins 8, Windjammer 9, Spectrum 10, Anti-Jello Crack 10, Red Mushrooms 10, Welcome to Dome Rock 11-, Between Nothingness and Eternity 11-, Just Barely 11, Asteroid Belt 12, Pipe Dream 12.
Ref: C 94; R 22; Guidebooks: Moser, Vernon, and Paul's *Needles: Southern Sierra Rock Climbing,* Joe and Leversee's *Stonemasher Guide to Kern River Canyon and Environs (Needles).*
Directions: From Springville go east on Hwy. 190 past Camp Nelson and then beyond past Ponderosa Lodge/store just south of Peppermint Campground. Turn left onto 21S70 to top of Dome Rock. Park. Descend to rock. (Also approachable from Kernville. Head north on Hwy. 190.)

170 Quality Cliff/Jackass Dome ✷✷✷
Quality Cliff is a fun, tiny 60' granite sport crag. Bring seven quickdraws or less. Jackass Dome has midrange routes on south face. Summer. USFS–Sequoia NF, (559) 784–1500.
Classics: Quality: Climbing and Lichen It 11b, Old Yeller 11c, Branching Out 11c, Total Equality 11d; Jackass Dome: Sounds of Silence 10c, Long Gray Line 10c.
Ref: SC 3/92-26; Guidebooks: Mayr and Sweeney's *Southern California Sport Climbing,* Mayr's *Sport Climbing Guide to Southern California,* Moser and Vernon's *Domelands.*
Directions: Quality Cliff: From Kennedy Meadows go west on Sherman Pass Rd. for 6 mi. On left across Fish Creek. Zero approach walking across creek. Jackass Dome: Past Quality Cliff, find road 21S01, north of Fish Creek Campground. Drive north approximately 1 mi. on 21S01. Hike approximately thirty minutes to obtain dome.

171 The Sportsman's Grotto ✷✷✷
Small crag (less than 12 routes) with 5.10 and 5.11 sport routes. Summer. USFS–Sequoia NF, (559) 784–1500.
Classics: Gun Play 10d, The Dual 11a, Sportsmen's Arête 11, No Dice 11c, Taking Bets on Your Future 11+.
Ref: SC 3/92-26; Guidebooks: Mayr and Sweeney's *Southern California Sport Climbing,* Mayr's *Sport Climbing Guide to Southern California,* Moser and Vernon's *Domelands.*
Directions: From Kernville go north 18 mi. on Kern River Rd., then east on Sherman Pass Rd. (22S05). Park at first 15 mph hairpin after 8,000' elevation sign. Skirt mountain east/southeast at same level as parking area (stay below rocky treeless ridge), following stone piles for fifteen to twenty minutes to creek and The Sportsman's Grotto.

172 Limestone Campground ✷✷✷
The winter sport crags, Chouca Wall and Cave Area, harbor popular gymnastic overhangs. Check for road conditions. Winter. USFS–Sequoia NF, (559) 784–1500.
Classics: Chouca of the Kern 12a, Under Attack 12b, Holey Power 13a.
Ref: C 134, SC 3/92-23; Guidebooks: Mayr and Sweeney's *Southern California Sport Climbing,* Mayr's *Sport Climbing Guide to Southern California,* Moser, Vernon, and Paul's *Needles: Southern Sierra Rock Climbing,* Joe's *Stonemasher Guide to Kern Slabs.*
Directions: From Kernville lunge north on Kern River Rd. (passing en route Kern Slabs/New Directions Cliff on right) to Limestone Campground (approximately 10–20 mi.). Crag across road to east on a broken formation of limestone. Follow obvious trail to routes.

173 Kern River Road Areas (Kernville Rock, New Directions) ✷✷✷
Numerous partially to well-developed granite cliffs with approaches less than one hour. Cliff notes: Kernville Rockslabs and New Directions, popular winter sports crags; Roadkill, well-chalked 5.11 crack; Book Rock, forty-five-minute approach, eleven routes up to three pitches; Parker Bluffs, difficult but classic face; Sentinel Rock, Elephant Knob, beware rattlers; K&L Wonderbluff, named for Kodas and Laeger, sports excellent routes. The Slides is popular party spot. Peppermint USFS Campground with waterfalls and plunge pools east of campground. Rattlesnakes. Hot in summer, try autumn. USFS–Sequoia NF, (559) 784–1500.
Classics: Parking Lot Rock Anonymous Tip 12a; New Directions: Palpitations 11c, Morpheus 11c; Roadkill: 5.11; Book Rock: For All the Dreamers 10a, Novel Approach 10a, Footnote 10b, Over Booked 10d, Dyslexia 11, Book End 11d; Elephant Knob (southeast): Elephantiasis 7+, Wild Kingdom 9, Mumbo Jumbo 11; (east face): Perfect Memory 8; K&L Wonderbluff.
Ref: C [94, 92], R 33(39), SC 3/92; Guidebooks: Mayr and Sweeney's *Southern California Sport Climbing,* Mayr's *Sport Climbing Guide to Southern California,* Moser, Vernon, and Paul's *Needles: Southern Sierra Rock Climbing,* Vernon's *Book Rock.*
Directions: From Kernville go north on Kern River Rd. Each following approximate distance is from Kernville: 5 mi. to 500' Kernville Rock/Slabs (on right); 5 ½ mi. to New Directions Cliff (on right); 11 mi. to Roadkill (on right); 12 mi. to Book Rock (300' wall with dihedral on right,

forty-minute hike, via Salmon Falls viewpoint, 1 ^{8}/10 mi. north to Calkin Flats Campground, then dirt road 1 ^{7}/10 mi. southeast below rock), Sequel Wall/ Writers Block above and right; 24 mi. to Parker Bluffs (200' crag above Johnsondale, go left 1 mi. on California Hot Springs Rd. to trailhead and camping); 29 mi. to Sentinel Rock (on left above BSA camp); 30 ½ mi. to Elephant Knob (hidden on right, approach via road 22S53); 32 mi. to K&L Wonderbluff (on left via Dry Meadow Creek Rd. 22S83 to creek after second gate).

174 Miscellaneous Kernville Crags (Bohna Peak/Harley Rock) ✩✩✩

Miscellaneous granite crags around Kernville.
Autumn–spring. USFS–Sequoia NF, (559) 784–1500.
Ref: Guidebook: Moser, Vernon, and Paul's *Needles: Southern Sierra Rock Climbing.*
Directions: Kernville area. These seldom-visited crags exist: Bohna Peak (west of Greenhorn Summit), Split Mountain (northwest of Lake Isabella), Phoscheck Pinnacle (reddish pinnacle east of Kernville, seen from Kern River Bridge), and Harley Rock (above Owens Boys' Camp).

175 Owl Rock ✩✩✩

A granite crag south of Lake Isabella. Spring/autumn. Free camping. USFS–Sequoia NF, (559) 784–1500.
Classics: Owl Attack 9.
Ref: Guidebook: Moser, Vernon, and Paul's *Needles: Southern Sierra Rock Climbing.*
Directions: From Kernville it is several miles west of town on south side of Hwy. 178 at 2,000' elevation. (From Bakersfield it's 20 mi. east on Hwy. 178.) Steep trail to prominent Owl Rock buttress.

176 The Gymnasium ✩✩✩

Granite sport crag for Bakersfield climbers. Autumn/ winter. USFS–Sequoia NF, (559) 784–1500.
Ref: Guidebook: Moser, Vernon, and Paul's *Needles: Southern Sierra Rock Climbing.*
Directions: From Kernville go south on Hwy. 178 to mm 24 in lower Kern Canyon. The Gymnasium is above the river on north side of highway. Requires a stygian crossing of the Kern River, which is only feasible in fall.

177 Domelands Wilderness–Approaches via Kernville ✩✩✩

Beautiful 800' granite crags at altitudes of 8,000' up to 10,000'. Obtain USGS quads maps/Sequoia NF map to aid approaches, Kernville, Hockett Peak, Monache Mtn. cattle country—purify your water (i.e., drinking untreated water here could have same effect as downing a pound of psyllium seeds with two quarts of water). Call (760) 373-3781 for Sherman Pass conditions. Wilderness wonderland of granite outcroppings and exfoliation domes on the Southern Kern Plateau. Noteworthy areas include Bart Dome (800' of crystals, dikes, and water grooves), Church Dome, Trout Creek Domes, Rockhouse Basin, and Jackass Creek. Church Dome formations have most developed routes. Typically, formations have less than six routes. Abundant new route potential. See *Domelands* or R&I guide for complex approaches. Approach hikes vary from twenty minutes to 8 mi. Spring–autumn. Free camping. USFS–Inyo NF, (760) 873–2400.
Classics: Bart Dome routes, Church Domes; Poison Dome: Ebola Zaire 11.
Ref: AAJ 97-140, C [178-56 (topo), 94, 92, 91, 47], R 33(9/89)-insert; Guidebooks: Moser and Vernon's *Domelands,* Jenkins's *Southern Sierra,* vol. #1.
Directions: This is the west side approach for Domelands: From Kernville, the Domelands lies northeast between Kern River and its south fork. Go north on Kern River Rd. 18 mi. to Sherman Pass Rd. (22S05). (Sherman Pass Rd. is the north boundary of Domelands and major access road to Domelands' trailheads). Turn south onto Cherry Hill Rd. (22S12) and follow distances for turnoffs to domes: Brush Creek Spires, 7 ^{7}/10 mi., then up 23S14; Salmon Creek Wall, 9 ^{2}/10 mi. then west; Bart Dome, 11 ^{6}/10 mi. via trails from Manter Meadow Trailhead; Taylor Dome, 13 ^{3}/10 mi. via trails; Neanderthal Wall, 21 mi., then right on 22S12; Church Dome (Taj Mahal et al.), 21 mi., then left on 24S13 to end. Poison Meadow Domes off Sherman Pass Rd. via 22S19 to end.

178 Domelands Wilderness–Approach via Ridgecrest ✩✩✩

This is a second approach for granite Domelands-bound climbers. Dihedral Wall is on west side of river a couple miles south of parking. White Dome is very high quality. Spring–autumn. USFS–Inyo NF, (760) 873–2400.
Classics: Radiant Dome: Dike Hike 10, Gamma Rays 11; White Dome: White Lightning 10c; Rockhouse Basin; Dihedral Wall: Spread Eagle 9, Bitter End 10b.
Ref: C [94, 92, 47], R 33(9/89)-insert; Guidebooks: Moser and Vernon's *Domelands,* Jenkins's *Southern Sierra,* vol. 1.
Directions: This is east side approach for Domelands. From Ridgecrest (the junction of Hwy. 395 and Hwy. 14), go north on Hwy. 395 approximately 10 mi. Turn west on Nine Mile Canyon Rd. It's 21 mi. west and north on J41 (Kennedy Meadows Rd.) to Kennedy Meadows formations: Quality Cliff, Granite Knob, and Jackass Dome. To Rockhouse Basin Trailhead: Go west on Nine Mile Canyon Rd. as above, but turn west 11 mi. from Rockhouse Basin sign. These areas can be accessed via hiking (approximately one and a half hours) across south fork of Kern River: Trout Creek Domes (Columbia, Radiant, Moon, Sardine, Steamship), Rockhouse Basin, White Dome. These could also be approached from Kernville, especially early in season when south fork of Kern River is high.

179 Fossil Falls (aka Scott's Bluff) Inyo County ★★★

Fine, short, 40′ columnar basalt areas. Good intermediate routes 5.9–5.11. Vertical to overhanging cracks and roofs. Hard boulder problems down canyon. Camping to east of parking. Autumn–spring. BLM, (916) 978-4400.
Classics: Twilight of the Gods 11a.
Ref: N. Kaptain; C 92, R 14(5/86); Guidebooks: Moser and Vernon's *Domelands*, Lindgren's *Fossil Falls*.
Directions: From Little Lake (on Hwy. 395 north of Ridgecrest), tow the line approximately 3 mi. north on Hwy. 395. Fossil Falls is on the east side of the highway. One mi. past a big pullout on right of Hwy. 395, turn right onto Cinder Rd. Follow road to BLM sign. Hike south short ways to rock in small river gorge.

180 Little Lake (near Ridgecrest) ★

Twenty-foot granite highball bouldering. Spring/autumn. No camping. Private land. Uncertain if this is trespassing.
Directions: Ridgecrest. Little Lake is south of town on road through town.

181 County Line Crags

High quality, hillside 300′ granite crags and boulders that sit right on the Inyo and Kern County line. Nice Mojave Desert views. October–April. Free camping. Los Angeles Department of Water and Power.
Classics: Inyo Face 10/11, Inyo County Sheriff 11, Barney Fife Boulder B1.
Ref: R 78-94 (guide); Guidebook: Moser and Vernon's *Domelands*.
Directions: From Pearsonville (northwest of Ridgecrest) and Burger King, follow Hwy. 395 south for 1 ½ mi. Turn west on Brown Rd. for about a mile. Turn left, then right shortly. Go for 1 ¼ mi. and turn right, going about 2 mi. to south parking area and Inyo face area. Bouldering just before road's end. For north parking access, instead of going 1 ¼ mi., go about ½ mi. and turn north at second right, following Los Angeles Aqueduct and going left twice. This accesses the Speedway Wall.

182 Great Falls ★★★

Joshua Tree–like granite domes, sport routes, bold leads, and one 300′ rock, the Condome. Condome is largest formation (up and right from parking) with more than a dozen routes, some two pitches. Best rock near parking. Inyo County. Camping. BLM, (916) 978-4400.
Classics: The Inscrutable 7, The Inconceivable 7, Work of the Devil 10+, Stiletto 11, Seasons in the Abyss 12c, Bad Blood 12c.
Ref: N. Kaptain; Guidebook: Moser and Vernon's *Domelands*.
Directions: From Ridgecrest go east on Hwy. 178 past Trona Airport (4 mi. past Trona) to last street (Stockwell Mine Rd./Valley Wells). Continue on Hwy. 178 for approximately ½ mi. northeast of Stockwell Mine Rd. to

dirt road marked by large cairn of red-painted rocks. Go west on this dirt road, going right at each of two forks, to Great Falls box canyon (approximately 3 ³/₁₀ mi.). The last mile is very sandy; drive four-wheel-drive vehicle or walk.

183 SB★-(San Bernadino County) Poison Canyon ★★

Short 60′ granite leads and topropes. Winter. BLM, (916) 978-4400.
Classics: Flatfingers 10, 12+, The Pit Arête 11.
Ref: R 14(5/86); Guidebook: Fry's *Southern California Bouldering Guide*, Moser and Vernon's *Domelands*.
Directions: From Ridgecrest push 10 mi. northeast on Hwy. 178 to Poison Canyon.

184 SB-School Rocks (aka Heller Rocks) ★★

Bouldering reminiscent of boulders in Yosemite and cragging classroom for China Lake Mountain Rescue Group. Some good lines though gritty rock. Autumn–spring.
Ref: G. Barnes 1/98; R 14(5/86).
Directions: From Ridgecrest go 7 mi. west on Hwy. 178 and then north on Hwy. 14. Now turn west at Indian Wells Lodge to left on L.A. Aqueduct. Go south on aqueduct for 1 ½ mi. Turn west onto dirt road for 2 mi. to School Rocks. School Rocks are now in wilderness; the directions are correct but now you must walk the last 2 mi., which is a 1,000′ elevation gain on an easy road for a one-hour hike.

185 SE-Owens Ridge (Owens Peak Area) ★★★

Multipitch granite formations that have had activity for years. Bouldering near creek. Described as rock like Joshua Tree; rock gets more solid with increase in elevation. Home of the China Lake Mountain Rescue Group. The Power and The Glory (4p) 11. Spring/autumn. Free camping. Government land.
Ref: C [126, 120, 94, 92]; Guidebooks: Moser and Vernon's *Domeland's Guide, Climber's Guide to Owens Ridge*.
Directions: Northwest of Inyokern-Ridgecrest and west of Hwy. 395. From Ridgecrest go west on Hwy. 178, then north on Hwy. 14 to Indian Wells Lodge. A few hundred yards past lodge, turn west approximately 9 mi. up Indian Wells Canyon high-clearance dirt road. Owens Ridge is the 6-mi. ridge of exposed granite flowing from Owens Peak.

186 SB-Trona (Searles) Pinnacles ★

Wild landscape of more than 500 gritstone pillars but yeeoww . . . sharp holds! Training circuit of short climbs (60′) on overhanging pocketed faces. Searles Lake is dry. National Natural Landmark of geologic interest. Winter. Free camping. BLM, (916) 978-4400.
Ref: C 186-84, R 14(5/86); Guidebook: Moser and Vernon's *Domelands*.

Directions: From Trona go south on Trona Rd. to south side of Searles Lake. Then go 4 $^8/_{10}$ mi. east on dirt road to Trona Pinnacles.

187 SB–Wagonwheel Bouldering ☆☆☆☆

A premiere California bouldering area. Scenic, high desert bouldering and 40′ topropes on hundreds of granite boulders extend for mi. Designated BLM motocross, especially popular on weekends. Autumn–spring. Enjoyably free camping. BLM, (916) 978-4400.

Classics: Walter's Crack 10-, Still Life Arête B1-, The Eradicator B1+, Tit Rock, Barsinister Boulder, The Terminator.

Ref: C [186-84, 92], R 14(5/86); Guidebooks: Fry's *Southern California Bouldering Guide,* Moser and Vernon's *Domelands.*

Directions: From Red Mountain take Hwy. 395, then go 15 $^4/_{10}$ mi. north on Trona Rd. Turn right on dirt road 2 $^7/_{10}$ mi. to Wagonwheel Boulders.

188 Red Rock Canyon State Park

Seventy-foot basalt pillars. Colorful clay cliffs. Petroglyphs. Spring/autumn. State park, (661) 942-0662.

Directions: From Cantil go north on Hwy. 14. Red Rock Canyon is just east of highway.

189 Bishop's Peak ☆☆☆

Good dacite edge climbing northwest of San Luis Obispo along coast. Cracked Wall has the best climbs on the peak. P Wall, the largest at 180′, is named for big "P," short for Poly or Cal Poly, painted on rock, now covered over with second-generation paint to disguise it. Bring trad rack for more than sixty routes. Good bouldering problems. A popular student climbing area. Heaps of poison oak. Hollister Peak, northwest of Bishop Peak, also offers good climbing. It is the largest rock-walled mountain in a north-south chain of seven volcanic dacite peaks. Autumn. State/federal land.

Classics: Shadow 7, Flakes To Fresno 8, Rusty's Cave 8, P-Crack 8+, Stage Fright 9+, Out of Hangers 10-, Lama 10-, Camel 10, Battle of the Bulge 11, Opiate 12.

Ref: C 166-34, R 97-98; Guidebooks: Slater's *California Central Coast Climbing,* Slater's *Rock Climbs of San Luis Obispo's Seven Sisters,* Fry's *Southern California Bouldering Guide,* Tucker and Steele's *Tri-County Guide,* Gulyash's *Climber's Guide to Bishop's Peak,* Gulyash's *Completely Off the Wall,* Kroll's *Off the Wall.*

Directions: From San Luis Obispo (junction of Hwy. 101 and Hwy. 1), go north a short ways on Hwy. 1. Turn left on Highland to end. Bishop's Peak is to west. Areas are named Cracked Wall, Jam Crack Wall, Garden Wall, P Wall, Shadow Rock, and Summit Blocks. Fifteen-minute hike on trails. Bouldering can be found below cliffs on the Potato and Hummingbird Boulder. Other bouldering in area at Chorro Willows Overhang near Los Osos.

General Directions: Take Hwy. 1 to South Bay Blvd. heading toward Los Osos. Turn on Decrepit Rd. to parking. Walk on trail to boulder.

190 SB–Providence Mountains State Recreation Area

Spacious granite desert domes. Rumored to be closed to climbing. Autumn–spring. Free camping. State land.

Classics: Fang 5p.

Ref: S 7/73.

Directions: North of Essex and I-40. From Needles burn oil approximately 30 mi. west on I-40 to Essex Rd. exit. Go north approximately 15 mi. northwest to Providence Mountains State Rec. Area. Various areas.

191 SB–Granite Mountains (near Amboy)

Outback granite desert domes. Autumn–spring. Free camping. Government land.

Ref: S 7/73.

Directions: From Needles go approximately 50 mi. west on I-40 to Kelbaker Rd. exit. Head north approximately 9 mi. to Granite Mountains. Lots and lots of rock.

192 SB–Stoddard Ridge, Apple Valley, and Granite Mountains ☆☆☆

Large seas of granite with a world of isolated 100′ formations. Sport cragging and bouldering. One of these classic formations is called Hercules' Finger, a 60′ free-standing pinnacle. Some areas on private land may be closed. Please be courteous to landowners. Deep Creek Hot Springs. Autumn–spring. Camping nearby. Private land/BLM, (916) 978-4400.

Classics: Hercules's Finger (Pinnacle).

Ref: C 110(18), R [77-102 (topo), 61]; Guidebook: Yamin's *Sport Climbing in Southern California's High Desert.*

Directions: Stoddard Ridge areas are accessed via Hwy. 247 and gas pipeline road for 12 mi. going south out of Barstow. Apple Valley and Granite Mountains lie just east of Victorville. From Victorville go east on Hwy. 18 for about 2 mi. Go past Apple Valley to Joshua Rd. For Dead Zone turn left on Joshua Rd., then quick right on Yucca Loma for 2 mi. Then right turn again to road's end. Hike ten to twenty minutes to various cliffs. For BMX/Horseman's Center crags, continue on Hwy. 18 from Joshua Rd. a few more minutes to a left turn heading into Horseman's Center Park. After a hundred yards or so, bear right and then right again, parking south of BMX track at lot. Rider's Ready Wall is just north/northwest of track. Or, for Hercules' Finger, continue farther east on Hwy. 18 to Lucerne Valley and east on Old Woman Rd. Turn left on Camp Rock Rd. (junction Hwy. 247) for 8 $^6/_{10}$ mi. Then go east. At 1 $^7/_{10}$ mi., bear right. At 2 $^9/_{10}$ mi. go left on road (cairn). At 3 $^2/_{10}$ mi., go right until at Hercules' Finger.

193 StB☆–(Santa Barbara County) Brickyard/Lizard's Mouth ☆☆☆☆

Superb hueco bouldering twenty minutes from downtown Santa Barbara on ridge above town. More than 300 problems between the two areas: V7+: 10, V4–V7: 50, V2–V3: 80,

V0–V1: 200. Check out Steve Edwards's *Santa Barbara Bouldering* for detailed information on the problems. Landings go both ways, and a crash pad is helpful. The Santa Barbara area features sandstone on the hills east of town, among these Gibraltar Rock. Climbing is year-round, with summer being poorest. Much rock is difficult to access due to thick chaparral. Surfing. Mountain biking. State campgrounds on beaches at Refugio and El Capitan (both north of Santa Barbara) and Carpenteria (south of Santa Barbara). Or, camping in national forest. Some diners: Santa Barbara Roasting Co. (coffee) for armchair strategists; Cuca's and Freebirds (burritos). Autumn–spring. USFS–Los Padres NF, (805) 968-6640.

Classics: Lizard's Mouth: Goldak V0, The King is Dead V5, King Dinosaur V7, Breathless V3, Meilee V4, Experiment in Terror V2, Call Me V6, Take 5 V5, Mouth Traverse; Brickyard: Ant Traverse, Over, Grotesque Old Woman V7, Bug Traverse V6, Let's Troll V4, Red Heat V1, Sandanista V5, Yeti V3.

Ref: S. Edwards; R 55(5/93); Guidebooks: Edwards's *Rock Climbing Santa Barbara and Ventura*, Edwards's *Santa Barbara Bouldering*, Tucker's *Climbing Santa Barbara, Ventura, San Luis Obispo*, Fry's *Southern California Bouldering Guide*, Tucker's *Climbing in Santa Barbara and Ventura Counties*.

Directions: From Santa Barbara follow Hwy. 154 north. Turn left (west) on Camino Cielo (Kinevan Rd.) for 3 $^4/_{10}$ mi. to the Brickyard and 3 $^8/_{10}$ to Lizard's Mouth. Both areas are on the ocean side. The Brickyard trail starts opposite some boulders and heads past a small metal fence and downhill on a decent trail for about five minutes to the first boulders. Lizard's Mouth is just before the gun club, and the first boulders are just off the road and litter the entire hillside.

194 StB–Painted Cave ✮✮

Quick access and overhanging 15′ sandstone pumps on a few boulders. Sixty problems. Don't climb after rains, i.e., the wet rock is more susceptible to breaking then. Indian pictograph site $^1/_2$ mi. farther up road. Winter/spring. Private/government land.

Classics: Old Soft Hsu V3, Heavy Traffic 11 TR, Trojan War 5.12+ TR, Wedgie Roof V6, Break on Through V10.

Ref: C 103-11, R [70-34, 55(5/93)]; Guidebooks: Edwards's *Rock Climbing Santa Barbara and Ventura*, Artz's *The Best of Mother Rock*, Edwards's *Santa Barbara Bouldering*, Hellweg and Warstler's *Climber's Guide to Southern California*, Fry's *Southern California Bouldering Guide*, Tucker's *Climbing in Santa Barbara and Ventura Counties*.

Directions: From Santa Barbara take Hwy. 101 west to Hwy. 154 north (approximately 5$^1/_2$ mi.) to Painted Cave Rd. Go 1$^1/_2$ mi. up Painted Cave Rd. to two large roadside boulders after private property boulderfield. Park near boulder.

195 StB–Patterson Bridge Wall ✮✮

Traverses and straight-up 5.8–5.11 problems on sandstone railroad bridge. Popular with students seeking forearm excitement. Winter/spring. Government land.

Ref: Guidebooks: Fry's *Southern California Bouldering Guide*, Hellweg and Warstler's *Climber's Guide to Southern California*, Tucker's *Climbing in Santa Barbara and Ventura Counties*.

Directions: In Santa Barbara. From Hwy. 101 go south on Patterson Ave. Take first left past railroad. Park at end. Hike on bike trail north to railroad bridge, which is Patterson Wall.

196 StB–Gibraltar Rock, Cold Springs Dome, and Green Dome ✮✮✮

One-hundred-forty-foot soft sandstone topropes (anchors) and short leads. Each area has been rejuvenated with a handful of sport leads. Cold Springs Dome features steep jug hauls, i.e., good training wall. Green Dome is made of blue schist. Nearby Cathedral Peak also has climbing, but access is more difficult. Great views of the Pacific Ocean. Beware poison oak/rattlers. Autumn–spring. Camping on USFS land on East Camino Cielo. USFS–Los Padres NF, (805) 968-6640.

Classics: Gibraltar Rock: Rapture 9, T-Crack 10, The Soul 11b, Self Reflections 11, Sweating Buckets 12a; Cold Springs Dome: NH Direct 12b, Predators Keep the Balance 12; Green Dome (east): Dancing Fingers 10d; Green Dome (west): Stealing Fire 12d, Quartz Crystal 12d; Any Minute Now 6, T-Crack 9, The Nose 10+, Makumania 11.

Ref: C 103(8/87)-11, R 55(5/93); Guidebooks: Edwards's *Rock Climbing Santa Barbara and Ventura*, Mayr and Sweeney's *Southern California Sport Climbing*, Mayr's *Sport Climbing Guide to Southern California*, Hellweg and Warstler's *Climber's Guide to Southern California*, Tucker's *Climbing in Santa Barbara and Ventura Counties*.

Directions: From Santa Barbara (junction of Hwy. 144 and Hwy. 192), go west on Hwy. 192. Turn north on Mountain for $^1/_4$ mi., then turn north on Gibraltar Rd. for approximately 5 mi. Gibraltar Rock is on left. Cold Springs Dome is reached via trail (approximately 15 minutes) across the highway. Hike east. Green Dome is farther up Gibraltar Rd. Turn right on East Camino Cielo Rd. Follow pavement 7 mi. and 1 more mi. on dirt road to crag on left. Hike five minutes.

197 StB–San Ysidro Canyon ✮✮

Two walls: The lower one is most accessible. Low angle 200′ sandstone slabs in pretty canyon. Spring/autumn. USFS–Los Padres NF, (805) 968-6640.

Classics: Face Lift 7, Vanishing Flakes 10+/11a.

Ref: C 103(11); Guidebooks: Edwards's *Rock Climbing Santa Barbara and Ventura*, Artz's *The Best of Mother Rock*, Hellweg and Warstler's *Climber's Guide to Southern California*.

Directions: From Santa Barbara at Hwy. 101 go north on San Ysidro Rd. (approximately 1 mile). Then turn east on Hwy. 192 (approximately 1 mile). Then left at Park Lane. Turn left for $^1/_4$ mi. onto east Mountain Drive. Hike $^3/_4$ mi. to San Ysidro Canyon.

198 V☆–(Ventura County) Sespe Gorge ☆☆☆

Large wall (300') of good, sandstone multipitched beginner's cracks. Matilija Creek tunnels have begun to see some recent sport route development. Excellent climbs in a cool canyon along the double tunnel area. Climbs range from 5.10 to 5.12, on sandstone and conglomerate. Beefy bolts and much new route potential exist. Spring/autumn. USFS–Los Padres NF, (805) 968-6640.
Classics: Tree Line 5, Pipe Prime 6, Ending Crack 7.
Ref: C [163-52, 114-95], S 9/75; Guidebooks: Artz's *The Best of Mother Rock*, Hellweg and Warstler's *Climber's Guide to Southern California*, Tucker's *Climbing in Santa Barbara and Ventura Counties*.
Directions: From Ojai go west on Hwy. 150. Turn north on Hwy. 33 for 20 mi. to obvious wall on right. Park on west side of road for Sespe Gorge. Matilija Creek tunnels are 7 mi. outside of Ojai on Hwy. 33.

199 V–Ojai–The Foot ☆☆☆

Forty sandstone routes on 80' bolted faces. Thirty excellent, developed boulders up the trail. Setting for 1930s movie *Lost Horizon*. Good mountain biking. Beware poison oak. Autumn–spring. Free camping. USFS–Los Padres NF, (805) 968-6640.
Classics: Ruthless Poodles 10, Chummin' for Splatter 11b, Private Ojai 11.
Ref: C 114(6/89)-20; Guidebooks: Edwards's *Rock Climbing Santa Barbara and Ventura*, Fry's *Southern California Bouldering Guide*.
Directions: From Ojai go north on Foothill Rd. USFS access. Hike 100 yd. up Foothill Trail to The Foot. Take care to park away from residences.

200 V–Ojai–Jameson Field ☆☆☆

Twenty good sandstone boulders. Topropes, too. Autumn–spring. Landowners request no chalk use. Private land.
Ref: C 114(6/89)-20; Guidebooks: Edwards's *Rock Climbing Santa Barbara and Ventura*, Fry's *Southern California Bouldering Guide*.
Directions: Ojai. Follow Hwy. 150 northeast to Carne. Turn left on Carne, then right on Thacher to Thacher School. At Jameson Field.

201 V–Ventura River Wall ☆☆

Ventura River Wall is an artificial wall of cement with a 250' traverse wall (up to 5.12+) with glued-on holds. Autumn. State land.
Ref: C 114; Guidebooks: Fry's *Southern California Bouldering Guide*, Tucker's *Climbing in Santa Barbara and Ventura Counties*.
Directions: In Ventura, at junction of Hwy. 101 and Ventura River. Near Surfers Point. Under overpass next to bike path. Park to west.

202 V–Camarillo Grove Bouldering ☆☆

Steep 20' volcanic pocketed face climbs. Autumn. Park fee. Pay camping. Private land/county park.
Ref: C 114; Guidebooks: Edwards's *Rock Climbing Santa Barbara and Ventura*, Edwards's *Santa Barbara Bouldering*, Fry's *Southern California Bouldering Guide*.
Directions: From Camarillo go east on Hwy. 101 (north at Camarillo Springs exit) to Camarillo Grove County Park. Hike east to Camarillo Grove Boulders.

203 V–Point Mugu State Park (Mugu Boulder ● and Boney Bluff ☆☆☆)

One notorious 20' sandstone beachside boulder with 5.8-5.11 routes replete with graffiti and roadside noise from highway. Use nuts for toprope anchors if you have any. And more importantly, now features Boney Bluff 5.12-14 pocket pulling bolted area via a different approach. Rocky bluffs, surf fishing, sand dunes, and beachcombing. Autumn. Pay camping at state park (818-880-0350).
Ref: D. Gorman, Point Mugu Master; C 114, R 82-92 (topo); Guidebooks: Edwards's *Rock Climbing Santa Barbara and Ventura*, Anderson's *Sport Climbing in the Santa Monicas*, Katz's *Getting High in L.A.*, Fry's *Southern California Bouldering Guide*, Hellweg and Warstler's *Climber's Guide to Southern California*.
Directions: From Oxnard go south on Hwy. 1 to Point Mugu State Park. South of Mugu Beach Access. Large parking turnout on west side of Hwy. 1. For Boney Bluff: From Los Angeles escape on Hwy. 101 (Ventura Hwy.) northwest to Westlake Blvd. exit. Turn south on Hwy. 23 (Mulholland Hwy.). Turn right (west) on Mulholland for a short way to a right turn onto Little Sycamore Canyon Rd. for 4 mi. to Triunfo Pass. Pass the Mishe Mokwa Trailhead on right. (Park here for Echo Cliffs.) Continue 1 mi. farther for Backbone Ridge–Sandstone Peak Trailhead. Park. Hike one hour via Backbone Trail (1 mi. plus) to Tri-Peaks Trail (⅓ mi.). Follow climber's trail for Boney Bluff.

204 LA☆–(Los Angeles County) Leo Carrillo State Park ☆☆

Thirty-foot sandstone beach bouldering with overhangs. Uncertain if there's loose rock. Park named after 1950s movie actor. Autumn. Camping in state park (818-880-0350).
Ref: Guidebook: Katz's *Getting High in L.A.*
Directions: From Santa Monica go northwest on Hwy. 1 for approximately 26 mi. to Leo Carrillo State Park Beach.

205 LA–Russell Erickson Traverse (aka Sandbox) ☆☆☆

About a 100'-long 5.12+ sandstone bouldering traverse named after well-traveled climber Russell Erickson. Several 30' 5.12 topropes requiring long tie-off rope for anchor. This area is also known as The Sandbox. Autumn. State park.
Ref: N. Kaptain; R 82-92; Guidebook: Edwards's *Rock Climbing Santa Barbara and Ventura*.

Directions: From Santa Monica go northwest on Hwy. 1 for approximately 26 mi. to Leo Carrillo State Beach, then turn north on Mulholland Hwy. Go exactly 1 2/10 mi. and park just after the road cut. Hike along the crest of the ridge, straight down into the drainage for the Russell Erickson Traverse.

206 LA–Mulholland Boulders ☆

Two 15′ volcanic pocketed boulders. May not be terribly interesting. Autumn. Possibly private land.
Ref: N. Kaptain.
Directions: From Los Angeles mull west on Hwy. 101, then south on Kanan Rd., then right (west) on Mulholland Hwy. 2 4/10 mi. to volcanic Mulholland Boulders on left shoulder.

207 LA–Point Dume State Preserve (aka Zuma Beach) ☆

A 50′ metamorphic slab with ancient bolts. Soft rock. Remarkable beach scenery. Autumn. No camping. State park, (818) 880-0350.
Ref: N. Kaptain; Guidebooks: Katz's *Getting High in L.A.*, Hellweg and Warstler's *Climber's Guide to Southern California*.
Directions: From Santa Monica go approximately 18 mi. northwest on Pacific Coast Hwy. 1, through Malibu, to Point Dume State Park. Cliff at east end of Zuma Beach.

208 LA–Topanga Ridge (Twin Towers/Venice Slab/Boux Wall) ☆☆

Twin Towers has an enjoyable summit. Slab climb up to 200′ sandstone summit protected with bolts. Venice Slab has bouldering/toprope at base. Boux Wall has short topropes on steep bucketed wall called Bucket Brigade. Autumn. Government land.
Classics: Twin Towers: Superbowl Sunday; Venice Slab: Pocket Rocket 12; Boux Wall: Bucket Brigade 10, Arrecho 11, Jet Stream 11+.
Ref: Guidebook: Katz's *Getting High in L.A.*
Directions: Santa Monica. Twin Towers: Drive on Topanga Ridge Motorway from Saddle Peak Rd. Two unusual free-standing towers. Venice Slab: Across the Topanga Ridge Motorway from Twin Towers. Boux Wall: Park at cul-de-sac at end of Topanga Ridge Motorway. Boux Wall is obviously visible 100′ past parking. Bucket Brigade is directly below parking.

209 LA–Calabasas Peak/Castoff Rocks ☆☆

These are sandstone bouldering areas. Uncertain quality. Autumn. No camping. Government land.
Directions: Santa Monica. Calabasas Peak: From Stunt Rd. (200 yd. before Cold Creek Canyon Preserve), turn onto Calabasas Peak dirt road. At mi. 1.0, Arête Area consists of loose roadside slabs. At mi. 1.6 (high point of road),

downhill and right is Caves Area with 70′ red sandstone faces of better rock and good climbing potential. Castoff Rocks: Find this small sandstone boulder pile just off Stunt Rd., going up from Mulholland off large horseshoe. Take left for 150′ on dirt road to rocks.

210 LA–Piuma Road Boulders/Saddle Ridge Area ☆☆

Saddle Ridge has good bouldering potential, but access is gone. School Cracks are three classic 20′ sandstone vertical cracks. Stealth bouldering/topropes. For insiders only. Autumn. No camping. Possibly private land.
Classics: School Cracks.
Ref: Guidebook: Katz's *Getting High in L.A.*
Directions: Santa Monica. Piuma Road Boulders: Across from house at 24675 Piuma Rd. Saddle Ridge: Behind gated community on Piuma Rd.

211 LA–Malibu Creek State Park (aka Little Europe) ☆☆☆

Good pocket climbing depending on water levels. The 50′ sandstone sport crag, The Rock Pool; beyond it is the main attraction as well as expert bouldering. Autumn. Pay camping. State park closes at sunset (818–880–0367).
Classics: Apes Wall: Spider Monkey 11c; The Ghetto: Urban Struggle 12b, Stun Gun 12c; Maximum Ghetto 13a, Malibu Swinger 12.
Ref: N. Kaptain; C 141, R [82-92, 37]; Guidebooks: Mayr and Sweeney's *Southern California Sport Climbing*, Mayr's *Sport Climbing Guide to Southern California*, Katz's *Getting High in L.A.*, Fry's *Southern California Bouldering Guide*, Hellweg and Wartzler's *Climber's Guide to Southern California*.
Directions: From Hwy. 1 in Malibu, make tracks north 8–10 mi. on Malibu Canyon Rd. until Malibu Creek State Park appears on the left (west). Hike to the visitors center, cross concrete bridge, and turn left. The south-facing Planet of the Apes (so named from scenes shot there in the movie) toprope wall on right in 1/10 mi. Continue on past rock pool to reach bouldering and sport climbs on the north-facing Ghetto Wall. (One can park on Mulholland, just west of Las Virgenes, to avoid entrance fees.)

212 LA–Malibu Creek Tunnel Boulders ☆☆

Good 50′ sandstone pocket climbing. Autumn. No camping. State park.
Classics: Flyweenakis 11a, El Diablo 11, Arnold Palmer Mantle 11, Islands in the Stream 11+, Overlord B1-, Trash Compactor 11+, Avalon 12.
Ref: N. Kaptain; Guidebooks: Katz's *Getting High in L.A.*, Fry's *Southern California Bouldering Guide*.
Directions: From Malibu shred north on Malibu Canyon Rd. Park approximately 1 1/2 mi. south of park entrance. Hike southeast of road. The Malibu Creek Tunnel

Boulders are in drainage, just upstream (several hundred yards) from the north entrance of the tunnel. Legal parking is approximately ½ mi. north, on the left.

213 LA–Santa Susanna/Devil's Gate

These were Los Angeles practice climbing areas of the 1930/1940s. May be gone due to urban development. For a complete list of climbing guidebooks for California/Arizona and other states, see the thorough *The Climbing Guidebooks of the United States* by Randy Vogel. Private land.

Ref: Guidebooks: Vogel's *The Climbing Guidebooks of the United States*, Southern Cal RCS's *Climber's Guide to Santa Susanna*, Southern Cal RCS's *Climber's Guide to Devil's Gate.*

Directions: Los Angeles. Santa Susanna/Devil's Gate are old and possibly extinct Los Angeles climbing areas.

214 LA–Martian Landing ✰✰✰

Sixty-foot sandstone topropes and sport routes. Just west of Stoney Point on ridge. Autumn. No camping. Possibly private land.

Classics: The Martian Landing 5.11 roof.

Ref: N. Kaptain; Guidebook: Fry's *Southern California Bouldering Guide.*

Directions: Chatsworth. From Hwy. 118 turn south on Topanga Canyon Rd. Turn right and go ½ mi. on Santa Susanna Pass Rd. to Martian Landing.

215 LA–Stoney Point ✰✰✰

The historic crucible of southern California climbing offers a lifetime of contrivances and graffiti. Since 1935, when Glen Dawson led the Sierra Club mountaineering group here, Stoney Point became well known for its bouldering (Slant Rock, Turlock, and Angel Wings Boulders). Beethoven Wall and Beehive are popular for 80' topropes. The starting ground of famed American climbing pioneers Royal Robbins, Yvon Chouinard, Bob Kamps, Tom Frost, and T. M. Herbert. More than 250 routes. Soft sandstone can be friable after wet weather . . . let dry! Watch out for broken glass/soft rock. Crowded on weekends and afternoons. Brush clearing around the perimeter has revealed new boulders. Autumn–spring. City park is cited for major clean-up, and land to the north has been acquired for more bouldering potential. No camping. City land.

Classics: Beehive 4, Frosted Flakes 7, Mozart's 7, Paul's Hole 5.9, Composure 9, Center Route 9, Nutcracker 10a, Eye of Faith 5.10c, 747 10c, Sculpture Traverse 10d, Nabisco Traverse 11a, Maggie's Farm 11b, Ozymandias 11b, Vicious 12, The Flake/Turlock Boulder (Boulder II); B1 Boulder/Inside Out, Carousel Traverse V4 (B1), Master of Reality B1, Eat Out More Often, Split Rock, Iguana, 12a toprope, Hot Tuna Traverse V5, Expansion Chamber V5, Lion Head's Mantles.

Ref: Chris Owen 6/98; N. Kaptain; C [153-30, 141,74, 68], R 68-28, S 6/61; Sherman's *Stone Crusade,* Jones's *Climbing in North America;* Guidebooks: Owen's *Urban Rock: Stoney*

Point Climber's Guide, Fry's *Southern California Bouldering Guide,* Hellweg and Warstler's *Climber's Guide to Southern California,* Harlin's *West,* Hellweg and Fisher's *Stoney Point Guide.*

Directions: In Chatsworth (26 mi. northwest of downtown Los Angeles). Go south on Topanga Canyon Hwy. from Hwy. 118 to Stoney Point. On the corner of Hwy. 118 and Topanga Canyon. The big rock on east side of road, ¼ mi. north of traffic light at Chatsworth St.

216 LA–Chatsworth Park South (The Cell Block) ✰✰

Bolted sandstone leads climbs and bouldering at Chatsworth Park Quarry. City park.

Classics: Escape Artist 11 toprope, Birdman from Alcatraz 11+ toprope.

Ref: Guidebook: Fry's *Southern California Bouldering Guide.*

Directions: Chatsworth. From Hwy. 118 send it south on Topanga Canyon Blvd. Turn right on Devonshire St. to Chatsworth Park South. Just southwest of Stoney Point.

217 LA–Woolsey Canyon ✰✰

Sandstone bouldering and crag. Autumn. May be government land.

Classics: Rocketdyne Roof 11a, Indian Boulder topropes.

Ref: Guidebook: Fry's *Southern California Bouldering Guide.*

Directions: Chatsworth. Follow Hwy. 118 south to Topanga Canyon Blvd. Go right on Plummer. Go right up Woolsey Canyon Rd. to the Rocketdyne Gate. Park. Indian Boulder left of road. Roof across canyon.

218 LA–Purple Stones ✰✰

Quality 40' sandstone face bouldering problems in riparian forest setting. Topropes may be desired (anchor may be single old bolt). Bad landings could spell a trip to Paraplegiaville. Remember, he who hesitates is stoned. Exceptional rock quality. Some swampland. Declining popularity due to loss of access. Autumn. Possibly private land.

Classics: Topanga Lieback 9, The Water's Edge 10-, Flintlock 11, Asteroid Belt 12, Atlantis 12.

Ref: N. Kaptain; Guidebooks: Katz's *Getting High in L.A.,* Fry's *Southern California Bouldering Guide,* Hellweg and Warstler's *Climber's Guide to Southern California.*

Directions: Located ½ mi. south of town of Topanga (or a few mi. inland from Hwy. 1). Park at Calgas, on south side of town, and hike 6/10 mi. north on Topanga Canyon Blvd. to a turnout. (Illegal to park here, though some do anyway.) Go straight down trail into drainage, then hike ten minutes upstream to Purple Stones. Watch out for traffic.

219 LA–Sunset Stones ✰✰

Sandstone bouldering in chaparral above the Pacific Palisades. Reportedly good-quality rock with excellent problems. Autumn. No camping. May be government land.

Classics: Molarity of the Polarity 10+.
Ref: N. Kaptain; Guidebooks: Katz's *Getting High in L.A.*, Fry's *Southern California Bouldering Guide*.
Directions: From Santa Monica use Hwy. 1. Turn north on Temescal Canyon Rd. to end. Park. Hike north approximately 2 mi. on top of scenic trail to Sunset Stones.

220 LA–J. Paul Pebble ☆

Beachside 35' sandstone boulder topropes. Featured in John Long article. P.S. Nobody goes here anymore. No camping. Autumn. State land.
Ref: C 98(10/86)-41; Guidebooks: Katz's *Getting High in L.A.*, Fry's *Southern California Bouldering Guide*.
Directions: From Santa Monica surf it on Hwy. 1, just west of Sunset Blvd. J. Paul Pebble sits on beach.

221 LA–Bee Rock ☆

A 1930s and 1940s 200' sandstone practice crag closed around 1970. Potential for hard topropes. Access being negotiated. Uncertain rock quality. Spring–autumn. No camping. City park.
Ref: C 114-116; Guidebooks: Artz's *The Best of Mother Rock*, Katz's *Getting High in L.A.*
Directions: In L.A.'s Griffith Park, Bee Rock overlooks the zoo and downtown L.A.

222 LA–Eagle Rock

Crag next to major freeway, but little climbing due to poor rock and private property.
Ref: Guidebook: Southern Cal RCS's *Climber's Guide to Eagle Rock*.
Directions: West Pasadena at Eagle Rock. From I–210 and Hwy. 134, fly west on highway briefly. On right.

223 LA–Devil's Gate Dam Wall ☆☆

Leadable 65' routes on pillars under I–210. All routes now removed by Caltrans, and signs posted. Glue-on routes have obtained a certain practicality and vogue in the L.A. area for the after work crowd. As of 1991/1992, these routes would be removed by Caltrans and then local climbers would find new structures to place sport routes . . . an urban recirculating eddy. County land.
Classics: Pillar Society 12a/b.
Ref: N. Kaptain; Guidebook: Fry's *Southern California Bouldering Guide*.
Directions: From La Canada zip on Hwy. 210 east to Berkshire Place exit. Go east on Highland Dr. Devil's Gate Dam Wall on bridge south of reservoir. Ask locals for current guerilla crags.

224 LA–Eaton Canyon Park ☆☆

Artificial walls on bridge pillars offer 30' routes. County land.
Ref: Guidebook: Fry's *Southern California Bouldering Guide*.
Directions: Eaton Canyon Park is in Pasadena. Two areas: junction of Altadena Dr. under New York Dr. bridge and Altadena/Pinecrest. Hike to creek.

225 LA–Pacifico ☆☆☆

Granite topropes and ample scattered bouldering located at the end of a dirt road just before the long south-trending grade to the summit ridge (twenty-minute walk without four-wheel drive). Approach (past Horse Flats Campground). Pretty setting. Spring–autumn. Pay camping. USFS–Angeles NF, (626) 574-1613.
Ref: N. Kaptain; Guidebooks: Hellweg and Warstler's *Climber's Guide to Southern California*, Fry's *Southern California Bouldering Guide*.
Directions: From La Canada trace Hwy. 2N for 28 mi. Two mi. north of Newcomb's Restaurant, turn west on Santa Clara Divide Rd. (for 4 mi.). Turn left at Pacifico Campground sign for 4 $^2/_{10}$ mi. Turn right on dirt road. Turn left at Pacific Crest Trail sign for $^3/_4$ mi. (may be a four-wheel-drive road) to rock.

226 LA–Horse Flats Campground ☆☆☆

Wooded 40' granite boulder-loaded mountain escape from Los Angeles. Dimitrius Fritz writes, "There was 2 holds glued on Blank Generation. I think that's bad style, in fact that's NO STYLE. They have no class and no vision. Except for the idiot who did that, it's a good place to climb." Autumn. Pay camping; closed in winter. USFS–Angeles NF, (626) 574-1613.
Classics: Mr. Ed 8, Talk to Me Dirty 10, Bat Flake Arête 11+, Teflon President B1.
Ref: D. Fritz 6/98; N. Kaptain; C [174-84, 173-23], R 90-92 (topo); Guidebooks: Fry's *Southern California Bouldering Guide*, Hellweg and Warstler's *Climber's Guide to Southern California*.
Directions: From I–210 overpass in La Canada, follow Hwy. 2 north and east for 29 mi. Two mi. past Newcomb's Restaurant, turn west on Santa Clara Divide Rd. 2 $^4/_{10}$ mi. to Horse Flats Campground entrance. Toproping at sites 2 and 3 (tank with KW9 on it) and by hiking north across road from site 1 and north/northwest up trail in drainage approximately twenty minutes. For bouldering (best at southwest end of campground), drive farther, to trailhead halfway around the loop at campground site 7 on the right and hike for approximately fifteen minutes.

227 LA–Chilao (aka Sandy Bottom Boulders) ☆☆

Granite bouldering a la Horse Flats. Spring–autumn. Pay camping. USFS–Angeles NF, (626) 574-1613.
Ref: N. Kaptain; Guidebook: Fry's *Southern California Bouldering Guide*.
Directions: From La Canada follow Hwy. 2N for 28 mi. Turn left at Newcomb's Restaurant. Park at yellow gate on left for Chilao. Walk on trail downhill twenty minutes below waterfall. South of Horse Flats area.

228 LA–Devil's Punchbowl County Park ✩✩

Cup-shaped sandstone slabs give this area its name. Many sport climbs on these gritty, 50′ sandstone bolt-protected faces. Possibly access problems. No bolts. Spring/autumn. Closest camping at Lakeside Campground on Little Rock Reservoir. County park.

Classics: Tree Corner 8, Overhanger 8, Taboo 10b, Requiem 10 3p, Lower Bolt Route 10+; Attitude Wall: Best Seller 12a; Gorilla Face: Big Electric Cat 12a, Lunge Move 12a, Misguided 12c; Dog Wall: Mixed Breed 10b.

Ref: N. Kaptain; R [58-80 (topo), 57] C [141,108, 94]; Access Fund Notes; Guidebooks: Mayr and Sweeney's *Southern California Sport Climbing*, Mayr's *Sport Climbing Guide to Southern California*, Tidwell's *Devil's Punchbowl*, Hellweg and Warstler's *Climber's Guide to Southern California*, Bouclin et al.'s *Devil's Punchbowl Climber's Guide*.

Directions: From Antelope Valley Freeway (Hwy. 14) in Palmdale, go east on Hwy. 138 (Pearblossom Hwy.) to Pearblossom. Go south on Hwy. N6 (Longview Rd.) and follow signs to the Devil's Punchbowl County Park. Total mi.: 23 from Hwy. 14. Follow Burkhart Loop Trail south from parking lot to V.D. (Very Direct Wall) and Wallbanger Wall behind. From parking go north to Perverse Traverse, Attitude Wall, Gorilla Face, and Barking Dog Wall farthest north. Please avoid adjacent private land.

229 LA–Mt. Williamson Rock (aka Eagles Roost) ✩✩✩

Steep, quality climbing in a beautiful canyon offers 300′ metamorphic sport routes at all grades in the San Gabriel Mountains. Afternoon shade and 7,000′ elevation makes it a tolerable L.A. option in the summer. Buckhorn Campground (pay) is 3 mi. west. USFS–Angeles NF, (626) 574-1613.

Classics: Novus Ordo Seclorum 8, Golden Dawn 9, Totem Pole 10a, Dream Speed 11a, KAOS 11b, Guilty Being White 11, FSTD 11c; Freezer Burn Wall: 5.10-12, World on Fire 12b, Mythic Man 12b, The Pursuit 12b/c, Skeletons of Society 13a.

Ref: N. Kaptain; C [141, 127(8/91)-22], R 60, SC 9/91; Guidebooks: Mayr and Sweeney's *Williamson Rock*, Mayr and Sweeney's *Southern California Sport Climbing*, Mayr's *Sport Climbing Guide to Southern California*, Hellweg and Warstler's *Climber's Guide to Southern California*.

Directions: From La Canada (38 mi. from junction 210 and Hwy. 2), go north and east on Hwy. 2 (Angeles Crest Hwy.) approximately a half hour, passing two ski areas. After second ski area (Kratka Ridge) watch for Mt. Williamson Rock (large rocks) in drainage on left (approximately 2 mi.). From pullout above the rocks, hike northwest along ridge (tricky route finding) into the drainage. Or, from Wrightwood, 22 mi. west on Hwy. 2. Park at obvious dirt pullout. Crag visible. Hike approximately fifteen minutes down faint trail on the obvious knife-edged ridge.

230 SB–Mt. Baldy/Falling Rock Canyon ✩✩

Mt. Baldy: Access problems frequent this limited granite bouldering area. Owner has run climbers off . . . dicey. Private land. Falling Rock Canyon offers moderate topropes on USFS land.

Ref: N. Kaptain; Guidebooks: Artz's *The Best of Mother Rock*, Fry's *Southern California Bouldering Guide*.

Directions: From Claremont go north on Mills. Turn onto Mt. Baldy Rd. Park before junction with Glendora Ridge Rd. at school on right. Hike south of school to bouldering. Another climbing area is Falling Rock Canyon. Park at Icehouse Canyon lot. Hike up canyon ten minutes to first canyon on right and go past first waterfall to rock wall.

231 SB–Keller Peak Road ✩✩

Fun, roadside, 40′ granite overhanging sport cragging workout center for L.A. climbers. Bouldering, too. Spring-autumn. Free camping is available along road. USFS–San Bernadino NF, (909) 884-6634.

Classics: Brian's Song 10c, Joe's Problem 11a, Segments of Space 11c, Particle Acceleration 12a, Orange Tapestry 12a, Eve of The Ring 12d.

Ref: C 121-26, R 34; Guidebooks: Mayr and Sweeney's *Southern California Sport Climbing*, Mayr's *Sport Climbing Guide to Southern California*, Hellweg and Warstler's *Climber's Guide to Southern California*.

Directions: From Running Springs go 1 mi. east on Hwy. 330. Then right on Keller Peak Rd. 3 ½ mi. On right.

232 SB–Castle Rock/Roadside Rocks ✩✩✩

Beautiful 100′ granite walls near Big Bear Lake offer bouldering and sport cragging in the beauty of the cool mountain pines. Spring-autumn. USFS–San Bernadino NF, (909) 884-6634.

Ref: R 69-88; Guidebooks: Bartlett's *Oso Grande*, Hoffman's *Big Bear Valley: Climbing Routes of Southern California*, Hellweg and Warstler's *Climber's Guide to Southern California*.

Directions: From Big Bear Lake village, go just ¹/10 mi. west outside of town on Hwy. 18. Or 1 mi. east of dam. Turnout on north. Hike 1 mi. trail south to Castle Rock. Routes on south side. Also, bouldering/topropes ⁶/10 mi. east of dam south of highway on Roadside Rocks.

233 SB–Giant Rock ✩✩✩

Possibly one of the biggest boulders you'll ever see. Enormous 50′ granite boulders offer a Joshua Tree escape. Check out the wild history of George Van Tassel's The Integraton. Beware drunken bikers with guns on weekends. Autumn-spring. Free camping. BLM, (916) 978-4400.

Classics: Polished Steel 10+, Soldier of Fortune 11+, Fallen Angel B1-.

Ref: C 155 (10/95)- 79; Guidebook: Fry's *Southern California Bouldering Guide*.

Directions: From Yucca Valley hop 10 mi. north on Hwy. 247. Turn east on Reche to city of Landers. Travel north on Belfield to Integraton. From Integraton go east on dirt road (just north of Integraton), follow bend in road to north, then go northeast several miles to Giant Rock at base of hills near dry lakebed and airport.

234 SB–Joshua Tree National Monument ☆☆☆☆☆

Unique, zen-oramic, Joshua tree desert boasts more than 3,500 routes and many classic bouldering problems on white granite formations. More routes than in any North American rock-climbing area. This grainy quartz monzonite offers extremely good friction. History of colorful climbers, soloists, and international winter climbing scene. Climber camping popular at Hidden Valley and Ryan Campgrounds. Winters can be colder than anticipated. One million visitors per year. Raptor restrictions February–June.
Autumn/spring. NPS, (760) 367–5500.

Classics: Double Cross 7, Sail Away 8, Touch'n Go 9, Solid Gold 10a, Clean and Jerk 10b, Illusion Dweller 10b, Figures . . . 10, O'Kelley's Crack 10c, More Monkey . . . 11, Wangerbanger 11c, Leave It to Beaver 12a, Equinox 12d, Father Figure 12d, Pumping Hate 13a, Hydra 13c/d, Dihedron 14a; Bouldering: Slashface B1-, Gunsmoke Traverse B1-, Stem Gem B1, White Rastafarian B1, How's Your Mama B1, Orange Julius B1+, Gunsmoke B1+, Planet X B1+, Streetcar Named Desire B2-, So High B2, Caveman B2, Scatterbrain B2.

Ref: AAJ '70-124, C [192-20, 185-103, 183-36, 182-83, 181-111, 179-119, 178-110, 174-10/36, 170-112, 169-26, 167-78, 164-30, 162-122, 159-129, 158-84, 152-125, 150-54, 134, 125(4/91)-58, 123, 113, 111, 110, 109, 108, 107, 105, 104 to 95, 93, 90, 69(11/81), 65], M 83, R [101-78, 100-58, 93-34, 91-50, 83-26, 78-90, 76-40, 69-85], SC 6/92, S [1/89, 1/82, 1/72, 10/61]; Sherman's *Stone Crusade*; Guidebooks: Artz's *Turtle Rock Bouldering Guide*, Vogel's *Joshua Tree National Park Classic Rock Climbs*, Vogel's *Joshua Tree Sport Climbs*, Gingery's *Joshua Tree Bouldering*, Vogel's *Southern California Select*, Vogel's *Joshua Tree Rock Climbing Guide*, Bartlett's *Rock Climbs of Central Joshua Tree*, Bartlett's *Rock Climbs of Hidden Valley*, Bartlett's *Rock Climbs of Indian Cove*, Bartlett's *Rock Climbs of Lost Horse Valley*, Bard's *Rock Climbs of Lost Horse Valley*, Vogel's *Joshua Tree Select*, Vogel and Bartlett's *Joshua Tree Supplement*, Fry's *Southern California Bouldering Guide*, Hellweg and Warstler's *Climber's Guide to Southern California*, Harlin's *West*, Vogel's *Guide to Joshua Tree 1982*, Vogel's *Selected New Routes at Joshua Tree*, Wolfe and Dominick's *Climbing Guide to Joshua Tree National Monument*, Wolfe's *Climbing Guide to Joshua Tree National Monument 1970*.

Directions: From Joshua Tree spring south to Joshua Tree National Monument roads. The concentration of climbing areas in this vast desert rockland include Quail Springs, Hidden Valley, The Real Hidden Valley, Echo Rock, Wonderland of Rocks, Ryan Campground, and Saddle Rocks. Boulderers enjoy Hidden Valley Campground, Turtle Rock, Gunsmoke Area, and Asteroid Belt. Indian Cove (lower, sheltered from wind): From Joshua Tree go west on Hwy. 62, then south on Indian Cove Rd.

235 O☆–(Orange County) Hart Park ☆☆

Artificial 15'-high traverse walls for the dime edge specialist. This area consists of an Upper and Lower Wall. No camping. Autumn. Government land.

Classics: Barney Rubble Traverse B1.

Ref: Guidebooks: Fry's *Southern California Bouldering Guide*, Vogel's *Hunk Guide*.

Directions: North Santa Ana. Hart Park is on Glassell St., north of Hwy. 22.

236 O–Costa Mesa Artificial Walls ☆

A 150' traverse on natural rock holds. Some areas are more plastic than liposuction and silicon implants. Autumn. No camping. Government land.

Ref: Guidebook: Fry's *Southern California Bouldering Guide*.

Directions: In Costa Mesa. Costa Mesa Artificial Walls consists of these three areas: junction of 1) 405 overpass, 2)

Showing no signs of engine failure on When You're a Jet, 5.11+, Joshua Tree.

TIM TOULA

Adams Ave., and 3) Hamilton Ave. and Santa Ana riverbed.

237 O–UC-Irvine Campus Wall ☆
Bouldering on campus walls with long bouldering traverses. State land.
Ref: Guidebook: Fry's *Southern California Bouldering Guide.*
Directions: At UC-Irvine. On Campus Dr. under San Diego Creek bridge.

238 O–Turtle Rock ☆☆
Bouldering on a limestone matrix of fossil fragments in a city park. A sign has been posted at Turtle Rock stating that it is a Native American religious spot and please do not climb (or words to that effect). No camping. City park.
Classics: False Martin Quits, Beebop Tango, Latin Swing.
Ref: M. Baron 8/97; Guidebooks: Fry's *Southern California Bouldering Guide*, Vogel's *Hunk Guide.*
Directions: East of UC-Irvine. East on Campus Dr. Turn left on Turtle Rock. Turn left on Hillgate, then right on Rockview for Turtle Rock.

239 O–Corona Del Mar (aka The Beach or Pirate's Cove) ☆☆☆
Powerful climbing on 40′ oceanside formations of fine sandstone. Holds, often wet and greasy, are subject to breaking. Severely overhung problems that must be climbed by crook or by hook. Go at low tide and during weekdays. Fee area. Probably most popular Orange County area. Autumn–spring. No camping. Government park.
Classics: Ironman 11+, Sandman B1+, Annabel.
Ref: Guidebooks: Hellweg and Warstler's *Climber's Guide to Southern California*, Fry's *Southern California Bouldering Guide*, Harlin's *West*, Vogel's *Hunk Guide.*
Directions: In Newport Beach. From junction of Hwy. 73 and Hwy. 1, go south on Hwy. 1. Turn right on Marguerite and right again on Ocean Blvd. Park in park (fee) or on street. Corona Del Mar bouldering is just north of parking lot along beach.

240 O–El Toro Wall ☆
Artificial traverse bouldering wall under bridge. Government land.
Ref: Guidebook: Fry's *Southern California Bouldering Guide.*
Directions: In El Toro, at Normandale and El Toro Rd. Park at bridge above Alisos creek bed for El Toro Wall.

241 R☆-(Riverside County) Mt. Rubidoux/Riverside Quarry ☆☆☆
Mt. Rubidoux is a popular local Riverside boulder-strewn, 500′ hill. Razor edging and delicate footwork are required on hundreds of 50′ granite problems. Site of 1984 California Bouldering Championships. Riverside Quarry is a quarry near Mt. Rubidoux with lots of loose rock . . . one

excellent 5.11 crack, but mostly aid. Beware car break-ins. Autumn/spring. No camping. City park.
Classics: Beehive Crack 8, Fu Crack 10a, Circle Crack 11+, Hardy Boy Crack 12b, Flabob 12, In My Time of Dimes 12.
Ref: T. Reed; C 88; Sherman's *Stone Crusade*; Guidebooks: Artz's *Guide to the 1984 Bouldering Contest at Mt. Rubidoux, CA*, Fry's *Southern California Bouldering Guide*, Mackay and Vogel's *A Climber's Guide to Mt. Rubidoux*, Hellweg and Warstler's *Climber's Guide to Southern California*, Jensen and Smith's *Climber's Guide to the Riverside Quarry*, Kostinen's *A Guide to Miraloma Rocks.*
Directions: In Riverside. At junction of Hwy. 60 and Hwy. 91, go south on Hwy. 91. Exit west on Fourteenth St. Turn left on Redwood Dr. Bear right on Tequesquite. Turn right on San Andreas. Park opposite Mt. Rubidoux "exit." Areas from north to south include Superstar Slab, The Triangle, Smooth Sole Slab, Joe Brown Boulder, Half Dome, and The Island. At one time, the road up Mt. Rubidoux was open to driving; presently, it may be closed.

242 R–Big Rock (Bernasconi Ridge) ☆☆☆
Several granite areas (up to 200′) next to Lake Perris. Now saturated with sport routes as well. Here one can get satiated on high-quality, granitic friction climbs on large slab. Bouldering, too. Autumn–spring. Pay camping. Government land.
Classics: Trough 5, Northwest Passage 9, Edger Sanction 10a, Mushroom Boulders.
Ref: Guidebooks: Mayr and Sweeney's *Southern California Sport Climbing*, Mayr's *Sport Climbing Guide to Southern California*, Fry's *Southern California Bouldering Guide*, Cobb's *Guide to Big Rock Climbing Area*, Hellweg and Warstler's *Climber's Guide to Southern California*, Wise's *Big Rock*, Merrill's *Big Rock.*
Directions: From Riverside go south on Hwy. 215. Then head east 6 ½ mi. on Ramona Expwy. to south shore of Lake Perris. Big Rock is at Bernasconi Beach. Parking outside gate recommended. Park service locks gates . . . check times.

243 R–Nuevo Areas (Juniper Flats and Menifee) ☆☆☆
Nice granite bouldering areas. Autumn/spring. Pay camping. Private land.
Classics: Nuevos Rancheros 9+, Lizard King 10a, World's Best Thin Crack 12+, Women in Chains 13a.
Ref: Guidebook: Fry's *Southern California Bouldering Guide.*
Directions: From Riverside work your way south on I–215 to east on Nuevo. Then go south on Menifee. 1) Park at Ellis Ave. 2) Go west on Mountain Rd. to Gunther. Park at Juniper Flats rocks.

244 R–Hwy. 79 Glue On Boulder ☆
Bouldering with glue-on holds. Topropes.
Ref: Guidebook: Fry's *Southern California Bouldering Guide.*

Directions: From Beaumont go on I–10 to 3 mi. south on Hwy. 79. By roadside.

245 R–Hemet Bouldering ✪✪

Day's worth of fun granite bouldering. Autumn–spring.
Ref: Guidebook: Fry's *Southern California Bouldering Guide.*
Directions: In Hemet there are two approaches: 1) South on State to east on Gibbel Rd. 2) Hwy. 74 to south on Girard Ave. Then turn west on Pachea Trail to end. Don't trespass—you will be shot on sight.

246 R–I✪–(Idyllwild Area) Boulder Basin Campground (on Black Mountain) ✪✪✪✪

Sylvan 35′ granitic bouldering area appeals to the experienced boulderer. Summer/autumn. Fee area. Primitive camping on Black Mountain. USFS–San Bernadino NF, (909) 383–5588.
Classics: Where Boneheads Dare B1-, Moroccan Roll B1-, Largo Stem B1-, The Jewel (up road before YMCA).
Ref: C [174-84, 104, 59(3/80)]; Sherman's *Stone Crusade;* Guidebook: Fry's *Southern California Bouldering Guide.*
Directions: From Idyllwild meander north on Hwy. 243, 5 mi. past Pine Cove. Turn right on Black Mountain Rd. (4S01 closed until late May) for 5 3/10 mi. Parking fee to park at Boulder Basin.

247 R–I–OK Corral (on Black Mountain) ✪✪✪✪

Thirty-foot granite boulders in high pine forest. Road closed until May. Primitive camping on Black Mountain. USFS–San Bernadino NF, (909) 884–6634.
Classics: LARGO Scoop B1-, Hueco Problem, Arnould's Project.
Ref: C 59 (3/80); Guidebook: Fry's *Southern California Bouldering Guide.*
Directions: From Idyllwild meander north on Hwy. 243 5 mi. past Pine Cove. Turn right on Black Mountain (4S01) for 4 mi. OK Corral Boulders at hairpin.

248 R–I–Suicide Rock ✪✪✪✪✪

Tahquitz's 400′ granite companion, both with fantastic granite. Suicide features mostly slab climbing. Teething ground for second generation of California hardmen (Bachar, Long, Yaniro, etc). Autumn/spring . . . hot in summer. Weeping Wall is most popular. Pay camping. USFS–San Bernadino NF, (909) 884–6634.
Classics: Captain Hook 7, Mickey Mantle 8R, Flower of High Rank 9, Ten Karat Gold 10a, Sundance 10b, Valhalla 11a, Iron Cross 11a, Insomnia 11c, The Pirate 12c, Paisano Overhang 12c/d, Ishi 12d, Hades 13a.
Ref: R 19, C [134, 125, 118, 111, 110, 108, 106, 105, 104, 99, 98, 94, 88, 66], S [2/76, 12/73]; Guidebooks: Vogel and Gaines's *Climber's Guide to Tahquitz and Suicide,* Hellweg and Warstler's *Climber's Guide to Southern California,* Harlin's *West,* Vogel's *Rock Climbs of Tahquitz and Suicide*

Tahquitz Rock.

TIM TOULA

Rocks, Messick's *Rock Climbs of Tahquitz and Suicide Rocks,* Wilts's *Tahquitz and Suicide Rocks.*
Directions: From Idyllwild head northeast on Fern Valley Rd. to Humber Park. On left. Approach trail located at two water tanks. Pleasant half-hour hike. Suicide Rock has different named areas, which include Sunshine Face, Smooth Sole Wall, Weeping Wall, Eagle Pinnacle, and the Northern Area.

249 R–I–Humber Park ✪

One granite boulder problem between the bookends of Tahquitz and Suicide. Summer/autumn. USFS–San Bernadino NF, (909) 884–6634.
Classics: Nose Boulders, Weasels Ripped My Flesh B1, Spiral Tree Boulder.
Ref: Guidebook: Fry's *Southern California Bouldering Guide.*
Directions: From Idyllwild trend northeast on Pine Crest. Turn north on Fern Valley Rd. to park. Boulders at top of loop, outhouse, and above road at Humber Park. Trailhead for Suicide and Tahquitz.

250 R–I–Tahquitz ✪✪✪✪✪

One-thousand-foot granite teething ground for first generation of California hardmen (Robbins, Chouinard, Wilts, Galwas, Wilson, etc.). This mini-Yosemite in southern California was one of the first major climbing areas in the western United States. Tahquitz played a major role in California climbing evolution as early as the 1930s by the Rock Climbing Section (RCS) of the Southern California Sierra Club. Open Book, first climbed by Royal Robbins in 1952, is claimed to be the first 5.9 in the United States. Origin of the Tahquitz Decimal System, e.g., 5.7, which later became known as the Yosemite Decimal System (YDS). Ice in winter. Spring–autumn. Bivy at "P" loop or pay camping. USFS–San Bernadino NF, (909) 884–6634.
Classics: Angel's Fright 5, Fingertip 7, Open Book 9, Whodunnit 9, Super Pooper 10a, Fred 11a, The Vampire 11a, Green Arch 11a, The Edge 11b, Green Rosetta 11, Turbo Flange 11c, The Flakes 11c, Stairway to Heaven 12a, Constellation 12b.

Ref: C [125, 118, 111, 110, 108, 105, 104, 93, 88, 65], R [84-60, 67-58, 19], S 6/76; Climbing in North America; Guidebooks: Vogel and Gaines's *Climber's Guide to Tahquitz and Suicide,* Hellweg and Warstler's *Climber's Guide to Southern California,* Harlin's *West,* Vogel's *Rock Climbs of Tahquitz and Suicide Rocks,* Messick's *Rock Climbs of Tahquitz and Suicide Rocks,* Wilts's *Tahquitz and Suicide Rocks,* Mendenhall's *Strawberry Peak–North Wall (Tahquitz),* Shand's *A Climber's Guide to Tahquitz and Suicide Rocks,* Smith's *Climber's Guide to Tahquitz Rock.*

Directions: From Idyllwild go northeast on Fern Valley Rd. to Humber Park. On right. Hike a half hour up Ernie Maxwell Trail. Stiff approach. Tahquitz is *the* dominant dome above Idyllwild.

251 R–I–South Ridge ☆☆☆☆

Good landings at this 30′ granite bouldering area. Hot, sunny area . . . warmer than other Idyllwild areas. Four-wheel drive recommended. Autumn/spring. USFS–San Bernadino NF, (909) 884-6634.

Classics: South Ridge Arête B1, Mechanical Advantage B1+, Big Electric Cat B1.

Ref: Bud Couch; Sherman's *Stone Crusade;* Guidebook: Fry's *Southern California Bouldering Guide.*

Directions: From Idyllwild follow 243S to east on Saunders Meadow Rd. Turn north on Pine (sign). Turn right (east) on Tahquitz View for 3/10 mi. Turn right (south) on South Ridge Trail for 1 mi. to park at dead-end, or park sooner with two-wheel-drive car. Easy boulder problems in the turnaround. Other boulders 50 yd. southwest. South Ridge is south of Tahquitz.

252 R–I–Relativity Boulders (aka Pine Cove) ☆☆☆

Experimental area for testing the theory of relativity . . . the Speed of Light Dyno B2, an ethereal double lunge. Twenty-five-foot granite boulders. Access problems. Please keep this area noise and trash free to continue access. Spring–autumn. No camping. Private land.

Classics: Relativity Face B1, Speed of Light Dyno B2.

Ref: C (3/80); Sherman's *Stone Crusade;* Guidebook: Fry's *Southern California Bouldering Guide.*

Directions: From Idyllwild zoom for 2 mi. north on Hwy. 243. Turn west on Pine Cove Rd. 4/10 mi. to park. Relativity Boulders not seen from road. Go to historical marker on right, then downhill 150 yd. to west from monument. Please be quiet: residential area.

253 R–I–Sunrise Stones ☆☆☆☆

These and other Idyllwild areas are described in a classic 1980 *Climbing* article, "Pumping Granite" by John Long. Twenty-foot granite bouldering on private property (backyard). Owners don't give permission. Free camping. Private land.

Classics: Sunrise Boulder: Grandstaff Overhang.

Ref: C (3/80); Guidebook: Fry's *Southern California Bouldering Guide.*

Directions: From Idyllwild zoom for 2 mi. north on Hwy. 243. Turn west on Pine Cove Rd. to Park. Sunrise Stones are several blocks from Relativity Boulders (Pine Cove Area).

254 R–I–Idyllwild County Park ☆☆☆

Many mantle problems at this 30′ granite bouldering area. Park fee. Nice pay camping facilities. County park.

Classics: Mushroom Boulder, AH Boulder, Granite Wave.

Ref: Guidebooks: Vogel and Gaines's *Tahquitz and Suicide Rock Climbs,* Fry's *Southern California Bouldering Guide.*

Directions: West Idyllwild. At Idyllwild County Park. West side of campground.

255 R–The Tramway/Kaufman Crag ☆☆☆

Quite a few good granite routes and bouldering above 8,000′ elevation. Beautiful approach via pricey (approximately $20) tram, which is open year-round except for two weeks in August. Cool in summer. Free camping. USFS–San Bernadino NF, (760) 325-1391.

Classics: Boardwalk V9.

Ref: J. Christie; C [Mar 98-93, 189-134, 174-84].

Directions: From Palm Springs go west of town, following signs from Hwy. 111. Follow Tramway Rd. Take aerial tramway 2,000′ base to 8,500′ on Mt. San Jacinto's top. Hike 200 yd. downhill to 100′ Kaufman Crag (visible from tram on left).

256 R–Tahquitz Canyon ●

One-hundred-foot granite crag with detached plates. Hobo garden; take your chances. Winter. No camping. Indian Reservation.

Ref: R 19.

Directions: From Palm Springs, Tahquitz Canyon is west of town on Agua Caliente Indian Reservation.

257 R–Palm Springs Area ☆☆

Artificial bouldering traverses and short boulder problem on vertical wall with artificial holds.

Classics: Artificial bridge walls and topropes.

Directions: Palm Springs. Just east of town. Go off I-10 to south on Gene Autry Trail. Then east on Ramon at Whitewater River Wash to Palm Springs Area.

258 R–Chiriaco Summit ☆☆

Potential plentitude of Joshua Tree–type climbing amid tremendous cholla garden and 100′ granite crags. Site of General Patton's museum. Winter. Free camping. Uncertain if NPS land.

Classics: Zulu Dawn 10b, On the Warpath 11bR.

Ref: T. Roberts, J. Christie; R 59.

Directions: From Indio gallop east for forty minutes on I–10 to General Patton Museum exit (follow signs). From exit it is ten minutes on dirt road northeast to Chiriaco Summit rock.

259 R–Chuckwalla Mountains ●

Potentially good-looking 50' granite boulder piles, but there are many boulders made of extremely bad rock with possibly nothing or little to do. Free camping. Winter. BLM, (916) 978-4400.

Ref: Guidebook: Fry's *Southern California Bouldering Guide.*

Directions: From Blythe go 55 mi. west on I–10. Go south on Eagle Mountain Rd. exit to Chuckwalla Mountains.

260 Monument Peak (aka Old Squaw's Tit or Parker Needle)

Extremely rotten, 800' volcanic desert tower first done by J. Mendenhall, R. M. A. Johnson, and P. Estes in 1939 in Whipple Mountains. Route is 300', three pitches from west notch. The tower is an impressive 800' on its east side. Helmets (check life insurance policy?) are a must on this extremely rotten rock. Autumn–spring. Free camping. BLM, (916) 978-4400.

Ref: S. Baxter; *Desert* 1930-50; S 7/71; Guidebook: Zdon's *Desert Summits: A Climbing and Hiking Guide to California.*

Directions: From Parker head north across Colorado River and immediately turn right along river to Cross Roads. At Cross Roads, turn left into Whipple Mountains and base of Monument Peak. No specifics.

261 SD☆–(San Diego Area) Temecula Domes (aka Rainbow Valley) ☆☆☆☆

Worthy, Woodson-like, 150' granite boulders/domes. Traditional ethics. Stay on trails. Rattlers, poison oak, and deep brush threaten to drop many a good rock man and woman. Autumn–spring. No camping. Private land—access problems.

Classics: Maggie's Crack 9, High Voltage 11b, Rock Candy 11c.

Ref: R 31(5/89)-56; Guidebook: White's *Crags and Boulders of San Diego County.*

Directions: San Diego. Temecula Domes are 2 mi. south of Temecula on I–15. Both sides of freeway north of weigh station. Parking access at 1) ½ mi. south of Temecula on southbound side of I–15 pullout with guardrail, then head up dirt road to cairned trail to rock, 2) park just north of border check point on east side northbound lane of I–15, hike north 50 yd. to EMERGENCY PARKING ONLY sign and then 20 yd. more. Run west across I–15 (illegal) to ditch and trail up to rock, 3) Rainbow Valley exit to west and just north of weigh station. Park at where pavement ends. Hike dirt road going straight at sharp right to rock, and 4) east on Rainbow Valley Rd., then quick left (north) approximately 1–2 mi. to dirt pullouts on right.

262 SD–Mt. Woodson ☆☆☆☆

The white hillside boulders of Poway are noted as the best climbing in San Diego. Hundreds of classic 40' granite problems . . . one trip is never enough. Stonemasters bouldering site. Famous for stiff cracks and stiffer ratings. Developed in the 1960s. Winter. Near Ramona there is pay camping park. City park.

Classics: Bighorn 8, Robbins Crack 10-, Jaws 10+, Driving South 11+, Stairway to Heaven 11+, Uncertainty Principle 11d, I Hear My Train A Comin' 5.11+, Pruneface B1, Top Secret File B1, Head First in the Bushes B1, Mother Superior 12.

Ref: C [112(2/89), 111, 108, 96, 66], R [99-53, 13(3/86)-53; Sherman's *Stone Crusade;* Guidebooks: Vogel's *Southern California Select,* Fry's *Southern California Bouldering Guide,* Hellweg and Warstler's *Climber's Guide to Southern California,* Harlin's *West,* Paul's *Climbing Guide to Mt. Woodson,* Amick's *Mt. Woodson Boulder Maps,* Amick's *Mt. Woodson–Feb '87,* Brueckner's *Mt. Woodson Bouldering.*

Directions: From Poway go east on S4 and then 2 ½ mi. north on Hwy. 67. Turn left on Mt. Woodson Rd. Park on left at gated road (on the right just past Hedy Dr.). Hike up "yellow brick" road of 200 boulder problems following trail signs. Access sensitive.

263 SD–Rexrodes ☆☆☆

Trailside 40' granite boulders mainly to west of main trail on western flank of Mt. Woodson. Winter. No camping. City park.

Ref: Guidebooks: Fry's *Southern California Bouldering Guide,* Gomper's *Bouldering Guide to Rexrodes.*

Directions: From Poway go east on S4. Rocks at 2 mi. north on Hwy. 67. Park on south side of road. Hike south on Rexrodes Trail (sign) toward Lake Poway.

264 SD–Magnolia ☆☆☆

Scattered 40' granite boulders on dry hillsides: North, Main, and South Hills. Good area for beginners and intermediates. Topropes. Winter. No camping. Private land.

Classics: The Fin 10.

Ref: Guidebooks: Fry's *Southern California Bouldering,* Hellweg and Warstler's *Climber's Guide to Southern California,* Fry's *Southern California Bouldering Guide,* Schaffer and Walker's *Climber's Guide to Santee Boulders.*

Directions: East of Santee a couple mi. Mission Gorge Rd. to north on Magnolia Ave. to end. Hike to trail past dump.

265 SD–Santee Boulders ☆☆☆

Good 45' bouldering and topropes on solid granite in a small valley. Known for its face climbing. Pay camping at Santee Lake. Access sensitive. Summer/autumn. May be city land.

Classics: Mudball Boulder, The Pretzel B1, Batflake 11 toprope, Synchronicity 12b toprope.

Ref: R 13(3/86)-53; Guidebooks: Hellweg and Warstler's *Climber's Guide to Southern California*, Fry's *Southern California Bouldering Guide*, Schaffer and Walker's *Climber's Guide to Santee Boulders*.

Directions: Santee. From Mission Gorge Rd. turn north on Mast Blvd. Turn east on Carlton Oaks Drive. Then north on Leticia to left on Rumson. Park at Serres Court for Santee Boulders.

266 SD–Mission Gorge ★★★

Popular San Diego bouldering and cragging area since 1950. Fine 60' lines on slick granite. Autumn/winter. No camping. City park.

Classics: The Pump 7, Lunch Rock Jamcrack 8, General Dynamics 10+, Mission Impossible 11+, The Thumb 12c; Pink Boulder, Orange Cube.

Ref: R 13(3/86)-53; Guidebooks: Hellweg and Warstler's *Climber's Guide to Southern California*, Fry's *Southern California Bouldering Guide*, Gerberding's *Photo Guide to Climbs in Mission Gorge*, White and Van Belle's *Scumbag Digest*, Amick's *Free Climbs at Mission Gorge*, Lantry's *Climber's Guide to Mission Gorge*, Beck's *A Climber's Guide to Mission Gorge*.

Directions: In West Santee. From the junction of I–15 and I–8, go east on I–8, exiting onto Mission Gorge Rd. for 4 1/2 mi. Turn north on Father Junipero Serro Trail (at MISSION TRAILS REGIONAL PARK sign) to pullout at 6/10 mi. Mission Gorge rock on hillside to right, approximately ten-minute walk. Park road closes at dusk.

267 SD–La Jolla Beach (People's Walls and Boomer Beach) ★★

Sandy beach 30' bouldering at Boomer Beach. One can find face climbing and traverses on gritty, dirty sandstone. People's Wall is a 25' man-made wall. The Cave, below the wall on the beach, is a noteworthy classic. Best time: low tide and sunny. Cruxy parking. No camping. Possibly city land.

Classics: People's Wall: The Cave.

Ref: C 165(12/96)-116; Guidebooks: Hellweg and Warstler's *Climber's Guide to Southern California*, Fry's *Southern California Bouldering Guide*.

Directions: Northwest San Diego. From I–5 surf east on Ardath Rd., then west on Torrey Pines Rd. Turn right on Prospect, then right on Cave St. for Boomer's Beach in Ellen Browning Scripps Park at La Jolla Cove. People's Wall is 1/2 mi. south at junction of Coast and South Coast Blvd.

268 SD–Los Coches ★★★

Potentially good granitic bouldering area.

Ref: Guidebook: Fry's *Southern California Bouldering Guide*.

Directions: From San Diego wander east on I–8. Turn right off Los Coches Rd. exit to end. Hike uphill (obvious).

269 SD–Singing Hills (aka Crest) (closed?) ★★★

Classic, quality 50' granite boulders and topropes (maybe sport crag). No camping.

Classics: Big Dihedral 9, Classic Face 11c.

Ref: C 149-49; Guidebooks: Goode's *Climbing Guide to Crest San Diego, CA*, Fry's *Southern California Bouldering Guide*.

Directions: Take Hwy. 8 west to Crest Blvd. On top at church, go left. Then go left on small dirt road. Singing Hills rocks visible. Access through private land; may be closed.

270 SD–Pump Wall ★★

After-work 20' artificial training traverse. Featured on cover of *Climbing* 141. No camping. Government land.

Ref: C 141, R 17(1/87)-38; Guidebook: Fry's *Southern California Bouldering Guide*.

Directions: Ocean Beach. From west on I–8. Turn southwest on Sunset Cliffs Blvd. Park just south of Point Loma Ave. Hike to oceanside and look for the cement Pump Wall.

271 SD–Deerhorn Valley ★★★★

Mt. Woodson–like 50' granite boulders entwined in beguiling underbrush and private land with possibly changing access. Enticing splitter cracks on white hillside eggshells. Leading and toproping. As for routes, Full Moon Boogie 5.11a . . . send it! The cafe in Dulzura delivers the breakfast experience. Autumn–spring. No camping. Government/private land.

Classics: African Queen 10a, La Banda 10d, Full Moon Boogie 11a, Move to the Groove 11, Agent Orange 12.

Ref: R 16(10/86)-86; Guidebook: Olson's *Deerhorn Valley Topos*.

Directions: From San Diego sally southeast on Hwy. 94. Turn left (east) on Honey Springs Rd. (before Dulzura) for 4 mi. Deerhorn Valley consists of many areas. For Pinnacles Group area turn sharply at three oak trees. Several other areas past H.S. Ranch to rock. Problematic access.

272 R–The Falls/The Slab ★★★

Hillside and canyon fan of 40' granite boulders and short walls. Climbs out of the waterfall area. An area with more than thirty years of rock-climbing history. Disheartening litter. Spring/autumn. USFS–Cleveland NF, (858) 674-2901.

Classics: Elephant Boulder, Waterfall, 5.10+ finger crack.

Ref: Guidebooks: Hellweg and Wartsler's *Climber's Guide to Southern California*, Vogel's *Hunk Guide*.

Directions: From San Juan Capistrano fly 20 mi. northeast on Hwy. 74. Two mi. past a USFS campground, find a pullout on right with The Falls below highway to west. Hike five minutes. Also approachable via I–15, approximately 12 mi. west (west of Lake Elsinore). The Slab is on the north side of the road, just 2 mi. east of The Falls.

273 Pigeons Cliff

Great access 80′ basalt sport crag. Some fifteen to twenty climbs ranging from 5.9 to 5.13. Spring. Free camping. BLM, (916) 978–4400.

Directions: From Susanville go 2 mi. west of city limits off Hwy. 36. The pulloff on the left leads to Pigeons Cliff.

274 Tar Creek (aka The Swimming Hole) ✩✩✩

Difficult highball Jeff Johnson, Paul Anderson, and Wils Young bouldering problems with feared landings on beautiful 35′ conglomerate grit blocks often above the swimming ponds in a restricted access condor sanctuary. More than a hundred high-risk, off-the-deck, and therefore enjoyable problems await the first- and possibly last-time visiting climber. Spring/autumn. Camping nearby on Los Padres NF, (805) 968–6640.

Classics: Tarface 5.11, The Wave 5.11+, The Handicapper B2-, Entry Fee, Tar Baby, Naked Ape, Aquaman (très difficile).

Ref: R 77-96 (topo); Sherman's *Stone Crusade;* Guidebooks: Edwards's *Rock Climbing Santa Barbara and Ventura,* Edwards's *Santa Barbara Bouldering.*

Directions: From Fillmore (junction of Hwy. 126 and 23) go north on "A" St. Turn right on Goodenough Rd. Turn right at ROADS END sign. Wind up hillside 3 mi. At Oak Flat Fire Station, keep going another 1 ½ mi. After hairpin and straightaway, park on left at large lot. From left side of parking area, walk uphill past gate on road for 1 mi. to trail. Continue down to Tar Creek. Hike time, forty-five minutes.

275 New Jack City ✩✩✩

Winter sport climbing on smooth 100′ metamorphic rock similar to basalt. Eighty routes. This is an ORV area, so don't annoy the nonclimbers. Beware of nails and glass. Winter. Free camping. BLM, (916) 978–4400.

Classics: Crucified 10d, Brown Recluse 11b/c, Crossfire 12a, Lethal Weapon 12c, Double Knee Bar Ranch 12c/d, The Action 13a.

Ref: G. Barnes; Guidebooks: Mayr's *New Jack City Sport Climbing Guide,* Mayr and Sweeney's *Southern California Sport Climbing* (available at Nomad in Joshua Tree).

Directions: From Barstow go 14 ⁶/₁₀ mi. south on Hwy. 247. Take graded dirt road to right 1 mi. Follow various roads into rock basin on left. Approach time, ten to fifteen minutes. Higher-clearance vehicles can get closer to certain crags.

276 Box Springs

Sport climbing area with 5.9–5.11 leads.

Ref: Guidebooks: Artz's *The Best of Mother Rock,* Rough's *Box Springs Sport Climbing Guide.*

Directions: East of Riverside. From Riverside go east on third, which turns into Blaine east of I-215. Turn left onto Belvedere to right on Two Trees to left on Galaxie Heights. Up driveway to left at dirt road fork. Look for cliffs on left.

277 StB–Red Rock ✩✩✩

Nice volcanic bouldering area. More than one hundred bouldering problems. Popular recreation area. Minimal access fee. Government land.

Directions: From Santa Barbara follow Hwy. 154 north. Turn right onto Paradise Rd. for 10 mi. (turns to dirt). From Gateway parking area hike along trail to boulders.

278 Skofield Park ✩✩

Described as a little Fountainbleau. Fifty sandstone bouldering problems in city park closed on Tuesday/Wednesday. The Undertaker or To A Grave, both V6, offer two predominant challenges on the Undertaker Boulder. City park.

Ref: Guidebooks: Edwards's *Rock Climbing Santa Barbara and Ventura,* Edward's *Santa Barbara Bouldering.*

Directions: In Montecito.

279 Westmont College ✩

One sandstone boulder with a dozen or so problems on Westmont College campus between Page and Clark Residence Halls. Private land.

Ref: Guidebooks: Edwards's *Rock Climbing Santa Barbara and Ventura,* Edward's *Santa Barbara Bouldering.*

Directions: In Montecito.

280 Pine Mountain ✩✩✩✩

Wonderland of exploratory granite bouldering with classics already discovered like Sunkissed VO and The Jewel V1. Fall/late spring. Need to purchase pass for access. Camping on-site—bring water. USFS-Los Padres NF, (805) 968–6640.

Ref: C 176-72; Guidebooks: Edwards's *Rock Climbing Santa Barbara and Ventura,* Edwards's *Santa Barbara Bouldering.*

Directions: From Ojai go north for about 32 mi. on Hwy. 133 past Sespe Gorge to Pine Mountain Recreation Area sign. Turn right for 5 mi. to Pine Mountain Campground. Picnic Area boulders are in the campground opposite entrance. More bouldering a mile farther south to Reyes Peak Campground. Boulders are ¼ mi. south of the campground. Many boulders on ridgeline on the last mi. stretch of Pine Mountain Rd.

281 McCain Valley ✩✩✩

Great granite bouldering east of San Diego by one hour. Two areas: Lark Canyon with a hundred problems ¼ mi. south of campground entrance and Pinnacle Boulder Field (more extensive). Spring/fall. Pay campground. BLM, (916) 978–4400.

Classic: 200′ Lowenbrau Pinnacle 5.10 up visible from I-8.

Ref: C 168; Hubbard's *McCain Valley Bouldering.*

Directions: Take I-8 east to Campo Blvd., exit 66. Turn right on Hwy. 94 and drive south ½ mi. to intersection of

Old Hwy. 80. Turn left, going east for 1 ⁹/₁₀ mi. to McCain Valley Resource Conservation Area (sign). Turn left for 5 ½ mi. (turns to dirt at 2 ½ mi.) to 1) Lark Canyon Boulders on right. Park at third left entrance in Lark Canyon Campground. 2) Pinnacle Boulderfield: Drive past campground to obvious 100′ summit on left. Park on north side. Faint trail west from parking to Pinnacle Boulderfield.

282 Culp Valley (Anza-Borrego Desert Wildlife State Wilderness) ☆☆☆

Fine-grained gray granite 25′ boulders with black xenolithic knobs. State land.

Ref: J. Ludwig; R 99-54; Guidebooks: Zdon's *Desert Summits: A Climbing and Hiking Guide to California*, Lindsay's *Anza-Borrego Desert Region*.

Directions: At the top of the Montezuma grade, just east of Ranchita and north of I-8. Take CR 22 to SR 3.

283 Corte Madera

A quiet gem of the San Diego backcountry. A beautiful, remote multipitch 350′ granite crag with fine trad routes like South Buttress 10a. One to two hours east of San Diego. Raptor restrictions February–June. Also beware poison oak and large falling Coulter pine cones. Free camping by climber's path, or pay at Lake Morena County Park farther south on Bruckman Springs Rd. Fall–spring. USFS–Cleveland NF, (858) 674–2901.

Ref: R [99-54, 71-102 (topos)]; Guidebook: White's *Crags and Boulders of San Diego County* (guidebook virtually nonexistent).

Directions: From San Diego proceed east on I-8 one hour to Bruckman Springs exit. Take S-1 south for 3 ½ mi. to Corral Canyon Rd. For low-clearance two-wheel-drive drives, continue another 1 ³/₁₀ mi. to a trailhead near a steel gate. Park. Hike ten minutes to private-property signs. Follow Forest Service markers for 1 ½ mi. up to saddle (bouldering to north), then a ½ mi. down a jeep trail to climber's path, which is another thirty–sixty minutes.

284 Snow Valley Bouldering

Hundreds of granite boulder problems at 6,800′. Camping up Keller Peak Rd. USFS–San Bernadino NF, (858) 674-2901.

Classics: Ken's Arête, Tsunami, Sucking On a Dead Man's Brain.

Ref: See online guide or Outdoor Works in Cedar Glenn (909–336-0864).

Directions: From Running Springs go 5 mi. west on Hwy. 18 until 1 mi. west of ski area. Just north and west of parking area. Another area is just west of Little Green Valley Lake trailhead. Some boulders visible, others accessible by trails. Five-minute approaches.

285 Clark Mountain

Three-tiered limestone "wonder mountain" for all who seek true rad sport climbs. Discovered and developed by Randy Leavitt. Intense multipitched 5.13 sport routes out huge overhanging caves. More than 100 routes. Summer/autumn. Camping at trailhead. BLM, (916) 978–4400.

Classics: Religious Experience 12a/12c, Dios Mio 13c, Jumbo Pumping Hate 12/13d, Tusk 14a.

Ref: C [177-94, 173-23], R [81-18, 77-16]; Guidebook: McCray's *Welcome to Las Vegas Limestone*.

Directions: From Las Vegas, Nevada drive south on I-15 and into California. Clark Mountain is off to right. At first exit, Yates Well, turn right off ramp. Turn right after ⁷/₁₀ mi., then jag left, going past golf course. Continue on, pass water tank, and at 5 ³/₁₀ mi. bear left. Pass old houses on right, and at 8 ½ mi. turn right. At 9 ³/₁₀ mi. park at trailhead. Hike trail up gully to First Tier for forty-minute aerobic blast.

286 The Oasis

Steep bolted granite routes from 5.7 to 5.12, featuring Bad Blood 5.12d. Camping beneath.

Ref: C 186-89.

Directions: Near Trona.

287 Morro Rock (closed)

Morro Rock is *closed* to climbing—peregrine falcon nesting site. Volcanic outcropping at the entrance to Morro Bay, 576′ above sea level. Overlooks Morro Bay.

288 Silly Rocks

Bouldering.

Ref: R 97-98; Guidebook: Slater's *California Central Coast Climbing*.

Directions: In Santa Maria.

289 Cabrillo Peaks in Morro Bay

Ref: R 97-98; Guidebook: Slater's *California Central Coast Climbing*.

290 Big Sur Sea Stacks

Ref: R 97-98; Guidebook: Slater's *California Central Coast Climbing*.

291 Cerro Romualdo ☆☆☆

Sport crag on state land leased by Army National Guard. Only open to public when guns are cool. Check at guardhouse before entering for permission. Ten draws and trad rack for more than twenty routes.

Classics: Rainbow Ballet 7R, The Tube Shuffle 11a, The Phoenix 12.

Ref: R 97-98 Miniguide.

Directions: From San Luis Obispo (junction of Hwy. 101

and Hwy. 1), go north a short ways on Hwy. 1 into Camp San Luis (sign). Check for open or closed status at Building 738. Park at southwest end of complex in parking lot. Hike southeast along base on dirt road and on to rocks through trees.

292 Echo Cliffs ✫✫✫

These 200′ pocketed volcanic overhanging walls, caves, and arêtes extend for ½ mi. of pumping pleasure. Sixty-meter rope advisable. Santa Monica National Recreational Area.

Classics: Morning Glory 9, Bushed Coyote arête 10, Java 11d, Stain 12.

Ref: R 82-92; Guidebook: Edwards's *Rock Climbing Santa Barbara and Ventura.*

Directions: From Los Angeles escape on Hwy. 101 (Ventura Hwy.) northwest to Westlake Blvd. exit. Turn south on Hwy. 23 (Mulholland Hwy.). Turn right (west) on Mulholland for a short ways to a right turn onto Little Sycamore Canyon Rd. for 4 mi. to Triunfo Pass. Find the Mishe Mokwa Trailhead on right. Park. Hike forty-five minutes on Mishe Mokwa trail for 1 ⁷/₁₀ mi. Continue just 100′ past Split Rock, turning right on Access Fund Trail to cliffs.

293 SB–The Pinnacles (aka Coyote Crags)/North Shore Areas ✫✫✫

Climbed since the 1930s, these beautiful 100′ granite walls north of Big Bear Lake offer quality bouldering and sport cragging. Spring–autumn. Camping abounds. USFS–San Bernardino NF, (909) 884–6634.

Ref: R 69-88; Guidebooks: Bartlett's *Oso Grande,* Hoffman's *Big Bear Valley: Climbing Routes of Southern California,* Hellweg and Warstler's *Climber's Guide to Southern California.*

Directions: From Big Bear City go north on Hwy. 18 to junction with Hwy. 38. For North Shore Areas continue due north on Greenway to Pioneer Lane. Turn west 2 blocks and park. Bouldering all along Pioneer Lane. For The Pinnacles turn west on Hwy. 38. Turn north on Van Dusen Canyon Rd. Turn east on 3N16. Turn north on 3N32 for 1 mi. Turn left (southwest) down jeep trail for ⅓ mi. to rocks.

294 Happy/Sad Boulders ✫✫✫✫

Bishop's well-publicized and well-developed 30′ volcanic bouldering fields. Hundreds of routes and counting with many areas being developed. The West's winter alternative bouldering area. BLM, (916) 978–4400.

Classics: Sun Fire Majestic V0, Big Chicken V2, Mono Rail V3, many more.

Ref: M. Ryan; C [186-84, 185-28, 182-58 (topo)], R [92-39, 83-98].

Directions: From Bishop head north on Hwy. 395. Turn right on Rte. 6 for 1 mi., then left on Five Bridges Rd. to Gravel Works. Unpaved road splits in three; take left fork, Chalk Bluff Rd., for 2 ³/₁₀ mi. to parking area. Boulders are up the canyon across from the parking area. More bouldering areas are farther along Chalk Bluff Rd. including Chalk Bluff–Honorary Grit, Sacred Boulders, Pleasant Valley, as is Pleasant Valley Campground. Check with locals.

295 Druid Stones

Granite bouldering noted for the 70′ boulder known as the Druid Stone.

Ref: R 92-43.

Directions: Just west of Bishop. Take Hwy. 168. Turn left on Barlow Lane. Turn right on Chipmunk Canyon Rd. Turn left on second power line road, then first right. Park at corral. At second switchback, hike trail west uphill, then east. Forty-minute steep hike. Ask locals.

296 The Ashtray

Basalt bouldering. The Ashtray Boulder is a steep chunk of basalt not far from Truckee with a handful of classic, overhanging problems.

Classics: The Funk V8.

Ref: Rock and Ice online.

Directions: Near Truckee.

297 Rocklin Quarry ✫✫✫

Excellent basalt bouldering area with 15′ finger cracks, thin face climbs, and slabs on twenty to thirty routes.

Ref: S. Gallo.

Directions: Exit Hwy. 80 in East Roseville. Head east on Eureka Rd. Turn left on Taylor Rd. for 2 mi. Area is on left past Jiffy Lube.

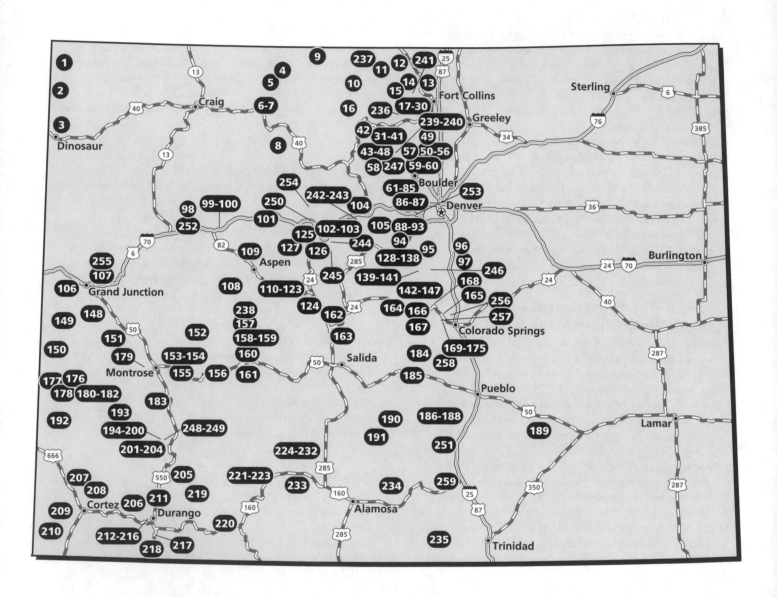

1
2
3 Dinosaur

13
4
5
6-7
Craig
40
13
8
40

9
237 11 12 241
10 14 13
15
16 236 17-30
239-240
42 31-41 49
43-48 57 50-56
58 247 59-60
Boulder
61-85
86-87
25
87
Fort Collins
Greeley
Sterling
6
76
385
34

254
242-243
104
98 99-100
252 250
101
125 102-103 105
127 126 244
109 245
Aspen
285
108 110-123
124
162
163
238
157
158-159
152
160
155 156 161
50
Salida
253
Denver
88-93
94
95
128-138
139-141
142-147
164 166
167
184
258
185
96
97 246
168
165
256
257
Colorado Springs
169-175
Pueblo
36
Burlington
24 70
40
24
50
287
Lamar

255
107
106 Grand Junction
149 148
150
151
179
153-154
Montrose
177 176
178 180-182 183
192
193
194-200
201-204
666
207
208
206 211
Cortez 209
210
205
219
212-216
218 217
220
550
221-223
233
248-249
224-232
285
160
160
Alamosa
285
190
191
234
259
25
87
186-188
251
189
235
Trinidad
50
350
287

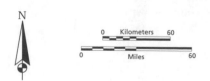

N

0 Kilometers 60
0 Miles 60

Colorado

Colorado

Just a reminder—this guide book is no substitute for skill, experience, judgment, or lots of tension. —From Charlie Fowler's *Telluride Rock*

From bouldering to big walls, sport crags to traditional strongholds, alpine cliffs to desert spires, Colorado is rich with rock. In addition, there's the scenic splendor of the Rocky Mountains, more than 250 climbing areas, and fifty-five peaks more than 14,000' tall. The only thing missing is sea cliffs. In the entire Lower 48, perhaps only California can match Colorado for diversity and number of climbing areas.

The Front Range sees the most climbing action due to its proximity to the growing megalopolis of Colorado Springs–Denver–Boulder–Ft. Collins.

Smooth, firm Dakota sandstone brings boulderers from across the nation to Ft. Collins's Horsetooth Reservoir. It's the state's premiere bouldering area and home of many legendary John Gill problems.

Perhaps no city has a higher per capita population of climbers than Boulder. Also, no city has such a variety and volume of nearby rock to climb. Boulder is blessed with a heap of granite crags up Boulder Canyon, the 1,000' sandstone Flatirons dominating the vista west of town, and world-famous Eldorado Canyon just 8 mi. to the south. The city is home to Colorado's climbing glitterati and also Colorado's most "politically correct." A long, rich history of climbing has taken place in the Boulder area, and visitors will find plenty to keep them occupied for as long as they stay, assuming they find somewhere to stay. Boulder is notoriously short on camping facilities.

Denver is fortunate to have the choice sandstone bouldering of Morrison, sport climbing at Clear Creek, and the expansive South Platte region of granite domes and pinnacles so close at hand.

Colorado Springs captivates the climber with two spellbinding landmarks: Garden of the Gods and Pike's Peak. The Garden's fantastically carved fins are beautiful to look at but terrifying to climb. At 14,110', Pike's Peak is home to splitter granite cracks that will pump the lungs as well as the arms.

South of Pike's Peak are the popular sport crags at Shelf Road, not far from the state pen at Canon City, and Penitente Canyon near Del Norte. Shelf Road is limestone, Penitente volcanic. If you drool over tips and clips, these are the crags for you.

Looking to the heights, The Diamond on Longs Peak rates tops over any other alpine wall in the state. Rocky Mountain National Park has many other alpine walls, as well as the conveniently accessible domes and buttresses of Lumpy Ridge. The serious nature of most routes in the park has helped keep it a traditionalist stronghold. For less serious amusement there's nearby Estes Park with its tourist hotels, trinket shops, and wax museums.

Speaking of mountain resorts, rich and ritzy Aspen and laid back (except for the prices) Telluride provide fun summer cragging and high mountain scenery.

For grade VI action on the big stones, try some of the Black Canyon's petrifying, metamorphic nail-ups. Heat, thirst, rockfall, big run-outs, and sheer difficulty make for a high failure to success ratio in the United States's steepest canyon. This is also home to the state's longest free climbs and most densely choked poison ivy descent gullies.

The West Slope has lots of desert-style sandstone climbing, though it's not nearly as famous or popular as Utah's nearby Canyonlands arena. Colorado National Monument and Dinosaur National Monument play host to climbing intrigue.

The semiarid climate combined with elevations ranging from 4,000' to 14,000' means there's an area ripe for climbing at any time of the year. Climbers have known this for a long time, giving Colorado one of the richest climbing histories of any state.

Colorado . . . if the summer thunderstorms or the occasional 100 mph Front Range winds don't blow you away, the climbing will!

1 Dinosaur National Monument–Brown's Park ★★

Eighteen-foot bouldering walls to spectacular 800' walls above the Green River. This remote (and can you say arid?) western national monument is better known for its world-class dinosaur fossils and white-water floats than rock climbing. Yet, you might dig the uncovered sandstone bouldering/short topropes in the Brown's Park Area of Dinosaur, where most white-water enthusiasts start off down the Green River. Autumn/spring. Private land/NPS, (435) 789-2115.

Classics: Steamboat Rock 9 A4, Emily's Crack 7, Warm Springs Bouldering.

Ref: B. Sautell; R 20(1/87).

Directions: From Dinosaur go 15 mi. north on Harper's Corner Rd. to Dinosaur National Monument. Or, from Maybell, go west on Hwy. 318 to Brown's Park. Bouldering can be found near the Gates of Lodore put-in or Warm Springs Campground on the Yampa. Cragging exists off Hwy. 318 or Irish Canyon.

2 Dinosaur National Monument–Steamboat Rock ★★★

Steamboat Rock V 5.9 A4 is a serious 700′ sandstone formation ascent first ascended by Layton Kor, Michael Covington, and Brian Marts in 1965. Short climbing season due to park restrictions. Ascent parties should check with rangers prior to an attempt for water-level conditions. Autumn/spring. NPS, (435) 789-2115.

Classics: Kor Route 5.9 A4.

Ref: B. Sautell; AAJ '66-146; R 20(1/87); Kor's *Beyond the Vertical.*

Directions: From Dinosaur drive north on Harper's Corner Rd. to Echo Park (four-wheel-drive road). Most attempts use boat to cross Green River at Echo Park to climb on Steamboat Rock. Or from Vernal go northeast on Hwy. 121 to rock located at Echo Park.

3 Plug Hat ★

Soft, white, 50′ sandstone bluffs stand as portals to Dinosaur National Monument outback. Autumn/spring. NPS, (435) 789-2115.

Ref: R 20(1/87).

Directions: From Dinosaur plug east on Hwy. 40 a couple miles. Turn left into Dinosaur National Monument and continue north for approximately 4 mi. where road cuts mesa. Plug Hat is white-cliffed mesa en route to Echo Park.

4 Hole in the Wall ★★★

Two-hundred-and-fifty-foot granite crags with bouldering. Leads and topropes from 5.7–5.12 on one- to three-pitch buttresses. Mt. Zirkel Wilderness is nearby to east. Summer. USFS–Routt NF, (970) 638-4516.

Classics: Siamese Twins 8+, Walmart–The Grand Opening 9+, Discount Heroism 11c.

Ref: Guidebooks: Breslaw and Dennis's *Steamboat Springs Rock Guide,* Breslaw and Dennis's *Saurian Detours.*

Directions: From Steamboat Springs (approximately 25 mi. total distance), romp north on Hwy. 129 to hamlet of Clark. Then just past town go northeast on 400 (Seedhouse Rd.) for 8 ¾ mi. Turn north (left) on four-wheel-drive road 431 (Diamond Park) before bridge to sometimes-locked gate (usually until July 1). Hole in the Wall Rock is 1 mi. past gate. Hang a left at fork in meadows where rock is visible.

5 Box Canyon ★★★

One-hundred-and-seventy-foot, south-facing granite crag. A couple handfuls of routes mostly 5.10 or the classic, Steel Nuts 5.8. Summer. USFS–Routt NF, (970) 638-4516.

Ref: Guidebooks: Breslaw and Dennis's *Steamboat Springs Rock Guide,* Breslaw and Dennis's *Saurian Detours.*

Directions: From Steamboat Springs (approximately 25 mi. total distance), romp north on Hwy. 129 to hamlet of Clark. Then just past town, go northeast on 400 (Seedhouse Rd.) for 8 ½ mi. Park on right at pullout. Box Canyon Rock adjacent.

6 Butcherknife ★★★

Good 30′ granite crag for a short toprope session. About six routes from 5.9–5.11c. You'll dispose of this fun area faster than a Bic shaver. Summer. City park.

Ref: Guidebooks: Breslaw and Dennis's *Steamboat Springs Rock Guide,* Breslaw and Dennis's *Saurian Detours.*

Directions: In Steamboat Springs. Follow Missouri Ave. east to Stehley Park, a small city park. Park where it makes a hard left. Hike dirt trail over bridge approximately 50 yd. to Butcherknife.

7 Blob Rock ★★★

A 30′ granite mini crag with bouldering. Enough rock for a few hours' worth of crankin', but good climbing with four short routes, like Tendon Tester 5.10d, from 5.7–5.11. Summer. USFS–Routt NF, (970) 638-4516.

Ref: Guidebooks: Breslaw and Dennis's *Steamboat Springs Rock Guide,* Breslaw and Dennis's *Saurian Detours.*

Directions: From Steamboat Springs go east of town to Fish Creek Falls. Before the parking for Fish Creek Falls, hike up two-track uranium mine trail on left for one steep ½ mi. to Blob Rock. Faces southeast.

8 The Domes/Silver Dome ★★★

A half-dozen 350′ granite domes with classics like Wings of Steel 5.11a on The Dome in the forest. At least seventy routes in the 5.6–5.11 range. Raptor restrictions April–July. Summer. USFS–Routt NF, (970) 638-4516.

Classics: The Dome: Wings of Steel 11a; Meadow Rock: Gluteus Maximus 10d.

Ref: Guidebooks: Breslaw and Dennis's *Steamboat Springs Rock Guide,* Breslaw and Dennis's *Saurian Detours.*

Directions: East of Steamboat Springs between Rabbit Ears Pass and Buffalo Park. From Steamboat Springs go south on Hwy. 40 toward Walden. Turn south on FR 100 (Buffalo Park Rd.). After 10 mi., park by cairn/flagging. Hike 1 ½ mi. west to The Domes. The Silver Dome is another 7 mi. south on FR 100. Park at Silver Creek Trailhead. Hike about 3 mi. west on Silver Creek Trail. Then cross-country to visible dome on ridge. Silver Dome has about ten routes up to 5.10.

9 Fugate Ranch ✫✫

These 50' crags with bouldering offer face and crack climbs on scattered granite outcrops near the highway and on the hillsides. Summer. Private land/USFS–Routt NF, (970) 638-4516.

Directions: From Walden plod north on Hwy. 125. Fugate Ranch is just past the junction of Hwy. 125 and Hwy. 127. Access to distant rocks possible via FR 896 and various others.

10 Rawah Range (Medicine Bows) ✫✫

Scattered granite outcrops near road and on ridge. Summer. Private land/USFS–Routt NF, (970) 638-4516.

Ref: Guidebook: Ormes's *Guide to the Colorado Mountains.*

Directions: From Walden, Rawah Range is the mountain range to east. Access from Hwy. 14 or Hwy. 27.

11 Red Feather Lakes Area (Creedmore Crag and Cinco de Mayo) ✫✫✫

Scattered 150' granite formations on open wooded slopes hold fine summertime climbing. Many fine 5.10–5.11 cracks. Fun exploratory area. USFS–Roosevelt NF, (970) 498-1100.

Classics: 3 Times a Lady 10, Mama Grande 11-, Brink of Madness 11, Another Form of Worship 11.

Ref: C. Luebben; Guidebook: Brink's *A Climber's Guide to Creedmore Crag and Cinco de Mayo.*

Directions: Northwest of Ft. Collins. From Ft. Collins drive north on Hwy. 287 to Livermore. Bear left (at sign) on Red Feather Lakes Rd. and continue onto Red Feather Lakes. (Creedmore Lake is approximately 5 mi. north of Red Feather Lakes.) Go north on 73C Rd. (Prairie Divide Rd.) to a left onto FR 181, which leads to Creedmore Lake. Hike to north ridge of lake for Creedmore Crag. From here, hike cross-country west across north fork of Poudre River to Cinco de Mayo Crag.

12 Virginia Dale Area (Haystack Mountain) ✫✫✫

Two-hundred-foot granite crags and boulders. A lifetime of potential climbing, but most land is privately owned by ranchers. Rock quality varies greatly between formations. Private land.

Classics: Circus Circus (roof crack) 12+.

Ref: T. Skinner, B. Scarpelli; Guidebook: Ormes's *Guide to the Colorado Mountains.*

Directions: Virginia Dale to Colorado/Wyoming border. From Wyoming/Colorado border go approximately 4 mi. south on Hwy. 287. A lot of rock exists along the highway. Haystack Mountain (200') is reached west of Virginia Dale, 2 mi. south of 2 Bar 7 Ranch.

13 Highway 287 Boulders (closed) ✫✫✫

Miles of privately owned Dakota sandstone hogbacks and blocks north of Ft. Collins visible along Hwy. 287, starting a few miles north of Hwy. 14. Many areas. Private ranchland—closed to climbing.

Ref: M. Wilford/J. Shireman.

14 Greyrock Mountain ✫✫✫✫

Quality 500' granite crags with more than one hundred routes 5.5–5.12, like The Greatest Route at Greyrock 5.8, above the scenic Poudre River Canyon. Details in Luebben's *A Rock Climber's Guide to Greyrock.* Visible from Ft. Collins to the northwest. Summer/autumn. USFS–Roosevelt NF, (970) 498-1100.

Classics: Simon 6, Sky Crack 7, Greatest Route at Greyrock 8, Mr. Gone 10, Jaminy Crackit 11d, Crago Corner 12a, Armed Response 12b.

Ref: C [156-66, 99], R 37(6/90)-47; Guidebooks: Green's *Rock Climbing Colorado*, Luebben's *A Rock Climber's Guide to Greyrock*, Ormes's *Guide to the Colorado Mountains.*

Directions: From La Porte (junction of Hwy. 287 and Hwy. 14), drive 8 1/2 mi. west on Hwy. 14. Park. Cross Poudre River. Hike north one hour up switchbacks on hiker's trail to Greyrock Mountain.

15 Poudre Canyon ✫✫✫

Miles and piles of 200' granite pinnacles, walls, and boulders . . . under attack. Fifty cool routes in 1993, like The Odyssey 5.11+. Greyrock is the biggest (and possibly most frequented) climbing area of the Poudre River Canyon areas. This white-water river canyon is in danger of being "damned" . . . Save the Poudre! Autumn/spring. USFS–Roosevelt NF, (970) 498-1100.

Classics: East of Eden 9, Sorcerer's Apprentice 11b, The Odyssey 11+, Fantastic Planet 9+/11c, Crossing Over 12b.

Ref: C. Luebben; C 72-6, R 54; Guidebooks: Benningfield's *Colorado Bouldering*, Hubbel's *Front Range Crags.*

Directions: From Ft. Collins pop 10 mi. north on Hwy. 287. From junction of Hwy. 14 and Hwy. 287, mileages are Greyrock (trailhead), 8 1/2 mi. (see previous entry, Number 14); Pine Vu (The Odyssey 5.11+), 9 1/10 mi.; Mishawaka Inn, 14 mi.; Crystal Wall (Fantastic Planet 9+/11c), 14 9/10 mi.; RA's Buttress (Sorcerer's Apprentice 11b), 18 7/10 mi.; Eden (East of Eden 9), 19 1/2 mi. Hatchery Rocks Bouldering area is 7 mi. past Hwy. 69 on right. Classic B5.12 problems next to road.

16 Nokhu Crags (Never Summer Range) ✫✫

Five-hundred-foot limestone/granite alpine crags. Climbing on jagged spires of badly weathered rock. These are the northernmost peaks of the Never Summer Range. Summer. Colorado State Forest land.

Ref: S 6/78; Delorme's *Colorado Atlas and Gazetteer*; Guidebook: Ormes's *Guide to the Colorado Mountains.*

Directions: From Gould go east on Hwy. 14 until west of Cameron Pass. Then go southwest 2 mi. on trails to Nokhu Crags.

17 Arthur's Rock (in Lory State Park) ⭐⭐

One-hundred-foot granite crag/bouldering. High granite formations at Lory State Park with an A3 route (and maybe a few bolted leads). Autumn/spring. State park, (970) 493–1623.

Directions: From Ft. Collins head 5 mi. west into Lory State Park. Hike twenty minutes up trail to the obvious Arthur's Rock.

18 Horsetooth Rock (Horsetooth Mountain Park) ⭐

Famous triple-toothed Ft. Collins landmark for which the Reservoir was named features this 300′ pegmatite granite crag. Routes are on west face. Not very popular with climbers, unlike the sandstone bouldering below at Horsetooth Reservoir. Private land/Larimer County Park, (970) 498–7000.

Ref: C. Luebben; Guidebook: Ormes's *Guide to the Colorado Mountains.*

Directions: From Ft. Collins go west around south end of Horsetooth Reservoir, then ³⁄4 mi. west of marina. Park at Horsetooth Mountain Park trailhead at top of hill. Hike up to Horsetooth Rock.

19 North Quarry and Horsetooth Reservoir Overview ⭐⭐⭐⭐

North Quarry area is a quarried sandstone area with tough problems like Magazine Face B1 and Cinch B2. Horsetooth Reservoir holds many areas of 40′ sandstone face bouldering in its 7 mi. of Dakota sandstone hogbacks on the east side of reservoir. Rotary Park is most famous area. Historic Gill, Holloway, Mammen, Wilford, and Sherman problems. The Tropics on LaPorte St. stay warmest in winter. Rock near south end is privately owned and closed to climbing. Camping at KOA in La Porte. Autumn/spring. Private land/Larimer County Park, (970) 498–7000.

Classics: Quarry: Motion Picture Slab B1, Magazine Face B1, Cinch B2; Torture Chamber: Torture Chamber traverse B1, Borgman's Bulge B1+, Nemesis Tower B2 toprope; Rotary Park: Mental Block Std Rt B1, Talent Scout B1+, Pinch Rt B2-, Eliminator Right B1, Left B1+, Meathook B3.

Ref: C [194-42, 161-44, 160(5/96)-98, 152-42, 130(2/92)-52, 128(10/91)-74, 67(7/81)], M 91, R 6(1/85), Sherman's *Stone Crusade,* Ament's *Master of Rock;* Guidebooks: Benningfield's *Colorado Bouldering,* Horan's *Front Range Bouldering: Ft. Collins Area,* Horan's *Front Range Bouldering, Horsetooth Hang Competition Guides.*

Directions: From Ft. Collins trot ten minutes west of town to several areas, mainly on the east side of Horsetooth Reservoir along Centennial Dr. (CR 23), described below. For North Quarry area: From Ft. Collins go west to the northwest side of Horsetooth Reservoir parking before entrance gate and road into Lory State Park. Hike down on faint path/gully past house/stable to classic corners and arêtes.

20 Horsetooth Reservoir–The Tropics (destroyed) ⭐⭐⭐

Once the most easily accessed and busiest bouldering area at Horsetooth, The Tropics has been destroyed.

Classics: Paradise Roof 10, The Arête B1, Roof B2, Triple A, Mega Traverse 5.12; Power Rock problems.

Ref: Guidebooks: Benningfield's *Colorado Bouldering,* Horan's *Front Range Bouldering: Ft. Collins Area,* Horan's *Front Range Bouldering, Horsetooth Hang Competition Guides.*

21 Horsetooth Reservoir—Land of Overhangs and Scoop Area ⭐⭐⭐

Twenty-five-foot sandstone bouldering wall. Variety of roof problems and face climbs, e.g., The Scoop B1. Larimer County Park, (970) 498–7000.

Classics: Scoop Area: The Scoop B1, Master of Disaster B1+; Land of Overhangs: Flakey Overhang B5.10, The Overhang.

Ref: Guidebooks: Benningfield's *Colorado Bouldering,* Horan's *Front Range Bouldering: Ft. Collins Area,* Horan's *Front Range Bouldering, Horsetooth Hang Competition Guides.*

Directions: From Ft. Collins follow Drake west. Turn right on Overland Trail, then turn left before CSU stadium on CR 42C up to Horsetooth Reservoir. At junction, go right for 1 ³⁄10 mi. along reservoir on Centennial, then up steep hill to parking pullout on left, which is for Rotary Park. Continue 1 mi. north to Sunrise Group Day Use Parking for Scoop Area. Hike south from car. Land of Overhangs is ⁶⁄10 mi. (2 ⁹⁄10 from junction) farther north from Scoop Area at a pullout on left and angler's sign. Rocks to west. Or, one can walk up from Tropics to southwest. Faces west.

22 Horsetooth Reservoir–Rotary Park ⭐⭐⭐⭐

Classic 35′ sandstone bouldering walls and blocks. The heart of the Horsetooth bouldering became famous with Pat Ament's book, *Master of Rock.* Many world-class bouldering routes such as John Gill's Mental Block B1 and The Eliminators B1s, Jim Holloway's Meathook Problem B3, and John Sherman's Mental Block Traverse. Larimer County Park, (970) 498–7000.

Classics: Rotary Park: Mental Block Std Rt B1, Talent Scout B1+, Pinch Rt B2-; Eliminator: Right B1/Left B1+, Meathook B3.

Ref: Guidebooks: Benningfield's *Colorado Bouldering,* Horan's *Front Range Bouldering: Ft. Collins Area,* Horan's *Front Range Bouldering, Horsetooth Hang Competition Guides.*

Directions: From Ft. Collins follow Drake west. Turn right on Overland Trail. Then turn left before CSU stadium on CR 42C road up to Horsetooth Reservoir. At junction, go right for 1 ²⁄10 mi. along reservoir on Centennial Dr. up steep hill to large parking pullout on left. Boulders below to the west. Formations and boulders include: The Ship's Prow, Bolt Wall, Pitch Penny Boulder, Mental Block, Meditation Boulder, Eliminator, and The Talent Scout. Faces west.

23 Horsetooth Reservoir–Sunshine Boulder/Marina Ridge ★★★

Twenty-five-foot west-facing sandstone bouldering walls and blocks. Nice views of the lake from the Sunshine Boulder. Private land/Larimer County Park, (970) 498-7000.

Classics: Sunshine Boulder: Standard Route B1, Muscle Undercling B1+, Piano Boulder Traverse B1.

Ref: Guidebooks: Benningfield's *Colorado Bouldering*, Horan's *Front Range Bouldering: Ft. Collins Area*, Horan's *Front Range Bouldering, Horsetooth Hang Competition Guides*.

Directions: From Ft. Collins follow Drake west. Turn right on Overland Trail. Then turn left before CSU stadium on CR 42C up to Horsetooth Reservoir. At junction, go left on Centennial Dr. uphill ⁴/10 mi. to SAIL N' SADDLE sign. Park on road and walk west down private drive very briefly, switching to trail to large Sunshine Boulder. Piano Boulder is ⁶/10 mi. farther south along road. On left. Faces west.

24 Horsetooth Reservoir–Duncan's Ridge ★★★

Extensive waterside 40′ sandstone band with good topropes/leads and limited bouldering starting at lake level. Water levels may hinder access. Larimer County Park, (970) 498-7000.

Classics: Leaning Cling B1-, Layaway B1, Regular Line 5.10.

Ref: R 70-84; Guidebooks: Benningfield's *Colorado Bouldering*, Horan's *Front Range Bouldering: Ft. Collins Area*, Horan's *Front Range Bouldering, Horsetooth Hang Competition Guides*.

Directions: From Ft. Collins follow Horsetooth Rd. west to Centennial Dr. At T intersection, turn right onto Centennial Dr., immediately crossing Spring Creek Dam. Park at north end of dam. Duncan's Ridge sits adjacent to waterline west of road. Faces southwest.

25 Horsetooth Reservoir–Torture Chamber ★★★★

Twenty-foot sandstone bouldering walls with good traverses, straight up bouldering, and toprope problems. The Torture Chamber Traverse B1 will drop the gas gauge on any climber's forearms. Larimer County Park, (970) 498-7000.

Classics: Torture Chamber Traverse B1, Borgman's Bulge B1+, Nemesis Tower B2.

Ref: Guidebooks: Benningfield's *Colorado Bouldering*, Horan's *Front Range Bouldering: Ft. Collins Area*, Horan's *Front Range Bouldering, Horsetooth Hang Competition Guides*.

Directions: From Ft. Collins follow Horsetooth Rd. (38E) west to Horsetooth Reservoir Rd. Torture Chamber is east of dam, just before (east of) the T intersection and Spring Creek Dam. A dangerous parking pullout sits at the entrance to this long bouldering band pointing downhill into Ft. Collins. Faces northwest.

26 Horsetooth Reservoir–Southeast Reservoir (closed) ★★★

Long 30′ sandstone cliffband with blocks below. Class problems exist like Flute Boulder B2, but this is private land—stay off!

Ref: Guidebooks: Benningfield's *Colorado Bouldering*, Horan's *Front Range Bouldering: Ft. Collins Area*, Horan's *Front Range Bouldering, Horsetooth Hang Competition Guides*.

Directions: From Ft. Collins follow Horsetooth Rd. west to Horsetooth Reservoir Rd. Go straight through T intersection onto CR 38E to southeast end of Horsetooth Reservoir. Boulders at South Reservoir's studded hillside lead up east to short cliffband. Faces southeast.

27 Chastine's Grove (closed) ★★★

One-hundred-foot granite crag presents face and crack challenges like Spinal Tap 5.13aX. Illegal, though good climbing. Climbers have been kicked out since 1990. Private land.

Ref: C. Luebben.

Directions: West of Loveland. Faces south.

28 Big Thompson River Canyon Areas ★★★

Metamorphic/granite bouldering/crags. Broken cliffs throughout canyon yield some classic lines, i.e., The White Dike 5.10R (obvious white dike across highway). Site of killer flash flood in early 1976. Autumn/spring. Private land/USFS-Roosevelt NF, (970) 498-1100.

Directions: Multitude of crags along Hwy. 34 between Estes Park and Loveland. Center of the Universe crags, ½ mi. up Big Thompson River Canyon on the right, features Massive Synapsial Response 5.11. Palisade Mountain is 13 mi. west of Loveland.

29 Combat Rock ★★★

An excellent 250′ granite buttress that is really fine face climbing and its own area exclusive of Estes Park. About twenty great routes like Eight Clicks to Saigon 5.10+. Good in winter, too. USFS-Roosevelt NF, (970) 498-1100.

Classics: Front Lines 10, Eight Clicks to Saigon 10+, Pearl Harbor 10d, Lizzard Warrior 11b, Blood for Oil 12a; Cedar Park Slab: Dogs in Beanland 8.

Ref: C 89, R 54 (topo); Guidebooks: Green's *Rock Climbing Colorado*, Hubbel's *Front Range Crags*, Gillet's *Rocky Mountain National Park Climber's Guide*, Kimball's *Lumpy Ridge*.

Directions: From Estes Park go 15 mi. east on Hwy. 34 to Drake. At Drake, go northwest on the Glenhaven exit. Turn right on the first dirt (forest access) road, ascending a series of switchbacks. Combat Rock is on west (left) side of road and faces south. Park on left at flat spot past small hilltop. Ten-minute approach. Elmer Fudd's Wok and S&M Wall are short walls just north of Combat Rock on same side of road. Faces south.

30 Cedar Park Slab ⭐⭐

Six-hundred-foot granite slab north of Combat Rock.
Couple beginner slab routes. Access is through private
property. Summer. USFS–Roosevelt NF, (970) 498–1100.
Ref: Guidebook: Hubbel's *Front Range Crags*.
Directions: From Estes Park go 15 mi. east on Hwy. 34 to
Drake. At Drake, go northwest on the Glenhaven exit.
Turn right on the first dirt (forest access) road, ascending
a series of switchbacks passing Combat Rock. Cedar Park
Slab is farther north in Roosevelt National Forest in
Cedar Park to west (visible from I-25). Easiest approach
via private property crossing (get permission). Faces
south.

31 Estes Park Area Overview–Sheep Mountain Rock ⭐⭐⭐

Sheep Mountain is a 350′ granite crag with multipitched
climbs like Double Fantasy 5.10a. Estes Park is the eastern
gateway to Rocky Mountain National Park and a host of
climbing areas. In summer, tourism is king and climbers
can expect a multitude of vacationers, shops, fantastic
scenery, and climbing areas. On Sheep Mountain, peregrine
falcon nesting may determine the climbing season; check
with park service. Camping in Rocky Mountain National
Park at Moraine Park. Summer/autumn. NPS, (970)
586–1206.
Classics: Double Fantasy 10a 3p; Gimmerton Corner 10b.
Ref: G. Asp, R. Joseph; AAJ '83, C 58; Mountaineering in
Colorado: Peaks about Estes Park; Guidebooks: Gillette's
Rocky Mountain National Park Climber's Guide, Kimball's
Lumpy Ridge, Harlin's *Rocky Mountain*, Bradley and
Hickeman's *Climber's Guide to Estes Park Area*, Ormes's
Guide to the Colorado Mountains, Fricke's *Climber's Guide to
Rocky Mountain National Park Area*.
Directions: For Sheep Mountain Rock: From Estes Park go
4 mi. north on Devils Gulch Rd., then go left on McGraw
Ranch Rd. to Rocky Mountain National Park Trailhead.
Go west to crag on right. A thirty-minute hike (½ mi.).
Faces south.

32 Estes Park Area–Eagle Rock ⭐⭐

A two-hundred-foot beginner granite slab. For those want-
ing easy routes near Estes Park like Spread Eagle 5.7 and
Left Dihedral. Summer. May be adventure trespassing (i.e.,
if you hear shots, duck). Private land.
Ref: Guidebooks: Gillet's *Rocky Mountain National Park
Climber's Guide*, Kimball's *Lumpy Ridge*, Fricke's *A Climber's
Guide to Rocky Mountain National Park Area*.
Directions: From Estes Park motor 1 mi. east on Hwy. 34 to
Dry Gulch Rd. Turn left for 1 ½ mi. Or, from Loveland,
go west on Hwy. 34 and north on Dry Gulch Rd. for 1 ½
mi. Crag on right. Eagle Rock is 1 mi. east of Alligator
Rock. Faces southwest.

33 Estes Park Area–Lumpy Ridge (Crescent Wall and Twin Owls) ⭐⭐⭐⭐

An intricate area of 600′ granite crags with boulders below.
Multiple formations along the stunning, rock-studded
ridge north of Estes Park include: Alligator Rock, Out West,
and Crescent Wall. From Old Parking Lot: Triangle Rock,
Gollum's Arch, Twin Owls, Rock One, Flounder Rock,
Christmas Crag, Checkerboard, Batman, Lightning, Book,
Bookmark, Lens, Pear, Sunshine, Citadel, Observ-atory,
Thunder Buttress, Parish, and Sundance. Incredible views
of Rocky Mountain National Park. Frequent summit visits
by lightning bolts. Limited parking, so arrive early on sum-
mer weekends. Good bouldering along Gem Lake Trail.
Check raptor restrictions. NPS, (970) 586–1206.
Classics: The Book: Osiris 7, Pear Buttress 8+, J Crack 9,
Thindependence 10c, Fat City 10c, Howling . . . 11b,
Corner Pump Station 11c, Dead Boy Dir. 11d, El Camino
Real 12c; Twin Owls: Wolf's Tooth 8, Crack of Fear 10+;
Crescent Wall: Conads 9, Finger Lickin' Good 11a,
Pressure Drop 11a, Flight for Life 12a; Bookmark:
Fantasy Ridge 9; L. Book: White Whale 7; Batman Rock:
Batman and Robin 6, Bat Crack 9; Checkerboard: Ziggie's
Day Out 10d; The Pear: Magical 6; Turnkorner 10b, The
Nose 10b; Kor's Flake 7+; Bouldering: Jaws V3.
Ref: AAJ '91-175, C [150, 126, 111, 110, 106, 104, 102, 99,
91, 88, 79(8/83)-22, 72, 71, 69, 66(5/81)-26, 67, 64, 63,
56], R [95-40, 68-44, 67-20], S 9/84; on-line guide
http://climbingboulder.com; Guidebooks: Benningfield's
Colorado Bouldering, Green's *Rock Climbing Colorado*, *Rocky
Mountain National Park: The Crag Areas*, Gillet's *Rocky
Mountain National Park Climber's Guide*, Kimball's *Lumpy
Ridge Estes Park Rock Climbs*, Harlin's *Rocky Mountain*,
Salaun and Kimball's *Thath-aa-ai-atah*, Ormes's *Guide to the
Colorado Mountains*, Fricke's *A Climber's Guide to Rocky
Mountain National Park Area*.
Directions: From Estes Park go 2 mi. north on Devils Gulch
Rd., then go left to Gem Lake Trailhead.

34 Estes Park Area–Hagermeister Boulders (aka Kingstone Boulders) (closed) ⭐⭐⭐

Forty-foot granite boulders in the pines. Historic John Gill
problems lost to housing development. Closed to climbing.
Private land.
Classics: Right Standard 6, Lubrication 9R.
Ref: Ament's *Master of Rock;* Guidebooks: Salaun and
Kimball's *Thath-aa-ai-atah*, Fricke's *A Climber's Guide to
Rocky Mountain National Park Area*.
Directions: In Estes Park, go uphill from Stanley Hotel in
housing development.

35 Estes Park Area–McGregor's Slab ⭐⭐

An array of 600′ granite slab climbs with about eight inter-
mediate routes. Private land/USFS–Roosevelt NF, (970)
498–1100.
Ref: S 5/88; Guidebooks: *Rocky Mountain National Park: The
Crag Areas*, Gillet's *Rocky Mountain National Park Climber's
Guide*, Kimball's *Lumpy Ridge*, Salaun and Kimball's *Thath-*

aa-ai-atah, Fricke's *A Climber's Guide to Rocky Mountain National Park Area.*

Directions: From Estes Park go west on Hwy. 34 to NPS Village. Park. McGregor's Slab is on north side of road, just east of Fall River entrance. Thirty-minute approach to hillside above Hwy. 34. Go through NPS campground and follow faint trail up left side of gully to right side of slab. Faces south.

36 Estes Park Area–Deer Ridge Buttress
★★

A 450' granite crag with beginner/intermediate routes. Concave wall of alpine granite in northwest flank of Deer Mountain. It sits across valley from McGregor's Slab. There are about eleven routes up to five pitches in length, e.g., Nun Buttress 5.8. NPS, (970) 586–1206.
Ref: C 64, S 5/88; Guidebooks: Gillet's *Rocky Mountain National Park Climber's Guide*, Kimball's *Lumpy Ridge*, Fricke's *A Climber's Guide to Rocky Mountain National Park Area.*
Directions: From Estes Park bound 6 mi. west on Hwy. 34. Turn left on Fish Hatchery Rd. Park at end of road. Deer Ridge Buttress is 1 mi. before park entrance. Approach: Forty-five-minute uphill. Faces northwest.

37 Estes Park Area–Castle Rock and The Window ★★

Two-hundred-and-fifty-foot granite crags with 5.10 routes. Private land.
Classics: Church Bells 10.
Ref: Guidebooks: Gillet's *Rocky Mountain National Park Climber's Guide*, Kimball's *Lumpy Ridge.*
Directions: From Estes Park spurt 2 mi. west on Hwy. 34. Castle Rock and The Window are on right above intersection of Hwy. 34 and west Elkhorn Drive.

38 Estes Park Area–The Thumb and The Needle ★★★

Granite crags with sport routes 5.10a–5.12 (e.g., Mind Over Matter 11c) on both rocks. USFS–Roosevelt NF, (970) 498–1100.
Ref: Guidebook: Salaun and Kimball's *Thath-aa-ai-atah.*
Directions: From Estes Park go south on Hwy. 7 to 1 mi. east on Peak View. Then go right ¼ mi. on dirt road. The Thumb and The Needle are on left (or west) side with marked trail for a three-minute hike.

39 Estes Park Area–Mary's Lake Boulders/Prospect Mountain (closed) ★★★

More than thirty routes on 30' granite formations called Needle, Thimble, Thumb, Fin, Shield Rock, and Dihedral Rock. Short bouldering and toprope cliff. Private—no trespassing.
Ref: Guidebooks: Benningfield's *Colorado Bouldering,*

Rossiter's *Rocky Mountain National Park: The Crag Areas,* Gillet's *Rocky Mountain National Park Climber's Guide,* Kimball's *Lumpy Ridge,* Fricke's *A Climber's Guide to Rocky Mountain National Park Area.*
Directions: From junction of Hwy. 36 and Hwy. 7 in Estes Park, go south on Hwy. 7 for 3 mi. Mary's Lake Boulders are on left (east) side of road by water tank. For Prospect Mountain (outcrops on south side): Turn right on Peak View Dr. Turn right at Churchill Boulder. Park at gate. Rocks on left.

40 Estes Park Area–Deville Rocks ★★
Three-hundred-fifty-foot granite crag with beginner/intermediate routes. Approach crosses private land. Summer. USFS–Roosevelt NF, (970) 498–1100.
Classics: Deville Three 7.
Ref: Guidebooks: Kimball's *Lumpy Ridge,* Fricke's *A Climber's Guide to Rocky Mountain National Park Area.*
Directions: From Estes Park go 4 mi. south on Hwy. 7. Park at Cheley Camp Junction. Hike south, then east on dirt road to structure. Hike ½ mi. east, Deville Rocks are on right. Approach crosses private land. Faces northwest.

41 Estes Park Area–Twin Sisters Mountain (aka The Crags) ★★★
Six-hundred-foot gneiss alpine crags. Although a bit of a hump to get to, many scattered crags and fins portend attention-grabbing climbing. Northcutt-Kor route done in 1959. Many routes put up by Scott Kimball. Exciting views of Rocky Mountain National Park and Longs Peak. Summer. USFS–Roosevelt NF, (970) 498–1100.
Classics: Shark's Fin: North Face 8, What's My Line 10.
Ref: C [89, 74, 69], S 5/88; Guidebooks: Rossiter's *Rocky Mountain National Park: The Crag Areas,* Gillet's *Rocky Mountain National Park Climber's Guide,* Kimball's *Lumpy Ridge,* Fricke's *A Climber's Guide to Rocky Mountain National Park Area.*
Directions: From Estes Park go south on Hwy. 7 for 7–8 mi. The Crags are ¾ mi. east of the road, ¼ mi. east of Wind River Pass. Park at Lily Lake Visitor Center, just past mm 6. Hike east 400 yd., then northeast to rocks. Several named formations include Upper and Lower Great Faces, Shark's Fin, Rib Rock.

42 Rocky Mountain National Park Overview ★★★★★
Alpine granite bouldering, cragging, big walls guaranteed to give one a Rocky Mountain high. Most Rocky Mountain National Park sojourns start from Estes Park on the east side or Grand Lake on the west side. Longs Peak, at 14,256', is the favorite focal point of rock climbers. Other great walls of interest include Chiefs-head, Hallett Peak, Notchtop, and Glacier Gorge. Cragging at East Portal at Cottontail crag and Windy Pass Rock. Rating high in the classics category is the Petit Grepon pinnacle, a lightning-bolt magnet. Bouldering enthusiasts can find challenges at

the Suzuki Boulder (1 2/10 mi. up Trail Ridge Rd. from Beaver Meadows Entrance Station), Hollowell Park Boulder (few minutes east up horse trail at Hollowell Park), Wild Basin Boulder (in Wild Basin District). Strong traditional ground-up ethic. Afternoon thunderstorms precipitate many an epic. Backcountry bivouac fee permit (970–586–1242) necessary for all overnight trips in park. Summer. NPS, (970) 586–1206.

Classics: Longs Peak: Casual Rt. 10-, Yellow Wall 11-, D-7 11, D-1 11, King of Swords 12a, Mt. Alice, Andrews Peak/Ptarmigan Towers, Hallett Peak, Petit Grepon; Notchtop Mountain: South Ridge III 9, Topnotch III 11c.

Ref: AAJ ['98>95, '89-157, 88-138, 85-200, 82>80, 78-534, 71, 69, 65-67], C [173-24, 166, 116, 111, 110, 106, 105, 89, 69, 64(1/81)-10, 63, 52, 49, 43(7/77)], R [93-100, 89, 85-152, 54, 31(5/89)-26, 13(3/86)], S [5/88, 8/85]; Mitchler and Covill's *Hiking Colorado's Summits,* Kor's *Beyond the Vertical,* Jones's *Climbing in North America;* on-line guide http://climbingboulder.com; Guidebooks: Benningfield's *Colorado Bouldering,* Rossiter's *Rock Climbing Rocky Mountain National Park: Volume 2 The High Peaks,* Rossiter's *Rocky Mountain National Park: The High Peaks,* Green's *Rock Climbing Colorado,* Gillet's *Rocky Mountain National Park Climber's Guide,* Knapp's *100 Select Classic Rocky Mountain National Park Climbs,* Roach's *Rocky Mountain National Park: Classic Hikes and Climbs,* Harlin's *Rocky Mountain,* Dumais's *Great American Rock Climbs,* Steck and Roper's *Fifty Classic Climbs,* Kimball's *Lumpy Ridge,* Garratt and Martin's *Colorado's High Thirteener's,* Fricke's *Climber's Guide to Rocky Mountain National Park,* Nesbit's *Longs Peak,* Ormes's *Guide to the Colorado Mountains,* Bueler's *Roof of the Rockies.*

Directions: Rocky Mountain National Park extends from Estes Park to Grand Lake, Colorado. East-side entrances include: 1) Estes Park Hwy. 36 via the trans-park highway Trail Ridge Rd. (closed in winter). 2) Long's Peak Rd. off Hwy. 7 south of Estes Park. 3) Wild Basin Entrance, farther south of Longs Peak Rd. along Hwy 7 south of Meeker Park. West-side entrances: 1) Usually from Grand Lake on Hwy 34. 2) A backcountry approach just south of Cameron Pass on Colorado Hwy. 14.

43 Rocky Mountain National Park–Moraine Park ☆☆☆

Two-hundred-foot granite crags. Summer. NPS, (970) 586–1206.

Classics: Days of Heaven 10.

Ref: Guidebooks: Kimball's *Lumpy Ridge,* Fricke's *A Climber's Guide to Rocky Mountain National Park Area.*

Directions: From Estes Park go to Rocky Mountain National Park to Moraine Park Campground. Go to Fern Lake Trailhead and go 1 mi. west to Arch Rocks on right. Faces south.

44 Rocky Mountain National Park–Hallett Peak (12,713') ☆☆☆☆

Popular 800' granite alpine wall for climbers due to the ease of access; numerous, pleasant climbs; and easy descents. The North Face is the main draw for technical rock climbers. Northcutt Carter Route III 5.7 was done in 1956, then the first pitch fell off and is now 5.10, renamed Just Got Harder, courtesy of Topher Donahue. NPS, (970) 586–1206.

Classics: Hallet Peak: Culp Bossier III 8, Jackson Johnson III 9, Northcutt Carter III 10.

Ref: R 80-144, R 95-20, S 3/83; Guidebooks: Rossiter's *Rocky Mountain National Park: The High Peaks,* Green's *Rock Climbing Colorado,* Gillet's *Rocky Mountain National Park Climber's Guide,* Roach's *Rocky Mountain National Park: Classic Hikes and Climbs,* Harlin's *Rocky Mountain,* Steck and Roper's *Fifty Classic Climbs,* Fricke's *A Climber's Guide to Rocky Mountain National Park Area.*

Directions: From Estes Park head west on Hwy. 36, then turn south on Bear Lake Rd. (just west of Beaver Meadow entrance to Rocky Mountain National Park). Proceed 8 mi. up to Bear Lake Trailhead for Hallet Peak, Flattop, and Notchtop. Hike up past Emerald Lake to base (one-and-a-half-hour approach).

45 Rocky Mountain National Park–Cathedral Spires (Petit Grepon) and Cathedral Wall ☆☆☆☆

The attraction here is the series of alluring 1,000' granite alpine spires and buttresses on the ridge running northeast from Andrews Glacier Valley. Petit Grepon's 5.9 route is a much sought-after route on a classic alpine pinnacle. Early starts a must or lightning will turn you into dust. NPS, (970) 586–1206.

Classics: Cathedral Spires–Petit Grepon: South Face 5.7–9; Saber: Southwest Corner 9; Sharkstooth: Northeast Ridge 6.

Ref: 169-66; Guidebooks: Rossiter's *Rocky Mountain National Park: The High Peaks,* Green's *Rock Climbing Colorado,* Gillet's *Rocky Mountain National Park Climber's Guide,* Dumais's *The High Peaks,* Steck and Roper's *Fifty Classic Climbs,* Bueler's *Roof of the Rockies,* Fricke's *A Climber's Guide to Rocky Mountain National Park Area.*

Directions: From Estes Park head west on Hwy. 36, then turn south on Bear Lake Rd. (just west of Beaver Meadow entrance to Rocky Mountain National Park). Proceed 7 ½ mi. up to Glacier Gorge parking area for the Sky Pond Trail, leading to climbing areas of Glacier Gorge, Pagoda Mountain, Chiefshead, Spearhead, and McHenrys Peak. The Cathedral Spires are an impressive site from Sky Pond. Cathedral Wall is 800' wall at southwest end of the Loch, near Sky Pond. Sharkstooth is farthest west of Cathedral Spires.

46 Rocky Mountain National Park–Spearhead (12,575') ★★★★

This stunning formation of excellent 800' granite alpine rock displays a pyramidal spearpoint. The wall sweeps from eighty degrees to near vertical. Spearhead sees a fair amount of climbers due to its classic routes like the easy North Ridge III 6 to more challenging routes like Sykes Sickle III 5.9 and Scimitar 5.10. Descent is to northwest. NPS, (970) 586-1206.

Classics: North Ridge III 6, Sykes Sickle III 9, Barb IV 10b, Three Stoners IV 11, Stone Monkey 12a, Barbarella.

Ref: C [132, 111, 105 (topo), 70], R 31(5/89)-26; Guidebooks: Rossiter's *Rocky Mountain National Park: The High Peaks*, Green's *Rock Climbing Colorado*, Gillet's *Rocky Mountain National Park Climber's Guide*, Roach's *Rocky Mountain National Park: Classic Hikes and Climbs*, Harlin's *Rocky Mountain*, Dumais's *The High Peaks*, Fricke's *A Climber's Guide to Rocky Mountain National Park Area*.

Directions: From Estes Park head west on Hwy. 36, then turn south on Bear Lake Rd. (just west of Beaver Meadow entrance to Rocky Mountain National Park). Proceed 7 ½ mi. up to Glacier Gorge parking area for the Black Lake Trail, leading to climbing areas of Glacier Gorge, Pagoda Mountain, Chiefshead, Spearhead, and McHenrys Peak.

47 Rocky Mountain National Park–Chiefshead ★★★★

Popular, backcountry, 1,000' granite, alpine, rock-walled mountain sports runout 5.10 climbs on featureless rock. NPS, (970) 586-1206.

Classics: Seven Arrows 10b, Path of Elders IV 10, Birds of Fire 10d.

Ref: C [146, 111, 103, 101, 88, 64], R 31(5/89)-26; Guidebooks: Rossiter's *Rocky Mountain National Park: The High Peaks*, Gillet's *Rocky Mountain National Park Climber's Guide*, Roach's *Rocky Mountain National Park: Classic Hikes and Climbs*, Harlin's *Rocky Mountain*, Dumais's *The High Peaks*, Fricke's *A Climber's Guide to Rocky Mountain National Park Area*.

Directions: From Estes Park head west on Hwy. 36, then turn south on Bear Lake Rd. (just west of Beaver Meadow entrance to Rocky Mountain National Park). Proceed 7 ½ mi. up to Glacier Gorge parking area for the Black Lake Trail, leading to climbing areas of Glacier Gorge, Pagoda Mountain, Chiefshead, Spearhead, and McHenrys Peak.

48 Rocky Mountain National Park–Longs Peak (14,256'), Mt. Meeker, and Chasm Lake ★★★★★

The Diamond, the monarch of the Front Range on the East Face of Long's Peak, is Colorado's premier 1,000' alpine wall and the Rocky Mountain siren of rock climbers and technical scramblers. Stunning plumb lines up alpine granite of impeccable quality. First summitted in 1868 by John Wesley Powell. In 1960, the landmark first ascent of the Diamond was completed by Dave Rearick and Bob Kamps in two days. Now a "long" day as a car-to-car trip or get one of the limited number of backcountry bivy permits. The Casual Route 5.10 is the most popular and easiest route on the Diamond. Eroica 5.12b is one of the more difficult. Longs is also extremely popular as a summit hike. Summer. NPS, (970) 586-1206.

Classics: Kiener's Rt. 3, Stettner's Ledges 7; Diamond: Casual Rt. IV 10-, Pervertical Sanctuary IV 10+, Yellow Wall V11, D-7 11, Diagonal Dir to D1 VI 11d, D-1 V 11+, King of Swords V 12a, Ariana 12a, Eroica 12b; Dunn: Westbay V 10 A3; Chasm View Wall: Directissima 10a; Mt. Meeker: Flying Buttress 9, famed north face.

Ref: AAJ ['97, '96, '91-175, '89-4, '77-192, '76-457, '75-138, 74-153, '69, '67-'65], C [186-118, 179-26, 161-66, 158-74, 152-42, 145, 126, 104, 88, 64, 48(5/78)], M 40, R [93-100, 75-86, 74-144, 72-23, 65-23, 54, 31(5/89)-26, 13(3/86), 1(3/84)], S [7/69, 5/67, 1/67]; Chapin's *Mountaineering In Colorado: Longs Peak Tales*; Guidebooks: Roach's *Colorado's Fourteeners*, Rossiter's *Rocky Mountain National Park: The High Peaks*, Green's *Rock Climbing Colorado*, Rossiter's *The Diamond of Longs Peak Classic Climbs*, Wadman's *Diamond Poster*, Gillet's *Rocky Mountain National Park Climber's Guide*, Roach's *Rocky Mountain National Park: Classic Hikes and Climbs*, Steck and Roper's *Fifty Classic Climbs*, Harlin's *Rocky Mountain*, Kimball's *Solitary Summits*, Borneman's *A Climber's Guide to Colorado's Fourteeners*, Robinson's *Technical Rock Climber's Guide to East Face of Longs Peak*, Dumais's *The High Peaks*, Ormes's *Guide to the Colorado Mountains*, Bueler's *Roof of the Rockies*, Fricke's *A Climber's Guide to Rocky Mountain National Park Area*.

Directions: From Estes Park follow Hwy. 7 for approximately 8 ½ mi. south to a right turn into Longs Peak Ranger Station and Campground (approximately 1 mi.). Eight mi. from trailhead to summit of Longs Peak. From the Diamond, Diagonal Wall sits below and left. Chasm View Wall is 600' face below Diamond to right.

49 Carter Lake ★★★

Challenging bouldering on 35' pebbly conglomerate sandstone faces with a sunny, western aspect above blue Carter Lake. Beware poor landings—short topropes advisable. The lovely bouldering testpiece, Great Kahuna Roof V5, is pictured on the cover of Bob Horan's Front Range Bouldering guidebook. First ascent, Mark Wilford. Entry fee required or tickets fired. Autumn/spring. Larimer County Park, (970) 498-7000.

Classics: Great Kahuna Roof V5, Scenic Boulder, Mighty Wall, Extension Block.

Ref: C [199-60, 179-21]; Guidebooks: Benningfield's *Colorado Bouldering*, Horan's *Front Range Bouldering*.

Directions: From Berthoud drive 6 mi. west on Hwy. 56 to Carter Lake Park entrance. Drive another 6/10 mi. to "junction." Go left another 1 4/10 mi. to rocks on east side of reservoir. Park at first lot overlooking lake. Boulders visible to right. Scenic Boulder is first prominent boulder. Bouldering along cliffband and on boulders below. The Great Kahuna Roof sits near the water's edge. Another area known as Biglandia is 1 ½ mi. north of the "junction," and to the east about fifteen-minute walk from road.

50 North St. Vrain Canyon–V-Slot Wall ✭✭✭

One-hundred-and-fifty-foot granite crag with the classic V-Slot 5.9+. USFS–Roosevelt NF, (970) 498–1100.

Directions: West of Lyons along Hwy. 36 for approximately 11 mi. Across from big bend in road where Little Thompson River flows into North St. Vrain River. Many granite outcrops between Lyons and Estes Park, mostly scruffy except for V-Slot Wall and Split Rocks. USFS.

51 Split Rocks (at North St. Vrain) (closed) ✭✭✭

Conspicuous blasted pink granite boulders next to road. One-hundred-foot granite crags to northeast. Closed to climbing—access negotiations in process. Animal Magnetism 5.12 is one of the most heinous of offwidths. Autumn/spring. Private land.

Ref: Ament's *Master of Rock.*

Directions: From Lyons, Split Rocks is west on Hwy. 36. Continue past Button Rock turnoff uphill until forest service sign and 20′ split boulders appear to left of road.

52 Steamboat Mountain (Ingleside Cliffs) ✭✭

Three-hundred-foot red cliffs of crumbly sandstone partially developed by employees of Lyon's now-defunct Latok climbing gear company. Autumn/spring. Private land.

Directions: From Lyons, Steamboat Mountain is 1–2 mi. west on Hwy. 36. To north and east of road.

53 Lyons Quarry ✭✭

Lyons Quarry is north of Lyons in Flagstone quarries. Good sandstone bouldering problems. Trespassing into tall, scary, occasionally loose problems with bad landings, aka Mark Wilford problems. Autumn/spring. Private land.

Ref: M. Wilford; C 89.

Directions: Lyons Quarry is north of Lyons in Flagstone quarries. Go north past post office ½ mi. on dirt road. Go west on more dirt roads for ¼ mi. Hard to find.

54 Rabbit Mountain/Pile Tor ✭✭✭

Twenty-foot overhanging bouldering on east side of Rabbit Mountain. Dakota sandstone hogback of quality traverses and topropes. Autumn/spring. Private land/City of Boulder Mountain Parks.

Ref: F. Saab; Guidebook: Benningfield's *Colorado Bouldering.*

Directions: From Lyons, Rabbit Mountain is a couple miles north/northeast of Lyons, just north of Hwy. 66. From the Old Prague Inn at 7521 Hwy. 66, go north on Seventy-fifth St. to a ninety-degree bend in the road (becomes Woodland Rd.). Park. Walk west on dirt road

(private land) to rock fin through obvious gap to west side of fin. Restricted seasonal access.

55 Button Rock Reservoir ✭✭✭✭

Sixty-foot granite crags and bouldering offering more than fifty face and crack climbs on roadside walls. Thirty classic routes to 5.13. Autumn/spring. Government land.

Classics: River Wall: Pocket Hercules 11d, Big Big Monkey Man 12b, New Horizons 12d; The Bullet: Finger Tattoo 12a, Pretty Blue Gun 12a, Lost Horizons 14a; Bouldering Wall.

Ref: C [142, 138, 105, 104, 94, 91], R 34(7/88); Guidebooks: Hubbel's *Lyons Area Classic Rock Climbs,* Green's *Rock Climbing Colorado,* Hubbel's *Front Range Crags,* Rolofson's *Boulder Sport Climber's Guide,* Rossiter's *Boulder Climbs North.*

Directions: From Lyons sally approximately 3 6/10 mi. west on Hwy. 36. Turn left at SHELLY'S COTTAGES sign (Co. Rd. 80). At ½ mi., Entryway Slabs on left, at 6/10 is Hitler's Sex Life and Buick Rocks on left, following good dirt roads until 2 3/10 mi. from Shelly's to locked gate (Aqueduct Rock on left) for Button Rock Reservoir. Hike five minutes up road to see The River Wall on right by little dam. Walking farther on road, The Bouldering Wall is next roadside wall on left and The Bullet is on right twenty minutes up.

56 South St. Vrain Canyon ✭✭✭

Strangely neglected 11-mi.-long canyon of 400′ granite cliffs. More popular with anglers for a while, but has now received attention from climbing enthusiasts. Fine assortment of one hundred trad and sport routes on many buttresses. Autumn/spring. Private land/USFS–Roosevelt NF, (970) 498–1100.

Classics: Five mi. up from Lyons and 1 mi. before Bavarian Village is 3p bolted 5.12d route on south side of canyon.

Ref: AAJ '83, 91, R 79-98; Guidebooks: Hubbel's *Lyons Area Classic Rock Climbs,* Hubbel's *Front Range Crags,* Rolofson's *Boulder Sport Climber's Guide.*

Directions: South St. Vrain Area is along Hwy. 7 between Lyons and Allenspark. Some formations on Hwy. 7 include (mileages from junction of Hwy. 36 and Hwy. 7 in Lyons): 3 8/10 mi., Mushroom Massif (The Mushroom 8) on left; 4 3/10 mi., December Wall (Caesar's Crack 10b) on right; 5 3/10 mi., Observatory Rock, North Narrow Slabs; 5 4/10 mi., North (The Hitcher 12b) South (Pon Scum 12-); 9 1/10 mi., The Fang (sport climbs, Perfect Stemetry 12d); 10 ½ mi., The Watchtower (The Corner 9-); and more.

57 Piz Badille ✭✭✭

This stately 600′ granite roadside buttress offers a handful of multipitch routes from 5.6–5.9. The Northwest Arête sports classic positioning and alpine scenery of Indian Peaks. Summer/autumn. USFS–Roosevelt NF, (970) 498–1100.

Classics: Northwest Arête 6, Reusable Love Bag 9.

Ref: Guidebooks: Hubbel's *Lyons Area Classic Rock Climbs*, Hubbel's *Front Range Crags*.

Directions: From Lyons go up Hwy. 7 through South St. Vrain Canyon. Turn left on Hwy. 72 (from junction with Hwy. 7) on left. The Piz is on prominent, west-facing buttress on left in 2⁸/10 mi. Parking strip on left. Short five- to ten-minute hike cross creek up talus to base. Descent to south.

58 Indian Peaks Wilderness Area ✪✪✪

Beautiful wilderness area with thirty peaks over 12,000'. See Roach's *Colorado's Indian Peaks Wilderness Area: Classic Hikes and Climbs,* which describes easy rock mountaineering routes on granitic peaks, e.g., Lone Eagle Peak (11,920'), North Face III 5.7. Many peaks named after Great Plains Indians: Apache, Arakaree, Ogallala, etc. Nice backcountry bouldering as well. Summer. Fee permits for backcountry camping. Arapaho NRA/USFS–Roosevelt NF, (303) 444–6600.

Classics: Mt. Toll (12,979'): North Ridge II 6, Dicker's Peak (13,170') I 5, Hiamovi Tower (12,700') III 4; Lone Eagle Peak (11,920'): North Face III 7, Devil's Thumb (12,080') I 4.

Ref: C 69, R [74-44, 70-81], S [10/78, 6/74]; Guidebooks: Roach's *Colorado's Indian Peaks Wilderness Area: Classic Hikes and Climbs,* Bueler's *Roof of the Rockies.*

Directions: Indian Peaks Wilderness Area encompasses the area between Granby on the west, Rocky Mountain National Park on the north, Hwy. 72 on the east, and East Portal to the south on the Arapaho National Forest. Various trailheads lead in from all directions. West of Ward, Brainard Lake is most popular. Four-wheel drive is a good idea for some trailheads. For Brainard Lake continue past the Piz (CO 57) for 7 mi. Turn right onto FR 112 for 5 mi. to the lake and parking.

59 Old Stage Wall (aka Left Hand Canyon) (closed) ✪✪✪

Ninety-foot granite roadside overhanging with four sport routes 5.11+ and up, e.g., Solstice 5.12d. Excellent climbing described by Paul Piana as "an island of fun in a sea of rubble." A 90' wall cut by roof system 10' off ground. Autumn/spring. Private land.

Ref: C 101, R 34(7/88); Guidebooks: Hubbel's *Lyons Area Classic Rock Climbs,* Rossiter's *Boulder Climbs North,* Rolofson's *Boulder Sport Climber's Guide.*

Directions: Northwest of Boulder. Up Left Hand Canyon Rd. on left. Faces west.

60 Mt. Sanitas ✪✪✪

A brief number of obvious Dakota sandstone traverse and straight-up problems adjacent to hiking trail on a north-south ridge of sandstone. Some topropes. Autumn/spring. City of Boulder Mountain Parks.

Ref: Guidebooks: Horan's *Best of Boulder Bouldering,* Benningfield's *Colorado Bouldering,* Horan's *Front Range Bouldering,* Ament's *High Over Boulder.*

Directions: In Boulder. Take Broadway (Hwy. 93) north. Turn left (west) on Mapleton Ave. for ½ mi. Park at picnic shelter ½ block past Memorial Hospital. Hike fifteen minutes up trail to west side of rock on Mt. Sanitas.

61 Boulder Canyon Areas ✪✪✪✪

Wealth of roadside granite crags and 250' domes in the scenic pines. An area of much historical significance in the Boulder climbing arena. Parking available at roadside pull-outs. River crossings more feasible by midsummer. Consult Rossiter's *Boulder Climbs North* for topos. Camping for Boulder Canyon lies up Hwy. 119 by Castle Rock. When climbing in Boulder, plan on paying for camping (KOA in northeast Boulder or Youth Hostel on 1107 Twelfth St.) or stay with friends in town. Autumn/spring. Private land/USFS–Roosevelt NF, (970) 498–1100.

Classics: Cozyhang 7, Empor 7+, Jackson's Wall Direct 9, Cosmosis 9+, Dementia 10a, Athlete's Feat 11a, Country Club Crack 11, Rude Boy 12-, Corinthian Vine 12d, La June 13a, Verve 13.

Ref: AAJ ['84 to 82], C [173-24, 169, 168-62, 117, 114, 110, 109, 108, 106, 104 to 93, 70, 64, 56, 48], M 86, R 54; Ament's *Master of Rock;* on-line guide http://climbingboulder.com; Guidebooks: Horan's *Best of Boulder Bouldering,* Benningfield's *Colorado Bouldering,* Rossiter's *Rock Climbing Boulder Canyon,* Green's *Rock Climbing Colorado,* Rossiter's *Best of Boulder Climbs,* Knapp and Steven's *100 Select,* Knapp's *Boulder Topropes,* Rolofson's *Boulder Sport Climber's Guide,* Harlin's *Rocky Mountain,* Rossiter's *Boulder Climbs North,* Ament's *High Over Boulder,* Erickson's *Rocky Heights,* Dornan's *Rock Climbing Guide to the Boulder, Colorado, Area,* McCrumm's *Boulder Rock Climbs.*

Directions: From Boulder, mileages from junction of Arapahoe and Canyon. Head ½–12 mi. up Boulder Canyon. Numerous small crags on either side of road. Parking available at roadside pullouts.

62 Boulder Canyon–Elephant Buttresses and The Dome ✪✪✪

First-seen climbing areas traveling up Boulder Canyon. Two-hundred-foot southwest-facing granite formations. Four towers and conspicuous Dome are very popular. One- to two-pitch sunny crags. More than forty intermediate 5.9–5.11 routes. USFS–Roosevelt NF, (970) 498–1100.

Classics: Second Buttress: Classic Finger Crack 9-; Third Buttress: Standard Route 7, Ah Maw 10a, Leftwing 10b, FM 11c; Fourth Buttress: Northwest Face 8, Zolar Czaki 10a; The Dome: East Slab 5, The Owl 7, Gorilla's Delight 9+, Supersqueeze 10d.

Ref: 168-62; Guidebooks: Harlin's *Rocky Mountain,* Rossiter's *Boulder Climbs North,* Ament's *High Over Boulder.*

Directions: From Boulder go ½ mi. west on Hwy. 119 (Canyon Blvd.). Area is on right (north). Cross stream (via steel pipe just to west during high water). Elephant Buttress is formation nearest to road.

63 Boulder Canyon–Brick Wall, Mental Rock, and Canyon Block (Milk Dud) ✰✰✰

Sixty-five-foot granite popular toprope cliffs. Sixteen routes. USFS–Roosevelt NF, (970) 498–1100.

Classics: Brick Wall: Perfect Route and South Face 10; Mental Rock: Manic Depressive 11+, Sleeper 12-; Canyon Block: Rude Boy 12a, Damaged Goods 12+.

Ref: Guidebooks: Rossiter's *Boulder Climbs North,* Ament's *High Over Boulder.*

Directions: From Boulder go 4 ^{7}/10 mi. west on Hwy. 119 (Canyon Blvd.). Brick Wall on north side of highway, 5 yd. from road. Canyon Block is west of Brick Wall on same side of road, fifteen minutes up a southwest-facing hill. Mental Rock is south of road, across bridge to north of creek and five minutes west (upstream).

64 Boulder Canyon–Eagle Rock Area ✰✰

Unpopular 350′ granite crag with six intermediate routes. USFS–Roosevelt NF, (970) 498–1100.

Ref: Guidebooks: Rossiter's *Boulder Climbs North,* Ament's *High Over Boulder.*

Directions: From Boulder go 6 ^{4}/10 mi. west on Hwy. 119 (Canyon Blvd.). Eagle Rock Area is on south side of creek.

65 Boulder Canyon–Blob Rock Area ✰✰✰

This 300′ south-facing granite crag sports approximately forty routes to 5.12d, Radlands of Infinity 5.12d. Good finger-tweakin' climbing, though unassuming appearance from road. USFS–Roosevelt NF, (970) 498–1100.

Classics: Blob Rock: Where Eagles Dare 9+, Bearcat Goes to Hollywood 11d, Limits of Power 12a, Radlands of Infinity 12d; East Blob: A Hike with Ludwig Dude 9+; Bitty Buttress: Bitty Buttress 8, Peapod 11b; Happy Hour: Dementia 10a.

Ref: Guidebooks: Rossiter's *Boulder Climbs North,* Ament's *High Over Boulder.*

Directions: From Boulder go 6 ^{7}/10 mi. west on Canyon Blvd. (Hwy. 119) on right (north). Blob Rock Area contains Bitty Buttress, Blob Rock, Happy Hour Crag, and Security Risk Crag.

66 Boulder Canyon–Cob Rock ✰✰✰

Two-hundred-foot granite crag with twenty routes. Creek crossing only sane at low water. Best 5.7s in the canyon, e.g., Empor 5.7+. Raptor restrictions. April–August. USFS–Roosevelt NF, (970) 498–1100.

Classics: Emptor 7, Huston Crack 8, Night Vision 10.

Ref: Guidebooks: Rossiter's *Boulder Climbs North,* Ament's *High Over Boulder.*

Directions: From Boulder, Cob Rock is 6 ^{8}/10 mi. west on Hwy. 119 (Canyon Blvd.) on left (south). Faces north.

67 Boulder Canyon–Boulder Falls Area ✰✰✰

Two-hundred-foot granite crag. Routes as hard as La June 5.13a. Popular tourist stop for Boulder Falls—watch for tourists wandering aimlessly in the middle of the highway. Winter ice climbing. USFS–Roosevelt NF, (970) 498–1100.

Classics: Iron Curtain 10+, The Threshold 11, The Prisoner 12-, La June 13a.

Ref: Guidebooks: Rossiter's *Boulder Climbs North,* Ament's *High Over Boulder.*

Directions: From Boulder go 7 ^{8}/10 mi. on Hwy. 119 (Canyon Blvd.) on right (north). Park at large pullout on south side of road. Boulder Falls Area includes Boulder Falls Wall, Chrome Dome, Plotinus, Berlin Wall, Wall of Winter Warmth, Krishna, Dream Canyon, and Boulder Slips. Faces south and east.

68 Boulder Canyon–Practice Rock and Aquarium Wall ✰✰✰

Practice Rock's 50′ granite wall is well known to all road-viewers and climbers for its Yosemite-like pinscar crack 5.11- or also used for clean aid practice A1. Three routes 5.9–5.11. Aquarium Wall sports seven classic 5.9–5.11 routes. USFS–Roosevelt NF, (970) 498–1100.

Ref: Guidebooks: Rossiter's *Boulder Climbs North,* Ament's *High Over Boulder.*

Directions: From Boulder go 8 mi. west on Hwy. 119 (Canyon Blvd.). Practice Rock is on right (north) side of road. Aquarium Wall is directly across on south side. Faces south.

69 Boulder Canyon–Bell Buttress ✰✰✰

Three-hundred-and-fifty-foot granite crag rings with approximately thirty routes of attractive variety. USFS–Roosevelt NF, (970) 498–1100.

Classics: Cosmosis 9+, Arm's Bazaar 12-, Verve 13.

Ref: Guidebooks: Rossiter's *Boulder Climbs North,* Ament's *High Over Boulder.*

Directions: From Boulder it's 8 ^{2}/10 mi. west on Canyon Blvd. (Hwy. 119) on left (south). Faces north/west. From parking ford stream . . . dicey when water is high to Bell Buttress.

70 Boulder Canyon–Vampire Rock, Black Widow Slab, and Animal World Rock ✰✰

Three-hundred-foot granite crag. Seldom visited, broken cliffs. Twenty routes. USFS–Roosevelt NF, (970) 498–1100.

Classics: Hands of Destiny 13a.

Ref: Guidebooks: Rossiter's *Boulder Climbs North,* Ament's *High Over Boulder.*

Directions: From Boulder go 8 ^{6}/10 mi. west on Hwy. 119 (Canyon Blvd.). On left (south). Black Widow Slab is just west across scree gully. Faces north.

71 Boulder Canyon–High Energy Crag Area ✪✪✪

Thirty-five-foot granite crag with nine short crack leads or topropes. Launch out on Star Span 5.11. USFS–Roosevelt NF, (970) 498–1100.

Ref: Guidebooks: Rossiter's *Boulder Climbs North,* Ament's *High Over Boulder.*

Directions: From Boulder go 9 $^2/10$ mi. west on Hwy. 119 (Canyon Blvd.). High Energy Crag Area is on left (south). Faces northwest.

72 Boulder Canyon–Nip and Tuck ✪✪

This 100′ granite crag features twenty routes like the classic Finger Crack 5.9. USFS–Roosevelt NF, (970) 498–1100.

Ref: Guidebooks: Rossiter's *Boulder Climbs North,* Ament's *High Over Boulder.*

Directions: From Boulder go 10 ½ mi. west on Hwy. 119 (Canyon Blvd.). Nip and Tuck is on right (north).

73 Boulder Canyon–Castle Rock ✪✪✪✪

A 250′ granite crag you can actually drive completely around. Boulder Canyon's best. Multipitch mixed crack and face climbs (approximately fifty routes) with bumper belays on first pitches. USFS–Roosevelt NF, (970) 498–1100.

Classics: Cussin Crack 5.7, Curving Crack 5.9, Athlete's Feat 5.11a, Country Club Crack 5.11, Gill Crack 12a, Never A Dull Moment 5.12-, Tourist Extravaganza 5.12+/13a, Aid Roof 5.14.

Ref: C [169-24, 166(2/97)-17, 99]; Ament's *Master of Rock;* Guidebooks: Horan's *Best of Boulder Bouldering,* Harlin's *Rocky Mountain,* Rossiter's *Boulder Climbs North,* Ament's *High Over Boulder.*

Directions: From Boulder go 11 $^9/10$ mi. west on Hwy. 119 (Canyon Blvd.) to Castle Rock on left.

74 Boulder Canyon–Cenotaph Crag ✪✪

One-hundred-foot granite crag with five routes, e.g., seek out Apparition 5.11a. USFS–Roosevelt NF, (970) 498–1100.

Ref: Guidebooks: Rossiter's *Boulder Climbs North,* Ament's *High Over Boulder.*

Directions: From Boulder go 12 $^4/10$ mi. west on Hwy. 119 (Canyon Blvd.) on right (north). Faces west, so hard to see when driving up canyon. Cenotaph Crag is approximately ½ mi. past Castle Rock.

75 Boulder Canyon–Suprising Crag ✪✪

Fifty-foot granite crag with eight intermediate routes. USFS–Roosevelt NF, (970) 498–1100.

Ref: Guidebooks: Rossiter's *Boulder Climbs North,* Ament's *High Over Boulder.*

Directions: From Boulder go 13 mi. west on Hwy. 119 (Canyon Blvd.). Suprising Crag is on left (south) side of road. Faces west.

76 Flagstaff Mountain ✪✪✪

Where Boulder boulders. Hundreds of problems/contrivances on good sandstone edges, sharp flakes, and greasy pebbles. Ament's *Climber's Playground,* if you can find a copy, is a photo album of the classic historic problems in a top-of-the-town setting. Many formations include Pumpkin Rock, Cookie Jar Rock, Nook's Rock, Capstan Rock, Cloud Shadow, The Alcove, Pratt's Overhang Area, Monkey Traverse Wall, Alamo Rock, Beer Barrel Rock, Pebble Wall, Flagstaff Amphitheater, and Overhang Wall. Autumn/spring. City of Boulder Mountain Parks, (303) 441-3408.

Classics: Monkey Traverse, Tree Slab, southwest corner of Beer Barrel Rock, King Conquer, Smith Overhang, Distant Dancer 12a.

Ref: C [170-23, 130(2/92)-52, 94, 3(9/70)], R 97-44, Sherman's *Stone Crusade,* Ament's *Master of Rock;* on-line guide http://climbingboulder.com; Guidebooks: Horan's *Best of Boulder Bouldering,* Benningfield's *Colorado Bouldering,* Horan's *Front Range Bouldering: Boulder Area,* Green's *Rock Climbing Colorado,* Horan's *Front Range Bouldering,* Ament's *High Over Boulder,* Ament's *Climber's Playground,* Dornan's *Rock Climbing Guide to the Boulder, Colorado, Area.*

Directions: From Boulder go west on Baseline Rd. to where it turns into Flagstaff Mountain Rd. (small stone bridge). Boulders scattered along Flagstaff Mountain Rd., most popular parking 1 $^6/10$ mi. up from stone bridge.

77 Walker Ranch–Meyer's Gulch ✪✪

One-hundred-foot granite domes between Walker Ranch and Gross Reservoir. Autumn/spring. Government land.

Ref: Guidebook: Hubbel's *Lyons Area Classic Rock Climbs.*

Directions: From Boulder follow Baseline Rd. west to Flagstaff Rd. (Baseline turns into Flagstaff Rd.). Drive over Flag-staff Mountain to Walker Ranch (signs) approximately 3 mi. past Boulder Mountain Parks boundary (top of Flagstaff grade).

78 Flatirons Area–The Amphitheatre ✪✪

Boulder's picturesque landmark tilted slabs bordering the west side of town offer beginner's slabs on the east front and advanced climbs on the west. Short approaches, neat routes. The Amphitheatre features more than thirty beginner's routes on a 150′ sandstone formation. Autumn/spring. City of Boulder Mountain Parks, (303) 441-3408.

Classics: First Pinnacle West Ridge 4, Class Second Pinnacle east face left 7, Siberian North Face 10.

Ref: AAJ ['84 to 82], C [C 166, 117, 111, 110, 109, 108, 107, 101, 74, 70], R 27; on-line guide http:// climbingboulder.com; Guidebooks: Horan's *Best of Boulder Bouldering,* Benningfield's *Colorado Bouldering,* Rossiter's *Rockclimbing The Flatirons,* Green's *Rock Climbing Colorado,* Knapp and Steven's *100 Select,* Rossiter's *Best of Boulder Climbs,* Rossiter's *Boulder Climbs North,* Roach's *Flatiron Classics: Easy Climbs and Trails,* Ormes's *Guide to the Colorado Rockies.*

Directions: In Boulder, go west on Baseline Rd. to base of Flagstaff Mountain. Go left after small stone bridge to Gregory Canyon trailhead. Hike southwest 200 yd. to The Amphitheatre.

79 Flatirons–1 through 5, Ironing Boards and Royal Arch ★★★★★

Renowned for the East Face of the Third Flatiron, which holds the longest climbs in the Boulder area up forty-five-degree, 1,000' sandstone. One of the best beginner rock-climbing resources in the United States. Many intermediate sandstone routes up back sides of Flatirons. More than 130 routes. The Ghetto offers pumping bouldering hidden on back side of the Third Flatiron. Restrictions on bolting, bicycles, dogs, and climbing due to raptor nesting March 15–July 15. Please check. Autumn/spring. City of Boulder Mountain Parks, (303) 441–3408.

Classics: First Flatiron: North Arête 4, Direct East Face 6; Third Flatiron: East Face 3, Velvet Elvis 11, Far Niente 12; Green Mountain Pinnacle: Death and Transfiguration 11, The Ghetto Bouldering, Arc de Triomphe 11b.

Ref: AAJ '82; Sherman's *Stone Crusade*; C 152-125; on-line guide http://climbingboulder.com; Guidebooks: Horan's *Best of Boulder Bouldering*, Benningfield's *Colorado Bouldering*, Green's *Rock Climbing Colorado*, Rossiter's *Best of Boulder Climbs*, Rossiter's *Boulder Climbs North*, Harlin's *Rocky Mountain*, Roach's *Flatiron Classics: Easy Climbs and Trails*, Ormes's *Guide to the Colorado Rockies*.

Directions: In Boulder, from junction of Broadway and Baseline, go west on Baseline to left on Kinnikinnic, which leads to Chautauqua Park. Park here. Map board displays Chautauqua Park trails. Hike times up to one-hour approaches to specific Flatiron formations.

80 Flatirons Area–Skunk Canyon and Dinosaur Mountain ★★★

More great rock on wild 600' sandstone formations in the Flatirons. Skunk Canyon treasured for fifty traditional routes e.g., Satan's Slab 5.8, and hard sport climbs, e.g., Five Year Plan 5.13 and Beware the Future 5.13+. Dinosaur Mountain holds many formations and at least ninety routes. One of the hardest bouldering problems in the states is Jim Holloway's Slapshot B3. Autumn/spring. City of Boulder Mountain Parks, (303) 441–3408.

Classics: Stairway to Heaven 4, Satan's Slab 8, Doric Dihedral 12-, Android Powerpack 12 toprope, The Guardian 12+, Five Year Plan 13, Beware the Future 13c, Slapshot B3; Dinosaur: Bidoight 9+, Touch Monkey 11c, Power Bulge 12c, Cornucopia 12c.

Ref: AAJ '85-211 C [114, 111, 99, 95]; on-line guide http://climbingboulder.com; Guidebooks: Horan's *Best of Boulder Bouldering*, Benningfield's *Colorado Bouldering: Boulder Climbs North and South*, Roach's *Flatiron Classics: Easy Climbs and Trails*.

Directions: Just west of Boulder. In Boulder, go west on Table Mesa Dr. to National Center for Atmospheric Research buildings. Park. Hike west to Mesa Trail. At this trail junction, Skunk Canyon is to north, Dinosaur Mountain/Bear Canyon to south. Numerous trails depart west from Mesa Trail to the various cliffs. Bear Canyon can also be reached by going west on Table Mesa to Lehigh, left to Bear Mountain Dr., right to Stoney Hill, right to cul-de-sac parking. Hike west to Mesa Trail, then south to Bear Canyon Trail.

81 Flatirons Area–Nebel Horn, Fern Canyon, Bear Peak North (Shanahan Canyon, The Slab, and Sphinx) ★★★★

Beautiful rock-studded canyons and wooded hillsides. Untempered sport-climb bolting led to bolting ban in all Boulder Mountain parks. Many beautiful sandstone sport routes and trad adventure routes and summits. Autumn/spring. City of Boulder Mountain Parks, (303) 441–3408.

Classics: Ruby Slipper 11a; Fern: Rip This Joint 10, Rude Welcome 11, Undertow 12a, Mentor 12b, Violator 13c.

Ref: C [114, 72-6, 71]; on-line guide http://climbingboulder.com; Guidebooks: Horan's *Best of Boulder Bouldering*, Benningfield's *Colorado Bouldering*, underground route list, Rossiter's *Boulder Climbs North*, Roach's *Flatiron Classics: Easy Climbs and Trails*.

Directions: In Boulder. From South Broadway turn west on Table Mesa Dr. Turn left on Lehigh St. Turn right on Cragmoor to dead end. Park. Hike west to Mesa Trail, then right to Fern Canyon. Can also be approached from Bear Mountain Dr.

82 Flatirons Area–Bear Peak South (Devil's Thumb, The Maiden, and The Matron) ★★★

Best 500' sandstone spires to bag in Boulder area. Cool summits. Fabulous routes like the Maiden's West Overhang 5.11, and freaky 120' free rappel into space. Raptor restrictions February–July. Autumn/spring. City of Boulder Mountain Parks, (303) 441–4142.

Classics: The Maiden: Standard Route 6, East Ridge 10, W. Overhang 11, The Matron: East Ridge 5, Warlocks 12a.

Ref: C [176-119, 88, 74, 69], S [1/88, 4/73]; on-line guide http://climbingboulder.com; Guidebooks: Horan's *Best of Boulder Bouldering*, Benningfield's *Colorado Bouldering*, Rossiter's *Boulder Climbs North and South*, Harlin's *Rocky Mountain*, Roach's *Flatiron Classics: Easy Climbs and Trails*, Ormes's *Guide to the Colorado Mountains*, Dornan's *Rock Climbing Guide to The Boulder, Colorado, Area*.

Directions: From Boulder go south on Hwy. 93 (Broadway) to Hwy. 170 (Eldorado Springs turnoff). Go west on Hwy. 170 approximately 2 mi. to dirt parking lot on north side of road for Bear Peak (Mesa Trail south end trailhead—easier and longer than Shadow Canyon). Shadow Canyon Trail provides access to Shadow Canyon and meets Mesa Trail.

83 Eldorado Canyon State Park ★★★★★

The Golden One of the Front Range. This venerable climbing canyon of Boulder offers a soup-to-nuts climbing experience. Slabby to thin vertical face to wildly overhanging roofs. Intricate multipitch leads and bolted sport climbs offer more than 500 routes up to 5.13. Bouldering challenges along rivercourse. Sandstone formations up to 700' include: Rotwand Wall, Wind Tower, Whale's Tail, Red Garden Wall, West Ridge, Bastille, Peanuts Wall, and Supremacy Rock. Cloud Nine is now a popular bouldering area above Eldorado. Colorful history of local wags. Entry fee. Raptor restriction is in effect February–July. Autumn/spring. State park, (303) 494-3943.

Classics: Wind Tower: Wind Ridge 6, Rainbow Wall 13a; The Whale's Tail: West Crack 2; The Bastille: Bastille Crack 7, West Buttress 9; Red Garden Wall: Ruper 8, Yellow Spur 9/10, Touch 'N Go 9, Rosy Crucifixion 10a, Superslab 10+, T2 10+/11-, Vertigo 11b, C'est La Vie 11, Naked Edge 11, Fire and Ice 11d/12a, Downpressor Man 12b, Scary Canary 12s, Psycho 12+, Genesis 12d, Desdichado 13; Rincon: Over the Hill 10b, Rincon 11a, Aerospace 11s, Wendego 12-, Evictor 12d; Supremacy Crack 11b, The Web 13b, French Fry 12b; Bouldering: Lunge Break B1, Germ Free Adolescence B1+, Milton Boulder: Never Say Never B2.

Ref: AAJ ['88-87, '85-209, 83, 82], C [196-76, 192-40, 187-70, 167-31, 159(3/96)-94, 158-104, 132, 129, 125, 118, 117, 114, 110, 109, 108, 106 to 94, 91, 88, 75 to 66, 61(7/80)-3, 55, 49, 10/72, 2(7/70), many Basecamps], M [92, 77, 55], R [93-128, 90-34, 85-36, 67-59, 65], S [6/80, 1/65]; Sherman's *Stone Crusade*, Kor's *Beyond the Vertical*, Jones's *Climbing in North America*, Ament's *Master of Rock*; on-line guide http://climbingboulder.com; Guidebooks: Horan's *Best of Boulder Bouldering*, Benningfield's *Colorado Bouldering*, Green's *Rock Climbing Colorado*, Knapp and Steven's *100 Select*, Horan's *Front Range Bouldering: Boulder Area*, Rossiter's *Best of Boulder Climbs*, Rossiter's *Boulder Climbs South*, Rossiter's *Front Range Bouldering*, Harlin's *Rocky Mountain*, Erickson's *Rocky Heights*, Dornan's *Rock Climbing Guide to the Boulder, Colorado, Area*.

Directions: From Boulder go 8 mi. south on Hwy. 93 (Broadway). Turn right (west) on Hwy. 170 and go 4 mi. to Eldorado Springs, following park signs to pay kiosk and parking. All canyon property east of park is private—no parking.

84 Mickey Mouse Wall (Industrial Wall) ★★★★

This remote 500' southern suburb of Eldorado is accessed via railroad tunnels. Climbing like Eldo's Red Garden Wall, but without the crowds. Fifty routes on serious sandstone trad leads like 5.11x's Krystal Klyr and Perilous Journey and the magnificent Red Dihedral 5.12+ R. Or, for those that don't want to explode their skinbag, classics like Simian's Way 5.11b. The Industrial Wall is a sport crag on the lower south end of Mickey Mouse Wall offering winter crankin' on 5.13 routes and the Suburbia Boulder below. Raptor

TIM TOULA

Pete Steres on Lunge Break, B1, Eldorado Canyon State Park.

restrictions February–July. Autumn. City of Boulder Open Space.

Classics: Captain Beyond 10, Perilous Journey 11x, Firecracker 12b/c, Red Dihedral 12+, Tunnel Vision 13a, TGV 13c, 14b.

Ref: C [176-30, 101], R [84-24, 70-34, 54]; Guidebooks: Horan's *Best of Boulder Bouldering*, Green's *Rock Climbing Colorado*, Rolofson's *Boulder Sport Climber's Guide*, Rossiter's *Boulder Climbs South*.

Directions: From Boulder go south on Hwy. 93 (Broadway) for 7 mi. past Eldorado Canyon exit to junction with Hwy. 72. Turn west on Hwy. 72 for 1 ½ mi. Turn north on dirt road toward Plainview. Park just east of railroad tracks. Hike north on tracks through four tunnels to Mickey Mouse Wall. Watch for trains coming through the tunnels and thick poison ivy along the base. Porthole South Crag between third and fourth tunnel (also Suburbia Boulder). Secret Crag above second tunnel. Faces south.

85 Coors Crag ★★★

West-facing sandstone/granite crag. Autumn. Uncertain if there is access through private land.

Classics: Rabid Rabbit 12a.
Ref: C 88.

Directions: From Golden (approximately 8 mi. north to northwest of Golden), go north on Hwy. 93, west on Hwy. 72, south on Blue Mountain Dr. to Fire Clay for Coors Crag.

86 Table Mountain (Golden Cliffs) ★★★

Smooth-textured, 50′ basaltic rimrocks make for enjoyable 5.8–5.12 sport cragging on face edges and cracks. South- and west-facing crags with a sunny disposition, especially in winter. Approximately 150 routes. Coors Brewery tours (ask for "short tour" if you want to go straight to the tasting room). Autumn–spring. No camping. The first major climbing area owned and operated by the Access Fund.

Classics: Politicians, Priests, and Body Bags 10a, Silver Bullet 10c, Bullet the Brown Cloud 11b, The Resolution 11c, Industrial Disease 11c, Electrocuticles 12a.

Ref: C 106, R [69-30, 67-93, 47(1/92)-39]; on-line guide http://climbingboulder.com; Guidebooks: Hubbel's *Golden Cliff's Rock Climbs*, Green's *Rock Climbing Colorado*, Hubbel's *Front Range Crags*, Rolofson's *Boulder Sport Climber's Guide*.

Directions: Golden. Table Mountain sits above the Coors Brewery. North Crags accessible via Ptarmigan Ave. Dirt parking lot. A fifteen-minute uphill hike to obvious volcanic rimrock. East Crags: Parking on Peery Peak for crags on east side of mountain is now endangering access.

87 Clear Creek Canyon ★★★★

Clear your mind, and your butt will follow you up some great sport routes. Close to 200 roadside overhanging sport routes in a complex canyon of 150′ granite buttresses like Sport Crag, Stumbling Block, Red Slab, New River Wall (Sonic Youth 13a, Public Enemy 13c), High Wire Crag, Wall of Justice, Monkey House, Anarchy Wall, Crystal Tower, Primo Wall, and Nomad's Cave. Great cranking. Autumn/spring. Private/government land.

Classics: New River Wall: Sonic Youth 13a, Public Enemy 13c; High Wire Crag: Hip at the Lip 12a; Anarchy Wall: Anarchitect 12d.

Ref: C [123(12/90)-27, 88], R 54, SC 3/91; on-line guide http://climbingboulder.com; Guidebooks: Rolofson's *Clear Creek Canyon*, Hubbel's *Clear Creek Classic Rock Climbs*, Green's *Rock Climbing Colorado*, Hubbel's *Front Range Crags*, Rolofson's *Boulder Sport Climber's Guide*.

Directions: From Golden (20 mi. south of Boulder), head just west of town on Hwy. 6 into Clear Creek Canyon. Developed crags on either side of road from 3 mi. west of first tunnel to 1/2 mi. west of fifth tunnel. New River Wall between first and second tunnels, north of road. High Wire Crag is on east side of second tunnel. Anarchy Wall (most popular) is on west side of third highway tunnel.

88 Morrison ★★★★

Top choice in the want ads of Denver/Boulder boulderers. Huge sandstone overhangs keep problems dry and arms swollen. Contortionistic problems in the Black Hole add new dialects to body language. Many 40′ toprope and boulder problem variations. Warm (southwest facing) on sunny winter afternoons and, for the matador of the morning, cool on early summer morns. Bring a toothbrush. Popular with geologists, bankers, nannies, and camel jockeys. Autumn–spring. Private land.

Classics: Hogback Mama, Wisdom Simulator, Cytogrinder, Helicopter, Black Hole, Magnum Force Slab, Dyno-Soar; south side: Breashears Finger Crack, Otis V12.

Ref: C [130(2/92)-52, 102], R [89, 68-30, 54, 14(5/86)]; Sherman's *Stone Crusade*; Guidebooks: Benningfield's *Colorado Bouldering*, Horan's *Front Range Bouldering: Southern Area*, Horan's *Front Range Bouldering*.

Directions: From Morrison park on east end of town on Hwy. 8. Rocks and climbers visible from parking slots. Walk 1/4 mi. east on Hwy. 8 up to Morrison rocks. North of Hwy. 8 is most used; more visible blocks on south side.

89 Bear Creek Canyon (aka Morrison–Evergreen Road) ★★

Forty-five-foot granite bouldering/crags. Great potential short crag climbs, if access allows. Autumn. Private/government land.

Directions: East of Kittredge. Bear Creek Canyon extends from Morrison to Evergreen along Hwy. 74.

90 Noel's Boulders ★★

Thirty-foot granite bouldering. Autumn. Private land.

Ref: Guidebook: Horan's *Front Range Bouldering*.

Directions: Noel's Boulders lie in Evergreen.

91 Lover's Leap ★★★

Ten multipitched routes from 5.6–5.10 above Hwy. 285 on a nice 500′ granite buttress. Other scattered rock formations exist. Any lover of classic routes should leap onto the five-pitch Lover's Leap 5.7+. Ice routes in winter.

Ref: Guidebooks: Hubbel's *Front Range Crags*, Hubbel and Rolofson's *South Platte Rock Climbs*, Harlin's *Rocky Mountain*.

Directions: From southwest Denver, at junction of Hwy. 285 and Soda Lakes Rd., go 3 1/10 mi. west on Hwy. 285. On south side of road. Park in pulloff directly under rock (largest formation on left side of road as one approaches from Denver). Hike up northwest scree field approximately fifteen minutes to Lover's Leap. Faces north.

92 North Turkey Creek (closed) ★★★

Instant "pop-top" rock climbing on this 100′ andesite crag and bouldering area. Twenty very fun routes for beginner and intermediate climbers, topropable with extendo runners on anchors. Limited bouldering, too. Access closed—posted *no* climbing. Autumn/summer. Private land.

Classics: Green Slab 7/9+, Queen of Hearts 6/9, 5.8 boulder hand crack; 5.12 Crack Wall: Routes from 8 to 12a.

Ref: Guidebooks: Hubbel's *Front Range Crags*, Hubbel and Rolofson's *South Platte Rock Climbs*, Harlin's *Rocky Mountain*.
Directions: North of Conifer. Faces north.

93 Ocelot Cliffs ✫✫✫

An old Denver standby 250′ granite cliff. Autumn. Government land.
Classics: Groove 7, Weebles Wobble 9, Cheeses of Nazareth 10, Weebles Wiggle.
Ref: C 58(1/80)-3.
Directions: South Denver. Ocelot Cliffs are at the junction of Hwy. 73 and North Turkey Creek Rd.

94 Arrowhead Rock and Eagle Cliff ✫✫✫

Lots of rock along roadway includes this 250′ granite crag. Summer. NPS.
Directions: This area is south of Conifer and west of Hwy. 285 before reaching Pine Junction. Arrowhead Rock and Eagle Cliff are not visible from road. Faces south.

95 Roxborough State Park (closed) ✫✫

Rock climbing is not allowed on the 70′ red rock formations at this state park. It is a state natural area, slated for day-hike-use only. It has no camping or picnic facilities. State park, (303) 973-3959.
Directions: From southwest Denver (junction of Hwy. 470 and Hwy. 85), pull south on Hwy. 85 a few miles. Turn west on Titan Rd. to Roxborough State Park.

96 Castle Rock Area ✫

From atop this prominent, volcanic landmark above the town of Castle Rock one can view the majestic panorama of the Front Range. Easy fourth-class scramble on east face leads to summit. Uncertain if there are some 80′ roped routes. Boulder-strewn hillside offers minimal bouldering, where holds have been known to break easier than fine china. Autumn/spring. City park.
Directions: At Castle Rock (on I-25 south of Denver). Depart I-25 at exit 182, going east on road to Castle Rock formation with flag and antennas on top.

97 Castlewood Canyon State Park (Cherry Creek Canyon) ✫✫✫

Multitudes of bouldering blocks and 60′ short bolted lead walls wind through this serpentine canyon of Castlewood Conglomerate. Good variety of more than sixty climbs with grades up to B2 and 5.12. Sharp rock warrants rope protection for topropes. Fixed anchors should be checked or backed up. Beware friable holds. No camping in park. More significantly, only 3.2 percent beer allowed in park . . . whoa, du-u-ude! Autumn/spring. State park, (303) 688-5242.
Classics: Hot Fudge 7, Gorilla Milk 9, Hot Tuna 10, Pretzel

Logic 11, You Name It 12-.
Ref: R 60; on-line guide http://climbingboulder.com; Guidebooks: Benningfield's *Colorado Bouldering*, Hanson's *Rock Climber's Guide to Castlewood Canyon State Park*, Horan's *Front Range Bouldering: Southern Area*, Green's *Rock Climbing Colorado: Front Range Crags*, Drysdale and Crooks' *Scenic Solitude*, Mosiman's *Climber's Guide to Castlewood Canyon*.
Directions: From junction of I-25 and Hwy. 86 in Castle Rock (thirty minutes from Denver), proceed approximately 6 ½ mi. east on Hwy. 86 to just ⁴/₁₀ mi. before Franktown (junction Hwy. 83 and Hwy. 86), then follow signs south to Castlewood Canyon State Park. From entrance, walls on right in order are 5+ Dime (private land) at first pullout, Grocery Store (most routes) at second parking area, and Porky's Wall/South Park Boulder at south entrance station. To east of road is Falls Wall. All are short hikes on trail to rock. Entrance fee.

98 Rifle Mountain Park ✫✫✫✫✫

It's far from quiet on the Western Front. Since 1990, Rifle has had a skyrocketing appeal with elite sport climbers and has become an international favorite in the gymnastic climbing arena. Cliffs run for approximately 2 ½ mi. on either side of a delicate riparian habitat. Most routes (approximately 230 in 1995) come out of caves/amphitheaters or severely overhung walls. Routes less than one hundred degrees are considered slabs, thus guaranteeing a burn that will melt diamonds. Pegg's *Bite the Bullet* (1997) is the definitive guidebook. Notably excellent ice climbing in winter. Showers/swimming at Rifle city pool. Fee camping at far end of canyon or free farther up in national forest. Check with rangers for current details. City of Rifle Park.
Classics: Hot Potato 9, PMS 10c, 80 Feet of Meat 11a, Primer 11b, Bolt Action 11d, Helpless Betty 11d, Pitchfest 12b, Pump Action 12c, Pumporama 12d, In Your Face 12d, Apocalypse 91 13a, Anti-Phil 13a, Vision Thing 13b, Fluff Boy 13c, Dumpster Barbecue 13c, Path 13c, Slice 14a, Zulu 14b, Tomfoolery 14b, Kryptonite 14.
Ref: C [179-25, 177-32, 172-27, 170-23, 164-28, 163-68/106, 162-76, 158-120, 157-34, 138, 136, 131(4/92)-20], R [98-24, 77-87, 75-18, 54]; SC [12/92, 12/91]; Guidebooks: Media West's *Climber's Guide to Rifle Mountain Park*, Pegg's *Bite the Bullet*, Green's *Rock Climbing Colorado*, Saab's *Climber's Guide to Rifle*.
Directions: From Rifle (approximately twenty minutes), go north shortly up Hwy. 13. Turn right on Hwy. 325 through Rifle Gap. Go right at Rifle Gap Reservoir. Continue on Hwy. 325 until ¼ mi. past State Fish Hatchery to obvious limestone walls in Rifle Mountain Park. Climbing walls marked with signs.

99 Glenwood Canyon ✫✫✫

This incredibly scenic canyon contains towering 1,000′ canyon walls of limestone and granite. Layton Kor made some of the first ascents. The limestone was once described as alternating layers of "Ry-Krisp and kitty litter." The

The beautiful Independence Monument in Colorado National Monument above Grand Junction.

Pukes sport climbing area is the most solid limestone at the east end of the tunnel, 1 mi. east of Glenwood Springs on the north side of I–70 where a large pullout allows parking. Also, solid granite near dam on south side of river. Amazing, hairboat white-water run. Autumn/summer. Private land/USFS–White River NF, (970) 945–2521.
Classics: International 10 pitch 5.9+, Sucking Wind 11 (granite).
Ref: AAJ ['86-174, '83, '77-196, '76-401], C [75, 72-6].
Directions: From Glenwood Springs follow I–70 east into Glenwood Canyon. Various access points.

100 No Name Canyon ✫✫✫

Tranquil canyon with 100' granite crags and trailside bouldering. Autumn. USFS–White River NF, (970) 945–2521.
Ref: Benningfield's *Colorado Bouldering*.
Directions: From Glenwood Springs follow I–70 east to No Name exit, number 119. Go north from exit past residences to parking area. Rock beyond in No Name Canyon. Bouldering areas are limited to trailside area at bridge. Poison Ivy Wall is to left. Other route areas above to right.

101 Wolcott Boulders/Cliffs (Eagle River Recreational Area) ✫✫✫

Two fun, 20' Dakota sandstone bouldering cubes feature intermediate problems and toprope bolts on top. Also some leads on the cliffs across the river. A nice I–70 traveler's bivy spot. Autumn–spring. BLM, (970) 947–2800.
Ref: J. Sherman; Guidebook: Benningfield's *Colorado Bouldering*.
Directions: From Wolcott (junction of Hwy. 6 and Hwy. 131), float 1 3/10 mi. west on US 6. Park/camp at obvious Wolcott Boulders in fisherman's camp on right. Short cliffbands accessible from above by going 8/10 mi. north on Hwy. 131 to pulloff on left. Hike west to cliff edge. Or, from junction, hike west along railroad tracks to rock.

Cragging is north of I–70 (park at mm 154 westbound, well off interstate), up gully. Nice wall on right.

102 Frisco Bouldering (aka Via Boulders) ✫✫✫

A 17' metamorphic bouldering wall for the thoroughbred boulderer. This laconic area has less than a dozen problems, but you'll turn as red as a pepper climbing them. The two Steve Mammen testpieces, Frisco Buttress (arête) V6 and Via the Hot One (concave face) V9 are among the tougher boulder problems along Colorado's noisy I–70. Bring earplugs. Summer/autumn. USFS–White River NF, (970) 945–2521.
Classics: Frisco Buttress V6, Via the Hot One V9.
Ref: S. Mammen; Sherman's *Stone Crusade;* Guidebooks: Benningfield's *Colorado Bouldering,* Astaldi and Gruber's *High Country Crags.*
Directions: Outskirts of Frisco. At I–70 westbound entrance ramp of exit 201. Park at pullout before getting onto westbound entrance ramp. Hike southwest on freeway entrance ramp, staying off pavement. Above the first lamppost and before the ramp ends and I–70 begins, a faint footpath leads 20 yd. up slope to the well-chalked, overhanging Frisco Bouldering Wall, a 20' granite wall visible 50' above road with aspen trees in front. Faces east.

103 Swan Mountain Road Bouldering ✫✫✫

Friendly 20' quartzite, west-facing practice wall in trees north of Dillon Reservoir offers good beginner and intermediate bouldering/short topropes. Fun intermediate problems—try the classic 5.11 overlap in left center of wall. Summer. USFS–White River NF, (970) 945–2521.
Ref: Guidebooks: Benningfield's *Colorado Bouldering,* Astaldi and Gruber's *High Country Crags.*
Directions: From Silverthorne exit (number 205) on I–40, go south on Hwy. 6 for about 4 mi. to traffic light for Swan Mountain Rd./Breckenridge. Turn right on Swan Mountain Rd. for 1 9/10 mi. (going past USFS Prospector Campground). Make right turn into Swan Mountain Recreation Area. Immediately after turn, park at gate (sometimes locked) on right. Find footpath and hike five minutes northwest through woods to hidden rock band. Toprope wall ten minutes farther north.

104 Silver Plume ✫✫✫

A goldmine of short 100' granite cliffs crag above mines. Early climbs done by Army's 10th Mountain Division. In the 1990s, routes put up to 5.13 above the drone of I–70. Ten routes. Summer. Private/government land.
Ref: C 105; Guidebook: Hubbel's *Front Range Crags.*
Directions: At Silver Plume (west of Georgetown on I–70). A goldmine of short rock cliffs lines I–70 in either direction from Georgetown. Routes done above the town of Silver Plume (use Silver Plume exit west of store to parking at

mine). Trails lead west and north up stream drainage to West Slabs and Monument Rock.

105 Mt. Evans (14,264') ★★★

Several good alpine granite cliffs at 13,000', the most renowned being the 700' Black Wall. Mt. Evans is billed as the highest paved road in the world. Raven Rock, across Grass Creek near Wildlife Preserve near Mt. Evans, is a cragging area. Summer. USFS–Arapaho NF, (970) 498-2770.

Classics: Good Evans III 11- 5p, Road Warrior III 11-, Rappel Route III 11.

Ref: AAJ ['97-161, '89-159]; C [105, 88], R [85-102, 32(7/89)]; Guidebooks: Roach's *Colorado's Fourteeners,* Hubbel's *Front Range Crags,* Ormes's *Guide to the Colorado Rockies.*

Directions: From Idaho Springs (at I-70 exit 240), drive 21 mi. south on Hwy. 103, then turn right (south) on Hwy. 5 (Mt. Evans Summit Rd.). Four climbing areas. From Chicago Lakes Overlook on the Mt. Evans Hwy. (near Summit Lake), a white, 700' granite wall is visible. Hike northwest around Summit Lake to Black Wall, containing challenging free climbing at the Road Warrior Buttress, Road Warrior 5.10d (Wild lightning bolt offwidths). Good Evans III 5.11- is also recommended. Also, more climbing at The Aprons (5.7 slabs/fins), north of the summit of the road or west of Summit Lake, and good crags above west end of Lincoln Lake back down the hill approximately 2 mi. from Summit Lake.

106 Colorado National Monument ★★★

Collection of colorful, timeworn 500' sandstone spires and sheer-walled cliffs viewed from a high plateau. Formations include Sentinel Spire, Pipe Organ Spire, Organ Pipe Tower, Independence Monument, and The Kissing Couple. Otto's Route III 5.9 is *the* popular ascent for first-time park climbers. Sentinel Spire's Medicine Man is a 5.12 crack classic. Scattered cragging and paltry bouldering lie north of visitors center. Historic climbing guide in visitors center. Prehistoric Indian cultures. Visit September–November/March–April. Pay campground at park or free BLM to south/west. NPS, (970) 858-3617.

Classics: Independence Monument: Otto's Route III 9; Sentinel Spire: Fast Draw 10/Medicine Man 12, Bell Tower 11, Devil's Kitchen Area, Pipe Organ Spire, Kissing Couple.

Ref: AAJ ['96, '94, '92-143, '89-159, '88-144, '87-70, 84], C [187-72, 111, 105, 102, 101, 95, 88, 74, 10/72, 48], R [75-46, 65, 60, 16(10/86)-56]; Guidebooks: Burns's *Selected Climbs in the Desert Southwest,* Green's *Rock Climbing Colorado,* Bjornstad's *Desert Rock III,* Knapp's *Fifty Select Classic Desert Climbs,* Bjornstad's *Desert Rock,* Harlin's *Rocky Mountain.*

Directions: West entrance (for scenic Rimrock Rd.): From Fruita at I-70 exit, go up switchbacks 4 mi. south to Colorado National Monument Rimrock Rd. Cliffs up road have routes, spires east/southeast of visitors center.

Rappel in. East entrance (for practice rocks and Independence Monument): Go farther east a couple miles past west entrance on Hwy. 340 to indistinct parking area. Hike by fenced-off swank houses into canyon one hour to Independence Monument.

107 Gas-Food Sign Boulders ★

These 30' roadside talus blocks present some intriguing, though limited sandstone bouldering challenges for all grades below large southern slope of Mt. Garfield's Mancos Shale. Autumn/spring. BLM, (970) 244-3000.

Ref: Guidebook: Benningfield's *Colorado Bouldering.*

Directions: From Grand Junction go just 5 mi. east of town on I-70 westbound lane. Parking only accessible via westbound lane! Gas-Food Boulders are at GAS-FOOD sign 5 mi. before town. Park by sign. Hike one or two minutes to rock. Difficult overhanging edge problem and easier slabs. This is only one area—other scattered bouldering areas exist along I-70 along this slope.

108 Redstone Boulders and Raleigh World ★★★

Redstone Boulders are a collection of four conglomerate boulders with more than one hundred variations. Difficult Jeff Achey and Duane Raleigh problems like the twisted Corkscrew Roof B1+. Sport crag twenty-minute hike up steep hill to west (ice slabs in winter). Topropes 2 mi. south on 50' crag next to waterfalls. Forest Service Campground just ¼ mi. across bridge to east. Summer. USFS–White River NF, (970) 945-2521.

Ref: J. Shireman; C [C 165(12/96)-124, 132]; Guidebook: Benningfield's *Colorado Bouldering.*

Directions: From Carbondale, Redstone Boulders are approximately 15 mi. south on Hwy. 133. Park on east side of road at boulders (visible in riverbed at mm 53). Raleigh World: Continue south on Hwy. 133 and take first turn into Redstone. Go to second dip in road (10 mph sign). Park at gray dirt road going uphill. Hike up this road until it bends right, then turn left onto trail for 300 yd. When you pass an 8' spruce on right side of trail, head uphill on faint trail to two huge boulders.

109 Gold Butte ★★★

Fifty-foot south-facing winter sandstone bouldering in Aspen during sunny spells. Dakota sandstone, but fairly soft. Some topropes. Landowners don't approve of climbing, i.e., no trespassing! Private land.

Ref: J. Sherman.

Directions: North of Aspen. Ask locals.

110 Patrol Boulder and Aspen Area Overview ★★★★

Patrol Boulder is a handy 15' roadside warm-up boulder 3 mi. east of town. At 8,000' starting elevation, Aspen climbing areas are characterized by numerous quality one- and two-pitch small routes in subalpine pageantry. Climbing during golden autumn days is almost better than slow dancing. The mainstays of Aspen climbing areas are dispersed along Hwy. 82 east to Independence Pass. Easy approaches, though not all are road visible. Bruce's *Rock Climber's Guide to Aspen* is good climbing information source. Camping at various USFS campgrounds (Difficult, Weller, or Lincoln Creek). USFS–White River NF, (970) 945-2521.

Classics: Zanzibar Dihedral 7, Ultra Edge 9, Cryogenics 10, Mind Parasite 11, Bicentennial Roof 12-.

Ref: C [136(2/93), 105, 63], R 54; Guidebooks: Benningfield's *Colorado Bouldering*, Green's *Rock Climbing Colorado*, Higgins's *Rock Climber's Guide to Aspen*, Harlin's *Rocky Mountain*, Bruce's *Rock Climber's Guide to Aspen*, Davis's *Aspen Rockclimbing: Selected Routes*.

Directions: Patrol Boulder: From Aspen go east until $9/10$ mi. west of Difficult Campground (3 mi. east of Aspen) on Hwy. 82. On north side of road 20 yd. uphill in the bushes. The mainstays of Aspen climbing areas are dispersed along Hwy. 82 east to Independence Pass.

111 Dragon Rock, Master Headwall, and Classy Cliff ✮✮✮

Fifty-foot granite crags. A small handful of climbs. Striking aid crack (uncertain if freeclimbable). Summer. USF–White River NF, (970) 945-2521.

Classics: Classy Cliff: Edge of Time 8, Shot Put 9, Arching Connection 10b, Unfinished Business 12c/d.

Ref: Guidebooks: Bruce's *Rock Climber's Guide to Aspen*, Harlin's *Rocky Mountain*.

Directions: From Aspen go east on Hwy. 82 to $7/10$ mi. east of Difficult Campground entrance (3 mi. east of Aspen). Dragon Rock, Master Headwall, and Classy Cliff are north of road. Avoid death slope by skirting right. Faces south.

112 Difficult Cliffs ✮✮✮

Eighty-foot granite crags. East and west cliffs. Difficult routes. West face has sustained, overhanging routes. Summer/autumn. USFS–White River NF, (970) 945-2521.

Classics: Difficult East: Daredevil 9, Pipeline 10+, Fast Twitch 11c; Difficult West: The Product 10d, B-Sharp 11+, Seventh Octave 12.

Ref: Guidebooks: Bruce's *Rock Climber's Guide to Aspen*, Harlin's *Rocky Mountain*.

Directions: From Aspen go 3 mi. east on Hwy. 82 to Difficult Campground entrance. Difficult Cliffs are across the creek from the campground via twenty-minute hike.

113 Wall Walls et al. ✮✮✮

A 120′ granite crag. Good climbing in the 5.9–5.11 range. USFS–White River NF, (970) 945-2521.

Classics: Emancipation Proclamation 9, Avant Garde 10-,

Carpetbagger 11b, Fish Worm Crack 12a.

Ref: Guidebooks: Bruce's *Rock Climber's Guide to Aspen*, Harlin's *Rocky Mountain*.

Directions: From Aspen, at Difficult Campground entrance (3 mi. east of Aspen) on Hwy. 82, go east for 3 $6/10$ mi. Wall Walls area is south of road. East and West Walls.

114 Guides Crack and Jaws Boulder ✮✮✮

Twenty-five-foot granite bouldering; crack and face. Good short, classic problems. Summer. USFS–White River NF, (970) 945-2521.

Ref: Guidebooks: Bruce's *Rock Climber's Guide to Aspen*, Harlin's *Rocky Mountain*.

Directions: From Aspen, at Difficult Campground entrance (3 mi. east of Aspen) on Hwy. 82, go east for 3 $9/10$–4 $1/10$ mi. Guides Crack and Jaws Boulder are north and south of road, respectively.

115 Weller Slab ✮✮✮

Scenic 200′ granite crag. Two-pitch routes from 5.7–5.11, e.g., Zanzibar Dihedral 5.7. Summer. USFS–White River NF, (970) 945-2521.

Classics: Zanzibar Dihedral 7, Ultra Edge 9, Apple Pie 10a, Three-Eyed Toad 10+, Generation of Swine 11d.

Ref: Guidebooks: Green's *Rock Climbing Colorado*, Higgins's *Rock Climber's Guide to Aspen*, Harlin's *Rocky Mountain*.

Directions: From Aspen, at Difficult Campground entrance (3 mi. east of Aspen) on Hwy. 82, go east for 4 $3/10$ mi. north of Weller Campground. Fifteen- to twenty-minute uphill hike to Weller Slab. Faces south.

116 Pass Walls and Whirlpool Rocks ✮✮✮

Two-hundred-foot granite crag. Short approaches and varietal climbs. Summer. USFS–White River NF, (970) 945-2521.

Classics: Pass Walls: Rascal 5.7, Hose Fossil Finish 5.11c, Might as Well Pump 5.12d; Whirlpool Rock: Flexible Flyer 5.10+, Flying Dutchman 5.11+.

Ref: C 91; Guidebooks: Bruce's *Rock Climber's Guide to Aspen*, Harlin's *Rocky Mountain*, Davis's *Aspen Rockclimbing: Selected Routes*.

Directions: From Aspen, at Difficult Campground entrance (3 mi. east of Aspen) on Hwy. 82, go east for 4 $7/10$–4 $9/10$ mi. north of road. Walk $1/2$ mi. east to Pass Walls from parking under Whirlpool Rock. Pass Walls are right next to highway. Radically overhung boulder (Ice Cube BJ V5) on south side of road.

117 Grotto Wall and Nude Buttress ✮✮✮

The most popular Independence Pass crag. Two-hundred-foot granite crag bouldering. Two-minute approach, fifteen minutes to upper walls. Deserves a visit. Bouldering in talus slope below . . . possibly bad landings. Summer. USFS–White River NF, (970) 945-2521.

Classics: Lower: Twin Cracks 5.8, Cryogenics 5.10c/11d, Wire and Fire 5.11-, Rocket Man 5.12a, Scene of the Crime 5.12d, Exotic Headache 5.13-; Upper: Plaque Right 5.9, Mind Parasite 5.11a, Bicentennial Roof 5.12-, Rock Candy 5.12a, Alison in Wonderland 5.12c; The Ineditable V9.

Ref: C 103; Guidebooks: Green's *Rock Climbing Colorado*, Bruce's *Rock Climber's Guide to Aspen*, Harlin's *Rocky Mountain*.

Directions: From Aspen, at Difficult Campground entrance (3 mi. east of Aspen), go east 5 4/10 mi. east on Hwy. 82. Park at hairpin turnout or up road at Lincoln Creek turnoff. Grotto Wall is north of road. Caution: Hwy. 82 sees lots of traffic.

118 Greaseball Slab and Lincoln Creek Crag ★★★

A 100' granite crag with bouldering. Traditional and sport routes. Summer. USFS–White River NF, (970) 945-2521.

Classics: Cramper 5.10c, Thrill-A-Thon 5.10+, Urinary Tract 5.11, Dean's Day Off 5.12a.

Ref: Guidebooks: Bruce's *Rock Climber's Guide to Aspen*, Harlin's *Rocky Mountain*.

Directions: From Aspen, at Difficult Campground entrance (3 mi. east of Aspen) take Hwy. 82 east 6 2/10 mi. to Lincoln Creek Rd. Turn right (south) on Lincoln Creek Rd, 1/4 mi. to campground (bouldering/topropes), 1/2 mi. more to Lincoln Creek Crag (fifteen-minute approach uphill to northeast).

119 Turkey, Wild Rock, and Bulldog Cliff ★★★

Three-hundred-foot good granite crag with bouldering. The Upper Boulderfield is the most popular Independence Pass bouldering. Good landings, easy and moderate problems. Super scenery. Summer. USFS–White River NF, (970) 945-2521.

Classics: Turkey: Nose 5.8, Identity Crisis 5.10d, Inner Limits 5.11d.

Ref: Guidebooks: Higgins's *Rock Climber's Guide to Aspen*, Harlin's *Rocky Mountain*.

Directions: From Aspen, at Difficult Campground entrance (3 mi. east of Aspen) on Hwy. 82, go east for 7 4/10 mi. Turkey, Wild Rock, and Bulldog Cliff lie north of road.

120 Independence Pass (Instant Karma Cliff)/Putterman's Dome ★★★

One-hundred-foot granite crag in grand, high mountain scenery. Summer. USFS–White River NF, (970) 945-2521.

Classics: Kundalini 10.

Ref: C. Burns; C [160-78, 136, 116, 98, 75, 52], S 9/74; Randall's *Vertigo Games*; Guidebooks: Perkins's *Independence Pass West Climbing Guide*, Wille's *Heinous Cling*, Green's *Rock Climbing Colorado*, Bruce's *Rock Climber's Guide to Aspen*.

Directions: From Aspen go east until 18 mi. east of Difficult Campground entrance (3 mi. east of Aspen) on Hwy. 82. Hike 1 mi. north to Instant Karma Cliff. Another cliff, Putterman's Dome, lies between Monitor Rock and crest of pass, almost invisible from highway. Putterman's is small dome the size of Grotto Wall. Faces west.

121 Independence Pass (East Side Boulders) ★★★

Two boulders, one on either side of road, saturated with variations every few feet. Amusing for an hour or two. Fifteen-foot gneiss bouldering. Summer. USFS–San Isabel NF, (719) 545-8737.

Ref: C [132-63, 116(10/89)-25]; Sherman's *Stone Crusade*; Guidebook: Benningfield's *Colorado Bouldering*.

Directions: From Independence Pass go east on Hwy. 82 to bottom of steep grade (last 10 mph switchback). Just 20 yd. past switchback, turn left onto dirt road and follow it approximately 1 mi. to the East Side Boulders.

122 Monitor Rock ★★★

This 500' polished granite buttress sits quietly amid the stunning Colorado mountain scenery. At 10,000' elevation; be prepared for cold mountain weather while cranking on sixty assorted routes. Camping off highway. Summer. USFS–San Isabel NF, (719) 545-8737.

Classics: Outward Bound South Arête 5.5, 10th Army Division 5.8, and many classic modern 5.10–12 sport routes.

Ref: R 74-102, S 9/74; Guidebooks: Aspen Climbing Guides' *Monitor Rock Select*, Topo sheet.

Directions: From Twin Lakes go 4 mi. west on Hwy. 82 or 12 7/10 mi. west from Hwy. 24. Monitor Rock is largest formation north of road. Most sport routes on west (main) wall.

123 Ellingwood Ridge ★★★

A classic, 1,500' mountaineer's goal on the alpine granite of the Sawatch Range's La Plata Peak (14,336'). Though easy class 5 on a technical scale, it is long. First ascended by Albert Ellingwood in 1921. Summer. USFS–San Isabel NF, (719) 545-8737.

Ref: C 2(7/70); Guidebooks: Dawson's *Guide to Colorado's Fourteeners Vol. 1*, Borneman and Lampert's *A Climber's Guide to Colorado's Fourteeners*, Bueler's *Roof of the Rockies*.

Directions: From Twin Lakes Village drive 8 mi. west on Hwy. 82 to junction of Lake Creek and its south fork. Cross bridge over Lake Creek to dirt road up west side of south fork to Ellingwood Ridge.

124 Arkansas River Granite (Granite Canyon) ★★★

Two cliffs 1/4 mi. apart. Scattered boulders and dispersed 400' walls of pink granite. Stay on public land. Summer/autumn. Private/government land.

Ref: C 132, S 9/74.

Directions: Granite Canyon: From Leadville go south on Hwy. 24 to town of Granite, then south 3 ½ mi. on Hwy. 24. Other granite areas can be found along the Arkansas River on down to Buena Vista.

125 Minturn Rock ☆☆

Two west-facing sandstone buttresses above town. Fun bolted faces. Very limited bouldering. Summer. Private land/USFS–San Isabel NF, (719) 545-8737.

Ref: Guidebook: Benningfield's *Colorado Bouldering*.

Directions: On Hwy. 24 above Minturn. Minturn Boulders are east of Hwy. 24 just ⁴/10 mi. south of I-70. Turn left, crossing railroad tracks for about ¹/10 mi. Also, routes on two prows east of Minturn and Hwy. 24.

126 Red Cliff Areas (Gilman Canyon, Roof Rock, Hornsilver) ☆☆☆

Gilman Canyon has mixed granite climbing and good potential. Roof Rock is a good toprope slab area with plenty of moderate routes. Hornsilver has the area's more exposed and technically difficult routes. The campground is a good place for a quick strike on the area's climbing. At Homestake reside quality intermediate routes. Many attractive, high-altitude summertime buttresses expose one to Colorado's mountain beauty. More information at Vail Mountaineer. Popular white-water area. Summer. USFS–White River NF, (970) 945-2521.

Classics: Gilman Canyon: Crack-A-Ono 10c, Air Gilman 11c; Roof Rock: Trouble With Normal 10b; Hornsilver (Lower): Luna C 12b; Hornsilver (Upper): Moonwalk 11a; Homestake: Wolfman Shuffle 11b.

Ref: R 54; Guidebooks: *Vail Rock Topo Sheets*, Benningfield's *Colorado Bouldering*.

Directions: Several areas near Red Cliff. From bridge at Hwy. 24 and Red Cliff junction, going south on Hwy. 24, areas include: Gilman Canyon, first right from bridge; Roof Rock, approximately 1 ¹/10 mi. from bridge; Hornsilver Cliffs, 1 ½ mi. from bridge (cliffs on hill above Hornsilver Campground); and Homestake crag, 2 ⁶/10 mi. from bridge and then right onto Homestake Rd. for ⁸/10 mi.

127 Mt. of the Holy Cross (14,005') (Sawatch Range) ☆☆☆☆

The great, white cross of snow, 1,200' high by 500' across, in the mountain's northeast face has become a symbol for climbers and Christians alike. Mixed rock and ice routes. For those who heed the hard-core mountaineer's motto, "Never pass up a chance to keep yourself out of breath," see the complete listing of 741 highest summits in the state of Colorado above 13,000', *Colorado's High Thirteener's* by Garratt and Martin. Holy Cross Couloir III east-facing snow route is the classic. Summer/autumn. USFS–White River NF, (970) 945-2521.

Ref: C 58(1/80)-3, S [11/80, 12/76, 5/70]; Guidebooks: Roach's *Colorado Fourteeners*, Garratt and Martin's *Colorado's High Thirteener's*, Borneman and Lampert's *A Climber's Guide to Colorado's Fourteeners*, Ormes's *Guide to the Colorado Mountains*, Bueler's *Roof of the Rockies*.

Directions: From Minturn go 2 mi. south on Hwy. 24, then turn west for 6 mi. to Tigawan Campground and 2 more mi. to Half Moon Campground. Hike 2 mi. to Half Moon Pass and then 2 mi. to East Cross Creek. Total distance: Half Moon Campground to summit of Mt. of the Holy Cross is 7 mi.

128 SP–South Platte Area Overview ☆☆☆☆/Etive Slabs ☆☆

South Platte Area is a seemingly endless celebration of granite domes in a fragrant ponderosa pine forest. A climber's crack-climbing heaven. South Platte's one rule of thumb: The longer the approach, the better the rock. The centerpiece of South Platte magazine articles has been the incredible 5.13 Sphinx Crack. Etive Slabs offer good guiding routes from 5.5–5.9 on a west-facing, insignificant 200' slab as far as South Platte rock goes. They are on private land and closed to climbing. Thus, no camping at Etive. Raptor restrictions March–July. Summer/autumn. Private land/USFS–Pike NF, (719) 545-8737.

Classics: South Platte Classics: Optical Illusion 9, Center Route 9 (Cynical Pinnacle), Whimsical Dreams 11, Wunsch's Dihedral (Cynical Pinnacle) 11+; Sphinx Rock: Lickey Split 7, Cheops 10c, Sphinx Crack 13; Etive Slabs: Parchment Farm 6R.

Ref: AAJ ['91-174, 85-210, 84, 83], C [151-58, 117, 111, 110, 107, 106, 104, 103, 102 (map), 99, 98, 97], R [80-48, 69-19, 25]; on-line guide http://climbingboulder.com; Guidebooks: Trout's *South Platte Rock: Selected Climbs*, Hubbel's *South Platte Rock Climbing*, Green's *Rock Climbing Colorado*, Hubbel's *Rock Climbing the South Platte*, Rolofson's *The Hard Stuff (Turkey Rock and South Platte)*, Hubbel's *Brown Book of Lies*, Cheney's *For Turkeys Only*.

Directions: South Platte is a large granitic wonderland encompassing rock from Pine to Woodland Park on Hwy. 87. For Etive Slabs: From junction of Hwy. 285 and Hwy. 126, go south 5 ⁶/10 mi. on Hwy. 126. Turnout on left (north).

129 SP–Ding Domes ☆☆

Two-hundred-foot intermediate granite crag with 5.7–5.9 face routes. Weekend paint-pellet war games may be encountered here. Summer. Private land.

Classics: Raindance 6R, Easy Streak 7R, Beeline 9-.

Ref: Guidebooks: Hubbel and Rolofson's *South Platte Rock Climbs*, Harlin's *Rocky Mountain*.

Directions: From Pine go 2 mi. north on Hwy. 83. Hike up valley to west (fifteen minutes) to Ding Domes. Faces east.

130 SP–Bucksnort Slabs ☆☆☆

Two-hundred-foot east-facing granite beginning to expert slabs. Crack of Anticipation 5.7+ is the classic dihedral and

Slippery When Wet 5.11 a wild face. Limited parking. No camping on-site. Famous Bucksnort Saloon ³/10 mi. farther up road. Twenty routes. Summer. Private land.

Classics: Classic Dihedral 7, Crack of Anticipation 7+, Shaken Bake 10+, Slippery When Wet 11b, Bouxsnort 5.11c, Hurricane Gloria 12-.

Ref: C 94; Guidebooks: Green's *Rock Climbing Colorado*, Hubbel and Rolofson's *South Platte Rock Climbs*, Harlin's *Rocky Mountain*.

Directions: From Pine go 2 ¹/10 mi. north on Jefferson County Rd. 83 (dirt). Park north of slabs for a one-minute approach to Bucksnort Slabs.

131 SP–Squat Rock ☆☆☆

One-hundred-and-fifty-foot intermediate granite crag with thirty routes from 5.7–5.11. Try getting Higher Education 5.10. No camping. Keyhole hangers may be needed for some routes. Summer. Private land.

Classics: Lichen or Not 9, Higher Education 10.

Ref: Guidebooks: Hubbel and Rolofson's *South Platte Rock Climbs*, Harlin's *Rocky Mountain*.

Directions: From Pine, Squat Rock is 1 ¹/10 mi. north on Jefferson County Rd. 83 in tight valley on east side of Elk Creek. Faces south.

132 SP–Sphinx Rock ☆☆☆☆

This 150′ southwest-facing granite crag contains the well-publicized Sphinx Crack 5.13, a dynamited finger crack; one of the hardest and most famous of the hardman cracks in Colorado first flashed by Yuji Hirayama in the 1990s. Eight routes total. Autumn. Private land.

Classics: Lickety Split 7, Cheops 10c, Sphinx Crack 13.

Ref: C [154-106, 136, 70]; Guidebooks: Green's *Rock Climbing Colorado*, Hubbel and Rolofson's *South Platte Rock Climbs*, Harlin's *Rocky Mountain*.

Directions: From Pine, Sphinx Rock is ⁴/10 mi. north on Jefferson County Rd. 83.

133 SP–Beach and The Wave ☆☆

Intermediate granite slab crag. Private land; climbing strongly discouraged. Summer.

Ref: Guidebooks: Hubbel and Rolofson's *South Platte Rock Climbs*, Harlin's *Rocky Mountain*.

Directions: From Pine go 2 ⁷/10 mi. north on Jefferson County Rd. 83 to Bucksnort Saloon. Turn on road to east. Follow this to dead-end sign. Take sharp right at this sign. Park at first major left switchback. The Wave is to the right (five-minute hike). The Beach is next to next switchback.

134 SP–Banner Peak ☆☆

Intermediate granite crag with some okay cracks. Sunny, but long, unpopular hike has made it seldom visited. Summer. Private land.

Ref: Guidebooks: Hubbel and Rolofson's *South Platte Rock Climbs*, Harlin's *Rocky Mountain*.

Directions: Banner Peak is a forty-five-minute hike west from back side of The Dome.

135 SP–The Dome/The Bishop ☆☆☆

The Dome offers 500′ south-facing granite crag climbing. Some steep, some slabby. Long friction pitches like Bishop's Jaggers 5.9 captivate. The Bishop Finger Crack 5.12c is the challenge of The Bishop, a two-pitch formation offering hard cracks. Summer. The BLM land may be sold to Jefferson County Open Space. BLM/Jefferson County Open Space/private land.

Classics: Bishop's Jaggers 9-, Topographical Oceans 10, Craftwork 11c, Bishop Finger Crack 12b/c.

Ref: Guidebooks: Trout's *South Platte Rock*, Green's *Rock Climbing Colorado*, Hubbel and Rolofson's *South Platte Rock Climbs*, Harlin's *Rocky Mountain*, Ormes's *Guide to the Colorado Mountains*.

Directions: From Conifer go west ⁶/10 mi. on Hwy. 285, then south on Jefferson County Rd. (JCR) 97 (Foxton/Reynold's Park Rd.) 8 ³/10 mi. Turn right and travel on JCR 96 for 3 ⁸/10 mi. to large parking area on west side of road next to old mining road. Hike up old mining road to The Dome or The Bishop for three-quarters to one hour.

136 SP–Malay Archipelago ☆☆☆

Four-hundred-foot granite face. The Malay Archipelago is a cluster of easy-access areas. Summer. USFS–White River NF, (970) 945-2521.

Classics: El Nino 10, Platte Magic 10.

Ref: C 169-120; Guidebooks: Trout's *South Platte Rock*, Hubbel and Rolofson's *South Platte Rock Climbs*, Harlin's *Rocky Mountain*.

Directions: From junction of Hwy. 285 and Jefferson County Rd. (JCR) 97, go south 8 ³/10 mi. on JCR 97 to junction with JCR 96. Go southeast (left) on 96 for 2 ¹/2 mi. to Jazz Dome (on left), and ⁸/10 mi. farther to Dome Rock (above town of Dome Rock). Atlantis Slab is 4 ⁸/10 mi. past Dome Rock (east of road).

137 SP–Cathedral Spires (Sunshine Wall, Poe Buttress, Cynical Pinnacle) ☆☆☆☆

Classic 350′ southeast-facing granite pinnacles and walls. Sunshine Wall, with five pitch routes, is known for its warm exposure in winter and wild cracks like Equinox 5.10+. Cynical Pinnacle is known for Wunsch's Dihedral 5.11+. The Poe Buttress is not known for the excellent Mississippi Half Step 5.11+. Entire area, including Dome and Bishop, closed March 1 to July 31 to protect falcon nesting. Summer. Jefferson County Open Space.

Classics: Cynical Pinnacle: Center Rt 9+ (no aid unless you traverse to the last pitch of Wunsch's), Center Rt 10 A0, Wunsch Dihedral 11 A0 or 11+R, Class Act 11; Poe Buttress: The Maelstrom 10+, Mississippi Halfstep 11+, Brother in Arms 12; The Standard Route on Sunshine Wall 5.10d—way classic.

Ref: R. Bradt 4/97; C [167-44, 95, 90]; Guidebooks: Trout's *South Platte Rock*, Green's *Rock Climbing Colorado*, Hubbel and Rolofson's *South Platte Rock Climbs*, Harlin's *Rocky Mountain*, Rolofson's *The Hard Stuff*.

Directions: From Conifer go west $^6/_{10}$ mi. on Hwy. 285. Then south on Jefferson County Rd. (JCR) 97 (Foxton/Reynold's Park Rd.) for 8 $^3/_{10}$ mi. Turn right on JCR 96 and go 3 $^1/_2$ mi. to parking. Hike straight up forty-five minutes. Cathedral Spires area includes Sunshine Wall, Poe Buttress, and Cynical Pinnacle.

138 SP–Noodleheads ☆☆

Three-hundred-foot granite crack crag . . . all sizes. Try Green Eggs and Ham 5.11. Semiremote. Summer. USFS–Pike NF, (719) 545-8737.

Classics: New Creations 10b, Green Eggs and Ham 11b.

Ref: Guidebooks: Hubbel and Rolofson's *South Platte Rock Climbs*, Harlin's *Rocky Mountain*.

Directions: Sprucewood. Continue 3 $^1/_2$ to 4 mi. to sharp turn with pullout and gate. Park here before road drops down hill. The Noodleheads are a forty-five-minute hike to west.

139 SP–Jackson Creek Areas (Jackson Creek Dome/Taj Mahal) ☆☆

Four-pitch, intermediate level scattered granite domes and faces. Forty-six routes. Summer. USFS–Pike NF, (719) 545-8737.

Ref: Guidebooks: Green's *Rock Climbing Colorado*, Hubbel's *Front Range Crags*, Hubbel and Rolofson's *South Platte Rock Climbs*, Harlin's *Rocky Mountain*.

Directions: From junction of Hwy. 285 and Hwy. 67 in Sedalia, go southwest less than $^1/_2$ mi. on Hwy. 67. Turn south on 105 (Perry Park Rd.) and go 5-6 mi. to Rt. 38 (Jackson Creek Rd.). Rt. 38 turns into FS 502. Turn west on Rt. 38, going west and south for 10 $^1/_2$ mi. to Taj Mahal (west of road), 1 mi. farther south to Jackson Creek Dome (east of road) and Spire Rock (west of road).

140 SP–Humphrey's Dome/The Castle ☆☆

The 550' granite Humphrey's Dome is of lesser South Platte quality. Some nice 5.10 routes like Small Talk 5.10b. Ownership is all Forest Service; however, easiest access to the Castle is from Wellington Lake. Well worth the fee. Summer. USFS–Pike NF, (719) 545-8737.

Classics: Humphrey's Dome: Sugar Magnolia 9+, Small Talk 10b; The Castle: Throne Room 10b.

Ref: Guidebooks: Trout's *South Platte Rock*, Hubbel and Rolofson's *South Platte Rock Climbs*, Harlin's *Rocky Mountain*.

Directions: From Buffalo Creek (Hwy. 126), stampede south along FS 543. In 3 $^1/_{10}$ mi., Humphrey's Dome is on right. Continue on 543 a few mi. to right turn to Wellington Lake's west side to The Castle and Dildo Rock. More than one-hour approach; fee charged for access. FS 543 is now closed to traffic between Buffalo

Creek and the junction with FS 550 due to forest fire/flooding. Access to Humphrey's Dome is now done via hike/mountain bike on 543. Access to The Castle is south on Hwy. 126 from Buffalo Creek to FS 550, west on Hwy. 550 to junction with FS 543, then south on 543 to junction with FS 560 at Wellington Lake. Alternate route to The Castle: Take FS 560 east from Bailey to Wellington Lake.

141 SP–Little Scraggy Dome/Asshole Rock ☆☆☆

Four-hundred-foot granite crag. Up to three pitch routes. Summer. USFS–Pike NF, (719) 545-8737.

Classics: Asshole: Cardiac Crack 9+, Psycho Killer/Wild West Show 11d; Little Scraggy: 5.10c

Ref: Guidebooks: Hubbel and Rolofson's *South Platte Rock Climbs*, Harlin's *Rocky Mountain*.

Directions: From Buffalo Creek scratch south on Hwy. 126 for 4 $^3/_{10}$ mi. Turn right (west) on Hwy. 550. For Asshole Rock go $^3/_{10}$ mi. west on Hwy. 550, then head south/southwest, bearing right and going as far as you can. Park. Asshole is largest rock and faces north. Check Cardiac Crack 5.9+. Almost Asshole Rock is to northwest fifteen minutes. For Little Scraggy Dome go 2 $^2/_{10}$ mi. west on Hwy. 550. Then follow a road south as far as your crate will allow, passing a field and two small streams. Little Scraggy is on left, five minutes from road. More granite domes exist in area: Da Butts Rock, Refugee Rock, and Skinner Mountain.

142 SP–Wigwam Creek Area ☆☆☆

The Wigwam Creek Area is the most alpine of the South Platte Areas at 7,000'–9,500' elevation. Six-hundred-foot granite face climbs like El Supremo 5.11b. Known for steep water grooves a la Tuolumne Meadows. Very scenic. This is in the Lost Creek Wilderness. No power drills, and minimize any use of bolts (use good judgment). Summer. USFS–Pike NF, (719) 545-8737.

Classics: Wigwam Dome: Rambling Rose 10a, Pow Wow Canal 11a, El Supremo 11b, Warpath 5.11b; The Sun: Better Lock Next Time 10b; Wigwam Tower: Pow Wow Wow 9+, Lady Liberty 10a.

Ref: Guidebooks: Trout's *South Platte Rock*, Hubbel and Rolofson's *South Platte Rock Climbs*, Harlin's *Rocky Mountain*.

Directions: From Deckers go west on Hwy. 126 for 2 $^8/_{10}$ mi. to FS 211. Go 2 mi. on FS 211 to fork and stay right on FS 211 (Little Wigwam Dome is seen to west) for 1 $^1/_{10}$ mi. to FS 560. Go west on 560 for 1 $^1/_2$ mi. to fork. Stay right on 560, heading north an additional 4 $^1/_{10}$ mi. to junction with FS 545. Turn left (west) on 545 (1 $^2/_{10}$ mi., take right fork at $^8/_{10}$ mi.) to Wigwam Creek trailhead. Two-mi. approach to Wigwam Dome, Sun, and Moon. Six mi. more to Wigwam Tower and Keystone Buttress. Beartooth Spire and associates thirty-minute hike southwest of parking.

143 SP–Tarryall Area ✮✮✮

Remote, moderate 350' granite crack area with long approach. McCurdy Park Tower has a high concentration of good beginner routes . . . good for a weekend outing. This is in the Lost Creek Wilderness. No power drills, and minimize any use of bolts (use good judgment). Summer. USFS–Pike NF, (719) 545-8737.

Ref: Guidebooks: Hubbel and Rolofson's *South Platte Rock Climbs,* Harlin's *Rocky Mountain,* Ormes's *Guide to the Colorado Mountains.*

Directions: From Lake George go 18 mi. west on Hwy. 24 to town of Twin Eagles. Park. Hike 6 mi. north on trail 607 to McCurdy Park Tower.

144 SP–Big Rock Candy Mountain et al. ✮✮✮

Big Rock Candy Mountain harbors multipitched expert routes up a massive, west-facing 1,300' dome. Features some of the longest granite face routes in state. Ten pitch routes like Field of Dreams 5.11d inspire. Sunshine Dome, right next door, is second highest at 900' and offers mixed crack and face routes. Helen's Dome Area consists of three substantial rock formations: Helen's Dome, 600' (Electric Koolaid 5.9+); Acid Rock (Charley Don't Surf 5.10); and Sheep Rock (Sheep Just Want to Have Fun 5.9R). Here one can expect steep, knobby face routes. Combine all three domes in a day for the Tour De Platte route. Summer. USFS–Pike NF, (719) 545-8737.

Classics: Big Rock Candy: Field of Dreams 11+, Childhood's End 11+; Sunshine Dome: Narrow Escape 10a, Shining Path 11a, Heart of Darkness 12b; Helen's Dome: Beam Me Up Scotty 10aR, Buffalo Tears 10a.

Ref: Guidebooks: Trout's *South Platte Rock,* Green's *Rock Climbing Colorado,* Hubbel and Rolofson's *South Platte Rock Climbs,* Harlin's *Rocky Mountain,* Rolofson's *The Hard Stuff.*

Directions: Big Rock Candy Mountain: From Lake George go 1 mi. west on Hwy. 24 to right on Tarryall Rd. (Hwy. 77) for 6 4/10 mi. Turn right on FS 211 for 8 ½ mi. Turn right on jeep road for 3 mi. to top of ridge. Park. Hike east downhill to river and cross (dangerous in spring, thigh-high in summer), then hike north to rock. Approach time: one hour. Tick Dome is on west side of river to north. For Sunshine Dome: Go 9/10 mi. farther north on FS 211. Turn right on dirt road. At 7/10 mi., take left fork 6/10 mi. to ridgetop. Hike trail north off east side of ridge approximately forty-five minutes. Hike to Helen's Dome is twenty minutes east of Molly's Campground farther north on FS 211. Dirt road to Sunshine Dome is now closed, and access requires one- to one-and-a-half-hour approaches from FS 211. Better approach for Big Rock is to take approach to Turkey Rock, but continue west on FS 360 (Cedar Mountain Rd.) to Metberry Rd. (FS 205). This is a four-wheel-drive road. Take road down to the river (exciting). This puts you a few minutes south of the base of Big Rock.

145 SP–Top of the World ✮✮✮

Cracks. Many formations high above the river bottoms. Ragnarok formation is 500', but most areas average 200–300'. Fun Climb #101 is one of best multipitch 5.7/5.8 climbs in South Platte. Only the Boulder Pile was burned over. Summer. USFS–Pike NF, (719) 545-8737.

Classics: Chair Rock: Toot Suite 11a; Lower Gemstone: Just Say No 11a; The Slabbo: My Pet Monster 9+; Ragnarok: Fun Climb #101 8; The Boulder Pile: Succubus 10b, Weasels Rip My Flesh 10c, Pirahnna 11a.

Ref: Guidebooks: Hubbel and Rolofson's *South Platte Rock Climbs,* Harlin's *Rocky Mountain.*

Directions: From Pine Junction (on Hwy. 285), go southeast 10 9/10 mi. to FS 538 (2 6/10 mi. past town of Buffalo). Go north on FS 538 for 1 7/10 mi. to fork. Right fork goes to campground. Left fork goes 1 7/10 mi. to a left turn. Chair Rocks are ½ mi. down left turn, facing south at dead-end parking. Spoof Rock is a ten-minute hike west down ridge on closed road. For Gemstones (Upper and Lower): 100' down Spoof Rock closed road, hike thirty minutes north on game trail below all rock on ridgetop to Upper Gemstone. Lower Gemstone is ten minutes farther down-hill. Other areas: The Slabbo, Ragnarok, and The Boulder Pile.

146 SP–Sheep's Nose ✮✮✮✮

Even the dyed-in-the-wool climber will make sheep's eyes at this formation. Good intermediate crack climbing on 500' granite dome with routes up to six pitches. Also, fine, bal-ancey face climbing. Bouldering in front and to the left. South facing; can be warm in winter. Camp at Turkey Rocks Campground. Summer/autumn. USFS–Pike NF, (719) 545-8737.

Classics: Ten Years After 9, Sheep's Dare to The Direct 5.9+, Lost in Space 9-/Ozone Direct 10a, Sheep's Dare 10b, Golden Fleece 10d, Seamis 11a, Psycho Babble 12-R.

Ref: C [150-26, 74]; Guidebooks: Benningfield's *Colorado Bouldering,* Trout's *South Platte Rock,* Green's *Rock Climbing Colorado,* Hubbel and Rolofson's *South Platte Rock Climbs,* Harlin's *Rocky Mountain,* Cheyney and Couchman's *For Turkeys Only,* Rolofson's *The Hard Stuff.*

Directions: From Woodland Park drive Hwy. 67 north to West Creek. Go south of town on Hwy. 68 for 1 2/10 mi. Turn right until parking access road for Sheep's Nose is found under rock. Park.

147 SP–Turkey Rocks Area ✮✮✮✮

Best selection of 250' granite cracks in Colorado with routes like Whimsical Dreams 5.11b. Three areas include Turkey Rock (good intermediate selection), Turkey Perch (easier cracks), and Turkey Tail (hardest cracks). Summer/fall. USFS–Pike NF, (719) 545-8737.

Classics: Turkey Rocks: Turkey Shoot, Southern Comfort 9, Straw Turkey 10-, Rasmussens Crack 10, Vanishing Point 10d, Great White Crime 11a, Shear Shark Attack 12b; Turkey Perch: 5.7–5.9; Turkey Tail: Drumstick Direct 10d, Whimsical Dreams 11b, Journey to Ixtlan 12a.

Ref: C [111, 80(10/83)-34]; Randall's *Vertigo Games;* Guidebooks: Trout's *South Platte Rock*, Green's *Rock Climbing Colorado*, Hubbel and Rolofson's *South Platte Rock Climbs*, Harlin's *Rocky Mountain*, Cheyney and Couchman's *For Turkeys Only*, Rolofson's *The Hard Stuff.*

Directions: From Woodland Park drive Hwy. 67 north to Westcreek. Go south of town on Hwy. 68 for 1 ²/10 mi. Then turn right, going beyond Sheep's Nose and following rough road to Big Turkey Campground (great crack splitter problem to south of campground). Turkey Rocks is a fifteen-minute hike from campground. (Better approach is to continue past campground about a mile, watching for a road to the left. Take this road to a parking lot and then follow the trail to the base of the ridge, shooting between the rocks.)

148 Unaweep Canyon Boulders ☆☆☆

Hundreds of Dakota sandstone boulders. Neat face bouldering on Fossil Rock and many more. Year-round. Free camping on BLM land. Private land/BLM, (970) 244–3000.

Ref: C [112, 108(6/88)-24], R 68-26; Guidebook: Baum's *Grand Junction Rock: Unaweep Canyon Area.*

Directions: From Whitewater go southwest on Hwy. 141 to first cattle guard (bouldering traverses V9? above road on right) and mm 150 for Unaweep Canyon Boulders and starting points to begin the multiday bouldering opportunities.

149 Unaweep Canyon ☆☆☆

The main part of Unaweep Canyon is a Black Canyon of the Gunnison removed from its canyon. The southeast-facing granite/gneiss walls loom more than 500' above the road. Access is split private and public. Wall of Plenty is only public cliff. Sunday and TV Wall are on private land. Access half public and half private for Mothers Buttress. Camping at mm 150 on Jacks Canyon Div. Rd. No camping along road due to private land. Raptor restrictions March 15–July 15. Summer. Private land/BLM, (970) 244–3000.

Ref: C 108(6/88)-24, R [75-90, 73-28]; Guidebooks: Green's *Rock Climbing Colorado*, Baum's *Grand Junction Rock: Unaweep Canyon Area.*

Directions: From Grand Junction motor on Hwy. 50 for 24 mi. and turn onto Hwy. 141 for 15 mi. Or, from Whitewater, go 15 mi. southwest on Hwy. 141 to Unaweep Canyon. Obvious crags to north of road and walls further west. Formations include Mothers Buttress, Wall of Plenty, Sunday, and TV Wall.

150 Dolores River Outcrops ☆☆

Desert sandstone walls flanking river with bouldering at base. Established routes. Some boulders may be on private land (patchwork of public and private lands along valley floor). Autumn/spring. Private land/BLM, (970) 244–3000.

Directions: From Gateway, Dolores River Cliffs are found along Hwy. 141 south of town.

151 Escalante Canyon ☆☆☆

A mini "Canyonlands" of 150' Wingate sandstone crack climbing. Cracks of all sizes, including the sweet dihedral Passion for Pumping 5.11+, one of developer Chuck Grossman's many firsts. Autumn/spring. Private land/ BLM, (970) 244–3000.

Classics: Cactus Practice 9, Mosquito Crack 10, Passion for Pumping 11+, Split Decisions 11+/12a, Pooh Corner 12.

Ref: AAJ '89-160; Guidebook: Bjornstad's *Desert Rock.*

Directions: From Delta go northwest on Hwy. 50 for 11 mi. Turn left to Escalante Canyon (signs) to Smith Cabin (approximately 11 mi.). After 1 ⁸/10 mi. from Hwy. 50, small area on right. The main attractions are the many crack climbs on the walls 1 mi. before, above, and 1 mi. beyond Smith Cabin. More climbs across the river.

152 Crawford Pinnacle (aka Needle Rock) ☆

Conspicuous 300' volcanic plug/pinnacle that commands center stage of the valley floor. First ascent in July 13, 1921, by Ward Ruble and Clyde Miller. Most ascents go to local Bill Housewert from nearby Hotchkiss. In early 2001, *Groove Kitchen* was put up by Courtney Scales and Keith Reynolds ascending the Southwest Arete.

Classics: *NE Gulch 4th class?*, Black Waterfall 7, Groove Kitchen 6p 5.11+. USFS-Gunnison NF, (970) 641–0471.

Ref: K. Reynolds; NPS Guide.

Directions: From Crawford flow a few miles northeast from town on CR East 50 (dirt roads) to Crawford Pinnacle on left. Signs. If you miss this one, don't even think about heading into the Black Canyon.

153 Black Canyon National Monument ☆☆☆☆☆

The "Wonder Bread" of climbing areas. A long, mesmerizing chasm with committing, multipitch-free/aid rock climbing on wildly striped walls. Painted Wall is tallest at 2,200'. Scenic Cruise V 5.10+ is the quintessential route. Be prepared: All Black Canyon climbs have a serious aura about them (i.e., finding the route, diverse routefinding, rockfall from above, poor protection, unadvisable leadouts, rotten rock, weather extremes, and approaches with ticks and poison ivy in the spring). Climbing views obscene, epic potential extreme! But remember, you never see the moon without the promise of the sun. In all, a must-experience for the well-rounded rock climber. Painted Wall raptor restrictions March 15–July 15. Free backcountry permits, (970) 249–1915, ext. 24. Season d'etre: Mid-September through October or April/May. Camping on North and South Rims. NPS, (970) 858–3617.

Classics: Russian Arête III 9, Porcelain Arête IV 10, Journey Home 10R, Scenic Cruise IV 10+, Escape Artist III 9+/11, Checkerboard Wall III 11R, Astrodog V 11+/12a, Stratosfear VI 11+/R/X, Air Is Free II 12-, Apparition IV 12b, The Free Nose V 12b, Hallucinogen Wall VI 11 A4, Dragon: Painted Wall A4; The Serpent VI 11+R.

Ref: A 1984, AAJ ['98>96, '91-175, '85-209, 84>81, '66-146],

C [194-32, 186-118, 171-24, 166(2/97)-15, 164-94, 105, 97, 93, 91, 78(4/83), 75, 69, 63, 62, 56, 55(7/79), 49, (7/73)-2, (5/72)-7, many Basecamps], M [79, 64-15, 56], OB 4(8/82)-45, R [98-24/81, 94-94, 81-98, 74-20, 72-144, 20], S [11/80, 9/73]; Kor's *Beyond the Vertical: Climbing in North America*; Guidebooks: Green's *Rock Climbing Colorado*, NPS office book, Harlin's *Rocky Mountain*.

Directions: North Entrance: Where most climbs begin. From Crawford filter south about thirty minutes on good dirt roads, following signs. Walls accessed from north Rim Campground area: 1) Via Cruise Gully: North Chasm View Wall (The Cruise, Hallucinogen Wall) and South Chasm View Wall (low-water crossing or Tyrolean), 2) Via SOB Gully: North Chasm View Wall, Russian Arête, Porcelain Arête, Painted Wall. For South Entrance: From Montrose go 8 mi. east on Hwy. 50. Turn north for 6 mi. on Hwy. 347 to rim. Entry to South Chasm View Wall. Complex descent off South Rim; South Rim is usually accessed via the Tyrolean via the Cruise Gully. Camping at South Rim Campground.

154 Marmot Rocks (in Black Canyon National Monument) ★★★

Incredible views of the Painted Wall from four excellent quartz monzonite boulders. Boulders creatively named A, B, C, and D. High problems with generally good landings. Problems to B5.12. *Bouldering Guide to Marmot Rocks* available in NPS office. Summer. NPS, (970) 858–3617.

Ref: Guidebooks: Benningfield's *Colorado Bouldering*, NPS guide *Bouldering Guide to Marmot Rocks*.

Directions: From Montrose scamper 8 mi. east on Hwy. 50. Turn north for 6 mi. on Hwy. 347 to South Rim of Black Canyon. The 20′ granite boulders lie visible between Painted Wall and Cedar Point Overlooks. (Ignore the rock below the rim . . . there isn't any climbing there—ha ha.) Park at Painted Wall Overlook. Hike west on road, then south to blocks 100′ off road to Marmot Rocks.

155 Cimarron Boulders ★★★

Classic B1 granite bouldering. Other 25′ problems exist intermingled in scrubby oak stands. Newberry's store in Cimarron is a source of Black Canyon information. Autumn. BLM, (970) 240–5300.

Ref: J. Newberry.

Directions: From Cimarron hop 1 mi. west on Hwy. 50 to pulloff on left for the Cimarron Boulders. Three boulders south across creek. Also slightly farther west, turn right on dirt road pulloff and park. Hike 50′ north from Hwy. 50 to Speed Limit B1 Boulder, which faces road.

156 Curecanti Needle (Gunnison River Canyon) ★★★

Curecanti Needle is a well-known pyramid-shaped landmark dramatically rising 800′ from the deep confines of the Black Canyon. Its name derives from the Ute Indian chief Curicata, who hunted in the area. Standard route III 5.9 is

Hallucinogen Wall, Black Canyon of the Gunnison.

TIM TOULA

on the west face. Other routes exist. Granite boulders and craglets spread out through arid sagebrush hills offer an area of potential. Hwy. 50 Crack 5.9 is at mm 8. Summer. BLM, (970) 240–5300/NPS, (970) 641–0471.

Ref: Guidebook: Scott's *Crested Butte Guide*.

Directions: For Gunnison River Canyon cracks: From Gunnison follow Hwy. 50 west for approximately 8–9 mi. On north side of road; a hard spit from the car will hit the route. For Curecanti Needle: South rim approaches require trespassing and a likely bust. Best legal access: Drive west from Gunnison on Hwy. 50 for about thirty minutes. Turn northwest onto Hwy. 92 for twenty to thirty minutes, going to Pioneer Lookout Point on left (south) side of road. Park. Hike with inflatable raft almost due north on only trail, then west into Curecanti Creek drainage. Drop down to gorge bottom. Inflate raft. Cross creek to Blue Creek. Hike up Blue Creek (best done in fall) and then around south to notch. Climb one mank pitch to giant ledge system, then around to northwest to begin Standard 5.9 obvious crack route near large tree. Loose rock—got helmet? Other routes exist. Rap two ropes west face to ledge, then back around one rap to notch. Questions? Call (999) Got–Beta.

157 Spring Creek Park (aka The Upper Loop Boulders or Skyland) ★★★

Rhyolite boulders in aspen stand at base of the west flank of Crested Butte. Classic 30′ problems in a beautiful setting. A couple of routes have been done on the treacherous walls of Mt. Crested Butte above. This is a local mountain bike trail and archery range. Summer. Government land.

Classics: High Time: Jug Watch B1-, Love Handle B1; Hone Stone: Weeping Warrior B2; The Long Shot V5, Atomic Tick Fever V7.

Ref: B. Bernholtz; R 93; Guidebooks: Benningfield's *Colorado Bouldering* (misnamed route names), Scott's *Crested Butte Guide*.

Directions: Southeast Crested Butte. From town drive approximately 2 mi. south on Hwy. 135. Turn left at Skyland golf course sign. After approximately ½ mi., turn left on paved road past houses and pond parallel to base of Crested Butte Mountain, i.e., north. Park at archery range. Hike north along local mountain bike trail. Spring Creek Park Boulders lie on either side of trail. One of the boulders is visible southeast from town and has the difficult Weeping Warrior Arête B2 on the southwest side. Love Handle B1 is the center route on the largest boulder to the southeast of Weeping Warrior and east of trail.

158 Cement Creek (aka Anarchy Wall) ★★

Local Crested Butte southwest-facing sport crags feature both limestone and granite in the same area. The obvious left-facing corner identifies the 180′ Anarchy Wall. Summer. Camping. USFS–Gunnison NF, (970) 874–6600.

Ref: C 102; Guidebook: Scott's *Crested Butte Guide*.

Directions: From Gunnison follow Hwy. 135 for 21 mi. north until 7 mi. south of Crested Butte. Turn east on FR 740 (signed) for limestone cliffs at 1 (The Caves) and 2 ⁷/₁₀ (Disco Inferno) mi. on left. Go approximately 4 mi. to Anarchy Wall's black granite sport climbs up valley on left after campground.

159 Taylor Canyon ★★★

The main local crag for the shredders of Crested Butte. Good 100′, east-facing granite cragging offers a variety of face, stately crack lines (Christine's Dream 5.11+), and a few wild roofs (Colorado musician Chuck Grossman's Doubletime at Sue's Place 5.12- and Welcome to China 5.12) employing natural protection. More crag (excellent new sport routes) and bouldering areas upstream along highway. Camping at North Bank Campground. Summer/autumn. USFS–Gunnison NF, (970) 874–6600.

Classics: Angles Away 9, Better the Second Time 11-, Christine's Dream 11+, Doubletime at Sue's Place 12-, Welcome to China 12.

Ref: Vertigo Games; Guidebooks: Benningfield's *Colorado Bouldering*, Scott's *Crested Butte Guide*.

Directions: From Almont drive 7 ½ mi. northeast to Harmel's Lodge. Just ¼ mi. past lodge. Main Taylor Canyon area lies at dirt parking lot on left. Rock climbing potential continues up canyon.

160 Almont Band (aka Lost Canyon Bouldering) ★★★

A couple obvious sandstone roadside boulder problems and the mainstay lengthy, east-facing, 25′ bouldering band lends itself to lengthy pumps. Good beginner/intermediate area. Summer. USFS–Gunnison NF, (970) 874–6600.

Ref: Guidebooks: Benningfield's *Colorado Bouldering*, Scott's *Crested Butte Guide*.

Directions: From Gunnison go approximately 8 mi. north on west side of Hwy. 135. Obvious rock band above road is the Almont Band, with a couple boulders below the main band near road.

161 Hartman Rocks ★★★

Colorado's mini–Joshua Tree. Granite boulders, pinnacles, and knobs spread out through arid sagebrush hills. Rock quality varies from marbled granite edging, cracks, and roofs to grainy choss. Some classic boulder problems (White Lightning B1, ¼″ Master B1-), though potentially hard to find without a warm-blooded local guide. Quintessential Pinnacle 5.10d is a 40′ bolted spike. Fun mountain biking. Autumn. Free camping. Private land/BLM, (970) 641–0471.

Classics: Quintessential Pinnacle 10d, ¼″ Master B1, Stone Groove B5.12, White Lightning B1-.

Ref: Guidebooks: Benningfield's *Colorado Bouldering*, Houck's *Bouldering in the G-Spot*, Scott's *Crested Butte Guide*.

Directions: From Gunnison follow Hwy. 50 for approximately 1 mi. to the south edge of town. Turn left on Gold Basin Rd. (CR 38) across from Holiday Motel and drive (past airport) for five to ten minutes. Turn right on Hartman Rocks Rd., then left up steep jeep trail. Or, farther south past Hartman Rocks Rd., Hartman Rocks appear on right side of road.

162 Buena Vista Crags (Bob's/Elephant Rock) and Bouldering ★★★

Bob's and Elephant Rock both have good climbs on coarse granite with instant roadside access. Bouldering and 100′ cragging are possible. Many routes from 5.7–5.12 like Bob's Crack 5.9 and the classic Power Pig 5.11d. Away in the distant hills lie miles of coarse granite studs. Spring/fall. Private land/USFS–Pike NF, (719) 545–8737.

Ref: P. Krainz, J. Bernhard; Guidebook: Green's *Rock Climbing Colorado*.

Directions: From Buena Vista, Buena Vista crags and bouldering lie east in granite-studded mountains. Elephant Rock (pinnacle) is just north of town 3 mi. on CR 371, on west side of road and Bob's Rock (face) on east side of road. More rock down CR 371 and 375 as well. Get maps.

163 Buena Vista Boulder ★★★

The Buena Vista Boulder is a single 20′, roadside, rhyolite boulder with shorter rocks nearby. Chained Heat V6 features overhanging pockets. An hour's worth for the expert. Summer. State land/possibly private land.

Ref: J. Sherman; C 132; Guidebook: Benningfield's *Colorado Bouldering*.

Directions: From Buena Vista (at junction of Hwy. 285 and Hwy. 24), go south on Hwy. 285 for approximately 3 mi. to Nathrop. Turn left and cross Arkansas River on Rd. 301. Continue ½ mi. north and then turn right on Hwy. 300 for approximately 2 mi. Buena Vista Boulder on left (east) of road. Also, from Buena Vista, much rock east in granite-studded mountains, but much of it is on private road. Various access roads. Get maps.

164 Eleven Mile Canyon ✫✫✫

Picturesque, slabby granite domes with roofs, steep walls, and canyon walls offer a mix of sport and trad routes. Fifty routes. Good bouldering, too. Turret Dome is highest formation at 450'. Used by Colorado Mountain Club and Air Force Climbing Club for practice. Renewed in the mid-1980s for sport climbing by D'Antonio, Kertzman, Gadd, and Goddard. Popular recreation area. The South Platte wanders through the canyon and provides excellent scenery as well as an icy dip after a warm day of climbing. Entrance and camping fees. Summer. USFS–Pike NF, (719) 545-8737.

Classics: Fingers Fun 10-, Canyon Classic 11c, Here's to Future Ways 12b.

Ref: C [150-26, 111, 108(6/88)-78, 100, 99, 97, 96, 95, 91, 88, 82(2/84)-7], R 54; Guidebooks: Benningfield's *Colorado Bouldering*, Green's *Rock Climbing Colorado*, D'Antonio's *Mueller State Park and Eleven Mile Canyon: Classic Rock Climbs*, Bamberger/Glaze's *Climber's Guide to Eleven Mile Canyon*.

Directions: From Lake George (approximately forty-five minutes west of Colorado Springs), go left at only gas station in town. Follow dirt road to sign for Eleven Mile Canyon. Rocks at various mileages from canyon entrance: Guardian Rock: ¹⁄₁₀ mi. (right), Secret Journey 9+; ²⁄₁₀ mi. (right), Mind Games 5.11+R; ⁶⁄₁₀ mi. (right), Fingers Fun 10- fingers. Bigot Rocks: 2 ⁶⁄₁₀ mi. (right) roadside, Will Power 12-. The Tooth: 2 ⁷⁄₁₀ mi. (left). Eleven Mile Dome: 2 ⁸⁄₁₀ mi. (right), Overleaf 8. Arch Rock: 4 mi. (left), Staircase 5. Turret Dome: 4 ³⁄₁₀ mi. (right). The Sentinel: 4 ⁴⁄₁₀ mi. (left). Hard Rock: 4 ⁶⁄₁₀ mi. (right), King for a Day 12+, 5.11c. Springer Gulch: 5 ³⁄₁₀ mi. (right), Here's to Future Ways 12b. River Boulders: 6 ½ mi. up canyon to pullout, wade creek. Pine Cone Dome: 8 ²⁄₁₀ mi. (right), Squid Face 5.9+ dihedral. Mt. Meredith: 8 ²⁄₁₀ mi. (left). Camp Rock: at 8 ½ mi. (right).

165 Ute Pass Boulders ✫✫✫

Big 40' granite boulders with large, sharp feldspar crystals offer challenging face and crack cranking interspersed throughout the scrub oaks. Many classics like the Megaton Boulder Traverse B1+. These boulders are part of Manitou Springs Watershed Area and private property. Autumn. Private land/ USFS–Pike NF, (719) 545-8737.

Ref: J. Dunn; C [154-102, 150-26].

Directions: From Colorado Springs flee west on Hwy. 24 to about 5 mi. out of town. Park on west side of road at Waldo Canyon USFS Trailhead. Boulders lie above parking lot (legal access) and more extensively across road beyond locked gate (trespassing).

166 Twin Rocks (closed) ✫✫✫

Small 150' intermediate granite crag with crack routes from 5.7–5.10. There is also a lot of bouldering and short topropes in the area. Summer. Private land.

Classics: Wild Raspberries 8.

Ref: Guidebooks: Hubbel and Rolofson's *South Platte Rock Climbs*, Harlin's *Rocky Mountain*.

Directions: From Divide drive a few mi. west on Hwy. 24. Turn right on dirt roads to Twin Rocks. Granite domes and boulders are visible from road. The land on which the rock lies was traded by the USFS to private landowners and thus the land is now off-limits to climbing.

167 Mueller State Park (Four Mile Dome) ✫✫✫✫

Largest 400' granite dome in this area. Summer. Pay camping in state park, (719) 687-2366.

Classics: She's A Dike 4p 10, Voyeur's Odyssey 11a, Cling-On Treachery 3p 5.12a.

Ref: C [111, 105, 103, 102, 101, 99, 95-10]; Guidebooks: D'Antonio's *Pike's Peak and Garden of the Gods Classic Rock Climbs*, Hubbel and Rolofson's *South Platte Rock Climbs*, Harlin's *Rocky Mountain*, Rolofson's *The Hard Stuff*.

Directions: From Florissant go 7 mi. south on dirt road at Thunderbird Inn. Turn left at fork for ¼ mi. Turn right ½ mi. Go south of town to Mueller State Park. Four Mile Dome is visible. Faces west.

168 Woodland Park Bouldering ✫✫✫

Good 30' crystalline granite boulders. Summer. Private land.

Ref: C [150-26, 111, 108(6/88)-78, 100, 99, 97, 96, 95, 91, 88, 82(2/84)-7], R 54; Guidebooks: Benningfield's *Colorado Bouldering*, Green's *Rock Climbing Colorado*, D'Antonio's *Mueller State Park and Eleven Mile Canyon: Classic Rock Climbs*, Rolofson's *Eleven Mile Canyon*, Bamberger and Glaze's *Climber's Guide to Eleven Mile Canyon*.

Directions: At Woodland Park turn north from traffic light at McDonald's. Continue up road until it splits. Go left for 1 ½ mi. Woodland Park boulders are above an obvious parking spot.

169 Green Mountain Falls ✫✫✫

One-pitch granite crag featuring the classic Sex Axe 5.12-. Summer. USFS–Pike NF, (719) 545-8737.

Ref: C 117.

Directions: Along Hwy. 24 northwest of Colorado Springs, before Woodland Park. Turn left to Green Mountain Falls parking at end of road. Hike up to cliffs.

Colorado Road Thoughts

One morning at T. Henry's apartment in Golden, T. Henry exclaims, "Look at this morning, it's beautiful! I can see Longs Peak from my living room!" Iron Mike bemoans, "All I can see from my apartment in Chicago is the warehouse across the street."

170 French Creek Crags

Directions: From Colorado Springs go west on Hwy. 24 to Waldo Canyon USFS Trailhead. French Creek crags are up Hurricane Canyon to French Creek. Approximately one-hour hike. Summer. USFS–Pike NF, (719) 545-8737.

171 Pikes Peak (14,110') (Bigger Bagger, Pericles, Cameron's Cone) ☆☆☆☆

Five-hundred-foot east-facing granite alpine/crags with stunning vistas and stunning climbs like The Flame, three pitch 5.10+. Involved, punch-drunk, talus/scree approaches—makes a Jane Fonda workout seem like a stroll to Baskin-Robbins. Fee road; no overnight parking. An immense alpine world. Summer. USFS–Pike NF, (719) 545-8737.

Classics: Pericles: Arching Jams 10-, Bigger Bagger Pinnacle; Bigger Bagger: Hidden Lines 11; Sphynx: The Flame 3p 10+.

Ref: AAJ '71-380, C [101, 95], R 95-96, S 11/88; *Vertigo Games*; Guidebooks: D'Antonio's *Pikes Peak Classic Rock Climbs*, Roach's *Colorado's Fourteeners*, Harlin's *Rocky Mountain*, Ormes's *Guide to the Colorado Mountains*.

Directions: While this is an impressive summit, rock climbers will be attracted more to the alpine climbs on pink granite at the 12,000' level. The climbing lies in separated cirques (called the North Pit–Flame/Bigger Bagger and Bottomless Pit–Pericles on the east flank of the peak). The Barr Trail is the 12 mi. classic hiker's approach to summit. From Colorado Springs go west on Hwy. 24 to Cascade. Turn south on Pikes Peak Rd. Park at mm 15 (at 12,500') for approach to Bigger Bagger Pinnacle, then a couple mi. of moderate walking, or park at mm 17 (at 13,000') for Pericles, then 2,000' talus descent. Approach options: 1) A shuttle drop-off is best technique—facilitates camping near climbs. Otherwise, camp in town or on USFS land. 2) Hitchhiking; may be slow. 3) Park and walk 2 mi. down road from summit. 4) Hike 10 mi. up Barr Trail. 5) Cog railway from Manitou Springs. The impressive granite of Cameron's Cone at 10,000' is reached up the cog tracks. On Cameron's north ridge are Gog and Magog Rocks. Cameron's Cone is another climbing area on its flank.

172 Pikes Peak Backside ☆☆☆

Granite crags with Earl Wiggen's crack routes present themselves on the back of Pikes Peak. Summer. USFS–Pike NF, (719) 545-8737.

Ref: Guidebook: Ormes's *Guide to the Colorado Mountains*.
Directions: Along dirt road between Cripple Creek and Colorado Springs. This road circumvents Pikes Peak to the south.

173 Garden of the Gods ☆☆☆

Picturesque red sandstone formations with a vertical tilt. Kissing Camels, largest of formations, has popular scramble up chute from parking area. Collection of 230 traditional and modern climbs on rock softer than your stools after a bottle of hot prune juice. Be prepared for sketchy pro and long runouts on older routes. Climbing started in the 1920s with Albert Ellingwood. Anaconda 5.11, on north Gateway, was the hardman's testpiece of the 1980s. Cathedral Rock (250') now holds many modern routes. Bouldering traverse on north Gateway Rock. No chalk or soloing. Mandatory sign-in at Thirtieth St. entrance. Colorado Springs is a famous tourist garden. Autumn. Private park, (719) 634-6666.

Classics: Montezuma Tower North Ridge 7; North Gateway (north): Pig Dream's 10-, Anaconda 11; North Gateway (west): Men at Work 11, Pete and Bob's 11; South Gateway (northeast): Silver Spoon 6, Mighty Thor 10, Cocaine 10+, Cold Turkeys 11; South Gateway (west): Credibility Gap 9+; Kindergarten Rock (east): New Era 7, End of an Era 7; Kindergarten Rock (west): Footloose 10; Cathedral Rock: End to End 10b, Diesel and Dust 11b, Anarchy 12; bouldering on west face base of North Gateway.

Ref: AAJ ['85-210, 84], C [170-114, 111, 102, 99, 95, 74, 69, 60, 48(5/78)], R [78-91, 73-98], S 9/64; Guidebooks: Heidenreich and Geiman's *50 Prime Climbs*, Geiman's *Garden Guide*, Benningfield's *Colorado Bouldering*, D'Antonio's *Pikes Peak and Garden of the Gods Classic Rock Climbs*, Rolofson's *Soft Touch III*, Green's *Rock Climbing Colorado*, Harlin's *Rocky Mountain*, Rolofson's *Soft Touch*, Rolofson and Hubbel's *South Platte and Garden of the Gods*, McCristal's *Rock Climber's Guide to the Garden of the Gods*, CMC's *Mountaineer's Weekend*, Ormes's *Guide to the Colorado Mountains*.

Directions: West Colorado Springs. Drive west on Hwy. 24 to north on Garden Dr. to Garden of the Gods Park. Major 400' sandstone formations include North Gateway Rock, South Gateway Rocks, Kindergarten Rock, Montezuma Tower, and Keyhole Rock.

174 North Cheyenne Canyon ☆☆☆

This scenic canyon offers a nice variety of granite cranking on walls up to 500'. The Army carried on practice sessions in North Canyon in the 1950s. Summer/fall. USFS–Pike NF, (719) 545-8737.

Classics: Tunnel Vision 7, Reality Check 8, Crow's Nest 9+, Black Science 10; Graduation Boulder.

Ref: J. Dunn; C 99, R miniguide, S 9/64; *Master of Rock*; Guidebook: Ormes's *Guide to the Colorado Mountains*.

Directions: Southwest Colorado Springs. Exit I-25 at exit 140A, going south on Hwy. 85. Turn right (west) onto

Gold Camp Rd., which turns into North Cheyenne Canyon Rd. at mouth. Find Graduation Boulder about 1 mi. on left (obvious) from gate at mouth of canyon. Other excellent boulder across creek. Also find the 60′ Crow's Nest 5.9+, a blunt arête route at notch left of spire on north side of canyon. And south above Graduation Boulder, look up at The Pinnacle North Face with about ten good routes, e.g., Tiger Snap 10d. The Sun Slab routes lie on east-facing wall around the corner from The Pinnacle North Face. More worthy climbing farther up road on nearby Eagle Perch (Vitamin G 13b) and Grand Specimen's six-pitch Directissima 10c. Ask locals or see Green's *Rock and Ice* miniguide.

175 St. Peter's Dome ✩✩✩
Classic crack/dihedral lines on 300′ north-facing granite crag of the 1960s mingle with sport routes of the 1990s. Some of the finer Pikes Peak area cragging located on its southeast corner at 9,500′. The Martyr 5.9, on the 300′ north face of Aiguille, is area's showpiece climb. Mountain Chalet in the Springs has more information. Free and fee camping on USFS lands. Summer. USFS–Pike NF, (719) 545-8737.
Classics: Abbey Road 7, Martyr 9, Oracle 11, Devotion 11+, Ascension 11+, Athenian 11+.
Ref: C 138(6/93)-28.
Directions: From Colorado Springs ascend north 18 mi. up Stage Rd. and Gold Camp Rd. to St. Peter's Dome Overlook. Continue ¼ mi. beyond the overlook and park in pullout on right. Hike north up steep hillside on faint trail. In ½ mi., back side of crags are visible. On west lies The Priory, Monastery, Hell, and Purgatory. Hike east for Sanctum, Pearly Gates, and Aiguille de St. Peter formations.

176 Dolores River Canyon Road ✩✩✩
Three-hundred-foot, west-facing sandstone crag. Intermediate to expert Wingate cracks. Historic hanging flume. Autumn–spring. BLM, (970) 240-5300.
Ref: Guidebook: Fowler's *Naturita and Paradox Valley Rock Climbs*.
Directions: Between Bedrock and Uravan. Roadside boulders and walls along Dolores River Canyon Rd. (dirt road).

177 Paradox Divide ✩✩✩
Fifty-foot Dakota sandstone crags. Good camping along CR X4 road. Autumn–spring. BLM, (970) 240-5300.
Ref: Guidebook: Fowler's *Naturita and Paradox Valley Rock Climbs*.
Directions: Paradox Valley is along Utah/Colorado border on Hwy. 90 (Hwy. 46 in Utah). Best climbing near intersection with CR X4 road, just west then south of Paradox off Hwy. 90.

178 Bedrock Cliffs ✩✩✩
One-hundred-foot sandstone crag with one-pitch crack climbs. Spring/autumn. BLM, (970) 240-5300.
Ref: Guidebook: Fowler's *Naturita and Paradox Valley Rock Climbs*.
Directions: Just south of Bedrock. Bedrock Cliffs are canyon walls cut by the Dolores River.

179 Shavano Valley Boulders/Dry Creek Area ✩✩
A large supply of varnished 40′ sandstone boulders. Some fine sandstone block bouldering and topropes, if one chooses rock quality wisely. But lots of loose, brittle rock. Indian petroglyphs on boulders. Brown Wall sports leads. Spring/autumn. Private land/BLM, (970) 240-5300.
Directions: From Montrose go 10 mi. west on Hwy. 90 (Spring Creek Park Rd.), then right on Shavano Valley Rd. to rock. Requires exploration. Farther west is Dry Creek area, where locals once used their bumpers for toprope anchors on 50′ climbs.

180 Naturita Bouldering/Calamity Bridge ✩✩✩
Naturita sandstone boulders and Speedway crags; can be particularly nice in winter on warm, sunny days due to their south faces. Nice problems, e.g., Beak Boulder, a 5.10- finger crack. On private land, so class behavior is in order. Check Charlie Fowler's latest guide for specifics on the Naturita area rock and calligraphy lessons. Please don't climb here after rains; holds break from water absorption. This goes for most of the desert sandstone. Spring/autumn. Private land/BLM, (970) 240-5300.
Classics: Beak Boulder: 5.10- finger crack.
Ref: C 118, SC 12/91; Guidebook: Fowler's *Naturita and Paradox Valley Rock Climbs*.
Directions: Surrounding Naturita. Naturita Boulders: Near water tank on road to Nucla, low bands on bluff northwest of town, and roadside cliffs immediately east of town. Calamity Bridge: West of Naturita approximately 4 mi. on Hwy. 141 to Calamity Bridge. Turn right just after bridge. Down by the San Miguel River. Abundant rock (Speedway crags) nearby to west—miles-long bouldering.

181 Long Park Area (Atomic Energy and Antenna Crags) ✩✩✩
The 150′ Atomic Energy Crag is the most prominent south-facing Dakota sandstone bluff. Quality routes tend to be most desperate. Must-do is Rancho Deluxe 5.10. Numerous cliffs beside the two mentioned here; although much of the rock can be dismissed as wasted sand. Prolific, quality bouldering along shorter cliffs scattered nearby may qualify as a greater attraction. Free camping. Spring/autumn. BLM, (970) 240-5300.
Classics: Pocket Change 10, Rancho Deluxe 10, On the Beach 11, Atomic Test Site 12, Guns or Butter 12-, Nuclear Free Zone 12, Sleazy Streak 12.

Ref: C 118; Guidebooks: Benningfield's *Colorado Bouldering*, Green's *Rock Climbing Colorado*, Fowler's *Naturita and Paradox Valley Rock Climbs*.

Directions: From Naturita go 2 mi. west on Hwy. 141, 5 mi. west on Hwy. 90, then right on CR EE22 approximately 5 mi. Just before junction with A18 sits Atomic Energy and Antenna Crag.

182 Lost World Crag and Sawtooth Ridge ✰✰✰

Out in the dry, sunny West can be found these tall, user-friendly, 100' Dakota sandstone bluffs. Bouldering exists along Sawtooth Ridge, seen from junction of Hwy. 90 and CR EE22. Holds can break after a rainstorm—best to refrain from climbing then. Roads gruesome when wet. Spring/autumn. BLM, (970) 240-5300.

Classics: Whispering Wind 6, Spaghetti Western 10+, Wounded Knee 10, Hendrix in the West 11, Tarantula 11, Do the Right Thing 11+, Psychedelic Hangover 12-, Have Gun Will Travel 12+.

Ref: C 118, SC (12/91); Guidebooks: Benningfield's *Colorado Bouldering*, Green's *Rock Climbing Colorado*, Fowler's *Naturita and Paradox Valley Rock Climbs*.

Directions: From Naturita go 2 mi. west on Hwy. 141, then 5 mi. west on Hwy. 90. Turn right on CR EE22 for 2 mi., then right on dirt road 1 mi. to Lost World Crag and Sawtooth Ridge.

183 Ridgway State Park ✰✰

South-facing 30' sandstone boulders and some topropes. Spring/autumn. State park, (970) 626-5822.

Directions: From Ridgway (south of Montrose) go just north on Hwy. 550 for 3–4 mi. north of Ridgway State Park.

184 Shelf Road ✰✰✰✰

This 80' winter limestone sport cragging haven features forearm-pumping faces. Shelf Rd. locals have taken a commendable front seat in the realm of land-management relationships, the public eye, and rock-climbing access. Access information boards and pay camping at Sand Gulch and The Bank. September–May. Private land/BLM, (719) 269-8500.

Classics: B.C. 9, Suburbia 5.10a, Lofus Farm Tools 10b, Under The Milky Way 10d, Lost Planet Airman 10d, Back to The Future 5.11c, Heavy Weather 11d, Future Fossil 5.12c, Surreal Estate 5.12c, The Example 5.13b.

Ref: C [178-52, 160, 159-42, 113, 111, 106, 105, 103, 101], R [103-98, 91-38, 69-94, 34(7/88), 26(7/88)], SC 9/91; Guidebooks: Benningfield's *Colorado Bouldering*, Van Horn's *Shelf Road Rock Climbs*, Green's *Rock Climbing Colorado*, Knapp's *200 Shelf Road Climbs*.

Directions: From Canon City (Hwy. 50), turn north on Reynolds St. (at Burger King), which turns into Field St. for approximately 13 mi. Follow Shelf Rd. signs to several named cliff areas, which include The Bank, The Dark Side, Sand Gulch, The Gallery, Dead Colt Canyon, Cac-tus Cliff, and Spiney Ridge. Bouldering at Sand Gulch Campground. Partial closure of climbing areas; please check bulletin boards.

185 Royal Gorge ✰✰✰

One-thousand-foot gneiss walls. Called "nearly forgotten" in 1979 (Mountain 68), even more so now, though not for lack of rock. Site of the climb called Tombstone Wall IV 5.7 A3. Illegal BASE jumping off bridge (possibly the world's highest suspension bridge). Late summer/autumn. Private land.

Ref: AAJ '65-433, C 56, M 68.

Directions: From Canon City follow signs to Royal Gorge, approximately 8 mi. west of Canon City.

186 Little Owl Canyon (closed) ✰✰✰

Historic John Gill bouldering problems on overhanging 15' Dakota sandstone. Mosquitoes may be as great a problem as the routes. Autumn/winter. No trespassing. Private land.

Ref: John Long's "Pumping Sandstone," Ament's *Master of Rock*, Sherman's *Stone Crusade*.

Directions: From Pueblo, Little Owl Canyon lies to the west. Ask locals.

187 Ripper Traverse Area (closed) ✰✰✰

Historic John Gill bouldering problems of the Dakota sandstone genre. Climbing here is trespassing. Autumn/winter. Private land.

Classics: Ripper Traverse B1, Little Overhang B1.

Ref: C 194-42; John Long's "Pumping Sandstone," Ament's *Master of Rock*, Sherman's *Stone Crusade*.

Directions: West of Pueblo.

188 Fatted Calf (closed) ✰✰✰

Historic John Gill bouldering problems on overhanging Dakota sandstone. In secluded, privately owned canyon—trespassing. Other rocks downstream include Chip Rock. Expert routes only. Autumn/winter. Private land.

Classics: Home to the Fatted Calf B2.

Ref: John Long's "Pumping Sandstone," Ament's *Master of Rock*, Sherman's *Stone Crusade*.

Directions: West of Pueblo. Fatted Calf is closed to climbers. Ask locals for details.

189 Badlands (closed) ✰✰✰

Historic John Gill bouldering problems on overhanging Dakota sandstone. Big-time trespassing—illegal! Beware quicksand, mosquitoes, and cow-pie landings. Popular with mathematicians, nuclear physicists, and candy company executives. Autumn/winter. Private land.

Classics: Juggernaut B1+, Penny Ante Boulder B1/B2.

Ref: John Long's "Pumping Sandstone," Ament's *Master of Rock*, Sherman's *Stone Crusade*.

Directions: East of Pueblo. Ask locals for details.

190 Schoolhouse Rock ☆☆☆

Ninety-foot granite crag on Hardscrabble Mountain.
Summer. USFS–San Isabel NF, (719) 545-8737.
Directions: Near Westcliffe.

191 Crestone Peaks (14,294') ☆☆☆☆

Abounding in alpine rock pageantry, this superb array of
1,500' alpine buttresses is a must for any mountaineer.
Crestone Needle was first climbed in 1916 via third-class
route; Ellingwood Ledges in 1925. Coarse conglomerate
rock with wild knobs. Quality varies from superb to shoddy.
Subject to volatile weather: Best to try in July through
September. Complex routes often make retreat difficult,
which has resulted in several deaths. The strong and brave
will come . . . and some may die. Summer. USFS–San Isabel
NF, (719) 545-8737.
Classics: Crestone Needle's Ellingwood Ledges III 7.
Ref: AAJ '95, C [99, 65, 63, 2(7/70)], R 85-102, S 31(5/85)-
26; Guidebooks: Green's *Rock Climbing Colorado: Fifty
Classic Climbs*, Borneman and Lampert's *A Climber's Guide
to Colorado's Fourteeners*, Ormes's *Guide to the Colorado
Mountains*, Bueler's *Roof of the Rockies*.
Directions: From Westcliffe drive south on Colfax Lane to
junction at Becks School. Turn west to end of road and
trailhead. Hike road for approximately 5 mi. to Colony
Lakes (often-used bivy spot) and proceed onto Crestones
for the "tourist route." Average ascent time from lake and
up 2,000' face is six hours with a two-hour descent down
southeast ridge to gully. Also approachable from west.
Challenging cluster of isolated 14,000' summits include
Kit Carson Peak, Crestone Peak, Humboldt Peak, and
The Crestone Needle.

192 Slick Rock ☆☆

Eighty-foot Dakota sandstone boulders above main cliff
band, i.e., upper tier (cattle guard). Autumn–spring. BLM,
(970) 882-4811.
Ref: Guidebooks: Fowler's *Naturita and Paradox Valley Rock
Climbs*.
Directions: From Naturita slide east on Hwy. 145 for 4 mi.,
then 38 mi. south on Hwy. 141 to town of Slick Rock.
The most worthy rock lies approximately 1 mi. northeast
of town, adjacent to Hwy. 141. Many other crags around.

193 Lower San Miguel River ☆☆☆

Excellent, 20' Dakota sandstone toprope cracks farther
north on right. High cliff and good bouldering at junction
of San Miguel River and Hwy. 145. Bouldering and
topropes. The Cove Boulders come recommended.
Autumn/winter. Private land/BLM, (970) 882-4811.
Directions: From Placerville, Lower San Miguel River is
along Hwy. 145 for 10 mi. west of town and east of highway. Areas include The Cove Boulders, 1/4 mi. north of
Specie Creek Rd.

194 Mill Creek Spire ☆

Mostly a stunning and rotten, though a classic, chimney
200' sandstone pinnacle. Enjoy the Alien Stem Route 5.8
A2+ three pitch. One rap. Summer/autumn. USFS–San
Juan NF, (970) 247-4874.
Classics: Beautiful Dreamer 10, Party Out of Bound 11;
Mill Creek Spire: Alien Stem Route 5.8 A2+ 3p 1rap.
Ref: C 124; Guidebooks: Sawyer and Fowler's *Telluride Rocks*,
Fowler's *Telluride Rock*, Harlin's *Rocky Mountain*, Pattie's
Telluride/Ophir Rock Guide, Kees's *Telluride Rock: An Interim
Guide*.
Directions: From Telluride, just west of town on Hwy. 145
south, hike north of the Hwy. via Deep Creek Trail up
switchbacks. At large meadow, the tower sits to the
northeast. Bushwhack on light trails.

195 Mill Creek Wall ☆☆☆

Antoine Savelli sport-trad crag with tough 80' sandstone
routes like Misty 5.12 and Starfire 5.13. Summer/autumn.
USFS–San Juan NF, (970) 247-4874.
Ref: Guidebooks: Sawyer and Fowler's *Telluride Rocks*,
Fowler's *Telluride Rock*, Savelli's *Telluride Hot Rocks*.
Directions: From Telluride light out just west of town
going north of Hwy. 145 south to Mill Creek Wall to
trailhead. Crag is next to creek.

196 Society Turn ☆☆☆

Obvious 35' sandstone rock band north above road.
Features bouldering traverses, roofs, and toprope anchors.
Good on sunny days even in winter. Camping at Telluride
Town Park. Access Fund Land.
Ref: R 70-34; Guidebooks: Sawyer and Fowler's *Telluride
Rocks*, Fowler's *Telluride Rock*, Harlin's *Rocky Mountain*,
Pattie's *Telluride/Ophir Rock Guide*, Kees's *Telluride Rock: An
Interim Guide*.
Directions: From Telluride drive 3 mi. west of town at junc-
tion with Hwy. 145.

197 Idarodo Mine (aka Mine Boulders) ☆☆☆

The best bouldering in the Telluride area? Okay. Colorado?
Nope. North America? Most certainly not. Still, well worth
any climber's time. Hillside 30' conglomerate chunks sport
views of spectacular Bridalveil Falls. The Falls Walls is
Telluride's hottest new sport climbing wall with a classic 5p
5.11 route, The High Lonesome. Possible trespassing in
patchwork of public and private lands—check locally about
access. Summer/autumn.
Ref: D. Raupp; Guidebooks: Benningfield's *Colorado
Bouldering*, Sawyer and Fowler's *Telluride Rocks*, Fowler's
Telluride Rock, Savelli's *Telluride Hot Rock*, Harlin's *Rocky
Mountain*, Kees's *Telluride Rock: An Interim Guide*.
Directions: From Telluride drive east on pavement. Turn
onto dirt road past Idarodo Mine buildings. Take sharp
left past first hard right to boulder. A trail leads through
bouldering circuit.

198 Ilium Valley Boulders/Bilk Creek Wall ☆☆☆

Ilium Valley Boulders offer pleasant 20' Dakota sandstone boulders with good landings. Pristine setting amongst aspens and firs. Bilk Creek Wall is a 60' toprope wall—good 5.10-5.11 climbing. Bring extendo runners. Summer/autumn. USFS–San Juan NF, (970) 247-4874.

Ref: C 132; Sherman's *Stone Crusade*; Guidebooks: Benningfield's *Colorado Bouldering*, Sawyer and Fowler's *Telluride Rocks*, Fowler's *Telluride Rock*, Pattie's *Telluride/Ophir Rock Guide*, Savelli's *Telluride Hot Rock*, Harlin's *Rocky Mountain*, Kees's *Telluride Rock: An Interim Guide*.

Directions: From Telluride drive west 3 mi. to Ophir/Rico Junction. Continue 2 ½ mi. west on Hwy. 145. Turn left at south Fork Rd./Ilium sign for approximately 1 ½ mi. Park at large boulder. Ilium Valley Boulders are a hike west 200 yd. on trail. For Bilk Creek Wall turn right shortly after getting on Ilium Valley Rd. before Ilium Valley Boulders.

199 Needle Rock ☆

This loose rock, 200' sandstone pinnacle presents a somewhat classic 5.8 crack climb on the west face of the formation. Nice views. Summer. USFS–San Juan NF, (970) 247-4874.

Ref: Guidebooks: Sawyer and Fowler's *Telluride Rocks*, Fowler's *Telluride Rock*.

Directions: From Telluride, Needle Rock is just south and above town. Access is easier during winter via ski lifts.

200 Bear Creek Boulder and Crags ☆☆☆

Big 35' south-facing conglomerate cube in beautiful valley below Bear Canyon Falls. High bouldering or topropes. Excellent-quality rock on cliffs. Private road provides access (not a problem), but please respect private property. Summer. USFS–San Juan NF, (970) 247-4874.

Ref: Guidebooks: Sawyer and Fowler's *Telluride Rocks*, Fowler's *Telluride Rock*, Harlin's *Rocky Mountain*, Kees's *Telluride Rock: An Interim Guide*.

Directions: From Telluride the dirt road starts just west of ski hill. Go 3 mi. south up road (four-wheel-drive if open; hike or bike otherwise). Bear Creek crags beyond boulder.

201 Ames Wall ☆☆☆

A sizeable 600' granite cliff with one handful of grade III adventure routes. Chossy and okay rock, like on Gravity's Deception 5.8. More noted for ice climbing, i.e., Ames Ice Hose. Summer–winter. USFS–San Juan NF, (970) 247-4874.

Classics: Gravity's Deception 8, Seamstress Corner 11+.

Ref: C [117, 69]; Guidebooks: Sawyer and Fowler's *Telluride Rocks*, Fowler's *Telluride Rock*, Harlin's *Rocky Mountain*, Kees's *Telluride Rock: An Interim Guide*, Rosebrough's *The San Juan Mountains*.

Directions: Ames. Just west of the town of Ophir and west of Hwy. 145. Park at historic power plant. Hike south then west on railroad grade running beneath Ames Wall. (Don't even think of parking at Ames and trudging directly through to the cliff through private property.) Changing access conditions likely.

202 Ophir Wall ☆☆☆☆

At 9,000', a splendid, 650' granite mountain crag. Ophir Wall is the centerpiece crag of the Telluride area near the Ophir post office . . . they could stick this face on a stamp. More than 120 routes. Summer. USFS–San Juan NF, (970) 247-4874.

Classics: Pork Shoulder 6, Easy Overhang 7, Hot Wee Wee 9, Hidden Secrets 9, Emotional Rescue 10b, Honey Pot/Y-Crack 10b, Dr. Gizmo 10d, Powder in the Sky 10d, Ophir Broke 12c, Morning Glory 12+/13a, Dingo Maniaque 13.

Ref: AAJ ['82, 81], C [124, 117(128), 106, 98, 97, 89, 63]; Guidebooks: Sawyer and Fowler's *Telluride Rocks*, Green's *Rock Climbing Colorado*, Fowler's *Telluride Rock*, Pattie's *Telluride/Ophir Rock Guide*, Savelli's *Telluride Hot Rocks*, *Ophir Wall Bums*, Harlin's *Rocky Mountain*, Kees's *Telluride Rock: An Interim Guide*.

Directions: At Ophir (10 mi. south of Telluride). Look up! Ophir Wall is the big crag above (north of) Ophir. Faces south.

203 Cracked Canyon and Dark Side ☆☆☆

Cracked Canyon is infamous for its steep talus approach to its famous 150' steep granite climbs on the left canyon wall. Right wall (east) has more moderate routes. The tricky overhanging routes here have airmailed many a good climber postage due. Eighty routes. Beware rockfall. Dark Side area now with about fifty routes. Uncertain if Dark Side crag's north-facing walls are sometimes wet. Summer. USFS–San Juan NF, (970) 247-4874.

Classics: Beginner's Luck 6, Chewbacca 8, Crack of Mind 8, Orange Peel 10, Free Box 10, Javelin 10+, Talusman 11, Superfresh 11-, Where Eagles Dare 11+; Dark Side crags: Destination Resort 10, End of Innocence 11, Greasy Sex Rap 11+, Lovesick Blonde 12-, Man Overboard 12+.

Ref: C [124, 117, 97, 63]; Guidebooks: Sawyer and Fowler's *Telluride Rocks*, Green's *Rock Climbing Colorado*, Fowler's *Telluride Rock*, Pattie's *Telluride/Ophir Rock Guide*, Rosebrough's *The San Juan Mountains: A Climbing and Hiking Guide*, Harlin's *Rocky Mountain*, Kees's *Telluride Rock: An Interim Guide*.

Directions: At Ophir. Cracked Canyon: 200 yd. past Ophir Post Office and just east of the Ophir Wall. Hike north up scree canyon just east of Main Wall of Ophir. The Dark Side is the wall due south of Cracked Canyon on the other side of the river.

204 Lizard Head Peak, Chimney Rock, and other San Juan Spires ☆☆☆

Lizard Head Peak (13,113'), with its notoriously loose, volcanic, 300' summit pinnacle, lends to its classic appearance. The South Face offers three routes, 5.7-5.8, the best of which is the corner wide crack to a fist and fart chimney at the top. Two rappels down Original Route. A genre of its own. Other San Juan Spires are similar flirts with loose rock and the unseen. Chimney Rock, another well-known climbing objective, was first climbed in 1934 by Melvin Griffiths and Robert Ormes. Mt. Sneffels has many pinnacles on its northwest ridge, including The Hand, The Penguin, The Thumb, and Purgatory Point, and on its southwest ridge lies Wolf's Tooth, Blue Needle, and The Monolith. Summer. USFS–San Juan NF, (970) 247–4874.

Classics: Lizard Head Peak 7, Chimney Rock, Sunlight Spire, Mt. Sneffels (pinnacles).

Ref: OB 41-41I, R [85-102, 79-47, 25(6/88)], S 1/68; Guidebooks: Sawyer and Fowler's *Telluride Rocks*, Roach's *Colorado's Fourteeners*, Green's *Rock Climbing Colorado*, Fowler's *Telluride Rock*, Rosebrough's *The San Juan Mountains*, Lavender et al.'s *San Juan Mountaineer's Guide*, Ormes's *Guide to the Colorado Mountains*, Bueler's *Roof of the Rockies*.

Directions: From Telluride skedaddle approximately 15 mi. south on Hwy. 145 to Lizard Head Pass. Hike west/northwest up to Lizard Head through scree to southwest corner of the Lizard Head Peak Pinnacle. Multihour approach. Many other backcountry spires exist throughout the San Juan Mountains and include Chimney Rock (from Ridgway go east on Owl Creek Pass Rd. [FR 858] for 13 mi. to top of pass. Go just beyond pass, turn south on FR860A, then up to southeast face [right up chimney and large chockstone southwest face]), Hand, Penguin, Thumb, and Wolf Tooth on West Ridge of Mt. Sneffels, Babcock and Lavender Spires in Tomahawk Basin of the La Plata Mountains, and Ominous Pinnacle, The Index, Little Finger, Twin Thumbs, Gray Needle, Noname Needle (Jagged Peak), and Sunlight Spire in the Needles/Grenadier Range.

205 San Juan Mountains (Needles/Grenadier Ranges et al.) ✶✶✶✶

Alpine, loose rock adventure spires, fourth-class mountaineering, and rocky ridge walking. The Needles-Grenadiers offers backcountry walls in the Weminuche Wilderness and is one of Colorado's finest mountain ranges. In the Grenadiers, five rock monoliths are of note among the overwhelming masses: The Trinity Peaks, Vestal Peak, and Arrow Peak. In the Uncompahgre Group, the north faces of the Wetterhorn (800'), Coxcomb, and Wildhorse Peak present rock-climbing challenges. In the Lower 48, no other mountain range contains as much land above 10,000' as the San Juans. Also, this is an area rich in gold and silver mining, so tote a gold pan in your climbing pack. Summer. USFS–San Juan NF, (970) 247–4874.

Classics: Needles (Monitor Peak): East Face 1,200' wall, Sunlight Spire (13,395') 5.10 fingers; Peak 18 Needles (Pigeon Peak): Broken Quill 11; Grenadier Range (Mt. Silex): East Face 18p 5.7, Storm King Peak 13p 7; Mt. Silex (West Trinity Peak): North Saddle 7p 7; Mt. Silex (Arrow Peak): North Ridge 6; Mt. Silex (Vestal Peak): Wham Ridge 4; San Miguel Range: Lizard Head, Wilson-El Diente Ridge;

Uncompahgre Range (Chimney Rock): South Face, Coxcomb; Uncompahgre Range (Uncompahgre Peak): North Face; Uncompahgre Range (Wetterhorn): North Face III 7, Matterhorn; Sneffels Range: Mt. Sneffels (pinnacles), Teakettle; Pilot Knob, US Grant Peak.

Ref: AAJ ['81, 75, 73-432, 36], 69-400, C [96, 63, (1/79), (1/78), (1/72), 5(1/71)], OB 41-41, R 25(6/88), R 76-144, S[7/88, 9/87, 7/83,1/71, 11/67], *Trail and Timberline* [11/69, 6/63,11/59]; Ikenberry's *Hiking Colorado's Weminuche Wilderness*; Guidebooks: Roach's *Colorado's Fourteeners*, Sawyer and Fowler's *Telluride Rocks*, Rosebrough's *The San Juan Mountains*, Garratt and Martin's *Colorado's High Thirteener's*, Pixler's *Hiking Trails of Southwestern Colorado (San Juan Mountains)*, Gebhardt's *Backpacking Guide of the Weminuche Wilderness*, Borneman and Lampert's *A Climber's Guide to Colorado's Fourteeners*, Ormes's *Guide to the Colorado Mountains*, Bueler's *Roof of the Rockies*.

Directions: Ouray/Telluride/Durango area. Various trailheads access extensive wilderness mountains. Needles/Grenadiers: 1) Vallecito Lake, northeast of Durango, being the most popular among climbers. 2) Molas Lake, south of Silverton on Hwy. 550, is another. 3) As an alternative, the Narrow Gauge Railroad of 1882 offers transit (though slow) from Durango through Silverton (May–October, reservations advised) into the heart of the Needles-Grenadiers and the Chicago Basin backcountry climbs. Molas Crag near Elk Park train stop in Animas Canyon is recommended for cragging. 4) The Uncompahgre Group (Chimney Rock, et al.) is accessed approximately 2 mi. north of Ridgway. Head east up Owl Creek Road to south on west Fork Cimmaron Rd. Or, go west from Lake City.

206 La Plata Mountains ✶✶

Alpine, loose rock adventure spires, fourth-class mountaineering, and rocky ridge walking. Several 13,000' peaks will appeal to climbers: Hesperus, Centennial, Lavender, Spiller, and Babcock Peak with its multiple summits and spires. Lavender Peak has a multiple-spired ridge of which ascents have been made on a pinnacle known as Lavender Spire. Summer. USFS–San Juan NF, (970) 247–4874.

Ref: Guidebooks: Rosebrough's *The San Juan Mountains*, Borneman and Lampert's *A Climber's Guide to Colorado's Fourteeners*, Bueler's *Roof of the Rockies*.

Directions: From Hesperus go ½ mi. west of downtown, then head north on Hwy. 124 into La Plata Canyon until the end of four-wheel-drive road. Hike at end of road up north side of creek takes one into Tomahawk Basin, from which Babcock and Lavender Peaks are accessed. Boren Creek, also up La Plata Canyon, provides access for Babcock. Other access points include Transfer Campground Rd., Owen Basin, and Rush Basin.

207 McPhee Reservoir ✶✶

Jumbled 100' sandstone crags with bouldering. Good potential if cleaned. Autumn. Government land.

Directions: From Dolores go west on Hwy. 184 for approximately 2 mi., then north on road to McPhee Reservoir. Cliffs near marina.

208 Dolores Boulders and Crags ✵✵✵

Scattered wreckage of soft 40′ sandstone boulders. Autumn. Private/government land.

Directions: From Dolores just north of town on Hwy. 145. Dolores boulders and crags are on left.

209 McElmo Canyon ✵✵

Dakota sandstone 90′ cliff similar to Naturita. Bouldering at main intersection a few miles west of Hwy. 666. Pay campground in Hovenweep National Monument. Lots of Dakota sandstone outcrops around Cortez. Routes have been done on Battle Rock, south side of road. Autumn. Private land/BIA.

Ref: C. Fowler; C 64.

Directions: From Cortez go south on Hwy. 666 for 2 6/10 mi. Turn west into McElmo Canyon (signs for Hoven-weep National Monument). Climbing for 20 mi. along canyon. Bouldering at 2 7/10 mi. past Hwy. 666. Battle Rock is 12 mi. west of Cortez.

210 Sleeping Ute Mountain (9,244′)

Rock appears on the toes of Sleeping Ute Mountain, though this lies on Ute Mountain Indian Reservation Land. BIA.

Directions: West of Towaoc, southwest of Cortez.

211 Golf Wall and Hermosa Valley Cliffs ✵✵✵

The Golf Wall has twenty-five limestone sport climbing routes on quality 60′ overhanging walls. For ski and rope sessions, one can ski in Purgatory and pump up at the Golf Wall in the afternoon. It's in shade until 2:30, when the sun opens its arms to climbers. That is, the Golf Wall is sunny in winter (T-shirts with water drips). Ask at Pine Needle Mountaineering in Durango for current route development. Summer/autumn. USFS–San Juan NF, (970) 247-4874.

Classics: Golf Wall: Greenskeeper Playground 10d, Double Bogey 10d, Gopher Hole 12a, Cinderella Story 12b, Golf Wars 12, Nine Iron 13a, Divotator 13b.

Ref: Guidebooks: Green's *Rock Climbing Colorado*, Kuss's *Durango Sandstone*.

Directions: The Golf Wall sport crag is approximately 14 8/10 mi. north of Durango on Hwy. 550 and is apparent on the right (just 1 3/10 mi. past Tamarron Resort). Park on west side of Hwy. 550 in small pullout across from north tip of visible roadside cliff couple hundred feet from road. Faces southwest. Hermosa Valley Cliffs: From Durango go 7 9/10 mi. north on Hwy. 550 through Hermosa to left on CR 203. Take right on CR 201 for 1 4/10 mi. Park at campground. Walk up on fence lines

(most people will want to walk on ground) to western end of rock called West Coast of the Hermosa Valley Cliffs. The Pinnacle is the main attraction. The cliffs are visible intermittently throughout the area.

212 Turtle Lake Wall Area ✵✵✵

Quaint boulder garden delivers a productive bouldering session on soft sandstone blocks with friendly landings or highball heinaland. Roped routes on dirty wall above boulders; Coyote's Tooth 5.8 (pinnacle at base of cliff) is recommended. Old nail ups on Turtle Lake Wall. Camping spots can be found farther up Junction Creek Rd. If you like what you tasted at Turtle Lake, ask locals about Sailing Hawk bouldering area. Summer/autumn. State/private land.

Ref: C 104; Sherman's *Stone Crusade*; Guidebooks: Benningfield's *Colorado Bouldering*, Kuss's *Durango Sandstone*, Kozak's *Southwest Rock*.

Directions: From Durango (3 mi. west), turn west off Main St. onto Twenty-fifth St., which turns into Junction Creek Rd. (CR 203). Go 2 9/10 mi. on Junction Creek Rd. Turn right (north) on CR 205 for 1 1/10 mi. Garden Area: Obvious roadside boulder on left side of road is start of tour of half dozen boulders. Park at small pullout on right. Chapman Lake Wall (5.8–5.10) is behind the Garden. Continue 4/10 mi. to beneath South Pillar of Turtle Lake Wall. A 1/2 mi. beyond is Great White Slabs, which holds pure friction fear to 5.10-.

213 X-Rock ✵✵✵

X-Rock consists of the following climbing walls: 1) Boxcar Boulder on trail with its 20′ tall overhanging is a five-star Dakota sandstone boulder (experts report to East Face), 2) Morgue Wall after Boxcar 5.5–5.11 up to 80′, 3) Gold Wall past Morgue up to 5.11, 4) X-Rock is past Gold Wall and is popular toprope practice wall, 5) Aid Wall 40′ north of X-Rock, 6) Rock of Afternoon Delights 250′ north of Aid Wall. This well-used practice area by Durango beginners also seduces experienced climbers with its overhanging bouldering and sixty-two classic lines. Good views of the Watch Crystal across the east Animas River valley to the east. Autumn/spring. Private land.

Classics: Beginner's Rock 4, Oxbow 7, Left X 8-, Diagonal Dihedral 9, Red Book 9, The Itch 9+, Gold Wall 10c, Morgue 11b, Gravity Storm 12b, School Room 12+?, Left side of X Rock 13-?; Boxcar Boulder B1-2s.

Ref: C 132; Sherman's *Stone Crusade*; Guidebooks: Benningfield's *Colorado Bouldering*, Rosebrough's *The San Juan Mountains*, Kuss's *Durango Sandstone*, Kozak's *Southwest Rock*.

Directions: From Durango strike north on Hwy. 550 to north edge of town. Just 1/10 mi. before the highway becomes divided. Park off highway. (Parking at north end of Health Center lot is frowned on.) Obvious trail leads west out of lot, then north to rocks (five minutes). X-Rock is obvious (the rock with the big X in it) when driving north on Hwy. 550 as one reaches the divided highway. Faces east.

214 Watch Crystal (East Animas) ✩✩✩✩

Durango's best leads and hardest route in '94 Space Boy Elroy 13c/d. One hundred and ten routes 1994. The 300' west-facing Watch Crystal formation has several midrange traditional leads and two pitch routes, featuring the namesake, Watch Crystal Crack 5.10d. Information on new development of sport routes available at Pine Needle Mountaineering. The Durango Silverton Narrow Gauge Railroad in Durango is a popular tourist attraction, splendid during golden fall colors. Camping is available on national forests around Durango. Autumn. USFS–San Juan NF, (970) 247–4874.

Classics: Yellow Pages 6, I Need a Shower 7+, Apple Cider 8, Simian's to the Sun 9, Push Me Pull You 10a, Durangatang 10b R, Crime and Punishment 11a, Punta Magna 11c, Overview 11+, Sweeney's Special 12-, Clown Face 12- toprope, Stargazer 12b.

Ref: C [99, 98, 97], R 14(5/86); Guidebooks: Kuss's *Durango Sandstone*, Kozak's *Southwest Rock*, Rosebrough's *The San Juan Mountains*.

Directions: From Durango (approximately 4 mi. northeast out of town), take Hwy. 550 north. Turn right onto Thirty-second St., following this to a left onto CR 250. East Animas Rocks access point is at 1 1/2 mi. Parking on right. Tenuous access as approach trail (at 1866 address) lies between private residences. Stay on trail. Steep approach.

215 Fort Wall ✩✩

Fort Wall is 20' brick wall lending itself to outdoor building on south end of gym. Hard on tips. Other Durango buildering at Kiva Theater (traverse, major bust) and Miller Jr. High cracks. Private land.

Ref: Guidebook: Kuss's *Durango Sandstone*.

Directions: At Ft. Lewis College in Durango.

216 Dry Fork ✩

Seldom-visited sandstone cliffs on mesa rim on left side of valley. Autumn. State land.

Ref: Guidebook: Kuss's *Durango Sandstone*.

Directions: From Durango go west on Hwy. 160 for 3 1/2 mi. (from Red Lion Inn to CR 207). Turn right on CR 207 for 1 1/10 mi. Park on right fork at junction with CR 208 for Dry Fork.

217 Bondad Cliff ✩✩

Cracks on sandstone softer than Charmin toilet paper—squeezably soft, but fun. Don't trust this rock. Handful of routes. Similar sandstone in softness to the Rimrocks in Billings, Montana. The Remington Roof Crack 12- is a fun challenge. The southern aspect of this cliff permits the donning of Bermuda shorts and bare chests on sunny days in winter. Ute Indian Reservation land.

Classics: Duke 11-, Remington Roof 12-.

Directions: From Durango (approximately 13 mi. south of town), from junction of Hwy. 160 and Hwy. 550, go south 12 1/10 mi. to CR 310. Go left (east) on CR 310 up road to cliffs for 1 2/10 mi. Short walk north to Bondad Cliffs.

Ref: AAJ ['88-144, '86-168]; Guidebooks: Kuss's *Durango Sandstone*, Kozak's *Southwest Rock*, Norton's *Durango Area*.

218 Ignacio Cliffs ✩✩

Eighty-foot sandstone cracks and bouldering. Rock may be too soft. Autumn. BIA.

Directions: Much rock from Bondad south to Aztec National Monument and east to Ignacio (and Ignacio Cliffs).

219 Pope's Nose ✩✩✩✩

A wilderness wall protected from climbers by its remoteness. This south-facing granite wall of 1,200' has routes up to eight pitches in the Weminuche Wilderness Area of the San Juan Mountains. At least five major routes like Thunder Road IV 5.9 A3 on this big wall. Climbing is good usually from mid-June to mid-September. USFS–San Juan NF, (970) 247–4874.

Classics: Brain Damage 5.9+ A3, Thunder Road IV 5.9 A3, Central Buttress 5.10- A3, Contraceptive Cracks 5.9 A3+.

Ref: AAJ '71-381, C [58(1/80)-3, 8(7/71)], S [11/82, 4/80]; Guidebooks: Kozak's *Southwest Rock*, Rosebrough's *The San Juan Mountains*.

Directions: From Durango (35 mi. east/northeast of town), go to Bayfield. Go north to Vallecito Lake Reservoir, turning right onto CR 603 before lake. Go east and north to Pine River Campground and trailhead. Park. A full day's hike 13 mi. to Flint Creek drainage and confluence of Los Pinos River. Hike 2 mi. upstream to base of 1,200' wall known as the Pope's Nose. Be sure to get a topo map or call (900) GUD-LUCK.

220 Martinez Creek Cliffs ✩✩✩

Good intermediate-grade climbing (Endless Summer 5.9) on this 60' sandstone crag though rock looks crosley. Summer/autumn. Private land. USFS–San Juan NF, (970) 247-4874.

Classics: Mugwump 7-, Endless Summer 9, Blues Incognition 9+.

Ref: Guidebook: Kozak's *Southwest Rock*.

Directions: From Pagosa Springs go 7 mi. west on Hwy. 160 (first obvious cliff on west side of canyon). Go to Martinez Creek Drainage, up canyon to concrete water gate. Cross stream to west. Angle uphill and west toward Martinez Creek Cliffs on west side of canyon. Fifteen-minute walk on land that may be private property. Descent to south end of cliff.

221 South Fork Rock–Cadillac Crack/ Collier Crag ✩✩✩

Many 150' rhyolite crags between South Fork and Wolf Creek Pass, and northwest of South Fork near Masonic

Park. The areas mentioned here are representative of area. Summer. Private land/USFS–Rio Grande NF, (719) 852–5941.

Ref: C 88(2/85)-31.

Directions: From South Fork (junction of Hwy. 160 and Hwy. 149), go west on Hwy. 149 4 $^6/_{10}$ mi. to Cadillac Crack, 5 ½ mi. for Collier crags. (South Fork Area is approximately 17 mi. west of Del Norte.)

222 Beaver Creek (Breakfast Boulders) ☆☆☆

A 150′ rhyolite crag with bouldering. The Breakfast Boulders offer one a much-to-do tour. Extensive potential, similar to Penitente, but taller and with more cracks. Summer/autumn. USFS–Rio Grande NF, (719) 852–5941.

Ref: C 88(2/85)-28; Guidebooks: Benningfield's *Colorado Bouldering*, D'Antonio's *San Luis Valley Rock Climbing and Bouldering Guide*.

Directions: From South Fork (junction of Hwy. 160 and Hwy. 149), go west on Hwy. 160 for 1 $^4/_{10}$ mi. Turn left via Beaver Creek forest access for $^3/_{10}$ mi. to Twilight crag on left, another ½ mi. for Guard Station crag parking, and $^4/_{10}$ mi. more to reach Breakfast Boulders (park in loop, in aspens). (These areas are approximately 17 mi. west of Del Norte.)

223 Big Meadows ☆☆☆

Unlimited bankroll of 150′ rhyolite crags between South Fork and Wolf Creek Pass. Extensive potential (Rhyolite Rain 5.10), similar to Penitente, but taller and with more cracks. Summertime area. USFS–Rio Grande NF, (719) 852–5941.

Ref: C 88(2/85)-28; Guidebook: Benningfield's *Colorado Bouldering*.

Directions: From South Fork (junction of Hwy. 160 and Hwy. 149), go west on Hwy. 160. At 3 $^7/_{10}$ mi. is Winnebago Crack; 4 $^9/_{10}$ mi., Moon Valley; 5 ½ mi. Roadside Boulder; and 10 $^4/_{10}$ mi., Big Meadows. Areas are east of Wolf Creek Pass.

224 La Garita Area–Rock Garden ☆☆☆

Rock Garden is a clone canyon of the more famous Penitente Canyon (see below). Plenitude of 60′ rhyolite sport climbs featuring eighty routes. Bouldering on ridge to west and Crocodile Rock. Ask permission from rancher Jim Spearman. The La Garita Area features a network of east-west-running rhyolite canyons with many sport routes. Autumn. Private land.

Classics: California Crack 5.10a, U2RINXS 5.11, Hot Chocolate 5.11c, Ready Rok 5.12, Just Do It 5.12+, Living Years 5.13b.

Ref: C [134, 119(4/90)-224, 101, 94, 91, 88(2/85)-28]; Guidebook: D'Antonio's *San Luis Valley Rock Climbing and Bouldering Guide*.

Directions: From La Garita drive ½ mi. west. Take right at Y for 2 $^3/_{10}$ mi. Find Rock Garden on left across from ranch.

225 Carnero Canyon ☆☆☆

Multipitched rhyolite sport routes, including a diagonal three-pitch 5.6. Summer. BLM, (719) 274–8971.

Classics: Jesus Liquid 10d, Plump and Luscious 11c, Step Out of Time 12a, Egotonic 12c, Ubiquitous Confusion 12c/d.

Ref: C 88(2/85)-28; Guidebook: D'Antonio's *San Luis Valley Rock Climbing and Bouldering Guide*.

Directions: From La Garita drive ½ mi. west. Take right at Y for 1 $^9/_{10}$ mi. Parking on right for Carnero Canyon.

226 Penitente Canyon ☆☆☆☆

Great, popular, 50′ rhyolite short sport craggin' area of media attention. Many routes established by "The Philadelphia Flyer," Bob D'Antonio. La Madonna is painting of Virgin Mary on wall left of the photogenic "Bullet the Blue Sky" arête. One hundred and twenty beautiful routes like Yah-ta-hei 5.10c, Los Hermanos de la Weenie Way 5.11, Bullet the Blue Sky 5.12+, Color of Emotion 5.13. Camp at Penitente Canyon Campground. Summer/autumn. BLM, (719) 274–8971.

Classics: Yah-ta-hei 10c, Bucket Slave 10, Los Hermanos de la Weenie Way 11, Not My Cross 11, Forever Young 12a, Bullet the Blue Sky 12+, Color of Emotion 13.

Ref: C [178-111, 176-120, 134, 109(8/88)-17, 107, 103, 101, 99, 88(2/85)-28], R [78-28, 29(11/89)-28]; Guidebooks: Benningfield's *Colorado Bouldering*, Horan's *Front Range Bouldering: Southern Area*, Green's *Rock Climbing Colorado*, D'Antonio's *San Luis Valley Rock Climbing and Bouldering Guide*.

Directions: From La Garita (north of Del Norte), drive ½ mi. west. Go left at Y for approximately $^8/_{10}$ mi. Take next right (at old wooden sign, WAGON TRACKS) into mouth of Penitente Canyon.

227 Witches Canyon ☆☆☆

Good bouldering on huecos. Forty short rhyolite routes like Plump and Luscious 5.11c. Summer. BLM, (719) 274–8971.

Ref: C [134, 88(2/85)-28]; Guidebook: D'Antonio's *San Luis Valley Rock Climbing and Bouldering Guide*.

Directions: From La Garita go ½ mi. west. Turn left at Y for 1 $^4/_{10}$ mi. (sign for Witches Canyon). Go right for 1 ½ mi., veering left into canyon and routes along it. Rough road. Witches Canyon outcroppings look like giant eye.

228 LG–Penis Rock/Balloon Ranch Boulders ☆☆

Remote, detached phallic pinnacle features the route Soul Pole 5.11d. Six routes. More unclimbed volcanic rock beyond. Summer. USFS–Rio Grande NF, (719) 852–5941.

Ref: C 88(2/85)-28; Guidebooks: Benningfield's *Colorado Bouldering*, D'Antonio's *San Luis Valley Rock Climbing and Bouldering Guide*.

Directions: From La Garita go ½ mi. west. Go left at Y for 1 ½ mi. Go right for $^8/_{10}$ mi., then left for $^6/_{10}$ mi. Turn west for $^7/_{10}$ mi. past Sidewinder Canyon and continue uphill south on main road. At 3 ²/10 mi. slice right until 3 ⁶/10 mi. Park and hike west ½ mi. up to rock. For Balloon Ranch Boulders go farther past Penis parking to gulley and go uphill ⁶/10 mi. On right.

229 Sidewinder Canyon ☆☆☆
Gorgeous Mudhoney Wall with routes like Mudhoney 5.13a. About fifteen routes. Pretty wooded canyon. Cool in summer. USFS–Rio Grande NF, (719) 852-5941.

Classics: Jesus Lizard 11, Spider Baby 12-, Mudhoney Wall 13a.

Ref: C [134, 88(2/85)-28]; Guidebooks: Benningfield's *Colorado Bouldering*, D'Antonio's *San Luis Valley Rock Climbing and Bouldering Guide.*

Directions: From La Garita go ½ mi. west. Go left at Y for 1 ½ mi. Go right for ⁸/10 mi. Then left for ⁶/10 mi. Turn west for ⁷/10 mi. Canyon on right. Hike into Sidewinder Canyon.

230 La Garita Creek Wall ☆☆☆
More rhyolite walls with about twelve routes. Respected for bouldering and cool climbs like Pocket Plethora 5.11c, SST Crack, and Book of Brilliant Things, the two latter both 5.12. Uncertain if closed by private landowner. Private land.

Ref: C [91, 88(2/85)-28]; Guidebooks: D'Antonio's *San Luis Valley Rock Climbing and Bouldering Guide.*

Directions: From La Garita drive ½ mi. west. Turn left at Y for Balloon Ranch Boulders at 3 ³/10 mi.

231 Shaw Springs ☆☆☆
Expert's 80' volcanic sport crag. Steep face edges. Forty routes. Good climbs like Lithium Christmas 5.12a await. Bouldering, too. Summer. USFS–Rio Grande NF, (719) 852-5941.

Classics: Lexicon Devil 10+, Eternal Thirst 11c, Lithium Christmas 12a, Venus Groovepusher 12d.

Ref: C 88(2/85)-28; Guidebooks: Benningfield's *Colorado Bouldering*, D'Antonio's *San Luis Valley Rock Climbing and Bouldering Guide.*

Directions: From La Garita drive ½ mi. west. Turn left at Y 7 mi. to right at cairn. Shaw Springs has two areas: one on right, and another on left at T.

232 Elephant Rock/Eagle Rock Boulders ☆☆
Wind-eroded glacial relics. Potential for 25' volcanic bouldering/hard topropes. Summer. Private land.

Ref: C 88(2/85)-28; Guidebooks: Benningfield's *Colorado Bouldering*, D'Antonio's *San Luis Valley Rock Climbing and Bouldering Guide.*

Directions: From La Garita drive ½ mi. west. Turn left at Y for 9 ⁷/10 mi. Where pavement begins, turn right ½ mi. to Elephant Rock bouldering. Eagle Rock: A few miles before reaching Elephant Rock, turn west on USFS 660 for 3 ½ mi.

233 Del Norte Rock (Courthouse Boulders/Hidden Gulch) ☆☆☆
Boulders and 100' volcanic cliffs offer good freeclimbing potential in a beautiful area of Colorado. Summer/autumn. USFS–Rio Grande NF, (719) 852-5941/BLM, (719) 274-8971.

Ref: D. Dyess; C 88; Guidebook: D'Antonio's *San Luis Valley Rock Climbing and Bouldering Guide.*

Directions: Cliffs lie south of Del Norte on forestlands. Courthouse Boulders: Just 2 blocks south of the traffic light in town, and then 1 ½ blocks east at courthouse. Hidden Gulch: 4 ½ mi. east of Del Norte on Hwy. 160 at top of hill, go south off Hwy. 160 on BLM land. Then go southwest on dirt roads a few mi. through fence to Hidden Gulch.

234 Sierra Blanca Range (Ellingwood, Blanca, and Little Bear Peaks) ☆☆☆
The Sierra Blanca range contains three 14,000' summits: Blanca (14,345'), Ellingwood (14,042'), and Little Bear Peak (14,037'). The 1,500' north faces of Blanca and Ellingwood Peaks are as spectacular as the east face of Little Bear. Summer. USFS–San Isabel NF, (719) 545-8737.

Classics: Blanca and Ellingwood Peaks.

Ref: C 8(7/71), S 31(5/85)-26, 10/83, 2/78]; Guidebooks: Roach's *Colorado's Fourteeners*, Steck's *Fifty Classic Climbs*, Garratt, Borneman, and Lampert's *A Climber's Guide to Colorado's Fourteeners*, Ormes's *Guide to the Colorado Mountains*, Bueler's *Roof of the Rockies.*

Directions: From Alamosa blast east on Hwy. 160. Turn north on Hwy. 150 for 3 mi. Then turn northeast, heading directly to Sierra Blanca Range and Blanca's Peak. In a couple miles, road turns to a knock-you-down and tear-your-undercarriage-out drive. Hike east to Como Lake and peaks beyond.

235 Stonewall Gap ☆☆☆
We're talking hogback! Plinths of 40' Dakota sandstone boulders and craglets. Culebra Peak (14,069') dominates the background. Summer. Private land/USFS–San Isabel NF, (719) 545-8737.

Ref: J. Gamertsfelder.

Directions: From Stonewall rock north along on Hwy. 12 to Stonewall Gap (mm 39) with its visible rock plates. This amazingly long Dakota sandstone hogback is rife with short topropes and boulders as it heads north out of Stonewall to North Lake. Some areas on government land, some on private land.

236 The Monastery ☆☆☆☆
Excellent granite sport climbing crag in a scenic remote setting with more than fifty bad-ass routes, including Tommy Caldwell's Dream Catcher 5.13c and Third Millennium 5.14a. Late spring to autumn. Camping at KOA in USFS–Roosevelt NF, (970) 498-1100.

Classics: Sex in the Wilderness 6, Kesey 7, Hot Zone 9, Rico

Suave 10, Contortionist Forte 11, Psychatomic 12, Dream Catcher 13c.
Ref: A. Salo; R [80-104], 79-16; Guidebook: Gillet's Monastery.
Directions: From Drake head west on Hwy. 34 and take a right on CR 43. After ³/10 mi., turn right and drive over a bridge onto FR 128. After 2 ½ mi., you will come to a T in the road; take the left. Take another left at a Y at 2 ⁶/10 mi. Go left again at a Y at 3 ⁶/10 mi. At 5 ²/10 mi. you will come to a right-hand switchback. Park on the uphill side. The trail leaves from here. It is hard to lose, and the walk southwest takes forty-five minutes.

237 Sitting Camel (aka Chimney Rock or Camel Rock) (formerly WY 95) ★★

One-hundred-foot, camel-shaped sandstone pinnacle features crack and face climbs. First ascent in 1937 via iron-spiked ladder. Head and Hump summits. Nearby animal traps from blowing winds (West Animal Trap), ½ mi. south from top of west ledges. Crumbly rock integrity. Possibly private land.
Classics: West Face 5, ESE Face 5 A2, East Crack 9.
Ref: See Bonney's Guide.
Directions: Southwest of Tie Siding.

238 Mt. Crested Butte ★★★

Eight-hundred-foot rhyolite, seven-pitch adventure wall routes on west face of Mt. Crested Butte. Summer/autumn. USFS–Gunnison NF, (970) 874-6600.
Ref: M. Laggis, K. Reynolds.
Directions: Rock flanks just east of Crested Butte.

239 Pinecliffe Rocks ★★★

One-hundred-and-fifty-foot granite cliffs above railroad tracks. Fifteen routes, 5.6–5.12. Summer. USFS–Roosevelt NF, (970) 498-1100.
Ref: Guidebooks: Hubbel's *Front Range Crags*.
Directions: At Pinecliffe bridge, go northeast along railroad tracks to parking. Cliffs east along tracks above Beaver Creek gorge.

240 Gross Reservoir (Zebra Rock) ★★★

Granite outcrops scattered about Gross Reservoir.
Ref: Guidebook: Hubbel's *Front Range Crags*.
Directions: West of Boulder. Bouldering around the Reservoir (1 mi. south of dam) and Zebra Rock 5.11c crack climbs south of Reservoir. From Boulder go south on Hwy. 93. Turn west on Hwy. 72 for 8 mi. Turn right at Gross Reservoir sign. Go 3 mi. to white NO CAMPING sign. Hike northeast five minutes to Zebra Rock. Government land.

241 Rist Canyon ★★★

Granite bouldering, e.g., Cocktail Boulder. Summer. Private land.
Ref: J. Shireman.
Directions: From Bellvue follow road up canyon to roadside Cocktail Boulder on right.

242 Arapahoe Basin Rock ★★

Gneiss schist crag with intermediate, one-pitch routes 5.6–5.10. Uncertain if rock is good rock. Summer. USFS–Arapahoe NF, (970) 498-2770.
Ref: Guidebook: Astaldi and Gruber's *High Country Crags*.
Directions: From Keystone Village go 8 mi. west on Hwy. 6. Park at west end of A-Basin Ski Area parking lot. Cross road to north and pick up trail for five minutes to crag.

243 Montezuma Valley ★★★

Lovely mountain valley of hillside boulders and one-pitch, gneissic-schist walls offering climbs of all grades. Summer/autumn. USFS–Arapahoe NF, (970) 498-2770.
Classics: Haus Rock: 5.7 (bolted slab), Crystal Ball 12, Macho Picasso 13.
Ref: Guidebook: Astaldi and Gruber's *High Country Crags*.
Directions: From Keystone Village go 1 mi. west on Hwy. 6. Then turn right on Montezuma Rd. On left side of road find parking areas for three different areas (five- to fifteen-minute walks): At 1 mi. on left, Porcupine Rock, 100' crag, five 5.8–5.11 routes, mostly choss. At 1 ²/10 mi., left Haus Rock, 5.6–5.11 trad/5.13 sport (Crystal Ball 5.12); Hummingbird Boulders, eight good 5.9–5.11+ short routes; and Alpenglow Wall, twelve 5.8–5.12 routes (Alpenglow Arête 5.11a). About forty routes. At 1 ⁸/10 mi. on left, Zuma Cliff 40' 5.6–5.12 (5.12 toprope). Ten routes; across road on right Morning Glory Wall, three 5.8–5.10 routes and a good 5.11 route.

244 Ten Mile Canyon ★★★

Six mi. of granite walls and buttresses (large conspicuous Mt. Royal directly above Frisco; multipitch, loose rock) feature one to multipitch beginner/intermediate climbs on either side (east or west) of I-70. Total of about seventy-plus routes from 5.5–5.11. Ice climbing, too. Good domes include: ⁴/10 mi. southwest of Frisco, The Dome and Sunshine Buttress, more than twenty routes, 5.6–5.11, and ⁸/10 mi. southwest of Frisco, White Cliff, thirteen routes 5.5–5.9. Summer. USFS–White River NF, (970) 945-2521.
Ref: Guidebook: Astaldi and Gruber's *High Country Crags*.
Directions: Between Frisco and Copper Mountain along I-70. Park carefully along I-70.

245 Blue Lakes Crags ★★★

Beautiful alpine valley beginner/intermediate craggin'. Classic short leads/topropes 5.4–5.10. Above parking area is Shriek Back Wall with steep 5.10 leads or toprope (chains). Down road 100 yd. then up to north is 165' Quandary Wall

with the 165′ classic 5.7 granite route Keystone Boys.
Summer. USFS–White River NF, (970) 945-2521.
Classics: Keystone Boys 7, 5.10 toprope.
Ref: Toula; Guidebook: Astaldi and Gruber's *High Country Crags*.
Directions: From Breckenridge drive 7 4/10 mi. south on Hwy. 9. After second sharp switchback, turn right onto Blue Lakes Dr. Proceed 2 mi. up mountain valley until end of road. Park. Bouldering wall at parking area. One hundred yd. down valley below road is The Diving Board with bolted route Robbie's Hammer 5.7. Snow blocks road till May/June.

246 Devils Head ✪✪✪

Granite sport crag in South Platte Area features sixty routes with many 5.11/12 routes. Great views of Pikes Peak. USFS–Pike NF, (719) 545-8737.
Classics: Eros 10c, The Epitaph 12d.
Ref: R 90-104; Guidebook: Anderson's *Devil Made Me Do It: Climber's Guide to Devil's Head, Colorado*.
Directions: From Sedalia go southwest on Hwy. 67. Turn south on Rampart Range Rd. (FR 300) to Devils Head Campground (fee). Hike Zinn Overlook trail forty minutes up to crags.

247 Upper Dream Canyon ✪✪✪✪

Above Boulder Canyon, granite sport climbing area sports dreamy multipitch clip-ups. Autumn. USFS–Roosevelt NF, (970) 498-1100.
Ref: Guidebook: Rossiter's *Upper Dream Canyon Classic Rock Climbs*.

248 Telluride Edge ✪✪✪

Red sandstone walls offer one-pitch leads, topropes, and bouldering. Good stuff near town. Summer. USFS–San Juan NF, (970) 247-4874.
Ref: Guidebook: Sawyer and Fowler's *Telluride Rocks*.
Directions: North of Telluride. Take Jud Wiebe Trail from Aspen St.

249 Fall Walls ✪✪✪

Three-hundred-foot conglomerate cliffs with 80′ climbs like Trickle Down Theory 5.11 and Heart of Gold 5.11+. Nice climbs established by Charlie Fowler. Summer. Private land/USFS–San Juan NF, (970) 247-4874.
Ref: Guidebook: Sawyer and Fowler's *Telluride Rocks*.
Directions: East of Telluride. On road up to Bridalveil Falls (psst, ice climbing!), park at second switchback and gander right toward cliff.

250 Vail

World-class limestone and ice alcove. Ice flows mainly in winter, but also mixed rock with the advent of harder ice climbs.

Ref: C 176-25.
Directions: South above East Vail.

251 Greenhorn Meadows Campground

Small bouldering and bivy area with a V4 roof problem and others. Summer. Private land.
Ref: Guidebook: Benningfield's *Colorado Bouldering*.
Directions: Near Colorado City. From I-25 (exit 74) go 3 mi. west on Hwy. 165 to Greenhorn Meadows Campground site 27. Trail to rocks.

252 Newcastle Boulders ✪✪✪

A pile of ten sandstone boulders features classics Stinkin' Linkin' V5 and Trabaharder V9.
Ref: Guidebook: Benningfield's *Colorado Bouldering*.
Directions: From Newcastle (exit 105 off I-70) follow Seventh St. out of town. Turn right onto CR 241 a few minutes to visible boulders. Roadside pullout available above boulders.

253 Matthews/Fuller State Park ✪✪✪

Several Dakota sandstone blocks like the Millennium Boulder offer climbing challenges up to V7 in a scenic Front Range setting just north of Red Rocks Music Arena. Autumn/spring. State park.
Classics: Millennium Boulder V1-V6.
Ref: R 89 (12/98)-100.
Directions: Southwest Golden. Exit I-70, going south toward Morrison on Hwy. 93. Follow signs to park. Twenty-minute uphill hike to boulders from two access points.

254 Gore Range

Peak C 8 pitch 5.7+ North Face by Cam Burns.
Ref: AAJ [98, 97].
Directions: West of Silverthorne.

255 Fortress/Turkey Neck

Syphilitic mudstone towers capped with sandstone blocks sits in the trenches at Mt. Garfield's base, visible from I-70 on the way into or out of Grand Junction. First climbed by Takeda, Arellano, and Raleigh. Great fun—for aid enthusiasts or phallic lovers. Bring long aid gear for slammin' em home. BLM, (970) 244-3000.
Ref: C 10/94-110.
Directions: From Grand Junction blast east to Palisade exit. Turn right onto dirt road that heads west for 2 mi. Turn right and go under I-70. Park. Hike west twenty minutes and into ravine with spires.

256 Williams Canyon ✪✪✪

Limestone sport-climbing area developed by famed guidebook author Stewart Green and son, Ian. Seventeen clip-up routes. Sixty meter or two 50 m ropes advisable. Fall. USFS–Pike NF, (719) 545–8737.

Ref: R miniguide.

Directions: From Colorado Springs go into Garden of the Gods, and just past Balanced rock turn left onto Rampart Range Rd. Take for 5 mi. of bumps to Williams Canyon, which starts on north side of water tower. Hike twenty minutes southwest from water tower to south on old road. Keep right at fork, descending into trail on north side of draw to Caveman Wall, where The Butter (11c/d) is.

257 Tall Boy Pinnacle ☆☆☆

Excellent granite, one-pitch climbing on about a dozen routes. Moss Wall sits on the back side of the pinnacle. USFS–Pike NF, (719) 545–8737.

Classics: Squeeze Boy 8, TallBoy 14a.

Ref: R miniguide.

Directions: In Manitou Springs. Go southwest on Ruxton to Barr Trailhead. Tall Boy Pinnacle lies to southwest of trailhead. Go back down Ruxton to first street and up to old trailhead, then across creek over dam. Follow tracks to zigzag trail to base of rock.

258 Table Mountain (7,423')

Beautiful Dakota sandstone offers small collection of more than twenty routes and many bouldering opportunities. State land.

Classics: I Ain't Blind 9, Sweet Thang 10, Twisted Travels 11, Magical Blend 12-.

Ref: R 67-94; Guidebook: D'Antonio's *Classic Rock Climbs: Garden of the Gods/Pikes Peak Colorado.*

Directions: From Colorado Springs head south on Hwy. 115. Approximately 15 mi. from Fort Carson entrance, turn right (west) onto Table Mountain Rd. Go 1 8/10 mi. for routes at Shambala, then hike north 3 2/10 mi. for bouldering at Ayurveda. Hike fifteen minutes north for both.

259 Lathrop State Park

Bouldering area on sandstone hogbacks. Pay camping. State park, (719) 738–2376.

Directions: From Walsenburg take Hwy. 160 west to Lathrop State Park.

Connecticut

Take a dog to obedience school, you'll both learn a lot. —Life's Little Instruction Book

Connecticut is tantamount to traditional climbing. This rural state's numerous mini crags, the central Traprock areas being the most famous, exemplify the vestiges of bold leads with minimal protection. Ratings are stiff and solid as the rock itself. The mindset here has gone as far as a few leaders using hooks tied off to the ground for protection. This hardcore approach has been dubbed a Traditionalist Conspiracy. On the other side of the coin, there are plenty of well-protected climbs at just about every grade in Connecticut. The state sports a host of genuinely beautiful areas that deserve a visit.

1 West Granby (Broad Hill) ✫✫✫
Sixty-foot quartzite crag. Fifteen routes with a 5.7 and 5.9 but mostly 5.10 and 5.11. Owned by Granby Land Trust.
Classics: Withy Windell 10c, Crazy Diamond 11c.
Directions: Near West Granby. Route 20 West. South on Simsbury Rd., right on Broadhill Rd. End of pavement continues up dirt road 200 ft. Cliff on right.

2 Pothole ✫✫
Pothole is a continuous cliff with the left and right ends being shorter and therefore popular with climbers for bouldering. Sharp rock. Private land.
Ref: A. Rubin; Guidebook: Perzel's *Climber's Guide to the 'Monks*.
Directions: From Storrs burn 3 mi. east on Gurleyville Rd. to Pothole. Park on side road on right just before the crag, not along Gurleyville Rd.

3 St. John's Ledges ✫✫✫
Low-angle 55' granite slabs reminiscent of New Hampshire granite. Nice forested area adjacent to the Housatonic River. Often wet. Possibly state land.
Classics: EMC: 13th Dwarf Crack 5, On The Edge 6, Dwarf Nebula 9-, Falling Bodies 9+, Little Jewel.
Ref: C 97.
Directions: In Kent. Short hike on Appalachian Trail from Route 341 gets one to the rock. St. John's Ledges has these three areas: Main Slab, Lower Cliff, and EMC (Eccentric Mountaineering Club) Wall.

4 West Hartford Reservoir (closed) ✫✫✫
Currently under negotiations to reopen. Good 35' basalt boulder problems up to B1+. Owned by Metropolitan District Commission (MDC).
Classics: Ultimate Crack 9, Croft Block B1-, Euro-weenies B1+.
Directions: In West Hartford. At West Hartford Reservoir.

5 TR (Traprock Crags)–Rattlesnake Rock et al. ✫✫✫✫
Traprock crags comprise a renowned band of basaltlike rock running north to south through the lowlands of central Connecticut and consisting of several cragging areas described below. The main ones are Pinnacle Rock, Ragged Mountain, and East Peak. Climbed on as early as 1930, it is solid rock, forming short cliffs ranging in height from 25' to 110'. Most are vertical cliffs between 40' to 70' with cracks, thin edges, and blocky overhangs. A strong, no bolts, ground-up lead ethic has led to leading with skyhooks tied off to the ground. (There are no sport routes here, that's for sure.) "Trap rock" is an old term used for the rock type, diabase. It originated from the German word *treppe,* meaning "step." Quarrymen used this term because the rock separated into large, spectacular blocks and was quarried in a series of steps. For the climber Traprock is the focal point of climbing history in Connecticut. Check Ken Nichols's guidebook *Traprock* for cliff details. There is *no* camping at any of the crags. Look for a motel or find a state or private campground. Unfortunately, encroaching housing developments and liability fears have made access difficult or changed. Climbers need to be extra courteous to landowners and choose parking spots wisely. Pinnacle Rock is privately owned.
Classics: Rattlesnake Rock: Hard Nut to Crack 5.9, Down to Earth 5.10-.
Ref: C [102, 90, 85(8/84)-8, 79(8/83)-14, 60-4]; Guidebooks: Nichols's *Traprock,* Harlin's *East.*
Directions: New Britain to Meriden. From I-84 slither 1 1/10 mi. west on Hwy. 6. Turn left past quarry and park. The three crags from north to south and in order of access: Porcupine Hole (not much), Green Wall (a few good ones), and Rattlesnake Rock (some good routes) are reached by using the blue-blazed Metacomet Trail. Trailhead is right next to the start of TV road. Porcupine

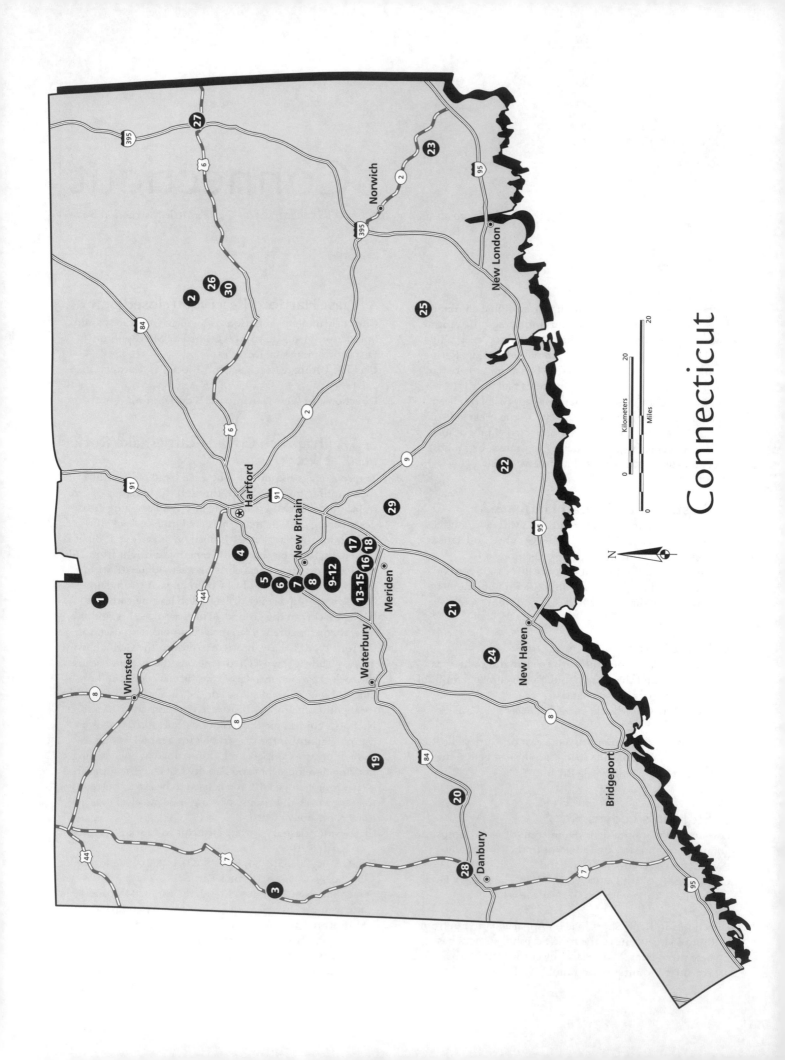

Connecticut

Hole and Green Wall face west. Rattlesnake is on other side of the mountain, faces east (and south), and is visible from I–84. Prepare to enter the suburban wilderness zone.

6 TR–Pinnacle Rock Ridge (Pinnacle Rock et al.) ✮✮✮

Holds some of the longer rock climbs in the Traprock area. Pinnacle Rock at 80′. Private land.

Classics: Zambezi Hatchet Head 7, Dream Weaver 9-, Psycho Path 9, Lost World 9, Supermantel 10-, Funshine 11-, Wild Kingdom 11-.

Ref: C [95, 93, 88, 60]; Guidebooks: Nichols's *Traprock,* Harlin's *East.*

Directions: From New Britain go west on Hwy. 72 (exit 34). At one time access problems were due to housing encroachment. No access problems at Pinnacle now, but people have to be quiet, courteous, and careful of where they park. Turn north on Crooked St. Take Hwy. 372 west. Turn north on Metacomet Rd. to parking. (Watch NO PARKING signs.) Hike northeast. The crags here are (from north to south): Lone Pine, Pinnacle Rock, Rock Garden, and Nike Base. Also approachable from Rattlesnake Rock: Follow Metacomet Trail east, then south approximately 2 mi. Approach Pinnacle from Metacomet Rd. as follows. In old dirt lot (blocked off—no parking here) on right side of Metacomet Rd. across from pond. Walk in here. Follow dirt road (old access road for Nike missile base). At set of concrete blocks, trail leads right uphill to area of Dream Weaver/Psycho Path. Continue past blocks uphill. Lone Pine will be visible on right. At top of hill road intersects blue-blazed Metacomet Trail. Head north (left) to reach Rattlesnake Rock. Head south (right) to reach summit of Pinnacle Rock. Beware of broken glass and trash from local party crowd.

7 TR–Cook's Gap (Stone Haven and Sounding Board) (closed)✮✮✮

This now-closed 50′ traprock crag had poorly protected leads. The Sounding Board has quality rock and is warm in winter. Highway noise is as soothing as punk rock. Owned by Tilcon-Tomasso quarry company, which doesn't want climbers there.

Classics: Stone Haven: Energy Crisis 10, Breath of Life 10+; Sounding Board: Centurion 10.

Ref: C 88; Guidebook: Nichols's *Traprock* .

Directions: New Britain. Cook's Gap has these two areas: 1) Stone Haven: On Hwy. 72, 7/10 mi. west of I–84. Hike trail a distance east/northeast to top of cliff. 2) Sounding Board: On the south side of Cook's Gap (junction I–84 and Hwy. 72). From I–84 take exit 33 east, going 9/10 mi. on Woodford Ave. Park. Shortest approach of any Traprock cliff.

---

8 TR–Bradley Mountain (Fire Wall et al.) (closed) ✮✮✮

Seventy-five-foot traprock crag. Fire Wall is the nicest of these walls and has overhangs and superb face climbs. Parking problems: Please park with regard for private landowners because you might want to climb here more than once. New Britain Water Company. Portions of Fire Wall owned by Town of Southington.

Classics: Sunset Rock: Sunset Crack 9, Super Natural 11; Fire Wall: Funeral Pyre 10, Firebird 10, Burned Beyond Recognition 11; Beatlejuice V4, Locksmith V5.

Ref: J. Nadeau 1/99; M. Siacca; C [88, 60-4]; Guidebook: Nichols's *Traprock.*

Directions: New Britain. Bradley Mountain Cliffs include: 1) Sunset Rock: From I–84 (exit 33) east, then south on Ledge Rd. for 3/4 mi. south of Woodford Ave. Park. Hike east 3/4 mi. on Metacomet Trail. 2) Sunrise Rock: Above east shore of Plainville Reservoir, reached farther on the Metacomet. 3) Fire Wall: Park at Shuttle Meadow Rd. and Plainville Reservoir. (Now very dicey parking here. Town of Southington now owns old Plainville Reservoir [Crescent Lake], which is operated as town park for fishing, nonmotorized boating, etc. A parking lot was built there, but at present you need to be a Southington resident to park there. Unfortunately, there is usually someone there checking IDs.) Hike along south shore, then southeast. Split Rock, Lost Wall, Hideout (from west to east) are on south end of Bradley Mountain. Located 1/2 mi. east of junction of Shuttle Meadow Rd. and Long Bottom Rd. and then 200 yd. north of road. But nearest parking at Water Deptartment lot on Andrews St.

9 TR–Shuttle Meadow (Spider Wall) (closed) ✮✮✮

Spider Wall comes highly recommended. These cliffs possess more of the sound, quality traprock. New Britain Water Company.

Classics: Graffiti Wall: Fire in the Lake 11, King of the Hill 11-; Spider Wall: Tarantula 8, Candle In the Wind 9, Aja 10, Cirith Ungol 11-, Grand Central 12-.

Ref: M. Siacca; C [88, 60]; Guidebook: Nichols's *Traprock.*

Directions: From New Britain carpool 6 mi. south on Hwy. 71A to Shuttle Meadow Reservoir Rd. then onto Andrews St. Park at Water Department lot (restrictions). Pretty involved to get a parking permit there. It is only good for six months, and application needs to be notarized. If you park in lot without a permit, you will get a ticket. Plus, from here you can look across the street at the 6′ by 10′

sign that says among other things NO ROCK OR CLIFF CLIMBING. Spider Wall is one of the crags that water department employees patrol the most since it is visible from the road. Cliffs (northeast to southwest): 1) Fiddle Buttress: 1/4 mi. south of lot. 2) Graffiti Wall (nice): 4/10 mi. south of lot. 3) Spider Wall (very nice): 6/10 mi. south of lot. 4) Grond Cliff (nice selection of mostly 5.8 and below): approximately 1 mi. south of lot on Metacomet Trail (just before power lines).

10 TR–Lost Valley (Molar Buttress et al.) (closed) ✬✬

One-pitch volcanic crag. The Lost Valley cliffs are found on the northeast finger of the reservoir. Don't miss Critical Mass 5.9 or Crack and Treat 5.8+, or Antimatter 11 for that matter. New Britain is home of Stanley Tools.
Classics: Fox Den: Crack and Treat 9-.
Ref: M. Siacca; C 88; Guidebook: Nichols's *Traprock*.
Directions: New Britain. Park at Water Department lot. Hike south 1 mi. to Wasel Reservoir. The Lost Valley cliffs are found on the northeast finger of the reservoir, located in a horseshoe starting at the northwest end and circling around to the southeast: 1) Molar Buttress (40′ tall, crap), 2) Cracked Block (approximately 25′ quality rock), 3) Fox Den (great), 4) Dam Wall (mostly crap), 5) Lakeside (not bad), and 6) The Outback (not bad).

11 TR–Ragged Mountain (Main Cliff et al.) ✬✬✬✬

The venerable crag of the state. Eighteen small crags offer intense cragging in an intensely climbed area. Unconquerable Crack 5.9 and Subline 5.11- are just two of the many exceptional routes here. Climbs date back to 1930. The area was one of the first crags where machine nuts were implemented. Be forewarned . . . vandalism has also been implemented. The Ragged Mountain Foundation owns most of the Main Cliff (which remains open); Town of Berlin owns the rest. The rest of Ragged areas owned by private landowners is closed: Small Cliff (clean good routes), May Crack (okay), Bloody Head Buttress (poor), The Citadel (poor). Outcrop is privately owned.
Classics: Weissner Slab 3, Serendipity 5, Diagonal 6, Broadway 8, Sisu 8+, Vajolet Corner 9, YMC 9, The Cage 10, Visions 10+, Cygnus X 11, Earthbound 11-, Enforcer 11c, Skull and Bones 11; Small Cliff: Diagonal 6, Shadow Wall 9, Mother's Lament 10.
Ref: J. Sargeant 11/00, M. Siacca; C [98, 95, 93, 91,90, 88, 60, 48], R [95-32, 78-28]; Guidebooks: Nichols's *Hooked on Ragged*, Harlin's *East*, Nichols's *Traprock*, Johnson et al.'s *Climber's Guide to Ragged Mountain*, Reppy and Streibert's *Climbing Guide to Ragged Mountain*.
Directions: Two options in Berlin: 1) Legal parking on West Lane in Berlin. From here can take the Ragged Mountain Loop Trail west (left) to get to the crags in thirty to forty minutes. 2) Park in Timberlin Park in Berlin (on Route 364) and take the trail from playground in rear of the park. Take a lime-green-blazed trail about fifteen minutes through woods until you reach Short Wall, just before intersection with blue-blazed Metacomet Trail. Join Metacomet Trail at bridge. Cross bridge to Mill-brook Lane. Follow Millbrook Lane to Carey St. Turn left on Carey St., then right up dirt driveway, following blue blazes all the way to cliffs. It's fifteen minutes from Timberlin Park to Millbrook Lane and another fifteen minutes to reach Main Cliff. Check with locals about road closures and parking.

12 TR–Short Mountain (Short Wall and Winter Wall) (closed) ✬✬✬

A 70′ beginner/intermediate traprock crag. Short Wall, buried in the woods, has moderate routes. Climbers' trail passes through huge chimney. (Chimney is at Winter Wall, which faces south and therefore has the sunny disposition.)
Classics: Winter Wall: Hot Line 9, Muscular Dystrophy 12.
Ref: M. Siacca; C 60-4; Guidebook: Nichols's *Traprock*.
Directions: New Britain. 1) Short Wall on northwest side of the mountain. Park in Timberlin Park on Route 364 in Berlin and take the trail from playground in rear of the park. Take a lime-green-blazed trail about fifteen minutes through woods until you reach Short Wall, just before intersection with blue-blazed Metacomet Trail. Follow Metacomet Trail south to Winter Wall. Walk north on Metacomet to reach Ragged Mountain. *No Parking on Carey Street.* Owner of Winter Wall will call police on you without fail.

13 TR–West Peak (Electric Rocks and Radio Forest, et al.) ✬✬✬

Ninety-foot traprock crag. Hard routes have better rock quality than beginner's routes.
Classics: Moment in the Sun 10, Plumb Line 10, Lord of the Rings 10, Scheherazade 11, Shock Treatment Variation 11, Arc de Triomphe 11.
Ref: M. Siacca; C [95, 63, 60]; Guidebook: Harlin's *East*.
Directions: Meriden. On the west side of West Peak, these cliffs (from north to south) appear: Electric Rocks, Valley View, Jumping Off Point, Hourglass, Chimney Rock, Cable Rock, Radio Forest, West Buttress. On the south side are the Windy Wall, Notch, and AMC Wall. Weird parking. From YMCA on East St., follow power lines to Electric Rocks Cliff. Or from I-691 take exit 5 north on Hwy. 71. Go right on Park and right on Percival Park Rd. to access cliffs on south end of mountain. Access to West Peak from this direction is quite long. If the park road is open, you can drive to top of East Peak by Castle Craig, park there, and hike over on Metacomet Trail to West Peak (approximately fifteen-minute walk). Police have been discouraging parking on top of West Peak because of commercial installations up there. Percival Park Rd. is barricaded by concrete blocks from this direction. Only access to the park road is from within Hubbard Park. If you choose to walk in this way, from the concrete blocks,

walk right and follow road to far side of reservoir. Follow blue-blazed hiking trail left into the woods. This is Metacomet Trail. This trail goes over summits of Merimere Face, Fall Wall, Amphitheater, etc. and reaches parking lot at Castle Crag *(don't boulder on the castle)*. To reach West Peak, you would have to continue farther north. From this direction you will go by AMC Wall, Notch, then Windy Wall. Quite a haul. Hiking time from concrete blocks to castle parking lot is thirty to forty minutes.

14 TR–East Peak (Amphitheater and Merimere Face, et al.) ✩✩✩✩

Another prized Connecticut cliff. Ninety-foot traprock crag just behind Ragged Mountain in popularity. Great variety of routes. Thor's Hammer 5.9 is one of the finest routes in Connecticut, and Dol Guldur 5.11+ is a must-do! City park.

Classics: Merimere Face: Thor's Hammer 9, Thunderbolt 11; Amphitheater: Cat Crack 10-, Rite of Spring 11, Volcanic Eruption 12; Castle Crag: Jaws 5; Fall Wall: Reflections of Fall 9, Stallion 11.

Ref: M. Siacca; C [98, 95, 90, 88, 63, 60-4, 48]; Guidebook: Harlin's *East*.

Directions: From Meriden follow Hwy. 71N. Turn west on Park Dr. Turn right on Percival Park Rd. to parking area above dissected buttresses. (Percival Park Rd. is closed for much of the year, so driving to the top of East Peak and accessing crags from top is not always an option that's available. During seasons when park road is open, it's open from about 9:00 A.M. to dusk, so watch the time or else you could get locked in. Other approach option is described above under West Peak, number 13. There is also an unpleasurable trudge up through the scree field below the crag.) East Peak Cliffs from south to northeast are Castle Crag, Amphitheater, Fall Wall, Alcove, and Merimere Face.

15 TR–South Mountain (Chopping Block and Prow) (closed) ✩✩✩

Great views of the Connecticut countryside from this 90' rotten traprock crag. Ariana on The Prow by Jim Adair is the reason to visit. Otherwise, few people climb here because of the junk rock. Land here is mix of private and City of Meriden, Meriden Land Trust. Word is that people have been kicked out recently.

Classics: Prow: Ariana 9+; Chopping Block: Far from The Maddening Crowd 8; Scylla 10+.

Ref: M. Siacca; C [95, 63, 60-4]; Guidebook: Nichols's *Traprock*.

Directions: From Meriden follow Hwy. 71N. Turn west on Park Dr. Turn right on Reservoir Ave. for approximately 1 mi. Parking lot on Reservoir Ave. Short trails east of road. South Mountain Cliffs from north to south are Hard Rock, Storm Shelter, Northwest Face, Prow, Chopping Block, Crumbling Ruin, Oasis Undercliff, and Rubble Pile.

16 TR–Cathole Mountain ✩✩✩

This 60' traprock crag with its two-minute approach is a good place if you only have a few hours.

Classics: Pegasus 8, Mindbender 9, Jaguar 10+, and Imperial Wizard 12-.

Ref: M. Siacca; C 93; Guidebook: Nichols's *Traprock*.

Directions: From Meriden paw 8/10 mi. north on Hwy. 71A. Cathole Mountain is on right up scree. Park in pulloff on right below the crag—not by the guard shack or entrance road. Follow clear but unmarked trail up hill to the cliff. Trail deposits you right at the base of Pegasus.

17 TR–Lamentation Mountain State Park (Evening Wall et al.) ✩✩✩

Fifty-foot traprock crag features good climbs at the Evening Wall. You may find yourself lamenting over the climbing as well as the hike to get to it. State land.

Classics: Wailing Wall: Climb Wave 10+; Arc Angel 7.

Ref: Guidebook: Nichols's *Traprock*.

Directions: Meriden. Lamentation Mountain State Park has three crags: Evening Wall, Wailing Wall, and Aviary. From I-91 (exit 19) wail west on Baldwin Ave. approximately ½

Bruce Dicks, second ascent of Dol Guldur, East Peak.

JEFF ACHEY

mi., then right on Bee St. to parking at south end of Bradley-Hubbard Reservoir. Hike north up dirt road to Mattabessett Trail, first to Wailing Wall and farther to Evening Wall. For Aviary turn north on Mattabessett Trail, then east and south.

18 TR–Chauncey Peak (Looking Glass and Prison Wall) (closed) ✩✩✩

Traprock 80' crags. Looking Glass sports best routes on Chauncey. Prison Wall has the highest concentration of hard roofs in Connecticut but requires a preamble through an unprotected band of vertical scree. Suspended Sentence here is good though. Training Ground is mostly okay beginner routes. The other walls are not worth visiting.

Classics: Hangman's Noose 9+, Suspended Sentence 10.

Ref: C [90, 63, 60-4]; Guidebook: Nichols's *Traprock*.

Directions: Meriden. From I–91 (exit 19) wail west on Baldwin Ave. approximately ½ mi., then right on Bee St. to parking at south end of Bradley-Hubbard Reservoir. Hike north up trail on eastern side of reservoir to rocks on right. From north to south the Chauncey Peak Crags are Buzzard Perch, Wildlife Sanctuary, Orange Spot, Looking Glass, Training Ground, and Prison Wall. The information kiosk in the parking lot of Giuffria Park (where the reservoir and parking is) lists climbing as prohibited. The park caretaker lives in the house by the parking lot and will present you with those rules if he sees visible climbing gear.

19 Orenaug Park ✩✩✩

This quiet, 100-yd.-long, disbanded, 55' traprock cliff sits at a duck pond. The private property adjacent to the trail is clearly marked by orange ribbons and at no point does the trail cross it. Was closed in 1995, but access issues seem cleared up. Was closed by town in 1994/1995 following some climbing accidents. Town was worried about liability. Ragged Mountain Federation and Access Fund were able to get crag opened again and are working with Woodbury right now to fix current (2001) dispute. An adjacent landowner has claimed ownership to the land at the base of the cliff and has closed access to approximately 60 percent of the climbing there, including all the best stuff. Private land/City of Woodbury land.

Classics: Rankin's Roof 8, Cedar Crack 7-8, Crocodile Tear's 10-, Cobalt 11.

Ref: R 69-30; Guidebooks: Ivanhoff and Nichols's *Woodbury Rock Climber's Guide*, Nichols's *Woodbury Cliffs*.

Directions: From Woodbury (west of Waterbury), Orenaug Park is off Hwy. 6. Please do not trespass.

20 Rocky Glen State Park (open?) ✩✩

State park crag.

Directions: From Newtown go north of I–84 to Rocky Glen State Park. Signs.

21 Sleeping Giant State Park ✩✩

This beginner/intermediate traprock crag of the 90' Chin Cliff Formation holds a famous Weissner Route, Weissner's Rib 5.6. The Chin has considerable bad rock, but the rock in the Tower area and the Right Knee (where Tempest is) is pretty good. One hundred routes. Nice views. State park, (860) 424–3200.

Classics: Weissner's Rib 6, Yvette 9, Frenchman's Cap 9, Rhadamanthus 10 et al., Way Rad 10, The Tempest 11-.

Ref: C [97(8/86), 60], R 79-49; Guidebook: Harrah's *Sleeping Giant*.

Directions: From Hamden slip north on Hwy. 10, following park signs. Sleeping Giant is visible from I–91 or Hwy. 15.

22 Chatfield Hollow State Park ✩✩✩

Just 8 mi. inland from Long Island Sound is strenuous climbing on 60' granite crag. Entry fee. No camping. State park, (860) 663–2030.

Classics: Forearm Frenzy 10+, Boyd's Void 12.

Ref: C. Tacy.

Directions: From Killingworth go just west on Hwy. 80 into Chatfield Hollow State Park. Park signs. While you can access the crag through the park, the climbing is actually most easily approached from the trailhead parking area for the Chatfield Hollow Trail on Route 80 (closer). This parking lot is about ⁸⁄10 mi. west of the state park entrance. From here walk west on Route 80 (uphill) for approximately ¹⁄10 mi. (Far end of the crag visible through the trees from here.) At the end of guardrail on right side of road is unmarked but clear path leading downhill into the woods. Turn left at bottom of hill and follow trail to the crag. For approach to the cliffs from within the park: Park on the west side of the pond and take one of the trails (possibly orange blazed) that leads to the cliffs. Check trail maps for the Chatfield Hollow trails available at the park entrance.

23 Wintechog Hill (aka Lantern Hill) ✩

Wintechog Hill is a 50' quartzite crag above a rockworks plant. Climb on weekends. Land of Pequot tribe—be respectful.

Directions: From Norwich go 10 mi. southeast on Hwy. 2 before Hwy. 201. On right. Wintechog Hill is above rockworks plant.

24 East and West Rock Park (closed/open) ✩

The impressive 69' traprock crag of East Rock is closed by city of New Haven decree. Trespassers arrested. West Rock is a state park open to climbing, but most of the rock is vegetated, loose, and seldom climbed. Watch for lobbed beer bottles . . . high school party zone. City/state park.

Ref: Guidebook: Harlin's *East*.

Directions: New Haven. West Rock Park is northeast of I–15 (exit 59) and north of Hwy. 63. East Rock Park is on Hwy. 5 just north of downtown New Haven.

25 Route 11 Crag ☆

This 40′ crag is an unfinished section of Hwy. Route 11. It was created when the DOT blasted through a hill to finish the highway. As of yet, it is undecided as to whether it will be finished. Due to the method of creation, extensive cleaning of routes is required. Good sections of rock are found on both south-facing cliffs. This crag also offers several good boulder problems. It is recommended that climbs be toproped due to the unpredictable nature of rock. State land.

Classics: Virgin Mary 3, Taz 5, Pine Tree 6, Flavor 6, Ice, Tea and Lemonade 7, Brain Scramble 8, Wacked 8.

Directions: From intersection of Route 82 and Route 85 in Salem, go south on Route 82 for approximately 1 mi. until you reach entrance ramp for Route 11 North. Just beyond entrance ramp is a DOT salt shed and a commuter parking area. Enter from here and hike up Route 11 northbound exit ramp (unfinished) approximately ½ mi. You will see four walls, each between 50′ and 85′ at highest points. Also accessible with four-wheel-drive vehicles, but Salem police disapprove.

26 Fifty Footer ☆☆

Intermediate- to expert-level 35′ granite crack climbs. Parts are overhanging; the easiest climb is a tough 5.8+ (some say it's actually a 5.9) with two crux moves and other routes to 5.12. Excellent for toproping, not much for lead climbing. Because of the strenuous uphill hike on the Nipmuck Trail, bring only the bare essentials. One rope and 25′ to 30′ slings ought to be sufficient for gear. State land.

Ref: Perzel's *A Climber's Guide to the 'Monks.*

Directions: From UConn take Hwy. 195 south to Chaffeeville Rd. about 5 ⅓ mi. to blinking yellow light. Take a left onto Chaffeeville Rd. The parking area is hard to find. It is about ½ mi. down Chaffeeville Rd. on the left. The entrance to the parking area is unmarked and is accessed between two mounds of dirt. The trail is likewise poorly marked, even though it is part of Connecticut's blue-blazed hiking trail system, more specifically the Nipmuck Trail. It is probably only a 500 m hike to the crag, but it's all uphill. Fifty Footer, Pot hole (see number 2), and Wolf Rock are all within ten minutes of each other.

27 Half Hill (aka Ross' Cliff) ☆☆

A fairly high cliff with some nice little crack climbs just above parking area. Most base areas are shaded. Some lead climbs, but most are topropable. Weekends tend to be busy with hikers, people fishing, and sometimes climbing and rappelling. At highest point the cliff is reported to be 120′ tall and overhanging. If it were, it would be tallest in Connecticut. Federal land.

Ref: B. Skonieczny.

Directions: From Danielson, at I-395, take exit 91 to Route 6 East. From I-395 drive up Route 6, and then take first road on right (South Frontage Rd.). Follow signs to Old Furnace State Park. Pass by the state park and take the first road on the right (Ross Rd.). Drive down road approximately ³⁄₁₀ mi. Turn right onto dirt road, you will see Ross Pond State Park sign on right. Follow this bumpy road to end and park in the shade near the obvious boulderfield. Good crack climbs are found straight up hill. Continue down road and take next right (Ross Rd.). Pass Old Furnace State Park. Road is on right. Dirt road will have sign at top for Ross Pond. Drive to end of road and park at end between two ponds. Hike straight up to bottom of small part of cliff or continue up left to gain access to clifftop trail.

28 Cache's Challenge

Expert 15′ quartzite bouldering with eight routes V0–V3. This climbing area was formed from construction in 1998. There is a bunch of boulders around the place and cliffs behind them. Enjoy the good climbing before it is gone.

Classics: Gus's Revenge on north side, V1; Cache's Cave on west side, V0.

Ref: A. Cotton 5/98.

Directions: Near Danbury, take I-84 to exit 7 onto Route 7. Get off first exit and turn left at light. Go through one light and turn left at second light (four-way intersection). Travel 100 yd., and cliffs and boulders are on the right. (Alpine Ski Shop across the street.)

29 Seven Falls Bouldering Area

Just south of Middletown. One mi. south of Aircraft Rd. and Saybrook Rd., pass under telephone lines to PARALLEL PARKING ONLY sign. Park. Look for trail to north of road to a dozen boulders.

Ref: www.wesleyan.edu/wsa/wmc/sevenfalls.html.

30 Wolf Rock

Day's worth of 25′ granite boulders. Two areas of climbing—upper and lower crags. Lower crag is fairly easy—an excellent place to bring beginners. The upper crag is more difficult but still pretty easy. Even a beginner climber will master most of the crag in a day or two. See also area number 26, Fifty Footer, which is nearby.

Directions: Take Route 195 south past UConn into Mansfield Center. This area is along the Nipmuck Trail.

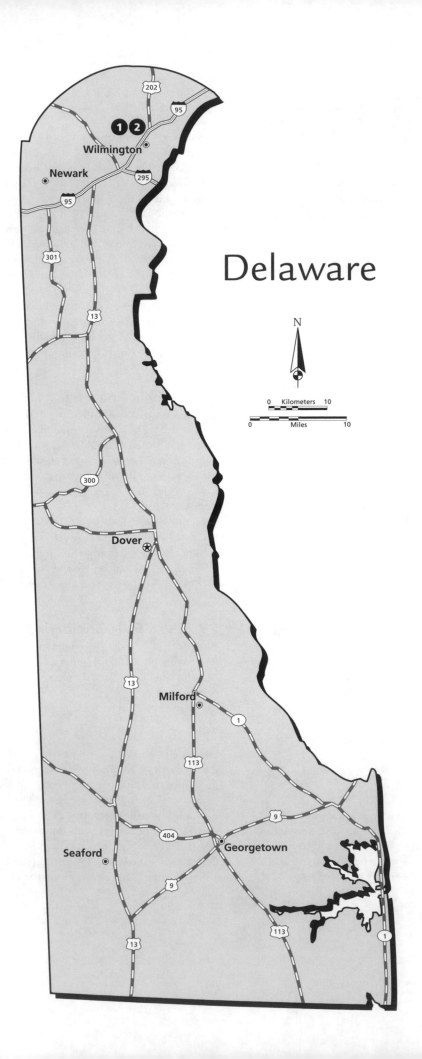

Delaware

Delaware

To a flea, the coyote is the whole world. —David Love, geologist

It's a small wonder people say Virginia when talking about rock climbing in Delaware. Still, these small wonders may make you aware of Delaware.

1 Rockford Park ✮✮

There are two separate and distinct parks in Delaware that have limited climbing. First, Rockford Park has a granite boulderfield located on the downhill slope across from the stone tower. There are presently approximately thirty-five documented problems in the park up to V5. City land.
Ref: C. Schaefer 2/99; Guidebook: Nick and Sloane's *New Jersey Crags.*
Directions: North of Wilmington. Take Route 52 West. Turn right on Rising Sun Lane, past Tower Hill School. Take last right before the old train bridge. Turn left into Rockford Park. Park behind tower. Rock is by the river.

2 Alapocas Woods (closed) ✮✮

There are a number of small granite crags/quarried areas located in this park that have been climbed in the past, as well as potential for additional development. Closed to climbing as of 1999, but access management plans are in the process. *Please* do not climb here until a management decision has been made. City land.
Ref: C. Schaefer 2/99.
Directions: Alapocas Park is across the Brandywine River from Rockford. From intersection of Kennet Pike and Hwy. 141, take 141 east. (The total distance off of Hwy. 141 to rock is probably 1 ½ mi.–2 mi.) Turn left into Barley Mill. It bends right at bottom of hill and turns into Henry Clay Rd. Driving in the downstream direction (south), this road bends right and turns into Rising Sun Lane. Turn left onto West Nineteenth Street heading southeast compasswise. Make a left onto Riverview Ave. Take first right onto William St. Take first left onto Rockford Rd. Take this down toward the creek and this will lead to a town house (nice, expensive) lane. Follow this through what looks like a security-guard gate (really it isn't, but appears so). At this point, the directions are kind of hit and miss, but you are probably 200 yd. from the parking lot. Keep heading toward an old abandoned factory. Drive right next to it. Head toward base of big smokestack (good landmark) and the parking lot. If problems with directions, stop at Rockford Park and spot the smokestack. It should be something like 200–300 yd. away. The access bridge across the creek is right at the parking lot (cliffs visible across the creek). Alternate directions: Take Route 52 west. Turn right on Rising Sun Lane, going past Tower Hill School. Take last right before the old train bridge. Turn left into Rockford Park. Park behind tower. Rock is by Brandywine Creek.

Delaware Road Thoughts

Chase rainbows, exceed the speed limit, and spoil your inner child rotten . . . someone is waiting to fall in love. . . .

Florida

N

| 0 | Kilometers | 75 |
| 0 | Miles | 75 |

Pensacola
29
10
1
231
98
Panama City
319
98
Tallahassee
19
75
10
Perry
301
Jacksonville
1
95
95
19
98
2
Gainesville
17
75
Daytona Beach
Ocala
40
41
27
95
19
Orlando
589
75
4
Melbourne
Tampa
192
St. Petersburg
Sarasota
17
27
Fort Meyers
75
80
27
95
Fort Lauderdale
75
41
Miami
3
Key West
1

Florida

There is nothing good or bad, but thinking makes it so. —Shakespeare

When it comes to rock, Florida climbers are so hungry they could eat the ass end out of a dead 'gator. The odd climbing areas in Florida are like attractions at Disneyworld: mainly for amusement in between visits to the next golf course.

Still, a visit to Silver Bluff, Florida Caverns State Park, or the Gainesville Quarry might put one in a whimsical mood, or should we say Goofy.

1 Florida Caverns State Park ✪

Got the bug juice? Be prepared for Jungle Joe, bio-bouldering where you might exclaim, "I've been slimed." Twenty-five-foot limestone bouldering formations. A 100' roof crack that if you could clean it out it would have grown back in by the time you got back to the other side. A maze of interconnected caverns used by Indians to hide from an expedition of Andrew Jackson's army. More climbing areas may exist in the Florida panhandle. Pay camping in state park (850–482–1228).
Ref: R 34.
Directions: From Marianna furrow north a few mi. on Hwy. 166 North, following signs to Florida Caverns State Park. Park at visitors center. Boulders are a short hike from the visitors center on the nature trail scattered along the Chipola River floodplain.

2 Gainesville Quarry ●

Several quarries present climbing opportunities with limestone walls up to 60'. The older ones have the most consolidated rock. The rock at the newer quarries is sand camouflaged as rock. Moccasin-infested pool at bottom. No camping. Private land.
Ref: R 34.
Directions: From Gainesville the quarry supposedly lies 10 mi. west of town on Hwy. 26, then possibly via dirt roads. Access is in question due to housing developments.

3 Silver Bluff (in Alice Wainwright City Park) ✪

Easy traversing on a 10' vertical, pocketed 200-yd. oolitic limestone band under the palm trees. For more difficulty try creating eliminate problems. Although Silver Bluff is small, the underlying geology is a limestone ridge that runs from southern Florida up to Georgia, but it is only exposed in a few areas and often on private land. City land.
Ref: R 34.
Directions: Southeast Miami. Follow I–95 south to Rickenbacker Tollway (which leads to Key Biscayne). Silver Bluff is a little limestone wall sitting at the junction of Federal Hwy. and Rickenbacker Tollway at Alice Wainwright City Park on the coastline.

4 Walt Disney World Resort Complex

The Magic Kingdom even has a climbing wall; be sure to fit it in the amongst the ride schedule. Pay camping. Walt Disney World Resort Complex (407–W–DISNEY) or climbing wall (407–WDW–PLAY).
Directions: In Orlando.

Florida Road Thoughts

I explored a strange and unusual place called Florida State Caverns. What was so strange about it? There were rocks. At first, we were of the opinion that we would be on a wild goose chase and we were . . .

Nobody really knew of any bouldering done or what it even was. So Caleb and I tromped around in the woods. They had what they called a bluff (you should have seen it; it was about 10' high at the most. It was so cute!). Anyway we got off the trail to check it out, and there were some pretty cool boulders down there, but very dirty with lichen and moss covering it. But I still couldn't find anything to supply a 100' roof crack. We might as well been searching for a pot of gold.

We hiked around for two hours and found some boulders, but nothing else. Nothing significantly overhanging; so disappointed I gave up. We started hiking back and I saw this sign pointing towards something called a Tunnel Cave. We checked it out. The Tunnel Cave was about one hundred feet deep with an opening at the end and running down this cave was a large crack from the beginning to the end. So we found the pot of gold. And lived happily ever after. The End.

Seeya, Janean

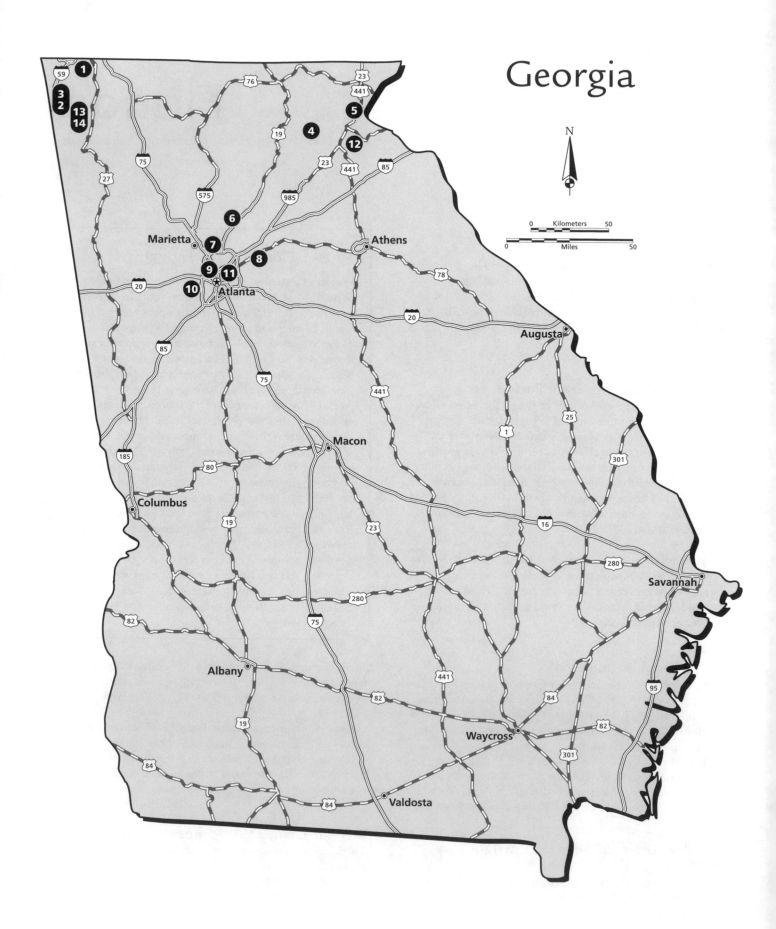

Georgia

It's not the award that counts, it's that I can still do it. Y'see, I didn't get it by laying back,
I got it by sweatin'! —James Brown, on accepting an American Music Award

Sorry for this pun, but if former president Jimmy Carter were a climber, he might say that the climbing in Georgia is peanuts compared to its northern and western neighbors. However, enough rock prevails to ensure a future for climbing in the state.

The southern half of the state is presently barren of established climbing areas. However, in Atlanta, the rock climber can don his shoes and begin to warm up in minor areas like Boat Rock and Allenbrook. Travelling farther north from Atlanta exposes one to Georgia's rugged northern hills, where climbing has been established in areas like Mt. Yonah and Tallulah Gorge.

The Appalachian Mountains visit Georgia before coming to a rest in Alabama, and it is here where the rock climber may pick the peaches of the state's climbing in new areas like Rock Town. Some of the fine Chattanooga, Tennessee, sandstone areas are actually in Georgia. With additional exploration in the sandstone belt, the state will surely yield fine crags in the future.

1 Patton Bluff ★★★

One trip to this 160' sandstone crag resulted in gunshot mirrors. Bring bulletproof vests, Dobies for the car, and slacjacs. Autumn. Private land.
Ref: P. Jarrard.
Directions: From Chattanooga tread south of Bee Rocks on Lookout Mountain Pkwy. past golf course. Park at nuclear power lines. Hike south along lines to Patton Bluff.

2 Rising Fawn Rocks ★★★

Undeveloped 80' sandstone cragging potential. Private land.
Directions: From Rising Fawn wander and boggle on I–59 south of Chattanooga to Rising Fawn exit. Go east to rocks.

3 Cloudland Canyon State Park (closed) ★★★

Stunning canyon vistas with 100' high sandstone crag extensions. An old rusty pin above the nature trail makes one wonder when the first rock climbers visited here. In the second week of April, the park offers an Outdoor Adventure Weekend in which climbing and spelunking are open to public—call for dates. Otherwise, for the rest of the year it is illegal to climb here. Kim Hatcher, public information officer for the Georgia Department of Natural Resources' State Parks Division, wrote *Rock 'n' Road* (1997), ". . . rock climbing is not allowed within the boundaries of this park . . . anyone caught rock climbing here will be cited by the DNR. Rock climbing is allowed at Tallulah Gorge State Park in northeast Georgia. Free permits (required) may be obtained at the visitor center." Park official Ed Reed wrote, "The reason that we offer rock climbing at Tallulah Gorge and not at Cloudland is primarily due to the rescue expertise that is available at Tallulah. The staff at Tallulah are well trained in high angle rescue and there is also a specially trained team in the local fire department that assists with rescues. This is not the case at this time at Cloudland Canyon. In addition the trails in Cloudland Canyon often pass directly beneath the canyon walls where visitors might be endangered by loosened debris from the canyon walls. There are no plans at this time to offer rock climbing at Cloudland." Hopefully this will change! As of 2000, $2.00 car entrance fee and pay camping at state park (706) 657–4050.
Ref: K. Hatcher 10/97; park officials.
Directions: From Trenton meander 8 mi. southeast on Hwy. 136 to Cloudland Canyon State Park entrance. Take park road north to overlook. Hike trail to obvious rimrock . . . don't climb!

4 Mt. Yonah ★★★

This mountainside exfoliated 150' granite dome offers good beginner's slab routes (seventy total) and good bouldering below the granite dome. Climbing since 1970 developed by Chris Hall et al. Also, training grounds for the Army Rangers and beginning climbers. (A reader tells us that "The property owner that lives at the top of the road has restricted access to the top except for the Army Rangers that frequently use the crags for mountain training.") As of 1997, the army has purchased enough land to cut an access road up to Mt. Yonah's parking lot. Currently, they are beginning to bulldoze a road. The army plans to open this to the public when they aren't training at the mountain (they train approximately 1 weekend a month). The road hadn't been completed by March 1999. The Access Fund has had a major hand in implementing this access situation; check with them for current information. Autumn. USFS–Chattahoochee National Forest, (770) 297–3000.

Classics: Dihedral 6, Army Routes B#8 6, Stannard's Crack 8, Orgasm 9, Lucy in the Sky . . . 10a, Afternoon Delight 11a, New Standard 12; The Boulder: Ringwraith 10.

Ref: C [C 166-35, 68-12], R [83-26, 78, 69-30]; Guidebooks: Watford's *Dixie Cragger's Atlas*, Robinson's *Deep South Climber's Companion*, Hall's *Southern Rock*.

Directions: From Cleveland light 4 mi. north on Hwy. 75. Just past Yonah Campground on right (granite face visible on right), turn onto dirt road on right. Hike up road for 2 7/10 mi. to Army hut and parking at Mt. Yonah. Access to the road is not open to the public. The Army has made no road; one must still park at the bottom and hike up the road all 2 7/10 mi.

5 Tallulah Gorge State Park ★★★★

This breathtaking 2-mi.-long chasm protects beautiful quartzite climbing on more than sixty routes on various formations in the canyon. Best climbing is on the east side. Buddy Price was one of the earlier climbing pioneers in the 1970s. Most routes established by climbers Rich Gottlieb and Shannon Stegg with others. Upper Falls at Tallulah Falls and Gorge has been permanently closed due to Peregrine Falcon's nests . . . only the Main Wall is open. Free climbing permits (required or pay $100 fine if caught without) may be obtained at the visitors center (open 8:00 A.M. to 5:00 P.M.). Twenty permits are available daily. The hike into the Main Wall area is extremely dangerous and aid ropes are recommended. The word *Tallulah* means "terrible" in Cherokee. Scenic waterfall, white-water boating (April/November), and tourist attraction. Autumn. As of 2000, $4.00 parking fee. Pay camping, $12. Hours: 8:00 A.M.–dark. State park, (706) 754–7970.

Classics: G.I. 6, Bee's Eye 7, Mescaline Daydream 8, Diagonal 9, Punk Wave 10a, Flying Frog 10, Stretch 10, The Prize 11, Heaven and Hell 12a.

Ref: C. Watford 2/01, C. Kimler 6/98; C 72; Guidebooks: Watford's *Dixie Cragger's Atlas*, Robinson's *Deep South Climber's Companion*, Price's *Carolinas Climber Guide*.

Directions: From Clarkesville (two hours northeast of Atlanta), spurt 12 mi. north on Hwy. 441/15 to Tallulah Falls. Park at the new Tallulah Gorge State Park Visitor's Center on the right. The trail leaves from the visitors center. Hike into Tallulah Falls and Gorge. Main Wall is on east side of ravine.

6 Allenbrook ★★

For the steep rock climber, an afternoon's entertainment (fourteen routes) at a small and very overhanging 45' sandstone creek bluff. The nearby mansion somehow remained unharmed by General Sherman's destructive march during the Civil War. NPS.

Classics: Beginner's Rt 6, The Groove 8, Rumors Roof 10/A1, Afterburner 11d, Flaming Fingers 12a.

Ref: Locals; Guidebooks: Watford's *Dixie Cragger's Atlas*, Robinson and Watford's *Deep South Climber's Companion*.

Directions: North Atlanta. Just south of Roswell on Hwy. 9 (2/10 mi. north of Riverside Rd.). Park at historical Allenbrook mansion lot and Chattahoochee River National Park Headquarters. Hike for five minutes north past charming house above creek to small bluff. This is approximately 1/4 mi. north of Chattahoochee River.

7 Chattahoochee River National Recreation Area (aka Morgan Falls) ★★

Sporadic riverside bouldering area along pleasant footpath. NPS, (770) 399–8070.

Classics: The Zipper 11d.

Ref: C 68; Guidebooks: Watford's *Dixie Cragger's Atlas*, Robinson's *Deep South Climber's Companion*.

Directions: North Atlanta. Follow Hwy. 9N to the Chattahoochee River. Three climbing areas can be found in the Chattahoochee River National Recreation Area: 1) Long Island: Hwy. 41 south from I-285 past Post Woods Apartment and Chattahoochee River. Park at bridge on left. Trail leads into hidden rock. 2) Palisades: East bank of Chattahoochee River at Powers Ferry Landing. From I-285 east take Powers Ferry Rd. exit onto Powers Ferry Rd. (parallels interstate back to river). Pull into Ray's on the River Restaurant and park at boat ramp in back. Start at Frog Boulder. Toprope face and crack routes. 3) The Zipper: Exit I-75 north on Windy Hill Rd., bearing sharply right onto Interstate North Pkwy. past Powers Ferry Rd. for 1 mi. to recreation area entrance on left before river bridge. Hike gravel running trail 200 yd. to quick right turn. Faint trail up and left into woods features the 11+ roof crack The Zipper. The access from Ray's on the River is now blocked by a gate that will make a statement but will not keep anyone from crossing and a sign that directs you to other places from which you may enter the area.

8 Stone Mountain Park (closed) ★★★

At 800' proud, this is the single largest piece of exposed granite in the eastern United States. This Southeast landmark and tourist park is well known for its confederate commemorative rock carving. No climbing allowed. Actually, good potential does exist for climbing here on the back end. Pay camping at park (770–498–5690 within the metro Atlanta area or 800–317–2006).

Ref: C [108, 68].

Directions: From Atlanta trot 16 mi. east on Hwy. 78 to Stone Mountain Park.

9 Georgia Tech Bouldering Wall ★★★

The original outdoor 30' bouldering wall of the 1980s was torn down to make room for the Olympics. A new wall was built as a replacement and is located on the Georgia Tech campus, in O'Keefe gym. It includes a bouldering wall and a variety of roped climbs. Prices vary according to involvement with Georgia Tech and ORGT (its outdoor program). Questions? Call (404) 894–7420.

Ref: C. Watford 2/01.
Directions: At Georgia Tech's O'Keefe Gym, at 801 Atlantic Dr. in Atlanta.

10 Boat Rock (closed) ★★★

Unfortunately, this former bouldering competition area, which stored some fun, 30' granite bouldering problems and short toprope material within its bowels, is now closed as landowners have enclosed the area with private homes. Autumn. Private land.
Classics: Left Side of Yellow Wall Arête.
Ref: C. Watford 2/01, S. Deweese 12/98; C [105, 97, 93]; Sherman's *Stone Crusade.*
Directions: Southwest Atlanta. Follow I-20 west. Go south on Fulton Industrial Blvd. Turn east 1 ½ mi. on Boat Rock Rd. (just past obvious front-yard roadside boulders). Avoid these first boulders at houses. Park at white gate on right. Hike approximately ten minutes on jeep roads/trails to Boat Rock boulders. Check with locals for current access issues. Two areas of rocks: one adjacent to the trail and another area diagonally left approximately ¼ mi. from these.

11 Emory University

Artificial 25' wall with varying overhanging, outcropping, and cave features.
Directions: Atlanta Emory University campus is north of downtown off I-85. Located inside of the Woodruff P.E. Center.

12 Currahee Mountain ★★★

There are two 75' granite cliffs here. One is a huge slab that offers many sport routes. Great place to learn balance and foot control. The other is straight up and also a bit negative in places. This cliff offers more challenging routes, including a nice water crack. County land.
Ref: C. Watford 2/01; T. Tate; Guidebook: Watford's *Dixie Cragger's Atlas.*
Directions: From Atlanta go north on I-85 to I-985. This will turn into Hwy. 23. Keep going north to the Toccoa exit. Take the Toccoa exit and continue on for about 2-3 mi. While on this road, you will see a high, pointed peak with several large microwave towers. This is where you are going. You'll come to a stoplight with a large log cabin-like Shell station on your left. Turn right here.

Head up this road for about 3 mi. until a rusted mailbox with a white arrow on it appears on the left. Turn left here. Head up steep hill approximately fifteen minutes. Park at the tower at top of mountain. Follow a footpath around the fence to the cliffs.

13 High Point

Trad sandstone climbing is now closed due to nonclimber vandalism. Owned by Georgia Power.
Ref: C. Watford 2/01; C 167-45.
Directions: Near Lafayette and 10 mi. south of Chattanooga. Main gate closed.

14 Lost Wall/Rock Town (on Pigeon Mountain, 2,220') ★★★★

Pigeon Mountain features secluded 120' sandstone routes at Lost Wall and great classic sandstone bouldering at Rock Town. November-April. Free camping around Rock Town Lane. State wildlife land; Crockford-Pigeon Mountain Wildlife Management Area, (706) 295-6041.
Classics: Rock Town: Leatherback V4, Smell My Finger V5, Bandies V7, Sherman Roof V8, Bionic Rats V9.
Ref: C 194-60, R 100-91; Guidebook: Watford's *Dixie Cragger's Atlas*
Directions: From Lafayette go west on Hwy. 193 for about 3 mi. Turn left onto Chamberlain Rd. for 3 ½ mi. Turn right into Crockford-Pigeon Mountain Wildlife Management Area up switchbacks to fourth switchback for Lost Wall at 1 9/10 mi. Continue up to top of Pigeon Mountain, bearing left onto Rock Town Lane. In less than a mi., turn left and park at lot. Walk about fifteen to twenty minutes, following white-blazed trail to the Rock Town boulders.

Georgia Road Thoughts

NEWS RELEASE:

The ingredients for Viagra have finally been released:
    2 percent aspirin,
    2 percent Ibuprofen,
    1 percent filler,
    95 percent "Fix a Flat"

Hawaii

Hilo

130

19

200

11

250

270

190

19

11

360

36

37

31

30

Wailuku

450

440

460

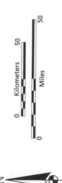

72

4

83

H3

3

H2

2

99

H1

1

93

Honolulu

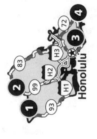

Lihue

56

50

550

Kilometers

0   50

Miles

0   50

N

Hawaii

Congratulations! Today is your day. You're off to Great Places! You're off and away!
—From Dr. Seuss's *Oh, the Places You'll Go*

Hawaii is not exactly a destination climbing area, despite the fact that the islands are composed entirely of basalt and concrete. Nevertheless, you're bound to get leied as soon as you step off the plane. Sea cliffs and lava tubes on the dry sides of the islands have potentially good bouldering and cragging areas. Best to get friendly with the natives.

1 The Mokuleia Wall ✰✰✰
Basalt climbs (70') from 5.8–5.12 on twenty-four bolted/toprope routes. Assorted cracks and bolted face leads on basalt columns. State land.
Classics: Beat the Burn 5.9, Spice of Life 5.10, Torpedo Youth 5.11.
Ref: *The Honolulu Advertiser.*
Directions: From Waialua go west on Hwy. 930, passing Dillingham Air Strip on left, then past Camp Erdman on right. After ¼ mi., find orange electrical box on left. On right is stone bunker on beach and a U-turn area. At this point, park at roadside. Hike south on trail into Waianae Mountains to Mokuleia Wall. It is just beyond Dillingham Airfield (about 1 mi.). Approach takes about twenty minutes (fairly strenuous).

2 Waimea Boulders ✰✰✰
Twenty-foot basalt bouldering on beach. Obvious boulders at Waimea Bay.
Ref: R 94-35.

3 Waahila State Recreation Area ✰✰✰
Eighty-foot basalt crags off road. Good, traditional gear climbing. State land, (808) 587–0300.
Directions: From Honolulu drive east on H1 to Waahila Ridge State Recreation Area. Turn north on one-way road into recreation area.

4 Makapuu Boulders ✰✰
Small amount of oceanfront 35' basalt bouldering on the shores of the Pacific. Routes on cliffs 500' above ocean. Very scenic setting with awesome views of islands and windward Oahu. Toproping with a couple of bolted routes.

Don't leave anything of value in your car! (Notorious rip-off spot.) State land, (808) 587–0300.
Ref: J. Lemes.
Directions: From Waimanalo Beach on the island of Oahu, drive south on Hwy. 72. Makapuu Boulders at Makapuu Point, on the coast of the Pacific Ocean, east of Hwy. 72. Follow cliffs ¼ mi. toward the Makapuu Lighthouse.

Other Hawaiian Climbing Areas
Makua Cave
40' basalt sport routes 3 mi. before Kaena Point on Hwy. 93 via H1 West. See http://employees. inline.com/jeff/oahu.htm.

Hanging out at Waimea Bay, Oahu.

JOHN SHERMAN

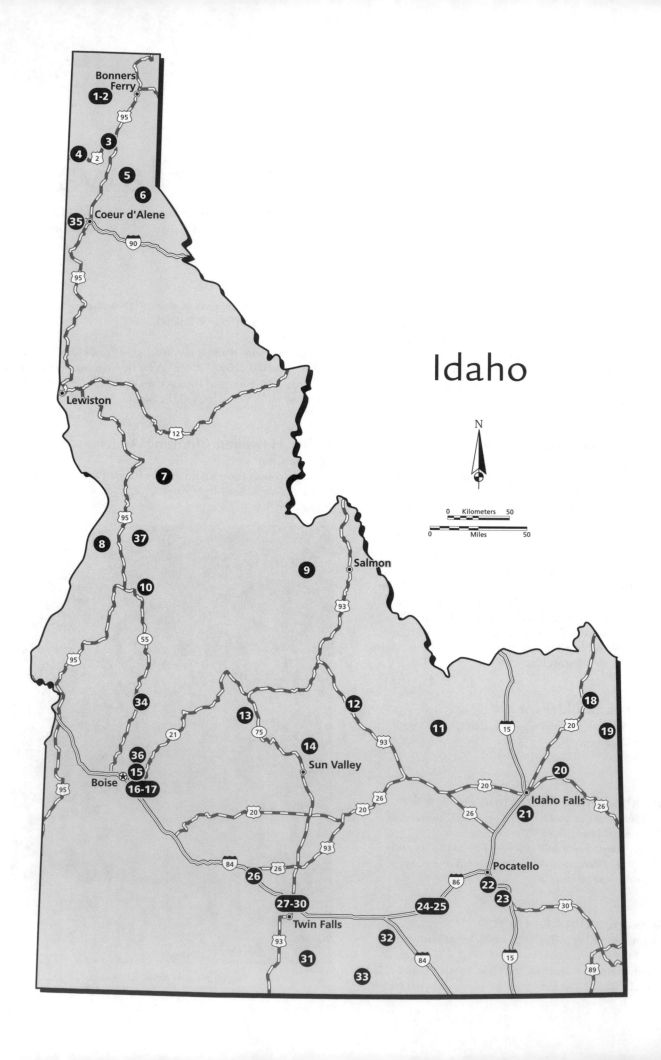

Idaho

Idaho

There never was a tater like the Idaho spud. —Kip Attaway

White granite, brown potatoes, and black basalt—what a colorful state is Idaho. The City of Rocks is the number-one area, a windy wonderland of granite domes that remind one of Joshua Tree but have sagebrush instead of yuccas. Until the late 1980s and early 1990s, the "City" was a sleepy Mormon ranching community, a runaway from a wax museum. From the late 1980s into the 1990s, it rose to the forefront of the summer sport climber's attention, attracting many international climbers.

Basalt bands consist of the remainder of southern Idaho areas. These tend to be short, sweet, and mafic. Whether it's on the Black Cliffs, Dierke's Lake, or Massacre Rocks—to name but a few—you are sure to find the tater of your choice.

If you yearn for longer climbs and higher elevations, go north to the stately Sawtooths or the scenic Selkirks. The Sawtooths offer backcountry beauty, where granite faces more than 1,000 feet can be found. Northern Idaho offers a list of scattered granite crags. At the top of this list is Chimney Rock in the Selkirks.

If you're a hungry climber, look to Idaho for sustenance in its rock piles and potatoes.

1 Selkirk Crest Range ☆☆☆

Eight-hundred-foot alpine granite faces. The Selkirk Mountain Range (at 7,000') provides climbers with several glacially carved granite faces, buttresses, and boulderfields on bear-grass slopes. Easy mountaineering routes to difficult rock climbs can be found. Most rock can be reached within a three-hour hike. Chimney Rock is most noteworthy for rock climbers. Other peaks with rock climbing that have received less attention or have been developed after Chimney Rock include Mt. Roothaan, Silver Dollar Peak, Harrison Peak, and the East Face Gunsight Peak 5.8. USFS–Idaho Panhandle NF, (208) 765–7223.
Classics: Harrison Peak: Standard Rt 7, Twin Flakes 8, Sunset Dihedral 9-, Keystone Rt 9, Chimney Rock (var.); Gunsight Peak: East Face Gunsight 8, Silver Dollar Peak West Ridge II 3, The Twins.
Ref: AAJ '76-454, C [106, 99, 94]; *Selkirks: Nelson's Mountains;* Guidebooks: Green's *Idaho Rock: Selkirk Crest and Sandpoint Areas,* Lopez's *Exploring Idaho's Mountains: Guide for Climbers and Hikers.*
Directions: From Sandpoint take Hwy. 95 north. Turn north on Pack River Rd. Pick up Selkirk Crest trailheads

off this road at West Branch Rd. or farther north to end of road. Or from Priest River, turn north to Coolin and continue beyond this town to one of two roads: 1) Turn east up Hunt Creek Rd. for Gunsight Peak or 2) take Horton Ridge Rd. (9 ½ mi. north of Coolin) to its end and hike east for Mt. Roothaan/Chimney Rock. Obtain a topo map.

2 Chimney Rock ☆☆☆☆

This popular, well-developed 450' granite crag on a Selkirk peak top is known as the Lightning Rod of northern Idaho. First ascent of the west face in the early 1930s. Many classic crack routes (more than twenty-six) established in the 1970s. USFS–Idaho Panhandle NF, (208) 765–7223.
Classics: Rappel Chimney 6/7, Cooper-Hiser III 9, Sancho's Direct 10, Fun Roof 10, Magnum Force 10b, Free Friends 10+, Sticky Fingers II 10d R, Yahoody 11, Tsunami 11d.
Ref: AAJ '92-142, C [111, 105, 102(6/87)-20, 99, 94, 66(5/81)-26, 60], S [10/72, 2/62]; Guidebooks: Green's *Idaho Rock: Selkirk Crest and Sandpoint Areas,* Lopez's *Exploring Idaho's Mountains: Guide for Climbers and Hikers.*
Directions: From Sandpoint (approximately 20 mi. northwest) take 95 north. Turn north on Pack River Rd. Turn west on West Branch Rd. onto left fork leading to trailhead. Park. Hike trail approximately 3 mi. Or, from Sandpoint follow Hwy. 2 west to town of Priest River. Turn north to Coolin and continue beyond this town several mi. to Horton Creek Rd. (Chimney Rock is visible from Priest Lake. Another option is to turn east up Horton Creek for trailhead to Mt. Roothaan and Chimney Rock beyond.

3 Schweitzer Rocks (aka Practice Rocks) ☆☆☆

Seventy-foot granite crags with boulders below. Routes from mostly 5.7–5.10. Sensitive access—probably doomed by houses. Please do *not* camp on premises. Private land.
Classics: Fern Crack 7, Definitely Maybe 9, Hi–Di–Do 10a, Stonemaster Delight 10c.
Ref: C [120-38, 111, 102(6/87)-20, 99, 94]; Guidebook: Green's *Idaho Rock: Selkirk Crest and Sandpoint Areas.*
Directions: From Sandpoint (visible from town) go 3 mi. north on Boyer Ave. (follow SKI AREA signs). Turn left on

ski area road. Turn right on first road after crossing railroad tracks. Park at second switchback. Hike up trail to Schweitzer Rocks. Faces east. New housing may make access difficult and threatens boulders. Good problem on Lot 4 boulder.

4 Laclede Rocks ☆☆☆

Several roadside buttresses tempt climbing motorists to stop and partake of their sport on 90' gneiss crags offering face and crack climbing as well as bouldering. Good stuff on sunny rock! Please stay off dangerous roadcut area. Blasted (man-made) routes next to the blue Pend Oreille River. Also, good swimming in the heat of summer. Private land.

Classics: New Sensations 8, The Dihedral 9-, Chicken McNubbins 10b, Road Kill 11c, Another Roof 12.

Ref: C [124, 111, 106, 105, 102(6/87), 99, 94]; Guidebook: Green's *Idaho Rock: Selkirk Crest and Sandpoint Areas.*

Directions: From Laclede (10 mi. west of Sandpoint) crank 2 mi. west on Hwy. 2. Park at pullout below Laclede Rocks on Hwy. 2 or above cliffs from road heading up on east side of rock. Faces south.

5 Granite Point (on Pend Oreille Lake) ☆☆☆

Two-hundred-and-fifty-foot granite bluffs offer solid 5.9–5.10 face/crack climbing, e.g., Main Line 10d, on southeast shore of Lake Pend Oreille (and south of Kilroy Bay). Fun exploration. Boat belays. Mountain goats. USFS–Idaho Panhandle NF, (208) 765–7223.

Idaho Road Thoughts

Ahhhhhhh. Home plate isn't there. Well, shit. If home plate isn't there; if it has gone the way of Ixtlan and innocence, then what drives us to drive through the night to a home? We keep leaving home in search of—what? Adventure? Amusement? Agreement? America? Is home there when we return? Thomas Wolfe told us you can't go home again, and that's true. And who doesn't know it? Old Chris Columbus knew it. Darwin knew it. Marilyn Monroe knew it. And Don Juan knows it. Ed Mitchell knows it. He has been further out there than anyone; and he came all the way back to earth from the dark side of the moon, searching to find home in Noetics. Me and my brother fuck-ups of the lost highway keep repeating those long drives through the night, heading for that mythical home our imaginations have placed out there in the future, that home which we have always left in a full-throttle search for whatever is down the road, around the next turn, over the next hill, at the end of the next long straightaway. What is it that the long distance driver and all other explorers suspect can be found somewhere else but where they are?

—From Dick Dorworth's essay "Night Driving"

Classics: Reasonable Alternative 9, Fingerling 10c, Main Line 10d.

Ref: C [105, 102(6/87)-20, 99]; Guidebook: Green's *Idaho Rock: Selkirk Crest and Sandpoint Areas.*

Directions: From Sandpoint take Hwy. 95 south. Turn east on Garfield Bay Rd. to end. Rent boat for 6-mi. ride across lake to Granite Point. Also accessible on FR 278 (High Dr.) north from Cedar Creek or west from Clark Fork, but with a bushwhack of some miles.

6 Kingston and Steamboat Rocks ☆☆☆

A large group of quartzite buttresses, six of which are 500' and hold classics like The Prow III 9. USFS–Idaho Panhandle NF, (208) 765–7223.

Classics: Prow III 9.

Ref: AAJ '77-186, C 102(6/87)-21.

Directions: From Kingston trek 20 mi. northeast of Kingston at northeast fork of Coeur d'Alene River to Kingston and Steamboat Rocks.

7 Huddleson's Bluff

Multipitched summertime crag. Huddleson's Bluff is on south side of Clearwater River. USFS–Nez Perce NF, (208) 983–1950.

Ref: AAJ '76-454.

Directions: From Grangeville follow Hwy. 13 east to Hwy. 14. Turn south on Hwy. 14 paralleling south fork of Clearwater River to FR 649. Cross cold river and hike downstream. Huddleson's Bluff is on south side of river.

8 Seven Devil Mountains ☆☆

One of the state's most precipitous ranges, with 200' volcanic crags. He Devil summit is the highest summit in the range at 9,393'. Devil's Tooth's north summit, 7,760' and north of Sheep Lake, is a technical rock climb, while south summit is third class. Most technical climbs are loose, blocky adventure summits. Climbing pioneering done by the Mazama mountaineering group in 1963. Beware rope munch and do not fall. NPS/USFS–Payette NF, (208) 634–0400.

Classics: Devil's Tooth: North Face; Twin Imps: North Peak.

Ref: AAJ '93, S 1/85; Guidebook: Lopez's *Exploring Idaho's Mountains: Guide for Climbers and Hikers*

Directions: From Riggins drive 1 mi. south on Hwy. 95. Turn west up Squaw Creek Rd. to Windy Gap Campground. Hike east/southeast to Seven Devil Mountains formations. Devil's Tooth (7,760') is north of Sheep Lake or access via 7 Devils Loop Trail. Topo necessary.

9 Bighorn Crags ☆☆☆

These 1,000' granitic alpine crags lie in a 10 mi. by 20 mi. long range of little renown but much beauty in a wilderness setting. Lying on the east side of the middle fork of Salmon River, the Bighorn Crags are part of the massive granitic intrusion called the Idaho Batholith. Trailheads take travelers into River of No Return Wilderness for granitic domes, pinnacles, and outcrops, e.g., Fishfin Ridge (Rusty Nail) above Welcome Lake, Cathedral Rock. Back-country lakes abound. USFS–Salmon NF, (208) 756–5100.

Classics: Sugarloaf Dome, Fishfin Spires, Heart Lake Area, Knuckle Peak.

Ref: *Mazama* Vol. 33, v13, *Mountaineers* Vol. 48 v13, R 15(7/86), S [1/89, 5/84]; Guidebooks: Mitchell's *50 Eastern Idaho Hiking Trails*, Lopez's *Exploring Idaho's Mountains: Guide for Climbers and Hikers.*

Directions: From Salmon go west via USFS Roads 021–101 to Cobalt. Go south of Cobalt on Panther Creek Rd. (055) and turn west onto Yellowjacket Rd. (112–118) to Yellowjacket Lake. Crags Campground is most popular trailhead. Others include Middle Fork, Waterfall Creek, and Panther Creek. Trailheads take travelers into River of No Return Wilderness for granitic domes, pinnacles, and outcrops of the Bighorn Crags.

10 Slick Rock ★★★★

This excellent 1,200′ east-facing granite formation offers beautiful, multipitched climbing amid splendid mountain scenery. The Regular Route 5.7 (nine pitches from toe to top) is a classic; look for the center crack splitting the center of the face leading to apex of summit. Descent off north side via trail in gully; stay left. Camping at Ponderosa State Park off Davis Rd. (see directions) or campground 1 mi. before reaching Slick Rock. USFS–Payette NF, (208) 634–0700.

Classics: Regular Route 7.

Ref: R 50 (7/92); Guidebook: Lopez's *Exploring Idaho's Mountains: Guide for Climbers and Hikers.*

Directions: Approximately 10 mi. northeast of McCall. From center of town (Hwy. 55) turn right on Thompson Rd. Turn left on Davis Rd. for 8/10 mi. Turn right on Lick Creek Rd. for 10 ½ mi. to Slick Rock, visible on left side of road. Park in small pullout. Cross the creek on a log jam directly below the pullout and climb the hillside for ten minutes to base.

11 Lemhi Range ★★★

One can find quartzite or limestone climbs in an alpine setting or lower area crags. The desert south end of the Lemhi Range features impressive cliffs in Box (limestone) and East Canyons. For more alpine climbs, Diamond Peak offers vertical tests on its flanks. Mainly easy routes. This is one of several northwest- to southeast-running ranges in Idaho. Diamond Peak is highest in range, approximately 12,200′. Scattered rock outcrops. Mostly rotten sedimentary rock, but good climbing at Bear Valley Lakes Trail at Bear Valley Lake. Good rock on the northeast face. Opportunities for technical climbs on solid dolomite. USFS–Salmon NF, (208) 756–5100.

Ref: AAJ '90-177, S [5/82, 5/65]; Guidebook: Lopez's *Exploring Idaho's Mountains: Guide for Climbers and Hikers.*

Directions: This range extends for 100 mi., south from Salmon to Howe. Diamond Peak: From Hwy. 28 near Lone Pine, go west on Hwy. 181, then right on Diamond Peak Access Rd. East Canyon: From Howe go north on Hwy. 22, then east to Bernice.

12 Lost River Range ★★★

Borah Peak, 12,662′, is highest point in Idaho. First ascent of Mt. Breitenbach's limestone North Face III 5.8 A2. Mostly easy fourth-class routes and winter mountaineering, but quartzite/limestone rock climbing potential does exist, e.g., Mt. McCaleb. Free camping. USFS–Salmon NF, (208) 879-4100.

Classics: Borah: East Face 2, North Face Snow Climb.

Ref: AAJ '83, R 92-112; S 9/82; Guidebook: Lopez's *Exploring Idaho's Mountains: Guide for Climbers and Hikers.*

Directions: Lost River Range fault block range extends 70 mi. southeast of Challias to Arco. Mt. Borah: Rock Creek to Double Springs Rd. Mt. Breitenbach: Reached via Dry Creek. Many access points. Get topos.

13 Sawtooth Mountains (Elephant's Perch) ★★★★★

Majestic 1,000′ granite alpine crags, spires, and walls offer summertime mountain climbers more than one hundred established routes in this extensive alpine wilderness area. The Elephant's Perch, approximately 3 mi. southwest of Redfish Lake, amongst others, sports classic, multipitched (up to ten p) climbing on its southeast to west faces. Its 1,200′ face is touted as the largest chunk of premium granite in the state, and rightly so. Thompson Peak, at 3,285 m, is the highest in the Sawtooths. Majestic Mt. Heyburn was first climbed in 1935 via Southwest Ridge by the Underhills/

TIM TOULA

The stunning Elephant's Perch.

William party. Summer attracts tourists; September may be less crowded. Route information in Ketchum at Elephant's Perch shop. USFS–Sawtooth NF, (208) 727-5000.

Classics: Elephant's Perch: Sideline II 9, Astro Elephant IV 10-, Myopia IV 11-, Fine Line IV 11, Direct Beckey V 11, Sunrise Book III 12; Mt. Heyburn: Stur Chimney, Warbonnet; Finger of Fate: Open Book III 8, Verita Ridge; Warbonnet: Petzoldt Route, Grand Aiguille, many others.

Ref: AAJ ['79-195, 77-186, 76-455, 75-133, 72-70, 66-138], C [132, 69, 10/72], OB 19(2/75), R [92-112, 44, 15 (7/86)], S [4/67, 11/61, 6/61]; Guidebooks: Mitchell's *50 Eastern Idaho Hiking Trails,* Elephant's Perch topos, Lopez's *Exploring Idaho's Mountains: Guide for Climbers and Hikers,* Kelsey's *Climber's and Hiker's Guide to the World's Mountains.*

Directions: Stanley. The Sawtooth Mountains lie west of Hwy. 75 and Hwy. 21. Several USFS trailheads begin at numerous alpine lakes west of Hwy. 75, which include Stanley Lake, Redfish Lake for Garden of Giants and Elephant's Perch, Upper Hell Roaring Lake via Decker Flats Road for Finger of Fate, Yellow Belly, Petit Lake for El Capitan, and Alturas Lake. The northern end of range has most accessible climbing with access via Iron Creek Rd. (2 mi. west of Stanley) and Redfish Lake for Elephant's Perch (approximately 5 mi. south of Stanley at mm 185, then 2 mi. west to Redfish Lake and take ferry at Lodge to save 5 mi. hike around lake, then 2 mi. west up Redfish Lake Creek Trail to 1 mi. south up side drainage to base). See Forest Service maps for other approaches. From Stanley many climbs can be completed in one day, but most climbers will want to enjoy several nights.

14 Sun Valley Crag ✭✭✭

Features 60' quartzite sport crag with twelve routes. A fine mountainous area of high-altitude boulders and crags with 5.13 Yaniro drilled routes on upper block. USFS–Challis NF, (208) 756-5100.

Ref: M. Laggis; Guidebook: Lopez's *Exploring Idaho's Mountains: Guide for Climbers and Hikers.*

Directions: From Sun Valley (just northeast of Ketchum), at junction of Sun Valley and Saddle Roads, rise and shine for 10 mi. (fifteen minutes) up Trail Creek Rd. until 1 4/10 mi. from the top of Trail Creek Summit on the Sun Valley side. Sun Valley Crag with extreme Tony Yaniro routes is on right just above road. Faces northwest. Small parking pullout is on left. More rock also below pullout. Bouldering and other routes above and back down road toward town.

15 Table Rock Quarry ✭✭✭

Site of first Southwestern Idaho Bouldering Contest. This favored Boise climbing hang sports 35' south- and west-facing, frictiony sandstone bouldering or short lead/ toprope walls. At least ninety face and crack routes/problems. Quarrying activities have destroyed some of the better routes. Private/public land.

Classics: Popeye 7, Bat Crack 9, Burning Bush 10a, Crystal 10d, Naked Edge 11a, Super Crack 11b, Master's Edge

11b, I Stone 11c, Propeller 11d toprope, Stem Corner 12a, Nuclear Sunset 12a/b, Crank Cream 12c, Roadrunner 12c (classics like 29 Potatoes 11a, Hakenkruez 12a, Vetikal Slur 12c are now destroyed).

Ref: C 107; Guidebooks: Epeldi's *Boise Climbs,* Bingham's *City of Rocks,* Lopez's *Exploring Idaho's Mountains: Guide for Climbers and Hikers.*

Directions: East Boise (fifteen minutes from downtown). Table Rock overlooks city to east of the capital. It sits below giant cross (lit up at night) and the giant letter B on slope below it. From junction of Hwy. 21 (Warm Springs Hwy.) and Broadway Ave., drive 2/10 mi. north on Broadway (Ave. B). Turn right on Reserve St. for 4/10 mi. Turn right on Shaw Mountain Rd. for 1 mi. Go right on Table Rock Rd. for 2 2/10 mi. (partially dirt) to junction on top of Table Rock. Proceed past two radio towers for 2/10 mi. to cliff top and parking above Table Rock Quarry. Descend to rock. The Quarry has areas of bouldering, short moderate routes, Big Times Area, the Main Bouldering and Toprope Area, and an active quarry area.

16 Black Cliffs (North) ✭✭✭

The Black Cliffs are the chief workout area of Boise rock hounds. Short 35' south-facing basalt walls put forward interesting routes with great face and crack opportunities. One hundred and seventy routes up to The Sting 5.12d. May get too hot in summer. Raptor restrictions February 1–June 30.

Classics: Round Table 8, Pabst Smear 9, The Scream 10a, Basic Training 10a, Beta Junkie 10c, The Spear 10c, Cool for Cats 11c, Wimp Roof 11c, Kaopectate 12c, The Sting 12d.

Ref: C [111, 107(4/88)-16]; Guidebook: Epeldi's *Boise Climbs,* Bingham's *City of Rocks, Black Cliffs Route Finder.*

Directions: Southeast Boise (fifteen minutes from downtown). From junction of Hwy. 21 (Warm Springs Hwy.) and Broadway Ave., drive for approximately 7 4/10 mi. to Black Cliffs (North) on the right above dam in visible canyon.

17 Black Cliffs (South Side) (aka The Dark Side) ✭✭✭

The Dark Side (or the South Side) routes represent the most difficult routes at the Black Cliffs, including Darius Azin's testpiece God 5.13b. There is a new 5.14a, Drunken Sailor to the left of the Dark Side on the cliff called Nixon's Head. Climbs are mainly face climbing and a cooler summer alternative to the North Side. These 40' basalt crags have face and crack climbing and fifteen routes from 5.10 up. This is essentially the same canyon as the Black Cliffs North but with a different driving approach.

Classics: Fairway to Heaven 10b, Virgin 11a, Groveler 11d, Wirebrush Haircut 11d, TVOD 12a, God 13b, Drunken Sailor 14a.

Ref: AC 107(4/88); Guidebook: Epeldi's *Boise Climbs, Black Cliffs Route Finder.*

Directions: Southeast Boise (fifteen minutes from downtown). Take I-84 east of Boise to Gowen Rd. exit. Go east on Gowen Rd. for $^3/_{10}$ mi. Turn right on Federal Way for approximately $^7/_{10}$ mi. Turn left on Columbia Rd. (before Micron Tech) dirt for 2 $^8/_{10}$ mi. Turn left on faint dirt road leading $^4/_{10}$ mi. to the top of Black Cliffs (South). Park above diversion dam. Climb down to right.

18 Upper Mesa Falls ☆☆

This scenic area features white, frothy waterfalls surrounded by basalt cap rock and offers only a few climbs on short 25′ basalt cliffs and a little pinnacle called Weeble Wobble 5.6 just south below walkway. Other basalt formations in area may afford good climbing. USFS–Targhee NF, (208) 652-7442.

Classics: Weeble Wobble Pinnacle 6R.

Directions: From Ashton follow Hwy. 47 northeast to scenic Mesa Falls. Limited short cliffs and pinnacle below waterfall.

19 Badger Creek ☆☆☆

This rural 25′ basalt bouldering area carries fifty challenging traverses and overhang problems like the B1 Overhang. Rough on skin. Buggy (ticks especially) in summer. At one time, bats in the roof crack problems. Green Canyon Hot Springs is fifteen minutes from Tetonia. No camping. Possibly private land.

Classics: Kauk Traverse, B1 Overhang, Roof problems.

Ref: Guidebooks: Sottile's *Jackson Hole: Sport Climbing and Bouldering*, Yanoff's *Full Circle*.

Directions: From Tetonia (approximately one hour from Jackson, Wyoming), dig $^6/_{10}$ mi. north on Hwy. 33. At StorMor silver silo, bear right approximately 2 $^7/_{10}$ mi. Turn right on Badger Creek Rd. for $^6/_{10}$ mi. of dirt. Badger Creek's obvious boulders are nestled on sunny, south-facing hillside above road on left (north).

20 Heise Boulder and Paramount Cliffs ☆☆☆

Heise Boulder is more than 40′ high and has about a dozen good clip-up routes to 5.12 like Seeking Sleazy Squeezes 11+. Possibly painful pockets. Paramount Formation possesses several nice climbs up to 5.10. Be sure to visit the relaxing Heise Hot Springs. Camping at Paramount. Government land.

Classics: Heise: Seeking Sleazy Squeezes 11+, Dark Justice 12a; Paramount: Chuck and Jed's Excellent Adventure 8.

Ref: Guidebook: Sottile's *Jackson Hole: Sport Climbing and Bouldering*.

Directions: From Swan Valley swoon 13 $^1/_2$ mi. northwest on Hwy. 26. Turn north (right) for approximately 4 mi., following signs to Heise Hot Springs. The Heise Boulder is $^1/_2$ mi. past the actual Hot Springs on roadside left and is more convenient than a 7 Eleven. The Paramount Formation sits visible 1 $^1/_2$ mi. farther on left at the mouth of Kelly Canyon. Both face south predominantly.

21 Blackfoot Canyon ☆☆☆

Reportedly good sport crag climbing. Government land.

Ref: Locals.

Directions: From Idaho Falls go south to mouth of Blackfoot Canyon.

22 Ross Park ☆☆☆

Site of the Pocatello Pump climbing competition. Short (40′) but plentiful basalt toprope pumps and good face bouldering that gets plentiful afternoon sun. More than ninety routes and 200 bouldering problems. Wildlife zoo above rocks. Autumn/spring. Pay camping in this City of Pocatello Park.

Classics: Eat My Shorts V4, Backbreaker V4.

Ref: C [180-43, 111, 105, 99]; on-line guide www.isu.edu/ outdoor/climbing/pokybldr.htm; Guidebook: Pocatello Pump topos.

Directions: South Pocatello. From I-15 and Fifth Ave. (exit 67), one small area exists right along Fifth St. on left as you exit I-15. Ross Park Main area: Go north on Fifth. Turn left on Fredregill. Turn left on second, continuing to rocks on left.

23 Marsh Creek (closed) ☆☆☆

These short (60′), excellent climbs at one time offered especially sweet overhanging basalt face climbing. Thirty routes. Now closed. Private land.

Ref: Locals.

Directions: From Inkom at I-15 and Inkom exit. Turn west on road at cement plant to Marsh Creek Rd. south for 2 $^8/_{10}$ mi. Park on left. Hike past farmhouse behind creek to craglets.

24 Massacre Rocks ☆☆☆☆

Some of the best basalt cragging in Idaho. Scattered 135′ cliffs and craglets amount to approximately 500 routes (1996) on vertical to slightly overhanging walls. The Main Wall above the Snake River is the mainstay attraction. Many safety bolts on routes. There may be rattlers. Autumn-spring. Free camping. BLM.

Classics: Main Wall: Debra Winger 11d, Danger Zone 12; Owl Cove: Nurse Ratchet 9+, Freudian Slip 11a; Something Wild 10d; Snakepit: Gangbang 10b, Switchblade 12+; Bouldering Wall: Happiness is a Warm Gun 11d/ 12a; Love Connection Wall 12-13; Le Petit Covette: This Smoo is for You 10c.

Ref: C 95(4/86)-58; www.isu.edu/outdoor/climbing/ pokybldr.htm; Guidebook: Spurlock's *Massacre Rocks Climbing Guide*.

Directions: From American Falls two access methods are possible: 1) Take Hwy. 39 north from town, then after crossing Snake River, take first left past dam/bridge. At second road on left (at $^2/_{10}$ mi.), turn left. Follow around curve to right and turn left over tracks at first possibility. Follow this road for a while, passing two silos on left. Then at farm building on right, turn left. Pass house (go slow!—dogs) to gate. Go through gate and onto lesser dirt roads for about 2 mi. to top of crags, staying left to several parking access points with trails always on left. Park/camp. 2) Boat access. Shoot west on I-86 to exit for Massacre Rocks State Park. Park/camp at park. Fees. The areas, Main Wall and Owl Cove, lie directly across river from park. Canoe over.

25 Massacre Rocks State Park ✯✯

Large 25' basaltic eggs in park offer tough, polished problems to crack. A limited circuit of twelve expert problems. Also canoe access for Main Wall across Snake River. This area named for skirmish in 1862 between Indians and settlers with wagon trains. Summer/autumn. Pay camping at state park (208-548-2672).

Ref: SC 12/91.

Directions: From American Falls go west approximately ten minutes on I-86 to Massacre Rocks State Park.

26 Malad Gorge State Park

This wild basalt river gorge offers some climbing potential on wild canyon 100' rimrock. How much is the question. Rock looks broken or loose most of the way downstream. Part of the Malad River Canyon, which is approximately 250' deep. Called the world's shortest river because it is only 2 1/2 mi. long. Devil's Washbowl is a natural feature below the unruly cataracts and waterfall. Wild white-water run. In the 1870s Malad was a stopover for wagons transporting gold from mines in northern Idaho and was referred to as the "gold road." Spring/autumn. Pay camping in state park (208-837-4505).

Directions: From Hagerman, Malad Gorge State Park is just north of town, off Hwy. 30 or I-86. Follow signs to park.

27 The Climbing Corral ✯✯

Fifty-foot basalt routes and toprope problems with safety-bolted anchors up to 5.11. Twenty routes. Spring–autumn. Free camping on BLM lands.

Ref: R 56; Guidebook: Weber's *Basalt Climbs of South Central Idaho*.

Directions: Twin Falls. From Blue Lakes Blvd. go north across bridge over Snake River. Turn right on the first road north of the bridge. After 2 6/10 mi., go right at a distinct fork in the road. The rocks lie just past this fork on right at Snake River overlook and telephone wires. The Climbing Corral is reached before getting to Canyon View Crag. Faces south.

28 Canyon View Crag ✯✯

Similar to Dierke's Lake, but this small 50' basalt crag area offers short, thin, technical cracks that can be difficult to protect. Good for the intermediate or expert. Spring/autumn. Private land.

Classics: Nermal's Revenge 8+, Screaming With Binky 10.

Ref: R 56; Guidebook: Weber's *Basalt Climbs of South Central Idaho*.

Directions: Twin Falls. From Blue Lakes Blvd. go north across bridge over Snake River. Turn right on the first road, north of the bridge. After 2 6/10 mi., go left at a distinct fork in the road for 1/4 mi. Turn right at green corral on faint road for approximately 200 yd. Canyon View Crag sits on rim overlooking Snake River with Dierke's Lake climbing area to the south across the river.

29 Pillar Falls ✯✯

Instant-access 70' basalt sport crag makes for a great in-town pump. Edges, pockets, and cracks on fifteen routes for 5.11–12 climbers. Pillar Falls is off to northeast in Snake River. Spring/autumn. Pay camping nearby. Please be mindful you're on private land.

Ref: Guidebook: Weber's *Basalt Climbs of South Central Idaho*.

Directions: Twin Falls. From junction of Pole Line Rd. East and Eastland Ave. North, follow Pole Line Rd. East for 1/4 mi. Park on north side of road in gravel pullout with access sign. A dirt road with locked gate lies adjacent. Walk down the dirt road for 75 yd. into Snake River Canyon. Obvious rock face is Pillar Falls.

30 Dierke's Lake Crag (in Shoshone Falls Park) ✯✯✯

Well-protected, athletic sport climbs good for rainy day or winter overhang climbing on 70' basalt walls. More than fifty routes, mostly 5.10 and up. Stick clips? Beware loose suspect rock. Belay carefully. Great basalt bouldering on small edges or pockets. Minimal entrance fee during summer. Also, long flows of basalt rimrock in the area. Shoshone Falls is called "The Niagara of the West." The 210' falls are actually higher than Niagara Falls. The falls span 1,000' and are best in spring. Autumn–spring. Pay camping. City of Twin Falls Park.

Classics: Casual Cruise 10a, Ziplock 11c, Citation 11d, Power Lunch 12c, Evil D 12c, My Life as an Indian 13a; best boulders along trail at Dierke's Lake.

Ref: C [186-50, 95], R 56; Guidebooks: Bingham topo sheet, Weber's *Basalt Climbs of South Central Idaho*.

Directions: From Twin Falls follow Blue Lakes Blvd. Turn east at Falls Ave. going for 3 mi. (park signs). Turn north on Champlin Rd. Just before Shoshone Falls, follow marked road that forks right to lake. Park. A few minutes' hike. Dierke's Lake Crag is obvious alcove across lake, with bouldering before it. For hard cragging (5.11–5.13) go left past boulders into the alcove; for natural pro (5.6–5.10) head right along lake.

31 Upper Rock Creek Canyon ✯

Abundant 80' rock walls in this scenic canyon unfortunately turn out to be mostly chossy rhyolite bands and strange pinnacles. This area is composed of naturally protected crack climbs with adventurous/frightening rock. Myriad of potential up canyon or higher on rimrock suggests there might be a few plums to be picked. Spring/autumn. A plentitude of USFS campgrounds nearby for your sleeping ease.

USFS–Sawtooth NF, (208) 737–3200.

Classics: Frozen Fingers 9+.

Ref: Guidebooks: Weber's *Basalt Climbs of South Central Idaho.*

Directions: From Hansen (7 mi. southeast of Twin Falls on Hwy. 30), speed south on Idaho G-4 (Rock Creek Canyon Rd.) for approximately 14 mi. Look for the climbing crags surrounding Schipper Campground or south of large paved pullout in Upper Rock Creek Canyon 1 $^7/_{10}$ mi. south of Schipper Campground.

32 Connor Columns (at Connor Creek Summit) ✩✩✩

Scenic columnar 85′ basalt cragging for the crack-climbing enthusiast on a high desert perch complete with golden eagles. A variety of cracks from OW to seams on mostly poor rock with about twelve good solid crack lines. Climbs for the beginner to hardman. Autumn/spring. Camping recommended at Lake Cleveland on Mt. Harrison (Pomerelle Ski Area). BLM.

Ref: C 95(4/86)-58; Guidebook: Weber's *Basalt Climbs of South Central Idaho.*

Directions: From Albion (east of Twin Falls and 12 mi. south of I-86), climb in your metal carriage southeast up Hwy. 77 for 8 mi. to Connor Creek Pass. At mm 11, turn left onto dirt road leading to Coe Creek Picnic Area. Go for 1 mi., parking close to ridgeline left of columns. Park in flattened spot off road. Hike south below ridgeline to Connor Columns. Faces southwest. (Other parking options exist; this is one of the closest options.)

33 City of Rocks National Preserve ✩✩✩

Climbing wonderland of 200′ granite gnomelike domes and twisted elfin pinnacles in a high, arid sagebrush desert. As late as 1986, one could visit here and find just a couple Rasta men and maybe a punk rocker. Then the area gained international attention when rap bolting swept through the "City" in the late 1980s, resulting in difficult sport climbs; however, many are closed now to climbing. Come with supplies and with "guns" loaded. Limited bouldering. Summer/autumn. Raptor restrictions April 15–June 15. Pay camping. BLM/private land/NPS, (208) 824–5519.

Classics: Norma's Book 6, Wheat Thin 7, Delay of Game 8, Scream Cheese 9, Thin Slice 10a, Bloody Fingers 10-, Bovine Guidance 11, Strategic Arms 11c, Electric Avenue 12a, Spuds In the Gym 12b, Amphibian (aka Biceps) 12c, Red Rum 13c, Dolphin Routes.

Ref: C [192-116, 125, 122, 118(2/90)-78, 112, 110, 109, 106, 104, 99, 98, 94, 89, 83(5/83)-44,], R [94-62, 92-119, 91-38, 90-34, 73, 69, 15(7/86)], SC (6/91), S 3/84; Ament's *Master of Rock;* Guidebooks: Calderone's *Rock Climbing Idaho's City of Rocks,* Forkash's *City of Rocks Select,* Davis's *City of Rocks: Idaho Classic Rock Climbs,* Bingham's *City of Rocks,* Lopez's *Exploring Idaho's Mountains,* Goodwin's Topo Sheets, Harlin's *Rocky Mountain.*

Directions: From Almo go 1 mi. south, then 4 mi. west on dirt roads, following signs. Multitude of roadside crags with various roadside parking spots. (Also accessible from Oakley via south on Birch Creek Rd.) Popular formations include Twin Sisters, Bread Loaves, Bath Rock, Parking Lot Rock, Elephant Rock, and Dolphin Rock. Many closures, access restrictions, and private property; check first with rangers. Please park on government land.

34 Banks

Seldom climbed and relatively unknown, this sport crag holds mostly 60′ granite face routes on large boulders. Eleven routes as of 1998. Many unclimbed routes possible. Route names unknown. Scenic timbered river environment. Summer. No camping. USFS–Boise NF, (208) 382–7480.

Ref: G. Parker 1/98.

Directions: From Boise take Hwy. 55 for 15 mi. north of Horseshoe to Banks. Turn right at Banks and then go 4 mi. toward Garden Valley. Park at Deer Creek boat ramp or in pullout by Bronco Billy rapid. Rocks located on north side of road. Faces south. Anchors visible from road.

35 Post Falls Rocks

New 50′ granite sport climbing area. No camping. City land.

Classics: Jude 11a, Flusher 12a, Fearless Leader 12a.

Ref: C. Haas.

Directions: Post Falls. Traveling east on I-90, get off in the city of Post Falls at the Spokane Street exit and hang a left at the stop and head south. Go across the bridge and turn right at the first right after the bridge. Go all the way to the end of the street. Head to Quemelin Trails and hike to the walls.

36 Mores Mountain ✩✩

Boise climbing area northeast of town. USFS–Boise NF, (208) 373–4100.

Ref: Epeldi's Boise Climbs.

37 Riggins Amphitheater ✩✩✩

Wild limestone sport climbs (some manufactured) offer cool summertime climbing on about thirty routes 5.11 to 5.13 like A Day in the Wife 5.11d and Chunder 5.13c. Free camping. USFS–Payette NF, (208) 634–0700.

Ref: R 56 (Jul 1993).

Directions: From Riggins go ½ mi. south on Hwy. 95. Turn east on USFS road to Seven Devils Campground. Go up switchbacks to mm 9. Park on right. Hike downhill ten minutes to north.

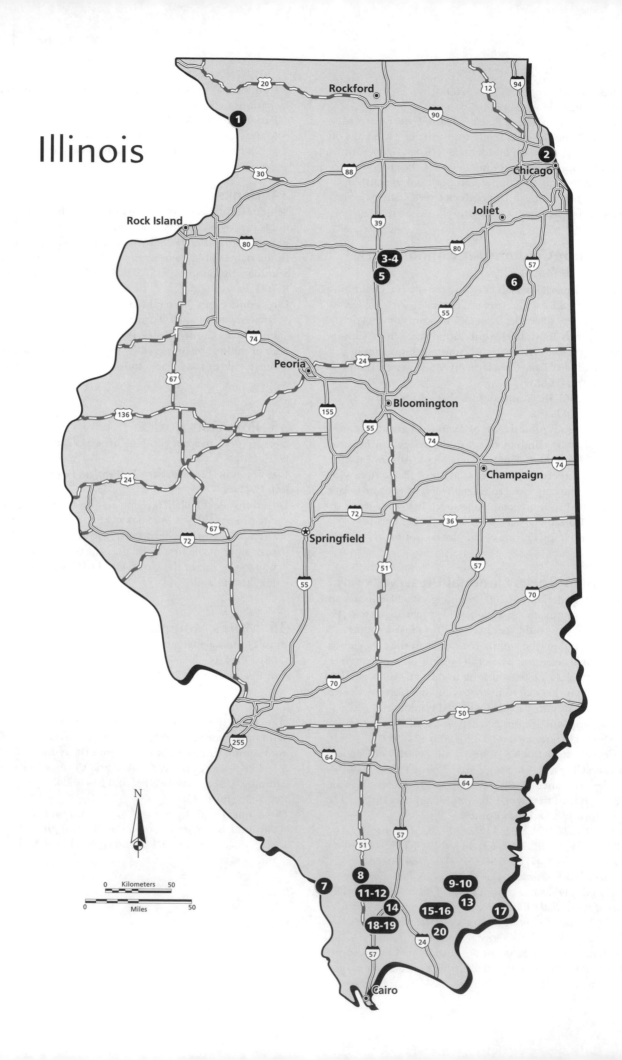

I banish fear with two words: "You lead." —Kolokotronis, Guide to Mississippi Palisades

Yes, the Midwest has more to offer than hours of endless prairies. Frequently bypassed by transcontinental climbers, the Land of Lincoln offers many alluring rock sport challenges as well as Chicago, Blues Capital of the World and home of one of the world's tallest buildings, the Sears Tower.

Unbeknownst to most climbers, northern Illinois has climbing in spots such as Mississippi Palisades and Kankakee River State Park. Central Illinois, the "Grand Prairie," offers rock enthusiasts little except the chance to burn the carbon buildup off their valves en route to the southern climbing areas of the state.

Southern Illinois, unlike its northern counterpart, is a blend of low mountains, steep hillsides, sparkling lakes, and sandstone bluffs. The headquarters for the southern Illinois sandstone tour begins in Carbondale at Makanda Bluffs and drifts east to such classic cliffs as Cedars and Drapers Bluffs and Jackson Falls. These are backed up by lesser visited, ancestral John Gill haunts like Dixon Springs, Bell Smith Springs, and Cave In Rock. The climbing is rustic, charming, and challenging. The cliffs in southern Illinois are a precious resource for all climbing enthusiasts. Please show support for their continued access to climbers. Act now! Get involved with the access process, otherwise we'll all be singing the blues.

1 Mississippi Palisades State Park ✮✮✮

These 80′ limestone bluffs and palisades exude much beauty along the lengthy Mississippi River on the Great River Road. More than eight climbing walls (see Classics). Climbs from as early as 1940 by the Iowa Mountaineers and Chicago Mountaineers. For its grade, Fear of Flying 5.9 is one of the finer park routes. Ask park officials for restrictions on climbing areas and bolting. Access sensitive—good climbing etiquette helpful for continued climbing in park. Everything south of south entrance remains open, except Sun Buttress and Forgotten Wall. T. Peterson writes, "Stay off of 'Monkey Swing' in the Quads because it has a rare and endangered fern growing on the rock. 'Fear of Flying' 5.9 has got to be harder than 5.9, especially the second pitch; I don't know how anyone can call it a 9." Wooded ravines. Geologically known as the "Driftless Area." Eleven mi. of hiking trails. Full camping hook-ups at state park, (815-273-2731).

Classics: Sentinel: East Face 4, Hellish Move 8, Pretzel 9, Blank Wall 10+, Buck Naked 12; Forgotten Wall: Deception 8+, Sidewinder 12; Sun Buttress: Labyrinth 9; Twin Sisters: Difficult Crack 8, Horrific 8; Indian Head: Bowline 9; Amphitheater Wall: Fear of Flying 9.

Ref: Ted Peterson 7/98; C 126(6/91)-47; Guidebooks: Collett's *River Rock: Climber's Guide to the Mississippi Palisades,* Taylor and Collett's *River Rock,* Kolokotronis's *Guide to Mississippi Palisades,* Bagg's *50 Short Climbs in the Midwest.*

Directions: From Savanna drive approximately 3 mi. north on Hwy. 84. Follow signs to south entrance of Mississippi Palisades State Park on Hwy. 84, where most developed climbing areas (and natural spring) are found. These

DAVID HART

Eric Ulner cranking tough on Detox Mountain, 5.12a, Jackson, Illinois.

Illinois Road Thoughts

"It's just a Monopoly Board out there, Tim. . ."
—worldly philosophy from Iron Mike

areas include (north to south): Sentinel (most popular, just south of south park entrance), Sun Buttress, Twin Sisters, Indian Head, Bee Wall, Amphitheater Wall, Butter Walls, and Upton's Cave. Cliffs in northern reaches of park are usually overgrown and rotten.

2 Sears Tower ☆☆☆

The world's largest tower (103 stories) first ascended *outside* by the infamous "Spider" Dan Goodwin in the 1980s, which almost ended with the Chicago Fire Department washing him off on the upper pitches. Chicago's famous museums and art institutes are renowned rest-day stops. Chicago hosts several fine climbing gyms (see list below) and is the home of the famed Chicago Mountaineering Club. Private land.

Ref: R 17(1/87)-38.

Directions: Chicago. Sears Tower is on 233 South Wacker Ave.

3 Buffalo Rock State Park ●

These 50′ sandstone bluffs drop right into the Illinois River, making access to the start of climbs fun and sporty. Historically since the 1600s it has been an Indian haunt, French outpost, religious sect camp, tuberculosis sanatorium, to now presently a state park. Atop the cliffs, wildlife park sports listless buffalo. Primitive camping requires permits. State park, (815) 433–2220.

Directions: From Ottawa tromp west on Ottawa Dr. (LaSalle CR 34) for approximately 1 mi. to Buffalo Rock State Park. Or, take exit 81 off I-80. Go south on Hwy. 178 briefly. Turn east onto LaSalle CR for approximately 5 mi. Turn right into park and follow road up hill to parking at picnic shelter. Riverside bluffs are below shelter. Rappel down, but don't go into the Illinois drink.

4 Starved Rock State Park (closed) ●

Scenic state park with eighteen canyons, bluffs 125′ high overlooking Illinois River, and twelve waterfalls. Named from a legend about a band of Indians who chose to starve on a sandstone butte rather than surrender to an enemy tribe. Ice climbing on twelve scenic waterfalls (e.g., Council Overhang) as well. Rock climbing at Starved Rock is presently illegal. Pay boat tours. Pay camping is available at Starved Rock State Park approximately 1 mi. east of Hwy. 178 on Hwy. 71 or there are classier accommodations at the Starved Rock Lodge. State park, (815) 667–4726.

Directions: From La Salle head east on I-80. Take exit 81 south on Hwy. 178 for approximately 1 mi. Just after crossing Illinois Waterway, turn left onto road for Starved Rock State Park. Several rock bluffs along water's edge in park (including the prominent soft sandstone bluff, Starved Rock) are off-limits to climbing/rappelling.

5 Matthiessen State Park (closed) ●

Seven mi. of scenic trails, moist canyons, and photogenic 80′ sandstone rock outcroppings. The rock here is really too green for minimum-impact rock climbing but could make for some scenic rappels. For ice climbers there are two waterfalls: Giant's Bath Tub (68′) and Cascade Falls (45′). Climbing at Matthiessen State Park is posted illegal. Pay camping is available at Starved Rock State Park, approximately 1 mi. east of Hwy. 178 on Hwy. 71, or there are classier accommodations at the Starved Rock Lodge. State park, (815) 667–4868.

Directions: From Utica (just east of La Salle on I-80), head for 2 6/10 mi. south on Hwy. 178, following park signs to Matthiessen State Park entrance. Turn right (west) for approximately 1 mi. into parking lot/trailheads for scenic ravines. (This park is directly south of Starved Rock State Park.)

6 Kankakee River State Park (closed) ☆☆

Kankakee means "beautiful river" in Illiniwek Indian language. This lovely, 35′ limestone stream corridor reads like a short-story anthology that has sat on a bookshelf for years. Lots of short topropes and bouldering (rocky landings) need a good dusting off. Budget rock quality, but some good climbs do exist. May need to check with rangers before climbing in this highly used urban recreation area. Pay camping available at state park (815–933–1383).

Classics: Hookasaurus 5.11/12.

Ref: Guidebook: Nicodemus's *Climber's Guide to Kankakee River State Park.*

Directions: From Kankakee, Kankakee River State Park is just northwest on Hwy. 102. Short walk to rock-lined waterway.

7 Fountain Bluff (aka Gorham) ☆

Steep 180′ sandstone crag, but rock quality is marginal—be careful. Among the first routes done was Leap Frog, by Joe Healy and Jim Foster in 1976. Please be discreet and respectful of landowners. The climbing, on private land, has taken decades to gain. Private land/USFS–Shawnee National Forest, (618) 253–7114.

Classics: Leap Frog 11 (4p).

Ref: Guidebooks: Ulner's *Vertical Heartland*, Thurmond's *SIC Routes.*

Directions: From Gorham go south on Hwy. 3 (follow signs) to large Fountain Bluff. Easy approach.

8 Southern Illinois University Buildering
⁕⁕

A variety of developed buildering problems that'll get your forearms mighty tight. State land.

Ref: Guidebook: Grosowsky's *The Gritstone Mountaineer.*

Directions: In Carbondale at Southern Illinois University Buildering. Climbing wall at Student Center and pool (beginner's areas); upper rear entrance to Pulliam Hall (intermediate/expert); and Church Wall, near the Van Netta Funeral Home, which offers the most difficult area and good landings.

9 Stoneface 1 and 2 (aka Cave Hill) (closed) ⁕⁕⁕

A long 40′ band of the hardest sandstone in southern Illinois. Good intermediate and beginner's area. Easy access. Stoneface 2 totes bigger cliffs but longer bushwhack. No bolting. This and Cave Hill are closed due to their designation as Research Natural Inventory Areas, involving the Meed's milkweed, which is on the federally endangered plant list. USFS–Shawnee National Forest, (618) 253-7114.

Classics: Graduation 7, Hangover Overhang 9+, Midnight Cowboy 10, V.S.O.P. 10, Sweatstack 11, Long Roof 11+.

Ref: Moers; C 68; Guidebooks: Detterline's *A Climber's Guide to the Mid-South,* Grosowsky's *The Gritstone Mountaineer,* Bagg's *50 Short Climbs in the Midwest.*

Directions: From Harrisburg head south on Hwy. 34. Turn left on dirt road (Stoneface sign) for 1 4/10 mi. Turn right at T for 6/10 mi. to right on dirt road. Follow signs and park at circle loop. Rock lies above parking.

10 Cave Hill (aka Stoneface) (closed) ⁕⁕⁕

A long 120′ sandstone band of good rock. Good intermediate and beginner's area and a good late fall/winter area. No bolting allowed here! USFS–Shawnee National Forest, (618) 253-7114.

Classics: Chrysalis 8, Hi Gene 8, Elaine's Disdain 8.

Ref: Moers.

Directions: South of Harrisburg. Access from Glen O. Jones State Park. From northwest point of car campground follow Cave Hill Trail along ridge approximately 2 1/2 mi. until you come to old fire tower pole in middle of trail. Turn right and follow to edge of bluff (100 yd.); climbs start here. Cave Hill is a northeast extension of the Stoneface crag line divided by FR 112.

11 Giant City State Park—Makanda Bluff (aka Shelter One Bluff) ⁕⁕⁕

Also known as "The City" or one of Illinois's best climbing areas. This could be as casual as cragging gets. Fun, challenging topropes (bring long extendo rope) up overhanging pocketed face on very frictiony 90′ sandstone. Forty routes. Good bouldering/traverses as well. City Limits, an early testpiece by Joe Healy, was done at the dawn of the hardman. Danger! Watch for UFOs (not the ones from 5.10) falling from above. Rock corridors known as "streets." Nearby Alto Wineries, the finest winery in southern Illinois. Pay camping. State park, (618) 457-4836.

Classics: Dead Dog 10+, Electric Acid Kool Aid Trip 11, Fiddler on the Roof 11+ (illegal area), Fear of Flying (illegal area), City Limits 12+, Return to Forever Bouldering Traverse B1; Razor Blade Rock.

Ref: C [68, (47) 1978], S 7/85; Sherman's *Stone Crusade;* Guidebooks: Floyd's *A Climber's Guide to the Midwest Metamorphic Forms,* Ulner's *Vertical Heartland, SIC Routes,* Detterline's *A Climber's Guide to the Mid-South,* Grosowsky's *Gritstone Mountaineer,* Bagg's *50 Short Climbs in the Midwest.*

Directions: From Carbondale take a giant's step 12 mi. south on Hwy. 51 past yellow happy-faced tower to Giant City State Park. Makanda Bluff at Shelter One is best cliff in park. Park at first cliff on left below pavilions. Razor Blade Rock (bouldering) is a couple hundred yd. south of Shelter One and adjacent to road. Park at small lot across from large field south of Stonefort Trail sign. Stonefort is an illegal climbing area. Devil's Standtable is another climbing area in the park. Other areas in park closed to climbing as fern preserves.

12 Devil's Kitchen Lake Area #3/Opie's Kitchen ⁕⁕⁕

Two quality sandstone bouldering areas near shores of Devil's Kitchen Lake with a plentitude of perilous, pumping pinch climbs on rowdy roofs and touchy traverses. A must-see for the boulderer. Camping at Devil's Kitchen Campground on north end of lake. Technically, one should have a Duck Stamp to legally get out of one's car within the refuge. Keep a low profile. Crab Orchard National Wildlife Refuge, (618) 997-3344.

Ref: Guidebook: Ulner's *Vertical Heartland.*

Directions: From Carbondale cook east on Hwy. 13 a short ways. Turn south (right) on Giant City Rd. (2800E). Go south until junction with 600N. Turn left (east), going past north shore of Little Grassy Lake. (600N turns into 300N.) At junction with 200E, turn right (south) to Hwy. 215 north. Turn left to Devil's Kitchen Lake loop parking. (Area number 3 is on west side of lake in northwest sector.) Rock is at water's edge. Opie's Kitchen is on east side of lake in northeast sector. Get there by taking 300 past junction with 200E to a right turn at Devil's Kitchen Campground at north end of lake. Park at Rocky Bluff Parking Lot. Across the road from the start of the Rocky Bluff Trail, hike on faint trail west toward spillway to walk down leading to overhanging traverse wall.

13 Garden of the Gods (closed) ⁕⁕

Colorfully swirled sandstone in wildly sculptured 40′ formations intrigues the eye. Limited topropes and bouldering. The Forest Service has requested of the Southern

Illinois Climber's Alliance that climbers not climb at Garden of the Gods due to its Natural Area designation. SICA agreed with them. Rocks are 300 million years old. USFS–Shawnee National Forest, (618) 253-7114.

Ref: Guidebooks: Detterline's *A Climber's Guide to the Mid-South,* Grosowsky's *The Gritstone Mountaineer.*

Directions: From Herod drive south on Hwy. 34. Follow signs east to Garden of the Gods.

14 Ferne Clyffe State Park ✩✩✩

Special park climbing regulations (1992). Many 90′ sandstone cliffs exist in park, but rock climbing is allowed only at Round Bluff (southern end of park) due to protected ferns. Topropes and bouldering total forty routes. Rock corridors known as "streets." Large overhanging/shallow caves in this 1,000 acre park. Hawk's Cave is just one of several in the park. Ferne Clyffe State Park rangers now regularly patrol Cedar Bluff. Unleashed dogs, camping, or building a fire will get you a $75 ticket, guaranteed. Hillside Convenience in Buncombe is no longer open. Great pizza can still be had at Dad's Pizza in Goreville. Pay camping in this state park (618-995-2411).

Classics: Hawks Beak 7, Missouri Breaks 9+, Rusty Pin 10.

Ref: E. Ulner 5/98; C 68; Guidebooks: Ulner's *Vertical Heartland,* Detterline's *A Climber's Guide to the Mid-South,* Grosowsky's *The Gritstone Mountaineer,* Bagg's *50 Short Climbs in the Midwest.*

Directions: From Marion go 8 mi. south on I–57. Take I–24 south, and then take Hwy. 37 south to Goreville. Ferne Clyffe State Park is 1 mi. southwest of Goreville. Head to south end of park road. From north end of lot, cross stream over rocks to main bluff with deep overhang at base. Faces east.

15 Bell Smith Springs ✩✩✩

Steep 50′ sandstone bouldering faces. An old John Gill bouldering haunt that may now be off-limits to climbers. Natural bridge. Bell Smith Springs is a source of spring water. USFS–Shawnee NF, (618) 253-7114.

Ref: Ament's *Master of Rock;* Guidebook: Grosowsky's *The Gritstone Mountaineer.*

Directions: From Harrisburg seep south on Hwy. 145 to Delwood. Turn west on Forest Service roads, following signs to Bell Smith Springs.

16 Glenn Street Falls Road (aka Jackson Falls) ✩✩✩✩

Southern Illinois's finest cragging. Like Twain, Faulkner, and Steinbeck, this area is an American classic. Cream-gray 65′ sandstone in a sylvan setting enhances the sport routes on unique formations. More than 200 routes and counting. Check out Bill and Terry's store at Ozark for good sandwiches and 25-cent pool tables. Or, The Coyote, 2 mi. from the Falls parking, has climbing information, gear, etc. Climbing west of railroad tracks is off-limits due to Natural

Area designation. Autumn. USFS–Shawnee NF, (618) 253-7114.

Classics: Munchkin 9, Group Therapy 10, Lovely Arête 11-, Digital Delicatessen 11+, Cro-Magnon Warrior 12-, Viking Blood 12, Wrecking Ball 12c, No Dogs Allowed 12, Butcher of Baghdad 13a.

Ref: E. Ulner 1/98; R 45; Guidebooks: Floyd's *A Climber's Guide to the Midwest Metamorphic Forms,* Cater's *Sport Crags of the East,* Ulner's *Vertical Heartland,* Simpson's *Jackson Falls Rock Climbing Guide,* Thurmond's *SIC Routes,* Grosowsky's *The Gritstone Mountaineer.*

Directions: From Ozark (total distance to crags, 6 8/10 mi.), off Hwy. 45 head east on McCormick Rd. Turn left at Zion Church. In approximately ¼ mi, take right (at first white house with knife shop) on Pope County Rd. (3130N) for 1 9/10 mi. to creek. Park in camping area. Hike south along creek to rock landing and down metal tree ladder (gone as of 1998—see below) to a pool and a magical little hollow. Jackson Falls climbing routes are along walls on either side of pond. Attention: Jackson Falls no longer has the ladder for canyon entry. Climbers must now either hike around to the "Dog Walk" gully or rappel in to the canyon. Climbers, at the request of the Forest Service, removed the ladder as it had become dangerous with age. Also, two key branches in the ladder's tree had been broken, creating a technical move to get onto the ladder.

17 Cave In Rock State Park ✩✩✩

Pictured in Ament's *Master of Rock,* these overhanging 80′ limestone bluffs along the scenic Ohio River greet visiting climbers with sustained tip violence traversing/cragging with 115-degree rock cliffs extending for ½ mi. The cave in this limestone bluff on the Ohio River is 55′ wide. The area was the first great example of highway robbery where souls were enticed with whiskey and "entertainment" but held up instead. Ferry shuttles cars across to Kentucky for a fee. Local Jim Thurmond says fishin's good, too: "They're jumpin' with their tails on the surface." Restaurant and pay camping in state park (618-289-4325).

Ref: Ament's *Master of Rock;* Guidebook: Grosowsky's *The Gritstone Mountaineer.*

Directions: At Cave In Rock State Park. East of town. Follow signs.

18 Draper's Bluff ✩✩✩

Draper's Bluff is a special natural area and one of the finer southern Illinois climbing areas. Higher in height and longer in length than neighboring Cedar Bluff; one can enjoy an orange sunset while clinging to one of its many classic long routes. In 1997 more than sixty routes, traditional and new sport routes. Some routes require rappel-in tactics. As this is an area of public and private land, please don't trespass. No camping anywhere. Public parking now allowed in alfalfa field directly in front of the south face. Hiking from the Cedar Grove Church parking lot is no longer necessary. Hillside Convenience in Buncombe now closed. Dad's Pizza in Goreville still open—great pizza. Southwest face of Draper's belongs to Ferne Clyffe State Park (also no camping allowed). South and north faces are privately owned.

Classics: Mike's Climb 8, High Over Camp 9+, Puppet Master 9, Ant Killer 9, The Outline 12a, Yabadabadew 13a.

Ref: E. Ulner 5/98; C 68, R 67-56; www. verticalheartland. com; Guidebooks: Floyd's *A Climber's Guide to the Midwest Metamorphic Forms,* Ulner's *Vertical Heartland,* Thurmond's *SIC Routes,* Detterline's *A Climber's Guide to the Mid-South,* Grosowsky's *The Gritstone Mountaineer,* Bagg's *50 Short Climbs in the Midwest.*

Directions: From Marion go 10 mi. south on I–57 to Lick Creek exit. Then go approximately 3 mi. east on Lick Creek Rd. Turn right and park at Cedar Grove Church in the far right (east) half of the lot (public). Hike (approximately forty-five minutes total) past west side of church to the northwest for 200 yd. to hill. Take trail marked with two posts. Cross meadow, turn left, and jump stream. Go uphill between two shacks. Skirt right shack and enter woods, crossing a wash to fork at bottom of Draper's Bluff. Turn right at fork for North Face, Yabadabadew. Turn left for South Face—and majority of routes.

19 Cedar Bluff ✫✫✫

Same classic 80′ sandstone cliff line as Draper's Bluff. Three dozen routes and beautiful basal bouldering. Please respect church affairs by refraining from camping at church. Cedar Bluff is a natural area. Bolting and primitive camping are no longer allowed on public portion of land, which is controlled by Ferne Clyffe State Park.

Classics: Mike's Meander 5, Unfinished Symphony 10a, Dizzy 12a.

Ref: C 68; Guidebooks: Floyd's *A Climber's Guide to the Midwest Metamorphic Forms,* Ulner's *Vertical Heartland,* Thurmond's *SIC Routes,* Detterline's *A Climber's Guide to the Mid-South,* Grosowsky's *The Gritstone Mountaineer,* Bagg's *50 Short Climbs in the Midwest.*

Directions: From Marion go approximately 15 mi. south on I–57 to Lick Creek exit. Then go approximately 3 mi. east on Lick Creek Rd. Turn left onto Cedar Grove Rd. and go ²/₃ mi. to Cedar Grove Church. Park in the far right (east) half of the lot (private.) From edge of woods behind church, hike northeast to Cedar Bluff for about five minutes. It was a tradition among southern Illinois climbers to point their cars in the direction of the cliff they are climbing on: right for Cedar Bluff and left for Draper's.

20 Dixon Springs State Park ✫✫✫

Quaint state park with old John Gill problems near picnic area and wooded ravines. Tallest sandstone formations (60′) found by hiking south into canyon from picnic area under Hwy. 146 bridge. Pay camping in this state park (618–949–3394).

Classics: John Gill boulder problems: Persian Wall B2.

Ref: C 68 Ament's *Master of Rock;* Sherman's *Stone Crusade;* Guidebooks: Detterline's *A Climber's Guide to the Mid-South,* Grosowsky's *The Gritstone Mountaineer,* Bagg's *50 Short Climbs in the Midwest.*

Directions: From Dixon Springs drive east on Hwy. 146 to Dixon Springs State Park. Park at swimming pool. Rocks located near picnic area and to south of Hwy. 146 under bridge.

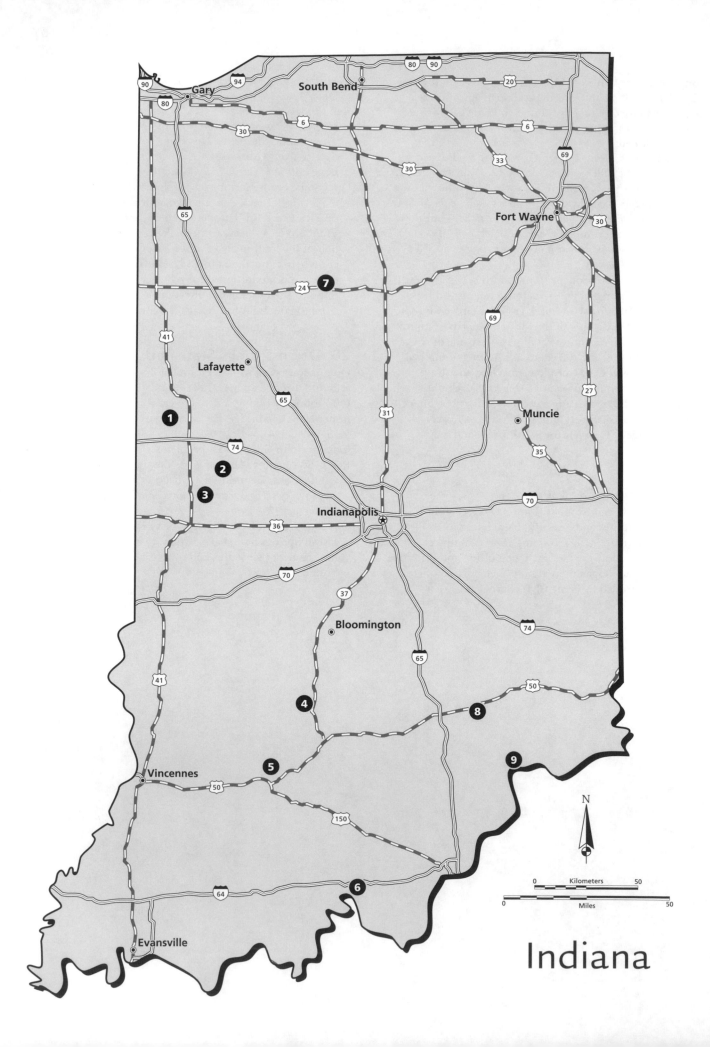

Indiana

Indiana

It makes me sick when I see a guy just watching it go out of bounds.
—Larry Bird, Boston Celtics star, from French Lick

Indiana has done much for the world of sports, if not for climbing itself. Kurt Thomas added "flair" to gymnastics. Larry Bird, once called "The Hick from French Lick," taught the city boys a thing or two about playing hoop in the process changing the lackluster NBA into the most exciting pro sports league around. And, of course, every Memorial Day the nation's sports fans tune in their television sets to the Indianapolis 500.

As far as climbing goes . . . well, optimism can only carry one so far. But you will find a few climbing endeavors before leaving the state.

1 Portland Arch (closed) ☆☆

You're a long ways from Oregon, Homer! Portland Arch is a 15′ natural bridge carved into the native 230-million-year-old Mansfield Sandstone rock formation. Closed by the state to rock climbers since 1974 because of a number of fatal accidents. This is truly a loss for Indiana climbers as Station number 21's south-facing crag is a good chunk of viable climbing rock and a resource for climbers. Possibly the best natural sandstone crag (80′) in Indiana. The Arch itself and much of the other sandstone in the area is too green and mealy for climbing. Rare and unusual plants amid steep ravines and rock walls along a self-guided nature trail. Also, this area has some of the best ice climbing (e.g., Yellow Fang) in Indiana along with Williamsport Falls area. No camping. Nature Conservancy of Indiana, Fountain County.

Ref: B. Moers; Guidebook: Zvengrowski's *Portland Arch.*

Directions: From Attica (southwest of Lafayette), go south on Hwy. 41 for approximately 6 mi. Turn west on Hwy. 650N and gas her for 5 mi. to the hamlet of Fountain. Portland Arch is just south of town. Turn left on Walnut for 1/10 mi. Then turn left on Scout Camp Rd. for 3/10 mi. to parking lot for Portland Arch. Hike trail to left for crag (best for climbing); right for Portland Arch (friable). If you can get a trail brochure: The cliff escarpment is at Station number 21 (at the giant beech), and Portland Arch is at Station number 11.

2 Shades State Park/Pine Hills Nature Preserve (closed) ☆

Skip it Clyde, skip it! An area of historical interest only for Indiana rock climbers. Deep sandstone canyons but no great loss to climbers other than rappellers because the rock is mostly green. Good hot-weather canoe runs on Sugar Creek; rentals available. All Indiana State Parks closed to climbing as of 1994. Pine Hills Nature Preserve also has impressive geological features. Pay camping in state park (765–435–2810).

Ref: B. Moers.

Directions: From Crawfordsville slide southeast on Hwy. 47. Turn west onto Hwy. 234, following Shades State Park signs to areas.

3 Turkey Run State Park ●

Sorry for this pun, bird lovers, but the rock here is foul tempered! Scenic sandstone gorges with minimal climbing on mank, green rock. Some bouldering on trails. Good hot-weather canoe runs on Sugar Creek. Rentals available. Go

---

Indiana Road Thoughts

It's not the first time I've had weird propositions from total strangers in foreign states. I'm sitting in my truck near French Lick, looking at the road map for a destination, when this old man comes up to my truck.

He must have thought it was retirement time for my truck, because out of the blue he asked if I'd like to buy a Ford LTD with 80,000 mi. on it for $600. "She's a fine runner," he assures me. Had I looked down at my speedometer with 240,000 mi. on it and thought about it, he was probably a guardian road angel. A couple hundred miles later my engine blew, costing me twice as much as the Ford.

—TNT

Indiana boys on an Indiana climb—Unlikely Wall.

TIM TOULA

in autumn, as with all Indiana areas. Pay camping in state park (317–597–2635).
Ref: Moers, Childs.
Directions: From Rockville peck north on Hwy. 41. Turn east on Hwy. 47. Follow Turkey Run State Park signs.

4 Unlikely Wall ✩✩✩

This two-tiered, 25′ limestone roadcut has become quite popular with Bloomington students, allowing for a quick pump after or when skipping class. In a class of its own, it features perhaps the best bouldering, short topropes, and sport clips you're gonna find in the Hoosier State, excluding rock gyms. There is a guidebook to this and other Indiana climbing areas available in town. Beware: Some loose rock! In fall 1996 signs were posted indicating car theft in the parking area. Possibly state land.
Classics: The Stain 12b.
Ref: Rice; Guidebook: *Guidebook to Unlikely Wall.*
Directions: From Bloomington speed 5 mi. south on Hwy. 37 to Harrodsburg Interchange. Park under Hwy. 37 overpass bridge on west side. Hike up obvious steep and well-traveled dirt path to north and up to rocks (five minutes). Faces east. There are many limestone cutouts along this highway.

5 McBride's Bluff ●

Dirty dancing on down-home climbing on rank 90′ sandstone cliffs. Traditional crack, toproping, and rappelling practice area. One-quarter mi. of cliffline, but the quality of rock would disgust a maggot. Private land.
Ref: Rice.
Directions: Near Shoals. Go north on Hwy. 450 by Dover Hill. Ask at Dover Hill Variety Store. (Involves turning right at burnt bus.)

6 Wyandotte Caves SRA ●

No doubt the Ohio River Valley has many limestone bluffs surrounding the river shores if one looks. Dirty limestone outcrops that might clean up. Great rest-day activities; wild cave tours available of five to eight hours in length. Showers available. Classic restaurant, the Overlook, in Leavenworth makes for a fabulous view of the Ohio River. State land.
Ref: Moers.
Directions: From New Albany strike west approximately 20 mi. on I-64 to exit 105. Turn south on Hwy. 135, then west on Hwy. 462 to Wyandotte Caves. Cliffs along the Ohio River in Harrison Crawford State Forest.

7 France Park (closed) ✩

Cass County has closed the area to climbing as of 1998. The Black Wall at the south end of the lake is the best and most solid. The 20′ limestone is generally bad, with the worst areas being directly above the lake. Climbers had to sign a waiver. Cost was $4.00. Pay camping at county park.
Ref: M. Durant 5/98.
Directions: From Logansport allez 3 mi. west on Hwy. 24. Turn at pseudo log cabin.

8 Muscatatuck County Park ✩✩✩

This charming wooded park features more than a few enjoyable and challenging limestone bouldering (possibly toprope) routes (to 30′) with a nice selection for all grades. Your enjoyment will depend on how aggressive you are with a Dustbuster as the holds can have their fair share of debris; still, some of Indiana's best bouldering. Modern and primitive camping. Jennings County Park, (812) 346-2953.
Classics: Hoosier Mama? V4.
Directions: North Vernon. Go south on Hwy. 7 to Muscatatuck County Park, just outside of town. A 20′ rock band is visible across the road as one drives and descends into a wooded ravine. Park at the parking lot and walk just a minute to the bouldering wall.

9 Clifty Falls State Park ✩✩✩

Good limestone bouldering such as that found on Cake Rock. Though limited, may be some of the cleanest limestone in the state. Pay camping in state park (812–265–1331).
Directions: From Madison follow signs west of town into park. Boulders along hiking trail.

Iowa

If you take a shower with your clothes on, it shows your crazy. If you take a shower with your clothes off, it shows your nuts. —Des Moines truck-stop graffiti

Can you say corn? The rural Iowa climbing crop is well below its plump harvest of corn. Still, for those willing to go milling, climbing can be found on limestone/dolomite bins in areas scattered about the eastern half of the state: Backbone State Park, Palisades-Kepler State Park, and Yellow River State Forest. These areas fit into the sport climbing genre, as well as the limestone area, Wild Iowa.

1 Yellow River State Forest ✩✩

These are 40′ solid limestone bluffs in a quiet, sylvan setting. Scenic camping and park headquarters are located near the Overlook Area number 2. Good pay camping in forest. Nearby Effigy Mounds National Monument provides an interesting side trip. Autumn. State land, (319) 586-2548.

Ref: Guidebook: Bagg's *50 Short Climbs in the Midwest.*

Directions: From Harper's Ferry, from junction with Hwy. 364 (Harper's Ferry Rd.) and Lansing Harper's Rd., one can find rock bluffs in either one of two places: 1) South of Harper's Ferry, high limestone bluffs (includes Hanging Rock, Eagle Rock; possibly too soft) face east along Hwy. 364 and the mighty Mississippi River. These bluffs, though plentiful, long, and tall, are of poorer quality than in state forest. 2) West of Harper's Ferry, take Lansing Harper's Rd. 3 mi. west. Turn left (south) on State Forest Rd. B25 for 3 mi. past campgrounds. Turn right up steep hill, and then bear left to overlook. Park at overlook. Walk 30′ south to top of limestone bluffs. Climbing is below.

2 Backbone State Park ✩✩

Several winding vertebra of vertical 70′ dolomite. The good climbs are not for the spineless. Expect dusty limestone topropes in amongst the highest bluffs in Iowa. One of the better areas is across from the main picnic area. The Backbone is the highest point in rural northeast Iowa. Climbers and rappellers must register at the park office. Autumn. Pay camping at state park (319-924-2527).

Ref: Guidebook: Bagg's *50 Short Climbs in the Midwest.*

Directions: From Strawberry Point drive 5 mi. southwest off Hwy. 410 (follow state park signs). Various climbing areas at Backbone State Park: Lower Picnic Area, The Backbone (North, Middle, and South Bluffs), and Richmond Springs Bluffs.

3 Ledges State Park (closed) ●

This lovely wooded stream corridor holds extremely soft 40′ sandstone walls in its sinuous grasp. Once home of the Iowa State "Wall Cleaners" Zipline Specialistes. There is no rock climbing or rappelling allowed anymore in this state park due to the inherently soft and fragile nature of the stone. (This is evident in the chopped steps and carved initials and handiwork of previous park users.) Pay camping at state park.

Ref: Guidebook: Bagg's *50 Short Climbs in the Midwest.*

Directions: From Boone drive 6 mi. south on county roads. Follow Ledges State Park signs. Two areas capture rock climbers' attention: Ledges/Big Wall and Sentinel Rock. Get a park map.

4 Wild Iowa (Picture Rocks Park) ✩✩✩

Quality dolomite sport cragging hiding below the cornstalks. Several short walls hold brief but steep sport routes on 35′ to 80′ dolomite bluffs along a quiet stream. No doubt Iowa's best sport crag to date. Ice climbing also. Camping at this government park.

Classics: Beginner route, The Old and the Decrepit 5, The Young and the Bold 8, Virgin Lemonade 10b, Bird in Hand 11b, Flash 11d , Lesbian Knife Fight 12a, Monkeyspank Mayhem 12b.

Ref: SC 92.

Directions: From Monticello at junction of highways (151 and 38), putt south on Hwy. 38 for 3 mi. At PICTURE ROCKS PARK sign, turn left for 2 4/10 mi. past Camp Courageous and wind down into cul-de-sac of Picture Rocks Park. Routes begin 25 yd. from car and continue along stream away from parking.

5 Maquoketa Caves State Park (closed) ✩✩

A land of impressive 80′ limestone sinkholes, caves, and amphitheaters amid Iowa's fertile farms. At one time, lime-

Iowa

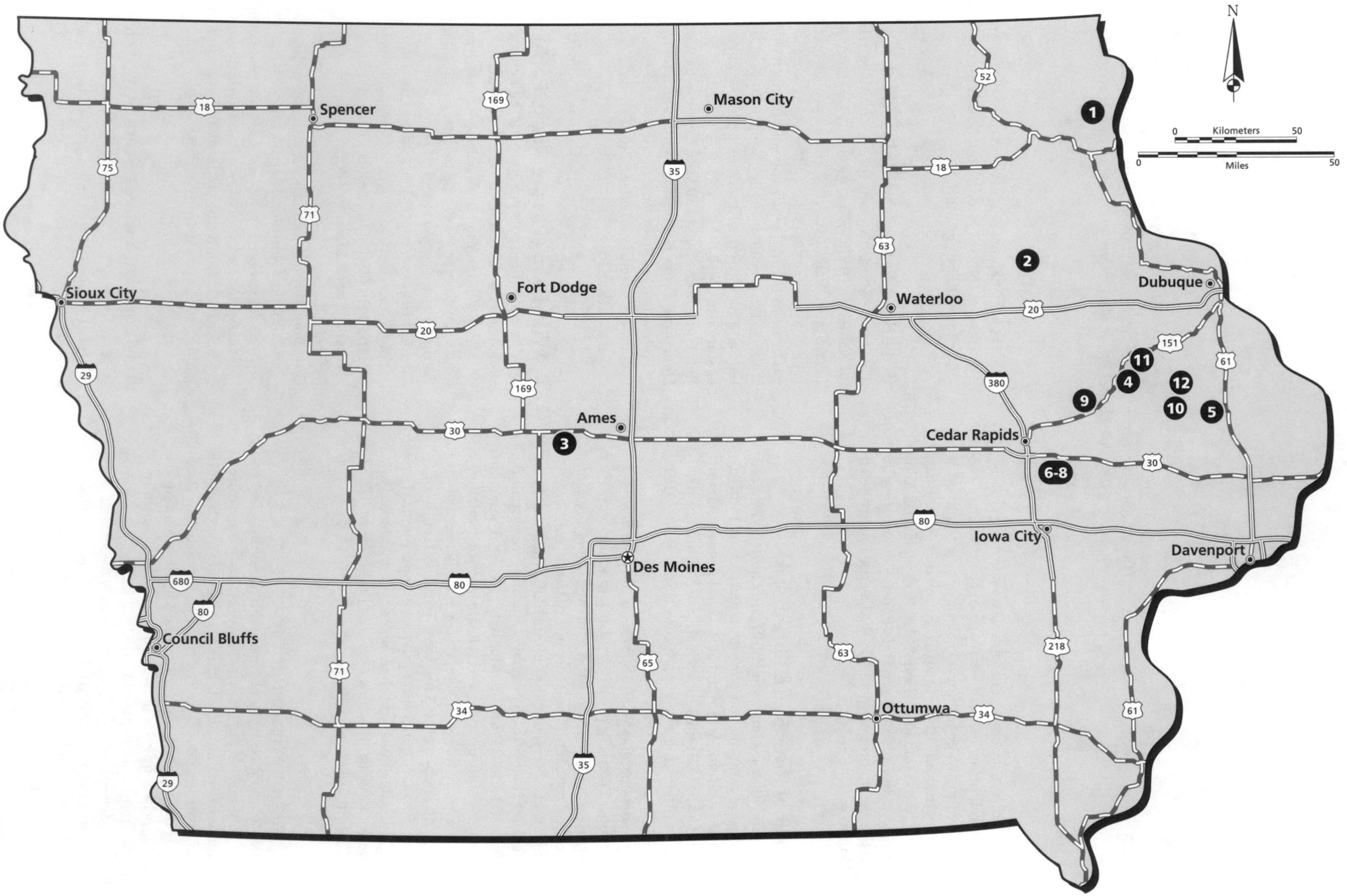

Kilometers

Miles

50

50

0

0

1

2

11

4

9

6-8

5

12

10

3

Dubuque

Davenport

Waterloo

Cedar Rapids

Iowa City

Mason City

Spencer

Fort Dodge

Ames

Des Moines

Ottumwa

Council Bluffs

Sioux City

52

18

63

35

169

20

71

18

75

29

680

80

29

71

34

65

35

80

34

63

218

61

30

380

20

151

61

stone topropes and bouldering were sent on this 1 mi. of cliffs. Now posted no climbing courtesy of Iowa State Parks. The rock tends to be mungy and damp overall for rock climbing. Dance Hall Cave is the largest in the park and was a popular climbing area. Dolomite caves offer spelunking as well. Pay camping in state park.

Ref: Guidebook: Bagg's *50 Short Climbs in the Midwest.*

Directions: From Maquoketa go west briefly on Hwy. 64. Turn north on Hwy. 61 for 9/10 mi. Turn left on Hwy. 264 for 6 mi. Turn left at park signs and park at Dancehall Caves. Follow staircase down to rock and magnificent caves and rock formations.

6 Palisades Kepler State Park ✯✯✯

The Cedar River provides the backdrop for what may be some of the best bouldering in Iowa. Interesting 80′ dolomite features some cool bouldering and toprope cragging potentials. Pay camping in state park.

Ref: Guidebooks: Ferguson's *Rock: The Climber's Guide to Palisades-Kepler State Park,* Bagg's *50 Short Climbs in the Midwest.*

Directions: From Cedar Rapids drive 8 mi. east on Hwy. 30. Follow park signs to various Palisades Kepler State Park areas. These include: Lookout Tower and Cliff Trail Area for toprope/lead cragging, and Quarry, near dam (fun bouldering pit) at south end of park.

7 Palisades Natural Area ✯✯

Short 30′ dolomite dirty wall. Limited potential. Loose rock. County land.

Ref: M. Wendling 11/98.

Directions: From Cedar Rapids go south on I–380. Take exit 13 (Hwy. 30 East) and go east on Ivanhoe Rd. Follow the signs to Palisades Natural Area.

8 Palisades-Dows Preserve ✯✯

Recently developed 40′ dolomite area; all ratings are tentative, as they are based on one or two ascents. County land.

Classics: Barking Spiders 7, Nubbin Buttress 8 R, Treehugger 10a, Silly Escapade, 10b R, Skippy Whipper 11b.

Ref: M. Wendling.

Directions: From Cedar Rapids drive east on Hwy. 30. Just past mi. 257, look for sign for Palisades Natural Area and Palisades-Dows Preserve. Turn right and follow signs 6 mi. to observatory. From parking lot find two faint trails behind observatory. Take right hand of two trails. When trail crosses creek, turn left and follow creek to crags. Approach hike is roughly 2/3 mi. to nearest crag. Approximately 1-mi. total to farthest.

9 Wapsipinicon State Park ✯✯

Potential for numerous short trad routes, 40′ dolomite walls. Pay camping at state park.

Ref: M. Wendling, 1/99.

Limestone walls at Wild Iowa (Picture Rocks Park).

Directions: Located immediately south of Anamosa on Hwy. 151. Follow signs into the park.

10 Pine Valley

Near Canton.

Ref: M. Weir.

11 Indian Bluffs Preserve ✯✯✯

One of Iowa's most secluded and scenic preserves is also home to the state's longest and arguably best climbs. Bouldering, traditional and sport climbing can be found at this area (mostly sport). Climbs range from 25′ to 90′, with great potential for new routes.

Classics: Ward Off 11b, C North Red 12a, El Diablo 12b.

Directions: From Monticello drive north on Hwy. 151 for 1 mi. Turn right onto CR D-65 (Richland Rd.). There are two options to get to the preserve from here. Either take Richland Rd. to Butterfield Rd., or take Jordan Rd. to the North Park boundary. Jordan Rd. is usually four-wheel-drive only but is shorter. Roads can be extremely muddy in spring.

Iowa Road Thoughts

My friend, Marty, from Iowa Falls doesn't understand this passion for climbing things. But being a hunter at least he has some respect for the heights . . . "Only way you're going to get me to climb that thing," he states fervently, "is if there is something to kill on top!"

—TNT

12 Hoot Bluff (Ozark) ★★★

Short but very steep climbing in a mini-amphitheater directly above a cornfield. Great place to climb on cold fall and even winter days as the crag is south facing.

Classics: Liberal Tendencies 11a, Deer Crossing 11b, Golden Showers 11d, Gravity Amp 12a, Back in the Groove 12d.

Directions: From Canton, off of Hwy. E–17, take Sixth Ave. west, then follow the signs to Ozark. The access road is on the right after crossing the Maquoketa River Bridge. Caution: Access road can be extremely muddy in spring or after a heavy rain.

Other Iowa Climbing Areas (Now Closed)

Wildcat Den State Park
Mines of Spain

Kansas

Curiosity is almost, almost the definition of frivolity. —Ortega y Gassett

Can you say wheat? Sure, I knew you could. Draw a line between the home of Budweiser in St. Louis and the Coors brewery in Golden, find the midpoint, and what do you have? Rock City, Kansas, a sprinkling of sandstone spheres in the heart of America's breadbasket. Enough rock to keep one busy for hours (using the plural loosely).

Driving through Kansas may make you want to go on a bender. If so, other areas you may wish to discover include Fall River, Salina Rock, and the western stacks at Monument Rocks. Still, if you don't like contriving, then keep on driving.

1 Rock City ✫✫✫
Spherical 25′ sandstone boulders with sloping holds and perfect lawn landings. Make a leg-stretching bouldering stop to break up the "Land of Ahs" drive along I–70. The rock du jour if you're in Kansas. You are approximately 90 mi. southeast of the Geographical Center of the USA at Lebanon, Kansas. Spring/autumn. Private park. Day use only.
Ref: C [155-123, 119(4/90)-53], R 99-68; Sherman's *Stone Crusade.*
Directions: From Salina drive north 16 mi. on I–135, then west, following signs for Rock City through Minneapolis. Open sunrise to sunset. Admission.

2 West Salina Area
Small outcrops with short toprope potential.
Ref: J. Thurmond.
Directions: From Salina drive west of town to the vicinity of the second exit (exit 244) on I–70. West Salina Rocks

Monument Rocks.

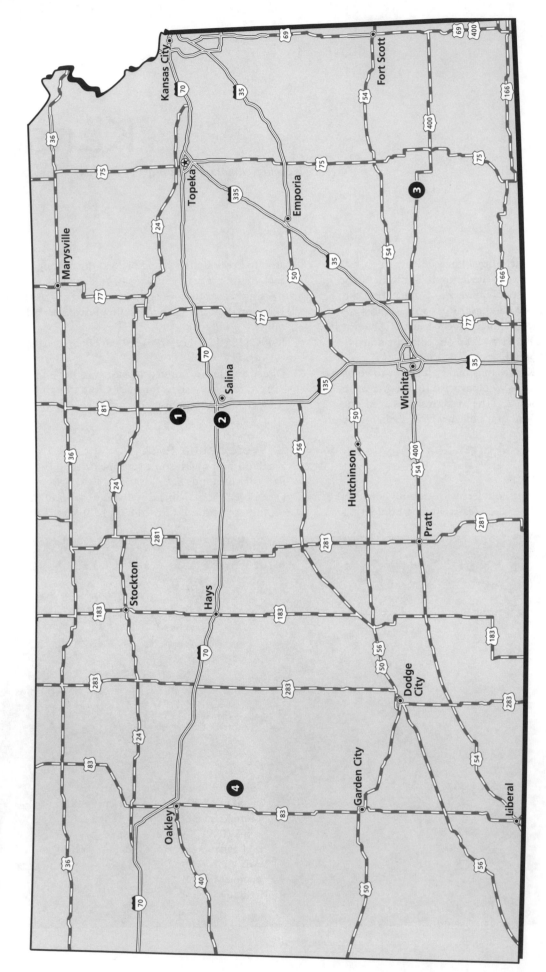

Kansas

Marysville
Kansas City
Topeka
Emporia
Fort Scott
Salina
Wichita
Hutchinson
Pratt
Stockton
Hays
Dodge City
Garden City
Oakley
Liberal

36
75
70
35
69
400
54
166
24
335
335
75
77
50
35
54
54
70
77
135
35
400
81
50
56
36
281
281
24
183
183
70
283
50
56
283
24
183
83
40
36
70
50
54
56
166

1
2
3
4

N

Kilometers
0   50
Miles
0   50

are supposed to be south of the interstate and visible from the interstate. Exact access unknown.

3 Fall River Cliffs ✦✦

A quaint old Kansas standby area featuring climbing by the tracks. At the current time legal access is only available for the western half of this 40′ sandstone crag. The landowner has a standard waiver to sign that can be obtained at Mountain High in Wichita. The better half of the crag unfortunately is not included in this access. The owner of this half of the crag has been known to escort climbers off of the land at gunpoint. There are excellent routes, including a classic 5.8 crack called Main Face Crack, or Cave Crack depending on whom you talk to. There are some short bolted routes on the legal half of the crag. The bolts are approximately four years old, which is not bad except that they are in sandstone. One more note about the owners: They like to hunt, so it is advisable not to climb in late fall during deer season. This area should not be mistaken for the state park northwest of town. Private land.
Ref: M. Downing; R 99-68.
Directions: Fall River. Follow Laurel east then southeast to baseball field. Park. Hike along railroad tracks approximately 1 mi. east to Fall River Cliffs, just south of and adjacent to tracks.

4 Monument Rocks (closed) ✦

A windy land of soft, white 50′ sandstone magical spires in the vast west Kansas prairie. This is a local climbing area for a group of three climbers from western Kansas who want to climb but can't because the local cops have caught on to Jared Bogard's bank-climbing antics. Mostly it's desert/aid

climbs, but most of the time it's solo and run out (from the ground). County land.
Classics: Sticky Rib Eats 6 crack, J. Bogard Mama made Gumbo 4, J. Bogard and K. Doubrava.
Ref: J. Bogard.
Directions: From Oakley send her south on Hwy. 83 about twenty minutes. Turn east, following signs.

Kansas Road Thoughts

Surely stranger things have happened on the road, but this is right up there . . .

Four of us guys are driving back from Arkansas across western Kansas stuck in a VW Rabbit. We've established a proper high rate of speed to make the drive go faster when a family of four pulls up to us in the passing lane; dad driving, mom in the passenger seat, with a boy and girl in the back. Halfway shocked that they are passing us at the current speed, it wasn't nearly as shocking as what happened next.

The mom gives us a sheepish grin and then says something to the dad. The next thing we know she lifts up her sweater and mashes her breasts against the passenger window. Holy Gheezus!

We must have been a pretty funny sight, four grown men with their eyes lit up like the northern lights and their jaws hitting the floor, cuz they were sure laughing at us.

So is this family entertainment in Kansas? I don't know, but the driver in our car did a heckuva' job holding the wheel straight.

—TNT

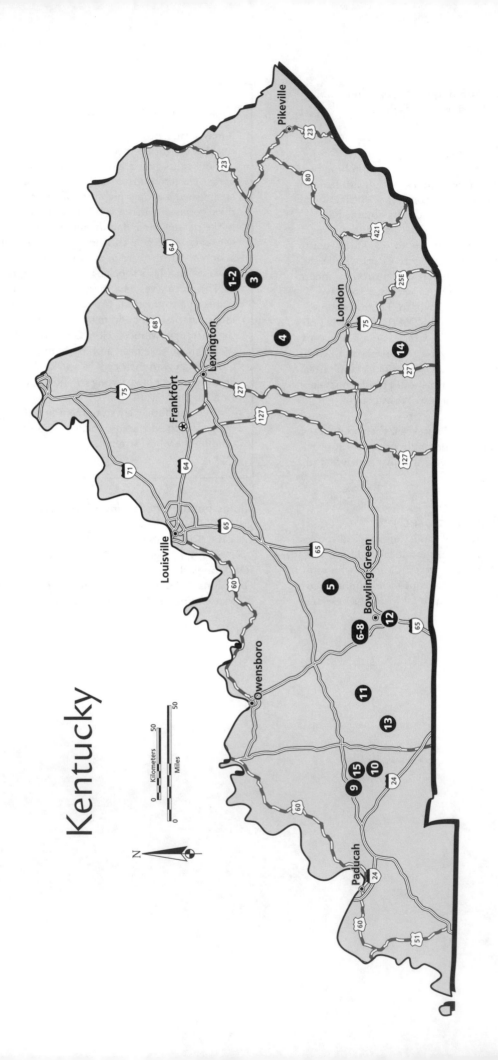

Kentucky

Kentucky

If a man listening will let it, bluegrass will transmit right into your heart. —Bill Monroe, Mr. Bluegrass

The Bluegrass State may conjure up thoughts of white rail fences bordering thoroughbred horses heading for the Kentucky Derby. Or, it may prompt thoughts of coal miners with weary, blackened faces on bleak, ravaged hillsides.

For rock climbers the state should elicit bright visions; namely, steep rock and plenty of it. Kentucky holds one of the great future reserves of overhanging, gymnastic rock climbing. For those amenable to a slightly softer sandstone than West Virginia's New River Gorge, the Red River Gorge allows rock climbers unlimited dreams for climbs of the future.

Until now, the word *marathon* has always denoted running via the legs. Now that climbers have discovered Red River Gorge, they will be running marathons with their forearms. The "Gorge" offers a climber some of the most continuously steep and overhanging rock to be found in America. Within the infinite, serpentine canyons lies a wealth of climbing to meet any climber's technical treasure hunt: pocketed face, waves of edges, roofs, and various cracks on long, sweeping walls of orange and gold sandstone.

There is a legend that says Eskimos possess more than fifty separate words to describe the word *snow*. When climbers discover the Red River Gorge, they'll have at least that many for the nuances of the word *pump*.

Abundant crags of the Appalachian hardwood forests are part of the great eastern sandstone preserve climbers will come to cherish for years. Both ends of the state hold great potential.

So, pick a crag and pump up the volume.

1 Western World (aka Spaas Creek) ☆☆☆
An area of 100′ sandstone cliffs in the Red River Gorge sandstone belt. See Hackworth's guide. Autumn/winter. USFS–Daniel Boone National Forest, (859) 745–3100.
Classics: Dark Star 8, Sand Blasted 10-, Invisible Barrier 11.
Ref: C 95; Guidebook: Hackworth's *Stones of the Years*.
Directions: Near Stanton. Sandstone rimrock lines the hills near Stanton.

2 Red River Gorge ☆☆☆☆☆
Superpumper! Possibly the largest concentration of the steepest sport-climbing rock in America. Vast sandstone-rimmed canyons feature 200′ overhanging walls along or within a short distance from the road. Softer sandstone than most Eastern big-name areas (e.g., New River Gorge) is the purchase tax for buying time on remarkably difficult, aggro-sport climbs first developed by the ubiquitous Porter Jarrard. Classic traditional Martin Hackworth leads as well. The Motherlode area has become known as the major sport-climbing pump palace with its tidal wave of unrelenting forearm challenges. "Pyrex" forearms are necessary to resist the burn. Many access issues due to archaeological and biological concerns; climbers should stay abreast of Forest Service management policies. Best season: Autumn. Food: Ernie's, Miguel's; restaurant at state park, Hemlock Lodge, has Monday–Thursday soup-and-salad dinner. Local information at Climb Time Gym in Lexington. Information at Miguel's Pizza, just south of Natural Bridges State Park entrance. Camping free on USFS lands or pay camping at nearby campgrounds, Miguel's. USFS–Daniel Boone National Forest, (859) 745–3100, Stanton Ranger District, (606) 663–2852 (climbing information).
Classics: Trad: Half Moon Arch: Full Moon 6; Chimney Rock: Chimney Direct 7; Duncan Branch: Frenchburg Overhang 8; Long Wall: Autumn 9; Jailhouse Rock: At Death's Door 10b; Fortress Wall: The Battlement 10c and Hollywood Boulevard 11a 30′ roof; Purple Valley: Burden of Dreams 11a offwidth roof; Nada Tunnel: Black Death 11, Negative Energy 11+ (forty-five-degree face splitter crack pumpfest); Pebble Beach: Welcome to Old Kentuck' (Nazi Bitch Crack) 13a. Sport: Military Wall: Fuzzy Undercling 11b, Gung Ho 12; Left Flank: Stunning The Hog 12d, Table of Colors 13b; Twinkie 12a, Phantasia 13a; Sky Bridge Ridge: King Me 11, Soul Ram 12; Funk Rock: Red Hot Chili Pepper 10d, Infidel 11d, Frugal Chariot 12a; Roadside: Crazyfingers 10; Ghetto Methods V10.
Ref: S. Smith 2/01, R. Ellington 3/98; P. Jarrard; C [198-122, 186-27, 182-100, 180-42/107, 165(12/96)-24, 161-94, 155-38/118, 150-132, 142, 134, 126(6/91)-25, 99(12/86)-54, 95, 68(9/81)-28, 56], R [95-90, 94-115, 91-60, 89-33, 76, 75-94, 74-28, 53(1/93)-51], SC 12/91; Guidebook: Redmond's *Red River Gorge Bouldering*, Bronaugh's *Red River Gorge Climbs*, Jarrard and Snyder's *Selected Climbs at Red River Gorge*, Cater's *Sport Crags of the East*, Hackworth's *Stones of the Years III*, Pearsall's *Climber's Guide to the Red River Gorge*, Becker and Blazy's *Red River Gorge*.

Directions: From Slade go north on Hwy. 15 and east on Hwy. 77 to tunnel above Nada. Climbing begins at tunnel, with crags scattered around the Red River Gorge. Areas include: At Martin Fork Parking Area on Hwy. 77 just 1 1/10 mi. east of Nada Tunnel, cross road and hike up Trail 221: Military Wall (up right) and Left Flank (on left). Phantasia: approximately 1 mi. north on Hwy. 77 (on left) from junction with Hwy. 715. Sky Bridge Ridge: 8 mi. east on Hwy. 715 from junction with Hwy. 77 (1/2 mi. past concrete bridge), trail north of road; parking pullout beyond on left. Funk Rock City: From previous pullout continue to first left turn onto rough road 6/10 mi. to end, cross Swift Camp Creek to east. Emerald City, Global Village, and Roadside Crag: Go south on Hwy. 11, 3 mi. past Miguel's Pizza for EC and GV (on left), 1 1/2 mi. farther for Roadside Crag (on left). Motherlode: Go south on Hwy. 11 for 12 1/2 mi. past Miguel's. Turn right on Hwy. 498. Go past Hopewell Church. At 1 2/10 mi, turn right on gravel/logging road, following it downhill steeply to its end at bottom. Hike dirt road/cairns five minutes for a maximal pump. Main cliffs to right.

3 Natural Bridges State Resort Park (closed) ✮✮✮

Sandstone bouldering blocks and walls near the natural bridge. All Kentucky state parks closed to roped rock climbing. Bouldering may still be allowed. Pay camping in state park (606–663–2214).

Classics: Natural bridge.

Ref: P. Jarrard.

Directions: From Slade go 2 mi. south on Hwy. 11 to Natural Bridges State Park (signs).

4 Pilot Knob ✮✮

A slew of sandstone cliffs and formations. Private land.

Directions: From Berea go east on Hwy. 21 to Big Hill. Pilot Knob is northeast of Berea and is obvious 100' sandstone circular knob in center of valley.

5 Dismal Rock ✮

One-hundred-eight-foot sandstone multipitch sport and trad crag; especially good for intermediate climbers. Pay camping. State land.

Classics: Standard Classic 8, Nitty Gritty Dam Jam 9, Finger Jam Crack 9.

Ref: J. Dickey; www.trpeople.com/climbing for Kentucky climbing information; Guidebooks: Detterline's *A Climber's Guide to the Mid-South*, Dickey's *Rock Climbs in South Central Kentucky*.

Directions: From Munfordville wander west on Hwy. 728 to Nolin River Dam. Park below spillway and make way across below dam to Dismal Rock. Climbed on since mid-1960s by Bill Holmes and others. Louisville climbers (the old guys) left wooden wedges in cracks and put in glori-

fied nails they called bolts. They also used plastic—yes, plastic—chocks. These plastic chocks were great until you fell on them. Then it took a double-bitted axe to get them out. These soon lost favor with the locals. (Guess it's really hard to get someone to follow you on a climb with a double-bitted axe.) More rock exists downstream. Nearby Mammoth Caves worthy of a rest-day visit.

6 Young's Ferry (aka Green River Bluffs) (closed) ✮

Very little development at this 50' sandstone crag since the bolting phenomenon. Private land.

Ref: J. Dickey.

Directions: From junction near downtown Bowling Green, amble north 6 2/10 mi. on Hwy. 185 (Gordon Ave.). Turn left on Hwy. 263 for 1 1/2 mi. Turn right after water tower (left goes to Greencastle Cliffs). Turn right on Ezra Whalen Rd. and take right fork for approximately 2 8/10 mi. (left fork for Devil's Sidesaddle). Hike downriver to expanses of cliffs and boulders.

7 Devil's Sidesaddle ✮

Twenty-foot sandstone bouldering wall. Uncertain rock quality. Private land. Possibly off-limits.

Ref: J. Dickey.

Directions: From junction near downtown Bowling Green, amble north 6 2/10 mi. on Hwy. 185 (Gordon Ave.). Turn left on Hwy. 263 for 1 1/2 mi. Turn right after water tower (left goes to Greencastle Cliffs). Turn right on Ezra Whalen Rd. and take left fork for approximately 3 mi. When you head uphill and enter trees look for dirt road on right, across from driveway. Park on road and walk dirt road until reaching open field. Cross field to trail; Devil's Sidesaddle cliffs are 100 yd. farther.

8 Greencastle Cliffs (near Mt. Zion Church) (closed) ✮✮

Sixty-foot sandstone crag with more than one hundred topropes in area. Toprope anchors are trees. Better than playing Monopoly on a rainy day. Three bolts on entire cliff, no bolted routes. The rock quality here is definitely suspect. Private land: Please be discreet.

Classics: Broken Glass 9, Return to Earth B5.9, Hand job 11, Journey to Ixtlan 11.

Ref: J. Dickey; C 68; Guidebooks: Detterline's *A Climber's Guide to the Mid-South*, Dickey's *Rock Climbs in South Central Kentucky*.

Directions: From junction near downtown Bowling Green, amble north 6 2/10 mi. on Hwy. 185 (Gordon Ave.). Turn left on Hwy. 263 for 1 1/2 mi. Turn left after water tower and zip for 1 3/10 mi. Turn right on Mt. Zion Rd. for 9/10 mi. Park in lot and walk along field (keep clean) in front of church to trail leading to Greencastle Cliffs. Hike right 1/4 to 1/2 mi. around edge of meadow into woods through a small drainage to super steep cliffs.

9 Pennyrile Cliffs (aka Pumpkin Center/Hunter's Bluffs) ✩✩✩

Up to 150′ sandstone cliffs are visible, but most seem to have too soft of rock for quality climbing. The amazing Thurmo-Nuclear (35′ roof crack) 5.12+ is quality and just a five-minute walk up to first small outcrop behind thickets. Probably about a dozen bolted routes, 5.6–5.12. Climb here before the trees leaf out, i.e., autumn–early spring. Private land/state wildlife land.

Classics: 5.8 Drug Helmet, 5.10 High Step, Thurmo-Nuclear roof crack 5.12+.

Ref: W. Hobbs 2/01; A. Carrier, J. Thurmond.

Directions: From Dawson Springs roll 5 mi. west on Hwy. 62 until just past KEENE WILDLIFE AREA sign. Just north of bridge, turn east off blacktop onto dirt road. Pennyrile Cliffs are visible.

10 Pennyrile Forest State Resort Park ✩✩✩

Two small 40′ sandstone areas in the park: 1) Indian Bluff (steep) on right along road from lodge to lake. 2) Gill's Overhang (now a "graffiti thinktank" for three generations since John Gill's classic overhang problem) and a novel amenity in the bouldering world across from the swimming area. Park at swimming area. Autumn. Pay camping. State land.

Classics: John Gill Dynamic B2 (see picture in Ament's *Master of Rock*).

Ref: C 68; R 95-57; Ament's *Master of Rock*; Guidebook: Detterline's *A Climber's Guide to the Mid-South*.

Directions: From Dawson Springs go south on Hwy. 109 to Pennyrile State Forest.

11 Lake Malone State Park

This state park holds 20′ sandstone crags. Pay camping. State park, (270) 657–2111.

Ref: W. Hobbs.

Directions: From Russellville hop north on Hwy. 431 to Lake Malone State Park (signs).

12 Western Kentucky University Buildering

When physical overcomes the mental, climbing students have preferred the outside of campus buildings to the inside, e.g., Tate-Page Hall: 60′ brick veneer to top, slim protection available; great traverse at steps on west side. State land.

Classics: Gordon Wilson Hall, Finger traverse, Garrett Ballroom Steps, Garrett Center Corners, Old Science Hall Wall, State St., Cherry Hall Wall.

Ref: W. Hobbs; Guidebook: Dickey's *Rock Climbs in South Central Kentucky*.

Directions: Bowling Green. Buildering on Western Kentucky University campus. Camping is coed.

13 Pilot Rock ✩✩

Damp, lichen-covered, 50′ sandstone sport routes possible. Two bolted sport routes 5.8 and 5.10. Possible OW horror classic in back. Very trashy, but hey, at least there's no access problem. Watch out for tourist projectiles. Visit Jefferson Davis historic site (fourth highest in nation) and learn some interesting facts. Free camping. Private land—please be respectful.

Classics: Yeah . . . Right!

Ref: J. Dickey; Guidebooks: Detterline's *A Climber's Guide to the Mid-South*, Irons's *Climber's Guide to Pilot Rock*.

Directions: From Hopkinsville fly east on Hwy. 68 to Jefferson Davis Monument. Turn left across from monument onto Britmart/Fairview Rd. Glide for 6 mi. on Hwy. 508. Turn left. Go 1 7/10 mi. to Honey Grove. Turn right onto Hayes Rd. (gravel) before Honey Grove Grocery. Go 1 4/10 mi. and turn right onto paved road Hwy. 189. Go 1 1/2 mi. to Pilot Rocks on left.

14 Cumberland Falls State Park (closed) ✩✩

A beautiful waterfall area sports sandstone riverside boulders and crag. Pay camping in state park (606–528–4121).

Directions: From Goldburg (on I–75) ramble 20 mi. west on Hwy. 25. Turn west on Hwy. 90, following signs to Cumberland Falls State Park. Boulders and short walls along river.

15 Fowler Ridge Road

Fifty-foot sandstone crag. Autumn. Federal land. No camping.

Ref: 11/97.

Directions: From Dawson Springs follow signs to Pennyrile State Park. Turn onto the first gravel road. Follow the road until you hit Fowler Ridge Rd. Where Fowler Ridge Rd. "Ys," find a parking area big enough for two cars. Walk down the left fork. After about 1/4 mi. there is a mile-long ridgeline.

Louisiana

Louisiana

Sometimes the road less traveled is less traveled for a reason. —Jerry Seinfeld

Which of the following best completes this sentence: Louisiana is to climbing

a) As Pee Wee Herman is to pro wrestling
b) As France is to beer
c) As Roseanne is to dieting
d) All of the above

Face it; Louisiana is composed of floodplain deposits from the Mississippi River, not rock. There is rumor of climbing in a limestone quarry, and we've heard of a 6'-tall meteorite in a city park; other than that, the climbing is solely on private backyard climbing walls. Nevertheless, the climber passing through Louisiana would do well to stop and sample the outstanding cuisine (if even just a bag of Zap's Cajun Crawtater potato chips), and if in New Orleans, the famous nightlife.

1 Sherman's Mystery Boulder
One lonely boulder. Made famous by John Sherman's Fab 50 slide-show tour.

Potential Louisiana Rock-Climbing Areas
Limestone Quarry
Possibly Meteorite Boulder

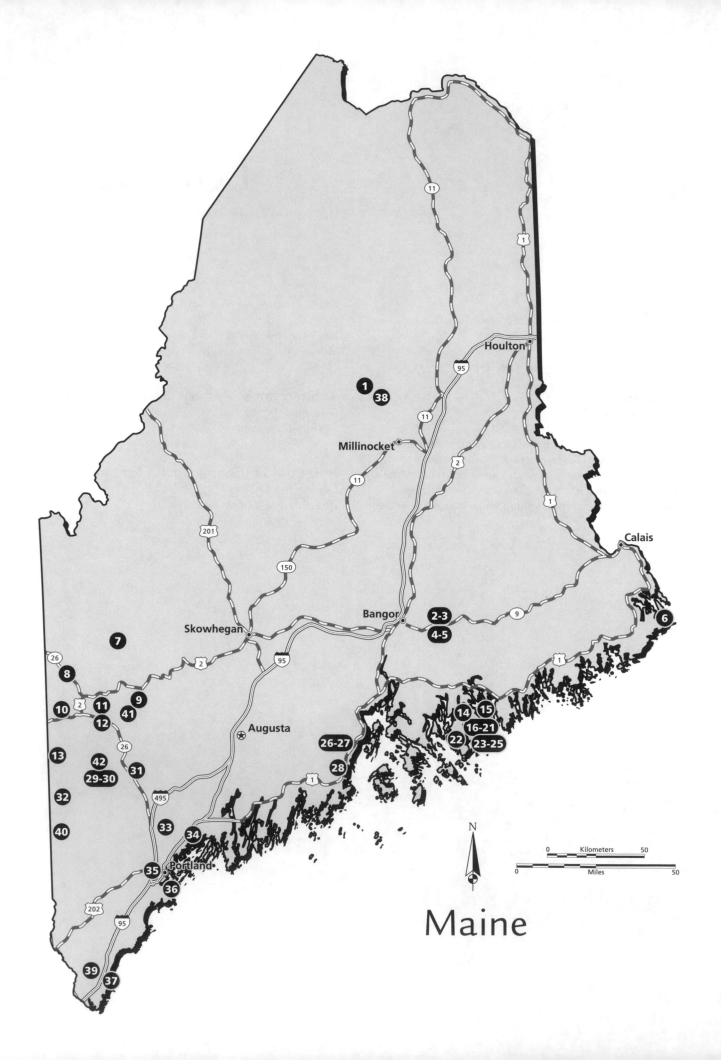

Maine

Maine

If you're going after Moby Dick, take along the tartar sauce. —Life's Little Instruction Book

Many climbers will never get closer to Maine than thumbing through an L. L. Bean catalog, which is a shame as L. L. Bean won't ship you a granite sea cliff or live lobster.

The state is sprinkled with areas, but the "Maine" attraction for visiting climbers is Mt. Desert Island's Acadia National Park. Beach bouldering and wave-lashed sea cliffs await the adventuresome in a pristine environment. Climbers may also find it hard to resist the other small oceanside areas.

However, the climbing doesn't stop at the Atlantic. For those willing to shop around the Maine woods, more deals abound than in the factory outlet stores along the coast. Climbing bargains in areas like Big Chick, Barrett's Cove, and Shagg Pond should be listed on any climber's shopping list.

Get there before the sale is over.

1 Baxter State Park (Mt. Katahdin) ✩✩✩
Mt. Katahdin features broken granite alpine cliffs up to 2,000′. Check out North and South Basins for rock. The great South Basin above Chimney Pond contains cliffs and slabs. Foul weather, loose rock. Katahdin is the highest point in Maine (5,268′) and the northern end of the Appalachian Trail. Camping at Roaring Brook Campground. Advanced reservations required! The Table Land is a glacial boulderfield 4,700′ above sea level. Summer/autumn. Pay camping in state park (207–723–5140).
Classics: Armadillo IV 7 (arête), long ice/snow routes.
Ref: C [122(10/90)-80, 89]; R 70-144, S 18(11/72)-10; Cole and Wilcox's *Shades of Blue* (ice); Guidebooks: Scofield's *High Peaks of the Northeast,* Harlin's *East.*
Directions: From Millinocket (check with rangers), go 28 mi. north to Roaring Fork Campground in Baxter State Park. Hike 4 mi. into South Basin for climbs on Mt. Katahdin.

2 Fletcher's Bluff ✩✩✩
Fletcher's Bluff is a 300′ granite subsidiary bluff of Big Chick. Route information is available through the University of Maine Outing Club. Summer/autumn. Camping nearby.
Classics: Meltdown 11+, Zebra 12a.

Ref: C [162-58, 84 (2/77)]; Guidebook: Ellison's *Clifton Rock Climbs.*
Directions: From Clifton (on Hwy. 9 east of Bangor), go ³/₄ mi. past Parks Pond on Hwy. 9. A dirt road is on left. Just farther east on Hwy. 9 past this dirt road, Little Chick is first on left, and then Big Chick. A fire tower sits north/northeast of Big Chick. Fletcher's Bluff is north of Hwy. 9, northeast of fire tower, 2 ⁸/₁₀ mi. down FR 09-13-0. Trail departs to northwest from Hwy. 9 just past right-hand bend in highway. Faces south.

3 Big Chick (aka Big Peaked) and Little Chick (aka Little Peaked) ✩✩✩
These 300′ south-facing granite crags have two caves at the east end of Little Chick. Up to three pitch routes. Great views of Katahdin and Cadillac Mountain. Route information is available through the University of Maine Outing Club. Summer/autumn. Camping nearby.
Classics: My Time 5, Ben's Balls, Layback 7 2p; now more modern sport routes.
Ref: C [162-58, 84 (2/77)]; Guidebook: Ellison's *Clifton Rock Climbs.*
Directions: From Clifton (on Hwy. 9, 18 mi. east of Bangor), go ³/₄ mi. past Parks Pond on Hwy. 9. A dirt road is on left. Just farther east on Hwy. 9 past this dirt road is a gravel road opposite highway department picnic area. (Little Chick is first formation on left, Big Chick on right. A fire tower sits north/northeast of Big Chick.) Turn north on gravel road for ⁷/₁₀ mi. Park. Hike ¹/₅ mi. to fire warden's camp (spring behind camp). Cliffs obvious, various trails.

4 Parks Pond Bluff ✩✩✩
A large face of seamless 380′ granite crag, i.e., few cracks. Most routes, on central portion of cliff, are steep angled face. The east end has overhangs. Overall, possibly a friction climber's paradise. Numerous boulders as well. Set in a New England pine-birch forest. Summer/autumn. Camping nearby.
Classics: Detour 6, D.C. 6, Maple Run.
Ref: C 84 (2/77); Guidebook: Ellison's *Clifton Rock Climbs.*
Directions: From Clifton (on Hwy. 9 east of Bangor), go ³/₄ mi. past Parks Pond on Hwy. 9. A dirt road is on left.

Park. Hike south across road, 100 yd. east of yellow house for ¹/₂ mi. Parks Pond Bluff overlooks Park Pond ¹/₄ mi. away.

5 Eagle Bluff ☆☆☆

This 200′ granite crag with knobby features offers a nice mixture of climbing on more than ninety routes. Camping at bivy sites near crag. Route information and other good road beta may be obtained from the University of Maine Outing Club in Orono. In Bangor, restaurants include Siam Garden (Thai) and Sea Dog Brewery. Parks Pond pay campground on Hwy. 9, 3 mi. east of Hwy. 180. April–May/August–October.

Classics: Open Book 4, Standard 6, Crossover 7, Crossover Dir 8, Eagle's Gift, Hard Stuff 9, Where Eagles Dare 10, Highlander 10, Excitable Boy 11, Amber Waves of Grain 11, Gait of Power 12a, Energizer 12.

Ref: Blair; C 84 (2/77), R 68-97; Guidebooks: Smith's *Low Budget Guide*, Ellison's *A Climber's Guide to Clifton 1974*.

Directions: Clifton. On Hwy. 9 (east of Bangor). Take Hwy. 180 east toward Otis for 2 mi. to pullout on left. Trail starts at large corner in road (at blue-marked tree) and leads east from pullout to top and bottom of Eagle Bluff. Cliff is somewhat visible from road. Hike twenty minutes.

6 Quoddy Head State Park (West Quoddy Head) ☆☆☆

Striking, wind-stunned spruce trees arise from 200′ gneiss cliffs that rise above water. Easternmost climbing area in the United States. Reportedly, some fine steep rock crags . . . Dan Goodwin 5.14 route Maniac? If you find this route hard, try this tongue twister, supposedly the world's hardest: The seething sea ceaseth and thus the seething sea sufficeth us. Summer/autumn. Park season: May 15–October 15. Pay camping in state park (207–733–0911).

Ref: P. Beal; C 84 (2/77).

Directions: From Lubec go south along coast on South Lubec Rd. to West Quoddy Head in Quoddy Head State Park. Rocks along shoreline.

7 Tumbledown Mountain (3,068′) ☆☆☆

Giant 600′ granite slab reminiscent of Cannon Cliff, New Hampshire, offers sport climbs. Nearby Tumbledown Chimney is a cleft in a rock cliff overhang by a balancing rock. Summer/autumn. Pay camping in state park.

Classics: AMC Route Var. 1 5.6 600′.

Ref: C [162-58, 84 (2/77)].

Directions: From Rumford rumble north on Hwy. 17 to Byron, then east on Byron Rd. Tumbledown Mountain is on north side of road. Faces south.

8 Grafton Notch (The Eyebrow and Table Rock) ☆☆☆

Roadside cliff—phantom area. Potential for a lot of climbing on 700′ granite formations. Rare plants in the area may curtail use of some areas. Popular hiking trails. Summer/autumn. Entry fee. Free camping. State park, (207) 824–2912.

Ref: J. Mallery, P. Beal; C 84 (2/77); Guidebook: Osgood's *White Mountains*.

Directions: From Newry slice northwest on Hwy. 26 to the Grafton Notch State Park area.

9 The Pinnacle ☆☆☆

A 500′ granite pinnacle in Maine?

Ref: C 84 (2/77).

Directions: From Rumford follow Hwy. 108 south, then turn right on Worthley Rd. (near East Peru) to another right on Greenwood Rd. via four-wheel-drive or logging roads. The Pinnacle lies ¹/₂ mi. west of the road.

10 Androscoggin River (Hwy. 2) Crags ☆☆☆

Scattered 300′ granite crags line the roadside north of the Androscoggin River, providing climbers lots of potential exploration. Summer/autumn. Free.

Ref: C 84 (2/77); Guidebook: Osgood's *White Mountains*.

Directions: From Bethel go just west of town on North Rd. and north of the Androscoggin River.

11 Bucks Ledge ☆☆☆

Two-hundred-foot granite crags with sport and multipitched routes. Summer/autumn. Camping.

Classics: Simian Strength 5.10.

Ref: C 84 (2/77); Guidebook: Osgood's *White Mountains*.

Directions: At Bryant Pond, go northwest on Hwy. 26. Shortly, turn right (north) before North Pond (a large pond) to cliffs. Bucks Ledge is visible from Hwy. 26 between Locke Mills and Bryant Pond. Faces west.

12 Payne Ledge ☆☆☆

Good climbing overlooking Twitchell Pond on this 150′ expert granite crag. Summer/autumn. Pay camping nearby.

Ref: C 84 (2/77); Guidebook: Harlin's *East*.

Directions: Locke Mills (5 mi. east of Bethel on Hwy. 26). Ask at Bob's Corner Store. From Bob's putt west across tracks and turn on first road to the left. Continue down a few mi. to second pond on left, which is Twitchell Pond. Payne Ledge visible.

13 Shell Pond (Evans Notch) ☆☆☆

Beautiful granite crags with forty routes. Summer/autumn. USFS–White Mountain National Forest, (207) 824–2134.

Ref: P. Beal; R [72-103, 66-17].

Directions: Southwest of Bethel. From Gilead go south on Hwy. 113 (approximately twenty minutes) to Evan's Notch.

14 A☆-(Acadia National Park) Overview ☆☆☆☆

The climbing in Acadia features short, 100′ granite ocean-side bouldering and short cragging opportunities. Here the climber will find an idyllic seacoast island accented with granitic climbs. There are many crags scattered throughout the park, of which Precipice Cliffs, Great Head, and Otter Cliffs are among the finest. Climbers must register. Paid NPS camping (Blackwoods and Seawall Campgrounds) replete with foghorns and "dance of the sugar plump raccoons" at night. For those willing to explore or island hop, an ocean of 450-million-year-old rocks await. And for those with an appetite, the proper way to eat lobster is within your fingertips. Raptor restrictions March 15–August 15. July–October. NPS, (207) 288-3338.

Classics: Old Town 7 to Return to Forever 9, Chitlin Corner 9+, A Dare By the Sea 10c, High Wire 11b, Maniacal Depression 11c, Pipe Dreams 12a.

Ref: C [198-97, 182-32, 172-32, 166(2/97)-53, 2/77, 84, 65, 48], R [92-82, 39(9/90)-64, 10(9/85)], S 9/82; Guidebooks: Warner's *Rock Climbing in Acadia National Park*, Elfring's *AMC Mountain Desert Island and Acadia National Park*, Harlin's *East*, Childs's *Climber's Guide to Mt. Desert Island*.

Directions: Bar Harbor. (From Ellsworth approximately 20 mi. southeast.) Acadia National Park headquarters just north of town on Hwy. 233. The rock climbing lies mainly to the south and southeast of town.

15 A-Frenchman Bay Islands ☆☆

Forested islands ringed with 50′ granite rock at their base. Some walls are steep and overhanging. Summer/autumn. Pay camping at park. NPS.

Ref: Guidebook: NPS.

Directions: From Bar Harbor find four islands out in Frenchman Bay. Boat approach is necessary.

16 A-Cadillac Mountain (Eagle Crag and The Gorge) ☆☆

Eagle Crag has modern 80′ granite sport routes and great views of the islands. Pinnacle in the gorge. Commanding views of Maine's landscape (including Mt. Katahdin) from the summit. The highest point (1,530′) on the eastern seaboard and the first place in the United States to catch the sun's rays in the morning. Summer/autumn. Pay camping. NPS.

Ref: P. Beal; Guidebook: NPS.

Directions: From Bar Harbor go through town on Hwy. 3 east for 2 mi. to NPS one-way loop road. Follow park loop to "Cadillac Mountain" summit. Hike between Cadillac and Dorr Mountain to The Gorge via trail. For Eagle Crag pick up south ridge of Cadillac Trail from Hwy. 3 opposite Blackwoods Campground.

17 A-Road Bridges ☆☆

Some of the best bouldering in the park may lie on these beautifully sculpted 30′ granite bridges. Summer/autumn. NPS.

The idyllic Otter Cliffs at Acadia.

TIM TOULA

Ref: Guidebook: NPS.

Directions: From Bar Harbor go through town on Hwy. 3 east for 2 mi. to NPS one-way loop road. Follow park loop to three different bridges of quarried granite. The first red granite Road Bridge is located just after turning onto the one-way loop.

18 A-Precipice Cliffs (on Champlain Mountain) ☆☆☆☆

Among Acadia's nicest rock, this complex of 150′ immaculate orange granite cliffs perches on a curved hillside above the Atlantic Ocean. Maniacal Depression has been dubbed the "Naked Edge" of Mt. Desert Isle. NPS has guidebook in visitors center. For the truly thrifty, this cliff allows one to climb at Acadia without paying the entrance fees. Raptor restrictions March 15–August 15. Summer/autumn. Camping at Blackwoods Campground or Seawall. NPS.

Classics: Precipice Cliffs: Old Town 7, London Bridges 8, Bartleby 8, Recollections of Pacifica 9, Scrimshaw 9+, Chitlin Corner 9+, Emigrant Cracks 10, Black Beard 10, Smooth Sailing 10, Connecticut Cracks 11, Maniacal Depression 11c, Pipe Dreams 12a.

Ref: Blair; R 92-82; Guidebooks: NPS, Harlin's *East*.

Directions: From Bar Harbor, Precipice Cliffs lie to the right off the loop road accessed via the Precipice Trail. Champlain is farther up the trail.

19 A-Bubbles ☆☆

One-hundred-foot east-facing granite crags on D-cup mounds bigger than Dizzie Gillespie's cheeks (as viewed from Jordan Pond). The South Bubble Erratic is a large, precariously perched boulder seen from the loop road, just east of South Bubble Peak. Summer/autumn. NPS.

Classics: Gargoyle 8.

Ref: Guidebook: NPS.

Directions: From Bar Harbor go through town on Hwy. 3 east for 2 mi. to NPS one-way loop road. Follow park loop to "Bubbles" parking lot. Hike south on trail to crag or north on trail to boulders.

20 A–Sand Beach, Great Head, and Beehive Boulders ☆☆☆

In a marvelous setting redolent of the ocean, these three 40' granite bouldering and short toprope areas are reached via the same parking area. The southern point of Great Head offers two routes, mainly from 5.10–5.12, put up by Jeff Butterfield. The Beehive is named for the unusual shape of its east cliff face. Summer/autumn. NPS.

Classics: The Head Arête 10d, Sedated 11c, Transatlantic 12d A0.

Ref: C 65, R 92-88; Guidebook: NPS.

Directions: From Bar Harbor go through town on Hwy. 3 east for 2 mi. to NPS one-way loop road. Follow park loop to "Sand Beach" parking area. Hike south to boulders along the sand beach. Or, go southeast to harder bouldering around the Great Head side. (Great Head can also be accessed via Schooner Head Rd.) Or, hike west across loop road on trail to Beehive Boulders.

21 A–Jordan Cliffs ☆

Scattered east-facing 60' granite chunks of climbable rock on the hillsides above Jordan Pond provide the boulderer or cragger with a cranking lunch. Raptor restrictions: March 15–August 15. Summer/autumn. NPS.

Ref: Guidebook: NPS.

Directions: From Bar Harbor go through town on Hwy. 3 east for 2 mi. to NPS one-way loop road. Follow park loop to "Jordan Pond" parking area. Jordan Cliffs obvious on east side of lake.

22 A–Echo Cliff ☆☆☆

One of the hardest routes in the park, Time's Arrow 13a, can be found here on these 60' granite sport crags. Good swimming at Echo Lake. Pay camping at Seawall Campground. Summer/autumn. NPS.

Classics: Time's Arrow 13a.

Ref: P. Beal; Guidebook: NPS.

Directions: From Somesville go south on Hwy. 102 to Echo Lake. Echo Cliff is ¼ mile south of lake and parking area.

23 A–Otter Cliff ☆☆☆

Fine 60' granite crags, superb oceanside setting. If you're going to pick a couple spots to climb in Acadia, this should be one of them, along with the Precipice Cliffs. First ascents were done here as early as 1920s by Fritz Weissner and the

Appalachian Mountain Club. The crashing waves of the Atlantic Ocean splash this terraced crag. Be sure to climb at low tide. Summer/autumn. NPS.

Classics: Wonder Wall 4, Appealing Ceiling 10+ (at Thunder Hole), High Tide Girdle 10+, A Dare by the Sea 10+, The Gallery 12a.

Ref: C [65, 64], R 92-82; Guidebooks: NPS, Harlin's *East*.

Directions: From Bar Harbor go through town on Hwy. 3 east for 2 mi. to NPS one-way loop road. Follow park loop to "Otter Cliff" pullout. The rest is obvious.

24 A–Blackwoods Bouldering Area ☆

Extremely small amount of shoreline 20' granite bouldering, but good enough to stretch your legs out of the campground. Summer/autumn. NPS.

Ref: Guidebook: NPS.

Directions: From Bar Harbor go through town on Hwy. 3 east for 2 mi. to NPS one-way loop road. Follow park loop to shoreline just south/southeast of Blackwoods Campground (easy hike from campground to the boulders). Park at unmarked pulloff by pedestrian crossing walk on loop road just west of Otter Cliff and viaduct.

25 A–Hunter's Beach ☆

Small 50' granite sea cliffs with some good routes, but difficult to pick them out. Summer/autumn. Private land.

Ref: Guidebooks: NPS, Harlin's *East*.

Directions: From Bar Harbor go through town on Hwy. 3 toward Seal Harbor. Go through mansions . . . on the outside of them. Climbing at cove west of Hunter's Beach proper. Faces east. Hard to find. Ask local climbers.

26 Maiden Cliffs ☆☆

Three-hundred-foot metamorphic beginner slabs with big white cross on top of cliff. A northern extension of Barrett's Cove rock. Affords views of Megunticook Lake. Driving Hwy. 1 through Maine could be dubbed the "Land of the Factory Outlet Store." Summer/autumn.

Ref: C 84 (2/77).

Directions: From Camden, at junction with Hwy. 1, take Hwy. 52 west out of town for 3 mi. Look for 200' buttress of Maiden Cliffs on right.

27 Barrett's Cove (The Verticals) ☆☆☆

Major 300' south-facing metamorphic slab buttress for this part of Maine. The Verticals, 60' buttress 500 yd. farther west, has many good topropes in 5.10–12 category (bring slings). Barrett's Cove is also known for its good ice climbing. More rock on nearby Mt. Baldy and others. Very hot in summer, but a nice beach at southeast end of Megunticook Lake. Also, scenic Atlantic Ocean coastline nearby. Summer/autumn. Pay camping in this state park (207-236-0849).

Classics: Good 5.6–5.8 on face. Charlotte's Crack 7, Templeton's Crack 8, good 5.12 boulder problem at base. The Verticals: Bolt Ladder 9, Brown Eye 10c, Chalk on the Wild

Side 11b toprope, Clash of the Tendons 12a; The Outback: Sunspot 11, Cracked Up 11; Borderline: 12 arête; Mt. Battie: Arête 10b, Prospero 10+, Dream Weaver 11a, Ariel 11d, Renascence 12c, Resonance 12d, Reconnaissance 13a.

Ref: Blair; C 84 (2/77), R [92-81, 62]; Guidebook: Townsend's *Rock and Ice Climbs in the Camden Hills.*

Directions: From Camden take Hwy. 52 northwest out of town for 2 1/2 mi. Look for 200' buttress on right. More rock before and after main crag. Parking/trailhead on right. Barrett's Cove: Walk up road to trail to boulder. The Verticals: Hike left from the top of the slab. Lost Valley: Take streambed above Verticals. On left wall. The Rampart is 1 mi. north of Camden on Route 52 at Old Carriage Rd. Park. Take trail left until a right at a stream. Head straight for rock through woods and up talus on right. Four good lines 5.11 to 5.12.

28 Rockport Harbor ✫

In our "for what it's worth" department . . . an east-facing traverse wall of bizarre, pocketed 25' limestone is here to play on. Summer/autumn.

Ref: Guidebook: Townsend's *Rock and Ice Climbs in the Camden Hills.*

Directions: Southeast Rockport. In Rockport Harbor.

29 Bear Mountain

More of a mountaineering route than classic rock-climbing route. First 50' in height is a fifty- to fifty-five-degree slope. Al Chase pitons. Some decent bouldering at bottom of mountain below cliffs. Summer/autumn. Private land.

Ref: S. Zanelli 11/98; C 84 (2/77), R 72-103.

Directions: From South Waterford bear south on Hwy. 37 a few minutes. Bear Mountain is east of Hwy. 37. Park near boat launch. Hike across road up to rock-finding trail.

30 Hawk Ledge ✫✫✫

This 300' granite slab offers three-pitch 5.8 friction climbs and other intermediate face climbs with routes rising to 5.12. Nice views from top. Summer/autumn.

Ref: C 84 (2/77).

Directions: South Waterford. Take Mill Hill Rd. east out of town. Turn right on Skunk Alley Rd. for 1/2 mi. When it turns to dirt, go for 100 yd., find parking on left. Hike up road across from parking to top of summit. Hike down left to base of routes. Alternative route: Soar south on Hwy. 35 past Bear Mountain a few more minutes. Hawk Ledge is on east side of road.

31 Rock-A-Dundee and Land of Overhangs ✫✫✫

At Rock-A-Dundee, the right half of the cliff is the only accessible portion of this southwest-facing 70' granite sport crag. All climbing on the left half is closed due to private land parcels. Land of Overhangs features blocky roofs and hang problems, if you can find it. Get pumped!

Autumn/winter. Private land.

Classics: Rock-A-Dundee: Bold Crow 10+, Bladebone Arête 12-.

Ref: P. Beal; C 84 (2/77).

Directions: Oxford/Welchville (northwest of Mechanic Falls). At junction of Hwy. 121 and Hwy. 26, go northeast off Hwy. 26 on Whittemore Rd. (name of road uncertain), continue to railroad tracks, turn left, and continue for 200 yd. to clear-cut. Walk back to edge of clear-cut. Rock-A-Dundee is visible from Hwy. 26.

32 Jockey Cap ✫✫✫

Good for a day's visit of hard or easy climbs on this 60' granite crag's west and south faces. If you try the Mako Roof, just remember, Mako sharks have a big bite. Good bouldering at right and left sides and below cliff itself on Molly's, Spiritual, and Peary Boulders. A monument lies on top to famed artic explorer, Admiral Peary. Summer/autumn. No on-site camping. Possibly private land.

Classics: Mako Roof 11+, Great White 12; Gorilla Traverse V8/9.

Ref: C [186, 99, 64], R 43; Guidebooks: Webster's *Rock Climbs in White Mountains,* Osgood's *White Mountains.*

Directions: Fryeburg. Gallop a couple minutes east of town (rock visible from Hwy. 302). From Jockey Cap General Store on Hwy. 302, a quick walk takes one to the base of Jockey Cap rock.

33 Bradbury Mountain State Park ✫✫✫

Excellent problems on 25' metamorphic boulders, though limited. Sports some of Maine's most difficult bouldering problems. Rough rock—pick up an extra bottle of Nu-skin at one of the many factory outlet stores in nearby Portland and Freeport. Summer/autumn. Private land/state park, (207) 688-4712.

Classics: Can't Get Theah From Heah 13a.

Ref: P. Beal.

Directions: From Brunswick take I-95 south to Freeport exit for Bradbury. Go north on Dyer to Hwy. 9 for approximately 4 mi. Turn right approximately 1/2 mi. to Bradbury Mountain State Park entrance. Park near picnic shelter. Hike (twenty minutes) west 1/2 mi., then south 1/4 mi. over stone wall to cliff and farther south 1/4 mi., leaving main park hiking trail past cliff to boulders in southwest side of park boundary. Patience (and a local climber) may be necessary to find these blocks.

34 Wolfe's Neck Woods State Park and South Freeport Bouldering ✫✫✫

At Wolfe's Neck, climbing is recommended at low tide. Hard 25' topropes on offshore boulder. Pay camping at state park. Summer/autumn. Private land/state park, (207) 865-4465.

Classics: Wolfe's Neck: Gold Coast 12d.

Ref: P. Beal: Guidebook in preparation for greater Portland area rock.

Directions: South Freeport. South Freeport Bouldering: Off

Pine Rd. going toward Freeport. A small cluster of rocks. Park at narrow pullout just past a boulder or at store back at intersection of Pine and South Freeport. For Wolfe's Neck: Follow Flying Point Rd. east. Turn right on Wolfe's Neck Rd. to Wolfe's Neck Woods State Park. Climbing is found in the remote west half at shoreline.

35 Rocky Hill (aka The Quarry) ☆

A local hangout with a quaint industrial ambience. This 80' metamorphic crag offers expert climbs with bouldering. Summer/autumn. Private land.

Classics: Horizontal 8+, Tips 9+, Grand Larceny 11a.

Ref: P. Beal; C [194-90, 84]; Guidebook: Beal's *Greater Portland Rock.*

Directions: In Portland. Forest Ave. to Bell to Read St. Turn left on Quarry Rd. to gates.

36 Portland Headlight, Willard Beach, and Two Lights State Park ☆☆☆

At Fort Williams, four different 30' metamorphic areas of bouldering and toproping areas with oceanfront views. Davey Jones Wall (first parking lot) has classic short top-ropes. Headlight Wall offers superb bouldering directly below the lighthouse. Casino Beach Cliff, perhaps best in Portland area, accessed by walking fifteen minutes north up coast. Seaside bouldering and toproping on unique white metamorphosed stone. Beautiful incut holds. South from the Headlight to Two Lights is known as the Forbidden City and contains a host of various rock cliffs. Portland Headlight is first lighthouse in the United States, commissioned in 1791 by George Washington. Summer/autumn. City/state park, (207) 799-2661.

Classics: Willard Beach: The Anvil: Get Your Wings 11a; Fort Williams: Harbor Lights 10, Tempest 12; Headlight Wall.

Ref: C [139, 84(2/77)-38]; Sherman's *Stone Crusade;* Guidebooks: Harlin's *East,* Beal's *Greater Portland Rock.*

Directions: South Portland. At Portland Headlight off Shore Dr. Short walls below lighthouse. The climbing continues along the coast in either direction. To the north, one may find access via Willard Beach. To the south, hike fifteen minutes along the shore from the lighthouse or via Two Lights State Park at Cape Elizabeth.

37 Bald Head Cliff (closed) ☆☆☆

This 80' granite beveled cliff pierces the shore of the Atlantic Ocean. This seaside cliff is owned by Cliff House Resort and is strictly closed to rock climbers.

Ref: Cliff House Resort 11/00; P. Beal; B. Wade 6/99.

Directions: South Ogunquit.

38 Fat Man's Woe

Fat Man's Woe is a great place to climb! Find overhangs, as well as some good 5.8 to 5.10 at this 200' granite crag.

Thirty routes. Summer/autumn.

Classics: Living Water 5.10.

Ref: Local.

Directions: In or near Baxter State Park, overlooking Rippegeneous Dam.

39 Mt. Agamenticus (Big A)

Numerous small 20' granite crags and boulders scattered throughout the woods on the mountain. No camping. York Parks and Recreation Department, (207) 363-1040.

Ref: Local.

Directions: Between Ogunquit and South Berwick, just west of Agamenticus Station. On Mt. Agamenticus (aka Big A), formerly a downhill ski area.

40 Devil's Den

Granite crags. USFS–White Mountain NF, (207) 824-2134.

Ref: J. Semple.

Directions: Near Porter. Go north on Hwy. 160, then hang a left on Porter Field Rd. Now turn left on Norton Hill Rd. Take a short drive up this dirt road to a house. Park at the house and take a short hike up the dirt road. This will take you to a large field on the top of a hill. Cross this field to the top of the cliffs. Trails on left and right lead down to rocks. From the top go left and down through a narrow ravine to find some short but interesting climbs.

41 Shagg Pond Crag ☆☆☆☆

Overhanging 250' granite crag with many good routes to 5.13 established by Delaney, Mushial, Baker, Parrott, and Graham. Summer/autumn.

Classics: Short Shagg 9+, Shaggin Wagon 12a, Ginseng 12b, Shagg It 12d.

Ref: C 162-58, R [95-68, 72-103, 71-23].

Directions: From Sumner go northwest on Redding Rd. to just past Shagg Pond. The parking is way up the road at a turnaround. Walk the dirt road until a pond appears. Use rightmost trail. It's a twenty-minute steep hike. Take a right at a hard-to-find "X," made out of trees. Walk a couple minutes more down this trail to the rock.

42 Pulpit Rock

Small compact crag; excellent crack slab and wall routes.

Ref: R 72-103.

Directions: From North Waterford go east on Hwy. 118. Then go north on Hunt's Corner Rd.

Other Maine Climbing Areas
Tumbledown Dick Mountain

Granite crag northeast of Gilead off North Rd.

Maryland

And so, my fellow Americans, ask not what your country can do for you; ask what you can do for your country. —John F. Kennedy

Maryland is a state often overlooked for its rock-climbing potential. However, rock climbing is sprinkled throughout the state. It ranges in elevation from sea level in its coastal and Chesapeake Bay regions to more than 3,300 feet in the western reaches of the state.

The Eastern Shore is predominantly low, rolling farmland and pine forests interspersed with marshy bottomlands. Little is found here in the way of rock climbing. However, as one moves west, the tempo picks up with fun climbing in areas such as Rocks State Park (a John Stannard playground).

In central Maryland the rich agricultural belt of the Piedmont plateau arises. The most used areas of the state are found here. These include Great Falls and Carderock, just outside of Washington, D.C. One can find more secluded climbing at Annapolis Rocks and Catoctin State Park, broken by the ridges of the Catoctin Mountains.

The Eastern Continental Divide passes through western Maryland, where the Youghiogheny River watershed drains north to the Ohio River System. Western Maryland has long been the guru garden of eastern kayaking. For climbers areas like Rocky Gap lend themselves to climbing development. With some rock sleuthing, other areas will hopefully be discovered in future years.

1 Rocky Gap State Park ✩✩

A 100' south-facing quartzite crag. An arc of cliffs on south side of gap. Discontinuous chunks of rock on north side. Spring/autumn. Pay camping in state park (301-777-2139).
Ref: Guidebook: Canter's *Nearby Climbing Areas.*
Directions: From Cumberland, go north on I-68 to exit 50. Turn left over bridge into park. Follow road in park veering left past lodge and continuing to two climbing areas: 1) Canyon Overlook Nature Trail: Walk five minutes to overlook; rocks below. 2) North end of dam and waterway rockcut: Cliffs to west of spillway. Cliffs line opening through south end of Evitts Mountain. Found on Evitts Creek 7.5' topo.

2 Catoctin State Park (Cat Rock, Chimney Rock, and Wolf Rock) ✩✩✩

That cat's a real scooter, man! Smooth 50' quartzite face and small pinnacle on southeast side of Cat Rock knob on topo. Detached pinnacle at north end is Wolf's Head. Many short, difficult climbs on this large broken plate. Park service states, "A rock climbing permit may only be issued for Wolf Rock." All other areas within the park are closed to rock climbing and rappelling. The permittee may call the visitors center up to five days in advance to make a reservation for rock-climbing groups. The party will pick up and sign the permit on the day they are scheduled to climb. Walk-in permits are issued depending upon site availability. Climbing helmets are required. Climbing is permitted 10:00 A.M. until 4:30 P.M. on weekdays and from 8:30 A.M. to 5:00 P.M. on weekends. Limit of twenty-five people total (families, individuals), or one organized group not to exceed twenty-five members. Permits are not issued on weekends in October due to high visitation park-wide. A climber writes of the bouldering at Cunningham Falls in Catoctin (1998): "Although there is a very limited quantity of rock here, the bouldering that does exist is of very high quality. Cunningham Falls quartzite bouldering (the best here) exists on the far or left side of the falls. Near the top of the falls (to the left of the boulder in the middle of the falls), there is a shallow cave that offers an extremely exciting finishing move, a dyno to the last jug, directly above the falls. Near the bottom of the falls, many harder problems with smaller holds exist. Cunningham Falls has problems up to V5. A nice day's worth of tugging. Most of the rock worth climbing is overhanging, some with jugs, some with crimpers. Be careful not to tick off the tourists at the falls, and use caution on some problems, there is a potential for a fall into the waterfall!" Check out Cat, Wolf, and Chimney Rock in Catoctin State Park while you are there. For more bouldering look at the Hog Rock Trail just across the road. Lots of good climbing can be found a little off the trail. Camping can also be found in several areas in Catoctin State Park (301-663-9330).
Classics: Bouldering and detached blocks.
Ref: 2/99; G. Collins; Mark's Guide to "Hidden" Climbing Areas on-line guide; www.we.comehome.org/climbing/in-house; Guidebook: Canter's *Nearby Climbing Areas.*

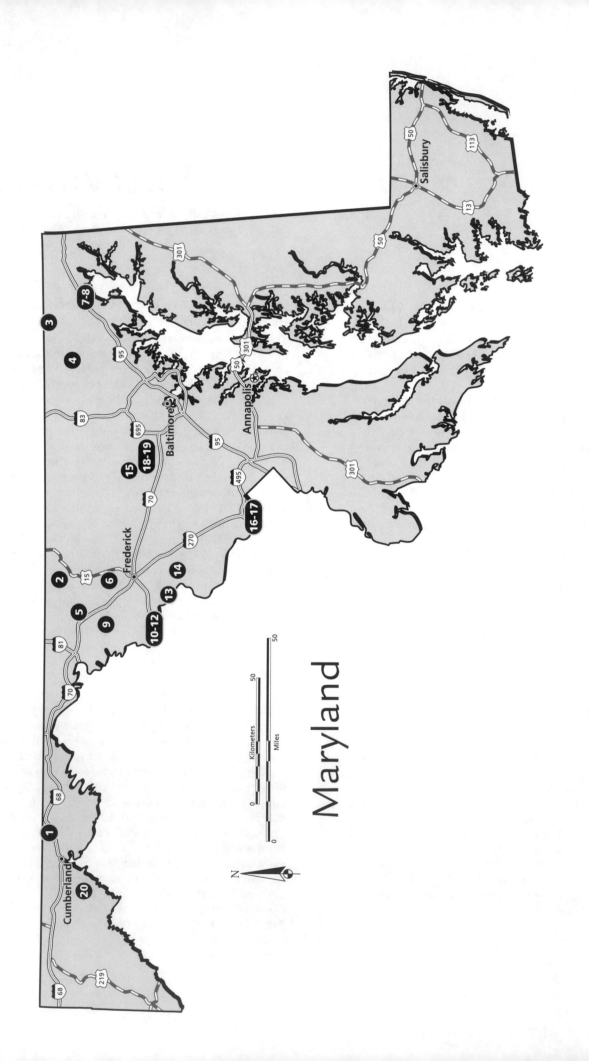

Maryland

Directions: From Thurmont pounce west on Maryland Hwy. 77 into Catoctin State Park. See park map or Catoctin Furnace 7.5′ topo. Wolf Rock is most popular and only legal climbing formation. From Wolf's Head parking area, ten-minute uphill hike. Cunningham Falls has best bouldering. Ask at ranger's office for more information.

3 Wilson (Wildcat) Point

Eighty routes on this 90′ granite crag. Spring/autumn. Private land.

Classics: Tremors, Get Mad, The Fringe.

Ref: E. Mistarka 9/98; Guidebook: Canter's *Nearby Climbing Areas*.

Directions: Between town of Peach Bottom and Bald Friar Rd. via dirt road along railroad tracks. Wildcat Point is found on Conowingo Dam 7.5′ topo. (The railroad personnel told us that the southern tunnel was called Wildcat, the middle tunnel Wilson, and the north tunnel Frazer. All the climbing development was nearest the middle tunnel and at the parking lot at Cooks Landing Rd.) Many sheer cliffs on railroad cuts on east side of river. Especially good cliff on ridge above the southernmost railroad tunnel. Ed Mistarka has been a primary developer of many sport climbs in this section of the Susquehanna Valley and is working with the Access Fund closely on access problems on the private land here.

4 Rocks State Park ★★★

Bust a move, ye terrapins, and all assorted others on this 110′ conglomerate crag with seventy-five routes. Two toprope areas. Uncertain if open to climbing. Check first with rangers. Spring–autumn. No camping in state park (410-557-7994).

Classics: Breakaway, Vertical, Golden Arches 5.10+toprope, Biceptstentials 5.10+ toprope.

Ref: Mistarka 9/98, G. Collins; C 160-38; www.nobeta.com/rocksair.html; Guidebook: Canter's *Nearby Climbing Areas*.

Directions: From Forest Hill rock north on Hwy. 24 to park. Found on Fawn Grove 7.5′ topo. Rocks State Park is roughly one hour northeast of Baltimore.

5 Annapolis Rocks/Black Rock ★★

Long 60′ quartzite crag cliff with many pinnacles and overhangs with a wide variety of routes and grades and featuring a huge roof. Spring–autumn. Camping and spring available on Appalachian Trail. Camping on forest land.

Classics: Pine Tree 9, Nixon's Nose A1, north side overhang 10, Twin Pyramids 10+, south end overhang on north end and overhanging crack/face on south end.

Ref: G. Collins; Mark's Guide to "Hidden" Climbing Areas on-line guide www.welcomehome.org/climbing/in-house/; Guidebook: Canter's *Nearby Climbing Areas*.

Directions: From Hagerstown go south on I–70 to South Mountain. Annapolis Rocks are at head of hollow, north of I–70 (visible) on South Mountain. Where I–70 crosses Alt. 40, find a parking area on Alt. 40 on north side of road. Hike north on Appalachian Trail (AT) 1 mi. Rocks on left. Black Rock is located farther north on AT from Annapolis Rocks. Found on Myersville 7.5′ topo.

6 White Rock (Yellow Springs Area) ★★

Three climbing areas to check out if you're near Yellow Springs. The first area here is a quartzite crag with a large ceiling and a few hard climbs. The sun warms up this cliff quickly. The second area is a small bouldering area north of Yellow Springs; good for kids since it is roadside. The third area is another small but interesting schist cliff area north of Frederick in a pleasant wooded streamside area. It's a nice teaching area with classic 45′ wall for toproping or leading, and a fun 5.10 overhanging boulder face. Camping pullouts along road. Spring/autumn. City of Frederick Water Conservation Area.

Ref: Guidebook: Canter's *Nearby Climbing Areas*.

Directions: From Yellow Springs (north of Frederick; take Rosemount Rd. exit off I–15, go north on Rosemount Rd. to Yellow Springs): 1) For the first area wend 1 ½ mi. northwest to a white-blazed trail leading to the prominent White Rock cliff on Catoctin Mountain. Found on Frederick 7.5′ topo. 2) For the second area follow Yellow Springs Rd. for 1 9/10 mi. to obvious roadside boulders (minimal). 3) The third area is found in one of two ways. Continue up road to first right. Turn right and follow a few miles to a T. Turn right and follow downstream for a short time till rocks appear on right. Or from Frederick at I–270 follow I–15 north for 9 mi. to Mountaindale Rd. Go north on Mountaindale Rd. for 2 7/10 mi. and veer left (still on Mountaindale Rd.) for 2 more miles, following road past lake to rocks on right. Park on left.

7 Velvet Rock

An outward-arching face marks this 70′ crag. Private land.

Ref: Guidebook: Canter's *Nearby Climbing Areas*.

Directions: North of Havre de Grace. Velvet Rock is on west side of Susquehanna River at I–95. Found on Havre de Grace 7.5′ topo.

8 Arundel Quarry

This quarry, owned by Arundel Corp., contains an overhanging wall and other faces on a coarse-grained, granite gneiss with an obvious foliation produced by black mica. The rock was used in early days by colonial settlers, but commercial use did not occur until about 1816, when stone was needed for the abutments to the Susquehanna River Bridge. Private land.

Ref: Guidebook: Canter's *Nearby Climbing Areas*.

Directions: Havre de Grace. Arundel Quarry is on west side of river and north of B&O Railroad tracks. Found on

Havre de Grace 7.5' topo. More small outcrops to north along Susquehanna River.

9 Washington's Monument State Park ✬

Round, man-made 40' block tower offers buildering. First monument to George Washington. Museum with slide presentation. Pay camping in this state park (301–791–4767).

Ref: Tourist brochure.

Directions: From Boonsboro forge east on Hwy. 40 to Washington's Monument State Park (signs). Cylindrical stone monument on the Appalachian Trail.

10 Maryland Heights (aka Elk Bluff) ✬✬

There is more to Maryland Heights than meets the eye. What usually meets the eye is the 400' quartzite face with the old powder sign painted on it. On the ridge surrounding the main cliffs is what climbers call Skink Rock—there are tons of skinks always seen there. Another set of cliffs yet unnamed, a two-tier bouldering area, currently has seventeen problems and the potential for about thirty more problems. Miscellaneous boulders sit off by themselves. One boulder, called Balc Junior, sits uphill and upriver from what we currently believe is the official Balcony Rock. This area has many harder routes. It is slightly overhanging face climbing with a bulge at the eastern end that has a cave area under it. This bulge of seemingly easy overhanging rock serves as a great place to toast your arms and force yourself to get some technique. There are also many other small faces in Maryland Heights that we simply haven't had enough time to work on. Watch for rock fall; bring helmets. Get permission from Harper's Ferry rangers. Free camping along canal or at Antietam to north. Spring/autumn. NPS.

Ref: C. Schaefer 6/98; Guidebook: Canter's *Nearby Climbing Areas*.

Directions: At Harpers Ferry, on north shore of Potomac River at confluence with Shenandoah River. Found on Harpers Ferry 7.5' topo. Register at Harpers Ferry NPS Ranger Station. More information: Take Hwy. 340 toward Harpers Ferry from Maryland. Turn left on Keep Tryst Rd., then a right after liquor store on Canal Rd. (name of road uncertain). This takes you down through Sandy Hook under a train trestle and along the Potomac River. Parking along Canal Rd. on right. Other options include parking in Harpers Ferry, West Virginia, and walking over the pedestrian bridge, which goes over the Potomac River and directly toward the main Maryland Heights's face. You must check in with rangers in Harpers Ferry if you are going to climb the Main Face or anything upriver of it. Uncertain if climbing on Balcony Rock is okay. Check in to be sure.

11 Balcony Rock ✬✬

Large overturned anticline composes this 40' quartzite crag. White Horse Rapids drowns out climbing signals. Sunny. Check in with rangers in Harpers Ferry. NPS.

Ref: Guidebook: Canter's *Nearby Climbing Areas*.

Directions: From Sandy Hook look just west of town to Balcony Rock, on north shore of Potomac River. Found on Harpers Ferry 7.5' topo.

12 Weverton Cliff ✬✬

Moderately high quartzite cliffs capped by large overhang.

Ref: Guidebook: Canter's *Nearby Climbing Areas*.

Directions: At Weverton, off Hwy. 340. Weverton Cliff is east of Harpers Ferry, at south end of South Mountain. Found on Harpers Ferry 7.5' topo.

13 Point of Rocks ✬

Overhanging 40' black schist cliffs overlooking the Potomac river. Upper cliffs are cleaner; lower cliffs near railroad tracks are overgrown. Questionable rock quality.

Ref: Guidebooks: Canter's *Nearby Climbing Areas*, C & O Canal Guide.

Directions: From the town of Point of Rocks at junction of Hwys. 15 and 28, go east on Hwy. 28 and immediately take right on road to C & O Canal Park and Trail (signs). Follow road around house and cross over bridge; then turn right to parking under tracks. Walk 100 ft. to cliff base. At end of Catoctin Mountain, Point of Rocks is found east of Hwy. 15 and south of Hwy. 28. See Point of Rocks 7.5' topo. Faces west.

14 Sugarloaf (1,282') ✬✬

This 140' quartzite monadnock is a popular practice area possessing short climbs of all difficulties. Scenic views of the distant Potomac River. Across the ridge, south-facing cliffs offer other climbs. Camping down road at canal. Private land of Stronghold Inc.

Classics: Butterfingers, Rhythm Roof, and The Prow 5.12 roof.

Ref: Lakey; Mark's Guide to "Hidden" Climbing Areas online guide www.welcomehome.org/climbing/in-house/; Guidebook: Canter's *Nearby Climbing Areas*.

Directions: From Frederick go approximately 15 mi. south on I–270 to exit 22. Turn left and go south on Hwy. 109. Turn right on Hwy. 95 for a few miles to Stronghold (great name for a town near a climbing area, heh?). Sugarloaf is featured just north of this small town. Turn right on Comus Rd. for about 2 mi. to Sugarloaf Mountain entrance. Follow road thru gate winding up mountain for a couple miles to East View Overlook. Two climbing areas exist: 1) Devil's Kitchen, just a few minutes walk west of East View Overlook, and 2) Summit Crags, just a few more minutes up road from East View to West View parking lot. Park. Follow trail past concession stand for 10-minute hike turning right before stairs into scree field to small cliffs. Good hi ball bouldering or short cragging exist to left of stairs as well. Found on Buckeystown 7.5' topo.

15 Bassard Rock

Mostly easy climbing on this gneiss crag, with an appealing open book. Rotten bands exist. Possibly government land.

Ref: Guidebook: Canter's *Nearby Climbing Areas.*

Directions: Bassard Rock lies west of Baltimore on north bank of Patapsco River approximately ½ mi. east of Bloedes Dam. Found on Relay 7.5' topo.

16 Great Falls ☆☆☆

Small 60' schist clifflets along peaceful Potomac River offer the D.C. climbers an enjoyable after-work climbing area. The rock on the Maryland portion of the Potomac Gorge is overall less steep than Virginia. The Virginia side offers more climbing and thus receives more attention. Climbing has gone on here since the 1920s. Free camping is available on "hike-bike" campgrounds. A "capital" climbing idea if you're touring Washington, D.C. NPS.

Classics: AAU Rock: AAU Crack 10+; The Bulges: G.F. Bulge 8, Super Bulge 11; Mather Gorge: Phrygian 10, Mixolidian 11; Purple Horse: Barn Roof.

Ref: G. Collins; Appalachia 6/43; Mark's Guide to "Hidden" Climbing Areas on-line guide www.welcomehome.org/climbing/in-house/; Guidebooks: Harlin's *East,* Eakin's *Climbers Guide to Great Falls of the Potomac,* Nelson and Grossman's *A Climber's Guide to Great Falls Park,* PATC's Map D, Potomac Gorge Climber's Edition.

Directions: From Washington, D.C., Great Falls is west on MacArthur Blvd. on north shore of Potomac River to Cropley parking at Old Angler's Inn. Hike west on tow-path to crags for: 1) Angler's Inn Rock: 150 yd. west on towpath on left. 2) Sherwin Island (Cupid's Bower): Hike west ¼ mi. on canal towpath. Cross (wade) at culvert on left in river to east side of Sherwin Island. 3) Spitzbergen (aka AAU Rock): From Old Angler's Inn, ¾ mi. and 200 yd. past bridge at Widewater to trail on left. Purple Horse: 100 yd. farther east. 4) Mather Gorge: 1 mi. from Old Angler's Inn, then to river. Or, continue to Great Falls Tavern Visitor Center parking. Go south for The Bulges: From Great Falls Tavern Visitor Center, go ½ mi. south and right off Billy Goat Trail. For Rocky Islands: North and south ends of isle west of Bulges.

17 Carderock ☆☆☆

Diminutive and venerable 30' schist microslab problems in a breath of fresh air outside the nation's capital. Dubbed the "Grease of the East," the climbing here is akin to driving on bald tires when it's raining cats and dogs. Expect weekday crowds and big challenges on small holds with many microvariations. More problems here than in the U.S. economy. Protect topropes from sharp edges with auxiliary webbing sheath. For multipitch climbs check out the four arêtes on the Washington Monument in D.C. (just kidding).

Classics: Easy Layback 4, Cripple's Crack 9, The Dream 10-12, Silver Spot 12/13.

Ref: C [93, 91]; Sherman's *Stone Crusade;* Guidebooks: PATC's *Carderock: Past and Present,* Canter's *Nearby*

Luis Gouffray enjoying Slow and Easy, 5.7, Sugarloaf Mountain

Climbing Areas, Harlin's *East,* Gregory's *Climber's Guide to Carderock.*

Directions: From Washington, D.C., go west on MacArthur Blvd. along north shore of Potomac River until Carderock is reached. Climbing along river a short leg stretch from parking area. (Great Falls climbing area is farther west along MacArthur Blvd.)

18 Patapsco Valley State Park (McKeldin Area)

The climbing here is a mixture of granite, sandstone, and quartzite. There is much more climbing throughout the park that needs to be established. Try Ilchester Rock. There are rumors of cliffs up to 50' high. When on the trail, watch out for speeding mountain bikers. State park, (410) 461–5005.

Ref: 2/98.

Directions: From Columbia take Hwy. 29 north to Hwy. 70 west. Get off at Marriottsville Rd. (exit 83). Follow Marriottsville Rd. until you see the turnoff for the McKeldin Area on the right. Follow the road all the way back to the rapids area. Park above the steep road going down the hill and walk down the road. Make a left onto a paved road/trail, and then get on the switchback trail. Follow the trail until you get to the climbing/bouldering areas. Also, bouldering and toprope area at Catonsville.

19 Woodstock Rock

Relatively unknown 40′ sandstone area offers some great climbing. There is a huge bouldering cave and several face routes. The climbing here is unique with many bulges. A great area that is close to the metropolitan area. BIA.

Classics: Bouldering in Cave.

Ref: 6/98.

Directions: From Columbia take Hwy. 29N to where it dead-ends at Route 99. At Route 99, go left for about fifteen minutes. Go right on Woodstock Rd. When you get to the Woodstock Inn, park in the lot on the left of the road. Follow the train tracks to the left for about ¼ mi. Rocks will be on left.

20 Dan's Rock ✭

Beautifully spray-painted, bomber-hard quartzite rock up to 40′ high with one 5.10 face route. Short, easy climbs to one bolted 5.10 face overhang. This place is trashed but nice views of the West Virginia mountain and valley country. County land and Department of Maryland Natural Resources.

Ref: Maryland Welcome Center information specialist.

Direction: From I-68 and exit 34 (southeast of Frostburg), roll 8 mi. south on Hwy. 36. Just before town of Midland (look for signs to Dan's Rock), turn left on Paradise Rd. for ²/10 mi. Turn left at signs for Dan's Rock Rd., southwest following up mountain for 3 mi. to parking area on right with steps. Climbing below. Faces east.

Massachusetts

Some men see things that are and ask why, I see things that are not yet and ask why not. —John F. Kennedy

Massachusetts has arguably the most well-known rock in America, amongst nonclimbers that is. Plymouth Rock figured big in the early history of the colonies. Ever since, Massachusetts has cranked out historical events and personages: witch hunts, the birth of basketball and volleyball, JFK, and Hot Henry Barber.

Boston has the Celtics, baked beans, and several urban crags, bouldering areas, and building climbs. Quincy Quarries and Hammond Pond are recommended. Cape Cod has sand, clam chowder, Martha's Vineyard and Nantucket. Western Massachusetts doesn't have Harvard, but it does have areas like Great Barrington and the Berkshire Mountains to lend charm to a climbing trip.

1 Pine Cobble ✫

Thirty-foot beginner/intermediate quartzite crag. Ask at Williams Outing Club for information. Spring/autumn. Government land.
Classics: S Crack 9.
Directions: Williamstown, off Cole Ave. Hike northeast through woods on abandoned logging roads to Pine Cobble. Good luck!

2 GB✫–(Great Barrington Area) Monument Mountain ●

A 120′ metamorphic, east-facing beginner/intermediate crag described as dirty and mossy; where nuts grind out of the rock. Also, loose, blocky razor-sharp rock . . . dangerous to ropes. Possibly "shall we gather at the river" potential. More information for Barrington areas available at Simon's Rock College in Great Barrington. Spring/autumn. Government land.
Ref: C [116, 107].
Directions: From Great Barrington go north on Hwy. 7 to Monument Mountain (signs). Hike ten minutes west on trail. Devil's Pulpit is a freestanding pinnacle above Monument Mountain parking lot. North Buttress is a sweep of rock with overhangs.

3 GB–Bung Hill ✫✫✫✫

This 45′ intermediate crag features uncrowded leads on 70′ routes and granite bouldering. Access sensitive—keep low profile. Spring/autumn. Private/government land.
Classics: Berkshire Sampler 10d, Sunnyside Wall (5.7–5.11 topropes/bouldering).
Ref: 4/98; C 107.
Directions: In Great Barrington. Bung Hill is rocky prominence above junction of Hwy. 7 and Hwy. 23E. Take trail west of billboards on Hwy. 7 north of Great Barrington. Park at East St. There is a gas station/car wash that allows climbers to access the crag from a trail next to its dumpster.

4 GB–Reservoir Rocks and East Mountain ✫✫✫

An uncrowded 100′ granite crag with twenty-five short leads. Other areas being developed along East Rock Trail, Brush Hill Slabs, and Icy Gulch (East Mountain State Forest). Access sensitive—maintain low profile. Best to consult with locals to find access routes on state property. And at Reservoir Rocks, you have to be careful where you park, because the natives tend to get restless. Spring/autumn. Private land.
Classics: Endeavor to Persevere 10.
Ref: 4/98; C [116, 107(4/88)-20].
Directions: Great Barrington. Park at Quarry St. near East St. Hike south along power lines to pole 52. Follow faint trail left into woods, then uphill and slightly right to Practice Cliff. Go around right end and up to main wall.

5 Black Rock

Inquire at Berkshire School for Black Rock information.

6 Rose Ledge ✫✫✫

The fragrance of the rose lingers on the hand that casts it. So does this 45′ gneiss toprope area with 151 routes. The bouldering is nice, too. Obscure guidebook by Williams College and Dartmouth. Spring/autumn. Government land.
Ref: A. Rubin; Guidebook: Rubin's *Rose Ledge Rock Climbs*.
Directions: From Miller Falls follow Hwy. 47N. Turn onto Hwy. 63N to Northeast Utilities Northfield Mountain Recreation Area on right. Hike twenty minutes on trail to Rose Ledges. See map at visitors center.

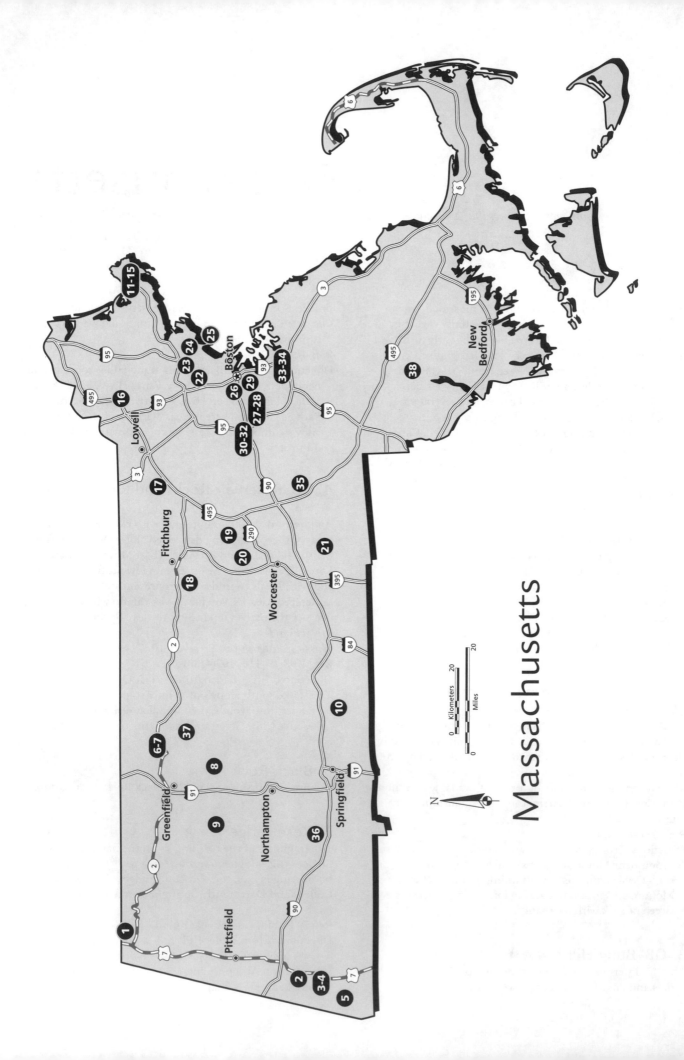

Massachusetts

11-15

25

24

23

22

16

Lowell

495

95

93

95

26

29

33-34

27-28

30-32

Boston

93

95

38

New Bedford

195

495

95

17

Fitchburg

495

19

290

20

Worcester

35

90

21

18

395

2

84

10

37

6-7

8

Greenfield

91

9

Northampton

36

Springfield

91

Pittsfield

90

1

7

2

3-4

5

7

N

0 Kilometers 20

0 Miles 20

7 Farley Ledge ✯✯✯✯

Best lead climbing in Massachusetts contains parallel-sided cracks, large roofs, and steep slabs on this 100' gneiss crag. Gorgeous rock mimics gritstone. Good ice climbing as well. Sensitive access. Spring–autumn. Government/private land.
Classics: 5.9 hand cracks, Middle Trinity Crack 11b, J-Crack 12a; The Thrill of Victory V8.
Ref: C [108, 106, 99].
Directions: Farley. On west edge of town north of Hwy. 2. Visible from road. Ask at Amherst climbing shops.

8 Rattlesnake Gutter ✯✯

Sixty-foot gneiss crag. Spring/autumn. Possibly private land.
Ref: C 108.
Directions: From Leverett go just north of town via Montague St. Tricky access to Rattlesnake Gutter—check locally.

9 Chapel Ledges ✯✯

Sixty-five-foot granite crag makes for good introductory climbing area. Great swimming. Spring–autumn. State park.
Classics: 5.3 classics, The Bulge 5.8, Forget-Me-Knot 11+.
Ref: P. Burton 7/98, R. Murnane; C 98; Guidebook: Wilcox's *Climber's Guide to Chapel Ledges*.
Directions: From Northampton go northwest on Hwy. 9 to center of Williamsburg. At flashing yellow light, take right on Ashfield Rd. for 11 mi. to Chapel Ledges.

10 Bunyan Mountain ✯✯

One-hundred-and-forty-foot metamorphic beginner/intermediate crag. Spring to autumn.
Classics: Good 10 and 11 cracks, Eyeless in Gaza 11.
Ref: C 116(10/89)-29.
Directions: At Monson. From Hwy. 32 go west on Bunyan Rd. Park at ROAD ENDS 500 FT sign. Hike along dirt road, going left at forks. When road ends, angle left through woods to Bunyan Mountain.

11 Dogtown Commons Bouldering ✯✯

Granite bouldering. Park and explore. Summer/autumn.
Ref: C; Guidebook: La Forge's *Boston Rolls*.
Directions: From Gloucester (Hwy. 1N from Boston to east on Hwy. 128), romp north on Hwy. 127 for 2 mi. Turn onto Dogtown Rd. east for 2 mi. to Dogtown Commons.

12 Atlantic Ave. (at Gloucester)

Twenty-foot-high wide cracks in a residential area. Spring/autumn. Private land.
Ref: Guidebook: La Forge's *Boston Rolls*.
Directions: Gloucester. From Concord and Atlantic Ave., go east on Atlantic Ave. Crag on west side of street. Slightly visible from road.

13 Concord St. (at Gloucester)

Forty-five-foot crag with two good cracks at far end of cliff. Spring/autumn. Private land.
Classics: Jammin, One Little Indian.
Ref: Guidebooks: La Forge's *Boston Rolls*, Hendricks's *Climbing in Eastern Massachusetts*.
Directions: Gloucester. Near Atlantic Ave. and Redrock. At Hwy. 128 exit 14 (0.0 mi.), go north on Hwy. 133. At 1 9/10 mi., turn right onto Harlow St. At 2 1/2 mi. veer right on Concord Rd. At 2 9/10 mi., park on left. Hike back toward Concord Rd. Cross field near house (uncertain if there is a small trail).

14 Redrocks ✯✯

Bring long 30' slings for anchors at this 70' granite top-rope area. Spring/autumn. Access trail on private land, crag is on City of Gloucester property.
Classics: Zipper 5, Toejams 5, Morning Glory 8+, Ray's Picture 10-, Rip Van Winkle 10.
Ref: Guidebook: La Forge's *Boston Rolls*.
Directions: From Gloucester hop west on Hwy. 128 to exit 14. Go west on Hwy. 133 for ten seconds and park on its west side at field abutting Hwy. 128. Hike west 4/10 mi. along Hwy. 128 to NO PARKING signs (old Redrock parking area). Enter woods to east of signs and then north 250 yd. to cliff. South and North Areas. Good bouldering in the woods.

15 Stage Fort Park ✯✯

Fun surfing the 40' granite slab routes on the beaches. Trees and bolts for anchors—long anchor slings necessary. Spring–autumn. City of Gloucester Park.
Classics: C Shell 7, The Deep Six 9, Jaws 10.
Ref: Guidebooks: La Forge's *Boston Rocks*, Hendrick and Striebert's *Climbing in Eastern Massachusetts*.
Directions: From Gloucester, at junction of Hwy. 127 Western Ave. and Hwy. 133 (Essex St.), turn west on Hwy. 127. Stage Fort Park entrance is near this junction on ocean side of Hwy. 127. Parking fee after 9:00 A.M. or park along Western Ave. 2/10 mi. west of entrance. Main Crag faces west away from shore. Beach Buttress is around to the northeast.

16 Denrock ✯✯

Beginner's topropes on these 30' granite walls. Good bouldering, too. Coarse rocks are rough on ropes. Summer/autumn. Pay camping a few mi. down Route 114.
Classics: Bulge 7, Finger Rippin' Good 10, Painted Lady 9/11.
Ref: C 166(2/97)-34; Guidebooks: Appalachian Mountain Club's *Rock Climbs North of Boston*, La Forge's *Boston Rocks*, Hendrick and Striebert's *Climbing in Eastern Massachusetts*.
Directions: In Lawrence. At I–495, take exit 42A. Turn east on Hwy. 114 for 4/10 mi. Park. Hike south away from shopping mall to Denrock.

> ## Massachusetts Road Thoughts
> F=MA
> —Sir Isaac Newton

17 Westford Quarries
These quarries provide slab climbing opportunities. Private land.
Ref: Guidebook: Duval's *Guide to Westford Quarries.*
Directions: Quarries in Westford.

18 Crow Hill (at Leominster State Forest) ☆☆☆
This 100' wooded, steep gritstone crag is very popular (possibly crowded). Early eastern U.S. 5.11s were put up here . . . bold Henry Barber leads. Spring–autumn. State forest, (978) 874-2303.
Classics: Open Book 5, Intertwine 8, Watusi 9, Melissa's Madness 10, Cro-Magnon Crack 10, Jane 11, Dune 13a R/X.
Ref: C [195-22, 122, (7/74), (11/75)], R 101-30; Guidebooks: Hall's *A Guide to Crow Hill,* Phillips's *Crow Hill,* Webster's *The Crow Hill Guidebook,* La Forge's *Boston Rocks,* Harlin's *East,* Rubin's *Central Massachusetts Climbing Areas,* Hendrick and Striebert's *Climbing in Eastern Massachusetts.*
Directions: From East Princeton (one hour from Boston), fly 2 mi. northwest on Hwy. 140. Turn 1 3/10 mi. on Hwy. 31. Park at Crow Hill Pond. Hike 1/2 mi. west.

19 Berlin Boulder ☆
Short, 12–18' granite boulder problems. Spring–autumn. Private land.
Classics: Jug or Not 6, Flea Bag 9.
Ref: Guidebook: La Forge's *Boston Rocks.*
Directions: From Worcester take Hwy. 70 northeast. Turn east onto Hwy. 62. Take West St. north for 1/2 mi. Turn on Randall Rd. east for 3/4 mi. Turn on Lancaster Rd. north for 1 mi. Park on left across from greenhouses for Berlin Boulder.

20 Boylston Quarry
Nobody climbs here; will you? Sixty-foot granite crag.
Classics: Hamstrung 9+.
Ref: Guidebook: La Forge's *Boston Rocks.*
Directions: From Worcester take Hwy. 70 northeast for 9 mi. (just before Hwy. 62 East and east of Wachuset Reservoir Dam). Park on left. Hike 1/4 mi. east on dirt road at end of guardrail for Boylston Quarry.

21 Purgatory Chasm State Park ●
Cool, shady 70' granite walls tend to be a bit dirty. Need a climbing permit. An episode of *Rescue 911* was filmed here

in 1992—watch your step! Spring/autumn. Pay camping in state park (508–234–3733).
Classics: The Apocalypse 4, Divine Comedy 10, Last Cornice 10, The Inferno 10+.
Ref: Guidebooks: La Forge's *Boston Rocks,* Hendrick and Striebert's *Climbing in Eastern Massachusetts.*
Directions: From Worcester take Hwy. 146 south to Purgatory Chasm State Park. Follow signs.

22 Black and White Rocks ●
Wait 'til you see it . . . possibly a 25' horizontal bouldering pile. Or as one climber put it, "There is no shame in poverty, but what am I doing climbing here?"
Classics: Easy Overhang 6, Madcap 4.
Ref: Guidebooks: La Forge's *Boston Rocks,* Hendrick and Striebert's *Climbing in Eastern Massachusetts.*
Directions: Melrose. At Felsway East and East Border Rd., go east on East Border Rd. Black and White Rocks are to the north between Woodland St. and Glen Rock Rd. on jeep trails.

23 Castle Hill ●
Beginner climbs on a rounded 40' dome. Obscure, low quality. State reservation land.
Ref: Guidebooks: La Forge's *Boston Rocks,* Hendrick and Striebert's *Climbing in Eastern Massachusetts.*
Directions: Saugus. From Hwy. 1 go northwest on Main St. to Breakheart Reservation. Park at power lines. Hike at power lines 100 yd. northeast to Castle Hill domes.

24 Lynn Woods (Lantern Rock) ●
Lantern Rock (25') is the big draw here. More climbing at Burr Hill Observation Tower. Municipal park.
Ref: Guidebooks: La Forge's *Boston Rocks,* Hendrick and Striebert's *Climbing in Eastern Massachusetts.*
Directions: Saugus. From Hwy. 1 and Walnut St., go east into park on Walnut St. Turn left onto Pennybrook St. Park just past gate at Birch Pond. Lantern Rock is to east.

25 Fort Ruckman (Nahant) ☆
Small 25' oceanside cliff for beginners. Possibly the only sea-cliff climbing in Massachusetts. Bring a long extension sling for topropes. Potentially loose rock. Government land.
Classics: Repeat Performance 6, Innovative Imitation 7.
Ref: Guidebooks: La Forge's *Boston Rocks,* Hendrick and Striebert's *Climbing in Eastern Massachusetts.*
Directions: From Lynn go south on Nahant Rd. onto peninsula. Turn right onto Castle Rd. Turn left onto Bass Point Rd. to end. Hike beyond gate to south on pavement over Bailey's Hill to Fort Ruckman Park (World War II vintage). Once inside the fort gate, follow paved road to south over Bailey's Hill to rocks bordering the ocean. (Parking close to cliff is a problem with police. Recommended option: Park at MDC lot on isthmus between Lynn and Little Nahant, then walk or cycle.)

26 Esoteric Boston Areas–MIT Domes, John Hancock Tower, et al.; Delle Ave. (Hyde Park); Northboro Arches, Rockport Quarries, Johnson's Quarries, Wachusett Dam (Clinton) ✮✮

Intellectual buildering at M.I.T. See Boston Rolls, the guidebook describing Boston buildering areas and the only climbing guidebook with really "exposed" climbers.

Ref: Guidebooks: La Forge's *Boston Rocks,* La Forge's *Boston Rolls,* Hendrick and Striebert's *Climbing in Eastern Massachusetts,* Hollerback and King's *MIT Boulderer's Guide.*

Directions: Esoteric Boston Areas–MIT Domes (various places on the M.I.T. campus); John Hancock Tower, et al.; Delle Ave. (Hyde Park); Northboro Arches, Rockport Quarries, Johnson's Quarries, and Wachusett Dam (Clinton).

27 Route 9 Boulder ✮

A single 15′ boulder to include on a Hammond Pond foray.

Ref: Guidebooks: La Forge's *Boston Rocks,* Hendrick and Striebert's *Climbing in Eastern Massachusetts.*

Directions: Newton (Boston suburb). On Route 9, Route 9 Boulder is ⁹/₁₀ mi. west of Hammond Pond Pkwy.

28 Hammond Pond ✮✮✮

"Bouldering at Bloomingdale's." Crank on sharp edges on novel 30′ conglomerate rock called "puddingstone" in this 300-acre nature preserve now sandwiched between mansions and shopping malls. Bouldering since the 1920s. Seven or eight cliffs—from difficult fingery cranks to easy topropes on slabs. Hardmen and -women will find the overhanging Alcove and Pusherman's Wall the most challenging. State reserve and city park.

Classics: Lower Walls: Cracker Jack 6; The Alcove: Over Easy 8, Breakfast of Champions 11, Hammond Eggs 12; Pusherman Wall: The Snort 9, Cold Turkey 5.11, Hepatitis 12, Goofball 12, Ecstasy 13 (Mallery Eliminate); The Dealer 11; Cutters 6.

Ref: C [186, 139, 138, 120], J 90-30, S 9/81; Sherman's *Stone Crusade;* Guidebooks: La Forge's *Boston Rocks,* La Forge's *Boston Rolls,* Hendrick and Striebert's *Climbing in Eastern Massachusetts.*

Directions: Go 5 mi. west of downtown Boston in Chestnut Hill. Several parking areas for Hammond Pond: 1) At junction of Hwy. 9 (Boylston St.) and Hammond Pond Pkwy. (HPP). Turn east on HPP and park at pond parking by the Chestnut Hill Shopping Center. Hike west up slope to The Alcove. Rocks visible. Main Wall to left of The Alcove. 2) Temple Boulders (Pusherman Wall) farther west along HPP. Hike north of Temple a minute to boulders in trees. (Don't park on Temple property.) 3) North of Temple between Beacon St. and Green Line. Park on west. Hike west. Boston road map and talisman recommended for unguided out-of-towners.

29 Kenmore Walls (near Kenmore Square)/Charlesgate ✮

Ornamentally cut 20′ granite walls. Thin face problems. Area for the homeless. City park.

Classics: Kenmore Square: Warmup 7, Hop Skip and Jump 8, Sequence 9, Pipeline 9, Spiderman 10, B.C. 12; Charlesgate: Abracadabra 8, The N.A. 10.

Ref: Guidebooks: La Forge's *Boston Rocks,* Hendrick and Striebert's *Climbing in Eastern Massachusetts.*

Directions: Boston. East of Kenmore Square. Located on overpass linking Storrow and Park Dr. on the south side of Commonwealth Ave. and on south side of Beacon St. Cruxy parking. For Charlesgate walk from the Kenmore Square up on the overpass across the Mass. Turnpike, at which point the road forks. This is a long retaining wall adjacent to the Charles River Bridge. The East Area is a long retaining wall for the overpass starting near the turnpike and ending at the east side of the bridge. The West Area is on the opposite side of bridge.

30 Bates Boulder (aka Fairy Rock) ●

Unbelievable! Horizontal 15′ pile—feeble. Eleven easy bouldering problems with variations.

Classics: Fruit Market 7, Iron Cross.

Ref: Guidebooks: La Forge's *Boston Rocks,* Hendrick and Striebert's *Climbing in Eastern Massachusetts.*

Directions: West of Boston. Take Elmwood Rd. east to Kelley Memorial Park. Hike north ¼ mi. to Bates Boulder.

31 Waban Arches (in Boston) ✮

Excellent finger burners on aqueduct of cut 35′ granite blocks. There may be a climber's social on Thursday.

Ref: S 9/81; Guidebooks: La Forge's *Boston Rolls,* Hendrick and Striebert's *Climbing in Eastern Massachusetts.*

Directions: Waban Arches are in Wellesley (west of Boston) at a golf course. Ask locally. Be very discreet to preserve access.

32 Echo Bridge ✮✮✮

Bridge climbing on cut 35′ granite block. Private land. State land. Illegal.

Ref: S 8/81; Guidebooks: La Forge's *Boston Rolls,* Hendrick and Striebert's *Climbing in Eastern Massachusetts.*

Directions: Echo Bridge is in Newton.

33 Quincy Quarries (in Boston) ✮✮✮

The "hoi polloi" area of Boston (along with Hammond Pond). Tons of off-route eliminates in this over-loved Boston practice area have been established since the 1930s. More than 175 routes on 60′ granite walls. Toproping on this area's miniscule fingertip edges and molecular footholds is the norm. Pugnacious urbanites and high car-theft area; throw a few dobies in the backseat. Don't miss Quincy in the springtime. At press time, access to the J-Wall will be limited while the quarry is being drained and filled with dirt from Boston's Big Dig Project. The area around the deep part of the quarry has been fenced off. Access to the C, D, E, and F walls can be approached by ground. There is no more water at the base of these walls. State land.

Classics: Layback 5, Flake Direct 6, Satisfaction 7, Pink Face Center 7, Sigma 8, Big Biner 8, Ripple 9, Blocks 9, Sour Grapes 10, Bigtop 10, Parabola 10, Ladder Line 10+, East of Eden 11, Knightline 11, Church of LSD 12, Life Sentence 12.

Ref: D. Tabor 10/98; C 157-45, 149-63, S 9/81; Guidebooks: Strand's *Blasted Rock, Harvard MC,* La Forge's *Boston Rocks,* Hollerback's *Bouldering Around Boston,* Harlin's *East,* Hendrick and Striebert's *Climbing in Eastern Massachusetts,* Crowther and Thompson's *A Climber's Guide to Quincy Quarries.*

Directions: Southeast of Boston (approximately 6 mi). In Quincy follow Hwy. 93S. Turn on Willard St. (exit 8), going southeast. Turn onto Riccuti Dr. Park on left before quarry or farther up road before microwave tower on right. Hike to Quincy Quarries.

34 Rattlesnake Rocks (in Blue Hills Reservation) ✩✩✩

One cool face roof on this 30′ granite crag. Less crowded than nearby Quincy Quarries. P.S. There are rattlesnakes in the Blue Hills, but not at this crag. State land.

Classics: White Face 5, Ship's Prow 7, Flying Circus 9+, Cruising for Burgers 11, Elementary School 10/Roof 12a; Burger Boulder.

Ref: Guidebooks: La Forge's *Boston Rocks,* Hendrick and Striebert's *Climbing in Eastern Massachusetts.*

Directions: Southeast Boston. Take Hwy. 93S. Turn onto Willard St. (mm 8) southeast. Turn on Wampatuck Rd. southwest. Turn on Blue Hills (before Chickatawbut). (Old parking area that no longer exists: Park on right. Hike north.) New parking area: Park at Shea skating rink on Route 37 in Braintree and hike to the cliff. Too long and confusing access for here; see guidebook. At least four areas of climbing on the Blue Hills Reservation: Ship's Prow, Burger's Boulder, The Overlook, and The Playground.

35 College Rock ✩✩

Bring bouldering/short 45′ granite toproping accoutrements. Hopkinton is renowned as the start of the Boston Marathon. Town park.

Classics: Wasted 10-, My Mind Is A Blank 11; 200′ bouldering traverse V3.

Ref: Guidebook: La Forge's *Boston Rocks.*

Directions: From Hopkinton spurt south on Hwy. 85 for 2 ½ mi. Turn left on College St. for ½ mi. College Rock is on right. Hike a little ways on trail.

36 Tekoa Mountain

Recently discovered, undeveloped (but will be soon) 65′ crag. Has two faces, one with a chimney—good beginner climb. Also has tough climbs. Government land.

Ref: J. Lorenzatti.

Directions: From Westfield go west on Route 20; behind Strathmore Woronoco Paper Mill. Follow train tracks until you can see the local golf course across from you. Can only be reached by four-wheel-drive vehicle.

37 Mormon Hollow

At Wendell.

38 Rocky Woods (Taunton Bouldering Area)

Twenty-foot puddingstone boulders feature a Chris Trautz problem, The Crack V3.

Ref: www.newenglandbouldering.com/mass/taunton.html.

Directions: From Taunton go west on Hwy. 44. Turn right on North Walker St. Turn left on Rocky Woods Rd. Park when road gets rough (approximately 3/10 mi.) Hike about 300′ to cairned path. Go left for 100′, and then right to another cairn to The Wall (The Crack V3) first and the Warmup Boulders behind.

Michigan

If you must drink and drive, drive a limo. —TNT

If it weren't for Michigan, you wouldn't need this climbing atlas. Michigan, Detroit in particular, put the world on wheels. It also gave it soul via recordings from Motown Records. So, let your wheels carry your soul to the short but steep stone at Grand Ledges in the Lower Peninsula.

Does Michigan have hard rock? Well, it's a free-for-all with the blistering guitar riffs, Motor City Madman, Ted Nugent, or Bob Seger. This kind of rock 'n' roll could float one up to the far reaches of the Porcupine Mountains or the Keweenaw Peninsula in Upper Michigan.

Michigan Rock: Listen for it!

1 Keweenaw Peninsula ✯✯✯

An isolated, 4-mi.-long escarpment above the shores of Lake Superior. One-pitch climbs on red-gray 100′ basalt overlooking the Huron Mountains to the south. Excellent beginner and intermediate rock-climbing area with forty-five routes. Camping below Obsession Cliff. Michigan's Upper Peninsula (locally called the U.P.) is a sportsman's paradise with miles of forests and lakes for hunting, fishing, and hidden rock climbing. Late summer–autumn.
Classics: Last Call For Alcohol 7, Obsession 7, Stairway to Heaven 9.
Ref: T. Hahn 9/98; C 109(8/88)-26.
Directions: From Houghton take Hwy. 41 north for 24 3/10 mi. Just before village of Phoenix, turn left onto Cliff Dr. on the Keweenaw Peninsula. Obsession Cliff, 1/2 mi. south; J.C. Area, 1 1/2 mi. south along Cliff Dr. Park on road.

2 Lake of the Clouds (Porcupine Mountain State Park) ●

Rubbly volcanic crag rock with lofty views on this easily accessible 3-mi.-long escarpment. One reader writes of the rock, "Lead climbing would have been insane. Even top roping, the climbing still sucked. It was like climbing on Oreo cookies. Every hold you grabbed pulled off and started an avalanche below. If there is a good place to climb there I would really love to know where it is. We saw the entire escarpment by Lake of the Clouds and couldn't find it. If you go to the Porcupine Mountains, please go for the scenery, not the climbing." Guidebook author Alan Bagg writes, "The cliff, however, is at least three hundred feet of excellent rock wall with cracks and slabs similar to the basalt-formed north shore of Minnesota." And there you have it. The "Porkies" contain 58,000 acres in one of the Midwest's few remaining large wilderness areas and sport 80 mi. of trails in rugged hills with scenic vistas of a mile-long inland lake from a 1,300′ escarpment. Summer/autumn. State park, (906) 885-5275.
Ref: Guidebook: Bagg's *50 Short Climbs in the Midwest.*
Directions: From Silver City go west on Hwy. 107 to end of road at Lake of the Clouds overlook near west end of lakes. Cliffs are visible.

3 Norwich Ledge ✯✯

The Norwich Ledge Escarpment is a 5-mi.-long cliff of 300′ basalt features overlooking the west branch of the Ontonagon River. Summer/autumn. Government land.
Ref: Guidebook: Bagg's *50 Short Climbs in the Midwest.*
Directions: From Silver City drive east on Hwy. 64 to Green. Turn south on Hwy. 64 (toward White Pine). Turn left on FR 219. Turn left on FR 178. Turn right on FR 219 for 4 mi. Park along road. Hike 1/2 mi. due south (tough during dense vegetation) to Norwich Ledge. Finding this place could prove more fun than solving a Rubik's Cube blindfolded.

4 M–(Marquette Area) Sugarloaf Mountain ✯

Commanding views of the Marquette area from the summit but minimal amount of rock. Forty-foot granite west-facing toprope walls and bouldering features make for a local teaching area. Summer/autumn. Government land.
Ref: Thompson.
Directions: From Marquette push north out of town on Hwy. 550 a few mi. until a sign entitled MT SUGARLOAF (hint) is encountered. Park on the right in pullout. Hike east up dirt trail ten minutes to very limited, 40′ rock bands. Farther north, a roadcut on the west side of the road offers steeper challenges.

5 M–Presque Isle Park (closed) ●

Fishing boats, seagulls, and superior views lend a fine atmosphere to a limited amount of roped climbing on the

Michigan

N

| 0 | Kilometers | 50 |
| 0 | Miles | 50 |

1

41

26

2

45

3

Ironwood

45

2

141

4-5

41

Marquette

Sault Ste. Marie

7

6

28

77

75

41

2

Iron Mountain

Escanaba

35

31

Alpena

75

Traverse
City

131

23

115

27

75

Ludington

10

10

Bay City

131

Saginaw

25

75

Muskegon

96

Grand Rapids

27

Flint

69

31

8

94

196

Lansing

96

75

94

Kalamazoo

94

Detroit

Benton Harbor

69

12

75

94

31

131

127

23

12

50′ basalt cliffs and bouldering on the lava flows. A small pinnacle (visible from one of the first overlooks) adds character to the climbing. Beginner's slab at water's edge. One wishes there was a greater quantity of this interestingly formed basalt. Closed by the city to rock climbing in 1998. Summer/autumn. City park.

Ref: Thompson.

Directions: North Marquette. Along the Lakeshore Blvd. Drive the loop in the Presque Isle Park to the east-side pullouts. Rock can be found on the east to northeast aspect of the isle at lakeside.

6 M–Mount Marquette ★★★

This 100-yd.-long cliff band offers beginner and intermediate climbers the opportunity to hone their skills on dimond-hard 80′ quartzite. The town of Marquette caresses the mesmerizing shores of Lake Superior and is the home of Northern Michigan University. Local climbers' dining adventures include: a pastry at Jean Kay's, Baby Cakes Bakery, Vango's Restaurant and Bar, or The Verling. Summer/autumn. Private land.

Classics: Sphincter 9.

Ref: Thompson.

Directions: From Marquette proceed out of town on CR 553 past ski area to a radio tower (just past dome house) on right (ten-minute drive). Turn right on dirt road leading to radio tower. Drive 50 yd. past tower and park. A trail on left leads up to Mt. Marquette cliff (five minutes).

7 M–Palmer Cliffs ★★★

Quartzite cliff with leads and topropes. Area information at Quick Stop Bike Shop or Down Wind Sports in Marquette. Summer/autumn. Private land.

Ref: Thompson 5/98.
Directions: Near Palmer. Access sensitive.

8 Grand Ledge ★★

Lower Michigan's rock-climbing training headquarters. Six-hundred-foot-long clifflet of short 40′ topropes composed of soft Eaton sandstone of the Saginaw Formation. One hundred and ten routes of fragile rock, but strenuously steep. Climbing is no longer permitted in Fitzgerald Park due to "liability insurance cost." Climbing is still allowed at the city-owned Oak Park, but it was heavily crowded, with locals reporting continuous lines every weekend. Please use padding under toprope anchors. No camping, but picnic tables have been installed. Spring/autumn. City park, (517) 821-8478.

Classics: The Nose 4, Overextension 5, Jay's Overhang F6, Building Blocks F7, Potato Chips 7, Despondency 9, Intimidation 9, Doug's Roof 10.

Ref: M. and P. Stailey 5/96, F. Abissi 10/98; R 60, S 10/75; Guidebooks: www.higround.com, Bagg's *50 Short Climbs in the Midwest*, Bright and Van Laar's *A Climber's Guide to Grand Ledge*.

Directions: Two ways: 1) From Lansing drive 10 mi. west on Hwy. 43 to town of Grand Ledge (4 mi. south of I–96). Climbing exists in both Fitzgerald Park (on Jefferson St.—now closed) and Oak Park (West Front St.—open). Turn north on Hwy. 100, going across Grand River. Turn left (west) on West Front St. to its end and park. 2) From Lansing take I–96 to the Grand Ledge exit (Route 100). Follow this about 3 mi. until just before the bridge over the Grand River. Turn right at West Front St. (sign for Oak Park). Follow this road to the end and park.

Minnesota

International
Falls

Virginia

Bemidji

Moorhead

Duluth

St. Cloud

Willmar

Minneapolis

St. Paul

Mankato

Rochester

Albert Lea

11
2
1
3-4
5-7
9-10
11-15
8
16
17
18
19
20
21
22
23
24

N

Kilometers   50

Miles   50

Minnesota

If you can put two rounds into the same hole from twenty-five meters, that's gun control! —Jesse Ventura, Governor of Minnesota

Minnesota, the Land of 10,000 Lakes, has roughly 400 lakes for every climbing area. While the fishing areas may outnumber the crags, there are some resemblances between the two sports. Some of the cliffs feel like fish, at least Taylor Falls, which can be as slick and slimy as a bucket of walleye entrails. Yet, the same cliff can be as tasty as a fine fillet of the same.

Casting over the state, one can expect more bites to bend your rod tip than during a spring hatch. In the southwest, Blue Mounds State Park offers pink quartzite to fill your creel. In the southeast, Barn Bluff will provide the catch of the day for hungry sport climbers.

Though off most climbers' trip itinerary, the beauty of the North Country crags makes for a pleasant destination. Superior shore areas like Palisade Head and Shovel Point greet climbers with pleasant lake views. Just inland from these, Carlton Peak and Johnson Lake areas offer a woodsman's delight and the chance to get a feeling for what it's like to rub your hand backwards over a walleye's dorsal fin.

So keep an eye on your tips; the fishing is good in Minnesota.

1 Carlton Peak ✩✩

The 70′ crag piques the curiosity as well as one's skin. Spectacular fall colors. Summer/autumn. Free camping on USFS–Superior National Forest (218–365-7561).
Classics: From 5.6 to 5.11.
Ref: Guidebooks: Pagel's *Superior Climbs: A Climber's Guide to the North Shore*, Bagg's *50 Short Climbs in the Midwest*.
Directions: From Duluth go northeast on Hwy. 61 to Tofte. Just southwest of Tofte, turn west on a "sparks-a-flyin'" gravel road for 1 mi. (staying right at fork) to old quarry at base of Carlton Peak. Hike 100 yd. up to south face.

2 Boundary Waters Canoe Area ✩✩✩

Exploratory granite crags and lake cliffs accessed by canoe in Boundary Waters Canoe Area. Strictly enforced regulations for canoe trips. Summer/autumn. Free camping. USFS–Superior National Forest, (218) 365-7561.
Directions: Ely is the departure point for most wilderness trips into the Boundary Waters Canoe Area.

3 Section 13 ✩✩

This 50′ intermediate crag sports clean rock with sharp crystals and about a dozen excellent routes up to 5.11. Locals request no-chalk-use ethics for North Country crags. Spring/autumn. Free camping. State land.
Classics: Rubble Trouble 7, Macho Pitchu 9+, Seam's Hard 11-.
Ref: M. Dahlberg; Guidebook: Pagel's *Superior Climbs: A Climber's Guide to the North Shore*.
Directions: From Tettegouche State Park go north on Hwy. 61 (past junction with Hwy. 1) to CR 6 at Little Marais. Turn right on Hwy. 6 for 2 mi. to gravel pits on right. Park in back northeast corner of second pit. Hike north on faint trail with divining rod for rock. After ⅓ mi., pass bog. Continue in line for another ⅓ mi. until rocks are visible on left. Turn ninety degrees and saunter ⅓ mi. up ridge to top of crag. Talus field west of Sec-tion 13 crag. (In eastern half of Section 13 on Finland USGS quad.) Faces north.

4 Sawmill Creek Dome ✩✩✩

This 50′ crag supports good short routes though rope- and skin-trashing rock. Fabulous scenery. Spring/autumn. Free camping at this state-owned land.
Classics: Afghanistan Banana stand 7, Birch Flakes 8+, A Farewell to Arms 11-, Once in a While 11.
Ref: M. Dahlberg; Guidebook: Pagel's *Superior Climbs: A Climber's Guide to the North Shore*.
Directions: From Tettegouche State Park go north on Hwy. 61 (past junction with Hwy. 1) to CR 6 at Little Marais. Turn right on Hwy. 6, going past Section 13 gravel pit parking for another mi. until a knob (Sawmill Creek Dome) appears behind a ridge on left. Continue past Roses Rd. on right and park on left at obvious right bend in CR 6. Hike east on dirt township road quietly past farmer's house to bog and then hillside and Sawmill Creek Dome. Faces north.

5 Johnson Lake Area ✩✩✩

Short 50′ west-facing anorthosite crags. Another one of those beautiful Minnesota lake sort of areas, eh?

Minnesota Road Thoughts

The Verm and I are barreling across the long open spaces of western Minnesota. Verm's in the back of the van sacked out in his sleeping bag when I go to pass a truck. Midway through the pass, a duck flies across the road and hits the left corner of the truck. There is an explosion of feathers so great, the next thing I know, the windshield is covered with prime Minnesota duck down. I rolled down the window and soon we had enough down to refill Verm's old sleeping bag.

—TNT

Summer/autumn. Free camping on state land. Possibly federal/state land.

Classics: Over the Rainbow 7+, Jack Be Nimble 8, Shriek Foot 9+, Cirith Ungol 11, Mephisto Waltz 11+.

Ref: M. Dahlberg; Guidebook: Pagel's *Superior Climbs: A Climber's Guide to the North Shore.*

Directions: From Tettegouche State Park drive west on Hwy. 1. Turn right on Lake CR 6 to Johnson Lake Area. Jericho Wall is south/southwest from west end of Johnson Lake, less than ½ mi. Thither and Yon Area is south of Jericho in the woods. Mystical Mountain and Johnson Lake sit on southwest side of lake. Navigating through the brush may prove difficult.

6 Shovel Point (aka Tettegouche State Park) ✩✩✩

A scenic, pointed finger-of-rock cliff that tickles the side of Lake Superior. Splendid setting in which 100′ rhyolite cliffs drop straight into lake. Rappel in. The most seasonal North Shore cliff due to its south-facing aspect. No-chalk ethic pervades the Northland. Spring–autumn. Pay camping at state park (218–226–6365).

Classics: The Great Yawn 6, Dance of Sugar Plump Fairies 7/9, Ross's Crack 10 toprope, Narcoleptic Epic 11+.

Ref: M. Dahlberg; C 151-106, S 1/80; Guidebooks: Farris's *Minnesota Rock: Selected Climbs,* Pagel's *Superior Climbs: A Climber's Guide to the North Shore,* Bagg's *50 Short Climbs in the Midwest.*

Directions: From Silver Bay scoop 6 mi. north on Hwy. 61 to Baptism River Rest Area, next to Tettegouche State Park Center. Hike trail ¼ mi. north to point (signs reading SHOVEL POINT).

7 Palisade Head (in Tettegouche State Park) ✩✩✩✩

This highly aesthetic 200′ rhyolite lakeside perch is part of the Lake Superior Palisades, which extends 40 mi. northeast and offers sheer faces and long cracks. Seasonal climbing bans due to peregrine falcon nesting. "Choice" is one of the better finger cracks in Minnesota. As with all North

Country areas, a strong no-chalk-use ethic is requested due to the naturally good frictional (abrasive) properties of the rock. Summer/autumn. Pay camping at state park (218–226–6365).

Classics: Quetico 7, Superior 8, Bluebells 9, Phantom Crack 10, Drivin' in Duluth 10+, Choice of a New Generation 11+, Soli Deo Gloria 12+.

Ref: M. Dahlberg; C 151-106, S 1/80; Guidebooks: Farris's *Minnesota Rock: Selected Climbs,* Pagel's *Superior Climbs: A Climber's Guide to the North Shore,* Bagg's *50 Short Climbs in the Midwest.*

Directions: From Silver Bay (one hour from Duluth), go just 2 mi. north of town on Hwy. 61. Turn right and head for the tourist overlook. Palisade Head Cliffs below.

8 Shelly and Hendrum Abutments ✩

For those seeking novelty . . . in a place where it's hard to find natural rock. These are 30′ sandstone bouldering/ toprope structures. Shelly abutments have more difficult climbs. No gluing, bolting, or chipping has been done in the past. Spring/autumn. Private land.

Classics: Shelly: Climax Corner 11.

Ref: D. Dokken.

Directions: Both areas lie under railroad tracks west of Hwy. 75. 1) From Hendrum drive 1 ½ mi. north on Hwy. 75 to several gritstone abutments to west of road (just south of Hwy. 200). 2) For Shelly Area: From Shelly go south on Hwy. 75 for ½ mi. to intersection of Marsh Creek. This area can be found where the creek and railroad tracks intersect.

9 Point of Rocks ✩

Urban 35′ intermediate level granite gabbro crag. Spring/autumn. No camping. City of Duluth Park.

Classics: Black Feather 10c.

Ref: Guidebook: Pagel's *Superior Climbs: A Climber's Guide to the North Shore.*

Directions: Duluth. Point of Rocks is just southwest of downtown. A few blocks above West Superior St. This rock hub separates West from East Duluth. Faces southeast.

10 Whope Wall (aka Maxim's Wall) ✩

This urban climbers' playground deals a nice mixture of problems on 35′ granite climbs. Mainly face climbing on short topropes and bouldering. Whope is pronounced "whoopee." No camping. Spring/autumn. City of Duluth Park.

Classics: Glacier Slide 9, Question of Balance 10d, Iron Bar 11, Several B1 boulder problems.

Ref: C 94; Guidebook: Pagel's *Superior Climbs: A Climber's Guide to the North Shore.*

Directions: West Duluth. From I–35 and Piedmont whoop it up to Piedmont and West First St. for Whope Wall.

11 Casket Quarry ●

This quarry contains steep 100′ granite walls that are as stable as a marble on a balloon. Got a helmet? Casket Quarry was once mined for headstones. Summer/autumn. No camping. Private land.
Classics: Strike Three 10.
Ref: Guidebook: Pagel's *Superior Climbs: A Climber's Guide to the North Shore.*
Directions: West Duluth. From I–35 (visible) exit at Central Ave. and go north. Turn left on Medina St. Turn right at 57th Ave. West, following north across railroad tracks and park. Hike path left and up to Casket Quarry.

12 Skyline Drive Boulders ✩✩✩

Series of small (up to 40′) boulders offering a variety of climbing. Look for west-facing "Party 80–82" rock. Center Face Direct 5.8 runs up the middle of the largest boulder to a pine growing on top. Summer/autumn.
Classics: The Crack 7+, Party 82 8, Kathy 9.
Ref: C 94.
Directions: Above the city of Duluth along Skyline Dr. Some climbing has also been done in Brewer Park along Skyline Dr.

13 Ely's Peak ✩

The city of Duluth's main climbing area has fairly stable and clean rock. Short 40′ basalt leads and topropes. Summer/autumn. Government land.
Classics: Tunnel Area: Dislocation Overhang 6, Bionic Finger Crack 11+; Northwest Bluff: Corner Geometry 6, First Blood 9+.
Ref: C 94; Guidebook: Pagel's *Superior Climbs: A Climber's Guide to the North Shore.*
Directions: Southwest of Duluth. Go 5 mi. southwest at exit I–35 at Midway Rd. and go 2 mi. south. Turn left into 123 Rd. Ave. West. Park just before railroad berm. Hike right on Willard Munger State Trail a few minutes, then angle left on path. Two areas for Ely's Peak. Tunnel Cliff above railroad tunnel. For Northwest Bluff hike northwest on trail at tunnel for several hundred yards north of the main area.

14 Nopeming Rocks

Series of small, 40′, west-facing boulders offer a variety of climbing for the beginner or intermediate climber. Summer/autumn.
Classics: Mud Crack 6, NW Face 7, Main Overhang 8.
Ref: C 94.
Directions: From Duluth head south along I–35 to Nopeming Rocks.

15 Jay Cooke State Park ✩✩

Volcanic bouldering and one-pitch crag. Pay camping at state park (218–384–4610).

Ref: M. Wilford.
Directions: From Carlton go just west on Hwy. 210 to Jay Cooke State Park. Rock is on right by waterway off hiking trail.

16 Banning State Park ●

Fifty-foot sandstone crag with bouldering. Spring/autumn. Pay camping at state park. Popular with kayakers as well.
Ref: M. Dahlberg.
Directions: From Sandstone go just north of town, following Banning State Park signs.

17 St. Cloud Quarries ✩

One-pitch granite sport crag. Autumn. Private land.
Ref: M. Dahlberg.
Directions: In St. Cloud area. Ask locals about St. Cloud Quarries.

18 Taylors Falls (Interstate State Park) ✩✩✩

Minnesota's most well-known climbing area. For beginner to expert. Basaltic elfin crags (up to 70′) and bouldering entertain climbers and onlookers alike along the scenic St. Croix River. Difficult boulder problems/short leads in the Boneyards and cliff climbs along the walkway. Also climbs on Wisconsin side (see Interstate Park, Wisconsin). Unique "potholes" from glacial action. Spring–autumn. Pay camping in state park (651–465–5711).
Classics: Sonny and Juanita 5, Old Man 8, Slick Slides 9, Number Six 10a, Batman 10, Walking on Air 11-, Sizzle Foot 12b; B2 Bomber.
Ref: M. Dahlberg, D. Dokken; C 107, S 1/80; Sherman's *Stone Crusade;* Guidebooks: Farris's *Minnesota Rock: Selected Climbs,* Swenson et al.'s *Midwest Mountaineering's Taylors Falls Guide,* Bagg's *50 Short Climbs in the Midwest,* Von Grossman and Scott's *Close to the Edge, Down by The River.*
Directions: At Taylors Falls. South of Hwy. 8 in Taylors Falls State Park.

19 North Winds Silo

World-class silo climbing on 45′ walls. Winter. Private land.
Classics: Grainbelt 12.
Ref: M. Dahlberg.
Directions: At Forest Lake. You'll have to ask local climbers about North Winds Silo.

20 Odessa Boulder (aka Intersection Boulder) ✩

You ain't gonna believe this one! Highly polished, roadside, 12′ granite glacial erratic that does have some challenging problems above vast swampy cornfields. Could make a good goose blind. Autumn. Possibly private land.
Classics: Corner flake 5.7, B1S.

Mark Strege on the quartzite at Blue Mounds State Park.

Ref: D. Dokken.

Directions: From Odessa blow west on Hwy. 7 to the Odessa Boulder, just 1 mi. past the intersection of Hwy. 75 and Hwy. 7. On south side of road. Yep, that's it. You drove this far, might as well climb it. Actually, some good routes.

21 High Bridge

Covert 100' artificial routes. Government land.
Ref: M. Dahlberg.
Directions: High Bridge is in St. Paul. Ask locals.

22 Barn Bluff (aka Red Wing) ✪✪✪

This weathered 80' dolomite/sandstone quarry overlooking the Mississippi River became popular with sport climbers in the 1990s. Beware soft rock, i.e., potentially dangerous loose rock at top of cliff. Especially good views of Mississippi River, Lake Pepin, and Red Wing fault. Home of Red Wing Shoe Co., makers of Vasque Ascenders. Autumn. No camping. City of Red Wing Park.

Classics: Vertical Vice 8+, Needles and Pins 9+, Sleeping Bat in a Zip-lock Bag 10a, Preemptive Strike 12c, Paradigm Shift 13b.

Ref: M. Dahlberg; Guidebooks: Farris's *Minnesota Rock: Selected Climbs*, Postma's *The Barnyard Boogie: Guide to Barn Bluff, Red Wing, Minnesota* (1990).

Directions: In Red Wing. Follow East Fifth north past Hwy. 61 to parking and trailhead. Barn Bluff overlooks the town of Red Wing. Faces south.

23 Pipestone National Monument (Pipestone Quarry) ✪✪

Short 15' quartzite boulder problems in interesting surroundings. Red stone quarried for peace pipes. An area of Dakota Indian history and archaeology. Autumn. Pay camping. NPS, (507) 825–5464.
Ref: D. Dokken.
Directions: Near Pipestone, at Pipestone National Monument.

24 Blue Mounds State Park ✪✪✪

This 1-mi. band of solid 50' tan and pink Sioux quartzite presents the traveling climber with an enjoyable climbing stop. The rock is easily viewed from Hwy. 8. No fixed gear allowed. This park is noted for its indigenous prairie plant life. The wind sweeping through the bluestem grasses and prairie smoke flowers give this area a *Little House on the Prairie* feel. Supposedly named for the bluish appearance to settlers as the sun set behind it. Autumn. Pay camping at state park (507–283–1307).

Classics: Seduction and Rejection 9, Purgatory 11, Dicks Dihedral (lb) 11+, Right Side of the Bulge 12.

Ref: M. Dahlberg, D. Dokken; Guidebooks: Farris's *Minnesota Rock: Selected Climbs*, Wurdinger's *A Rock Climbing Guidebook to Blue Mounds State Park* (1989), Hynek and Landmann's *Prairie Walls: Climber's Guide to Blue Mounds State Park*.

Directions: From Luverne (I–90) go 4 mi. north on Hwy. 75. Turn 1 4/10 mi. east on Hwy. 8. Park on left at fence. Hike north on trail to Quarry Area on high trail or on low trail to Prairie Area. From parking area, climbing areas in Blue Mounds State Park (south–north) include: South Quarry, North Quarry, Prairie Walls, Mini Fortress, and Receding Ramparts.

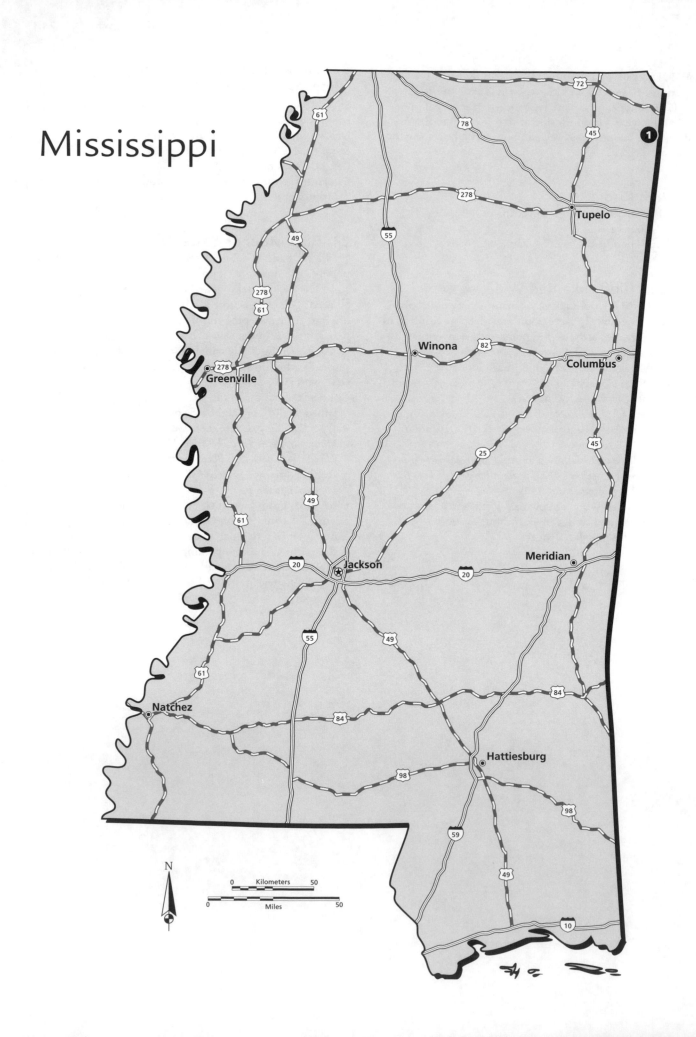

Mississippi

72

61

78

45

1

278

55

49

Tupelo

278
61

Winona

82

Columbus

278
Greenville

45

61

49

25

Jackson

Meridian

20

20

55

49

61

84

Natchez

84

Hattiesburg

98

98

61

59

49

10

N

0   Kilometers   50

0   Miles   50

Mississippi

If you don't like the direction the river is flowing, don't jump in. —From the book *Think*

Tennessee may be the home of Elvis, but his birthplace was Tupelo, Mississippi. As far as climbing goes, The King of Mississippi areas is Tishomingo State Park. Located in the northeast corner of the state, Tishomingo's 40-foot sandstone cliffs are worth a visit, if not to do the Jean's Overhang roof crack, then to be able to say, "I climbed in Mississippi."

To date, this is a claim you couldn't make elsewhere in the state, unless some unsuspecting farmer has just backed

As classic as roof cracks come, Jean's Overhang, 5.10d/11a, Tishomingo State Park.

TIM TOULA

his tractor into the back side of a new rock pile. Like neighboring Louisia na, most of Mississippi is covered in silt deposited by the mighty Mississippi River.

Don't forget to check out the catfish that make chef Paul Prudhomme look anorexic.

1 Tishomingo State Park ✮✮✮

A duffel bag full of fine short topropes on 40' sandstone walls. For the crack enthusiast, Jean's Overhang tempts one with one of the most classic 5.11- roof cracks in the United States. A pleasant rock-climbing teaching area. Along the Natchez Trace Pkwy. Autumn–spring. Entrance fee. Pay camping in state park (662–438–6914).

Classics: Muscle City 8, Challenger 9, Jean's Overhang 11a (roof crack).

Ref: C 68; Guidebooks: Detterline's *Tishomingo: A Climber's Guide to Mississippi Rock,* Detterline's *A Climber's Guide to the Mid-South.*

Directions: From Iuka scurry 25 mi. south on Hwy. 25, following signs into Tishomingo State Park. Park at playground. Cross swinging footbridge to right. Short rock walls adjacent to park trail. Jean's Overhang 5.10d/11a is first large roof crack above trail on left.

Missouri

Missouri

Don't go around saying the world owes you a living; the world owes you nothing, it was here first. —Mark Twain

While checking out the climbing in the Show Me State one might, at first glance, be compelled to shout, "Show me the next state." Nevertheless, rock junkies all need a fix at some time or another, and Missouri has many varied cragging areas waiting to supply you.

The climbing is plotted across Mark Twain's beloved countryside in little magical acres mainly south of I–70. The most concentrated climbing lies just east of Columbia along the wide Missouri River. Limestone bluffs from Rocheport down to Wilton have been developed by University of Missouri students. Access here has been a problem, though.

While discovering some of the other climbing curiosities, such as Elephant Rocks, Johnson's Shut-In, and Labadie, one has cause to impersonate Missouri native son Harry S Truman: "The truck stops here!" you'll say, "At least for an hour." These rural areas present some fun bouldering and short leads.

Perhaps many more climbing areas are costumed in the Ozark masquerade, but if not, there's always the 5.19 palming arête waiting to be done on St. Louis's Landscape Arch.

1 Cliff Drive ★★

These 40′ limestone north-facing craglets offer twenty sport and natural leads. Most popular routes are polished, while newer routes still have good edges. All routes easily toproped. Bluffs continue but are somewhat overgrown and loose. Possibly a high-crime area. Spring/autumn. No camping. City park.
Classics: The Book 5.7, The Big Crack 7, The Overhang 5.10, 5.12 roof toprope, The Bolt Route 12-.
Ref: B. Leo, C. O'Halloran; Guidebook: Floyd's *A Climber's Guide to the Midwest Metamorphic Forms.*
Directions: Northeast Kansas City, Missouri. From Independence Ave. (Hwy. 24), follow Cliff Dr. north. Park right in front of the cliff.

2 Swope Park ★★

A Kansas City locals' limestone bouldering area with six main boulders, the largest of which is The Room. Spring/autumn. No camping. City park.

Ref: B. Leo; Guidebook: Floyd's *A Climber's Guide to the Midwest Metamorphic Forms.*
Directions: Kansas City. From I–435 go west on Gregory Blvd. into Swope Park. Four separate bouldering areas in the vicinity of the stone bridge on Blue River Rd. (two south of bridge on Blue River Rd., one north of bridge on Gregory Blvd., and one east of bridge on Oldham Rd.).

3 Rocheport and I–70 Missouri River Bluffs ★★★

One-hundred-foot limestone bluffs; various crack and face climbs. May be closed to climbing due to the Katy Trail. Autumn. Pay camping. NPS.
Classics: Poop Chute 9, Rocheport Crack.
Ref: J. Karpowicz, G. Porter; Guidebook: Oliver and Taylor's *Boone County Climbs.*
Directions: From Rocheport exit on I–70, go north to Rocheport. Follow Katy Trail south to Rocheport Bluffs. Faces west.

4 Andromeda Sprain Area (closed) ★★★

One-hundred-foot Burlington limestone cliffs—many miles of it. Access to cliffs is via private land. Closed due to the Katy Trail. Andromeda Sprain is perhaps one of the more classic routes along the Missouri River. Sport climbing has been in these Missouri River bluffs since the 1980s. Around the Andromeda Sprain area are now at least twenty high-quality sport routes, like Katy's Trail, from 5.9 to 5.12, with the average difficulty being face climbing at 5.11 range. Spring/autumn. Pay camping. Private land.
Classics: Andromeda Sprain 2p 9, Katy's Trail 11d/12a.
Ref: C 59; J. Karpowicz, G. Porter; Guidebooks: Floyd's *A Climber's Guide to the Midwest Metamorphic Forms,*

Missouri Road Thoughts

How do they get the deer to cross at that yellow road sign?

—George Carlin

Mike Lissing on the Middle Traverse at Capen Park.

Detterline's *A Climber's Guide to the Mid-South,* Oliver and Taylor's *Boone County Climbs.*
Directions: From Rocheport exit on I-70 go south on dirt road for 3 2/10 mi. Park. Hike west through fields to top of Andromeda Sprain crag. Faces west.

5 Capen Park ✭✭✭/Rock Quarry ✭ (closed)

Local Columbia limestone toproping and bouldering area developed since the 1970s. Piton Crack Area to north off Rock Quarry Rd. behind warehouse is now closed for good. This, however, is just a small portion of what is available as the 70' cliffs along the creek side hold fun challenges; as does the short but steep bouldering traverse a minute from the car. In the spring and summer, shake hands with humidity. Autumn. No camping. City park/private land.
Classics: Capen: Apeman 5.8, Slicker than Owl Shit on a Barn Floor 10+, Swing Time 11-, Footloose Direct 11, Middle Traverse B1; Rock Quarry: Piton Crack, Prow B1.
Ref: J. Karpowicz, G. Porter; C 59; Guidebooks: Floyd's *A Climber's Guide to the Midwest Metamorphic Forms,* Detterline's *A Climber's Guide to the Mid-South,* Oliver and Taylor's *Boone County Climbs.*
Directions: Columbia (southeast of University of Missouri). From College Ave. go south to Capen Park. Park on left. Hike north three minutes along creek past bouldering and traverse wall to toprope bluff. The off-limits (i.e., closed) Rock Quarry, with its locally famous Piton Crack, is located behind warehouse and left of trail to Main Bluff of Capen Park. Main Bluff faces east.

6 The Rock (Fulton Pinnacle)

One 30' sandstone rock along creek with at least six routes. Power Failure 5.10 is a Fulton Pinnacle crack testpiece on

the stream side of the pinnacle. Access problem—NO TRESSPASSING signs. Autumn. Pay camping.
Classics: Power Failure 10.
Ref: J. Karpowicz; C 74; Guidebook: Floyd's *A Climber's Guide to the Midwest Metamorphic Forms.*
Directions: Near Fulton. The Rock is east of town along Route O in the creek on the right-hand side of the road.

7 Providence ✭✭✭

A continuation of Missouri's 100' limestone river bluffs. Autumn. Pay camping. NPS land.
Classics: Providence Crack 10.
Ref: J. Karpowicz, G. Porter; Guidebook: Floyd's *A Climber's Guide to the Midwest Metamorphic Forms.*
Directions: From Columbia go south on Hwy. 163, then take Rd. K into Providence. Providence Rocks are just south of town. Faces west.

8 Easley Bluff ✭

A continuation of Missouri limestone 100' river bluffs. One mud crack; when it rains, mud pours down the crack. Still, considered a classic of sorts amongst locals. Mainly a rappelling area. Autumn. NPS.
Classics: Warren Harding Memorial Bolt Rte 7 A4.
Ref: J. Karpowicz, G. Porter; Guidebooks: Detterline's *A Climber's Guide to the Mid-South,* Oliver and Taylor's *Boone County Climbs.*
Directions: Easley. Easley Bluff is just south of town. Faces west.

9 Devil's Backbone ✭

A beginner's/intermediate area. Autumn. No camping.
Classics: Star In My Pocket 9, Twenty-Two Skidoo 10.
Ref: J. Karpowicz, G. Porter.
Directions: From Columbia take left onto Airport Rd. Go straight until road dead-ends at bridge. Uncertain access—short hike along Devil's Backbone Trail across bridge to Devil's Backbone bluffs. Ask locally for detailed directions. Faces west.

10 Wilton Bluff (on Missouri River) ✭✭✭

Cliffs of intermittent good rock hold more than fifty routes. Access sensitive (owner threatening to start towing); may be closed. Although a continuation of same bluffs as Rocheport and Andromeda, these are set back farther from Katy Trail. Bluffs were closed for about one year until early April 1992, primarily due to death of a nonclimber on approach dirt fall affectionately known as the Khumbu Dirtfall. Autumn. Private land. Pay camping.
Classics: Meadow (aka 2 Pitch Climb) 7, Lamentations 9, Bong Eater 10, Streaker 10, Slingshot 10, Sickle 10, The Outer Edge 10, Trepidation 11, Desperado 11, Streaker 12a, Crossroads 12.
Ref: J. Karpowicz, G. Porter; C [122, 74, 67, 59]; Guidebooks: Floyd's *A Climber's Guide to the Midwest Metamorphic*

Forms, Detterline's *A Climber's Guide to the Mid-South,* Oliver and Taylor's *Boone County Climbs.*

Directions: From Wilton go north on road along railroad tracks until road turns away. Park. Hike across tracks up to rocks. Wilton Bluff is thirty minutes from Columbia.

11 Labadie (closed) ★★★

Short and fun bolted leads from 5.9 to 5.11 on 80′ sandstone wall. Potential bluffs in the distance. People arrested for rock climbing in 2000—best to not climb here. Be careful not to leave gear on railroad tracks. Autumn. No camping. Private land.

Classics: Antman 10, The Dance 12a.

Ref: Locals; Guidebooks: Floyd's *A Climber's Guide to the Midwest Metamorphic Forms,* WVOC: *A Climber's Guide to St. Louis.*

Directions: From Labadie go east on Hwy. T for 3 ³/10 mi. Turn left on Davis Rd. past pond. Take dirt road to railroad track/river bottoms. Curve around to right. Park in front of bridge. Hike across ditch to railroad tracks and Labadie bluff. Go with a local if possible. Faces west.

12 Rockwood Reservation State Forest (Rockwood Bluff) (closed) ★★

Seventy-foot sandstone bluff climbing and bouldering with a variety of climbing styles. Climbers must register and wear helmets. Autumn. State land, (636) 458-2236.

Ref: S 7/85.

Directions: From St. Louis rock west on I-44 to Eureka. Go north on Hwy. 109 to Rockwoods Reservation. Ask rangers about Rockwood Bluff.

13 Pevely Cliffs (Quarry) ★★

Old 80′ limestone quarry converted into a sport climber's area. Several hollowed-out hillsides with arch entrances and lanes large enough to drag-race two semi trucks. St. Louis is home of the Gateway Arch and the birthplace of Bigfoot, The Original Monster Truck—something every climber needs. Autumn. No camping. Private land.

Classics: Central Pillar Rt 12-?.

Ref: D. Braihland 5/98; Guidebook: WVOC: *A Climber's Guide to St Louis.*

Directions: At Pevely (thirty minutes south of St. Louis), go east on Hwy. Z, turning into Abbey Lane at light. Go for 2 mi. of pavement, turning to gravel at first major bridge crossing a stream. Park off road on right (past cliffs) at NO DUMPING sign or by stream. Hike back across stream to Pevely Cliffs/Walls and take any trail on left to jeep trail. Follow trail left to second set of cliffs. New trail cut to top.

14 Henley (closed) ★★★

Along the Osage River, the Forgotten Wall's 100′ limestone walls have some of the highest concentration of quality climbs in the state. Henley seems to be the dumping area for deer carcasses, cars, and other junk. Closed as of 1992. Greg Finnoff wrote, "Although access is questioned this is the best, most solid rock I've seen in Missouri. This fall [1997], 20 new routes were drilled ranging from 5.8 or so to 5.13a (Zeus, 12 bolts, 100′ overhangs 25′) with 3 projects waiting to be completed. This is a very worthwhile crag. If you're passing through the Midwest it's a must visit. There is plenty of room for development; all that's needed is man or woman power!! This is a 'must stop crag' for anyone in or passing through the Midwest. A couple of the routes listed below need redpoints because I spent most of my time bolting rather than climbing due to the lack of climbing partners in the area...." Autumn. No camping. Private land.

Classics: Carcass Crack 5, Up and Down 6, Sunset Boulevard 7, Homage to Bates 10, Born Again Hard 10/11, Men of Power 11, Lactic Pig 12 toprope, Zeus 13a, Pooh Bear 12a/b, Honey Pot 11d project, 13 project, Monkey Siren 13, Monkey Business 9, Monkey Woman 11d, Little General 10a, Old Easy 9, The Mule 12c/d, Power Wagon 12d/13a, Near Arch 10d, Square Roof 12, South Buttress 12a, Piglets Big Scare 8.

Ref: G. Finnoff 1/98, J. Karpowicz, G. Porter; Guidebooks: Floyd's *A Climber's Guide to the Midwest Metamorphic Forms,* Reed's *A Climber's Guide to Henley Forgotten Wall.*

Directions: At Henley. From I-70 take Hwy. 63S to Hwy. 54. Turn left on Hwy. E for 1 ²/10 mi. Veer right on Hwy. H for 5 ⁶/10 mi. (crossing one-lane bridge at 2 mi.). Turn left onto Hwy. South Teal Rd. At ⁷/10 mi., veer left and continue for 2 ⁴/10 mi. to parking on right. Three-minute hike from the road to Henley crag along the Osage River.

15 Collins ★★★

Overhanging 35′ sandstone bluffs with reportedly good climbing. Autumn. No camping. Private land.

Ref: J. Karpowicz, G. Porter, M. Stites.

Directions: From Collins go west on Hwy. 54 to river course and Collins crag. South of Roscoe.

16 Soest Road Bouldering ★★

A 25′ sandstone bouldering traverse wall that is sheltered by an angling ceiling. The main reason to stop is the 80′-long Ironman Traverse. Forget about trying to climb here when it's wet or raining. Wait until at least a couple days after a rain as the term "slimefest" comes to mind. Autumn. No camping. Private land.

Classics: Ironman 80′ overhanging technical traverse in 5.12–13 range.

Ref: M. Stites, A. Avenoso 12/97; Sherman's *Stone Crusade,* pp. 196–97.

Directions: From Rolla, from Pine St. and Tenth (at University of Missouri), go east on Tenth Street (aka Hwy. BB) for 5 mi. Turn right on Hwy. 3220 for ½ mi. Turn right on Hwy. 3000. Soest Road Bouldering/Bluffs on either side of bridge.

17 Devil's Elbow ☆☆

A small 150' limestone bluff close to I-44. Scary but possibly fun place to climb. Beware of poison ivy. Autumn. Free camping. USFS–Mark Twain NF, (573) 364–4621.

Classics: Mike's Crack 9, Pocket Pool 10, Open Throttle 11, Swingset 12.

Ref: S. Maynard 3/98; C 59; Guidebooks: Floyd's *A Climber's Guide to the Midwest Metamorphic Forms*, Denise's *A Climber's Guide to Devil's Elbow*.

Directions: At the town of Devil's Elbow, bluffs are unmistakable above the river. (From Rolla bend southeast on I-44 to exit 169 [Hwy. T] to west on Hwy. Z [old Route 66] to bridge. Turn left before bridge and follow road to town of Devil's Elbow.) Faces south.

18 Paddy Creek Wilderness Area ☆

Many hiking trails lead to numerous high-quality 30' sandstone boulders in a beautiful setting. Excellent bouldering. Autumn/winter. Free camping. USFS–Mark Twain NF, (573) 364–4621.

Ref: Guidebook: Denise's *A Climber's Guide to Devil's Elbow*.

Directions: From Rolla course south on Hwy. 63 to town of Licking. Paddy Creek Wilderness lies west off Hwy. 32 in the Mark Twain NF. Faces south.

19 Elephant Rocks State Park ☆☆☆

How did the elephant hunter get a hernia? Carrying the decoys! Coarse 30' granite boulders, a billion years old, stand end-to-end like a line of circus elephants. More than one hundred boulder problems. Potential in nearby quarries and other boulder areas around; Pink Rock, etc. A reader tells us that technical climbing is now allowed. Autumn–spring. Pay camping. State park, (573) 546–3454.

Classics: Gill problem B1-, EBGB's B5.10, many more.

Ref: J. Karpowicz, G. Porter; C 68, S 7/85, Ament's *Master of Rock*; Guidebooks: Floyd's *A Climber's Guide to the Midwest Metamorphic Forms*, Detterline's *A Climber's Guide to the Mid-South*.

Directions: From Ironton go 7 mi. north on Hwy. 21, then 1 mi. west on NA (signs) to Elephant Rocks State Park. Hike on Braille trail.

20 Graniteville Quarry

Steep 50' granite quarry walls. Possibly off-limits. Autumn. No camping. Private land.

Ref: S 7/85; Guidebook: Floyd's *A Climber's Guide to the Midwest Metamorphic Forms*.

Directions: Graniteville Quarry is at Graniteville.

21 Royal Gorge

Forty-foot rhyolite crags. Autumn. Free camping.

Ref: J. Karpowicz, G. Porter.

Directions: From Arcadia, Royal Gorge is 1 mi. south on Hwy. 72.

22 Johnson's Shut-ins State Park ☆☆☆

Short, 40' pithy rhyolite topropes at a quaint riverine setting. Harder climbs require some contriving on microholds. Good practice area for novices. Open to climbing September–May. Registration permit required. Some of the oldest exposed rock in the United States. Good swimming, crowded in summer. "Shut-ins" means canyonlike gorge. Autumn. Pay camping. State park, (573) 546–2450.

Classics: Long Arm 7, Electric Green Bikini 9+, Arrowhead 10, Steppin' Out 9 (Dir.) 11, Brain Dead 11/12.

Ref: J. Karpowicz, G. Porter; C 68, S 7/85; Guidebooks: Floyd's *A Climber's Guide to the Midwest Metamorphic Forms*, Hagen's *Johnson's Shut-ins State Park Climbing Guide*, Detterline's *A Climber's Guide to the Mid-South*.

Directions: From Lesterville go west on Hwy. 21 to north on Rd. N to Johnson's Shut-ins State Park. From parking lot near park office, short hike along east fork of Black River on park trail to short cliffs.

23 Prairie Creek Hollow

At the scenic Current River stand these 100' rhyolite cliffs. Autumn. Free camping. State/federal land.

Ref: C [122-104, 116(10/89)].

Directions: From Eminence go east on Hwy. 106 to north on Hwy. V to Jack's Fork and Prairie Creek Hollow.

24 Williamsville

One-pitch limestone crag. Autumn. USFS–Mark Twain NF, (573) 364–4621.

Ref: J. Karpowicz, G. Porter.

Directions: Near Williamsville.

25 Linden ☆☆

Forty-foot limestone formations lend themselves well to bouldering. Springfield is home of Bass Pro Shop, one of the largest sporting-good shops in the world. Nearby Branson is home to a large country-music store. Autumn. No camping. Private land.

Classics: Smooth Groove B1, Round is Good B1+.

Ref: J. Karpowicz, G. Porter.

Directions: From Springfield go east on Hwy. 60, then go south on Hwy. 125 to Linden. Turn left onto Lindenlure Rd. Rock is at end of road on north bank of Finley Creek.

26 Shoal Creek

Quartzite toprope and bouldering area. Private land.

Ref: J. Karpowicz, G. Porter; Guidebook: Floyd's *A Climber's Guide to the Midwest Metamorphic Forms*.

Directions: From Joplin go just southwest of town off I-44 exit 6 to Hwy. 86 on Shoal Creek. Rocks visible from interstate to south. Enter Wildcat Park entrance to cliff parking.

27 Southeast Missouri State Buildering

The hallway under Academic Hall offers an excellent opportunity when it's raining on your parade. State land.

Directions: From St. Louis take I–55 south and get off at exit 99. Take a left onto Hwy. 61. About 5 mi. up the road, take a left on Broadway for 2 mi. Take a left on Henderson across from Imo's Pizza. Go 1 block and the buildering is on your left. Take a left. Academic Hall is right across the street, and the hallway is directly under the stairs.

28 Truman Lake ✯✯✯

Fun sport climbs on solid limestone from 5.8 to 5.12+ developed by Jim Thurmond and others. Not much trad, but bring a few stoppers just in case. Autumn. Pay camping. State land.

Ref: C. Brooks 3/98; Guidebook: Floyd's *A Climber's Guide to the Midwest Metamorphic Forms.*

Directions: From Warsaw drive west on Hwy. 7. Turn right on the last road before you cross the first bridge to Truman Lake. Follow the road until you come to a stop sign. Turn left. Take the road to the golf course and turn left. Park on the gravel road immediately on your right. Hike down the road until you find a decent trail leading to the left. Follow the trail, staying to the right until the cliffs. Faces west.

29 Schuler's Ferry ✯✯✯✯

This sport crag is along the Osage River. It is actually only 4–5 mi. downriver from Henley. Uncertain rock quality. If this crag were in Colorado, there would be 600 to 700 routes. There is one huge cave in particular, very featured and very steep. At the end of summer 1998, Missouri got it's first mid-5.13 here. The potential for literally hundreds more exist. Come with your drill! It's very easy to get to the top of the routes, facilitating top-down bolting. The only difficulty is top down when it's so steep! Autumn. Private land.

Classics: First Bluff: Classic Corner 10, Estella Luna 10, Black Face 11a, The Pear 12; Second Bluff: Classic Crack 9, Balancing Act 9, Barrow Head Face 10c, Baby Face 12.

Ref: G. Finnoff 4/98.

Directions: From Jefferson City go south on Hwy. B through Wardsville and St. Thomas. About 4 mi. beyond St. Thomas, Schuler's Ferry will be a right turn onto a gravel road. This road drops down a steep hill and continues along the valley, coming to the Osage River in approximately ½ mi. Park, get out, and look up and down the river. The main series of bluffs are off to the right as you are facing the river. Faces west. Hike on up there and have fun.

30 Earthquake Hollow ✯✯✯

Great problems are concentrated in a small area of boulders. Most of the landings are wonderful. You might want to bring along a pad! Ask about the twenty routes and more information by contacting Columbia's Rock Climbing Gym at (888) 4–A–BELAY. The main features are a Main Wall with several problems, good landings, and a "spectator boulder"; two hallways parallel to and behind the Main Wall; a free-standing Pinnacle; the forty-five-degree Phoenix Boulder behind and below the Main Wall's spectator boulder; and the Twister Boulder, between the Phoenix and the Pinnacle. Autumn. No camping. Although access from Missouri Department of Conservation land, the boulders are on private property.

Classics: Phoenix Boulder: Phoenix Prime V5+, short steep with direct finish; Frogger V4, add the arête to Phoenix. Main Wall: Albatross V3, high 'n' classic near the right end. Twister Boulder: Twister V5, arcing left to right traverse with a deadly horizontal throw. Hallway behind Main Wall: Hot Tamale V3+, at the entrance; Pinball V7, farther in; look for the wicked mono near the top.

Ref: B. Gilbert 10/98; Guidebook: Floyd's *A Climber's Guide to the Midwest Metamorphic Forms.*

Directions: From Jefferson City (southeast of Columbia), follow Hwy. 54 north 10 mi. to Hwy. TT. Turn right (east) down Hwy. TT to a sharp right turn. Look for Conservation Department sign. Exit Hwy. TT and go 8 mi. down gravel road to an obvious parking area. Park. Hike on grass path approximately ¼ mi. across field into forest to the boulders.

31 Clifty Creek

There is a beautiful 100' rock bridge a mile down the creek. You have to cross the creek three or four times, but it is a shallow one. Great day hike. Autumn. Free camping. State land.

Ref: R. Holmes 6/98.

Directions: From Dixon take Hwy. 28 north for about 6 mi. to signs for Clifty Creek. Follow road to parking area. Follow trail down to creek. Follow creek downstream for 1 mi. to rock bridge. There are several areas along the way to climb. Faces south.

Other Missouri Climbing Areas

Monegaw Springs

Scenic south-facing sandstone bluffs up to 65' along the Osage River. Go south of Monegaw Springs to parking area above river.

Mammoth Cave

Limestone cave with arching wave and a handful of sport routes put up by Jim Thurmond. From St. Louis take Hwy. 21 southwest to the small town of Desoto. Turn west onto Hwy. H for a few mi., then turn south on Mammoth Creek Rd. to Mammoth Rd. to its intersection with Big Creek. Mammoth Bridge is just south of the hwy. on east side of creek.

Devil's Tollgate

For a more wilderness setting, Devil's Tollgate is a unique bouldering stop northeast of Johnson's Shut-in and southwest of Tom Sauk Mountain State Park on the Tom Sauk Trail. Drive north from Glover on Hwy. 21 to Hogan and turn left on Hwy. AA. Hwy. AA eventually winds north and turns into Mikan Rd., dead-ending at a trail. Hike trail north to the Tollgate.

Montana

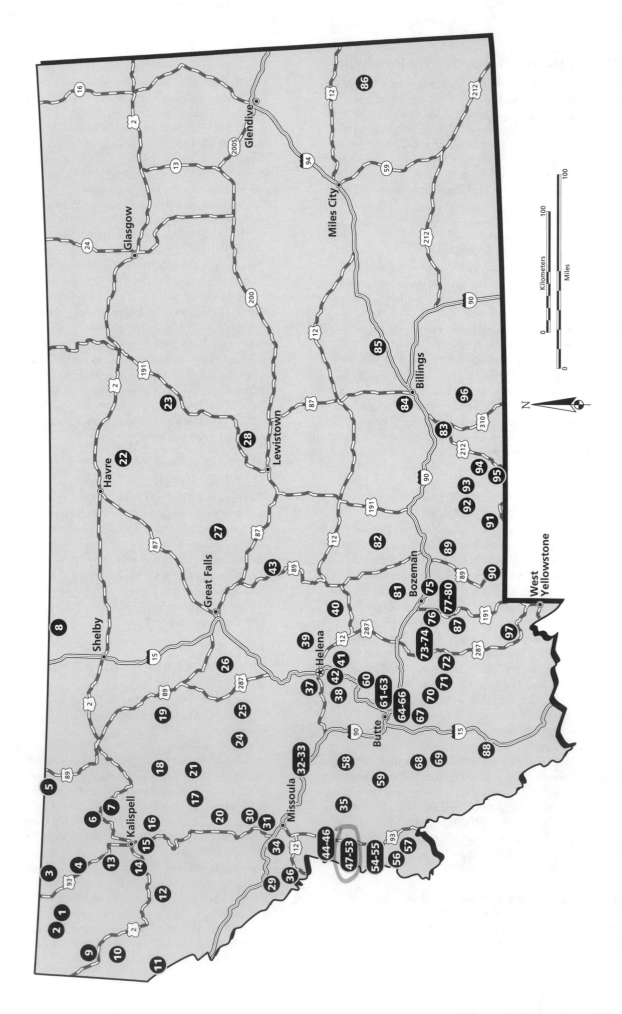

Montana

In a recent weather report that described the snow in the Northwest, the announcer on KHAR, Alaska, said: "And Helena got six inches during the night . . . Helena, Montana, that is! —from Kermit Schafer's Best of Bloopers

As some climbers from Montana will tell you, "Shhhh, there is no climbing here." As the land will tell you should you visit here, seek and ye shall climb.

1 LK☆-(Lake Koocanusa Area) Stone Hill/Overview ☆☆☆☆

The happy rock-hunting ground of northern Montana. West-facing 160′ quartzite cragging on small but positive edges above the blue waters of Lake Koocanusa. Most of the Hold Up Bluffs North is developed. Many first ascents by Gary Phoenix. Good potential for new routes. Home of the Koocanusa Crank Competition. Free camping fifteen minutes north of Stone Hill at Camp 32 (USFS). Pay camping at lake. USFS–Kootenai NF, (406) 293-6211.

Classics: Fantasyland 8, Room with a View 8+, Clark's Nutcracker 10-, Nightflyer 10b, Solid Courage 10c, Phoenix/Bailey 11a, Fade to Black 11b, Widow Maker 12- Wish for Dish 12, No Rest for the Wicked 12.

Ref: C 119(4/90)-43, R [99-87, 55(5/93)]; Guidebooks: Green's *The Rock Climber's Guide to Montana,* Stenger's *Stone Hill: Rock Climbs of Lake Koocanusa,* Caffrey's *Climber's Guide to Montana.*

Directions: From Eureka take Hwy. 93N. Turn onto Hwy. 37S to bridge. Stone Hill is 3 ^{1}/10 mi. south, where lies the popular roadside area known as Hold Up Bluffs on left. This area has highest concentration of established routes. Most development has been on east side of lake. Developed climbing above and below road.

2 LK–Lake Koocanusa West Side (Land of the Lost) ☆☆☆

More beautiful lakeside 100′ quartzite cragging. Developed after the east side. USFS–Kootenai NF, (406) 293-6211.

Classics: Decomposure 9, Obsession 10a, Butterfingers 11a, Separate Reality 11c.

Ref: Guidebooks: Green's *The Rock Climber's Guide to Montana,* Stenger's *Stone Hill: Rock Climbs of Lake Koocanusa,* Caffrey's *Climber's Guide to Montana.*

Directions: From Eureka take Hwy. 93N. Follow Hwy. 37 south to bridge at Lake Koocanusa. Go over bridge to west side of Lake Koocanusa. Following areas exist going

south of bridge: Ginseng Rock, ³/4 mi.; Upper Jock Rock/Tomahawk Rock, 1 ¹/2 mi. uphill; Land of the Lost, 2 ¹/2 mi. below road.

3 Krag and Stahl Peaks (in Whitefish Range)

On Krag and Stahl Peaks lie exposed one-pitch limestone rocks and cliffs. Possibly dubious rock quality. A backcountry experience—we're talking way up in the mountains. Much rock up in northern Montana. Summer. USFS–Flathead NF, (406) 758-5200.

Ref: Guidebook: Caffrey's *Climber's Guide to Montana.*

Directions: Krag Peak: From Fortine go north on Hwy. 93, then northeast on FR 114, then right on Williams Creek (FR 7019). Stahl Peak: Continue up FR 114 instead of turning right, then onto 7022.

4 Stryker/Point of Rocks ☆☆☆

Abundant, 50′ black metamorphic west-facing roadside rocks and blocks. Summer. USFS–Flathead NF, (406) 758-5200.

Directions: From Stryker strike south on Hwy. 93 to Point of Rocks.

5 Glacier National Park ☆☆☆☆

Unsurpassed grandeur amid glacially carved mountain summits. Most alpine routes are on dangerously loose rock bands of limestone, diorite sills, and/or shale bands. Some peaks with technical (roped) routes include: Kinnerly Peak: East Face, Longfellow Peak, Mt. Cleveland, Chief Mountain; Ipasha Peak: Northeast Arête; Mt. Wilbur: East Face; Mt. Siyeh: 3,500′ North Face, Reynolds Mountain, Walton, and the west face of Mt. Saint Nicholas. Mt. Siyeh's 3,000′ north face is especially impressive. Peaks up to 10,000′ elevations. Check Edwards's guide for detailed information. Come prepared to deal with bears (i.e., grizzlies with sharp claws and big teeth), glacial travel, permits, and harsh weather (hopefully good). Summer. Backcountry fee permits. NPS, (406) 888-7800.

Classics: Mt. Siyeh 3,000′ North Face, Garden Walls Spires, Citadel Spire on Porcupine Ridge, Avalanche

Campground area between Logan and Avalanche Creeks at base Mt. Cannon 6-pitch broken cliffs, Mt. St. Nicholas, Mt. Stimson.

Ref: AAJ '98, S [5/81, 10/79, 8/78, 3/75, 12/69, 5/68, 4/68, 4/64], *Trail and Timberline* (1958) #479 (147-152); Reese's *Montana Mountain Ranges*, Nelson's *Hiker's Guide to Glacier National Park*, Molvar's *Hiking Glacier and Waterton Lakes National Parks*; Guidebooks: Edwards's *Climber's Guide to Glacier National Park*, Caffrey's *Climber's Guide to Montana*.

Directions: From Kalispell go northwest on Hwy. 2 onto Going-to-the-Sun Rd. Hwy. 2 borders the park on its west and south sides, while Hwy. 89 is main road on the east. Splitting the center of Glacier National Park is the stunning Going-to-the-Sun Hwy. Besides the big peaks mentioned below, other technical rock-climbing areas can be found on smaller undertakings like Garden Wall Spires, Citadel Spire (Porcupine Ridge), and Avalanche Campground Crag (between Logan and Avalanche Creeks), crags north of St. Mary's Lake. Mt. Oberlin, amongst the myriads of peaks, makes for a quick summit run from Logan Pass.

6 West Glacier Rocks ✯✯

These 150′ granite crags lie just outside of the southern boundary of Glacier National Park along the Flathead River. Summer/autumn. USFS–Flathead NF, (406) 758-5200.

Ref: Guidebook: Caffrey's *Climber's Guide to Montana*.

Directions: From West Glacier go east on Hwy. 2 to small cliffs within 10 mi. of town. West Glacier Rocks visible on right. Faces north.

7 Skiumah Creek Walls

North-facing limestone crags lie just outside of the southern boundary of Glacier National Park along the Flathead River. Rescue and Skiumah Creeks offer ice climbing also. USFS–Flathead NF, (406) 758-5200.

Ref: Guidebook: Caffrey's *Climber's Guide to Montana*.

Directions: From West Glacier go east on Hwy. 2 to Skiumah Creek. Walls on high flanks of canyon. Small cliffs on Hwy. 2 within 10 mi. of town.

8 West Butte (The Sweet Grass Hills)

A rock-rimmed butte visible for miles on the expansive Montana prairie. The southeast face has the most exposed vertical faces. The Sweet Grass Hills are laccoliths of twenty-five-million-year-old volcanics. Mentioned in *Climber's Guide to Montana*, as are most of these areas. Climbers should use caution with this guidebook, as some areas may not be quality rock climbing. Possibly government land.

Ref: Guidebook: Caffrey's *Climber's Guide to Montana*.

Directions: From Sunburst go 13 mi. east. Turn north to West Butte. Rock on southeast face of West Butte.

9 Kootenai Falls ✯✯

Fifty-foot granite crags. The Kootenai Falls area is considered a practice crag but is noted as rotten rock. Near class 5 and 6 rapids along the Kootenai River, which were the film site of the movie *The River Wild*, starring Meryl Streep. USFS–Kootenai NF, (406) 293-6211.

Ref: Reese's *Montana Mountain Ranges*; Guidebook: Caffrey's *Climber's Guide to Montana*.

Directions: From Libby go 12 mi. south on Hwy. 2 to Kootenai Falls.

10 Cabinet Mountains ✯✯✯

Alpine granite crag and walls. The following is a representative overview of some of the possibilities of rock climbing in this range: The middle fork of Ross Creek has smooth granite cirque headwalls. Bad Medicine Area, west side of Bull Lake in Cabinet Mountains, holds impressive cliffs and spires, albeit reportedly rotten. Technical rock climbing may also be found on Ojibway Peak: West Face; Elephant Peak: East Ridge; Rock Peak: East Face; Lentz Park: Southeast "A" Peak: large North Face (may be rotten). St. Paul Peak may be one of the best long routes (ten pitches). "A" Peak (at Granite Lake) has a 2,800′ limestone face. Reputedly, famed mountaineer John Roskelley's favorite range. Check out Toby's Grill in Noxon. USFS–Kootenai NF, (406) 293-6211.

Classics: St. Paul Peak: East Face Direct.

Ref: AAJ '83, S 12/62; Guidebook: Caffrey's *Climber's Guide to Montana*.

Directions: From Libby the Cabinet Mountains lie southeast of town, east of Hwy. 56 and west of Hwy. 2. Several access points include northeast of Noxon Dam up Rock Creek.

11 Devil's Gap/Noxon Reservoir ✯

Assorted east-facing 200′ metamorphic buttresses. Uncertain rock quality. USFS–Idaho Panhandle NF, (208) 765-7223.

Ref: Guidebook: Caffrey's *Climber's Guide to Montana*.

Directions: From Noxon go south along Noxon Reservoir, then west up Marten Creek (on west side of Noxon Reservoir). Cliffs are north along Devil's Gap. Cliffs north of Noxon on west side of reservoir visible from junction of 200 and 56. Other cliffs are visible north up junction of 200 and 56.

12 SM✯–(Salish Mountains) Thompson River Cliffs and Overview ✯✯

The Salish Mountains provide alpinists no real backcountry rock climbing except for fringe areas mentioned here. The Thompson River has angling broken cliffs of 200′ sedimentary rock. USFS–Lolo NF, (406) 329-3750.

Ref: Guidebook: Caffrey's *Climber's Guide to Montana*.

Directions: Near Kalispell. Along lower Thompson River at mouth.

13 SM–Tally Lake Crags ✩✩

A Kalispell 300′ metamorphic practice crag in scenic lakeside forests. If you pine for adventure, Tally Lake offers multipitched climbing, though rock may be green. Summer/autumn. USFS–Flathead NF, (406) 293-6211.
Ref: Guidebook: Caffrey's *Climber's Guide to Montana*.
Directions: From Kalispell go northwest on Tally Lake Rd. to Tally Lake. Crags at southeast side of Tally Lake. Other climbable formations (6 mi. from Tally Lake) to south could yield good climbs; visible traveling northwest from Kalispell.

14 SM–Kila Cliffs ✩✩

A sunny roadside cliff with interesting short topropes/leads. One-pitch routes on metamorphic rock. Caged Indian paintings at base of cliff at approximately mm 107.6 are similar to those found near Spokane's Indian paintings and Tumwater's pictograph rocks. State and private land.
Ref: Guidebook: Caffrey's *Climber's Guide to Montana*.
Directions: From Kalispell go west on Hwy. 2 just past town of Kila. Kila Cliffs on roadside left. Faces south. State land at mm 108, private land mm 107.

15 SM–Somers Cliffs ✩✩

A small 80′ metamorphic crag with some steep routes. Permission may be necessary to climb here. Private land.
Ref: Guidebook: Caffrey's *Climber's Guide to Montana*.
Directions: Somers (northwest part of town at the old dump). From junction of Hwy. 93 and Hwy. 82, go south on Hwy. 93 for 7/10 mi. Turn right onto Best View Dr. for 3/10 mi., then go down a couple hundred yards to old dump site on left and Somers Cliffs. Faces southwest. Not visible from Hwy. 93.

16 Big Fork Cliffs ✩

Super panorama of Flathead Lake from top of this 45′ metamorphic practice rock with short overhangs. Needs some TLC, but would be an okay little beginner's crag. Summer/autumn. Possibly private land.
Ref: Guidebook: Caffrey's *Climber's Guide to Montana*.
Directions: From Big Fork (southeast of Kalispell), at junction of Hwy. 35 and Hwy. 209, drive south 3/10 mi. on Hwy. 35. Turn left for 1/10 mi. to trail leading to left side of Big Fork Cliffs. Faces west.

17 Swan Range (Swan Peak)

Technical scrambling in the Swan Range, which contains lots of shale and limestone cliffs mostly south of Big Salmon Lake Area in the Gordon Creek Area. Rock quality is suspect. Summer. USFS–Flathead NF, (406) 293-6211.
Ref: Guidebook: Caffrey's *Climber's Guide to Montana*.
Directions: From Kalispell, the Swan Range lies to the east/southeast. Swan Peak has involved approach.

18 Great Bear Wilderness (Gunsight Rock)

Gunsight Rock is a remote limestone crag in the Flathead Range. Summer. USFS–Flathead NF, (406) 293-6211.
Ref: Guidebook: Caffrey's *Climber's Guide to Montana*.
Directions: From Hungry Horse on Hwy. 2, follow roads southeast of town along Hungry Horse Reservoir to Spotted Bear Ranger Station. Gunsight Rock is way east of station. Total time is approximately two hours on USFS roads and then two hours' hike to crumbly rock.

19 Bynum Reservoir (Antelope Butte)

Limestone spires and a weird, black, igneous rock known as Shonkinkite occurs here in the outlying buttes as climbable palisades. Government land.
Ref: Guidebook: Caffrey's *Climber's Guide to Montana*.
Directions: From Bynum go west of Bynum Reservoir at Antelope Butte.

20 Mission Range (Garden Wall)

Technical routes can be found on various mountains: Mt. Harding (9,061′) from Summit Lake, Eagle Pass Monolith (gendarme south of Harding), Gray Wolf Peak, and the Garden Wall. Broken faces of shale; uncertain rock quality. Other areas include Sunset Crag's extensive vertical cracks and pinnacle formations near Freeman Pass. Travel on Flathead Indian Reservation lands requires the use of permit. Grizzly bears. Summer. BIA/USFS–Flathead NF, (406) 293-6211.
Ref: Reese's *Montana Mountain Ranges;* Guidebook: Caffrey's *Climber's Guide to Montana*.
Directions: From St. Ignatius pursue Hwy. 93 north to Ninepipe (5 1/2 mi. south of Ronan) and turn east for 4 mi. Turn left (north) 1/8 mi. and then turn right up to Eagle Pass in Mission Range, getting as far as possible before hiking Garden Wall.

21 Bob Marshall Wilderness (Chinese Wall)

An incredible wilderness area with extensive bands of limestone and shale walls, rotten in nature. The Chinese Wall, a 10-mi.-long limestone fortress, is a standard photo in most classic geology textbooks. USFS.
Ref: Guidebook: Caffrey's *Climber's Guide to Montana*.
Directions: From Swan Lake go east/southeast of town via various USFS roads. The Bob Marshall Wilderness lies on the Flathead NF (406-293-6211) and Lewis and Clark NF. Obtain USFS maps.

22 Bear Paw Mountains

The Bear Paws are a mixture of weird igneous rocks sandwiched by volcanic extrusives on the north and south. Manshead Rock is typical of the one-pitch formations. Government land.
Ref: Guidebook: Caffrey's *Climber's Guide to Montana*.
Directions: From Havre go south to Lloyd. Manshead Rock,

near Lloyd Butte, holds volcanic outcrops in the Bear Paw Mountains.

23 Natural Bridge State Monument (Little Rocky Mountains) ✯✯

Meager portions of historic John Gill bouldering problems. Granite rock may be more abrasive than Andrew Dice Clay. Private/government land.

Ref: Ament's *Master of Rock;* Guidebook: Caffrey's *Climber's Guide to Montana.*

Directions: Natural Bridge State Monument is at Zortman or through town of Hay.

24 Scapegoat Wilderness (Scapegoat Mountain)

An incredible wilderness area with extensive bands of limestone and shale walls, rotten in nature. Scapegoat Mountain maintains a colossal buttressed plateau. Uncertain rock quality. Summer/autumn. USFS–Flathead NF, (406) 293-6211.

Ref: Guidebook: Caffrey's *Climber's Guide to Montana.*

Directions: From Augusta (west of Great Falls), escape southeast via USFS road to Sky Mountain Lodge. Obtain USFS maps.

25 Dearborn River Cliffs ●

Bizarre 200′ rhyolite cliff bands. Caution: Rock is rather soft for climbing. Small potential. More cliffs in mountains to west, e.g., Sawtooth Ridge and Haystack Butte. Government/private land.

Ref: Guidebook: Caffrey's *Climber's Guide to Montana.*

Directions: From Augusta follow roads south until intersection of Dearborn River.

26 Crown Butte ✯

Laccolith of 60′ Shonkinkite (volcanic) rock. Some good crack climbs for the beginner or intermediate climber, but mostly dirty rock. Beware of Mr. No Shoulders (i.e., rattlers). Owned by Nature Conservancy.

Ref: Guidebook: Caffrey's *Climber's Guide to Montana.*

Directions: From Simms top out 4 mi. south on Simms-Cascade Rd. on Crown Butte. Approach from north off small dirt road encircling base.

27 Square Butte

Square Butte is a fluted laccolith of black Shonkinkite rock rising dramatically from the Montana prairie lands. Aesthetic, but rock quality uncertain. Featured in more than one Charlie Russell painting. Highwood Mountains also have rock on South Flanks. Shonkinkite fins in fields to north of town. BLM.

Ref: Guidebook: Caffrey's *Climber's Guide to Montana.*

Directions: Square Butte on Hwy. 80. Follow BLM road for 5 mi. to west side of Square Butte.

28 Judith Mountains (Judith Peak/Black Butte)

Black Butte also has resistant igneous outcrops on south side. Exploratory areas.

Ref: Guidebook: Caffrey's *Climber's Guide to Montana.*

Directions: Judith Peak: From Lewistown go 10 mi. north on Hwy. 191, then east on pavement through Maiden to top of peak. Igneous formations lie on south side of mountain.

29 M✯–(Missoula Area) Cache/Pebble Creek

Solid granite comprises this large-toothed outcrop on canyon slope. Climbers from the University of Montana have sampled these haunts for years. Eats in Missoula: Mustard Seed, Old Town Cafe, The Shack, Mammoth Bakery, and Dos Lobos. USFS–Lolo NF, (406) 329-3750.

Classics: Cache Creek Tooth.

Ref: Guidebook: Caffrey's *Climber's Guide to Montana.*

Directions: West of Missoula on I-90. Exit at Tarkio and go south back through Rivulet to Fish Creek Drainage. Take south fork of Fish Creek (FR 343) to Cache Creek. Also accessible via Lolo Hot Springs by heading north over to FR 343.

30 RR✯–(Rattlesnake Range) Finley Creek

Three-hundred-foot tower in Finley Creek. Uncertain rock quality.

Ref: Guidebook: Caffrey's *Climber's Guide to Montana.*

Directions: From Arlee go east/southeast on Hwy. 8. Finley Creek is west of Seeley Lake.

31 RR–High Falls Creek

Crags of uncertain rock quality.

Ref: Guidebook: Caffrey's *Climber's Guide to Montana.*

Directions: From Missoula spring 4 mi. north up Van Buren St. (with junction of I-90). Turn right on Rattlesnake Creek Rd. to High Falls Creek (east of Stuart Peak).

32 M–Bearmouth Canyon ✯✯

Lots of south-facing limestone crags.

Directions: From Missoula go east on I-90 for approximately thirty minutes to Bearmouth Canyon, west of Drummond.

33 M–Rattler's Gulch/Mulkey's Gulch ✯✯✯

Limestone one-pitch sport climbing on walls, spires, and hobnobs along the interstate.

Ref: R 99-82; Guidebook: Green's *The Rock Climber's Guide to Montana.*

Directions: From Drummond (east of Missoula on I-90 approximately thirty minutes), exit I-90 and head 2 mi.

west on frontage road to Rattler's Gulch. Mulkey's Gulch is slightly farther west.

34 M–Harper's Bridge

One-hundred-and-fifty-foot granite crag. USFS–Lolo NF, (406) 329-3750.

Ref: G. Copenhaver 4/98; Guidebook: Caffrey's *Climber's Guide to Montana.*

Directions: Just west of Missoula, get on to Big Flat Rd. Follow signs to Deep Creek Shooting Range. You will come to an intersection just past a gravel pit. Above the intersection, there is an outcropping of cliffs that are a short uphill hike to get to. If you take a right at the intersection, it will take you to Harper's Bridge. From there you can head north and come across another outcropping of rock outcrops.

35 M–Redtail Rocks

One-pitch volcanic crag and volcanic tuff towers. USFS–Bitterroot NF, (406) 363-7117.

Ref: Guidebook: Caffrey's *Climber's Guide to Montana.*

Directions: From Rock Creek go approximately 7 mi. east. Go up first creek east of Ravenna Railroad tunnel to Redtail Rocks. From Missoula go east on I-90 to Rock Creek exit. Turn south to Squaw Creek or in area of Dalles Campground.

36 M–Lolo Hot Springs–Fish Creek and Granite Creek Domes ✰✰✰

Various-quality 180′ granite crags, spires, and boulders scattered throughout larch-forested hills between Lolo Hot Springs and Lolo Pass. A wide variety of good routes and boulders. Rock tends to be steep face with edges or rounded, coarse-grained crimpers to flared cracks. Still lots to discover and climb. Easy access has made this a popular Missoulan climbing area. Nearby attractions include Lolo Hot Springs and the Lumberjack Saloon. USFS–Lolo NF, (406) 329-3750.

Classics: Tor Rock: Accelerator 10, Deceptor 10, Guajanator 12a; Elk Rock: F 104 11, Elk Fart 11.

Ref: R 99-82; Guidebooks: Green's *The Rock Climber's Guide to Montana,* Hutcheson's *Climber's Guide to Lolo Pass,* Torre's *Bitterroot Climber's Guidebook,* Torre's *Bitterroot Bouldering Guide,* Torre's *A Rock Climber's Guide to the Bitterroot Valley,* Caffrey's *Climber's Guide to Montana.*

Directions: From Lolo Hot Springs cook west to three areas of rock climbing: 1) Granite boulders/crags west along Hwy. 2 (mm 1 and 2) to Lolo Pass and east fork of Lolo Creek. 2) ¼ mi. west from Lolo Hot Springs, take right on Fish Creek Rd. Turn left on FR 4200 to Bobcat Loop for Reef, Bonzai, and Elk Rock (ten minutes). 3) Back on Fish Creek Rd., continue ½ mi. farther up (past FR 4200) and turn left onto Granite Creek Rd. in a couple miles for Tor Rock (good bolted routes) on left (trail) and other formations (fifteen minutes). Keep your eyes open.

> ## Montana Road Thoughts
>
> Any state where you can buy automatic weapons, drive as fast as you can, and has gambling and big skies has a lot going for it.
>
> —TNT

37 Blue Cloud Spires/The Schoolhouse ✰✰✰

Stacks of granite boulders and 100′ pinnacles are northern terminus of Boulder Batholith. Classic intermediate problems at the Schoolhouse. A nice place to earn your intermediate bouldering diploma. USFS/private land.

Ref: 9/97; Guidebook: Caffrey's *Climber's Guide to Montana.*

Directions: From Helena drift just west on Hwy. 12 for approximately 8 mi. (fifteen minutes from downtown Helena). In the timber and scrublands at Blue Cloud and Sweeney Creeks are granite formations. Some private access. The Schoolhouse was a white schoolhouse on the north side of road at mm 34.5 before it was removed in 1997. Look for gravel parking area on north side of highway. Hike northwest (angle left) to granite boulders in two minutes. More rock beyond fifteen minutes.

38 Rimini (Ten Mile Creek)

Thirty-foot granitic bouldering. USFS–Helena NF, (406) 449-5201.

Ref: Guidebook: Caffrey's *Climber's Guide to Montana.*

Directions: From Rimini (southwest of Helena, go west on Hwy. 12 to left turn on Rimini Rd.), go just south to rocks along Ten Mile Creek.

39 Helena Limestone–Hellgate Canyon/ Beaver Creek Canyon ✰✰✰✰

Possibly Montana's finest limestone sport crag. Hellgate Canyon harbors 150′ limestone sport crags with some fine routes and finer scenery. Some notable routes include Batteries Not Included 5.8, Bassackwards 5.10, This Ain't Nuthin' 5.12-. USFS–Helena NF, (406) 449-5201.

Ref: R 99-84; Guidebooks: Green's *The Rock Climber's Guide to Montana,* Caffrey's *Climber's Guide to Montana.*

Directions: From Helena proceed east on Hwy. 12, then north on Hwy. 284 to east side of Canyon Ferry Lake. Hwy. 284 goes southeast to Hellgate Gulch. Other limestone cliffs exist in Trout Creeks, Magpie Creek, and to Avalanche Creek.

40 The Needles (in Big Belt Mountains) ✰✰✰

One-hundred-and-fifty-foot limestone crag. Spring/ autumn. USFS–Helena NF, (406) 449-5201.

Ref: AAJ '87-182; Guidebook: Caffrey's *Climber's Guide to Montana.*

Directions: The Needles are on the east side of the Big Belt Mountains. Access through private ranch.

41 McClellan Creek Boulders ☆☆
Twenty-five-foot granite boulders and pinnacles. Possibly private land.
Ref: Guidebook: Caffrey's *Climber's Guide to Montana*.
Directions: From Helena drift just east on Hwy. 12 to East Helena. Go south on Hwy. 518 to McClellan Creek Boulders.

42 Sheep Mountain (in Boulder Batholith) ☆☆☆
Popular with Helenite and dyed-in-the-wool climbers, these 200' spirelike outcrops and crags are on the south side of Sheep Mountain. Quality bouldering roadside and at base of mountain, too. Formations include Devil's Thumb, Left Rock, Upper Rock, Middle Rock, and Right Rock. Seventy routes to 5.12. BLM/private land.
Ref: Guidebooks: Green's *The Rock Climber's Guide to Montana*, Caffrey's *Climber's Guide to Montana*.
Directions: From Clancy (south of Helena on I-15, visible from interstate), Sheep Mountain is approximately 2 mi. northwest of town on east.

43 Neihart (Carpenter Creek) ☆☆
A nice supply of worthy one-pitch granite and metamorphic formations. Sound rock makes for enjoyable climbing in the pine forests. USFS-Lewis and Clark NF, (406) 791-7700.
Ref: Guidebook: Caffrey's *Climber's Guide to Montana*.
Directions: From Neihart: Drive south to Memorial Falls quartzite crag (50'). Saw north on Hwy. 89 between mm 45 and 46 to solid, granite outcrops. Limestone bands at mm 47. Cliffs lie to east of road. Best quartzite cliff (150') in Neihart above town.

44 BM☆-(Bitterroot Mountains) Bass Creek Crags ☆☆☆
Fun granite cragging. Major concentration of crags at Lappi Lake includes: Sawtooth Ridge, The Turret, and Mickey Mouse. Also on south side of Bass Creek. USFS-Bitterroot NF, (406) 363-7117.
Classics: Bombay Boogie 7, Flashdance 8, Waltz to Hands 9, Bop Til You Drop 10.
Ref: AAJ '94-148; Guidebooks: Torre's *Bitterroot Climber's Guidebook*, Torre's *Bitterroot Bouldering Guide*, Torre's *A Rock Climber's Guide to the Bitterroot Valley*, Caffrey's *Climber's Guide to Montana*.
Directions: From Florence (18 mi. south of Missoula on Hwy. 93), fish 5 mi. south on Hwy. 93W on Bass Creek Rd. (dirt) to dead-end. Park. Hike west to large slab 2 or 3 mi. up canyon.

45 BM-Kootenai Canyon ☆☆☆☆
Best quick rock-climbing fix from Missoula (thirty minutes). Fun overhanging gneiss/schist one-pitch routes, e.g., Venus De Milo. An area of crags and more; Easter Rock is ½ mi. up trail north of diversion dam. Ramparts 1,800' above offer longer routes: 600' route on Chief Charlo 1 2/10 mi. up trail. Well-developed area presents many routes to visiting climbers. USFS-Bitterroot NF, (406) 363-7117.
Classics: Chief Charlo 6, Classic Crack 7, Outermost Limits 8, Wiener Pigs 10+, Eleventh Commandment 10, Flying Time 10, Uncontrollable Desire 11, Venus De Milo 11+, Venus Fly Trap 12.
Ref: R 99-82; Guidebooks: Green's *The Rock Climber's Guide to Montana*, Torre's *Bitterroot Climber's Guidebook*, Torre's *A Rock Climber's Guide to the Bitterroot Valley*, Caffrey's *Climber's Guide to Montana*.
Directions: From Stevensville (south of Missoula on Hwy. 93), coast ½ mi. north on Hwy. 93. Turn west approximately 1 mi. on Kootenai Canyon Rd. (dirt) to obvious canyon. Park at dead-end. In no time flat, the rock at mouth of Kootenai Canyon north of creek appears. Most routes on right side of trail, though some on other side of creek.

46 BM-Big Creek
Massive series of long arêtes. Summer. USFS-Bitterroot NF, (406) 363-7117.
Ref: R 99-82; Guidebook: Caffrey's *Climber's Guide to Montana*.
Directions: West/northwest of Victor. Below Big Creek Lake on north side of creek.

47 BM-Gash Ridge Needles
Backcountry ridge of spires and pinnacles. USFS-Bitterroot NF, (406) 363-7117.
Ref: Guidebook: Caffrey's *Climber's Guide to Montana*.
Directions: West of Victor. Gash Ridge Needles are at head of Sweathouse Creek. Northwest of Gash Point.

48 BM-Bear Creek
South-facing crag up the middle fork of Bear Creek. Summer. USFS-Bitterroot NF, (406) 363-7117.
Ref: Guidebook: Caffrey's *Climber's Guide to Montana*.
Directions: Southwest of Victor. Between north and middle forks of Bear Creek. Ubiquitous hidden cliffs from Bear Creek south to Nez Perce fork of Bitterroot River.

49 BM-Fred Burr Creek
South-facing granite pinnacle. USFS-Bitterroot NF, (406) 363-7117.
Ref: Guidebooks: Torre's *Bitterroot Climber's Guidebook*, Torre's *A Rock Climber's Guide to the Bitterroot Valley*, Caffrey's *Climber's Guide to Montana*.
Directions: Southwest of Victor. Hike 2-3 mi. up trail to spires on north side of Fred Burr Creek. Crosses over private property at first.

50 BM–Sheafman Creek

South-facing granite summer crags with climbs of varying length. USFS–Bitterroot NF, (406) 363-7117.

Ref: Guidebooks: Torre's *Bitterroot Climber's Guidebook*, Torre's *A Rock Climber's Guide to the Bitterroot Valley*.

Directions: South of Missoula. In the Bitterroots. Distant approaches up Sheafman Creek Trail.

51 BM–Mill Creek ★★★

This glacially carved canyon and wilderness area holds high-quality granite crag/buttress near trailhead; has several 5.10/11 165′ climbs like Neutered Rooster and Chickenhoist. USFS–Bitterroot NF, (406) 363-7117.

Classics: No Sweat Arête III 5.9 at west end of spires.

Ref: R 99-82; Guidebooks: Green's *The Rock Climber's Guide to Montana*, Torre's *Bitterroot Climber's Guidebook*, Torre's *A Rock Climber's Guide to the Bitterroot Valley*, Caffrey's *Climber's Guide to Montana*.

Directions: From Corvallis (south of Missoula off Hwy. 93), go west on Hwy. 54. Hike ½ mi. up trail to north side of Mills Creek. Prominent buttresses are visible from Hwy. 93. One mi. north of Blodgett Canyon. Faces south.

52 BM–Blodgett Canyon ★★★★★

First exposed in John Harlin's Climber's Guide to North America (Rockies). Several miles of granite arêtes and buttresses up to 1,000′ have attracted more and more climbers to this scenic Rocky Mountain canyon. Many multipitched routes. Campground bouldering. The weather in the Bitterroot Mountains varies dramatically. It's possible to climb in winter on south-facing slopes or suffer heat prostration in the July sun. Be wary of sudden thunderstorms. Abundant tick population in May requires frequent body checks. Breakfast: Coffee Cup Cafe in Hamilton. USFS–Bitterroot NF, (406) 363-7117.

Classics: Nez Perce Spire: Southwest Buttress IV 10; Shoshone Spire: South Face III 8, In Memoriam III 10; Flathead Spire: South Face IV 10d, Direct 12, Larry's Leisure Suit 10; The Prow: Time Binder IV 11b; Parking Lot Wall bolted routes, Campground Boulder.

Ref: AAJ ['93, 88-143], C 132, R [99-82, 6(1/85)]; Guidebooks: Green's *The Rock Climber's Guide to Montana*, Torre's *Bitterroot Climber's Guidebook*, Torre's *Bitterroot Bouldering Guide*, Torre's *A Rock Climber's Guide to the Bitterroot Valley*, Caffrey's *Climber's Guide to Montana*, Harlin's *Rocky Mountain*.

Directions: From Hamilton bop 6 mi. west on Main St. Follow signs to Blodgett Canyon. Buttresses and spurs that line the north side of the canyon include The Prow and Stegosaurus Ridge, which are dark in color. Then, four light buttresses: Blackfoot Dome (Beehive) with Kootenai Buttress, Nez Perce Buttress, Shoshone Spire, and Flathead Buttress. Fantastic views of Blodgett Canyon available from Overlook Trail from forest road just south of Blodgett Canyon proper.

53 BM–Canyon Creek

On the north side of creek are prominent south-facing granite towers. An obvious dihedral lies on Morning Glory Wall. When climbing in the Bitterroot Mountains in May–June, be on guard for ticks, carriers of the disabling Rocky Mountain Spotted Fever. Checking your clothing frequently and your body at night will prevent acquiring this unwanted buddy. USFS–Bitterroot NF, (406) 363-7117.

Ref: Guidebooks: Torre's *Bitterroot Climber's Guidebook*, Torre's *A Rock Climber's Guide to the Bitterroot Valley*, Caffrey's *Climber's Guide to Montana*.

Directions: From Hamilton bop 6 mi. west on Main St. Just before Blodgett Canyon, turn left on USFS road. Hike up trail 2 mi. to wilderness boundary sign to Canyon Creek. To the southwest up the ridge is the prominent Morning Glory Wall. Towers lie on north side of creek, e.g., Canyon Peak.

54 BM–South Fork Lost Horse Creek

Observation Point cliffs are 70′ high and horizontally fractured. Series of granite buttresses on ridge to north. USFS–Bitterroot NF, (406) 363-7117.

Ref: AAJ '93; Guidebooks: Torre's *Bitterroot Guidebook*, Torre's *Bitterroot Bouldering Guide*, Torre's *A Rock Climber's Guide to the Bitterroot Valley*, Caffrey's *Climber's Guide to Montana*.

Directions: From Hamilton trot south on Hwy. 93. Turn right (west) on Hwy. 79 to Lost Horse Observation Peak. Climbing at the observation point. Or, on ridge to north of south fork up canyon, and pinnacle at confluence of Lost Horse Creek and north fork. Bouldering areas: ¼ mi. past the Lost Horse Saloon and beyond on FR 5621 and 62945. Bouldering also at Lake Como Recreation Area (hiking trail) and several areas east of Hamilton, one of which is located on Hwy. 38, east of Skalkaho Pass.

55 BM–Rock Creek

South-facing granite spurs and pinnacles. USFS–Bitterroot NF, (406) 363-7117.

Ref: Guidebook: Caffrey's *Climber's Guide to Montana*.

Directions: From Darby go northwest to Lake Como. Then go up Rock Creek. On the north side of creek stand granite spires.

56 BM–Trapper Peak Area

The centerpiece of attention here is the North Face Direct Route on Trapper Peak (9,801′), a Montana classic. The Antonilli Route (original route) and North Face Direct were done back in 1971. The area also holds a variety of backcountry granite pinnacle and face-climbing opportunities. USFS–Bitterroot NF, (406) 363-7117.

Classics: Antonilli Rt III 8, North Face IV 10, Lowe Rt IV 11.

Ref: AAJ '82, R 79-144; Guidebooks: Brunckhorst's *Alpine Ice and Rock Guide to Southwest and Central Montana*, Caffrey's *Climber's Guide to Montana*.

Directions: Southwest of Hamilton. Spires west of Trapper

Peak, the Peak, and outcrops in Trapper and Boulder Creek drainages. Pinnacles in Crow Creek and Gem Lake.

57 BM–Eagle Rock

Obvious 5.9 dihedral and other difficult short routes can be found on this south-facing crag. USFS-Bitterroot NF, (406) 363-7117.

Ref: Guidebook: Caffrey's *Climber's Guide to Montana*.

Directions: From Medicine Hot Springs soar 1 mi. south to Eagle Rock.

58 Granite Mine Boulders ✮

Good 30′ granite bouldering opportunities. USFS-Deerlodge NF, (406) 683-3900.

Ref: Guidebook: Caffrey's *Climber's Guide to Montana*.

Directions: From Phillipsburg go 4 mi. east at the Granite Mine. In Flint Creek Range. Also in area, Mt. Powell has fractured cliff. Big cliffs farther north on Hwy. 1.

59 Warren Peak (in Anaconda Range)

Exposed granite buttresses. Quality climbing—faces and spires. Peak (10,259′) above Warren Lake. Also, nice northeast ice/snow couloir. Warren Lake/Rainbow Lake areas have granitic boulders. USFS-Deerlodge NF, (406) 683-3900.

Ref: Guidebooks: Brunckhorst's *Alpine Ice and Rock Guide to Southwest and Central Montana*, Caffrey's *Climber's Guide to Montana*.

Directions: Warren Peak is south of Anaconda in the Anaconda Range.

60 Boulder Boulders (Muskrat Creek) ✮✮

Woodland 30′ granite boulders and hobnobs in Elkhorn Mountains. USFS-Deerlodge NF, (406) 683-3900.

Ref: Guidebook: Caffrey's *Climber's Guide to Montana*.

Directions: From Boulder go up McClellan Creek or slopes east of Muskrat Creek.

61 Maxwell Point ✮✮

Granite bouldering and rock climbing near TV towers. Access problems with locked gates. Possibly private land.

Ref: Guidebook: Caffrey's *Climber's Guide to Montana*.

Directions: Overlooks Butte, east of town. Maxwell Point is also called X-L Heights.

62 McClusky Mountain ✮✮✮

One-hundred-foot granite rock face on the south side of the mountain delivers rewarding climbing and views. Some nice intermediate routes. This area is northeast of Homestake Pass. USFS-Deerlodge NF, (406) 683-3900.

Ref: Guidebook: Caffrey's *Climber's Guide to Montana*.

Directions: From Butte go east on I-90. Exit north on ramp Hwy. 241. Go on FR 222 to Delmoe Park. Hike north to the south side of the McClusky Mountain. Hour approach.

63 Spire Rock/Roof Rock ✮✮✮

Wealth of 150′ granite climbs at Spire Rock on the King and Queen formations. Roof Rock sports a feast of overhangs, including the Long Wall area. Good potential. USFS-Deerlodge NF, (406) 683-3900.

Classics: King Spire: Cerebral Stem 10b, Blood Sport 11, Catabolism 12; Queen Spire: Dream Weaver 9, Cruise Control 10b, Nuclear Energy 12; Roof Rock: Montana Street 8, Kurt's Unemployment Benefits 9+, Black Streak 12.

Ref: Guidebooks: Green's *The Rock Climber's Guide to Montana*, Krueger and Calhoun's *More Climbs in Butte*, Bishop's *A Climber's Guide to Butte*.

Directions: Spire Rock: From Butte take I-90 east over Homestake Pass to Pipestone exit. Go northwest 5 4/10 mi. on Delmoe Lake Rd. King and Queen Spires are main formations. Roof Rock: Double back along the interstate by turning left 4 mi. Before Spire Rock, turn onto Whitetail Creek Rd. for 3/4 mi. to notch. Just before the notch, turn left onto a faint road for 1/4 mi. (a cattle guard means you've gone 1/4 mi. too far). Park. Hike road steeply to ridge. Traverse ridge on road through mining claim. Go another 1/2 mi. on road (small drop, then up) to trail (thirty-minute hike to here) on right (blazes on two separate trees and rock cairn) for fifteen minutes.

64 Homestake Pass (Dragon's Back) ✮✮✮

This vast expanse of granite is part of the geologic province known as the Boulder Batholith. For climbers this translates to 100′ granite bouldering grounds ad infinitum. These decomposing granite climbs straddle the Continental Divide. Butte liveries: M and M Cafe, Gamers Cafe, Silver Dollar Bar. USFS-Deerlodge NF, (406) 683-3900.

Classics: Gillette Edge 7, Crackster's Unite 8, Town Pump 10b, Hot Wings 11b, Killer Whale 11c, Simian Rage 13; Dragon's Back: Bishop's Surprise 7+, Proboscis 8, Heinous Anus Cookies 9, Dream Weaver 9, Power Pusher 9+, Touch and Go 10, Cruise Control 10b, Slipperman 11a.

Ref: Guidebooks: Green's *The Rock Climber's Guide to Montana*, Bishop's *A Climber's Guide to Butte*, Caffrey's *Climber's Guide to Montana*, W. Hough's guidebook.

Directions: From Butte go 5 mi. east on I-90. Nearly 100 square miles of granite boulders. Best parking for Homestake Pass climbing is on I-90 Westbound (north side) rest area. Hike east along railroad tracks. Scattered formations include Split Pinnacle, Gillette Edge, Aid Boulder, and Moby Dick. All rocks more than 50′ tall have routes. Hot Wings is found north of mm 236 pullout. Dragon's Back, obviously named, is 2 mi. east of rest area.

65 Timber Butte ✮✮

Small western hillside covered with minimal 50′ bouldering opportunities. USFS–Deerlodge NF, (406) 683–3900.
Ref: Guidebook: Caffrey's *Climber's Guide to Montana*.
Directions: From Butte pop south on Montana St. toward small local ski area. Timber Butte Boulders are on west-facing hill approximately 1 mi. east of the ski area.

66 Pipestone Pass ✮✮✮

An expansive area of 150′ granite crags in this forested and easily accessed area south of Butte. USFS–Deerlodge NF, (406) 683–3900.
Classics: Our Rock: Central Corner 7; Mahogany Rock: Gravity's Child 10; Roadside Rock: 5.12 crack.
Ref: Guidebooks: Krueger and Calhoun's *More Climbs in Butte*, Bishop's *A Climber's Guide to Butte*, Caffrey's *Climber's Guide to Montana*.
Directions: From Butte go southeast on Hwy. 2 to east of pass. Various crags along road over Pipestone Pass. Our Rock (the prominent white-finned formation) is just east of the top of pass. Below pass, turn right into willows at nondescript dirt road, cross dilapidated wooden plank bridge, cross over old railroad bed, following road up past private cabin below formation. Short, steep hike. Mahogany Rock: Farther east, turn right at Fish Creek Rd. (sign) for approximately 4 mi. to parking at left switchback. Hike fifteen minutes up gulch traversing to rock. (Visible from Pigeon Creek Campground). Road-side Rock is located still farther east on Hwy. 2 past Rader Creek Rd., where a bolted 5.12 crack stares at the roadside and you may find yourself on the pavement without the right skills for the job.

67 Humbug Spires ✮✮✮

Multiples of 300′ to 600′ coarse-grained granite spires. The highest is The Wedge (7,045′) at 600′. The Wedge has a number of good routes 5.7 to 5.10 on southwest and 5.12s on north face. The Crown overhangs on all sides. Unreliable patches of white granite. Check for suspect bolts. Vast amounts of untouched rock in a scenic wilderness area. Summer/autumn. BLM.
Classics: The Wedge: Butterknife Route II 8, Tiny Tim 10.
Ref: C 168-68, R [99-82, 26(7/88)-55], S 3/67; Guidebooks: Green's *The Rock Climber's Guide to Montana*, Krueger and Calhoun's *More Climbs in Butte*, Caffrey's *Climber's Guide to Montana*.
Directions: Southwest of Butte. Go 26 mi. south on I-15. Exit at Moose Creek exit. Go east for 3 ½ mi. to parking at the Humbug Spires BLM Trailhead. (East of the town of Divide.) Popular formations include: The Wedge (4 ½ mi. hike), The Finger, Baldy, The Thumb, The Dome, and The Wall. Other approaches up Tucker Creek and Lime Gulch require private land access.

68 Wise River Cliffs (in Pioneer Mountains) ✮✮✮

Stunning, 300′ quartzite cliff in beautiful canyon. Elkhorn Hot Springs is farther south. USFS–Beaverhead NF, (406) 832–3178.
Ref: Guidebook: Caffrey's *Climber's Guide to Montana*.
Directions: From Wise River, approximately 8 mi. south from town, 300′ cliff on west side of Wise River. Cross creek at old wooden tree-trunk bridge. Surmount short talus field to base of cliff. Other cliffs farther south up above road to Lodgepole Campground. Faces east.

69 Mt. Tweedy/Mt. Torrey (in Pioneer Mountains)

Three-hundred-foot granite alpine crag. Also spires on ridge between Elkhorn and David Creeks. Highboy Mountain has a climbable east buttress above Tub Lake. Good technical granite on North Ridge. Summer/autumn.
USFS–Beaverhead NF, (406) 832–3178.
Classics: North Ridge III 7 A1.
Ref: AAJ '88-138; Guidebooks: Brunckhorst's *Alpine Ice and Rock Guide to Southwest and Central Montana*, Caffrey's *Climber's Guide to Montana*.
Directions: West approach for Pioneer Mountains: From Wise River go south from town on FR 484 to access roads out of Elkhorn area. East approach: Go northwest from Dillon on I-15 to Apex, then west on USFS road (road uncertain). Range of rock south from Mt. Tahepia to Tent Mountain.

70 South Boulder River Cliffs (in Tobacco Root Mountains) ✮✮✮

A prosperous ambience of scattered 200′ granite outcrops. USFS–Beaverhead-Deerlodge NF, (406) 287–3223.
Ref: Guidebook: Caffrey's *Climber's Guide to Montana*.
Directions: From Cardwell go south on Hwy. 359, then south on South Boulder River Rd to upper reaches. Climbing can be found west of Hollow Top Mountain or at north ridge of Manhead Mountain.

71 Leggat Peak (in Tobacco Root Mountains)

Metamorphic rock is on north face of Leggat (10,089′) and a route called Legacy II 7. USFS–Beaverhead NF, (406) 287–3223.
Ref: Guidebooks: Brunckhorst's *Alpine Ice and Rock Guide to Southwest and Central Montana*, Caffrey's *Climber's Guide to Montana*.
Directions: From Sheridan go east on forest roads to Branham Lakes. Hike east to Leggat Peak's east face.

72 Revenue Flats (in Tobacco Root Mountains) ✮✮✮

Scattered, dark 100′ granite spires. Classic short one-pitch climbs and bouldering. Scattered bolted routes. Unless you're partial to picking buckshot out of your backside, make sure you're on public lands. Beartrap Hot Springs to east of Norris are worth a soak. Private/BLM.

Ref: Guidebook: Caffrey's *Climber's Guide to Montana*.

Directions: From Norris head approximately 5 mi. west of town on good dirt road from junction (near old Revenue Mine).

73 Madison River Cliffs (Neat Rock/Bushy Boulder) ✮✮✮

Small, easily accessed 150′ granite south-facing crag. About twelve routes. Bushy Boulder has several fun toprope/boulder lines. Eagle nesting area. Blue-ribbon trout fishing along the Madison River.

Classics: Neat Rock: Standard Rt 9, Rock Lobster 10+.

Ref: Guidebooks: Green's *The Rock Climber's Guide to Montana*, Dockins's *Bozeman Rock Climbs*, Caffrey's *Climber's Guide to Montana*.

Directions: From Norris (approximately 33 mi. west of Bozeman), migrate 7 mi. east on Hwy. 84. Turn left on dirt before Beartrap Bridge for 2 ½ mi. to Neat Rock. Drive-up access. Bushy Boulder is obvious roadside block 1 ¹⁄₁₀ mi. south of west of bridge. More cragging along roadside south toward Norris from this boulder.

74 Madison River Boulders ✮✮

Twenty-five-foot granite bouldering blocks offer solid opportunities. Climbs on buttresses above boulders and along road as well. Part of the cliff has been blasted—caution advised.

Ref: Guidebooks: Dockins's *Bozeman Rock Climbs*, Caffrey's *Climber's Guide to Montana*.

Directions: From Norris (approximately 33 mi. west of Bozeman), trot 8 mi. east. Take first right (Bozeman side) across Beartrap Bridge and go for 1 ⁸⁄₁₀ mi. on bumpy dirt road to roadside blocks along Madison River.

75 B✮-(Bozeman Area) Bozeman Pass ✮✮✮✮

Bozeman Pass quickly has one roping up on 80′ overhanging pocketed limestone leads. Bozeman hosts several crags and bouldering areas within a one-hour drive of town. Fine climbing in several areas includes Bozeman Pass (sport), Hyalite Canyon (leads/toprope), The Grove (bouldering), and Gallatin Canyon (leads). Home of Montana State University. Eats: Spanish Peaks Brewery and Italian Cafe, Western Cafe, and John Bozeman's Bistro. Spring/autumn. Private land/USFS–Gallatin NF, (406) 587-6701.

Classics: Bozeman Pass: Ethos Burned 10, Fright Train 11b, Moments Away from Manhood 11+, many more good leads.

Ref: C 108, R 99-84; Guidebooks: Green's *The Rock Climber's Guide to Montana*, Dockins's *Bozeman Rock Climbs*, Caffrey's *Climber's Guide to Montana*.

Directions: From Bozeman go 6 mi. east on I-90. Requires driving past Bozeman Pass area and then heading back

west toward Bozeman. Parking on north side of highway at pullout below alcove of limestone.

76 B–The Grove ✮✮✮

Inconspicuous 30′ granite bouldering area, micro-edge crankin'. Go with a local escort. Hold on tight . . . the problems here are like taking a tough bronc to the buzzer. Private land.

Classics: The Project B1.

Ref: B. Dockins; Guidebook: Caffrey's *Climber's Guide to Montana*.

Directions: From Bozeman go southwest of junction of Hwy. 84 and Hwy. 191. The Grove is not obvious from Hwy. 191. Ask local climbers.

77 B–Hyalite Canyon–Practice Rock ✮✮✮

Local Bozeman "pet" crag. The 100′ metamorphic Practice Rock is very popular. Other good rock treats exist, with about eighteen routes. Spring/autumn. USFS–Gallatin NF, (406) 587-6701.

Classics: Jerry's Route 8, Theoretically 10, Practice Wall 11, Cardiac Arête 12, Last of the Wild Ones 12.

Ref: C 108, R 99-84; Guidebooks: Green's *The Rock Climber's Guide to Montana*, Dockins's *Bozeman Rock Climbs*, Caffrey's *Climber's Guide to Montana*.

Directions: From Bozeman (ten minutes) go 6 mi. south on Nineteenth Ave. Turn left on Hyalite Canyon Rd. At 3 ¹⁄₁₀ mi. park on left for Practice Rock.

78 B–Crocodile Rock ✮✮

Quick 'n' easy 50′ granite roadside climbing. The Overhangatang Boulder, a one-time classic, was sanctioned during road-widening construction. USFS–Gallatin NF, (406) 587-6701.

Classics: Black Corner 10, Crack of Tripe 12.

Ref: Guidebooks: Dockins's *Bozeman Rock Climbs*, Caffrey's *Climber's Guide to Montana*.

Directions: From Bozeman go 6 mi. south on Nineteenth Ave. Turn left on Hyalite Canyon Rd. for 4 ⁴⁄₁₀ mi. Park on left for Crocodile Rock.

79 B–Gallatin Canyon Main Area and Towers ✮✮✮✮

Local Bozeman climbers' playground with one hundred fine routes. Tricky climbing and funky pro makes for mentally stimulating climbing in this classic river canyon with 200′ gneiss. You won't find this one in the classifieds, but it's well worth the time! USFS–Gallatin NF, (406) 587-6701.

Classics: Skyline 6, Standard Rt 8, First Best 10-, Black Line 10b, Butthole Surfer 11+; Cube Routes.

Ref: C 108, R 99-84; Guidebooks: Green's *The Rock Climber's Guide to Montana*, Dockins's *Bozeman Rock Climbs*, Caffrey's *Climber's Guide to Montana*.

Directions: From Bozeman burn pavement southwest for 8

mi. on Hwy. 84. Turn 17 mi. south on Hwy. 191. (Coming from south on Hwy. 191, Gallatin Canyon area lies just a few minutes north of Big Sky.)

80 B–Gallatin Canyon Limestone (aka Storm Castle Mountain) ✯✯

Undeveloped, light-potential, intermittent 200′ limestone rock. Spring/autumn. Private land/USFS–Gallatin NF, (406) 587-6701.

Classics: Dr Z 9.

Ref: Guidebooks: Dockins's *Bozeman Rock Climbs,* Caffrey's *Climber's Guide to Montana.*

Directions: From Bozeman wend 20 mi. south on Hwy. 191 to 6 mi. south of Gallatin Gateway between mm 64–65. Turn 1 mi. up Squaw Creek Rd. for Gallatin Canyon Limestone.

81 B–Bridger Range (Ross Peak–NE) ✯✯✯

Granite alpine walls in the Bridger Range. USFS–Gallatin NF, (406) 587-6701.

Classics: 5.9 A4.

Ref: AAJ '77-187; Guidebook: Caffrey's *Climber's Guide to Montana.*

Directions: From Bozeman go north on Hwy. 86 for 20 mi. to Bracket Creek. Turn left onto Bracket Creek Rd. (dirt road) through clearcuts toward the saddle of Ross Peak in the Bridger Range.

82 Crazy Mountains (Twin Lakes) ✯✯

Climbs on 1,000′ quartzite/granite alpine buttresses (e.g., The Dogtooth's Brother Bear Route IV 8 A2) in an easily overlooked range. Crazy Peak (11,209′) and Iddings Peak (just under 11,000′) are the two highest in the range and offer couloirs to climb. USFS–Gallatin NF, (406) 587-6701.

Ref: AAJ '98-203; Guidebooks: Brunckhorst's *Alpine Ice and Rock Guide to Southwest and Central Montana,* Kelsey's *Climber's and Hiker's Guide to the World Mountains,* Caffrey's *Climber's Guide to Montana.*

Directions: From Big Timber fire 27 mi. northwest via Big Timber Creek Rd. to Half Moon Campground. Hike to Twin Lakes. Alpine rock routes lie on the ridge south of Twin Lakes. Formations offering rock include Crazy, Iddings, and Granite Peaks.

83 Joliet ✯✯

Prominent bluffs of 150′ soft sandstone. Private land.

Ref: Guidebook: Caffrey's *Climber's Guide to Montana.*

Directions: From Joliet, bluffs just east of town on Hwy. 212. May require private ranch access.

Rimrock near Billings.

TIM TOULA

84 Billings Rimrocks ✯✯✯

Long chain of 50′ sandstone minicrags on the north fringe of this big sky town. Due to the soft rock nature, leading is chancy because protection will blow out quicker than a bald tire on August blacktop. Hence, toproping is the norm. After rain, refrain from climbing. Faces south; on a sunny summer day, you'll be sweatin' like a sinner in church on Sunday. Scenic views of Billings and shredder mountain biking on the terraces at the top of the rock.

Eats: Dos Machos, George Henry's, Miyajima, Vinnie's. City land.

Classics: Welcome to Billings 8, Elephant's Memory 10a, Lizard Cracks 10, The Gem 11?, Full Sail 5.12 toprope.

Ref: Guidebooks: *Rimrock Beach,* Caffrey's *Climber's Guide to Montana.*

Directions: Sandstone bluffs that rim the city of Billings on Rimrock Dr. Best areas: Wilshire Heights subdivision; Suncliffs, below city's radio towers; Indian Cliffs, east of town; and bouldering at Gregory Hills subdivision.

85 Pompey's Pillar ✯

Historic landmark of the Lewis and Clark expedition with Clark's signature in stone. Named after Sacajawea's son. Soft 200′ sandstone formation, uncertain if climbing is

allowed. Closed October 3 and from 9:00 A.M. to 5:00 P.M.
BLM.
Ref: Guidebook: Caffrey's *Climber's Guide to Montana*.
Directions: From Billings, Pompey's Pillar is 25 mi. east off
I-94.

86 Medicine Rocks State Park ●
Chossy 40' sandstone crag. Possibly good frontpointing.
Pay camping in state park.
Ref: Guidebook: Caffrey's *Climber's Guide to Montana*.
Directions: From Ekalaka, Medicine Rocks State Park is 7
mi. north on Hwy. 7.

87 Spanish Peak Wilderness Area
Summer alpine backcountry cliffs. USFS–Gallatin NF,
(406) 587-6701.
Classics: 5.9 A4.
Ref: AAJ '96-168.
Directions: Big Sky Area. Pack in from Big Sky Ski Resort
via Beehive Basin in Spanish Peak Wilderness Area.

88 Pipe Organ Rock (in Beaverhead Mountains)
Unique 100' volcanic flutes on I-15 hillside. May or may
not deliver good climbing. Spring/autumn. Possibly government land.
Ref: Guidebook: Caffrey's *Climber's Guide to Montana*.
Directions: Southwest of Dillon. Pipe Organ Rock is on
west side of I-15. Faces southeast.

89 Absaroka Range (Mt. Cowen) ★★★☆
An immense variety of backcountry granite rock in a cold,
alpine setting. Mt. Cowen Cirque, the Needles (Eeny, Mee-
ny, Miney, and Moe), and the Black Spire are just some of
the select rock massifs to dance across. The Mt. Cowen area
was climbed as early as the mid-1950s by Bob Witters and
Ed Anaker. Several modern routes established by Tom
Kalakay and others. Check out Brunckhorst's guide for
topos. USFS–Gallatin NF, (406) 587-6701.
Classics: Mt. Cowen Northeast Arête III 6; Eenie: Passive
Aggressive Disorder III 10+, Montana Centennial Route
IV 11-, Mark of the Beast III 12A0; Black Spire: Arrow
Arête II 8.
Ref: AAJ '87-181; Gallatin NF map; Guidebooks: Brunck-
horst's *Alpine Ice and Rock Guide to Southwest and Central
Montana*, Caffrey's *Climber's Guide to Montana*.
Directions: From Livingston go south on Hwy. 89 to Pray,
then southeast on Mill Creek Rd. to East Mill Creek Rd.
to Elbow Lake (Snowy Range Ranch) trailhead. About a
9-mi. hike gets one to Elbow Lake and the beginning of
the Needles and Mt. Cowen. Another area, Rubber Hose
Buttress, is found southeast of Chico Hot Springs down
the Emigrant Creek Rd., just past the station known as
White City. Or, go south from Big Timber to Hicks Park
for other Absaroka Range climbs.

90 Yankee Jim Canyon ★★
Various small 100' metamorphic bluffs and boulders.
USFS–Gallatin NF, (406) 587-6701.
Ref: USFS map.
Directions: From Gardiner go north on Hwy. 89. Yankee
Jim Canyon is on left. Just north of Rigler Bluffs.

91 BR☆–(Beartooth Range) Granite Peak ★★★★★
From crags to classic 1,000' alpine granite faces on abundant walls, such as Silver Run Peak and Beartooth Peak, the
Beartooths ensure climbing drama. The Shark Fin, 12,500',
is the highest spire in the state. Granite Peak, the highest
point in Montana at 12,799', has a popular class 5.6 East
Ridge. Abundant ice/snow routes as well. Great climbing,
but beware of some loose rock. Severe weather—coming well
prepared may be the difference between a good night's sleep
and chattering teeth. USFS–Gallatin NF, (406) 587-6701.
Classics: Silver Run Peak: Book of Power IV 9; Granite Peak:
East Ridge III 6, Sawtooth Mountain, Beartooth
Mountain, Metcalf Mountain, Beartooth Spire; Glacier
Peak: Beckey Rt IV AI3, 7.
Ref: AAJ ['72-132, 70-131, 68-146, 67, 65], R 66-20, S [9/84,
4/68, 4/66, 12/64]; Ament's *Master of Rock*, Schneider's
Hiking the Beartooths; Guidebooks: Brunckhorst's *Alpine Ice
and Rock Guide to Southwest and Central Montana*, Green's
The Rock Climber's Guide to Montana, Jacobs's *Climbing
Granite Peak: Beartooths*, Caffrey's *Climber's Guide to
Montana*.
Directions: From Red Lodge to the west lie several trailhead
entrances to the Beartooth Mountain Range. Granite
Peak can be reached via East Rosebud Creek. Other
entrances include: West Rosebud Creek or Rock Creek
from Alpine, southwest of the town of Roscoe. All are
backpacking approaches.

92 BR–West Rosebud Creek ★★★☆
Five-hundred-foot granite walls. Both are near Mystic
Lake Hydroelectric Plant, south of the creek. Multi-
pitched routes. Lots of rock, sometimes loose. A few
smaller excellent-quality crags. USFS–Gallatin NF, (406)
587-6701.
Classics: Balls of Fire 3p 10, Concentration Crack 11b, Thin
Crack.
Ref: Guidebooks: Brunckhorst's *Alpine Ice and Rock Guide to
Southwest and Central Montana*, Caffrey's *Climber's Guide to
Montana*.
Directions: From Billings it's a two-and-a-half-hour drive
southwest in Beartooth Range. South of Nye, Montana.
Long approaches. The Bulge and Power of Tower are the
two most popular buttresses in West Rosebud Creek.

93 BR–East Rosebud Creek ★★★☆
The gateway to the amazing Beartooth Wilderness. One-
thousand-foot granite/metamorphic rock buttresses and
towering turrets. Beautiful multipitched routes. Limited

bouldering in area. Come with a partner. Lots of rock, often loose. Radical kayaking. The Grizzly Bar in Roscoe comes recommended. USFS–Gallatin NF, (406) 587-6701.

Classics: Tower of Innocence 10 5p, Three Sisters, The Doublet, Camel's Hump, Chocolate Drop. A Classic Route Description: Heading from Roscoe to Alpine, after the Jimmy Joe Campground (free). Cross a metal bridge with some pulloff areas after it, park here, and look up toward the right. You will see the large round buttress called The Ramp, a 5.7 classic five-pitch route with many variations. Down slope and to the right of that is the double dihedral known as Double Book Dome with a 5.8, 5.9, 5.10c(?). All nice and used to be bolted before the fires of 1996.

Ref: R. Koehler 6/98; Guidebooks: Brunckhorst's *Alpine Ice and Rock Guide to Southwest and Central Montana*, Green's *The Rock Climber's Guide to Montana*, Caffrey's *Climber's Guide to Montana.*

Directions: From Billings it's a two-and-a-half-hour drive southwest in Beartooth Range. Three Sisters offer closest multipitch routes. Phantom Creek for roadside cragging. Up by the East Rosebud Lake, climbing is on east side of lake on large prominent buttresses known as Camel's Hump and Chocolate Drop. The Doublet is up near Snow Creek.

94 BR–Red Lodge Limestone Palisades ✮

This 200' limestone palisade is highly visible from road. There may be loose rock. Government land.

Ref: Guidebook: Caffrey's *Climber's Guide to Montana.*

Directions: From Red Lodge it's just west of town. For Point of Rocks amble just south on Hwy. 212. Lo-o-ong line of limestone bands.

95 BR–Rock Creek (Beartooth Valley) ✮✮✮✮

Beautiful alpine valley lined with substantial 1,000' granite rock walls, white boulders, and wilderness trailhead into Beartooth backcountry. Ice falls in winter. Summer.

USFS–Gallatin NF, (406) 587-6701.

Classics: Roadside walls, Gill and Sherman bouldering problems.

Ref: Ament's *Master of Rock;* Guidebook: Caffrey's *Climber's Guide to Montana.*

Directions: From Red Lodge head 10 mi. south on Hwy. 212. Turn west on Rock Creek Rd. Before trailhead, you'll encounter roadside bouldering and obvious walls in the distance. Trailhead at the end of the road offers various backcountry climbing areas.

96 Castle Rocks ✮✮✮

These prominent 200' limestone thrones have probably never seen any climbing, especially since they are on the Crow Indian Reservation. BIA.

Ref: USFS map; Guidebooks: Caffrey's *Climber's Guide to Montana.*

Directions: From Pryor jaunt south approximately 5 mi. to triune of visible buttes (Castle Rocks).

97 Mt. Hilgard (in Madison Range) ✮✮

Classic climbs on alpine buttresses. Technical traverses on ridges to north of Hilgard: The Wedge, Sawtooth Ridge, and Tunnel Ridge. USFS–Gallatin NF, (406) 587-6701.

Classics: Mt. Hilgard, 11,316; Northeast Direct, West Face routes, The Beehive.

Ref: Guidebooks: Brunckhorst's *Alpine Ice and Rock Guide to Southwest and Central Montana*, Kelsey's *Climber's and Hiker's Guide to the World Mountains*, Caffrey's *Climber's Guide to Montana.*

Directions: From West Yellowstone travel north on Hwy. 287/191 to west on Hwy. 287 to Earthquake Area Visitor's Center. Just east of center, go north on Beaver Creek Rd. along east flank of Mt. Hilgard to Polmgeton Trailhead. Hike Sentinel Creek for 7 mi., then Hilgard Basin Trail for 2 mi. Rock routes on east faces.

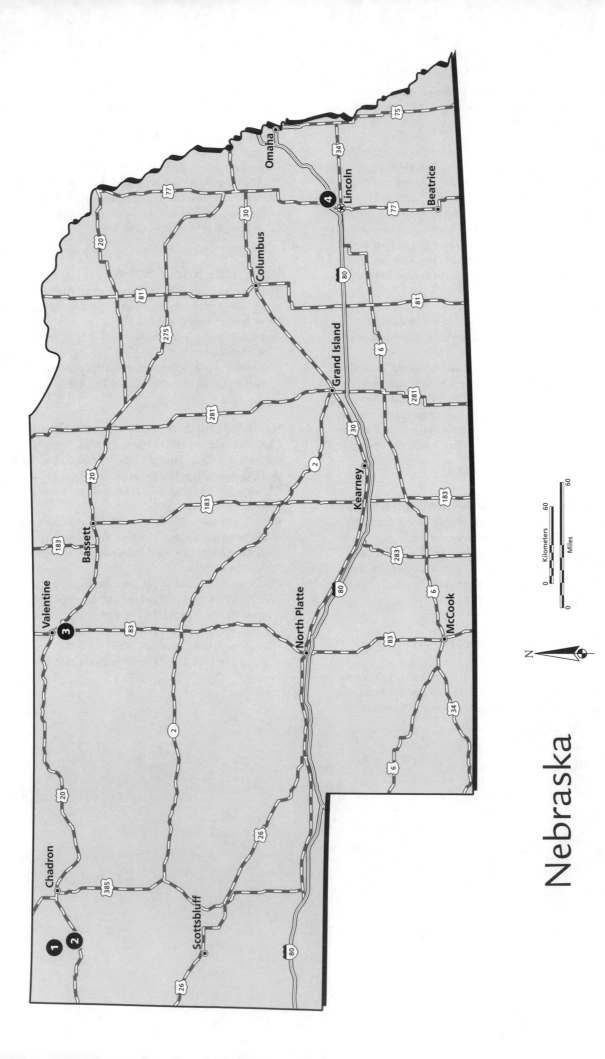

Nebraska

Nebraska

Give me chastity, but not yet. —Augustine

You whiz past one small farm town after another. You saunter through miles of flats and kilometers of ups and downs. As you drive over a spacious prairie land, imagine the perfect climbing area: a 1,200′, sheer-walled formation of perfectly clean granite in the shape of Gina Lolabridgida. Cracks of every imaginable size tantalize the climber's eye. More lines pop up than at a Henny Youngman standup act. Can you expect to find this vision in Nebraska? Not. Imagine it, but do not expect it.

While you're at it, imagine miles of overhanging sport climbs. Dream of virgin boulder gardens. When suddenly the reflector pole alarm clock goes off, you'll realize that the miles of endless Nebraska blacktop has metamorphosed you into road toast.

With any luck, the clear blaze-orange sunset, dust devils, and whirling tallgrass prairies will captivate you until you reach the next climbing area, i.e., the next state.

On a more real note, the state has geologic potential in the northwest corner, near South Dakota's Black Hills, where unverified reports of Dakota sandstone have arisen.

1 Toadstool Park

Sandstone bouldering the size of toadstools.
Directions: Northwest Nebraska. Northwest of Crawford. Take Hwy. 2 north. Turn west onto road for Horn and Toadstool Park (signs).

2 Fort Robinson State Park ●

Dramatic 200′ white volcanic fortresses arises in contrast to the surrounding prairie. The soundness of this ash rock makes the Fisher Towers seem like marble statues. Summer/autumn. Pay camping in this state park (308–665–2903).
Directions: At Fort Robinson. White bluffs surround Fort Robinson State Park.

3 Niobrara Canyon ✯✯

A real Nebraska climbing area; 80′ limestone face climbing. Possibly federal land.
Directions: Valentine, Nebraska. Go to US Hwy. 83 and US Hwy. 20 intersection.

4 University of Nebraska–Lincoln Climbing Gym

Conquering the heights at Toadstool Park.

JOHN SHERMAN

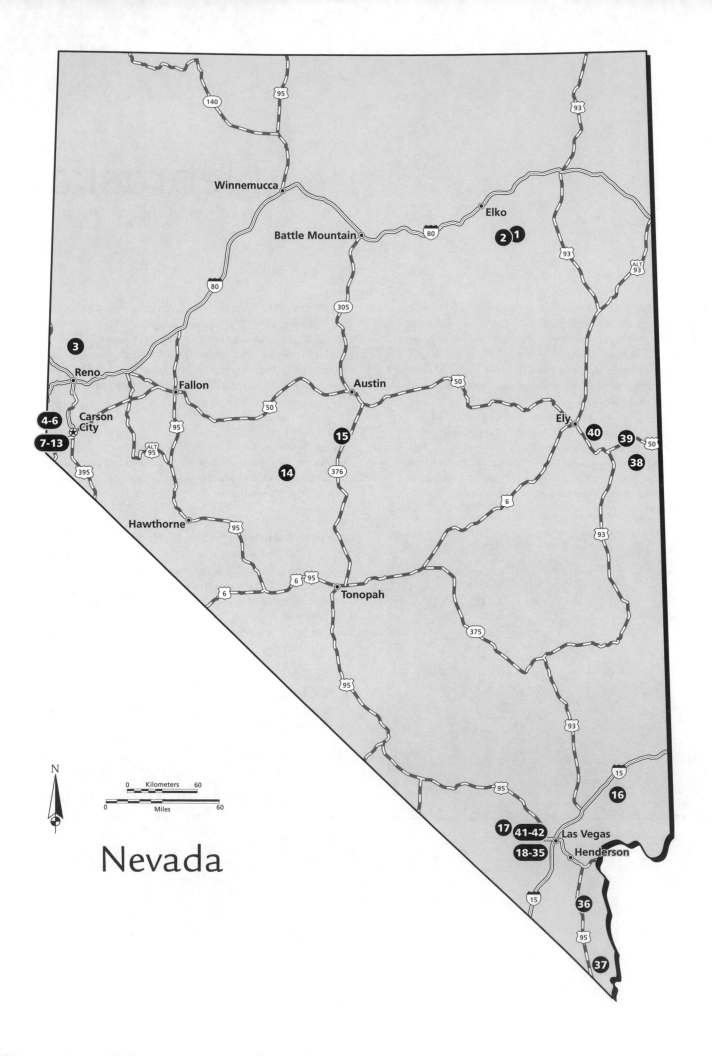

Nevada

Winnemucca

Elko

Battle Mountain

2 1

3

Reno

Fallon

Austin

Ely

40
39

4-6

Carson
City

7-13

38

15

14

Hawthorne

Tonopah

16

17 41-42

Las Vegas

18-35

Henderson

36

37

N

Kilometers 0 — 60

Miles 0 — 60

Nevada

When the going gets weird, the weird turn pro. —Hunter S. Thompson

A trip to the casinos or legal brothels of Nevada is no sure bet, but a trip to the Silver State's climbing areas is a winner every time. Tops amongst Nevada areas is Red Rocks, near Las Vegas. Red Rocks has everything from five-move boulder problems to grade V free climbs, all on exciting (read, sometimes friable) Aztec sandstone. And now, Mt. Charleston heads up the limestone revolution. Vegas is also known for its showgirls, Wayne Newton, and some of the best limestone sport climbing in the country. Of even more interest to climbers are the numerous all-you-can-stand buffets at the casinos.

Lake Tahoe also attracts the climbers. Of many small areas, the most popular currently is Cave Rock, a radically overhanging expert crag at lakeside. A snappy selection of other nearby areas on the California side of this big, deep lake also draws climbers.

The sparse population and remote nature of the central and eastern parts of the state have kept development to a minimum in these areas. This is Basin and Range country, however, and each adjacent mountain range has a character all its own. Nevada is known for rich strikes like the Comstock Lode. Doubtless there will be climbers striking it rich here in the future.

1 Lamoille Canyon (Ruby Mountain Range) ✩✩✩

The Ruby Mountains are a 100-mi.-long by 12-mi.-wide fault block of stunning, impenetrable 1,300' gneiss/granite cliffs. Alpine walls of veined gneiss exist in the lower canyon; ghostly white granite is in the upper canyon reaches. Both are ruby hard. Little is known about the history of rock-climbing ascents in these western mountain canyons. A *Mazama* 1970 article notes many class 2 through 5 ascents (hike-ups for modern hard-core rock climbers) of many of the range's rock-climbable peaks. Jim Shepherd writes,

> USFS campground is a fee area most of the year. Area supports year around climbing, there is some amount of technical ice available in the winter. The higher peaks out of the canyon can have snow approaches well into August. The really big walls have seen virtually no climbing activity, and first ascents are for the asking. As in any new area, there are eons of loose stuff on ledges, so brain

buckets are mandatory. At the lower (north) end of the canyon there have been some bolted sport routes put up in the last couple of years, mostly in the area around the first turnout. A trail to the bottom of the rocks contours up from the turnout, and local climbers have been improving and ducking it on each trip. Further up the canyon, across the road from the upper end of the Thomas Creek Campground, is one of the biggest faces (1,300'+) on a side canyon. Just below the campground is the Colossus Wall, and there is a waterfall for a few weeks in the spring. Most of the big stuff has walk down the back side or scree filled gullies.

Elko was rated the numero uno small town in the United States in 1993 and is home to Cowboy Poetry, several casinos, and, of more interest to rock climbers, the Ruby Mountain Range. Pine Lodge, near the mouth of Lamoille, has good eats. Spring–autumn. Free/pay camping. USFS–Humboldt-Toiyabe NF, (775) 738–5171.

Ref: J. Shepherd; S. Clemens; *Mazama* 12/70, S 12/63.

Directions: From Elko burn 30 mi. southeast of Elko on Hwy. 227 to Lamoille Canyon cutoff, and then turn southwest up Lamoille Canyon Rd. Rock climbing greets one at the mouth of canyon with roadside bouldering and cragging. Backcountry formations include Ruby Dome, Mt. Silliman, Mazama Peak, Mt. Gilbert, Tibia Dome, Ruby Tower, Mt. Thomas, Scott Peak, Mt. Fitzgerald, and Snowflake Peak. Camping at Thomas Canyon 7 mi. up canyon or free off Camp Lamoille Rd. Road's end is 12 mi. up canyon. Road may be blocked by snow until June. Except for scattered roadside cliffs, approaches are up steep, rugged hillsides.

2 Ruby Dome ✩✩✩

Yosemite-like, 500' granite cliffs. Ruby Dome sits at 3,471 m. Ruby Mountains are a very rugged range. As of 1993, Te-Moak Indian Reservation does not grant access. Spring–autumn. Free camping. USFS–Humboldt National Forest, (775) 738–5171.

Ref: S. Clemens; *Mazama* 12/70, S 12/63; Guidebook: Kelsey's *Climber's and Hiker's Guide to the World Mountains.*

Directions: From Elko shine southeast on Hwy. 227, then turn right (south) to Lee. Just before Lee, head east up

Echo Creek to Ruby Dome Trailhead Parking. Hike northeast on trail. This trailhead is currently off-limits to public access unless Te-Moak Indian Reservation permit is purchased (expensive). Option: Long approach from Lamoille Canyon.

3 Pig Rock ✦✦

Chiseled, 70' volcanic pocket pulling and swinish glued-flake cranking. Good finger training area. Possibly Euro graffiti. Fragile rock—climb here only when rock is dry. This could be the closest rock climbing to Nevada's famed Mustang Ranch. Autumn–spring. Free camping. BLM, (775) 623–1500.

Classics: Dentist 12a, Plant Food 12b, Blade Runner 12c, Ton-Ton 13a.

Ref: C 121-40, SC 12/92; Guidebooks: Thornburg's *Quickdraw Guide to Northern California Sport Climbing Areas,* Carville's *Climber's Guide to Tahoe Rock.*

Directions: From Reno grovel out on I-80. Turn north on (exit 18) Pyramid Ave./Hwy. 445 for 25 ⁶/10 mi. Past 40' bridge (low culvert) over wash, turn left (approximately ten minutes or 2 ⁶/10 mi.) on dirt road to small canyon (Pig Rock). From dirt go for ⁷/10 mi., taking left at fork. After 1 ⁷/10 mi. fork left, staying on main road. Pointed spire (Wolf's Tooth) is on right. Stay on main road to Pig Rock at 2 ⁶/10 mi. from pavement. Pig Rock is wall on left. Warning: May be difficult to find.

4 LT✦-(Lake Tahoe Area) Trippy Rock (aka Incline Rock) ✦✦

Incline Rock is a 75' andesite plug that creates a good toprope area. Overhanging north faces 11a–12a. Top anchors. Nice views of Lake Tahoe. Spring–autumn. Free/pay camping. USFS-Toiyabe National Forest, (775) 752–3357.

Ref: R 38; on-line guide www.kgt.net/rockclimb/ lake_tahoe_east_side/trippy_rock/; Guidebooks: Carville's *Climber's Guide to Tahoe Rock,* Jenkewitz-Meytras's *Tahoe Rock Climbing,* Dexter et al.'s *Climber's Guide to Lake Tahoe Region,* Beck's *Climber's Guide to Lake Tahoe and Donner Summit.*

Directions: From Incline Village go 3 ½ mi. north on Hwy. 431. Turn left before prominent vista point. Park. Hike 100 yd. uphill and right for Trippy Rock.

5 LT-Lycra Eliminator ✦✦✦

Excellent overhanging face. Five topropes (with anchors) from 5.11c to 12a. Summer. USFS-Toiyabe National Forest, (775) 752–3357.

Ref: R 38-39.

Directions: Lycra Eliminator is in Incline Village, above the ski area off Tyrol Dr.

6 LT-Crystal Bay Boulder ✦✦

Bouldering can be found on the 40' Crystal Bay Boulder. Crystal Tower, up and left of Crystal Bay Boulder, has 80'

granite topropes. Crystal Cracks has short topropes below Crystal Bay Boulder. Summer/autumn. USFS-Toiyabe National Forest, (775) 752–3357.

Classics: Crystal Bay Boulder: Left-10a and (R)-11; Crystal Tower: Dir 11d, Crystal Eyes 10a; Crystal Cracks: Hand of Doom 10b, Master of Reality 11c, Snowblind 11c, Crystal Meth 10c.

Ref: R 38; Guidebooks: Carville's *Climber's Guide to Tahoe Rock,* Jenkewitz-Meytras's *Tahoe Rock Climbing,* Dexter et al.'s *Climber's Guide to Lake Tahoe Region,* Beck's *Climber's Guide to Lake Tahoe and Donner Summit.*

Directions: Halfway between King's Beach and Incline Village. Shine on Hwy. 20. Turn on Amagosa St. Turn right on Warsaw Rd. Park at end for Crystal Bay Boulder.

7 LT-Sand Harbor State Park ✦✦✦

Thirty-foot granite bouldering. Spring–autumn. Pay camping in state park (775-831-0494).

Ref: Guidebooks: Carville's *Climber's Guide to Tahoe Rock,* Jenkewitz-Meytras's *Tahoe Rock Climbing,* Dexter et al.'s *Climber's Guide to Lake Tahoe Region,* Beck's *Climber's Guide to Lake Tahoe and Donner Summit.*

Directions: From Incline Village go 4 mi. south on Hwy. 28 to Sand Harbor State Park. Signs. Go 8 mi. north from Spooner Summit. Small cluster of boulders lies north of park. Best bouldering at east end of park.

8 LT-Ballbuster Rock ✦✦✦

An excellent boulder with 50' granite topropes. Anchors on top. Summer. Free camping. USFS-Toiyabe NF, (775) 882–2766.

Ref: Guidebooks: Carville's *Climber's Guide to Tahoe Rock,* Jenkewitz-Meytras's *Tahoe Rock Climbing,* Dexter et al.'s *Climber's Guide to Lake Tahoe Region,* Beck's *Climber's Guide to Lake Tahoe and Donner Summit.*

Directions: From Spooner Summit, at junction of Hwy. 50 and Hwy. 28, go 3 mi. north and 50 yd. uphill to west. Ballbuster Rock is 100' west of Hwy. 28.

9 LT-Spooner Crag ✦✦✦

South-facing volcanic 50' tuff formations with good edge and pocketed sport climbs. Ten routes. Bring a handful of quickdraws. Spring–autumn. USFS-Toiyabe NF, (775) 882–2766.

Classics: Jello Wars 11a, Hits Per Minute 12b.

Ref: Guidebook: Carville's *Climber's Guide to Tahoe Rock.*

Directions: From junction of Hwy. 28 and Hwy. 50, go just west of junction. Turn onto side road at junction, heading west. Park halfway down road. Hike uphill 75 yd. to Spooner Crag.

10 LT-Shakespeare Rock ✦

Beginner's crag. A north-facing 350' andesite plug with steep black wall above highway. Cave at lower right of Shakespeare has routes as well. Uncertain face potential.

May be breakable holds. Lichens form outline of Shakespeare. Spring-autumn. USFS-Toiyabe NF, (775) 882-2766.

Classics: The Tempest 6.

Ref: SC 12/92; Guidebooks: Carville's *Climber's Guide to Tahoe Rock*, Jenkewitz-Meytras's *Tahoe Rock Climbing*, Dexter et al.'s *Climber's Guide to Lake Tahoe Region*, Beck's *Climber's Guide to Lake Tahoe and Donner Summit*.

Directions: In Glenbrook, on Hwy. 50. Several miles southwest of Spooner Summit. Dirt roads to base. Shakespeare Rock is the prominent formation.

11 LT–Castle Rock ☆☆☆

Tri-summited 200′ granite formation of knobby rock is good for an afternoon of climbing. West-facing expert crag. Summer. USFS-Toiyabe NF, (775) 882-2766.

Ref: Guidebooks: Carville's *Climber's Guide to Tahoe Rock*, Jenkewitz-Meytras's *Tahoe Rock Climbing*, Dexter et al.'s Climber's *Guide to Lake Tahoe Region*, Beck's *Climber's Guide to Lake Tahoe and Donner Summit*.

Directions: Kingsbury Village. From Kingsbury Grade go 1 ½ mi. north on Hwy. 207 (visible from road). Turn north on Benjamin to Andria to dirt road for Castle Rock.

12 LT–Cave Rock (closed) ☆☆☆

Extremely overhanging, 100′ basalt sport-climbing cove that makes Garden of the Gods in Colorado look solid. About two dozen difficult sport routes starting at 5.11c. Success on these power routes requires an extremely large vocabulary of tricks, from knee bars to toe scums. Access sensitive: As of 1997, the Forest Service is planning to pull out all the bolts, thereby eliminating climbing. Cave Rock is closed to climbers. Climbers should stay away from the main cave and make their requests to the Forest Service legally. See the Access Fund page. Autumn-spring. Free camping on USFS-Toiyabe NF (775-882-2766).

Classics: Over the Falls 10c, Asylum 11d, Impact Zone 11d, Port of Entry 12a, Concave 12d, Psycho 13a, Shut up and Climb 13b, Phantom Lord 13c, Slayer 14a.

Ref: C [169-45, 143, 142, 123-39, 121-40, 114], R [80-28, 79-28, 38], SC 12/92; Guidebooks: Thornburg's *Quickdraw Guide to Northern California Sport Climbing Areas*, Carville's *Climber's Guide to Tahoe Rock*, Jenkewitz-Meytras's *Tahoe Rock Climbing*.

Directions: From south Lake Tahoe dig 8 mi. north on Hwy. 50. Park at turnout ¼ mi. before rock or park at boat ramp in park (fee). Cave Rock above and below highway. Faces south.

13 LT–East Shore Bouldering ☆☆☆

Thirty-foot granite boulders. USFS-Toiyabe NF, (775) 882-2766.

Ref: Guidebooks: Carville's *Climber's Guide to Tahoe Rock*, Jenkewitz-Meytras's *Tahoe Rock Climbing*.

Directions: East Shore Bouldering is between Cave Rock and Glenbrook on Hwy. 28.

14 Sherman Peak Granite Dome ☆☆☆

Granitic big walls up to 1,000′. Spring/autumn. Free camping on BLM (775-635-4000)/USFS-Toiyabe NF (702-964-2671).

Ref: R 18(3/87)-35.

Directions: From Gabbs go west toward Sherman Peak.

15 Wild Granites ☆☆☆

Soaring granite buttresses and solid canyon walls offer rock climbing. This area is truly wild, undeveloped, and remote. Summer/autumn. Free camping. USFS-Toiyabe NF, (702) 964-2671.

Ref: Guidebook: Kelsey's *Climber's and Hiker's Guide to the World Mountains*.

Directions: South of Austin. Go east past Austin on US 50 over Toiyabe Summit and Bob Scott Summit. Turn south into the Big Smokey Valley and drive past Kings-ton Canyon and a small store/gas station until you see the Granites. Drive up the dirt road that seems to go as close as you can. Get out of your car, start walking, and count on getting lost. Bring shovels, boards, jacks, and right chemicals. Although the approach is not far in miles, it is a hard uphill hike in rough country, and the trail is tenuous at best.

16 Valley of Fire State Park

Twenty-mile-long canyon of 200′ sandstone cliffs, buttes, and thingamabobs. Intermittent manganese varnish on rock offers so-so climbing. Climbing is legal, but with restrictions as to where and how—check with rangers in this, Nevada's oldest state park. Indian petroglyphs. Pay camping. Autumn-spring. State park, (702) 397-2088.

Ref: AAJ '86-160, C [101, 96].

Directions: From Las Vegas smoke 31 mi. north on I-15. Turn east at exit 75, following signs to Valley of Fire State Park.

17 Mt. Charleston ☆☆☆☆☆

Incredible fish-in-the-barrel opportunity for sport climbing on the beautiful limestone flanks of Mt. Charleston. Incredibly hard limestone (may need three holes per Bosch battery). Probably the best limestone sport climbing in America. Many areas include: Robber's Roost, The Cove, The Hood, Convenience Cliff, The Imagination Wall, Mom's Cave, Roadkill Boulders, Universal Wall, and Angel Falls. Buttresses seen from Lee Canyon Ski Area were climbed in the 1970s by Fred Beckey. If you're looking for easy climbs, you're outta luck. Everything here is 5.11 and up. At 8,000′, mainly a summer area. Free camping at Lee Canyon, Mary Jane Falls Canyon, or Archery Range or pay camping on USFS-Toiyabe NF (702-873-8800).

Classics: Rapping Boys 11d, Bloodline 12a, Boys in the Hood 12c, Straight Out of Compton 12d, Straight Out of Compton 13a, Borderline 13a, Ghetto Boys 13c, Soul Man 13d, Hypersoul 14a.

Ref: C [192-21, 177-94, 176-25, 171-28, 167-31, 165(12/96)-

24, 161-40, 149-(12/94)-565 142], R [89, 81-18, 77-86, 74-20, 72, 57], SC [12/92, 9/92]; Guidebooks: McQuade's *Vegas Rocks: Rock Climbs,* McCray's *Welcome to Las Vegas Limestone.*

Directions: From Las Vegas (thirty minutes), take Hwy. 95 toward Reno. Turn left on road (Hwy. 157) to Mt. Charleston. After much winding and 20 mi., reach the Mt. Charleston Hotel. From here continue on Hwy. 157 west to several crags: For Robber's Roost turn right on Hwy. 158. Cliff up on left, parking on right. Go back west on Hwy. 157 for remaining areas: For Pirate's Cove park on left past fire station. Hike across road northwest. For The Hood follow Hwy. 157 and turn right onto Echo Rd. to parking area and board for North Loop trail. Trail leads to Convenience Cliff and The Hood. Other areas being developed as well.

18 RR☆–Red Rock Canyon National Conservation Area Overview ☆☆☆☆☆

You've hit the jackpot! Long (up to 1,800') free climbs, sport routes, bouldering—a lifetime and then some on soft, adventurous sandstone in kaleidoscopic canyons. More classic routes than Kmart has blue-light specials. Camping at Red Rocks before (east of) visitors center. Note: Loop Rd.

Bob DuBois pulling the crux, Levitation, 5.11-, Red Rocks.

now has gate locked at night that doesn't lend itself to alpine starts on long routes. Get a guidebook for multipitched routes. May be trouble with car break-ins. Vegas buffets, gambling, Circus Circus, and showgirls. You probably won't want to miss Desert Rock Sports for local climbing information or the Wayne Newton shows for local entertainment. Autumn–spring. Camping is only at two areas in Red Rocks. Free/pay camping. BLM, (702) 647-5000.

Classics: Multipitch: Lotta Balls 8, Crimson Chrysalis 9, Prince of Darkness 10, Dream of Wild Turkeys 10, Levitation 29 11-, Ixtlan 11, Rainbow Wall V 12; Sport: Running Man 11b, Fear and Loathing 12a, The Gift 12d.

Ref: AAJ ['89-157, 86-161, 77-185], C [186-118, 179-20, 168-62, 167-25, 159-130, 138, 131, 128(10/91)-26, 114, 109, 104], M 140, R [94-100, 69-28, 66-143, 53(1/93)-51, 49, 36(3/90)-18, #18 (possibly incorrect topos), 1], R 90-136, SC [6/91, 9/92], S 9/87; *Rocks Around the World,* Hart's *Hiking the Great Basin;* Guidebooks: McQuade's *Vegas Rocks: Rock Climbs,* Swain's *Red Rocks Select,* Faulk's *Red Rocks,* Harlin's *Rocky Mountain,* Urioste's *Red Rocks of Southern Nevada.*

Directions: From Las Vegas roll approximately 15 mi. west on Charleston Blvd. See below for various directions to several Red Rocks areas listed here: Calico Basin (Craft Rocks), First Pullout, Gallery/Wall of Confusion, Sandstone Quarry, White Rock Spring (Angel Food Wall/Sheep Skull Crag), Willow Springs, Icebox Canyon, Pine Creek Canyon, Juniper Canyon, Oak Creek Canyon, Mt. Wilson, First Creek Canyon, Mustang and Sandstone Canyons, Black Velvet Canyon, Mud Spring Canyon, Windy Canyon, and Chocolate Rocks. If you plan to use areas on the Scenic Loop Rd., the gate is open 6:00 A.M.–8:00 P.M. April 18–October 28 and 6:00 A.M.–5:00 P.M. in winter (as of December 2001).

19 RR–Calico Basin (Cannibal Crag et al./Kraft Rocks) ☆☆☆

Cannibal Crag and others are short leads on friable rock. Problems change year to year. Kraft Rocks maintains challenging Neapolitan 30' sandstone bouldering blocks, perhaps the best and certainly the most developed in Red Rocks area. Topropes on big cube; leads on cliffs above. Please respect private land and petroglyphs. Free camping. BLM, (702) 647-5000.

Classics: Cannibal Crag: The Fox 10+; Kraft Rocks: Couldn't Be Schmooter 8+, High Class Hoe 10-, Stoney Point 5.10 Arête, Winter Heat 11+, Monkey Bars Boulder, The Cube.

Ref: AAJ ['89-157, '86-161, '77-185], C 128(10/91)-26, SC (6/91), R [53(1/93)-51, 49, 36(3/90)-18, 18], S (9/87); Sherman's *Stone Crusade,* Hart's *Hiking the Great Basin;* Guidebooks: Swain's *Red Rocks Select,* Faulk's *Red Rocks,* Harlin's *Rocky Mountain,* Urioste's *Red Rocks of Southern Nevada.*

Directions: From BLM Visitor Center go back east approximately 2 mi. toward Las Vegas on Hwy. 159. Turn left to Red Spring Picnic Area on Calico Basin Rd., for 1 2/10 mi.

Turn right. Then turn left after a "private property" gate. Cannibal Crags: Go $^1/_{10}$ mi. bearing left to a wash and locked gate (leave unblocked). Crags are west of gate. Kraft Rocks: Go $^1/_{10}$ mi. and bear right going for $^4/_{10}$ mi. Turn right for $^1/_{10}$ mi. Turn left for $^2/_{10}$ mi. Hike north to rocks. Beware changing access conditions due to home buildings.

20 RR–First Pullout Walls (Universal City/Fixx Cliff) ☆☆☆☆

More than a half dozen small 100′ sandstone sport crags. Fixx Cliff led the way of developing other Red Rocks sport crags. Winter sport crag. But bring traditional gear. Beware loose rock. Free camping. BLM, (702) 647–5000.

Classics: Dog Wall: Cat Walk 10-, It's A Bitch 10; Fixx Cliff: Saved By Zero 11, Free Base 11+.

Ref: AAJ ['89-157, '86-161, '77-185], C 128(10/91)-26, R [53(1/93)-51, 49, 36(3/90)-18, 18], SC 6/91, S (9/87); Hart's *Hiking the Great Basin;* Guidebooks: Swain's *Red Rocks Select,* Faulk's *Red Rocks,* Harlin's *Rocky Mountain,* Urioste's *Red Rocks of Southern Nevada.*

Directions: At first pullout on BLM Scenic Loop (1 $^1/_{10}$ mi.). Walk a short distance to First Pullout Walls. Faces south. The Scenic Loop Rd. gate is open 6:00 A.M.–8:00 P.M. April 8–October 28 and 6:00 A.M.–5:00 P.M. in winter. Check in with rangers for overnight trips.

21 RR–Second Pullout (Gallery and Wall of Confusion) ☆☆☆☆

Hot iron of Las Vegas winter sport cragging. One-hundred-foot sandstone crag. Free camping. BLM, (702) 647–5000.

Classics: The Gallery: The Gift 12+, Glitch 12+; Wall of Confusion: Fear and Loathing 12a; Buck's Muscle World 9, Dancin' with A God 10a, Pump First Pay Later 10c, Rebel Without A Pause 11-.

Ref: AAJ ['89-157, '86-161, '77-185], C 128(10/91)-26, SC (6/91), R [53(1/93)-51, 49, 36(3/90)-18, 18], S (9/87); Hart's *Hiking the Great Basin;* Guidebooks: Swain's *Red Rocks Select,* Faulk's *Red Rocks,* Harlin's *Rocky Mountain,* Urioste's *Red Rocks of Southern Nevada.*

Directions: At second pullout on BLM Scenic Loop. Walk up and left to the two most popular sport walls, The Gallery and Wall of Confusion. The Gallery is 150′ right of Wall of Confusion. Stratocaster Wall is behind these. Many other sport crags straight ahead and to right as well. The Scenic Loop Rd. gate is open 6:00 A.M.–8:00 P.M. April 8–October 28 and 6:00 A.M.–5:00 P.M. in winter.

22 RR–Sandstone Quarry (Running Man Wall) ☆☆☆☆

A toprope 200′ sandstone area rejuvenated into sport cragging areas. Many climbs in the shade. Autumn–spring. Free camping. BLM, (702) 647–5000.

Classics: Running Man Wall: Red Heat 10+, Running Man 11b, Graveyard Waltz 11+; Stratocaster Wall: Cut Loose 11a, Stratocaster 12a, The Choad Warrior 12c; Sonic

Youth 11+, Just Shut Up and Climb 11; Trophy: Keep Your Powder Dry 12b, Pet Shop Boy 12d, Shark Walk 13a.

Ref: AAJ ['89-157, '86-161, '77-185], C 128(10/91)-26, SC (6/91), R [53(1/93)-51, 49, 36(3/90)-18, 18], S (9/87).

Directions: At 2 $^3/_4$ mi. on Scenic Loop (sign), past The Gallery. Park in Sandstone Quarry lot. Hike west 75 yd. to thirty minutes. Crags network in all directions. Running Man Wall/Stratocaster Wall is back in the direction of the second pullout. The Scenic Loop Rd. gate is open 6:00 A.M.–8:00 P.M. April 8–October 28 and 6:00 A.M.–5:00 P.M. in winter.

23 RR–White Rock Spring (Angel Food Wall and Sheep Skull Crag) ☆☆☆

Seven-hundred-foot sandstone west-facing formations. Good for early season climbs. Autumn–spring. Free camping. BLM, (702) 647–5000.

Classics: Angel Food Wall: Tunnel Vision III 7.

Ref: AAJ ['89-157, '86-161, '77-185], C 128(10/91)-26, SC (6/91), R [53(1/93)-51, 49, 36(3/90)-18, 18], S (9/87); Hart's *Hiking the Great Basin;* Guidebooks: Swain's *Red Rocks Select,* Faulk's *Red Rocks,* Harlin's *Rocky Mountain,* Urioste's *Red Rocks of Southern Nevada.*

Directions: At 5 $^9/_{10}$ mi. on Scenic Loop. Sheep Skull Crags at 6 $^3/_4$ mi. on loop. Twenty-minute hike. The Scenic Loop Rd. gate is open 6:00 A.M.–8:00 P.M. April 8–October 28 and 6:00 A.M.–5:00 P.M. in winter.

24 RR–Willow Springs ☆☆☆☆

Easy-access canyon with one-pitch routes. Good 300′ sandstone bouldering near outhouse. More of a traditionalist area but now the site of The Promised Land sport climbing cave with twenty-five routes from 5.11–5.13. Autumn–spring. Free camping. BLM (702-647-5000).

Classics: Ragged Edges I 8, Nadia's Nine I 9, Sheep Trail 9, Black Track I 9, N'Plus Ultra 10-, Chicken Eruptus 10, Left Out 10+, Big Iron 11, Bighorn Buttress 4p 11; The Promised Land: Confrontation 13b.

Ref: AAJ ['89-157, '86-161, '77-185], C 128(10/91)-26, SC (6/91), R [83-97, 53(1/93)-51, 49, 36(3/90)-18, 18], S (9/87); Hart's *Hiking the Great Basin;* Guidebooks: McCray's *Welcome to Las Vegas Limestone,* Vertical Brain's *Vegas Rocks,* Swain's *Red Rocks Select,* Faulk's *Red Rocks,* Harlin's *Rocky Mountain,* Urioste's *Red Rocks of Southern Nevada.*

Directions: At 7 $^1/_2$ mi. on Scenic Loop Rd. (signs) to Lost Creek parking. Five-minute walk. Ragged Edges Cliff is most obvious varnished cliff angling right from parking. The Promised Land is a one-hour hike up canyon. Four-wheel-drive road continues onto Pahrump. The Scenic Loop Rd. gate is open 6:00 A.M.–8:00 P.M. April 8–October 28 and 6:00 A.M.–5:00 P.M. in winter.

25 RR–Icebox Canyon (Sunnyside Crag/Refrigerator Wall et al.) ☆☆☆☆

Three-hundred-foot sandstone "Icebox" in winter. Frigid Aire Buttress is 800′ and largest. Necromancer area has shorter routes. Many one-pitch routes as well as multi-pitched adventures. Autumn. Free camping. BLM, (702) 647–5000.

Classics: Sunnyside Crags: Spring Break 11+, Tarantula 12-, Gotham City 12-; Frigid Aire Buttress IV 9+, Unfinished Symphony 10+, Breakaway 2p 10+; Sensuous Mortician 9.

Ref: AAJ ['89-157, '86-161, '77-185], C 128(10/91)-26, SC (6/91), R [53(1/93)-51, 49, 36(3/90)-18, 18], S (9/87); Hart's *Hiking the Great Basin;* Guidebooks: Swain's *Red Rocks Select,* Faulk's *Red Rocks,* Harlin's *Rocky Mountain,* Urioste's *Red Rocks of Southern Nevada.*

Directions: Icebox Canyon is at 7 ⁹/₁₀ mi. on Scenic Loop Rd. The Scenic Loop Rd. gate is open 6:00 A.M.–8:00 P.M. April 8–October 28 and 6:00 A.M.–5:00 P.M. in winter.

26 RR–Pine Creek Canyon (Beer and Ice Gully/Dark Shadows) ☆☆☆☆

Popular area because of the short and easy access. Mescalito's red-tipped pyramid is a popular target and marks north/south split in canyon. Good single-pitch to multipitch 600′ sandstone routes. Autumn. Free camping. BLM, (702) 647–5000.

Classics: Straight Shooter 9+, Out of Control 10, 29 Posers 11+, Dark Shadows III 7, Centerfold III 10, Negro Blanco IV 10+, Heart of Darkness IV 10d, Risky Business III 10+, Terminal Velocity 5p 13-.

Ref: AAJ ['89-157, '86-161, '77-185], C 128(10/91)-26, SC (6/91), R [53(1/93)-51, 49, 36(3/90)-18, 18], S (9/87); Hart's *Hiking the Great Basin;* Guidebooks: Swain's *Red Rocks Select,* Faulk's *Red Rocks,* Harlin's *Rocky Mountain,* Urioste's *Red Rocks of Southern Nevada.*

Directions: At 10 ½ mi. on Scenic Loop Rd. Follow sign to parking on right for Pine Creek Canyon. Hikes of thirty minutes to three hours. The Scenic Loop Rd. gate is open 6:00 A.M.–8:00 P.M. April 8–October 28 and 6:00 A.M.–5:00 P.M. in winter.

27 RR–Juniper Canyon (Cloud Tower/Rainbow Mountain) ☆☆☆☆

Classic, long up to 1,500′ sandstone, shady multipitch routes. Crimson Chrysalis climbs a 1,200′ bolt-protected tower—eight raps. The 5.11d to the right of Crimson Chrysalis on Cloud Tower is considered the "Astroman" of Red Rocks. Viewable from Cloud Tower, the colorful thirteen-pitch Rainbow Wall V/VI 5.12b rates high on the list of serious Red Rocks aid routes. Spring/autumn. Free camping. BLM, (702) 647–5000.

Classics: Cloud Tower: Crimson Chrysalis IV 9, Cloud Tower IV 11+/12a; Rainbow Wall: Regular Rt 13p 12b, Sergeant Slaughter 11p (12 freed) or 10A3, Desert Solitaire 8p 9 A3+.

Ref: AAJ ['89-157, '86-161, '77-185, '76-452], C [167-25, 128(10/91)-26], SC (6/91), R [87-30, 77-18, 53(1/93)-51, 49, 36(3/90)-18, 18], On Sight v.1. Number 2, S (9/87); Hart's *Hiking the Great Basin;* Guidebooks: Swain's *Red Rocks Select,* Faulk's *Red Rocks,* Harlin's *Rocky Mountain,*

Urioste's *Red Rocks of Southern Nevada.*

Directions: At 10 ½ mi. on Scenic Loop Rd. (signs). Park at Pine Creek parking area. Approach: One to one and a half hours to Cloud Tower routes and Rainbow Mountain. The Scenic Loop Rd. gate is open from 6:00 A.M.–8:00 P.M. April 8–October 28 and 6:00 A.M.–5:00 P.M. in winter.

28 RR–Oak Creek Canyon (Mt. Wilson/ Rainbow Buttress) ☆☆☆☆

Classic 1,000′, sunny multipitch routes on beautiful south-facing sandstone walls. The marvelous and popular route Levitation 29 IV 5.11 should not be missed. Autumn/winter. Free camping. BLM, (702) 647–5000.

Classics: Solar Slab 13p 6, Catwalk 7p 6+, Rainbow Buttress IV 8, Levitation 29 IV 11-, Black Orpheus IV 10, Eagle Dance IV 10 or 12; Celebration Wall: Solar Slab III 6, Coltrane III 9, Resolution Arête 20 p 11.

Ref: AAJ ['89-157, '86-161, '77-185], C 128(10/91)-26, SC (6/91), R [53(1/93)-51, 49, 36(3/90)-18, 18], S (9/87); Hart's *Hiking the Great Basin;* Guidebooks: Swain's *Red Rocks Select,* Faulk's *Red Rocks,* Harlin's *Rocky Mountain,* Urioste's *Red Rocks of Southern Nevada.*

Directions: From BLM Visitor Center shoot south on main road. Turn right at signs for Oak Creek Canyon on rough, rocky, bone-shaking dirt road soon to be paved. Hike one hour plus. Get map/topos for routes.

29 RR–Mt. Wilson (Aeolian Wall) ☆☆☆☆

The enormous 2,000′ East Face is Nevada's biggest wall and the high point in Red Rocks. Remote overnight climbs. Autumn. Free camping. BLM, (702) 647–5000.

Classics: Lady Wilson's Cleavage IV 8, Woodrow V 10, Aeolian Wall V 9A3, Resolution Arête V 10 A2.

Ref: AAJ ['89-157, '86-161, '77-185], C 128(10/91)-26, SC (6/91), R [53(1/93)-51, 49, 36(3/90)-18, 18], S (9/87); Hart's *Hiking the Great Basin;* Guidebooks: Swain's *Red Rocks Select,* Faulk's *Red Rocks,* Harlin's *Rocky Mountain,* Urioste's *Red Rocks of Southern Nevada.*

Directions: Approach via First Creek or Oak Creek Canyons for Mt. Wilson.

30 RR–First Creek Canyon (Lotta Balls) ☆☆☆

The second pitch of Lotta Balls is a "marblelous" climb. Shaded routes in afternoon. Spring/autumn. Free camping. BLM, (702) 647–5000.

Classics: Lotta Balls II 8, Rob Roy I 10-.

Ref: AAJ ['89-157, '86-161, '77-185], C 128(10/91)-26, SC (6/91), R [53(1/93)-51, 49, 36(3/90)-18, 18], S (9/87); Hart's *Hiking the Great Basin;* Guidebooks: Swain's *Red Rocks Select,* Faulk's *Red Rocks,* Harlin's *Rocky Mountain,* Urioste's *Red Rocks of Southern Nevada.*

Directions: From BLM Visitor Center shoot south on main road. Turn right at signs for First Creek Canyon Trailhead, ⁷/₁₀ mi. south of Oak Creek turnoff. Follow road west. Take the Upper Trail (left) and left fork again when trail splits again. Stay on south side of drainage. Hike is forty-five minutes.

31 RR–Mustang and Sandstone Canyons ✩✩✩

Uncertain development on these 1,000′ sandstone walls. Check at access. Spring/autumn. Free camping. BLM, (702) 647–5000.
Ref: AAJ ['89-157, '86-161, '77-185], C 128(10/91)-26, SC (6/91), R [53(1/93)-51, 49, 36(3/90)-18, 18], S (9/87); Hart's *Hiking the Great Basin;* Guidebooks: Faulk's *Red Rocks,* Harlin's *Rocky Mountain,* Urioste's *Red Rocks of Southern Nevada.*
Directions: Mustang and Sandstone Canyons are north of Mud Springs.

32 RR–Black Velvet Canyon ✩✩✩✩✩

Black Velvet Wall is a renowned, black-stained 1,600′ curtain of sandstone. Classic, long, and shady multipitch routes speak of adventure. Concentration of high-quality Red Rock climbs. Dream of Wild Turkeys is one of the more popular Red Rocks routes on the 2,000′ sheer north face of the Velvet Wall. The Monument Area, forty-five minutes to the right (north) of the mouth of the canyon, contains classic hardman's testpieces, including the aesthetic roof crack Desert Gold 13-. Spring/autumn. Free camping. BLM, (702) 647–5000.
Classics: Mazatlan I 10+, Epinephrine (18p) IV 9, Triassic Sands III 5.10b, Prince of Darkness III 5.10b, Rock Warrior IV 10R, Dream of Wild Turkeys IV 10, Fiddler on Roof 7p 10+, Ixtlan IV 11, American Ghostdance 12-; Monument: Desert Gold 13-.
Ref: AAJ ['89-157, '86-161, '77-185], C [128(10/91)-26, 96], SC (6/91), R [53(1/93)-51, 49, 36(3/90)-18, 18], S (9/87); Hart's *Hiking the Great Basin;* Guidebooks: Swain's *Red Rocks Select,* Faulk's *Red Rocks,* Harlin's *Rocky Mountain,* Urioste's *Red Rocks of Southern Nevada.*
Directions: From junction of Hwy. 159 and Hwy. 160, drive west on Hwy. 160 for 4 7/10 mi. Turn right (north) on dirt roads approximately 2 mi. to second dirt road on left. Turn left and go 1/2 mi. to T. Turn right for 3/10 mi. to end of road. Hike into large, black, varnished walls of Black Velvet Canyon. Approaches of one hour. Rough, rocky entrance road, but cars make it.

33 RR–Mud Spring Canyon ✩✩✩

The 800′ domal north face of Global Peak contains the delicate face route Chuckwalla. Spring/autumn. Free camping. BLM, (702) 647–5000.
Classics: Chuckawalla III 9.
Ref: AAJ ['89-157, '86-161, '77-185], C 128(10/91)-26, SC (6/91), R [53(1/93)-51, 49, 36(3/90)-18, 18], S (9/87); Hart's *Hiking the Great Basin;* Guidebooks: Swain's *Red Rocks Select,* Faulk's *Red Rocks,* Harlin's *Rocky Mountain,* Urioste's *Red Rocks of Southern Nevada*
Directions: Mud Spring Canyon is at 4 7/10 mi. past Blue Diamond Cutoff on Hwy. 160. Go right to Mud Springs.

34 RR–Windy Canyon ✩✩✩✩

The 1,000′ sandstone south face of Windy Peak stirs up climbers. Good winter climbing. Free camping. BLM, (702) 647–5000.
Classics: Jubilant Song III 7.
Ref: AAJ ['89-157, '86-161, '77-185], C 128(10/91)-26, SC (6/91), R [53(1/93)-51, 49, 36(3/90)-18, 18], S (9/87); Hart's *Hiking the Great Basin;* Guidebooks: Swain's *Red Rocks Select,* Faulk's *Red Rocks,* Harlin's *Rocky Mountain,* Urioste's *Red Rocks of Southern Nevada.*
Directions: At 4 7/10 mi. past Blue Diamond Cutoff on Hwy. 160, go right to Windy Canyon.

35 RR–Chocolate Rocks ✩✩✩

The southernmost area in Red Rocks harbors good winter climbing at this 100′ crag. Short one-pitch, southeast-facing routes. Joshua trees and barrel cactus. Free camping. BLM, (702) 647–5000.
Classics: Combination Corner 8, Gallows 10.
Ref: AAJ ['89-157, '86-161, '77-185], C 128(10/91)-26, SC (6/91), R [53(1/93)-51, 49, 36(3/90)-18, 18], S (9/87); Hart's *Hiking the Great Basin;* Guidebooks: Swain's *Red Rocks Select,* Faulk's *Red Rocks,* Harlin's *Rocky Mountain,* Urioste's *Red Rocks of Southern Nevada.*
Directions: From Las Vegas smoke approximately 17 mi. west on Hwy. 160 (6 8/10 mi. past Blue Diamond turnoff). Park at pullout. Hike twenty minutes up to Chocolate Rocks.

36 Keyhole Canyon ✩✩✩

A consolation prize for Vegas climbers. Fun short leads on 50′ granite walls. Site of the Keyhole Classic. Nice rock art at this state archaeological site—please don't climb on petroglyphs. Autumn/spring. State land.
Ref: Guidebook: *Keyhole Canyon Guide.*
Directions: From Boulder City take Hwy. 93 west to Hwy. 95. Aim south on Hwy. 95 (past road to Nelson) for 15 8/10 mi. to mm 41. South of mm 41, turn left at dirt road with a culvert for 3 mi. Turn right at second power line road approximately 2 mi. Turn left around line to Keyhole Canyon for 1/4 mi.

37 Christmas Tree Pass (in Newberry Mountains) ✩✩✩

A desert array of white, slabby 200′ domes and towers (Space Needle, Dali Dome, and Nixon Towers) in a surreal landscape. The bold lead outs on "grainitic," "crunchy, Kellogg's cornflake" friction climbing may take some adjustment—like rollin' the dice in Laughlin. Sporadic development since the 1970s. Petroglyphs. Winter. Free camping. NPS.

Classics: Dali Dome: Wilkinson Sword 7, MC 18, Might As Well 9+, Surreal Peel 10, Exhibition 10; H&R Block: Prime Interest 9; Space Needle: Grand Visener's Garden Party 10, Dark Side of the Moon 10, Jaws 11a, Separate Reality 11d.
Ref: C [94 (photos), 54(5/79)-19], R 66-58, S 10/76.
Directions: From Laughlin slide west on Hwy. 163. Turn north (before hill and left curve) on dirt road to domes. Or, from Searchlight take Hwy. 95 south and east 9–10 mi. on Christmas Tree Pass Rd. to domes.

38 Wheeler Peak (Great Basin National Park) ✭✭

This national park was signed into law by President Reagan in 1987. The main focus of this park is Wheeler Peak's 2,000' north face; the first-ascent route, Stella by Starlight, was done solo 5.8 A3+ Ice 9 by Wade Mills in June 1977 as reported in Kelsey's guide. A 1987 *Summit Magazine* reports an ascent by Robbins and Chouinard. Upper bowls contain quartzite climbs (may be rotten). Also ice climbs. Bristlecone pine forests in the Wheeler Peak Area contain perhaps the oldest known living tree on Earth. The park also contains Lexington Arch, 75' high, one of the world's largest limestone spans and limestone cragging. Summer/autumn. Pay camping at Baker and Lehman Campgrounds. NPS, (775) 234-7331.
Classics: Stella by Starlight 8 A3 I9, Northwest Couloir, IV, 5.5, AI 3, 8 pitches, Robbins/Chouinard Route?
Ref: S (7/87); Guidebooks: Garrett's *Ibex and Selected Climbs of Utah's West Desert*, Grubbs's *Hiking Great Basin National Park*, Kelsey's *Hiking and Climbing in the Great Basin National Park*.
Directions: From Baker (on Hwy. 487), go west into Great Basin National Park. Climbers' attentions have been drawn to the north face of Wheeler Peak and its cirque with Jeff Davis Peak. Park at the Wheeler Peak Campground and hike via the Bristlecone Pine Trail. Other areas of interest to rock ascentists accessed via different roads include: Lexington Arch in the south fork of Lexington Creek, south fork of Big Wash, Mt. Moriah north slope cliffs, Osceola Arch, and Red Bat Caves.

39 Crankenstein Corral ✭✭✭✭
Multipitched limestone sport crag. East of Ely.

40 Table Rock ✭✭✭
Multipitched limestone sport crag in Cave Lake State Park (702-728-4460).
Directions: East of Ely.

41 La Madres North/South (The Trenches)
Limestone sport climbing a short distance from town in wild canyons.
Classics: Catch a Fire 12b.
Ref: C 177-94, R 83-96.
Directions: In Las Vegas, from Hwy. 95, follow West Alexander west to its junction with Jensen at southeast base of Lone Mountain. Turn north on Jensen. Turn left on Lone Mountain Rd. Turn left shortly onto dirt road, following this 3 mi. and passing gravel pits on right. Stay left to a pullout on right. The Trenches are across the road.

42 Lone Mountain (Sin City)
Wintertime city crag with a potpourri of twenty limestone climbing routes and some bouldering. City land.
Ref: R 83-97; Guidebook: McCray's *Welcome to Las Vegas Limestone*.
Directions: In Las Vegas, from Hwy. 95, follow West Alexander west to its end. Turn right on Jensen for 1 4/10 mi. to parking at bottom of Lone Mountain and climbing cave up on the hill. Or, park at adjacent city park. Faces south. Heading farther west on Alexander via construction road to the next range of mountains will get one to The Gun Club Crags and The Strip.

Other Nevada Areas
Potosi Mountain ✭✭✭
Limestone cranking featuring the Killer Cave with 5.11–5.14 sport routes, just thirty minutes outside of Vegas. Winter/fall/spring.
Classics: Pinched Loaf 11b, Moment of Clarity 12a, Lawnmower Man 13b, Reverse Polarity 14b, Annihilator 14c.
Ref: C [195-23, 191-80], R 91-22; Guidebook: McCray's *Welcome to Las Vegas Limestone*.
Directions: From Las Vegas head west on Hwy. 160 for about 20 mi. to Hwy. 159 (Blue Diamond Cutoff). Continue west on Hwy. 160 for another 6 mi. even. Turn south for 7 1/2 mi. Park it, unless four-wheel-drive equipped, then keep gunning it. Hike south 2/10 mi. Then head west 1 2/10 mi. on dirt road. Go another 1/2 mi. up steep hill, then west to wash and south-facing cave.
Shaman Caves
Overhanging limestone sport routes in restricted wildlife area in the Sheep Range. Climbers asked not to climb here. Desert National Wildlife Range.
Ref: C 176-44, R 83-26.

New Hampshire

Too much of a good thing is wonderful. —Mae West

A trip through New Hampshire in the fall is sweeter than maple syrup on honey wheat pancakes. Brilliant fall colors accent quaint white colonial houses, posing the urgent question, "Do New Hampshire stores only sell paint in white, green, and red?" Crisp rock and sparkling temperatures invigorate any climber's spirits. During this quintessential time of year, a climber will discover a world of rock climbing packed into this one little state, a state of unending beauty.

The White Mountains offers climbers an abundance of climbs and history. Any psyched climber will want to visit the long-standing Cathedral and Whitehorse Ledges, Franconia Notch, Cannon Cliff, and the Kancamagus Highway. Still, for sport climbers, areas like Rumney and Joe English Hill are becoming more popular than white paint and deserve a visit.

After one trip to the Granite State, you'll discover why they say, "It's all right here in New Hampshire."

1 Androscoggin River Areas (Artist Rock) ✩✩✩

Abundant granite crags line this river valley. Summer/autumn. Pay camping. Private/government land.

Directions: From Gorham multitudes of visible crags lie north of Hwy. 2 along the Androscoggin River Valley leading east into Maine. Artist Rock is a named feature to the south of Hwy. 2, about 2 mi. east of the Maine border.

2 Twin Mountain Boulder Crack ✩✩✩

This bitchin' 18′ granite 5.12 bouldering crack problem taunts passing motorists every day. Summer/autumn. No camping. Government land.

Ref: J. Mallery.

Directions: At junction of Hwy. 302 and Hwy. 32 in Twin Mountain; boulder sits northeast of intersection. Obvious aesthetic hardman's crack, viewable from road to northeast of intersection. Faces southwest.

3 Zealand Valley (Mt. Oscar Southwest Face North and Middle Sugarloaf) ✩✩✩

Mt. Oscar is a small granite cliff with a ground-up ethic. Routes up to three pitches (Life by Numbers 8R) have been established also on North and Middle Sugarloaf (southeast face). Fantastic views of Mt. Washington and Presidential Range. For all your White Mountain climbs, consult Rock Climbs in the White Mountains (third edition). Summer/autumn. USFS–White Mountain NF, (603) 528–8721.

Classics: North: Fissure Hop 8, Rich's Roof 9+; Middle Sugarloaf: Saber 6, Skyline Promenade 9R.

Ref: C [197-146, 118-106, 109, 105, 101, 99, 84-(6/84)-7]; Guidebook: Webster's *Rock Climbs in the White Mountains of New Hampshire* (third ed.).

Directions: From Twin Mountain ride east on Hwy. 302 a few minutes. Turn right on Zealand Valley Rd. for 1 mi. Park at Sugarloaf Trailhead in Zealand Valley. For Mt. Oscar: Go east from campground up forest road until slabs visible above old clearcut. For Sugarloaf: Hike 1 ½ mi. west on Sugarloaf Trail. From col go left for Middle and right for North. Faces southwest.

4 Mt. Washington (Huntington Ravine) ✩✩

The site of one of New England's first rock climbs, The Pinnacle. It was first climbed in 1910 and was "yardstick climb" for aspiring mountaineers when it became famous from Kenneth Henderson and others' 1928 ascent of the Northeast Ridge. Renowned as an ice-climbing area, but good 600′ granite rock routes exist. Information and shelter available at the Pinkham Notch Hut. Site of the world's highest wind speed, 232 mph. Hold on tight! Perhaps these words from Osgood's *White Mountains* will do justice to its grandeur: "The austere and majestic crest of Mt. Washington was both the Ararat and the Carmel of the most ancient Indian traditions, sanctified by centuries of reverent memories, and regarded by the inhabitants of the valleys of Pequawket and Ossipee as a sacred and stainless shrine." Summer. USFS–White Mountain NF, (603) 528–8721.

Classics: Old Route 5, Northeast Ridge of the Pinnacle 7, Independence Line 8, Pinnacle Dir 9, Roof of the World 11; Central Buttress: Henderson Ridge 4.

Ref: AAJ '70-139, C [141, 109, 105, 64, 59], R [74-44, 43(5/91)-48], S 12/69; on-line guide www.chauvinguides.com/guidebook.htm; Guidebooks: Cole and Wilcox's *Shades of Blue*, Scofield's *High Peaks of the Northeast*; Webster's *Rock Climbs in the White Mountains: East Volume*,

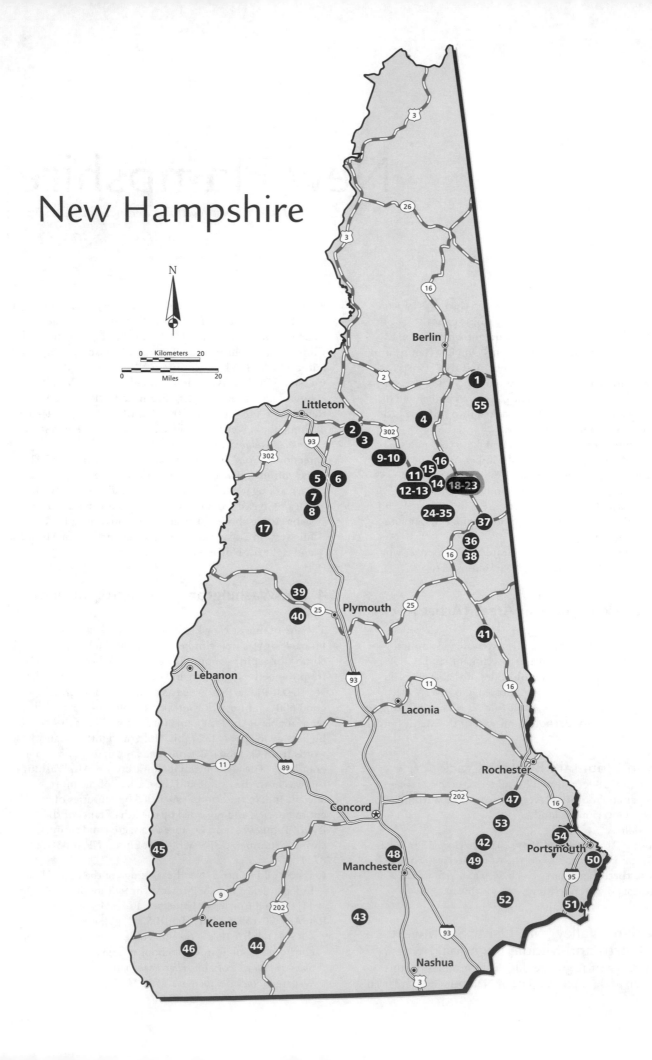

New Hampshire

N

Kilometers 0 — 20

Miles 0 — 20

Berlin

1
55

Littleton

4

2
3

9-10

15 16
11
12-13   14   18-23
24-35

5   6

7
8

37

36
38

17

39

40

Plymouth

41

Lebanon

Laconia

Rochester

11

89

47

Concord

53

42

45

48

49

54
Portsmouth

Manchester

50

95

9

52

202

51

43

Keene

46

44

Nashua

3

Webster's *Rock Climbs in the White Mountains,* Barber's *Climber's Guide to Mt. Washington Valley,* Ross and Ellms's *Cannon, Cathedral, Humphrey's, and Whitehorse: A Rock Climber's Guide,* AMC, Osgood's *White Mountains.*

Directions: From North Conway go north on Hwy. 16. Follow Mt. Washington Auto Rd. and signs to top. (Mt. Washington Auto Rd. is open on a seasonal basis and carries a fee.) Before summit, hike twenty minutes down Huntington Ravine Trail. Or, approached via Pinkham Notch AMC Camp via Tuckerman Ravine to Huntington Ravine Trail (approximately 3 mi.).

5 FN☆–(Franconia Notch) Artist's Bluffs/Overview ☆☆☆☆

This gorgeous setting is home of the Old Man of the Mountains, the state symbol. The venerable 1,000′ granite of Cannon Cliff offers a variety of climbs: long aid to short hard free routes at base. Old Cannon first route done in 1928. Cannon Slabs on the north end offer New England's severest friction climbs. This is alpine rock climbing: Beware loose rock, protean weather, tricky route finding, and old pitons. Climbers required to sign in and out at same checkpoint. Preferred descent is at north end past the Old Man. Camping at Lafayette Campground, south of Boise Rock. Supplies at North Woodstock or Franconia. Artist's Bluffs is popular with beginners, classes, and rappellers. Summer/autumn. Free camping. USFS–White Mountain NF, (603) 528–8721.

Classics: Lakeview 5, Whitney-Gilman 7, Sam's Swan Song 7, Moby Grape 8, Vertigo 9, Slip of Fools 10a, VMC Direct 10+, Duet Direct 10d, Labyrinth Wall V 11c, Walk on the Wild Side 11, Fall From Grace 12b.

Ref: AAJ ['70-139, 67] *Appalachia* [6/65, 6/71, 6/72], C [88, 61]; Guidebooks: Cole and Wilcox's *Shades of Blue,* Webster's *Rock Climbs in the White Mountains of New Hampshire* (third ed.), Harlin's *East,* Peterson's *Cannon: A Climber's Guide,* Ross and Ellms's *Cannon, Cathedral, Humphrey's, and Whitehorse: A Rock Climber's Guide,* Hall's *Revised Guide to Cannon Cliff,* Whipple's *Climbing Routes on Cannon Cliff,* Osgood's *White Mountains.*

Directions: The majesty of Franconia Notch is found in these historic areas (north to south): Artist's Bluffs, Eagle Cliffs, Eaglet, Cannon Cliff, and Indian Head. The main access road is I–93, running right through the notch. For Artist's Bluffs: From junction of I–93 and Hwy. 18, go north from the notch to pullout just beyond junction on the right side of Hwy. 18.

6 FN–The Eagle Cliff (Eaglet) ☆☆

This 200′ granite rock spire played an important role in New England climbing history when it was first ascended in 1930. Now infrequently visited. Peregrine falcon nesting site. Summer/autumn. Free camping. USFS–White Mountain NF, (603) 528–8721.

Classics: West Chimney 6.

Ref: C [101, 70]; Guidebooks: Webster's *Rock Climbs in the White Mountains of New Hampshire* (third ed.), Osgood's *White Mountains.*

Directions: From Woodstock go north on Hwy. 93. Start east across from Cannon Mountain tramway parking. Head northeast across from Cannon Cliff. Hike approximately forty-five minutes up steep uphill bushwhack cairns and faint trail to The Eagle Cliff.

7 FN–Cannon Cliff ☆☆☆☆

The home of the Old Man of the Mountains. The venerable 1,000′ granite east face of Cannon offers a variety of climbs: long aid to short hard free routes at base. Old Cannon first route done in 1928. Cannon Slabs on the north end offer New England's severest friction climbs. This is alpine rock climbing: Beware loose rock, protean weather, tricky route finding, and old pitons as exemplified by The Labyrinth, the longest 5.11 climb in the Northeast. Climbers required to sign in and out at same checkpoint. Preferred descent is at north end past the Old Man. Summer/autumn. Free camping. USFS–White Mountain NF, (603) 528–8721.

Classics: Cannon Slabs: Lakeview 5, Consolation Prize 8, Odyssey 10; Whitney-Gilman 7, Sam's Swan Song 7, Moby Grape 8, Vertigo 9, Slip of Fools 10a, VMC Direct 10+, Duet Direct 10d, Labyrinth Wall V 11c, Walk on the Wild Side 11, Fall From Grace 12b, White Iceberg 12, Ghost Roof A4, One Drop of Water A3.

Jimmy Dunn on VMC Direct, Cannon Mountain.

JIM DUNN COLLECTION

Ref: AAJ ['70-139, 67]; *Appalachia* [6/65, 6/71, 6/72], C [186-118, 171-34, 167-78, 132, 121, 112, 111, 105, 93, 90, 75, 71, 67, 61, 60, 59, 54, 11/75), R [79-56/66, 70-28, 69-144, 67-58, S [11/88, 9/84]; on-line guide www.chauvinguides.com/guidebook.htm; Guidebooks: Harlin's *East*, Webster's *Rock Climbs in the White Mountains of New Hampshire* (third ed.), Peterson's *Cannon: A Climber's Guide*, Ross and Ellms's *Cannon, Cathedral, Humphrey's, and Whitehorse: A Rock Climber's Guide*, Hall's *Revised Guide to Cannon Cliff*, Whipple's *Climbing Routes on Cannon Cliff*, Osgood's *White Mountains*.

Directions: From North Woodstock trend 7 mi. north on Hwy. 93. Park at Profile Lake Trailhead on left (below the Old Man). Sign in. Three trails assist climbers in reaching the different sectors of Cannon Cliff: Lakeview for Cannon Slabs, Reppy's Crack for middle of cliff, or Whitney-Gilman for south end.

8 FN–Indian Head ⭐

This 100′ granite crag sees limited traffic but sports two beautiful 5.10+ finger cracks at the top of the mountain. Summer/autumn. Free camping. USFS–White Mountain NF, (603) 528-8721.

Ref: Guidebooks: Webster's *Rock Climbs in the White Mountains of New Hampshire* (third ed.), Osgood's *White Mountains*.

Directions: From North Woodstock take Hwy. 93 north a few minutes. Park at Flume Visitor Center. South of Franconia Notch. Hike west through tunnel under interstate to trail up to top of Indian Head Mountain. Faces southeast.

9 CN⭐–(Crawford Notch State Park) Mt. Willard et al. ⭐⭐

The routes on the south face of 800′ granite Mt. Willard are among New Hampshire's tallest walls. Frankenstein Cliff is the most popular cliff within the "notch." Mt. Willard and Frankenstein are also noted ice-climbing areas. Elephant Head Crag is a practice/teaching cliff. The Crawford Slabs are typical low-angle granite slabs. Appalachian Trail access. Be aware: peregrine falcon nesting from May to mid-July with a "no climbing" request by Fish and Game Department. Summer/autumn. Pay camping. State park, (603) 374-2272.

Classics: Of Mice and Men 3p 7; Mt. Willard: Across the Universe III 10; Frankenstein Cliffs: Bride of Frankenstein 10-, Tressle Buttress, The Green Room 11+, Upper Tier sport routes. Check I.M.E. Route Book.

Ref: C [93, 88, 75, 65, 61], R [103-144, 43, 29(1/89)], *Appalachia* 1928-33; Guidebooks: Cole and Wilcox's, *Shades of Blue*, Webster's *Rock Climbs in the White Mountains of New Hampshire* (third ed.), Ross and Ellms's *Cannon, Cathedral, Humphrey's, and Whitehorse: A Rock Climber's Guide*, Osgood's *White Mountains*.

Directions: From Bartlett drive north on Hwy. 302 to Crawford Notch State Park (signs). The splendor of this famed area includes Mt. Willard, Frankenstein Cliff,

Elephant's Head, and Crawford Slabs. Elephant's Head: Top of notch. Mt. Willard: At top of notch. On west side. Parking pullout on west. Hike south to base. Frankenstein Cliff: Turn left to Arethusa Falls. Park at end by railroad tracks. Hike north along tracks. Cut left before trestle and up hill. Crawford Slabs (Ethan's and Abel's): west side of notch via Webster Cliff Trail bushcrashing left after crossing Saco River.

10 CN–Frankenstein Cliff ⭐⭐

The 300′ granite Frankenstein Cliff is the most popular cliff within the "notch." Upper tier has seen a rejuvenation of interest due to sport routes. Frankenstein is also noted for Chia ice climbing route. Summer/autumn. Pay camping. State park.

Classics: Frankenstein Cliffs: Bride of Frankenstein 10-, Tressle Buttress, The Green Room 11+; Upper tier sport: Dark Lord 8, Shakin' up the Orange Street 11-, Stem Like a Barstand 11-, Whispering Forest 11d, Attila the Nun 12a, Rocky Horror Show 12-.

Ref: *Appalachia* 1928-33, C [105, 71], R [43, R 29(1/89)]; Guidebooks: Cole and Wilcox's *Shades of Blue*, Webster's *Rock Climbs in the White Mountains of New Hampshire* (third ed.), Ross and Ellms's *Cannon, Cathedral, Humphrey's, and Whitehorse: A Rock Climber's Guide*, Osgood's *White Mountains*.

Directions: From Bartlett drive north on Hwy. 302 to park (signs). Frankenstein Cliff: Turn left to Arethusa Falls. Park at end by railroad tracks. Hike north along tracks. Cut left before trestle and up hill, following trail that leads up through lower cliff bands. Higher up the upper tier sport climbing cliffs come into view. Quick bushwhack to base. Faces southeast.

11 Missing Wall and Texaco Slab ⭐⭐

Warm, south-facing 100′ granite cliffs. Sweet New England is 250′ left of Texaco Slab. The continuous three-pitch Obelisk is recommended route of the cliff. Spring/autumn. USFS–White Mountain NF, (603) 528-8721.

Classics: Sweet New England 11, The Obelisk 11.

Ref: Guidebook: Webster's *Rock Climbs in the White Mountains of New Hampshire* (third ed.).

Directions: From Bartlett trend north on Hwy. 302 to Inn Unique. Park at Davis Path parking. Hike across river via suspension bridge and bang the brush north (left) for Texaco Slab (low-angle slabs) or circle around right end of slab and broken cliff band. Hike up left at easiest point to talus, then diagonal left to Missing Wall.

12 Hart's Ledge ⭐⭐

Triple-tiered obscure granite cliff. Lower tier has worst-quality rock. Upper tier is rounded. Interesting boulder caves on left side. Summer/autumn. Pay camping. USFS–White Mountain NF, (603) 528-8721.

Classics: Hart Attack 10+, Hart of the Night 12, 12d.

Ref: C 101, R 43; Guidebooks: Webster's *Rock Climbs in the*

White Mountains of New Hampshire (third ed.), Osgood's *White Mountains*

Directions: Just northwest of Bartlett. Cross the Saco River in town and head west (left) 2 mi. Turn right over railroad tracks for ¼ mi. to housing development. Park at end of road, following logging roads west to Hart's Ledge (fifteen minutes). Ask locals or see guidebooks. Visible at Silver Springs from north on Hwy. 302.

13 Cave Mountain ☆

Good small 75′ granite crag. Bring tape. Summer/autumn. Pay camping. May be private land.

Classics: Leaves of Grass 8, Roofer Madness 12a.

Ref: Guidebook: Webster's *Rock Climbs in the White Mountains of New Hampshire* (third ed.).

Directions: From Bartlett go 1 mi. from town off Hwy. 302. Hike Mt. Langdon Trail ¼ mi. (veer left on faint trail). Cave Mountain is due north of Bartlett across the Saco River.

14 White's Ledge/Pick of the Litter Cliff ☆☆☆

Across valley from Attitash Ski Area, the 300′ granite White's Ledge has seen climbers' tracks since the early 1930s. It is a peaceful cliff. Pick of the Litter is a recent sport crag. More information in Webster's *Rock Climbs in the White Mountains of New Hampshire.* Spring/autumn. Pay/free camping. USFS–White Mountain NF, (603) 528-8721.

Classics: Endeavor 7, The White Streak 8, International Mountain Crack 9+, Inside Straight 10-; Pick of Litter: Pick of the Litter 8, Pumping Pockets 9+, Forchristsake 10b, Top Dog 11a, By Bosch! By Gully! 11b.

Ref: C 112, R 43; Guidebook: Webster's *Rock Climbs in the White Mountains of New Hampshire* (third ed.).

Directions: From Glen (junction of Hwy. 302 and Hwy. 16), go 2 mi. east on Hwy. 302 to chalets (Birchview by the Saco). Turn into development and turn left on Covered Bridge Lane, passing houses until ledge outline is to your left. Park on shoulder. Scramble to cliff over talus. For Pick of the Litter, from Birchview by the Saco, follow the river, turning left at GARLAND sign. Follow river until in front of White's Ledge. Park at clearing. Hike north on road, paralleling dirt road. When road splits, walk farther north five to ten minutes, looking for streambed on right. Cliff is uphill ten minutes at top of wash. Faces south.

15 Stairs Mountain (Giant Stairs/Back Stairs) ☆☆

Remote, less frequented 300′ granite cliffs. Uncleaned routes. Spring/autumn. Free camping. USFS–White Mountain NF, (603) 528-8721.

Classics: Natural Order 8.

Ref: C 105; Guidebook: Webster's *Rock Climbs in the White Mountains of New Hampshire* (third ed.).

Directions: From Glen go northwest on Hwy. 302. Turn right on Jericho Rd. to end. Hike or bike approximately 2 mi. on Rocky Branch Trail to shelter. Giant Stairs are west up Stairs Col Trail to col. Back Stairs are 1 ½ mi. up same trail, then bushwhack north twenty minutes to southeast-facing main cliff.

16 Popple Mountain ☆

A lightly climbed 175′ granite crag. Summer/autumn. Free camping. USFS–White Mountain National Forest, (603) 528-8721.

Classics: Aku Aku 6, Where Eagles Dare 11-.

Ref: Guidebook: Webster's *Rock Climbs in the White Mountains of New Hampshire* (third ed.).

Directions: From North Conway go north on Hwy. 16 to Jackson. From Jackson continue on Hwy. 16 north toward Pinkham Notch. Shortly, look on left on high hillside for cliff. Park on side of road. Cross stream and bushwhack to base of Popple Mountain—difficult to find. Faces east.

17 Owl's Head ☆☆☆

Large, impressive, but little-known 800′ granite slab with climbing the likes of Cannon Cliff. Spring/autumn. No camping. Government/private land.

Classics: Diamond Head 10.

Ref: Locals; Guidebook: Osgood's *White Mountains.*

Directions: From East Haverhill fly south on Hwy. 25 to Oliverian Notch. Park at Owl's Head to north. Obvious on east side of road. Faces south.

18 Cemetery Crag ☆☆

Obscure 100′ granite cliff renewed with sport climbs. Spring/autumn. Free camping. USFS–White Mountain NF, (603) 528-8721.

Classics: Saco Cracker 11, Muscle Beach 12b, Bloodsport 12d.

Ref: Guidebook: Webster's *Rock Climbs in the White Mountains of New Hampshire* (third ed.).

Directions: From North Conway drive northwest on West Side Rd. past Saco Crag to first hill. Turn left on first narrow dirt road. Park at old cemetery for Cemetery Crag. Faces northeast.

19 Saco Crag ☆☆☆

Little 30′ granite cliff down by the river. Cool in the summer, with the added advantage of a nearby swimming hole. Spring/autumn. Free camping. USFS–White Mountain NF, (603) 528-8721.

Classics: Overtime Crack 11a, Saco Cracker 11, Muscle Beach 12b, Bloodsport 12d.

Ref: C 109; R 43; Guidebook: Webster's *Rock Climbs in the White Mountains of New Hampshire* (third ed.).

Directions: From North Conway drive northwest on West Side Rd. just past Humphrey's Ledge. On left across road is the Saco River swimming hole, which lies right across the street from Saco Crag. Faces northeast.

> ### New Hampshire Road Thoughts
>
> A good plan executed right now is far better than a perfect plan executed next week.
>
> —George S. Patton

20 Humphrey's Ledge ⭐⭐⭐

This 300′ granite crag totes about fifty routes up to three pitches long. It's been noted for its crumbly rock, but good climbs (e.g., Robinson Crusoe) can be had. Good bouldering at base. Summer/autumn. Pay camping. USFS–White Mountain NF, (603) 528–8721.

Classics: Cakewalk 6, Weissner Route 7, Dedication 7+, Sole Survivor 9, Robinson Crusoe 10R-, The Procession 5.12c.

Ref: C [109, 75, 64, 60], R 43; Guidebooks: Cole and Wilcox's *Shades of Blue*, Webster's *Rock Climbs in the White Mountains of New Hampshire* (third ed.), Ross and Ellms's *Cannon, Cathedral, Humphrey's, and Whitehorse: A Rock Climber's Guide*, Osgood's *White Mountains*.

Directions: From Conway go approximately 2 mi. north of Cathedral Ledge on West Side Rd. Humphrey's Ledge is on left. Uncertain if there is parking at Lady Blanche House.

21 Cathedral Ledge ⭐⭐⭐⭐⭐

The major Northeast crag. Nearly 400 routes on Cathedral and Whitehorse Ledges. Beautiful 400′ granite climbing featuring traditional climbs, sport routes up to 13d (e.g., The Mercy), and desperate aid in the Cathedral Cave. Classic multipitch lines as well. Home of the first "canoe-lean" traverse. Try the Morning Dew for awesome coffee, juices, etc. Beware: Black-fly mania in April–June. Try late summer/autumn. No camping or fires at base. Find pay camping near town or on Kancamagus Hwy. The White Mountain Hostel, 36 Washington St. in Conway, is also a friendly base camp for climbing ventures. Raptor restrictions May–July. State park.

Classics: Thin Air 6, Refuse 6, Funhouse 7, Three Birches 8, They Died Laughing 9, Recompense 9, Nutcracker 9+, Book of Solemnity 10-, Intimidation 10, Recluse 10+, The Arête 11R, Camber 11, Women In Love 11+, The Possessed 11+, The Prow 12a, Tourist Treat 12, Mordor Wall 12- (IV 7, A4), Liquid Sky 13, Edge of the World 13c, The Mercy 5.13d; Cote Boulder.

Ref: AAJ '68-155, C [195-22, 170-58, 167-78, 165(12/96)-68, 164-30, 159(3/96)-66, 114, 112, 109, 105, 101, 99, 93, 88, 75, 71, 65, 64, 61, 60, 59, 43(7/77), 10/72], M 118, R [87, 81-144, 76-19, 43]; on-line guide www.chauvin guides.com/guidebook.htm; Guidebooks: Cole and Wilcox's *Shades of Blue*, Webster's *Rock Climbs in the White Mountains of New Hampshire* (third ed.), Handren's *Rock Climbing Guide to Cathedral and Whitehorse Ledges*, Cathedral Ledge topo print, Harlin's *East*, Cote's *A Climber's Guide to Mt. Washington Valley*, Ross and Ellms's *Cannon, Cathedral, Humphrey's, and Whitehorse: A Rock Climber's Guide*, Osgood's *White Mountains*.

Directions: North Conway. Go west on River Rd., then north on West Side Rd., following signs for approximately 2 mi. Various access points to different cliffs of Cathedral Ledge. All with short approaches. Gates close at 6:00 P.M. for road to top—don't get locked in!

22 Guide's Wall ⭐⭐

A dozen 100′ granite climbs 5.7–5.9 that are usually overlooked when one sees Cathedral and Whitehorse Ledges. Summer/autumn. Pay camping. USFS–White Mountain NF, (603) 528–8721.

Classics: A Stitch in Time 9.

Ref: C [167-78, 71]; Guidebook: Webster's *Rock Climbs in the White Mountains of New Hampshire* (third ed.).

Directions: North Conway. Guide's Wall is small cliff between Whitehorse and Cathedral Ledge. Visible on the approach to the Whitehorse Slabs. Approached one of three ways: 1) Bushwhack from Bouchard Cabin. 2) After doing Whitehorse Ledge Route. 3) Via Bryce Path to crag top. Faces east.

➤ 23 Whitehorse Ledge ⭐⭐⭐⭐

Parlez-vous slab? You will at this big-time New Hampshire slabbing area. Whitehorse possesses 800′ granite slabs for friction lovers or the 650′ South Buttress for steep face climbers. For more cragging of a steeper genre, Where in the Blazes Cliff is found on the far left end of the South Buttress, as well as popular, one-pitch Steak Sauce Crag and Cosmic Crag. Summer/autumn. Pay camping. USFS–White Mountain NF, (603) 528–8721.

Classics: Slabs: Standard Rt 5, Sliding Board 7, Interloper 10; South Buttress: Inferno 8, Children's Crusade 9/11-, Last Unicorn 10, Ethereal Crack 10, Total Recall 11, Future Shock 11, Unforgettable Fire 11, Whip Finish 11c, The Eliminate 11+, Wonder Wall 12-, Science Friction Dir. 12; Steak Sauce 12+.

Ref: C [167-78, 112, 109, 105, 99, 97, 93, 88, 70, 64, 60, 59], OB 46(8/79)-30, R 43; on-line guide www. chauvinguides.com/guidebook.htm; Guidebooks: Cole and Wil-cox's *Shades of Blue*, Webster's *Rock Climbs in the White Mountains of New Hampshire* (third ed.), Handren's *Rock Climbing Guide to Cathedral and Whitehorse Ledges*, Harlin's *East*, Cote's *Climber's Guide to Mt. Washington Valley*, Ross and Ellms's *Cannon, Cathedral, Humphrey's, and Whitehorse: A Rock Climber's Guide*, Osgood's *White Mountains*.

Directions: North Conway. West on River Rd. to south on West Side Rd. Whitehorse Ledge is just ½ mi. south of Cathedral Ledge on dirt road. Parking at Whitehorse Lot. (Possibility of car break-ins.). Or one can park on main Cathedral Ledge Rd. and walk over. To get to base of slabs, hike up Bryce Path from parking. Faces east and south.

24 K☆–(Kancamagus Hwy. Area) Overview ☆☆☆

Scattered 300' granite woodland crags and slabs on the well-traveled and scenic Kancamagus Hwy. The more popular ones are listed here. Some crags are difficult to find—local assistance recommended. Sundown is the cliff of choice for a one-day visit. Camping at Covered Bridge area. Amenities are abundant at North Conway, factory-outlet capital of New Hampshire. If it's raining, there's always the Mt. Cranmore Recreation Center climbing wall. Summer/autumn. Pay camping. USFS-White Mountain NF, (603) 528-8721.

Classics: Crack in the Woods 10d, Romper Room 12a, Eyeless in Gaza 12b, Yellow Matter Custard 13a/b.

Ref: C [61(7/80)-18, 60(5/80)-14], S 7/82; Guidebooks: Cole and Wilcox's *Shades of Blue*, Webster's *Rock Climbs in the White Mountains of New Hampshire* (third ed.), Osgood's *White Mountains*.

Directions: From North Conway go west on Hwy. 112 (Kancamagus Hwy.). Several crags at various points along "Kanc" include (east-west): Woodchuck Ledge, Found Ledge, Lost Ledge, Sundown Ledges, Painted Walls, Rainbow Slabs, Crack in the Woods, Table Mountain Slab, Bear Mountain Slab, Mt. Hedgehog, and Green's Cliff. Cliffs are easier to locate when trees are barren of leaves.

25 K–Woodchuck Ledge ☆☆

Good crack climbing and unusual face climbing on 250' syenite crag. Sits on the south slope of Mt. Haystack. Summer/autumn. Pay camping. USFS-White Mountain NF, (603) 528-8721.

Classics: Zanzibar 5, Aspiring 10, Terminator 11d, Screaming Yellow Zonkers 11+, Bucket Loader 12a, Zonked Out 12, 13c?.

Ref: C [112, 109, 105, 101, 95], R 43; Guidebook: Webster's *Rock Climbs in the White Mountains of New Hampshire* (third ed.).

Directions: From Conway drive a few mi. west on the Kancamagus Hwy. (Woodchuck Ledge is first visible cliff when going west) until ½ mi. past Dugway Picnic Area. Park at pullout. (Parking is 2-3 mi. east of Covered Bridge Campground at pullout on north side of road.) Approach: Follow wide, grass-covered logging road north for approximately twenty minutes. Negotiate a large, raspberried, marshy field in front of the crag. Faces south.

26 K–Found Ledge ☆☆☆

Short and steep 80' granite crag with terrific face climbing. As difficult to find as is its sibling, Lost Ledge. Summer/autumn. Pay camping. USFS-White Mountain NF, (603) 528-8721.

Classics: Short but Sweet 10+, Lumberjack Crack 11c, Inquisition 11d, Walkabout 5.12a, Hanger Lane 5.12b.

Ref: C [109, 105], R 43; Guidebook: Webster's *Rock Climbs in the White Mountains of New Hampshire* (third ed.).

Directions: On the Kancamagus Hwy., set back ½ mi. from road. From Conway go 4 9/10 mi. west on Hwy. 112 before Covered Bridge to a two-car pullout on the south of the Hwy. Walk in for 50'. Now go left along riverbed that heads right and uphill. Stay in channel, keeping right at any forks, for fifteen minutes. Look for huge boulders on right and main cliff. Go past to slab, and then up and 100' beyond is Found Ledge. Faces south.

27 K–Lost Ledge ☆☆

Bolt-protected 80' granite slab routes. This area is just west of Found Ledge. Summer/autumn. Pay camping. USFS-White Mountain NF, (603) 528-8721.

Ref: C 109; Guidebook: Webster's *Rock Climbs in the White Mountains of New Hampshire* (third ed.).

Directions: From Conway go west on Hwy. 112 to covered bridge. Park at roadside turnout on south side of Hwy. 302, ½ mi. east of bridge. Follow a brook uphill from parking until Lost Ledge is visible through trees. A gully lined with trees splits cliff in two halves. The Carpet Slab on right is low-angled beginners' area. The left side is clean granite like Whitehorse Ledge. Faces south.

28 K–Sundown Ledges, Far Cliff, and Outback Cliff ☆☆☆

Super-popular 80' granite Kancamagus cliffband. A recommended first stop along the Kancamagus Hwy. Eyeless in Gaza is one of the best routes in the area for its grade. Yellowmatter Buttress has several sport routes. Many hard routes. Sports some of the best camping near Conway. Summer/autumn. Pay camping. USFS-White Mountain NF, (603) 528-8721.

Classics: Main Cliff: Rough Boys 10-, Vultures 10+, Dikenstein 11c, End of Tether 12-, Toothless Grin 12-; Yellowmatter Buttress (sport): Carrion 11+, Romper Room 12a, Eyeless in Gaza 5.12-, She's Crafty 12c, Yellowmatter Custard 13a, Pastry Works 13-; Far: Superba 5, Thwarthog 9, Pressure Drop 11, Scorpion Arête 11a, Gill's Groove 12; Outback: Three Stars 7, Hyperspace 10, Iron Lung 11a, Love Crack 12b.

Ref: C [112, 109, 105, 101, 99, 97, 93, 88, 75, 71, 64, 59], R [95-68, 43R]; Guidebooks: Cater's *Sport Crags of the East*, Harlin's *East*, Webster's *Rock Climbs in the White Mountains of New Hampshire* (third ed.).

Directions: From Conway drive approximately 12 mi. west on Hwy. 112 to covered bridge. Cross bridge and park on right (or in campground in back). Three main cliff areas include: 1) Sundown Ledges Main Cliff behind campground. 2) Far Cliff on the right. 3) Outback Cliff: Left (west of) and behind Main Cliff. For Main and Far Cliffs: Hike Boulder Loop Trail five minutes (past junction to cliff top) over small streambed through trees to scree. Turn left at first scree to Main Cliff's left end. Gill's Groove Crag is between Main and Far Cliffs. Far Cliff is farther along Boulder Loop and visible on left. For Outback (thirty minutes): Hike west from bridge on dirt logging road for five minutes, then turn right on first old logging road. Follow road across stream and continue to follow stream twenty minutes to crag. Faces southeast.

29 K–Painted Walls ☆☆

This 100′ granite cliff sits right of Rainbow Slabs and is recognized by its black streaks. Rock can be crumbly. Most popular route and main reason to visit this cliff is the four-pitch Windjammer route. Summer/autumn. Pay camping. USFS–White Mountain NF, (603) 528–8721.

Classics: Windjammer III 11.

Ref: C [99, 88, 75]; Guidebook: Webster's *Rock Climbs in the White Mountains of New Hampshire* (third ed.).

Directions: From Conway go west on Hwy. 112 to covered bridge. From bridge follow logging road upstream and get on Nanamocomuck Ski Trail, passing four small wooden bridges. Turn right at fourth bridge and go uphill via stream to overgrown lumber road to Painted Walls's 300′ granite slabs. Or, park at Crack In the Woods pullout 1 ³/₁₀ mi. west of bridge, cross river, and hike toward Rainbow Slabs on logging roads, then bushwhack diagonally right to Painted Walls. Faces south.

30 K–Rainbow Slabs ☆☆

Total slab climbing on 200′ swaths of granite with sparsely protected 5.3 to 5.9 routes. Routes two pitches in length. Long runouts abide. Summer/autumn. Pay camping. USFS–White Mountain NF, (603) 528–8721.

Classics: Face Dances 6, Take A Giant Step 8+.

Ref: C [93, 75]; Guidebook: Webster's *Rock Climbs in the White Mountains of New Hampshire* (third ed.).

Directions: From Conway go west on Hwy. 112 to covered bridge and then beyond another 1 ³/₁₀ mi. (if river is low). Wade Swift River, continuing right along logging road on bank, then left on more roads. Bushwhack to base. Or (the dry approach) from bridge follow logging road upstream and get on Nanamocomuck Ski Trail, passing four small wooden bridges. Continue past bridges until opposite Lower Falls. Bushwhack on old lumber roads to Rainbow Slabs. This area is visible from Lower Falls parking on Hwy. 112: Rainbow Slabs on left, Painted Slabs on right. Faces south.

31 K–Crack in the Woods Cliff ☆☆☆

Two routes make finding this 100′ granite cliff a must for the intermediate and advanced climber: The Crack in the Woods, New Hampshire's most classic crack, and Pumping Station, an exercise in overhanging climbing. Summer/autumn. Pay camping. USFS–White Mountain NF, (603) 528–8721.

Classics: The Crack in the Woods 10+, Pumping Station 11+.

Ref: Guidebook: Webster's *Rock Climbs in the White Mountains of New Hampshire* (third ed.).

Directions: From Conway go west on Hwy. 112 to 1 ³/₁₀ mi. past covered bridge. Ford Swift River to logging road, heading briefly right, then turning left into woods in

small drainage for short way. Look hard for cliff going uphill and left. Or (the dry approach), use Nanamocomuck Ski Trail, passing Rainbow Slabs (see Rainbow Slabs, above) and continuing right up drainage to Crack in the Woods Cliff. Faces south.

32 K–Table Mountain Slab ☆☆

Scenic, remote 150′ granite slab featuring friction scoop climbing. Long walk . . . goes well with a nice merlot and aged cheese. Of a handful of routes, Merlin is most popular. Summer/autumn. Pay camping. USFS–White Mountain NF, (603) 528–8721.

Classics: Merlin 8.

Ref: Guidebooks: Webster's *Rock Climbs in the White Mounztains of New Hampshire* (third ed.), Osgood's *White Mountains*.

Directions: This remote slab on the Kancamagus Hwy. is located at top of first drainage northwest of Rainbow Slabs. From the Kanc it's a long hike. Best approach for Table Mountain Slab: From Conway drive 17 mi. west on Hwy. 112 past covered bridge. Drive south up Bear Notch Rd. and park on left (east) side of road at pullout below crest. Hike approximately forty minutes up Attitash Trail to summit of Table Mountain. As you approach center of slab, veer a little right, and rap two ropes down Merlin route to base. Faces south.

33 K–Bear Mountain Slab ☆☆

A little-used granite beginner's slab above the Kancamagus Hwy. Still, like a literary classic that never gets read, it's nice to know it's there. Summer/autumn. Pay camping. USFS–White Mountain NF, (603) 528–8721.

Classics: Say Mr. Congressman II 8.

Ref: Guidebook: Webster's *Rock Climbs in the White Mountains of New Hampshire* (third ed.).

Directions: From Conway drive west on Hwy. 112 past covered bridge. As you drive past Rainbow Slabs, Bear Mountain Slab is first large south-facing slab/cliff on right above Swift River. Drive south up Bear Notch Rd. and park on left (east) side of road at pullout below crest. Hike east to mountain. Faces south.

34 K–Mt. Hedgehog ☆☆

Climbing history dates back to the 1920s on these 200′ granite slabs. East Ledges have the most climbs. The North Ledge offers the most classic climb of the area, Avatar. Summer/autumn. Pay camping. USFS–White Mountain NF, (603) 528–8721.

Classics: MacDougal's Variation 7, Avatar I 8+.

Ref: Guidebook: *Webster's Rock Climbs in the White Mountains of New Hampshire* (third ed.).

Directions: From Conway drive approximately 17 mi. west on Hwy. 112 well beyond covered bridge. Pass Bear Notch Rd. to Passaconway Historical Site. Go 1 ³/₁₀ mi. further west, parking at Mt. Hedgehog Trail. Take trail up left branch for 2 mi. to summit. Four separate granite ledges reside here for climbers: Summit Cliff, East Ledges, North Ledge, and Helms Deep Gully. Faces south.

35 K–Green's Cliff ★★

Long walk into one of the most remote Kancamagus granite cliffs. Seldom visited. Summer/autumn. Pay camping. USFS–White Mountain NF, (603) 528–8721.

Classics: Stewart's Crack 8.

Ref: Guidebook: Webster's *Rock Climbs in the White Mountains of New Hampshire* (third ed.).

Directions: From Conway drive 17 mi. west on Hwy. 112 past covered bridge onto Bear Notch Rd. Continue a few more mi. west past Mt. Hedgehog to south and Sabbaday Falls. At falls, begin looking north of Hwy. 112 for Green's Cliff, which sits approximately 2 mi. north of Hwy. 112. On this approach, one becomes a member of the pro bushwhacking tour. Of the Kancamagus Areas mentioned here, this is the farthest area from North Conway. Faces south.

36 B and M Ledge (aka B&M Ledge) ★★★

Coarse, crystalline 300′ granite crag with a list of some forty wild and treasurable routes to savor. Summer/autumn. Free camping. USFS–White Mountain NF, (603) 528–8721.

Classics: Bandit 9, If Dogs Run Free 11-, Sacred Space 2p 12a, Heavy Weather Sailing 12-, Nightflyer 5.12-, Flesh for Fantasy 13a.

Ref: C [109, 105, 101, 99, 93, 88, 75, 71], R 43; Guidebook: Webster's *Rock Climbs in the White Mountains of New Hampshire* (third ed.).

Directions: From Conway head south on Hwy. 16 to Madison. Turn left at sandpit. Band M Ledge can be seen from Hwy. 113 past gravel pits.

37 Redstone Quarry ★★

Eighty-foot granite crag. Summer/autumn. Private land.

Ref: Locals.

Directions: Near Conway. Ask local climbers about Redstone Quarry. Touchy access.

38 Madison Boulder ★★

If God can do anything, could he create a boulder so big even He couldn't lift it? This one might be the one! This glacially shipped granite boulder is one of the largest in the world, boxed with dimensions of 83′ long, 37′ wide, 23′ high, and weighing in at just a little more than your typical sport climber at 4,662 tons. The largest glacial erratic in New England. Problems up to 5.12 on the south face. Watch for splinters on your shimmy down the tree route descent. Autumn. Day use only. State natural area, (603) 323–2087.

Classics: Love Search Arête 12a, North Face.

Ref: J. Mallery; C 109.

Directions: From Conway (approximately ten minutes) roll south on Hwy. 113 toward the hamlet of Madison. About ⅔ of the way between Madison and Conway, turn west at MADISON BOULDER sign for approximately 1 ½ mi. Madison Boulder is a noteworthy glacial erratic that rests back in the trees 50 yd. from the road's end.

39 Rumney ★★★★

Surprise! This may be the best sport cragging and bouldering in the state. Sport and trad routes on the 100′ metamorphic schist walls of the Main Cliff/Meadows area and above the Black Jack Boulders at the beautiful Waimea Wall, Bonsai and Northwest Territories. Crags are surrounded in country charm and visible from Hwy. 25. Fine bouldering at the Black Jack and the Town Pound Boulders. Thanks to locals Shimberg, Hammond, Stevenson, Handren, Damboise, Mallery, Smith, Graham, et al. for great routes. For current information check at the Rock Barn on Hwy. 25, a couple of miles west of Plymouth; the only climbing barn of its kind. Eateries: Steve's at Rumney, Elvio's in Plymouth. Described in Osgood's White Mountains guidebook in 1876 thusly, "The long and rugged

Playing at the Town Pound Boulders.

TIM TOULA

ledges are starred with small but brilliant sheets of mica; and clusters of hardy evergreens along the narrow plateau interfere with the prospect." Raptor restrictions. Spring–autumn. Free/pay camping. Private/USFS–White Mountain NF, (603) 528–8721.

Classics: Beginner's Route 5, Holderness School Corner 8, Town Pound Crack 10b, Black Jack Crack 10-, Peer Pressure 10d, Espresso 11a, Flying Hawaiian 11a, Retrospade 11c, Flea Surgeon 12a, Technosurfer 12b, Venus on a Half Shell 12c, Hope for Movement 12d, Urban Surfer 13a, Neptune 13a/b, China Beach 14a, Jaws 14b, Livin' Astro, The Fly 14.

Ref: E. Mushial, J. Mallery; C [196-22, 191-17, 188-26, 186, 185-33, 177-40, 143, 142, 139, 126(6/91)-28, 115(8/89)-28], R [101-20, 95-68, 87, 68-89 (topos)]; Sherman's *Stone Crusade;* Guidebooks: Smith's *Rock Climbing Guide to Rumney,* Cater's *Sport Crags of the East,* Danna's *Schist Another Hangover: Rumney Rock Notes,* Webster's *Rock Climbs in the White Mountains of New Hampshire* (third ed.), Osgood's *White Mountains.*

Directions: At Rumney Village (west of Plymouth on Hwy. 25, then just 7/10 mi. north of Hwy. 25 on Stinson Lake Rd.). Town Pound Boulders approximately 1 8/10 mi. east of Rumney Village on Quincy Rd. (obvious roadside); Main Cliff et al. (Orange Crush, Kennel Wall): approximately 1 1/10 mi. west of Rumney Village on Buffalo Rd. Main cragging is here. Black Jack Boulders and sport cragging (Waimea Wall, Bonzai Crag): approximately 1 1/2 mi. west of Rumney Village on Buffalo Rd. Park roadside. Hike north at telephone pole number 38. Sensitive access; park respectfully in the Meadows Lot. Cliffs face mainly south.

40 Polar Caves (closed) ✮✮✮

Rumney-like 100′ schist cliffs visible from road in this roadside tourist attraction. Included to let climbers know it is highly illegal to climb on these tempting taste treats. Private land.

Ref: E. Mushial.

Directions: Just west of Plymouth on Hwy. 25 at Polar Caves Park (you can't miss it).

41 Brown's Ridge ✮✮

Secluded 200′ granite beginner/intermediate slabbin' cliff, similar to Whitehorse Ledge, New Hampshire. Pay camping. Summer/autumn.

Classics: Shine Your Helmet 7.

Ref: Guidebook: Webster's *Rock Climbs in the White Mountains of New Hampshire* (third ed.).

Directions: From Conway drive 25 mi. south on Hwy. 16. Turn right on Brown's Ridge Rd. and park at small bridge and pullout. Thrash west 1 mi. to Brown's Ridge cliff. This cliff can be viewed from road driving south from Conway. Look southwest at "Ossipee Owl." Faces east.

42 Pawtuckaway State Park ✮✮✮✮

Taste treat of an excellent bouldering pâté followed by a main course of saucy 100′ granite leads. Devil's Den has the highest cliffs. Lower and Upper Slabs have 40′ short leads—most opt for topropes. Scenic free camping. Black flies from mid-May to mid-June. Guiding from Vertical Concepts (Durham). Spring/autumn. Pay camping. State park.

Classics: The Flake Rt 4, Microwave Crack 6, Lakeside Jamcrack 6, The Book 8, Mounds 9-, The Horn 9-, The Whip 9+, China Dragon 9+, Heat Wave 11b, The Exorcist 2p 11+, Sympathy for the Devil 13a, Bouldering: Chuck's Torture B1+, Taco Bell, Indiana Jones V8/9.

Ref: C 139, R 51(10/92); Guidebook: Saball's *Pawtuckaway Rock Climbs,* Swain's *A Climber's Guide to Pawtuckaway State Park and Southeast New Hampshire,* Harlin's *East, Guide to Bouldering at Pawtuckaway.*

Directions: Two approaches. From Manchester follow Hwy. 101 east to exit 4. Go north to little town of Raymond. Get on Hwy. 27/107 northwest a few miles out of town. Then veer onto Hwy. 107 north for 2 8/10 mi. Turn east on Reservation Rd. (at Pawtuckaway sign) for approximately 3 mi. to fire tower trailhead. Continue driving 1 3/10 mi. past this, following BOULDERS markers on rocks into Pawtuckaway State Park. Park at BOULDERS in white paint on horizontal log, following the trail behind log into Devil's Den boulders/cliff. Or continue driving past this to pond and park. (Note that a reader has submitted the following: "Due to extreme overuse during the past two years, this parking area is no longer accessible.") Lower and Upper Slabs sit across the water on east side of pond. Good boulders include the Natural Boulders and The Whip Area. Approach two: From Manchester follow Hwy. 101 east to exit 5. Turn north on Hwy. 156 for 5 1/10 mi. (go past state park entrance). Turn left on Old Deerfield Rd. at "Cilley" soldier statue for 2 9/10 mi. Turn right onto "Class 6" road at blue/gray mobile home on left for 3/10 mi. (signs). Hike 3/4 mi. on road to the rock or risk oil-pan annihilation with low-clearance vehicle.

43 Joe English Hill ✮✮✮

Possibly New England's best-kept secret. Climbing here probably began in 1916 when H. L. Emerson and a friend first pulled their way up a rope on the cliff. Excellent 200′ granite crag offers a pleasing variety of climbs; mostly face climbing. Overhanging sections feature sport lines. Though on a military installation, climbing seems to be tolerated. So choose your weaponry, lock on target, then fire! This is one New Hampshire climbing area that may deserve more attention. Summer/autumn. No camping. Private land.

Classics: Bolted face roofs, bouldering.

Ref: B. Askins 3/98; locals; C 111(16).

Directions: From New Boston spin south on Hwy. 13 a couple mi. Turn left at Meadow Rd. for 9/10 mi. Turn right onto Joe English Rd. and veer immediately left for 2/10 mi. (veering right on pavement leads to good view of crag at cul-de-sac). Park before Air Force fenced gate. Follow road (southeast) just beyond the gate. Joe English Hill Rocks on the hillside on left. Faces south.

44 Monadnock State Park

Mount Monadnock (3,165'), with its 80' schist/quartzite slab, is an example of a geologic phenomenon that bears the same name. It rises 1,500' to 2,000' above the surrounding countryside. Besides being a premier example of a monadnock, the area also has examples of roches moutonnes, sillimanite crystals, glacial erratics, folds, pegmatite veins, an old graphite mine, and dipping beds of the Littleton formation. A two-and-a-half-hour round-trip hike on White Arrow Trail takes one to the summit. Many other hiking trails. Summer/autumn. Pay camping. State park, (603) 532–8862.
Ref: S 1/73; Guidebook: Baldwin's *Monadnock Guide.*
Directions: From Marlborough head southeast of town on Hwy. 124 to Monadnock State Park. Signs. Bouldering and short climbs may be found at the following areas in and around the park: Bald Rock and Pulpit, Sarcophagus Rock, Black Precipice (largest vertical cliff), Parker Trail Erratic Boulder, Doric Temple, cliff between White Dot Trail and Fire Warden's Cabin, The Tooth, south side of Mt. Monadnock, Hello Rock, and Jumbly Rocks.

45 Fall Mountain

Twenty-foot granite bouldering. More than one hundred problems. Bring a spot pad and at least one spotter in case of poor landings. Free camping. State land.
Classics: Godsmack! V4, Jugular Vein V3, M.D. 84 V3.
Ref: M. Kmiec 8/97; R 99-36.
Directions: North Walpole. Go north on Route 123 until you pass the Jiffy Mart in North Walpole. Park in the pulloff to the left. Cross the road and hike up the mountain.

46 Mt. Caesar

One-hundred-foot granite crag. Autumn. No camping. County land.
Classics: Pocket Full of Wasps (5.4)★★★ 100': Starts directly below the tallest section of the cliff. Climb 30' up the thin face right next to a quartzite rib (poor protection) to a large ledge with a tree. Climb straight up and over the exfoliated slab layer (two bolts) to another taller exfoliation (possible belay stance 50'). From here go left around the exfoliation, then finish straight up the remainder of the cliff (small trees for belay). This route can be done in one or two pitches.
Ref: 11/97.
Directions: From Keene take Route 12 south to Route 32. Continue south on Hwy. 32 to Monadnock Regional High School and Mt. Caesar Elementary School. Parking available in school parking lot. Walk up to far right-hand corner of the cemetery and get on trail to top of Mt. Caesar. From top of Mt. Caesar, walk down and left to

the slabs (obvious). Slabs can be seen from Route 32 North. Face south.

47 Stonehouse Pond

Small but excellent 100' conglomerate crag with a half dozen sport routes. This crag, which lies on private property, has had access problems in the past. May be closed to climbing currently. Autumn. No camping. Private land.
Classics: The Roost 6, The Nose 7, The Joke 9+, BBB 10, new sport routes?
Ref: 11/97; M. Laggis; Guidebook: Swain's *A Climber's Guide to Pawtuckaway State Park and Southeastern New Hampshire.*
Directions: In Barrington. From junction of Hwy. 125 and Hwy. 9, go west on Hwy. 9, turning left just past Hwy. 202 before white house. Follow dirt road to crag sitting on west side of Stonehouse Pond.

48 Rock Rimmon

One of the fastest-drying granite cliffs in New Hampshire. Some one hundred great routes in the middle of the city, though quite a bit of broken glass. Summer. No camping. City land.
Classics: Angel 6.
Ref: 11/97.
Directions: Manchester. On west side of city, but well within city limits.

49 Dumplington Hill

Small 40' granite cliff in the trees similar to but smaller than Pawtuckaway. Forty routes. Summer. No camping. Private land.
Ref: 11/97.
Directions: West of Raymond. Take Hwy. 27 west to a left turn onto Langford. Follow Langford to the hill. Access from side roads, then along power line and railroad track.

50 Wallis Sands State Beach

Possibly the only sea-cliff climbing in New Hampshire. Part of the 20' gneiss cliff was buried in the late 1980s by a parking lot. Boulder at low tide. Toprope advisable. Summer. No camping. State land, (603) 436–9404.
Ref: 11/97; Guidebook: Swain's *A Climber's Guide to Pawtuckaway State Park and Southeastern New Hampshire.*
Directions: Near Rye. On Route 1 at Wallis Sands State Beach. Park ½ mi. north of entrance at pulloff at top of small hill. Descend to bottom of sea cliffs. Faces east.

51 Carr's Cove

Obscure 20' granite beginner's area historically used by local high school. This area is on the edge of a saltwater marsh. Best to visit at midday when tide is low. Look out for possible car theft. Summer. No camping. Private land.
Classics: Traverse of the Crag 5.7.

Ref: 11/97; Guidebook: Swain's *A Climber's Guide to Pawtuckaway State Park and Southeastern New Hampshire.*
Directions: Seabrook. From junction of Hwy. 1A and Hwy. 286, go south on Hwy. 286. Turn left on Brown Ave. to stream crossing and then curve in road. Take a left at curve onto a dirt road and private yard. Follow a dirt road until a clearing is reached. Park off to side. A quick walk down the well-traveled road gets one to a marsh and south-facing Carr's Cove.

52 Rock Rimmon
Small 30' granite crags and boulders below the fire tower. Another obscure beginner area. No camping. State land.
Ref: 11/97; Guidebook: Swain's *A Climber's Guide to Pawtuckaway State Park and Southeastern New Hampshire.*
Directions: In Kingston. Follow Rock Rimmon Rd. to below the fire tower. Ledges down and left of fire tower. Faces north.

53 Priest Rd. Cliff
A small but quality practice area. South-facing 60' conglomerate crag with thirty routes under a high-tension power line, so no vegetation—it dries quickly. No camping. On private property; climbing may or may not be allowed.
Classics: Disneyworld 5, Arch 6, The Priest's Pulp, Kingfish 5.7+ traverse.
Ref: 11/97; Guidebook: Swain's *A Climber's Guide to Pawtuckaway State Park and Southeastern New Hampshire.*
Directions: In Nottingham. Just off Hwy. 152, directly below high wires. On Priest Rd. (of course).

54 Dame Rd. Boulder
Several small crags and 20' granite boulders along the road, one of which (the Dame Rd. Boulder) has nine small toprope routes up to 5.9. Pine tree provides a toprope anchor. Good after-work climbing place for locals. Summer. No camping. Private land.
Ref: 11/97; Guidebook: Swain's *A Climber's Guide to Pawtuckaway State Park and Southeastern New Hampshire.*
Directions: In Newmarket. On Dame Rd. on right side approximately 2 7/10 mi. from Hwy. 108 and Newmarket Center. More bouldering exists off Dame Rd. and Bay Rd. in Newmarket.

55 Wild River (Bonney Cave) ☆☆☆
A wonderfully steep granite crag featuring more than a dozen unrelenting and memorable climbs, such as the cliff's impressive central crack, Big Red. July–September. Camping at Wild River Campground. USFS–White Mountain NF, (603) 528-8721.
Ref: R 72-102.
Classics: Big Red 5.12 100' crack, Wildlife 12b, Get A Life 12c, Wild Thing 13a.
Directions: From Gilead, Maine, drop south on Hwy. 113. Turn southwest on Wild River Rd. for 5 1/2 mi. to Wild River Campground. Park at trailhead. Hike forty minutes south along Blue Brook to wall on right.

Other New Hampshire Climbing Areas
Trollville (Anti-Vail)
Ref: C 186-31.

New Jersey

The trail stretches out in front of me like something about to dissolve, and I go tracking down it like someone possessed. —Tom Brown, The Tracker

Yo! The Garden State, which in New Jerseyite used to translate as the "Armpit of the East," has actually become a flowerbed of climbing areas. While there are more areas upcoming than listed here, please be sure to check out the boulders at Princeton and the cliffs at the Gunks-like Delaware Water Gap for some enjoyable cranking.

1 Pine Paddies (in Norvin Green State Forest) (closed) ✩✩

A small, 80′, Arkose sandstone, casual, off-the-beaten track climbing area. Local guidebook installed at trail box. The area containing Pine Paddies has been taken over by a man named Sam Braen. It is now illegal to go back there to climb or hike. Supposedly this area is to be destroyed and used for quarries. This is a shame because this is an excellent climbing area for New Jersey due to its leadable climbs and difficult routes, but this area may not be around for too long. Autumn. Private land.

Classics: Count Crakula 8+, OOBLIK 11d.

Ref: Guidebooks: Nick and Sloane's *New Jersey Crags, Pine Paddies local guidebook.*

Directions: Near Wanaque (Hwy. 511). Take a left onto West Brook Rd. for 2 mi. Take another left onto Snake Den Rd. for ½ mi. Park at Weiss Ecological Center. Walk up Snake Den Rd. a few minutes to Blue Dot Trail. Hike forty-five minutes on Blue Dot Trail to top of Pine Paddies cliff past scenic overlook. Closed to climbing!

2 Yards Creek Reservoir (closed) ✩✩✩

Closed by the power company because of a climbing accident. At one time, this 100′ sandstone crag was a frequented climbing spot on a New Jersey map. Autumn. Private land.

Ref: Locals; Guidebook: Nick and Sloane's *New Jersey Crags.*

Directions: North of Blairstown. Between Upper and Lower Yards. Creek Reservoirs.

3 Delaware Water Gap National Recreation Area (aka Mt. Tammany) ✩✩✩

This prominent landmark sports a 200′ quartzite Gunks-like cliffband diagonalling conspicuously above I–80 with a variety of one hundred gymnastic routes. These are the tallest cliffs in New Jersey. One no longer needs to register with the Park Service to climb as in the past. A climbing guide may be purchased at the Kittatinny Point Visitor Center. Best climbing here is in winter, when wasps and poison ivy are gone. May have dirtier rock and more traffic than Pennsylvania side. Camping at Worthington State Forest, 4 mi. north of cliffs on Old Mine Rd. NPS, (908) 496-4458.

Classics: Trapdoor Chimney 5, Sobriety Test 7, The Gauntlet 8-, Double Overhang 8, Dead Man's Curve 9-, Corkscrew 9-, Say Your Pwayers Wabbit 10-, Ride of the Valkyries 10, Real Rangers 10+, Premature Exasperation 11, Rad Dudes from Hell 12 toprope.

Ref: C 109, R 75-38; Guidebooks: Nick and Sloane's *New Jersey Crags,* Steele's *A Climbing Guide to the Delaware Gap,* Harler's *Climb Pennsylvania,* Dougher's *Rock and Ice in the Gap.*

Directions: At Delaware Water Gap, New Jersey side. Off I–80 before bridge into Pennsylvania. Park at I–80 highway rest area. Walk east along highway to base of Mt. Tammany cliff. Rough Grey Dot Trail is descent or via rappel.

4 Allamuchy State Park (Buzzard Mountain) ✩✩

Traditionally, a small, 50′ sandstone bouldering and toprope area. Now with some bolted leads (approximately twenty routes) on arkose sandstone. Guides available at Mountain Sports in Clinton and through Monmouth County Park System. Camping at Stephen's State Forest Campground. Autumn. Pay camping in state park.

Classics: Salty Tears 6/7, Classic Route 9+, Blowout 10, A Year in a Life 10a/11d.

Ref: 2/99; E. Meudt, Miller; Guidebook: Nick and Sloane's *New Jersey Crags.*

Directions: From Netcong (I–80, exit 25), go north on Hwy. 206 for 1 mi. Turn left on Waterloo Village Rd./604 for just less than 2 mi. to picket fence. Allamuchy State Park main rocks are 150 yd. on northwest side of road; not visible in summer. Various walls face mainly southeast.

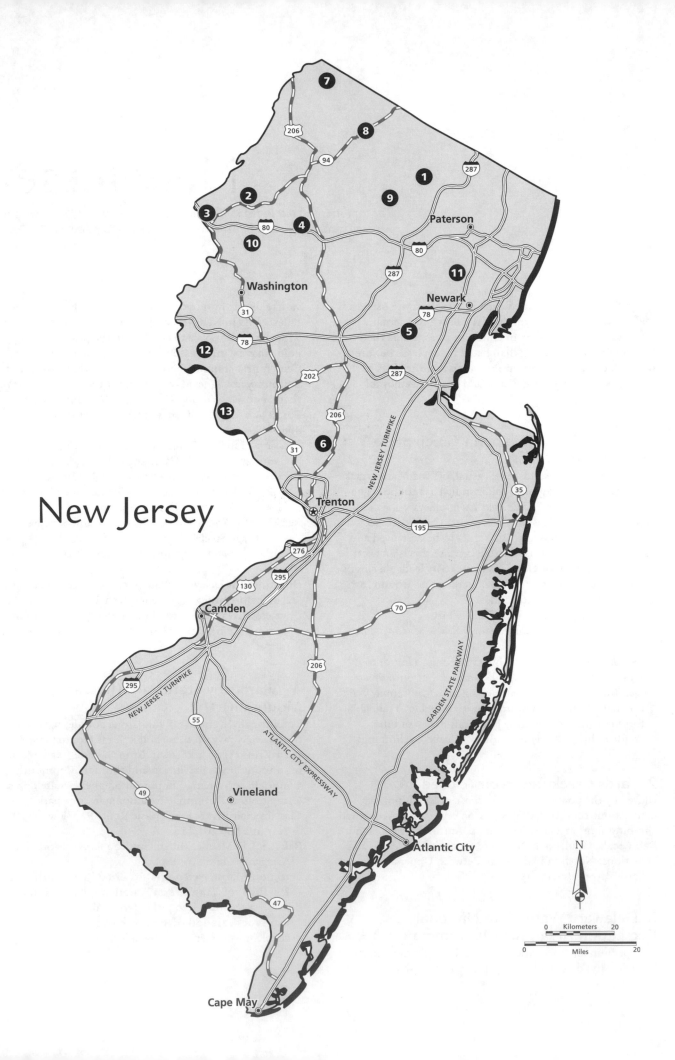

New Jersey

5 Watchung Cliff ✪✪✪ (closed?)

Pumpy, 105-degree 30′ basaltic gabbro walls with sucker jugs give way to bouldering and toproping. Good for training . . . once known as Jersey Jeff's training area. Routes done by R. Raffa in the 1970s and Shockley in the 1950s. In the early 1990s, no climbing statute was enforced. Check locally before climbing. Autumn. No camping. Union County park.

Classics: Zipper 6, Frog Leg Crack 10, Triple Overhangs 10d, Credit Card Climb 11, Watchung Traverse B 5.11.

Ref: M. Freeman; C 115(52); Guidebook: Nick and Sloane's *New Jersey Crags.*

Directions: Central New Jersey. Northwest of Scotch Plains. From I–78 take exit 43, going east. Turn right onto Glenside, then right on Valley Rd. to parking for Seeley's Lake on left. Cliffs are south of Lake. Faces west.

6 Cradle Rock Boulder Field (aka Princeton Boulders) ✪✪

Long-standing and well-loved bouldering garden of Princeton. Bitch Boulder has hard problems (up to 5.12), other boulders have more moderate low-angle or vertical tweakin' on 20′ basalt boulders. Newly established Funk Fuzz V10 on Shipwreck Rock is latest testpiece. Early routes established by Bob Palais, Doug Gray, and Jeff Achey. Popular among Princeton students. Threatened to be blown up by Elizabethtown Water Company to make room for storage tanks. This area could be recognized as one of the first climber's parks in the country, with activity beginning as early as 1930. Also known as the Mt. Rose Natural Area. Autumn. No camping. Private land.

Classics: Granite Enema V0, Static Cling V2, Fusion Boots V6, Funk Fuzz V10.

Ref: C [128(10/91)-55, 94], R [98-26, (11/91)R]; Sherman's *Stone Crusade;* Guidebook: Nick and Sloane's *New Jersey Crags.*

Directions: Northwest Princeton. West approach for Princeton Boulders: From junction of Hwy. 206 and Great Rd., follow Great Rd. west, turn left (south) onto Cherry Valley Rd., then turn left onto Providence Line Rd. for approximately ½ mi. Park on left. Faint trail to Bitch Boulder starts just left of sharp turn in large trail and 30′ left of an unclimbable boulder. Other trail to right heads south to Cradle Rock (Burt and Carol) Boulder, Birch's Tooth, and Slab Boulders. East approach: From Great Rd. (mentioned above), turn south on Pretty Brook, and then right on Providence Line Rd. Turn right on Honey Brook Dr. and park on left. Hike west on Providence Line Rd. into woods.

7 High Point State Park ✪

Small 30′ quartzite wall on Appalachian Trail offers a few beginner's lines. State land.

Ref: Guidebook: Nick and Sloane's *New Jersey Crags.*

Directions: From Sussex head north on Hwy. 23 to High Point State Park. A couple hundred feet before park office, park on left at Appalachian Trail. Hike ten minutes south on Appalachian Trail. Faces east.

Ed Van Steenwyk hugging the Cradle Rock.

JOHN SHERMAN

8 Dinosaur Crag

A small 50′ metamorphic crag with very limited activity to date. There is still some development potential here, but it requires extensive cleaning of lichen and loose rock. The crag was developed by the former mountain manager of Vernon Valley/Great Gorge ski area and some coworkers during 1994–96. The owners of the property are fully aware of the development of the crag and are supportive of climbing there. Summer. No camping. Private land.

Classics: By far the best climb here is Out There 5.10c, a face climb that ascends a semi-detached pillar. The cleanest piece of rock at this crag. Other routes of good quality include Puke and Cry 5.10b, Freak Scene 5.10a, and Green Mind 5.6.

Ref: E. Youmans.

Directions: McAfee. Route 94 to Great Gorge Village Condominiums. Go through the security gate in front of "the Spa" and make a right immediately after going through the gate (tell the guard you're going to play golf). Follow this road until it ends at a gate. Park here and walk the dirt road until you reach a less-developed road on the right (about 1,000′ after you pass a large building on the right). Follow this road a short distance until you see the crags on the right.

9 Green Pond and Craigmeur Ski Area

Green Pond offers extensive 100′ sandstone cliffs offering lead climbing up to two pitches. Much loose rock. Requires Newark Watershed Permit from office on Echo Lake Rd., just south off Hwy. 23. Craigmeur Ski Area also has similar crags. Private land.

Ref: Locals; Guidebook: Nick and Sloane's *New Jersey Crags*.

Directions: Cliffs are above the town of Green Pond and farther at Craigmeur Ski Area on Hwy. 513.

10 Jenny Jump State Forest

This 35′ granite toprope area features about a dozen routes of mixed grades. State land.

Ref: Guidebook: Nick and Sloane's *New Jersey Crags*.

Directions: From Hope (just south of exit 12 on I–80), follow Hwy. 519 north 1 mi. and signs to Jenny Jump SF via a right onto Shiloh Rd for 1 mi. Then follow State Park

Climbing class.

JAMES M. BURWICK

Rd. 1 mi. to a left into main entrance. An overhanging boulder is present across from office on hill. Main cliff area and more bouldering are south on trail from campsite 19. Park at restrooms.

11 Mills Reservation (Montclair Cliffs) (closed)

The 50′ basalt cliffs border right on private property. Be courteous and keep the climbing clean. Under access attack—please do not climb here. Summer. No camping. County land.

Classics: The Crack 5, Right face direct (aka Krimp City) 9+, The Overhang (left side) 10.

Ref: Stadinski (3/97); Guidebook: Nick and Sloane's *New Jersey Crags*.

Directions: Turn right at Montclair State College onto Normal Ave. Continue past light and make left-hand turn onto Highland Ave. Park at bottom of small clearing on the right and walk up the middle to trail. Cliffs are within sight from here. Faces east.

12 Musconetcong Gorge Nature Preserve ☆

Five 25′ granite outcrops along Musconetcong River.

Ref: Guidebook: Nick and Sloane's *New Jersey Crags*.

Directions: From Riegelsville go northeast on CR 627 to its junction with CR 519. Go south on 519, crossing river, and shortly turning onto Dennis Rd. for ¼ mi. to nature preserve sign. Park. Twenty-minute hike on path east along river through ravine and then past metal gate.

13 Buzzard's Butte ☆

Twenty-five-foot shale toprope/5.10 lead area overlooks small waterfall. Private land.

Ref: Guidebook: Nick and Sloane's *New Jersey Crags*.

Directions: From Frenchtown go 6 mi. south off Hwy. 29. Park at pullout on left. Hike a football field up trail.

Other New Jersey Climbing Areas

At least twelve more small bouldering and/or toprope areas are described in Paul Nick's and Neil Sloane's *New Jersey Crags*. Some of these may be open to climbing. Many of these have questionable access. Please consult this fine book for specific access information and detailed route names and topos. Areas include:

South Mountain Reservation ☆

Basalt bouldering walls at Hemlock Falls on South Orange Ave. and at Turtle Back Rock on Northland Ave. In South Orange.

Riegelsville Cliffs ●

One-hundred-eighty-foot chossy cliffs above Delaware River. Few routes. At Riegelsville.

Pyramid Mountain Park ☆

Ample bouldering 4 mi. north of Boonton.

Tourne County Park ☆☆

Numerous granite boulders offer short problems. Near Mountain Lakes.

New Mexico

If all men are created equal, why are there passing lanes? —Bud Dry billboard in Albuquerque

In the Wild West, New Mexico is at the heart of it: Billy The Kid and range wars, Southwest culture and cooking, Santa Fe.

The west is still wild as far as climbing in New Mexico goes. For finger-tendon torture try the pockets at the sport crags of Cochiti Mesa, Enchanted Tower, and Box Canyon. To shred the tips, spend an hour at City of Rocks. To build up legs on which Lycra won't flap, approach a climb in the Sandias or Organ Mountains. And to get arrested, try climbing on the Spanish Land Grants or Indian Reservations.

Drive down any road in New Mexico and even today you'll discover plenty of unfingered rock to last a lifetime. Here are several places to enchant the traveling rock climber.

1 Sugarite Canyon State Park ★★★

Scenic, 7,800′ mesa topped by a long rim of volcanic caprock featuring 100′ vertical basalt cracks and steep face routes (more than one hundred). The 1990s saw lots of activity that led to sport routes via motorized drilling. The State Park Service outlawed bolting while still allowing climbing. Bring traditional crack gear or toprope equipment (i.e., extendo toprope runner). Spring/autumn. Pay camping at state park (505–445–5607).

Ref: Guidebook: Jackson's *Rock Climbing New Mexico and Texas.*

Directions: From Raton take exit 452 off I–25. Proceed east on Hwy. 72 for 3 mi. Turn north on Hwy. 526, following signs to Sugarite Canyon State Park, with visitors center on right in less than 2 mi. After visiting about park climbing regulations, go 2 2/10 mi. farther on Hwy. 526. Turn left and drive 1 3/10 mi. to Soda Pocket Campground, where the climbing area begins. Hike north on Little Horse Mesa Trail. Upon attaining rim, turn right and go to marshy lake. From lake head south to rappels off rimrock.

2 Shiprock (7,178′) ★★★★★

Spectacular, 1,700′ high, fifty-million-year-old volcanic plug visible for more than 50 mi. away. Colorful history: In the 1930s, considered the last great mountaineering problem of the United States. First ascent in 1939 by Brower,

Dyer, Bedayan, Robinson. FFA: 5.10 in 1959 by Rogowski and McCalla. Didactic route finding. Dangerous stacked blocks. Two-hour hike to circumnavigate Shiprock, aka Tsa-Beh-Tai (Navajo for "rock with wings"). The 1962 rock-climbing ban by the Navajo Indian Nation still applies today, i.e., illegal to climb. Clandestine bivy at north end of south dike. Volcanic weather patterns. Spring/autumn. BIA.

Classics: West Face 9+, Sherman's all free route 10+ (in Long's Couloir).

Ref: A (5/70), AAJ ['69-398, 66-52], C 83(4/83)-34, OB 55(2/81), R [91-28, 89-48, 79-56, 68-28], S [17(5/71)-1V, 6/71, 5/70, 9/64, 1/69]; Jones's *Climbing in North America;* Guidebooks: Bjornstad's *Desert Rock,* Ungnade's *Guide to New Mexico Mountains,* Steck and Roper's *Fifty Classic Climbs.*

Directions: From Shiprock travel 6 2/10 mi. south on Hwy. 666. Turn west on road to Red Rock for 8 mi. to east side of South Dike. Turn right on dirt road to southwest base of Shiprock, crossing over to west side of radiating dike when almost at the base (most frequent bivy spot). Possible to app-roach from other dirt roads to west of Hwy. 666.

3 Blanco Bouldering Canyon ●

Canyon of giant 25′ sandstone sugar cubes and lots of 'em. But poor reports of rock quality make one want to say, "I'm sicka than a dog!" To clarify: One *Rock 'n' Road* reader wrote (1997): "While this area is very beautiful and looks like a climber's paradise from the road, it is actually a very poor site.... On my visit, however, the rock in every part of the canyon was poor at best. The sandstone is too loose and crumbly for climbing. There are occasional short finger cracks that might be marginally entertaining, but they are not worth searching for, and I was unable to find any worthwhile places to boulder. If someone knows of a specific point in the canyon that is climbable, then that might be useful, but I found the canyon as a whole to be a bad use of my day." Now you know. Or, as we say here, a bad day out climbing is still better than a great day in the office. Autumn–spring. BIA.

Ref: A couple of stoners.

Directions: From Blanco go east on Hwy. 64. Much roadside rock through Blanco Canyon. Better bouldering in

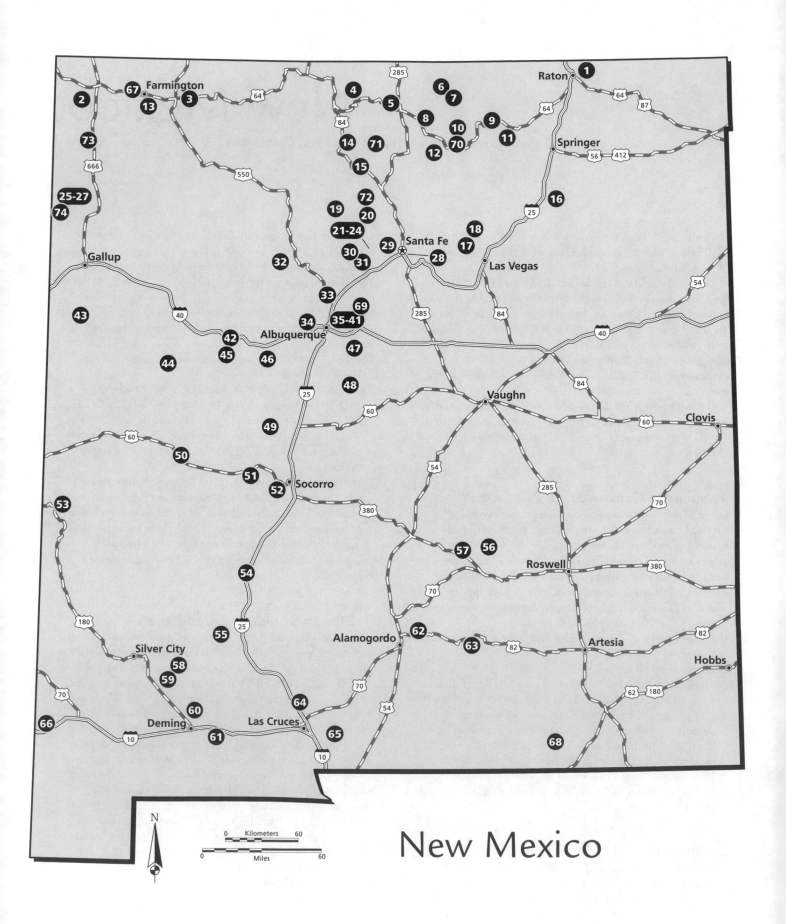

New Mexico

Farmington, head west out of town on Thirtieth St. After going through small pass, take first right. Before crossing stream, take right toward cliff line. Obvious 20' roadside boulder V4/V6 low traverse.

4 Brazos Cliffs (11,250') ✯✯✯

Postcard quartzite cliffs of gigantic proportion. This prodigious, seventy-million-year-old fault scarp provides excellent, 1,500' multipitched routes of varying nature in an incredible box canyon. Route information in *American Alpine Journal.* El Choro Waterfall flows down the 2,200' cliff during spring runoff from Vega de la Miranda Lake. Lodging only in pay cabins (start at $145 per night) at Corkins Lodge. Call ahead. Prime months September–October. This canyon is privately owned by Corkins Lodge and is accessible to guests only. For reservations call (800) 548-7688.
Classics: Easy Ridge 13p, Great Couloir 17 p (both routes lie right of Big Gully), Gothic Arches Buttress IV 7A2?.
Ref: AAJ '68-155, C 8(7/71); Guidebook: Ungnade's *Guide to New Mexico Mountains.*
Directions: From Brazos, Brazos Cliffs omnipresent to east. Follow State Road 512 east of town for 7 mi. Access by renting cabins from management at canyon mouth. Or approach possible from top (Tierra Amarillo) to brink of Encinad Wedge via Hwy. 64 to 3 mi. northwest. Cliffs face mainly south/southwest.

5 Tres Piedras ✯✯✯

Shake your congas! These small, easily accessible 165' granite outcrops amongst the pines hold some sixty bueno one-pitch routes on different formations. Tectonics 5.11c is an earth-shaking beauty. Autumn/spring. Note: Partially on private land. Landowner requests no fires, chalk, soliciting; and please close gates. Also, must sign a waiver through Los Alamos Mountaineers. Camp only on USFS land. Private land/ USFS–Carson National Forest, (505) 758- 8678.
Classics: South Rock: Surface Tension 11-; Mosaic Rock: Clean Green Dream 9, Hothouse to Hell 10, Tectonics 11c; Middle Rock: Cowboy Bob's Chickenhead Delight 9+.
Ref: Guidebooks: Jackson's *Rock Climbing New Mexico and Texas,* Weber and Jamarillo's *Taos Rock III.*
Directions: From Tres Piedras (junction of Hwy. 285 and Hwy. 64), drive 8/10 mi. west on Hwy. 64. Just past Carson NF Ranger Station, turn right at silver water tower onto dirt road for approximately 3/10 mi. to fence/locked gate. Park. Hike north briefly to South Rock. Seven clustered formations at Tres Piedras include: South Rock, Mosaic Rock, Middle Rock, North Rock, and West Rocks.

6 Questa Dome (on Bear Mountain) ✯✯✯✯

Golden 500' granite dome on a high mountain ridge. Beautiful multipitch routes (up to six pitches) and addictive New Mexico beauty. Much more rock below highest

Studying Plate Tectonics, 5.11c, at Tres Piedras.

main dome. Bring a full rack of gear. Summer/autumn. Free camping at mouth of canyon in USFS–Carson National Forest (505–586-0520).
Classics: Questa Dome: A Question of Balance 4p 10, Another Pretty Face 11, Aero Questa 12-.
Ref: R 73 (5/96)-143; Guidebooks: Jackson's *Rock Climbing New Mexico and Texas,* Weber and Jamarillo's *Taos Rock III.*
Directions: From Questa drive approximately 3 mi. north of junction of Hwy. 522 and Hwy. 38. Questa Dome is visible to the east of highway on north side of mountain valley. Turn right at El Rito sign for a mile past houses. Continue due east toward rock on El Rito Road. Jog right at house; this turns into a four-wheel-drive road (parking spots available as road gets rockier). Turn right at T. Go up road a few hundred yards to indiscreet opening on left with USFS trailhead sign and two parking slots. (If you reach the streambed, you've gone too far.) Hike forty-five minutes uphill on trail to base of dome. Faces south/southwest. Climbing on other rock formations possible en route to base of Questa Dome.

7 Red River Canyon

Large mountainside of many rock formations. Good 100' basalt routes. Ice climbing along Hwy. 38. Spring–autumn. Camping in USFS–Carson National Forest, (505–586-0520).

Ref: C. Burns; Guidebook: Weber and Jamarillo's *Taos Rock III*.
Directions: From Questa drive east on Hwy. 38 a few miles. Assorted rocks on slopes of Red River Canyon to right.

8 Arroyo Hondo (aka John's Wall or Rio Hondo) ★★★

Approximately twenty routes on a small 50' basalt wall with some clean, aesthetic lines. Riverside hot springs on Rio Grande River approximately ¼ mi. downstream on right from junction with end of road. Spring–autumn. Free camping on USFS land. Private land/USFS-Carson NF, (505) 758-8678.
Classics: Memory Lane 8, The Bulges 9, The Nose 10a, Bulges 10-, Nice Guy Syndrome 12.
Ref: Guidebooks: Jackson's *Rock Climbing New Mexico and Texas*, Weber and Jamarillo's *Taos Rock III*.
Directions: From Taos go north on Hwy. 522 to Arroyo Hondo, approximately 10 mi. Turn left (west) at Arroyo Hondo. Follow dirt road approximately 2 mi., bearing right at fork. Almost down at the Rio Grande River, John's Wall is a small basalt roadside wall that appears on right at small bridge.

9 Cimarron Canyon State Park ★★★

Canyon choked with 200' sandstone and granite rock pinnacles inspire one to jump right out of the car and start roping up. But rock quality is good to questionable. Elkabas Wall has 5.6–5.9 crack climbs. Mr. Putterman, I Presume 5.10 is classic sport route halfway through canyon. Climbing allowed on the palisades with a special-use permit from the park. Cimarron Canyon State Park is part of the 33,000-acre Colin Neblett Wildlife Area, the largest wildlife area in the state. Autumn/spring. Pay camping. State park, (505) 377-6271.
Classics: Cimarron Dihedral 8+, Mr. Putterman 10.
Ref: C. Burns.
Directions: From Cimarron drive 13 mi. west on Hwy. 64. At Cimarron Canyon in wildlife area.

10 El Salto Dome (on Lucero Peak) ★★

El Salto is a prominent 800' toothed monolith viewable north from Taos. Both rotten and good granite present. Difficult approach (possible bushwhacking)—best to go with locals. Descents are difficult and require raps. Nice two-pitch ice climbing. Summer. Free camping in USFS-Carson NF (505-758-6329).
Classics: Star Wars 7, Empire Strikes Back 7.
Ref: Guidebook: Weber and Jamarillo's *Taos Rock III*.
Directions: From Taos drive north on Hwy. 522. Turn right and go to Arroyo Seco. Head east past school on El Salto Rd. (before road to Taos Ski Area). El Salto Dome looms above. From parking a 2- to 3-mi. trail hike gets one to base. Begin to head to face when it is clearly in view via ravine.

11 Tooth of Time (at Philmont Boy Scout Ranch) ★★★★

The Tooth of Time, 9,003', is a stunning 500' granite face and selection of pinnacles towering above the Philmont Ranch. Routes done at least as early as 1972 by Davis, Wright, and Barrett. Assorted outcroppings in nearby vicinity to the south. Permission must be granted to climb or must be active scout (or active trespasser, argh). Site of National Boy Scout Jamboree. Summer/autumn. Private land.
Classics: Tooth: South Face IV 7 A4; Cathedral Rock: Southwest Face II 7.
Ref: C 10/72.
Directions: From Cimarron drive south on Hwy. 21 to Philmont Boy Scout Ranch. Inquire at office. Access by special request only. Formations include Tooth of Time and Cathedral Rock.

12 Taos Junction (Dead Cholla Wall) ★★★

Fine climbing on this 70' basaltic rim of the dramatic Rio Grande River chasm. At least twenty-five rap bolted lines. Primitive camping or pay at Orillo Verde Recreation Area along Rio Grande. Spring/autumn. USFS-Carson NF, (505) 758-6329.
Classics: Jamtime 10, Esmerelda 11, Blind Faith 11, Lava Flows 11.
Ref: J. Whitney; Guidebooks: Jackson's *Rock Climbing New Mexico and Texas*, Weber and Jamarillo's *Taos Rock III*.
Directions: From Taos drive south on Hwy. 68 to the south end of town. Turn right onto Hwy. 570 (96) (becomes rough dirt road). Follow down to bridge over Rio Grande River and up to west rim on Hwy. 567. Once on west rim, take first dirt road on right to the canyon's rim and park above rim. Walk couple minutes to rim, bearing right to Dead Cholla Wall. Faces east. Optional access, now only access, is via the small town of Pilar (15 mi. southwest of Taos). From Pilar go north along river on Hwy. 567 to Taos Junction Bridge. Then left over bridge to Canyon Rim, following previous instructions.

13 Kokopelli Spire ★

Soft, 200' sandstone tower first done by Cameron Burns and Mike Baker in 1991. Spring/autumn. Government land.
Ref: C. Burns; AAJ '92-139.
Directions: Farmington. South of town and south of the San Juan River. Kokopelli Spire was called Needle Rock by locals. This is private land and private wildlife preserve. Climbing by special arrangement with landowner only. Ask first!

14 Ghost Ranch Spires ●

Soft, 200' sandstone towers that make Fisher Towers look like marble. Routes reportedly pushing the limits of soft rock, making this area as popular as a repo man. Spring-autumn.

Classics: Ghost Tower III 5.10X, Mt. Ethan Putterman III 5.9R A4+, Animas Spire, Cracker Jack Tower, Coyote Pinnacle, King Rudi 8 A2+.
Ref: C. Burns; AAJ ['93, 92-139].
Directions: From Abiquiu go north on Hwy. 84 to Ghost Ranch. These towers lie north of Ghost Ranch.

15 Abiquiu
Eighty-foot basalt climbing crag.
Ref: R 40.
Directions: Near Abiquiu.

16 Wagon Mound
Basaltic layers at tops of mesas around town. Scattered clumps from 100′ basalt flows lend themselves to short toprope bouldering in northern New Mexico. Can be good, sound rock. Possibly government land.
Directions: Rocks visible near town of Wagon Mound near exit 387 off I–25.

17 Hermit Peak ✭✭
Big 1,200′ southeast-facing granite walls await the rock climber on this large landmark visible west from Las Vegas. Reports are of poor granite. Las Vegas area has an abundance of undeveloped Dakota sandstone as well, though much is on privately owned land. Spring–autumn. USFS–Santa Fe NF, (505) 425-7697.
Ref: J. Gamertsfelder, J. Delataillade; Guidebook: Ungnade's *Guide to New Mexico Mountains.*
Directions: From Las Vegas shy approximately 20 mi. northwest on State Road 65 to El Porvenir Campground. Two trail approaches for Hermit Peak: Trail 223, approximately 3 mi. to east side, and Trail 247, approximately 4 mi. to southwest side.

18 The Limestone Block ✭✭
A geologic anomaly, this 25′ limestone block sits alone on a volcanic floor. Fun climbing. Private land.
Ref: J. Gamertsfelder.
Directions: From Sapello drive en route to Raciada. Limestone Block sits just off the road on the other side of a fence.

19 Las Conchas ✭✭✭
In the cool mountain forests, several short, 60′, one-pitch rhyolite walls (Roadside Attraction, Cattle Call Wall, Gallery Wall, Leaning Tower, etc.) wander from the pavement into a canyon. Nice grassy teaching area below face. Campground just slightly east down road. Reminiscent of Penitente Canyon, Colorado. Nearby Spence Hot Springs worth a visit. Summer. USFS–Santa Fe NF, (505) 438-7840.
Classics: Hollywood Tim 9, Donkey Show 10c, Presumed To Be Modern 12a, Happy Entrails 12d, Leaning Tower Crack A2+.
Ref: AAJ '90-176, C 124; Guidebooks: Jackson's *Rock Climbing New Mexico and Texas,* Samet's *Sport Climbing in New Mexico North.*
Directions: From San Ysidro go north on Hwy. 4. At La Cueva (watch speed—cops), turn right on Hwy. 4 for 9 8/10 mi. to East Forks Box Canyon parking area on left. Hike north along drainage into Las Conchas Canyon. Los Conchas Campground just farther to east. (This area is approximately 20 mi. west of Los Alamos.)

20 Capulin ✭✭
Extensive 150′ volcanic crack crag. Two cliffs developed. Capulin has tremendous potential for the endangered species, aka the adventure crack climber. The walls are long and clean, perhaps the best welded tuff in New Mexico. Hunters in fall. Access road may be closed in spring. Check locally. Spring/autumn. USFS–Santa Fe NF, (505) 438-7840.
Classics: Zozobra 10, Barracuda 11, Psycho Killer 12.
Ref: L. Sheftel, Gamertsfelder, Bradley Mountain Wear, Santa Fe; C 117(34); Guidebook: Ungnade's *Guide to New Mexico Mountains.*
Directions: From Los Alamos head toward Jemez Springs on Hwy. 4. Take left on straightaway after climbing the switchbacks on forest road toward St. Peters Dome Lookout. Follow signs toward lookout. Take lookout trail on left down toward canyon until Capulin's obvious cliffs come into view across canyon. (Thirty-minute to one-hour bushwhacks.) Stay on trail and double back along the canyon (long way) or drop down steep canyon side toward cliffs (shorter way). Total of about 55 mi. driving from Santa Fe and forty minutes hiking.

21 White Rock Canyon (Overlook, Playground, et al.) ✭✭✭
White Rock Canyon is an area of at least eleven small but separate 80′ basalt crags lining the Rio Grande River Gorge. Many routes—the popular south-facing Overlook alone has sixty-five routes. Some crags designated traditional and some are sport—ask locals. Small amount of bouldering around bases of crags. Camping at Bandelier NM. Nuclear research nearby; is drinking the water from the waterfall at the Overlook safe? Splendid views of Sangre de Cristo Range to east. Other climbing information at Trailbound Sports in Los Alamos. Excellent winter/year-round climbing at The Overlook and Below the Old New Place when sunny. County park.
Classics: Overlook: Cholla Wall 9+, Thorazine Dream 11d, Face Off 12a; Below Old New Place: Putterman Cracks 9, Scandinavian Airlines 10c, Flesh-Eating Gnats 11a/b, Wailing Banshees 11-, Monsterpiece Theater 12-; Playground: Blowhole 10b, Flying A 10+, Unrelenting Nines 11, First Strike 12c; Lounge: Bud Light 10c, Orangaboom 11c, Negro Modela 12a; Pajarito Gorge: Shake It Up 12d.
Ref: Bradley Mountain Wear; C [124, 117, 62], R 40; online guide http://home1gte.net/jgchen/rockguide;

Guidebooks: Jackson's *Rock Climbing New Mexico and Texas*, Jett's *Sport Climbing In New Mexico North*, Ungnade's *Guide to New Mexico Mountains*.

Directions: From White Rock go east/southeast of town along canyon rim on Rover St. Three main access points for White Rock Canyon: 1) For Overlook Access follow signs to "Overlook." Park. Hike east to rim. Follow ridge north down well-used climber's trail to second cliff band (lots of bolts). 2) For Old New Place, Below Old New Place, Sununu Place, Playground: Via public access trail between 719 and 721 Rover Ave. 3) For New New Place, Lounge, Pajarito Gorge cul-de-sac at end of Kimberly off Rover. Hike south to rim. Pajarito Gorge is right near New New Place.

22 The Y ✫✫✫

Very fine basalt climbing, mostly 50' cracks. Much other rock exists in a fingery system of canyons. Climbing in The Y done in 1970 by Margolin and Porter. A highly restricted government area. Obey all No Trespassing signs or get nuked. Also, no bolting by authority of NPS. Nearby Jemez Caldera is world's largest volcano. Bandelier NM named in honor of Adolph Bandelier, first southwest ethnologist of the 1880s. Spring/autumn. Government land.

Classics: North Wall: Open Book 8+, Wisconsin 10-R, Ringjam 10+, Spiral Staircase 11b, The Nose 12aX toprope; South: Cavemantle 10a.

Ref: R 40; Guidebook: Jackson's *Rock Climbing New Mexico and Texas*.

Directions: Just east of Los Alamos. At junction of Hwy. 502 and Hwy. 4, park. Not visible. Hike 200 yd. to east. Follow steep trail into canyon. In Bandelier NM. Most climbing at The Y is on a south-facing wall.

23 Back Rocks/Los Alamos Canyon ✫✫✫

Many rhyolite crags offer fun sport climbing. Climbing in the Los Alamos area as early as 1951 by Los Alamos Mountaineer members Don Monk, Kermith Ross, George Bell, and Harry Hoyt. Back Rocks was one of the first areas in Los Alamos to receive rock climbing and now has excellent sport routes. Possibly hazardous waste site at Los Alamos Canyon. Bring the Geiger counter! USFS–Santa Fe NF, (505) 667–5120.

Classics: Back Rocks: Ewoks 8, Black Velvet 9, Tapdancing on a Land Mine 10a, Piranha in a Pocket 11b; Los Alamos Canyon: Officer Paco 11d.

Ref: C. Burns; R 40.

Directions: At Los Alamos. Back Rocks are located on west edge of town.

24 Potrillo Cliffs (White Rock Canyon) ✫✫✫

Good 50' southwest-facing toprope basalt training area for beginners. Twenty routes. In 1950s famed for Pillars of Hercules, locally respected as a hard climb. Spring/autumn. No camping. BLM, (505) 758–8851.

Classics: Coors Crack 9, Pillars of Hercules 9, Fool on the Hill 12b/c.

Ref: R 40; on-line guide http://home1.gte.net.jchen/rockguides; Guidebooks: Jackson's *Rock Climbing New Mexico and Texas*.

Directions: Southern outskirts of Los Alamos. Potrillo Cliffs is a subsidiary canyon of White Rock Canyon, southwest of main White Rock area. At junction of Hwy. 502 and Hwy. 4, go south on Hwy. 4. Turn left on Monterey Dr. south. Turn right on Potrillo for approximately 1 mi., then right again on Estante Way until you come to a pullout on the right side of the road (³/10 mi.), just past a fire hydrant on the right side of the road. Park. Follow the obvious trail south. At split, take right branch to U.S. Government Property sign. Turn left. Walk straight back to cliffs.

25 Cleopatra's Needle ✫✫✫

Stunning 275' sandstone pinnacle with quintessential sugary rock and "expando cracks" that could, thus, turn a sweet ascent into a real sour experience. Do not confuse this Cleopatra's Needle with the Cleopatra's Needle located on the Thames Embankment in London close to the embankment Underground station. That obelisk was actually constructed for Tuthmose III and is carved with hieroglyphics praising Tuthmose and commemorating his third *sed* festival. Sorry, just a brief side note for those who like trivia. First ascent: M. Powell, J. Galwas, D. Wilson in 1956. Autumn. No camping. BIA.

Classics: East Face 10 A2.

Ref: A (5/70), C 83(4/83)-34; Kor's *Beyond the Vertical*; Guidebook: Bjornstad's *Desert Rock*.

Directions: From Fort Defiance, Arizona, drive 17 mi. north into New Mexico on Hwy. 12. Turn east on dirt road (next to a sawmill and a sign reading *Camp Asaayi*, etc.). In a few miles, towers will be on left. Drive past Cleo and turnoff with "829" on rock until the base of Venus Needle. For Cleopatra's Needle hike back along cliff base. Cleo looks like a wide pinnacle from west side, a slender toothpick from south.

26 Navajo Needle ✫✫

This 275' sandstone pinnacle abuts a mesa on the Navajo Indian Reservation. First ascents in 1971 by two different parties via South Buttress and West Face. Three pitches. Both 5.10 A4. Spring/autumn. No camping. BIA.

Ref: C 83(5/83)-34; Guidebook: Bjornstad's *Desert Rock*.

Directions: From Fort Defiance drive 17 mi. north on Hwy. 12. Turn east on dirt road (next to a sawmill and a sign reading CAMP ASAAYI, etc.). In a few mi., towers will be on left. Drive past Cleopatra's Needle and turnoff with "829" on rock until the base of Venus Needle. Navajo Needle sits to north of Venus Needle, adjoining mesa.

27 Venus Needle ✯✯

Another Navajo Indian Reservation, very sugary 275' sandstone pinnacle. First ascent: Kor and Magary in 1962. Spring/autumn. No camping. BIA.
Ref: A (5/70), C 88; Guidebook: Bjornstad's *Desert Rock*.
Directions: From Fort Defiance drive 17 mi. north on Hwy. 12. Turn east on dirt road (next to a sawmill and a sign reading CAMP ASAAYI, etc.). In a few mi., towers will be on left. Drive past Cleopatra's Needle and turnoff with "829" on rock until the base of Venus Needle.

28 Cameltrack Canyon (aka Asshole Canyon) ✯✯

Thirty-foot basalt crag. No bolting please—toprope or solo only. Spring/autumn. No camping. BLM, (505) 758-8851.
Classics: Tap Dancing on Glass 12.
Ref: Bradley Mountain Wear (now out of business).
Directions: Cameltrack Canyon is a "locals secret area."

29 Diablo Canyon ✯✯

Features long adventure basalt climbs. An excellent 5.11 corner can be found here on this 200' basalt crag. Thick face potential. Loose rock. Some caving. No camping. Spring–autumn. BLM, (505) 758-8851.
Ref: Bradley Mountain Wear (out of business).
Directions: Between Santa Fe and Los Alamos. Access for Diablo Canyon is via La Tierra Rd., 10 mi. on dirt road.

30 Cochiti Mesa (Cacti, Jimmy Cliff, Eagle Canyon et al.) ✯✯✯✯

Several different 80' rhyolite cliff bands overlooking fantastic, "Land of Enchantment" super scenery at 7,000' offer steep crack and pocketed face. East-facing Eagle Canyon cliffs shady in summer with lots of moderate routes. Crack climbs in the Dihedrals area done in the 1970s by Hesse, Pandroni, and Roybal. Many sport routes by Delataillade, Read, and Bentley. Winter climbing good if roads accessible—try skiing if they're not. Summer too hot by afternoon. Camping at Bland Canyon (south of Dixon's Apple Farm) or roadside pulloffs. Hot springs at Jemez Springs. Autumn–spring. Free camping along FR 289. USFS–Santa Fe NF, (505) 829-3535.
Classics: Adolescent Fantasy 9, Monkey Lust 10, O.M.S. 11, Balance of Terror 12a, Gunning for the Buddha 12, Shadow Dancer 12c, Izimbra 13-, Touch Monkey 13.
Ref: Bradley Mountain Wear, L. Sheftel; C [138, 133 (topos), 124, 117, 110, 107], R [40, 31(5/89)-38], SC vol. 2, number 1(J 92); on-line guide http://home1.gte.net/jgchen/rockguide; Guidebooks: Jackson's *Rock Climbing New Mexico and Texas,* Jett and Samet's *Sport Climbing in New Mexico North*.
Directions: From Cochiti at I-25 (exit 259), trend west on Hwy. 22 to town of Cochiti Lake. Continue past town (avoid taking road to Dixon's Apple Farm unless you want apples). Go 5 mi. right on FS 289 (rough road—high-clearance may be desirable) to Cochiti Mesa. Several areas along road. In order they are: Eagle Canyon (on right), Jimmy Cliff (on left), Main Cochiti Cliffband (on left), Vista Point (on left), then, past gate, Cacti Cliff (on left), and Disease Wall (on left).

31 Cochiti Canyon ✯✯✯✯

Awesome 100' basalt cracks in scenic canyon closed to climbing by Cochiti Pueblo Tribal Council in late 1980s. Santa Fe, capital of New Mexico, offers rest-day climbers the options of gallery/museum hopping or crystallizing with the natives. Climber's food hangs at Dave's Not Here, Diego's, El Primo Pizza, Pasquals, and Subscription Coffee House. Other Santa Fe camping areas include the ski area east of town and the high and wild Pecos Wilderness Area. Spring/ autumn. Private land/BIA.
Ref: Bradley Mountain Wear; R 40; Guidebooks: Jackson's *Rock Climbing New Mexico and Texas,* Jetts and Samet's *Sport Climbing in New Mexico North*.
Directions: At Cochiti Pueblo. Hike down the wash from golf course ten minutes to Cochiti Canyon.

32 Cabezon Peak (7,785') ✯

Tallest volcanic peak in Rio Puerco Valley south of Cuba rises 2,000' above valley floor. Easy class 3 West Face to vertical rock offers fun summit. Spring–autumn. Private and government land.
Classics: Oven Route?
Ref: J. Gamertsfelder; S [5/69, 7/68]; Guidebook: Ungnade's *Guide to New Mexico Mountains*.
Directions: From San Ysidro head 20 mi. north on Hwy. 44. Turn southwest on secondary roads for 9 mi. to San Luis and 5 mi. to ghost town of Cabezon. Go past town to mesa to southwest edge of Cabezon Peak. Hike east.

33 Bernalillo ✯✯

Topropes on ½ mi. of volcanic rock band. Miles of 40' basalt rims, though it may be illegal to climb here. Great views of the Sandias/Cabezon Peak. Picnicking. Spring/autumn. No camping. BIA/government land.
Ref: B. Murray.
Directions: From Albuquerque burn 17 mi. north on I-25. Then turn west on Hwy. 44. Shortly (after approximately 2 mi.), turn right, following signs for Jemez Dam approximately 6 mi. to Bernalillo Cliffs on right.

34 West Mesa (aka Petroglyph National Monument, Ninety-Eighth St.) ✯✯✯

This extensive north-south 35' basalt mesa hosts beautiful bouldering and topropes and a mother lode of 20,000 petroglyphs that stretches for 17 mi. along Albuquerque's West Mesa escarpment. The rock inside the Petroglyph National Monument is off-limits to climbers, though area to north of monument boundary may still be used. A bouldering buffet and an important archaeological area. Possible car vandalism. Autumn–spring. Entrance fee for monument.

No camping. Managed by City of Albuquerque/NPS (505–899–0205).

Ref: P. Davidson, NPS.

Directions: West Albuquerque. For Petroglyph National Monument (closed to climbing), from I–40 take Unser Boulevard exit north 3 mi. to park visitors center; 5 mi. north to Boca Negra Unit. Areas to north of park boundaries may still be open to climbing—access unknown at this time.

35 SM☆-(Sandia Mountains, 10,447') Overview ☆☆☆☆☆

The Sandias present a formidable and rugged, 1,200' granitic crest flanking the east edge of Albuquerque. Many (more than forty) climbing formations with excellent adventure routes, though loose rock is a constant concern. Got helmet? The Shield is one such formation, 1,000' high and ½ mi. in length. Consult locals for approach details as epics can occur very easily before getting started on routes. Approaches alone will burn more calories than a Twist 'n' Ski. Wilderness camping at top of the limestone band (see directions). Highest point: 10,687'. Recommended carbohydrate recharge at Ron's Camino Real (mexy) in Albuquerque. The Sandia Crest is also a popular hang gliding launch site. Raptor restrictions March–August 15. Spring–autumn. Free and pay camping. USFS–Cibola NF, (508) 281–3304.

Classics: Shield: Procrastination 8 11p, Rainbow Dancer 9p 11a slab; Torreon Wall: Mountain Mama 6p 10c vertical crack; Needle: Southwest Ridge 9; Muralla Grande: Warpy Moople 10 8p; Voodoo Child 11d.

Ref: Stone Age Climbing Gym; C [117, 110, 107, 2/85], R [75-26,43(5/91)-31], S [4/70, 7/68]; Guidebooks: Schein's *Sandia Select,* Jackson's *Rock Climbing New Mexico and Texas,* Harlin's *Rocky Mountain,* Hill's *Hiker's and Climber's Guide to the Sandias,* Ungnade's *Guide to New Mexico Mountains,* Loucks's *Climber's Guide to the Lower Sandias,* Kyrlach's *Guide to the Sandia Mountains.*

Directions: From Albuquerque go east of town via La Luz Trail approaches. Torreon, Muralla Grande, and The Shield should be approached from the Sandia Crest. From parking go through fence and directly down to the limestone band for Torreon and several other formations. The most prominent formations include Shield, Needle, Muralla Grande, Yataghan, and The Thumb. Route finding a problem, though good guides for Sandia Mountains access/approach map in Hill's guide, listed above.

36 SM–Juan Tabo Campground and La Luz Trail (Bottom) ☆☆☆

This is the low-elevation entry to Sandia Crest climbs on the Shield, etc. Some granite bouldering and topropes near parking. Gate closed 10:00 P.M. to 8:00 A.M. Summer/autumn. Free camping. USFS–Cibola NF, (508) 281–3304.

Classics: Pulpit: Cave Route 7.

Ref: R 43(5/91)-31; Guidebooks: Hill's *Hiker's and Climber's*

Guide to the Sandias, Loucks's *Climber's Guide to the Lower Sandias.*

Directions: Albuquerque. From I–25 go north on Tramway Blvd. (past tram cutoff). Turn right at Juan Tabo turnoff. Go for approximately 3 mi. Turn right past second stone pillar set to La Luz Trail signs.

37 SM–La Cueva Canyon ☆☆☆

Bouldering on 30' granite chunks near the rockhouses; west and east of paved road. Spring/autumn. Pay camping. USFS–Cibola NF, (508) 281–3304.

Classics: Gemstone 8.

Ref: C 107, R 43(5/91)-31; Guidebooks: Hill's *Hiker's and Climber's Guide to the Sandias,* Loucks's *Climber's Guide to the Lower Sandias.*

Directions: Albuquerque. Go north on Tramway Blvd. 1 mi. past Sandia Peak Tram. Turn right to La Cueva picnic area. Then turn right on FS 3333B.

38 SM–Fat City and Embudo Spring Boulders ☆☆☆

Local Albuquerque bouldering areas on west foothills of Sandias. Thirty-foot granite boulders reminiscent of an armadillo's shell. Autumn–spring. USFS–Cibola NF, (508) 281–3304.

Ref: R 43(5/91)-31; Guidebooks: Hill's *Hiker's and Climber's Guide to the Sandias,* Loucks's *Climber's Guide to the Lower Sandias.*

Directions: From Tramway Rd. go east on Indian School. Go 1 mi. to Fat City or end of road to Embudo. Great beginner's practice rock at mouth of canyon.

39 SM–U-Mound ☆☆☆

Popular local bouldering area above the urban sprawl of Albuquerque at the southwest edge of the Sandia Foothills. Coarse 25' granite face problems. Commanding vista of Albuquerque and views of the West Mesa on western horizon. Autumn–spring. No camping. Government land.

Ref: R 43(5/91)-31; Mayer's on-line guide www.cs.nmt.edu/andy/rocks.html; Guidebook: Hill's *Hiker's and Climber's Guide to the Sandias.*

Directions: Albuquerque. From I–25 go north on Tramwood exit. Turn right on Copper (heading toward mountains) to road's end. Hike five minutes northeast past lot to three clusters of U-Mound Boulders. Boulders are on left side of cone-shaped hill. Access may change due to housing developments and urban sprawl of Albuquerque at the southwest edge of the Sandia Foothills.

40 SM–Three Gun Springs/Tijeras Canyon ☆☆☆

Solar bowl of 80' granite rock offer bolted leads (now chopped, only topropes) on boulders up to 5.12. Headwall leads and big cluster of boulders (visible from parking) below south Peak Buttress. Copious amounts of rock adja-

cent to I–40 (Tijeras Canyon) offer adventure bouldering. Hawk-watching area in spring. Climbable all year. Autumn–spring. Free camping. USFS–Cibola NF, (508) 281–3304.
Ref: R 43(5/91)-31; Guidebook: Hill's *Hiker's and Climber's Guide to the Sandias.*
Directions: Just east of Albuquerque. Take I–40 and go north at Carmel exit to Monticello Estates (big sign). Follow FS 552 signs to trailhead. At Three Guns Trailhead, hike north 1 mi. Boulder cluster on right below South Peak Buttress. Tijeras Canyon is area adjacent to I–40 at Three Guns exit. Rock scattered throughout Tijeras Canyon, mostly large boulders.

41 SM–Sandia Crest (La Luz Trail-Top) ★★★★
Upper, high-elevation (best) entry to west flank of the Sandia Crest climbs. Summer escape from the Albuquerque heat. Tons of granite up to 1,200' and even limestone bands. The Shield is closed spring and summer due to peregrine falcon nesting. Summer/autumn. Free camping. USFS–Cibola NF, (508) 281–3304.
Classics: Shield: Procrastination 8 11p; Needle: Southwest Ridge 9; Muralla Grande: Warpy Moople 10 8p; Echo Canyon: Krankenstein 12a, Date with Death 13d; Yucca Flower Tower: Rawhide 10c; Tombstone: 5.5 Traverse.
Ref: R 43(5/91)-31; Guidebooks: Schein's *Sandia Select,* Harlin's *Rocky Mountain,* Hill's *Hiker's and Climber's Guide to the Sandias,* Loucks's *Climber's Guide to the Lower Sandias,* Ungnade's *Guide to New Mexico Mountains.*
Directions: From Albuquerque go east on I–40. Turn north on Hwy. 14. Go west on Hwy. 44 to trailheads at top of the Crest of the Sandias (signs). Drop down to several impressive rock formations via various trails. Map and route topos a must.

42 Casa Blanca Bouldering ★
Bouldering and topropes on soft, 30' Dakota sandstone cubes along I–40. On BIA–Laguna Indian Reservation. Permission needed. Spring/autumn. No camping.
Directions: East of Grants. On south side of I–40 near Casa Blanca Cubero exit 104 (mm 104). Rocks visible.

43 Zuni Bouldering/Zuni Needle
Thirty-foot Dakota sandstone east of town. Rock varies in quality—poor to middlin'. For locals or happen-to-be-theres. Zuni Tower is 270'. Spring/autumn. Pay camping. BIA.
Ref: C. Burns.
Directions: Bouldering east of Zuni, visible from road. Zuni Needle is just south of junction of Hwy. 602 and Hwy. 53.

44 El Malpais National Monument and National Conservation Area ★
Big Zuni 250' sandstone cliffs. Dakota capstone 40'. Wilderness permit for primitive campground. Spring/ autumn. Free camping. NPS/BLM/private land. El Malpais is managed by a joint effort between the National Park Service and the Bureau of Land Management. BLM, (505) 287–7911. NPS, (505) 876–2783.
Classics: Crack of Heroclites 5.11c 3p.
Ref: B. Murray, NPS.
Directions: From Grants drive 5 mi. west on I–40. Go south on Hwy. 117 approximately 10 mi. to cliffs on east side of road. Cliffs for 20 mi. Boulders at mm 44. Climbing may not be allowed in the El Malpais National Monument. Cliffs visible from I–40 on a clear day.

45 Enchanted Mesa (closed) ★★
Called Katzimo, these large 500' sandstone rock islands and imposing cliffs sit in a lonely mesa environment on the Acoma Indian Reservation. Featured sandstone mesas, buttresses, and towers. Acoma Pueblo, inhabited since the twelfth century, is the oldest continuously inhabited city in America. Guided tours of the pueblo. Ancient carved holds and removable stake ladder allowed first ascents by Indians in ancient times. Off-limits to climbing. Spring/autumn. BIA.
Classics: Scanlan's Laguna 10+.
Ref: T. Skinner; Su 18(5/72)-120.
Directions: From Grants drive east on I–40 approximately 25 mi. Go south approximately 12 mi. from Casa Blanca exit to the Acoma Pueblo and Enchanted Mesa. Cliffs everywhere.

46 The Grotto (closed) ★★★
Great sport climbing and petroglyphs on black 50' basalt gorge. Closed—no trespassing. Autumn–spring. No camping. Private land.
Ref: R.
Directions: From Albuquerque travel west on I–40 to exit 126. Go southeast on Hwy. 6 for 4 3/10 mi. Turnout where two bullet-ridden vehicles (now gone?) are on south side of road. Top of The Grotto visible 100 yd. to north. Do not climb here.

47 Big Block Wall ★★★
Short, broken 40' limestone sport crag in small canyon with desperate tiered roof bouldering at base and a few sparse lines. Easy access. Cool; shaded in summer. Lots of limestone nearby. Spring–autumn. Pay camping. USFS–Cibola NF, (505) 281–3304.
Ref: J. P. Gamertsfelder; Guidebook: Jett and Samet's *Sport Climbing in New Mexico South.*

New Mexico Road Thoughts
A three-legged dog walks into a saloon in the Old West. He slides up to the bar and announces: "I'm looking for the man who shot my paw."

Directions: From junction of I-25 and I-40 in Albuquerque, blast 13 mi. east on I-40 to Tijeras exit (number 175). Turn south approximately 4 mi. on Hwy. 337. Park at bend with big roadcut. Big Block Wall visible to south below road. Pine Flat Campground farther south down road.

48 New Canyon (in the Manzano Mountains) ✮✮✮

Quality, though sharp, 40' limestone sport cranking on incuts and pockets. Solid rock. Bouldery routes starting at 5.11. Developed by the Millers, Samet, and Hadfield. Climbable most of the year and good in winter. Autumn. USFS–Cibola NF, (505) 847-2990.

Classics: The Pervert and The Hammer 11d, Shortest Straw 12c, Last Straw 12d.

Ref: C 124; Guidebook: Samet's *Sport Climbing in New Mexico South.*

Directions: From Manzano (on Hwy. 55, north of Mountainair on Hwy. 60), forge west on FS 245 approximately 3 mi. (½ mi. past USFS building). Turn right, going for ¼–½ mi. to New Canyon rocks.

49 Ladrones Mountain (Ladron Peak 9,176') ✮✮

Clumps of rock visible from as far as I-25. Abrupt 500' granite escarpments, large canyons, and box canyons offer technical rock climbing. Summer/autumn. Free camping. BLM, (505) 761-8700.

Ref: J. Detaillade.

Directions: From Magdalena go west on Hwy. 52, then east/northeast on dirt roads for many mi. to Ladrones Mountain. Get a topo map.

50 Enchanted Tower (aka Thompson Canyon or Datil) ✮✮✮✮

Overhanging, big-hold, sport-route pump climbing. Come with good forearm endurance or you'll melt faster than a watered-down witch, e.g., Zee Wicked Witch. A 60 m rope is helpful on some Tower routes developed by Bertrond Gramont. Free camping below bluffs on leased grazing land from the USFS. Please park just off road, avoiding the trampling of the grass. And also be courteous when crossing private land. Bring water. Good cafe in Datil: Friday (Mexican, Saturday salad bar, otherwise very beef-oriented menu). Spring/autumn. Free camping. USFS–Cibola NF, (505) 854-2281.

Classics: Ugly Duckling 9, Cheshire Cat 10, Golden Stairs 11, Once Upon a Time 11c, Sleeping Beauty 11d, Rumplestiltskin 12a, Tinkerbell's Nightmare 12b/c, Jabberwackey 12d, Zee Wicked Witch 12+, Goliath 13a, Ripped Van Winkle 13-, Mad Hatter 13a, Child of Light 14a.

Ref: R. Steed, L.Sheftel, J. Detaillade; C [163-40, 133, 110(10/88) 24-5, R [74-96, 63], SC 12/91; Guidebooks: Jackson's *Rock Climbing New Mexico and Texas,* Jett and Samet's *Sport Climbing in New Mexico South.*

Directions: From Datil drive approximately 5 mi. west on Hwy. 60. Turn right (past mm 72) at Cleaveland-Gatlin sign onto dirt roads. Turn left onto Thompson Canyon (USFS) road before a ranch house, following dirt road for approximately 1–2 mi. to Enchanted Tower on right at roadside. Mainly faces west. More rock 5 mi. farther on Hwy. 60. Turn right onto FR 6A for 4 mi. then right on FR 25 for 1 mi.

51 Water Canyon

Highly scenic area with abundant 100' volcanic rock. Spring–autumn. Free camping. Private land/USFS–Cibola NF, (505) 854-2281.

Directions: From Socorro drive west on Hwy. 60 for 20 mi. Water Canyon is visible to the south. Turn south onto paved road following signs.

52 Box Canyon ✮✮✮

B5.13 bouldering on sweeping, powerful, pocketed roof problems immediately in arroyo below bridge and mostly bolted 80' volcanic sport climbs on sanguine cliff faces. Recommended walls: Alcohol Wall has moderate routes, Major Wall 5.11 and up (The Demon 13a), Ride the Lightning Wall (5.11 and up). Free, convenient camping on south end of canyon. Bad bugs from April to September— try autumn/winter. Free camping. BLM, (505) 835-0412.

Classics: Diamond Clutch 5.7, Little Overhang 5.8, Nowhere to Go 5.10+, Little Red Wall 5.11, TNT 5.11+, Highway 60 5.12, The Luge 12b/c, Almost Blue 12c, Fair Trade 5.13b; Arroyo bouldering roofs: Left to Roof V5, Streambed Traverse 11+ (low), The Ultimate Boulders V0-V4 .

Ref: L. Sheftel; C [133, 107, 96(6/66)-20]; SC vol. 2, number 1(J 92); Sherman's *Stone Crusade;* Guidebooks: Jackson's *Rock Climbing New Mexico and Texas,* Jett and Samet's *Sport Climbing in New Mexico South,* Hufnagel and Gramont's *Climber's Guide to Box Canyon.*

Directions: From Socorro drive approximately 7 mi. west of town on Hwy. 60 to bridge with canyon on left. Park at pulloff on southwest side of bridge. Walk into Box Canyon, passing bouldering arroyo walls to reach cliffs. Another parking/camping area at south end of canyon accessed by turning left on first dirt road west of bridge and following to south canyon mouth. From north to south on east side, crag walls include: North Wall, Red Wall, Waterfall, Minor, and Major. On the west side is the East Wall.

53 Luna Crags and Boulders

Potential volcanic cragging areas. Spring/autumn. USFS–Apache-Sitgreaves NF, (520) 333-4301.

Directions: Volcanic crags to the east of town of Luna.

54 San Jose Canyon ★★

A sinuous canyon with cracks and volcanic pocketed faces as well as less than vertical routes. Loose tops require caution and cleaning may be necessary. 5.8 to 5.11 climbing. Ask Rex Klietz at ranch house for access permission to climb. Spring/autumn. No camping. Private land.
Ref: J. Gamertsfelder.
Directions: From Truth or Consequences drive approximately 20 mi. north on I–25 to Redrock exit 100. Turn left at exit and follow old Hwy. 85 north approximately 1 1/2 mi. to the Old Pankey Ranch House on left and canyon on right. Park at house. Hike more than 1/4 mi. downstream of the red barn across from house into obvious rock-lined San Jose Canyon.

55 Hillsboro (Horses Joe Canyon) ★★

A small canyon area with short, 40′ quality routes on welded tuff. Farther west on Hwy. 152 exist funkazoid pinnacles and Devil's Backbone. Be sure to stop in Hillsboro at the Three Angels Bakery for some heavenly bread. Autumn–spring.
Classics: 5.8 crack, 5.8 dihedral, 5.10b face, 5.11 face.
Ref: D. Hardin.
Directions: From Hillsboro drive five minutes west on Hwy. 152. Park at first pulloff past steel angle bridge. Hike down into Horses Joe Canyon.

56 Capitan Mountains (Sunset Peak) ★★★

Alluring granitic crags and boulders on the southern and southeastern buttresses of 9,335′ Sunset Peak. The height of the crags range from 150′ to approx 800′, with the bigger cliffs in the canyon to the North of Hale Canyon. The cliffs lie at an elevation of 7,200′ to 8,800′. *Capitan* means "mountain that stands alone." Famous Fort Stanton Caves "Hall of Velvet" nearby. Spring–autumn. Free camping. Private land/USFS–Lincoln NF, (505) 854–2281.
Ref: T. Atwood.
Directions: From Tinnie head north from town on Hwy. 368 until Capitan Mountain boulders and crags are visible to northwest. There are two main crags, one at the head of Hale Canyon and one at the head of the unnamed canyon just north of Hale Canyon. Access difficult due to private roads and landowners. Approaches range from 3 1/2 mi. to 5 1/2 mi. with elevation gains of 1,500′ to 2,500′.

57 Capitan Bouldering ★★

Dakota sandstone roadside climbs with one prominent 25′ roadside crack. Near site of 1950 Smokey the Bear (U.S. Forest Service mascot) rescue. Spring/autumn. No camping. Private land/USFS–Lincoln NF, (505) 854–2281.
Directions: From Capitan it's on the east edge of town on Hwy. 380. Capitan Bouldering Band on right.

58 Dwyer ★★

Small volcanic cragging area.
Ref: Fish.
Directions: Near town of Dwyer on Hwy. 61. Ask locals for crag directions. Approximately 5–10 mi. northeast of City of Rocks State Park.

59 City of Rocks State Park ★★★

In this mile-high, fairytale gnome land of 35′ volcanic pinnacles, be prepared to find lancet-filled pockets and flakes sharper than Miracle 3 blades. Temper your discoveries with powerful pulling on more than one hundred routes. Check descents before getting summit locked. Best rock at north suburb. Thick calluses a must or be willing to volunteer some skin. Nice hot springs (uncertain if still open) to stew in yer own juices 2 mi. south of park . . . but wait until after a session. Spring/autumn. Pay camping. State park, (505) 536–2800.
Classics: Garbage Can Traverse.
Ref: C [191-83, 187-103, 114]; Sherman's *Stone Crusade;* Guidebook: Jackson's *Rock Climbing New Mexico and Texas.*
Directions: From Deming drive northwest on Hwy. 180 for approximately 23 mi. Turn right (east) on Hwy. 61 for approximately 4 mi., turn north (left) on road to City of Rocks State Park (signs). Gate locked at dark.

60 Labyrinth and Jumble ★★

Sandstone boulders up to 25′—easy on tips. A good break from nearby City of Rocks sharpness. May be buggy in May. Nearby Cooke Peak (8,408′) is obvious largest rock (possibly granite or rhyolite) summit. Don't miss the Deming Duck Race every third week in August. Spring–autumn. Free camping. Private land/BLM (505) 525–4300.
Ref: B. Murray.
Directions: North of Deming on southwest side of Massacre Peak. Take Hwy. 180 north 1 mi. to Hwy. 26. Go east on Hwy. 26 approximately 6 mi. to Krolls. Turn north at Krolls on dirt road approximately 8 mi. to road branching right over dam. After crossing dam, take left fork 2 mi. to boulders. Labyrinth hard to see atop hill, 1/4 mi. right (northeast) of road. As locals for directions.

61 Rockhound State Park ★★

A mountainside full of rock at 4,500′. Only development so far is a few marginal problems on a large, jasper boulder. Uncertain if there are other routes. Bring a hammer and you might find a thunder egg or geode in the rock beds. This is one climbing area and park where "chipping" is allowed. Spring/autumn. Gate open 7:30 A.M.–sunset. Pay camping at state park (505–546–6182).
Classics: Jasper Boulder.
Directions: From Deming go south on Hwy. 11 for 5 mi. Turn east on road, following Rockhound State Park signs. One prominent boulder with difficult problems sits right out of the campground on hillside. Cliffs are

mostly friable rhyolite, but more bouldering exists above the first palisades.

62 Cloudcroft Canyon (aka High Rolls) ✩

Overhanging 100′ limestone, topropes, and sport climbs arise from vestiges of old aid lines. Possibly dirty rock. Other areas. Good mountain-biking area. Alamogordo Space Hall of Fame. Spring–autumn. Free camping. USFS–Lincoln NF, (505) 434-7200.

Classics: Pleasure Victim 11a, One Arm Bandit 12.

Ref: J. Gogas.

Directions: From Cloudcroft drive approximately 8 mi. west on Hwy. 82 into Cloudcroft Canyon, with limestone rock walls.

63 Rio Penasco ✩

Small, dirty dolomite crag with few redeeming features—go there with a brush! Fifty-foot dolomite crag. Spring-autumn. No camping. USFS–Lincoln NF, (505) 434-7200.

Ref: J. Gogas.

Directions: From Mayhill drive 11 mi. east on Hwy. 82 to Rio Penasco. At NFS boundary sign.

64 Dona Ana Peak (5,899′) ✩✩✩

Scenic, remote, and peaceful drive-up bouldering, topropes, and lead climbs on volcanic rock. Routes on ridge to east of campground. More routes at Checkerboard area on the east side of Dona Ana Peak. Easy routes tend to be runout. Nice camping to north of peak and at base of hills near boulders. High-clearance vehicles recommended. Petroglyphs. Southwest Mountaineers at Bike's Plus has more information. Spring/autumn. Free camping. BLM, (505) 525-4300.

Classics: Bear Boulder: Bare Bulge (east face) V4; Checkerboard Wall: Knight's Move 8, et al., Full Tilt Boogie 10.

Ref: J. Gamertsfelder, D. Hardin; R 48(3/92)-37; Guidebooks: Jackson's *Rock Climbing New Mexico and Texas,* Ungnade's *Guide to New Mexico Mountains, Hiking Guide to Dona Ana County, New Mexico.*

Directions: From Las Cruces go east on Hwy. 82 approximately 5 mi. Turn north on Jornada del Muerto Rd. (look for Jornada Experimental Station signs) to Dona Ana Peak (approximately 6 ½ mi.). At rock pillar and USDA sign, turn west for approximately 2 mi. to north side of peak and parking/camping. Boulders/cliffs are scattered at foot of and tops of peaks. Checkerboard is the obvious, prominent face to east, visible during drive-in. It is best accessed from northwest (back side) of its visible face. Hike thirty minutes. Approach to the southwest and drop packs off at cairn and pick up on descent.

65 Organ Mountains (9,012′) ✩✩✩✩

The Organ Mountains are a fault block rising 5,000′ above the valley floor. Approaches are steep and long (more than one hour), but the payoff is a clean array of spectacular ridgeline pinnacles reaching 1,500′ toward the heavens. Most approaches made from west side of mountains as east side is very brushy. Synopsis: Tooth is best rock and highest concentration of harder routes. Southern Comfort for a fun afternoon. Sugarloaf Peak and East Slabs are Tuolumne-like. Citadel has quite a few 10s, good routes. Lambda Wall is blocky. The high peaks (Rabbit Ears and High Horns) are blissful, easy routes. The first ascent of the highest summit, Organ Needle (9,012′) occurred in 1904. More than one hundred significant routes—many multipitched affairs on beautiful quartz monzonite. Spring- autumn. Pay camping. Government land.

Classics: The Tooth Formation: Tooth Extraction III 10, Tooth or Consequences III 10, Tooth Fairy III 10, Southern Comfort Wall: Margaritaville 8, Black Velvet 9; Sugarloaf Peak: Left Eyebrow 6, Left Eye 9, Science Friction 12; North: Boyers Chute 6, Awful Buttress 11; Rabbit Ears: North Dihedral of ORP 10.

Ref: D. Hardin, Bowling; C [174-64], R 48(3/92)-37, S 4/75; Guidebooks: Jackson's *Rock Climbing New Mexico and Texas,* Ungnade's *Guide to New Mexico Mountains.*

Directions: From Las Cruces, Organ Mountains have two main approaches: 1) West side (usual approach): Take Hwy. 70 east to below San Agustin Pass. Turn right onto dirt road, paralleling mountains to south. Two main trailheads accessed off this: a) Turn left to Topp Hut for Rabbit Ears approach or b) go farther south, then turn left (before reaching University Ave. Rd., another access road) for Tooth approaches. 2) East Side (brushy, for Sugarloaf/East Slabs): Take Hwy. 70 east over San Agustin Pass. Turn right onto road leading to Aguire Springs Campground. Park at trailhead in campground. Hike south for Sugarloaf. Camping at Rabbit Ears Canyon mouth, at Topp Hut, Modoc Mine Rd. top. Aguirre Spring Campground, base of Tooth, Sugarloaf's north saddle. Route guide at visitors center outside of Las Cruces on west side of range.

66 Stein's Pass ✩

Loose, scabby boulders and 200′ volcanic crags. Included here because of its alluring proximity to the interstate. A handy "crash"/bivy spot between Hueco Tanks and Tucson. No water. Spring/autumn. Free camping. BLM, (505) 525-4300.

Ref: J. Gamertsfelder.

Directions: From Lordsburg go 23 mi. west on I-10 to Arizona/New Mexico border. Take Stein's Pass exit. Go north on dirt road and pull in left. High-clearance vehicles helpful.

67 The Heap ✩✩

A 20′–30′ sandstone bouldering area. Can climb year-round. No camping. Private land.

Classics: Petro Traverse (go high V-4, stay low V-6).

Directions: From Farmington drive west out of town on Thirtieth St. Go through small pass between two small hills. Drop out of pass and take first right. If you cross over small stream, turn around and take the first right. Take dirt road toward the cliff line. Stop at obvious boulder with chalk on it by road.

68 Sitting Bull Falls ★★★★
Limestone sport crag features wild steep routes next to Sitting Bull Falls. Gates open 8:00 A.M.–sunset. Minimum entrance fee. USFS-Lincoln NF, (505) 434-7200.
Classics: Kootenai Cruiser 5.13d.
Ref: C 162-44; Guidebook: Jackson's *Rock Climbing New Mexico and Texas.*
Directions: West of Carlsbad.

69 Palomas Peak ★★★
Vertical to overhanging 50' limestone crag mixes trad routes developed by Whitelaw and Groth and sport routes like Timmy Fairfield's Turbo Trad 13a. Eighty routes. Autumn/spring. Camping at KOA in Bernalillo. USFS-Cibola NF, (505) 281-3304.
Ref: C 155-68; Guidebooks: Moret's *Palomas Peak,* Jackson's *Rock Climbing New Mexico and Texas.*
Classics: Kyle's Crack 7, Classic Jam Crack 9, Smoked Salmon 10c, Quickdraw McGraw 11b, Gunslinger 12a, Turbo Trad 13a, Entertaining Mike Tyson 13b.
Directions: From Bernalillo get off I-25 at exit 242. Take Hwy. 165 through Placitas up to just past Las Huertas Picnic Area and switchbacks. Park at area with three concrete blocks on left. Hike is thirty minutes across valley. Find a path 60' up road and parallel road. Then head down to valley to junction and clearing where cairns mark uphill route to base.

70 Heart of Stone Rock ★★★
A 350' granite crag with up to three-pitch routes like Laid Back Limey 5.9+. Runout adventure climbing. Fee required to enter private land.
Ref: Guidebook: Jackson's *Rock Climbing New Mexico and Texas.*
Directions: North of Taos. Ask locally.

71 El Rito
Funky cobblestone sport climbs up to 5.13 developed by Ed and Rich Strang and others. Camping 1/4 mi. up road. USFS-Carson NF, (505) 581-4554.
Classics: Jug-or-naut 10, Bolting Barbie 12a.
Ref: R [84-96, 83-86]; fine on-line guide www.losalamos.org/climb/el_rito_guide.htm.

Directions: From El Rito (northeast of Abiquiu), go east out of town and turn north on Hwy. 247 for 3 3/4 mi. to Y intersection past Canada del Potrero sign. Park. Twenty-minute hike starts 15 yd. back down road. Go south along road through meadows and trees. In 1/4 mi., cross stream. Go through meadow, uphill through trees, heading toward private fence line. From fence turn left over hill into gully. Climb up hill to cliffs.

72 The Dungeon
Los Alamos's summertime sport crag features forty rhyolite sport routes up to 5.13. Main rock developers include Gram, Strang, Detaillade, and Laeser. Bring 60 m rope and fifteen draws. Area burned during 2000 fire, but climbs are okay. Camping up ski road or pay at nearby Bandelier. USFS-Santa Fe NF, (505) 438-7840.
Classics: Loose Cannon 13a, Honky Serial Killer 13d.
Ref: R 101-84; Guidebook: Wehner's guide.
Directions: From Los Alamos follow Hwy. 502 west a couple mi. Turn left onto Diamond Dr. for almost 1/2 mi. Then turn right onto West Jemez Rd. following it west 2 mi. past Los Alamos National Lab and ski hill road. Park at dirt pullout on right. Hike downhill north past gate on jeep trail for fifteen minutes to large cliff (Main Wall) on left.

73 Bennett Peak, Ford Butte, Church Rock
Desert volcanic plugs similar to and south of Shiprock. Bennett Peak first ascent by Laeser and Burns in 1992. Ford Butte first ascents: Main Peak in 1970s by M. Dalen and D. Nordstrom; North Peak by Baker and Burns in 1990; Church Rock by Rosebrough, Baker, and Burns in 1990.
Ref: AAJ '94.
Directions: From Farmington go south on Hwy. 666 just north of BIA road 13/outpost of Newcomb. Bennett Peak is to west; Ford Butte to east.

74 Angel Wing (closed) ★★
A 180' soft (XX—we're not talking Dos Equis) three-pitch sandstone spire II 5.10 A3. First ascent: 1982 Banditos. Private land.
Ref: AAJ '91-168, C 83(4/83)-34; Guidebook: Bjornstad's *Desert Rock.*
Directions: From Fort Defiance, Arizona, wing it 10 mi. north on Hwy. 12 into New Mexico. Angel Wing is south of Navajo on the west side of road.

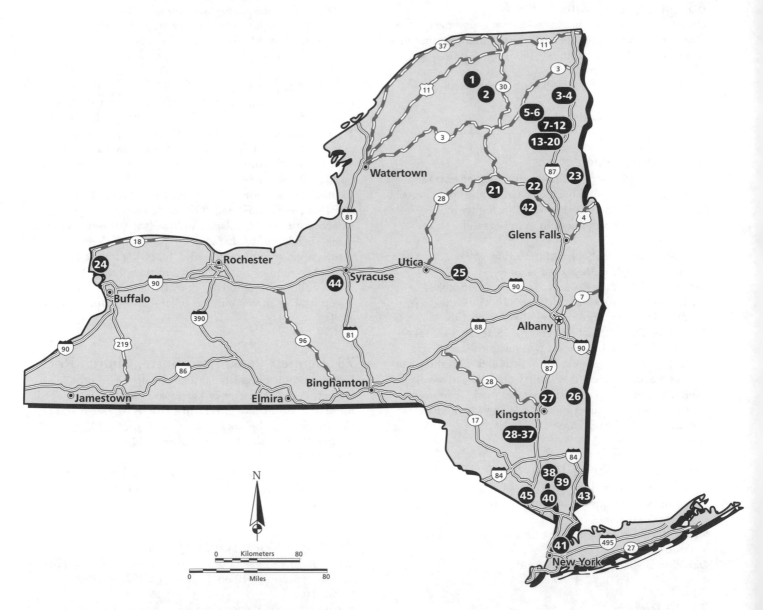

New York

New York

Drive fast, the life you save may be your own. —Rodney Dangerfield on New York City neighborhoods

Climbing in New York started in the 1930s, when King Kong and Fay Wray scaled the Empire State Building. Since then, most New York climbers have dissed that objective, signing off Kong's success to his tremendous ape index. The focus of New York climbing is on the Shawangunks; mile after mile of bullet-hard, quartzite conglomerate famous for roof climbs, stiff grades, and an all-star cast of climbers including Weissner, Stannard, Barber, Hill, Wunsch, Bein, Franklin, and, of course, the naughty Vulgarians. It also has the friendliest atmosphere in the climbing realm.

The Gunks certainly took away the limelight from the Hudson Palisades, which was once a New Yorker's standby. Farther north, the Adirondacks bow quietly to the Gunks. Classic granite, lush vegetation, and stately scenery await ascendeurs in the "Daks."

Of question are areas of limestone near Niagara Falls and sandstone in the western part of the state that may contribute to New York's popularity in the future.

For classic urban bouldering New York City's Central Park has Rat Rock. When in New York City, be sure to take in a Broadway show, a Yankees game, and the de rigueur mugging for an adrenaline rush on par with the climbing.

New York, you'll want to be a part of it.

1 A☆–(Adirondacks State Park Area) Overview ☆☆☆☆

Upstate New York's mountainous mix of crags, slabs, and 700′ granite cliffs. An enormous amount of rock and beauty, and sometimes, unfortunately, rain. The "Daks," the largest state park in the United States, has a rock-climbing history dating back to 1916. Camping at Poke-O-Moonshine and also 1 mi. north of Moss Cliff (both pay) or free across road from Spider's Web parking (Chapel Pass Area). Breakfast at Filling Station in Keene or Noonmark Diner in Keene Valley. Adirondack Park Visitor Interpretive Centers located in Paul Smiths (518-327-3000) and Newcomb (518-582-2000). Black flies from May to June. Summer/autumn. Private land. State park, (518) 897-1291.
Ref: J. Belser, Scofield's *High Peaks of the Northeast;* C 158, R 67-55; S [9/88, 6/64]; Guidebooks: Mellor's *Climbing in the Adirondacks: Rock and Ice Routes* (third ed.), Rosencrans's *Adirondack Rock and Ice Climbs,* Harlin's *East,* Vandiver's *Rock and Routes of the North Country New York,* Healy's *Climber's Guide to the Adirondacks: Rock and Slide Climbs in the High Peaks,* Goodwin's *Climbs in the Adirondacks.*
Directions: Various areas scattered throughout upstate New York's Adirondacks State Park include: Azure Mountain, Haystack, Poke-O-Moonshine, Baker Mountain, Moss Cliff, Pitchoff Cliff, Pitchoff Chimney Cliffs, Cascade Cliff, Owl's Head, Pitchoff 9N (Spruce Hill), Mountain Shadows, Mt. Jo, High Peaks Region, Wallface, Chapel Pond Pass Cliffs, Roaring Brook Falls, Sunrise Cliff, north fork of Bouquet River, King Phillip Spring Wall, Sugarloaf, Moxham Mountain, and Roger's Rock.

2 A–Azure Mountain ☆

Though this 250′ granite cliff is spectacular to look at, it is mostly devoid of free climbing but conducive to aid climbing. Summer/autumn. Free camping. State land.
Ref: Guidebooks: Mellor's *Climbing in the Adirondacks: Rock and Ice Routes* (third ed.), Rosencrans's *Adirondack Rock and Ice Climbs.*
Directions: From St. Regis Falls turn south on Blue Mountain Rd. before Santa Clara. Approach via dirt road opposite Blue Mountain Inn to Azure Mountain. Ask locally.

3 A–Haystack

Steep 250′ granite bump of rubble. Lots of 5.8–5.10. First routes done in the late 1960s. Government land.
Classics: Paul's Delight 4.
Ref: Guidebooks: Mellor's *Climbing in the Adirondacks: Rock and Ice Routes* (third ed.), Healy's *Climber's Guide to the Adirondacks: Rock and Slide Climbs in the High Peaks.*
Directions: On 9N (Hwy. 86) to east of road between Jay and Au Sable Forks. Cross Au Sable River 2–3 mi. south of Au Sable Forks on iron bridge. Follow road 2 ½ mi. to Haystack cliff (stay left at the fork).

4 A–Poke-O-Moonshine ☆☆☆☆

Top-gun Adirondack cliff. The granite/gneiss slab is identified by its prominent arch. The main face is a fault scarp 600′ tall by 1 mi. wide above the campground. Bloody

JIM DUNN COLLECTION

Jim Dunn at Poke-O-Moonshine.

Mary may be one of the best 5.9s on eastern granite. First climbs done in 1957 by John Turner. Raptor restrictions May–July. Pay camping. Government/private land.

Classics: Catharsis 6, FM 7, Gamesmanship 8, The Sting 8, Bloody Mary 9+, Great Dihedral 9+, Homecoming 10-, Fastest Gun 10, Freedom Flight 10, Moonshine 10+, Summer Solstice 11-, The Howling 12b, Salad Days 13-.

Ref: C [183-33, 123(12/90)-83, 90]; *Climbing in North America*; Guidebooks: Mellor's *Climbing in the Adirondacks: Rock and Ice Routes* (third ed.), Harlin's *East*, Healy's *Climber's Guide to the Adirondacks: Rock and Slide Climbs in the High Peaks.*

Directions: From Elizabethtown wax 16 mi. north on Hwy. 9. On left Poke-O-Moonshine Cliff is north of slab. Approach from campground to avoid crossing private land. Faces east.

5 A–Baker Mountain ☆☆

The 70′ granite cliff is visible from Bloomingdale Rd. over the river. Good crack climbs. No camping. State land.

Ref: Guidebooks: Mellor's *Climbing in the Adirondacks: Rock and Ice Routes* (third ed.), Rosencrans's *Adirondack Rock and Ice Climbs.*

Directions: From Saranac Lake go north on Pine St. Turn onto East Pine. Then go to Moody Pond. Park at far end of pond at power lines. Hike on Baker Mountain Trail, going left at fork ten minutes to left-branching path. Faces west.

6 A–Moss Cliff ☆☆☆

Classic splitter cracks on this 400′ granite crag. Right side has vertical cracks up to 400′. Pay camping. State land.

Classics: Touch of Class 9, Hard Times 9+, Fear of Flying 10, Coronary Country 10, Aerie 11+.

Ref: Guidebooks: Mellor's *Climbing in the Adirondacks: Rock and Ice Routes* (third ed.), Harlin's *East.*

Directions: From Lake Placid go 6 ½ mi. north on Hwy. 86. Head toward Whiteface Ski Area. Moss Cliff is prominent, 400′ buttress on north side of road. Ford good-size stream and bushwhack to cliff. Faces southeast.

7 A–CL☆–(Cascade Lake Cliffs Area) Pitchoff Cliff ☆☆

Pitchoff Northeast Cliff (160′ granite crag) is recognized by the Dog House, a huge leaning boulder at base of cliff. For Cascade Lakes, Pitchoff Chimney Cliffs is most recommended area. Free/pay camping. State land.

Classics: Overdog 8, Finger It Out 9.

Ref: Guidebooks: Mellor's *Climbing in the Adirondacks: Rock and Ice Routes* (third ed.), Harlin's *East*, Healy's *Climber's Guide to the Adirondacks: Rock and Slide Climbs in the High Peaks.*

Directions: From Lake Placid follow Hwy. 73 to Cascade Lakes before Keene. The following areas are in the Cascade Lakes area: Pitchoff Northeast Cliffs, Pitchoff Chimney Cliff, and Cascade Cliff. To get to Pitchoff Northeast Cliff: From Keene go north on Hwy. 73, turning onto Barkeater Ski Lodge Rd. Follow the road a few miles past lodge to Mountain Rd. Ski Trail. Hike trail a mile until cliff is visible on left.

8 A–CL–Pitchoff Chimney Cliffs ☆☆

A 300′ granite cliff detached from a cliff. Good routes cleaned of lichens offer good pro in lipped horizontal cracks. The Great Chimney serves as a climber's landmark. Free/pay camping. State land.

Classics: The Great Chimney 3-6, The El 7, Pete's Farewell 7, Dynamo Hum 8, Roaches on the Wall 10, Run Higher Jump Faster 10+, Star Sailor 10+.

Ref: Guidebooks: Mellor's *Climbing in the Adirondacks: Rock and Ice Routes* (third ed.), Healy's *Climber's Guide to the Adirondacks: Rock and Slide Climbs in the High Peaks.*

Directions: From Lake Placid (approximately fifteen minutes), follow Hwy. 73 to lower end of Lower Cascade Lake before Keene. Park at southernmost of two good pullouts. Hike trail up to Pitchoff Chimney Cliffs. Faces south.

9 A–CL–Cascade Cliff ★★

Easy access; poor quality, loose rock with wandering 600′ granite broken routes for the adventurous beginner. Pitchoff Chimney Cliffs across road recommended. Free/pay camping. State land.

Classics: The Overhanging Gutter 7, Lichen Delight 7+.

Ref: Guidebooks: Mellor's *Climbing in the Adirondacks: Rock and Ice Routes* (third ed.), Healy's *Climber's Guide to the Adirondacks: Rock and Slide Climbs in the High Peaks*.

Directions: From Lake Placid follow Hwy. 73 before Keene. Park at picnic area between upper/lower Cascade Lakes on south side of road. Cascade Cliff's huge wall forms the southeast side of Cascade Notch above the mile-long Lower Cascade Lake.

10 A–Owl's Head ★★★

Most popular Adirondack 60′ granite toprope crag. Bring extendo rope for anchors. Popular teaching area, with plenty to do up to 5.9. No camping. Private land—use good behavior.

Ref: Guidebook: Mellor's *Climbing in the Adirondacks: Rock and Ice Routes* (third ed.).

Directions: On Hwy. 73, between Lake Placid and Keene, 1 mi. south of Lower Cascade Lake. Take dirt road through development. This dirt road starts directly across from house marked "1981." Hike twenty minutes up trail to Owl's Head. Faces southwest.

11 A–Pitchoff 9N (Spruce Hill) ★★★

A 250′ granite crag. Not to be confused with Pitchoff Cliffs near Cascade Lakes. No camping. State land.

Classics: PSOC Rt 7.

Ref: Guidebooks: Mellor's *Climbing in the Adirondacks: Rock and Ice Routes* (third ed.), Healy's *Climber's Guide to the Adirondacks: Rock and Slide Climbs in the High Peaks*.

Directions: Between Keene and Elizabethtown. From junction of Hwy. 9 and Hwy. 73, pitch off east on Hwy. 9N for 5 mi. toward Elizabethtown. Pitchoff 9N cliff is the impressive buttress north of road. Park below and hike north twenty minutes up through woods.

12 A–Mountain Shadows

Beginner 200′ granite crag. State land.

Ref: Guidebook: Mellor's *Climbing in the Adirondacks: Rock and Ice Routes* (third ed.).

Directions: Just west of police barracks between Elizabethtown and Hwy. 87. Mountain Shadows restaurant is 1/2 mi. east of cliff.

13 A–Mt. Jo ★

Topropes on this 80′ beginner granite crag make it an Adirondack Mountain Club teaching cliff. Access problems. Private land.

Classics: Reunion 5.

Ref: Guidebooks: Mellor's *Climbing in the Adirondacks: Rock and Ice Routes* (third ed.), Healy's *Climber's Guide to the Adirondacks: Rock and Slide Climbs in the High Peaks*.

Directions: From Lake Placid follow Hwy. 73 south to Heart Lake Rd. and turn right. Go until behind Adirondack Loj. Mt. Jo Wall is visible from hiker's building parking. A half mile hike. Faces southeast.

14 A–High Peaks Region ★★

Most of these are long 900′ granite slab adventure routes. New cliffs appear as vegetation slides off, old cliffs get overgrown. Mt. Marcy is highest point in New York at 5,344′. The area is known for "slide" climbing—somewhere between actual rock climbing and technical hiking on large slabs. Sticky rubber may make trekking here more enjoyable. Noonmark Mountain is a toprope area as well. Giant Mountain is known for its novel "slide climbs" in its western cirque: the Bottle, Question Mark, Eagle, Finger, and Tulip. Lots of potential for the adventure climber. If you can't figure out the angle, use a slide rule . . . duh. State/private land.

Classics: Big Slide: Sliderules 7; Gothics: 1,000′ 5.7 slab runout; Colden, E Dix, McComb; Roger's Slide: Little Finger 5.

Ref: C 143, S [5/87, 7/86, 4/72]; Guidebooks: Mellor's *Climbing in the Adirondacks: Rock and Ice Routes* (third ed.), Rosencrans's *Adirondack Rock and Ice Climbs*, Healy's *Climber's Guide to the Adirondacks: Rock and Slide Climbs in the High Peaks*.

Directions: Novel slab and cliff climbing on exposed, backcountry Adirondack High Peaks include: Big Slide, Gothics, Panther Gorge, Porter, Noonmark Mountain, Indian Head, Rooster Comb, The Brothers (number of cliffs facing John Brook Valley), Giant, and Wallface (listed separately). For the Gothics's Rainbow Slide, take Gothics trail from dam of Lower Ausable Lake past Rainbow Falls. Long slide routes on mountain slabs. Get a topo or backcountry map of the "Daks." Most formations are accessed west of Keene Valley via different trails in the heart of Adirondack beauty.

15 A–Wallface ★★★

At 800′, largest cliff in New York and highest precipice east of Rockies at 1,200′. A most serious Adirondack cliff. Free and mixed free/aid routes begin with slabs and end in sheer to overhanging walls on the upper reaches of the cliff. Four-mile pass loaded with huge boulders. Backcountry camping. State land.

Classics: Weissner Rt 4, The Diagonal 7, No Man's Pilot 8+, Pleasure Victim 11a, Mental Blocks 12a.

Ref: S 1/88; Guidebooks: Mellor's *Climbing in the Adirondacks: Rock and Ice Routes* (third ed.), Harlin's *East*, Healy's *Climber's Guide to the Adirondacks: Rock and Slide Climbs in the High Peaks*.

Directions: Need Adirondacks High Peaks trail map, available at local outdoor shops. Hike either from Adirondack

Loj at Heart Lake south of North Elba (Lake Placid) approximately 5 mi. or from Tahawas. Five-mi. backcountry approach for Wallface. Faces predominantly north.

16 A–Chapel Pond Pass Cliffs (Spider's Web and Washbowl Cliffs) ✩✩✩✩

Chapel Pond Pass consists of various granite cliffs up to 700′ offering a variety of climbing conditions: Chapel Pond Slab, Emperor Slab, King Wall, Chapel Pond Gully, Washbowl Cliff, Lower Washbowls, Spider's Web. Spider's Web offers exceptionally fine and strenuous crack climbing for the "Daks." It is a steep wall with interlocking cracks. Free camping across the street from the Spider's Web. Washbowl Cliffs closed in spring due to peregrine falcon nesting season. Roaring Brook Falls, north of Chapel Pond on Hwy. 73, also offers practice area on 120′ wall next to scenic falls. State land.

Classics: CPS: The Empress 5, Thanksgiving 7; Washbowl: Partition 8, Master Charge 11; Spider's Web: Slim Pickens 9, Yvonne 9+, Drop Fly or Die 11, Romano's Route 11, White Night 11+, It's Only Entertainment 11+, Zabba.

Ref: C 90; Guidebooks: Mellor's *Climbing in the Adirondacks: Rock and Ice Routes* (third ed.), Harlin's *East,* Healy's *Climber's Guide to the Adirondacks: Rock and Slide Climbs in the High Peaks.*

Directions: From junction of I–87 and Hwy. 73, go 6 mi. west on Hwy. 73 to Chapel Pond Pass. South of Hwy. 73 lies Chapel Pond Slab (good), Emperor Slabs (choss), and King Wall. North of Hwy. 73, Spider's Web is on the right coming from I–87, a ten-minute hike. Washbowl Cliffs has twenty-minute approach on faint trail. Beer Walls just downhill toward Keene from Spider's Web—park on west side of road and take trail up drainage to top of west- and south-facing crag.

New York Road Thoughts

We're all coming out of The Bacchus in New Paltz on a Halloween Night. As we walk across the parking lot, a car starts pulling out, when all of a sudden a guy starts running out of the bar across the street screaming, "Get the license plate on that car! Get the license plate on that car!"

We start to walk over to check out the number when from the shadows this guy just jumps toward the rear of the vehicle and rips the license plate clean off the car. An impressive effort for sure.

If that wasn't good enough, he then proceeds to punch his fist right through the driver's side door window. Whoa, even more impressive!

But the car speeds off, leaving the guy behind. The car may have got away, but not with its license plate.

When you go to get someone's license plate number in New York, don't mess around!

—TNT

---

17 A–Roaring Brook Falls ✩

Roaring Brook Falls is a beginner's practice area on 120′ granite wall of loose, rotten rock next to scenic falls. State land.

Ref: Guidebook: Healy's *Climber's Guide to the Adirondacks: Rock and Slide Climbs in the High Peaks.*

Directions: From junction of I–87 and Hwy. 73, go 6 mi. west on Hwy. 73 to Chapel Pond Pass. Roaring Brook Falls is north of Chapel Pond on Hwy. 73.

18 A–Sunrise Cliff (on Mt. Gilligan)

Interesting little 80′ granite crag. State land.

Ref: Guidebook: Mellor's *Climbing in the Adirondacks: Rock and Ice Routes* (third ed.).

Directions: On Hwy. 9, 3 ½ mi. north of junction of Hwy. 9 and Hwy. 73. Sunrise Cliff is east of road on Mt. Gilligan.

19 A–North Fork of Bouquet River ✩✩✩

Granite lead/toprope problems up to at least 5.11. State land.

Ref: Guidebooks: Mellor's *Climbing in the Adirondacks: Rock and Ice Routes* (third ed.).

Directions: From Keene go on Hwy. 73 south until approximately 2–3 mi. south of Chapel Pond. Park at river crossing and cross river. Hike right along bank of north fork of Bouquet River for ½ mi.

20 A–King Phillip Spring Wall ✩

A 120′ granite slab similar to Chapel Pond Slab, featuring topropes at all beginner-level routes. No camping. State land.

Ref: Guidebook: Mellor's *Climbing in the Adirondacks: Rock and Ice Routes* (third ed.).

Directions: From Keene go south on Hwy. 73 to I–87 (exit 30). Park at King Phillip Spring, just west of exit 30 on I–87. Walk to highway up entrance ramp, past roadcut, and turn right to cliff. Don't park on I–87.

21 A–Sugarloaf ✩✩✩

Potential for exploration on this 400′ granite crag. State land.

Ref: Guidebook: Mellor's *Climbing in the Adirondacks: Rock and Ice Routes* (third ed.).

Directions: Near town of Indian Lake. From Hwy. 28 and Cedar River Rd., take Cedar River Rd. for 8 mi. Sugarloaf is on right.

22 A–Moxham Mountain

Sport-route potential surrounding mountain. Many easy granite slab routes on dome as well. State land.

Ref: Guidebook: Mellor's *Climbing in the Adirondacks: Rock and Ice Routes* (third ed.).

Directions: On Hwy. 28 North, 5 mi. north of North Creek. Moxham Mountain is on left.

23 A–Roger's Rock ★★★

Picturesque 800' granite slab rising out of Lake George. Boat approach, long runouts. Little Finger is most obvious crack route on an otherwise nondescript slab. Pay camping. State land.

Classics: Little Finger 7, Screaming Meaney 8+.

Ref: Guidebook: Mellor's *Climbing in the Adirondacks: Rock and Ice Routes* (third ed.).

Directions: From Hague go just north on Hwy. 9N. Approach by boat from north end of Roger's Rock Campground on Lake George. Paddle past Juniper Island north for ten more minutes. Faces south.

24 Niagara Falls State Park (Niagara Glen) ★★★

The 200' limestone Niagara scarp runs through here, creating cliffs and boulders. There is 20' high bouldering downstream of Niagara Falls at the area known as Niagara Glen. Restricted climbing areas—best to check with local climbers for current status. Do not climb on the Headwall! Climb only on the boulders. Look for guidebook at Lumber City Rock Gym in Buffalo. American Falls (185') and Horseshoe Falls (175') on Canadian side. Autumn. Pay camping. State park.

Ref: C. DeSouza 1/99; C [140, 120(104)]; *Roadside Geology of New York*, p. 44; Guidebook: Check with Lumber City Rock Gym in Buffalo.

Directions: Follow Hwy. 190 west over bridge into Canada. Immediately after the toll, bear right. At stop sign, turn right. This takes one under the bridge and along the river. The Niagara Glen is approximately 1 mi. on your left. Park in lot and descend metal stairs to boulders. Faces predominantly east.

25 Little Falls (Moss Island) ★★★

Precambrian 40' gneiss walls called "Pothole Disneyland" at Moss Island in Little Falls between the river and Lock 17 of the canal. A long climbing history since 1950s of colorful locals and sandbaggers, including Stolz, Lin, Vrooman, Randall, and Skibinski. The overhanging crack, The Virgin 5.12c, is the local testpiece. Fifty routes. Baseball Hall of Fame down the road in Cooperstown. Spring–autumn. KOA camping in Herkimer. NPS.

Classics: Poof! You're a Pomegranite! 8, Looking Glass 10, Fred P. Jones 10, Freddy Krueger 12-, Fred Flintstone 12a, The Virgin 12c.

Ref: C 155 (10/96)-63, R 74-28; *Roadside Geology of New York* p. 182; Guidebook: Stolz and Davis's *Little Falls: A Rock Climber's Guide*.

Directions: Little Falls walls exposed along the Mohawk River. Moss Island is a friendly, accessible area. From I-90 take Hwy. 169 north to Little Falls for 2 mi. Just before bridge, turn left and park underneath it. Go up lock stairs to 40' crag. Watch out for sandbags along the lock. Faces south.

26 Taconic State Park

Metamorphic cragging and bouldering. Access being negotiated in 1990. Bash Bish Waterfalls. Part of an overthrust fault known as the Taconic Klippe. State park, (518) 329-3993.

Ref: C 120-105; *Roadside Geology of New York* p.106.

Directions: From Copake go approximately 5 mi. south. Taconic State Park is along Hwy. 22, approximately 3 mi. west of Massachussetts/Connecticut/New York border intersection.

27 Kingston Quarry ★★★

A 60' limestone quarry sporting manufactured holds on glabrous stone. Demanding routes from 5.12d to 5.14a are strictly for fit sport climbers. No camping. Spring–autumn. City park.

Classics: Public Enemy 12d, Penis Envy 13, It's a Guy Thing 13c.

Ref: M. Freeman; SC 3/92.

Directions: In Kingston (just twenty minutes north of the Gunks). Park at intersection of Gill St. and Treemont St. (northeast of East Strand St. and Thompkins Ave.). Kingston Quarry is 50 yd. north from parking. Just west of the Hudson River. Faces southeast.

28 S★–(Shawangunks Area) Overview ★★★★★

The climbing at the Gunks can put a smile on your face that could light up New York City. For years this series of creamy 200' quartzite cliffs has been the number-one choice of East Coast craggers. In the early 1990s, the New River Gorge in West Virginia became the "bottom line." Still, the Gunks, with 7 mi. of crags, boast a regal variety of stunning quartzite climbs. A colorful history of rock-climbing development that included the off-color Vulgarians. Fun climbing and gracious climbers. More than 1,000 one- and two-pitch routes. Famous stepped overhangs of all difficulties. Sometimes rusty fixed pro. Good nutcraft essential to protect in horizontal breaks. Current ban on all bolting. German inns. Great apples. Spring/autumn. Daily/ yearly user pass charged by Mohonk Preserve private land trust (914–255-0919).

Classics: High Exposure 6, CCK 7, Birdland 8, Directissima 9, Mellow Yellow 10, Transcontinental Nailway 10, Matinee 10+, Kligfield's Follies 11+, Nectar Vector 12a, Kansas City 12, Project X with Projectile Finish 12b, Intruders 12d, Survival 13a, The Zone 13a; Bouldering: Gill Egg B1, Outbreak Boulder: Child's Play V9, Boxcar Arête V8.

Ref: M. Siacca; C [194-113, 183-22, 159-106, 127, 114, 102, 99, 98, 95, 83(5/83)-26, 73, 54], M [117, 111, 73-20], OB 43(2/79), R [101-40/83, 94-108, 79-106, 63], S 1/86; Sherman's *Stone Crusade, Vulgarian Digest, Climbing in North America, Shawangunk Rock Climbs;* www.gunks.com/. Guidebooks: Greene and Russo's *Bouldering in the Shawangunks*, Williams's *Gunks Select*, Swain's *Gunks Guide*, Williams's *Shawangunks Rock Climbs, vol. 1, 2, and 3*,

TIM TOULA

Al Diamond dancing with Clairvoyance, 5.13b, Shawangunks.

Harlin's *East, Climbing In Southern Ontario,* Rezucha's *Shawangunk Grit,* Gran's *Climber's Guide to the Shawangunks,* Crother's *Shawangunk Climbs List.*

Directions: From New Paltz go west on Hwy. 299. Turn right at German Inn on Hwy. 44/55 and wind up switchbacks (may be necessary to park at switchbacks on busy weekends) to the bridge (camping) where the base of main cliffs lie. Less than one and a half hours from New York City (ten minutes from New Paltz). Major Shawangunks cliff areas include: Bonticou, Sky Top, Trapps, Near Trapps, Millbrook, Giant's Workshop/ Cope's Lookout, Hemlock Rock, and Lost City. Cliffs face mainly southeast.

29 S–Bonticou/Cybernetic Wall ✩✩✩✩

This 60' quartzite crag is known amongst the Gunks elite for rad and bad overhanging routes. Mohonk Preserve private land trust.

Classics: Bonticou: Artificial Intelligents 13a, Running Man 13c; Cybernetic Wall: Love Muscle 13a, Cybernetic Wall 13d.

Ref: C 99, 98; Guidebooks: Williams's *Gunks Select,* Swain's

Gunks Guide, Williams's *Shawangunks Rock Climbs, vol. 1, 2, and 3.*

Directions: From Mountain Rest Rd. out of New Paltz, turn right on Bonticou Rd. to Bonticou crag. For Cybernetic Wall it's approximately 2 mi. farther north. Ask locals for specifics.

30 S–Skytop ✩✩✩✩

Scenic 100' quartzite cragging with many Gunks classics adjacent to the Mohonk House. Lofty views and sunny cragging. Sees less use than the Trapps but still a mainstay area. Parking at Mohonk Lodge for guests and employees only. It may now be closed.

Classics: Sound and Fury 8, Jekyll and Hyde 9, No Exit 10, Mellow Yellow 10+, Open Cockpit 11+, Foops 11+, Supercrack 12, Vandals 13-.

Ref: C [105, 95, 94, 93]; Guidebooks: Hill, Williams, Swain, Harlin's *East.*

Directions: From parking at bridge for Trapps, walk north/northwest along carriage road beyond Trapps for 4 mi. to Skytop. Also accessible from Mohonk Lodge by walking south around lake, but only if you're a lodge guest.

31 S–Giant's Workshop/Cope's Lookout ✩✩✩

Sweet, overhanging 80' quartzite climbs, though less extensive than other Gunks cliffs. Mohonk Preserve private land trust.

Classics: Intruders.

Ref: Guidebooks: Williams's *Gunks Select,* Swain's *Gunks Guide,* Williams's *Shawangunks Rock Climbs, vol. 1, 2, and 3.*

Directions: Giant's Workshop/Cope's Lookout are between the Trapps and Skytop. Ask locals.

32 S–Trapps ✩✩✩✩✩

The longest 250' quartzite cliffband in the Gunks and the meeting place for Gunks climbers. Uberfall is congregational point for climbers, ranger information, water, and rescue site. Free camping traditionally near bridge. Check locally for details. Mohonk Preserve private land trust.

Classics: High Exposure 6, Shockley's Ceiling 6, Classic 7, MF 9, Directissima 10, The Yellow Wall 11, Kligfield's Follies 11+.

Ref: C [99, 94, 93], R 79-106; Guidebooks: Williams's *Gunks Select,* Swain's *Gunks Guide,* Williams's *Shawangunks Rock Climbs, vol. 1, 2, and 3.*

Directions: From New Paltz go west on Hwy. 299. Turn right at German Inn on Hwy. 44/55 and wind up switchbacks (may be necessary to park here on busy weekends) to base of main cliffs. Park near bridge if possible, same as for Near Trapps. From parking at bridge, walk north along carriage road a few minutes to Uberfall and Trapps. Faces southeast.

33 S–Lost City ★★★★

The hidden 60′ quartzite crag of the Gunks. Beautiful routes that include the groundbreakers of their era, Persistence 11+ and Survival of the Fittest 13a. Mohonk Preserve private land trust.

Classics: Stannard's Roof 10, Persistence 11+, Resistoflex 12-, Survival of the Fittest 13a, Clairvoyance 13b.

Ref: C 99; Guidebooks: Williams's *Gunks Select*, Swain's *Gunks Guide*, Williams's *Shawangunks Rock Climbs, vol. 1, 2, and 3.*

Directions: Continue past the Trapps parking in the Gunks on Hwy. 44/55. Park at Coxing Swimming Area off Clove Rd. Hike west to Lost City. Faces southwest. Ask locals.

34 S–Near Trapps/Bayards ★★★★

Classic Gunks 150′ quartzite climbing across the road from the crowds in the Trapps. Mohonk Preserve private land trust.

Classics: Disneyland 6, Yellow Ridge 7, Broken Sling 8, Roseland 9, Criss Cross 10-, Kansas City 12.

Ref: C 93; Guidebooks: See number 33, Harlin's *East.*

Directions: From parking at bridge walk south along trail (Trapps to north). Near Trapps are first obvious cliffs on right. Bayards are cliffs farther south. Faces southeast.

35 S–Millbrook ★★★★

Beautiful climbing on the longest quartzite routes in the Gunks and possibly the scariest. Raptor restrictions May–August. Mohonk Preserve private land trust.

Classics: Westward Ho 7, Time Eraser 10-, Bank Shot 11, Happiness is a 110° Wall 12, Nectar Vector 12+.

Ref: C 99; Guidebooks: See number 33.

Directions: From New Paltz go west on Hwy. 299. Turn right at German Inn on Hwy. 44/55 and wind up switchbacks (may be necessary to park on switchbacks on busy weekends) to base of main cliffs. Park near bridge if possible, same as for Trapps. Hike south forty-five minutes on top on trail to rap from tree in middle of Millbrook cliff. Faces southeast.

36 S–Hemlock Rock ★★★★

Access-sensitive, 60′ quartzite crags. Be quiet or get the bullhorn from the landowner.

Classics: Rockabye Baby 10+, 11c crack, Hemlock Rocker 12a.

Directions: Ask locals for Hemlock Rock.

37 Minnewaska State Park (Peter's Kill Area) ★★★

Illegal to climb in this state park adjoining the Mohonk Preserve. Numerous 200′ cliffs of Gunks-like quartzite nature. Only Peter's Kill Area is opened to rock climbing. A letter of 1996 from Thomas L. Cobb, Palisades Interstate Park Commission states, "It is illegal to rock climb in the Palmogat Ravine area of Minnewaska State Park Preserve . . . we will be opening up a portion of Minnewaska for rock climbing this fall, with seasonal closure ending this year on or about Dec. 15, 1996. We will limit climbing to an average of fifty permits per day, and anticipate a $5.00 per person climbing fee." Josh Lowell writes in 1998, "The Peter's Kill area of Minnewaska State Park is now officially open to climbing, thanks to the efforts of the Access Fund. The focus in the past year has been on bouldering, and Peter's Kill now hosts the best concentration of quality bouldering in the East. There are quality problems at all grades, but it's the hard problems that make Peter's Kill unique. There is a $5 fee for day use. Bring a crash pad and a spotter." Pay camping. Autumn. State park, (914) 255–0752.

Classics: Lightning Blade V1, Tree Bola V3, Mentos V4, V5 Traverse V5, Mad Lion V6, Tiger Style V7, The Terrordome V8, Silence V9, Khadejha V10.

Ref: J. Lowell; T. L. Cobb, *Access Fund Report;* C [192-118, 164-46, 150-54, 120(105-7)], R [95-87, 79-106]; Guidebooks: See number 33.

Directions: From New Paltz go west on Hwy. 44 to Minnewaska State Park. Check at office about Peter's Kill Area fees/permits.

38 Storm King State Park (Hudson Highlands) (closed)

Technical rock climbing is not permitted as a sanctioned activity on the metamorphic crags in this state park. Autumn. Pay camping. State park, (845) 786–2701.

Ref: T. L. Cobb, Guidebook: *Student's Guide to Storm King.*

Directions: From West Point go north along Hudson River to palisades in Storm King State Park.

39 Hudson River Palisades (Highland Falls) ★★★

Solid, slate walls 150′ tall and eighty-five degrees with bolted faces. Part of the Hudson Palisades, an incredible cliff line that extends for 40 mi. from West Point, New York, to Englewood, New Jersey. The state line lookout, 532′ above the river, offers good views of columnar jointing in cliff face. Hudson Palisades off-limits to climbing both in New York and New Jersey. Autumn. Pay camping. Government land.

Ref: D. Dyess.

Directions: Along the Hudson River from West Point south to Palisades at New York and New Jersey state line, cliffs line the bank of the Hudson River. Several areas dependent on access. From Highland Falls go north to West Point Military Academy. South of the Academy. Go to Grand Union Grocery Store and take road left down to railroad tracks. Walk north on tracks; Hudson River Palisades on left. Other walls along railroad tracks. Faces east.

40 Palisades Interstate Park (closed) ★★★

Hudson Palisades 300' gneiss cliffs are off-limits to climbing both in New York and New Jersey. Technical rock climbing is not permitted as a sanctioned activity in this state park. Autumn. No camping. State park, (845) 786–5003.
Ref: T. L. Cobb; C 120-105, S 2/62.
Directions: From West Haverstraw, Palisades Interstate Park is west on Hwy. 202 to near Ladentown. Faces south.

41 Central Park Boulders (Rat Rock, Umpire Rock, and Cat Rock) ★★

Schist bouldering (Rat, Cat, and Chess Rocks) in the middle of New York City. An experience. Rat Rock has a long traverse and is slightly more pleasant than fondling a dull razor. Also, the Harlem (aka Worthless) Boulder is at the shady end of Central Park. Enjoy people-watching. Possibly thieves, riffraff, and rats. Guinness Book of World Records is in nearby Empire State Building. Autumn. No camping. City park.
Ref: C [189-111, 127(8/91)-32, 111]; Sherman's *Stone Crusade;* Guidebooks: Nick and Sloane's *New Jersey Crags,* Harlin's *East.*
Directions: Manhattan. In Central Park. Rat and Cat Rocks on Sixty-third St. Rat at west side of park near baseball fields, Cat on east side near bridge and pond. Other New York City bouldering includes: Riverside Dr. (in Riverside Park) retaining walls, Seventy-second St. Wall in park out of tunnel, and Boat Basin (easy) at end of Seventy-ninth St.

42 Crane Mountain

Adirondack mountain crag. Summer. Free camping. State land.
Classics: Daybreak 3, Cornerstone 5, Straits of Fear 8, Sundogs 9+, Fifi Fingers 10, I'll Fly Away 10.
Ref: J. Harrison 2/98.
Directions: From Albany take I–87 (Northway) to exit 23. Head north on Route 9. Turn left on Route 28. Go west on Route 8. Turn left (south) on South Johnsburg Rd. Crane Mountain is prominently visible to the west. Access is 7 mi. south of Johnsburg off Garnet Lake Rd. Note also that Huckleberry Mountain is right next door, with many rad-man routes. Faces south.

43 Mud Hole

If you can't make it to the illustrious Gunks, this is a nice 60' granite hideaway that gets little traffic during the week. Climbing dates back to the 1970s with an old rusty piton to prove it. Most of the twenty-two climbs are in the 5.9–5.12 range. The best reference 5.10 in New York is Canutility. Excellent traverse. Guaranteed pump. All climbs, except two, are vertical to overhanging (slightly). Excellent community. Beware, land recently sold to new landowners. Not sure about access. Autumn. No camping. Private land.

Classics: The Drip 5.8, Open Book 5.9, Can-u-tility 5.10, Unknown 5.11, Crescent Crack 5.11, S & B 5.12b, Mono-Mania 5.12c.
Ref: T. Jung 2/99.
Directions: Near Armonk. Start at Hwy. 684 to exit 3. Take Route 22 North toward Bedford. Left at the blinking yellow light onto Cox Ave. Go down 1 mi. over a bridge. Park on the right-hand side in a dirt parking lot. Walk across and take path starting with concrete. Path diverges. Follow the bend to the right. Leads up to cliff in 100 yd. Faces east.

44 Split Rock Quarry

The area is in a turn-of-the-twentieth-century stone quarry. In the 1900s, while being used for munitions storage, the whole place exploded and has not been used since. It is really the only climbing of any substance in the Syracuse area. The climbing here is on a rough stone-blocked structure resembling Mayan ruins. The structure is made up of large rough-cut blocks of limestone about 50' high. Thirty routes. Pete and Dave Wiezalis have climbed this area since 1992. It offers mixed grades from short 25' 5.4s (Lollygag Wall) to 50' pump runs at about 5.11 (Crazy Finger Wall). This is also a popular party spot, with much glass and miscellaneous junk around. *Bring a good tarp for your rope* (and tape for your fingers). In summer, the place can get quite wild, with bikers, four-wheel-drive enthusiasts, shooters, and partygoers. Police will come on occasion and kick people out (especially if people are shooting). On several occasions, the police have kicked people out, but left us to climb. Also, please be thoughtful of the locals near the dead-end. And you thought this was just a quarry.
Classics: Lollygag 4, The Bike Wall 6, Black Thumb 8.
Ref: P. Wiezalis 4/98.
Directions: Onondaga (southwest Syracuse). Take I–90 to I–690 East to I–695 exit at Route 5 West. Take left onto Warner's Rd. (Hwy. 173). At third light, take right onto Onondaga Blvd. After 1/3 mi., the road sort of dead-ends (with no more houses), and the old quarry road rises up to the left. Park either at the base of the hill (at the end of the road) or drive up Quarry Rd. Be nice to the neighboring house folk as they determine when the police get called (tickets have been issued in the past). Hike up hill, looking left for old 50' rock crusher.

45 Ramapo Transit Cliffs (closed) ★★★

Cliffs with a variety of slabs and overhangs. Routes since the 1970s.
Classics: 5.9+ crack, Sciatic Hang 10R, Roof Hopper 12a.
Ref: Guidebook: Nick and Sloane's *New Jersey Crags.*
Directions: Just north of the junction of Hwy. 17 and the New York Thruway at Ramapo. Behind the Ramapo Transit Bus Company.

North Carolina

Never eat anything with a shelf life of under two years. —Russell Erickson's climbing dietary guidelines

1 Roxboro Boulder ✫✫

Two quartzite rocks up to 45': The main boulder and a side bluff that holds many difficult cracks and faces. Many climbs are only noticeable by bolts. The owner doesn't mind if you walk up, but cars will be taken if they are parked on his land. Favorite place for locals to get drunk and drive four-wheelers. Best to find other places to camp. Autumn–spring. Private land.

Classics: Devils Tower: The Bluffs; Senseless Appearance, The Bluffs (may be unclimbed); Crimp Fest: Main Boulder.

Ref: J. Bittner, Moore.

Directions: At Roxboro. Go north on Hwy. 501 until you reach Woodsdale Rd., then make a left. Drive approximately 1 mi. to the bottom of a hill. There you stop at a road with a red fence on the left. Park without blocking access. Hike up the gravel road. Make all right-hand turns until you reach the top of the hill.

2 Umstead State Park (Durham Bouldering) ✫✫

William B. Umstead area. A very small area of 20' quartzite bouldering problems. Autumn–spring. State park, (919) 677-0062.

Directions: Near Durham. Take Cary exit off I-40. Or, Umstead Park: From Raleigh take I-40 north to Harrison Ave. exit. Five minutes from interstate. Hidden in forest. Easiest access across airport property to a single boulder. Ask local climbers for more details.

3 Faux Rock ✫✫✫

A man-made climbing wall with a price tag of $75,000 at North Carolina State University. State land.

Ref: S 5/87.

Directions: Raleigh. Faux Rock is at North Carolina State University.

4 Moore's Wall ✫✫✫✫✫

The overhanging pump palace of North Carolina. Beautiful, diamond-hard 300' quartzite crag with thin edges to Nell Carter buckets. Excellent bouldering/ topropes at Zschiesche's Corridor along trail en route to

cliff or Howie's Roof atop Moore's. The routes here are better than hitting a grand slam in the bottom of the ninth with two out and a full count. Please respect the privilege of camping at road's end because it is on private land. (Please, no fire rings and keep turnaround clear.) Breakfast at Demon Rock Restaurant. Spring/autumn. State land.

Classics: Zoo View 7, Air Show 8, Blue Chock 10a, Bimbo's Bulge 10c, Quaker State 11a, Pooh Corner 11, Wild Kingdom 11d/12-, Go Dog Go 12a, Underdog 12b, POV 12d, Zeus 13b, Zeus 14a; Bouldering: Zschiesche's Corridor: Zen Spasm, Duck Soup; Grandstand Boulder: Titan Traverse, Piss and Vinegar.

Ref: C [177-26, 174-106, 169-30, 147, 116, 97, 75(12/82), 68, 63], R 42(3/91)-32, S 10/64; Sherman's *Stone Crusade;* Guidebooks: Cater's *Sport Crags of the East,* Harlin's *East,* Kelley's *The Climber's Guide to North Carolina,* Hall's *Southern Rock: A Climber's Guide,* Price's *Carolinas Climber's Guide.*

Directions: From Winston-Salem go 16 7/10 mi. north on Hwy. 66. Turn right on Moore's Spring Rd. Go right on Mickey Rd. Go right on Charlie Young Rd. Turn right on Mountain Road to top. Park. Hike on climber's trail to cliff base of Moore's Wall. Areas include: Wall of Fire, Sentinel Buttress, Circus Wall, and The Amphitheater.

5 Hanging Rock State Park (closed) ✫✫✫

This 150' quartzite crag with topropable climbs from summit is closed to climbing. Pay camping in state park (910-593-8480).

Classics: Three Beers 7, Five Eight Wall 8.

Ref: P. Jarrard; C 68, S 10/64; Guidebooks: Hall's *Southern Rock: A Climber's Guide,* Price's *Carolinas Climber Guide.*

Directions: From Winston-Salem follow Hwy. 311 north to Hwy. 89 through town of Danbury. Follow until park signs appear. Turn left off Hwy. 89 to park. Then follow obvious trail from parking lot to Hanging Rock State Park.

6 Cook's Wall ✫✫✫

This 300' quartzite crag is similar to nearby Moore's Wall but different in that it is not as steep. Good potential for moderate routes. Rock quality tends to vary. Autumn–spring. Pay camping nearby. Private land.

Classics: Emla 13d.

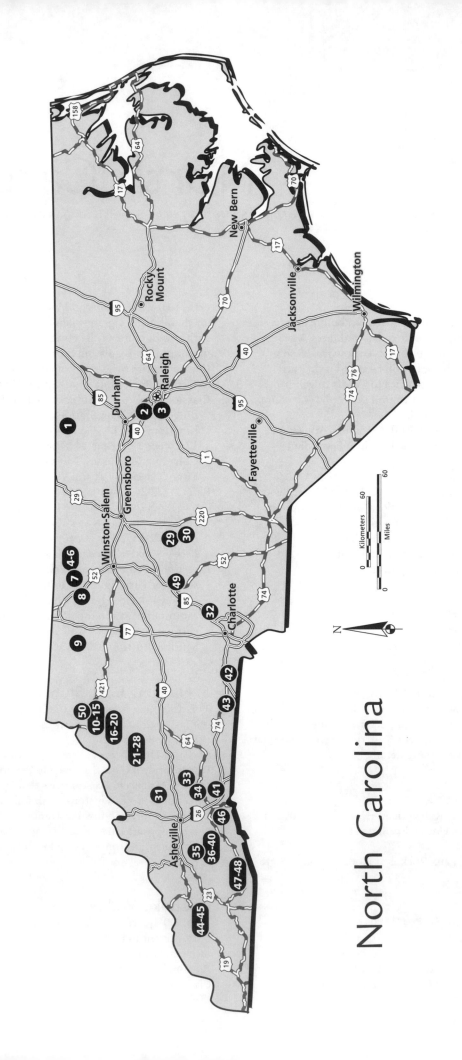

North Carolina

Ref: P. Jarrard; C 146 (64); Guidebook: Hall's *Southern Rock: A Climber's Guide.*
Directions: Access from Hanging Rock State Park via Cook's Wall Trail. Hike 1.5 mi. uphill. Cook's Wall is on the other side of ridge from Moore's Wall.

7 Sauratown (closed) ✫✫✫✫
As of 1996, this 150' quartzite crag area is officially closed by the property owners (YMCA Camp Hanes). Also, people parking at the top of the mountain at the turn-around risk being towed. Camp Hanes no longer approves of climbers using camp for access. Great steep, south-facing winter area that receives ample sun. Sourballs still may be one of the best 5.11s on the East Coast. Twenty-three new sport routes (many 5.10s). Camp at Moore's Wall, just a short drive away. Autumn–spring. Private land.
Classics: Leisure World 9-, Aid Raid 10+, Orange Dihedral 10+, Stokes County Monkey Trial 10, Sourballs 11a, Channel 12 12b.
Ref: C [139, 116, 63]; Guidebook: Kelly's *Climber's Guide to North Carolina.*
Directions: From Winston-Salem go 25 mi. north on Hwy. 66. Turn left at Faith Baptist Church and go ½ mi. Turn left for 3 mi. on Sauratown Mountain Rd. Park. Hike south of towers, picking up climber's trail.

8 Pilot Mountain State Park ✫✫
Pilot Knob, a giant rock-walled knob, is a regional landmark. Presently, there is no climbing allowed on it. The climbing area here is a short 60' quartzite wall below summit parking. Mostly a toprope area and with some sport routes on average to poor rock. Popular on weekends. Great views of the North Carolina landscape. Autumn–spring. Pay camping in state park (910-325-2355).
Ref: S 10/64; Guidebooks: Cater's *Sport Crags of the East,* Kelley's *The Climber's Guide to North Carolina,* Hall's *Southern Rock: A Climber's Guide,* Price's *Carolinas Climber's Guide.*
Directions: From Winston-Salem go 20 mi. north on I-52 to Pilot Mountain State Park exit. Follow signs to top of road. Rock climbing is on Little Pinnacle, just below top of park road to the south. Big Pinnacle "The Pilot" is an obvious short hike from there on the Ledge Springs Trail.

9 Stone Mountain State Park ✫✫✫✫✫
This 500' granite dome offers some of the best slab climbing on the East Coast. Spectacular, death-defying runouts on sparsely bolted routes have gained a reputation for groundfall potential. Thus, known as the "Home of the Running Belay," whereby the belayer runs away from the cliff to remove slack from the system and hopefully catch the leader's fall enough before he or she hits the ground. Makes for spectating more exciting than an overdose of rhino horn. Not an area for those allergic to slabs. No new routes allowed. North Carolina Mountain Rescue School site. Check for gate closure in evenings. Spring–autumn. Pay camping in state park (336-957-8185).
Classics: The Great Arch 6, No Alternative 6, Yardarm 8, The Pulpit 8, Grand Funk Railroad 9-, Fantastic 9, Yankee Go Home 10, Mercury's Lead 10, Strawberry Preserves 10, Purple Daze 11, The Last Dance 11, The Discipline 12.
Ref: C [192-52, 157-60, 68(9/81)-18, 63, 48], R [67-60, 9(7/85)]; Guidebooks: Cater's *Sport Crags of the East,* Harlin's *East,* Kelley's *The Climber's Guide to North Carolina,* Hall's *Southern Rock: A Climber's Guide,* Waddle's *Dixie Crystals: A Climber's Guide to Stone Mountain, North Carolina,* Price's *Carolinas Climber's Guide.*
Directions: From Elkin take Hwy. 21 north to west on Stone Mountain Rd. (NC 1002). Follow park signs. South Face is most popular, but North Face also has more for hard-core friction enthusiasts.

10 Hebron Colony ✫✫✫
This cool bouldering area is located adjacent to sunbathers and waterfalls. The climbing is okay, too.
Classics: Four V3s by main waterfall.
Ref: J. Henson.
Directions: From Boone go approximately 7–8 mi. on Hwy. 105 South to Hound Ears. Take dirt road at country store. Park in 2 mi. at hairpin. Hike 1 mi. down trail to Hebron Colony.

11 Grandma's Boulders ✫✫✫
In a beautiful mountain meadow, these 20' giant egg boulders have thin cranks on solid crystals. Autumn. Private land.
Classics: Classic V1-V5s; Jon Woodruff V7 testpiece.
Ref: Locals.
Directions: From Boone, Grandma's Boulders is 10 mi. west on Laurel Branch Road. Ask local climbers.

12 Winkler's Creek Boulders ✫✫
Ten classic 15' conglomerate creek-side problems. Cool swimming hole downstream. Spring–autumn. Private land.
Classics: "Raise Hell" crack! V2, V4 traverse with finish over creek! Undone B2 (looks classic).
Ref: Locals.
Directions: Near Boone. Ask locals. One mi. up Winkler's Creek Road, 50 yd. above reservoir.

13 The Knob Boulders (aka Howard's Knob) (closed) ✫✫✫✫
A great bouldering area with a variety of more than 200 boulder problems on solid, mostly 25' metamorphic overhanging, dark rock in the Appalachian forest. Great landings. Numerous dynos. Long, classic traverses (>V6). Spring–autumn. Private land.
Classics: Base Crack V0, Two Fingers V0, The Chain V2, Thumblock V3, Poppy Pitch V4, Metalica Traverse V5, Heinous Rock V2-V6.
Ref: J. Henson; C [147, 140(11/93)]; Sherman's *Stone Crusade;* Guidebook: Henson topo.

Directions: Near Boone. On Blue Ridge Pkwy. Access problems. Ask local climbers or at rock-climbing shop if open. From Boone, The Knob Boulders are northeast of town, north off Hwy. 321.

14 Blowing Rock Boulders ☆☆☆☆

A variety of classic 25′ boulder problems (approximately one hundred) just below the crest of the Blue Ridge Mountains. Good landings. NPS camping on Blue Ridge Pkwy., 2 3/10 mi. south of junction BRP/Hwy. 221. Autumn–spring. Private land/NPS.

Classics: 45M-! and Classic Wall problems, Sporty V0, Reach and Lunge V3, Maddox Wall Testpiece V5, Roof of Death V5, Raw Terror V6, Desperate Bitch V7.

Ref: J. Padden; C 147; Sherman's *Stone Crusade;* Guidebook: Henson topo.

Directions: From Blowing Rock (just south of Boone), go south 1 7/10 mi. on Hwy. 221. Park at rest area. Follow trail ten minutes southwest out of parking lot. The trail starts at the far end of the parking area (the end closest to saddle hills) and leads straight to the boulders. This is the only trail used now, as the other was causing potential access problems.

15 Morphine-Endorphine Wall ☆☆☆

Fifteen classic 60′ quartzite sport climbs (5.10 and up). Autumn. Private land.

Classics: Last Glitch Effort 12a/b.

Ref: Locals; Guidebook: Cater's *Sport Crags of the East.*

Directions: From Blowing Rock go south 14 mi. on Hwy. 221. Look left for pulloff with NO DUMPING sign. Walk across road and up trail one minute to Morphine-Endorphine Wall . . . recommended area for those afraid of bulking up legs.

16 GM☆-(Grandfather Mountain Area) Grandfather Mountain ☆☆☆☆☆

Best summer climbing in North Carolina. Many good 150′ quartzite cragging areas, but unfortunately Shiprock is the only one legally open (as of 1992). Closed due to protection of several endangered species. Owned by the Nature Conservancy. Boone has many good eateries: for breakfast, The Bagelry, Melanie's (natural foods); more beer, Murphy's/ Savanna Joe's; Tumbleweed for microbrews, chips, carbo reloads. Klondike laundry, Red Onion salad bar; natural food stores: Razzberry's, Bare Essentials. Summer/autumn. Private land. USFS–Pisgah NF, (828) 652-2144.

Ref: C [189-32, 122]; Guidebook: Kelley's *The Climber's Guide to North Carolina.*

Directions: From Boone wend south on Blue Ridge Pkwy. Climbing is atop Grandfather Mountain (closed). The Boone Bowl Area describes a crag-studded area from Grandfather Mountain to Boone east along Hwy. 105. Bushwhack craghopping requires tree jumping to and fro to reach scattered crags. Check with locals.

17 GM-Indian Rock (closed) ☆☆☆☆

Satellite 100′ quartzite crag west of Ship Rock known as "The Undiscovered Indian." Beautiful climbing. The Jewels Area (closed) is fifteen to twenty minutes above Indian Rock. Ten routes 5.9-5.11+. Unrepeated routes. Buy hiking permit. Summer–autumn. Private land.

Classics: Stingray 10d, Mako 10+, Catfish 11+, Fishhead Sandwich 11d.

Ref: Guidebook: Kelley's *The Climber's Guide to North Carolina.*

Directions: From Linville wind north on Blue Ridge Pkwy. to parking area at third Wilson Creek Overlook. (Ship Rock is west back 1/4 mi. on left.) Hike west approximately 3/4 mi. on road by going uphill on Tanawna Trail (Wilson Creekbed), then bearing right. Indian Rock is the first of three roadside crags coming from Grandfather Mountain followed by Ship Rock, then Pilot Knob.

18 GM–Ship Rock ☆☆☆☆

Possibly the best cool summer climbing area in the South. This southwest-facing, 150′ quartzite crag is a beauty of the Blue Ridge Pkwy. Autumn–spring. NPS.

Classics: Boardwalk 8, Airly Gardens 9+, Linn Cove Lullaby 10a, Harpoon 10-, Special Forces 11-R, Anguish of Captain Bly 11, The Broach 11d, Razor Boy 12, The Link 12, Alternative Man 12c.

Ref: C [189-32, 108]; Guidebook: Kelley's *The Climber's Guide to North Carolina.*

Directions: From Linville meander north on Blue Ridge Pkwy. to parking area at Wilson Creek Overlook. Hike south approximately 1/2 mi. on road past the bridge to Ship Rock. Access sensitive.

19 GM–Pilot Knob (closed) ☆☆☆☆

Hear about the three eggs? Two bad. What a shame these 60′ quartzite eggs are locked up. For 5.10 climbers and up, these are super-good overhanging routes featuring difficult short testpieces. Summer–autumn. Private and government land.

Classics: No Thugs 11, The Big Hein 12+, Network Nine 12d.

Ref: P. Jarrard; Guidebook: Kelley's *The Climber's Guide to North Carolina.*

Directions: From Linville glide north on Blue Ridge Pkwy. past Grandfather Mountain. Park at Raven Rocks Overlook. Hike north uphill ten minutes to Pilot Knob. It is now closed.

20 GM–Mildred Boulders (closed) ☆☆☆

Small area of 20′ sylvan roadside quartzite boulders. Like a Polaroid camera, it takes about one minute to get the picture of the problems here. Summer. Private land.

Classics: "500 feet too short" V2, Hall of Horrors V3/4, Henson Testpiece V5.

Ref: Guidebook: Kelley's *The Climber's Guide to North Carolina.*

Directions: Just south of Grandfather Mountain on Hwy. 221, shortly south of the intersection of Blue Ridge Pkwy. and Hwy. 221S. On left. Mildred Boulders are roadside boulders. Faces west.

21 LG☆-(Linville Gorge) Sitting Bear ☆☆/Overview ☆☆☆☆☆

Linville Gorge is a 14-mile gorge of steep, metamorphosed rock buttresses reaching 600′ in height. Many crags line the East Coast's deep (2,000′), rugged, and highly scenic wilderness gorge. A base-camp area of Outward Bound School. Sitting Bear is a pillar on same ridge as the landmark Table Rock with a handful of 5.9–5.11 face routes. Good summer climbing. Camping recommended on road between Gingercake Acres and Table Rock, not at Table Rock parking itself. Largest stands of virgin timber in North Carolina. Raptor restrictions January–July. Summer– autumn. Free camping. USFS-Pisgah NF, (704) 652-2144.

Classics: Helmet Buttress Wall, The Amphitheater.

Ref: C [174-108, 91, 68, 63, 50]; Guidebooks: Kelley's *The Climber's Guide to North Carolina*, Harlin's *East*, Hall's *Southern Rock: A Climber's Guide*, Price's *Carolinas Climber's Guide*.

Directions: From Morgantown go 21 mi. north on Hwy. 181. Turn left at sign for Gingercake Acres on dirt road. For Sitting Bear: Go approximately 1 mi., pull off on right, and park by a stream running under road. Walk up hill through orchard to ridge. Stroll north for approximately fifteen minutes. For other Linville Gorge areas: Continue down road to Table Rock parking area.

22 LG–Hawksbill ☆☆☆

Shady, summer 300′ granite crag for the intermediate and expert climber. More than forty routes, many of which overhang. Spring-autumn. Free camping. USFS-Pisgah NF, (704) 652-2144.

Classics: Hawksbill Traverse 9, Lost in Space 10, Time Avenger 10d, Fat Lady 11b, Encore 11c, The Diving Board 11d, No Funk . . . 12, Ice Cream Direct 12c, Conventional Warfare 12d.

Ref: Guidebooks: Kelley's *The Climber's Guide to North Carolina*, Harlin's *East*, Hall's *Southern Rock: A Climber's Guide*.

Directions: From Morgantown go 21 mi. north on Hwy. 181. Turn left at sign for Gingercake Acres on dirt road. Go approximately 2 mi., pulloff on left by wood bumpers. Hop across road and follow trail uphill for approximately fifteen minutes. At flat spot, turn left for a ways to a right onto a less obvious trail down to the base of Hawksbill. This area is also on same ridge as Table Rock.

23 LG-Table Rock ☆☆☆☆

The most popular beginner/intermediate 325′ cliff at Linville Gorge. Shortest approach at Linville and thus the most visited cliff in the Gorge. Bring water and supplies. Home to the North Carolina Outward Bound School. Spring-autumn. Free camping. USFS-Pisgah NF, (704) 652-2144.

Classics: Jim Dandy 4, Peek-A-Boo 5, Skip to My Lou 6, Helmet Buttress 6, Blood, Sweat, Tears 7, True Grit 8+, Cracker Jack 8, Second Stanza 9, Look Ma no Bolts 10, On Misty Edge 11c, Peterbuilt 12.

Ref: C 75; Guidebooks: Kelley's *The Climber's Guide to North Carolina*, Harlin's *East*, Hall's *Southern Rock: A Climber's Guide*, Price's *Carolinas Climber's Guide*.

Directions: From Morgantown go 21 mi. north on Hwy. 181. Turn left at sign for Gingercake Acres on dirt road. Go approximately 8 ½ mi. to Table Rock parking area. Take obvious trail to the right. (North Carolina Wall is to left.) Little Table Rock and Devil's Cellar are smaller satellite cliffs below Table Rock proper.

24 LG-The Chimneys ☆☆☆

A 50′ granite crag toprope and kids' teaching area. Spring-autumn. Free camping. USFS-Pisgah NF, (704) 652-2144.

Classics: 5.4–5.5 topropes, The Humbler, The Tumbler.

Ref: Guidebooks: Kelley's *The Climber's Guide to North Carolina*, Harlin's *East*, Hall's *Southern Rock: A Climber's Guide*.

Directions: From Morgantown go 21 mi. north on Hwy. 181. Turn left at sign for Gingercake Acres on dirt road. Go approximately 8 ½ mi. to Table Rock parking area. Take main trail to the left. The Chimneys are on the left. Faces west.

25 LG-North Carolina Wall ☆☆☆☆☆

An impressive and popular 500′ high by 2,000′ long wall with only a few classic routes due to the impenetrability of the rock. Approach from the top rather than below to avoid a raging bushwhack. Caution advised in approach gully; steep, narrow road. Lengthy approaches—allow extra time for the pleasantries of bushwhacking. See Kelley's guide for specifics. Raptor restrictions. Summer–autumn. Free camping. USFS-Pisgah NF, (704) 652-2144.

Classics: The Corner 7, Bumblebee Buttress 8, Tarantula 9, Apricot Jam 9+, Rinky Dink 10 Dir 11b, Pixie Wall 11d.

Ref: C [75,68]; Guidebooks: Kelley's *The Climber's Guide to North Carolina*, Harlin's *East*, Hall's *Southern Rock: A Climber's Guide*.

Directions: From Morgantown go 21 mi. north on Hwy. 181. Turn left at sign for Gingercake Acres on dirt road. Go 8 ½ mi. to Table Rock Park. Hike south along east ridge of gorge. Just past the Chimneys, turn right, follow it to the edge of the cliff. At fork, go right and drop down gully to Apricot Jam on right and left for Main North Carolina Wall (rough trail). (If you go left at fork, you'll hike along top of North Carolina Wall. In a while, an alternative descent goes down left of obvious Mossy Monster Buttress to base of North Carolina Wall.)

26 LG-Amphitheatre (Prow/Mummy) ☆☆☆☆

This area is basically a southern extension of the North Carolina Wall. Great exposure. About forty routes with some classics any climber will want to do on a visit. Fantastic scenery. Summer–autumn. USFS–Pisgah NF, (704) 652-2144.

Classics: Amphitheatre: The Prow 4, Open Book 11, Turkey Beard 12a; Mummy Buttress: The Daddy 6, Land of Little People 11a.

Ref: C 68; Guidebooks: Kelley's *The Climber's Guide to North Carolina*, Harlin's *East*, Hall's *Southern Rock: A Climber's Guide*.

Directions: From Morgantown, go 21 mi. north on Hwy. 181. Turn left at sign for Gingercake Acres on dirt road. Go approximately 8 ½ mi. to Table Rock parking area. Hike south on main trail past the Chimneys for approximately twenty minutes. Go right at small pine (with paint markings) to head of Amphitheatre. Follow poor trail down middle of gully. Open Book 5.11 is halfway down on left, high on hanging block. The Prow 5.4 is on left skyline on North Face out on tree ledge. Mummy Buttress, separated by obvious chimney, is farther down trail on left (south side). Land of Little People 5.11a starts high up at base of chimney. The Daddy 5.6 starts below trees. Reggae Wall, a short wall of 5.9–5.11 climbs, sits above Mummy Buttress. A trail on top of cliffs leads southwest to it.

27 LG–Wiseman's View ★★★

This 250′ granite crag is on the west side of Linville Gorge. Spring–autumn. Free camping. USFS–Pisgah NF, (704) 652-2144.

Classics: Double Indemnity 7 four pitch.

Ref: Guidebooks: Kelley's *The Climber's Guide to North Carolina*, Harlin's *East*, Hall's *Southern Rock: A Climber's Guide*, Price's *Carolinas Climber's Guide*.

Directions: From Morgantown go 24 mi. north on Hwy. 181. Turn left onto Hwy. 183 going west. Hang another left on Kistler Memorial Hwy. Go 4 mi. on dirt road. Hike up to Wiseman's View cliffs on left.

28 LG–Shortoff Mountain ★★★

Good summertime area. Good routes (approximately fifty) up to four pitches on sound 400′ rock. Most routes from 5.9–5.11. Maginot Line 5.7+ is an acclaimed North Carolina classic. Camping past a spring. Lengthy approach. Raptor restrictions January–July. Summer–autumn. USFS–Pisgah NF, (704) 652-2144.

Classics: Maginot Line 7+, Serentripitous 7, Paradise Alley 8+, Dopey Duck 9, Built to Tilt 10, Straight and Narrow 10a, Help Mr. Wizard 11a, Pinball Wizard 11.

Ref: Guidebooks: Kelley's *The Climber's Guide to North Carolina*, Harlin's *East*, Hall's *Southern Rock: A Climber's Guide*, Price's *Carolinas Climber's Guide*.

Directions: From Morgantown go 2 mi. north on Hwy. 181. Turn left onto Jamestown Rd. Turn right onto Hwy. 126, go 11 mi. to Wolf Pit Road (may be impassable when wet). Drive 2 ½ mi. to the end. (From here it's a 2-mi. hike to clifftop.) Take larger trail to the left uphill for five minutes. Turn right and walk for approximately twenty-

five minutes, ignoring trail splits until you reach a perpendicular road. Go straight across road onto the "Mountains-to-the-Sea-Trail" (white paint marks) for approximately fifteen minutes to the top. Walk clifftop approximately ten minutes to a spring (might be dry), follow gully (one rappel?) down to base of Shortoff Mountain. (Alternative approach: Hike 5 mi. past North Carolina Wall on trail.)

29 Green Mountain (aka Asheboro Boulderfield or Stack Rocks) ★★★

Unique, green 25′ granite boulders feature thin edge cranks on very solid rock. Fifty to sixty problems. Hot in summer; try autumn. Extremely sensitive access—be low-key or . . . watch out for the gun club! No camping. Private land.

Classics: Johnny Quest 10, Lightning Bolt Crack 11, Blue Moon 14a? (Zschiesche's Route).

Ref: Locals.

Directions: From Asheboro follow Hwy. 64 west for 7 mi. Turn left at Delks Surplus for ½ mi., then turn right on first dirt road going for 1 ½ mi. Look for farm pond on right. Go right on dirt road at ponds for ¾ mi. Park on right. Follow path up hill to Green Mountain Boulders.

30 Uwharrie National Forest ★★

Miscellaneous green rhyolite bouldering somewhere along Uwharrie Trail features nice edges, pockets, cracks, arêtes, and long roof traverses. Autumn. USFS–Uwharrie NF, (910) 576-6391.

Directions: In the Uwharrie National Forest. South of Asheboro.

31 Snake's Den ★★

Small 180′ cragging area. A dozen or so routes, most 5.7 or less. Caution: Top of cliffs are loose. Also, watch out for flying mammals (i.e., bats) coming out of cracks. Camping along road in forest. Autumn. USFS–Pisgah NF, (704) 652-2144.

Classics: Wasp Flake 5, Bookends 6.

Ref: Guidebooks: Kelley's *The Climber's Guide to North Carolina*, Hall's *Southern Rock: A Climber's Guide*, Price's *Carolinas Climber's Guide*.

Directions: From Asheville cruise north on Hwy. 19/23 for approximately 12 mi. to Jupiter/Barnardsville exit. Go east on Hwy. 197 to Barnardsville. Take a right onto Dillingham Road for 10 mi. to base of rock. Snake's Den climbs start from road.

32 Poplar Tent ★★★

Scattered 15′ granite boulders. One hundred problems. Autumn. No camping. Private land.

Classics: First obvious boulder. Red Giant crack: V0 diagonal crack. Red Giant traverse: V3 traverse from start of crack right and top out on Red Giant. Red Giant: V3. Start opposite of crack at low undercling. Foot Floater: V2, back side of same boulder, start at head height under-cling. Levitation: V4. Back area of boulderfield. Locate low roof crack. Eliminator : V2. Very last boulder. Locate obvious crack up the middle.

Ref: P. Jarrard.

Directions: From Charlotte take I–85 north to Poplar Tent Rd. Take right at end of ramp and go 1/4 mi. until you pass baseball field on left. Take an immediate left past the field onto Woodhaven Rd. Follow the road to the end and park in the lot of the Frito Lay distribution plant. It's okay to park here, but don't block the driveway or any trucks. From the parking area go northeast up into the woods and follow a trail below the quarry (a crane is visible). This trail ends at the boulders (three-minute walk).

33 Rumbling Bald ✫✫✫✫

Best winter climbing in North Carolina. Good boulderfield to left of approach to Screamweaver. Beautifully etched, 500′ granite formations. Absolutely no camping on premises. Pay campgrounds nearby. Please respect the fact that this is private land—access sensitive. Closed fall 1993—uncertain if reopened.

Classics: Fruit Loops 7, Granola 8, Chickenhead City 9, Lakeview Slab 10, Breakfast of Champions 10+, Shredded Wheat 11a, Wild Hickory Nuts 11b, Southern Boys Don't Wear Plaid 11c, Spiders and Snakes 12a, Hanging Chain 12b, Battery Brides 12d, Fairhope 13a, Love Wig 13a.

Ref: C [174-104, 142]; Guidebooks: Kelley's *The Climber's Guide to North Carolina*, Price's *Carolinas Climbers Guide*.

Directions: From Lake Lure, at 5 mi. west on Hwy. 74, go 1 4/10 mi. north on Boy's Camp Rd. Park on right past Lure Woods housing entrance. Hike north on trail to Rumbling Bald (which is on left).

34 Chimney Rock

Chimney Rock's 300′ sandstone flanks of rock loom overhead in this rugged, mountainous valley. Autumn. Totally privately owned park. Professional rock-climbing demonstrations by invitation only.

Ref: P. Jarrard.

Directions: From Asheville follow southeast on Hwy. 74-A to the west arm of Lake Lure. Chimney Rock sits south of Hwy. 74-A. This area lies across from Rumbling Bald Mountain to the north.

35 Pearson's Pebble ✫

Boy Scout beginner toprope area and granite slab boulder. USFS-Pisgah NF, (828) 877-3265.

Ref: A. Van Steen.

Directions: From Canton follow Hwy. 215 south for 13 mi. to Camp Daniel Boone. Hike 1/2 mi. northeast on Art Loeb Trail to Pearson's Pebble.

36 Victory Wall/Small Wonders Wall ✫✫

A small 240′ granite wall with routes up to three pitches in the North Carolina highlands. Autumn. Raptor restrictions. USFS-Pisgah NF, (828) 877-3265.

Classics: Fabulous Thunderbird 7, Insufficient Firepower 11a; Small Wonders 10d.

Ref: Guidebook: Kelley's *The Climber's Guide to North Carolina.*

Directions: From Brevard head north on Hwy. 276. Turn southwest on Blue Ridge Pkwy. until junction of Hwy. 215 (Beech Gap). Turn north on Hwy. 215 toward Canton for 3 mi. Park at sharp left curve before stone bridge. Ascend steep trail in bank to old road. Go left on road 1/2 mi. to Sam's Branch stream. Cross it up to base of rock. Small Wonders Wall is approximately 1/2 mi. north of parking pullout for Victory Wall on north-facing cliff on hillside across stream.

37 Devil's Courthouse (closed) ✫✫✫

From a prominent perch on the scenic Blue Ridge Pkwy., this busy beginner's teaching area is also popular with rappellers and tourists. Beautiful, quality 240′ gneiss rock and views. Possible potential expert routes. Uncertain if there are falling rocks. Use a helmet. Nice summer or autumn area. Campground at Graveyard Field en route to Asheville. Illegal to camp on Blue Ridge Pkwy.! Raptor restrictions May–August. NPS, (828) 271-4779.

Classics: Tourist Route 3, Zig Zag 5, Nine Lives 9.

Ref: C 68; Guidebooks: Kelley's *The Climber's Guide to North Carolina*, Hall's *Southern Rock: A Climber's Guide*, Price's *Carolinas Climber's Guide*.

Directions: From Brevard head north on Hwy. 276. Turn southwest on Blue Ridge Pkwy. until 1 mi. east of Hwy. 215 (Beech Gap). Devil's Courthouse Rock is on your left. Park. Hike approximately fifteen minutes uphill on paved trail. (Forty-five minutes south of Asheville.)

38 LoG✫-(Looking Glass Area) North Face/Hidden Wall ✫✫✫✫✫

This clean, 300′ white granite dome, consisting of three areas, is another superb North Carolina area. Excellent varied climbing on approximately forty routes. The north side of the mountain is characterized by classic crack lines and aid pitches. Cornflake Crack 5.11a is the highly touted classic. Its overhanging nature makes it climbable in hard rain. Many hard aid lines with freeclimbable first pitches. Autumn/spring. Free camping on USFS-Pisgah NF (704-877-3350).

Classics: Sperm 9+, Seal 10, Cornflake Crack 11a, The Womb 11+, Safari Jive 11c, Rubber Duck 11d; First pitch of Glass Menagerie, Waste Not Want Not 12, Glass Menagerie IV 13a.

Ref: C [186-118, 181-108, 155 (10/95)-90, 63], R [97-48, 89-136, 39(10/90)-53]; Guidebooks: Kelley's *The Climber's Guide to North Carolina*, Harlin's *East*, Hall's *Southern Rock: A Climber's Guide*, Price's *Carolinas Climbers Guide*.

Directions: From Brevard ride north ten minutes on Hwy.

276 to Sliding Rock parking area. Below falls 100 yd., find trail and hike thirty minutes uphill to North Face. Hidden Wall is 300 yd. left of Main North Face and sports a dozen good routes.

39 LoG–Looking Glass (Nose) ✫✫✫✫

This 500′ granite cliff is characterized by unique horizontal slots known as "eyebrows." The area classic and first route on Looking Glass, The Nose, was done in 1966. Spring–autumn. Free camping on USFS–Pisgah NF, (704) 877-3350.
Classics: Sundial Crack 8, The Nose 8, Hyperbola 10, Odyssey 11, Predator 12.
Ref: C 174-105; Guidebooks: Kelley's *The Climber's Guide to North Carolina,* Hall's *Southern Rock: A Climber's Guide,* Price's *Carolinas Climber's Guide.*
Directions: From Brevard go north on Hwy. 276 (4 mi. past Pisgah Ranger Station). Turn left on Fish Hatchery Rd. (USFS 475). Turn right on 475B for 3 mi. to top of hill. Park. Hike southeast fifteen minutes to Nose.

40 LoG–Looking Glass (South Face and Sun Wall) ✫✫✫✫

The most popular South Face of Looking Glass offers well-protected 600′ granite slabs and good beginner's climbs. Excellent moderate routes. Sun Wall has tricky protection in horizontal slots known as "eyebrows." Also, one can find less-climbed, though good, routes. Spring–autumn. Free camping on USFS–Pisgah NF, (704) 877-3350.
Classics: South Face: Second Coming 7, Gemini Crack 8-, Rats Ass 8, Unfinished Concerto 9, Dingus Dogs 12a; Sun Wall: Tits and Beer 9, Nick Danger 10, Pat Ewing 10, Aerospace Cadet 10d, The Odyssey 11a.
Ref: R 99-46; Guidebooks: Kelley's *The Climber's Guide to*

Looking Glass.

TIM TOULA

North Carolina, Hall's *Southern Rock: A Climber's Guide,* Price's *Carolinas Climber's Guide.*
Directions: From Brevard go north on Hwy. 276 (4 mi. past Pisgah Ranger Station). Turn left on Fish Hatchery Rd. (USFS 475). Turn right on 475B for 1 ²/₁₀ mi. Park. Hike north to South Face. The Sun Wall is reached by hiking left along base of South Face from the large corner route, Southender (or right along base of the Nose area).

41 Bradley Falls ✫✫✫

Easy-access quartzite crag and good swimming. Spring–autumn.
Classics: Fallsview 10, Carolina Lightning 10, Disarmament 11.
Ref: C 114-23.
Directions: From Hendersonville go a few mi. south on I-26. Take exit 28 north, heading northeast on Holbert Cave Rd. to Bradley Falls.

42 Crowder's Mountain State Park ✫✫✫

The nickname "Crowded Mountain" (elev. 1,625′) bespeaks of its popularity on weekends—may be the most popular climbing area in all of North Carolina. Many hillside 100′ quartzite craglets (such as the nearby Hidden Wall with unique huecos and weird cracks). Slimebelly Snakeass Sodhole Skunkpie is a climb worth traveling for, if for no other reason than to say you climbed it—if you can say it at all. Beware local populace with guns. Remove all valuables from car. Check for current access restrictions and follow park regulations. Autumn–spring. Pay camping in state park (919-853-5375).
Classics: Eyesocket Roof 10+, Axis 11+; Practice Wall: The Burn 10, Slimebelly Snakeass Sodhole Skunkpie 5.12-, Black Flag Direct 13; The Hidden Wall: The Snag, The Whining 12a, Slabsters Lament Dir 13.
Ref: C [114, 68]; Guidebooks: Cater's *Sport Crags of the East,* Kelley's *The Climber's Guide to North Carolina,* Hall's *Southern Rock: A Climber's Guide,* Price's *Carolina's Climber's Guide.*
Directions: From Gastonia shoot 5 mi. west on I-85 to Edgewood Rd. exit. Go south off exit. Follow Whiteside Rd. just past SR 1122 to parking on right (state park signs) at gated road. Do not block. (Possible car vandalism.) Hike on jeep trail twenty minutes uphill. Crowder's Mountain State Park crags lie south/southeast of towers.

43 King's Mountain Boulders ✫✫

Good bouldering challenges on coarse-grained 30′ granite rock five minutes from the interstate. "Rocky" graffiti holds a certain "error" of pulchritude. Autumn. No camping. Now owned by Crowder State Park.
Classics: Rocky Graffiti Lunge B1-.
Ref: S. Cobourn, R. Turan.
Directions: From Gastonia it's a short drive on I-85 west to the last North Carolina exit. Go south off exit ½ mi. Turn left onto county road, going 1–2 mi. King's Moun-

tain Boulders visible ahead on knoll off road to left. Look carefully. New parking area under way. (Old parking: Park on grass at side of road. Pick up faint trail to rocks for five minutes in direction of I–85.)

44 Ducky Rock ✯✯
Day's worth of cranking on this 40′ granite formation. Depending on water level either good bouldering or good treading. Autumn. USFS–Nantahala NF, (828) 479–6431.
Classics: South Arête 8, Luka Roof 10, Psychodelic Delusions 11.
Ref: A. Van Steen.
Directions: From Wesser motor 5 mi. east on Hwy. 19 to bridge. Park under bridge. Hike 1/4 mi. south on east bank of Nantahala River to Ducky Rock.

45 Stockholder's Rock ✯✯
Forty-foot granite bouldering and Boy Scout toprope area. Good beginner's teaching area. Spring–autumn. USFS–Nantahala NF, (828) 479–6431.
Classics: Stockholder's Crack 12.
Ref: A. Van Steen.
Directions: From Wesser go 2 mi. west on Hwy. 19. Hike north on swinging footbridge. Go east 100 yd. to Stockholder's Rock. At Nantahala Gorge.

46 Cedar Rock Mountain ✯✯✯
Steep 400′ West Face has been site of renewed activity in late 1980s with multipitched granite routes up to 5.12. Low-angle face and groove climbing on North Face. Wilderness area setting. Spring–autumn. Free camping. USFS–Pisgah NF, (828) 877–3265.
Classics: Toads-R-Us 9+, Details at Ten 10, Miracle Whip 11a, Wild Ginger Root 11, Ghouls . . . 11d, Surfin' with the Alien 5.12a, Passion and Warfare 12c.
Ref: C [114, 89–90]; Guidebook: Kelley's *The Climber's Guide to North Carolina.*
Directions: From Brevard go north on Hwy. 276 for 6 mi. Turn left on 475 (Fish Hatchery Rd.) and go 4.6 mi. Turn left at Gloucester Gap on Cathy's Creek Rd. Go 2 2/10 mi. and park. Walk through gate, follow main road through Low Gap to Butter Gap and then go straight until the road ends. Go left up short trail to base of Cedar Rock Mountain to Surfin' with the Alien 5.12a.

47 Cashiers Valley ✯✯✯✯
Big 1,000′ walls and granite slabs in mountainous forests. This expanse of granite gives one the feeling of Glacier Point Apron multiplied by 1,000. (In 1997 Keith A. Robinson wrote the following: "The feeling of the local climbers is if you can't keep an extremely low profile then don't come here.") Autumn. USFS–Nantahala NF, (704) 526–3765.
Classics: Ask locally.
Ref: Guidebooks: Harlin's *East,* Kelley's *The Climber's Guide to North Carolina.*

Directions: From Cashiers go west to Highlands. Cashiers Valley is granite-choked valley with many fantastic slabs with various access points. Special care should be taken not to trespass.

48 Whiteside Mountain ✯✯✯✯
What do Whiteside Mountain routes have in common with the movie *The Exorcist?* They're both long and scary. The largest wall in the south features bold, runout, mixed aid, and free climbing up to ten pitches in length on an incredibly devious, 800′ granite big wall. Original Route is most popular route on cliff. Thunderstorms from north can take climbers by surprise. Seasonal (February 15–August 15) cliff closure due to peregrine nesting. Camping in USFS campgrounds on Hwy. 64 between Highlands and Franklin. Nice fall climbing. Summer is hot. USFS–Nantahala NF, (704) 652–2144.
Classics: Bungle In the Jungle 10 7p, New Diversions 10, Gom Jabber (Original Route) 10, Volunteer Wall V 12a or 10 A4S, Blarney Stone A4.
Ref: AAJ 97-167, C [186-118, 170-82, 165(12/96)-26, 68, 54], R [75-144, 15(7/86); Guidebooks: Kelley's *The Climber's Guide to North Carolina,* Hall's *Southern Rock: A Climber's Guide,* Price's *Carolinas Climber's Guide.*
Directions: From Cashiers drive 4 6/10 mi. to Whiteside Mountain Rd. Park on left at sign. Difficult hike (approximately one hour total) to south via ridge footpath to saddle crest. At ridge crest, leave main trail where it makes sharp left at sign. A small faint trail goes through rhododendron thickets down to base of Whiteside Mountain's cliffs. Thirty minutes along base to Original Route.

49 Dunn's Mountain
Forty-foot granite boulders. Twenty routes. Autumn. No camping. Private land.
Ref: C. Petty.
Directions: From I–85 in Salisbury, exit on Hwy. 52 south. Go a few mi. and exit left on Dunn's Mountain Rd. Travel a few mi. on this road and you will see a couple of obvious 40′ boulders right off the road.

50 Hound's Ear Boulders
Bouldering area only open once a year for special bouldering contest.
Ref: C 182-55.
Directions: Boone area.

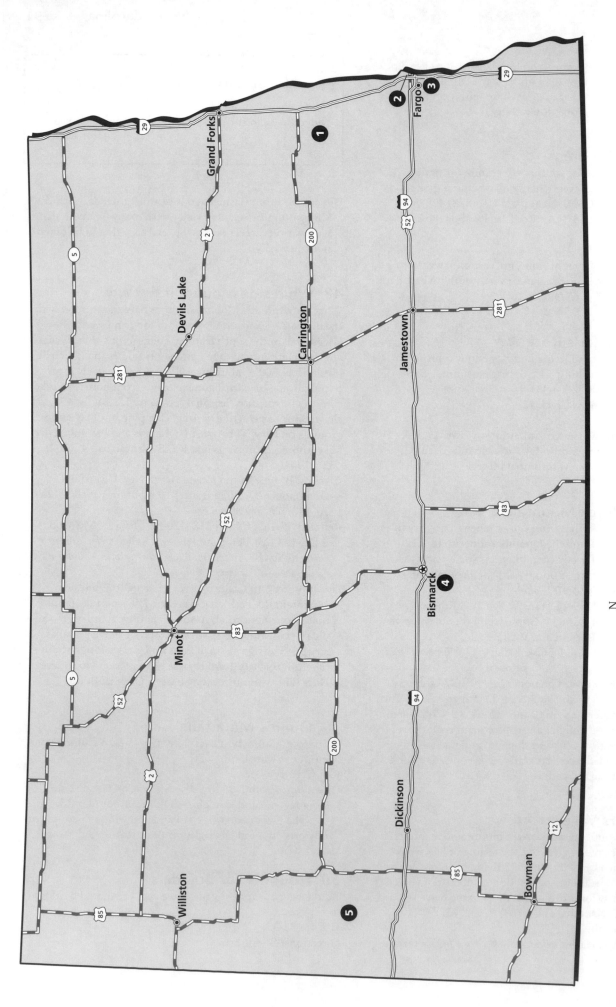

North Dakota

North Dakota

Buffalo chips is all it means to me. —Unknown

For the fervent traveling rock climber desperately seeking sustenance from another first-rate climbing area, the drive across North Dakota will have one beckoning, "Is there a God?" The Fishing Hall of Fame and the geographic center of North America lies in North Dakota. But if you're fishing for climbing, prepare to get skunked.

We know of no natural climbing areas in this state with the possible exception of some boulders, but chances are you may find the structures listed here a challenge. If you know of rock climbing in North Dakota, please contact us at Misguided Guidebook Authors of America, Cando, North Dakota.

1 KTHI-TV Tower ☆☆☆

At 2,063′, KTHI-TV Tower is North America's tallest structure— "The Half Dome of the Prairies." It may be that only a structure in Russia is taller. Now an early-morning stealth mission for crazed BASE jumpers; highly illegal to climb and potentially dangerous to one's health, i.e., temporary sterility, radiation burns, etc. The Red Pepper (Mexican eatery) at Grand Forks recommended for an alternative "burn." No camping. Private land.
Ref: M. Strege.
Directions: From Blanchard, KTHI-TV Tower is just south.

2 Shakedome (aka Fargo Abutments) ☆☆

The main climbing walls in North Dakota. Note that using corners or cracks between the blocks is considered poor style. Urban climbing on gritstone and concrete abutments done in the 1970s. Solution pocket routes on 12′ high concrete. Gritstone 20′ high (traverses, spirals, etc.). Bridge ethics: No bolting, gluing, or chipping. Some good problems—really! Okay, so we're stretching it here a bit, but have you ever been to Fargo, North Dakota? In case you're wondering where the closest real rock is, it's 600 mi. west to the Needles of South Dakota, 250 mi. south to Blue Mounds, Minnesota, and 250 mi. east to the Twin Cities, and don't even think about going due north. Spring/autumn. No camping. Private land.
Classics: Center route on concrete B2, Spiral route 100′ 5.10, Benzel-Wenner low traverse 5.11.
Ref: D. Dokken.
Directions: From Fargo exit I-94 in Moorhead, Minnesota. Go several mi. north on Eighth St. to First Ave. North. Turn left and cross Red River. Turn right at first intersection. Turn right again (after underpass) at Sixth Ave. North. Go east 2 blocks to Oak St. and make a right and follow railroad tracks to river and Fargo Abutments.

3 Fargo YMCA

It's fun to climb at the YMCA! Indoor walls.
Ref: J. Eide 12/97.
Directions: In Fargo at Center and I-94.

4 Bismarck Boulder

A report of a granite boulder somewhere near Bismarck. Can it be true?
Ref: D. Dokken.
Directions: Just south of Bismarck. Or so rumor has it— exactly where we have yet to find out.

5 Roosevelt National Park (Blue Butte?)

A 250′ developed sandstone crag—but uncertain rock quality. Virtually unknown. Watch for rattlesnakes! Summer. Pay camping. NPS.
Ref: G. Rohmer 7/98.
Directions: From Dickinson go west on I-94 to the South Unit of Theodore Roosevelt National Park. Or, take I-94 Williston exit at Hwy. 85 at Belfield. Go north 60 mi. to the North Unit of Theodore Roosevelt National Park.

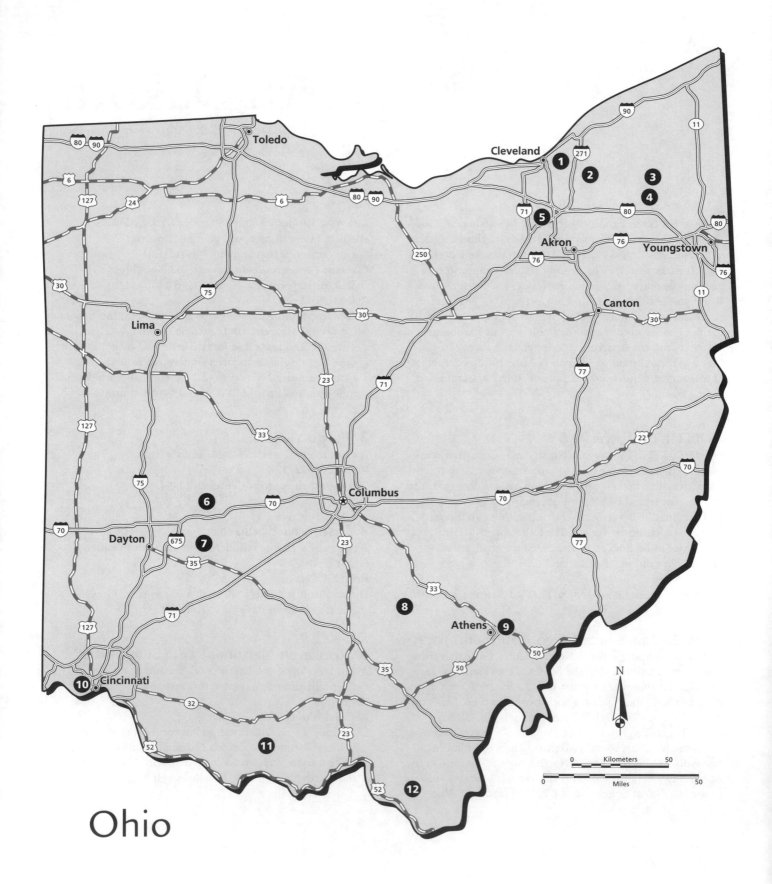

Ohio

Ohio

I fail my way to success. —Thomas Alva Edison

With more miles of paved roadway than any other state, Ohio grants easy access to its climbing areas. Alas, there are more buckeyes in this urbanized state than climbing areas. Still, some fine stopover cragging awaits one at Whipp's Ledges and Springfield Gorge. Clifton Gorge State Park is one of the old Ohio mainstay areas.

What's that you say? You didn't log enough "airtime" while visiting Ohio? A visit to Cedar Point's Magnum XL-200 in Sandusky or King's Island's King Cobra near Cincinnati will prepare you for the longest whipper on El Cap.

1 Roxboro ☆☆
A funky little south-facing crag in a ravine on the Cleveland Heights/Shaker Heights border. A couple of nice roof topropes and some long traverses on this 40' sandstone wall developed by Fletch. About eight routes. No camping. City land.
Ref: R. Head.
Classics: Root Beer Roof 11+, Indica Out.
Directions: Cleveland Heights. Off Roxboro Rd. and north. Park across road from school.

2 South Chagrin Falls Reservation ☆
A small rock-climbing (mostly rappelling) area in Cleveland Metroparks that does have some marginal 30' slippery sandstone topropes and bouldering. Squaw Rock is a focal point in the reservation. A "squaw," rattlesnake, infant, and other images were carved into the side of this sandstone boulder in 1885 by Henry Church. Small walls along and across stream present other challenges. Rock is sandy! Autumn. No camping. City park, (440) 243–7860.
Ref: R. Head.
Directions: Near Chagrin Falls. From junction of Hwy. 422 and Hwy. 91, go north for 1 3/10 mi. on Hwy. 91. Turn right (east) on Hawthorn Pkwy. for 1 2/10 mi. to parking area. Hike down trail in South Chagrin Reservation to Squaw Rock.

3 Geauga/Portage County Areas
Outcroppings up to 100' that are mainly on private land—get permission from landowner(s). Rock is mainly Sharon Conglomerate. Autumn. Private land.
Ref: Guidebook: Bagg's *50 Short Climbs in the Midwest*.
Directions: Crags lie around Geauga and Portage Counties. Crags lie on private and public lands, e.g., Nelson-Kennedy Ledges State Park. No specifics.

4 Nelson-Kennedy Ledges State Park (closed)☆
Conglomerate sandstone 25' short walls and boulders make for potentially good climbs but fall short of hoped-for rock quality. Still, this scenic wooded area does have a few fun beginners' climbs if you happen to be there. Autumn. State park.
Directions: From Warren go northwest on Hwy. 422. Turn west on Hwy. 305. Turn north on Hwy. 282 to Nelson–Kennedy Ledges State Park. Cliffs on left. Parking area on right.

5 Whipp's Ledges (in Cleveland Metroparks) ☆☆☆
A small but fun "street" of vertical 45' topropes on classic sandstone face edges and quality bouldering. Seventy-five routes. One classic 5.6 crack, Hinckley Crack, challenges beginning climbers. The little bouldering wall just downhill from main area offers good, though limited, vertical problems and a nice traverse. No chalk use requested. Cliff named after Robert Whipp, who was almost strangled by his wife and brother in the 1800s. Canoe rental at lake for anglers. Return of the buzzards (turkey vultures) on Buzzard Day (March 15) is an annual springtime event. Autumn. No camping at park, but local pay campground nearby. Cleveland Metroparks (216–351–6300) for required climbing permit.
Classics: Hinckley Crack 6, The Banana 10, Snoopy 10d, Dunes 11, Buzzard 11, O-Wall Direct 11b, Me and Mr. Moozam 12a.
Ref: R. Head.
Directions: From Hinckley whip west on Hwy. 303, continuing past Hwy. 94 to CR 44. Turn south on CR 44. In a few mi., turn left into Whipp's Ledges Picnic Area. Hike five minutes east from parking lot uphill to rocks. There is also an upper parking lot area. To access: Go south on CR 44 from junction with Hwy. 303. Turn left on Bellus

Hinkley Crack, 5.6, an anomaly crack amongst the fine short face climbs at Whipp's Ledges.

Rd. After a short way, turn right into Top of Ledges Rd. Park. Hike southwest on trail for a few minutes to top of rock.

6 Springfield Gorge (closed)☆☆☆

Good limestone rock features overhanging pocketed top-rope challenges. Developed by Mike Johnson. Camping ten minutes away at John C. Bryan State Park.

Classics: Phone Booth 6, Crankenstein, 10, Oh Well 11, Battle of the Bulge.

Directions: In West Springfield. Located on Hwy. 68, south of Hwy. 41.

7 Clifton Gorge (in John C. Bryan State Park) ☆☆☆

Compelling problems at this rare Ohio 50′ limestone toprope and overhanging pocketed climbing area. Once closed to climbing, this area is opened under heavily restricted one-year trial conditions thanks to the work of the Ohio Climber's Association. Climbers wishing to practice their craft in Ohio's state parks should expect restrictions (mandatory registration, no lead climbing) and seek current information from rangers before heading to crags. This National Natural Landmark was cut by the Little Miami River and is 100′ at its deepest point. Autumn. Pay camping. State park, (513) 767-1274.

Classics: Red Spider 5/7, Mickey Mouse 8, Markwell's 10-, Roar 10+, Bong Direct 11, Double Overhang 12.

Ref: C 120-107, S 8/79; Guidebooks: DeGuiseppi's *A Climber's Guide to Clifton Gorge*, Bagg's *50 Short Climbs in the Midwest*.

Directions: From Springfield go south on Hwy. 72 to Clifton Gorge in John C. Bryan State Park. Faces south.

8 Hocking Hills State Forest (Conkles Hollow)

Quartzitic 200′ sandstone crag with some high amphitheaters. Climbing allowed in the state forest, not in the state park. Ninety-nine acres of forestland have been set aside for rock climbing and rappelling. Pay camping. Hocking State Forest, (740) 385-4402.

Ref: Guidebook: Bagg's *50 Short Climbs in the Midwest*.

Directions: From Logan go 2 mi. west on Hwy. 33 and turn south on Hwy. 664. Turn north on Hwy. 374. Turn right onto CR 11 (Big Pine Rd—C11) to Conkles Hollow. The area is located on Big Pine Rd., 1 mi. east of Conkles Hollow. A parking area is within easy walking distance of the rock and cliff face. Use the parking area off Big Pine Rd., cross the road, find the green bridge, and hike up the hill. Please register to show area is used and use the chemical toilets.

9 Pepsi Rock ☆☆

This 35′ sandstone rock has ten routes. Summer. Pay camping. Private land.

Ref: C 149-50.

Directions: In Athens, take Hwy. 50 onto East State St. exit. Follow for ¼ mi., then park on right of road next to the Pepsi Distributor. Rock face is directly up from the road.

10 Eden Park (aka "Old Reservoir Wall") ☆☆

Old reservoir wall in this Cincinnati city park offers a 25′ high limestone traverse that goes for hundreds of feet. An after-work pump area. Pace yourself so you'll be able to enjoy the Cincinnati Art Museum, the Krohn Conservatory horticultural center, and the Museum of Natural History. Autumn. No camping. Call city park (513-352-4080) for permit.

Classics: The Cave 9.

Ref: C 80(10/83)-14; Guidebook: Bagg's *50 Short Climbs in the Midwest*.

Directions: Cincinnati. At Eden Park. Just north of downtown at Twenty-second off Columbia Pkwy. in the Mt. Adam cultural arts district.

11 Adams County Dolomite Cliffs

Reported rock climbing in Adams County on 80′ limestone crags. Autumn. Private land.

Ref: Guidebook: Bagg's *50 Short Climbs in the Midwest*.

Directions: There are crags around Adams County. Opportunities at Buzzard Roost Rock southwest of Lynx and at Shawnee State Park. No specifics.

12 Lake Vesuvius National Recreation Area ☆☆☆

Lake Vesuvius is in Wayne National Forest. There are a few good cracks, nice faces, awesome bouldering, and lots of untouched rock at this 50′ sandstone crag. Ten to twenty routes are frequently used. Most are 5.6 to 5.9+. Most climbers are local. While climbing is allowed, no bolting is permitted. Different pay campgrounds. NPS, (614) 532-0151.

Directions: From Ironton drive north on Hwy. 93 for 7 mi. to park entrance. From US 52 take Route 93 from

Ironton, Ohio. Travel north for 7 mi. to park entrance. Drive 1 mi. to parking lots on main road and park. Climbing is located by parking lots across road. Most cliffs are located out the trails past the dam and spillway around the lake and Furnace shelter baseball diamond.

Other Ohio Climbing Areas
Hemlock Falls
Forty-five-foot sandstone crags with two routes. A reader reports that the falls are a rappelling area only now due to conservation attempts by the owner, the Mohican Outdoor School. Autumn. No camping. Private land.

Ref: Dunlap 6/98.
Directions: Need to ask to climb at Hemlock Falls.
Paint Creek Lake
Located at Paint Creek Lake between Hillsboro and Chillicothe along US Hwy. 50. Under the supervision of U.S. Army Corps of Engineers. No lead climbing.
Directions: From Bainbridge go west on Hwy. 50 a few miles. Turn north on CR 1 (Rapid Forge Rd.) to two designated climbing areas: Harmony Trail Walls and Spillway Walls, east and southeast of Army Corps of Engineers Office on southeast finger of lake.

Oklahoma

Quality is never an accident; it is always the result of high intention, sincere effort, intelligent direction, and skillful execution; it represents the wise choice of many alternatives. —Oklahoma truck-stop wall plaque

In Oklahoma, where the wind comes sweeping down the plain, you might be surprised to find more than just a Will Rogers expression and endless highway. Oklahoma climbers have developed interesting areas for the climbing motorist. A stop at Chandler Park will certainly get the auto-shackled climber to stretch out his legs and tendons on some lengthy finger-pumping traverses.

Hopefully, one can carry this pump until western Oklahoma, where the mainstay of Oklahoman climbing lies. Beautiful scenery, buffalo, and bird life abound in and amongst the traditional friction routes of the Quartz and Wichita Mountains. Don't let the scenery lull you into thinking the climbing isn't difficult, intimidating, and scary or you'll stay longer than planned. For technical difficulty, the "Quarry" offers freestyle slabbing on glasslike granite . . . if it's still accessible.

1 Chandler Park/Avery Dr. Areas ★★★

Long, fingery traverses in a small, 30'-high limestone labyrinth make for an easy-access stop for the cross-country driver. Problems up to 5.13. Avery Dr. area features short and hard climbs—pockets to credit-card edges on boulder problems and topropes. Bring a Frisbee for the fun Frisbee golf course above the rocks in Chandler Park. Autumn. No camping. City park.

Classics: Ordeal 11, Herpes 12b, Sam and the Dialtones 12d; Little G: Swinging Richard 12a; Lost C: J.B. Trout 10, Dusted 13+; Vice Grip: Instigator 11d; Prattville C: Mean Street 13.

Ref: C [127(8/91)-26, 116, 91, 88(2/85)-16]; Sherman's *Stone Crusade*; Guidebooks: Lohn's *The Oklahoma's Climber's Guide*, Floyd's *A Climber's Guide to the Midwest Metamorphic Forms*, Mosel's *Tulsa Rock '90*.

Directions: In West Tulsa. From I-75 (exit 3) proceed west on Twenty-first St., following signs into Chandler Park. Rock becomes apparent. Other areas are farther west ten minutes along Avery Dr., then a five-minute hike. One can find four separate bouldering areas here: Little Germany, Lost City, Vice Grip, and Prattville Crag.

2 Tenkiller State Park ★★★

More than a dozen bolted 5.12 and 13s sport leads on beautiful overhanging 35' sandstone. Best quick-access

The crags at Tenkiller State Park.

TIM TOULA

sport climbing for the traveling climber drumming along I-40. Problem: A reader tells us it is closed now, and if you get caught climbing there the "gov't guys will take your climbing equipment . . . all of it." Proceed with care. The rock came into existence by the Corps of Engineers. Merrill Danner writes, "I have seen the water running full bore over the bulk of the climbing . . . once in two different years." Still, the sandstone resulting from the dynamite is very nice, clean, and vertical with some nice overhangs. Autumn/spring. Pay camping. State park, (918) 489-5643.

Classics: The Dihedral 10, Bowling for Dollars 12, Acropolis 13b, La Famine 13c.

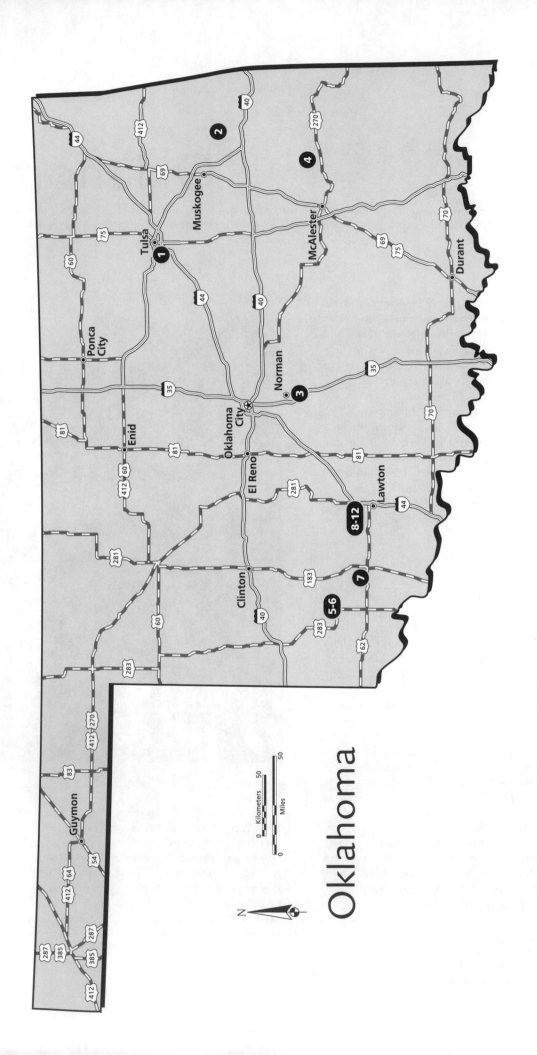

Oklahoma

Ref: M. Danner 10/98, 1/98; Wilson; C 127-26; Guidebook: Mosel's *Tulsa Rock '90.*
Directions: From Vian stomp north on Hwy. 82 to Tenkiller Reservoir and dam. Cliffs with bolted lines are below dam at the end of the spillway.

3 University of Oklahoma–Hal Neiman Wall and Andrews Park

Get smart! Sandstone campus buildering. State land.
Ref: *Outside* 9/85 picture.
Directions: In Norman. At Hal Neiman Wall. Also at Andrews Park, north of post office in downtown Norman.

4 Robber's Cave State Park ★★

Small area of interesting and excellent boulder problems on varied, fine-grained sandstone formations. Most of the longer climbs (60′ max) are in the Stone Corral area, 100 yd. from the cave parking lot. No-chalk area due to high visual impact, i.e., expect an audience of local nonclimbers. Autumn, but avoid the crowded mid-October leaves festival. Pay camping. State park, (918) 465-2562.
Classics: Slider 6, The Corral 8, The Cave 8, Entrance Boulders 1 & 2 5-11.
Ref: E. Anderson 11/98; Wilson; Guidebook: Lohn's *The Oklahoma's Climber's Guide.*
Directions: From Wilburton steal approximately 6 mi. north on Hwy. 2. Follow park signs into Robber's Cave State Park. Campground on road to right. Climbing west of Hwy. 2 at Cave Parking Lot.

5 Baldy Peak (aka Quartz Mountain) ★★★

This area would rate high in any Nielsen rating. For zee friction specialistes, this 160′ granite dome of lead-out routes could be called the "Tuolumne of the Midwest." Interesting crack routes as well as some bouldering at base, especially near campground. Eighty routes, 5.7–5.12. This is private land: Please keep clean and start no fires! Try Luigi's Italian food in Blair. Autumn/spring. Camping and showers at Quartz Mountain State Park (405-563-2238). Private land.
Classics: Bourbon St. 8, Hobbit 8, S-Wall 9, Amazon Woman 10b, Moosehead 10c, Good Guys 10c, Wild Child 11b, LA Woman 11c, Master Race 12a.
Ref: Wilson; C [127, 116(10/89)-92, 106, 69, 68(9/81)-24]; Guidebooks: Lohn's *The Oklahoma's Climber's Guide,* Floyd's *A Climber's Guide to the Midwest Metamorphic Forms,* Frank, Wurster, and Raleigh's *Oklahoma On the Rocks II,* Raleigh and Thomas's *Southern Exposure.*
Directions: From Granite skim 4 mi. south on Hwy. 6. Turn left on E1460 Rd. into Baldy Mountain parking. Or, from Altus go 17 mi. north on Hwy. 44. Turn left on Quartz Mountain State Park campground turnoff (Hwy. 44A). Before campground, follow CR E1470 west past CR N2050 and turn right (north) on CR N2040. After cross-

ing small culvert, turn right on a dirt road and stay right to parking area.

6 YCC Quarry (closed) ★★★

Short, broken granite wall. Closed to climbing. Private land.
Ref: Guidebook: Raleigh and Thomas's *Southern Exposure.*
Directions: From Altus rock 18 mi. north on Hwy. 44 to 1 mi. east of Quartz Mountain turnoff. Turn south on dirt road (YCC sign). Quarry down road with gate (sometimes closed). YCC Quarry is northeast of buildings.

7 Rock of Ages Quarry (aka The Ghetto) (closed) ★★★

Slippery, steep, 100′ granite slabs; manufactured holds; sport climbing for experts. Uncertain if it's legal to climb here. Need parking permit for Rock of Ages Quarry. May or may not be open. No camping. Autumn. Private land.
Classics: Rand's Dihedral 10c, Reagan Youth 11a, Body by Jake 12b, Stonehinge 12c, Z-Man 12c, Adonis 12+, Pocket Hercules 13b, Poseidon 13c.
Ref: C [167-105, 113(4/89)-24]; Guidebooks: Floyd's *A Climber's Guide to the Midwest Metamorphic Forms,* Frank, Wurster, and Raleigh's *Oklahoma On the Rocks II,* Raleigh and Thomas's *Southern Exposure.*
Directions: From Mountain Park slip west of Hwy. 183 to Rock of Ages Quarry on southeast side of mountain to large low-angle dome. May be closed or strict parking rules.

8 WM★–(Wichita Mountains Wildlife Refuge) Overview ★★★

Wonderful granite climbing in a large federal wildlife reserve with free-roaming buffalo. Several fine areas from slabs to steep 450′ granite walls on more than 300 routes. The Narrows, Elk Slabs, and Charon Gardens are all within Wichita Wildlife Refuge. The Narrows and Charon Gardens are best for those with a penchant for steep rock. Charon Gardens is the place to go for good hard cracks and sport climbs, although it's limited. "The only backcountry camping on the Refuge is in the Charon Gardens Wilderness Area (backcountry camping is $2.00 per person for a three-day pass), but only ten people total are allowed in the wilderness at a time. There is no climbing fee. Just some funny regulations about when and where you can camp, etc. The park officials can't tell you where the climbing areas are, just general areas listed here. I stress this information, because we almost received $100 fine by camping where we weren't allowed . . ." writes J. Johnson in 1997. Everything else is day use only. The only other nearby campground is at Doris Campground (tent, RV, quieter semiprivate sites are $6.00 per night as of 1997). Meers Restaurant recommended. Autumn/spring. Access sensitive–ban/restrictions on climbing may have been instituted in 1994. Wichita Mountains Wildlife Refuge, (405) 429-3222.

Classics: Arrowsmith 7, Crazy Alice 8, Dihedral/Flying Nun 9, Wild and Crazy 10b, Aerial Anticipations 11+, Desperate Reality 12-, Nubian Dance 12.

Ref: C [160, C 150-54, 142, 116, 91, 69], S 3/86; J. Wilk's on-line guide http://fusian47.webclimbing.com/areas.html; Guidebooks: Lohn's *The Oklahoma's Climber's Guide,* Floyd's *A Climber's Guide to the Midwest Metamorphic Forms,* Frank, Wurster, and Raleigh's *Oklahoma On the Rocks II,* Raleigh and Thomas's *Southern Exposure.*

Directions: From Lawton romp 12 mi. west on Hwy. 62. At Cache, turn north (right) on Hwy. 115 to Hwy. 49. Turn west on Hwy. 49. The three major rock-climbing areas in Wichita Mountains Wildlife Refuge lie south of Hwy. 49 in this order: The Narrows, Elk Mountain Slabs, and Charon Gardens/Lost Dome. Other areas to find on a refuge map with minimal rock include: Mt. Scott (bouldering/The Rock Pile), Osage Lake.

9 WM–Charon Gardens Wilderness Area (Lost Dome) ☆☆☆

Hard 80′ granite cracks and sport climbs, especially on Lost Dome's south face. Bolted sport leads. Limited, but worth the hike if you're there. Autumn/spring. Pay camping. Wichita Mountains Wildlife Refuge, (405) 429-3222.

Classics: Claw 10d, Lost My Religion 11a, Tap Dancers 11c, R.A. 11d, Serpentine 11d, Slime of the Century 11d, Yellowbeard 12a, Tied to the Whipping Post 12b.

Ref: Wilson; C 127-26; Guidebooks: Frank, Wurster, and Raleigh's *Oklahoma On the Rocks II,* Raleigh and Thomas's *Southern Exposure.*

Directions: From Cache romp north on Hwy. 115. Turn west on Hwy. 49 and motor to Sunset Picnic Area, 1 mi. west of park headquarters on far west side of refuge. Hike west on trail to Crab Eyes and Lost Dome Area, a forty-five minute hike.

10 WM–Elk Mountain Slab ☆☆☆

Clean, west-facing 450′ granite slabs with runout leads. Site of probably the first technical rock leads in Oklahoma in 1940. Desperate Reality 5.12- is this area's testpiece roof crack. Autumn. Free/pay camping. Wichita Mountains Wildlife Refuge, (405) 429-3222.

Classics: Great Expectations 6, Buns Up 8, Desperate Reality 12-.

Ref: C 68; Guidebooks: Frank, Wurster, and Raleigh's *Oklahoma On the Rocks II,* Raleigh and Thomas's *Southern Exposure.*

Directions: From Cache (just west of Lawton), stampede north on Hwy. 115 for 5 $7/10$ mi. to junction with Hwy. 49. Go 5 mi. west on Hwy. 49 to park headquarters. Go south, then west on Indianhoma to Post Oak Lake Rd. Go north on Post Oak Lake Rd. 1 mi. to parking. Hike 2 mi. north for Elk Mountain Slabs.

11 WM–The Narrows ☆☆☆

Steepest rock in the Wichitas. If you're looking for rock other than slabs, The Narrows and Lost Dome (300′ granite crags) are best bets. Autumn. Free/pay camping. Wichita Mountains Wildlife Refuge, (405) 429-3222.

Classics: Kirplunk 7, Crazy Alice 8, Ice Box Crack 9, Dihedral/Flying Nun 9, League of Doom/Space Balls 11a, Aerial Anticipations 11d.

Ref: Wilson; Guidebooks: Frank, Wurster, and Raleigh's *Oklahoma On the Rocks II,* Raleigh and Thomas's *Southern Exposure.*

Directions: From Cache head north on Hwy. 115 for 5 $7/10$ mi. to junction with Hwy. 49. Go 3 mi. west on Hwy. 49. Turn south for 1 mi. on Lost Lake Rd. to closed gate. Park. Hike 2 mi. south down road to huts, then east past water pump to creek in canyon. Follow creek 1 $1/2$ mi. to The Narrows walls.

12 WM–The Meadows ☆☆☆

Great, easy, bolted leads to desperate overhanging sport climbs on 85′ granite crags. Thirty to fifty routes. Also some nice trad cracks. Autumn. Pay camping. Wichita Mountains Wildlife Refuge, (405) 429-3222.

Classics: Taco Time 8, Creek Show 10c, Barter Town 11b, Briar Rabbit 11d, Blockade 11a, Aqua Man 12b.

Directions: From east refuge entrance gate, go west on main road until you reach a three-way intersection. At this stop, go right (north), then take the next left (west). Follow the gravel road that goes beside the lake until its end. Park and follow trails to the southwest, passing streambeds. The climbing is along the stream on separated walls. The second wall is called the Thunderdome (from *Mad Max*). This is the highest concentration of routes that exist so far. There are routes on every other wall.

Oregon

I am so ripped! They should put a mirror over Chain Reaction to see how pumped up I become . . . . —Polish climber at Smith Rock

If you were going to choose one word to describe rock climbing in Oregon, it would be volcanic. Volcanoes or their remains comprise three-fourths of the state.

Not too long ago, Beacon Rock was called "the best climbing in Oregon," even though it was in Washington. Then came the introduction of sport climbing to the United States. Smith Rock's loosely welded tuff made for scary clean climbing, but it was well suited for bolted face climbing. Hence, Smith Rock became one of the first popular sport crags in America.

Though Smith Rock gets most of the attention in Oregon, the state is spiced with climbing areas. If a week at Smith has you yearning to pull on some solid stone, try the good basalt in the nearby Crooked River Gorge. This gorge is unique in that climbers have respected varying styles there; one side is reserved for traditional ground-up climbing, while on the other side anything goes. Also, in the Bend area is unusual bouldering inside lava tubes.

The Eugene area is well known in the world of track and field for its runners. In the climbing world, it can claim Skinner Butte as the most contrived crag in the world. Plus, just up the road, adventure climbers will discover a goulash of formations at the Menagerie or Wolf Rock to please their crotchets.

While the state is not blessed with the quality of alpine rock supermarkets like that of California's Sierra Range, one may find stores of rock (albeit crumbly) in the Cascades. The Central Cascades have incredible amounts of snow six months of the year pouring in at 180′ of annual precipitation. It, along with most of the state, is an area of volcanic flavors featuring andesite, basalt, and rhyolite cones. Farther east, in the central arid deserts, lie Stein's Pillars, The Steeple, and the Twickenham/Clarno Areas. And to the north, the Columbia River Gorge shows climbers more of this volcanic behavior.

Still, other areas add variety to Oregon's climbing menu. For the discerning rock gourmand, the Wallowa and Blue Mountains serve one of Oregon's more flavorful granitic meals and afford fine fares at any price.

Finally, a trip to Oregon coast provides climbers a chance to stand on a precipice, view the wildest rocks they've seen anywhere, and know they'll never want to partake of them. Sodden sea stacks and sometimes grotesque shoreline features provide only the esoteric personality with the quintes-sential "je ne sais quoi" climbing experience.

So when it comes to Oregon climbing, bon appetit!

1 Rocky Butte ★★

Popular, accessible, after-work 70′ basalt toprope crags offer fine climbs on Toothpick and Breakfast Crack Walls, despite traffic noise, poison oak, and litter. One hundred routes. Two areas: On top (artificial rock wall) and northeast side (rock quarry—toprope cracks). Hard one-pitch crack climbs. Possibly Oregon's first 5.12—Close to the Edge. Best routes in the 5.10–5.11 ranges. Portland eats: B. Moloch-Heathman Bakery, Jake's Crawfish, Macheesmo Mouse, Hamburger Mary's, Tad's Chicken 'n' Dumplins. Spring/autumn. No camping. City park.

Classics: Blueberry Jam 9, Emotional Rescue 10b, White Rabbit 10b, Blackberry Jam 10b, Birds of Paradise 10d, Wizard 11a, Crack Warrior 11b, Phylynx 11b, Toothpick 11c, Close to the Edge 12-.

Ref: C [111, 54]; Guidebooks: Olson's *Portland Rock Climbs*, Pajunas's *Rocky Butte Quarry Guide*.

Directions: Northeast Portland. Take I-84 east. Exit Eighty-second Ave. (eastbound), driving north. At junction of Freemont and Eighty-second, turn right for ½ mi. (the road curves north and becomes Ninety-first St.). Cliffs are found on north side of road near Bible Temple Church. Faces north. Several dirt pullouts offer parking. Bouldering traverses at the top of Rocky Butte.

2 Broughton Bluff (aka Troutdale Head) in Lewis and Clark State Park ★★★

Thirteen separate cliffs of 150′ basaltic lava rock overlooking Sandy River ascended as early as the 1950s. Mostly short routes, occasionally made into two pitches. Winter climbing. Spring/autumn. Pay camping. State park/private land.

Classics: The Sickle 8, Loose Block Overhang 9, Gandalf's Grip 9+, Classic Crack 9+, Sheer Stress 10a, Physical Graffiti 10d, Demian 10d, Superstition 11a, Critical Mass 11c, E. Pluribus Pinhead 11d, Dracula 12a, Bloodline 12b, Bad Omen 12b.

Ref: C 73(6/82); Guidebooks: Olson's *Portland Rock Climbs*, Jones's *Columbia River Gorge: A Complete Guide*, Thomas's

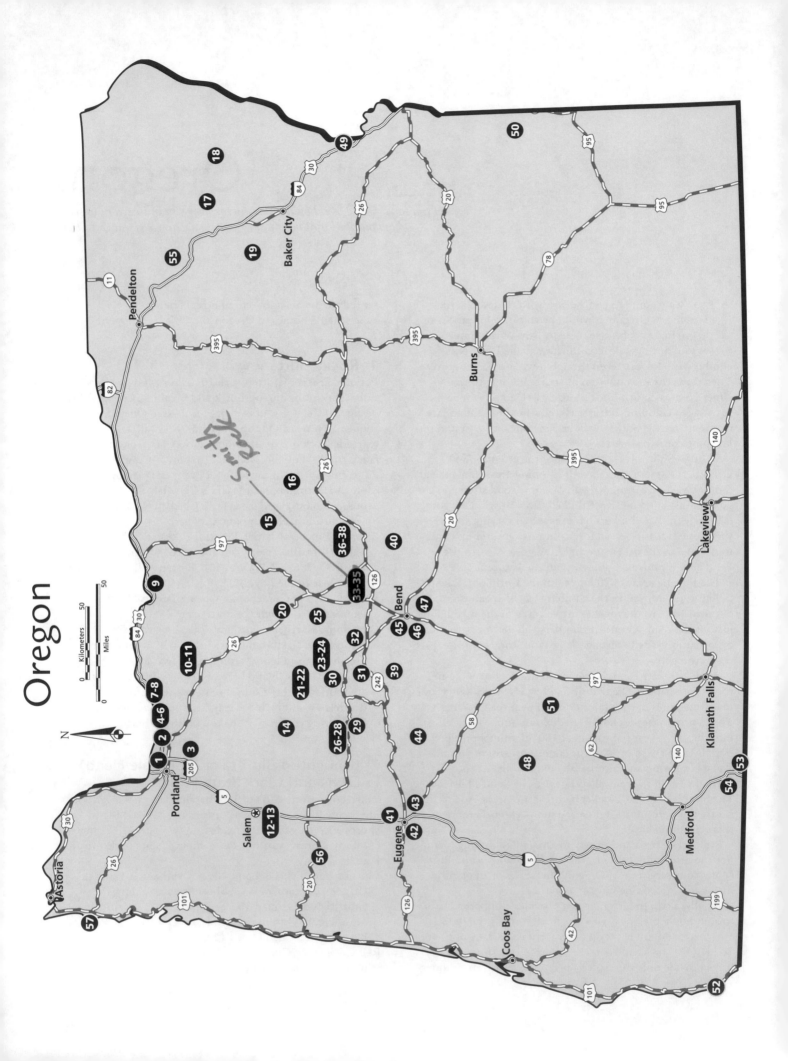

Oregon

Oregon Rock, Dodge's *A Climbing Guide to Oregon.*

Directions: From Portland's eastern outskirts take exit 18 off I-84 at Lewis and Clark State Park (signs). Go under railroad tracks. Park at day-use area for Broughton Bluff. Faces southeast. Hike south on trail to path angling right to Hanging Gardens Wall (The Sickle 8). Other walls include: North Face (Gandalf's Grip 9+), Red Wall (Classic Crack 9+/Pinhead 11d), and Bat Wall (Dracula 12a).

3 Carver Bridge Cliff and Madrone Wall ✯✯✯

Carver Bridge Cliff: Bunches of sport climbs and cracks on a scrubbed, private basalt cliff. Please respect private land. Madrone Wall: A light-duty, hardman wall developed in the late 1980s. Also known as the Hardscrabble Rock Quarry, this crag sheds beautiful views of the Clackamas River Valley. About one hundred steep routes. Please sign release waiver available through the Portland Rock Gym. Ants, wasps, and poison oak in summer—visit in winter. No camping. Private land.

Classics: Carver Bridge Cliff: New Generation 9+, Scotch and Soda 10d, Smerk 11a, Notorious 11b, Uncola 11c, Chariots of Fire 11c, Rites of Passage 11c, Sea of Holes 12a, Wally Street 12a, Angular Motion 12a; Madrone Wall: Ant Abuse 10a, Sheesh 10c, Mr. Noodle Arms 11b, Beam Me Up, Mr. Scott 11, Divine Wind 11c, Wild Things 11d, Full Spank Mode 12a, Shining Wall 12a, Scott Free 12b.

Ref: R 72-30; Guidebook: Olson's *Portland Rock Climbs.*

Directions: Southeast of Portland. 1) Carver Bridge Cliff: Ask at Portland Rock Gym. Must be a member of the Portland Rock Gym or sign waiver. Faces east. 2) Madrone Wall: Just 2 2/10 mi. east of little community of Carver, park on highway shoulder at gate with No Shooting signs. Hike to clearing at Shining Wall. Left trail goes to Madrone Wall, right to Hardscrabble Wall. Faces west.

4 Crown Point State Park ●

Vista House atop 300' basalt bluffs uphill across railroad tracks from Rooster Rock State Park. First recorded ascent, 1950. Mixed dirt and rock scrambling. Crown Point rises 700' above the river. Scenic views of the Columbia River Gorge. Two climbs of note: Zucchini Route (Northeast Face, 5.6 A2) and West Chimney 5.5. Bring hard hats. Autumn. No camping. State park, (503) 695-2240.

Ref: OB 23(10/75); Schneider's *Hiking the Columbia River Gorge;* Guidebooks: Olson's *Portland Rock Climbs,* Jones's *Columbia River Gorge: A Complete Guide,* Dodge's *A Climbing Guide to Oregon,* Nenburger's *A Climber's Guide to Columbia River Gorge.*

Directions: From Portland go on I-84 approximately 20 mi. east of town to Crown Point State Park.

5 Rooster Rock State Park ✯✯

Popular 100' basalt pinnacle standing in Columbia River. Several easy routes climbed in 1917 by Ray Conway, a Mazama mountaineer, and even earlier by daring sailors. South Face route is reasonably stable. Historic 1805 Lewis and Clark campsite. Spring–autumn. Day-use fee $3.00. No camping. State park, (800) 551-6949.

Classics: South Face 4.

Ref: C 73(6/82), OB 23(10/75); Guidebooks: Olson's *Portland Rock Climbs,* Jones's *Columbia River Gorge: A Complete Guide,* Dodge's *A Climbing Guide to Oregon.*

Directions: From Portland (approximately 25 mi. to Rooster Rock State Park), crow east on I-84 at exit 25. Park at Rooster Rock State Park. Hike 300' north of highway.

6 Pillars of Hercules (aka Speelyei's Columns) ✯✯

Collection of chimney climbs on 120' basalt towers and cliffs. Five routes as easy as 5.4. First ascents in the 1940s. Much of the information in Dodge's *A Climbing Guide to Oregon* on Cascade rock and Columbia River basalt is geared toward the rockaneer. These areas may be a big disappointment to twenty-first-century sport climbers but may excite the adventure climber. Spring–autumn. Pay camping.

Classics: Hairpin Spire, Pinochle Pinnacle.

Ref: *Mazama* [10/87, 1985], OB 23(10/75); Guidebooks: Olson's *Portland Rock Climbs,* Jones's *Columbia River Gorge: A Complete Guide,* Dodge's *A Climbing Guide to Oregon.*

Directions: Pillars of Hercules is just 3 mi. east of Rooster Rock State Park on I-84. Park at Bridalveil exit (HM1E).

7 Cougar Rock, Little Cougar, and Winema Pinnacles ●

Theses areas are comprised of 1950s rockaneering routes on 120' of rotten basalt rock. Spring–autumn. Pay camping.

Ref: Guidebooks: Jones's *Columbia River Gorge: A Complete Guide,* Dodge's *A Climbing Guide to Oregon,* Nenburger's *A Climber's Guide to Columbia River Gorge.*

Directions: Along Columbia River between Multnomah and Oneonta Creeks. Park at Multnomah Falls. Hike Larch Mountain Trail past two upper falls for Cougar Rock and others.

8 St. Peter's Dome

Pointed, crumbling 200' basalt turret with standing dirt and loose rock. Oregon's first long aid climb done by Everett Darr/Joe Leuthold and the Wy'east Climbers in the 1940s. Spring–autumn. Pay camping.

Ref: Guidebooks: Jones's *Columbia River Gorge: A Complete Guide,* Dodge's *A Climbing Guide to Oregon,* Nenburger's *A Climber's Guide to Columbia River Gorge.*

Directions: From Dodson float 2/10 mi. west on Hwy. 30 to Ainsworth State Park. Hike logging road and trail to south for St. Peter's Dome.

9 Apocalypse Needles

Fire Spire (½ mi. east of Tottering Tower) is the highest Apocalypse Needle and was first ascended in 1953. Tottering Tower was first ascended in 1963. Other volcanic pinnacles in area. Pay camping.

Classics: Tottering Tower, Apollo Column, Fire Spire.

Ref: Guidebooks: Jones's *Columbia River Gorge: A Complete Guide*, Dodge's *A Climbing Guide to Oregon*, Nenburger's *A Climber's Guide to Columbia River Gorge*.

Directions: From Dalles Bridge junction go 6 ½ mi. east on I–84. Tottering Tower visible to south. Other pinnacles of the Apocalypse Needles difficult to see.

10 French's Dome ☆☆☆

A peaceful 100′ basalt crag amongst a forest of evergreens on the lower west side of Mt. Hood. Fifteen routes with fun bolted leads up to 5.12. Giant's Staircase 5.6 is highly favored route of the crag. Because the best routes are on the north side of the pillar, they can be very cold if it is not a hot day. All routes are well protected, but there are a couple of routes with some runouts. All routes have chains at the top connected to three bolts. A 60 m rope is helpful for a couple of the climbs on the lower face. Thirteen draws will get you up almost every route. USFS–Mt. Hood NF, (503) 622–7674.

Classics: Giant's Staircase 6, Alpha Centauri 8, Tin Tangle 8, Silver Streak 10b, China Man 11b, Crankenstein 11d.

Ref: Peter Franzen 10/98; Guidebooks: Olson's *Portland Rock Climbs*, Dodge's *A Climbing Guide to Oregon*.

Directions: From Portland go east on Hwy. 26. Travel east on Hwy. 26 until you reach the town of Zigzag. Turn left on the road on the opposite side of the highway of the Zigzag Inn. Follow this road for 6 ²/10 mi. and park at the turnout on the right. The turnout is a little past where the power lines cross the road. There is a trail that leads down the hill into the trees. French's Dome is about 200′ down the trail.

11 Mt. Hood Area (Illumination Rock) ☆☆☆

Mt. Hood (11,235′) is most often climbed up its south side from Timberline Lodge. This is more of a snow/ice hike than a technical rock climb. The first known ascent was done in 1857. Illumination Rock (9,643′) is a stunning 400′ volcanic rock pinnacle on the West Face first ascended in 1913; called by some the "best rock on Mt. Hood." This translates as "rotten volcanic rock." Also on West Face, Yocum Ridge, a Beckey/Scheiblehner route, is most technical class 5 rock route. For loose rock specialists. Beware: Very high accident rates. Got helmet? Though now a dormant volcano, the last activity was back in 1907. Summer. USFS–Mt. Hood NF, (503) 622–7674.

Classics: Razorblade Pinnacle: Gillette Arête III 10; Summit Trekking Routes: South side (easiest), Wy'east, Cooper Spur; Technical rock: Illumination Rock; Lamberson Butte Complex: Great Pig Iron Dihedral 10 A2, Bag of Tricks 10c, Headhunters 11b.

Ref: AAJ ['92-130, '91-166, '85-190], C 187-44, R 100-78, S

10/61; Grauer's *Mount Hood: A Complete History;* on-line guide www.uac.pdx.edu; Guidebooks: Barstad's *Hiking Oregon's Mt. Hood and Badger Creek Wilderness*, Olson's *Portland Rock Climbs*, Smoot's *Summit Guide to Cascade Volcanoes*, Thomas's *Oregon High*, Dodge's *A Climbing Guide to Oregon*, Mazama's *A Climber's Guide to Mt. Hood*, Sullivan's *Exploring Oregon's Wild Areas*.

Directions: In and around Mt. Hood Wilderness Area, several rock-climbing options: 1 and 2 are northeast from Zigzag: 1) Razorblade Pinnacle (350′): three-hour hike via Top Spur to Bald Mountain Trail into Sandy River Basin. Hike up southernmost drainage of Muddy North Fork Sandy River. Multipitch routes with new potential. 2) Ramona Falls Crag: 150′ cliff 1 ½ mi. up Ramona Falls Trail number 797. 3) Salmon River Slab: From Zigzag go 3 ⁸/10 mi. south on FR 2618 for 80′ slab. 4) Illumination Rock: From Zigzag go east on Hwy. 26 to just past Gov-ernment Camp. Turn left up to Timberline Lodge. Park and begin three- to four-hour hike up southwest slope to 9,600′ alpine peak. Classically unstable rock. 5) Mirror Lake/Multorpor Mountain Area: Crags just southeast of Government Camp (Hwy. 26). East of Government Camp on Hwy. 35, park at Hood River Meadows lot for numbers 6 and 7: 6) Newton Pinnacles: From gate hike ski run, angling right (thirty minutes total) to middle (best) of three pinnacles (80′). 7) Lamberson Butte/Gnarl Ridge: Hike northeast on trail number 645 to 646 to number 600 for one and a half hours (3 mi.) to 200′ walls in photogenic subalpine valley dubbed the "Leavenworth of Oregon."

12 Salem Boulders

Obscure boulders.

Ref: C. Jones.

Directions: Salem. Ask locals for directions to Salem Boulders.

13 Eastgate Park–The Playhouse ☆☆

Artificial boulder with twelve routes and playhouse designed to teach kids climbing. Slide descent. Autumn. No camping. County land.

Directions: In Salem at Eastgate Park.

14 Detroit Area ☆

A cluster of adventure climbs on volcanic chess pieces (domes/spires) on the ridges surrounding Tumble Lake. Composed of andesite "sardine" lava. Classic-looking formations include Dog Tooth Rock, Dome Rock, Needle Rock, Spar Rock, Tumble Rock, Elephant Rock, and Whitman Rock. (Two mi. west of town is USFS ranger station. Inquire there for more information.) Summer/ autumn. Free camping. USFS–Mt. Hood NF, (503) 622–7674.

Ref: Guidebook: Dodge's *A Climbing Guide to Oregon*.

Directions: From Salem fly west on Hwy. 22 to small village of Detroit. From Detroit Reservoir approach via French Creek Rd. (FR 2223) (starts at west end of Detroit at Breitenbush River Bridge). Turn north onto FR 2207 for

Dog Tooth Peak. Turn south onto FR 501 for Dome and Needle Rock.

15 Clarno Group ☆

Volcanic cluster of spires with first ascents as early as 1963. Easy pinnacle bagging on short routes. Spring/autumn. Possibly BLM land.

Classics: Steigomaster, Old Fossil, Hancock Tower.

Ref: Guidebook: Dodge's *A Climbing Guide to Oregon.*

Directions: From Clarno go 2 ½ mi. east on Hwy. 218 to Camp Hancock. Clarno Group lies east of the road. Formations include Steigomaster, Old Fossil, Hancock Tower, and The Bottle.

16 Twickenham Group ☆

Dozens of pinnacles, some bagged as early as 1966. Easy climbing routes on questionable rock. Some of the formations include Twilight Tower, Red-Tail Spire, and Rotten Fingers. The area between Twickenham and Clarno holds many outback rock formations. Spring/autumn. Possibly BLM land.

Classics: Redtail Spire, Rockin' Rock, Rotten Fingers.

Ref: Guidebook: Dodge's *A Climbing Guide to Oregon.*

Directions: From Fossil go south 10 mi. on Hwy. 19. Take Twickenham Rd. 13 mi. west to mouth of Dry Hollow. Turn north for 1 mi. on poor road to small intermittent stream crossing. Cross main streambed northeast to row of towers known as the Twickenham Group.

17 High Valley et al. ☆☆

Quality 80′ basalt cragging on the rimrock of Little Creek Canyon. Nice cracks. A 20′ high bouldering band a short walk to north of main area. A lot of the rock here is like slightly burnt oatmeal—you only want to taste small portions. More information from Eastern Oregon State College Outdoor Program. Spring/autumn. Free camping.

Classics: High Valley: Master Blaster 9, Do or Fly 10; Star Boulder; Grande Ronde: Fletcher the Stretcher 12a, Logger's Loveth 12.

Ref: C [119-43, 114, 100(2/87)], S 7/87.

Directions: From Union light east on High Valley Rd. en route north to Cove until High Valley cliffs are met on left past bridge. Areas include Bridge Crag and Central Elgin Wall. Also, basalt rimrock in Powder River Canyon (may be closed) and Grande Ronde River west of La Grande have good climbing. Faces east.

18 Wallowa Mountains (Eagle Gap Wilderness) ☆☆☆

Up to 1,000′ granite cliffs in a wilderness area. Eagle Cap, at 9,595′, is a major attraction. Areas include Greenstone at Wallowa Lake, Flagstaff Point, Chimney Point at Brownie Basin, and Benthos Buttresses at Scotch Creek Cirque. As for most mountain ranges at this latitude, best climbing weather is from July to September. Excellent rock present on steep, alpine faces. Summer. Free camping. USFS–Wallowa-Whitman NF, (541) 523-6391.

Classics: Benthos Buttress: Cutty Sark 4p 10, Bachelor Party 700′ 10d.

Ref: C [119-47, 100(2/87)], S (7/87, 6/64); Barstad's *Hiking Oregon's Eagle Cap Wilderness;* Guidebook: Dodge's *A Climbing Guide to Oregon.*

Directions: From Enterprise go south on Hwy. 82 to Wallowa Lake or northwest on Hwy. 82 to south on Lostine River Rd. to Flagstaff Point in the Wallowa Mountains. Flagstaff Point provides closest access to the Matterhorn and Eagle Cap. Pack into Lake Basin via backcountry trails.

19 Anthony Lakes (In Elk Horn Mountains) ☆☆☆

Ramp climbing on series of alpine granite peaks: Van Patten Butte, Gunsight Peak, Lee's Peak, and Lookout Peak. Consists of 200′ granite routes up to 5.12 on south face of Lookout Peak. Spectacular views. Ice climbing, trout fishin', and good skiing. Summer. Free camping. USFS–Wallowa-Whitman NF, (541) 523-6391.

Ref: C [100(2/87), 119-47], S (7/87).

Directions: From North Powder go approximately 20 mi. west of town. Go west to south of Anthony Lakes Ski Resort. Anthony Lakes sits at 7,000′.

20 Bill's Columns ☆☆

Good 'n' hard, 100′ columnar basalt crag. Spring/autumn. Free camping. Possibly BIA land.

Ref: Locals; C 73; Guidebook: Dodge's *A Climbing Guide to Oregon.*

Directions: In Warm Springs, Bill's Columns is on Hwy. 26. Faces south.

21 Triangulation Peak (Spire Rock) ☆☆

Steep alpine volcanic rock in the High Cascades. Summer. Free camping. USFS–Deshutes NF, (541) 383-5300.

Classics: Spire Rock, X Spire.

Ref: Guidebook: Dodge's *A Climbing Guide to Oregon.*

Directions: North Whitewater Rd., 3 mi. above Hwy. 22. Hike Cheat Creek Trail 2 mi. to Jefferson Peak Trail, then 2 mi. to Spire Rock.

22 Mt. Jefferson ☆☆

Adventure rockaneering on the second highest peak in Oregon is mainly a loose-rock scramble with a looser pinnacled summit. Got helmet? Best months are July to September in the High Cascades. May need wilderness permit. Summer. Free camping. USFS–Deshutes NF, (541) 383-5300.

Ref: AAJ ['98-185, '71, '66-136], OB 11(10/73), S [3/71, 4/64]; Guidebooks: Smoot's *Summit Guide to Cascade Volcanoes,* Thomas's *Oregon High,* Dodge's *A Climbing Guide to Oregon.*

Directions: From Idanha go 6 ½ mi. east on Hwy. 22. Turn on Whitewater Rd. (2243) to end. Hike on trails to Jefferson Park approximately 5 mi. Routes for Mt. Jefferson via Whitewater or Jefferson Park Glaciers as well as others.

23 Shepard Fork of Metolius River ☆
Easy fifth-class routes on volcanic formations. Named in 1961 for astronaut Allen Shepard. Summer. USFS–Deshutes NF, (541) 383-5300.
Ref: Guidebooks: Dodge's *A Climbing Guide to Oregon.*
Directions: From Camp Sherman (approximately 30 mi. northwest of Bend), go north 15 ³/10 mi. on Metolius River Rd. Campground on left. Shepard Tower is ¼ mi. east in woods.

24 Gothic Rock ☆
Cluster of 350' towers near northwest end of Green Ridge. 1960s rockaneering; uncertain recent developments. Summer. USFS–Deshutes NF, (541) 383-5300.
Directions: From Sisters go northwest on Hwy. 20 to Indian Ford. Turn north on Hwy. 11 and follow series of Forest Service roads north along Green Ridge to Alder Springs lookout for Gothic Rock.

25 The Cove Palisades State Park
Obscure bouldering area near park. Spring–autumn. Pay camping. State park, (541) 546-3412.
Directions: From Redmond blast north on Hwy. 97 for approximately 17 mi. to Culver. Go west from Culver to The Cove Palisades State Park.

26 The Menagerie ☆☆☆
More than two dozen 300' phantasmagoric pinnacles in a Pacific Coast forest setting. These volcanic formations, named after animals, are on a southern slope. Rooster Rock (solid rock) sports several routes to 5.8, with Roosters Tail, Chicken Rock, and Hen Rock nearby. Big Arch and The Rabbit Ears are 1 mi. north. A half mi. east of Rabbit Ears are Turkey Monster (by Dodd, Jensen, and Pratt in 1966), Porpoise 5.8, and The Bridge 5.9 plus several other crags and spires. Summer/autumn. Raptor restriction in effect Feb. 1–August 15. Protected wilderness area on USFS land, Willamette NF (541–465-6521).
Classics: Turkey Monster, South Rabbit Ear III 5.7; North Rabbit Ear: South Face dihedrals, Rooster Rock 5.8, Chicken Rock South Face 8.
Ref: C [75(12/82), 73(6/82)], S [5/82, 6/77, 2/76]; Guidebooks: Olson's *Portland Rock Climbs,* Dodge's *A Climbing Guide to Oregon,* Thomas's *Oregon Rock,* Sullivan's *Exploring Oregon's Wild Areas.*
Directions: From Cascadia (east of Sweet Home), go approximately 10 mi. east on Hwy. 20. From Cascadia State Park go 2 ⁴/10 mi. east on Hwy. 20, then north on FS 134. After milepost 9, turn right on FS 134A. Go ³/10 mi. on 134A, then right at junction and follow to dead-end for The Menagerie.

27 Santiam Pinnacle ☆
Minimal fifth-class scramble on a volcanic pinnacle. Routes to 5.6. Free/pay camping. USFS–Willamette NF, (541) 465-6521.
Ref: Guidebooks: Dodge's *A Climbing Guide to Oregon,* Sullivan's *Exploring Oregon's Wild Areas.*
Directions: From Sweet Home travel east on Hwy. 20 to a few mi. west of FR 15 (east of The Menagerie and west of Iron Mountain). North above Hwy. 20, and opposite north of Jumpoff Joe Mountain, a Forest Service road leads to Santiam Pinnacle.

28 Iron Mountain ☆☆
Picturesque Cascade peak with rock routes on a 300' cliff. Trail ascends west slope. Summer. Free/pay camping. USFS–Willamette NF, (541) 465-6521.
Classics: Maidenhair Fern Crack.
Ref: Guidebooks: Dodge's *A Climbing Guide to Oregon,* Sullivan's *Exploring Oregon's Wild Areas.*
Directions: From Cascadia (east of Sweet Home), go approximately 16 mi. east on Hwy. 20, east of Tombstone Pass. From Hwy. 20 go, ¼ mi. east of Deer Creek Rd. (15). It's a one-hour hike north to Iron Mountain's rock. Faces southeast.

29 Wolf Rock ☆☆☆
Adventure climbs on the dramatic walls of a 900' volcanic pinnacle, the largest monolith in Oregon. Barad-Dür (Dark Tower) was landmark climb for Oregon done in 1972 by Wayne Arrington and Mike Seely via the monstrous South Face. Traditional, runout routes with a big-wall feel may bite harder than Jack Nicholson's Wolf character. Summer/autumn. USFS–Willamette NF, (541) 465-6521.
Classics: Barad-Dür IV 9 A3 (11a), Caligula 7, Hogback Chimney 1960 Route 5.0.
Ref: C [75(12/82), 73(6/82)]; Guidebooks: Olson's *Portland Rock Climbs,* Dodge's *A Climbing Guide to Oregon,* Thomas's *Oregon Rock.*
Directions: East of Eugene in Cascades. Go east on Hwy. 126 to Blue River. Continue east on Hwy. 126 to just past town of Blue River. Turn north on FR 15 and proceed past Blue River Lake to Wolf Rock. Fifteen-minute approach. (Long drive on gravel road.)

30 Three Fingered Jack (7,841')
Featuring steep alpine rock in the high cascades, this basaltic shield volcano is suited more for the adventurist than the technical rock enthusiast. Loose rock—bring some cement. Summer. Free camping. USFS–Deschutes NF, (541) 383-5300.
Ref: Guidebooks: Smoot's *Summit Guide to Cascade Volcanoes,* Thomas's *Oregon High.*

Directions: From Santiam Pass on Hwy. 20, hike Pacific Crest Trail north for approximately 4 mi. to Three Fingered Jack.

31 Mt. Washington (7,794') ✯✯

Numerous routes, two to eight pitches, go up this well-known, alpine basalt summit. First ascended 1923 fourth-class route. This and other Cascade areas are geared toward the rockaneer and may be a big disappointment to the twenty-first-century climber seeking technical difficulty. Beware rock fall. Only year-round water source is Cold-water Spring (along PC trail). Summer. USFS-Deschutes NF, (541) 383-5300.

Classics: North Ridge, West Ridge, SE Spur 13p 9+.

Ref: AAJ '85-190, C [89, 75(12/82), 73(6/82)], S 5/63; Guidebooks: Smoot's *Summit Guide to Cascade Volcanoes,* Thomas's *Oregon High,* Dodge's *A Climbing Guide to Oregon,* Sullivan's *Exploring Oregon's Wild Areas.*

Directions: From Santiam junction of Hwy. 22 and Hwy. 126, take Hwy. 20/126 east to Hoodoo Ski Bowl/Big Lake turnoff. Forge south on FS 2690 for 2 mi. Turn left onto FS 500 for ½ mi. to junction with Pacific Crest Trail. (Alternative trailhead on west side of Big Lake.) Hike south via Pacific Crest Trail for approximately 3 ½ mi. and then east on climber's trails one and a half to two hours to north ridge of Mt. Washington.

32 Sisters Bouldering Area ✯✯✯

Could be the Buttermilks of the Northwest. Twenty-foot volcanic boulders with sharp holds. Got tape? Spring/autumn. Free camping. USFS-Deschutes NF, (541) 383-5300.

Directions: From Sisters go approximately 5 mi. north of town on dirt roads to Sisters Bouldering Area.

33 Smith Rock State Park ✯✯✯✯✯

Once an aid climbing practice area for Yosemite Wall adventurers, Smith is now a world-class sport climbing Mecca: the hacienda of hangdogging. This once-sleepy central Oregon crag, often dismissed by traveling climbers as 300' of volcanic choss, rose to international fame when Alan Watts et al. began cleaning and rapbolting improbable-looking face climbs surrounding the once-popular cracks and corners of the Dihedrals. Of the several walls, the Dihedrals, Christian Brothers, and the 300' Monkey Face tower are main modern climbing attractions. By May, heat forces serious attempters into alpine starts. Check out www.spiritone.com/~summit for the sweet on-line guide. Bend amenities: Cafe Sante, West Side Bakery, Mexicali Rose, Deshutes Brewery (not necessarily in that order). Spring/autumn. Pay camping at Smith or Skull Hollow Campground, 8 mi. east on Lone Pine Rd. Raptor restrictions February 15–July. State park, (541) 548-7501.

Classics: Super Slab 6; Monkey Face: West Face 8, Monkey Space 11b, Backbone 13a, East Face 13c/d, Just Do It 14c; Spiderman 7; Smith Rock Group: Phoenix 10a, Kunza Corner 10c; Split Image 12+; Morning Glory: Pack Animal Dir 10b, Kings of Rap 12d, Churning in the Wake 13a; Dihedrals: Moonshine Dihedral 9, Karot Tots 11b, Sunshine Dihedral 11d, Wats Tots 12b, Latest Rage 12b, Chain Reaction 12c, Darkness at Noon 13c, To Bolt or Not to Be 14a; Christian Brothers: Wartley's Revenge 11b, Dreamin' 12a, Boy Prophet 12b, Rude Boys 13c, Scarface 14a; Bouldering: The Cave, Red Wall Boulders.

Ref: C [182-30, 173-60, 169, 164-32, 158-70, 153-46, 145, 138, 136, 112, 110, 109, 108, 106, 103, 100, 99, 98, 95, 75(12/82), 74, 73(6/82), 72, 58, 54], M [117, 107], R [103-66, 94-26, 93-30, 85-24, 80-28, 76-30, 75-84, 73-22, 53(1/93), 20(1/87)], S [1/82, 9/64]; Sherman's *Stone Crusade, Rocks Around the World;* www.smithrock.com; Guidebooks: Watts's *Climber's Guide to Smith Rock,* Thomas's *Oregon High: A Climbing Guide,* Staub and Carlson's *Red Point: Smith Rock 1989,* Harlin's *West,* Dodge's *A Climbing Guide to Oregon.*

Directions: From Terrebonne send it approximately 3 mi. east to Smith Rock State Park (signs) on Crooked River Dr. More than 500 routes on several walls and areas of climbing, which include Picnic Lunch, Wooden Ships, The Gullies, Morning Glory, The Dihedrals, Christian Brothers, Smith Rock Group, West Side, Monkey Face, Red Wall, The Monument, Staender Ridge, and Marsupial Crags. Crooked River Gorge covered separately.

34 Crooked River Canyon–Upper Gorge (North) ✯✯✯✯

Beautiful 110' columnar basalt hosting stemming problems, arêtes, technical face, and cracks of all grades. The Upper Gorge is a sport climbing area that hosts the majority of the modern action. Autumn–spring. Pay camping. State land.

Classics: Colorsplash 10b, E-Type Jag 11a, Hieroglyphics 11d, Mojomatic 12a, Shark Infested Waters 12b, Playing In Traffic 12, The Urge 12d, Peruvian Skies 12d, Feminazis 13a, Big Tuna 13b.

Ref: R 38(7/90)-28; Guidebooks: Watts's *Climber's Guide to Smith Rock,* Dodge's *A Climbing Guide to Oregon.*

Directions: From Smith Rocks Crooked River Dr., go east on Northeast Wildox Ave. for ½ mi. Park off road before canal bridge. Hike north at canal over spectacular arch bridge about 400' above river. Use the farthest left of three roads once across. To maintain low visibility and thus the area's viability, do not walk along canal. Hike downstream (north approximately 800 yd.) twenty minutes. Rap at big riverbend (anchors). Crooked River Canyon is on left. Some routes are marked from above. Or, faint trail goes left into canyon. Faces south.

35 Crooked River Canyon–Lower Gorge (South) ✯✯✯✯

Classic 110' columnar basalt crack climbs. A traditional area of the gorge. Spring/autumn. Pay camping. State land.

Classics: West: Cruel Sister 10a, Wildfire 10b, Badfinger

ANDREAS ROSSBERG

Jen Goings hanging on with Pure Palms, 5.11a, at Crooked River Gorge.

10b, Blood Clot 10b, Last Chance 10c, On the Road 11a, Pure Palm 11a, White Trash 12a, Try to be Hip 12a, Catalyst 12-, Masquerade 12b; East: Margot's Madness 10b, Brothers Child 10c, Master Loony 11a, Zealot 12a; Drilling Zona 11c.

Ref: R 38(7/90)-28; Guidebooks: Watts's *Climber's Guide to Smith Rock*, Dodge's *A Climbing Guide to Oregon*.

Directions: From Smith Rocks turnaround parking area (past main parking area), hike east 50 yd. on trail to basalt rim edge of Crooked River Canyon. Where rungs are glued into rock, chimney down gully. Hike upstream five minutes to West Columns. The West Side Columns are most accessible and thus have most traffic. East Side, with good moderate routes, is most easily visited during low water by hopping across rocks. Otherwise, long hike.

36 The Steeple, Jannu, and Altar ☆

One-hundred-and-forty-foot volcanic pinnacles. Temple of Jannu and Altar Pinnacles lie to the east of Steeple. Spring/ autumn. USFS–Ochoco NF, (541) 416-6643.

Ref: Guidebook: Dodge's *A Climbing Guide to Oregon*.

Directions: From Prineville go 12 ½ mi. northeast on McKay Creek Rd., keeping to main stem of creek. Steeple is 4/10 mi. past national forest boundary, on north side of stream. Jannu is ½ mi. west of Steeple (possibly off FS land). Altar is on south side of stream at FS boundary.

37 Twin Pillars

Eroded volcanic remnants standing approximately 200′ above the pine forest in the Mill Creek Wilderness. A lot of rock exists in the Ochoco Mountain range. Spring– autumn. Free camping. USFS–Ochoco NF, (541) 416-6643.

Ref: Guidebook: Dodge's *A Climbing Guide to Oregon*.

Directions: From Prineville go more than 11 mi. north on Mill Creek Rd. (CR 33). Twin Pillars are northeast of Stein's Pillar. Reached by 8 ½ mi. trail from Wildcat Campground. Other formations include Cougar Rock to the northwest and Rooster Rock to the northeast.

38 Stein's Pillar ☆☆

Aid/adventure climbing on freestanding 400′ rhyolite pillar. First ascents in 1950 by Baars and the Richardsons. At least three aid routes on east and south faces. Spring/ autumn. Free camping. USFS–Ochoco NF, (541) 416-6643.

Classics: Southwest Face 10d, northeast face Firefly III 11a, east face aid route.

Ref: AAJ ['67, 63], *Mazama* ['66, 50], M 66-14, S [6/77, 12/64]; Guidebooks: Dodge's *A Climbing Guide to Oregon*, Thomas's *Oregon Rock*, Beckey's *Cascade Alpine Guide* (Columbia River).

Directions: From Prineville blast east on Hwy. 26. Turn approximately 8 mi. north on Mill Creek Rd. You can't miss it. Hike trail to Stein's Pillar.

39 Sister's Group (North, Middle, South) ★★

Characterized by snowfields, glaciers, and rock gendarmes. These routes are mostly snow/ice routes with minimal rock climbing characterized by climbing through bands of unstable rock. Included here for its alpine value. Other peaks in the vicinity: Husband, Wife, Broken Top. North (10,085'), South Ridge. First ascent: 1910. East Face 5.4 et al.; Middle 10,047' Northeast Face 5.4, East Face 5.3; South Sister 10,358'—Prouty Glacier Route. Summer. Free camping. USFS-Deschutes NF, (541) 383-5300.

Ref: AAJ '77-173, S [10/68, 7/64, 5/64]; Guidebooks: Grubbs's *Hiking Oregon's Three Sisters Country,* Smoot's *Summit Guide to Cascade Volcanoes,* Thomas's *Oregon High,* Dodge's *A Climbing Guide to Oregon.*

Directions: Approaches: North and Middle Sisters: From McKenzie Pass go 6 mi. southwest on Hwy. 242 to Frog Camp Creek. Hike Obsidian Trail 3528 for 3 ½ mi. to Trail 3528A for 1 mi. to backcountry trails for approximately 2 mi. or more. South Sister: From Bend go 27 mi. west on Cascade Lakes Hwy. (Hwy. 46) to Devil's Lake. From Devil's Lake, South Sister Climber's Trail 36 is most-used trail. Alternative: Park at Sparks Lake and take Green Lakes Trail to east side of South Sister.

40 Prineville Cliffs ★★
Volcanic crags.

Ref: Guidebook: Dodge's *A Climbing Guide to Oregon.*

Directions: From Prineville travel south on Juniper Canyon Rd. to Prineville Reservoir. Go approximately ¼ mi. past boat landing and small bridge. Prineville Cliffs are on right.

41 Coburg Caves (closed) ★★★
Steep, weird volcanic bouldering in West Caves, Middle Caves, East Caves. The East Caves are 100', steep, with routes to 5.11+ and some aid routes. The Whale Boulder has many expert bouldering problems on 14' tall boulder. All these areas are on private land—do not trespass!

Classics: East Caves, Whale Boulder, Raspberry Route.

Ref: J. Jaqua 5/97, locals.

Directions: From Eugene go north on Coburg Rd. to town of Coburg. Turn east on McKenzie View Dr. for ½ mi. For Coburg Caves hike north of road approximately 1 ½ mi. to West, Middle, Whale, and East Caves.

42 Skinner Butte Columns ★★★
Concentration of difficult lead or toproped 80' finger crack basalt dihedrals with specific on-route, off-route rules. Guide at Eugene Recreation Department. C1-C4 contrivance scale. The 300 "routes" will hone your crack skills. For soloists, finger locks or wooden box! Autumn. No camping. Government land.

Ref: C 84(6/84)-35; Guidebooks: Olson's *Portland Rock Climbs,* Thomas's *Oregon Rock,* Harlin's *West.*

Directions: In Eugene, just south of the Willamette River on Lincoln Ave. Take I-5 to I-105 West until it ends at Seventh Ave. Turn left and go east for 3 blocks. Turn left onto Lincoln, going for 6 blocks to the columns below west side of Skinner Butte.

43 Cock Rock ★
A ridge of 50' columnar basalt to the north offers cracks and pinnacles. Routes established in the 1950s. Beware poison oak. Autumn. No camping. Government land.

Ref: Locals.

Directions: East Eugene. Cock Rock is just north of the burg of Jasper, to left (east) of highway.

44 Flagstone ★★★
Thirty (and counting) bolted basalt sport routes on solid rock. Mostly 60 m and two-rope climbs. Autumn. Free camping. USFS-Willamette NF, (541) 465-6521.

Classics: Scarface 8, Apache Acid 8, The Hydrotube 9, Games without Frontiers 10b, Walt's Wall 10b, Sibling Rivalry 11a.

Ref: M. Sugarbaker 6/98, locals; Guidebook: Olson's *Portland Rock Climbs.*

Directions: From Eugene take Hwy. 126 east of town to hamlet of Finn Rock. Turn south on FR 2618 along Quartz Creek for 14 ½ mi. At junction with FR 350, turn onto FR 350 to Flagstone crags. Faces southwest.

45 Awbrey Butte (closed) ★★
One of numerous 25' volcanic bouldering areas and lava caves near Bend. Dain Smoland writes, "Locals said that access is extremely bad, and that people should not go out there. Apparently they built a golf course or something around the boulders, and they'll chase you away if you try and climb there." Central Oregon Community College has a gym, showers, and indoor wall. Private land.

Classics: Classic arêtes and steep pocketed face.

Ref: D. Smoland 1/99, locals; Sherman's *Stone Crusade.*

Directions: West Bend. Just 2 mi. past Central Oregon Community College. On left, 100' from road. Park in main lot at far end of Awbrey Butte cliff. Sensitive parking—be excellent to private landowners.

46 Meadow Picnic Area ★★★
Thirty-foot basalt toprope climbs and bouldering are downstream from parking. Signs went up in 1999 prohibiting the use of chalk. USFS-Deschutes NF, (541) 383-5300.

Ref: D. Smoland, K. Lawlor.

Directions: From Bend go 6 mi. southwest on Cascade Lake Hwy. (sign) to Meadow Picnic Area. Faces east.

47 Bend Lava Tubes (Skeleton Caves) (closed?) ★★
Long, hard bouldering roof and traverses in a unique basalt bouldering cave. Chalk is banned. So special that directions

are no longer given by locals' request to save it. Also used by local cavers. USFS–Deschutes NF, (541) 383–5300.

Ref: C 165(12/96)-45, R[81-32, 78-28]; Sherman's *Stone Crusade*.

Directions: Near Bend.

48 Umpqua Area (Eagle Rock et al.) ☆

Several volcanic pinnacles, the most prominent being Eagle Rock with four-pitch routes. Others include: Rattlesnake, Gartersnake, Dome, Old Woman, and Old Man. Summer. Raptor restrictions February 15–August 15. USFS–Umpqua NF, (541) 672–6601.

Ref: S 12/66; Guidebook: Dodge's *A Climbing Guide to Oregon*.

Directions: From Roseburg go approximately 50 mi. east on Hwy. 138 to Eagle Rock Campground. Several formations lie north of hwy.: Eagle Rock, Dome Rock, Rattlesnake Rock, Old Man, and Old Woman. Pulley cart on cable across river for Eagle Rock approach.

49 Huntingdon Limestone Cliffs

Potentially good, large, 300′ limestone cliffs. Spring– autumn.

Directions: Huntingdon. Huntingdon Limestone Cliffs are on I–84, north of exit 345. Faces west.

50 Leslie Gulch ☆☆

Many steep, narrow canyons of varicolored tuff in dry sage hills. Tony Yaniro's manufactured sport crag area. Free camping. BLM, (541) 473–3144.

Directions: From Caldwell, Idaho, go south on Hwy. 95 just inside Oregon state line. Turn west onto Leslie Gulch Succor Creek Byway. Follow road into Leslie Gulch.

51 Mt. Thielsen (9,182′) ☆☆

Called the "Lightning Rod of the Cascades," the attraction here is seeing if you can climb to the summit and back before lightning turns you into splinters. The summit is noted for fulgurites (lightning-caused deposits). Named after pioneer railroad builder. Thielsen is the central plug of an ancient volcano. Potential exists for new technical routes. Many other rock-type mountains exist in the area but are considered worthless piles of vertical scree. Summer. Free camping. USFS–Umpqua NF, (541) 672–6601.

Classics: North Face: McLaughlin Memorial III 7.

Ref: S 7/71; Guidebooks: Smoot's *Summit Guide to Cascade Volcanoes*, Thomas's *Oregon High*, Sullivan's *Exploring Oregon's Wild Areas*.

Directions: From Diamond Lake parking take Trail 1456 for 3 mi. east past Pacific Crest Trail to north side of Mt. Thielsen pinnacle. Other sides (West Ridge is popular) are four- to six-hour scrambles. Faces east.

52 Sea Coast Rocks

Various oceanside bouldering areas, crags, and 800′ sandstone pinnacles. State land.

Ref: Guidebooks: Olson's *Portland Rock Climbs*, Sullivan's *Exploring Oregon's Wild Areas*.

Directions: Astoria to Brookings. Many abstract rock formations exist along the coast of Oregon. Rock quality is uncertain. For the adventurous looking for the je ne sais quoi climbing experience, the following areas north to south are mentioned to check out: Tillamook Head, north of Cannon Beach (and Tillamook Lighthouse); Hug Point (from Cannon Beach, 4 mi. south on Hwy. 101—tall cliffs and caves); Neahkahnie Mountain (north of Manzanita, at viewpoint); Twin Rocks (near town of Rockaway—ocean formations, need boat); Salmon River Headlands (at Three Rocks—ragged coastline rocks, cliffs 100′); Fogerty Creek State Park, north of Newton; Seal Rocks (north of Waldport on Hwy. 101—pinnacles in sandy beaches); Sunset Bay (south of Coos Bay); Seven Devils Beach Pinnacle (near Whiskey Run Point); Bandon Needles (at Bandon—some of the most spectacular rock needles on the Oregon coast); Blacklock Point (near Cape Blanco State Airport—cliffs, waterfall, offshore rocks); Humbug Mountain (south of Pt. Orford—steep cliffs); Sisters Rocks (north of Ophir—beach boulders and other formations); Cape Sebastian State Park (south of Gold Beach—large monoliths several hundred feet and one of the most spectacular overlooks on the Oregon coast); Harris Beach State Park—Twin Cousins and possibly a 500′–800′ sea stack (all near Brookings). Quality of routes varies drastically. Fixed pro should be used with caution due to sea salts.

53 Pilot Rock ☆☆

This columnar basalt tower offers short rock routes at 5,910′. Summer. Free camping. BLM, (541) 618–2200.

Classics: Upper West Face 5.4 A1, South Face 5.6, West Gully class 3; Pinnacle Rock: I 5.7.

Ref: D. Cole 3/98; Guidebooks: Sullivan's *Exploring Oregon's Wild Areas*, Dodge's *A Climbing Guide to Oregon*.

Directions: From Ashland soar south on I–5 to within 1 mi. of Siskiyou Summit. (Pilot Rock is east of I–5.) From the Mt. Ashland exit, go south on old Hwy. 99 for approximately 2 mi. under freeway. Turn left on Pilot Rock Rd. Go on FR 40-2E-33 for 1 mi. Park at Pacific Crest Trail crossing. Hike south to rock. Pinnacle Rock is located just 200 yd. southeast of Pilot Rock at end of a logging road. Pilot Rock Rd. may have a locked gate across it. The local landowners, Nancy and Marshall Cole, allow you to access Pilot Rock via the Pacific Crest Trail, which crosses Pilot Rock Rd. Park and walk Pilot Rock Rd. to its crossing at the Pacific Crest Trail, respecting the reforestation efforts on the Coles' land, which the previous landowner clearcut in 1998.

54 The Greensprings

This 80′ basalt crag holds twenty-five routes. Watch for loose scree when setting up topropes. Access to the top of the crag is available to the left of the "Marge's Hairdo" formation at the far left side of the cliff, up a somewhat dirty

5.0 easy solo. Highly recommended! No camping. USFS–Rogue River NF, (541) 858–2200.

Classics: Mexican Summer, a stunning 5.11c arête is an excellent climb with good moves and position. Other classics include Hairway to Steaven (10c) and the classic 5.9 crack Sky Patrol, usually toproped, occasionally led by those unafraid of shaky gear and death runouts from hell. Well, maybe it's not that scary.

Ref: 11/97; Guidebook: A guidebook by local Ashland hardman Mahlon Valentic is available from either of Ashland's outdoor stores.

Directions: From Ashland follow Hwy. 66 (may be 99 and alternately known as the Greensprings Hwy.) south from Ashland for about 17 mi. to Tolman Creek Rd. and turn right (it's a sharp turn down a gravel road). The crags are visible to your right up on a hill. Proceed down the road about 200 yd. to an obvious parking area on the right. Hop across the ditch and suffer up the short, yet heinously steep, approach trail, which splits at the crags. Most routes lie up to the left, a few more up to the right.

55 Spring Mountain

One-hundred-foot andesite crag. Fifty routes. Can be buggy in mid- to late summer. Autumn. Free camping. USFS–Umatilla NF, (541) 278–3716.

Classics: Exterminailer 5.7, Welcome to Spring Mountain 8, Flaked Out 9, By Hook or by Crook 11a, Chubby Hubby 12a, Blister in the Sun 12d.

Ref: 12/97.

Directions: From La Grande head west on I–84. Take the "Summit Rd." Mt. Emily exit. Turn right (northeast) and drive 8 mi. on Summit Rd. until you see a sign that says WHITMAN ROUTE OVERLOOK. Turn left at this sign and go about a mi. to a meadow where a dirt road angles off to the right. Follow this sometimes-rough road for 300 yd. until it is blocked by some large boulders. Park here. The trail begins on the left, 50' past the large boulders. Hike 200 yd. or so to get to the cliff. Faces south.

56 Harlan Roadside Quarry

Potentially good 70' basalt crag needs much cleaning. Lots of blackberry bushes at the base of cliff.

Classics: Slightly overhanging route under the tree (5.11a).

Ref: Tim Nam 6/98.

Directions: Near Philomath. Faces south.

57 Ecola State Park

Oceanside conglomerate bouldering. Day-use fees. State park, (503) 436–2844 or (800) 551–6949.

Ref: R 89–90.

Directions: Just outside of Cannon Beach.

Pennsylvania

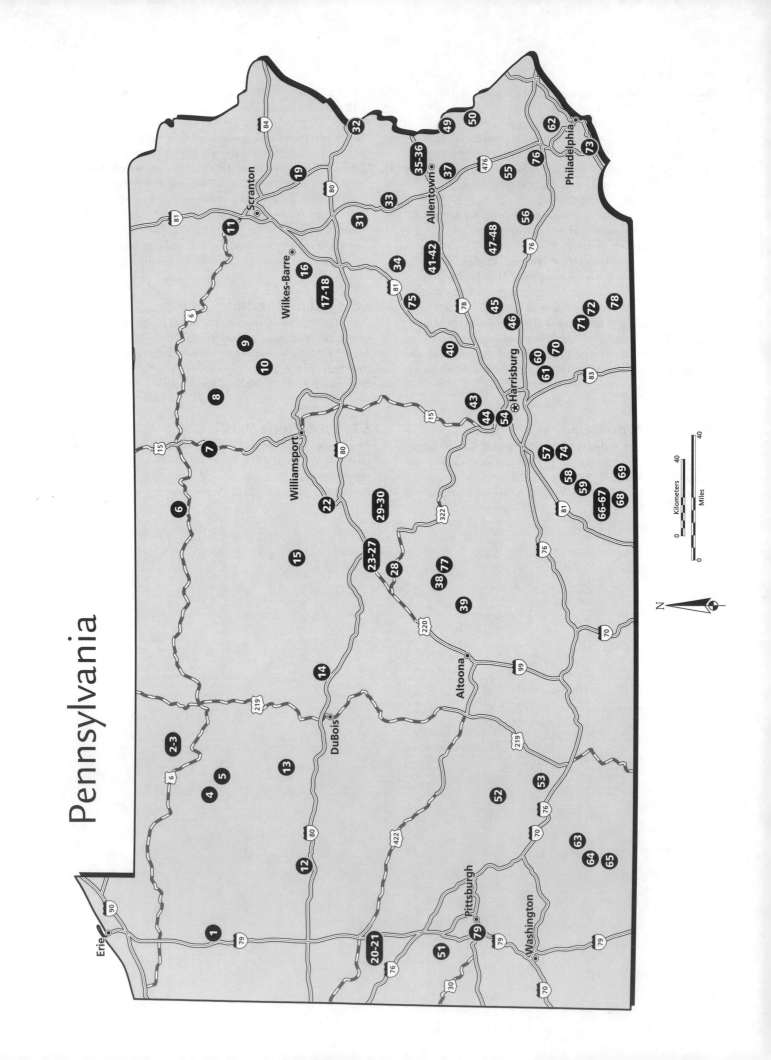

Pennsylvania

Only last week I murdered a rock, injured a stone, and hospitalized a brick. —Muhammad Ali

Rocky. Rocky. Rocky. This describes Pennsylvania, not just for Hollywood pugilism, but for climbers as well. More than four score climbing areas dot the geologically complex state. Sandstone, shale, quartzite, schist, traprock, and limestone form the crags and quarries. The majority of these areas are less than a rope length tall, but they're quality meters nonetheless.

Pittsburgh, America's steel capital, is a tough western Pennsylvania city surrounded by tough climbing areas. The rock is mostly cobbly sandstone, locally called gritstone. White Rock and the Chestnut Ridge area, south of Pittsburgh, are the best of these areas. Far to the north of Pittsburgh are the Allegheny Mountains, with good bouldering on sandstone in a remote forest setting.

Penn State, home of Joe Paterno's perennial pigskin powerhouse, Nittany Lions, is in the center of the state and surrounded by limestone quarry action. Bellefonte Quarry received nationwide attention for a questionable ethical experiment when a half-pitch finger crack was carved in the rock with a masonry saw. Thankfully, this tactic has not caught on in more natural areas.

Philadelphia, "The City of Brotherly Love," is in the east half of the state, as is Gettysburg, where brother killed brother in one of the Civil War's bloodiest battles. For good overhanging quartzite to attack, try Shickshinny, the Pennsylvania Gunks. Pennsylvanian sport climbers have much to talk about now with the revamping of old climbing areas into new wave sport crags, e.g., Safe Harbor. Also popular are the red shale cliffs of Ralph Stover State Park.

If you like to get in the ring with some tough short climbs, you'll find Pennsylvania a good match for you.

1 Meadville Quarry

Quarry climbing. Private land.
Ref: C 69(11/81).
Directions: Near Meadville.

2 Jake's Rock ☆

Someone's idea of a bad joke? Exceedingly limited and soft, 30′ sandstone rimrock. Geologically speaking, this area is known as a "rock city" of Pennsylvanian Pottsville sandstone. Rock cities are common in the Pottsville Formation because it contains massive sandstones and conglomerates that tend to slump away from main rimrock into huge blocks. These rock cities can be found around the western New York, northeast Pennsylvania, and northwest Ohio regions. Designated archaeological site. Autumn. Pay/free camping. USFS–Allegheny NF, (814) 723–5150.
Ref: C 69(11/81), R 79-28; *Roadside Geology of Pennsylvania.*
Directions: From Warren (approximately twenty minutes), go east approximately 7 mi. on Hwy. 59 to Allegheny Reservoir. Just past Kinzua Information Center, turn right onto FR 262 for 1 3/10 mi. Then turn right onto FR 492 for 1 1/10 mi. to Jake's Rock Overlook. North-facing outcrops a few minute's walk from parking area at overlook. A short day's worth of climbing.

3 Rimrock Overlook ☆☆☆

Wild cliffs of 50′ steroidal cobblestone. Just one of several areas of classic gritstone climbing in the realm of the scenic Allegheny National Forest. Fine views of Kinzua Branch of Allegheny Reservoir. Some downtown Warren eateries include Jefferson House and Snuffy's (sandwiches). Autumn/spring. No camping. USFS–Allegheny NF, (814) 723–5150.
Ref: C 69(11/81), R 79-28.
Directions: From Warren (approximately thirty minutes), go east on Hwy. 59 for approximately 7 mi. to Allegheny Reservoir. Cross bridge past Kinzua Information Center and continue uphill to Rimrock sign. Turn right onto FR 454 for approximately 3 mi. to Rimrock Overlook. Follow wooden steps down a few minutes to cliffs and boulders. Faces west.

4 Heart's Content

Climb to your heart's content in the beautiful Allegheny National Forest. Some nice overhanging sandstone formations offer a variety of face climbs in the form of bouldering problems and topropes. Snappy/sandy holds may need cleaning and/or testing. Prime climbing times are those sunny, crisp autumn and spring days when leaves crack underneath your feet. White pines up to 400 years old. Autumn/summer. Free camping. USFS–Allegheny NF, (814) 723–5150.
Ref: C 69(11/81).
Directions: From Warren (approximately twenty minutes),

drive southwest on SR 3005 to SR 2002 to Heart's Content Recreation Area. From Heart's Content Campground go north for 6/10 mi. to Tanbark Trail, passing Hickory Creek Trail en route. Hike via white blazes on Tanbark Trail northwest (to left, if driving from campground) for approximately 1/2 mi. into valley. Larger formations are approximately 1/4 mi. past initial boulder tunnel on trail across creek on other side of valley.

5 Minister Creek ✬✬✬

Abundant ferns and mosses reminiscent of an Olympic rain forest make a rock climber want a minister to pray for a miracle to clean the vegetation off the rock. A clean swath of climbable rock is the exception. Some exceptions do exist on this soft conglomerate. Best not to climb after a rain. Described in a *Climbing* magazine article in 1981 by Eric Guerrein. There was no sign of climbers in 1994 when the author visited. Toprope area. Bring a partner. Nearby Heart's Content makes a better traveling climber's choice. Nice pay campground or free camping away from parking area. Autumn/spring. USFS–Allegheny NF, (814) 723-5150.

Classics: Arête Boulder, Slab Boulders.

Ref: C 69(11/81) .

Directions: From Mayburg drive northeast on Hwy. 666 to Minister Creek Recreation Area. Park across from campground in parking area. One slab boulder in campground. For cliffs and boulders hike north above west side of campground on blazed Minister Creek Trail for twenty minutes. At fork (trail sign), go left to cobblestone boulders and walls above.

6 Blue Run Rocks ✬✬✬

This is a little diamond in the rough in the Tioga State Forest. Three freestanding 40′ sandstone boulder blocks and short cliffs of excellent New River Gorge quality sandstone. Difficult face climbing more concentrated than a can of frozen orange juice. Rusting bolt ladder, pins when visited in 1994. Bring a toprope, brush, and partner to enjoy. Autumn/spring. Free camping. Tioga State Forest, (570) 724-2868.

Classics: La Rocka 7, Gatorade 7 A1, Campfire Boulder Problem.

Ref: Guidebook: Harler's *Climb Pennsylvania*.

Directions: From Wellsboro (twenty-five minutes), drive 14 mi. west on Hwy. 6. At Manhattan (railroad caboose), turn right for 5 1/2 mi. north on Shin Hollow Rd. Park at Blue Run Trail. Hike in beautiful sylvan glade 2 mi. to top of cliff, following orange blazes. Blue Run Rocks are to right of trail. May be hard to see with leaves on trees. Faces mainly south/west.

7 Blossburg ●

Better known as "Chossburg." Flakey, striated 50′ sandstone bands create an effect of "stunning choss." One roof with fixed pins and a couple of boulder problems challenge the advanced climber. Otherwise, this area would better be known as a local rappeller's teaching area. Autumn/spring. Free camping. Tioga State Forest, (570) 724-2868.

Ref: Guidebook: Harler's *Climb Pennsylvania*.

Directions: From Blossburg go 1 mi. south on Hwy. 15. At junction of Hwy. 15 and State Route 2016, find Blossburg cliff line on northwest side of road above Tioga State Forest and Bloss Township sign. Hike up white-blazed trail a couple of minutes. Faces south.

8 Cedar Ledge (Canton) (closed) ✬

The southwesterly 70′ sandstone ledge is privately owned, and its new owners strictly forbid trespassing. The owners will not grant permission on any terms, even with liability wavers. No camping. Private land.

Ref: D. Wonderlich 4/98; Guidebook: Harler's *Climb Pennsylvania*.

Directions: From Canton plod 2 mi. south on Hwy. 14. Park at cemetery. Cedar Ledge is prominent bluff line on left well above road. As of 1998 the cliffs are off-limits to rock climbing. Do not trespass or climb here!

9 Canyon Vista Rocks (Rock Garden or Labyrinth) ✬

For the boulderer only, a very limited 15′ conglomerate bouldering wall of Gunks-like conglomerate offers a stretch stop for a one-time visit. There are other small bouldering/toprope outcrops in area (e.g., above Mineral Spring Rd.) that offer more climbing possibilities. Very scenic valleys. Autumn. Pay camping. World's End State Park, (570) 924-3287.

Ref: Guidebook: Harler's *Climb Pennsylvania*.

Directions: From LaPorte drive northeast on Hwy. 154 to World's End State Park. From park office drive south on Hwy. 154 to Mineral Spring Rd. Turn left up to Canyon Vista/Rock Garden Park at Canyon Vista Turnout. After you admire the sweeping panorama, saunter across road 1/10 mi. south into Rock Garden.

10 Angel Falls ●

Forget it, Frank, forget it! Fractured 70′ sandstone bands offer little except for maybe a beginner's belay/rappel climbing class or ice climbing. As of 1998, access to the climbing and rappel area is discouraged by the State Forestry agency. Overuse has caused erosion, so access has been restricted to allow the area to recover. Autumn. Free camping. Wyoming State Forest, (570) 387-4255.

Ref: D. Wonderlich 4/98; Guidebook: Harler's *Climb Pennsylvania*.

Directions: From Montoursville wing it north on Hwy. 87 to Brunnerdale Rd. (turn right [east] at Camp Lycogis) for 1 1/2 mi. of dirt. Park on right at red dirt lot. Hike 1/4 mi. up Falls Run (Loyal Sock Trail—yellow-red blazes). Alternate parking area is at Angel Falls parking a little farther up Brunnerdale Rd. on left but requires a 3/4 mi. farther hike.

11 Clarks Summit (closed) ✩✩✩
This fine area is closed by wishes of private landowners. No camping. Private land.
Ref: E. Slacktish 9/98, D. Hubbard 4/98; Guidebook: *Obscure Alternatives.*
Directions: Just north of Scranton. Ask locals.

12 Emlenton Quarry
Quarry climbing. Private crag.
Ref: C 69 (11/81).
Directions: Emlenton Quarry is in Emlenton.

13 Beartown Rocks
Sandstone rock city offers bouldering.
Ref: Guidebook: Harler's *Climb Pennsylvania.*
Directions: From Sigel tramp 3 1/2 mi. northeast on Hwy. 949. Turn on dirt road to a trail. Hike along Trap Run, then Woods Rd. back right to Beartown Rocks.

14 Panther Rocks
Crag with beginner's topropes.
Ref: Guidebook: Harler's *Climb Pennsylvania.*
Directions: From Anderson Creek (north of I-80, exit 18), drive 3 mi. east on Four Mile Rd. Panther Rocks is on right.

15 Big Rocks
Several boulders overhanging from slight to severe; a few up to V9. Good if you want to get away from it all. Autumn. Camping nearby. Sproul State Forest, (570) 923-6011.
Ref: Anonymous climber.
Directions: From Snowshoe (I-80 at exit 22), drive west on Hwy. 53. Turn north on Hwy. 144 for approximately 30 mi. Turn left at Barney's Ridge Rd. and follow to Big Rock's Vista Rd. Turn right and follow to Big Rocks on left.

16 Tilbury ✩✩✩
This 75' conglomerate crag offers topropes on fine rock with an impressive overhang 10'-15' long. Routes start at 5.11. Autumn. Private land.
Ref: Guidebook: *Obscure Alternatives.*
Directions: From Shickshinny go approximately 10 mi. east on Hwy. 11. Across road north of Stookey's BBQ. Tilbury is about 10 mi. from Mocanaqua.

17 Five Finger Rock Area (aka Paradise or Mocanaqua) ✩✩✩
Good conglomerate bouldering and 40' cragging. The Five Finger Cliff (Paradise) faces north, then wraps around to form a U shape, a lot like Skytop at the Gunks. There are high concentrations of sport routes at the Library and more than a dozen at Paradise. Some of the bolted routes require a few traditional placements. There is still a lot of new route potential. Paradise has huge overhangs that go at A3ish. Autumn. There is good pay camping at Ricketts Glen State Park (very scenic place, lots of waterfalls). Private land.
Classics: Champ's Chimney 4, Claustrophobia 4; Table Rock: Mercury (1' crack), Iodine (hard sport face).
Ref: J. Lantz 2/98; Guidebook: Harler's *Climb Pennsylvania.*
Directions: From Shickshinny drive east on Hwy. 239 across Susquehanna River. Immediately after crossing bridge, turn left onto small lane before railroad bridge. Park at first small pullout on right. Hike up to visible rock. Five Finger Rock Areas include Paradise Cliff for topropes and Big Wall for leads. Other access: From burg of Mocanaqua follow SR 3004 to visible rock cliffs and boulders left of road. Park at Mocanaqua sewer treatment area. Hike up dirt road to hilltop. Go left for 1/4 mi. Five Finger Rock Area is up left. The locals call it Paradise because it is suitable for climbing even in the dead of winter. This includes multiple areas: The Library, Paradise, and a few other minor crags.

18 Shickshinny (aka Table Rock) ✩✩✩
Possibly one of the best crags in Pennsylvania. A mini Gunks of 60' conglomerate quartzite except unlike the Gunks, bolts are allowed. Fine bouldering, too. Pay camping at Glen Ricketts State Park to north. Autumn. Private land.
Classics: Pizza Route 5, SOB 8, Easy Dreaming 9, Phasers In Stun 10, Colonel Red 12.
Ref: J. Lantz 2/98; Guidebooks: *Obscure Alternatives,* Harler's *Climb Pennsylvania.*
Directions: Near Shickshinny. If you are traveling west on Hwy. 11, take the left over the first bridge after Shickshinny (stoplight at the bridge). Then take your first left; it takes you to Paradise (see Pennsylvania number 17). If you follow the road you are on for 3 mi. (instead of taking the left), there will be a small, concealed pulloff on the left. This is Table Rock, with routes up to 5.12, both sport and traditional. Two good climbs there: Mercury (1' crack) and Iodine (hard sport face). There are also large boulders there, with problems up to V8. This crag runs for 1 1/4 mi. and is mostly very clean (like Paradise).

19 Prospect Rock (at Gouldsburg State Park)
Sandstone (20') bouldering on horizontal cross bedding. No camping. State park, (570) 894-8336.
Ref: Guidebook: Harler's *Climb Pennsylvania.*
Directions: South of Scranton on I-380. At exit 6, go north on Hwy. 507 for 2 mi. to Gouldsburg State Park. Go to far end of road. Hike southwest to Prospect Rock.

20 McConnell's Mill State Park ✩✩✩
McConnell's Mill State Park contains a 4 mi. gorge up to 400' deep with excellent 60' rimrock cliffs. A nice climbing/

bouldering area. Very popular and crowded on weekends. Also, popular white-water area. No camping. State park, (724) 368–8091.
Ref: C 69 (11/81); on-line guide www.geocities.com/ millsbouldering/; Guidebooks: Value's *McConnell's Mill State Park Classic Rock Climbs,* Harler's *Climb Pennsylvania.*
Directions: From Newcastle go 13 mi. east on Hwy. 422. Follow road above mill to Rim Road Climbing Area cliffs.

21 M–Breakneck Bridge Rock ✯✯

In McConnell's Mill State Park, this 50′ west-facing sandstone area is more of an overflow area for rescue practice and rappelling but does offer a few climbs/topropes. No camping. State park, (724) 368–8091.
Ref: Guidebooks: Value's *McConnell's Mill State Park Classic Rock Climbs,* Harler's *Climb Pennsylvania.*
Directions: From McConnell's Mill State Park, follow signs for 2 mi. to Breakneck Bridge. No rappelling from bridge.

22 Castanea Slab (closed)

This 160′ sandstone roadside slab is closed to climbing. Private land.
Classics: Save The Seals 8.
Ref: Guidebook: Bowers's *Bellefonte Climbing.*
Directions: At Castanea (south of Lock Haven), Castanea Slab is on Hwy. 220.

Tyrolean traverse at McConnell's Mill State Park.

23 Bellefonte Quarry (closed) ✯✯✯

Do not climb here! This long-standing Penn State climber's hangout with a certain error of pulchritude has been closed since 1992. These areas are listed for historical-use information only. Bellefonte was known in the 1980s as a friction/micro-edge master's dream area—new shoes were necessary for the hard routes. It also became noted for a controversial 5.11 finger crack sawed into the limestone with a masonry drill. While it was open, it was worth visiting for its novelty, some classic climbs, and its swimming in the quarry pools in the summer. Private land.
Classics: El Crackitan 9+, White Line Fever 12a, Autumn Arch 13.
Ref: Guidebooks: Bowers's *Bellefonte Climbing,* Harler's *Climb Pennsylvania.*
Directions: Bellefonte. Specific directions withheld upon owner's request.

24 Death Star Quarry (closed) ✯✯✯

Charming satellite of main Bellefonte area with a couple of beautiful, but difficult, climbs.
Classics: Darth Vader 11d, SDI Crack 12.
Ref: Guidebooks: Bowers's *Bellefonte Climbing,* Harler's *Climb Pennsylvania.*
Directions: Bellefonte. Directions withheld upon owner's request.

25 Friction Quarries (Compressor and Silent) (closed) ✯

Classics: Clam Sandwich 9.
Ref: Guidebooks: Bowers's *Bellefonte Climbing,* Harler's *Climb Pennsylvania.*
Directions: Bellefonte. Directions withheld upon owner's request.

26 Double Secret Quarry (closed) ✯

Classics: Butterflies 9-.
Ref: Guidebooks: Bowers's *Bellefonte Climbing,* Harler's *Climb Pennsylvania.*
Directions: Bellefonte. Directions withheld upon owner's request.

27 Pleasant Gap Quarry (closed) ✯

Classics: Hypoxia 11c.
Ref: Guidebooks: Bowers's *Bellefonte Climbing,* Harler's *Climb Pennsylvania.*
Directions: Bellefonte. Directions withheld upon owner's request.

28 Penn State Campus ✯✯✯

Most geologically varied artificial climbing wall in the United States. Local legend says it will crumble if a virgin walks by. Go to Appalachian Outdoors for climbing information. State.

Classics: Hammond Wall (90′ traverse), The Obelisk (left of Old Main).
Ref: Guidebook: Harler's *Climb Pennsylvania*.
Directions: Find Penn State campus at State College, Pennsylvania.

29 Coburn ✩
Scenic forested area with 35′ sandstone bouldering and cragging. Old Penn State climbing club site. Autumn.
Classics: George of the Jungle 10.
Ref: Guidebook: Harler's *Climb Pennsylvania*.
Directions: From Coburn (south of Hwy. 45), cross bridge in town over Penns Creek. Follow road to rock on right. Coburn Rocks at roadside and above.

30 Pinnacle Rock (Coburn Area) ✩
Sandstone micro area.
Classics: Pinnacle Direct 6.
Ref: Guidebook: Harler's *Climb Pennsylvania*.
Directions: Go 1 mi. south of Coburn Rock. Park and cross railroad trestle. Hike on path to left for Pinnacle Rock.

31 Lehigh Gorge State Park ✩✩
Nice 80′ Shawangunks conglomerate crag. Not a summer cliff. Autumn. Free camping. State park, (570) 443-0400.
Classics: 18′ roof crack (freed).
Ref: Guidebook: *Obscure Alternatives*.
Directions: From Jim Thorpe go briefly west on Hwy. 209. Go northwest on Hwy. 93. Turn northeast (right) to town of Weatherly and go through onto Lehigh Gorge. Park across from rifle range sign. Hike east on main trail crossing, taking left turn at second stream. When trail forms T, go to the right and top of Lehigh Gorge cliff. Cliff is near railroad tracks and Lehigh River. (Giving accurate directions here is like trying to teach Punjabi—get a map or local.) Faces south.

32 Delaware Water Gap National Recreation Area (Mt. Minsi) ✩✩✩
The "Little Gunks" is composed of the same Shawangunks quartzite as that of the famed area, The Shawangunks, outside of New Paltz, New York. Nice 280′ multiple-pitch climbing on tilted east-facing strata with more than one hundred routes. Compared to New Jersey side, Minsi is less traveled and therefore quieter, and the rock is of better quality. Also, some good ice climbs exist: The Minsi Curtain and The Minsi Flume. Dingman Falls, at 130′, is the highest waterfall in Pennsylvania. No longer need to register with the Park Service to climb here as in the past. A nameless man suggests "helmets are the in thing here," but that we shouldn't say he said it. E-mail him at . . . . Autumn. Pay (Dingman's Ferry Campground April–October)/free camping river road. NPS, (570) 588-2435.
Classics: Drifting Arrow 5, Hell and High Water 5+, Dancing Fool 7, Flying Circus 8, Chieftain 8+, High Falls 9, Elders

of the Tribe 9, Great Big Billy Goat Gruff 10-, Raptor of the Steep 10, Voyage of the Damned 11, Razor's Edge 11.
Ref: C 121-120, S 11/82; Guidebooks: Nick and Sloane's *New Jersey Crags*, Steele's *Climber's Guide to the Delaware Water Gap*, Harler's *Climb Pennsylvania*.
Directions: From Delaware Water Gap go 2 mi. south on Hwy. 611. Park at Cold Air Cave parking lot. Hike up from parking area. Cold Air Cave has topropes. For Mt. Minsi cliffs take blue-blazed trail up from the cave to Practice Face and climbs. Or, park at Point of Gap and take longer trail up.

33 Stoney Ridge ✩✩✩
Pennsylvania's Pump Palace. A 113-degree, "lean mean" 70′ wall with more than eighty beautiful routes on solid quartzite. More information at Whitehall. Have a pleasant pump if it's open—closed to climbing as of 1993. Access sensitive. Cliff is a microwave in summer, icebox in winter. No camping. Private land.
Classics: Doc's Dilemma 6, Stump Crack 8, Astra 9, Worm Surgeon 10c, Next Edition 10d, Pariah 11, Activator 11+, Maalox Power 12a.
Ref: C [143, 142, 112, 94, 86(10/84)-46], S 11/82; Guidebooks: Pleiss's *Stoneyridge*, Harlin's *East, Obscure Alternatives*.
Directions: At Bowmanstown (north of Lehigh Gap). Follow Hwy. 248. Turn north on White St. Go east on Fireline Rd. (curvy!). Then head south on Craig. Turn west on Oak. Park past Stone Ridge Manor Apartments. (Please do not park at apartments!) Stoney Ridge Cliff visible behind apartments.

34 Tamaqua Cliff ✩
Seneca Rock nuance cliff with detached pinnacle. Forty-foot quartzite crag and bouldering. Bring toprope setup. Autumn. No camping.
Ref: Guidebook: *Obscure Alternatives*.
Directions: From Tamaqua (junction of Hwy. 309 and Hwy. 209), go south on Hwy. 209. Park at gas station. Tamaqua Cliff is up on east side of road. A cut gorge is opposite on west side of highway.

35 Lehigh Parkway ✩✩
A 30′ wall with steep, thin face climbing mostly 5.10 or harder. Bouldering or topropes. Do not fix pins. Autumn. No camping. City park.
Directions: In Allentown. Between Fifteenth St. and Twenty-fourth St. Just south of Hamilton Blvd. and north of Lehigh St. Bouldering problems lie just west of Little Lehigh Pkwy. entrance sign on Fifteenth St. Also bouldering on bridge walls farther west of second parking area.

36 South Mountain Boulders ✩✩✩
A dozen high-quality 30′ gritstone boulders. Autumn.
Classics: Hunk Boulder, Jeff's Arête.

Ref: Guidebook: *Obscure Alternatives*.

Directions: In Allentown. Take Fourth St. south to East Rock Rd. Park at Mountain Top Lane. Hike south 100 yd. for South Mountain Boulders.

37 Emmaus Boulders ✵✵

Good 30′ conglomerate bouldering area with about ten good boulders. Autumn. No camping. Private land.

Classics: Main Boulder 5.9–5.11, Ultra Friction Boulders 5.12.

Ref: Guidebook: *Obscure Alternatives*.

Directions: In Allentown. Follow Emmaus Ave. west (passing Commix Hotel on right) to Alpine St. At the end of Alpine St. (before underpass) for Emmaus Boulders, hike south. Don't park at end of Alpine St. (tickets given!).

38 Donation Rocks ✵

Toproping on plenty of overhangs at this 60′ sandstone crag. Autumn. Private land.

Classics: Damnation Wall (8–10), Royal Delight 10a, Pancakes 11, Royal Pain 12.

Ref: Dave McCormack II 10/98; Guidebook: Harler's *Climb Pennsylvania*.

Directions: From Huntingdon go north on Hwy. 26 to Donation. Take left before a large white building on the left coming from Huntingdon that may have once been a general store. (If you get to a large gravel parking lot with a phone booth on the right, you went too far.) Donation Rocks located in gap of the ridge.

39 Huntingdon Rocks ✵

Good 120′ quartzite crag offers topropes on face routes. Autumn. Pay camping. Private land.

Ref: Guidebook: Harler's *Climb Pennsylvania*.

Directions: Huntingdon Rocks are in Huntingdon above Juniata River and railroad tracks. Ask locals. Please don't trespass.

40 Boxcar Rocks (aka Chinese Wall) ✵

"Snappy" conglomerate holds on this 100′ crag. Short 5.9 cracks. Private land.

Classics: Margie's Curves 2, Moby Neil 4, Russell's Ruin 5.

Ref: Guidebook: Harler's *Climb Pennsylvania*.

Directions: From Tower City Hwy. (209), drive south on Hwy. 325. Turn left (south) on Gold Mine Rd. At second ridge, park at turnout (strip mine). Hike east on ridge for ½ mi. to Boxcar Rocks.

41 Pinnacle Rock (Near Albany) ✵✵

A 50′ beginner quartzite crag. Autumn. Free camping.

Classics: Cave 3.

Ref: Guidebook: Harler's *Climb Pennsylvania*.

Directions: From Albany drive south on Hwy. 143. Park at ski area. Hike one hour to northeast skyline. From Eckville hike south on Appalachian Trail to Pinnacle Rock Trail to pinnacle.

42 Pulpit Rock

Topropes at this beginner quartzite crag. Autumn. Free camping.

Ref: Guidebook: Harler's *Climb Pennsylvania*.

Directions: Northeast of Hamburg. At Hamburg Reservoir off I-78, follow Reservoir Rd. to rock. Can also access Pinnacle Rock number 41 above from here via Appalachian Trail to Pinnacle Trail.

43 Table Rock ✵

Beginner sandstone sport crag. Summer. Free camping.

Classics: Center Crack 2.

Ref: Guidebook: Harler's *Climb Pennsylvania*.

Directions: From Dauphin go north on Hwy. 225 to Appalachian Trail. Hike 2 mi. north on trail to Table Rock.

44 Dauphin Narrows

Very limited sandstone bouldering and crag area.

Classics: Linoy Buttress 1, Joint Point 6.

Ref: Guidebook: Harler's *Climb Pennsylvania*.

Directions: From Dauphin drive south on Hwy. 322. Dauphin Narrows visible to east.

45 Brickyard Quarry

Forty-foot quartzite quarry.

Classics: Divine Comedy 5, Savage Slit 8.

Ref: Guidebook: Harler's *Climb Pennsylvania*.

Directions: From Newmanstown go 1 mi. south on Hwy. 419 to watershed. Park. Hike on path up to ridgeline and Brickyard Quarry.

46 Brickerville Rocks ✵✵

Conglomerate bouldering and topropes. Autumn.

Ref: Guidebook: Harler's *Climb Pennsylvania*.

Directions: From Brickerville go 2 mi. west on Hwy. 322 to Brickerville Rocks.

47 Mt. Penn Bouldering Wall (aka Reading) ✵

A 25′ quartzite bouldering retaining wall below the overlook. Autumn. City park.

Ref: D. Newton.

Directions: Reading. At Japanese pagoda atop Mt. Penn overlooking Reading.

48 Neversink Mountain

Seventy-foot sandstone topropes on priable rock.

Classics: Chimney 5.0, Steam Head 5, Muscle Head 6, Scheizenhole.

Ref: Guidebook: Harler's *Climb Pennsylvania*.

Directions: At Mt. Penn, follow Hwy. 422 to Twenty-fifth. Turn on Fairview to Twentieth St. Go up Neversink Mountain. At third hairpin to right is dirt road to left. Go on dirt road for 50 yd. On right.

49 Tohickon Creek Cliffs ✩✩

A scenic 300' shale crag above a scenic creek. Ice climbing, too. Pay camping. Private land.

Ref: S 11/82.

Directions: Tohickon Creek Cliffs are just north of Ralph Stover State Park. From Kintersville go south of junction of Hwy. 611 and Hwy. 32. On Hwy. 32 for approximately 1 mi.

50 Ralph Stover State Park (aka High Rocks) ✩✩✩

Rejuvenated, overhanging 120' sport climbing area and difficult bouldering. The rock, argillite shale, tends to be dirty but very steep. The site of a water-powered grain mill owned and operated by Ralph Stover in the late eighteenth century. The Stover heirs gave this as a gift to the Commonwealth in 1931. An additional property known as the "High Rocks" was added through the donation of the late noted author James A. Michener. This area is popular for its spectacular views, and its sheer rock face offers a unique challenge to the experienced climber. Beware of tourist UFOs from overlook. Scenic area. Autumn. State park, (610) 982-5560.

Classics: Hummingbird 6, Neanderthal 8, Phonebooth 10, Welcome to Stover 10+.

Ref: *Appalachia* 12/65, S 11/82; Guidebooks: Nick's *Ralph Stover State Park, Pennsylvania: Classic Rock Climbs,* Reilley's *A Climber's Guide to Tohickon Gorge: High Rocks,* Harlin's *East,* Harler's *Climb Pennsylvania,* Kolman and Ellis's *A Climber's Guide to Boileau Rocks,* Chambers's *Stover Park Rock Climbs*.

Directions: From Doylestown drive north on Hwy. 611 to Plumsteadville. Turn right on Stump Rd. (SR 1010) to Ralph Stover State Park, following state park signs. Just one hour north of Philadelphia.

51 Dickson Quarry

This 60' sandstone quarry with pit caves has had ongoing access problems for more than twenty years. Quarry is on private land owned by cemetery.

Classics: Jerry's Malaise 5, The Alcove 7, Scorpio 11c.

Ref: C 69(11/81); Guidebooks: Jirak's *AK Handbook,* Harler's *Climb Pennsylvania*.

Directions: At Sewickley. Take Nevin Rd. to Dickson Rd. Park before hairpin turn. Hike past fireplug into woods to Dickson Quarry.

52 High Rocks (Derry Rocks) (closed) ✩✩✩

Quality Pennsylvania stone! A great little 40' quartzite cliff with a cluster of classic climbs. Ten Crack is the eye-grabbing classic crack. Other fine overhanging face climbs.

The bad news is that it's private land. No trespassing! Closed as of 1994. Lots of litter. Perhaps climbers can keep this area open by offering to clean it up? Derry High Rock was declared a no-trespassing zone in 1998 by the gun club that owns it. Some drunk fell off of it, and he sued the owners. Owners now posted it and fine people they find on or around the area.

Classics: Pegboard 5.0, Sloth 7, Ten Crack 10+, Der Kommissar 12, Jimi Hendrix 12.

Ref: J. Hensberger 4/98; C 69(11/81); Guidebook: Stryker's *Red Rock: A Climber's Guide to High Rocks*.

Directions: Derry (east of Latrobe, Pennsylvania). From corner of Second St. and Ligonier St. in Derry (at St. Joe's School), head up Ligonier St. for 1 3/10 mi. Just past Twin Maples Hunt Club, turn right into sharp-angling road. Follow this dirt road a minute, veering left, and park. Hike trail a couple of minutes to High Rocks, the small cliff with steep climbs. About one hour east of Pittsburgh.

53 Beam's Rocks ✩✩

A neat 60' gritstone area that probably does not see as much climbing action as it could. It does see graffiti from spray cans. Some classic beginner's boulder problems and intermediate climbs on bizarre pockets and edges. Popular sport rappelling/teaching area in Forbes State Forest. Popular hiking area. Autumn. Free camping. Forbes State Forest, (724) 238-1200.

Ref: C 69(11/81); Guidebook: Stryker's *Red Rock: A Climber's Guide to High Rocks*.

Directions: From Ligonier follow Hwy. 30 southeast to Laurel Mountain Summit ski areas. Take right off Hwy. 30 onto Laurel Summit Rd. for 2 1/10 mi. to ski area. Go past entrance to ski area for another 2 1/10 mi. Parking for Beam's Rocks Trailhead is on left (parking slots for five cars), just before brown dome house. Hike 3/4 mi. to top of cliffs. Faces east.

54 Forster St. Bridge

Bridge bouldering. No chalk, EB's, or three-piece business suits. No camping without a cardboard box.

Classics: Bloody Bulge.

Ref: Guidebook: Harler's *Climb Pennsylvania*.

Directions: Forster St. Bridge is in central Harrisburg, just east of Harvey Taylor Bridge (north) over the Susquehanna River.

55 Wolf Rock

Diabase rock bouldering.

Ref: Guidebook: Harler's *Climb Pennsylvania*.

Directions: From Pottstown go east on Hwy. 422. Turn left at Nieffer Rd. (at airport). Turn right on Highland Dr. (at Herstein Church). Take left at T. Park at second pulloff over hill crest (by tower). Hike to house, then go left at T; back on level ground. Hike right to Wolf Rock boulderfield.

56 St. Peter's ✯✯✯

West-facing 80′ diabase crags enclosed in three quarries with sharp-edged face climbing. Please obey all signs. Autumn. Pay camping. Private land.
Classics: Poison Ivy 9, Burnt Turkey 9.
Ref: S 11/82; Guidebooks: Detterline's *Climbing at St. Peter's,* Harler's *Climb Pennsylvania, Obscure Alternatives.*
Directions: From Pottstown go south on Hwy. 100. Then go west on Hwy. 23. Turn north to St. Peter's village (before French Creek). Turn east on Rock Run Rd. to trailer park. St. Peter's three quarried areas are found just north.

57 White Rocks (Cumberland Co.) ✯✯

One-hundred-foot quartzite crag with crack and steep slab climbing. It may be of use for climbers to obtain maps from Michaux State Forest. Also on the forest are multiple bouldering areas of varying size and quality. Most of these can be found with the state forest map. Private land/ Michaux State Forest, (717) 352-2211.
Classics: Jim's Throne 3, Thin Crack 7.
Ref: J. Baker 3/98; Guidebook: Harler's *Climb Pennsylvania.*
Directions: In Boiling Springs, from Hwy. 174 turn left on Butcher Hill Rd. Keep left over bridge and left at fork. Turn right on Creek Rd. and right on White Rocks Dr. Park on right and hike up old Appalachian Trail (blue blazes). A housing development has gone in nearby.

58 Hammond Rocks

Short routes on this conglomerate crag and popular local party place. Rocks are covered with graffiti, broken bottles, and litter. Michaux State Forest, (717) 352-2211.
Ref: J. Baker 3/98; Guidebook: Harler's *Climb Pennsylvania.*
Directions: From Mt. Holly Springs pop 5 ½ mi. south on Hwy. 34. Turn southwest onto Ridge Rd. Hammond Rocks appear on left before junction with Cold Springs Rd. on ridge of south mountain.

59 Pole Steeple (in Pine Grove Furnace State Park) ✯✯

Interesting short climbs on this 100′ quartzite crag. A good beach at Laurel Lake below cliff. Solid Montalto quartzite contains a wealth of fossilized Scolithus worm burrows. Autumn. Pay camping. State park (717-486-7174).
Ref: Guidebooks: Harler's *Climb Pennsylvania,* Canter's *Nearby Climbing Areas.*
Directions: From Mt. Holly Springs go south on Hwy. 34. Turn southwest on Hunters Run Rd. to Laurel Lake at Pine Grove Furnace State Park. Go to south shore of Laurel Lake at Pole Steeple parking lot. Hike up Pole Steeple Trail. Faces northwest.

60 Elizabethtown Pillar ✯

Free and aid climbing on 70′ bridge trestle. Rock type: Early Amtrak. Private land.
Ref: Guidebook: Harler's *Climb Pennsylvania.*
Directions: In Elizabethtown, take Hwy. 230. Go west at MTA truck school. Take first left past railroad. Park at bridge. Elizabethtown Pillar is at creek.

61 Governor's Stables (closed) ✯✯✯

Now closed, this limited woodland bouldering area offered quality problems and warranted a visit. Classic and difficult Eric Horst problems up to V8, many V0 to V5. Autumn. No camping. Private land.
Classics: Overhanging corner B1, Arête B1.
Ref: E. Horst; Guidebook: Harler's *Climb Pennsylvania.*
Directions: From Harrisburg go south on Hwy. 441 past Three Mile Island. Go left at Elizabethtown Rd. Go right at Governor's Stables Rd. to an old gate on right where downslope of road becomes wooded. Park at gate. Hike southwest five minutes past gate to Governor's Stables, a small cluster of black diabase boulders in woods.

62 Livezey (aka Lutz) Rock ✯✯✯

Forty-foot schist crag with good topropes and bouldering. Information at Basecamp store in Philly (Chestnut and Eighth). Autumn. No camping. Government land.
Classics: Steven's 7.
Ref: Sherman's *Stone Crusade;* Guidebook: Harler's *Climb Pennsylvania.*
Directions: Northwest Philadelphia. Off Wissahickon Dr. in Fairmount Park on Livezey Lane in Chestnut Hill parking. Short hike to Livezey Rock.

63 Kralack (aka Krahlick) Rock ✯✯✯

This 60′ sandstone crag features mostly overhanging topropes. Autumn. Free camping. Private land.
Ref: C 69(11/81); Guidebook: Harler's *Climb Pennsylvania.*
Directions: From Connellsville at Laurel Run go west of Youghiogheny River at raft takeout. Follow Creek Rd. for approximately 1–5 mi. west of river. Kralack Rock is on left (visible).

64 Coll's Cove

Ref: C 69(11/81).
Directions: Coll's Cove is a crag near Uniontown.

65 White Rocks (at Uniontown) ✯✯✯

This 50′ quartzite crag has been closed since 1994. Solid and well climbed; gritstone boulders and walls. Some of Pennsylvania's finest face climbs. Autumn. No camping. Please help keep good relations with establishment. Private land of the Sportsman's Club.
Classics: Infinity 5, Post Office 6, The Grooves 7, Orangatang 10, A Crack Too Far 11.
Ref: J. Govi; C 69(11/81); Guidebooks: Harler's *Climb Pennsylvania,* Webster's *Gritstone Climbs,* Explorers' Club's *Guide to White Rocks.*
Directions: From Uniontown go south on Hwy. 119, then

take Hwy. 857 to Fairchance. Turn left at Friends Roller Rink. Past railroad tracks, the road splits right to White Rocks (1 mi., uphill) or left to Fairchance Rod and Gun Club (possibly on Elm St.). Hike 1 mi. on White Rock Creek Trail to White Rocks. (Approximate directions.)

66 Brown Rocks ☆
Vertical face topropes. The Pennsylvania Bureau of Forestry manages this area. Michaux State Forest, (717) 352-2211.
Ref: Guidebook: Harler's *Climb Pennsylvania.*
Directions: Brown Rocks is visible from road to right of White Rocks and Pond Bank.

67 White Rocks (Pond Bank) ☆☆
A west-facing 60′ quartzite crag with lots of bouldering on Appalachian Trail. No camping. Michaux State Forest, (717) 352-2211.
Classics: Zombie 7; Bouldering.
Ref: J. Baker 3/98; Guidebook: Harler's *Climb Pennsylvania.*
Directions: From Mechanicsburg go south on Hwy. 641 to Hwy. 174. Turn left at Allen (Appalachian Trail). Cross railroad. Go after bridge to right at fork. (Dirt road is White Rocks road.) Park at Appalachian Trail on right. Hike to ridgeline for White Rocks.

68 Hermitage (aka Shaffer or Monument Rock) Rock ☆☆
Massive 100′ quartzite pinnacles—a crazy mix. Cliffs above Hermitage Cabin. The rock is vertical with sparse handholds. The "monument" is the detached pinnacle. The area sits deep in a gorge and is very shaded. The Pennsylvania Bureau of Forestry manages this area. Michaux State Forest, (717) 352-2211.
Classics: Rappel Crack 5, Ten Pins 8, Spider Man 10.
Ref: J. Baker 3/98; Guidebooks: Harler's *Climb Pennsylvania,* Canter's *Nearby Climbing Areas.*
Directions: Near South Mountain. From Route 30 turn south on Route 233. Turn left at T and go through town of South Mountain. Turn right on Anitietam Rd. Go about 3 mi. and turn on Ron Swift Run Rd. Park at sharp turn and follow blue blazes for Hermitage Rock. Look for Hermitage Cabin on Michaux State Forest map.

69 Devil's Den (at Gettysburg National Military Park) ☆☆
Battlefield bouldering on a 35′ andesite wall holds many good problems up to V8/V9 between cannons and cavalry on quality diabase rock. Bouldering should be kept low-key and should not be done while large groups (especially kids) are about. No ropes can be used at any time, and groups of climbers should be kept small (five or fewer). This is the most accessible bouldering area in midstate Pennsylvania. This is where Confederate sharpshooters fired on Union soldiers stationed on Little Round Top. Good for an hour's diversion if you're visiting Gettysburg.

Autumn. Pay camping. NPS, (717) 334-1124.
Ref: E. Horst; Guidebooks: Harler's *Climb Pennsylvania,* Canter's *Nearby Climbing Areas.*
Directions: In Gettysburg National Park. Follow park service loop road south of visitors center for approximately five minutes. Rocks are on right at Devil's Den sign and a score of cannonballs from the road. Excellent bouldering at "hairpin" turn. Faces south.

70 Chickies Rock ☆☆☆
This solid, 220′ quartzite cliff is capped by large overhangs and has oddly slanting holds. A good practice area for beginners' classes. Some classic routes and a couple of classic overhanging bouldering problems in cave at base of cliff. Beware: This area can be a flying-bottle war zone due to tourists. Unique fossil Scolithus tubes. Airy views of the Susquehanna River, where, down on the river, fishing guide Scott Goldsmith says the bass jump right into your creel—just don't eat 'em as Three Mile Island is upstream!
Autumn. No camping. Lancaster County park, (717) 684-5249.
Classics: For Madmen Only 7, Milt's Roof 9+, Boulder Cave 10 to 13-.
Ref: E. Horst; C 109, S 11/82; Guidebooks: Holland's *A Guide to Climbs at Chickies,* Harler's *Climb Pennsylvania,* Canter's *Nearby Climbing Areas.*
Directions: From Columbia go 2 mi. north of Hwy. 30 on Hwy. 441. On left. Two parking areas: 1) At top of hill with bulletin board. Walk five to ten minutes to top of cliff. Hike down steep trail to railroad tracks and base. 2) At bottom of hill, small park at small pullout. Hike trail west to railroad tracks and base of Chickies Rock. Faces west.

71 Safe Harbor (closed) ☆☆☆☆
Ain't safe to climb here no more: closed. A 1970s 120′ schist crag rejuvenated into 1990s sport crags—could be Pennsylvania's best. Cemetery Wall (shady, dries faster) lies north of Conestoga Creek, while the ½-mi.-long South Crags lie to the south. (Drive car along base.) Slabs, vertical, and some overhung face on solid stone. Mostly thin face. Good winter area. Indian burial sites and rock carvings. Pay camping. Private land/county park.
Classics: South: Two Pines 8, Public Service 8+, Autumn Arches 10b, Super Slab 10d, Machismo 11c, Expose 12a, Wonderama 12b; Cemetery: Leap of Faith 12-, Dry Bones Dance 12d.
Ref: R 51(10/92), C [139, (8/92)]; Guidebooks: Horst's *Susquehanna River Rock,* Harler's *Climb Pennsylvania.*
Directions: Safe Harbor. Two crags on east shore of Susquehanna River: 1) Cemetery Wall: From Safe Harbor Park go north on River Rd. for 2 mi. Turn left (southwest) on Observation Rd. for 2 mi. Anchor your rig at pullout across from communication tower. Hike paved road past gate 200 yd. to "mowed road" on right going to railroad bed, then 200 yd. upstream. 2) South Crags: From Safe Harbor Park go south on River Rd. for

approximately 1 mi. Take right on Green Hill Rd., then right down "No Outlet" drive slowly to railroad bed. Park along bed.

72 Tucquan Overhangs ★★

Twenty-five-foot schist bouldering on short overhangs. Spring–autumn. Private land. Ask permission from landowner.
Classics: Classic 7, Dynamesh 10.
Ref: E. Horst; Guidebook: Harler's *Climb Pennsylvania*.
Directions: From Martic Forge (south of Lancaster), go 3 8/10 mi. left (at Martic Forge Hotel) on River Rd. to small bridge. Tucquan Overhangs is on left in woods.

73 Swarthmore Quarry (destroyed—no longer exists)

Now a freeway, but in the 1970s, this 50′ sandstone crag was one of the best short crag areas in Pennsylvania before being filled in.
Classics: Four Strong Winds 12+.
Ref: M 94; Guidebook: *Obscure Alternatives*.
Directions: Southwest Philadelphia. At Swarthmore, follow Hwy. 320 to Twenty-second St. East. Take Fairview Rd. Go north on Seventh St. Go west on Blackrock Lane to end. Park. Hike north of ball field to cliff.

74 Whiskey Springs ★★★

Excellent 30′ bouldering problems. The rock is quartzite (Weverton Formation). The season extends from about March until late fall. Autumn/summer. Free camping. Government land.
Classics: Flesh Eater: Climb the northeast corner of the obvious big overhang.
Ref: T. Garland 4/98.
Directions: In Boiling Springs (southwest of Harrisburg). From the four-way stop facing dentist office in town, take a left down Park Dr. Drive past municipal building and take a left on to Petersburg Rd. Go to four-way stop and keep going straight until you come across the Appalachian Trail. Park (spring on left). Hike west up Appalachian Trail ten minutes until you get to boulders and rocks all along ridge.

75 Minersville

A unique 50′ crag with lots of little conglomerate boulders. Two bolted lines and routes up to 5.12d. It's a lot like Maple Canyon, Utah, in that it has a pebble-type conglomerate. Many of the routes here have been protected by a static line and redpointed on lead. We just started developing it this year. A few local kids decided to bolt it, so that accounts for the two bolted routes. They (the kids) didn't know about toproping and had no experience bolting—so en garde! One of the lines that they bolted is a classic steep 5.10. face. The crux is grabbing this fist-size pebble, then turning it into a high-step and a reach to a shatty crimper.
Ref: J. Lantz 2/98.

Directions: Near Harrisburg, right off I–81 just past the Frackville exit.

76 The Rim

Possibly one of the better bouldering spots in Pennsylvania. Steep face moves on Gunks-like conglomerate.
Ref: J. Lantz 2/98.
Directions: Near Philadelphia. Ask locals about access and parking problems.

77 Hunter's Rock

Terrific new 15′ sandstone bouldering area with new routes going up at every outing. Great for beginners and/or those who think they can pull. Summer. Free camping. State land/private land.
Classics: Mojo V2, Resin Run V5, Blood Orchid V5, Knob Goblin V6, Standard American Accent V6/7, Sabotour V6/7, Rock Hugger V7, Hooker Traverse V7, Classic Girl V7/8.
Ref: E. Harrison 1/99.
Directions: Near Donation. Ask locals.

78 Peavine Island

Forty-five-foot granite crag. Private land.
Ref: E. Mistarka 9/98.
Directions: Delta, Pennsylvania. Take Hwy. 372 to Norman Wood Bridge and go south on River Rd. on south (York County) side of bridge. At 6/10 mi. there is a small pullout on left. Follow the trail across water and then go right. Crag visible when atop the small hill.

79 Oakwood Park

An old reservoir made of 15′ sandstone blocks, now converted to a park. The wall offers a crimpy traverse about 400′ in length, only a few minutes from downtown Pittsburgh. There are also a number of boulder problems on the wall, using only shallow pockets for handholds. Quite comfortable on sunny, forty-degree days in the winter. No camping. City land.
Classics: 5.9? Traverse.
Ref: Chris Leger 6/98.
Directions: From downtown Pittsburgh take 279 south to the Green Tree exit. Take the left fork at the exit and make a left. Turn right at the light onto Poplar St., then left at the next light onto Noblestown Rd. Go straight through the next light and make a sharp turn onto Durbin St. Park at the playground a few hundred feet down the road on the right.

Other Pennsylvania Climbing Areas
Henry Bridge
In Philadelphia.
Haycock Mountain (Nockamixon State Park)
Diabase bouldering ridge about 16 mi. north of Doylestown.

Rhode Island

It's not that I am so smart, it's just that I stay with problems longer. —Albert Einstein

ood things come in small packages. Good thing, because packages don't come any smaller than Rhode Island. America's smallest state has what some call "the best bouldering on the East Coast"—Lincoln Woods. In keeping with the state's small size, the other Rhode Island climbing areas cater mostly to bouldering and toproping on short-order cliffs.

Look for good things in Rhode Island and you'll find them.

1 Diamond Hill Park (closed) ✩

Local 60′ granite crag frequented by rappellers now closed to rock climbing. Routes from 5.7 to 5.10. Bring extendo toprope runners. Summer/autumn. Entry fee. No camping. Once a state park, now run and closed by the Town of

Cumberland Recreation Department (401–728–2400).
Ref: Guidebook: Rocha and Li's *A Climber's Guide to Diamond Hill, Cumberland, Rhode Island.*
Directions: Diamond Hill Park is at Diamond Hill off Route 114, just a few mi. north of I–295.

2 Lincoln Woods State Park ✩✩✩

Pure white 35′ granite boulders in a beautiful sylvan setting. Some topropes at Goat Rock and Lost Crag. Lots of bouldering linkups stimulating the nickname "Linkin' Woods." Also known as "Green Rock." There are probably sixty popular boulders varying from two to six routes depending on their size. One reader writes, "You can't even see all the boulders in a day let alone do every route on them that suits you. . . . Some of the old-timers have been

Andrew Sornberger puts his touch on a classic at Lincoln Woods.

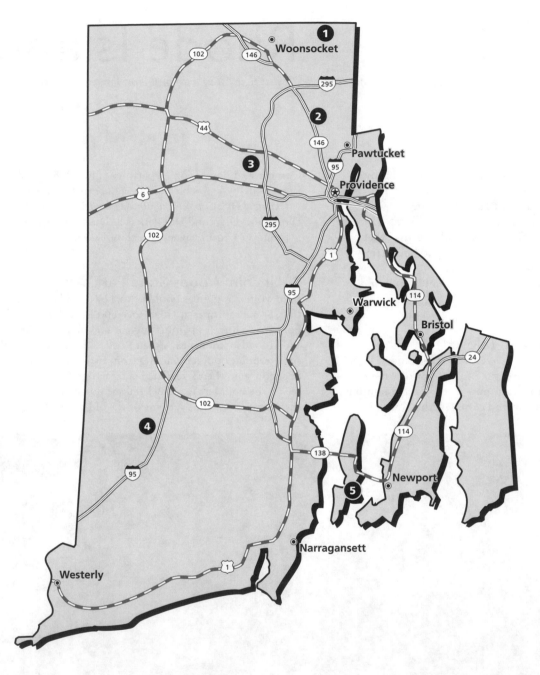

1
Woonsocket

102
146

295

2

146
Pawtucket

95

Providence

44

3

6

102

295

1

95

Warwick

114

Bristol

24

102

4

114

95

138

Newport

5

1

Narragansett

Westerly

N

0 Kilometers 10

0 Miles 10

Rhode Island

climbing there for fifteen years and there are routes they still can't send." Check Providence Rock Gym for Xerox map. Summer/autumn. No entrance fees (as of 1998), but picnic fees. No camping. State park, (401) 723-7892.

Classics: The Wave 7, Mark's Traverse 11, Iron Cross B1+; Latex Sheath 11+, Zero Gravity 11+, The Nose 11, Iron Cross B2, Try Again B2; Die Harder V8, Midnight Lichen V9, Trojan Horse V9, Conquest of the Irrational V10.

Ref: Locals 3/98; C [186, 139, 114, 104(10/87)-20], R [99-94, 90-22]; Sherman's *Stone Crusade;* on-line guides http://home.ici.net/~rufus/Lincoln.Woods/Boulders/ Boulders.html and www.newenglandbouldering.com; Guidebooks: Harlin's *East,* 1970s hard-to-find guidebook.

Directions: From Providence (twenty minutes from downtown), go just north on Hwy. 146 to Lincoln Woods State Park (signs). Park on right after turning onto Loop Rd. Hike left up road to rocks.

3 Snake Den State Park

As the area's guidebook states, this is "decent rock for desperate climbers." Snake Den's 35' granite/gneiss formation features some of the hardest toprope problems on its overhangs. Check out the 20' roof crack. The Rhody Loadies put up first climbs in the late 1970s, even though some climbs were done as early as the 1960s. Contrary to the area's name, snakes are not a problem, although car theft is. Also, watch out for intermittent loose rock. Autumn/winter. State park, (401) 222-2632.

Classics: Venom 10+, Battle of the Bulge 10+, Rattlesnake 12+ toprope.

Ref: C 114(6/89)-26; Guidebook: Sewall's *Rock Climbs of Snake Den State Park.*

Directions: West Providence. Snake Den State Park is in town of Johnston. From junction of I-295 and Hwy. 6, slither west on Hwy. 6 (Hartford Ave.) for approximately 2 mi. Turn right on Brown Ave., passing Dame Farm on right. In 1 more mi., park at dirt lane blocked with boulders on right. Walk a mere 100 yd. to first of seven small crags arranged northwest to southeast. Another set of cliffs is 400 yd. past first cliffs to old stone wall, then a corner. Cross a small brook until the left end of outcrop is reached.

Rhode Island Road Thoughts

And David put his hand in his bag, and took thence a stone, and slang it, and smote the Philistine in his forehead, that the stone sunk into his forehead; and he fell upon his face to the earth.

—I Samuel 17:49

4 Arcadia Management Area (Mt. Tom Trail) ✫✫✫

Topropes and bouldering in Rhode Island's most aesthetic setting. Crags may be hard to find, most popular being around Mt. Tom Ridge. In a quarried area on the east side of the ridge, Halloween 13a is one of the hardest topropes in the state. Mountain biking. State wildlife area, Arcadia Check Station, (401) 539-7117.

Classics: Mac Man 11, The Drip 11, Football and Toast 11; Halloween 13a.

Ref: http://users.ids.net/~brianps/crags.htm; C 114-28.

Directions: Near Arcadia. Arcadia Management Area Cliff is about 4 mi. west on Hwy. 165. Go south on Mt. Tom Rd. to Mt. Tom Trail. Hike north to cliff and a few minutes to crags on left.

5 Fort Wetherill State Park ✫✫

Bouldering and 40' granite beginners topropes above the Atlantic waves. Cliff diving. Spring–autumn. No camping. State park, (401) 423-1771.

Ref: Guidebook: Harlin's *East.*

Directions: From Jamestown go 1 1/2 mi. southeast on coast to Fort Wetherill State Park (signs). Across bay from Newport.

Other Rhode Island Rock Climbing Areas
Dinosaur Rock

Large boulder face. West of Hope Valley on Yawgoog Rd. to Narragansett Trail parking. Half mi. down yellow Narragansett Trail.
Durfee Hill

Thirty-foot granite crag in management area south of junction of Hwy. 44 and Hwy. 94, 1 1/2 mi on right.

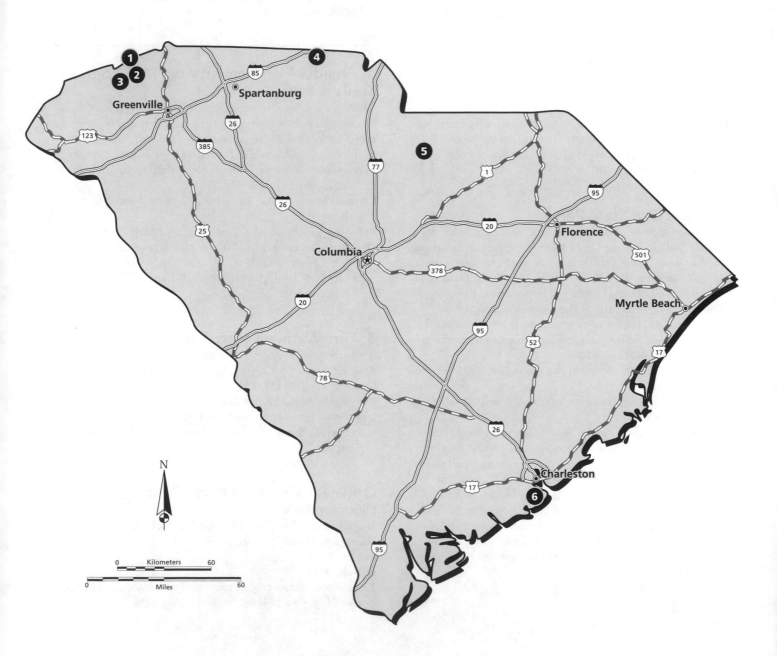

South Carolina

South Carolina

If inside there is no enemy, the enemy outside can cause us no danger. —African Proverb

With a nickname like the Palmetto State, South Carolina squelches the urge for rock climbers to visit the state faster than CB reception in an Appalachian tunnel. In fact, taking a vacation from rock climbing along the Atlantic shoreline at say Myrtle Beach or Hilton Head might be the only reason for a climber's sojourn to this Southland. Yet, long before climbers can relax at the most popular vacation spots in the state, rock bastions along the northern border arise to halt the swing of any climber's putter.

Beckoning walls, like those found at Table Rock, will widen any climber's eye. While in the past South Carolina has been outshined by its analog to the north, the recent openings of these rock worlds by state-park officials should prepare the way for future climbing trips.

1 Jones Gap State Park (closed) ✮✮✮
Located in one of South Carolina's most pristine wilderness areas; climbing at this 200' granite crag is opened only to rescue team members (as of 2000). Obtain climbing permit. Autumn/winter. Trailside pay camping $2.20/night. Office open 11:00 A.M.–noon. State park, (864) 836-3647.
Ref: *Access Fund Notes.*
Directions: From Greenville haul it northwest on Hwy. 276 for 25 mi. to Jones Gap State Park (signs).

2 Caesar's Head State Park (closed) ✮✮
Spectacular vistas erupt from sandstone boulders on top of a mountain. Closed to climbing (as of 2000). Three parties of climbers are rescued here each year. Rescues are paid for by those rescued. Site of Raven Cliff Falls—one of the highest waterfalls (400') in the eastern United States. Autumn. Trailside pay camping $2.20/night in state park (864) 836-6115.
Ref: T. Parlier 10-97; *Access Fund Notes.*
Directions: From Greenville shoot north on Hwy. 276 for 37 mi. to Caesar's Head State Park, near the North Carolina border.

3 Table Rock State Park ✮✮✮✮
Table Rock, at 3,124', features beautiful granite rock with fist-size quartz crystals dotting the surface. There are some

Caesar's Head.

TIM TOULA

nice cracks and face climbing to thrill all climbers. The average climbable route here is 5.9+ and up. Bring the trad gear. There are a few bolts that start at about 25' up. These routes are very run-out. At one time the incredible 600' rock face of Table Rock and all other state parks in South Car-olina were closed to rock climbing. Now half of this South Carolina big wall is opened from September to December. Climbers must obtain free permit. Office open daily from 8:00 A.M. to 6:00 P.M. No climbing from January through June due to peregrine falcon nesting. Further information can be obtained via Table Rock State Park, 246

Table Rock State Park Rd., Pickens, SC 29671; (864) 878-9813. Autumn. As of 2000, entrance fee is $1.50/person. Pay camping $16/night. State park/private land.
Classics: Reflections 5.8 A3 7p.
Ref: C 68; Guidebooks: Hall's *Southern Rock,* Price's *Carolinas Climber's Guide.*
Directions: From Greenville go north on Hwy. 276. Turn west on Hwy. 11 to Table Rock State Park. Follow park signs to ranger's office. Check in for permit. Hike starts at trail at 1,160' and goes to the summit of Table Rock at 3,124'. It's a hard hour-and-a-half hike in to the South Wall. A fourth of that time is spent bushwhacking.

4 Kings Mountain State Park (closed)

No climbing amongst scattered outcrops and bouldering. En route through Spartanburg, South Carolina, bop into the Beacon Drive-in for the world's largest hamburgers and onion rings. Careful, the food is slippery but makes for an effective weight-training belt. Autumn–spring. Pay camping. State park, (888) 887-2757.
Ref: R. Turan.
Directions: From Bethany wield north to Kings Mountain State Park.

5 Heath Springs

Famous area for Civil War battle fought here. Many, many boulders up to 25' that are largely undeveloped. Some of the rock is crumbly. Autumn. No camping. County land.
Classics: Southern Cross V3, Sonic Youth V5, Boss Hog V2.
Ref: Chris Petty.
Directions: From the town of Lancaster, go south on US 521 to the small town of Heath Springs. US 521 bears a sharp left at the end of town; go straight here onto SR 15 and go 1 7/10 mi. Take left at historical marker sign. This is SR 467, but the sign may not be there. Go 1 2/10 mi. and park on the right at pulloff. Follow trail from here 100 yd. into the woods where boulders are.

6 James Island County Park (The Climbing Wall)

A 50' bouldering wall with "Full Moon" climbing programs to escape the heat. Rock classes and instruction. Passes and daily fees $8.00 and up, noon–8:00 P.M. weekdays and 9:00 A.M.–8:00 P.M. weekends during summer. Water-slide feature in the park. Primitive camping or cottages available. Autumn. James Island County Park, (843) 795-7275.
Ref: Holly Luther 6/98; www.ccprc.com/jicp.htm.
Directions: Located by Charleston, South Carolina, on James Island. Take Folly Rd. to Riverland Dr. Park is on your left.

South Dakota

The world asks one question: Did you do your job? The answer is not: I would have done it if people had been nicer . . . if I'd had the money . . . if I hadn't died; if's don't count. The answer must be: yes! —Korczak Kiolkowski, Crazy Horse inventor

Every summer, 25,000 Harley-Davidsons chain together for the Black Hills Motorcycle Rally. Riding hogs and picking up chicks, these zealous cyclists fervently state, "I'll give up my bike when they pry it from my cold, dead fingers." In similar fashion, Black Hills rock climbers under the spell of the "Hills" for years would also exclaim, "I'll give up my rock when they pry it from my cold, dead, skinless fingers."

Go to the hills, from whence the climbs cometh. The Needle's Eye, Cathedral Spires, and Ten Pins are all traditional areas with a special caveat for the visitor: The climbs are bold and scary. Conversely, the Rushmore Needles area now holds the attention of sport climbers. As any climber who has spent much time there knows: The Black Hills are a special place. Though the Needles arena has received the spotlight of attention, it is just one area. Much more rock exists in the Hills—quartzite, shale, sandstone, and limestone . . . yes, even gold. (And if you find some gold to climb on, give us a call for a free belay.) There will be plenty of climbing for years to come.

The middle of the state is a climber's wasteland until one hits the Palisades at the eastern border. On your way to the East Coast, stop in and pick up an ear of corn at the Corn Palace in Mitchell—you may need it for "Bridge Night" at New River Gorge.

1 Center of the Nation Boulders ☆

A climber's and geographer's novelty. A couple classic, 10′, limestone, sit-down boulder problems at the geographical center of the United States. Actually, the center of the nation is 10 mi. west of here. Don't expect too much. Autumn. No camping. Government land.

Classics: Stone Johnny B5.9.

Ref: D. Dokken.

Directions: From Belle Fourche go approximately 27 mi. north on Hwy. 85. Turn right, following old paved road ¼ mi. to the geographical center of the United States. Center of the Nation Boulders are 3 mi. south of junction with Hwy. 168.

2 BH☆-(Black Hills Area) Overview ☆☆☆☆

Unique and varied bouldering and cragging in ponderosa pine forests. Bold, traditional leads in the Needles. Sport routes behind Mt. Rushmore. Scattered small bouldering areas abound. Geologically, the "Hills" are a domal uplift. Various formations of sandstone (e.g., Edgemont) and limestone (e.g., Spearfish Canyon) are positioned in concentric rings around the ancient pegmatitic granite of the

The daunting Vertigo Spire 5.11+, the Needles.

TIM TOULA

South Dakota

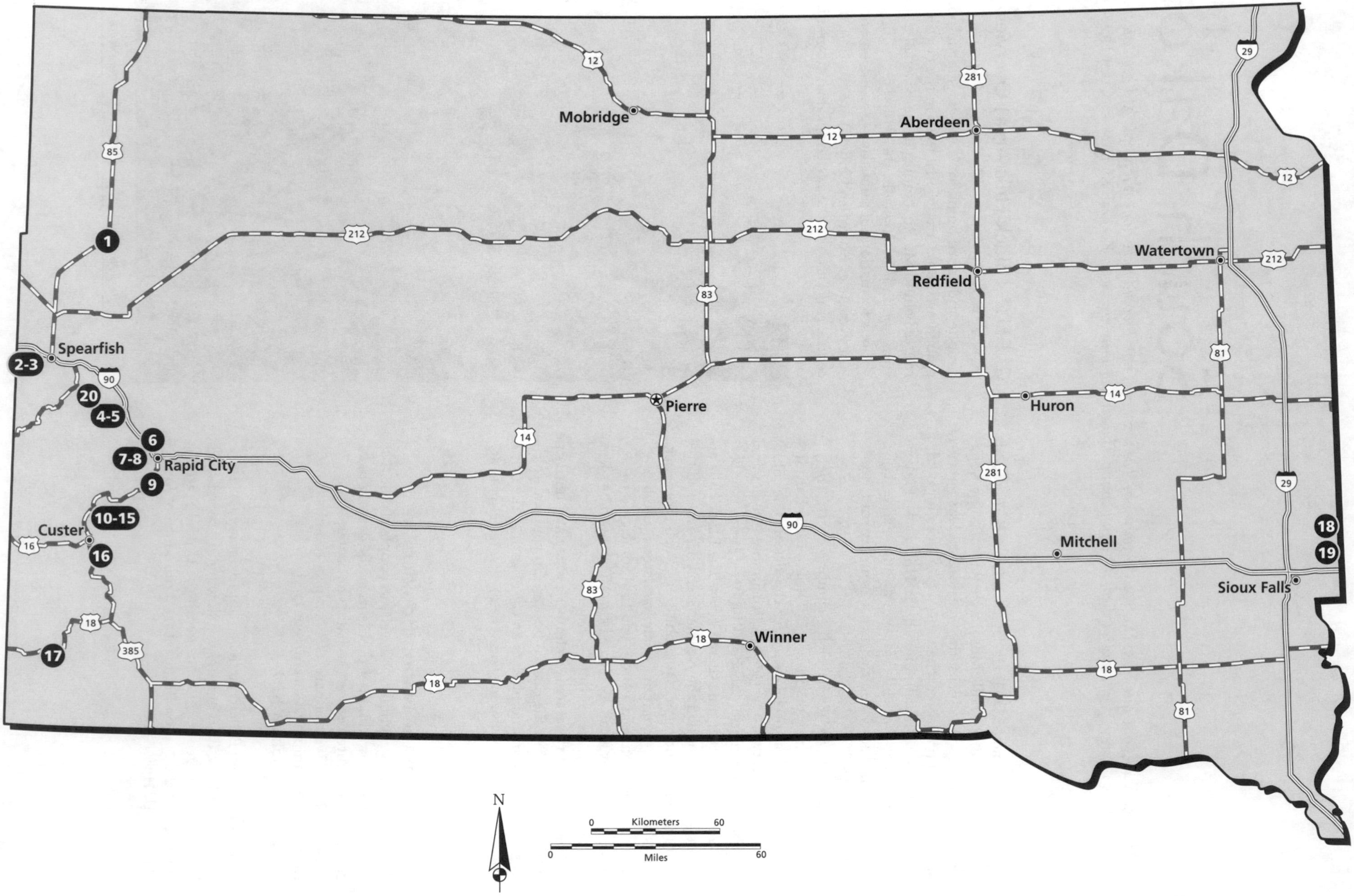

Mobridge

Aberdeen

Watertown

Redfield

Huron

Sioux Falls

Mitchell

Pierre

Winner

Spearfish

Rapid City

Custer

12
29
212
81
29
14
281
281
90
18
81
18
212
12
281
212
83
12
85
212
83
14
18
18
385
90

1
2-3
20
4-5
6
7-8
9
10-15
16
16
17
18
19

N

Kilometers
0   60
Miles
0   60

Needles Area. With a double lifetime's worth of rock, the Black Hills still lends itself to the discovery of many unestablished small cragging and bouldering areas. Remember, fires are allowed only in established grates in campgrounds and not on open Forest Service land. Summer/autumn. Free/pay camping. Private/state/USFS–Black Hills NF, (605) 673-9200.

Classics: Needles Eye 8, Four Little Fishes 9, Superpin 10b, Vertigo 11+, Forbidden Colors 13, Walking The Plankton 13a, The Thimble B1 (see individual listings).

Ref: C [143-99, 142, 133-90, 129, 122(10/90)-64, 116, 115, 114, 110, 95, 74, 69], R [101-46, 95-57, 83-28, 37(6/90)]; Gildart's *Hiking South Dakota's Black Hills Country*; Guidebooks: Phinney's *Mt. Rushmore Memorial Climber's Guide*, Page's *Needles of Custer State Park in the Black Hills of South Dakota*, Horning's *Black Hills Needles: Selected Free Climbs*, Mountain Mania's *Rushmore Needles Climbing Guide*, Piana's *Touch The Sky*, Harlin's *Rocky Mountain*, Dingus McGee's *Poor Person's Guide to the Black Hills' Needles*, Kamps's *A Climber's Guide to the Needles*, Conn's *Rock Climbs in the Needles*.

Directions: From Rapid City the Black Hills expand west from town northeast to Spearfish and southeast to Hot Springs.

3 BH–Spearfish Canyon ✪✪✪

One-pitch limestone sport cragging in an amazingly bee-yoot-ee-full canyon. More than one hundred routes. This area has been heavily developed in the last few years of the late 1990s. The main area is the Mohican Wall, which has a good selection of 5.11-5.13+. Skeletal Remains is not as good, but you can climb there on sunny days in the winter. Potentially good bouldering. Good ice climbing in winter. Contact Mountain Mania or Adventure Sport in Spearfish for more detailed information. Autumn/winter. Free/pay camping. USFS–Black Hills NF, (605) 642-4622.

Ref: A. Gram.

Directions: From Spearfish hook south on Hwy. 14A to roadside Spearfish Canyon walls. Go to the local climbing shop right off the highway in Spearfish. They're super cool and will set you up with directions to the crag.

4 BH–Nemo Boulders ✪

Sandstone bouldering maze of 20' walls. A few good problems for the beginning to intermediate climber. Spring-autumn. Free camping. USFS–Black Hills NF, (605) 578-2744.

Directions: From Nemo go just south of town on Hwy. 2335. Park at Steamboat Rock pullout. Hike west to rock. Nemo Bouldering is in corridors and may require a little snooping around to find.

5 BH–Experimental Forest ✪✪

Incredible-quality quartzitic bouldering and short, east-facing, 30' toprope walls. This quartzite band is seemingly unusual for the Black Hills. Huecoesque overhang. Summer–autumn. Free camping. USFS–Black Hills NF, (605) 578-2744.

Classics: Quartzite Overhang.

Directions: From Rapid City follow Hwy. 44 west. Take Hwy. 385 north (going 4 ½ mi. past Trout Haven and FR 237). Turn left (west) onto FR 616 (good dirt) for 7/10 mi. Turn left onto FR 663 for 2 mi. Turn right onto FR 658 for 6/10 mi. Experimental Forest Rocks are on left on high point of landscape. Quartzite boulders near parking. Walk uphill to cliff band. Inconspicuous.

6 BH–Meat Packing Plant ✪✪

Some meaty problems on low parking-lot boulder. Other 15-20' Dakota sandstone boulders and west-facing top-ropes "a cut above" these. For the real rock hounds, the South Dakota School of Mines's Museum of Geology is well worth the visit. Spring/autumn. No camping. Possibly private land.

Classics: Problems by Meat Packing Plant, Mark's Lunge B1+.

Ref: M. Jacobs.

Directions: Rapid City. Head just west of downtown. When you smell fresh beef from West Omaha St., turn north onto Chicago St. Parking (which may have changed) just past the meat packing plant where obvious 20' overhanging sandy sandstone boulder with bolts looks at your car. Hike north past building to more rock on slope. These Dakota boulders are visible when driving west on west Omaha St. to north of road.

7 BH–Johnson Siding (closed?) ✪✪✪

If you'd like to start out with a clean slate, try this stunted, unique 45' slate outcrop with some classic lines for the intermediate climber. A dozen excellent, short, west-facing climbs from 5.8 to 5.11. Instant access. (A reader reports that this area is now closed.) Spring–autumn. No camping. May be private land.

Classics: 5.9 Corner, Centerpiece (crack) 10+, Bein Roof B1.

Ref: S. Fossen.

Directions: From Rapid City slide west on Hwy. 44 to restaurant/bar at Johnson Siding (don't blink!). Just past store, take first turn left and look immediately right for this small but quaint area. Park off road, a cheater's stick away from the rock.

8 BH–Falling Rock ✪✪✪

Small pockets and edges. Seventy-five-foot limestone winter sport training wall. Pay camping. USFS–Black Hills NF, (605) 343-1567.

Ref: C 90s; Guidebook: printed sheet.

Directions: From Rapid City plummet 4 mi. west on Hwy. 44 to Falling Rock. Check with locals for more details/guide.

9 BH–Boulder Hill ✩✩

Granite cragging. USFS–Black Hills NF, (605) 343–1567.
Ref: M. Jacobs.
Directions: From Rapid City scamper southwest on Hwy. 16. Turn north on Hwy. 358. Hike east to Boulder Hill rocks.

10 BH–Keystone Areas ✩✩✩

The 80′ granite/metamorphic cragging area west of Keystone was developed by Mark Jacobs and others. Some fun, pumpy routes. Summer/autumn. Free/pay camping. USFS–Black Hills NF, (605) 574–2534.
Classics: 5.11 bolted route.
Ref: M. Jacobs.
Directions: From Keystone sneak approximately 1 mi. west on Hwy. 353. Hike up steep hill to routes on back of rock. Also, more rock approximately 1 mi. southeast of town on Hwy. 16 tying into Hwy. 244. On right is roadside slate pinnacle.

11 BH–Mt. Rushmore (Chopping Block/Middle Marker) ✩✩✩✩

Sylvan cranking behind the back of Mt. Rushmore. This area has become known as the sport-climbing alternative to the Needles since its renewed energy in 1985 by Black Hills rogues Phinney and Engle. So, if you want a workout, stay here. If you want to get a workout and get scared shitless, go to the Needles. Classic 100′ granite face routes on beautiful stone. In summer, holds can be slicker than a South Dakota snake-oil salesman. Remember, no climbing is allowed within posted boundaries of Mt. Rushmore. These are intricate areas, so consult literature references for topo maps or hire Paul Piana as a guide. Mt. Rushmore is just 17 mi. from Crazy Horse—where the chipping never stops! Summer/autumn. Free camping. USFS–Black Hills NF, (605) 574–2534.
Classics: Gossamer 8, Star Dancer 9, Baba Cool 10a, Ankles Away 10, Mr. Critical 11, Double Chin 11c, Twelve White Sticks 11d, Yuppie Warfare 12-, Ladies in Love 12, Forbidden Colors 13, Tomcat Tracer 13a, Jackknife Matinee 13, Lizzie Beams Desire 13+.
Ref: C [122(10/90)-64, 116, 107, 95], R 37(6/90)-38; Guidebooks: Phinney's *Mt. Rushmore Memorial Climber's Guide*, Horning's *Black Hills Needles: Selected Free Climbs*, Mountain Mania's *Rushmore Needles Climbing Guide*, Piana's *Touch the Sky*.
Directions: From Keystone nose your way up Hwy. 244 behind Mt. Rushmore Monument. Wind west past visitors center on Hwy. 244 for one minute. When you see George Washington's nose in profile to your right, you're getting close to the start of the main sport-climbing development. In two minutes, on the back of the presidents' backs, just past the no-climbing boundary, is Emancipation Rockphormation. By minute three or four, on the right side of the road are the main areas Middle Marker, Monster, and South Seas (adjacent to old gravel road). Chopping Block is on left side of Hwy. 244 across from South Seas before very sharp left bend. Slightly farther west is Horse Thief Lake. Various parking pullouts service each climbing area. Check with NPS at Mt. Rushmore. Intricate areas—consult a guidebook or local.

12 BH–Harney Peak ✩✩✩

The highest point in South Dakota, at 7,242′, offers 80′ granite bouldering/crags along the way through the Cathedral Spires. Great for exploring and its views of the Black Hills. The Marina Area is up on the slopes of Harney Peak. There is a rather large rock wall, approximately 300′–400′, with lots of new route opportunities, and ice climbing in the winter WI3. Some routes are listed in Piana's *Touch the Sky*. Summer. Free camping. USFS–Black Hills NF, (605) 574–2534.
Ref: A. Gram; Guidebooks: Page's *Needles of Custer State Park in the Black Hills of South Dakota*, Horning's *Black Hills Needles: Selected Free Climbs*, Mountain Mania's *Rushmore Needles Climbing Guide*, Piana's *Touch the Sky*, Harlin's *Rocky Mountain*, Dingus McGee's *Poor Person's Guide to the Black Hills' Needles*, Kamps's *A Climber's Guide to the Needles*, Conn's *Rock Climbs in the Needles*.
Directions: From Custer drive approximately 8 mi. north on Hwy. 89 to Cathedral Spires parking area. Hike north approximately one hour, passing the Cathedral Spires and Picket Fence. En route to Harney Peak are scattered formations. Another way: From US 385 south of Hill City, turn left toward Hill City. Turn left again on Palmer Creek Rd. (dirt). Park by a large meadow below large rock north face of Harney Peak. Find an abandoned trail and hike for about 2 mi.

13 BH–Needles (Outlets, Ten Pins, Cathedral Spires) ✩✩✩✩✩

Grass roots, ballsy (i.e., runout), traditional granite ascents—the way Americans used to climb. A fall from one of the runout routes could answer the long-standing enigma, "Does pain have meaning?" Any climber seeking a real perspective of the words *traditional ascent* can get it from routes like The Thimble, Vertigo, Hairy Pin, and Superpin. From first ascents by Fritz Weissner in 1936; to the Conns in the late 1940s; to Rearick, Kamps, Gill, and Cleveland in the 1960s; Muehl, Bein, Black, Piana, and Archbold in the 1970s; and many colorful others, such as Delannoy, Lewis, Smedley, and Jacobs on into the 1990s. Many brave climbers have honed their face skills or at least been on "pins and needles" in the magical Black Hills. Spring/autumn. Pay camping. USFS–Black Hills NF, (605) 574–2534/Custer State Park, (605) 255–4515.
Classics: Spire Two 3, Innercourse 5, Rum Room 7, Tent Peg 7, Tricouni Nail 8, Trojan Determination 8, Behind the Door 9, Four Little Fishes 9, Hardrocker 9, Needle's Eye 5.10-, Nantucket Sleigh Ride 10, Superpin 10bR,

Farewell to Arms 10+, For Whom the Bell Tolls 11a, Limited Immunity 11b, Vertigo 11+ , Leaning Jowler 12a, Walking the Plankton 12b; Bouldering: Thimble B5.12a, Outlet/Campground Boulders, Campground Boulder (Yellow Wall B1).

Ref: C [174-118, 115(8/89)-68, 50(10/78)-22], R 8(5/85); Sherman's *Stone Crusade, Master of Rock;* Guidebooks: Page's *Needles of Custer State Park in the Black Hills of South Dakota,* Dickerson and Whittle's *Custer State Park/Needles Climbing Guide,* Horning's *Black Hills Needles: Selected Free Climbs,* Mountain Mania's *Rushmore Needles Climbing Guide,* Piana's *Touch the Sky,* Harlin's *Rocky Mountain,* Dingus McGee's *Poor Person's Guide to the Black Hills' Needles,* Kamps's *A Climber's Guide to the Needles,* Conn's *Rock Climbs in the Needles.*

Directions: From Custer wheedle 7 mi. north on Hwy. 89. Four areas of historical significance in the Needles: 1) Sylvan Lake: This area is at junction of Hwy. 89 and Hwy. 87 and contains the Outlets northwest of lake, Campground Boulder on east shore, and Photographer's Peak ¼ mi. southeast. 2) Needle's Eye: 1 ¼ mi. east of Sylvan Lake and famous for the Thimble, adjacent to the Needle's Eye, and many classic routes. 3) Ten Pins: Go further east past Needle's Eye where sharp switchbacks arise. The Ten Pins lie in between hairpin turns. Classic! 4) Cathedral Spires and Picket Fence: ½-mi. hike north from Ten Pins to this land of more than multipitched summits en route to Harney Peak. Many more formations in the Needles await development. Local guide or guidebook a must for this complex area.

14 BH–Iron Mountain Hwy. ⭐⭐⭐
Obvious roadside granite boulders developed partially by bouldering specialist Bob Murray. Sixty-foot cragging formations as well. Giant rose quartz specimens. Postcard tunnel views of Mt. Rushmore. Summer–autumn. USFS–Black Hills NF, (605) 574-2534.

Ref: M. Jacobs; Guidebook: Piana's *Touch the Sky.*

Directions: From Keystone wind south on Alt. Hwy. 16 through scenic tunnels to top of Iron Mountain Hwy. switchbacks. Climbing lies at crest of road, mainly on right.

15 BH–Raspberry Rocks ⭐⭐⭐
Fine 200′ granite cragging. Smoother-quality granite than the pegmatite of the Needles. Excellent, challenging routes. Developed by Kertzman, Jacobs, Engle, et al. Summer–autumn. Free camping. USFS–Black Hills NF, (605) 574-2534.

Classics: Carl's Bad Cavern 7, Garden of Eden (two roofs) 9, Horn Route 10, left Face of Eve 11b, RIP Diagonal 11d.

Ref: M. Jacobs; C 95-13; Guidebook: Dingus McGee's *Poor Person's Guide to the Black Hills' Needles.*

Directions: From Keystone pick your way up Iron Mountain Rd. (Hwy. 16A) through scenic tunnels up to crest. Three mi. past crest find Iron Creek Rd. Go ⁸/₁₀ mi. farther on Hwy. 16A. Turn right (west). Go to end of road. Continue in same direction on foot for ten minutes on ridge, then down and right to base (talus) of Raspberry Rocks.

16 BH–Custer Area ⭐⭐⭐
Many scattered granite bouldering and 40′ toprope areas with short, steep walls. A lot of other rock (possible understatement) exists near the town of Custer. The only problem may be answering the question, "Am I on private land?" Next question, "Do they own shotguns?" Summer/autumn. Pay camping. Private land/ Black Hills NF, (605) 673-4853.

Classics: Custer's Last Hang 10+.

Ref: P. Muehl; Guidebook: Piana's *Touch the Sky.*

Directions: Custer. Many formations extend out from town in all directions. Custer's Last Hang: Above town to south: At small grocery store on east side of town, follow roads south/southeast to obtain the crest of the hill above town where signs loom over town. Park near crest. Walk north to roof crack and other rock. Scattered crags south on Hwy. 385, visible from road. Also, more short roadside areas/boulders west of town on Hwy. 16. Not to mention a truckload north on Hwy. 385. May need to ask landowner permission for some areas.

17 BH–Edgemont Sandstone ⭐
Scattered 30′ bands of Dakota sandstone bouldering walls and blocks. Exploration necessary.

Ref: D. Hoover.

Directions: Edgemont. North of town lies Dakota sandstone bouldering similar to Whiterock, Wyoming.

18 Devil's Gulch Historic Site ⭐⭐⭐
A quaint, narrow chasm with limited 40′ topropes or high solos on red quartzite. Potential for extremely good gymnastic challenges. May require brushing off the dust. First aerial traverse in 1876 by outlaw Jesse James and horse while escaping a guns-a-smokin' posse. Free camping at nearby Split Rock Municipal Park on the west side of the railroad tracks. Autumn. Pay camping. Government park, (605) 594-6721.

Classics: Dick's Roof B5.10, Rattlesnake Traverse 5.8+.

Ref: D. Dokken.

Directions: From Garretson roam just north of town, going north on Main St. and following signs. Turn right at railroad tracks. Follow signs to Devil's Gulch Park and parking. A quick walk from the car on a little footbridge over the gulch. Rocks below.

19 Palisades State Park ⭐⭐⭐
Pleasant climbing along forested watercourse with 60′ cracks and face edging reminiscent of Devil's Lake slippery quartzite. Riverside pinnacles. Park policy: no bolting. Rock of 1.8-billion-year-old Sioux quartzite composes the

Rock-lined waterways of Palisades State Park.

bedrock of southeast South Dakota and Southwest Minnesota in Devil's Gulch Park, South Dakota, and Blue Mounds, Minnesota. Spring/autumn. Minimal entrance fee. Pay camping. State park, (605) 594–3824.

Classics: Bachar Cracker 5.11+.

Ref: D. Dokken.

Directions: From Sioux Falls (20 mi. northeast), follow I–90 east. Exit on Hwy. 11 north for 8 ⁴/₁₀ mi. to Garretson. Turn right (south) on Split Rock Creek Rd. for approximately 2 mi., following Palisades State Park signs to visible rock along waterway inside park. Climbs on either side of creek.

20 Deadwood ☆☆☆

These 40′ limestone climbs vary in difficulty from 5.9 to 5.11–12. Spring and early summer are the best seasons because the wasps aren't out and later in the summer people have been spotting rattlesnakes. Free camping. USFS–Black Hills NF, (605) 578–2744.

Directions: From Deadwood go toward Sturgis on Hwy. 14A. Just out of town you will go down a hill. When you reach the bottom, take a left on a gravel road. Cross a bridge and go for approximately 3 mi., crossing a couple more bridges. If you get to a tunnel, you went too far. Park on the left side of the road. Head down hillside on the right side of the road and cross the creek. Find the trail that angles left to right up the hillside across the creek to the rock.

Tennessee

You can't buy a 5.12. —Rob Robinson

Tennessee has been blessed with high-quality sandstone crags and an abundance of them. Inspiring roofs, overhanging face, cracks, and hangs destroy a vertical climber's sense of balance. But who needs it? Better to pick up a bottle of Jack Daniels, watch old movies of Elvis Presley's hip rotations, get charged up at the nuclear reactor at Oak Ridge, and then launch to the rocks.

Longtime Chattanooga local Rob Robinson dubs Tennessee "the Fort Knox of sandstone." Truth is, you'll find the climbing here worth its weight in bullion. It is powerful, gymnastic sandstone as superb as any in the United States. Chattanooga's traditional areas, Sunset Park and Tennessee Wall, are typical of the quality cragging and cliff base bouldering this Civil War state volunteers. The climber with a keen eye for discovery may find similar marriages in more than a dozen (and counting) bluffs radiating north from "Nooga," the buckle of the sandstone belt.

A Sunday drive through the state demands a climber to query if any climbing has been done on "this crag or that one ova thar." The Cumberland Plateau is such an area. As is true throughout the Southeast, any exploration should be done with a careful regard toward "local" rapport. Yet once you discover how friendly state residents really are, you might just discover what they mean when they say, "Down South in Tennessee, there's really living."

1 Clarksville Cliff (King's Bluff) ✮✮✮

Quaint, white 40'–75' limestone river bluffs overlook the Cumberland River. Most of the 151 routes are short, vertical four-bolt clip-ups on poor to decent rock quality up to 5.13b. Walter Wilkinson developed 85 percent of the area while living in Clarksville from 1991 to 1995. The other real developer of the area was Terry (Rainman) Parker, who also wrote the first guidebook. Routes range from 5.4 to 5.13. King's Bluff. Since 1995 Eman Lacoste has been developing the new routes and says while the area is access sensitive, climbers are still welcome. It ain't no Rifle, Colorado, but then Rifle ain't no Clarksville! En route through Nashville to southern Tennessee crags, don't miss the Grand Ole Opry and the world's largest collection of soda and beer cans (more than 25,000) at Soda Mart/Can World on Ridgecrest Dr. in Goodlettsville. The season is year-round, but summers are hard and winters cold—fall is just about right. No camping. Private land—please be respectful.

Classics: 5.7+ Captain Hook, three bolts; 5.8+ Baby Kangaroo, three bolts; 5.8- The Natural, crack; 5.9+ Crow's Nest, four bolts and 5.9+, 5.10a Born to be Freed, all natural broken corner and face; First Plumb, four bolts; 5.10c Ritz-Bits, four bolts; 5.10d Plum Tuckered Out; 5.11a Murphy's Law, four bolts #5 Super Rock; 5.11b/c Baby I'm Ten Inches Long, five bolts; 5.12b/c For Girly Girls Only, four bolts, 5.13b? Three Wishes, bolted.
Ref: E. Lacoste 11/00, J. Dickey; Guidebooks: Wilkinson's guidebook, Porter's *Searching for Stone.*
Directions: Clarksville. Take exit 11 west off I-24. Follow Hwy. 76 (Ashland City Rd.) 6 $^1/_{10}$ mi. west, passing Hwy. 41A en route. At Glendale Car Wash, turn left onto Max Ct. for $^1/_{10}$ mi. and park below huge power lines—climbers with pacemakers, take note! (Gray building with "Woodmen of the World" is adjacent to west.) Climb hill, following power lines for less than five minutes to King's Bluff and Cumberland River. Anchors at the top of every route. All the land is privately owned, so climbers must use rappel bolts as walking off the cliff is not allowed by landowners' requirements.

2 SCP✮-(South Cumberland Plateau) Bee Rock/Overview ✮✮✮

The South Cumberland Plateau holds an amazing profusion of sandstone walls that line canyon bluffs throughout many river valleys. This region of rock extends triangularly from Nashville to near Knoxville and down to the small town of Jasper. Bee Rock is one such 80' sandstone cliff. Pay camping. Private land.
Classics: Three Teeth 6, Life's a Beach 10, Love Monster 11+, Tuff Enuff 13-.
Ref: E. Whittemore; C [112, 107, 101]; *South Cumberland and Falls Creek Falls: A Hiker's Guide;* Guidebook: Whittemore's *Heart of Stone.*
Directions: From west of Monterey buzz off exit 300 on I-40. Turn south (right) on Hwy. 70 for $^1/_{10}$ mi. Turn left onto Bee Rock Rd. for $^4/_{10}$ mi., parking outside of campground on left in gravel lot. Bee Rock is south of campground, ten minutes. Hike on dirt road to rock. Spider Rock and Hidden Rock are past campground. Bear right on dirt road in front of campground gate.

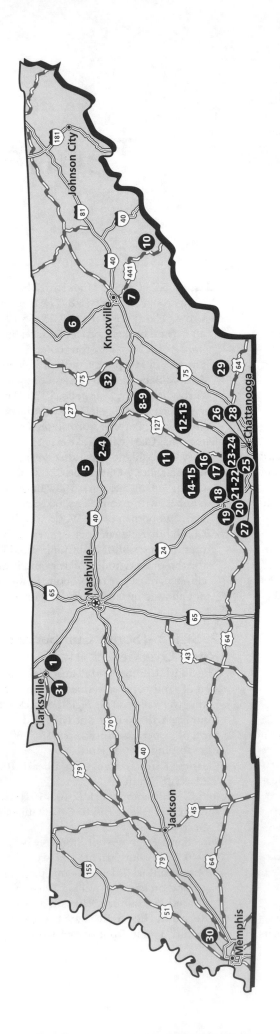

Tennessee

181

Johnson City

81

40

40

441

10

7

Knoxville

6

75

32

75

29

64

27

8-9

Chattanooga

127

12-13

26

28

2-4

23-24

5

11

16

25

14-15

17

21-22

18

19

20

27

40

24

Nashville

65

65

43

64

1

31

Clarksville

70

40

79

Jackson

45

79

64

155

51

30

Memphis

N

0   Kilometers   60

0   Miles   60

3 SCP–Spider Rock/Hidden Rock (closed) ★★★

Sorry, she's a goner . . . closed down. Access problems have caused the closure of these one hundred sandstone cliffs to climbing. Free/pay camping. Private land.

Classics: Spider Rock: Retro Vex 11d, Confessor 12b; Hidden Rock: Radial Extension 8+, Volunteer Jam 10c, Future Mettle 11+, Blankenstein 12.

Ref: C [131(4/92), 112, 107, 101]; Guidebook: Whittemore's *Heart of Stone.*

Directions: From west of Monterey buzz off exit 300 on I-40. Turn south (right) on Hwy. 70 for ^{1}/10 mi. Turn left onto Bee Rock Rd. for ^{4}/10 mi., parking outside of campground on left in gravel lot. Bee Rock is south of campground, a ten-minute hike on dirt road to rock. Spider Rock and Hidden Rock are past campground. Bear right on dirt road in front of campground gate for ^{3}/10 mi. to parking on right. Spider Rock below parking. Hidden Rock picks up at old barn and chimney.

4 SCP–The Boulderfield (closed) ★★

Sandstone boulder garden. Autumn. Pay camping. Private land.

Ref: E. Whittemore; C 101; Guidebook: Whittemore's *Heart of Stone.*

Directions: Between Cookeville and Monterey.

5 Superslab (closed) ★★★

Sandstone slab/crag. Superslab is on the Cumberland Plateau. Private land. Ask locals.

Ref: E. Whittemore; Guidebook: Whittemore's *Heart of Stone.*

6 Devil's Racetrack (near Cove Lake State Park) ★★★

Face climbing on routes up to 5.12 on mini "Seneca Rocks" 200′ sandstone blades. Pay camping at Cove Lake (423) 566-9701. Autumn/winter. Private land.

Ref: A. Ilgner.

Directions: North of Knoxville. From Knoxville take I-75 to Cove Lake exit. Drive to Cove Lake State Park. There are two entrances into Cove Lake Park. Take the second one and you'll be right on the road that exits the park on the back side. Pass stop sign. Devil's Racetrack Rock on gravel before creek crossing to rocks. After the stop sign, look for the first left gravel road, about ^{1}/4 mi. Go up the gravel road about 200 yd. and park on the right side near a wide spot in the road and next to the small creek. Walk up the creek and the hill to gain the cliffs. These fins are viewable from I-40 on the east side of the interstate at mm 137.

7 Cherokee Bluff ★★

This 100′ craglet yields more than thirty short, quality routes on rare limestone. Most topropes and sport leads are 5.10–5.11. Expect steep face edging with a couple zesty 5.12 overhang problems on the far right end. Watch the houseboats motor upstream from this climber's aerie. Knoxville offers the University of Tennessee Volunteers and a cultural cornucopia of eateries in famed Old Town. Spring/autumn. No camping. Private land.

Classics: Static Cling 11.

Ref: J. Latendresse; C 131(4/92)-24; Guidebooks: Watford's *Dixie Cragger's Atlas*, Robinson and Watford's *Deep South Climber's Companion*, East Tennessee Climber's Association guide.

Directions: From Knoxville follow Hwy. 129 from downtown for approximately ten minutes. Just past hospital and then Marine Reserve, take first right onto Mont Lake into a small residential area. Follow and take another first right onto Craghead to dead-end. Hike to Tennessee River, where lies Cherokee Bluff's split-level crag. Top tier is 40′ high and is split by exposed foot-trail traverse. Bottom tier (approximately 60′) requires a rappel down to water level.

8 SCP–Ozone Falls ★★

Bouldering opposite serene woodland falls. Possibly routes on 80′ soft sandstone amphitheater. A scenic gorge with 110′ high waterfall creating pools in this State Natural Area.

Ref: E. Whittemore; Guidebook: Whittemore's *Heart of Stone.*

Directions: From Crab Orchard (I-40) take exit 329 and travel east on US 70 about 4 ^{1}/2 mi. to the parking area for Ozone Falls, just west of Ozone. The overlook of the falls is about 100 yd. down a trail.

9 SCP–Black Mountain ★★★

Fun 50′ sandstone bluffs and massive boulders popular with Knoxville locals. Sixty routes up to 5.12. Developed by Glenn Ritter and Tony Robinson in the early 1990s. Autumn. No camping. Private land.

Classics: Beta Daddy V6, many routes.

Ref: R. Turan; C 131(4/92); Guidebooks: Watford's *Dixie Cragger's Atlas*, Robinson and Watford's *Deep South Climber's Companion*, East Tennessee Climber's Association guide.

Directions: From Knoxville (one and a half hours), take I-40 west to Crab Orchard exit to the south on paved road. After ^{3}/10 mi., take a right onto gravel road for 1 ^{7}/10 mi. At three-way junction, turn left, going up the flanks of Black Mountain to obvious tower. Front Area is just before tower, and Back Area is at base of tower both off to south.

10 Look Rock ★★

A small area of numerous short 40′ topropes and minimal bouldering on bomber quartzite rock one hour from Knoxville and just outside Great Smoky Mountains National Park. Fifty routes. A nice beginner area with some surprises to be found for experts. This area makes for a nice escape from the Smoky Mountain summer tourist mania.

Rob Turan is Beta Daddy V6, Black Mountain.

Inspiring views of the Great Smokies combine with fun, short cranks. Spring–autumn. Free/pay camping. Uncertain land ownership.

Ref: J. Latendresse.

Directions: From Maryville (approximately thirty minutes), look to the Smokies, then rock south on Hwy. 336 to Sixmile. At Sixmile (wide spot in the road), get on Montvale Rd., then get on Forrest Hill, which takes one under Foothills Pkwy. overpass. From the overpass it's $^3/_{10}$ mi. on Happy Valley (aka Montvale Rd.) to base-camp sign and road junction. Take left at junction onto Butter Gap Flats for $^7/_{10}$ mi. Go left for $^3/_{10}$ mi., then right for $^1/_{10}$ mi. to obtain the Foothills Pkwy. Turn left onto parkway for $^4/_{10}$ mi. to Look Rock Tower parking area. Two areas: 1) Short cliffs below parking area. 2) Hike trail across road $^1/_2$ mi. up to Look Rock Tower. Bouldering and short topropes underneath tower to west.

11 SCP–Fall Creek Falls State Park ★★★

Amid rhododendron and laurel thickets, sparkling streams, and wild cascades sits Fall Creek Falls, which at 256′ is the highest waterfall east of the Rockies. Fields of giant boulders and abundant, unyielding 200′ quartzite monoliths on the Fall Creek Falls Trail and side trails of the Lower Cane Creek Loop. Climbing monitored by park—check with rangers. Autumn. Pay camping. State park, (423) 881–5298.

Ref: P. Jarrard; C 68; *South Cumberland and Fall Creek Falls: A Hiker's Guide;* Guidebooks: Watford's *Dixie Cragger's Atlas,* Detterline's *A Climber's Guide to the Mid-South,* Hall's *Southern Rock.*

Directions: From Spencer trickle east of Spencer on Hwy. 30 for several mi. Turn south on Hwy. 284 (State Park Rd.) to Fall Creek Falls State Park. Also accessed from Hwy. 111 (399 on maps). Rock walls line the waterfall area. Climbing at waterfalls and Millikan Overlook.

12 SCP–Laurel Falls (Laurel Snow Pocket Wilderness) ★★★★

Excellent, plentiful rock in scenic wooded hollows. Buzzard Point, the most popular 80′ area, holds a heap of sport routes (5.11a–13) developed by Jarrard, Chesnutt, Robinson, Ritter, and Stegg. Try a ride on Monkey Boy 5.11d to get a feel for the beauty of lines here. Thirty-one routes in early 1990s. Great potential for excellent bouldering on trails. Laurel Falls is a farther walk and thus a quieter cliff area away from Buzzard Point. The quality of rock of this white, diamond-hard sandstone will surprise you more than a trout in your bathwater. This is Bowater Inc. land. Dayton was the site of the 1925 Scopes Monkey Trial, which challenged the state law against the teaching of evolution in schools. Autumn–spring. Free camping. Private land/Rhea County land.

Classics: Harder 10, Classical Crack 11c, Monkey Boy 11d, Evolution Number Nine 12a, Origin of Species 12a, Webs We Weave 12b, Shallow Water 12b, Annie Sprinkle's Christmas 12+.

Ref: P. Jarrard; *South Cumberland and Fall Creek Falls: A Hiker's Guide;* Guidebooks: Robinson's *The Insider's Guide to Southern Sandstone, Vol. 1* (see www.southernsandstone.com), Watford's *Dixie Cragger's Atlas,* Robinson and Watford's *Deep South Climber's Companion.*

Directions: From Dayton shoot northwest of town, following signs. Several access points including this one for Laurel Falls: From medical center in Dayton, go west on Walnut Grove Rd. in Dayton for approximately 1 $^1/_2$ mi. Turn left at T where Pocket Wilderness sign lies onto Back Valley Rd. Go approximately 1 mi. more and turn right onto dirt road (Richland Creek Rd.) for 1 mi. to parking. Hike 1 $^1/_2$ mi. (approximately forty-five minutes) on good trail with abundant cliffs and boulders along way, bearing right after crossing old bridge. This trail takes one to cliff line at Laurel Falls. Routes begin to left of waterfall and continue down cliff for $^1/_2$ mi. or so.

13 SCP–Buzzard Point ★★★★

Scenic orange-and-white 100′ sandstone composes this sports crag. The beauty of this rock deserves more superlatives than space will allow. Tweaky face lines with occasional roofs, lots of good 5.10 climbing, and desperately aesthetic 5.13s add up to more than 115 routes. Autumn–spring. Free camping at parking area. Bowater resource land.

Classics: Dakota Blues 8, Jungalistic 9, 900′ Jesus 10a, Just Another Crack In the Wall 10d, King Jesus 11a, Crankasauraus 11a, Tall Cool One 11d, Incredalocks 12a, Gargantua 12a, Off to the Wild Blue Yonder 12a, Shake, Rattle, and Hum 12c, Oh Man 13a, Soul Sounds 13a, Au Natural 13, Pieta 14a (heavily drilled pockets).

Ref: P. Jarrard, J. Gruenberg; C [134, 121(4/92)-24]; *South Cumberland and Fall Creek Falls: A Hiker's Guide;* Guidebooks: Robinson's *The Insider's Guide to Southern Sandstone, Vol. 1,* Watford's *Dixie Cragger's Atlas,* Cater's *Sport Crags of the East,* Robinson and Watford's *Deep South Climber's Companion,* Ritter's *Buzzard Point Route Log.*

Directions: From Dayton shoot northwest of town, following signs. Several access points including this one for Laurel Falls: From medical center in Dayton, go west on Walnut Grove Rd. in Dayton for approximately 1 ½ mi. Turn left at T where pocket wilderness sign lies onto Back Valley Rd. Go approximately 1 mi. more and turn right onto dirt road (Richland Creek Rd.) for 1 mi. to parking. Hike more than two hours on good trail to main point with abundant cliffs and boulders along way. Or, hike a short distance, cross creek, and scramble up slope to base of wall.

14 SCP–Great Stone Door (Savage Gulf State Natural Area) ★★

Another scenic Tennessee climbing area, the Stone Door probably has the oldest history of rock climbing of any crag in the area. Two hundred foot sandstone crags. Most routes end at loose rock band 65′ up. The Nose Route 5.5 is closed. Climbing only on state park land; climbers must register. Autumn. Free camping. State park, (931) 692–3887.

Classics: Cornflake Crack 5, High and Dry 9, Campsite Dihedral 10.

Ref: P. Jarrard; C [93, 68]; *South Cumberland and Fall Creek Falls: A Hiker's Guide*; Guidebooks: Watford's *Dixie Cragger's Atlas,* Detterline's *A Climber's Guide to the Mid-South.*

Directions: From Beersheba Springs go east on paved road, following signs to park. Follow trail to Great Stone Door.

15 SCP–Savage Gulf State Natural Area ★★★★

This is a wild area of primeval forests, beautiful waterfalls, and a world of 100′ sandstone-rimmed canyons. Autumn. Pay camping. State land, (931) 779–3532.

Ref: *South Cumberland and Fall Creek Falls: A Hiker's Guide;* Guidebooks: Detterline's *A Climber's Guide to the Mid-South,* Hall's *Southern Rock.*

Directions: Several areas present rock within the Savage Gulf State Natural Area (besides the Stone Door). A map should be obtained to navigate in this area of big cliffs and boulders. On the east side: Savage Falls Day Loop or North Rim (northwest of Dunlap on 8, then south on Hwy. 111 [aka Hwy. 399] to signs). On south: Collins Gulf. On east: Greeter Trail.

16 SCP–Rollin's Cove ★★★

Great cranking on this 100′ sandstone crag. Rob Robinson, who has been climbing at a multitude of nearby crags in recent years, reports many classic climbs, including one of the best sandstone cracks in the south, The Trumpet Unblown 5.12+, and, according to him, two of the best sandstone arêtes anywhere, Phenomenon 5.12 and Melting Point 5.12+. This is part of the Cumberland Plateau. Autumn/winter. No camping. Private land.

Ref: *South Cumberland and Fall Creek Falls: A Hiker's Guide.*

Directions: From Whitwell go 10 mi. north on Hwy. 28.

Rollin's Cove Cliffs on left. Access is difficult due to mining operations on top and logging on bottom unless you're traveling with Robinson, the access master. Faces southeast.

17 SCP–The Chimneys ★★

Eighty-foot, south-facing sandstone crag. Autumn/winter. Free camping. Government park.

Ref: P. Jarrard.

Directions: From Whitwell amble north on Hwy. 108. The Chimneys is west off highway. Ask Chattanooga locals.

18 SCP–Fiery Gizzard (Grundy Forest)/Raven Point ★★★★

Spectacular views and climbing to match at these 200′ sandstone sport crags. The Dutch Maid Bakery (Tracy City) has fantastic bread. Autumn–spring. Free camping. Government/private land.

Ref: P. Jarrard; *South Cumberland and Fall Creek Falls: A Hiker's Guide.*

Directions: Fiery Gizzard is a canyon system extending south from Tracy City. Raven Point is an eastern overlook. Two access points: 1) From Tracy City go west on Hwy. 56 to left turn at Grundy Forest sign. Follow this to north tip of Fiery Gizzard. 2) From Tracy City go south at Don's Drug Store for 2 7/10 mi. to straight at Y to white house and parking area. Hike trail to Raven Point.

19 SCP–Sewanee Area (Proctors Hall, Easle, and Morgan's Steep) ★★★

Good steep sandstone crags. Routes in the Sewanee area first developed in the 1950s by Jim Scott. Further developed in the 1980s by Earl, Bean, Henderson, et al. Also impressive boulderfields, e.g., Morgan's Steep. Land is part of the University of the South. Check with Sewanee University Outing Club for more route details. Autumn–spring. Private land.

Classics: Streamline 9+, Power Tie 10, Little Easle 11-, Neurasthenia 11b.

Ref: C 118; *South Cumberland and Falls Creek Falls: A Hiker's Guide.*

Directions: Near Sewanee. Ask locals.

20 SCP–Buggytop Trail (Sewanee Natural Bridge) ★★★

Limestone boulderfields and overhanging outcrops blossom within 2 mi. of the trailhead. Autumn/winter. Private land.

Ref: P. Jarrard; C 118; *South Cumberland and Fall Creek Falls: A Hiker's Guide.*

Directions: Near Sewanee (west of Chattanooga). Buzz south on Hwy. 56 past Sewanee Natural Bridge turnoff at 2 mi. (there is rock here as well). At 6 ½ mi. from Sewanee, turn left at Carter State Natural Area sign.

21 SCP–Foster Falls (aka Fiery Gizzard) ★★★★

More than eighty pumping routes on 120' of superb sandstone. Many Eddie Whittemore sport climbs in overhung caves like the Bunkers Area. Having trouble getting up these routes? Try Arno Ilgner's Warrior's Way Course (see guides below). The Smokehouse (Monteagle) offers hearty Southern breakfasts, and the Dutch Maid Bakery (Tracy City) has fantastic bread. Autumn–spring. Free camping (April–October) with showers in nearby campground. (Chas Hawkins has a great deal: camping with showers and cabins available, call 804–559–4629.) Pay camping on state land.

Classics: Ankles Away 9, Twist and Shout 9+, Mrs. Treated 11a, Standing Room Only 11a, So What 11b, Welcome to Foster Falls 11b/c, Wristlets 11c, Framed 12a, Thieves 12b, Reptile 12a, Satisfaction 12a/b, Darkie the Rum Beast 13a, Snatch 13b, Kill or Be Killed 13d, The Conflict 14a.

Ref: P. Jarrard, E. Whittemore; C [174-50/105, 165(12/96)-44], R [100-91, 82-34, 79-24, 74, 73, 68-26]; *South Cumberland and Fall Creek Falls: A Hiker's Guide*; Guidebooks: Robinson's *The Insider's Guide to Southern Sandstone, Vol. 1*, Watford's *Dixie Cragger's Atlas*, Cater's *Sport Crags of the East*, Robinson and Watford's *Deep South Climber's Companion*, Detterline's *A Climber's Guide to the Mid-South*.

Directions: From Jasper go north on Hwy. 41 for a few miles. Turn left at Foster Falls Scenic Area (brown sign). Take paved road for ³/4 mi. to parking at large picnic shelter. From the parking lot take the trail on the left and follow signs on the trail, which takes you down to a swinging bridge and the base of the falls. Continue walking downstream to access the cliff.

22 SCP–Castle Rock ★★★★

This prominent 120' southeast-facing sandstone sport crag faces the town of Jasper. Expect overhanging face climbs. Autumn–spring. Private land.

Classics: Kindred Spirits 11, Glue Sniffer 11c, Lone Justice 11d, The Prow 5.11+, Pump and a Half 5.11+, Love Is 12b, Bugzapper 12b, Redline 12c, Apes on Acid 14a.

Ref: P. Jarrard; C 187-31, R 11(11/85).

Directions: From Jasper go up Hwy. 41 to top of plateau (approximately 2 mi.). Take first right to right at first stop (½ mi.). Park. Hike 1 mi. down along road to Castle Rock. Tricky to find; it's best to go with knowledgeable Chattanooga local.

23 C☆–(Chattanooga Area) Suck Creek ★★★★

Easy to find, south-facing roadside sandstone cliffs treat one to short but tasty 80' rock snacks. Gardner, Robinson, and Henley amongst the primary ascentists. About 150 routes total. Additional climbing throughout the canyon, but you'll need Robinson's new guide to locate—don't leave home without it! Wearing an NRA cap, a crewcut, and a neck with ample solar radiation will help the out-of-town climber blend. Site of car break-ins—leave the jewelry at home. River's Inn restaurant at junction of Suck Creek and River Canyon Rd. Autumn–spring. No camping. State forest land, (423) 634–3091.

Classics: Rockwork Orange 9+, The Rose 10a, Commandant's Choice 10, Pete and Rob's 10+, The Obsessed 11, Special Olympics 11d, Rainbow Delta 11b, Confetti Fingers 11+, The Cauldron 11+, Milky Way 12c/d; Mr. Big Stuff 10a, Pleasure Burn 11, Going off the Deep End 5.12-, Any Way You Slice It 12-, many more!

Ref: R. Robinson; C [100, 75(12/82), 72, 65], R [100-89, 11(11/85)]; Guidebooks: Robinson's *The Insider's Guide to Southern Sandstone, Vol. 1*, Watford's *Dixie Climber's Atlas*, Robinson and Watford's *Deep South Climber's Companion*, Robinson's *Southern Sandstone*, Detterline's *A Climber's Guide to the Mid-South*.

Directions: From Chattanooga (fifteen minutes) follow Hwy. 127/27 north. Turn 7 mi. west on Suck Creek Rd. to 2 mi. past T-Wall's left turn. Park at pulloff on right. Roadside Wall (I don't get it . . .) is adjacent to road on right. The Upper Passes are farther up and right (back toward "'Nooga" as one looks at hillside), a bit of a steep hike. To prevent theft, park where you can keep an eye on your car.

24 C–Little Rock City (closed) ★★★

This small 30' sandstone bouldering area has above-par boulders but double-bogie access. Private land: No trespassing. Awesome traverse potential. Autumn–spring. No camping.

Classics: Behind the Barndoor B1+.

Ref: J. Sherman.

Directions: From Chattanooga go north of town. Ask locals for specifics.

25 C–Tennessee Wall (aka T-Wall) ★★★★★

Renowned 3-mi. wall of complex, imposing 120' sandstone hangs, and roof cracks on orange, Arapilean rock. There's just about no finer rock and no finer climbing. More than 250 quality routes guaranteed to increase the size of your carotid artery. Most routes developed by southern sandstone hangmasters Rob Robinson and Forrest Gardner et al. since 1984. Some camping below trail and en route/at wall itself. Autumn–spring. Free camping. Prentice Cooper State Forest, (423) 634–3091.

Classics: Jay Walker 7, Golden Locks 8+, In Pursuit of Excellence 9, Hidden Assets 10a, Super Slide 10b, Points O'Contact 10+, Stone Wave 11a, Come and Get It 11, Steepopolis 12-, Only On Earth 11d, Twistin' in the Wind 12, Stone Hinge 12c, Wrectum Recker 12c, Celestial Mechanics 12+, Grand Contusion 13-, Tamper Proof 13a, Defender of the Crown 13a, Psychopath 13b, many more!

Ref: R. Robinson; C [199-80, 174-110, 164-70, 134, 106(2/89)-76, 100, 96], R [100-84, 11(11/85)]; Guidebooks: Robinson's *The Insider's Guide to Southern Sandstone, vol. 1*, Watford's *Dixie Cragger's Atlas*, Cater's *Sport Crags of the East*, Robinson and Watford's *Deep South Climber's*

Companion, Harlin's *East*, Robinson's *The Illustrated Underground Guide to the Tennessee Wall*.

Directions: From Chattanooga ramble on Hwy. 124/27N. Turn west (left) on Suck Creek Rd. (Hwy. 27) for 4 mi. to country store and bridge. After passing bridge, turn left onto River Canyon Rd. for 6 8/10 mi. Park on left past big boulder and large oak. Trail begins 75' before pullout. Hump up trail (good VO2 max assessment) to rock fifteen minutes up to Tennessee Wall.

Tennessee Road Thoughts

As we were taking a "rest-day" tour of the Jack Daniels Factory, Randy, our tour guide, says, "Now, every Friday we are given a pint of Jack Daniels for being employees . . . and that's what we call 'Good Friday'."

—TNT

---

26 C–Sunset Park (on Lookout Mountain) (minimally closed) ✯✯✯✯

Long-standing, quality Chattanooga crag since 1940. *Chattanooga* is derived from the Cherokee word meaning "rock rising to a point." Here, where 250 beautiful routes ascend west-facing walls and quality bouldering (workout traverses) sits at the base, you'll find your forearms rising to a pump. Above all, steep, first-rate 130' sandstone climbing. Cliff developers included Kimbrough and Martin in the 1960s, Gardner, Robinson, Eiseman, and Chesnutt in the 1980s. About a half dozen routes between the base of Alpha Omega and Prisoner of Zenda are closed. Of these, only Rattlesnake Route and the Headwall constitute any great loss. Beware: Do not tie into trees at the top unless you pad them with a shirt or something. $50 fines imposed. Most of the routes around Sunset Rock have fixed anchors at the top. Rob Robinson says, "Don't feed the rangers, they bite." No camping. Autumn. NPS, (423) 821-7786.

Classics: South: Blonde Ambition 7, Walk in the Park 8, Wind Walker 9, Black Magic 10, Agripa 10+, Black Street Revelations 11a, Train Time Dir 11, Raiders . . . 12, North: Bill's Route 8, Stan's Crack 9, Rattlesnake Route 9, Scream Wall 10-, Alpha Omega 10b, Flagstone 11a, Traintime Direct 11b, The Pearl 11b, The Prow 11+, Space Ranger 12-, Jennifer's World 12-, Edge of Might 12c, Dance of the Demon 13c; bouldering at base.

Ref: A. Ilgner 00, T. Waddle 3/99, R. Robinson; C [150-54, 100, 75(12/82), 72, 68], R [100-90, 89-44, 11(11/85)]; Sherman's *Stone Crusade*; Guidebooks: Watford's *Dixie Cragger's Atlas*, Robinson and Watford's *Deep South Climber's Companion*, Robinson's *The Insider's Guide to Southern Sandstone, vol. 1*, Harlin's *East*, Detterline's *A Climber's Guide to the Mid-South*, Hall's *Southern Rock*.

Directions: Above Chattanooga via Hwy. 148, on Lookout Mountain. Take West Brow Rd. to Sunset Park NPS parking area. Hike west five minutes past big house on trail from lot to tops of cliffs. More climbing exists at northeast tip of Lookout Mountain along West Brow Rd. at Point Park, though access has been a problem. Check significant rules before climbing.

27 C–Europa ✯✯✯

Good steep, creamy 100' north-facing limestone climbing. Lots of new wave (a few with the odd drilled pocket) sport routes. If you have drilled holds, recite Psalm 51 three times aloud. Autumn. No camping. May be on private land.

Classics: Add Fish Out of Water 11-, Necrophilia 12+, Transportergasm 13a, Savage Heart 13a, The Flamer 13.

Ref: P. Jarrard, R. Robinson; Guidebooks: Cater's *Sport Crags of the East*, Robinson's *Insider's Guide to Southern Sandstone, Vol. 1*.

Directions: From Chattanooga take I-59 to I-24 (approximately 20 mi.). Turn south on Haletown/New Hope Rd. (1 mi.). Go to east side of Nickajack Lake and Europa above railroad tracks.

28 C–Bee Rock Cliffs (aka The Markhams) ✯✯✯

These beautiful, 200' east-facing sandstone crags harbor wild routes. The Puppet Wall is a grid of sport routes (5.11-13b). Watch for bees. Autumn/winter. No camping. Private land.

Classics: Cornered Rats 11b, Trinity Site 11b, Both Sides Now 12-, The Host 12, Cryptical Envelopment 12c, Vector Analysis 13a, Theater of Madness 13c.

Ref: R. Robinson; C 100, R 11(11/85); Guidebooks: Robinson's *Southern Sandstone*, Detterline's *A Climber's Guide to the Mid-South*.

Directions: Bee Rock Cliffs are on the east side of Lookout Mountain above Chattanooga. This classic area is just ten minutes from Sunset Park on the southeast side of Lookout Mountain. It's been closed intermittently due to private landowners' wishes. Ask Chattanooga locals.

29 Hiwassee River Crags (aka Starr Mountain) ✯✯✯

Short but classic south-facing cragging and topropes up to 5.12 on short 60' sandstone bands. Scenic Hiwassee River valley popular with kayakers/boaters. Autumn/winter. Free camping. USFS-Cherokee NF, (423) 476-9700.

Classics: Pleasing to the Touch 6, Lucky Strikes 9+, Big Men, Small Airplanes 10, Vulcans Do Not Bluff 11, Excalibur 10+, I've Got the Power 11+, Fight the Power 11+; bouldering.

Ref: R 100-91; Guidebooks: Watford's *Dixie Cragger's Atlas*, Robinson and Watford's *Deep South Climber's Companion*.

Directions: From Etowah float south on Hwy. 411. Turn east before Hiwassee River. Drive for approximately 2 mi. past Gee Creek campground to parking near large culvert pipe. The Hiwassee River Crags are the visible bands above road on left. Hike uphill five minutes.

30 Memphis Buildering ★★

Areas are described in comical buildering guide to the Memphis area buildings. For a comfortable bivy check in at the Marriott Inn. For music check out B. B. King's Blues Club on Beale St. Be there. Private land.

Classics: Memphis buildings, Elvis's Airplane.

Ref: Guidebook: *An Underground Climber's Guide to Above Ground Memphis.*

Directions: Buildering in Memphis. Various buildings include: Fred P. Gattas, 5000 Summer Ave.; Kroger, 5110 Summer Ave.; 3272 Austin Peay; 550 Stateline; 2700 Getwell; Four Seasons Apartments on Mendenhall Rd.; Madison Heights United Methodist Church, 1300 Monroe at Claybrook; St. Elizabeth's Episcopal Church, 4780 Yale Rd.; Harahan Bridge on the Mississippi River via Riverside Dr.; Martin Luther King Park; Memorial Park Cemetery, 5668 Poplar Ave.; Eastwood Building, 6209 Poplar Ave.; Stone Faces at 2878 and 2811 Fairview; and Southwestern at Memphis South Pkwy. If you get caught by the authorities, tell 'em you're Elvis back from the dead.

31 Trice's Landing (closed) ★★

Now closed to climbing—do not climb here. A lot of short, 50' routes but good place to work on technique and teach a new partner. Twenty-five routes. Summer. Private property.

Classics: Not!

Ref: E. LaCoste 11/00; 11/97.

Directions: Clarksville. From Hwy. 41A (New Providence Blvd.), turn south onto Oak St., which is directly across from The Pack Rat pawn shop. Drive straight until you reach the Trice Landing Boat Ramp. Park in the area in front of the crappy picnic area. *Lock your car!* Now walk west through the picnic area until you hit the intermittent stream. Find a way to cross it. Once you cross it there is an old trail. Follow this back toward the river; it will skirt west along the top of the cliff by the river. Follow this for about 150 m until you find a cut that takes you south down to the river where you will see the climbing routes.

32 South Clear Creek/Obed River ★★★★★

Southern sandstone crags at their best line the amazing South Clear Creek and the Obed River. These are 200' sandstone cliffs with both wild trad and sport crags. Glenn Randall's Tierrany 5.12a led the way to many exciting overhanging climbs. Also features the famed Lilly Boulders with twenty-three bouldering formations, originally developed by rad ranger Rob Turan. Awesome white-water runs as well. Fall. NPS, (423) 346-6294.

Classics: Blue Sky Green Water 11d, Tierrany 12a, Scalded Dog 5.12b, many, many more!

Ref: C [174-109, 169, 168-121], R [100-91, 77-68]; Guidebooks: Robinson's *The Insider's Guide to Southern Sandstone, Vol. 1*, Watford's *Dixie Cragger's Atlas.*

Directions: For Obed: From Wartburg follow Hwy. 62 to Lansing. From Lansing go 3 mi. to Ridge Rd. Turn left on Ridge Rd. Once you turn on Ridge Rd., continue past Lillie Bridge and to Lillie Overlook. Park here and hike to the Obed. For South Clear Creek: Take Ridge Rd., heading to Lilly Bridge. After about 2 mi. look for Doc Howard Rd. on the left (at green-tinted trailer). Look for a field on the right which is the parking area and the trailhead. Follow the trail about 1 ½ mi. to the bottom of the cliff line and make a left, following the cliff line. Start looking for bolts.

Other Tennessee Climbing Areas

Toxic Wall

Nashville. Superb bouldering ¾-mi. long.

Ref: E. LaCoste 11/00.

Warfield Wall

Clarksville. Ten routes, 5.11–12c.

Ref: E. LaCoste 11/00.

Texas

Looks like fun . . . 'til you get up there, then you don't feel like drinking beer, so you drink Gatorade . . . ugh . . . screws your whole lifestyle up . . . —Harley biker on rock climbing, Hueco Tanks, Texas

Varied and wonderful and open, Texas possesses rock from the gracious sweeping cloud-lit panoramas of west Texas to the steep, vegetated limestone crags near Dallas and San Antonio with a little granite sprinkled in between. Yes, Hueco Tanks is not the end of Texas climbing—though it is some of the finest. Hueco has earned a reputation as the best bouldering area in the country. It also sports dozens of bolted face climbs, mostly in the 5.9–5.10 ranges, as well as retaining a few of the runout pitches that initially gave Hueco a reputation. Now, its strict climbing regulations add to its rep.

Also in west Texas is Big Bend Country. A trip there will delight the adventurous rock climber with some surprising finds along the Texas/Mexico border.

In central Texas, not far from LBJ's ranch, Enchanted Rock is a fun granite slab area. From San Antonio up to Dallas, overhanging pocketed limestone has been discovered and developed, including totally manufactured climbs in the Belton vicinity (apparently, some chuckleheads have decided to mess with Texas).

With all that climbing, world-famous barbeque, and Tex-Mex cuisine, legends like the mythical Pecos Bill, the real hanging judge Roy Bean, and pro golf's "Supermex" Lee Trevino, Texans have plenty to be proud of. No wonder they say, "Don't ask a man if he's from Texas. If he isn't, there's no use embarrassing him. If he is, he'll tell you."

1 Texas Tech Climbing Wall
Directions: Texas Tech Climbing Wall is at Texas Tech in Lubbock.

2 Lake Mineral Wells State Park (Penitentiary Hollow) ☆
Toproping only on 45′ sandstone, conglomerate blocks. Face climbs ranging from jughauls to pebble pinchfests on roughly eighty climbs. Bring 25′ extendo runners for toprope anchors. Climbers are asked not to climb when walls are wet. Rock climbing and entry fees ($5.00 in 1999). Autumn. Pay camping at state park (940–328–1171).
Classics: Penitentiary Hollow 6, Diving Board . . . 5.9, Peewee's Playhouse 10c, Recently . . . 10d, Finger Stinger 11a, Keith's Way 11b.
Ref: 1/98; *Texas Wildlife* 1992; on-line guide www.sss.org/

%7Eshred/climb/m_wells/mwells.htm; Guidebooks: Jackson's *Texas Limestone II: A Climber's Guide,* Jackson's *Rock Climbing New Mexico and Texas,* Jackson and Gallagher's *Central Texas Limestone.*
Directions: From Mineral Wells drive 2 mi. east on Hwy. 180 to Lake Mineral Wells State Park (signs). Signs in park point the way to the rock formations. Climbers must sign in at park.

3 Plano Pyramids (Dallas Buildering) ☆
Manufactured climbing on a good 25′ of cement. Private land.
Classics: Snake Crack V2-, See You In Nogales V3, Disney Fignus 12a.
Ref: Guidebooks: Jackson's *Texas Limestone II: A Climber's Guide,* Jackson and Gallagher's *Central Texas Limestone.*
Directions: From Dallas drive north on Hwy. 75 through Plano to Spring Creek exit. Cruise down access road past Spring Creek. Park at dirt road on the right at pyramidal concrete buttresses, aka the Plano Pyramids.

4 Renner Road (Dallas Buildering) ☆
Buildering problems on railroad trestle and flagstone pillars. Private land.
Classics: Razor's Edge V2, Super Lounge V5, Tarzan V6.
Ref: Guidebooks: Jackson's *Texas Limestone II: A Climber's Guide,* Jackson and Gallagher's *Central Texas Limestone.*
Directions: From Dallas drive Hwy. 75 north to Richardson. Get off at Renner Rd. and turn right. Take another right into the office-building parking lot. Park at southeast corner. Hike downhill to a railroad trestle.

5 Matilda Bridge/Trammel Trestle (Dallas Buildering) ☆
Short, vertical glue-on traverses. Good cement pocket bouldering. Private land.
Classics: MB: Razor's Edge V2, Super Lounge V5, Tarzan V6; TT: Track Crack 7, Dark Man 9, Stylin' 10, Jesus Rules 11.
Ref: Guidebooks: Jackson's *Texas Limestone II: A Climber's Guide,* Jackson and Gallagher's *Central Texas Limestone.*
Directions: From Dallas take Hwy. 75 north to

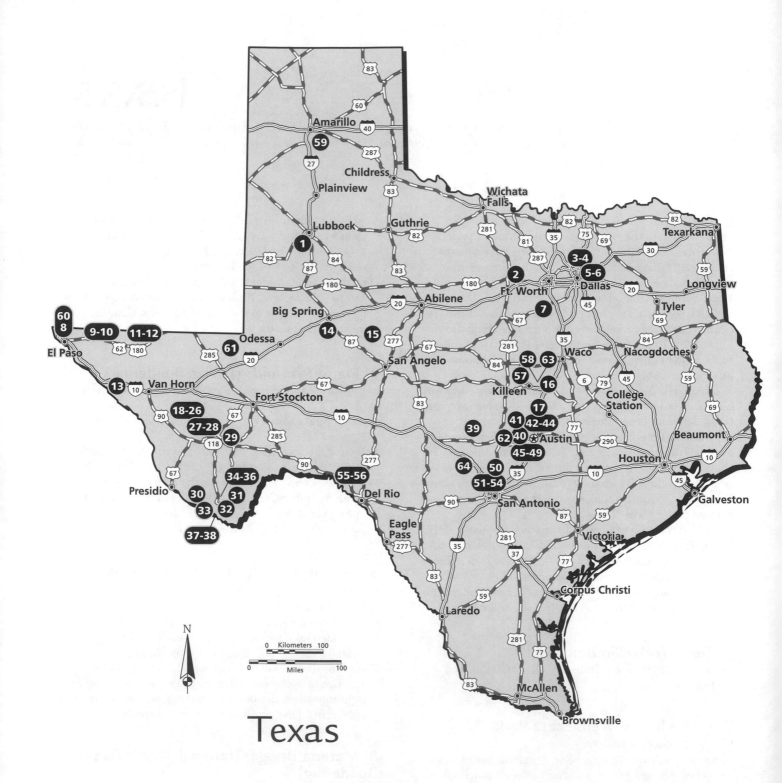

Texas

Mockingbird exit. Turn right, then left on Matilda. Hang a left on the first concrete drive. Hop over curb and drive under the bridge. Hike to far side of Matilda Bridge to climb. For Trammel Trestle Bouldering: Take Hwy. 75 north to Mockingbird exit. Turn right and go 3 mi. Turn left on Rockaway, then left on Fisher. Cross railroad tracks and park at tennis courts on left. Hike under railroad trestle to buildering/topropes.

6 Tietze Park (Dallas Buildering) ☆

Thirty-foot flagstone buildering traverses. Private land.

Ref: Guidebooks: Jackson's *Texas Limestone II: A Climber's Guide,* Jackson and Gallagher's *Central Texas Limestone.*

Directions: Dallas. Take Hwy. 75 north to Mockingbird exit. Follow Mockingbird east to a right turn on Skillman to Vanderbuilt. Park in Tietze Park.

7 Cleburne ☆☆☆

This overhanging 40′ limestone crag has been described as a mini-Frankenjura. Tough climbs for expert crankers. Private land.

Classics: Blue Velvet 12, Calypso 13a, Mariner 13a.

Ref: C 149-54, R 63.

Directions: From Cleburne go southwest on Hwy. 67 to Brazos River. (For detailed climbing information see locals or ask Ross Perot for a chart.)

8 Mini Hueco (in Franklin Mountains State Park) ☆☆☆

Fine bouldering on the oldest volcanic rock in El Paso. Approximately 120 extra-abrasive 60′ routes with sporty landings and chickenheads. Autumn–spring. Pay camping. State park, (915) 566-6441.

Classics: Saturation Boulder, The Heathen V3, Poodles Under Fire V3, Smokin Guns V4 toprope, Spill the Wine V4 toprope, The Wave V5.

Ref: D. Hardin.

Directions: From El Paso take I-54 north. Go 3 mi. west on Trans Mountain Rd. Park on roadside pulloff on right. A short five- to ten-minute hike to boulders up ravine to Mini Hueco area.

9 Castle Rocks (closed?) ☆☆☆

An enjoyable and still free (as of 1995) 60′ satellite crag of Hueco Tanks. Private land—may be closed by order of Smith and Wesson.

Classics: Bust-a-Move 10-, Your Sister 10, Finger Pockets from Hell 11+, Roof Crack 12-, The Scoop 12+.

Ref: J. Gamertsfelder.

Directions: From El Paso drive 24 mi. east on Hwy. 180. Turn north on Rd. 2775 for 8 mi., following Hueco Tanks State Park signs. Just before state park entrance, turn left on dirt road, following park boundary fence north and then east (Hueco Tanks ranger station visible to south). Continue east for approximately 3 mi. Park right next to rocks. Castle Rocks are visible to the northeast of Hueco Tanks State Park.

10 Hueco Tanks State Park (restricted access) ☆☆☆☆☆

The beacon of world-class rock climbing renowned for its huecos (holes) and multitude of overhanging boulder problems, rad leads, and moderate retro bolted routes. Many first routes put up by Mike and Dave Head, James Crump, Bob Murray, Les Harmon, Todd Skinner, and John Sherman. Perhaps no other climbing area builds a climber's power base and calluses like Hueco. Fine 300′ syenite rock, fair winter weather, and Mexican food attract climbers from around the world. Also, the home of world-class Native American rock paintings and world-class park mismanagement. Camping at the state park (call ahead to make sure) and Hueco Pete's (1 mi. south of park). Rock Rodeo Contest in February now kaput. Origin of John Sherman's V-scale bouldering rating system. State park, (915) 857-1135.

Classics: Cakewalk 6, Uriah's Heap 7, Indecent Exposure 9+, Sea of Holes 10a, Pigs to Pork 10+, Optical Promise 11+, Secret Sharer 11d/12a, Stardust 12b/c, Tarts of Horsham 12d, The Terminator Roof Crack 12a, Gunfighter 13a, When Legends Die 13a, Mother of the Future 13, Boystown 14a; Mushroom Boulder V0-V10, 45-Degree Wall V5, Bucket Roof V6, Crash Dummy V7, Slashface V14.

Ref: *Texas Parks and Wildlife* (6/98), C [195-22/84, 187-45, 183-67, 181-40, 177-21, 176-30, 171-28, 169, 168-46, 167-26, 165-60, 161-134, 160-48, 152-36, 134, 116(10/89)-72, 108, 104(10/87)-22, 103, 101, 100, 96, 95, 92], M 116, R [90-44, 85-22, 83, 82-32, 78, 74-89, 53(1/93) 51, 41(1/91)-31, 36, 34(7/88)-32, 26], SC [(6/91), 12/92]; Sherman's *Stone Crusade;* Guidebooks: Sherman's *Hueco Tanks State Park Classic Rock Climbs,* Jackson's *Rock Climbing New Mexico and Texas,* Piana's *Great Rock Hits, Sherman's Hueco Tanks,* Sherman et al.'s *Hueco Tanks: A Climber's and Boulderer's Guide,* Toula's *Rock Climber's Map to Hueco Tanks,* Head and Crump's *Indian Heights.*

Directions: From El Paso drive 24 mi. east on Hwy. 180. Turn north on Rd. 2775 for 8 mi., following Hueco Tanks State Park signs to ranger station. Entrance fee plus climber's daily fee as of 1995. Also, climbing now requires having a state park guide follow climbers around the park.

11 Guadalupe Peak (Guadalupe Mountains National Park) (closed) ☆☆☆

Friable, 1,000′ limestone rock and unexplored walls and crags of Texas-size magnitude. Guadalupe Peak is highest point in Texas at 8,749′. Gary Neptune and Peter Berney reported the first ascent of El Capitan in *Climbing,* March 1972. Potential rock climbing lies along the flanks of Guadalupe and El Capitan Peaks (spectacular hikes) as well as McKittrick Canyon (day use only). No motorized bolting. Backcountry permits necessary. Pay camping at NPS sites (915-828-3251).

Exploring the cool recesses of Hueco Tanks.

Ref: Schneider's *Hiking Carlsbad Caverns and Guadalupe Mountains National Parks*; C 3/72 (16).

Directions: From El Paso go 90 mi. east on Hwy. 62 to Guadalupe Mountains National Park. Two areas/entrances off Hwy. 62/180: Pine Spring Campground (park headquarters) and McKittrick Canyon.

12 McKittrick Canyon (Guadalupe Mountains National Park) (closed) ✭✭✭

Potential 300' limestone rock climbing lies along the flanks of McKittrick Canyon (day use only). Bouldering near streambed. No motorized bolting. Pay camping at NPS.

Directions: From El Paso go 90 mi. east on Hwy. 62. Then from Pine Spring Campground, head north on Hwy. 180, turning left into McKittrick Canyon. Rock is up canyon.

13 Lasca Rd. Picnic Area (Quitman Mountains) ✭✭✭

Potentially interesting 80' granite walls. The Quitman Mountains contain a wealth of rock. The rock remains questionable and should be checked. Autumn–spring.

Directions: From Van Horn drive 40 mi. west on I-10 to Lasca Rd. Picnic Area at exit 99. Short climbs/boulders on south side of interstate. Higher domes to south require long hikes, difficult access.

14 Big Spring State Park ●

Very small 15' limestone area on mesa overlooking hospital—and they get $2.00 for it. Fine Mexican restaurants in the area. State park, (915) 263-4931.

Ref: J. Gogas.

Directions: West Big Spring. At Big Spring State Park.

15 Coke County Cliffs ✭✭

Eighty-foot limestone crag. Private land.

Ref: J. Gogas.

Directions: From Robert Lee drive Hwy. 158 west until 5 mi. northwest of E. V. Spence Reservoir to Coke County Cliffs. Access may be private.

16 Miller Springs (aka Belton) ✭✭✭

Overhanging 50' limestone cliffs with sculptured sport routes feature unique holds (as fake as silicon implants, but fun/serious nonetheless). Routes for the dedicated sport climber only. See Jackson's guidebooks for all the details. Open in cooperation with the city of Belton and Army Corps of Engineers. Access sensitive—closed from April through August for cliff-swallow nesting. Climb elsewhere during this time or seek political asylum in a foreign country. Camping at Temple Lake State Park 3 mi. away. Owned by Army Corps of Engineers.

Classics: Steel Wheels 12b, Kinetics 12c, Concentrics 12c, De La Soul 12d, Reason d'etre 13a, Mister Sir 13a, Desert Shield 13, Desert Storm 13d.

Ref: R 63, C [189-94, 9/92]; Guidebooks: Jackson's *Texas Limestone II: A Climber's Guide*, Jackson and Gallagher's *Central Texas Limestone*.

Directions: At Belton (69 mi. north of Austin). Depart I-35 at exit 293A. Turn left at stop sign. Turn right onto Hwy. 317 (Main St.) through Belton for 2 mi. Just after crossing Little River, turn left into obvious pullout and park. Leave gate unblocked. Hike down paved road. Shortly, Front Wall Cliff will be on right.

17 Blue Hole Bouldering ✭

A great swimming hole with sporty (potentially wet) bouldering on steep, pockety, 30' limestone. No camping. City land.

Ref: Guidebooks: Jackson's *Texas Limestone II: A Climber's Guide*, Jackson and Gallagher's *Central Texas Limestone*.

Directions: From Georgetown (approximately thirty minutes north of Austin). Going north on I-35, take Southwestern University exit and turn right. Turn left at Scenic Dr. and follow signs to Blue Hole. Take a left at the graveyard to a parking area.

18 Boy Scout Ranch ✭

Crumbly 80' volcanic rock. Private land.

Classics: Wilkins 7, Needle Rock 9+.

Ref: Guidebook: Eggleston's *Climber's Guide to Point of Rocks and Environs*.

Directions: From Balmorhea go south on Hwy. 17 to Boy Scout Ranch. Get permission at ranch.

19 Church Rocks ✭✭

Cragging and "Three Pull" bouldering: three pulls and you're done for the day. Volcanic 50' rock so pungent and coarse grained it'll turn your tips into a fine puree—pray for more skin at the adjacent church. Private land.

Ref: J. Gogas; Guidebook: Eggleston's *Climber's Guide to Point of Rocks and Environs*.

Directions: In Fort Davis, park at cliff base near white First Presbyterian Church. Church Rocks are obvious.

20 Davis Mountains State Park ✭✭

This 40' rhyolite band could make a fun bouldering run (4 ½ mi. on trail) between Ft. Davis State Park and Ft. Davis Historical Site. The world-famous McDonald Observatory is farther up the road. Autumn–spring. Pay camping at state park (915-426-3337).

Ref: Guidebook: Eggleston's *Climber's Guide to Point of Rocks and Environs*.

Directions: From Fort Davis go 4 mi. west on Hwy. 118, following Davis Mountains State Park signs. Hike trail southeast.

21 Tumbolia ✭✭✭

Classic roadside 30' rhyolite face edge bouldering, summit jumping, and traversing. A few old toprope bolts exist. High solos and low traverses. For a real thrill drive the "Squeeze" at 50 mph. Winter. State land.

Ref: Guidebook: Eggleston's *Climber's Guide to Point of Rocks and Environs.*

Directions: From Fort Davis go approximately 2 mi. west on Hwy. 118 at Tumbolia picnic pullout on left. More rocks in the general vicinity.

22 Rock Pile Park ✮✮

Eighty-foot syenite rock piles. Autumn–spring. No camping. Private land.

Ref: Guidebook: Eggleston's *Climber's Guide to Point of Rocks and Environs.*

Directions: From Fort Davis go approximately 30 mi. west on Hwy. 166 to Rock Pile Park. May be closed to climbing at this time.

23 Sawtooth Mountains ●

Reportedly much more pleasing to look at than to actually climb, i.e., poor syenite rock. Autumn–spring. Private land.

Ref: Guidebook: Eggleston's *Climber's Guide to Point of Rocks and Environs.*

Directions: From Fort Davis go approximately 25 mi. west on Hwy. 166 to Sawtooth Mountains.

24 Wofford Rock ✮✮

Small, 120′ syenite crag—road visible. Ask permission. Cueva de Leon Saturday-night Mexican Buffet recommended. Autumn–spring. Private land.

Classics: Blue Hiway 2p 10, Hard Living 11.

Ref: Guidebook: Eggleston's *Climber's Guide to Point of Rocks and Environs.*

Directions: From Fort Davis take Hwy. 17 south for 2 mi. Go approximately 13 mi. west on Hwy. 166 (past Point of Rocks). Turn right at Davis Mountain Resort sign for 1 mi. Wofford Rock is on left.

25 Point of Rocks ✮✮✮

A gentle blend of syenite bouldering and 180′ face and crack climbs in the open-aired Trans Pecos region of Texas. Fun climbing. Pete, one of three landowners who own parts of Point of Rocks, wrote Rock 'n' Road in 1997: "The area facing the highway is a state rest stop, and state extends part way up the south face only. The west face, north faces, and the top, which are used frequently by climbers, are most definitely private land. We have had terrible experiences with people who trespass on the land (climbers, too), including major brush fires set by careless campfires and lots of litter. I was there today and climbers had torn down my neighbor's fence. NOBODY ever calls to ask permission to climb. We fear a major brush fire—the area is tinder dry, and even the catalytic converter from a car parked in tall grass can start a fire." For Pete's sake, let's get it together out there. Contact Pete at petesz@overland.net with any

questions. Autumn–spring. No camping. Private/state land.

Classics: Lucky Ledges 6/9, Palomino Gals 11, Bouldering.

Ref: Guidebooks: Jackson's *Rock Climbing New Mexico and Texas,* Eggleston's *Climber's Guide to Point of Rocks and Environs.*

Directions: From Fort Davis drive Hwy. 17 south for 2 mi. Go 10 mi. west on Hwy. 166. Park on right at picnic pull-out for Point of Rocks. Bouldering rock piles 10′ from car and up hillside. Crags around at West Face with bouldering below its face.

26 Carpenter Mountain (closed) ✮✮

A mini Point of Rocks. One-hundred-foot syenite crag. Private land.

Ref: Guidebook: Eggleston's *Climber's Guide to Point of Rocks and Environs.*

Directions: From Fort Davis follow Hwy. 17 south approximately 2 mi. Go 10 mi. west on Hwy. 166. Carpenter Mountain Rocks on left. South across from Point of Rocks. No access as of 1992.

27 Mitre Peak Area ✮

Multitude of boulders and 50′ volcanic rimrock on private ranchland. No camping. Autumn–spring. Private land.

Ref: Guidebook: Eggleston's *Climber's Guide to Point of Rocks and Environs.*

Directions: From Fort Davis, Mitre Peak Area is 6–10 mi. south on Hwy. 118 toward Alpine.

28 Boujuillas Dome ●

A 250′ crusty crag.

Classics: Silver Lining 8.

Ref: Guidebook: Eggleston's *Climber's Guide to Point of Rocks and Environs.*

Directions: From Fort Davis drive 15 mi. south on Hwy. 118 for Boujuillas Dome.

29 Iron Mountain ✮✮✮

This 300′ granite crag is the site of 1950s Sul Ross State University rock climbing classes. Autumn–spring. Private land.

Ref: Guidebook: Eggleston's *Climber's Guide to Point of Rocks and Environs.*

Directions: From Marathon go approximately 10 mi. north (from Exxon station) of town on gated dirt road. On Iron Mountain Ranch. The brown rock of Iron Mountain is visible to north from town. Must obtain permission from ranch.

30 Big Bend Ranch State Park ✮✮

Twenty-five-foot volcanic roadside boulders and rocks stationed on this scenic hillside. Winter. Pay camping in state park (915-229-3416).

Directions: From Lajitas drive approximately 10 mi. west on Hwy. 170 for Big Bend Ranch State Park.

31 Big Bend National Park Overview ☆☆☆

A wild and spacious southwestern park of desert, 1,000' limestone rock-walled canyons and volcanic peaks bordered to the south by the Rio Grande River. More climbing information can be obtained from Far Flung Adventures or Outward Bound. Four campgrounds in this national park. Autumn–spring. NPS, (915) 477–2251.

Classics: The Boot, The Deal.

Ref: M. Ziebell, J. Gogas; AAJ '65-434; Parent's *Hiking Big Bend National Park;* Guidebook: Jackson's *Rock Climbing New Mexico and Texas.*

Directions: From Study Butte roads lead into the Big Bend National Park east/northeast. Ask locally.

32 Chisos Basin ☆☆

A rugged basin of volcanic 700' rock. A world-class climbing center if all the rock were sound. Miles of hiking trails in these rugged wild lands. NPS, (915) 477–2251.

Classics: The Boot, The Deal (a perfect 5.11 crack somewhere on the South Rim).

Ref: S 11/68.

Directions: From Study Butte roads lead into the park east. Then follow serpentine roads up into Chisos Basin (well signed), where park headquarters is located. A small practice area sits roadside near the visitors center.

33 Santa Elena Canyon ☆☆

Giant 1,000' walls with possibly both good and dangerously loose limestone rock. Pick your way through the good rock to beautiful multipitched routes on the Mexican side, some requiring rafting explorations. Unique riverside bouldering. Large boulders feature 50' aid seam near canyon mouth. NPS, (915) 477–2251.

Directions: From Study Butte drive 3 mi. east on Hwy. 118 to 14 mi. south on dirt NPS road to Santa Elena Canyon (follow signs). Also possible as a scenic river trip bouldering circuit.

34 Wild Horse Mountain ●

Impressive amount of 200' volcanic rock. A few routes, but mostly junk rock. Winter.

Classics: Anal Khadafy.

Directions: From Study Butte drive north on Hwy. 118 to Wild Horse Mountain on right. Easily viewed from highway.

35 Willow Mountain ☆

Impressive 400' columnar jointed basalt. A few routes, but mostly poor rock. Winter. Private land.

Directions: From Study Butte drive 12 mi. north on Hwy. 118 to Willow Mountain. Park at gate number 3.

36 Study Butte (aka Indian Head) ☆☆☆

Tepid bouldering and 80' rhyolite cragging. The Argyle Wall contains more than a few sporty traditional leads. Nice climbing. Please do not climb on Indian artwork! The nearby town of Terlingua is famous for its chili cook-offs held every year. Winter. Free/pay camping nearby. Private/NPS land.

Classics: All Stars 6, Small Wall 10, Glass Image 11+, Feats in Space 12, Man from Midland 12+/13a.

Ref: J. Gogas.

Directions: Indian Head is just northeast of Study Butte and east of landfill. Ask locally.

37 Tuff Mountain ☆

Thirty-five-foot volcanic boulders on hillside. NPS.

Directions: From Castolon drive 3 mi. north on NPS road to Tuff Mountain on right.

38 Mule's Ears ☆☆

Volcanic 300' breccia pinnacle rockaneering. Historic ascents. NPS, (915) 477–2251.

Ref: AAJ?

Directions: Mule's Ears is located in Southern Big Bend National Park northwest of Castolon at Mule's Ears Overlook. Check with rangers for backcountry hiking information.

39 Enchanted Rock State Park (aka E-Rock) ☆☆☆☆

This island of granite rising 400' in the ocean of Texas is most noted as the birthplace of the state's rock climbing. Features 500 routes up to 5.12+ on mostly domes and slabs of vertical face and crack climbing. Coarse granite can be slicker than the scum off a Louisiana swamp on humid central Texas days. Rock texture defines the word *gnarlee*. Climber's guide sheet at the park office, but *Dome Driver's*

Enchanted Rock State Park.

Manual is the guide. Spring Peach Festival. Before you and your partner split that last carton of mac 'n' cheese, try the German atmosphere in nearby Fredericksburg. October–April. Pay camping in state park (915-247-3903).

Classics: Owl Crack 8, Middle Crack 8, Becky's Crack 9, Texas Crude 10, Stranger Than Friction 10b, Tonka Toys from Hell 11a, Texas Radio 11, Velvet Elvis 11d, Missing Link 12a, Altered States 12, Top Gun 12c, El Carnivore 13.

Ref: C [189-97; 158-70, 75], R 57; Guidebooks: Jackson's *Rock Climbing New Mexico and Texas*, Crump, Price, and Harris's *Dome Driver's Manual*, Bergeron and Crump's *Stranger than Friction*, Walker and Richards's *Climbing at Enchanted Rock*.

Directions: From Fredericksburg go 17 mi. north on Hwy. 965 to Enchanted Rock State Park.

40 Reimer's Fishing Ranch ✸✸✸

Go fishin' for this 60′ pocketed limestone sport crag on a private ranch with especially good routes in the 5.10–5.11 ranges and up to 5.13. Nice steep (overhanging!) routes in the Sex Cave. Open Wednesday–Sunday. Entrance fee (pay right at crag), $3.00 in 1998. Also, good fishing. Pay camping nearby at Pedernales Falls State Park or Pace Bend Park. Park closes at night—please leave on time. Private land, (512) 264-1923.

Classics: Dead Cats 10b, Crack Attack 10d, Bolt Talk 11a, Telegraph Road 11b, Crankenstein 11c, Liposuction 12a,

---

Texas Road Thoughts

So, there is a fair amount of rock in the state. Unfortunately, more than 90 percent of the Texas land base is privately owned—a fair amount of climbing in Texas is on private land. Ask permission from the landowners first.

On asking a Texas landowner permission to climb:

First, be optimistic! It's a vast land; you'll need optimism as big to match it!

Second, inquire locally as to who owns the land with the chunk of rock you'd like to ascend. That is, get the name and phone number of the owner and use it before you touch the rock. A polite no to your reprisal is better than a shotgun pointed at your chalk bag for trespassing.

Third, be polite, honest, and courteous! (You're setting precedence for other rock climbers. If you are not getting through, try that Texas ten-gallon drawl you've practiced.)

Four, talk slowly.

Five, if conversation fails to achieve a desired outcome, resort to a bribe.

Six, if after all your attempts permission is still denied, go climb in Colorado.

Lastly, keep breathing . . . it'll be a fatal climb if you quit.

—TNT

Body Wax 12, Head 12d, House of Pain 13a; World's Greatest Boulder.

Ref: J. Valdez; R 63; Guidebooks: Jackson's *Texas Limestone II: A Climber's Guide*, Jackson and Gallagher's *Central Texas Limestone*.

Directions: From Town Lake take Mopac south and turn right onto Southwest Pkwy. At dead-end, turn right onto Hwy. 71. Turn left onto Ranch Rd. 3238 (Hamilton's Pool Rd.), passing two low water crossings. One mi. after second crossing, turn right at Reimer's Ranch sign. On dirt road, stay left to a gate. Pay small admission fee at house. Proceed to Sano-can, then to rock.

41 Pace Bend Park/Thurman Cove ✸✸✸

Steep 60′ limestone sport crag. Reached only via boat. Pay camping at Pace Bend Park. Private land/Travis County Park, (512) 264-1482.

Classics: Voyage of the Boat People 12c.

Ref: J. Valdez; Guidebooks: Jackson's *Texas Limestone II: A Climber's Guide*, Jackson and Gallagher's *Central Texas Limestone*.

Directions: From Town Lake take Mopac south and turn right onto Southwest Parkway. At dead-end, turn right onto Hwy. 71. At FM 2322, turn right to Pace Bend Park.

42 Bull Creek Park (aka Library/Bonzo Walls) ✸✸✸

A chance for Austin city slickers to grab the bull by the horns and take a ride on overhanging 15′ pocketed limestone walls. Fine steep sport climbing (drilled) and bouldering. Approximately twenty bolted routes in this city park. Recommended in Austin area: Lake Austin Metro Park, Pace Bend Park (climbing), and Reimer's Ranch (climbing). Also, Chuy's Tex-Mex, Austin International Hostel. Good in summer.

Classics: Bedtime for Bonzo 11b, Raging Bull 12a, Metaphysics 12b, Atlas Shrugged 12c, Gulliver's Travels 12d/13a; Boulders: The Classic V0, Nude Edge V1, Water Weed Shuffle V5, Tiny Dancer V7.

Ref: C [140(11/93), 129], R [97-105, 63]; "Edge and Smear"; on-line guide www.sss.org/%7Eshred/climb/greenbelt.htm; Guidebooks: Jackson's *Texas Limestone II: A Climber's Guide*, Jackson and Gallagher's *Central Texas Limestone*.

Directions: From Town Lake in Austin, take Mopac Loop 1 north. Turn left on Rd. 2222 for several mi. Turn right on Lakewood to Bull Creek Park. Park across low water crossing. Cruise along creek downstream to rope climbs on Library/Bonzo Walls and high boulders or upstream for main boulders.

43 Mt. Bonnell/Frank's Meat Market (aka Eagle's Nest) ✸✸

Great views from top of Mt. Bonnell. Climbing ban sporadically enforced at Mt. Bonnell. Frank's has classic crack climbing, 40′ limestone, and only a handful of routes, 5.7 to 5.12. Private land.

Classics: Mt. Bonnell: Torts 10a, Tree of Woe 12a; Frank's: Frank's Crack 9/11 (roof), Frank's Meat Market 11b.

Ref: C 140(11/93); Guidebooks: Jackson's *Texas Limestone II: A Climber's Guide,* Jackson and Gallagher's *Central Texas Limestone.*

Directions: Mt. Bonnell: From Town Lake in Austin, take Mopac Loop 1 north. Turn left on Rd. 2222. Turn left on Mt. Bonnell Rd. Drive uphill to parking lot. Hike down short trail to climbs at the north end. For Frank's: Stay on Rd. 2222 to Hwy. 360 west. Pull off Hwy. 360 at dirt parking, just before big arching bridge. Cross to north side, walk up ramp to top, and cut left through trees to cliff base. When you see graffiti reading FRANK'S MEAT MARKET surrounded by roofs and cracks, you've arrived.

44 Bucket Cave/The Grot (closed) ★★★

Now closed, this was at one time Austin's best bouldering, offering steep, powerful 30′ limestone problems. Access-sensitive recreation and anthropological site. Government park.

Classics: Stinkfoot V3, Cane Toad V4, Gleam in Her Eye 4/5, Bone Fetish V6, Mercy Kill V6, Slacker 13.

Ref: A. Greyling 2/97; C 140(11/93); Guidebooks: Jackson's *Texas Limestone II: A Climber's Guide,* Jackson and Gallagher's *Central Texas Limestone.*

Directions: Austin. From Town Lake grope on Mopac (1) north. Turn left onto Spicewood Springs Rd. Turn left onto Mesa. Turn right onto Burney and right again onto Rim to dead-end at guardrail. Hike down paved trail, turning right onto worn trail to caves. The Grot comes first, and beyond is the Penal Cove and Bucket Cave.

45 Waller Creek/University of Texas ★★

Waller Creek hosts intermediate problems on vertical limestone walls.

Ref: C 140(11/93); Guidebooks: Jackson's *Texas Limestone II: A Climber's Guide,* Jackson and Gallagher's *Central Texas Limestone.*

Directions: In Austin. Waller Creek is at Martin Luther King and San Jacinto. Stroll past the old oil pump to the creek. On the University of Texas campus, buildering enthusiasts may find the following areas of interest: Jester Dormitory, PCI Library, and the Football Stadium.

46 Gooch Boulder ★★

This one good, white, 15′ limestone boulder with an overhang and traverses is a downtown novelty. City land.

Ref: C 140(11/93); Guidebook: Jackson and Gallagher's *Central Texas Limestone.*

Directions: In Austin, at the southwest corner off Lamar and Twenty-ninth St. Gooch Boulder lies northwest of the capital building.

47 Tenth St. Bridge/Mosquito Bridge ★

The Tenth St. Bridge has pumping, overhanging limestone workout traverse. At Mosquito Bridge find two cracks—5.8 hands and 5.10- fingers.

Ref: Locals; C 140(11/93); Guidebook: Jackson and Gallagher's *Central Texas Limestone.*

Directions: In Austin. Tenth St. Bridge is located at Tenth St. and Lamar Blvd. Park behind 7-Eleven on Tenth St. and walk under bridge. From Town Lake the Mosquito Bridge is located near the intersection of Lamar and First St. at north abutment of railroad tracks.

48 Sunken Gardens ★★★

An old Austin standby buildering area. Pumping workout traverse in city park.

Ref: C 140(11/93); Guidebook: Jackson and Gallagher's *Central Texas Limestone.*

Directions: In Austin. From Town Lake go south on Lamar. Turn right on Barton Springs. Turn left on Robert E. Lee to Wright Baseball Field. Sunken Gardens traverse walls at pool west of baseball field. These directions should, at least, put you in the ballpark.

49 Barton Creek Areas (New Wall/ Gus Fruh et al.) ★★★

These walls are characterized by steep, pumpy, 90′ limestone sport routes. Routes may be slightly sandy but are fun workouts. Close to one hundred good routes in this Austin city park.

Classics: New Wall: Flintstones 9, Hysteria 11a, Walk the Dog 11b, Buddha 12a; Great Wall: Through the Looking Glass 11a, Tunnel Vision Direct 12a, Iron Man 12b, Power Monkey 12c; Gus Fruh: MC2 13; Campbell's Hole: Hank's 12b; Ka'nee Knee's Wall: Ka'nee Knee's Bane V3; Urban Assault Wall: Cell Block 11b, Starfish 12c, Plate Tectonics 13b.

Ref: C [140(11/93), 111(12/88)-33 (map)]; R 63; Guidebook: Jackson and Gallagher's *Central Texas Limestone.*

Directions: In Austin. Along Barton Creek are found several limestone walls. From Town Lake drive south on Mopac and turn left on Barton Skyway to a dead-end (junction with Spyglass Rd. and Stop 'N' Go convenience store). Trail starts in drainage below store at guardrail. At the T, hike 1 mi. east (right) on hiking trail along Barton Creek to New Wall and Great Wall and ½ mi. farther to Gus Fruh. Urban Assault Wall is across creek. For Campbell's Hole turn left and hike to opposite side of bank to rock. For Ka'nee Knee's Wall: From Town Lake go south on Lamar, then turn right at Barton Springs. Turn left into Barton Springs Pool parking lot. Park near Hillside Theater. Trail leaves south end of lot.

50 The Academy (aka Guadalupe River State Park Crags) ★★★

An abundance of short 25′ gymnastic powerhouse limestone climbing. Developed by Alex Catlin, Jacob Valdez, Joe

Lowe, et al. Use caution during hunting season. Please be respectful of private lands on which lies the mainstay of climbing. Keep out of sight of houses. Private land/state park (pay camping), (830) 438-2656.
Ref: R 76-30; Guidebooks: Catlin's *Selected Climbs at the Academy (Austin)*, Jackson and Gallagher's *Central Texas Limestone*.
Directions: From San Antonio go north to Guadalupe River on Hwy. 281. Then go west on Hwy. 473 to Kendalia. The crags sit along the Guadalupe River and its intersection at Route 1376, Route 474 (through Kendalia), Route 3160 (through Kendalia), and at Guadalupe River State Park (accessed from Boerne, on I-10 northwest of San Antonio). Go northeast on Hwy. 46 for 27 mi. to park ranger station.

51 Cub Cave (closed) ✮✮
A 50' limestone sport crag with overhanging face climbs. Owner has closed off cave and will not let people climb there (as of 1996).
Classics: Genetic Drift 12b, Fisher King 13a.
Ref: Guidebook: Jackson and Gallagher's *Central Texas Limestone*.
Directions: San Antonio.

52 Olmos Wall/Olmos Dam Wall ✮✮✮
After-work artificial traverses and straight-up problems. Government land.
Ref: Guidebook: Jackson and Gallagher's *Central Texas Limestone*.
Directions: From San Antonio go north on Hwy. 281. Still inside city limits, turn left at Stone Creek Canyon (before Mouses convenience store). Next, turn right at Champion Stables. Go left at first gravel road. At boulders, park. Hike down trail to Olmos cave, sheltered by trees.

53 Shavano Roof ✮✮✮
Shavano Roof is known as the grandpappy of San Antonio roof climbs. Twenty-five-foot limestone crag. Private land/state park.
Classics: Shavano Roof 5.11+.
Ref: Guidebook: Jackson and Gallagher's *Central Texas Limestone*.
Directions: San Antonio. Take I-35 south to 1604 West. Follow Northwest Military Hwy. (1535) south past DeZavala Rd. to Cliffside Dr. Turn left. Past a left bend, park. Shavano Roof is located just off the east side of road.

54 Rolling Stone Wall ✮✮✮
Overhanging 25' limestone toproping crag.
Classics: Butch Roof V6.
Ref: Guidebook: Jackson and Gallagher's *Central Texas Limestone*.
Directions: San Antonio. Take I-35 south to 1604 West. Follow Northwest Military Hwy. (1535) south past

DeZavala Rd. to Huebner Rd. Turn left on Huebner Rd. to Salado Creek. Park. Rolling Stone Wall is found 150 yd. south of Huebner on the west side of creek. Butch Roof is 100' right of wall.

55 Pecos River Crags (closed?) ✮✮✮
Many routes have been developed by climbers here—80' sport routes, mainly. However, the area around White Shaman Cave is *closed* to climbing due to landowners' wishes. Other areas of limestone bluffs on private land may still be open. Area of Native American sites (White Shaman Cave) and artifacts. Winter. Pay camping at Seminole Canyon State Historical Park (915-292-4464). Private land.
Classics: Lady Remington 10a, Misfire 11a, Heat Seeker 11, Master of Disaster 12a, Sky Shaman 13a.
Ref: C 152-66; Access Fund Notes; Guidebooks: Jackson's *Rock Climbing New Mexico and Texas*, Lewis and Valdez Route List.
Directions: From Langtry drive south on Hwy. 90 to its intersection with the Pecos River and continue to the east bank. Turn south at the Chevron station onto a dirt road that leads down the east bank and to parking at the Pecos River Campground. Hike north of parking area, following trail to a picnic table where rappel anchors await two ropes. Check in at the Chevron station at the east side of the river for current accessible cliffs that are on private land.

56 Seminole Canyon State Park ✮✮
Hueco Tanks–like bouldering in impressive limestone canyons with highly treasured Native American rock paintings in the Fate Bell Shelter and Panther Cave. Climbing was once done here on these 80' cliffs. May be outlawed now due to Indian paintings. Pay camping in state park (915-292-4464).
Directions: From Langtry drive south on Hwy. 90 to Seminole Canyon State Park.

57 Fort Hood ✮✮
These 30' limestone crags support fifty routes. Winter. Free camping on federal land.
Classics: Basic Training 9, Silver Surfer 10d, Security Threat 11c, Mellow Gold 12b, Inferno 13a, Free Radical 13.
Directions: Near Killeen. Try the First Cavalry store in Killeen or Austin gear shops.

58 Beggar's Tomb ✮✮✮
Beggar's Tomb offers a small concentration of 50' gymnastic limestone sport climbs on the shores of Lake Belton. The routes are steep and powerful. To reach the climbing you must paddle across the lake from Temple Lake Park in Belton, Texas. Federal land.
Classics: Mellow Gold 5.12a, Soul Myth 5.12d/13a, Free Radical 5.13b.
Directions: From Dallas take I-35 south to Temple. Exit

and make a right on CR 2305. Follow this road for a couple of miles to Temple Lake Park. Enter the park and paddle across the lake to reach the climbing.

59 Palo Duro State Park ✯✯✯

Scenic canyon dubbed "The Grand Canyon of Texas" with nice views and some 75' routes. A good stop for the late-night road warrior looking for a place with a couple of routes to crash. Soft sandstone rock should be led only by the brave, will not hold much pro. Pay camping at state park (806–488–2227).
Classics: Hand Crack 5.9, Two Pin Boulder.
Ref: M. Cota 2/98.
Directions: From Amarillo go south on I–27. Turn west on Hwy. 217 for approximately 12 mi. to Palo Duro State Park.

60 Sneed's Cory (in Franklin Mountains State Park) ✯✯✯

Beautiful 40' granite area with facilities at parking area. Makes a nice day area in which to relax and practice after climbing at Hueco Tanks. Approximately twelve sport routes and various boulder problems. The park offers nearby undeveloped climbing opportunities a short hike farther up the mountain. There is also a mining hole blown out of the mountain farther up that offers more bouldering opportunities. The fee-station attendants are friendly and helpful—they have route maps if you ask. Area also contains numerous mountain-bike trails, so take your bike if you have the inclination. Pay camping at state park (915–566–6441).
Ref: L. Gonzalez 1/99.
Directions: Take I–10 west to Trans Mountain Rd. North to Franklin Mountains State Park. Go to fee station and ask directions to Sneed's Cory (first parking area on left followed by short walk on paved path to sunken climbing wall).

61 No Trees ✯✯

Unbelievably solid for sandstone bouldering. Twenty routes. Private land.
Classics: Thunderbird V2, Moby's Mantle V5, Eye of the Whale V5.
Ref: M. Ontiveros.
Directions: From Odessa get on Hwy. 302 and go west about 25 mi. until you get to a farm market road 1092. Go until paved road becomes a dirt road. Then take the first right after you cross over the first cattle guard.

62 Pedernales Falls State Park ✯✯✯

Limestone bouldering in the canyons. Sixty problems and counting. Pay camping at state park (830–868–7304).
Ref: C 189-32.
Directions: From Austin go west to Dripping Springs on Hwy. 290. Turn right (north) on Rd. 3232, following signs to park. Find bouldering along Wolf Mountain Loop Trail at mi. 1 on Bee Creek and at mi. 2 $7/10$ on Tobacco Creek.

63 Roger's Park

Bodacious pocketed limestone bouldering near Lake Belton. One hundred problems.
Ref: C 194, R&I.
Directions: At Belton (69 mi. north of Austin). Depart I–35 at exit 293A. Turn left at stop sign. Turn right onto Hwy. 317, then left onto FM 439. Pass over Belton Dam, staying on FM 2271. Turn right at Roger's Park Rd. Park at boat dock. Hike along shore and up the hill. On the right, find a trail off the road. Hike fifteen minutes to walls behind the trees.

64 Red Bluff ✯✯✯

Bouldering only (no ropes) area along Medina River. Seventy problems. Camping/use fees. Private land.
Ref: C 189-32.
Directions: Near San Antonio. Ask locals.

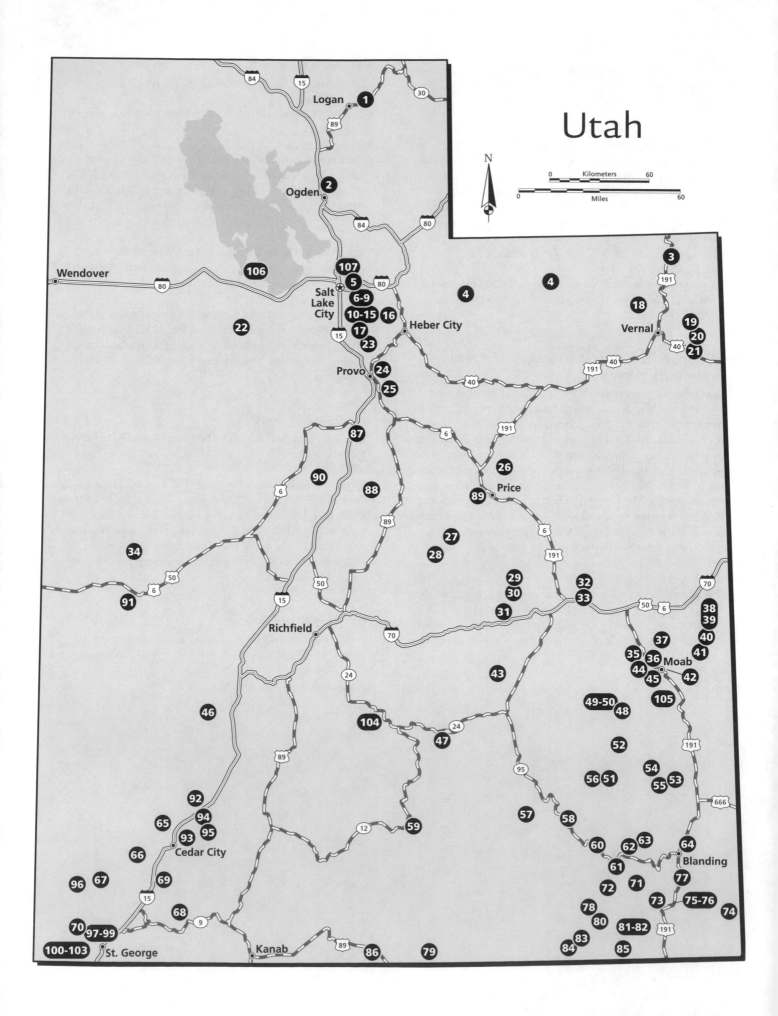

Utah

N

| 0 | Kilometers | 60 |
| 0 | Miles | 60 |

Logan ①

Ogden ②

Wendover ⑩⑥

Salt Lake City ⑩⑦ ⑤ ⑥-⑨ ⑩-⑮ ⑯ ⑰ ㉓

Heber City

④ ④ ③ ⑱ Vernal ⑲ ⑳ ㉑

㉒

Provo ㉔ ㉕

⑧⑦

⑨⓪ ⑧⑧

㉖ Price ⑧⑨

㉗ ㉘

⑨① ㉞

⑨① ㉙ ㉚ ㉜ ㉝ ㉛

Richfield ㉞ ㉟ ㊱ Moab ㊳⑨ ㊴ ㊶ ㉟ ㊱ ㊹ ㊺ ㊷ ㊸

⑩⑤

㊹⑨-⑩ ㊼ ㊸

㊺

㊻

⑩④ ㊲ ㊼ ㊺ ⑤④ ㊽ ㊾ ㊿ ⑤③ ㊼ ⑤① ⑤⑤

㊷ ⑤⑥ ⑤① ⑤⑤

⑨② ⑤⑦ ⑤⑧ ⑤⑨

⑥⑤ ⑨④ ⑨⑤ ⑥① ⑥② ⑥③ ⑥④

⑨③ Cedar City ⑥⓪ Blanding

⑥⑥ ⑥① ⑦⑦

⑨⑥ ⑥⑦ ⑥⑨ ⑦② ⑦① ⑦③ ⑦⑤-⑦⑥

⑦⓪ ⑨⑦-⑨⑨ ⑥⑧ ⑦⑧ ⑧⓪ ⑧①-⑧② ⑦④

⑩⓪-⑩③ St. George Kanab ⑧⑥ ⑦⑨ ⑧④ ⑧③ ⑧⑤

Utah

All climbers be assured that the more "good fights"
a climber has had, the richer he becomes. —Harvey T. Carter

While mapping Utah areas, I was tempted to just slap one big number on the state and call it good. Then I noticed the Great Salt Lake and decided to break it down. The Beehive State is loaded with rock (practically everywhere you look) and busy drones to develop it.

If one were to draw a line from Vernal through Price and down to Zion National Park, chances are 9.9 out of 10 that the area would be part of the great Four Corners sandstone belt. The quality of the sandstone here ranges from scary yet climbable to a cat box–grade nightmare. Still, this soft sandstone has created one of the most challenging crack climbing venues in some of the most scenic and wild areas of the United States (and the world).

It's hard to pick a place to begin to list some of these areas, yet Indian Creek or Canyonlands and Zion National Parks would have to rank first in popularity as climbing choices. And, any climber intrigued by the sandstone genre would enjoy visits to Arches, Moab, Dinosaur, San Rafael Swell, Capitol Reef, and shhhh—desert . . . climbers are screaming out the back door with knives and guns . . . .

The other not-so-small slice of the state is the backbone of "hard rock" hard rock climbing. The Salt Lake City area boasts most of the developed climbing so far, with clean areas like the granite in Little Cottonwood Canyon, the quartzite in Big Cottonwood, and the limestone power-cranking at American Fork. Yet even considering all that has been developed, Utah still has a federal reserve of rock in its great western bank.

1 Logan Canyon ✪✪✪

The politically correct canyon features year-round, 100′ limestone sport cragging. Site of the federally protected Maguire Primrose, especially at the Greenhouse Wall—tread with angel's feet. A National Forest Scenic Byway. Free camping at the mm 383 right-hand fork or USFS fee areas. Spring/autumn. USFS–Wasatch-Cache NF, (801) 753-2772.

Classics: Hobbit Hole 7, Preston's Pinnacle 7, Mighty Mouse 8, Community Effort 9, Kentucky Fried Penguin 9, Babe-a-licious 10, Bonnie 10a, Order and Chaos 10+, Begging for Bolts 11a, Limestone Cowboy 11c, Nuclear Fingers 12a, Paleface 12c/d, Vulcan Crawl 13a, Super Tweak 14b.

Ref: C [152, 131(4/92)]; R [76-22, 50(7/92)]; Guidebooks: Green's *Rock Climbing Utah,* Monsell's *Logan Canyon Climbs,* USFS sheet map.

Directions: From Logan there are scattered crags at various mile markers in Logan Canyon on Hwy. 89. Mini-Pinnacle Pullout, 375.3; Greenhouse Wall, 376.1; Second Practice Wall (toprope only), 376.5; Kentucky Fried Penguin, 381.7; Preston Valley Pinnacle, 382.3; Fucoidal Quartzite, 383.2; China Wall Turnoff, 383.4; 385/Chimney Crag, 385.1; Five Minutes from Fighting, 385.8.

2 Ogden Areas (Ninth St., Ogden Canyon, Schoolroom Wall) ✪✪✪

This extensive cliff above Ogden was the playground for the Lowe clan. Greg Lowe's Macabre Wall may have been first 12+ in United States (early 1970s). Fine bouldering on primo quartzite at Schoolroom Boulders. Camping areas in Ogden Canyon. Spring/autumn. USFS–Wasatch-Cache NF, (801) 625-5112.

Classics: Ninth St.: 11a, 11b, Gibbon Man 13b, Shotgun 6, Nuts and Bolts 7, Rohgar Stoddard Routes 8, Chouinard Crack 9, No Nuts 10a, Banghor 10b, Double Indemnity 11, Tree Crack 11a, Pass or Flail 11d, Heart of Darkness 12a; Warmwater Canyon: Double Indemnity 10-, Roadside Attraction 10+.

Ref: C [103,70]; Guidebooks: Mecham's *Ogden Rock Climbs,* local Schoolroom bouldering guide.

Directions: Ogden. Exit I–15 at Hwy. 39 and go east to Hwy. 203. For Ninth St. turn north (right) on Hwy. 203, then turn right on Ninth to end. Two short walls with some fun sport leads sit above parking area. Ogden Canyon: Follow Twelfth St. up into canyon for various walls along the length of canyon. For Twenty-fourth St. turn south on Hwy. 203, then east (left) on Twenty-fourth St. to end for Schoolroom Wall/Boulderfield, or continue farther south to Twenty-seventh St. and turn left to rock at road end.

3 Flaming Gorge Dam ✪✪

A shipload of small, friable, as well as good 80′ quartzite rock bands surrounding the reservoir. Though some of the rock is untrustworthy, you can trust you'll have a good time exploring for climbing challenges. Spring/autumn. NPS, (435) 784-3445.

Classics: Flying Bat Boulder.

Directions: Dutch John Area. From Flaming Gorge Dam on Hwy. 191, just south of dam $^8/10$ mi. to rocks at bridge. More rock north of dam approximately 1 mi. at roadside rock bands. Other areas exist—explore to your heart's content.

4 Uintah Mountains (Kings Peak, 13,528')

High, alpine granite mountaineering. This huge range presents climbable walls of varying quality for those willing to explore for them. Kings Peak is the highest peak in the range and Utah. Cragging can be found off Hwy. 150 east from Kamas at Soapstone campground and farther north at Ruth Lake. Summer. USFS-Wasatch NF, (435) 783-4338.

Ref: S [31(5/85)-1, 8/62]; Wharton and Huff's *Hiking Utah's Summits;* Guidebook: Baldwin's *A Rock Climbing Guide to the Uintas.*

Directions: From Mountain Home roads lead north onto Wasatch National Forest. Various hiking trails lead to Kings Peak alpine area and various backcountry walls.

5 SL☆-(Salt Lake Area) Parley's Canyon ☆☆☆

A quartzite fin similar to half of Seneca Rocks, West Virginia. Easy access for Salt Lakers. Cool, north-facing sport face climbs, but bring earplugs for the I-80 hum. Salt Lake City offers climbers many amenities, such as Great Harvest Bread, Brachman's Bagel, dollar movies, the Pie Pizzeria. Spring/autumn. USFS-Wasatch NF, (801) 733-2660.

Classics: Riptide Wall: Riptide 9, Astro Projection 11d; Iron Curtain Wall: Out of Touch 9, Iron Curtain 10, One with the Rock 11c.

Ref: S. Petro; Guidebooks: Ruckman's *Rock Climbing Utah's Wasatch Range,* Ruckman's *Wasatch Rock Climbs,* Calderone's *Climbs of the Northern Wasatch: A Supplement.*

Directions: Northeast Salt Lake City. Parley's Canyon wall is visible on south side of I-80 where the canyon mouth empties into Salt Lake City. Go east on Thirty-third. Turn north on Wasatch Blvd. to end. Hike up dirt road (four-wheel-drive) to square boulders and descend east to walls. A trail to east leads down to walls: Riptide Wall to west, Iron Curtain to east.

6 SL-Grandeur Peak ☆☆

Two 100' limestone cragging areas: The Quarry and The Reef (lowest limestone area on hill past first quarry to southeast). Spring/autumn. USFS-Wasatch NF, (801) 733-2660.

Classics: Public Anemone 11b, Leviathan 12+.

Ref: Guidebooks: Ruckman's *Rock Climbing Utah's Wasatch Range,* Ruckman's *Wasatch Climbing North.*

Directions: Northeast Salt Lake City. Between Parley's and Mill Creek Canyon. Go east on Thirty-third past freeway

entrance until it bends north and joins Wasatch Blvd. Turn north on Wasatch. Turn right on Palisade Dr. Turn right on Teton Dr. Park between 3161 and 3181 Teton Dr. Hike between houses, going north on dirt road for Grandeur Peak areas. Go north to Quarry. For The Reef, head up trail at first quarry southeast through sage. Reef is lowest limestone on hill.

7 SL-Mill Creek Canyon ☆☆

Small, 60' east-facing limestone toprope area. Sharp rock. Spring/autumn. USFS-Wasatch NF, (801) 733-2660.

Classics: Itchy Stitches 9.

Ref: Guidebooks: Ruckman's *Rock Climbing Utah's Wasatch Range,* Ruckman's *Wasatch Crags,* Ruckman's *Wasatch Climbing North,* Calderone's *Climbs of the Northern Wasatch: A Supplement.*

Directions: East Salt Lake City. Go east on 3800 South. From four-way stop (fees) at mouth of Mill Creek Canyon, go 1 $^9/10$ mi. to Stitches Wall, or 2 $^9/10$ mi. to Church Fork Wall.

8 SL-Mt. Olympus ☆☆☆

Impressive and massive 600' quartzite peak east of Salt Lake City harbors mountain goats and lengthy mountaineering routes with impressive views of Salt Lake City. Check guidebooks. Spring/autumn. USFS-Wasatch NF, (801) 733-2660.

Classics: Great Chimney 5, West Slabs 5, Kamp's Ridge II 6.

Ref: R 98-53; Guidebooks: Ruckman's *Rock Climbing Utah's Wasatch Range,* Ruckman's *Wasatch Climbing North,* Gottman's *Wasatch Quartzite.*

Directions: East Salt Lake City. From Wasatch Blvd., torque east on Oakview (Cumorah). Turn left on Zarahemia, then turn onto Park Terrace Dr. Go right on White Way. Park at trailhead. Hike one to two hours to Mt. Olympus.

9 SL-Pete's Rock ☆☆☆

Local urban assault toprope area overlooking Salt Lake City. This 80' quartzite rock pile has been the classroom for the Wasatch Mountain Club since 1930. Routes numbered according to difficulty. Of the numbered routes, 15 represents the most difficult, 1 the easiest. No camping. Spring/autumn. USFS-Wasatch NF, (801) 733-2660.

Ref: Guidebooks: Ruckman's *Rock Climbing Utah's Wasatch Range,* Ruckman's *Wasatch Climbing North,* Gottman's *Wasatch Quartzite.*

Directions: East Salt Lake City. From I-80 go south on I-215 to exit 4. Go south 2 $^3/10$ mi. At 5500 South Wasatch Blvd. 100' east of road. Parking below rock. Faces southwest.

10 SL-Big Cottonwood Canyon ☆☆☆☆

What's more complex than a Zappa song? The many cragging areas of the winding Big Cottonwood have yielded above-average trad and fine sport climbs in this easily accessible and scenic canyon just east of Salt Lake. Shady summer climbing on 100' quartzite walls like the Psychobabble Wall. Steep overhanging routes like Dog Eat Dog at the S-Curve await pining rock rounders. See Ruckman's guides for the intricate details. Autumn/spring. Pay camping up canyon at Spruces Campground. USFS–Wasatch NF, (801) 733-2660.

Classics: Jam Crack Route 6, Steort's Ridge 6, Narcolepsy 8, Margin for Air 10a, Life Sentence 10-R, Psychobabble 10b, Goodro's Wall 10c, Black Monday 11a, Right Pile 11d, The Enemy Within 12a, Cell Life 12a, Padded Cell 12-, Savage Dance 12, Cross-eyed and Painless 13-, Dog Eat Dog 13d.

Ref: S. Petro; C [113, 111, 109, 104, 103], R 32(7/89); on-line guide www.thedeadpoint.com/guides/bc.html; Guidebooks: Ruckman's *Rock Climbing Utah's Wasatch Range*, Green's *Rock Climbing Utah*, Ruckman's *Wasatch Range Classic Rock Climbs*, Ruckman's *Wasatch Climbing North*, Ellison and Smoot's *Wasatch Rock Climbs*, Calderone's *Climbs of the Northern Wasatch: A Supplement*, Gottman's *Wasatch Quartzite*.

Directions: Southeast Salt Lake City. Follow Hwy. 190 east to Big Cottonwood Canyon. Mileage to roadside cragging: Dogwood Crag (Cross-eyed and Painless), 1 3/10 on right; Ledgemere Picnic Area, 1 6/10 mi., The Wave, 1 7/10 mi., Narcoleptic Dreamscape, 2 6/10 mi.; the popular Storm Mountain Picnic Area (main parking—Goodro's Wall et al.), 2 9/10 mi. on left; and popular S-Curve Area, higher up the canyon at 4 4/10 mi. Park right in middle of S-Curve. Hike up to wall above.

11 SL–The Millstone and The Sundial ★★★

The Millstone is a large, east-facing slab obvious on the approach to The Sundial. Look carefully; you may see a few white mountain goats. More than thirty good routes in the 5.10–11 range. Sundial is a large, north-facing 500' quartzite buttress set in an alpine atmosphere. Numerous routes blanket the face. Figure on a full day's outing for most climbs. Descent is on west side below summit via high-angle ramp. Symbol of the Wasatch Mountain Club. Summer. USFS– Wasatch NF, (801) 733-2660.

Classics: The Millstone: Eraserhead 11a, Stone Ground 11b; Sundial: North Face II 6/7.

Ref: Guidebooks: Ruckman's *Rock Climbing Utah's Wasatch Range*, Ruckman's *Wasatch Range Classic Rock Climbs*, Ruckman's *Wasatch Climbing North*, Ellison and Smoot's *Wasatch Rock Climbs*, Gottman's *Wasatch Quartzite*.

Directions: From Salt Lake City head up Big Cottonwood Canyon 4 3/10 mi. to Mill D South Parking Area and Trailhead. Hike 3 mi. up Lake Blanche Trail to Sundial, just south of Lake Blanche (2 1/2 mi.). For Millstone stay right at first bridge up trail.

12 Brighton Boulders/Shiva Wall ★★★

White granite alpine bowl set behind Brighton. Also, good climbs on 30' boulders behind Girl Scout Camp include 5.11 and 5.10. Summer. USFS–Wasatch NF, (801) 733-2660.

Directions: From Salt Lake City take Hwy. 190 east to Brighton above Big Cottonwood Canyon. Park at Brighton Lakes Trailhead. Walk past picnic tables to boulders. For Shiva Wall hike up trail past Lake Martha to buttresses.

13 SL–Ferguson Canyon ★★★

Short, pumpy, 50' granite routes with about one hundred routes. A prominent granite tower that nobody ever climbs known as the Hound's Tooth sits above the canyon. Cool in summer, but spring and autumn best. USFS–Wasatch NF, (801) 733-2660.

Classics: Extreme Unction 10a, Bats in Belfry 10+, Get a Pump or Jump 11d, Fuego 12-.

Ref: C [113, 111, 104, 81(12/83)-4]; Guidebooks: Ruckman's *Rock Climbing Utah's Wasatch Range*, Ruckman's *Wasatch Climbing North*, Ellison and Smoot's *Wasatch Rock Climbs*, Gottman's *Wasatch Quartzite*.

Directions: Southeast Salt Lake City. Just south of Big Cottonwood Canyon. From junction of Big Cottonwood Canyon Rd. and Wasatch Blvd., go 1/4 mi. south on Wasatch Blvd. Turn left onto Prospector Dr. Turn left on Timberline to parking at gated dirt road on right. Hike up dirt road past water tank into Ferguson Canyon for thirty minutes. Many formations along trail.

14 SL–Little Cottonwood Canyon ★★★★★

The spotlight area of Salt Lake, with a long history of climbing on the white 500' granite cliffs above Salt Lake City and below Snowbird Ski Area. Unlike the soft sandstone in southern Utah, this is a rock-solid bet for good climbing (i.e., among the best granite in the state). Fine cracks mixed with bumpy multipitched slabs and a variety of roadside bouldering satiates any climber's rock appetite. Snowbird's artificial wall farther up the road has been the host of several international climbing contests. April–May/mid-September– November. Private land is posted no trespassing. Mixed private LDS Church and USFS–Wasatch NF land (801–733-2660).

Classics: Perhaps 7, Beckey's Wall 7, Satan's Corner 8+, Green Adjective 9-, Half a Finger 9, Coffin Crack 9, S-Crack Direct 9+, Plumbline 10a, Mexican Crack 10a, Fin Arête 10, Catalyst 10c, The Black Streak 10+/11a, Equipment Overhang 11a, Bitterfingers 11d, All Chalk . . . 12a, Coffin Roof 12, Meat Puppet 12c, Trinity Cracks 12a–13a, Trench Warfare 13a, Fallen Arches 13a; Bouldering: Standard Overhang V3/10, Barn Door V3, Crystal Pinch V6, The Buzz V9, All Thumbs V10, Wormhole V12; Hogum's Heroes 11d; Hellgate Cliffs: Social Realism 10a, Desp-arête 10d, Medusa 11b.

Ref: S. Petro; AAJ ['96, '79-198, 65-419], C [177-41/126, 173-24, 160-60, 113, 111, 109, 105, 104, 103, 97 to 93, 91, 88, 75, 68, 66, 61(7/80)-81, 58, 54], R [98-48, 85-36, 32(7/89)], S 4/77; on-line guide www.thedeadpoint.com/ guides/little.html; Guidebooks: Ruckman's *Rock Climbing Utah's Wasatch Range*, Green's *Rock Climbing Utah*, Ruckman's

Wasatch Range Classic Rock Climbs, Ruckman's *Wasatch Climbing North*, Ellison and Smoot's *Wasatch Rock Climbs*, Calderone's *Climbs of the Northern Wasatch: A Supplement*, Harlin's *Rocky Mountain*, Smith's *Wasatch Granite*.

Directions: Southeast Salt Lake City. Go east of Sandy on Hwy. 210. (Above junction with Hwy. 209, mileages start.) The rock begins with several parking areas on both sides of road. The popular cragging areas in the first few mi. of the canyon include: Crescent Crack, ¼ mi. on left; Trench Warfare, ⁴⁄₁₀ mi. on right; The Fin, ⁹⁄₁₀ mi. on left; The Dihedrals (approximately two dozen routes 5.6–5.12) 1 ³⁄₁₀ mi. on left; and Green Adjective Gully/Gate Buttress (approximately three dozen routes 5.6–5.13), 1 ³⁄₁₀ mi. on left. Many other buttresses and gullies ensure the need for Ruckman's latest guidebook. Bouldering is fairly obvious on left roadside. Hellgate Canyon/Cliffs (400' limestone) is farther up canyon just past Snowbird between Snowbird and Alta to north of road. Face climbing on prominent rock towers. Other areas up canyon include the Pfeifferhorn via the Red Pine Trail and Hogum Fork via the power-plant crossing. On the creek's south side, The Coal Pit Buttress and others allow for cool, shady slabbing in summer.

15 SL–Snowbird Wall ✪✪✪

First world-class competition wall in the United States to sponsor an international climbing event.

Ref: AAJ '89-123, C [122, 116, 61(7/80)-81].

Directions: Southeast Salt Lake City. East of Sandy on Hwy. 210. Park at Snowbird Lodge. On south face of the Snowbird Lodge.

16 Bell Canyon (Bell Towers) ✪✪✪

The Bell Towers are white, 600' granite buttresses that are just right (south) of Little Cottonwood Canyon's opening. Multipitched routes 400'–600' long in a textbook, U-shaped, glacially carved canyon. Camping in nearby Little Cottonwood Canyon. Spring/autumn. USFS-Wasatch NF, (801) 733–2660.

Classics: Ellsworth: McQuarrie Route 7, Beckey Route 9, Butcher Knife 10+ A0/11c, The Nerve 11a, Arm and Hammer 11c.

Ref: C [94, 75, 68], S 11/63; Guidebooks: Ruckman's *Rock Climbing Utah's Wasatch Range*, Green's *Rock Climbing Utah*, Ruckman's *Wasatch Climbing South*, Calderone's *Climbs of the Northern Wasatch: A Supplement*, Ellison and Smoot's *Wasatch Rock Climbs*.

Directions: Southeast Salt Lake City. Bell Canyon is next canyon parallel to and south of Little Cottonwood Canyon. Park on South Little Cottonwood Rd. 200 yd. east of Wasatch Blvd. Bell Towers are approximately 4 mi. (one-and-a-half-hour hike with bushwhacking) up canyon on south side. Approach crosses private land that is the town of Granite watershed. Get permission to cross from Granite Water Master.

17 Lone Peak Cirque (Big Willow Cirques and Question Mark Wall) ✪✪✪

High-angle knob and crystal face climbing in sensational alpine setting and rock at more than 10,000'. Lone Peak Cirque, Big Willow Cirque, and Question Mark Wall are steeper than your average Little Cottonwood climbs. The west face of Lone Peak is a pristine 700' granite cirque. Big Willow Cirque is a 1/2-mi. hike from Lone Peak Cirque but is best approached as separate approach from Big Willow Canyon. Bivy at base is a common practice. Late summer. USFS-Wasatch NF, (801) 733–2660.

Classics: Three- to six-pitch routes (5.6 to 5.10); four to five routes with A2–A3 pitch; Open Book 7, Gold Wall 3p 9, Out of the Question 10b; Question Mark Wall: Pika Paradise 7, Lowe Route 8 and QM Wall Route 3p 5.12a/b small nuts; Hyperform 10-.

Ref: S. Petro; AAJ '96-165, AAC [113, 75, 68, 64, 58], R 55-96, S [1/87, 12/62]; Guidebooks: Ruckman's *Rock Climbing Utah's Wasatch Range*, Smith's *Wasatch Granite*, Ellison and Smoot's *Wasatch Rock Climbs*, Ruckman's *Wasatch Climbing South*, Calderone's *Climbs of the Northern Wasatch: A Supplement*.

Directions: From Draper go up Draper Ridge Trail along west ridge of Lone Peak massif. Or exit I–15 at Hwy. 287. Turn left at country store. Go to town of Alpine and find trailhead by going north on Grove to Aspen Drives. A four- to six-hour, complex approach hike. Big Willow Cirque lies ½-mi. hike north from Lone Peak Cirque. Best to talk with someone who has been there or check Ruckman's *Rock Climbing Utah's Wasatch Range*.

18 Dry Fork Canyon ✪✪

Dry Fork Canyon harbors 200' spires/pinnacles of soft Weber sandstone. Cracks on desert varnished walls, too. First climbs established in 1969 by Brent Boren and Terry Pierce. Ask permission on private land. Climbing information may be hard to come by in these parts . . . . This is the kind of "inside information" that could only be found in one place: the Gateway Saloon (possibly in east Vernal) or the *American Alpine Journal*. Spring/autumn. Private land/USFS-Ashley NF, (801) 789–1181.

Classics: Red Twister Spire, Tyrolean Towers, Vulture's Roost.

Ref: AAJ '84-174, R 20(1/87).

Directions: From Vernal take Hwy. 44 north. Turn west on Hwy. 121. Turn north on Dry Fork Canyon Rd. Towers appearing on left in order: Vulture's Roost, 100' directly across from Remember the Maine County Park (yep, that's really the name); Tyrolean, 150'; and Red Twister Spire. The Uintah Mountains lie to the north.

19 D✪–(Dinosaur National Monument) Overview ✪✪✪

Geologic heaven of soft (rotten) sandstone, amazing formations, dinosaur remains, and white-water treks. Steamboat Rock (see Colorado chapter) is most well-known, big attraction for adventure climbers. Dry lightning storms in sum-

mer, but it may be too hot to climb then anyway. Best time to climb is in the fall. Check with rangers for details. Spring–autumn. NPS, (970) 374–3000.
Classics: Quarry Area, Prophecy in Stone Area, Split Mountain, Elephant Toes Tower.
Ref: AAJ 84, R 20(1/87); Guidebook: Burns's *Selected Climbs in the Desert Southwest.*
Directions: From Jensen mosey northeast on Hwy. 149. Several areas (on the Utah side) along road include: The Quarry Area, Prophecy in Stone Area, Split Mountain, and Elephant Toes Tower off Blue Mountain Rd.

20 D–Quarry Area ★★★
Overhanging sandstone/conglomerate boulder problems and 30' topropes near the bones of dinosaurs. Most problems near the Swelter Shelter, an overhang once inhabited by prehistoric Indians. Spring/autumn. NPS, (970) 374–3000.
Classics: Bullwinkle's Wrinkle 11.
Ref: R 20 (1/87).
Directions: From Jensen follow Hwy. 149 north. Near Swelter Shelter area and Quarry Housing Area. Bouldering a short walk from the Quarry.

21 Cliff Ridge/Indian Overhang ★★★
Face climbs featuring solution pockets on 400' Weber sandstone with delicate flakes and loose rock. Doubled bolts. First climbs established in 1988. Pick Pocket one of the longest climbs at three pitches. The Dinosaur National Monument is a few miles away. Camping at Cliff Ridge costs nothing, and there are no rest rooms or potable water, so haul your own. Camping is in the cedars and willows. Also, since the base of the cliff is a bit more than 5,400' in elevation, it never really gets hot, just up into the nineties. Climbing year-round except for the winter months. BLM, (801) 539–4001.
Classics: Pick Pocket II 8, Boltergeist 8+, Emperor's New Clothes 9+, Bloody Fingers 10.
Ref: Gudmundsen 1/98; R 20 (1/87); Guidebook: Gudmundsen's Web site guide www.geocities.com/Pipeline/7615/CliffRidgeRockClimbingLink.htm.
Directions: From Jensen (twenty minutes east of Vernal), follow Hwy. 40 east to corral. At black-and-white striped sign (gone as of 1998) on telephone pole on right (¼ mi. past mm 168), turn east/north (approximately 2 mi.) on dirt road (Cliff Ridge is in front of you). Turn left at Y, then stay right up hill to Indian Overhang and White Wall. Bouldering under the Indian Overhang and adjacent to it are routes on cliffs. More directions (excerpted from Scott Gudmundsen's guide): Cross over the Green River and continue toward the Colorado line. About ¼ mi. past mm 168 (6 mi. from state line), at wire and wooden sheep pens, turn east to your left at right angle to highway. Cliff Ridge is visible in front of you. Turn left at the Y to get to Indian Overhang. (Stay to the right once you have turned left at the Y.) Turn right and drive up the steep hill instead of driving past the cow pond (Davis Springs). If your car can't make it up the hill, continue on past the pond. Continue on this rough dirt road as far as you can go. You will have to hike a couple hundred yd. to the Indian Overhang and the White Wall. If you can make it up the hill, stay left on the dirt road and until within 200 yd. or so of the overhang. Note: The road from the highway turns to peanut butter after a substantial soaking. The roads in the cedars are sandy and drain well, however.

22 Deseret Peak (in Stansbury Mountains) ★★★
The northeastern face of Deseret Peak reportedly has fine limestone rock climbing routes. USGS topo recommended. Camping at Loop Campground. Summer. USFS–Wasatch-Cache NF, (801) 524–3900.
Ref: Guidebook: Kelsey's *Utah Mountaineering Guide.*
Directions: From Grantsville go south, following signs into south Willow Creek Drainage approximately 20 km. Limestone climbs at roadside before Loop Campground. Park at end of Loop Campground to approach Deseret Peak.

23 American Fork ★★★★
Site of the American limestone revolution. This favored Salt Lake 160' limestone sport climbing area showcases the deeply overhanging Hell Cave Area (Burning 13b), which stays dry but rains jugs, and the Membrane (License to Thrill 11c)—two of the more popular sport climbing areas. The Billboard, with more than thirty hard routes to 5.14a (Blue Mask/Hard Blues), is favored winter wall with a healthy forty-five-minute hike but special views. Please respect campers' privileges, especially at site 33 in Little Mill campground (pay). Free camping and swimming up road at Tibble Fork Reservoir via Hwy. 44 or pay camping in canyon. Summers, though doable, can be humid for sport climbing. Try fall or spring. USFS–Wasatch NF, (801) 524–3900.
Classics: Caress of Steel 10a, License to Thrill 11c, Step Right Up 11d, Pigpen 12a, Beeline 12b, X 13a, Hell Cave 13–14s, I Scream 14c, Monkey Brains 13a, The Shining 13c; House Boulder.
Ref: C [198-32, 176-28, 173-21, 131(4/92), 126, 123(12/90)-53, 118-111, 116], R 66-89 (topos); www.thedeadpoint.com/guides/af.html; Guidebooks: Ruckman's *Wasatch Range Classic Rock Climbs,* Green's *Rock Climbing Utah,* Ruckman's *Climber's Guide to American Fork Canyon/Rock Canyon,* Ruckman's *Wasatch Climbing South,* Boyle's *Wasatch Pickles,* Gottman's *Wasatch Quartzite.*
Directions: From Salt Lake City fire 25 mi. south on I-15. Turn east at exit 287 toward Timpanogos Cave and American Fork Canyon. Four main areas: 1) Hell Cave, 6/10 mi. past visitors center to pullout, then walk north of road. 2) Membrane, 1 mi. from visitors center to south. Little Mill Campground has good climbing at campsites 33 and 44. 3) The Billboard, 1 ½ mi. from V.C. just past Little Mill campground pull-in. 4) Division Wall 2 3/10 mi. from visitors center, located behind campsite 64. Avoid going through campsites . . . and campfires, argh.

24 Rock Canyon ☆☆☆

Rock Canyon features more than one hundred routes on both 80' slick quartzite in Lower Rock Canyon and great secluded limestone sport climbs in Upper Rock Canyon put up by Jeff Pedersen (Hey Whitey 13d) and Bill Ohran. Many bouldering challenges exist as well in the canyon, e.g., Chicago Boulder. One reader writes, "There have been restrooms and a drinking fountain put in, as well as a small amphitheater for concerts. The City of Provo for some reason or another has put a gate in front of the old road, and motorized vehicle traffic is prohibited. Bikers, hikers, and climbers of course can still go up the canyon, though. I believe their reason for shutting off the canyon to motorized vehicle travel was environmental in nature." Spring/autumn. USFS–Wasatch NF, (801) 524–3900.

Classics: Main Crack 7, Green Monster 9, Green Monster Aid Crack 10d, Edge of Night 10d, Green Hornet 11b, Learning to Fly 11d, Meadow Muffin 12, Valhalla 13.

Ref: Guidebooks: Ruckman's *Climber's Guide to American Fork Canyon/Rock Canyon*, Adams and Mickelson's *A Climber's Guide to Rock Canyon*, Ruckman's *Wasatch Climbing South, Beyond the Green Gate*.

Directions: From Provo go northeast out of town into mountains via North Temple Dr. Park where pavement ends in Rock Canyon. Parking is now in a designated parking lot below Rock Canyon right off the main road that leads there on the left side of the Provo LDS Temple. Fifteen-minute hike to upper limestone climbs.

25 Hobble Creek Canyon ☆☆☆

More 80' limestone sport cliffs—5.11/12 sport routes. Impressive-looking roofs. Good spring/fall climbing area. USFS–Wasatch NF, (801) 524–3900.

Ref: Guidebook: Ruckman's *Wasatch Climbing South*.

Directions: Canyon east of Springville. From Springville hobble east on Hwy. 77 (aka 400 south) to junction of 400 south and 1300 east. Continue along Canyon Rd. to a Y and go left into Hobble Creek Canyon. Take right fork after golf course for 2 8/10 mi. Pullout on right. Rocks to north. Hike approximately fifteen minutes.

26 Nine Mile Canyon ☆

Small 30' sandstone roadside wall and boulders. Soft rock. Roadside petroglyphs and free camping farther up canyon. Autumn. Private land/BLM, (435) 636–3600.

Classics: Black Seam 10+.

Directions: From east Wellington go north of town, following signs up Nine Mile Canyon just past processing plant on left.

27 Huntington Canyon ☆☆

Lots of sandstone crags and boulders in canyon, may be too soft in quality. Summer. USFS–Manti La Sal NF, (435) 637–2817.

Directions: From Huntington go west on Hwy. 31 into Huntington Canyon.

28 Joe's Valley/New Joe's ☆☆☆

Home of the "highball" bouldering problem and itinerant "Mattress People." Bifid sandstone canyon with 100' soft sandstone walls, which have seen no action, and the main-emphasis sporty face boulder problems like Nerve Damage V7X up to V11, e.g., Resident Evil. Pay camping up at Joe's Valley Reservoir. Spring/autumn. USFS–Manti La Sal NF, (435) 637–2817.

Classics: Entrance Crack B5.10, Better than Coffee V1, Slaberriffic V2, Stand Up Comedian V4, Three Weeks V7, Finger Hut V10, Imperial Stout V11, Black Lung V13.

Ref: C [192-26, 191-19, 11/98 (topo) 187-28, 180-56], R; online guide www.thedeadpoint.com/guides/joes.html; Guidebook: Baldwin's *A Bouldering Guide to Joe's Valley*.

Directions: From Orangeville go west on Hwy. 29 into Joe's Valley. The canyon is split into a left and right fork. Areas up Left Fork (Hwy. 29 to Joe's Valley Reservoir) include: Mining Cart Area, 1 9/10 mi., and Riverside Area at 3 3/10 mi. on left. Big Joe and Maneater are uphill across road. Areas up Right Fork (up Cottonwood Canyon Rd.) include: Mansize, 1 mi. up on left; Buoux Area, 2 4/10 mi. on left. New Joe's is about 3 ½ mi. north up Hwy. 57 to oil rig road on right side of road. Turn right into dirt road to parking at oil-rig platform. Hike up to various boulders.

29 SRS☆–(San Rafael Swell) Overview ☆☆☆☆

San Rafael Swell is a remarkable uplift in the remote central Utah desert featuring climbs on a mixture of scattered bouldering blocks, soft sandstone pinnacles/buttes, and Wingate buttresses of Buckhorn Draw. Of the many large formations, a few of the more obvious include: Bottleneck Peak (6,235'), Assembly Hall Peak (6,395'), Window Blind Butte (7,030'), Mexican Mountain (6,393') in the Northern Swell, and Family Butte (6,575') and Factory Butte (6,358') in the Southern Swell. Approaches may include long, steep talus slopes. Visit this region for its wild, remote, and daring endeavors. Includes challenging canyoneering, among which the most famous is the Black Box. Bring ample water/food. March–May/September–November. Free camping. BLM, (435) 636–3600.

Classics: Bottleneck Peak: IV Tippin' the Bottle 11+; Assembly Hall Peak: Lactic Stackidosis I 10+, Window Blind Butte II 9; Wingate Buttresses: Scenic Byway (first pitch) 9, Bad Obsession 11d; Dylan Wall Cracks: One More Cup of Coffee 10d, Idiot Wind 11c, Blood on the Tracks 12b; Sex Wall: Safe Sex 12a; Lone Rock: Owl Eyes 11c; Mexican Mountain IV 5.0, White Knight I 5.9; Turkey Tower II 11-, Factory Butte IV 9+R/X.

Ref: J. Garrett; AAJ ['98>94, '92-136], R 68-26; Guidebooks: Burns's *Selected Climbs in the Desert Southwest*, Green's *Rock Climbing Utah*, Bjornstad's *Wall Street to San Rafael Swell 1997*, Allen's *Canyoneering: San Rafael Swell Guidebook*, Bjornstad's *Desert Rock*.

Directions: San Rafael Swell's triangular (80 mi. wide by 35 mi. long) uplift cut by a flatiron ridge is situated from Price to Green River to Hanksville in central Utah. Access gained by I-70, which cuts the Swell in half; Hwy. 6 on the west, or Hwy. 10 on west and Hwy. 24 on east. Many areas besides the classics listed. Topo and road maps necessary. White Knight (spire) is north of I–70 between mm 118 and 119.

30 SRS–Bottleneck Peak and Window Blind Butte ✹✹

These sandstone beauties are up to 700′ soft sandstone adventure-climbing formations. More climbing of a cragging crack/dihedral nature at Buckhorn Draw. Free camping. Spring/autumn. BLM, (435) 636–3600.
Classics: Bottleneck Peak III 5.7 A3, Tippin the Bottle III 11+, Window Blind Butte III 5.9.
Ref: Guidebooks: Burns's *Selected Climbs in the Desert Southwest*, Bjornstad's *Wall Street to San Rafael Swell 1997*, Bjornstad's *Desert Rock*.
Directions: From Green River scope 32 mi. west on I–70. Turn north on exit 129 for 17 mi. to Bottleneck Peak sign. Hike southeast to Bottleneck Peak and east to Window Blind Butte. Or, approach via Cleveland through Buckhorn Wash.

31 SRS–White Knight ✹✹

This classic chess piece is a two-pitch spire featuring 180′ of soft sandstone. Free camping nearby. Spring/autumn. BLM, (435) 636–3600.
Classics: East Ridge I 9 (2p).
Ref: AAJ '82, S 7/81; Guidebooks: Bjornstad's *Wall Street to San Rafael Swell 1997*, Bjornstad's *Desert Rock*.
Directions: From Green River go approximately 42 mi. west on I–70. Visible between mm 118 and 119. Between mm 118 and 119, go north, then northwest on dirt road for 8/10 mi. toward Eagle Canyon. Hike north to White Knight spire behind outcrop.

32 Green River Boulderfields ✹

Scattered 25′ sandstone blocks along river road near Swasey's Rapid. Popular daily run among kayakers. Free camping in area. Spring/autumn. BLM, (435) 636–3600.
Directions: From Green River go north along Green River on dirt roads to sporadic boulders.

33 Battleship and Gunnison Buttes ✹

These prominent 300′ soft sandstone riverside landmarks comprise the exit portals to Desolation/Gray River trips. Don't miss the sweet melons at Green River in September. Free camping in area. Spring/autumn. BLM, (435) 636–3600.
Classics: Battleship Butte North Face II 5, Gunnison Butte Northeast Face II 5.
Ref: Guidebook: Bjornstad's *Desert Rock*.
Directions: From town of Green River, shoot north for 6 mi. on Long St. until the pavement ends and where the Green River opens into the valley. Battleship Butte is left of road in 4 mi., and Gunnison Butte is on right in 6 mi. via dirt roads.

34 House Range (Notch Peak and Swasey Peak) ✹✹✹

In Hiking the Great Basin, John Hart describes Notch Peak as "an improbable looking sheer-walled peak, an upthrust angle of stone unlike anything else the West Desert landscape contains." Thirty-five mi. of pale, sheer, unexplored crags, canyons, and walls. The 3,000′ north face on Notch Peak, at 9,725′, is one of the United States's largest limestone walls. More than a lifetime's worth of rock. Obtain topos. Fossil hunting. No services for at least 50 mi. Not only that, it's desolate. Summer. BLM, (435) 743–3100.
Classics: NW Ridge II 8 8p, North Face 2500′ V 5.10+ A3 (18p poor rock), Book of Saturday 5.11-R 12p route.
Ref: AAJ '87-178, C 104, S 5/86; Guidebooks: Garrett's *Ibex and Selected Climbs of Utah's West Desert*, Kelsey's *Utah Mountaineering Guide*, Hart's *Hiking the Great Basin*.
Directions: From Delta's only traffic light, travel west for 50.1 mi. on Hwy. 50. At BLM's Ibex Well sign continue straight on Hwy. 50 for a few more miles to the first major dirt road on right, Tule Valley Rd. Turn right here and continue north until about even with the obvious north face of Notch Peak and the canyon mouth below (the target). Turn east toward canyon when obvious jeep road junctions with Tule Valley Rd. Follow to mouth of canyon—four-wheel-drive and high clearance helpful here. Good granite climbing below north face of Notch Peak in Sawtooth Canyon and at Painter Springs Campground further north up Tule Valley Rd. Notch Peak summit hike is completely different approach via Miller Canyon (park at cabin). For Swasey Peak follow signs to peak. Get BLM maps.

35 Airport Towers (Courthouse Pasture) ✹✹✹

Soft Entrada sandstone spires up to 225′ high. Merrimac Butte's wild lightning-bolt, off-width crack leads to summit. Monitor and Merrimac Buttes named after the armored Civil War ships that engaged in battle. Spring/autumn. BLM, (435) 259–6111.
Classics: Merrimac Butte: The Hyper-crack on the Anchor Chain 11 . . . major off-width.
Ref: AAJ ['97-154, '94, '87-76, '86-165], 98-88; Guidebooks: Bjornstad's *Wall Street to San Rafael Swell 1997*, Bjornstad's *Desert Rock*.
Directions: From Moab go 12 mi. northwest, just north and west of junction of Hwy. 191 and Hwy. 313. This area holds four main towers: Echo Pinnacle, Aeolian Tower, Monitor, and Merrimac Butte. At mm 142, Echo Pinnacle and Aeolian Tower are visible from road. Monitor and Merrimac visible after Sevenmile Canyon switchbacks. Turn west onto dirt road off Hwy. 191 at mm 142. Cross railroad tracks, going west to second canyon visible to south. Echo is farthest to south. Beyond Echo and Aeolian, Monitor is to east (closest to Hwy. 191), and Merrimac is to right at south end of Courthouse Pasture.

36 Arches Bouldering (aka The Gym) ✯✯
Roadside 30′ Wingate sandstone bouldering blocks and short walls with south-facing aspect. Easy pickin's. Year-round. BLM, (435) 259-6111.

Classics: B5.10 arête nearest road.

Ref: C 88; Sherman's *Stone Crusade;* Guidebooks: Knapp's *Fifty Select Classic Desert Climbs,* Bjornstad's *Desert Rock.*

Directions: From Moab drift approximately 5 mi. north on Hwy. 191 (⁶/10 mi. north of Arches entrance, 2 ⁶/10 mi. north of junction of Hwy. 191 and Hwy. 128). The Gym Rocks on right at pullout.

37 Arches National Park ✯✯✯✯
Pinnacles, buttes, and arches in a kaleidoscope of 500′ sandstone configurations. Hard crack and clean aid climbing in a superb setting with stunning views of the La Sal Mountains. Lengthy crack lines in soft, desert sandstone. Climbing on all named arches on USGS topo maps is prohibited. The abundance of arches in the park has prompted the hiker's game of arch bagging. Delicate Arch is perhaps the most beautiful. Landscape Arch is one of the wildest and is the longest span of unsupported rock in the world. See *Arch Bagger* by Gerry Roach. Restrictions—check with rangers. Pay camping at Devil's Garden. Spring and fall offer excellent weather. NPS, (435) 719-2299.

Classics: Owl Rock 8, Zippy Zebra 10a; Three Penguins: Right Chimney 10c, Dark Angel 10, Mr. Sombrero 11c, Three Gossips 11, Sheep Rock (aid), The Organ (aid), Argon Tower (aid), Tower of Babel (aid).

Ref: A (5/70), AAJ ['96>93, 92-138, 91, 88-140, 87-70, 80, 77-85], C [182-72(topo) 139, 111, 106, 102, 100, 96, 94], R [98-88, 75-46], S 12/62; Schneider's *Exploring Canyonlands and Arches National Parks;* Guidebooks: Green's *Rock Climbing Utah,* Bjornstad's *Desert Rock: National Parks* (1996), Knapp's *Fifty Select Classic Desert Climbs,* Bjornstad's *Desert Rock,* Roach's *Arch Bagger.*

Directions: From Moab toddle 5 mi. north on Hwy. 191. Most approaches are visible from roadside. Popular climbing formations include: Three Penguins, 100 Yard Wall, Zippy Zebra Wall, Park Avenue areas (Queen Victoria Rock, Candelabrum, Jello Tower, Argon Tower), Court-house Towers (Organ northeast/southwest towers, Tower of Babel, Three Gossips, Sheep Rock, Lamb, Daisy Tower), Bubo, Off Balance Rock, Owl Rock, Buccaneer Rock, Sentry Rock, Dark Angel, Devil Dog Spire, and The Marching Men. Dark Angel Spire requires a dazzling 2 ½-mi. hike past Landscape Arch.

38 Westwater Canyon Spires ✯✯✯
Multiple 300′ Wingate sandstone spires. First ascensionists include famed river guide Dave Dawson et al. The climbs are followed by an exciting float past the "Room of Doom" and "The Rock of Shock" farther down the river. Spring/autumn. BLM, (435) 259-6111.

Ref: D. Dawson.

Directions: In Westwater Canyon. Requires white-water raft trip down the Colorado River. Park rafts at confluence with the Little Dolores River, then hike east for approximately 1 mi. to cluster of twisted spires.

39 Fisher Towers (The Titan) ✯✯✯✯
The Fisher Towers comprise approximately twenty soft rock or viscous mud spires. A list of the big ones includes: Dunce Rock, Forming Tower, Dock Rock, King Fisher, Ancient Art, Cottontail Tower, Echo Tower, The Titan, Sidekick Spire, The Oracle, Broadsword Rock, and Mystery Towers (Gothic Nightmare, Citadel, and Doric Column—³/4 mi. east of The Titan). The Titan, the largest freestanding spire of the Southwest at 900′, saw its first ascent up the northeast ridge by Kor, Huntley, and Ingalls in 1965. These spires are a true test of one's aid climbing abilities and are a place an aid climber can earn his "metal." Bring air voyagers for the protection, a sombrero for belays, and big cahones for the leads. One may incur a poignant karma check by trusting fixed gear here. Inexperienced aid climbers may find these towers as pleasant as spending a night on El Cap Towers with the Harpies. Spring/autumn. BLM, (435) 259-6111.

Classics: The Titan (largest free-standing pinnacle in the United States at 900′): Finger of Fate 8 A3, Sundevil Chimney 8 A4; Ancient Art 8 A0 or 10; Kingfisher: Colorado Northeast Ridge; Cottontail: West Side Story A3; Echo Tower: Phantom Spirit A3.

Ref: A (5/70), AAJ ['98>94, '92-139, 91-172, 91-176, 88-138, 87-70, 81, 78, 72-128, 67], C [181-32, 176-27, 156-86, 139, 136, 111, 106, 102, 96, 68, 7/71, 3(9/70) many Basecamps], R 75-46, S [18(7/72)-1, 7/72, 7/67]; *Beyond the Vertical, Climbing in North America;* Guidebooks: Burns's *Selected Climbs in the Desert Southwest,* Green's *Rock Climbing Utah,* Bjornstad's *Desert Rock III,* Knapp's *Fifty Select Classic Desert Climbs,* Roper and Steck's *Fifty Classic Climbs,* Bjornstad's *Desert Rock.*

Directions: From Moab (approximately thirty minutes) take Hwy. 191 north. Turn north on Hwy. 128 for approximately 21 mi. Turn right at mm 21 (signs) on dirt road for 2 mi. to parking. Hike east on trail. One-hour hike for Fisher Towers approach. About a 2-mi. hike to Titan and this historic, one-of-a-kind area. The Mystery Towers (Doric Column, et al.) are approached best from Onion Creek off Fisher Valley Ranch Rd. via one-and-a-half-hour gully hike past first bridge (see Onion Creek Towers).

40 Onion Creek Towers and Mystery Towers ✯✯✯
The Onion Creek Towers (Mongoose, Sari, and Hindu, aka Totem Pole) are sharp, 300′ spires met visibly along Onion Creek Rd. and are easy-approach, one-day attempts. The Mystery Towers (Gothic Nightmare, Citadel, and Doric Column) are the eastern extension of the Fisher Towers. They challenge the climber with the most difficult of the Fisher Towers aid ascents and are not the best place for a greenhorn to get a start at aid on hard mud spires. First ascents on all these towers date back to the 1960s. Citadel got second ascent after twenty-three years in 1992 by Slater and Sherman. Bring a trash-can lid, big culyons, and self-

cleaning jockey shorts. Also, air voyagers for the anchors. Any fixed gear may be untrustworthy at best. At worst, you'll use it. Spring/autumn. BLM, (435) 259-6111.

Classics: Sari: East Face 6; Doric Column A4.

Ref: AAJ ['95, '92-139, '91-172, '91-176, '88-138, '87-70, '72-128], C [176-27, 140(11/93), 102, (7/71), 3(9/70)], R 74-94, S 18(7/72)-1; A (5/70); Guidebooks: Burns's *Selected Climbs in the Desert Southwest,* Bjornstad's *Desert Rock III,* Bjornstad's *Desert Rock.*

Directions: From Moab (approximately thirty minutes) take Hwy. 191 north. Turn north on Hwy. 128 for approximately 20 mi. Turn right at mm 20 (signs) on dirt road for Onion Creek. Onion Creek Towers are hard sandstone, unlike Fisher Towers's mud. These small attractive poles are obvious from road after many small stream crossings. The Mystery Towers are reached beyond the Onion Creek Towers and are not visible from road. Park ½ mi. beyond bridge in deep gorge. Hike left up canyon creekbed for one-and-a-half-hour gully hike (tricky!). Take left fork into box canyon (past perched block); right fork is longer and harder.

41 Castle Valley (Castleton Tower/Nuns/Priest) ☆☆☆☆☆

This ridge hosts Moab's most famous towers. Four-hundred-foot Castleton Tower, at 6,656', is famous as the site of several car commercials and motion pictures. Formations are characterized by white calcite glaze, e.g., the north face of Castleton. Calcite crystals in cracks resemble dull piranha teeth, e.g., Crack Wars. Castleton Tower, with its fine cracks and even better views of the La Sal Mountains, is the most frequently climbed tower in Moab region. Uncertain if there's free camping at base. Spring/autumn. BLM, (435) 259-6111.

Classics: Castleton Tower: Kor-Ingalls 9, North Face 11 3p; Rectory: Fine Jade 11 6p, J. Smith's 11; The Priest: Honeymoon Chimney 10+.

Ref: AAJ ['96, '94, '89-155, '82], C [106, 56], R [98-87, 94-74, 92-94, 75-46, S [1/82, 9/70, 7/62]; *Beyond the Vertical, Canyon Country Climbs;* Guidebooks: Green's *Rock Climbing Utah,* Knapp's *Fifty Select Classic Desert Climbs,* Bjornstad's *Desert Rock,* Roper and Steck's *Fifty Classic Climbs.*

Directions: From Moab take Hwy. 191 west for approximately 15 mi. north on Hwy. 128. Turn right on Castleton Rd. approximately 1 mi. Park below Castleton Tower. Hike southwest shoulder for one-hour "shredder" talus app-roach. Climbed formations include: Castleton Tower, Rectory, Nuns, Priest, Sister Superior, Convent, and Parriot Mesa.

42 Colorado River Road ☆☆☆

Several areas of desert sandstone bouldering, 300' face and crack climbs, and spires adjacent to the scenic Colorado River. Quick access from road. BLM pay camping along road. Spring/autumn. BLM, (435) 259-6111.

Classics: Sorcerer 11+, Dihedrals, Negro Bill, Dolomite Tower; Lighthouse Tower: Lonely Vigil 9+, Big Bend Boulders, Richardson Amphitheatre.

John Mattson tugging hard at Big Bend Boulders.

Ref: AAJ ['97, '95, '89-153, '88-134, '77-184], C [182-72(topo), 100, 96]; Sherman's *Stone Crusade, Canyon Country Climbs;* Guidebooks: Burns's *Selected Climbs in the Desert Southwest,* Green's *Rock Climbing Utah,* Bjornstad's *Desert Rock III,* Knapp's *Fifty Select Classic Desert Climbs,* Bjornstad's *Desert Rock,* Harlin's *Rocky Mountain.*

Directions: From Moab follow Hwy. 191 west. Scattered routes 0–23 mi. north on Hwy. 128 (Colorado River Rd.) at various mi. markers include: Sorcerer, 1; Dihedrals, 2.8; Negro Bill, 3; Dolomite/Lighthouse Towers, 7.5; Big Bend Boulders, 8; and Richardson Amphitheatre, 23.

43 Goblin Valley State Park ☆

Test your fortitude on this decrepit hobnob of 150' sandstone spires that turn into freakish figures at sunset. Entrance/camping fees. Spring/autumn. State park, (435) 564-3633.

Directions: From Hanksville go north on Hwy. 24 to Goblin Valley State Park.

44 Moab Area ☆☆☆☆

The Moab Area is a dreamscape of sandstone spires, walls, boulders, and world-class mountain-bike terrain.

Spring/autumn. BLM, (435) 259-6111.

Classics: Monticello Rock I 7; Two Tortoise Rock: West Tortoise 9+, II Rhino Horn 9, Gooney Bird II 10, The Pinkie II 11, The Bride, The Crack House 13a.

Ref: AAJ ['94, '88-138, 86-171, 78-530, 76-452, 72-129], C [189-74/78, 182-72, 177-23, 173-107, 111, 106, 100, 94], R [75-81, 33(9/89)-32], S 11/71; Guidebooks: Bjornstad's *Wall Street to San Rafael Swell 1997,* Knapp's *Fifty Select Classic Desert Climbs,* Bjornstad's *Desert Rock,* Harlin's *Rocky Mountain.*

Directions: Around Moab, many climbing areas present excellent climbing opportunities not specifically mentioned as individual numbered units here. Formations and areas not listed elsewhere in this guide include: Barebutte Dome/Tombstone (Hwy. 313 toward Deadhorse Point), The Pinkie, The Bride, The Gooney Bird, Two Tortoise Rock, Monticello Rock, and the Crack House (northwest of town off Hwy. 191 via Little Canyon Rd. or Gemini Bridges Rd.), The Pickle (northeast of mm 130 on Hwy. 191), Mill Creek (La Sal Mountain Loop Rd.), Point of Moab, King's Hand, Raptor and Bootleg Towers (off Hwy. 279), Rhino Horn (La Sal Mountain Loop Rd., mm 108), Disappearing Angel (end of Hance Rd., south of Moab), Seraph (Kane Spring Rest Area, 14 mi. south of Moab), and Dead Horse Point State Park (Dream of Dead Horses IV 9 A2).

45 Potash Mine Road (Wall Street and Long Canyon Area) ☆☆☆

Wall Street features Navajo sandstone cracks softer than the Indian Creek Wingate; just 6' from road. Careful: Don't scratch the paint on your car door. Also bolted faces at Wall Street. Some need two—count 'em, two—ropes to lower off. The spectacular slanting Wingate cliffs at Long Canyon have a lifetime of crack potential for those willing to hike up steep talus slopes several hundred feet. Spring/autumn. BLM, (435) 259-6111.

Classics: Wall St.: Seibernetics 8, Flakes of Wrath 10-/11, Nervous in Suburbia 10a, Steel Your Face 10, Honors Odyssey 11b/c, Last Tango in Potash 11, Something Nasty 12; Long Canyon: (Maverick Buttress: Hot Toddy 10, Tequila Sunrise 11-, Miss Kitty 11+) Sidewinder 11, The Warrior 12a, Shipyard Wall.

Ref: AAJ ['97-154, '95, '94, '92-157], C [106, 102], R [98-86, 33(9/89)-32]; Guidebooks: Green's *Rock Climbing Utah,* Bjornstad's *Wall Street to San Rafael Swell 1997,* Copeland's *Climbs to Nowhere: Guide to Wall Street/Wall Canyon,* Bjornstad's *Desert Rock.*

Directions: From Moab run approximately 3 mi. north on Hwy. 191. Turn left on Hwy. 279 (Potash Mine Rd.). Once on Hwy. 279, it's approximately 3 mi. to Wall St. (defines the term "roadside cliff"). Drive 10–12 mi. farther from Wall St. to Long Canyon turnoff. Go west at Jughandle Arch into Long Canyon to abundant Wingate Cliffs. Shipyard Wall is in first side canyon. At the start of the switchbacks, The Warrior 5.12a spire is up and left, and the Maverick Buttress (at 4 8/10 mi. from Potash Rd.) is the most popular wall (shortest approach) up switch-

backs on left closest to road. Four-wheel-drive may be useful toward top of canyon. The road continues up to Hwy. 313 and Deadhorse Point State Park.

46 Mineral Mountains ☆☆☆

What's Joshua Tree doing here? White hillsides of Josh-like granite, but possibly somewhat grainier than Joshua Tree. Formations loom up to several pitches. Spring/autumn. BLM, (435) 586-2401.

Ref: www.climbrock.com; C 95.

Directions: From Milford, Mineral Mountains lie east on BLM dirt roads to prominent rock escarpments.

47 Capitol Reef National Park ☆☆☆

The Gorge offers a plentitude of rock in a vast and beautiful area of desert sandstone. Cliffs reach 500' in places with white domes above. Classic crack cragging is found across from the campsite, in Grand Wash, and at the mouth of Capitol Gorge. Classic bouldering is at Everett Reuss Memorial Boulder (Slapshot B1+), and Capitol Gorge Boulders—all are on left side of Scenic Dr. at 2 8/10, 3 7/10, and 8 1/10 mi. respectively south from visitors center. The Golden Throne is a stunning 400' dome with a beautiful 2-mi. hike. The route features extremely soft rock, and climbers should not trust their protection will hold, i.e., don't fall. The views from the top are fabulous, however. Some climbing areas closed due to historical rock art—check at NPS office. Please, no climbing near petroglyphs. Pay camping at Fruita campground near visitors center. Spring/autumn. NPS, (801) 425-3791.

Classics: Golden Throne II 8xx, Classic Hand crack 10-, Capitol Roof 11+, 13 crack.

Ref: R. Olevsky; AAJ ['98, '95, '82], S [7/81, 3/63]; Guidebooks: Green's *Rock Climbing Utah,* Bjornstad's *Desert Rock: National Parks* (1996), Bjornstad's *Desert Rock.*

Directions: From Torrey go east on Hwy. 24 to Capitol Reef National Park.

48 C☆-(Canyonlands National Park) Overview ☆☆☆☆☆

Unlimited climbing and beauty in one of the world's most special geologic landscapes—the greatest earth on show! The park has three districts: Island in the Sky (most climbed Wingate sandstone spires), The Needles, and The Maze. Most of the climbing attention has been given to the park's unique spires, though crags and walls exist as well. As of 1995, hammerless aid only and no new bolts, a policy that closes off a number of old routes and new lines. Other special climbing/camping restrictions (white chalk/reservations, etc.)—check with rangers. While there, obtain maps. Pay camping at various NPS sites, or free on BLM. Spring/autumn. Raptor restrictions: Airport Tower. February–June. NPS, (435) 259-4351.

Classics: Moses: Primrose Dihedrals 11+, Dunn Rt 10+, Pale Fire first two pitches 12; Zeus: Sisyphus 11; Monument

Basin Towers: Standing Rock 11+; Washer Woman: In Search of Suds 10+; Charlie Horse Needle 11a.

Ref: A 4(5/70)-37, AAJ ['97>94, '92-137, '88-138, '87-70, '87-179, '86-171, '85-200, 84, 82, 81], C [182-72(topo), 136, 128(10/91)-74, 126, 113(4/89)-45, 111, 94, 79(6/83)-38, 73, 68(9/81)-28, 56], M 64(11/78)-32, OB 55(2/81), R [98-88, 78-46, 23, 16, 10-33], S [4/77, 9/69, 1/65]; Molvar and Martin's *Hiking Zion and Bryce Canyon National Parks,* Schneider's *Exploring Canyonlands and Arches National Park,* Kor's *Beyond the Vertical, Canyon Country Climbs;* Guidebooks: Burns's *Selected Climbs in the Desert Southwest,* Green's *Rock Climbing Utah,* Bjornstad's *Wall Street to San Rafael Swell 1997,* Bjornstad's *Desert Rock: National Parks* (1996), Knapp's *Fifty Select Classic Desert Climbs,* Bjornstad's *Desert Rock,* Harlin's *Rocky Mountain, Fifty Classic Climbs.*

Directions: From Moab there are two entrances via Hwy. 313 and Hwy. 211. From Hanksville go via dirt roads. These remarkable areas draw climbers: Needles (Gilbey's Tower/innumerable spires), Island in the Sky, along the White Rim (Crow Head Spires, Monster Tower and Washer Woman Islet-In-The-Sky and Blocktop, Candlestick Tower), Taylor Canyon (Moses, Zeus), Monument Basin (fourteen spires including Standing Rock, Shark's Fin, Mars), Maze District (Standing Rock—inaccessible puzzle box, silence).

49 C–Taylor Canyon (Moses) and Hell Roaring Canyon ✰✰✰✰

Moses, the prophet of the desert, speaks with classic climbing lines and incomparable light shows. Breathtaking! Many walls in this vicinity beckon. NPS requires permit—please check in. Spring/autumn. NPS, (435) 259-4351/BLM, (435) 259-6111.

Classics: Moses: Primrose Dihedrals IV 11+, Pale Fire IV 12; Zeus: Sisyphus III 11.

Ref: AAJ ['97-153, '96, '92-138, 78-531], C [111, 68, 56], R 10(10/85), S [1/82, 4/73]; *Heroic Climbs;* Guidebooks: Burns's *Selected Climbs in the Desert Southwest,* Bjornstad's *Wall Street to San Rafael Swell 1997,* Bjornstad's *Desert Rock: National Parks* (1996), Bjornstad's *Desert Rock,* Knapp's *Fifty Select Classic Desert Climbs,* Harlin's *Rocky Mountain.*

Directions: From Moab spurt 9 mi. north on Hwy. 191. Turn west on Hwy. 313. Turn west before mm 10, following Horsethief Trail into Mineral Bottoms (spectacular switchbacks). Go south along Green River for 4 1/2 mi. into Taylor Canyon. Caution: Sandy washes. Stunning spire formations from river to rimrock include: Thracian Mare, Moses, Zeus, and Aphrodite. The magnificent Hell Roaring Canyon is to the north of Mineral Bottoms on BLM land and holds The Witch and Warlock Spires (down toward mouth) and Kachina Towers (at top of canyon).

50 C–Green River Wingate Cliffs ✰✰✰

Eternity of Wingate sandstone cracks along the Green River accessible via boat or White Rim Trail. Spring/ autumn. BLM, (435) 259-6111/NPS, (435) 259-4351.

Classics: BFE 11, Circle of Quiet 11d, Glad to Be a Trad 13a.

Ref: Guidebook: Bjornstad's *Desert Rock: National Parks* (1996).

Directions: From Moab go 9 mi. north on Hwy. 191. Turn right on Hwy. 313 for about 12 1/2 mi. Turn right on Mineral Bottom road, dropping into Mineral Canyon via switchbacks. Turn left at river just like going to Moses. North of park boundary, crack routes have been done on the Boundary Cliffs to the left. Or, from Green River float south along Green River to confluence with Colorado River. Pick a line, any line.

51 C–Needles District ✰✰✰

Trippy terrain of innumerable 400′ sandstone summits. Some areas closed at certain times of year. Druid Arch is now off-limits to climbing. Pay campground at Squaw Flat campground. Spring/autumn. NPS, (435) 259-4711.

Classics: Druid Arch III 9 A2, Gilbey's Tower III 10, Conehead I 8.

Ref: Guidebooks: Burns's *Selected Climbs in the Desert Southwest,* Bjornstad's *Desert Rock: National Parks* (1996), Bjornstad's *Desert Rock.*

Directions: From Moab ride 40 mi. south on Hwy. 191. Turn west on Hwy. 211 for 31 mi. to NPS ranger station. Check in. Needles District areas beyond at Elephant Hill. Gilbey's Tower is in Chesler Park.

52 C–Monument Basin (Standing Rock) ✰✰✰

Monument Basin contains many hard-core aid ascents on the kitty-litter rock of these freestanding towers. Fourteen towers have been ascended as of 2000. Standing Rock (freed via face climbing by Shipley and Reynolds at 5.11c—yes!) is the most sought-after pinnacle. The outlandish Shark's Fin is just one more of this area's wild possessions. NPS, (435) 259-2652.

Classics: Standing Rock (5.9 A3+)/11c, Shark's Fin A4.

Ref: A (5/70), C [142, 138, 129], M 92; Guidebooks: Burns's *Selected Climbs in the Desert Southwest,* Bjornstad's *Desert Rock: National Parks* (1996), Bjornstad's *Desert Rock.*

Directions: In Monument Basin in Canyonlands. Approach Standing Rock via White Rim Rd. via the Schaffer Trail from Island in the Sky by going north of Moab on Hwy. 191 to Hwy. 313 through park to Schaffer Trail.

53 ICC✰–Indian Creek Area Overview ✰✰✰✰✰

Set up your tent and learn to crack climb right in your own red-rock living room! This amazing mixture of hardman and hardwoman cracks, spires, and even adventure bouldering is respected for its purity of lines. Hundreds of sustained cracks from 5.10 to 5.13. Be sure to bring a punty to massage your forearms after pumping up these seriously strenuous cracks. Bring ample food and water. Camping no longer permitted in the cottonwoods across from the Battle

Climbers electrified on the airy Fingers in a Light Socket, Indian Creek.

of the Bulge Buttress, i.e., camping on public land only, which is now mainly Beef Basin Rd. Spring/autumn. Private land/BLM, (435) 587-1500.

Classics: Supercrack 9+/10, Incredible Hand Crack 10, Pente 11-, Coyne Crack 11+/12-, King Cat 11+, Supercorner 12-, Ruby's Cafe 12d, Pink Flamingo 13-, Belly Full of Bad Berries 13-, Tricks are for Kids 13; Bridger Jack Mesa: Rites of Passage, Six Shooter Peaks.

Ref: S. Petro; AAJ ['97, '89-153, '88-138], C [195-23, 192-115, 176-58, 174-115, 173-105, 139, 138, 128 (74), 118, 111, 100, 95, 88, 68, 60], R [98-46/55, 92-94, 77-28, 75-46]; Guidebooks: Burns's *Selected Climbs in the Desert Southwest*, Green's *Rock Climbing Utah*, Cornacchione's *Indian Creek Climbs*, Knapp's *Fifty Select Classic Desert Climbs*, Harlin's *Rocky Mountain*, Knapp's *200 Select Classics: Indian Creek Climbs*, Bjornstad's *Desert Rock*.

Directions: From Moab go 40 mi. south on Hwy. 191. Turn 16 mi. west on Hwy. 211 past Newspaper Rock. Indian Creek areas and buttresses include (south–north) as one enters from Newspaper Rock: Orion's Bow, Blue Gramma Cliff, Supercrack Buttress, Battle of the Bulge Buttress, Fringe of Death Canyon, Fringe of Life Canyon, Paragon Prow, and Bridger Jack Mesa. Get a guidebook.

54 ICC–Sixshooters (North and South) ★★★★

The North and South Six Shooters are those two obvious landmark spires past Supercrack in Indian Creek. The North Sixshooter is famed for the 5.11 lightning-bolt cracks on the east face and the South for its blocky easy route to the top. Free camping below spires. Spring/autumn. BLM, (435) 587-1500.

Classics: North Sixshooter: Lightning Bolt Cracks 11; South: 8.

Ref: C [182-72 (topo), 106, 88, 56]; Guidebooks: Burns's *Selected Climbs in the Desert Southwest*, Green's *Rock Climbing Utah*, Bjornstad's *Desert Rock*.

Directions: From Moab go south on Hwy. 191. Turn west on Hwy. 211, following road past Newspaper Rock past the many Wingate Buttresses to mm 7. Six Shooters visible to left. North is to the right. Dirt roads lead into spires via Davis Canyon. Accessibility changes with the wetness of the year.

55 ICC–Bridger Jack Mesa ★★★

Seven separate spire summits with climbs of 5.10-5.12. Spring/ autumn. BLM, (435) 587-1500.

Classics: Numbers of Persuasion 6p 5.11-, Rites of Passage 7p 5.11+.

Ref: S. Petro; C 120; Guidebooks: Burns's *Selected Climbs in the Desert Southwest*, Green's *Rock Climbing Utah*, Bjornstad's *Desert Rock*.

Directions: From Moab go south on Hwy. 191. Turn west on Hwy. 211, following road past Newspaper Rock past the many Wingate Buttresses to Beef Basin Rd. Turn left onto Beef Basin Rd. and cross creekbed shortly after

turning. Then turn right onto dirt road to Bridger Jack Mesa, which is the prong of spires west of Dugout Ranch and Indian Creek Canyon.

56 Cataract Canyon (on Colorado River) ★★

An exciting river trip of Wingate sandstone river shore boulders and towering cliffs and spires, especially down toward Lake Powell. Wild rapids (approximately twenty-three) on the Colorado River include the evil Satan's Gut. Spring/autumn. NPS, (435) 719-2313.

Ref: C 106.

Directions: Cataract Canyon starts at the confluence of the Green and Colorado Rivers. Hop on a boat at either Moab or Green River for the flatwater preamble.

57 Henry Mountains (Mt. Hillers and Mt. Holmes) ★★★

The Henry Mountains are a laccolithic range made of diorite porphyry surrounded by lowlands of sedimentary sandstone. Two accessible areas to start climbing are near Star Spring Creek (best campground) at south flank of Mt. Hillers and the west face of Mt. Holmes. Explore heartily in this rocky megalopolis just west of the Hite Crossing of Lake Powell. The Horn in the Henry Mountains is one good cragging area. The Henry Mountains claim free-roaming, buffalo herds. Summer/autumn. BLM, (435) 896-1500.

Classics: The Horn cracks 5.10/5.11, sport routes.

Ref: C 183-101; Guidebook: Kelsey's *Utah Mountaineering Guide*.

Directions: From Hanksville go south on Hwy. 95, then south on Hwy. 276 toward Bullfrog Basin. Turn west on road to Star Spring between mm 11 and 12. Obvious exposures lie in the Henry Mountains. Mt. Holmes area is at mm 16. Turn southeast. Four-wheel drive recommended.

58 Glen Canyon National Recreation Area (Hite Crossing Area) ★★★

Wilderness area features 500' Wingate sandstone buttes, pinnacles, mesas, and rimrock views of the Green River desert areas on the west side of Canyonlands National Park. Camping near Lake Powell. Spring/autumn. NPS, (520) 608-6404.

Classics: Ekker Butte, Bathtub Butte, Buttes of the Cross, Cleopatra's Chair, Trail of Tears 13b, No Way Jose 13+.

Ref: C 185-106, R 84-22; Guidebook: Bjornstad's *Desert Rock*.

Directions: On Hwy. 95, Hite Crossing is just north of Lake Powell crossing, south of picnic area. Cliffs above. Also, from Hanksville travel east on BLM and NPS roads. Obtain maps. Four-wheel drive is wise, as are maps.

59 Escalante Canyon Area ★★★

Soft sandstone, Wingate sandstone cracks. Great exploring in a landscape of the soul. Beware zippering all your gear when rock is damp/wet from rain or crack-soaking fog. Spring/autumn. BLM, (435) 679–8980.

Ref: Adkison's *Hiking Grand Staircase: Escalante and the Glen Canyon Region.*

Directions: From Escalante skate east on Hwy. 12 to Escalante Canyon and Calf Creek area. Roadside and backcountry areas offer rock climbing. Wingate Walls down the Burr Trail.

60 Jacob's Chair ☆☆

The first free ascent of this little-known 270′ sandstone spire was done in 1976 by Hurley and Forrest. Free camping nearby. Spring/autumn. BLM, (435) 587–1500.

Classics: West Face II 10.

Ref: AAJ ['94, '82]; Guidebooks: Bjornstad's *Desert Rock.*

Directions: From Fry Canyon Store (50 mi. west of Blanding), go 5 mi. northwest on Hwy. 95. Turn right on mining road (left fork at shack) for 5 mi. Jacob's Chair is the obvious needle in center of valley.

61 The Needle ☆☆

A 165′ sandstone pinnacle. First ascent done by A. M. Dudley and B. Bingham in 1985. Bouldering and cragging exist here as well if one explores. BLM, (435) 587–1500.

Classics: South Face II 5.11 A0.

Ref: Guidebook: Bjornstad's *Desert Rock.*

Directions: From Fry Canyon Store wheel south on dirt 200 yd. Take left fork for 3 mi. The Needle is on left. Hike 1 mi.

62 Bear's Ears ☆☆☆

Bear's Ears is a regional landmark of southern Utah at 9,000′. Wingate crack lines and wonderful views abound. Free camping in area. Summer/autumn. USFS–Manti La Sal NF, (435) 587–2041.

Ref: AAJ '89-156, C 111.

Directions: From Blanding amble south on Hwy. 191. Turn west on Hwy. 95, going just west of Hwy. 261. Turn right (before Natural Bridges National Monument) on dirt road to top of pass. Bear's Ears are the obvious, twinned Wingate caps on commanding hillside.

63 Texas and Arch Canyons ☆☆☆

Wild canyon wonderland of spires and classic 700′ sandstone towers. Cutler White Rim sandstone found here is of a softer breed than the diamond-hard (cough!) Wingate sandstone to the north in Indian Creek Canyon. En garde! Consider that all climbs here have a *serious* potential for protection-ripping falls due to the soft, sandy nature of the rock. Unless you possess a stout, sand-eating four-wheel drive, it's best to fix rappels from the rim for Texas Tower and other towers. Scenic camping sites. Late spring/ autumn. BLM, (435) 587–1500.

Classics: Texas Tower South Face 11+/12-R, Dream Speaker Spire 11c-R.

Ref: AAJ ['97, '96, '92-139, '88-138, '86-168], C 106, R 95-30; Guidebooks: Burns's *Selected Climbs in the Desert Southwest,* Bjornstad's *Desert Rock.*

Directions: From Blanding follow Hwy. 191S. Take Hwy. 95 west for 20 mi. Turn north on Texas Flat Rd. (TFR) 263. For Dream Speaker Spire go 3 ^{2}/10 mi. on TFR 263 to white wall. Park. Hike to white wall, then go east (right) down side canyon past granaries and circumnavigate the tower to its northwest side. For Texas Tower go 6 ^{2}/10 mi. on TFR 263 to 1 mi. before its end, turning right on dead-end road to rim. Fix two short rappels above the junction of Texas and Arch Canyons (see USGS topo maps). A good rappel point is down slabs just west of this junction past USGS benchmark (hard to find) where gullies mark the way down. Hike approximately one hour west up Texas Canyon to base. Also possible to access canyon via charming and sandy Arch Canyon (four-wheel drive only!) road—figure on two-hour drive from mouth.

64 Recapture Reservoir ●

Undeveloped soft Dakota sandstone boulders and short bluffs around picturesque lake. Rock may be too soft for most climbers' tastes. Spring/autumn. BLM, (435) 587–1500.

Directions: From Blanding chart a course a short way north on Hwy. 191 to Recapture Reservoir.

65 Bubble Rocks ☆☆

An abundance of andesite bouldering. On the southwest side of the pile there is a pretty cool wraparound traversing problem that starts from a huge jug about 12′ off the ground. Summer. County land.

Ref: P. Grimshaw 1/98; C 95-15.

Directions: From Cedar City drive north down Main St. Continue out of town past prison, under freeway, and past gas stations/truck stop. The road turns into Minersville Hwy. (you'll see mileage sign). Continue north for approximately 2–3 mi. until you reach four-way intersection with Midvalley Rd. Turn left (west) and continue down Midvalley Rd. for approximately 5 mi. The road surface turns to dirt after a while. You'll be getting closer to a series of low peaks called The Three Peaks on USGS topos. The Bubble Rocks are a low outcropping just southeast of the tallest peak. There are numerous dirt roads branching off the main road. Pick the likeliest looking one when you get close to the rocks and go.

66 Juniper Butte ☆☆☆

Quartz monzonite similar to Joshua Tree on a miniature scale. Bouldering at nearby Bubble Rocks. Spring/autumn.

Classics: Jump Back Pat Rat Crack 8, Jam Session 9, Iron Man 9.

Ref: C [100, 95-15].

Directions: Juniper Butte is supposed to be just west of Cedar City. (No specifics.)

67 Pine Valley Reservoir

Volcanic bouldering and cragging area. Camping available at Pine Valley campground. USFS–Dixie NF, (435) 865-3200.

Ref: C 95-15.

Directions: From Enterprise go along road to Pine Valley Reservoir. Spring/autumn. USFS.

68 Zion National Park ★★★★★

The most spectacular, big wall, desert sandstone arena, where 2,000′ sandstone walls loom overhead. Loose sandstone, sketchy pro, vertical bushwhacking, and extreme climate: a perfect setting for gourmet adventure climbing! The trend is for clean aid wherever possible, i.e., not considered sporting to carry a hammer on Touchstone Wall, Prodigal Son, Monkeyfinger Wall, Moonlight Buttress, Iron Messiah, and Catharsis. Zion climbing has a continually expanding history. Big wall ascents by Lowe, Olevsky, Middendorf, et al. The Zion Narrows is one of the most famous canyon hikes in the world. Regulations/fees (for bivies) and guidebook at NPS office. Possibly peregrine falcon closures. Driftwood Restaurant in Springdale will satisfy the empty, big-wall belly. Spring/autumn. Two pay campgrounds: South and Watchman. Raptor restrictions: February 1–August 15. NPS, (801) 772-3256.

Classics: Casual Sex I 7, Tourist Crack I 9+; East Temple; Iron Messiah 10, Spaceshot IV 10 C2, Touchstone Wall IV 11-R AO/ C2+; Angel's Landing: North Face VI 5.8 A2, Days of No Future VI 9 A3+, Northeast Buttress IV 11a, Swiss-American Route VI 9A4, Monkeyfinger V 12, Moonlight Buttress V 5.8 C1/5.13-; Kolob Canyon (Paria Point): Wind, Sand, and Stars 12+, Great Rib, Catharsis.

Ref: S. Petro, J. Middendorf, R. Olevsky; AAJ ['98>94, '92-137, 91-172, 87-178, 85-1/200, 82-80, 79-196, 78-531, 75-132, 72-129, 68-9], C [194-114, 190-116, 189-107, 186-128, 180-90, 179-23/120, 177-28, 158, 141, 133(8/92), 124, 111, 109, 102, 100, 96, 94, 93, 86(10/84)-26, 60, 52(1/79), many Basecamps]; On Sight Vol. 1, number 2; R [98-70/144, 93-28, 78-74, 77-20, 68-26, 66-75 (topos), 21(9/87)-41, 7(3/85)], S 10/83; Molvar and Martin's Hiking Zion and Bryce Canyon National Parks; Guidebooks: Burns's Selected Climbs in the Desert Southwest, Green's Rock Climbing Utah, Bjornstad's Desert Rock: National Parks (1996), Harlin's Rocky Mountain, NPS office copy (call 801-772-3256).

Directions: From Rockville zigzag on Hwy. 9 to Zion National Park (follow park signs). Main buttresses include (south to north): West side of Scenic Dr.: Mt. Kinesava, West Temple, The Sentinel, Three Patriarchs (Abraham, Isaac, and Jacob), Angel's Landing/The Organ, Moonlight Buttress, and The Pulpit; east side of Scenic Dr.: The Watchman, Tunnel Crags Area, East Temple, Great White Throne, Touchstone Wall, Leaning Wall (Spaceshot), Monkeyfinger Wall, and Temple of Sinewava. Down O' the Mouth cragging is just south of junction of Hwy. 9 and NPS road on east side of road. Bouldering opportunities present themselves along road-side near South Entrance campground junction as well. Practice Cliffs are on Scenic Dr. to Narrows just north of junction with Hwy. 9 on right.

69 Kolob Canyon ★★★★

Kolob Canyon is Zion's remote northwest satellite canyon with equally spectacular 1,500′ Navajo sandstone cliffs. A 1982 Summit magazine describes it auspiciously, "It is a rare person who succeeds the first time on a new route in Kolob Canyon." Visitors center offers backcountry permits during business hours. Autumn–spring. NPS, (435) 772-3256.

Classics: Great Rib VI 9 A2, Paria Point-!V 9 name?, Wind, Sand, and Stars V 12+; sport routes.

Ref: R. Olevsky, S. Petro; AAJ ['81-79], C [138, 95], S 7/82; Guidebooks: Green's Rock Climbing Utah, Bjornstad's Desert Rock: National Parks (1996); NPS office copy (call 801-586-9548).

Directions: From Cedar City go south on I-15 to exit 40. Proceed east up Kolob Canyon with God's speed to the parking area on right between Taylor Creek Trailhead and Lee Pass Trailhead. Park and walk five minutes up dry creekbed and obvious amphitheater to Wind, Sand, and Stars Route and others that lie just up trailhead on massive buttress. Bouldering areas can be found above visitors center at 1 7/10 mi. (left side), at Paria Point at 3 9/10 mi. (right side), and roadside boulder at 4 mi.

70 Snow Canyon State Park ★★★

Snow Canyon offers 800′ Southwestern sandstone aid/free walls . . . grade VIs. Soft rock. Home of HAFWEN (hammered anchors fixed when necessary). Ask at Outdoor Outlet in St. George for specific route information. More rock is being developed to west of park in various areas west of Santa Clara. It is reported that a $4.00 fee is now being charged for entrance to the park. Thirty-eight routes. Spring/autumn. Johnson's Canyon closed March–November for Mojave Desert tortoise. Pay camping in state park (435-628-2255).

Classics: A Thousand Pints of Lite II 7, Pygmy Alien 8-, Full

Metal Jockstrap 9, Jimmy the Geek 9, Babes in Thailand III 10a, Roar of the Greasepaint 10a, Highlander 10d, Clairvoyance 11b, Doghouse Arête 11b, Aftershock 11c 4p, Richness of It All 12a.

Ref: Beck; AAJ ['87-74/179, '79-196], C [111, 102, 96(6/66)-17, 74], *On Sight* Vol. 1, number 2; R 77-144; Guidebooks: Goss's *Rock Climbs of Southwest Utah*, Green's *Rock Climbing Utah*, Bjornstad's *Desert Rock: National Parks* (1996), Kindred, Goss, and Duck's *A Guide to Climbing in Snow Canyon;* USPS office copy (call 801-628-2255).

Directions: From St. George float northwest on Hwy. 18 for a few minutes. Turn west, following signs to park. Island in Sky has been focus of development and contains most routes. Popular areas include Circus Wall, Circus Maximus Area, The Wall of Tiers, Johnson Canyon, and West Canyon.

71 Valley of the Gods ☆☆☆

For soft-rock spire fanciers. Appropriately named, 400′ sandstone spires in this scenic Southwest valley. All spires are dangerously soft (whole towers have toppled) grade II and IIIs. Hot in summer. If you're ever asked why you climb here, the best response might be, "Because it might not be there tomorrow." The route Milk Crates from Hell 5.4 A3, on Eagle Plume's north face pretty much sums up the potential of the climbing hazards. Actually, many of the routes are quite manageable. Spring/autumn. Free camping. BLM, (435) 587-1500.

Classics: North Tower: NE Rt II 10.

Ref: AAJ ['88-138, 82, 76-452], C [195-125, 111, 106, 83(4/83)-34, S (7/81, 3/62); Guidebooks: Burns's *Selected Climbs in the Desert Southwest*, Bjornstad's *Desert Rock*.

Directions: From Mexican Hat crank 7 mi. north on Hwy. 163. Turn left (sign) on 27 1/2-mi. dirt loop road (number 242). Towers scattered along road. Valley of the Gods formations with routes include: Petard Tower, North Tower, Eagle Plume Tower, Tom-Tom Tower, Angel's Fear (aka Lady-in-a-Bathtub—you can't miss it), and Hidden Pinnacle. Loop road ends out on Hwy. 261 northwest of the San Juan Goose Necks and at the base of the Mokie Dugway.

72 Muley Point Overlook (aka Mokie Dugway) ☆☆☆

Ethereal panorama overlooking the San Juan River drainage, Monument Valley (farther south) and Valley of the Gods to east. Five star "bivy" spot. Short 30′ sandstone cliff bands deliver short leads and bouldering, God delivers the views. Bring friends! Spring/autumn. BLM, (435) 587-1500.

Classics: Many crack climbs.

Ref: T4.

Directions: From Mexican Hat take Hwy. 163 north. Turn northwest on Hwy. 261 to the top of Mokie Dugway switchbacks. At top of rim, a dirt road cuts southwest (left) for approximately fifteen minutes to cul-de-sac and Muley Point Overlook. Crack climbs finish at top of rim.

73 Comb Ridge Boulders and Crags ☆☆

Good, off-the-deck sandstone bouldering with usually good landings. Crack and face cragging. Indian rock art. Spring/autumn. BLM, (435) 587-1500.

Ref: Guidebook: Burns's *Selected Climbs in the Desert Southwest*.

Directions: From Bluff roam west on Hwy. 163 to the base of Comb Ridge Bluffs (major geological west-facing ridgeline extending south into Utah). Turn north on dirt road, heading north to Hwy. 95. For 15 mi. roadside Wingate blocks and crags capture the climber's gaze.

74 Hovenweep National Monument ☆

Sandstone topropes and bouldering amongst ancient Indian ruins. Please note: NPS requests no chalk and no bolting or other fixed gear. Pay campground. Spring/autumn. NPS, (970) 562-4282.

Directions: On Colorado/Utah border west of Cortez. Drive from Cortez through McElmo Canyon into Utah, then northeast to Hovenweep National Monument.

75 Bluff Cliff Bands ☆

Myriad of soft sandstone crack climbs in 200′ soft-rock cliffs. Some wild and wicked crack climbing lines—no bluffin'. Pick and choose. Spring/autumn. BLM, (435) 587-1500.

Ref: C 83(4/83)-34; Guidebook: Bjornstad's *Desert Rock*.

Directions: Obvious fortresses north of the town of Bluff. Also, go southwest from Bluff on Hwy. 191 for approximately 4 mi. (turning south on Hwy. 191) to find cliffs above road on left.

76 Navajo Twins (closed) ☆

Brotherly 150′ sandstone pinnacles easily viewed from the road. Uncertain ascents. Spring–autumn. Private land.

Directions: From Bluff go just north on Hwy. 191. On left sits Navajo Twins, twin spires behind the trading post.

77 White Mesa Overlook ●

Roadside boulder band. Soft rock, but some okay problems. Spring/autumn. BLM, (435) 587-1500.

Directions: From Bluff go 12 mi. north on Hwy. 191. White Mesa Overlook sits just north of junction with Hwy. 262.

78 Grand Gulch Spire (aka Shima Sani Spire) ☆☆☆

A 400′ classic-sculptured sandstone tower in the shape of a wizened old grandma, hence the Navajo name Shima Sani. Most accessible by river (BLM permit required). Only route as of 1992, the Corso De Gallo Route III 5.11 (first ascent in 1992 by D. Insley, B. Hatcher, and T. Toula) ascends from chimney notch on west side between main canyon wall and spire. Five interesting and varied pitches. Big friends and crack-climbing gear necessary. Spring/autumn. BLM, (435) 587-1500.

Classics: Corso De Gallo Route 5.11.

Ref: AAJ '94.

Directions: From Mexican Hat a classic, remote white-water float takes one 42 river mi. to the mouth of Grand Gulch. Shima Sani sits ½ mi. up Grand Gulch on left just off the east side of the west canyon wall. Visible from San Juan River.

79 Glen Canyon NRA (Lake Powell Area) ✫✫✫

Lake Powell is 186 mi. long and the second largest man-made lake in the world. Though recreational boating and swimming are its primary uses, 1,800 mi. of sandstone walls, buttes, arches, and pinnacles await the adventurous climber within its shoreline. Rainbow Bridge, "The Rainbow Turned to Stone," is the world's largest natural bridge at 290′ high. The town of Page, Arizona, provides the most facilities. Spring–autumn. NPS, (520) 608–6404.

Classics: Tower Butte (in Arizona): West Face (Keith/Insley Route) 8p 9 A3.

Ref: AAJ ['96, '95, '88-140, '76-453]; Kelsey's *Boater's Guide to Lake Powell*, Jones's *Spectacular Lake Powell Country*.

Directions: Accessible from several access points in the Lake Powell Area: Hite Crossing, Halls Crossing, Bullfrog, and Page. A ferry is available from Bullfrog Marina across Hall's Crossing, saving 130 mi. of driving. Boating is really a great way to access Lake Powell's many climbing secrets.

80 San Juan River ✫✫

Riverside bouldering on algal bioherms (unique, though sharp) and cracks on short sandstone/limestone walls, and sandstone pinnacles down toward Lake Powell. Shima Sani is a wilderness adventurer's rock spire at the mouth of Grand Gulch. This area is part of the large reserve in the San Juan Oil Fields which boomed in the 1950s and 1960s. Spring–autumn. BLM, (435) 587–1500/BIA.

Classics: Cracks at Snake House Crag (south bank), Shima Sani 5.11 at Grand Gulch, Mexican Hat.

Directions: Along the San Juan River, from Bluff all the way down to Lake Powell. Four-day river trip.

81 Mexican Hat ✫✫✫

This perfect rock imitation of a Mexican's hat is a proverbial tanning bed that at one time elicited various responses from summiting parties when they stared at a picture from a biker magazine of a well-endowed, topless female on a black Harley. Now gone—okay, so who took the picture? Bandito bolt ladder (southwest) is standard ascent. Now freed at 5.12 by Jeff Achey. Spring/autumn. BLM, (435) 587–1500.

Classics: Bolt Route A1, Robbins A2, Achey's Route 12.

Ref: A (5/70), C 83(4/83)-34, R [89-48, 75-46]; Guidebooks: Burns's *Selected Climbs in the Desert Southwest*, Green's *Rock Climbing Utah*, Bjornstad's *Desert Rock*.

Directions: From Mexican Hat go approximately 1 mi.

north on Hwy. 163. Turn right (sign) at dirt roads to the south side of Mexican Hat.

82 Gooseneck Overlook State Park ✫✫

Limestone bouldering band (25′ high) with captivating views of the twisting San Juan River goosenecks, one of the most striking and impressive examples of entrenched meanders (1,000′) in North America. Viewing these through an 18 mm fish-eye lens is a test of one's sense of reality. A view of 380 million years of geologic history. Spring/autumn. Camping. State park, (435) 678–2238.

Ref: C 88; Guidebook: Bjornstad's *Desert Rock*.

Directions: From Mexican Hat (7 mi. total distance), hop north on Hwy. 163. Turn west on Hwy. 261. Follow Hwy. 316 (park signs) for 3 mi. to Gooseneck Overlook. Bouldering on rock bands just below rim.

83 Organ Rock ●

Soft "potato chip" rock, certain-death 300′ shale spire. Marker from which the geologic formation Organ Rock Shale derives its name. First ascent by Shipley and Middendorf. Remember, your brain is your best survival organ. Spring/autumn. BIA.

Classics: Organ Grinder 10xxx = classic death!

Ref: J. Middendorf; R 42(3/91)-65.

Directions: From Mexican Hat, Utah, follow Hwy. 163 south to state line. Turn right (west) to Gouldings Lodge and go fifteen to thirty minutes beyond to visible Organ Rock pinnacle north of blacktop.

84 Jacob's Ladder ✫✫✫

Jacob's Ladder is a 300′ sandstone pinnacle. The Teapot (III 5.8) is another formation nearby. Spring/autumn. BIA.

Classics: North Face III 7 A3, NE Face III 10 A2.

Ref: AAJ ['88-142, 82, '74-149]; Guidebook: Bjornstad's *Desert Rock*.

Directions: From Olijeto Junction follow highway from northeast to San Juan Branch of Lake Powell for 6 mi. until Jacob's Ladder is visible approximately 3 mi. to west of road.

85 Monument Valley ✫✫✫✫✫

The Southwest's (and possibly the world's) most stunning collection of sandstone spires and mesas. Illegal to climb on the Navajo Reservation. Still mentioned as part of American climbing history and with the hopes that, one day soon, these may be legally climbable. A place with a presence. Spring/autumn. BIA.

Classics: Bear IV 5.10 A2, Rabbit, King on His Throne, Big Indian, Sentinel Spire, Setting Hen II 5.8.

Ref: AAJ ['92-137, '89-157], C [111, 83(4/83)-34]; Guidebook: Bjornstad's *Desert Rock*.

Directions: From Mexican Hat follow Hwy. 193 south to Arizona state line. The Utah/Arizona state line divides

Monument Valley in north and south halves. Formations in Utah include: Eagle Rock Spire, Setting Hen, Brigham's Tomb, King on His Throne, Stagecoach, Bear and Rabbit, Castle Butte, Big Indian, and Sentinel Spire. Other famed formations (e.g., Totem Pole) lie to south in Arizona. See Arizona listings.

86 Big Water Bluffs ●
Could this be the slipperiest, softest, standing sandstone in the world? To find out, try the enticing slabs seen from the highway. Note: Some of the appealing crack lines are softer than Charmin. Take-your-life-in-your-own-hands climbing experience. Spring/autumn. Possibly private land/BLM, (435) 644-4600.
Ref: D. Houchin.
Directions: From Page, Arizona, slide 16 mi. northwest on Hwy. 89. Big Water Bluffs are the obvious cliffs on left (south) side of highway.

87 Santaquin Canyon ✩✩✩
Limestone cliffs with difficult routes. Some of the first bolted routes done by James Garrett. Pay/free camping up canyon. USFS-Uinta NF, (801) 342-5260.
Classics: Santaqueen Prom Queen 10, As the Circle Turns 10.
Ref: C [176-28, 171-22].
Directions: From Santaquin follow road south into Santaquin Canyon.

88 Maple Canyon ✩✩✩✩
Utah's unique, must-stop sport crag features power pulling on sloping cobbles. There is no other place like it and no way to explain it. Box Canyon area, "the sport climbing gym in a box," has many excellent routes; 260 routes in 1999. Good weather spring, summer, and fall. Private land/USFS-Uinta NF, (801) 342-5260.
Ref: J. Stevens 11/98, S. Biggs 11/97; C [197-66, 177-22, 173-107], R 82-32; Guidebooks: Green's *Rock Climbing Utah,* Stevens's *Maple Canyon Rock Climbing 1997,* Steven's *Central Utah Climbing.*
Directions: From Nephi, at the junction of I-15 and exit 225, head east to a small town named Fountain Green. As you drive through, watch for a sign on the west (right) side of the road. Follow the signs the rest of the way to Maple Canyon. For your traveling pleasure, another reader's directions: From I-15 go east on I-132 to Fountain Green. Turn right on 400 South. Go 6 mi. to Freedom Rd. (Route 2478). Turn right on Gravel Canyon Rd.

89 Indian Rock ✩✩✩
Carbon County public-use area. Sixteen bolted routes to 5.11.
Ref: C 166.
Directions: From Price go 6 mi. north at Helper, then go west at gas station.

90 The Notch ✩✩
Volcanic tuff bouldering and short topropes in an open windswept grassland setting. Private land/possibly BLM.
Ref: pusher.com site.
Directions: From Nephi whip it west on Hwy. 132 for a ways until you see abundant cluster of rocks on the south side of road. Parking pullout across the road at mm 19.3. Other boulders, The Red Warrior Boulders, north of mm 19, to the northwest through grass from pullout about twenty minutes.

91 Ibex ✩✩✩
Beautiful Arapiles-like quartzite in a most desolate western Utah setting hoards diverse bouldering prospects and pleasurable cragging pursuits. Boulders like the Red Monster V6 and climbs like Severity Disparity 5.10+ will engender one to this Saudi Arabian setting. Many first ascents by James Garrett. Bring water and supplies. Windy . . . ever had to stake down your van? Rattlesnakes April–October: en garde! Camping abounds. Try September–November or March–May. BLM, (435) 743-3100.
Classics: Snakeskin 5.9-, Severity Disparity 10/11-, Quartermoon 10-, Quarter Inch from Falling 11, Ewe. F. O. 11+/12a, Long Shadow 5.12- (4p), Nose Shadow 12c, Cornucopia 12+, Children of the Corn 13-; Red Monster Boulder V6-V9.
Ref: J. Garrett, J. Sherman; R 98-74/100; Guidebook: Garrett's *Ibex and Selected Climbs of Utah's West Desert.*
Directions: From Delta's only traffic light, set 'er on cruise control at 100 mph west for 50 1/10 mi. on Hwy. 50 (loneliest highway in America). At BLM's Ibex Well sign, turn left onto dirt road for exactly 2 mi. Turn right, crossing dry lake bed for 2 2/10 mi. due west to base of the 40' Red Monster boulder and the Main Ibex Wall's white and brown tarnished cliffs. (If dry lake bed is wet, continue west on Hwy. 50 another mile or so and turn left, passing Rock Corral [more climbing] on right. Continue south and turn left at junction to attain main wall). Other satellite areas (e.g., Topus) also offer good bouldering/short cragging. For Topus go approximately 4 mi. south from BLM sign/Hwy. 50 to island of rock on left. More rock farther southwest.

92 Shinobe (Parowan Gap Wall) ✩✩✩
Sixty-meter bolted cobble climbing. Routes 5.8-5.12. Raptor nesting in spring—please don't climb here then. Respectfully view the petroglyphs. BLM, (435) 586-2401.
Directions: From Cedar City head north on I-15 to Parowan exit. Go west off Parowan exit from I-15 for 11 mi., following signs for petroglyphs. Park at south-side pullout. Hike north on trail to far right side of formation.

93 Cedar Canyon ✩✩✩
Short limestone walls offer quick access climbing up to 5.12. Free camping. Summer. Campground in canyon.

USFS–Dixie NF, (435) 865–3200.
Ref: Guidebook: Goss's *Rock Climbs of Southwest Utah*.
Directions: From Cedar City go east on Hwy. 14 for 9 ³/₁₀ mi. (Cetacean Wall on right, Graveside Matter on left) and just before mm 10 to Ten Mile Wall on right. Couple-minute approaches.

94 The Overlook (at Brian Head) ★★★

Summertime volcanic crag at 10,000′ with traditional crack and bolted routes mostly from 5.10 to 5.12. Beautiful views from the cool forests. Camping in trees. USFS–Dixie NF, (435) 865–3200.
Ref: Guidebooks: Goss's *Rock Climbs of Southwest Utah*, Green's *Rock Climbing Utah*.
Directions: Northeast of Cedar City. Take Hwy. 14 east to Hwy. 148 north to Hwy. 143 east. Go east on Hwy. 143 for a little less than 5 mi., turning left onto Sidney Valley Rd. for 4 ½ mi. to the overlook.

95 Running Scared Wall (aka Ravens Crag) ★★

Summertime 60′ basalt crag just past The Overlook with short face leads from 5.7 to easy 5.12. Camping in woods. USFS–Dixie NF, (435) 865–3200.
Ref: Guidebook: Goss's *Rock Climbs of Southwest Utah*.
Directions: Northeast of Cedar City. Take Hwy. 14 east to Hwy. 148 north to Hwy. 143 east. Go east on Hwy. 143 for 5 ½ mi. to visible cliffs on left. Parking just farther up road.

96 Crawdad Canyon Climbing Park ★★★

This sport climber's park in a beautiful basalt canyon is the vision of Jim Bosse. Unfortunately, Jim has passed on to higher climbing grounds, but his legacy remains for climbers to enjoy. More than 150 fun 60′ bolted routes. Complete with pay campground and other recreational facilities. Open year-round. Privately owned, (435) 574-2416.
Classics: Catwalk 7, Road to the Sun 8, Transcend and Include 9, Father Time 10c, The Procedure 11d, Operation 12c, Aerial Dentistry 13a.
Ref: Guidebooks: Goss's *Rock Climbs of Southwest Utah*, Green's *Rock Climbing Utah*.
Directions: From St. George zoom north on Hwy. 18 for 20 mi. Turn right and park at end of road. Short stroll to office to register. Bring I.D.

97 Cougar Cliffs ★★★

Sandstone canyon with a small selection (fifteen) of 5.9–5.13 sport routes.
Ref: Guidebook: Goss's *Rock Climbs of the Southwest*.
Directions: From St. George go north on Hwy. 18 to mm 6. Park on left and walk toward cliffs. Rappel in off chains.

98 Black Rocks ★★★

Very popular 40′ bolted basalt crag with thirty-two routes mostly 5.8–5.13. South- and north-facing walls. Check locally for climbing closures. Owned by Red Cliff Preserve.
Ref: www.sginet.com/users/sgish/black.html; Guidebook: Goss's *Too Much Rock, Not Enough Life*.
Directions: North of St. George. Go about 2 mi. north on Hwy. 18. Before crossing canyon, park on west side of road. Follow trail through fence and into canyon.

99 Chuckwalla Wall/Turtle Wall ★★★

Chuckwalla Wall is a 60′ bolted southwest-facing sandstone wall with fifteen routes 5.10–5.13. Try The Pilgrimage or Second Coming, both 5.12a. Turtle Wall is a 60′ bolted east-facing sandstone wall with eighteen routes up to 5.13. Cave routes like Banana Dance 5.11c make for fun climbing. Check locally for climbing closures. For all the beta on St. George climbing routes, pick up a copy of Todd Goss's *Rock Climbs of Southwest Utah and The Arizona Strip*. Autumn–spring. Owned by Red Cliff Desert Preserve and home to the desert tortoise.
Ref: www.sginet.com/users/sgish/climbing.html; Guidebooks: Goss's *Rock Climbs of Southwest Utah*, Green's *Rock Climbing Utah*, Goss's *Rock Climbs of Southern Utah: A Guide to 35 Crags*, Goss's *Too Much Rock, Not Enough Life*.
Directions: Just north of St. George. Go north on Hwy. 18 (Bluff St.) about ³/₄ mi. north of Skyline Dr. Park at pullout. Hike a few minutes to Chuckwalla Wall on right and twenty to thirty minutes farther down, making all right turns when necessary for Turtle Wall.

100 Green Valley Gap/The Point ★★★

Small, almost in-town canyon of sandstone boulders and short 35′ toprope/sport routes 5.9–5.12. Enjoy the Sand Stoner Reverse 5.12a face route.
Ref: Guidebooks: Goss's *Rock Climbs of the Southwest*, Goss's *Too Much Rock, Not Enough Life*.
Directions: Just west of St. George. From junction of Sunset and Dixie, go south on Dixie. Turn right on Canyon View Dr. following it as far into canyon as the rough road will allow. The Point is another area 2 mi. north of The Gap, with harder manufactured sport routes on soft sandstone.

101 Welcome Springs (Sumo, Wailing, and Cathedral Walls) ★★★

One-hundred-and-twenty-foot east-facing (Sumo) and north-facing (Wailing/Cathedral) limestone crags with more than thirty bolted routes to 5.13. BLM, (435) 688-3200.
Classics: Pagan Rituals 10b, Worshipping the Limestone Gods 11b, Natural Born Drillers 12, The Infidels 13a.
Ref: Guidebooks: Green's *Rock Climbing Utah*, Goss's *Too Much Rock, Not Enough Life*.
Directions: West of St. George. Follow Hwy. 8 west for 11

mi. Turn south at turnoff for Gunlock onto Hwy. 91 (toward Arizona). Turn right at 11 ½ mi. at High Desert Bird Ranch sign. Then turn right again in 2 mi. In 2 more mi., park on right. Walk ½ mi. up, then left up draw is Sumo Wall, followed by Wailing and Cathedral Walls on right.

102 Gorilla Cliffs/Simeon Complex ★★★

You'll go ape over these cliffs. Sorry for the pun, but just monkeying around. More than forty fun 60' sport routes (5.10–5.14a) between these two north-facing limestone crags and plenty more. Rattlers! Camping in situ. BLM, (435) 688–3200.

Ref: Guidebooks: Goss's *Rock Climbs of Southwest Utah*, Goss's *Too Much Rock, Not Enough Life*.

Directions: West of St. George. Follow Hwy. 8 west for 11 mi. Turn south at turnoff for Gunlock onto Hwy. 91 (toward Arizona). At 8 ½ mi., turn left for 2 mi. Take another left. Gorilla Cliff is first on right; Simian Complex is second on right. More bolted cliffs past these two farther east, notably the Soul Asylum and the Diamond.

103 Black and Tan Wall/Kelly's Rock ★★★

The Black and Tan Wall has about twenty east-facing limestone 70' sport routes; mostly 5.11 and up to powerful lines like Talking Smack and Sniffing Glue, both 5.13. Kelly's Rock has eight sport routes on a 70' north-facing limestone cliff. Try K8 5.11b for a fine line. BLM, (435) 688–3200.

Ref: Guidebooks: Goss's *Rock Climbs of Southwest Utah*, Green's *Rock Climbing Utah*, Goss's *Too Much Rock, Not Enough Life*.

Directions: Southwest of St. George. Follow Hwy. 8 west for 11 mi. Turn south at turnoff for Gunlock onto Hwy. 91 (toward Arizona). At 14 ½ mi., turn left at Woodbury Desert Study Area. In 3 mi., pass over cattle guard. Kelly's Rock is up wash on left. Black and Tan Wall is farther up road on right.

104 Van Belle Boulders (aka Loa Boulders) ★★★

Good volcanic tuff boulders discovered by Rock Ranger Bob Van Belle. BLM, (435) 896–1500.

Ref: B. Van Belle.

Directions: South of Loa.

105 Kane Creek Rd.

Variety of short to long dramatic 500' sandstone walls (Cirque Wall) just outside (southwest) of Moab. Instant access. BLM, (435) 259–6111.

Ref: C 191-82; Guidebooks: Burns's *Selected Climbs in the Desert Southwest*, Green's *Rock Climbing Utah*, Bjornstad's *Desert Rock III*.

106 Stansbury Island

Limited though fun bouldering west of Salt Lake.

Classics: Yo Mama V5.

Ref: R 98-95.

107 City Creek Canyon ★★

Limestone and conglomerate sport cragging with routes up to 5.13. Special visitation times. No camping. City park, (801) 483–6797.

Ref: Guidebook: Ruckman's *Rock Climbing Utah's Wasatch Range*.

Directions: North of downtown Salt Lake City. Follow one-way "B" Rd. to canyon. Fee gate. Open for cars (6-mi. drive) only during June–September on even-numbered days. Otherwise, hike 6 mi. up road to get to crags year-round. Most routes just past bridge on right.

Other Utah Climbing Areas
Moe's Valley

Fine sandstone bouldering on southwest fringe of St. George, northeast of junction of Dixie Drive and Tonaquit

Vermont

Persistence and determination alone are omnipotent. —Calvin Coolidge

While most climbers would not choose Vermont as their first destination, once they find themselves on the cliffs they will discover many enjoyable routes. Most local climbers are happy to welcome new climbers and pass on what information they have about climbing here.

Vermont's climbing is basically on small crags, 50 to 300 feet in height. While many of the areas are fun, none have the appeal of the Shawangunks. Vermont crags are viewed as training areas for challenges in other areas, with climbers utilizing the areas for a quick after-work climb or a weekend jaunt. This may account for the low-profile climbing scene in the state.

Some cliffs are undergoing access problems, so please do your best to give climbers a good reputation. Late summer and September are sweet times to visit.

1 St. Albans I–89 Crag

Metamorphic 80′ cliff band. Summer/autumn. Possibly private land.

Directions: From St. Albans go south on I–89. At mm 103.5, look east to visible St. Albans Crag. Between exit 17 and 18 near Arrowhead Lake.

2 Lake Willoughby State Park (Wheeler Mountain) ☆

Famous for premiere ice climbing (possibly the best in the Northeast) but little for its 300′ rock crag. Private campground at south end of lake. There may be nude sunbathers at beach—bring some extra tanning lotion in case you make friends. According to Diane Carter (1997), "There are peregrine falcons seasonally at Mt. Pisgah on Lake Willoughby and climbers are advised to respect any posted restrictions." Summer/autumn. Pay camping in state park.

Classics: Moosehead Crack 8, V.J.'s 7, Right Stuff 5.9, Wine and Cheese 9, Sticky Finger 10b, Wall Street (Great Corner Route 11a).

Ref: Locals; C 64, R 77-62; Guidebook: Cole and Wilcox's *Shades of Blue*.

Directions: From Lyndonville get off from I–91 at exit 23. Take Route 5 north to Wheeler Pond Rd. Park in hiker or climber parking areas. Hike in via climber's trail that resembles a logging trail. Do *not* drive down hiking trail.

3 Smuggler's Notch State Park (Elephant's Head) ☆☆☆

Remote and very alpine in nature, The Notch is home to several 300′ granite rock buttresses, e.g., Elephant's Head. Descent from Quartz Crack is tricky—look for the old Bear Pond Trail. Also, Vermont's "top-notch" bouldering area in the heart of Vermont ski country. Bouldering immediately adjacent to the road in The Notch. Fine ice climbing in winter. Great views. (May be closed summers for peregrine nesting.) Swimming in Brewster River Gorge, 3 mi. south of Jeffersonville. Vermont's renowned hiking trail, the Long Trail, cuts right through the Notch. Mt. Mansfield, the

JOHN SHERMAN

Bouldering at Smuggler's Notch.

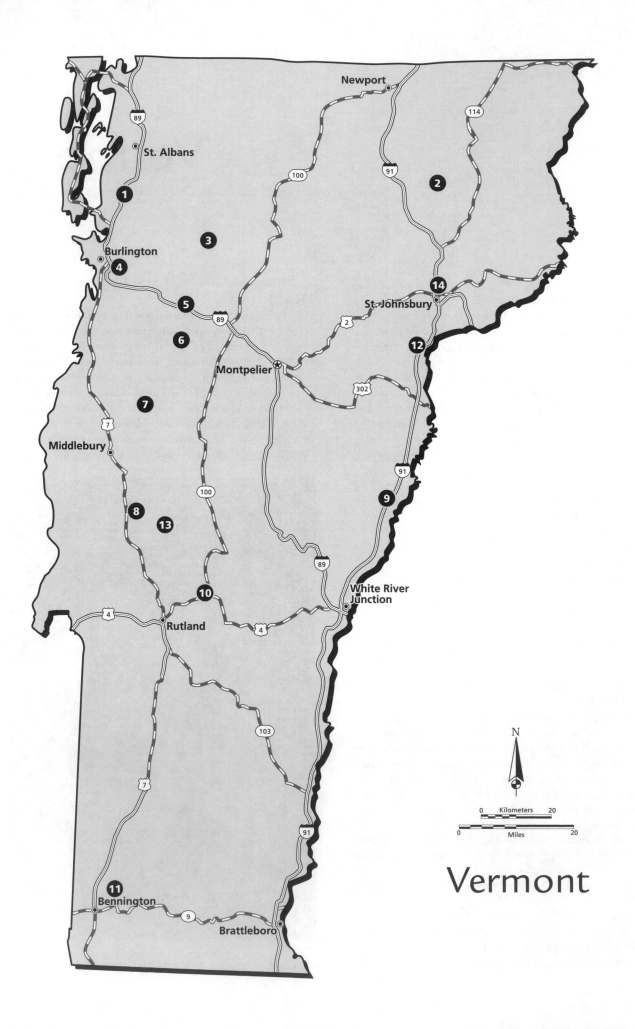

St. Albans

Newport

1

89

114

2

100

91

3

Burlington

4

14

5

St. Johnsbury

89

6

2

Montpelier

12

302

7

91

Middlebury

7

100

9

8

13

10

White River
Junction

4

Rutland

4

103

91

7

11

Bennington

9

Brattleboro

N

0   Kilometers   20

0   Miles   20

Vermont

highest point in Vermont at 4,393′, is just to west, accessed via toll road to south. Climbing can be found there also. Arctic flora. Autumn. Raptor restrictions March–August. Pay camping at state park (800-658-6934).

Classics: Quartz Crack 8, Elephant Head Buttress 10; Green Mountain Gringo B1.

Ref: Locals; C [139, 138], S 3/71; Sherman's *Stone Crusade*; Guidebooks: Viljanen's *Local's Guide to Smuggler's Notch Ice*, Duke of Jeffersonville's *Select Bouldering Problems in Smuggler's Notch*, Vermont, Cole and Wilcox's *Shades of Blue*.

Directions: From Stowe go 8 ½ mi. north on Hwy. 108 to top of Smuggler's Notch. Park at stone caretaker's hut that is surrounded by boulders. Several buttresses. Quartz Crack Buttress is directly over your head on the south side of The Notch. Elephant Head Buttress is on the north side of The Notch as you start down hill toward Stowe.

4 Winooski Cut (aka The Cut) ✮✮

The entertaining climbing on this vertical 50′ limestone cliff was exposed by a railroad cut. Topropes, traverses, and high solos. Burlington-area climbers have been using this well-polished limestone cut for years. In the evenings, one can be pretty certain of finding fellow climbers. No longer climbing in the adjacent quarry—fenced off and closed. The limestone tends to accumulate dust from above after rains, so bring the Glass Cleaner Plus. Autumn. Private land.

Classics: Left Crack 9, Hole in the Wall Direct 10.

Ref: Locals; Guidebook: Clune topo.

Directions: In Winooski, across from St. Michael's College. From exit 15 on I-89, go east on Hwy. 15 for approximately ½ mi. Turn right at light onto Lime Kiln Rd. Park just before the first bridge. Follow path along fence and then drop down to railroad tracks. Follow tracks for approximately 100 yd. to Winooski Cut on right. Faces south. A small area!

5 Bolton Rocks ✮✮✮

Green 300′ schist formations laced with quartz veins. Some good routes (best climbs are short cracks behind trees). Quite a bit of potential for more. More information on Shelburne Rd. at Climb High. Richmond is nearest town with supplies, i.e., good bakery. Upper: If kids are selling lemonade at trailhead, buy some. Don't miss the Ben and Jerry's factory tour in nearby Waterbury. Autumn. No camping. Raptor restrictions March–August. Private land.

Classics: Lower: Wavy Goodbye 7, Harvest Moon 8, Orgasmic 9, Sticks and Stones 10 (50′ left of H.M.), The Chalk Stops Here 11; Upper: Rose Crack 10 (overhanging on right end), The Thorn 11 (just right of Rose).

Ref: Locals; C 138(6/93)-32.

Directions: Bolton (west of Waterbury on I-89). Three areas: 1) On Route 2, just 1 mi. east of town on Route 2 behind Fernwood Manor Trailer Park. Obvious rock. Access sensitive. Consult locals first. *Closed* as of 1992—stay off. 2) Lower West Bolton: 2 mi. west of Bolton on Route 2. Turn

right on Bolton Notch Rd. up hill for 2/10 mi. Park at pulloff on right. Hike approximately 200 yd. in on trail. 3) Upper West Bolton: 4 ½ mi. west of Bolton on Route 2. On left above Duck Brook C. housing. Park on main road. Pick up trail at double row of pine trees. Take right branch.

6 Camel's Hump (closed) ✮

Obvious summit cliffs 4,083′ in elevation. Very remote with limited climbing in an environmentally sensitive area.

Ref: Locals.

Directions: South of Bolton. Accessed via Huntington Center. Go east from Huntington Center to trailhead for Camel's Hump.

7 Deerleap (near Bristol) ✮✮✮

Difficult, 200′, committing, loose crag. Pick a winner. Not to be confused with Deerleap Mountain outside of Rutland or with Bristol Cliffs at Bristol, which have little, if any, climbing on them. Cliff closed spring/summer for peregrine nesting. Good restaurants/stores in Bristol. Good swimming in New Haven at Lincoln. According to Diane Carter (1997), "This climbing area should be avoided March–October. Peregrine falcons nest there and the Vermont Department of Fish and Game has posted signs there for people not to disturb the area." Autumn. Private land.

Ref: Locals.

Directions: From Bristol bound approximately 1 mi. east on Route 116. Cliff on left back from the road. Turn in on dirt road just before the roadside diner below the Deerleap cliff. Park. Bushwhack. Avoid posted land.

8 Branbury State Park (aka Middlebury College Area) ✮✮

Locals have tried to keep this 100′ quartzite crag clean via limited use of fixed gear. Please respect this ethic to ensure

---

Vermont Road Thoughts

We were driving hard, hell bent for the best climbing treat of our lives. Over hill and dale, we sped past Vermont dairy farms knowing that soon we would be smacking our lips and the haste would be worth it! But when we arrived the sign read closed. Thousands of miles, and we had missed our chance to check it out. Fortunately, though we missed the tour, the clerk at Ben and Jerry's was still nice enough to open the locked door and hand us the end product—a pint of lip-smacking Chocolate Chip Cookie Dough. Who cared if we couldn't pull off the couch the next day? Life was good . . . . Thank you Ben and Jerry's!

—TNT

access. Rock can be wet well into summer. Mosquitoes looking for donors. Autumn. Pay camping at state park (800–658–1622).

Classics: Reptilian 10.

Ref: Locals.

Directions: From Middlebury go 10 mi. south on Hwy. 7. Turn east on Hwy. 53, following signs to park. Located in Branbury State Park on the shores of Lake Dunmore.

9 Fairlee Palisades

Handsome silver 100′ metamorphic cliffs on hillside. Autumn.

Ref: Delorme's *Vermont Atlas and Gazetteer.*

Directions: At Fairlee. Fairlee Palisades rise predominantly west above town, donating views of the Connecticut River to the west of I–91.

10 Deerleap Mountain (near Rutland)
☆ ☆ ☆

Lots of weekend activity at this 80′ metamorphic crag. Upper cliff is mostly for beginners. Lower cliff ranges from 5.4 to 5.10. Local climbers ask that chalk not be used on this cliff. Please use only established paths, i.e., don't bushwhack. Camping at nearby Gifford Woods State Park, 2 mi. east on Hwy. 4, then north on Hwy. 100 for 1 mi. Autumn. Private land.

Classics: Center Crack 6, Monkey Route 7, Monkey Direct 9+.

Ref: Locals.

Directions: From Rutland spring 9 mi. east on Hwy. 4. Park at top of Sherburne Pass. Hike north on Long Trail, then go on the Deerleap Trail a couple of hundred yards to the Deerleap Mountain cliff.

11 Route 9 Crag ☆

Rarely visited 30′ toprope area.

Ref: Locals.

Directions: From Bennington go east on Route 9. Route 9 Crag visible to north from road.

12 SGS Climb

West-facing 50′ granite cliffs.

Directions: From Barnet. Behind the Barnet Middle School (you can see the cliffs from there) about ¼ mi., there is a set of cliffs. You must cross a little stream and some woods to get to the base. From there, there are many routes one can take.

13 Mt. Horrid Cliffs

Steep 1,500′ rise in ¼-mi. distance in from roadway on Long Trail in Vermont. Summertime face climb. Spectacular views. Raptor restrictions March–August.

Ref: James Mullaney 1/98.

Directions: From Brandon go east on Hwy. 73 to Brandon Gap. Hike north on Vermont's Long Hiking Trail to Mt. Horrid (3,126′).

14 Under Cliff

This 30′ volcanic area is known by residents all over St. Johnsbury, but nobody goes to the area. Brendan Beirne and friends first started really climbing here in the spring. It's a great area for beginners to learn or an expert to freshen up on. Private land.

Classics: Jammen and Pushin!!! (First Ascents: Brendan Beirne, Mike Sherman, John Barkanic, Jake Hope.)

Ref: Brendan Beirne 4/98.

Directions: In St. Johnsbury. At I–91 and Hwy. 2, take exit 21 south on Hwy. 2. Turn left onto Central, left onto Cliff, and left on Underclyffe. The cliff is off of Woods and Underclyffe. Go up Underclyffe St. and turn onto Woods St. There's a green house on the right. It's the second house. Walk behind the house until you hit the trail. Walk up the trail. The cliffs will be on your right.

Virginia

True hope is swift and flies with swallow wings, Kings it makes gods, and meaner creatures kings. —Shakespeare

Virginia. The state breathes farmlands, rolling hills, and clandestine mountains. A traveling climber might be tempted to stay and become a farmer amid the rolling hills of the Blue Ridge Mountains. But is there that much rock to keep one here?

Great Falls, along the Potomac near Washington, D.C., holds perhaps the greatest history. This minicrag area continues to please the D.C. after-work crowd. A little more distant but equally worthy is Old Rag up in the Blue Ridge Mountains at Shenandoah National Park.

Other climbing areas like McAfee's Knob, Moorman's Boulders, and Bull Run show up in quiet, charming areas of Virginia.

1 Crescent Rocks (aka Raven Rocks) ✶✶✶
A 50' south-facing basalt crag for experts near the Virginia/West Virginia state line. Detached block is called the Pulpit. According to one local, the closest McDonald's is at Purcellville; got that, J.S.? Autumn–spring. Free camping along Appalachian Trail.
Classics: Popeye's Last Crank 12-.
Ref: G. Collins; Guidebooks: Watson's *Virginia Climber's Guide,* Canter's *Nearby Climbing Areas.*
Directions: From Purcellville follow Hwy. 7 west to Hwy. 601 north at Snickers Gap. Parking problems. New directions: Park west of gap on Hwy. 7, on south side of road. Hike west along highway to reach Appalachian Trail North. Hike north for 2 1/2 mi. to rocks. (Old directions: Go north on Hwy. 601 just inside Jefferson County. [Good map recommended]. Park. Hike northwest for 1/2 mi. on Appalachian Trail past MCI Radio Tower.)

2 Bull Run Mountain (closed?) ✶✶✶
Solid, white, west-facing 50' quartzite crag and bouldering on ridgetop in foothills of the Blue Ridge Mountains. Rusty old pins from 1940s. Access sensitive. Potomac Appalachian Trail Club has worked with landowners to keep open and provide parking access. Autumn–spring. No camping. Private land.
Classics: Airplane Overhang 11, The Block 11.
Ref: G. Collins, Lakey; Guidebook: Canter's *Nearby Climbing Areas.*

Directions: From Middleburg go north of Haymarket on Hwy. 626. Bull Run Mountain cliffs are on the northern, higher summit of the ridge running north from Thoroughfare Gap (some climbing here as well). A jumble of buttresses. Peak Gambs, the largest block overhangs on three—count 'em—three sides. Complicated access due to private ownership could leave one on the horns of the bull. West side closed off, so approach from east side. See Thoroughfare Gap USGS Quad (B.Y.O.T.—Bring Your Own Topo).

3 Great Falls ✶✶✶
Short, fun, and scenic 70' metamorphic Potomac River toprope crags. The Virginia side is the steeper side of the river and sees more climbing action. Echo Rock is home of the Phenomenal Plunge. Downstream Cliff features the classic climbs Silver Scream 10- and Waldorf Astoria 11. Historical D.C. climbing area since the 1920s. Climbing is also available on the Maryland side. Park restrictions apply. (See more under Great Falls, Maryland, listing.) Spring/autumn. Pay camping. NPS, (703) 285-2965.
Classics: Microdome: B29 6, M16 11-; Flat Iron: Bikini 5, The Pox 7; Dihedrals: Take Five 5, Die-hedral 10, The Roll 11+; Dike Creek: Balcony Corner 5, Right Stuff 7, Mantelpiece 10+; Seclusion: Stan's Lead 5, Sickle Face 10, The Demon 12+; Aid Box: Lost Arrow 10, Monkey Fingers 12-; Bird's Nest: Bird's Nest 7, Tiparillo 11+; Dr. Needlepoint: Conroy 7, Blitzkrieg 11+.
Ref: G. Collins; *Appalachia* 6/43; Guidebooks: Watson's *Virginia Climber's Guide,* Harlin's *East,* Eakin's *Climber's Guide to Great Falls of the Potomac,* Canter's *Nearby Climbing Areas,* Nelson and Grossman's guidebook, Potomac Appalachian Trail Climb (PATC).
Directions: Thirteen mi. northwest of Washington, D.C. Follow I–495 west for 6 mi. west on Old Georgetown Pike. Go 1 mi. right on Old Dominion Dr. Park at Great Falls Park Visitor Center. Eleven cliffs line Potomac River along River Trail just south of visitors center, beginning with Microdome (150 yd. east of picnic pavilion), then Flat Iron/Sand Box, Dihedrals, Dike Creek/Juliet's Balcony, Seclusion/Romeo's Ladder, Aid Box/Canal Cut, Bird's Nest/Cornice, Dr. Needlepoint/Degree 101, Downstream Cliffs, Cow Hoof, and ends with Echo Rock, 1 mi. downstream from visitors center.

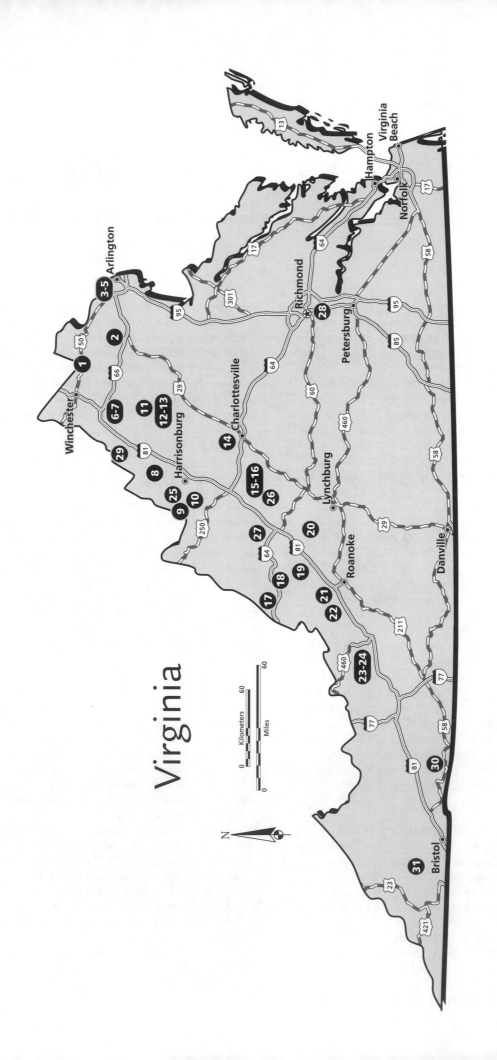

Virginia

4 Boucher Rock (and Eagle Rock) ★★★

This small, south-facing 45' metamorphic toprope crag lies along the Virginia side of the Potomac River, southeast of Carderock, thirty minutes from D.C. Spring–autumn. No camping. Government land.

Classics: Long Corner 8, Seeds and Stems 10; Arch: Still Start 11.

Ref: Guidebooks: Watson's *Virginia Climber's Guide*, Brinkworth's *The Complete Great Falls Climbing Guide*, PATC, Canter's *Nearby Climbing Areas*.

Directions: From junction of Hwy. 193 and I–495, go east on Hwy. 193 and quickly turn north on Balls Rd. Then turn north on Live Oak Rd. to end parking circle. Hike west to Boucher Rock (fifteen minutes) and farther west to Eagle Rock.

5 Ripe Mango

Tiny 60' schist crag on the Potomac River. Faces northwest. Autumn–spring. Free camping. NPS, (703) 285–2965.

Classics: Ripe Mango 10+, R.M. Direct A2.

Ref: Parker; Guidebook: PATC.

Directions: Southeast of Carderock. Ripe Mango is at northwest corner of intersection of George Washington Parkway and Plum Run.

6 Talking Headwall ★★

Small, 50' east-facing roadside crag offers some tough overhangs. Camping at Elizabeth Furnace Campground, south on SSR 678. USFS–George Washington NF, (888) 265–0019.

Classics: Little Creatures 10d, Great White Shark 12d.

Ref: G. Collins; Guidebook: Watson's *Virginia Climber's Guide*.

Directions: From Front Royal go west on Hwy. 55 to Waterlick. Drive south on Hwy. 678 about 2 mi. Talking Headwall is on right at roadside.

7 Little El Cap ★★

Top-of-ridge, west-facing 90' slab with about twenty routes. Summer/autumn. Camping at Elizabeth Furnace Campground, south on SSR 678. USFS–George Washington NF, (888) 265–0019.

Classics: 5.8.

Ref: G. Collins; Guidebooks: Watson's *Virginia Climber's Guide*, Canter's *Nearby Climbing Areas*.

Directions: From Front Royal go west on Hwy. 55 to Waterlick. Drive south on Hwy. 678. Little El Cap lies south of Talking Headwall and on opposite side of Hwy. 678 and creek.

8 Chimney Rock ★★

Climbing is on the east and west faces of this 60' wide, 80' high, freestanding 80' quartzite pinnacle. A 5.8 crack gets climbers to the anchors. Tuscarora sandstone a la Seneca Rocks. This is a VFW 9660 crag—obtain a written permit before you even think of standing under the stone here. Spring/autumn. Free camping. Private land.

Ref: Lakey; Guidebook: Watson's *Virginia Climber's Guide*.

Directions: From Luray go west on Hwy. 211 to Timberville. Proceed west on Hwy. 259 just past Cootes Store. Chimney Rock is on right (north) side of road.

9 Hone Quarry ★★

Ridgetop 20' quartzite bouldering and toprope area with twenty routes; great for the beginner/intermediate climber. Spring/autumn. Free camping in wilderness sites. USFS–George Washington NF, (888) 265–0019.

Ref: Guidebook: Watson's *Virginia Climber's Guide*.

Directions: From Harrisonburg go southwest on Hwy. 42. Then turn west on Hwy. 257 continuing past Briery Branch to Hone Quarry picnic area. Rocks are across the road and about twenty minutes up trail.

10 Hidden Cracks ★★

Bouldering and cragging on 75' south-facing formations. Autumn. Free camping. USFS–George Washington NF, (888) 265–0019.

Classics: Intrados, Rainy Day Woman, The Whale.

Ref: G. Collins.

Directions: From Harrisonburg follow Hwy. 42 south to Hwy. 257 west. Then go south of little yellow house to Hidden Cracks.

11 BRP–Blue Ridge Pkwy. (Shenandoah NP) ★★★

The Blue Ridge Pkwy. offers the quintessential scenic "drive of a lifetime" plus several rock-climbing areas at which to get out and stretch the legs and arms over miles of panorama on the Skyline Dr. The better areas are listed here. Most areas are short climbs of 20'–30' with occasional longer one-pitch routes. Routes range to 5.13. The Devil's Stairs area has lead climbs. Big Devil's Stairs canyon walls have some lead climbs on greenstone rock. Stony Man's eyebrow, a columnar jointed rock fin, has short climbs. Down the mountain is the Nose, a 70' cliff with overhang at top. Little Stony Man has leadable cliffs also of greenstone. Naked Creek Falls offers slab climbing next to waterfalls. (What could be more pleasant than a slab climb next to a waterfall?) Kettle Canyon contains high cliffs. White Rock Canyon is highly popular, and, though not exactly right on the parkway, Old Rag is a favored area for many a Blue Ridge mountaineer. Bearfence Mountain has fine bouldering. Spring–autumn. Free camping. NPS, (540) 999–3500.

Ref: Lakey; Gildart's *Hiking Shenandoah National Park*; Guidebooks: Watson's *Virginia Climber's Guide*, Heatwole's *Guide to Skyline Drive and Shenandoah National Park*, Canter's *Nearby Climbing Areas*.

Directions: From Front Royal there are many areas of rock climbing on the super-scenic Blue Ridge Pkwy. These include: 1) Fort Windham Rocks, mm 10.4 at Compton Gap Parking Lot; ½-mi. hike to post then left ¼ mi. to rocks. 2) Mount Marshall, mm 15.9; ½-mi. hike up trail. 3) Big Devil's Stairs, mm 17.7; 1 6/10 mi. hike up Bluff Trail. 4) Little Devil's Stairs, mm 19.4; hike via Little Devil's Trail. 5) Marys Rock, mm 31.5 at Thornton Gap; 1 ½ mi. hike up Marys Rock Trail. 6) Little Stony Man Cliffs, mm 39.1, L.S.M. parking lot; ½–1 mi. hike. 7) Crescent Rocks at C.R. Overlook; short hike south. 8) White Oak Canyon, mm 42.6; varied hike (see below). 9) Cedar Run Falls, mm 45.6 at Hawksbill Gap Parking Lot; hike trail to falls. 10) Hawksbill Mountain, mm 45.6 at Hawksbill Gap Parking Lot; trail to mountain. 11) Blackrock, at mm 51 parking at Big Meadows Lodge; cliffs below. 12) Bearfence Mountain (bouldering), mm 56.5; hike up Appalachian Trail. 13) Loft Mountain, mm 79.5 via Deadening Trail. Kettle Canyon and Naked Creek Falls are in the Big Meadows area.

12 BRP–White Oak Canyon (Shenandoah NP) ✩✩✩

A beautiful area with up to 80′ southwest-facing basalt crags featuring more than 150 routes. Good rock and ice climbing. Spring–autumn. Free camping. NPS, (540) 999-3500.

Ref: G. Collins; Guidebook: Watson's *Virginia Climber's Guide*.

Directions: From Sperryville travel west on Hwy. 211. Turn south on Skyline Dr. (Blue Ridge Pkwy.) to mm 42.6 or 43. Hike White Oak Canyon Trail to rocks. Farther south at mm 45.6 is another similar area, Cedar Run Falls. Or, from Sperryville travel 10 mi. south on Hwy. 231 to the town of Etlan. In Etlan, turn west on Hwy. 643 for 5 mi. Then go west on Hwy. 600 (Berry Hollow Rd., which continues to trailhead for Old Rag Mountain). Find trailhead for White Oak Canyon. Park. Hike 3 mi. west on White Oak Canyon Trail.

13 Old Rag Mountain (Shenandoah NP) ✩✩✩✩

If you can't find peace in the valley, try here. A mountain-side sanctuary of numerous granite bouldering, 125′ routes, and exploratory climbing on an Appalachian ridge crest. Stupendous, clean, white cracks and gritty slabs. The quality of climbing tempers the 3 ½-mi. hike in. Perhaps Washington, D.C.'s best crag. Autumn. Free camping. NPS, (540) 999-3500.

Classics: Eagle's Gift 9, Oh My God Corner 10b, Duck Walk 10c, Bushwhack Crack 10c, Good Friday 10d, Strawberry Jam 11a, April Fool 11, 5.13 crack.

Ref: R [44, 8(5/85)-6]; on-line guide www.contactclimbinggear.com./; Guidebooks: Watson's *Virginia Climber's Guide*, Harlin's *East*.

Directions: From Sperryville travel 10 mi. south on Hwy. 231 to the town of Etlan. In Etlan, turn west on Hwy. 643 for 5 mi. Then go west on Hwy. 600 (Berry Hollow Rd.), which fords two streams to trailhead for Old Rag Mountain. Hike beyond Old Rag Shelter to get to four areas of rock climbing. Another approach is off Blue Ridge Pkwy. on White Oak Canyon Trail. Intricate, difficult-to-find areas—leave your conscious mind behind or go with a local.

14 Moorman's Boulders ✩✩✩✩

Instant access to many excellent 20′ sandstone problems. Extremely sensitive access with private landowner—please be respectful of landowner's request. Swimming in river to cool the tips. Spring–autumn. No camping. Private land.

Ref: K. Parker; Guidebook: Watson's *Virginia Climber's Guide*.

Directions: From Charlottesville go approximately 12 mi. west on Barracks Rd. (which turns into Garth Rd.). Turn right on Hwy. 671 for 1 ½ mi. to Millington. Turn at large iron bridge that crosses Moorman's River. Moorman's Boulders are on right at bridge. Parking along road.

15 Raven's Roost ✩✩

Good views, nice rock, and hang glider's launch from this 80′ northwest-facing sedimentary crag with two dozen routes up to 5.13. Spring/autumn. Pay camping. USFS–George Washington NF, (888) 265-0019.

Classics: Black Streak, Wise Crack, White Punks on Dope, Swinging in the Trees, Total Control.

Ref: K. Parker; Guidebook: Watson's *Virginia Climber's Guide*.

Directions: From Waynesboro drive west for 11 mi. south on Blue Ridge Pkwy. to Raven's Roost Overlook.

16 Love Gap (aka Bell Coney) ✩✩

Just off scenic Blue Ridge Pkwy. sits this 80′ south-facing granite crag. Originally developed by Darrow Kirkpatrick in 1981. Autumn. Free camping. Government land.

Classics: Summer Soliloquy 9, Expecting to Fly 10.

Ref: Kirkpatrick, Parker; Guidebook: Watson's *Virginia Climber's Guide*.

Directions: From Waynesboro go south on Blue Ridge Pkwy. to mm 16. Turn left onto Virginia Rd. 814 for ½ mi. Park on right. Love Gap Cliff on left, north of road. Follow faint trail (possible bushwhack) about 200 yd. north to base of cliffs.

17 Covington Cliffs

Long band of 100′ sandstone cliffs visible to north of highway. Other rock outcrops in valley. Autumn. USFS–George Washington NF, (888) 265-0019.

Directions: From Covington go west on I-64. Covington Cliffs are on north side of highway.

18 Clifton Forge

Obvious 100′ sandstone roadside crag with thirty-five routes. Hot tip: Climb on the roadside during the summer and across the river (in the sun) in the winter. The roadside crag is private, while the riverside crag is USFS. Iron Gate is a good crag for locals in the Roanoke Valley region looking for an abundance of moderate routes with quick access. Please be very careful about loose rocks rolling down into the roadway; this area was once closed because of this problem. The wall across the river does have some established lines, but the access to the wall is difficult without trespassing on private property. The closest camping area is at Douthat State Park. If you need more information, contact either eangel@mindspring.com or someone at Blue Ridge Outdoors. The Lynchburg Climbing Club has published an on-line guide at www.lynchburgclimbingclub.com. Autumn. Private land/USFS-George Washington NF, (888) 265-0019.

Classics: Leather and Latex 5.7: crack climbing natural pro to cold shuts; Happiness in Slavery 5.9: face climbing, mixed, three bolts to cold shuts; Pretty Poison 5.10a: mixed, great exposure, and a bit run out in places; #0 TCU placement at roof, before final moves; Bip Bam Boom: 5.10b, short, sequency, fun three bolts to cold shuts; Clown Attack: 5.11b, big bolted roof to face six bolts to cold shuts, watch that first bolt placement once you pull the roof—it tends to cut the arm a bit.

Ref: Eric Angel 10/98, H. Allen 11/97; Guidebook: Watson's *Virginia Climber's Guide.*

Directions: From Clifton Forge just south on Hwy. 220. Clifton Forge Cliffs are visible on left. (Or north of Iron Gate on 220.) The well-developed crag is on the same side of the river as the road. Park at the Furnace and locate trail 50 yd., north of parking and hump to the base. Also, the opposite side of the river has lots of routes, not as developed. Access is tricky through private land to reach base, so please be respectful. Usually the folks aren't home, but watch out for snakes and buckshot.

19 Eagle Rock ✫

Southwest-facing 100′ sandstone crag. Autumn. Free camping. Private land.

Ref: K. Parker; Guidebook: Watson's *Virginia Climber's Guide.*

Directions: From Roanoke follow Hwy. 220 north to town of Eagle Rock and cliffs at James River. Park in picnic area. Two hours from Seneca Rocks.

20 Tunstall's Tooth ✫✫

This 225′ limestone pinnacle has good climbing on both river and land sides. First ascent of river side in 1972. Spring–autumn.

Classics: A2 line, moderate free routes.

Ref: AAJ '70-139; Guidebook: Watson's *Virginia Climber's Guide.*

Directions: From Big Island (20 mi. northwest of Lynchburg), chew through 2 ½ mi. of blacktop on Hwy. 501 to Tunstall's Tooth across the James River. Past the Georgia Pacific Plant is a bridge to access cliffs.

21 McAfee's Knob ✫✫✫✫

Two large bouldering areas, east and west of summit of the knob. A maze of many excellent 20′ sandstone problems (many 5.9), one area of which is called the Devil's Kitchen. For the answers to all your climbing questions, check with Blue Ridge Mountain Sports in Blacksburg or Roanoke. Spring–autumn. Free camping.

Ref: K. Parker; Guidebook: Watson's *Virginia Climber's Guide.*

Directions: From Roanoke drive 10 mi. north on Hwy. 311 to top of Catawba Mountain. Park on road 2 mi. before Hwy. 785. Hike 2 ½ mi. north on Appalachian Trail to McAfee's Knob.

22 Dragon's Tooth ✫✫

One-hundred-foot sandstone crags with mostly 50′ climbs and bouldering. Great views! Spring–autumn. Free camping. Private land, owned by the Appalachian Trail Conference.

Classics: Split Bulge 4, Rhapsody in Red 8, Hokie in Space 9.

Ref: K. Parker; Guidebook: Watson's *Virginia Climber's Guide.*

Directions: From Roanoke go approximately 12 mi. northwest on Hwy. 311. Park on left ¼ mi. past Hwy. 624. Hike south 2 ½ mi. to Dragon's Tooth. Fins of rock wait at the end of a scenic hike.

23 Fool's Face ✫✫

Small 45′ sandstone outcrops, but good climbing. More climbs uphill. Railroad land—please don't disturb railroad property and please, no whippers onto the tracks. The climbing area known as White Face sits directly across the New River. Swimming. Spring–autumn. No camping. Private land/USFS-Thomas Jefferson NF, (540) 552-4641.

Classics: Overlaps 6, Nutcracker 9+, Ravenous Roof 12-toprope.

Ref: K. Parker; Guidebook: Watson's *Virginia Climber's Guide.*

Directions: From Blacksburg drive approximately 10 mi. west on Prices Fork Rd. to McCoy Falls. Cliffs along railroad tracks. Parking area comes before rocks. Fool's Face and other climbs are scattered up the hill.

24 White Face ✫✫

Southeast-facing 145′ sandstone slab for beginners. Autumn. No camping. Private land. Toproping not easy. USFS-Thomas Jefferson NF, (540) 552-4641.

Classics: Magic Moments 7, Hard Drugs 10.

Ref: K. Parker; Guidebook: Watson's *Virginia Climber's Guide.*

Directions: From Blacksburg go west on Hwy. 114, then north on Hwy. 600 (Belspring Rd.) at Fairlawn to road's end. Park at cul-de-sac. Hike up trail, it's a short, steep hump to base of climbs. White Face is across the New River from Fool's Face.

25 The Fridge

South-facing 30′ sandstone bouldering. The Fridge is the biggest rock that is by itself near the second outcrop of boulders. Autumn. Free camping. USFS–George Washington NF, (888) 265-0019.

Classics: One Move Ecstasy, Two Move Ecstasy, Nut Slicer Corner, The Dimple Route.

Ref: Local.

Directions: From Harrisonburg take Hwy. 33 west. Before the mountains, turn left on road to Rawley Springs. Follow this road, going to Lower Rawley. At the end of the road, park in a parking area to the right. Hike up trail on left-hand side of the road.

26 Crabtree Falls

Probably the best ice climbing area in Virginia. This place is also supposedly the highest terraced waterfall east of the Mississippi. More than 1,500′ total vertical drop. Multiple falls of 20′–400′ tall. Mostly WI 2 and 3. No grade 4. Plan on an early start, especially in questionable weather. The top ice falls have been known to break off with no previous warning if it starts to heat up. Takes about a half day to climb from bottom to top with a couple of climbers. Winter. USFS–George Washington NF, (888) 265-0019.

Classics: The whole place is awesome! A great place to climb ice and bring newbies.

Ref: H. Allen 11/97; Guidebook: Watson's *Virginia Climber's Guide*.

Directions: From Colleen take Hwy. 29 to Route 56; follow west to Crabtree Falls Parking Area, on left on the climb to Montebello.

27 Goshen Pass

Any VMI cadet can give you more specific directions to Goshen's 80′ crags. The first crag on the east side of the river as you enter the valley (dubbed "Castle Rock") offers several opportunities for top belay, short lead, and short artificial climbs. Be careful—the rock suffers from weather action. No camping. State land, Goshen–Little North Mountain Wildlife Management Area.

Classics: On Castle Rock: Classic is straight up the middle to the obvious shelf. Then up through the crack. Welcome to Goshen: Straight up the middle to the obvious shelf. Then out to the left and straight up. Usually requires one aid

move. Python: On the left side below the protrusion (Bonehead). Climb straight up the crack below bonehead and over the top.

Ref: R. Lahue 1/98; Guidebook: Watson's *Virginia Climber's Guide*.

Directions: From Lexington take SR 39 north toward Goshen. Once you cross to the west side of the river you will be in a long valley. The hills have exposed rock on the top. Park at Goshen Pass Wayside Area or at confluence of Laurel Run and Maury River.

28 Manchester Bridge ✮✮✮

Old blocked bridge abutments compose a premiere Richmond sport climbing and toproping area with ticks from 5.5 to 5.10. One and a half hours south of Washington, D.C., near downtown Richmond on the James River.

Ref: W. Hobbs.

Directions: From D.C. get on I-95 south and head toward Richmond. At I-95, exit at 76B, Belvidere Rd. Follow Route 1 south. After James River, turn left at first light on Semmes Ave. for 2 blocks and make a left into the Flood Wall parking area. Follow the sidewalk fifteen minutes under the Manchester Bridge to the pedestrian bridge over the train tracks. When the path splits, make a right and head toward the river to an overlook. Turn right before the overlook to stairs to the base of the abutment.

29 Big Schloss ✮✮✮

These 100′ sandstone cliffs are no pile of "schloss." Good climbs up to 5.13 overhangs challenge climbers. Camping. USFS–George Washington NF, (888) 265-0019.

Ref: Locals; Guidebook: Watson's *Virginia Climber's Guide*.

Directions: From Edinburg (I-81, exit 279) follow Hwy. 675 west to Wolf Gap Campground. Park. Hike up ridge past site 9, bearing left twice to base of cliffs.

30 Grayson Highlands State Park

West of Volney off Hwy. 58.

31 Hanging Rock Picnic Area

North of Dungannon on Hwy. 72.

Washington

Good timber does not come with ease; the stronger the wind, the stronger the trees. —J. Willard Marriott

When you gaze at Washington, you behold an expanse of climbing variety. Climbers need only lift Fred Beckey's compendium of Cascade Alpine Guides to realize they will have a big rope bill. For one, the North Cascades capture the whim of the alpine rock climber with classics such as the Liberty Bell and Early Winter Spires. Two pleasant surprises await visitors to areas like Darrington and Static Point. And more, Mt. Rainier, and its volcanic associates, are the glacial calling cards for any mountaineering spirit.

Craggers have their fill in store when they visit Leavenworth and Index. These excellent granite areas are considered Washington's finest granite crags. More and more climbers are coming to appreciate the arid basalt climbing found in areas like the Tieton River Canyon and Champs de Brionne. Still, Beacon Rock, Little Si, and the Spokane area invite those seeking novelty.

Amazingly, even with all that's been done in the state; climbers can still find enough new rock to fill another pair of Fred Beckey's shoes.

1 Van Zandt ✮✮
Black-and-white-streaked, 600' sandstone walls and slabs on forested slopes above the town of Van Zandt. Looks impressive, but very soft sandstone a la Peshastin Pinnacles, Washington. Spring/autumn.
Ref: Guidebook: Kloke's *Climber's Guide to Lowland Rock in Skagit and Whatcom Counties.*
Directions: In Van Zandt, drive 7/10 mi. east on Potter Rd. Turn 3/10 mi. east on dirt road. Park. Hike up road to trail in woods, following right fork to Van Zandt Cliffs.

2 Sehome Hill ✮
Popular Bellingham practice area. Short 50' sandstone slab and bouldering routes make for a quick lunch break of topropes. Check out the go-go espresso drive-throughs that are so plentiful in town. Spring/autumn.
Ref: Guidebook: Kloke's *Climber's Guide to Lowland Rock in Skagit and Whatcom Counties.*
Directions: Just south of Bellingham College near College Pkwy. and Twenty-fifth St. Drive 3/10 mi. on Twenty-fifth

St. Hike 200' on a dirt road on left to a series of lower and upper Sehome Hill cliffs.

3 Larrabee State Park ●
Unique, 40' sandstone beach bouldering by the bay—get there before it's washed away. After doing the Moonwalk Traverse, you might be saying, "That's one small moon, doll-face!" Also more bouldering along the railroad tracks. More sandstone climbing on 30' towers exists just north off Hwy. 11 at Chuckanut Bay. Beachcombing. Great sunsets. Panoramic views of San Juan Islands. Spring/autumn. Pay camping in state park (800–452–5687).
Classics: Moonwalk Traverse.
Ref: Guidebooks: WMA's *Traveler's Guide Puget Sound,* Henrie's *Bellingham Rock,* Smoot's *Washington Rock Climbs,* Kloke's *Climber's Guide to Lowland Rock in Skagit and Whatcom Counties.*
Directions: From Bellingham the park is approximately 5 mi. south on Hwy. 11. Follow Larrabee State Park signs. Rock is located along the shore south of the boat dock and west of the railroad tracks.

4 Chuckanut Cliffs ✮
On Blanchard Mountain: Two 200' sandstone walls, Samish (150') and San Juan Wall (200'). Summer/autumn. Private/government land.
Ref: Guidebook: Kloke's *Climber's Guide to Lowland Rock in Skagit and Whatcom Counties.*
Directions: From Burlington drive 11 mi. north on Hwy. 11. Go right at cafe 2/10 mi. to gate. Hike Lily Lake Trail for approximately 2 mi. Chuckanut Cliffs right along Hwy. 11 as well.

5 Turtle Rock ✮
Smooth, steep slabs of slippery 120' metamorphic rock. Spring/autumn.
Ref: Guidebook: Kloke's *Climber's Guide to Lowland Rock in Skagit and Whatcom Counties.*
Directions: From Burlington drive north on Hwy. 11 to the southern end of Chuckanut Dr. Just north of the Chuck-

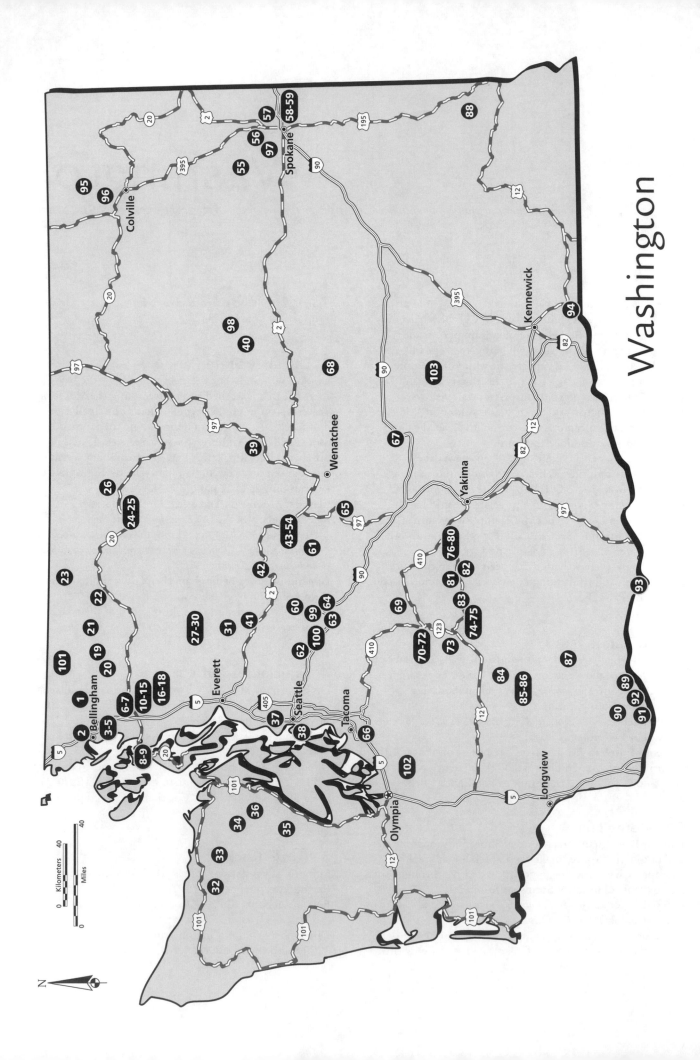

Washington

anut Manor Restaurant. Turtle Rock is right next to the highway and east of road.

6 Echo Rock ●
Loose, smooth, and slabby 100′ crag. Most climbing done on south face.
Ref: Guidebook: Kloke's *Climber's Guide to Lowland Rock in Skagit and Whatcom Counties.*
Directions: From Burlington take Hwy. 9 north. Turn right on Prairie Rd. for 2 ½ mi. Go right on Gripp Rd. for approximately 2 mi. Park. Hike south on railroad tracks to power lines. Follow lines ¼ mi. west to Echo Rock.

7 Butler's Bluff ✩
Vertical and overhanging rock on the north and east sides of this crag. Spring/autumn.
Ref: Guidebook: Kloke's *Climber's Guide to Lowland Rock in Skagit and Whatcom Counties.*
Directions: From Burlington drive on Hwy. 99N (several miles). Turn right for 2 mi. on Prairie Rd. Turn right on F and south Grade Rd. for approximately 1 mi. Hike east on gated road. Go east of old lookout on Butler Hill to Butler's Bluff.

8 Cap Sante Point ✩
Loose, 75′ sedimentary friction slabs. Things to do: San Juan Island sea kayaking, whale watching (June), whale museum Friday Harbor, and San Juan Island kickin' around. Things not to do: Wrestle a whale, fire multiple rounds at sea kayakers, or detonate atomic warhead. Spring/autumn. Camping in government park.
Ref: Guidebook: Kloke's *Climber's Guide to Lowland Rock in Skagit and Whatcom Counties.*
Directions: In Anacortes, drive north on Commercial Ave. Turn right on Fourth St. for ½ mi. to a right fork and wind up hill to parking on top. Two outcrops are found on east and south side of Cap Sante Point.

9 Mt. Erie ✩✩✩
Most popular area of Skagit County climbers, especially for teaching beginner and intermediate climbers. Fun 250′ granite walls surrounded by tall, thick forests command an outstanding view of the bay. Sport climbers have rejuvenated this area. With a new guidebook by Dallas Kloke (put out by the Skagit Valley Mountaineers), there are more than 150 new routes, including a lot of moderates. A lot of toprope routes and many natural leads. Mt. Erie is the highest point on the island. Summer. City land.
Classics: Zig Zag Direct 7, Nose Direct 10a, Women are from Venus 10c/d, Outer Space 7, Roaring Lions 7, Smashing Pumpkins 11a, Pinhead 11b, Karnage 12a.
Ref: 12/97; Guidebooks: Smoot's *Rock Climbing Washington*, WMA's *Traveler's Guide Puget Sound*, Mountain Rescue Unit's *Climbing Guide to Mt. Erie*, Kloke's *Climber's Guide to*

Lowland Rock in Skagit and Whatcom Counties, Smoot's *Washington Rock Climbs.*
Directions: From Anacortes take a right on Commercial until Thirty-sixth St. Take a left. Take another left on H St. Go about 2 ½ mi. to the turnoff. All climbs are reached from the top, following numerous trails. This prominent landmark is divided into Upper and Lower Cliffs. The Powerline Wall is found by following the power line down. Look for bolted top anchors for routes.

10 Spectator Rock ✩
A single 70′ beginner's bouldering slab. Don't blink. Spring/autumn. No camping.
Classics: Spectator Slab.
Ref: Guidebook: Kloke's *Climber's Guide to Lowland Rock in Skagit and Whatcom Counties.*
Directions: From Mt. Vernon go approximately 5 mi. east. Follow Hwy. 538. Then go for approximately ½ mi. north on Hwy. 9. Spectator Rock is on right above road.

11 Big Rock ✩
Beginner 40′ crag. Spring/autumn.
Ref: Guidebook: Kloke's *Climber's Guide to Lowland Rock in Skagit and Whatcom Counties.*
Directions: From Mt. Vernon drive 5 mi. east on Hwy. 538. Turn south for ³/10 mi. on Hwy. 9. On right above highway. Follow trail behind gravel pit leading to south base of Big Rock. A beginner's and rescue practice site. Easy roadside access.

12 Lunchhour Boulder ✩
Small, 25′ beginner bouldering area included in Kloke's guide to Skagit County areas. Of interest only for climbers looking to visit obscure areas. Spring/autumn.
Ref: Guidebook: Kloke's *Climber's Guide to Lowland Rock in Skagit and Whatcom Counties.*
Directions: From Mt. Vernon take Hwy. 538 to Hwy. 9. Go for ⁴/10 mi. north on Hwy. 9. Turn right 2 ³/10 mi. on Gunderson Rd. Lunchhour Boulder is on right. Routes on the east side.

13 Nookachamps Pinnacle ✩
A 25′ pinnacle. Spring/autumn.
Ref: Guidebook: Kloke's *Climber's Guide to Lowland Rock in Skagit and Whatcom Counties.*
Directions: From Mt. Vernon take Hwy. 538 to Hwy. 9. Go for ⁴/10 mi. north on Hwy. 9. Turn right on Gunderson Rd. for 5 ⁴/10 mi. Or, go south of Clear Lake on Beaver Lake Rd. for 3 mi. Nookachamps Pinnacle is visible on a hilltop above the Nookachamps River just west of road.

14 Equinox Rock ☆

The large boulders at the south and west face may be the redeeming feature of this area. Spring/autumn.

Ref: Guidebook: Kloke's *Climber's Guide to Lowland Rock in Skagit and Whatcom Counties.*

Directions: From Big Lake go south approximately 1 mi. to Walker Valley Rd. Turn east for 3 mi. on Walker Valley Rd. Then a 2-mi. hike to rock on a road that goes close to the east side of Equinox Rock. Refer to Clear Lake USGS Quad. (On map, rock is on the line between Sections 21 and 28.) Poor directions—proceed with genuine uncertainty.

15 Split Rock ☆

For locals only, excellent chimney climbing in a backwoods area on solid andesite rock. For those willing to do a little cleaning, the rewards are tremendous. Free camping. BIA.

Ref: 11/97; Guidebook: Kloke's *Climber's Guide to Lowland Rock in Skagit and Whatcom Counties.*

Directions: South of Big Lake. Drive on Lake Cavanaugh Rd. for 9 6/10 mi. Turn left on GA Pacific Logging road for 1 mi. Turn northeast on same logging road for 6 mi. (turning left, then right, and left once past main intersection) to Split Rock. (On Section 25 of Clear Lake USGS topo quad.)

16 Walker Valley Boulders (aka Devil's Rock Pile) ☆

Possibly moss covered. Spirelike 60' boulders. Spring/autumn.

Classics: Blockhouse Tower.

Ref: Guidebook: Kloke's *Climber's Guide to Lowland Rock in Skagit and Whatcom Counties.*

Directions: From Mt. Vernon drive 7 mi. east. Take Hwy. 538. Turn onto Hwy. 9S for 3 7/10 mi. Turn left on Walker Valley Rd. for 3 mi. Park at gate if locked. Hike east on spur road ½ mi., then head northeast on another spur road for ½ mi. through woods to south side of boulderfield of Walker Valley Boulders. Possibly difficult route finding.

17 Bald Mountain ☆

A prominent rock of vegetated rocky walls. Take your chances.

Ref: Guidebook: Kloke's *Climber's Guide to Lowland Rock in Skagit and Whatcom Counties.*

Directions: This area lies 3 mi. north of Lake Cavanaugh at the south base of Bald Mountain. From Big Lake go south on Hwy. 9 to its junction with Lake Cavanaugh Rd. Turn onto Lake Cavanaugh Rd. for 9 6/10 mi. Turn left onto logging road for approximately 1 mi. Drive 8/10 mi. north. Turn right on spur road to south base of Bald Mountain.

18 Cougar Rock ☆

East and North Face of Cougar Rock measure up to 175'. Uncertain rock quality.

Ref: Guidebook: Kloke's *Climber's Guide to Lowland Rock in Skagit and Whatcom Counties.*

Directions: From town of Big Lake, take Hwy. 9 south to the south end of Big Lake (the body of water, not the town). Turn onto West Big Lake Blvd. for 2/10 mi. and park. Hike up to east face of Cougar Rock. Jungle vegetation. Be wary of brambles thicker than flies on you-know-what.

19 Mt. Baker ☆☆☆☆

What is the snowiest place in the world? It's now officially Mt. Baker in Washington (United States), which endured a whopping 95' of snow during the 1998–99 winter season. A colossus of ice and snow, Mt. Baker (10,778') is Washington's northernmost stratovolcano. For the climber Mt. Baker is mainly a glacial challenge. Of the peak's several glaciers, the Parks Glacier is most magnificent. Camping on USFS–Mt. Baker NF (360-856-5700).

Classics: Mt. Baker: Boulder Glacier Route.

Ref: AAJ '97, C 125, CAJ 3(1911), *Mazama* 3, no. 1(1907), OB 8 '76; Guidebooks: Beckey's *Cascade Alpine Guide, Volume 3: Rainy Pass to Fraser River,* Nelson and Potterfield's *Selected Climbs in the Cascades,* Beckey's *Cascade Alpine Guide.*

Directions: Mt. Baker is most often approached south of Glacier, Washington, via FR 36 to Coleman Glacier. Or, east from Glacier via Hwy. 542 to the Ptarmigan Ridge. Or, southeast from Birdsview, Washington, via Baker Lake Rd. to Sulphur Creek and Easton Glacier.

20 Twin Sisters Mountains ☆☆☆☆

Twin Sisters Mountains are a collection of glacial cirques, spires, and horns on the western flanks of North Cascades. South Twin (6,932') and North Twin (6,570'), especially the West Ridge Route, measure prominently. Fred Beckey describes the Twin Sisters as some of the best rock in the Cascade Range. Free camping on USFS–Mt. Baker NF (360-856-5700).

Classics: North Twin (West Ridge).

Ref: AAJ '68, *Mountaineer* 1916, S 11/61; Guidebook: Beckey's *Cascade Alpine Guide.*

Directions: Twin Sisters Mountains are southwest of Mt. Baker, north of Hamilton, or southeast of Kendall.

21 North Cascades National Park (Mt. Shuksan, Forbidden Peak) ☆☆☆☆

North Cascades National Park is an enormous wilderness area extending from Glacier/Mt. Baker Ski Area in the north to the north tip of Lake Chelan in the south. Various access points within North Cascades National Park and Mt. Baker National Forest. How do you describe an encyclopedic wonderland of alpine rock and ice routes in one line of print? Simple! See Fred Beckey's Cascade Alpine Guides.

Mt. Shuksan (9,127′) with its 10 square mi. of real estate, was first ascended in 1906 and is probably the most celebrated mountain in the state of Washington, often called "The Showpiece of the Cascades." It is typical of numerous North Cascade mixed ice, snow, and rock routes. Forbidden Peak, in the southern end of the park, offers similar challenges. Washington Pass has one of the best concentration of rock climbs, i.e., Liberty Bell, Early Winter Spires, etc. Free backcountry permits, (360) 873–4500. Camping on NPS, (360) 856–5700/USFS–Mt. Baker- Snoqualmie NF, (360) 856–5700.

Classics: Mt. Shuksan: Price Glacier Route; Forbidden Peak: West Ridge 5.2, 1,700′ Northwest Face 5.7, Early Morning Spire; Mt. Goode: Northeast Buttress 5.5; Mt. Triumph: Northeast Ridge, Liberty Bell, Wine Spires, North Twin, American Border Peak, Nooksack Tower, Hozomeen Mountain; Cathedral Peak: Southeast Butt III 9, Amphitheater Peak, Mt. Baring 5.12-.

Ref: AAJ ['98, '97, '95>93, 92-129, 91-165, 90-162/165, 89-142, 88-129, 86-151, 85-188, 84 to 78, 76-340, 75-125, 74, 72, 69-65, 47], C [183-22, 171-68, 164-76, 144, 125, 115, 103, 97, 95, 93, 70], *Mountaineer* '46, OB 10(8/73), R [90-24, 74-44], S [11/87, 3/87, 8/85, 8/77, 4/73, 10/71, 9/70, 7/69, 5/68, 3/67, 5/65, 11/64, 5/64, 1/63, 3/61]; Jones's *Climbing in North America,* Beckey's *Challenge of the North Cascades,* Molvar's *Hiking the North Cascades;* on-line guide www.ac.wwu.edu/~berdind; Guidebooks: Smoot's *Rock Climbing Washington,* Beckey's *Cascade Alpine Guide Volume 3: Rainy Pass to Fraser River,* Nelson and Potterfield's *Selected Climbs in the Cascades,* Steck and Roper's *Fifty Classic Climbs,* Beckey's *Cascade Alpine Guide,* Beckey's *Cascade Alpine Guide II.*

Directions: Most areas reached off Hwy. 20 west of Mazama and east of Sedro Woolley. Or, northeast of Sedro Woolley on Hwy. 542 (Mt. Baker Hwy.).

22 Newhalem Rock ☆☆☆

This highway is lined with loads of high-quality granite. Dam releases may warrant a watchful eye if climbing in the river corridor. Free and pay camping in area. Summer/autumn. Private land/USFS–Mt. Baker- Snoqualmie NF, (360) 856–5700.

Directions: From Newhalem rock-climbing possibilities start on Hwy. 20 along Skagit River and continue to town of Diablo.

23 North Cascades National Park (Picket Range) ☆☆☆☆☆

An isolated northwest/southeast range of serrated rock peaks up to 8,200′ in elevation that have gained their appel-

Mt. Shuksan, a showpiece of the North Cascades.

TIM TOULA

lation from their resemblance to a picket fence. Mt. Challenger is the obvious peak of the Northern Pickets. Prominent formations include: Mt. Challenger, East Peak, West Peak, Inspiration Peak, Chopping Block, Twin Needles, Himmelhorn, Luna Peak, Bear Mountain, and Twin Spires. Expect long (up to two days) approach hikes. NPS.

Classics: Himmelhorn; Mt. Terror: North Face III 8; Inspiration Peak: South Face III 8, Luna Peak; Mt. Redoubt: Northeast Face; Bear Mountain: North Buttress west IV (seventeen pitches) 9.

Ref: *Appalachia* 6/'52, AAJ '[75, 69, 62, 59], C [141, 10/72], *Mountaineer* '71, 63, 62, 58, S [4/71, 7/63, 1/61, 6/60]; Guidebooks: Beckey's *Cascade Alpine Guide, Volume 3: Rainy Pass to Fraser River*, Nelson and Potterfield's *Selected Climbs in the Cascades*, Beckey's *Cascade Alpine Guide*.

Directions: The Picket Range is located in North Cascades National Park wilderness area north of Newhalem, west of Ross Lake, and approximately 13 mi. east of Mt. Shuksan.

24 Washington Pass (Liberty Bell and Early Winter Spires) ☆☆☆☆☆

A North American classic. "Roadside" alpine rock climbing on several granite towers, including the 1,200' east face of Liberty Bell. Relatively instant access on the best rock in the North Cascades makes this a choice area amongst climbers. Good views of climbs from Washington Pass Overlook Trail. Weather warning: Four-day pisses to total deluges. Summer. Free and pay camping. USFS–Okanagan NF, (509) 662–4335.

Classics: Liberty Bell: Beckey (1947) Route 6, Liberty Crack 9 A2 or V 11b A3 (5.13a), Thin Red Line V 9 A4; Concord Tower NF 6, Lexington Tower East Face IV 9; South Early Spire: West Face 5.10+, Dir East Buttress IV 11-.

Ref: Petroske; AAJ ['92-129, 91-165, 90-166, 89-142, 79-183, 69-66], C [129, 125(4/91)-74, 115, 97], R [84-144, 67-57], S [9/72, 10/69]; Guidebooks: Nelson and Potterfield's *Selected Climbs in the Cascades*, Smoot's *Washington Rock Climbs*, Harlin's *West*, Steck and Roper's *Fifty Classic Climbs*, Beckey's *Cascade Alpine Guide 3*.

Directions: Go 15 mi. west of Mazama on Hwy. 20 to Washington Pass. Hike south one hour from pass to these prominent formations: Early Winter Spires, Concord Tower, Lexington Tower, and Liberty Bell (three access trails). Another major area, Silver Star Mountain/Wine Spires, is ten minutes east down Hwy. 2 at signed pullout.

25 Wine Spires/Silver Star Mountain/ Snagtooth Ridge ☆☆☆☆

Overlooked because of nearby Liberty Bell, this glaciated mountain fortress impresses travelers east of Washington Pass with 1,200' granite walls. Silver Star Mountain (8,876') is highest formation. Summer. USFS–Okanagan NF, (509) 662–4335.

Classics: Burgundy Spire: North Face II 8; Chablis Spire: East Face III 10.

Ref: AAJ ['96-147, '94, '67, '53, '36], C [125, 115];

Guidebooks: Nelson and Potterfield's *Selected Climbs in the Cascades*, Beckey's *Cascade Alpine Guide 1*.

Directions: From Washington Pass go ten minutes east down Hwy. 2 at signed pullout. Approaches are via Willow Creek or Cedar Creek Routes—five hours. The Wine Spires consist of (north-south) Burgundy, Chianti, Pernod, and Chablis Spires. Kangaroo Ridge is to the south.

26 Goat Wall ☆☆☆☆

South-facing 1,000' metamorphic wall visible as you head up the Methow Valley from the Mazama general store. Large wall, generally undeveloped. Rock is of variable quality and generally brittle with few opportunities for natural protection. Long history of climbs. See Beckey's guidebook (listed below). Beautiful valley setting. Apples in the fall. USFS–Okanagan NF, (509) 662–4335.

Classics: Fun Rock and Dog Rock are roadside crags. Inspiration Route (5.9) follows blunt skyline buttress below and right of steep white main wall. Rumors of a long 5.11 exist.

Ref: S 5/87; Guidebook: Beckey's *Cascade Alpine Guide 1*.

Directions: From Mazama find Fun Wall 1 ½ mi. northwest of town. Continuing northwest, follow Mazama Rd. west under the long wall of Goat Wall.

27 D☆-(Darrington Areas) Squire Creek Wall/Overview ☆☆☆

Complex of mountainous, multibuttressed, slabby, 1,000' knobby faces. Expect long runouts, especially on older 5.7–5.8 routes. The 5.10 cruxes are usually protected, but with old ¼" bolts. The type of climbs here referred to by the locals as "knob trotting." Long, hard approaches, and thus, traditionally an area of low visitation. Good potential exists for new routes. Summer/autumn. USFS–Mt. Baker–Snoqualmie NF, (360) 436–1155.

Classics: Three O'Clock Rock: Silent Running 5.9; Blueberry Hill: West Slab 5.8; Green Giant Buttress.

Ref: AAJ ['79, 71, 70-118], R 97-39; Guidebooks: Gunstoke's *Climbing Guide to Darrington*, Smoot's *Rock Climbing Washington*, WMA's *Traveler's Guide Puget Sound*, Beckey's *Darrington and Index Rock Climbing Guide*, Smoot's *Washington Rock Climbs*, Beckey's *Cascade Alpine Guide 2*.

Directions: From Darrington several large granitic domes lie to the south of town. Squire Creek Wall: Follow Squire Creek Rd. southwest from town for approximately 5 mi. to Squire Creek Wall on right. Wall is to west and involves stream crossing. Other domes: From town drive south on Mountain Loop Hwy. for approximately 3 mi. Turn right (before Clear Creek Campground) on FS 2060 for 5–6 mi. to junction with FS 2065. At junction to southeast is Exfoliation Dome. Follow FS 2065 to southwest past Three O'Clock Wall, Comb Buttress on right, and then at end of road is Green Giant Buttress. See area map in guidebooks for layout of buttresses.

28 D–Green Giant Buttress ✯✯✯

This 1,100′ granite face is one of Washington's most impressive walls. Lots of ancient 1/4′ bolts, now being replaced with newer ones. Some eight- to nine-pitch slab routes. Summer. Free camping. USFS–Mt. Baker–Snoqualmie NF, (360) 436–1155.

Classics: Dreamer IV 9, Fast Lane 11b/c.

Ref: Guidebooks: Gunstoke's *Climbing Guide to Darrington,* Nelson and Potterfield's *Selected Climbs in the Cascades,* Beckey's *Darrington and Index Rock Climbing Guide,* Smoot's *Washington Rock Climbs,* Beckey's *Cascade Alpine Guide 2.*

Directions: From Darrington drive south on Mountain Loop Hwy. for approximately 3 mi. Go right (before Clear Creek Campground) on FS 2060 approximately 6 mi. to road end. Hike trail up Copper Creek to Green Giant Buttress (approximately one hour or 2 mi.).

29 D–Three O'Clock Rock and The Comb ✯✯✯

The "casual" 200′ granite crag of Darrington. More for intermediate and beginner climbers. Summer. Free camping. USFS–Mt. Baker–Snoqualmie NF, (360) 436–1155.

Classics: South Buttress: Big Tree 7, Conan's Crack II 8, The Kone II 9, Tidbits II 10b; Comb: Skyrider 10a.

Ref: AAJ '79, C 56; Guidebooks: Beckey's *Darrington and Index Rock Climbing Guide,* Smoot's *Washington Rock Climbs,* Beckey's *Cascade Alpine Guide 2.*

Directions: From Darrington drive south on Mountain Loop Hwy. for approximately 3 mi. Turn right (before Clear Creek Campground) on FS 2060 for 5 mi. to rock on right fork. Hike a half hour up trail to Three O'Clock Rock and The Comb.

30 D–Exfoliation Dome ✯✯

Serious adventure mountain rock climbs on this 1,000′ granite wall. Difficult descents. Summer. Free camping. USFS–Mt. Baker–Snoqualmie NF, (360) 436–1155.

Classics: Witch Doctor Wall: grade V aid wall; Blueberry Hill: West Buttress 8.

Ref: Guidebooks: Beckey's *Darrington and Index Rock Climbing Guide,* Smoot's *Washington Rock Climbs,* Beckey's *Cascade Alpine Guide 2.*

Directions: From Darrington drive south on Mountain Loop Hwy. for approximately 3 mi. Turn right (before Clear Creek Campground) on FS 2060 for 5–6 mi. to rock. Take FS 2065 (left fork) for approximately 1/2 mi. before Squire Creek Pass Trailhead. One-hour hike to Exfoliation Dome.

31 Static Point ✯✯✯

Granite buttress of high-angle, sustained 400′ friction slabs with long runouts. A remote cliff "discovered" by airplane. Summer. Free camping. Private land.

Classics: American Pie 10a R, On Line 10b, Shock Treatment III 10c.

Ref: Guidebooks: Smoot's *Rock Climbing Washington,* Cramer's *Sky Valley Rock 1999,* WMA's *Traveler's Guide Puget Sound,* Smoot's *Washington Rock Climbs,* Whitelaw's *Private Dancer,* Beckey's *Cascade Alpine Guide 2.*

Directions: From Sultan drive approximately 18 mi. north on Olney Rd. (following left fork) to southeast side of Spada Reservoir. Park near hairpin at southernmost end of reservoir. Hike southeast at logging road thirty minutes. Static Point is in Sultan Basin Recreation Area.

32 O✯–(Olympic National Park) Overview ✯✯✯

Most of the rock in the Olympic Range is friable except for the volcanic outcrops, which tend to be much sounder rock. Glacial wilderness peaks to 8,000′, the king of which is Mt. Olympus at 7,965′. Some parts of the park lie in the rain shadow and receive far less precipitation than others. Be prepared for glacier travel. Backcountry permits required. Varied rock, scenic rainforest, record rainfall, and record trees. Entertainment: Bob's Java Jive in Tacoma. Summer/autumn. Free/pay camping. Backcountry pay permits. NPS, (360) 452–0330.

Classics: Sawtooth Ridge: Mt. Cruiser, The Horn; Royal Basin: Needles Area; Mt. Constance Massif, Mt. Olympus.

Ref: AAJ ['77, 72, 69, 68], OB 4(8/72)-3, S [5/74, 4/70]; Molvar's *Hiking Olympic National Park;* Guidebooks: Olympic Mountain Rescue's *Climber's Guide to the Olympic Mountains,* Beckey's *Climber's Guide to the Cascade and Olympic Mountains of Washington,* Wood's *Olympic Mountains Trail Guide.*

Directions: Olympic Peninsula. Northwest Washington. The most popular of the various areas in the park include: Hurricane Ridge, The Needles, Sawtooth Ridge, and Mt. Constance.

33 O–Hurricane Ridge (Steeple Rock) ✯✯✯

Two-hundred-foot volcanic/metamorphic pinnacles amongst an alpine rock massif. Aptly named weather-wise. Summer. NPS, (360) 452–0330.

Classics: Steeple Rock: Southwest Face 2, Wings 8.

Ref: OB 4(8/82)-19; Guidebooks: Olympic Mountain Rescue's *Climber's Guide to the Olympic Mountains,* Beckey's *Climber's Guide to the Cascade and Olympic Mountains of Washington,* Wood's *Olympic Mountains Trail Guide.*

Directions: From Port Angeles head south on the Hurricane Ridge Rd. Scattered routes off the 17 1/2-mi. Hurricane Ridge Rd. make for easy access.

34 O–The Needles (Gray Wolf Ridge) ✯✯✯

The highest collective group of summits in the Olympics and focal point of alpine activity. Routes of varying length. Also known as the Royal Basin Area. Summer. Free/pay camping. NPS, (360) 452–0330.

Classics: The Incisor, Sundial, Arrowhead 6.

Ref: OB 4(8/82)-22; Guidebooks: Olympic Mountain

Rescue's *Climber's Guide to the Olympic Mountains*, Beckey's *Climber's Guide to the Cascade and Olympic Mountains of Washington*, Wood's *Olympic Mountains Trail Guide*.

Directions: Olympic Peninsula. Northwest Washington. Approach via the Dungeness River Rd. by heading south from Sequim on Hwy. 101 for a few miles. Then turn south onto FS Rd. 2909 to Dungeness River Rd. (usually not free of snow until May–June) to trailhead for The Needles. Hike approximately 7 mi. up Royal Creek.

35 O–Sawtooth Ridge (Flapjack Lakes Area) ✫✫✫

"The pillow lava playground" is the most popular area in the park. Mt. Cruiser is the most popular rock climb in the Olympics. Steep faces with rounded volcanic holds. Summer. Free/pay camping. NPS, (360) 452-0330.

Classics: Mt. Cruiser II 5, The Fin I 5, The Horn I 5, Trylon and Picture Pinnacles.

Ref: OB 4(8/82)-18; Guidebooks: Olympic Mountain Rescue's *Climber's Guide to the Olympic Mountains*, Beckey's *Climber's Guide to the Cascade and Olympic Mountains of Washington*, Wood's *Olympic Mountains Trail Guide*.

Directions: Olympic Peninsula. Northwest Washington. Several approaches to Hurricane Ridge, the most popular ones being through Hamma Hamma on FR 25 to Mildred Lakes north from Hoodsport via Hwy. 119, approaching via Flapjack Lakes (approximately 5 mi.).

36 O–Mt. Constance Massif ✫✫✫

Mt. Constance has approximately 2,000' north-facing volcanic walls. Beginner and intermediate level routes consist of steep gullies and chimneys with sinuous route finding. Summer. Pay camping. NPS, (360) 452-0330.

Classics: Red Dike III 5, West Arête III 4.

Ref: AAJ, OB 4(8/82)-20; Guidebooks: Olympic Mountain Rescue's *Climber's Guide to the Olympic Mountains*, Beckey's *Climber's Guide to the Cascade and Olympic Mountains of Washington*, Wood's *Olympic Mountains Trail Guide*.

Directions: Olympic Peninsula. From Brinnon follow the Dosewallips Rd. 15 mi. up to trailhead access for the Mt. Constance Massif. Leave plenty of time for the Constance Lake Trail hike 4,700' elevation gain.

37 University of Washington Climbing Rock ✫✫

Built in 1975, this artificial 30' outdoor wall was one of the first in the United States before the climbing-wall explosion of the early 1990s. You are supposed to be accompanied by University of Washington student as a guide. The Mountaineers in Seattle are a good source for climbing-library information—open to the public. Vertical Club is a good hangout for the best local rock talk, climbers' meet, etc. Possibly a bootleg guide at Swallow's Nest Shop. State land.

Ref: C 84(6/84)-35; Guidebooks: Smoot's *Rock Climbing Washington*, Smoot's *Washington Rock Climbs*.

Directions: University of Washington Climbing Rock is on the campus of the University of Washington, south of football stadium.

38 Schurman Rock (aka Monitor Rock) ✫✫

Cemented pile of small boulders built in 1939 by WPA. Artificial wall named after Rainier head ranger. Parklike atmosphere. Possibly the first artificial climbing wall in North America.

Ref: R 17(1/87)-44; Guidebooks: Smoot's *Rock Climbing Washington*, Smoot's *Washington Rock Climbs*.

Directions: West Seattle. Schurman Rock is at 5200 Thirty-fifth St. Southwest at Camp William G. Long.

39 Chelan Boulders ✫✫✫

Good 30' granite bouldering and topropes. Great apple harvests in the fall. Wild graffiti on bridge. Autumn–spring. No camping. Private/government land.

Classics: The Cookie 11 toprope.

Ref: M. Cook.

Directions: From Chelan follow Alt. Hwy. 97 to Apple Acres Rd. Hillsides covered with the Chelan Boulders's good rock sit above the apple orchards. Mainly private land—permission necessary. Or, take Hwy. 150 west and turn right into Chelan Station (on switchback) before Hwy. 150 turns right to bridge. An old dam release channel probably has best bet for accessible, good rock climbing in Chelan.

40 Banks Lake Area (Steamboat Rock State Park) ✫✫✫

Steamboat Rock is a columnar basaltic rock rising 1,000' above Banks Lake and a natural landmark used by pilots. Though a climbing backwater, this area has a lot of unclimbed rock—above and below the water. The rock has a tendency to be crumbly. Warm, desert area. Spring/autumn. Free camping. Private land/state park, (800) 452-5687.

Classics: Perfect Basser 11.

Ref: C 102(6/87)-26; J 87(26); Guidebooks: Smoot's *Rock Climbing Washington*, Smoot's *Washington Rock Climbs*.

Directions: From Grand Coulee drive 6 mi. south on Hwy. 155 to several areas near the shore of Banks Lake (bouldering on north shore of second cove, cragging at Highway Rock/Northrup Canyon Rd. across from rest area and at Steamboat Rock State Park). Also Eagle Rock and other isles offer good climbing by boat.

41 Index Town Walls (Upper and Lower) ✫✫✫✫

One of Washington's finest granite crags perched above the green forests of the scenic Skykomish River. Sheer, black-and-white-stained 600' walls rain with steep crack climbs. Stout ratings. Beware the spells of abundant precipitation.

Summer/autumn. Free camping. USFS–Mt. Baker–Snoqualmie NF, (360) 677–2414.

Classics: Lower: Toxic Shock 9, Slow Children 10d, Japanese Gardens 11c, Fifth Force 12b, City Park 13c (A1); Upper (Davis): Holland III 10c, Earwax 11b, Clay 11d; Diamond: Centerfold III 10+, Dark Crystal 11b.

Ref: C [128(11/91)-28, 124, 117, 6/90, 112, 110, 108, 104, 98, 93, 90(6/85)-28, 88, 65], M [125, 117], AAJ ['77, 68, 67], R 38(7/90)-70, S 5/71; Guidebooks: Smoot's *Rock Climbing Washington,* Cramer's *Sky Valley Rock,* WMA's *Traveler's Guide Puget Sound,* Nelson and Potterfield's *Selected Climbs in the Cascades,* Cummins's *Index Town Wall Guide,* Beckey's guides, Smoot's *Washington Rock Climbs,* Harlin's *West,* Smoot and Cranner's *Index Town Walls,* Carlstad and Brooks's *Rock Climbing Leavenworth and Index: A Guide.*

Directions: In Index. Upper Town Walls: Obvious, largest wall above town. Park at area adjacent to junction of road opposite city park and northwest side of railroad tracks. Then cross tracks to north and hike trail past boulderfield to Upper Walls. Lower Town Wall (quickest access—couple of minutes): 1 mi. west on paved road to a right turn into parking lot with trashed milk truck (now gone?). Camping along the river.

42 Steven's Pass (aka Ramone Rock) ✮✮✮

A small, granite, one-pitch crag—a fun pit stop. Hot Springs nearby at pass. Summer. Free camping. USFS–Mt. Baker–Snoqualmie NF, (360) 677–2414.

Classics: Troglodyte in Freeflight 9+, Son of a Pitch 10b, Teenage Lobotomy 11a.

Ref: AAJ '95; Guidebooks: Smoot's *Rock Climbing Washington,* Smoot's *Washington Rock Climbs.*

Directions: From Skykomish drive east on Hwy. 2. At top of Steven's Pass parking lot, drive north on dirt road past cabins and microwave station. Just past microwave station, follow trail north leading to the rock.

43 L✮–(Leavenworth Area) Overview ✮✮✮✮

Superb granite climbing up to 750' for the boulderer, cragger, or multipitched master. Central Washington's mainstay for hard-core rock climbers. Campground at Icicle Canyon. Heavily used area by climbers. Leavenworth is noted for its Bavarian atmosphere—good pie at Der Pizza. Spring: ticks; summer: rattlers; fall: hunters! Backcountry climbs like Prusik Peak under permit entry system—check with USFS in spring/autumn. USFS–Wenatchee NF, (509) 548–6977.

Classics: Castle Rock, Midnight Rock, Every Inch Is Hard 12; Prusik Peak: West Ridge II 7.

Ref: AAJ '68, C [111, 104, 83(5/83)-40, 63, 58, 54], R [99-48, 24, S 1/89; Guidebooks: Beckey's *Cascade Alpine Guide* (Columbia R.), third ed., Smoot's *Rock Climbing Washington,* Kramar's *Leavenworth Rock,* Nelson and Potterfield's *Selected Climbs in the Cascades,* Kramar's *Leavenworth Rock Climbs,* Smoot's *Washington Rock Climbs,*

Harlin's *West,* Carlstad and Brooks's *Rock Climbing Leavenworth and Index, A Guide,* Beckey and Bjornstad's *Guide to Leavenworth Rock Climbing Areas.*

Directions: Leavenworth. Rock described here is within a 10-mi. radius of town.

44 L–Chumstick Snag ✮

An isolated 80' sandstone pinnacle with two routes to the summit. Free camping. Spring/autumn. USFS–Wenatchee NF, (509) 548–6977.

Classics: Standard Route 7, Southwest Face 8 A1.

Ref: Guidebooks: Smoot's *Rock Climbing Washington,* Kramar's *Leavenworth Rock 1996,* Smoot's *Washington Rock Climbs.*

Directions: From Leavenworth drive 4 mi. on Plain Rd. Take a left up Spromberg Canyon. Park at end. Hike up meadow and 1/2 mi. up ridge to Chumstick Snag.

45 L–(TC✮–Tumwater Canyon) Overview and Waterfall Column et al. Jupiter Rock ✮✮✮

The most impressive rock features (1,000' granite big walls) of Tumwater Canyon. A two- to three-day day affair; long, strenuous three-hour approaches with river crossing; difficult descents. Spring/autumn. Free/pay camping. USFS–Wenatchee National Forest, (509) 548–6977.

Classics: Waterfall Column: Original Route III 8, Endgame IV 9; Jupiter Rock: King's Indian IV 8; Raft Rock: Raft Crack 10c.

Ref: AAJ ['82, 80], C 88; Guidebooks: Smoot's *Rock Climbing Washington,* Kramar's *Leavenworth Rock,* Nelson and Potterfield's *Selected Climbs in the Cascades,* Smoot's *Washington Rock Climbs.*

Directions: From Leavenworth drive 7 mi. west of town on Hwy. 2 at mm 94. Waterfall Column and Jupiter Rock (north of Waterfall) sit perched high above Wenatchee River on left. Both are sizeable approaches. Raft Rock directly across river from mm 94, but a boat is necessary to cross Jolanda Lake to get there. Other Tumwater Canyon approaches are usually more approachable.

46 L–Swift Water Picnic Area ✮✮✮

Excellent 20' granite bouldering in the immediate vicinity of the picnic area and on the opposite side of the highway. Perhaps one of Leavenworth's better bouldering circuits. Spring/autumn. No camping. USFS–Wenatchee National Forest, (509) 548–6977.

Ref: Guidebook: Kramar's *Leavenworth Rock.*

Directions: From Leavenworth drive 7 mi. west of town on Hwy. 2 to mm 92.3 to Swift Water Picnic Area. Park. Bouldering problems a stone's throw from car and also across highway to left.

47 L–TC–Rattlesnake Rock and Piton Tower ✷✷

Piton Tower is a detached granite pinnacle beside Rattlesnake Rock. Spring/autumn. Free camping. USFS–Wenatchee National Forest, (509) 548-6977.

Classics: Rattlesnake: Tubbing at Der Ritterhoff 11a, Rock 'n' Rattle 11c, Zweible 12b; Piton: East Face Notch 10-, West Face- 10+.

Ref: Guidebooks: Smoot's *Rock Climbing Washington*, Kramar's *Leavenworth Rock*, Smoot's *Washington Rock Climbs*.

Directions: From Leavenworth slither west up Hwy. 2 to approximately mm 95.7 (or 8/10 mi. upriver from Castle Rock). Park at roadside pullout south of crags Rattlesnake Rock and Piton Tower, which are perched 600' above river on right side of road. Grunt twenty minutes uphill.

48 L–TC–Castle Rock ✷✷✷✷

Most popular crag in Leavenworth, hence, popular on weekends. Beautiful 300' granite routes. History of climbs dates back to 1940s. Camp at Icicle Creek Canyon. Spring–autumn. Free camping. USFS–Wenatchee National Forest, (509) 548-6977.

Classics: Upper: Canary 8, Crack of Doom 9+, MF Direct 11b; Lower: Saber 4, Midway 5, Canary 8, South Face Jello Tower 8, Saints 8+, The Bone 9, Angel 10a, Brass Balls 10b.

Ref: C 63; Guidebooks: Smoot's *Rock Climbing Washington*, Kramar's *Leavenworth Rock*, Christensen's *The Royal Columns: A Rock Climber's Guide*, Smoot's *Washington Rock Climbs*.

Directions: From Leavenworth drive approximately 3 mi. west on Hwy. 2 to mm 96.5 and large parking area on right. Castle Rock is visible roadside. Midnight Rock is higher up but follows the trail past Castle Rock.

49 L–TC–Midnight and Noontime Rocks ✷✷✷

A premiere 150' granite Washington crag. Midnight Rocks has the best concentration of steep Leavenworth cracks, aka the "Cookie Cliff" of Washington. Noontime is small, flawless wall right of Midnight with difficult climbs. Raptor restrictions May–July (uncertain; call ahead). Spring/autumn. Free/pay camping. USFS–Wenatchee National Forest, (509) 548-6977.

Classics: Yellowbird 9, Curtains 10a, Sometimes a Great Notion 10d, Spellbound 11b, R.O.T.C 11c, Steven's Pass Motel 11d, Supercrack 12c; Noontime: Gulliver's Travels 12a.

Ref: C [93, 88, 65, 56, 54], S [31(5/85)-31, 7/64]; Guidebooks: Smoot's *Rock Climbing Washington*, Kramar's *Leavenworth Rock*, Smoot's *Washington Rock Climbs*.

Directions: From Leavenworth drive approximately 3 mi. west on Hwy. 2 to mm 96.5 and large parking area on right. Hike up and above Castle Rock on the Castle Rock Summit Trail for one hour to Midnight and Noontime Rocks. Fierce approach to fierce climbs.

50 L–TC–Tumwater Tower and Torture Chamber Bouldering ✷✷

Tumwater Tower: Small granite pinnacle obvious on hillside directly across river from mm 98. Every Inch Is Hard, a 5.12 testpiece by the worldly Dick Cilley, is very short crack directly above first pullout on left 3/10 mi. west of Icicle Creek Canyon Rd. Tumwater Tower is seldom visited because of the approach, but Torture Chamber Bouldering is roadside and easily accessed. Beware traffic on Hwy. 2. Spring/autumn. Free/pay camping. USFS–Wenatchee National Forest, (509) 548-6977.

Classics: Normal Route 5, Highway Route 8, Every Inch Is Hard 12.

Ref: C 63; AAJ ['82, 80]; Guidebooks: Smoot's *Rock Climbing Washington*, Smoot's *Washington Rock Climbs*.

Directions: From Leavenworth drive 2 mi. west on Hwy. 2. Park. Cross bridge at Boulder Picnic Area. Hike south along river. Torture Chamber Bouldering is just 4/10 mi. west on Hwy. 2 from Icicle Canyon Rd. on right.

51 L–Sandy Slab ✷

Conspicuous 250' sandstone roadside bolted slab, but loud and noisy. Loose rock. A beginner's climbing area from another era, i.e., possibly the Paleozoic. Autumn. Government land.

Classics: Suncups 8+.

Ref: Guidebooks: Smoot's *Rock Climbing Washington*, Kramar's *Leavenworth Rock*, Beckey and Bjornstad's *Guide to Leavenworth Rock Climbing Areas*, Smoot's *Washington Rock Climbs*.

Directions: From Leavenworth drive 2 2/10 mi. east on Hwy. 2. Sandy Slab is across from wide parking area.

52 L–Icicle Creek Canyon ✷✷✷✷✷

Potpourri of bouldering, 200' granite craglets, topropes, and exploring in forested river canyon. Stacked cliffs between benches offer climbers pseudo-multipitch routes as they proceed up large hillside. Some areas within canyon are on private land. Please respect private land by staying off. Ticks bad in spring. Summer/autumn. Free camping. Private/USFS–Wenatchee National Forest, (509) 548-6977.

Classics: At Snow Creek parking area: Deb's Crack 10c, Air Roof 11b; 8 Mile: Classic Crack 8+; Alphabet Rocks: Dog Leg Crack 8+; Rat Creek Boulder: 10d; Careno Crag: Regular Route 10b; Goat Rock: Knobs of Shame 10a, Great Outdoors 10d, Shitz on a Ritz 11a; Givler's Dome: Givler's Crack 8, Bo Derek 10b, Mastodon Roof 11, Pivotal Moment 11+, Never Never 12d; Duty Dome: Off Duty 10a; The Sword Area: 4th of July: Facelift 10a.

Ref: C [161-70, 93, 92, 88, 71, 63], S 7/70; Guidebooks: Smoot's *Rock Climbing Washington*, Kramar's *Leavenworth Rock*, Kramar's *A Topo Guide to Icicle Canyon Rock Climbs*, Smoot's *Washington Rock Climbs*.

Directions: From Leavenworth, on the west side of town on Hwy. 2, turn left onto Icicle Creek Rd. At second ninety-degree turn, climbing areas begin with the Playpen up and right (from barn and fence). From the Playpen mileages are Mountaineer's Dome, $^9/_{10}$ mi. on right (north); Bolt Rock, 1 $^3/_{10}$ on right; Snow Creek, 1 $^1/_2$ mi. on right; Deb's Crack, 1 $^9/_{10}$ mi. on right; Bruce's Boulder, 2 $^8/_{10}$ mi. on left; Domestic Dome, 2 $^9/_{10}$ mi. on right; Givler's Dome, 3 2/10 mi. on right; Warrior Wall, 3 $^1/_2$ mi. on right; Icicle Buttress, 3 $^7/_{10}$ mi. on right; 8-Mile Campground, 4 $^3/_{10}$ mi. on left; 8-Mile Buttress, 4 $^4/_{10}$ mi. on right; Classic Crack, 4 $^8/_{10}$ mi. on left and down; Bridge Creek Camp-ground, 5 $^7/_{10}$ mi. on left; The Sword, 6 mi. on right; Egg Rock, 6 $^2/_{10}$ mi. on right; and 4th of July Rock, 6 $^8/_{10}$ mi. on right. Camp at 8-Mile or Bridge Creek Campgrounds.

53 L–Snow Creek Wall ★★★★

At 750', largest granite wall in Icicle Creek Area. Routes up to seven pitches. Super-popular on weekends—prepare to queue up. Descent from top is hike off left side. Summer. Free camping. USFS–Wenatchee National Forest, (509) 548–6977.
Classics: Outer Space III 9, Orbit III 9, Hyper Space 10d, Edge Of Space 11c, Iconoclast 11b/12.
Ref: AAJ ['72-114, 66-131], C [88, 4(11/70)], S [7/70, 12/64]; Guidebooks: Smoot's *Rock Climbing Washington*, Nelson and Potterfield's *Selected Climbs in the Cascades*, Harlin's *West*, Smoot's *Washington Rock Climbs*.
Directions: From Leavenworth drive 4 mi. south on Icicle Creek Canyon Rd. Park at Snow Creek parking. Hike one hour from Snow Creek Wall Trailhead.

54 L–Peshastin Pinnacles State Park ★★

Magical, cream-colored 250' sandstone slabs and pinnacles tilt their backs above luscious apple orchards. Peshastin Pinnacles is the well-known "dry" area of Leavenworth. Main formations of Peshastin Pinnacles include: Orchard Rock, Martian Tower/Slab, Dinosaur Tower, Sunset Slab, Grand Central Tower, and Sickle Slab. Friable sandstone rock, e.g., 50' Trigger Finger Spire (toppled in 1978). Access Fund purchase reopened area. Washington's first climbing park managed by State Parks Office. Gate closes at dusk. In September–October, apple orchards yield their bounty. Spring–autumn. State park, (800) 233–0321.
Classics: Dinosaur: Washboard 10b, Dr. Leakey 11b; Sickle Slab: Windward Dir. 8; Austrian Slab: Fakin' It 10a; Grand Central: Lightning Crack 8, West Face 8/10, White Lightnin' 11a R.
Ref: AAJ '68; C [126, 116, 91, 88], S [18(5/72)-1, 6/72]; Guidebooks: Smoot's *Rock Climbing Washington*, Smoot's *Washington Rock Climbs*.
Directions: From Leavenworth go a few mi. east on Hwy. 2 just north past Dryden and visible from road. Follow signs from Hwy. 2 onto north Dryden Rd. approximately $^3/_{10}$ mi. past apple orchards to gate.

55 Tum Tum Canyon and Painted (Pictograph) Rocks ★★★

Steep, 200' overhanging granite for pump prospecting. Scenic recreational lake area. Spring/autumn. Pay camping. Government/private land.
Classics: U Name It 6, R.H. Factor 8, Pygmalion 9, Slim Line 10, Smooth Move 10, Lightening Line 11, Battle Star Galactica 11+.
Ref: C 102(6/87)-22; Guidebooks: Smoot's *Rock Climbing Washington*, Speaker's *Spokane Rock Climbs*, Loomis's *A Guide to Rock Climbing in the Spokane Area*.
Directions: From Spokane drive thirty minutes west on Hwy. 291 past town of Tum Tum. Continue west to Tum Tum Canyon and turn right (sharp diagonal) at houses. Just beyond (5 $^8/_{10}$ mi. from town) is Indian Painted Rocks before Corkscrew Canyon Rd.

56 Little Spokane River Natural Area (Indian Painted Rocks) ★★

An abundance of 50' granite outcrops, though some can be grainy. Needs exploration. Indian paintings of same origin as Kila Cliffs and Tum Tum's Indian Pictograph Rocks. Rattlesnakes abundant in summer. Spring/autumn. Government/private land.
Ref: I. Hickman; Delorme's *Washington Atlas and Gazetteer*.
Directions: Northwest Spokane. Take Waikiki west. Turn west on Rutter Pkwy. to parking at Indian Painted Rocks parking. Trail leaves parking area. Rocks obvious on hillside. More rock above private estates east of park along Rutter Pkwy. Possibly private land and access.

57 Minnehaha Park and Beacon Hill ★★★

Minnehaha Park is popular city crag with a history of good bouldering and short 80' granite lead climbs. Spring/autumn. Camping at Riverside State Park in northwest Spokane. City of Spokane Parks, (509) 625–6758.
Classics: Bat Crack 6, Diagonal 8, Don Quixote 10, Screaming Finger; Bouldering: Tarantula Traverse V2, Maginot Line V2, Battle of the Bulge V3, To Have and 2 Hold V8.
Ref: C [124, 120-125, 110-35, 102, 94, 70, 63, 60], R 76-30; Sherman's *Stone Crusade;* Guidebooks: Smoot's *Rock Climbing Washington*, Speaker's *Spokane Rock Climbs*, Loomis's *A Guide to Rock Climbing in the Spokane Area*.
Directions: In Spokane. Drive 2 mi. east of Spokane Community College on Spokane Rd. Rocks in Minnehaha Park lie 1 $^9/_{10}$ mi. east of Green St. Bridge over Spokane River or across from Upriver Dr. Dam on Spokane River. Other small bouldering areas to check out in Spokane include: 1) 1 $^2/_{10}$ mi. east on Upriver Dr. from Minnehaha parking. 2) North of junction I-90 and Pines Rd., good. 3) Along Little Spokane River near Wandermere Golf Course, a north-facing crag.

58 Dishman Hills Recreation Area (aka Dishman Rocks) ★★★

Several 90' granite walls in nice forested area. Spring/autumn. Pay camping. City park, (509) 477–4730.
Classics: Kling-on 11a, Rock 106 11a, Firestone 11b, Slave Labor 12a, Body Scarfer 12a.

Ref: C [110, 102]; Guidebooks: Smoot's *Rock Climbing Washington,* Speaker's *Spokane Rock Climbs 1996,* Loomis's *A Guide to Rock Climbing in the Spokane Area.*

Directions: In east Spokane. At corner of Sprague and Dishman. Dishman Rocks lie southwest of intersection. One access is south of Sprague on Sargent. After short way, park on left. Another approach is 1 $^6/_{10}$ mi. south on Dishman from junction with Sprague.

59 Rocks of Sharon ✫✫✫

Local 80′ granite crag with 5.6 to 5.9 routes. Spring/ autumn. County park.

Ref: Guidebook: Loomis's *A Guide to Rock Climbing in the Spokane Area.*

Directions: In southeast Spokane. Take Palouse Hwy. to Ben Burr Rd. to Jamieson Rd. to Krell Hill. Hike east to Rocks of Sharon.

60 Alpine Lakes Wilderness (approximately 7,700′) ✫✫✫

From scrambling to 500′ volcanic sheer rock walls, e.g., 2,200′ east face of Mt. Index, Alpine Lakes Wilderness offers a panoply of climbing discoveries in a vast collection of alpine peaks. Expect varied rock conditions—loose, vegetated. Summer. Free camping. Call ahead for backcountry permits. USFS–Wenatchee NF, (509) 548-6977.

Classics: Chimney Rock, Lemah Peak, Three Queens, Mt. Index.

Ref: AAJ ['61, 52, 46], *Mountaineer* ['70, 54, 52, 30], S [10/71, 5/65, 9/62]; Guidebook: Beckey's *Cascade Alpine Guide* (Columbia River), third ed.

Directions: Alpine Lakes Wilderness Area expands north from just north of Snoqualmie Pass on north side of Hwy. 90 to Hwy. 2 at Scenic. This immense backcountry area in the Central Cascades of Washington holds old and potential rock climbs in its reaches. Look to the following peaks for climbing sojourns: Three Queens, Chimney Rock, Lemah Peaks, Mt. Daniel, Cathedral Rock, Garfield Mountain, and Mt. Index.

61 Wenatchee Mountains (Mt. Stuart/Cashmere Crags) ✫✫✫✫

The Wenatchees are generally known as a more arid range of the Pacific Mountains; hence, generally drier weather for rock climbers. Mt. Stuart is a renowned alpine classic and the second highest granitic peak in the state at 9,415′. Nearby Dragontail Peak's Backbone Ridge offers a classic IV 5.9 route. But, "draggin' tail" here could result in a "lightning bolt" from the top. Summer. Free/pay camping. USFS–Wenatchee NF, (509) 548-6977.

Classics: Mt. Stuart: North Ridge IV 6 (big wall), Dir North Ridge 8; Dragontail Peak: Serpentine Arête 8, Backbone Ridge IV 5.9; Prusik Peak: West Ridge, South Face II 9; Cashmere Crags.

Ref: AAJ ['89-141, 89-128, 84, 77, 68, 66, 63, 60, 51, 49], C [132, 125(4/91)-74], *Mountaineer* ['70, 67], S [7/84, 7/70,

11/67]; Beckey's *Challenge of the North Cascades;* Guidebooks: Beckey's *Cascade Alpine Guide* (Columbia River), third ed., Nelson and Potterfield's *Selected Climbs in the Cascades,* Steck and Roper's *Fifty Classic Climbs.*

Directions: From Leavenworth follow Icicle Creek Canyon Rd. 8 ½ mi. to Stuart Lakes Trail at Bridge Creek campground. Turn left on Eightmile Rd. for 4 mi. to Stuart Lakes Trail. Hike south/southwest for approximately 5 mi. for Mt. Stuart/Dragontail climbs. Also accessible via Jack Creek off Icicle Canyon or Ingalls Creek off Hwy. 97 (both with longer approach time). The Wenatchees are a huge region of granite west/southwest of Leavenworth. Mt. Stuart: Cashmere Crags encompass a broad back-country area of innumerable, polished, granite spires ranging from Icicle Creek on the north, Mill Creek on east, Ingalls Creek on south, and Snow Creek glaciers on west. Several access points. Obtain area maps.

62 Little Si ✫✫✫

Possibly the best sport-climbing crag in the state. About sixty steep, 200′ volcanic sport routes on "rhino rock" feature hard small hold moves in-between jugs with routes up to 5.13 on the classic World Wall. Nice 4-mi. hike up Mt. Si. Summer/autumn. Denny Creek Campground (pay) farther east on I-90. Department of Natural Resources, (360) 902-1001.

Classics: Reptiles and Amphibians 8, Jug or Not 10, Goddess 10c, Godflesh 11c, Rainy Day Women 12a, Orgasmatron 12, Bust the Rhythm 12c, Technorigine 12c, Hydrophobia 12d, Chronic 13b.

Ref: C 180-29, R [100-115, 62]; Guidebooks: WMA's *Traveler's Guide Puget Sound,* Smoot's *Rock Climbing Washington: Selected Sport Climbs in Western Washington,* Burdo's *Exit 32* (Little Si), Smoot's *Rock Climbing Washington.*

Directions: Little Si is located at exit 32 on I-90. From North Bend go southeast on Hwy. 202 to Mt. Si Rd. Follow Mt. Si Rd. across Snoqualmie River and turn left, following to parking for Little Si. Hike down 434th Ave. southeast ¼ mi to signed trailhead. Go up trail to second step; turn left onto small path (bog). Turn left at next trail for ½ mi. to The Woods, World Wall, and Canopy Crag. Approach time: twenty minutes.

63 Denny Creek Area (approximately 5,600′) (Snoqualmie Pass) ✫✫✫

On the 400′ east face of Chair Peak sits its best rock climbing (death pianos—but good ice climbing). The Tooth's 500′ east face is its longest. Mostly sound volcanic rock. Nearby Guye Peak also offers technical rock through intermittent bands via the Improbable Traverse and Kennedy-Crooks Route (II 5.7). Room for more difficult routes on sound rock. Summer. Free camping. USFS–Mt. Baker–Snoqualmie NF, (360) 677-2414.

Classics: Chair Peak: East Face 5, Tooth Rock.

Ref: *Mountaineer* ['31, 11/28, '20]; Guidebooks: Beckey's *Cascade Alpine Guide* (Columbia River), third ed., Smoot's *Rock Climbing Washington.*

Directions: Just west of Snoqualmie Pass on north side of I–90. Take Denny Creek exit. Go north on Denny Creek Trail. The rock-lined ridge above Denny Creek includes Chair Peak and The Tooth.

64 Snoqualmie Pass (aka Fun Forest) ★★★

Fun, though noisy, tiny top-of-the-pass granite crags. Highway visible. Summer. Free camping. USFS–Mt. Baker–Snoqualmie NF, (360) 677-2414.

Classics: Wild Mouse 10d, Clash City Crack 11b, Scarab 12.

Ref: C [104, 88]; Guidebooks: Smoot's *Rock Climbing Washington*, Smoot's *Washington Rock Climbs*, Beckey's *Cascade Alpine Guide* (Columbia River), third ed.

Directions: Just west of Snoqualmie Pass on north side of Hwy. 90. Take Denny Creek exit. Go northeast about 1 mi. Park. Hike through tunnel under I–90 to the Fun Forest.

65 Swauk Pinnacles ●

Sandstone spires similar to Peshastin Pinnacles, but higher (200'), hence cooler, elevation and much farther from the nearest tavern. Though routes are established, rock may be mostly poor. Bring water—hot in summer. Primitive camping or established USFS sites at Swauk or Tronsen Camp-grounds. K. Dwight writes, "With the obvious lack of attention over the years, anyone who puts forth the effort to climb the sandstone mayhem available in this desert alpine setting will surely be disappointed. Plagued by 1/4" hardware store bolts and a nasty tendency to exfoliate major portions of existing climbs, the area will appeal to only a special breed. The previous two star rating is far overstated, and this area deserves a Black Hole rating because it indeed sucks the limelight from such nearby areas as Leavenworth and Vantage." Spring–autumn. Pay/free camping. USFS– Wenatchee NF, (509) 548-6977.

Classics: Northarctus Rock.

Ref: K. Dwight 7/98; C 114(6/89)-24; Guidebook: Boyle's *Swauk Pinnacles: A Climber's Guide*.

Directions: From Leavenworth go 5 mi. east on Hwy. 2 to Hwy. 97. Take Hwy. 97 south to Swauk Pass. Swauk Pinnacles are approximately 2 mi. west of pass. Approach via FS 7340 for north areas: Northarctus Rock (thirty minutes) or FS 7324 (Scotty Creek Rd.) to FS 7234-500 for south areas (Sphinx/Red Dike/Sentinel).

66 Spire Rock ★★

A man-made 25' spire of natural rock. May be reserved from 6:00 A.M. to 3:00 P.M. for group use. No chipping allowed . . . huh. Spring–autumn. County park.

Ref: Petroske; S 2/74; Guidebooks: Phillips and Webster's *Spire Rock, Washington (Seattle)*.

Directions: Tacoma. Spire Rock is at Sprinker Recreation Center at 14824 South C St.

Cranking vertical French fries at Frenchman's Coulee.

67 Frenchman's Coulee (aka Champs de Brione or Vantage) ★★

Bon Roche! Several walls of 90' basalt columns will cool your cragging fever. The signature "French fry" columns here have a colorful, yellow-green lichen coat. Watch out! Some entire columns have pitched off eliciting the natural question, "Do shakes come with those fries?" More than 300 routes up to 5.12 in a raw, beautiful high desert environment. Routes developed as early as 1953. As this area is arid and usually dry, it's a good place to head when it's wet in Seattle. Indian Feathers camping at 1 mi. This area is also known as Indian Nations. Camping at boat launch. Rattlers in summer. Autumn–spring. Free camping. BLM, (509) 665-2100.

Classics: Party in Your Pants 5.8, Pioneer 5.8, Spinach Before Dessert 5.9, Silhouette 5.10a, George and Martha 5.10a, Sex Party 5.10, Sinsemilla 5.10c, Desert Dessert 5.11a, Stems and Seeds 5.11b, Corner Stone 5.11+, Red M&M's 5.12, Jihad 5.12, Lingerie 5.12+.

Ref: C [187-58, 117-131, 6/87, 102]; Guidebooks: Smoot's *Rock Climbing Washington*, Ford and Yoder's *Frenchman Coulee: A Rock Climber's Guide*, Stanley's *Vantage Rock: A Climber's Guide to Frenchman's Coulee*, Eminger and Kittel's

The Washington Desert: A Rock and Ice Climber's Guide to Frenchman Coulee.
Directions: From Vantage go 6 mi. east on I–90 to exit 143 (Champs de Brione Winery). Turn left off exit for 8/10 mi. and turn left on Old Vantage Hwy. (road to Wanapum Dam Reservoir). Several named areas: Indian Feathers at 1 mi., Agathla Tower at 1 ½ mi. on left, Kingpins Columns at 2 mi. Other areas include Middle East, Zig Zag Wall, and Outland.

68 Gloyd Seeps Wildlife Area ☆☆☆

Repetitively tiered terraces of 80′ basalt columns in North Columbia Wildlife Basin Area. Routes developed by Intermountain Alpine Club, Pasco. Good potential for new routes. Autumn–spring. Free camping. Government land.
Classics: Hard-headed Woman 10a.
Ref: J. Bernhard.
Directions: From Soap Lake seep east on Hwy. 28 and in a few miles turn south on dirt road to Adrian. Continue past Adrian to basalt columns in Gloyd Seeps Wildlife Area.

69 Fife's Peaks (6,917′) ☆☆☆

Two mi. of 200′ andesite outcrops and pinnacles on forested ridge named after placer miner. Fife's Peaks exist in the likes of: Cannonhole Pinnacle, Mainmast, Mt. Aix, Buffalo Hump, Bootjack Rock, and Spectator Spire. Described best as crumbling, loose rock. Summer/autumn. Free camping. USFS–Mt. Baker–Snoqualmie NF, (360) 825–6585.
Ref: *Mountaineer '52*; Guidebook: Beckey's *Cascade Alpine Guide* (Columbia River), third ed.
Directions: From junction of Hwy. 123 and Hwy. 410, go east on Hwy. 410 to Pleasant Valley. Spectacular formations can be accessed via Crow Lake Trail or Fife's Ridge Trail.

70 Cayuse Pass/Cupola Rock (6,600′) ☆☆

One- to two-pitch routes on good volcanic rock. Super scenic views of Rainier on a clear day. Summer. Free camping. NPS, Mt. Rainier, (360) 569–2211, ext. 3314.
Ref: Guidebook: Beckey's *Cascade Alpine Guide I.*
Directions: Cayuse Pass: Short one-pitch opportunities on good rock also available from Cayuse Pass at junction of Hwy. 120 and Hwy. 410 and east up Hwy. 410. Cupola Rock: From Chinook Pass on Hwy. 410, go 3 mi. north past Sheep Lake, ¼ mi. east of Sourdough Gap.

71 Mt. Rainier National Park (14,410′) ☆☆☆☆☆

Visible from more than 100 mi. away, Mt. Rainier is the highest point in Washington (14,410′), with more than 35 square mi. of ice and six glaciers. Though not technically a rock climb and definitely not a sport route, Rainier is included here for its title of the renowned summit and highest point of Washington. To reach the summit, twenty-five routes exist. For the inexperienced in glacial travel, guide services are available locally. First ascent recorded as early as 1857 to the summit area, 1870 to the top. (Crummy rock, but good shoveling.) Emmons Glacier is notably the largest glacier in the Lower 48. If glacier climbing appeals to your senses, try Mt. Adams (12,276′) or Mt. St. Helens (9,677′) to the south along the Pacific Crest chain. Little Tahoma is a high satellite of Rainier. Small areas, like Tokaloo Rock, exist in park for rock climbing. May/September. Pay climbing permits and pay camping. NPS, (360) 569–2211 ext. 3314; www.nps.gov/mora/.
Classics: Mt. Rainier: Liberty Ridge, Emmons Glacier, Disappointment Cleaver, Ptarmigan Ridge.
Ref: AAJ ['98, '97, '94, '76-441, 74, 66-69], C [185-92, 105 (routes), 72], OB 17(10/74), R [100-71, 84-76, 81-18], S [5/88, 7/86, 5/73, 3/73, 5/72, 9/71, 7/71, 4/71, 10/69, 9/68, 11/67, 3/67, 11/66, 5/66, 11/65, 9/65, 4/65, 6/64, 1/63]; Filley's *Big Fact Book About Mt. Rainier, The Challenge of Rainier;* Guidebooks: Beckey's *Cascade Alpine Guide* (Columbia River), third ed., *Mt. Rainier High Traverse Tour Climbing Guide Number 3, Mt. Rainier Climbing Guide Number 2, Mt. Rainier Climbing Guide Number 1,* Nelson and Potter-field's *Selected Climbs in the Cascades,* Smoot's *Summit Guide to Cascade Volcanoes,* Smoot's *Adventure Guide to Mt. Rainier: Hiking, Climbing, and Skiing in Mt. Rainier National Park,* Steck and Roper's *Fifty Classic Climbs,* Molenaar's *Climbing History and Routes of Mt. Rainier,* Meany's *Mt. Rainier: A Record of Exploration.*
Directions: From Seattle drive south on Hwy. 410 to Mt. Rainier National Park. Several access points around park.

72 Cowlitz Chimneys (7,600′)/Governor's Ridge (6,614′) ☆☆☆

Cowlitz Chimneys and Governor's Ridge: eastern 200′ rhyolite flank of Mt. Rainier National Park. Mainly rock scrambles. Cowlitz Chimneys and Governor's Ridge are both rows of pinnacled summits overshadowed by Mt. Rainier. Pay camping. NPS, (360) 569–2211, ext. 3314.
Ref: *Mountaineer* 1915; Guidebook: Beckey's *Cascade Alpine Guide* (Columbia River), third ed.
Directions: From Cayuse Pass on Hwy. 410, hike west. See Beckey's guide.

73 Tatoosh Range (approximately 6,900′) ☆☆☆

This satellite of volcanic peaks to the south of Mt. Rainier generates interest among rock scramblers seeking different perspective of Washington's famed 14,000′ peak. Pinnacle Peak, called the "Matterhorn of the Cascades," catches the spotlight, although Unicorn Peak (6,917′), a good early season route, is the highest. Most rock climbs are scrambles on enjoyable fourth- or easy fifth-class rock. Summer. Pay camping. NPS, (360) 569–2211, ext. 3314.
Ref: S 9/65; Guidebooks: Beckey's *Cascade Alpine Guide* (Columbia River), third ed.

Directions: From Packwood go north on Hwy. 12, then north on Hwy. 123. Turn left on Stevens Canyon Rd. to Reflection Lakes. Hike to Pinnacle-Plummer Saddle in the Tatoosh Range. Other approaches available.

74 Goat Rocks Wilderness (8,200') (The Palisades) ✮✮✮

Your old goat legs ain't what they used to be? Try climbing amongst the snowfields, glaciers, and 450' pinnacle rocks harbored in rugged terrain. An area of technically easy but adventuresome mountaineering routes with glacier travel and minimal rock climbing involved to reach classic summit features. Summer. USFS–Gifford Pinchot NF, (360) 891-5000.
Ref: *Mazama* ['56, '61]; Guidebook: Beckey's *Cascade Alpine Guide* (Columbia River), third ed.
Directions: Just west of the town of White Pass on Hwy. 12. South of road. Complicated approaches. From east via South Fork Tieton River to Conrad Falls. From west start at Packwood on Hwy. 12 and go south on FR 21 to Snowgrass Flat. Hike west to Goat Rocks Wilderness. Prominent formations include: Big Horn, Little Horn, Black Thumb, Goat Citadel, and Mt. Curtis Gilbert.

75 The Palisades ✮

An impressive, 450' columnar jointed basalt wall up to 486' high along the Clear Fork River. Unfortunately, mossy rock. Incredible large trees with grade 6 tree trunks into Mt. Rainier National Park. Summer. USFS–Gifford Pinchot NF, (360) 891-5000.
Ref: *Mazama* ['56, '61]; Guidebook: *Beckey's Cascade Alpine Guide* (Columbia River), third ed.
Directions: Just west of the town of White Pass on Hwy. 12. The Palisades are south of road. Signed pull-in.

76 T✮-(Tieton River Area) Overview ✮✮✮✮

Columnar 200' andesite crack crags along the Tieton River with several areas to keep craggers busy. One can leave the Washington rains behind in these arid sage lands. Heat and rattlesnakes in summer. Spring/autumn. Free/pay camping. Oak Creek Wildlife Recreation Area, (509) 653-2390.
Ref: C [124-42, 122-30, 110-32]; Guidebooks: Smoot's *Rock Climbing Washington*, Christensen's *Tieton River Rock: A Climber's Guide.*
Directions: From Yakima go northwest to junction of Hwy. 410 and Hwy. 12. Tieton River area rock columns extend from 2–20 mi. west on Hwy. 12 to Rimrock Lake.

77 T–Royal Columns ✮✮✮

Many columnar, 90' andesite cracks and sport routes along the Tieton River. Raptor restrictions February–July. Spring-autumn. Free camping. State Wildlife Area, (509) 653-2390.
Classics: Inca Roads 9, Orange Sunshine 10, Solar King 11, 12a.

Ref: C 10/88-32; Guidebooks: Smoot's *Rock Climbing Washington*, Christensen's *Tieton River Rock: A Climber's Guide*, Christensen's *The Royal Columns: A Rock Climber's Guide*, Smoot's *Washington Rock Climbs.*
Directions: From Yakima trend northwest to junction of Hwy. 410 and Hwy. 12. Then go 2 mi. more on Hwy. 12. Across road from Oak Creek Game Range Headquarters. Cross bridge (sign reads ROYAL COLUMNS) and cut right through deer fence. Reasonable trail on switchbacks to rocks.

78 T–The Bend (aka The Crack House) ✮✮✮

Fine, one-pitch 170' columnar basalt crack climbing. Spring-autumn. Free camping. Oak Creek Wildlife Recreation Area, (509) 653-2390.
Classics: Ed's Jam 8, Introductory Offer, Hot Botany 10.
Ref: C (10/88)-32; Guidebook: Christensen's *Tieton River Rock: A Climber's Guide.*
Directions: From Yakima drive northwest to junction of Hwy. 410 and Hwy. 12. Then proceed 3 ½ mi. west on Hwy. 12 to The Bend.

79 T–Moon Rocks ✮✮✮✮

This crag offers 110' feet of andesite that features some volcanic cracks and a few nice face climbs. Ban on climbing during falcon season (February to July)—check with local officials. Spring-autumn. Free camping. Oak Creek Wildlife Recreation Area, (509) 653-2390.
Classics: Straight Talk 10, Moonstruck Pillar 11c.
Ref: C [10/88, 122]; Guidebooks: Smoot's *Rock Climbing Washington*, Christensen's *Tieton River Rock: A Climber's Guide*, Smoot's *Washington Rock Climbs.*
Directions: From Yakima go northwest to junction of Hwy. 410 and Hwy. 12. Then drive 5 ¹⁄₁₀ mi. west on Hwy. 12. Park. Hike on river footbridge to the west to Moon Rocks.

80 T–Rainbow Rocks ✮✮

More 60' andesite basalt columns. Spring/autumn. Free/pay camping. Oak Creek Wildlife Recreation Area, (509) 653-2390.
Classics: Black Celebration 11-.
Ref: Guidebooks: Smoot's *Rock Climbing Washington*, Christensen's *Tieton River Rock: A Climber's Guide*, Smoot's *Washington Rock Climbs.*
Directions: From Yakima go northwest to the junction of Hwy. 410 and Hwy. 12. Then drive 12 mi. west on Hwy. 12. Go north of road. Rainbow Rocks are east of Trout Lodge Cafe.

81 T–Wildcat ✮✮✮

More 200' columnar rock, though maybe not as solid as other areas. Spring/autumn. Free/pay camping. USFS.
Classics: Wildcat Crack 11, Anaphylactic Shock 11+.

Ref: C 10/88-32; Guidebook: Christensen's *Tieton River Rock: A Climber's Guide.*
Directions: From Yakima drive northwest to the junction of Hwy. 410 and Hwy. 12. Go 20 ½ mi. west on Hwy. 12. Then go 2 ⁹/₁₀ mi. north on Rd. 1306. Park for Wildcat.

82 T–Kloochman Rock (4,532') ✰✰✰

This stunning landmark visible across Rimrock Lake from Hwy. 12 is a northwest to southeast 200′ oval-shaped rock hump with distinct peaks on its northwest side. Unhealthy volcanic rock resembles vertical oatmeal. *Kloochman* is Chinook for "wife." Easy though loose technical rock scrambles make for an interesting summit. Spring/autumn. Free/pay camping. USFS–Gifford Pinchot NF, (360) 891–5000.
Ref: C 10/88-32; Douglas's *Of Men and Mountains* Guidebooks: Beckey's *Cascade Alpine Guide* (Columbia River), third ed., Christensen's *Tieton River Rock: A Climber's Guide.*
Directions: From Yakima drive northwest to junction of Hwy. 410 and Hwy. 12. Go 20 ½ mi. west on Hwy. 12. Just past Riverbend Campground and before the town of Rimrock, turn left onto Tieton Reservoir Rd. (FR 12), then turn left onto Lost Lake Rd. (FR 1402). Kloochman Rock is on the right after several mi. Two mi. east of the southeast arm of Rimrock Lake. Hike in from southeast ridge to base. The southeast Arête (Hickman/Toula Route, 5.6x) offers dangerous but interesting technical climbing. Got helmet? Easier hike-up routes up gully ramps to left. Also, Goose Egg Mountain on FR 12 (Tieton Reservoir Rd.) has potential climbing.

83 T–The Talon ✰

An oval-shaped 90′ andesite rock mass with distinct peaks. Spring/autumn. Free/pay camping. USFS–Gifford Pinchot NF, (360) 891–5000.
Ref: Guidebook: Beckey's *Cascade Alpine Guide* (Columbia River), third ed.
Directions: From Yakima drive northwest to junction of Hwy. 410 and Hwy. 12. Go west on Hwy. 12 until 5 mi. east of White Pass. The Talon is a splinter on north side of Round Mountain, directly south of Hwy. 12. Best approach from Clear Lake Rd., then west on FR 1330 or 1360 (uncertain about road name).

84 Tower Rock (3,337') ✰✰✰

Solid 400′ basalt crack crag. Summer. USFS–Gifford Pinchot NF, (360) 891–5000.
Ref: Guidebook: Beckey's *Cascade Alpine Guide* (Columbia River), third ed.
Directions: From Randle, Tower Rock is south on Hwy. 131, then southeast (approximately 7 mi.) on Cispus Rd. NFD 23 to Cispus River. From Tower Rock Campground, Tower Rock is due south.

85 Pinto Rock (5,123') ✰✰

A 300′ volcanic breccia duet offers face climbing on tuff knobs. A crater vestige with varied quality and lots of cobbles embedded in welded tuff. One modern bolted route (1997) on South End possibly looks 5.10. Beautiful location. Great huckleberry picking. Summer. Free camping. USFS–Gifford Pinchot NF, (360) 891–5000.
Classics: Spectacle Route 5, South End Bolted Route 10?
Ref: Off White 11/97; Guidebook: Beckey's *Cascade Alpine Guide* (Columbia River), third ed.
Directions: From Randle go south on Hwy. 131, then southeast on Cispus Rd. (NFD 23) to FR 28 to Mosquito Meadows. Then turn north (right) onto FR 77 and onto Pinto Rock.

86 Kirk Rock (5,597') ✰✰✰

Solid 400′ basalt outcrops for the adventurous rock climber. Spring/autumn. USFS–Gifford Pinchot NF, (360) 891–5000.
Ref: Guidebook: Beckey's *Cascade Alpine Guide* (Columbia River), third ed.
Directions: From Randle (approximately 26 mi.), go south on FR 25. Hike to Badger Peak Lookout, then south to Kirk Rock, Shark Rock, and others. Bring good topo/ USFS maps.

87 Sleeping Beauty Mountain (5,076')

Four-hundred-foot basalt crack crag for the adventuring rock climber. Spring/autumn. USFS–Gifford Pinchot NF, (360) 891–5000.
Ref: Guidebook: Beckey's *Cascade Alpine Guide* (Columbia River), third ed.
Directions: From Trout Lake (on Hwy. 141, north of White Salmon), go northwest on FR 23 for approximately 8 mi. Turn left on Rd. 2360 to Sleeping Beauty Mountain.

88 Granite Point (at Lower Granite Lake) ✰✰✰

Granite 30′ pimple, larger before dam flooded lower faces. Site of the Snake River Rock Rodeo April 18—contact University of Idaho Outdoors Program, (208) 885-6810. Lots of rock to develop. Spring/autumn.
Classics: Steep Face 5, Layback Crack 7.
Ref: University of Idaho Recreation Department map.
Directions: From Pullman follow Wawawai Rd. for 30 mi. to Granite Point at Lower Granite Lake. Faces north.

89 Rabbit Ears

A small pinnacle on a basaltic broken ridge.
Ref: Petroske; Guidebook: Dodge's *A Climbing Guide to Oregon.*
Directions: From Bonneville Dam north entrance, drive ²/₁₀ mi. east on Evergreen Hwy. Turn on CR 32 for 1 ⁹/₁₀ mi. Then go 1 mi. on right fork of Aldrich Butte Rd. Continue

1 mi. north along beaver marsh to slide. Hike up slide twelve degrees true azimuth to Rabbit Ears. This area is very close to Beacon Rock.

90 Chimney Rocks ✫✫✫
Castellated andesitic erosion needles. Sound rock. Similar rock formations found farther north on the Gifford Pinchot National Forest include: Pyramid Rock, Sturgeon Rock, Saturday Rock, Twin Rocks, Sister Rock, Cougar Rock, and Three Corner Rock. The area around Chimney Rocks purportedly has old mines and prospects. Scenic area—good views of Mt. Adams and St. Helens and Columbia Gorge Basin. Private land.
Ref: Petroske; S 5/65; Guidebooks: Olson's *Portland Rock Climbs,* Dodge's *A Climbing Guide to Oregon.*
Directions: From Washougal on Hwy. 14, go 6 ½ mi. on Hwy. 140. Go 3 ⁹/10 mi. on Larch Mountain Rd. A dirt road (four-wheel-drive) leads to Chimney Rocks, which are east of the west fork of the Washougal River.

91 Cigar Rock
Basalt pinnacle.
Classics: Tyrolean Spire.
Ref: Guidebook: Dodge's *A Climbing Guide to Oregon.*
Directions: From Camas drive 13 ½ mi. east on Evergreen Hwy. Turn 1 ⁶/10 mi. south on paved road (across from junction with Hwy. 140) to railroad. Park. Hike west to tunnel down to beach to prominent pinnacle, Cigar Rock. Spires on beach.

92 Beacon Rock State Park ✫✫✫✫
Long called the best rock climbing "in Oregon," the 400' basaltic Beacon Rock has some of the finest technical rock in the Columbia River Gorge. At 848', second largest monolith in world surpassed only by the Rock of Gibraltar. First ascent in 1901. Sixty routes on south face. Beware of poison oak/falling rock. Or, is it falling oak/poison rock? Got helmet? Mandatory sign-in at east end of parking lot. Named by the Lewis and Clark expedition of 1805. Raptor restrictions February–July. Spring–autumn. Pay camping. State park, (509) 653–2390.
Classics: Cruisemaster I 7, Southeast Face III 7, Free for All 8, Little Wing I 8, Right Gull III 8/10a, Blownout 10a, Dod's Jam 10c, Blood, Sweat, and Smears 10c, Seagull 10c, Flying Swallow 10d, Free for Some 11a, Pipeline 11b, Steppenwolf 11+, Ground Zero 11d, Stone Rodeo 12a, Excalibur 12b.
Ref: AAJ ['90-166, '85-188], C [93, 73, 54], OB 23(10/75); Guidebooks: Smoot's *Rock Climbing Washington,* Olson's *Portland Rock Climbs,* Jones's *Columbia River Gorge: A Complete Guide,* Harlin's *West,* Thomas's *Oregon Rock,* Dodge's *A Climbing Guide to Oregon.*
Directions: From Skamania (approximately 30 mi. east of Portland, Oregon), go just east of town on Hwy. 14 to Beacon Rock Park. Follow signs. Register at bulletin board at east end of rest area. Hike climber's trail to south side of formation. The 400' vertical face on the south side is only side climbing is allowed. East side is illegal. A separate hiker's trail leads to summit. Please do not park at boat ramp or camping area.

93 Horsethief Butte (in Horsethief Lake State Park)✫✫✫
Mostly 40' basalt topropes and bouldering. Teaching area. Nice mid-winter area because of its reprieve from Portland rains. The area is above Horsethief State Park. Pay/free camping is available at the park, not at climbing area. Spring/autumn. State park, (509) 767–1159.
Ref: OB 23(10/75); Guidebooks: Olson's *Portland Rock Climbs,* Jones's *Columbia River Gorge: A Complete Guide,* Thomas's *Oregon Rock.*
Directions: From The Dalles, Oregon, drive 3 mi. north across Columbia River. Go 2 ½ mi. east on Hwy. 14 to small bridge. After crossing small bridge, park on left (or at state park historical marker to west). Hike path south to hidden amphitheater in Horsethief Butte.

94 Twin Sisters (aka Two Sisters) ✫✫✫
Good climbing at these twinned 60' basalt pillars. Thick steel cable around base of the pillar makes for good belay anchor for routes up to mainly 5.10. Endless cliffs along roadside overlooking the Columbia River feature short bands of sound rock. Spring/autumn. No camping. Private land/BLM, (509) 536–1200.
Ref: J. Bernhard.
Directions: From Walla Walla glide west on Hwy. 12 to Wallula junction. Change onto Hwy. 730 for 2 mi. The Twin Sisters are a double-towered formation on left with interpretive sign. Also, quality routes behind these formations on distant cliffs.

95 China Bend ✫✫✫
Overhanging pocketed limestone sport crag with around fifty routes. Watch for rattlers. October/November. Camping along road or pay campgrounds nearby.
Classics: Tonto 11a, Lone Ranger 11a, Shut Out 12d.
Ref: R 84-100 (topo); Guidebook: Smoot's *Rock Climbing Washington.*
Directions: From Kettle Falls go north on Hwy. 395 for 3 ½ mi. After crossing the Columbia River, turn right on Northport Flat Creek Rd. for 17 mi. to China Bend Rd. Turn right for 2 mi. until crags are visible. Park on right by two pine trees. Hike trail up to crag. Faces south.

96 Marcus ✫✫✫
This ¼-mi. long limestone sport crag is relatively unknown. Locals have been putting a lot of work into it, with more than thirty routes ranging from 5.9 to 5.13. Wild Walls climbing gym in Spokane can give you the beta.

April–October. Free camping up road or pay at Evans Campground.
Classics: Blow of Choss 11a, Citizen Kaned 12d, Natural Born Puller 13a.
Ref: R 84-100(topo); Guidebook: Smoot's *Rock Climbing Washington.*
Directions: From Marcus (Hwy. 395 north of Spokane), go 3 mi. northeast on Hwy. 25 to Evans Campground. Before campground ⅕ mi., turn right by brick house on dirt road for about ½ mi. by roped tree. Hike trail to crag. Continue up road, using right fork to camping area. Faces west.

97 Deep Creek (Riverside State Park) ★★★

If you like juggy overhanging sport climbs on smooth basalt, this is a pretty cool place to go. There is development continuing throughout the canyon. More than twenty-five routes in 1998. Deep Creek is now included in updated Spokane Area Climb Guide by Jim Speaker. This version has photos instead of drawings and is much more informative. Not for inexperienced climbers as there is a lot of loose rock and some mossy and wet areas. Brain buckets strongly recommended, especially for belayers. Best source of information is Wild Walls in Spokane or locals at Deep Creek. This is a day-use-only area. Pay camping at state park (509-738-3964).
Classics: Mental Warfare 12c, Twenty-one Run 13a, Quiver 13b.
Ref: J. Brown 6/98; R 84-100 (topo); Guidebooks: Smoot's *Rock Climbing Washington,* Speaker's *Spokane Rock Climbs.*
Directions: From northwest Spokane take Hwy. 291 out of town. Turn left onto Seven Mile Rd. for 2 ½ mi. Turn right on State Park Rd. to a gate and parking area. Hike ten minutes into canyon via streambed to shady rock walls.

98 Banks Lake Golf Course ★★

A good climb for beginner and intermediate climbers looking for good technical practice. Excellent to pass the time when visiting the Grand Coulee Dam Area. About 1 ½ mi. down the road Northrup Canyon offers many opportunities for wall climbing and bouldering.
Classics: Golf Ball Wall 5.10.
Directions: In the area of Coulee Dam there is a little town by the name of Electric City. It lies between Grand Coulee and Steamboat Rock State Park. Just outside of Electric City there is a golf course by the name of Banks Lake Golf. By the end of the second hole/third hole tee-off, there is a 40′ face visible.

99 The Falls ★★★

Good-quality 20′ andesite hard bouldering near waterfalls. Advisable to boulder here when the falls are pretty low, otherwise bring a wet suit. Great sandy landings and very hard problems. Access would appear to be unthreatened, but climbing on the cliffs above is definitely off-limits. Problems ranging from about V3 to "futuristic." Rock is generally excellent, though lacking holds. No camping. City land.
Ref: 11/97.
Directions: From Fall City go to the Snoqualmie Falls tourist vista. From there hike down to the base of falls. At the wooden platform (end of trail) descend to the riverbed, and there is a small traverse wall immediately below the platform. Head toward the falls, and the main bouldering area is situated on the left and very near the falls.

100 Exit 38 ★★★★

Seventy-foot sport crag. One hundred routes.
Classics: Traffic 11b hand crack.
Ref: Guidebooks: Smoot's *Rock Climbing Washington,* WMA's *Traveler's Guide Puget Sound,* Burdo's guidebook.
Directions: North Bend. The Exit 38 Crag is located at exit 38 off I-90.

101 Baker Crags ★★★

The 30′–180′ sport routes start at the intermediate level, 5.9, and go up to 5.12. Some of the climbs stay dry all year (a true blessing in northwest Washington) due to the overhanging rock in certain areas. A guide to Baker Crags and other areas near Bellingham can be purchased at the "Great Adventure" in Bellingham or by sending $13.50 plus $3.00 shipping to: Jason Henrie Cory Bennet, 515 East Myrtle #4, Bellingham, WA 98225. Check it out! USFS-Mt. Baker NF, (360) 856-5700.
Classics: Cobblestone Wall: Mean Streak 5.9 (eight bolts/75′), Warts 5.10a (nine bolts/75′), Speaking Spanish 5.8 (nine bolts/75′), Big Daddy Wall: Learning to Fly 5.11a (2 pitches/bolted/180′), Go Go Gadget 5.11b (five bolts/35′), Across the House 5.11d (six bolts/45′), Super Bad 5.11d (six bolts/65′), The Pump House: Shorty 5.12c (five bolts/30′).
Ref: J. Bennett 11/97.
Directions: From Bellingham at I-5 take the Sunset Rd./Hwy. 542 exit east. Follow Hwy. 542 past the town of Maple Falls (last stop for gas) to the smaller town of Glacier. Baker Crags are at ½ mi. past mm 33 on the north (left) side of the road. Parking is available 200′ farther up on the right.

102 Fossil Rock ★★★

Ever hear of Smith Rock, Oregon? Good, because this area is similar to its Oregon brother Smith Rock, but with a touch of Washington Moss. The area is made of 85′ volcanic welded tuft rock, giving it the characteristic "knobs." The area is located on Department of Natural Resources (DNR) and Weyerhauser land. Some of the climbing has been closed by DNR due to access/use issues. These closed areas are a hot topic with DNR—climbers are urged to avoid confrontation with DNR or Weyerhauser due to the tricky access issues. Most routes are bolted (well), steep, and mostly range from 5.7 to 5.9, with a few easier, and a handful of 11s and 12s. Touchy land-use problems in the area, so tread lightly and be friendly. Pack your gun, everyone else does. Fifty routes. Summer. Free. State land.

Classics: Pump and Rest 9, Perfect Lovers 10a, Battle of the Bulge 11a, Poppa Oscar Tango 11b.

Ref: K. Dwight 2/99; Guidebooks: Smoot's *Rock Climbing Washington,* Yoder and Ford's *Rock Climber's Guide to Fossil* (a worthwhile guide to the area published in 1996; available at climbing shops in Olympia and Tacoma).

Directions: Near Yelm. Please see guidebooks for access issues and directions.

103 Potholes

Short 35′ basalt walls give way to endless fun vertical challenges.

Ref: Guidebook: Smoot's *Rock Climbing Washington.*

Directions: From Spokane drive west on I–90 for 100 mi. to exit 179 for Moses Lake. Go south on Hwy. 17 through McDonald. Turn west on Hwy. 262 to O'Sullivan Dam. Just before dam, go south on roads past Goldeneye and Chukar Lakes. Turn southwest to northeast end of Upper Goose Lake. Rocks on right of road just northeast of lake.

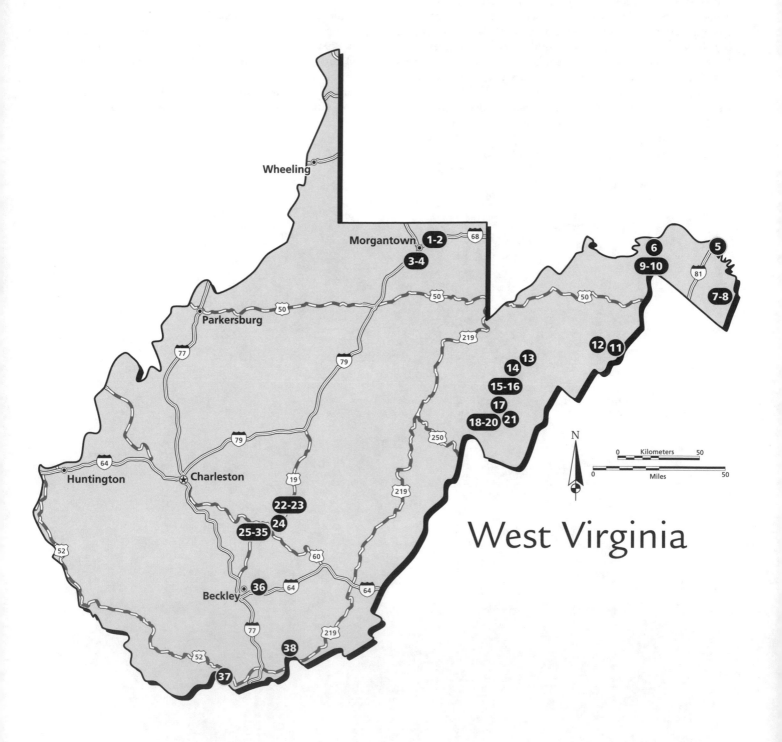

Wheeling

Morgantown **1-2**
3-4

68

6
9-10
5
81
7-8

Parkersburg

50

219

12 **11**

50

77

13
14
15-16

79

17
18-20 **21**

250

79

64

Huntington

Charleston

19

219

22-23
24
25-35

60

52

36

Beckley

64

64

219

77

38

52

37

N

Kilometers

0 50

Miles

0 50

West Virginia

West Virginia

A man hates to lose a good bivouac. —Anonymous climber upon hearing a Fayetteville lover had gotten married

In 1980, if you asked rock climbers heading to West Virginia where they were going climbing, they would unanimously respond, "Seneca Rocks." This quiet and scenic hollow boasted some bold leads. In 1987, Seneca's famous Gendarme formation toppled over, and with it, the area's popularity seemed to follow. For there was other earthshaking news from central West Virginia.

Once a sleepy Appalachian state, West Virginia became an eastern powercragging center when New River Gorge became known to the U.S. climbing populace in the late 1980s. For climbers, New River's seemingly endless and clean sandstone crags presented the opportunity for steep, fine lines. It is "almost heaven."

World class are the words for New River: the rock, the longest arch bridge above the crags, and class 5 white water below that. What more could you ask for in an area? Even after more than a dozen years, climbers are still putting in new routes today. For the climber interested in power sport climbing, New River and its neighboring canyons are a must. Visit in autumn for one of your most memorable falls.

And if you can pull yourself away from the "New" long enough to visit the other areas of the state, you'll find rock to expand your mind and trim your waist.

1 Mont Chateau ✩✩✩

Large 40′ sandstone outcrop with many huge overhangs. There is an upper and lower cliffband.

Classics: Garden 7, The Yellow Pages 8, Incredible Layback 9, Army Crack 10 (crack with black overhang), Nervous Disorder 10, Burley Bouldering Traverse.

Ref: Guidebook: Webster's *Gritstone Climbs.*

Directions: From Morgantown leap north on I—68. Exit at Hwy. 857, exit 10. Turn right on Fairchance Rd. (Hwy. 857) and go for ²/10 mi. Turn left following road past Lakewiew Resort; this road will curve left and continue under I–68 and straight to a stop sign. Continue for another ⁹/10 mi. to Mont Chateau USGS building. Find Mont Chateau rock 200 yds. south from the building, adjacent to Cheat Lake. Faces southwest.

2 Cooper's Rock State Forest ✩✩✩

Outstanding gritstone climbing on Dresden-like, short sandstone walls and bouldering maze. Cooper's Rock provides airy views of the Cheat River. For the explorer more climbing exists on surrounding Chestnut Ridge where rocks (lots of large sandstone boulders) exist in Darnell and Johnson Hollows. Find time in your schedule to visit this area. Five hundred climbs. Pay camping in state forest (304–594–1561).

Classics: Helen's Climb 6, Wing and a Prayer 8, Burned Image 9, Black Sunday 10, Slapstick 10; Sunset Wall: Copenhagen 9; Rock City: Death to Klingons 12a. Ask someone for the Rock City Alleyway. It's the last climb on the left. (Major overhang. Big swings. Hard hits. Many bruises. Very cool.) Picnic Table Boulder B1 in picnic area.

Great gritstone bouldering prevails at Cooper's Rock.

TIM TOULA

Ref: C. Garman 4/98, J. Govi; C 88(2/85)-26; Sherman's *Stone Crusade;* on-line guide www.climbpa.com/coopers.htm; Guidebooks: Thompson's *Cooper's Rock West Virginia Classic Rock Climbs,* Webster's *Gritstone Climbs,* Harlin's *East, Climb Pennsylvania,* Clark's *Climbing Guide to Cooper's Rocks.*
Directions: From Morgantown (about twenty-five minutes east), drive east on I-68 to Cooper's Rock exit. Follow park signs south to end of road and picnic area. Four immediate areas: Overlook Rock, Haystack, Island Rock, and Rock City. Areas below overlook have best climbing but are now closed (as of 1998). Another great area is Sunset Wall: Walk left out of the left-hand main parking lot and down the trail, backward parallel to the road you came in on. Also: Junction Rocks. Take the Rhododendron Trail until you hit the T intersection. Stop and look straight ahead. Small, but worth the hike.

3 White Day ●
Large 100' sandstone cliff. Sandy loose rock, vegetated. Atrocious quality. May be good for rappelling only.
Ref: Guidebook: Webster's *Gritstone Climbs.*
Directions: From Morgantown go south on Hwy. 73, just past White Day Golf Course on right. Look up!

4 Pioneer Rocks and Decker's Creek ☆☆☆
Part of the gritstone ridge of rock known as "Chestnut Ridge" in Pennsylvania and West Virginia. Fun, steep, and challenging 50' sandstone climbs.
Classics: Knobby Wall 4, Nemesis 6, Fear 8, Burn 'em Up 10.
Ref: Guidebooks: Harlin's *East,* Webster's *Gritstone Climbs.*
Directions: From Morgantown take I-68 east to Hwy. 7, exit 4. Go 3 3/10 mi. south on Hwy. 7 past Tyrone Rd. (CR 75). Go 1/4 mi., past Tyrone Rd. and Pioneer Rocks Market sign and park. Pioneer Rocks are only a few feet off Hwy. 7. Cliffs lie parallel to road for a mile. Decker's Creek is a continuation of Pioneer Rocks (mank) just north of Hwy. 7 paralleling Decker's Creek, east of Dellslow. Faces west.

5 Indian Church
This long, limestone cliff winds on the east side of Miller's Bend on the Potomac River. Possibly quarried away.
Ref: Guidebook: Canter's *Nearby Climbing Areas.*
Directions: Indian Church is 1 3/10 mi. northwest of Marlowe.

6 Edes Fort ☆☆☆
Beautiful large cliff of Tuscarora sandstone in wooded mountainside valley near Great Capacon. Private land makes canoe access only reasonable access.
Ref: Guidebook: Canter's *Nearby Climbing Areas.*
Directions: From the town of Great Capacon, drive south on Rockford Rd. (Hwy. 7) for 3 mi. to bridge. Edes Fort is visible to the north downstream from bridge. Float downstream in canoe to rock. For Edes Fort see Great Capacon 7.5' USGS topo.

7 Jefferson Rock ☆☆
Cliffs with 60' of Harper's phyllite. Quarried and natural rock from vertical to overhanging in nature. Friction slab as well. Sharp (!) edges. NPS, (304) 535-6298.
Ref: Guidebook: Canter's *Nearby Climbing Areas.*
Directions: Jefferson Rock is at Harpers Ferry, east of Hwy. 340 above the Shenandoah River.

8 Split Rock and Chimney Rock
The north side of Loudon Heights has several metamorphic outcrops suitable for climbing. The largest is Split Rock, a high but broken cliff. Chimney Rock is a fractured pinnacle of Harper's phyllite overlooking the junction of the rivers. There are other outcrops, visible from Harpers Ferry, west of Chimney Rock. Harper's Phyllite is the rock type. Autumn. Government land.
Ref: Guidebook: Canter's *Nearby Climbing Areas.*
Directions: From Harpers Ferry take Hwy. 340 southeast across the Shenandoah River until south of confluence of Potomac and Shenandoah Rivers. Formations are to south of Hwy. 340. Split Rock is western formation.

9 Capacon Gorge
Two mi. upriver from Caudey's Castle, the river cuts a gap through this 200' quartzite sandstone fold. Low cliffs on the south side, higher cliffs on north side. Best climbs at top of cliff with overhangs.
Ref: Guidebook: Canter's *Nearby Climbing Areas.*
Directions: For Capacon Gorge use Capon Bridge 7.5' topo. 3/4 mi. southeast of Caudey's Castle.

10 Caudey's Castle (closed)
A large sandstone tower. Posted and closed.
Ref: Guidebook: Canter's *Nearby Climbing Areas.*
Directions: For Caudey's Castle see Capon Bridge 15' USGS topo.

11 Devil's Garden
Quartzite crag near Wardensville.
Ref: Guidebook: Canter's *Nearby Climbing Areas.*
Directions: For Devil's Garden see Wardensville 7.5' USGS topo. On the south side of the gap in Anderson Ridge is a cliff with a series of deep chimneys. Permission necessary for road access.

12 Baker's Rocks (aka Hanging Rock) (closed?) ☆☆☆
A huge roof overhangs the highway. Unfortunately, this fine 100' quartzite crag near Wardensville now may be closed due to private landowners.

Ref: J. Govi; C 1980s; Guidebook: Canter's *Nearby Climbing Areas.*
Directions: From Wardensville (approximately one hour drive north/northeast of Seneca Rocks), hang it out for 8 ½ mi. on Hwy. 55. Baker's Rocks is on north side of road. See Moorefield 15′ USGS topo.

13 Smokehole Cavern Cliffs ☆☆

A 100′ sandstone crag with climbs from 5.10 to 5.12 as well as bouldering and topropes.
Ref: T. Cecil.
Directions: From Seneca, Smokehole Cavern Cliffs are twenty minutes north on Hwy. 55 near Smokehole Caverns. Park.

14 Champe ☆☆

Incredible Seneca Rocks 330′ sandstone satellite crag. A vertical to overhanging fin. These 330′ sport climbs are called some of the best face climbing in West Virginia. Autumn. Private land/USFS-Monongahela NF, (304) 636-1800.
Classics: Psychotic Reaction 5.9 (two-three pitches), Fintasia 11+, Enchampement 11+.
Ref: T. Cecil, J. Govi.
Directions: From Seneca Rocks go north on Hwy. 55 for 7 mi. Champe Rocks are east of highway. Limited access—must cross private land to get to USFS land. Check locally with Seneca Rock Guides before accessing land. Access is dicey.

15 Seneca Rocks ☆☆☆☆

A bastion of tried and true, gutsy, ground-up leads on fine Tuscarora sandstone. A fading star now that New River has dominated the West Virginia climbing scene, but still great climbing. Locals were crestfallen when The Gendarme, the centerpiece pinnacle between the two 300′ rock fins, tumbled after a jet blast on October 22, 1988. Game over, man, game over! Now, perhaps, better known as the "Gone Down." Pay camping at USFS Seneca Shadows campground (800-280-2267). USFS-Monongahela NF (304) 636-1800.
Classics: Conn's East 6, West Pole 7, Ecstasy 7, Triple S 8, Alcoa Presents 8, Castor/Pollux 9, Malevolence 10b, The Changeling 11b, Mr. Jones 11c, Terra Firma 11c, The Bell 11+, Psycho Driller 12c, Bonsai 12a, Bray to the Lord 12d, Black Mamba 12c, Fine Young Cannibals 13a.
Ref: T. Cecil; C [174-110, 140(11/93), 138, 106, 100, 95, 94, 75(12/82), 73(6/82), 68, 54, 48, Basecamps], OB 8(4/73), R [94-80, 85-70, 77-28, 67-52], S [9/63, 3/61]; Guidebooks: Barnes's *Seneca Rocks Guide,* Cater's *Sport Crags of the East,* Webster's *Seneca: The Climber's Guide,* Harlin's *East,* Bercaw et al.'s *Seneca,* Robinson's *A Climber's Guide to Seneca Rocks,* Jirak's *Seneca Rocks Route Sketches.*
Directions: At Seneca Rock. Obvious sandstone blade dominates the valley view. Ten-minute hike across river and then up short, steep trails to Seneca Rocks. Though Seneca Rocks is essentially one long fin, climbs are divided into South and North Peaks (both with routes on West and East Faces).

TIM TOULA

The hallowed Seneca Rocks.

16 Church (closed?) ⭐⭐
Several unnamed lines exist at this 70′ sandstone crag. Beware poison ivy. Ask at Seneca Rock Guides. Private land.
Ref: J. Govi.
Directions: Near Seneca Rocks. Church Rocks are right across road from church.

17 Riverton ⭐⭐
A beautiful little 80′ sandstone crag. Private land.
Classics: Almost Heaven 9+, Tree Crack 10c, Hillbilly 12.
Ref: J. Tuszynski 1/98, J. Govi.
Directions: From Seneca Rocks swerve 10 mi. south on Hwy. 33. On left to little town of Riverton. Good outcrop just east of town. Turn left at Riverton. Park beyond bridge. Hike up steep hill. Crossing private property is necessary.

18 Judy Gap ⭐⭐
Short but good 50′ sandstone crag. State land.
Classics: Test Pilot 11+ crack/face.
Ref: T. Cecil.
Directions: From Seneca Rocks go 11 mi. south on Hwy. 33 to north of Hwy. 33 at Judy Gap. Best climbing on east side.

19 Nelson Rocks Preserve ⭐⭐⭐
The preserve is a nonprofit, privately owned and funded organization dedicated to the preservation of Nelson Rocks as a natural and scenic resource operated by Stu Hammett and family. These beautiful 200′ Tuscarora quartzite crags offer thirty great routes on six distinct walls. Bolted routes on west side. Traditional routes on east side. Climbing on both fins north of Nelson Run. Nelson Rocks Preserve opened May 1998 for day use: $5.00 day-use fee, $30.00 annual pass. New parking area, bathroom, and 2 mi. of new trail. Rustic cabins. Lots of new route potential. Contact Nelson Rocks Preserve (301-627-5301; shammett@erols.com) or Seneca Rocks Mountain Guides (304-567-2115; Senecatrad@aol.com) for development guidelines and other information. Good luck, Stu!
Classics: Crescendo 5.10a, Stone Gallows 2-3p 5.10, Merlin 11a, Written in Stone 11+, Porcelain Pumphouse 11c.
Ref: S. Hammett 4/98, J. Tuszynski 1/98, T. Cecil; R 85-77; Guidebook: www.nelsonrocks.org/guide.html.
Directions: From Seneca Rocks go south approximately 11 mi. on Hwy. 33. Turn right on 28S for approximately 1 mi. toward Circleville. Turn left for ½ mi. on Nelson Gap Rd. to Nelson Rocks. Most climbs are located on fin,

West Virginia Road Thoughts
Remember, it's not, "How high are you?" it's "Hi, how are you?"
—Seen at rest stop off Route 81, West Virginia

north of small parking area. Entrance station on right—pay and sign in. Parking area down hill on right (no parking on Nelson Gap Rd.). Trailhead on left in gap.

20 Spruce Knob ⭐⭐
A dozen white 15′ sandstone conglomerate boulders in a scenic mountain meadow. These are short boulders. Also, highest point in West Virginia at 4,861′ and the most beautiful spot in the state. Visit in summer or fall.
USFS-Monongahela NF, (304) 636-1800.
Classics: Way Rad Gnarly Slap Move.
Ref: J. Tuszynski 1/98, G.Collins, T. Cecil; S 9/63.
Directions: From Seneca Rocks go approximately 10 mi. south on Hwy. 33. Turn west off Hwy. 33, following signs to top of Spruce Knob to lookout tower. Hike pebbled trail to view of meadow with scenic boulders.

21 Franklin Gorge ⭐⭐⭐
The Franklin Gorge has been divided into two areas: Contact/Impact Zone has limestone/SS overlap with thirty routes, and Riverbend (on river) is delightful winter/spring area with approximately twenty routes. All 80′ sport climbs—don't even bring a nut. Please respect climbing privilege here by picking up your own and others' trash. Most climbs put up by Harrison locals. General store has necessary foodstuffs and brews.
Ref: J. Tuszynski 1/98, T. Cecil, M. Gray.
Directions: From Franklin drop 2 mi. east on Hwy. 33E to first major stream crossing and general store. Turn right (north). Contact/Impact Zone (rocks and parking) are ½-1 mi. north on road. Hike a few minutes to Franklin Gorge rock. Riverbend Area: Drive to end of dirt road and hike along river to cliffs approximately ten minutes.

22 Summersville Lake ⭐⭐⭐⭐
Once an unknown climbing backwater, this area is now the lyceum of eastern rock climbers. An incredible inverted sandstone hang for climbing on clean, white 100′ sandstone crags. Sixty sport routes between 5.10-5.13. Several walls have been developed, with more to come. Swimming and waterskiing, too. Lake water level drops every September during Gauley River season when dam is released. Fall. Government land.
Classics: Bsiage 11a, Walk the Plank 11b, Mutiny 11+, Under the Milky Way 11+, Armada 12c, Apollo Reed 13a/b, Mercy Seat 13b.
Ref: Freeman; C [189-32, 143], R [95-32, 92-60]; Guidebooks: Cater's *Sport Crags of the East*, Cater and Saab's *Take Me to the River*.
Directions: From Summersville shuttle south on Hwy. 19 to bridge over Summersville Lake. At north end of bridge, park at rest area pulloff. (Also, safer parking at boat ramp approximately ½ mi. north.) Hike approximately fifteen minutes down trail from rest area under bridge to walls to the east along the lakeshore. The rock is visible when crossing the bridge northbound from Fayetteville.

Summersville Lake is approximately 20 mi. north of New River Gorge Bridge.

23 Gauley River Cliffs ✮✮✮
New development on 100' sandstone cliffs. The dam output from Summersville Lake is awesome, as is the famed white-water run of the Gauley River. Government land.
Ref: R. Turan.
Directions: From Fayetteville drive north on Hwy. 19 until signs point the way to Summersville Dam. Gauley River Cliffs downstream below output of dam.

24 Meadow River (Gauley River National Recreation Area) ✮✮✮✮
A scion of the noble house of the New River Gorge. The Meadow features first-class rock above class 6 rapids. These 100' cream-white sandstone cliffs feature fine overhanging face, arêtes (Mango Tango) and roof challenges (Puppy Chow/Greatest Show) above the purl of the Meadow River. At least three classic 5.12 roof problems along cliff base (E.T. Roof B1+, Ground School B1). Private land/NPS, (304) 574-2115.
Classics: Orange Crush Wall 5.11-12, Puppy Chow 12c, Greatest Show on Earth 12+/13a, Mango Tango 13-; Bouldering: Ground School B5.11+, ET Roof B1+.
Ref: K. Parker.
Directions: From Fayetteville float north on Hwy. 19 to Meadow River Bridge (cliffs visible to left when crossing over bridge). Turn left just after bridge, and then in 100' turn left again and go uphill ¼ mi. Park at slight road incut. Hike down jeep trail to cliffs on right for ten to fifteen minutes.

25 Cotton Hill (aka The Drys) ✮✮✮
Also known as "The Drys" (below the dam), this area stores a lot of rock. Typical New River Gorge–genre sandstone cliffs.
Ref: R. Turan.
Directions: From Fayetteville drive north on Hwy. 16 from Hwy. 19 until the Cotton Hill Bridge is crossed (approximately 5 mi.). Just after bridge, pull in on right by locked gate. Hike on road up to Cotton Hill cliff bands.

26 NR✮–New River Gorge National River Overview ✮✮✮✮✮
The New River Gorge embraces world-class cragging and white-water rafting. From sequestered anonymity to worldwide acclaim, the "New" became the "Roman Candle" of eastern U.S. rock climbing in the late 1980s when word of the climbing explosion led people to the crag above the river. The solid Nuttall sandstone of the New River forms into first-class face climbing, from thin edges to pumping overhangs, and fine cracks of all shapes and sizes. Now around 1,500 routes. Developed by the likes of Skidmore, Howard, Swoager, Barry, Artz, Horst, Reed, Jarrard, and Thompson. Rains ropes on the weekends and buckets during the spring and summer. Free camping under the bridge. Nearest facilities: Fayetteville. World's longest arch 1700' steel span bridge—876' high. Best season: September–November. and April–May. NPS, (304) 574-2115.
Classics: More classics than in a Greek library—see individual listings.
Ref: C [194-117, 163-84, 136, 133, 115, 113, 112, 109, 108, 106, 105(12/87)-36, 103, 102(6/87)-56, 85(8/84)-32]; R [103-48, 92-55, 84-92, 66-46, 36(3/90)-39, 29(1/89)-38, 12(1/86)], SC 9/91; Guidebooks: Cater's *New River Gorge: Rock Climbers' Handbook,* Brock's *Best Sport Climbs of the New River Gorge, Featuring the Cirque,* Cater's *Sport Crags of the East,* Cater and Saab's *Take Me to the River,* Harlin's *East.*
Directions: From Fayetteville drive 2 mi. north on Hwy. 19. Turn right and wind down below bridge to Bridge Buttress and New River Gorge NPS bulletin board. Many crags lie on both sides of river along various access roads. These include: Bubba City, Junkyard Wall, Bridge Buttress, Ambassador Buttress, Endless Wall, Fern Point, Beauty Mountain, Sunshine Buttress, Kaymoor Wall, and South Nuttall Wall.

27 NR–Bubba City ✮✮✮✮
Developed mainly by Eric Horst late 1980s. Good sunny exposures. Many classic, vertical face edging routes with some cracks thrown in for good measure. Close to 200 sport and trad routes. NPS, (304) 574-2115.
Classics: Boschtardized 11c, Rites of Summer 12a, Masterpiece Theatre 12c, Diamond Life 13a.
Ref: C [108(6/88)-38, 106, 105 (map)], R 29(11/89); Guidebook: Cater and Saab's *Take Me to the River.*
Directions: East side of gorge. North of Bridge Buttress. Bubba City is most northerly crag on east side. From Fayetteville float north on Hwy. 19 across bridge to Ames Height Rd. Turn left for 1 4/10 mi. to parking pullout on left. Hike dirt road for three rope lengths and take trail on left to crags. Note: Also approachable via Old Ames Mine Rd. and accessed beyond Bridge Buttress Rd. (road leading down to river). Take dirt road past old mines to end and hike up to crags. Many sub wall divisions include (south–north): Bubba Buttress, Central Bubba, Ames Wall, Head Wall, Little Head Wall, Ameless Wall, Sandstonia, Kingfish, and Rubble Rock.

28 NR–Junkyard Wall ✮✮✮
Junkyard Wall (80') seems to attract climbers like two magnets with the same poles. Why this is so strange is since the climbing is fine. Approximately one hundred routes. The name of the wall originated from the heinous collection of junk at the cliff base, since removed. NPS, (304) 574-2115.
Classics: New Yosemite 9, Team Jesus 10b, Childbirth 11c, Fat Cat 13a.
Ref: Guidebook: Cater and Saab's *Take Me to the River.*
Directions: East side of gorge. North of Bridge Buttress. From Fayetteville float north on Hwy. 19 across bridge to Ames Height Rd. Turn left for 6/10 mi. Turn left again to

parking pullout at sharp turn. Hike down road to Junkyard Wall. Note: Also approached by parking at first hairpin turn past Bridge Buttress and hiking five minutes.

29 NR–Bridge Buttress ✩✩✩

The most instant-access and longest-developed climbing area of the New River. Also, a good meeting spot for climbing and others. Some good rainy-day routes. More than 150 good routes. The gigantic New River Bridge rises overhead. If you're camping at the Bridge Buttress, don't drop the soap! NPS, (304) 574–2115.

Classics: Angel's Arête 10-, Stratagem 11c, Marionette 11c, Agent Orange 11d.

Ref: C 106; Guidebooks: Cater and Saab's *Take Me to the River*, Harlin's *East*.

Directions: East side of gorge. Bridge Buttress is almost directly below the bridge and just north. From Fayetteville float north on Hwy. 19 across bridge. Turn right at Visitor's Center Rd. Continue past visitors center and take two sharp right turns until below bridge. Parking roadside. Alternative access routes for Junkyard Wall and Bubba Buttress on road reached beyond.

30 NR–Ambassador Buttress ✩✩✩

An easy-access and generally quiet 80′ sandstone cliff with twenty-four routes. Named after a local elderly black gentleman whose charismatic manner led to his nickname, The Ambassador. Slightly less than two dozen traditional routes, including the beautiful Dragon in Your Dreams. NPS, (304) 574–2115.

Classics: Dragon in Your Dreams 11.

Ref: C; Guidebook: Cater and Saab's *Take Me to the River*.

Directions: East side of gorge. South of Bridge Buttress. From Fayetteville float north on Hwy. 19 across bridge. Shortly, turn right on Lansing Rd. for ½ mi. Turn right at store. Take Hwy. 82 (first left fork) for 7/10 mi. to parking pullout on left. Hike down below to Ambassador Buttress cliff via a right turn before creek. (Going straight takes one to Monolith Buttress on Endless Wall.)

31 NR–Endless Wall ✩✩✩✩✩

At 4 mi. in length, this is the longest wall in New River Gorge. Approximately 500 routes and maybe one or two classics—ha ha. The Cirque Area especially challenges hard route sport climbers. Fantastic! NPS, (304) 574–2115.

Classics: Celibate Mallard 10b, Leave It to Jesus 11c, Sacrilege 12b, Land That Time Forgot 12c, Welcome to Conditioning 13a, The Racist 13b.

Ref: C [187-31, 177-58, 126], R 36(3/90)-36; Guidebooks: Brock's *Best Sport Climbs of the New River Gorge Featuring the Cirque*, Cater and Saab's *Take Me to the River*, Harlin's *East*.

Directions: East side of gorge. Endless Wall is south of Bridge Buttress. Three well-used access points (north–south): 1) Fern Buttress: From Fayetteville float north on Hwy. 19 across bridge. Turn right on Lansing Rd. for ½

mi. Turn right at store. Take Hwy. 82 (first left fork) for 6/10 mi. to parking pullout on left. Hike down trail and cross creek. Continue on ten minutes to buttress. 2) Fern Point: Go 1 3/10 mi. east of Hwy. 19 to parking lot. Past lot, trail on right takes one twenty minutes to cliff. A fixed rappel is to the right, or better, down and right 35′, a slot provides a climb down via an old ladder. 3) Central Endless: Same as number two. Then walk Lansing Rd. 4/10 mi. away from Hwy. 19 to a two-car pullout with electric box. (Do not park here!) Pick up trail on right into woods (five minutes) to a fixed rappel on left.

32 NR–Beauty Mountain ✩✩✩✩

A beautiful 150′ sandstone crag with many fine routes (approximately one hundred) both crack and face. Wetter than most New River cliffs. Travesty, one of the more difficult routes at the gorge, is here at 5.13c/d, and the beautiful 5.12 roof and crack Genocide. NPS, (304) 574–2115.

Classics: Supercrack 9+, Welcome to Beauty 11, Mensa 11b, Son of Thunders 11c/d, Genocide 12a, Chunky Monkey 12a, Night Train 12a, Super Mario 13a, Travesty 13c/d.

Ref: Sherman's *Stone Crusade*; Guidebook: Cater and Saab's *Take Me to the River*, Harlin's *East*.

Directions: East side of gorge. South of Bridge Buttress. Southernmost Cliff on east side of the gorge. From Fayetteville float north on Hwy. 19 across bridge. Turn right on Lansing Rd. for 2 4/10 mi. to parking on left (school bus stop). Park well off road. Hike across street on dirt road past two houses, picking up trail down to rocks in approximately five minutes. Short toprope cliff (Garbage Wall) and block boulder (Super Mario) are encountered first. Then veer left to main Beauty Mountain area.

33 NR–Sunshine Buttress ✩✩✩

A small, sunny 90′ sandstone crag a short distance from Fayetteville. Good in cold weather. NPS, (304) 574–2115.

Classics: Disco Apocalypse 12c, Original Crankster 13a.

Ref: C 121(4/92)-26, SC 6/92; Guidebook: Cater and Saab's *Take Me to the River*.

Directions: West side of New River Gorge. From Fayetteville go north on Hwy. 19. Shortly before New River Gorge Bridge. Turn left onto Hwy. 82. Go 1 ½ mi. to Sunshine Buttress on right.

34 NR–Kaymoor ✩✩✩✩✩

Most overhanging section of New River Gorge—pumpus maximus sport climbs. The Glory Hole, where lactic acid showers down on unknowing belayers, was developed in 1991 by Doug Reed and others. At least one hundred routes. NPS, (304) 574–2115.

Classics: Lactic Acid Bath 12d, Burning Cross 13a.

Ref: C 121(4/92)-26, SC 6/92; Guidebooks: Cater and Saab's *Take Me to the River*, Cosby's *Kaymoor Guide*.

Directions: West side of New River Gorge. From Fayetteville go south from downtown on Court St. Past Sherrie's

Store, turn left onto Gatewood Rd. In 1 9/10 mi., turn left at Kaymoor #1 sign. It's 1 mi. to parking (large pulloff) at end of road. Trail five minutes to top of Kaymoor cliffs. The super overhang, Glory Hole, is off to right. Other walls to the north.

35 NR–South Nuttall Wall ✮✮✮✮
More steep 150' sandstone walls with fine crack lines like New Traditionalists. NPS, (304) 574-2115.
Classics: The Beckoning 11c, New Traditionalists 12c.
Ref: Guidebook: Cater and Saab's *Take Me to the River*.
Directions: West side of New River Gorge. From Fayetteville, go south from downtown on Court St. Turn left onto Gatewood Rd. Go past Kaymoor cliffs. Turn left at Elverton Rd. and follow it until road turns to dirt at top of rim. Park. Walk north along rim and stomp brush to get to South Nuttall Wall cliffs in thirty minutes or less.

36 Glade Creek ✮✮✮
Interstate sandstone crags similar to New River Gorge.
Directions: From Beckley go east on Hwy. 64. Visible on left. Glade Creek Cliffs above I-64.

37 Pinnacle Rocks State Park ✮✮✮
This Civil War commemorative rock features 100' sandstone walls with diverse aspects. Very steep south face. No camping. State park, (304) 589-5307.
Directions: From Bluefield shoot west on Hwy. 52 from town to Pinnacle Rocks State Park. Adjacent to highway on south side of road.

38 Bozoo Rocks ✮✮✮
"Climbing at Bozoo is like small potatoes: they're little, but they're damn good if you eat enough of 'em," says guidebook author Paul Sullivan. Vertical to overhanging crack climbing predominates on New River Gorge–quality 40'–80' sandstone features. Most routes are gear leads or topropes; a few mixed routes exist. Of the more than one hundred routes, Paul Sullivan and fellow climber Paul Delappe have put up 80 percent of the first ascents from the ground up. Excellent bouldering has just begun to be explored. This area is in the later stages of its "golden age," and most of the classic crack lines have been led. Also, home to the infamous "Trad Avengers." Bolts placed next to gear placements will not be tolerated (unlike the NRG) and will be chopped. This area is not sport-climber friendly, and all leads take at least some natural protection. Toproping is easy anywhere at Bozoo. Private land.
Classics: Tastes Like Chicken 7, Thru-Mortice 8, Bart 9, Diamonds Are Forever 9+R, Savory Truffle 9, Chunks 9+, Bovine Crack 10, Rigormortise 10, Recycle Your Sole 10, Necromancer 10+, Necrophelia 11r, Marge 11, The Furrowed Brow 11, Bone Machine 11, Osmosis.
Ref: P. Sullivan (4/96), Guidebook: Sullivan's *Bozoo Rocks*.
Directions: From Blacksburg, Virginia, head west on Route 460 to Rich Creek, Virginia. Then continue toward Peterstown, West Virginia. Once in town, take the second left for 1 to 2 mi. to Bozoo Rd. on the left. Follow it to Shanklins Ferry. Bear right on dirt road. Go to top of the first field on the left. Follow the trail. (Locals are very friendly and can give directions to Bozoo and Shanklins Ferry.)

Other West Virginia Climbing Areas
Woodland Wall
Ref: C 156-32, R 70-34.

Wisconsin

Wisconsin

Thew is no tomowwow! —Pete Cleveland, legendary Wisconsin climber

Upon entering Wisconsin, the traveling climber braves getting fat. This dairy-land state sways the touring cragger with cheese factories, ice cream, and farm-fresh eggs; not to mention brewery tours, including the home of the world's largest six-pack at G. Heileman's.

Only if you can avoid turning into a cow will you stand a chance of pulling the classic squarecut edges at Devil's Lake. Here, the climbing gods invented friction after they created this quartzitic crag. But Devil's Lake is the cragging area of Wisconsin and after a visit you too might be saying, "I love a good dime edge."

If you stay a spell, locals just might take you to other farmland sandstone areas where one can harvest a small crop of crag climbs.

Go in the fall when the colors are rich and the photos colorful. Be sure to smile and say, "Cheese!"

1 Interstate State Park ✩✩✩
Basalt bluffs lining the St. Croix National Scenic Riverway; especially colorful in fall. Testpiece thin-edge cranking (and I do mean thin) face, bouldering specialist problems on Mike's Boulder down at river (old bolt on face). Short meaty, 45′ climbs. The Old Man of the Dalles is a famous face in the rock, a la the Old Man of the Mountains at Cannon Cliff, New Hampshire. Wisconsin Outdoor Access is an organization intended for preserving Wisconsin climbing areas; see www.climbingcentral.com/WOA/WOA.html. Full facilities at park. Ice Age Interpretive Center. Golden Eagle Passport accepted. Pay camping. Spring–autumn. State park, (715) 482-2747.
Classics: Inside Corner 8, Walking On Air 11, Joint Project 13, Red Wall 13a; Mike's Boulder B2s.
Ref: M. Dahlberg, D. Dokken, C. Eklund; Sherman's *Stone Crusade;* Guidebooks: Farris's *Minnesota Rock: Selected Climbs,* Swenson et al.'s guidebook, Bagg's *50 Short Climbs in the Midwest.*
Directions: From St. Croix go just south on Hwy. 35. Cliffs at river's edge. Free access by walking over the bridge from Taylor's Falls, Minnesota. Several areas in Interstate State Park include: Old Man's Area, River Bluffs Area, and Summit Rock.

2 High Cliff State Park ✩
Limestone bouldering and crag. Several Indian effigy mounds. Spring to autumn. Camping in state park (920-989-1106).
Directions: From Sherwood go south on Hwy. 5, then follow signs to High Cliff State Park. On east shore of Lake Winnebago. Trailhead through old limestone quarry.

3 Necedah ✩✩✩
This 60′ sandstone crag sits along the Wisconsin River. Bolted leads. More small rock outcrops in the surrounding area, but one should ask climbing locals for more information. Fabulous fall colors and crisp conditions make up for the very humid and buggy summer conditions. No camping. Spring/autumn. State land.
Classics: Wide Crack 10+, Straight and No Chaser 11+, Rebel Yell 12a, Whiskey-A-Gogo 12c.
Ref: B. Werntz, D. Groth.
Directions: From Necedah wing it east on Hwy. 21 for about 8 mi. to Wisconsin River. Just past Woodbine Inn, turn right before Wisconsin River and follow a short ways to south end of Necedah Crag. Pull off on left and park. The Y-Crack Wall (expert area) is here.

4 Psamead Hollow ✩✩✩
Small 40′ sandstone crag, with others like it in the area. No camping. Spring–autumn. State lands.
Ref: B. Werntz, D. Groth.
Directions: From Coloma, Psamead Hollow is at rest area on west side of Hwy. 51, just south of its junction with Hwy. 21.

5 Mill Bluff State Park ✩✩
Flat-topped, cliff-sided rock rises abruptly from plain. Slender sandstone pinnacles range up to 100′. Keep a low profile. Petroglyphs and swimming in area. Spring/autumn. Pay camping in state park (608-427-6692).
Ref: B. Werntz, D. Groth.
Directions: From Tomah go 8 mi. southeast on Hwy. 12/16. Signs direct one to Mill Bluff State Park.

Brinton's Buttress at Devil's Lake.

JON BERNHARD

6 Granddad's Bluff ☆☆

This 60' sandstone bluff overlooks the La Crosse and Mississippi Rivers and offers a scenic view of the city of La Crosse. Local bouldering hang. Spring–autumn. No camping in this city park.
Classics: Fellowship 9.
Ref: B. Werntz, D. Groth.
Directions: In La Crosse, Granddad's Bluff is 2 mi. east at city park.

7 Abelman's Gorge (aka Rock Springs Narrows) ☆

Rock-quarry climbable on its west side. Spring/autumn. Check locally. Private land.
Ref: Guidebook: Bagg's *50 Short Climbs in the Midwest.*
Directions: Abelman's Gorge is at north edge of Rock Springs. Park at turnout on Hwy. 136.

8 Devil's Lake State Park ☆☆☆☆

The Midwest's most popular climbing area (aka, a Chicago suburb). Home of the 70' glassy, red quartzite surrounding

the charming Devil's Lake and the Devil's Lake Fuckness Association (DLFA). Hundreds of short routes either toproped or led. Don't miss the fine climbing at the Old and New Sandstone areas on private land. Autumn sports a red wonderland of colors. This 6,000-acre state park in the Baraboo Range has full camping accommodations—make reservations early. State park, (608) 356–8301.
Classics: West Bluffs: Son of Great Chimney 11, Coup d'etat 11, Match of the Snatch 12; East Bluffs: Brinton's Buttress 7, Birch Tree Crack 9, Sometimes Crack 9, Congratulations 10b, Thoroughfare 11b, Acid Rock 12a, Bagatelle 12d, Rubberman 13b/c, Gill's Flatiron B1; Old Sandstone Area: Kingsbury Cruise 11+, Donkey Dihedral 12b.
Ref: C [187-45, 185-28, 125, 102, 90, 73, 71, 67 (7/81)], R [99-100, 93-48]; Ament's *Master of Rock;* Guidebooks: Swartling's *Climber's Guide to Devil's Lake, Wisconsin,* Hemacinski's *Extremist's Guide,* Widule and Swartling's *Climber's Guide to Devil's Lake,* Smith and Zimmerman's *Climber's and Hiker's Guide to Devil's Lake,* Bagg's *50 Short Climbs in the Midwest,* Morris's *A Climber's Guide to Devil's Lake,* Gardiner's *Devil's Lake: East Bluff,* Primak's *Chicago Mountaineering Club Guidebook to Local Practice Areas.*
Directions: From Baraboo drive 3 mi. south on Hwy. 12, following signs to south shore of Devil's Lake. Five main areas: 1) West Bluffs: On the park road just west from the south shore beach and concessions stands, a trail leads north to the West Bluff. 2) Railroad Tracks and Watermarks Wall: From south shore concessions hike north on railroad tracks to side trail to Watermarks and farther north to Railroad Tracks Wall. 3) East Bluffs (most number of routes and popular): Park at CCC cabin. Hike north up trail. 4) Old Sandstone Area: Go 1 mi. farther east from east Bluffs. 5) New Sandstone Area is just a tad farther east of the Old Sandstone Area.

9 Gibraltar Rock (closed?) ☆☆

One of the larger Wisconsin climbing areas composed of sandstone crags and boulders. More than one hundred traditional routes and bolted lead climbs from 5.11 to 5.12 up to 120' high. Also, a "Broken Beer Bottle Biker Zone." The area has been closed by local authorities because of expenses incurred by two rescues during the summer and fall of 1995. Spring–autumn. Pay camping in county park.
Classics: Cedar Jest 7, Locomotive 8, Dave's Dive 8, Scott's Roof, Radical Empiricism 11, Road to Nowhere 11.
Ref: C [187-45, 160-36], R 73-32, S 9/75; Guidebooks: Landmann and Hynek's *Gibraltar Rock,* second ed., Zschiesche's *The First Sport Climbing Guidebook and Coloring Book to Gibraltar,* Weigand et al.'s *Climber's and Fisherman's Guide to Gibraltar Rock,* Bagg's *50 Short Climbs in the Midwest.*
Directions: From Lodi go 4 mi. north on Hwy. 113. Turn left on Hwy. V (signs to park). Shortly, turn left into park. Short hike to Gibraltar Rock.

10 Alumni Wall

Traversing and problems on this coed building.
Directions: Alumni Wall is at the University of Wisconsin Alumni Center.
Ref: B. Werntz.

11 Governor Dodge State Park ☆☆

Five thousand acres of steep hills, valleys, and 40′ sandstone bluffs. Spring to autumn. Full recreational facilities in state park (608–935–2315).
Classics: Cilley's Iron Face B1.

Ref: D. Groth.
Directions: From Dodgeville go 3 mi. north on Hwy. 23 to Governor Dodge State Park (signs).

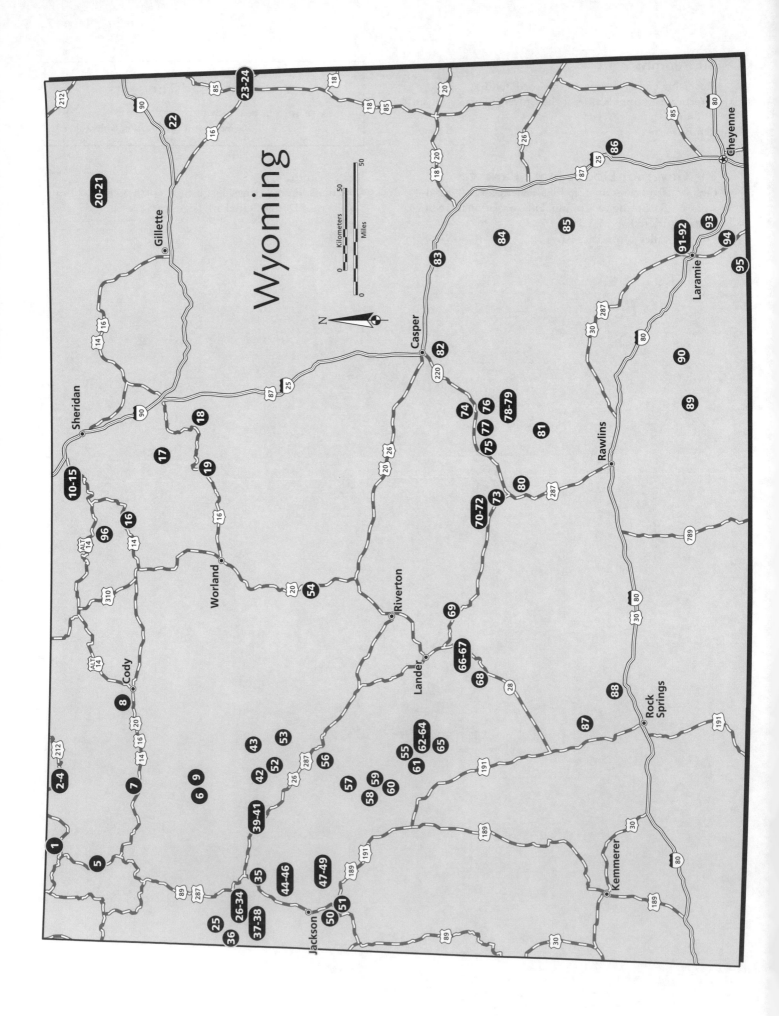

Wyoming

Wyoming

If wishes were wings, climbers would fly. —Don Hoover, Whiterock boulderer

The first clue that the traveling rock climber has entered Wyoming is the HOWDY! WELCOME TO BIG WONDERFUL WYOMING! sign. Next to come are weathered cowboys herding cattle on twenty-five million acres of rolling sagebrush plains spread out between mountain ranges of purple majesty. Not until climbers sally past this overburden will they realize that a wealth of rock-climbing jewels exists, and enough sheep to slow down any approach.

With an average elevation of more than 6,000 feet, the Cowboy State's climbing locales lie mainly in and around its famed mountain ranges. The Grand Tetons are the most famous, holding alpine treasures in its reaches and climbers in its spell. An ascent of the Grand Teton is still a treasured summertime event. The less-talked-about Wind River and Bighorn mountain ranges also hold incredible stores of climbing wares. The climber can find a lifetime of walls, crags, and boulders on a canvas of granite, limestone, or sandstone in these two ranges alone.

The Wind River Mountains (the original Rocky Mountains) feature many alpine climbing areas, the Cirque of Towers and Titcomb Basin being extremely popular. Mt. Hooker is just one of the Winds' finer big-wall challenges. Presently, the Sinks Canyon and the Wild Iris are two of the more popular cragging centers.

To the northeast, the Bighorns mirror the Winds in climbing charm. The Cloud Peak area offers alpine granite climbs, while Tensleep, Crazy Woman, and Little Tongue River Canyons provide cragging thrills. Beware, both mountain ranges have weather patterns that climbers may find unaccommodating for their lofty plans (including clouds of mosquitoes).

For close encounters of the rock-climbing kind, Devil's Tower in northeast Wyoming tests climbers' perseverance with columns of sustained cracks and stemming routes. The granitophiles of the world can ride the plutonic wave of granite that extends from Jeffrey City to Douglas to Laramie. Vedauwoo and Fremont Canyon are the two most popular areas that presently ride its crest. Attempting some of the renowned, gnarly cracks at Vedauwoo, potential ascentionists may find that they are indeed an "earth-bound" spirit. Farther to the west, Fremont Canyon offers one a magnificent chance for a dip "above" the river on clean granite.

Indeed, climbers will find Wyoming big and wonderful.

Hard-core locals claim fine winter conditions. Still, would anyone object to moving the state a little farther south for the winter?

1 Y☆–(Yellowstone National Park) Slough Creek ✩✩✩

Slough Creek offers decent, 150′ granite crags and boulders spread throughout the hilly woodlands. Trout fishing, too. Yellowstone, America's first national park since 1872, is a virtuoso ecosystem: grizzly bears, geysers (e.g., Old Faithful), thermal pools, buffalo, and one hundred species of mosquitoes. Should the rock climbing not offer enough excitement: remember, buffalo weigh 2,000 pounds and can sprint at 30 mph, three times faster than you can run! Pay camping in the park. Summer. NPS, (307) 344-7381.

Directions: From Tower Junction go approximately 8 mi. east on NPS road. Turn north to Slough Creek Trailhead and Campground. Crags visible to northeast of campground. Also roadside boulders and small walls farther east of Slough Creek turnoff and visible north of main park road.

2 Pilot Peak and Index Peak ✩✩✩

These distinguished, Alps-like pinnacles dominate the panorama just south of Cooke City on Hwy. 296. High, scenic alpine hike with easy fifth-class rock 300′ summits. Loose rock. Grizzly bear country. Summer. USFS–Shoshone NF, (307) 527-6241.

Classics: Pilot Peak (11,708′): Southwest Face 5; Index Peak: West Face 4.

Ref: Guidebook: Bonney's *Guide to the Wyoming Mountains and Wilderness Areas.*

Directions: From Cooke City go ⁸⁄10 mi. east on Hwy. 212. Hike south on Rays Trail to Hays Trail to Woody Creek Trail up to Pilot and Index Peaks.

3 Limestone Palisades

Lo-o-ong band (i.e., miles) of 200′ limestone starting below Index Peak and heading south. Rock is questionable. Needs exploration. Summer. USFS–Shoshone NF, (307) 527-6241.

Directions: From Cooke City 5 mi. east on Hwy. 212. Limestone Palisades is a lengthy band south of roadside.

4 Clarks Fork Granites ✯✯✯

Red 100′ granite outcrops a hop, skip, and a jump from pavement. "Pick and choose," one-pitch, granite climbing. Shotaro is a remarkable, 90′, overhanging, 5.12 finger crack at Junction Rock first freed by Hickman and Toula in the early 1990s. It's the first rock south of intersection of Hwy. 212 and Hwy. 296. Summer. Private land/USFS–Shoshone NF, (307) 527-6241.

Classics: Junction Rock: Shotaro 12.

Ref: J. Kanzler.

Directions: From Cooke City, Montana, stampede 14 mi. east on Hwy. 212 toward junction with Hwy. 296. Rock climbing begins north of junction and continues south on Hwy. 296. Rock outcrops are on east side of road—some bolted routes. Long, multipitched granitic walls in Clarks Fork River Canyon have seen ascents by Jim Kanzler and others.

5 Y–Yellowstone Falls Erratic ✯✯✯

One large, challenging, 16′ granitic boulder adjacent to a photographer's dream location. Spring to autumn. NPS, (307) 344-7381.

Ref: J. Sherman.

Directions: At Yellowstone Falls. Roughly ½ mi. before dead-end at Yellowstone Falls viewpoint. Marked with sign reading GLACIAL ERRATIC, on left side of road when driving toward viewpoint.

6 A✯–(Absaroka Mountains) Overview ✯✯✯

Scenic mountain range, but reportedly dicey rock in the backcountry. Brilliant ice climbing. Remote peaks. Large population of grizzly bears. Summer. USFS–Shoshone NF, (307) 527-6241.

Classics: Shoshone Canyon, Sunlight Basin.

Ref: C [199, 156-54]; Guidebook: Bonney's *Guide to the Wyoming Mountains and Wilderness Areas.*

Directions: From Cody, Absaroka Mountain range lies to the west from approximately the Montana border down to Younts Peak (near Togwotee Pass).

7 A–Chimney Rock (Yellowstone Hwy.) ✯✯

Obvious, popular landmark on Yellowstone Hwy. Abundance of other 300′ volcanic rock formations along Hwy. 16. Rock may be loose. Summer. USFS–Shoshone NF, (307) 527-6241.

Classics: Chimney Rock.

Ref: Guidebook: Bonney's *Guide to the Wyoming Mountains and Wilderness Areas.*

Directions: From Cody fire approximately 40 mi. west on Hwy. 16 to Chimney Rock. Chimney Rock is a 125′ pinnacle, first climbed in 1958 by Kamps and Rearick.

8 A–Shoshone Canyon ✯✯✯

Classic granite and limestone (Bridge Bands) cragging (close to 200 sport routes and many old trad routes) and one hundred or so Dakota sandstone boulder problems. Mostly one pitch. Many routes developed by the Cozzens brothers. Classic boulder problem (Wilford Wretch) at Dakota sandstone boulder garden. Five-star ice climbing down the South Fork, and fifth-class white water on the Shoshone River, too. A little-used opportunity in Wyoming. Cody is "The Rodeo Capital of the World." Spring/autumn. Private/government land.

Classics: Inner Gorge Granites; Tunnel Area: Arrowhead 5.11c; Boulder Garden: Parking Boulder B1+; Sphinx Boulders: The Sphincter.

Ref: C 198-54 (topos); Guidebooks: Aune's *Guide to Shoshone Canyon 1998,* Cozzens's *Shoshone Topographics,* Bonney's *Guide to the Wyoming Mountains and Wilderness Areas.*

Directions: From Cody float 2–5 mi. west of Cody on Hwy. 20 to Shoshone Canyon. Several areas: 1) The Boulder Gardens (Dakota sandstone boulders and crags): Go up Cedar Mountain Rd. (dirt) to third switchback, then west. 2) Sphinx Boulders: North of silver tube across river hiking east from Bridge Bands. 3) Bridge Bands: North of bridge. 4) The Island: Between second and third tunnels. 5) Inner Canyon and Dam Area (Gorge Granites): East of dam at river level below tunnels.

9 A–Castle Rock ✯

Obvious, 200′ volcanic plug at road's end at private ranch. Possibly other climbable volcanics in the area. Remarkable ice climbing in this area described in South Fork Water Ice by Todd Cozzens. Summer/autumn. Private land/USFS–Shoshone NF, (307) 527-6241.

Ref: R [68, 53]; Guidebook: Bonney's *Guide to the Wyoming Mountains and Wilderness Areas.*

Directions: From Cody stampede 1 mi. west on Hwy. 16. Turn southwest on Hwy. 291 for 19 mi. to Castle Rock.

10 BM✯–(Bighorn Mountains) Overview ✯✯✯✯✯

A climber's jewel sparkling with many facets of the sport: big-wall granite, limestone bluffs, and boxcar boulders with many sides waiting to be polished. Mid-July–early September. USFS–Bighorn NF, (307) 674-2600.

Classics: Cloud Peak VI 5.11, Fallen City, Crazy Woman Canyon, Ten Sleep Canyon, Shell Canyon.

Ref: AAJ [97-166, '79-200, 77-190, 74-153, 72-136, 71, 68, 65], C 166(2/97)-17, S 5/68; Guidebooks: Catlin's *Bighorns East,* Melius's *Cloud Peak Primitive Area,* Bonney's *Guide to the Wyoming Mountains and Wilderness Areas,* Bonney and Bonney's *Field Book: Bighorn Range.*

Directions: The 80-mi.-long Bighorn Mountain Range extends from the Montana border well below Ten Sleep Pass.

11 BM–Little Tongue River Canyon ★★★

Limestone cragging. Popular with Sheridan climbers. Spring–autumn. USFS–Bighorn NF, (307) 674–2600.
Ref: Bighorn Mountain Sports.
Directions: From Dayton travel up Hwy. 343 north of town to Little Tongue River Canyon. Hike into canyon to rock.

12 BM–Twin Buttes ★★★

The name says it all. These two prominent 300′ limestone buttresses capture a climber's eye to the north when approaching south from Greybull toward Burgess Junction. Bare Back 10+ is an overhanging hand crack in a dihedral, and Ring of Fire 10+ is a dihedral through two roofs. Summer/autumn. USFS–Bighorn NF, (307) 674–2600.
Classics: Bare Back 10+, Ring of Fire 10+.
Ref: M. Wilford; C 89; Guidebook: Bonney's *Guide to the Wyoming Mountains and Wilderness Areas.*
Directions: From Burgess junction head 2 ⁶/10 mi. north of junction on FS dirt roads (past picnic area). Turn right on dirt road past USFS ranger station to Twin Buttes.

13 BM–Burgess Picnic Area ★★

Pump while you picnic. A little 75′ granite outcrop with some short climbs and boulder problems adjacent to the creek in Burgess Picnic Area. Summer/autumn. USFS–Bighorn NF, (307) 674–2600.
Classics: Firepit route.
Directions: From Burgess junction flip 1 ½ mi. north of junction on FS dirt roads to picnic area signs. Right in the Burgess Picnic Area.

14 BM–Steamboat Rock ★★★

Routes on the 150′ limestone cliff and difficult boulder problems have been done below cliff. Lookout railings on top. Summer/autumn. USFS–Bighorn NF, (307) 674–2600.
Classics: Suicide Jockeys 12-.
Ref: C 89, R 48(3/92)-72.
Directions: From Dayton go west a few mi. on Hwy. 14 past Fallen City. Steamboat Rock has a prominent rock rampart on right with house-size boulders below. Faces south.

15 BM–Fallen City ★★

A geologic phenomenon and a rock climber's maze of climbs. Close to the road bouldering and 150′ limestone cragging. Summer/autumn. USFS–Bighorn NF, (307) 674–2600.
Classics: Wall of Voodoo 11X.
Ref: M. Wilford; C.
Directions: From Dayton zip west up on Hwy. 14 to Fallen City.

16 BM–Shell Canyon ★★★

A scenic world of 80′ dolomite with a granitic inner gorge. The granite climbing at Shell Falls is suggested as a place to start, though walls of dolomite envelop one. Summer. USFS–Bighorn NF, (307) 674–2600.
Ref: E. Sawyer.
Directions: From Shell wind east up Hwy. 14 in Shell Canyon to USFS Shell Falls area.

17 BM–Cloud Peak Wilderness Area ★★★★★

This heavenly, glacial, granitic wilderness peaks area of the Bighorns is a slightly scaled-down analog of the Wind River Range, also in Wyoming. Cloud Peak's 1,600′ east face is the most stunning although it's certainly not all. Black Tooth, second highest peak in the range, saw one of the first rock-climb ascents in 1933 by Rawles and Wilcox party. Black Tooth is third. All have large, dramatic faces. Much early exploratory climbing done by the Chicago Mountain Club in 1949. The imposing east face of Cloud Peak first freed via Ilgner and Petro's Shimmering Abstraction route. Plan on full-day hike-ins to reach these remote peaks. August. USFS–Bighorn NF, (307) 674–2600.
Classics: Cloud Peak: East Face, A Shimmering Abstraction IV 11, Woolsey South Ridge 5 (third highest), Black Tooth (second highest), Triple-summited Innominate.
Ref: AAJ '88-143, C [C 166(2/97)-17, 104]; Molvar's *Hiking Wyoming's Cloud Peak Wilderness;* Guidebooks: Bonney's *Guide to the Wyoming Mountains and Wilderness Areas,* Melius's *Cloud Peak Primitive Area.*
Directions: From Buffalo go one hour west via various access points to the backcountry of Cloud Peak Wilderness Area. Cloud Peak routes on east face accessed via the following: From West Ten Sleep Lake, walk to summit of Cloud Peak approximately six hours. Walk north five minutes to top of route. Then continue 100 yd. north to descend the second couloir down to glacier—approximately one hour to base of wall. Black Tooth/Woolsey area accessed via Kearney Lakes.

18 BM–Crazy Woman Canyon ★★★

Compact and 200′ plumb-steep canyon setting with rock as close to the road as it can get. More than thirty routes in 1999. Other areas expand up canyon. Primitive camping at 8,000′. June–October. Private land/USFS–Bighorn NF, (307) 674–2600.
Classics: Big Horn Roundup 12b, Psychodrama 12.
Ref: R 93-94 (topos); Guidebook: Catlin's topo sheet.
Directions: From Buffalo fly approximately 10 mi. south on Hwy. 196, then approximately 7 mi. west (at ranch sign, don't miss it) on Crazy Woman Canyon Rd. Other areas include: Elgin Park Wall on Rd. #460, Blue Chuck Cliff, Rd. #463; TLC Wall, Rd. #473, and walls at Rd. #466.

19 BM–Ten Sleep Canyon ★★★

Impressive length of 300′-plus dolomite walls in a wide dramatic mountain canyon. Developing amounts of one-pitch routes (more than one hundred in 1999) by Stan Price and Tod Anderson. June–September. Pay campgrounds at Ten

Sleep and Leigh Creek. USFS–Bighorn NF, (307) 674–2600.
Classics: If Dreams Were Thunder 12a, Superfly 12+.
Ref: D. Newton; R 93-94 (topos).
Directions: From Ten Sleep saunter 6 mi. east on Hwy. 16
to Ten Sleep Canyon. Climbing areas can be found near
mm 34, 35, 36, and between 41 and 42.

20 Missouri Buttes (5,372') ☆

Four 400' buttes of phonolite porphyry (same rock as
Devil's Tower). Spring-autumn. Private access. Ask permission.
Ref: Guidebook: Bonney's *Guide to the Wyoming Mountains
and Wilderness Areas.*
Directions: From Hulett prowl approximately 10 mi.
west/southwest on jeep roads to Missouri Buttes.

21 Devil's Tower National Monument
☆☆☆☆☆

This 600' monolith has to be seen to be believed; or, perhaps, believed to be seen. More than 160 classic, sustained
stemming cracks require prolonged endurance and mental
concentration. Thin fingers are handy and strong quads
and calves a must. Bring multiple RPs and wires. Challenging, though limited, bouldering scattered at base on broken columnar fragments of the rock known as phonolite
porphyry. Fun facts: First ascent in 1893 by Willard Ripley
and Will Rogers by long wooden pegs (A1?). First free
ascent by F. Weissner, L. Coveney, and B. House in 1937. In
1992, the popular Durrance Route 5.6 had received 16,810
climbers' ascents since 1937. First national monument in
the United States. Film site of *Close Encounters of the Third
Kind.* Some climbs may make for close encounters of the
wrong kind. In the heat of summer, a standard tactic is to
start on southwest routes and move west and on to the
north to avoid the heat of the sun. During June, a voluntary
climbing closure shows respect for the Native American culture. Autumn. Raptor restrictions March–July. Pay camping. NPS, (307) 467–5283.
Classics: Durrance Route 6, Bon Homme Var. 8, Everlasting
8+, Soler 9-, Assemblyline 9-, Walt Bailey Memorial 9,
Belle Fourche Buttress 10b, One-way Sunset 10c, Carol's
Crack 11a, Mr. Clean 11a, El Matador 11a, Direct
Southwest 11b, McCarthy West Face 11c, Deli Express
11d, Brokedown Palace 12a, Let Me Go Wild 12b,
Seamstress 12, Space Challenger 12+.
Ref: AAJ ['96-167, '77-179, '74-153, 70-68], C [198-94, 167-
44, 154-54, 141, 122(10/90)-61, 114, 108, 95, 91,
75(12/82), 73(7/82), 72, 54], M [118, 74], R [95-143, 86,
79-28/46, 73-32, 69-30] S 12/79; *Devil's Tower: Stories in
Stone,* Jones's *Climbing in North America;* Guidebooks:
Horning and Marriott's *A Poor Person's Guidebook: Free
Climbs of Devil's Tower,* Harlin's *Devil's Tower Wyoming and
Black Hills, South Dakota Classic Rock Climbs,* Guillmette's
Devil's Tower National Monument Climbing Handbook,
Gardiner and Guilmette's *Devil's Tower New Mexico: A
Climber's Guide,* Rypkema and Haire's *A Climber's Guide to*

Devil's Tower, Harlin's *Rocky Mountain,* Steck and Roper's
Fifty Classic Climbs, Bonney's *Guide to the Wyoming
Mountains and Wilderness Areas.*
Directions: From Devil's Tower junction hotfoot it 6 mi.
north on Hwy. 24, following park signs into Devil's
Tower National Monument past campground up to visitors center. Sign in. A paved trail begins at the visitors
center and circles the base of the Devil's Tower, serving as
a jump-off point to get to the base of the routes.

22 Inyan Kara Mountain (6,368') ☆☆

Volcanic cragging up to 200' and bouldering. Access from
private land. Spring/autumn. BLM, (307) 332–8447.
Ref: D. Hoover.
Directions: From Sundance scuttle 15 mi. south on Hwy.
585. Turn west on Inyan Kara Creek Rd. to base of rock
at southeast end of Inyan Kara Mountain.

23 Whiterock ☆☆☆

Boulderers who like to lunge or gliding lemurs will discover
fine dynamic bouldering on pygmaean, sandstone cubes.
Climbers shorter than 6' will find some of these blocks the
most challenging; boulderers taller than 6' should check
out Twin Rocks. Problems developed by the Hoover brothers, Bein, Devine, and Murray. Some good 80' cragging, too.
Nearby historic site of first hand-dug oil well in the United
States. Spring/autumn. Private land.
Classics: Problem Rock, Aerial Swoop B1, The Hoover
Maneuver B1+, Jaws B2, Den's Aerial B2, Twin Rocks,
Cactus Rock, Soul Bro.
Ref: D. and D. Hoover, P. Piana; C 79(6/83)-38; Sherman's
Stone Crusade; Guidebook: Toula's *Whiterock Bouldering
Guide.*
Directions: From Newcastle (junction of Hwy. 85 and Hwy.
16), glide 1 9/10 mi. east on Hwy. 16. Turn 1/2 mi. north
on Salt Creek Rd. Park on right just past meadow on
right at start of driveway to house trailer. Jump across
mini creek on trail. Contour to right around hill to base
of Whiterock Cliff. Bouldering areas are broken up into
Heaven, Hell, and Purgatory depending on ease of
access. Heaven has best bouldering and landings and is
directly below the northwest side of cliffs. Purgatory
and Hell are beyond in the rougher landscape.

24 Whoopup Canyon (closed) ☆

Features a classic black 50' sandstone crack. Most of the
rock here is soft sandstone. Petroglyphs. Cyndi Wertz, State
Office of External Affairs, reports that Whoopup is closed
to climbers (1997). Please do not climb here. Spring-
autumn. Private/government land.
Ref: D. Hoover.
Directions: From Newcastle whoop it up 8 mi. east on Hwy.
16. Turn 4 mi. south on dirt roads to short, rock-walled
Whoopup Canyon.

25 GT☆-Grand Teton National Park (GTNP) Overview ☆☆☆☆☆

Spectacular alpine mountaineering, sport cragging, and bouldering in the "Wyoming Alps." Arduous hiking app-roaches required of climbers. The Grand Traverse (Teewinot; Mt. Owen; Grand, Middle, and South Teton; and Nez Perce in-a-day) revered as an alpinist's fitness test. Also, home to Mt. Moran, the overlooked immense one along with many other alpine tests. NPS permits required for various Teton Routes. Check with rangers. NPS campgrounds are located at Jenny Lake or Gros Ventre Campgrounds. American Alpine Climber's Ranch (307-733-7271) also shelters climbers in park south of Jenny Lake. Or, camping found on more distant Forest Service lands. Nearest outdoor supplies, chuck wagon, and conversation sans libation area at Dornan's (Moose) near NPS headquarters. Summer. NPS, (307) 739-3300.

Classics: Death Canyon: Snaz 8–10a, Caveat Emptor 10; Grand Teton: Owen/Spalding 4, Exum Ridge 6–8, North Ridge 7, North Face 8, Gold Face 10-, Emotional Rescue 11-, Black Ice Couloir; Irene's Arête 8–10, Open Book 9; Cascade Canyon: Guide's Wall 8–10c; Symmetry Spire: Southwest Ridge 7; Baxter's Pinnacle: South Ridge 8–10; Mt. Owen: East Ridge 6; Mt. Moran: CMC 4, South Buttress Right 11a, Skillet Glacier; Blacktail Butte: Time Flies 10d, Graceland 11b (Upper), Do the Right Thing 11d, Arch 12a, Waterstreak 12b; Jenny Lake Boulders: Cutfinger Rock B1, Red Cross Overhang B2; Death Canyon: The Snaz 9/10a, Caveat Emptor 10.

Ref: AAJ ['98>96, '94, '89-160, 87-48/179, 85-205, 84, 82 to 80, 78, 77-188, 75-134, 74, 72-65], C [191-81, 179-88, 168-76, 136, 132, 111, 110, 88, 69], OB 44(4/79), R [100-98, 91-36, 20(1/87), 19, 18(3/87)], S [3/86, 4/77, 12/73, 6/71, 1/70, 6/67, 6/66, 3/63, 11/62]; Schneider's *Hiking Grand Teton National Park,* Jones's *Climbing in North America,* Bueler's *Teton Controversy: Who First Climbed the Grand;* Guidebooks: Rossiter's *Teton Classics,* Ortenburger and Jackson's *A Climber's Guide to the Teton Range* (third ed.), Ortenburger and Jackson's *Teton Range Climber's Guide,* Ortenburger and Jackson's *A Climber's Guide to the Teton Range, Vol. I and II,* Gill's *Guide to Jenny Lake Boulders, Alpenglow Teton Routes Guides,* Ortenburger's *A Climber's Guide to the Teton Range,* Steck and Roper's *Fifty Classic Climbs,* Fryxel's *Mountaineering in the Tetons,* Bonney's *Guide to the Wyoming Mountains and Wilderness Areas,* Bonney and Bonney's *Field Book: Teton Range and Gros Ventre Range,* Bonney and Bonney's *Guide to Jackson's Hole and Grand Teton National Park,* Gill and Chouinard's *Guide to Jenny Lake Boulders,* Coulter and McLane's *Mountain Climbing Guide to the Grand Tetons.*

Directions: From Moose go 8 mi. northwest on NPS road into Grand Teton National Park. Various access points. Check in at Jenny Lake Ranger Station for climbing information and permits. Lupine Meadows (for Garnet Canyon) is the most popular trailhead for the Grand Teton.

A successful summit party atop the Grand Teton.

TIM TOULA

26 GT-Boulder Island Boulder (at South Leigh Lake) ☆☆☆

An enjoyable morning's worth of 40′ topropes on this gla-cial erratic island. If you're canoeing to Mt. Moran, this rec-ommended pit stop is right on the way. Two sets of bolted anchors on top service nine routes. NPS, (307) 739-3300.

Classics: Boulder Island Boulder: Gunks problem 5.10, 5.11/12 topropes.

Ref: R. Collins; Guidebook: Sottile's *Jackson Hole: Sport Climbing and Bouldering.*

Directions: From Moose go north on NPS road. Park at String Lake parking area. Follow signs to String Lake/Leigh Lake portage. The portage and Boulder Island are at the southern end of Leigh Lake. Canoe north for 50 yd. across to small island. One giant boulder awaits your arrival. Note: Unless you're Christ or Jim Olson, you'll want a canoe for this approach!

27 GT-String Lake Boulder ☆☆☆

A 40′ glacial erratic and an hour's worth of topropes. Problems up to 5.11+. Bring wires and small friends for toprope anchors. NPS, (307) 739-3300.

Classics: 5.11c.

Ref: R. Collins, Guidebook: Sottile's *Jackson Hole Sport Climbing Guide.*

Directions: From Moose go north on NPS road. Park at String Lake parking area. Proceed 1 mi. north to String Lake Bridge. Turn left for Paintbrush Canyon (sign). Go 200 yd., and then turn left on faint game trail for 75 yd. to String Lake Boulder.

28 GT–Cascade Canyon (Hidden Falls)
✯✯✯

Hidden Falls is the Exum Mountain Guides practice rocks location. A fine beginner's area if no classes are being taught, i.e., go in the evening. Other classic, "short approach" (by Teton standards), 700' granite rock routes (e.g., Baxter's Pinnacle and Guide's Wall) lie higher up in Cascade Canyon. Summer. NPS, (307) 739-3300.

Classics: Practice Rocks: Open Book 5, Tree Route 6, Impossible Wall 10; Cascade Canyon: Guide's Wall 9/10c, Baxter's Pinnacle 9, Symmetry Spire III 7.

Ref: C [154, 153-64]; Guidebooks: Ortenburger and Jackson's *A Climber's Guide to the Teton Range*, Ortenburger's *A Climber's Guide to the Teton Range*, Bonney's *Guide to the Wyoming Mountains and Wilderness Areas*, *Alpenglow Teton Routes*, Rossiter's *Teton Classics*.

Directions: From Moose dodge 8 mi. north to Jenny Lake. Either hike thirty minutes or take a boat ride (fee) across Jenny Lake. For Hidden Falls: Hike ten minutes up Cascade Canyon. Cliffs are just west of Hidden Falls. Baxter's Pinnacle and Guide's Wall require thirty- or sixty-minute approaches farther up Cascade Canyon.

29 GT–Boulder City ✯✯✯

An enjoyable area, better if you have a partner and a 50' length of cord with which to toprope. Several good challenging granite boulders with bolted toprope anchors. Mosquito-esque setting. Nearby Jenny Lake Lodge (a little farther west) sports a fine gourmet breakfast until 9:00 a.m. Spring–autumn. NPS, (307) 739-3300.

Ref: Guidebook: Sottile's *Jackson Hole Sport Climbing Guide*.

Directions: From Moose drive north on NPS road about ten to fifteen minutes. Turn left at sign for North Jenny Lake. After 8/10 mi., park at Cathedral Group Pullout. Hike 2/10 mi. farther west on road. At APPROACHING TURNOUT sign on road, hike north into woods (fifteen minutes) passing an isolated cluster of pines in the meadow and using Mt. Moran's sweeping right shoulder in the distance as a directional sight. Boulder City lies hidden in the Lodgepole pines. Where the meadow hits the trees, pick up a faint trail (if you are lucky) over a small hill. On the other side of this hill (ridge) lie the boulders scattered in the trees. Good topropes over to east through talus.

30 GT–Jenny Lake Campground Boulders
✯✯✯

A tote bag of classic lakeside problems first ascended in 1950s. The Gill and Chouinard bouldering guide available at Jenny Lake Ranger Station provides a detailed tour of specific problems. As it states in the original guide, "These are big boulders, they make their own weather." The test-piece problem is Red Cross Overhang B2, especially when done dynamically in its original style. Stiff edging shoes and steel fingers help. In the heat of the summer, boulders tend to be greasier than Brylcream. Fifteen bouldering routes. Spring–autumn. NPS, (307) 739-3300.

Classics: Falling Ant Slab: no hands problems, Cutfinger Rock B1 Center Route, Red Cross Overhang B2 (the one you can climb—just kiddin').

Ref: C 127; Ament's *Master of Rock;* Sherman's *Stone Crusade;* Guidebooks: Sottile's *Jackson Hole Sport Climbing Guide,* Yanoff's *Full Circle,* Gill's *Bouldering Sheet* (available at Jenny Lake Ranger Station), Gill and Chouinard's *Guide to Jenny Lake Boulders.*

Directions: From Moose drive 8 mi. north to Jenny Lake Campground and nearby Jenny Lake Ranger Station. From ranger station saunter 100 yd. west to bicycle path and then north approximately a football field to three historic boulders (Cutfinger Rock, Falling Ant Slab, and Red Cross Rock) at Jenny Lake Campground. Cutfinger Rock's south face is seen first left of path, and Falling Ant Slab is just west, 15 yd. west toward Jenny Lake. Red Cross Rock is 30 yd. north of Cutfinger Rock, adjacent to bike path on left.

31 GT–Teewinot Boulders (at Lupine Meadows) ✯✯

Twenty-five-foot gneiss boulders scattered at the basal slopes of the lengthy east face of Teewinot. Summer. NPS, (307) 739-3300.

Ref: Guidebook: Ortenburger's *A Climber's Guide to the Teton Range.*

Directions: From Moose drive 8 mi. north. Turn left on Lupine Meadow Rd. (before Jenny Lake) to Lupine Meadow parking lot. Hike up main trail to Garnet Canyon/Grand Teton for ten minutes to big glacial erratics visible on trail to right. More boulders at base of Teewinot.

32 GT–Grand Teton (13,770') ✯✯✯✯✯

This classic, beloved alpine summit is the focal point of all Teton mountaineers. The Grand is characterized by rugged approaches, unsettled weather, and numbing temperatures all offset by one-of-a-kind views. Prized classics are listed below. The approach to the Grand via Garnet Canyon possesses many opportunities for climbing as well. Here, routes like Irene's Arête and bouldering in the Garnet Meadows area add enjoyment to any "Grand" excursion. Approaches for the Grand Teton's South Ridges (Exum, Petzoldt, and UnderHill) and Enclosure/Black Ice Couloir routes usually made from campsites on the Lower Saddle or Middle Teton Morainal Zone. North face routes usually approached from Teton Glacier. Obtain NPS permit. Long history of ascents. First to touch the top is still under scrutiny—possibly Owen Spalding in 1898. Or maybe Langford Stevenson in 1872? An Indian prior? Your guess. Mid-July through August the surest weather bets for a Teton summit success. NPS, (307) 739-3300.

Classics: Grand Teton: Owen/Spalding 4, Petzoldt Ridge 6, East Ridge 7, Complete Exum Ridge 7, North Ridge 7, Italian Cracks 7, North Face 8, Loki's Tower 9, Gold Face 10a, Emotional Rescue 5.11-; ice classics: Black Ice Couloir, Enclosure Couloir; Garnet Canyon: Irene's Arête 8/9, Open Book 9, Bouldering in the Garnet Canyon Meadows.

Ref: C [66, 63, 5(1/71)], R [67-44, 18], S 7/88; Bueler's *Teton Controversy: Who First Climbed the Grand;* Guidebooks: Ortenburger and Jackson's *A Climber's Guide to the Teton Range,* Rossiter's *Teton Classics,* Ortenburger's *A Climber's Guide to the Teton Range,* Bonney's *Guide to the Wyoming Mountains and Wilderness Areas,* Alpenglow Teton Routes, Steck and Roper's *Fifty Classic Climbs,* Coulter and McLane's *Mountain Climbing Guide to the Grand Tetons.*

Directions: From Moose drive 8 mi. north on NPS road. Turn left on Lupine Meadow Rd. (before Jenny Lake) to Lupine Meadow parking. Two approaches: 1) Trailhead for Garnet Canyon to Lower Saddle (for south ridge routes or Valhalla Traverse for Enclosure/North Face routes). 2) Amphitheater Lakes (to Teton Glacier/North Face routes) begins at Lupine Meadow parking area. Of the two, Garnet Canyon sees the most use for parties bound for the Owen Spalding/Exum Ridge routes. A third approach is via Cascade Canyon to Valhalla Canyon.

33 GT–Climber's Ranch Boulder ★★★

In summer, this 35′ gneissic boulder can be slicker than scum off a Louisiana swamp. Toprope problems or sporty solos. The Climber's Ranch (June–September) is a climber's social gathering spot for Teton ventures and Teton Tea. It's also a good deal and a good place to round up climbing partners. Run by the American Alpine Club, NPS, (307) 739-3300.

Ref: C 97; Guidebooks: Ortenburger's *A Climber's Guide to the Teton Range.*

Directions: From Moose go 5 mi. north on Park Rd. Turn left into American Alpine Club Climber's Ranch (sign). Climber's Ranch Boulder is the large, hillside boulder visible 100 yd. uphill to the west of the picnic pavilion.

34 GT–Death Canyon (Snaz Buttress) ★★★★

A popular Teton canyon of classic 1,000′ routes, e.g., The Snaz and Caveat Emptor. Swift climbers will often do two routes in a day. Popular with climbers because of the relatively short approach . . . for the Tetons. Camping at road's end. Summer. NPS, (307) 739-3300.

Classics: Snaz 10a, Caveat Emptor 10+.

Ref: R 19(5/87)-26; Guidebooks: Rossiter's *Teton Classics,* Ortenburger and Jackson's *A Climber's Guide to the Teton Range* (third ed.), Bonney's *Guide to the Wyoming Mountains and Wilderness Areas.*

Directions: From Moose ride approximately 3 mi. south on NPS road to Death Canyon Trailhead. Hike approximately one hour up canyon. Several buttresses to one's right, the Snaz Buttress being the most popular. See Ortenburger and Jackson's guide for intricate details.

35 GT–Blacktail Butte ★★★

Possibly the crag with the "Grandest" views in the United States. Until the late 1980s, this 60′ limestone crag was renowned as a fine, vertical, local toprope, microedge face-climbing area with just a single old ¼″ bolt route up the main face. Now, this popular Jackson crag, adorned with sport routes, evokes the name "Blacktail Buoux." Testpieces require precision footwork and steel tips. Twenty-five routes. Jackson is host of several fine coffeehouses/eateries, including Pearl Street Bagels and Shades Cafe. Spring-autumn. NPS, (307) 739-3300.

Classics: Lower: Time Flies When You're Alive 10c, Bolt Route 11a, Diagonal Crack 11, Do the Right Thing 11c, The Arch 12a, Water Streak 12b, Low Bouldering Traverse B5.12; Upper: Muy Macho 10d, Graceland 11b.

Ref: C 127, R 100-122; Ament's *Master of Rock;* Guidebooks: Sottile's *Jackson Hole Sport Climbing Guide,* Yanoff's *Full Circle, Blacktail Butte Topo Sheet* (free at Teton Mountaineering).

Directions: From Jackson drive 12 mi. north on Hwy. 191 (1 mi. north of Moose). Blacktail Butte is east of road. Main Area (North): Indiscreet stairway leads past low bouldering traverse/topropes up to the main bolted crag. For South (Upper) Cliffs: From parking lot follow worn foot-trail fifteen minutes southeast and then left up talus.

36 GT–Teton Canyon (Grand Wall) ★★★

Grand Wall is a 165′ granite cliff of sport climbs—a tip of an iceberg. Fun climbing and scenic views on the west side of the Grand Tetons. Thirteen sport and trad routes. Gives one a different perspective of the Teton Range. Reportedly good ice climbing as well in winter. Take in the quintessential Friday-night movie experience at The Spud Drive-in theater in Driggs. Summer. Pay and free camping. USFS-Targhee NF, (208) 354-2313.

Classics: 5.7 wall, 5.9 Route, Bambi 11a, Munger Crack 11+, Ninjitsu 11c, Dr. Hole 12a, Mayday 12a, Arms Deal 13a.

Ref: Guidebooks: Sottile's *Jackson Hole Sport Climbing Guide,* Yanoff's *Full Circle.*

Directions: From Driggs, Idaho, at main intersection head east on Targhee Ski Rd. Turn right at 5 9/10 mi. (Lost Horizons Restaurant on left—easy to miss) and take dirt road to road's end in Teton Canyon at 4 7/10 mi. Hike five minutes up trail. Grand Wall veers left up trail 100 yd. on left. Perhaps more striking are the limestone buttresses seen while driving into canyon.

37 GT–Corbett's and S&S Couloirs (The Tram) ★★

In summer cool, 70′ dolomite sport climbs in the mountains help beat the valley heat. By winter these are way-rad ski jumps. Corbett's Couloir's east face has pronounced water stain and is where the Ravin' Roof Bypass route lies. Rappel into either crag or fourth-class gully into Corbett's. Bring medium-size pro. Don't miss the last scheduled tram down. Calico Pizza and Vista Grande Mex Restaurant are popular hangs with Teton climbers. Summer. USFS-Bridger-Teton NF, (307) 739-5500.

Classics: Corbett's: Sky Pilot 11, Ravin' 12; S&S: New World 10c.

Ref: R. Collins; Guidebooks: Sottile's *Jackson Hole Sport Climbing Guide,* Yanoff's *Full Circle.*
Directions: Above Teton Village. Ride tram (smashing views) to top (fee: approximately $13 per person in 1993). Hike downhill south, then east, with tram cables to your left. First rock gully is Corbett's Couloir. The second is S&S Couloir.

38 Fish Creek Boulder (closed) ☆☆

This 30' granite practice boulder is included here for its historical value. Now no trespassing! Wilson is home of great breakfasts at Nora's Inn and fine western music at the Stagecoach Bar, where every Sunday the boys in the band whoop it up. Spring–autumn. Private land.
Ref: J. Jacobowski; Guidebook: Ortenburger and Jackson's *Teton Range Climber's Guide.*
Directions: From Wilson (approximately five minutes from town), drive ⁴/10 mi. north on West, then north 1 mi. on Fish Creek Rd. On left behind the BIG BOULDER sign. Fish Creek Boulder is visible to left 100 yd. from road, west of road near ranchette driveway.

39 A☆–Angle Mountain ☆

Roadside limestone bands (40') of dubious quality, although some routes possible. Summer. USFS–Bridger-Teton NF, (307) 543-2386.
Directions: From Moran drive up approximately 19 mi. east on Hwy. 287 past Teton overlook. Angle Mountain's obvious rock bands northeast of road requires steep hike.

40 A–Ramshorn

Spectacular horn prominently visible from Hwy. 287 north of Dubois. Mainly an alpine hike/climb. Ice axes and ropes may be necessary. Summer. USFS–Shoshone NF, (307) 527-6241.
Ref: Guidebooks: Bonney's *Guide to the Wyoming Mountains and Wilderness Areas,* Bonney and Bonney's *Field Book Yellowstone and Absaroka Range.*
Directions: From Dubois go approximately 10 mi. west of Dubois from Hwy. 287. Go northwest of Horse Creek campground. Long hike to Ramshorn.

41 A–Washakie Needles

Remote, alpine peak at 12,518'. Wilderness cluster of fifth-class rock—possibly mostly technical hiking. Summer. USFS–Shoshone NF, (307) 527-6241.
Classics: East Face 5.
Ref: Guidebooks: Bonney's *Guide to the Wyoming Mountains and Wilderness Areas,* Bonney and Bonney's *Field Book Yellowstone and Absaroka Range.*
Directions: From Thermopolis wheel west on Hwy. 120. Turn onto Hwy. 170, then follow dirt roads. Long hike involved to Washakie Needles. Also approached via Meteestse or Morton. All approaches require backcountry hiking.

42 Breccia Cliffs ☆

Alluring "butt" treacherous 600' breccia. Possibly few, if any, rock-climbing ascents. For the adventuresome climber who wants to push the limits of choss. Free camping. Summer. USFS–Shoshone NF, (307) 527-6241.
Ref: Guidebooks: Bonney's *Guide to the Wyoming Mountains and Wilderness Areas,* Bonney and Bonney's *Field Book Yellowstone and Absaroka Range.*
Directions: From Moran shred 23 mi. east on Hwy. 287. High escarpments northeast of road are the Breccia Cliffs.

43 Pinnacle Buttes (11,516') ☆

Treacherous and alluring 700' breccia spires. "Those dramatic cliffs can be seen from US 287 in all their dangerous looking glory" (from Bonney's *Guide to Wyoming Mountains and Wilderness Areas*). Free camping. Summer. USFS–Shoshone NF, (307) 527-6241.
Ref: Guidebooks: Bonney's *Guide to the Wyoming Mountains and Wilderness Areas,* Bonney and Bonney's *Field Book Yellowstone and Absaroka Range.*
Directions: From Dubois go approximately 24 mi. northwest on Hwy. 287. Then approximately 4 mi. north on Brooks Lake Rd. Hike east to Pinnacle Buttes.

44 GV☆–(Gros Ventre Mountains) Overview ☆☆☆

Gros Ventre Mountains is a forested mountain range, often overlooked because of its proximity to the Grand Tetons. The rock that does exist has seen little to date, but potential exists. New areas will probably require hikes of forty-five minutes or more from the road. Home of the 1925 Gros Ventre Slide, visible from parts of Jackson Hole and Grand Tetons. Summer. USFS–Bridger-Teton NF, (307) 739-5500.
Classics: Hoback Shield, Chimney Rock, and Granite Hot Springs Float.
Ref: S 12/62; Guidebooks: Bonney's *Guide to the Wyoming Mountains and Wilderness Areas,* Bonney and Bonney's *Field Book Teton Range and Gros Ventre Range.*
Directions: Gros Ventre Range extends from Kelly to Bondurant, east of Hwy. 191.

45 GV–Slide Lake Area ☆

Boulderfield just downstream of lake has limited climbable boulders. Finding boulders high enough to climb is like jumping through a minefield in a gunnysack. Some short but climbable roadside walls along the north side of the road. Good views of the 1925 Gros Ventre Land Slide. Gros Ventre River is popular kayak run. Free/pay camping along road. Summer. USFS–Bridger-Teton NF, (307) 739-5500.
Ref: D. Insley.
Directions: From Kelly go approximately 5 mi. east on paved FS road past Kelly Warm Springs. Slide Lake Area boulderfield on right. Short cliff bands on left offer more climbs.

46 GV–Jackson Peak (10,741') ✵✵

Five-hundred-foot gneiss alpine walls—with potential cragging. Summer. USFS-Bridger-Teton NF, (307) 739-5500.
Ref: Guidebooks: Bonney's *Guide to the Wyoming Mountains and Wilderness Areas,* Bonney and Bonney's *Field Book Teton Range and Gros Ventre Range.*
Directions: From Jackson zoom 10 mi. east on Flat Creek Rd. Park at Curtis Creek campground. Hike 5 mi. south on Goodwin Lake Trail to Jackson Peak.

47 GV–Pinnacle Peak (aka Weaver's Needle)✵

A 300' alpine Devil's Tower at 10,808'; first done in 1960 by Breitenbach, Krebs, Shepard, Sinclair, and Buckingham. Free camping. Summer. USFS-Bridger-Teton NF, (307) 739-5500.
Classics: South Chimney 5.5 (Rotten) 1960, west arête 5.5, 2001.
Ref: Guidebooks: Bonney's *Guide to the Wyoming Mountains and Wilderness Areas,* Bonney and Bonney's *Field Book Teton Range and Gros Ventre Range.*
Directions: From Jackson go south to junction of Hwy. 89 and Hwy. 189. Turn on Hwy. 189 for 11 mi. south on Hwy. 189. Turn left at Granite Creek Hot Springs (sign) to end. Hike north/northwest on trail. Pinnacle Peak is northwest of Granite Hot Springs. Use topo maps/

48 GV–Granite Creek ✵✵

Three different roadside boulders on left side of road. What's more piquant is the incredible limestone cliff band potential as well. Incipient sport climbing routes done around the statuesque Chimney Rock. Stew in your own juices at the classic hot springs below the waterfall or pay above (daily hours). Free camping. Summer. USFS-Bridger-Teton NF, (307) 739-5500.
Classics: Chimney Rock.
Ref: Guidebooks: Bonney's *Guide to the Wyoming Mountains and Wilderness Areas,* Bonney and Bonney's *Field Book Teton Range and Gros Ventre Range.*
Directions: From Jackson trend south to junction of Hwy. 89 and Hwy. 189. Turn south on Hwy. 189 for approximately 11 mi. Turn left at Granite Creek Hot Springs sign. Intermittent sharp boulders are dispersed along dirt road on left. Large cliff bands visible from road and Chimney Rock visible above end of road.

49 GV–Hoback Shield ✵✵✵

This 180' hillside southwest-facing limestone slab is a popular teaching and intermediate climbing area. Beware of ever loose rock as one nears the summit. In the heat of the summer, the Hoback in the morning and the Rodeo Wall in the afternoon make for a nice, one-two climbing punch. Twenty-four routes. Fun kayak run below on Hoback River. Camping just to north or south. Summer/fall. USFS-Bridger-Teton NF, (307) 739-5500.

Classics: The Bulge 8/10a, Thousand Cranes 9, Fandango 10c, Nervhus Sheep 10+, Electric Shower 11b.
Ref: C 128, R 100-122; Guidebooks: Sottile's *Jackson Hole Sport Climbing Guide,* Yanoff's *Full Circle, Hoback Shield Topo Sheet* (free at Teton Mountaineering).
Directions: From Jackson go south to junction of Hwy. 89 and Hwy. 189. Turn south on Hwy. 189 for 10 9/10 mi. Hoback Shield's limestone bowl is on left. Parking pull-out on right. (One mi. farther south on Hwy. 189 is Granite Hot Springs turnoff.) Short ten-minute uphill approach.

50 GV–Rodeo Wall ✵✵✵

Decidedly fun pulling on classic, lipped crimpers at this slightly-above-the-road, 70', east-facing limestone sport crag. Good cliff for intermediate climbers—just watch the runouts! Bring the quickdraws for the ten-plus routes. Astoria Hot Springs and campground is across the Hoback River: bonus! Spring-autumn. USFS-Bridger-Teton NF, (307) 739-5500.
Classics: Betty Tendonblaster 9, Buck Dancer 10c, Bulldog 11b.
Ref: R 100-122; Guidebooks: Sottile's *Jackson Hole Sport Climbing Guide,* Yanoff's *Full Circle.*
Directions: From junction of Hwy. 89 and Hwy. 189 (south of Jackson), buck 2 2/10 mi. south on Hwy. 89. On right at mm 139. Obvious, short, but s-s-steep ten-minute approach (reminiscent of a mini-hike up Garnet Canyon) to base of Rodeo Wall.

51 GV–Heechee Wall ✵✵

Untapped, east-facing vertical wall. Campgrounds nearby. Summer. USFS-Bridger-Teton NF, (307) 739-5500.
Classics: Easy Travel to Other Planets 12b.
Ref: Guidebooks: Sottile's *Jackson Hole Sport Climbing Guide,* Yanoff's *Full Circle.*
Directions: From Jackson go south to junction of Hwy. 89 and Hwy. 189. Turn 6 2/10 mi. south on Hwy. 189. On right (just beyond the Stinking Springs turnout). Hike south fifteen minutes up limestone talus to Heechee Wall.

52 A–Horse Creek ⭐⭐

Short-rein 40′ limestone toprope problems. Summer.
USFS–Shoshone NF, (307) 527–6241.

Directions: From Dubois trot approximately 10 mi. north.
Forty-foot wall is just northwest of Horse Creek
Campground. Roadside.

53 A–East Fork Valley ⭐⭐

Small, one-pitch, 60′ granite ranch outcrop. No camping.
Summer. Private land.

Directions: From Dubois travel approximately 10 mi. south
on Hwy. 287, then turn left (north) onto East Fork Rd.
for approximately 10 mi. East Fork Valley Rocks visible
on right.

54 Wind River Canyon ⭐⭐⭐⭐

Incredible wealth of 200′ sedimentary, dolomite, and metamorphic walls in this 10 mi. canyon carved by the Wind
River. Possibly a forty-foot sport crag at far north end of
canyon. Climbing is illegal on the Wind River Indian Reservation lands, which is most of the canyon. Please get permission from reservation or stay off private land. Hot
springs/camping in Thermopolis at state park. Nice class 3
kayaking/rafting run through canyon. Get permit. Spring–
autumn. BIA/private land.

Classics: 180′ Wind River Pinnacle 7 (by Walt Bailey and
Dave Sturdevant 1956).

Ref: Guidebook: Bonney's *Guide to the Wyoming Mountains
and Wilderness Areas.*

Directions: From Thermopolis wind ten minutes south on
Hwy. 20. Potential climbing begins east of road at north
end of canyon. Wind River Canyon rock starts near picnic
shelter and short cliffs on left. At mm 125, sandstone
cliffs fade to long stretch of dolomite bands. Past mm
124, Wind River Pinnacle on left. At mm 121, easy access
to roadside Dolomite Boulders (sharp), whose texture
gives the same feeling as lying down in a bed of coral.
Metamorphic lands begin at 117.3 and continue to mm
116 at south end of canyon. Campground at end of three
tunnels near mm 116.

55 WR⭐–(Wind River Mountains) Overview ⭐⭐⭐⭐⭐

The original Rocky Mountains and part of the Continental
Divide. A prime rock and alpine experience awaits all
climbers with myriad granite peaks and walls. Classic alpine
routes, like Wolf's Head, have been known to contribute to
many a climber's midsummer's night dream. The highest
point in Wyoming, Gannet Peak at 13,804′, is one of the
most remote alpine summits in the Lower 48. Range named
from the Wind River, which originates here. Summer.
USFS–Bridger-Teton NF, (307) 367–4326/Shoshone NF,
(307) 527–6241.

Classics: Wolf's Head: East Ridge II 5, Ellingwood Peak NF
IV6; Pronghorn: Antelope Arête III 8, Pingora Northeast
Face III 9, Warbonnet 5.10, Black Elk III 11-; Squaretop:

West Face V 10, Lost Temple Spire Southwest Arête 10,
Mt. Hooker NF VI 12; Sinks Canyon, The Wild Iris.

Ref: AAJ ['98-202, '96-167, '95>93, 92-142, 91-173, 90-177,
87-181, 86-172, 85-205, 84, 82 to 79, 78-74, 72-65], C [151-
58, 132, 97, 89, 70, 63, 10/72], R [82-76, 67-61], S [3/89,
8/76, 7/84, 11/81, 3/81, 9/75, 5/75, 12/72, 9/71, 6/70,
4/68, 11/66, 4/65, 5/64, 8/62]; Adkison's *Hiking Wyoming's
Wind River Range,* Kor's *Beyond the Vertical,* Kelsey's *Wind
River Mountains;* Guidebooks: Kelsey's *Climbing and Hiking in
the Wind River Mountains,* Jacobs's *Climbing Gannett Peak: The
Wind Rivers,* Steck and Roper's *Fifty Classic Climbs,* Bonney's
Guide to the Wyoming Mountains and Wilderness Areas, Bonney
and Bonney's *Field Book: The Wind River Range.*

Directions: From Lander to Pinedale, the Wind River Mountain range in west-central Wyoming extends for 90 mi. in a
northwest to southeast direction. A few selected areas are
shown here. Sixteen different road heads leading to various
wilderness trails. On the west side, the most popular are:
Green River, Elkhart Park, and Big Sandy. On the east side,
Trail Lake Ranch, Dickinson Park, and Sinks Canyon are
most popular. Most approaches are long and arduous
affairs to which more than one climber, buckling under a
one-hundred-pound pack load, has said, "Include me out."

56 WR–Trail Lake Ranch Road ⭐⭐

Scattered granitic boulders/80′ dolomite/granite craglets en
route to a wilderness trailhead. Summer. USFS– Shoshone
NF, (307) 527–6241.

Ref: Mitchell's *Wind River Trails,* Kelsey's *Wyoming's Wind
River Range;* Guidebooks: Kelsey's *Climbing and Hiking in
the Wind River Mountains,* Bonney's *Guide to the Wyoming
Mountains and Wilderness Areas,* Bonney and Bonney's *Field
Book: The Wind River Range.*

Directions: From Dubois take Hwy. 287 south. Turn west
on Trail Lake Ranch Rd. (high-clearance vehicle recommended) to scattered roadside rocks.

57 WR–Squaretop ⭐⭐⭐⭐

At 11,690′, Squaretop is one of the most photographed
peaks in the Winds. Just one of many alpine walls in the
Winds, though few have as spectacular and sheer of a 1,500′
west face. Routes range from hikes to beginner/ intermediate to grade IV and V. Coke Bottle is an aesthetically named
formation just west of Squaretop with yet another Fred
Beckey route. Many climbable formations in area. Summer.
USFS–Bridger-Teton NF, (307) 367–4326.

Classics: Squaretop: Southeast Face; West Face Routes: V
10; Coke Bottle.

Ref: Guidebooks: Kelsey's *Climbing and Hiking in the Wind
River Mountains,* Bonney's *Guide to the Wyoming Mountains
and Wilderness Areas,* Bonney and Bonney's *Field Book: The
Wind River Range.*

Directions: From Pinedale take Hwy. 191 west for a few mi.
to Cora cutoff. Turn north on Hwy. 352, following signs
to Green River Lakes. At road's end. Hike 8 mi. on trail or
make an approximately 6-mi. canoe trip to base of
Squaretop.

58 WR–New Fork Lakes Buttress ✮✮✮

A nice, weekend 700′ mountain crag, aka China Wall. The sustained first pitch of Toula and Valdez's Knucklebuster is as fine as finger cracks come in the Winds. Summer/autumn. USFS–Bridger-Teton NF, (307) 367-4326.

Classics: Bull's Horns Spires 9, Knucklebuster III 11d/12a.

Ref: Mitchell's *Wind River Trails;* Guidebooks: Kelsey's *Climbing and Hiking in the Wind River Mountains,* Bonney's *Guide to the Wyoming Mountains and Wilderness Areas,* Bonney and Bonney's *Field Book: The Wind River Range.*

Directions: From Pinedale take Hwy. 191 west for a few miles to Cora cutoff. Turn north on Hwy. 352. Turn right on FR 107 for 2 mi. to New Fork Lakes. Park at trailhead. Hike 6 mi. east on trail to visible New Fork Lakes Buttress to north. Two-hour approach.

59 WR–Titcomb Basin ✮✮✮✮

The most popular trailhead in the Winds leads to a most popular and spectacular alpine area. The 1,000′ Ellingwood Arête IV 5.6-8 is one of the better long climbs in the Winds for its grade. Mt. Helen's ice couloir is often compared to the Black Ice in the Tetons. Fremont's West Flank also offers many classic climbing challenges. Summer/autumn. USFS–Bridger-Teton NF, (307) 367-4326.

Classics: Fremont Peak: various; Mt. Helen Ice route, Ellingwood Arête IV 5.6.

Ref: C [132, 97], R 94-152, S 18(11/72)-35; Mitchell's *Wind River Trails;* Guidebooks: Kelsey's *Climbing and Hiking in the Wind River Mountains,* Bonney's *Guide to the Wyoming Mountains and Wilderness Areas,* Bonney and Bonney's *Field Book: The Wind River Range.*

Directions: From Pinedale follow Fremont Lake Rd. to Elkhart Park (twenty-five minutes). Hikes into Titcomb Basin/Fremont Peak area require a one- or two-day approach.

60 WR–Fremont Lake Boulders ✮

Small 25′ roadside granite boulders and mini crags. More even farther up road scattered in woods to east of road. Summer. USFS–Bridger-Teton NF, (307) 367-4326.

Ref: C. Rollins.

Directions: From Pinedale drive north on Fremont Lake Rd. Park. Hike east of road and south of Half Moon Lake to Fremont Lake Boulders.

61 WR–Burnt and Boulder Lake Boulders ✮✮

Granite boulders at Burnt Lake north and 2 mi. before public campground. Summer. USFS–Bridger-Teton NF, (307) 367-4326.

Classics: The Roadside Boulder.

Ref: T. Skinner.

Directions: From Boulder drive 2 ½ mi. east on Hwy. 353. Turn 10 mi. north on dirt road left or right fork to Burnt and Boulder Lake Boulders (signs). Boulders at Burnt Lake north and 2 mi. before public campground.

62 WR–Mt. Hooker and East Fork Valley ✮✮✮✮✮

Mt. Hooker, at 12,504′, is the major 2,000′ granite wall of the Wind River Range, with wild climbing and potentially cold, savage weather. Three classic free climbs IV/V 5.12s and five hardy A4 lines as of 1996. McCracken, Robbins, and Raymond did Original Route in 1964. In 1990, Ritchie, Rolofson, and Whitehouse freed all but 50′ due to weather on Jaded Lady Route. Shortly thereafter, completely freed by Piana, Rowell, Skinner, and Toula. First one-day free ascent of the entire wall in 1992 via the Red Light District by Luebben and Toula. Come provisioned for a several-day stay. Musembeah, to the northeast of Mt. Hooker, offers IV 5.8-5.9 climbing on sunny West Face. Several long, climbable walls in the East Fork Valley (Raid, Ambush) as well as Midsummer's Dome (multipitched crag with classic 5.9s) beckon Hooker-bound East Fork Valley climbers. Summer. USFS–Shoshone NF, (307) 527-6241.

Classics: Mt. Hooker: The Jaded Lady VI 5.12-, Red Light District IV 12-, Brain Larceny V 12R, Third Eye VI10 A4; Raid Peak, Ambush Peak.

Ref: AAJ ['96-167, '94-149, '93, 91-131/173, 79-199, 65-347], C [186-118, 123, 56(9/79)-16], R [82-81, 45], S 12/69; Piana's *Big Walls,* Mitchell's *Wind River Trails;* Guidebooks: Kelsey's *Climbing and Hiking in the Wind River Mountains,* Bonney's *Guide to the Wyoming Mountains and Wilderness Areas,* Bonney and Bonney's *Field Book: The Wind River Range.*

Directions: From Big Sandy Campground, it's a full day's hike up to East Fork Valley over Hailey Pass to Mt. Hooker. Mt. Hooker is also accessed from Dickinson Park (may be longer) via the Bear's Ears Trail. Local horse packers offer reasonable alternatives to humping back-breaking loads.

63 WR–Scab Creek Buttress ✮✮✮

Secluded, though fairly accessible, beginners' and intermediates' 200′ granite crag in the western Wind River Range. A National Outdoor Leadership School training rock. Free camping. Summer. USFS–Bridger-Teton NF, (307) 367-4326.

Classics: 5.7 slabs, The Prow 10+X, 5.10+ hand crack.

Ref: D. Hohl; C 102-30; Guidebook: Bonney and Bonney's *Field Book: The Wind River Range.*

Directions: From Boulder drive 6 mi. east on Hwy. 353. Turn north on dirt road BLM 5423 (take left fork). From road's end hike to right on faint foottrail. Hike 1 ½ mi. east past beaver ponds up first drainage on left to Scab Creek Buttress (thirty–forty-five minutes total hike). Difficult to find—check with USFS in Pinedale or topo map.

64 WR–Cirque of the Towers ✮✮✮✮✮

Undoubtedly one of the most stunning, rock-climbable, and overloved cirques in the Lower 48. Pingora's northeast face and Mitchell's north face are just two of the stunning, 1,000′ alpine features and classic, alpine (approximately ten pitch) rock climbs. Dangerously popular: Beware long spells of wet weather, lightning bolts, tent-eating bears, and birds with teeth (i.e., mosquitoes)—and mind-shattering views. Free camping. Summer. USFS–Shoshone NF, (307) 527-6241.

Classics: Wolf's Head Ridge 6, Pingora NE Face 9, Mitchell's Wind River Trails North Face 9, Warbonnet 10, Black Elk 11-.

Ref: AAJ 95-167, C 173-64; Mitchell's *Wind River Trails;* Guidebooks: Kelsey's *Climbing and Hiking in the Wind River Mountains,* Steck and Roper's *Fifty Classic Climbs,* Bonney's *Guide to the Wyoming Mountains and Wilderness Areas,* Bonney and Bonney's *Field Book: The Wind River Range.*

Directions: From Boulder take Hwy. 353 east to Big Sandy Trailhead (follow signs). Other roads lead in from Farson area. A 9-mi. hike takes one into Cirque of the Towers. Panoply of formations greets the climber at Jackass Pass. These include counterclockwise from northeast to southwest: Lizard Head Peak, Bollinger Peak, Pingora, Wolf's Head, Shark's Nose, Overhanging Tower, Block Tower, Watch Tower, Warrior Peaks, War Bonnet, and Mitchell Peak.

65 WR–Big Sandy Campground and Lodge ✵✵

These 50′ granite clifflets make for a pleasant diversion when awaiting the arrival of a climbing partner for a trip into the Cirque of the Towers. Free camping at Big Sandy campground. Summer. USFS–Bridger-Teton NF, (307) 367-4326.

Classics: Campground Crack 7.

Ref: Guidebook: Bonney and Bonney's *Field Book: The Wind River Range.*

Directions: From Boulder (approximately 1 1/2 hours), head east on Hwy. 353. Follow signs for Big Sandy Opening approximately one hour from blacktop (very muddy when wet). Small crags and bouldering in Big Sandy Campground and west of horse corral behind Big Sandy Lodge.

66 WR–Sinks Canyon ✵✵✵✵

For tenderfoot or buckaroo, the sport-climbing cow camp of western Wyoming and, for years, the hobbyhorse of National Outdoor Leadership School (NOLS) climbers, especially, Collins, Hess, and Dusl. In order of appearance from Lander: sandstone, dolomite, and granite all within 3 mi. of one another in this mountain canyon. For this reason an extraordinary climbing area. Traditional and sport leads with cryptogrammic sequences. Roadside boulders. Features the Sinks—where the Popo Agie River actually disappears and reemerges 1/4 mi. downstream. Bighorn sheep, rattlers (especially in Sawmill Canyon) and poison ivy in summer. Pay sites in lower canyon at state park or USFS campgrounds, or free in upper (USFS). Or, Country Fare Bed 'n' Breakfast in town is popular. USFS–Shoshone NF, (307) 527-6241/state park, (307) 332-6333.

Classics: Sawmill Canyon: Drifter 11, Born to Be a Cowboy 12a; SS: Std Route 6, Royal Edge 7, Gunky 8, Dab Nab It 11a; The Mitten: R side 9; Dolomite: Fun Planet 9, December's Children 10+, Burly 11+, No Impact 11d, Hardware 12a, Killer 12c, Full Tilt 12d, Dogs of War 13a, White Heat 13a; Cheesegrater Boulders; Granites: 9+ roof, Big Smoke 11c, Get Wacky 12a, Full Tilt 12d.

Ref: C [147, 129(12/91)]; Guidebooks: Bechtel's *Lander Bouldering,* Collins's *Sinks Canyon Sandstone and Limestone,* Toula's *Rock Climber's Map to Sinks Canyon,* Axthelm's *Sinks Canyon Climbs.*

Directions: From Lander rove 8 mi. west on Hwy. 131 into Sinks Canyon. Sandstone walls start immediately on right at canyon's mouth. Dolomite bouldering (Punk Rock, Cheesegraters) begins approximately 2 mi. up on right where dirt meets pavement. Dolomite sport climbs are obvious above boulders. Granite boulders and crags start in upper reaches of canyon just before bridge and road switchbacks. Granite buttresses on right just five minutes up Middle Fork of the Popo Agie River Trail.

67 WR–Ridgecrest Boulders ✵✵

Above-the-road ridgeline of 20′ sandstone blocks. A few small boulder problems and topropes. Sunny in winter. Spring–autumn. Private land.

Directions: From Lander go approximately 15 mi. south on Hwy. 28 to Ridgecrest Boulders. Hike up to sandstone ridge of boulders west of Hwy. 28.

68 WR–Wild Iris Wall (on Limestone Mountain) ✵✵✵✵

Pocketed, marbled dolomite bluffs provide classic, 80′ limestone sport climbing. A TFA (Tendon Fortification Area) and a hell of a good place to win one's spurs at pocket pulling. So much stone, one could wind up with too many irons in the fire. First routes developed by Richard Collins. Mainstay of routes developed by Valdez, Skinner, Piana, Badaracco, Jarrard, Whisler, and Delannoy. Though a high-elevation area, temperatures can get exceedingly hot in summer . . . or cold . . . wait a minute. Campsites available near quarry area or BLM campground en route to Atlantic City. Summer/fall. USFS–Shoshone NF, (307) 527-6241.

Classics: Rose 9+, Indian Country 10c, Devil Wears Spurs 10d, Pale Face Magic 11, Wild Horses 11+, Hot Tamale Baby 11d, Wind and Rattlesnake 12-, Gun Street Girl 12b, Rode Hard . . . 12+, Cow Reggae 13a, Adi-Goddang-Yos 13-, Throwin' the Houlihan 14a; Frankenstein B1+; OK Corral: Red As a Blooming Rose 10+, Zorro 12a.

Ref: C [181-24, 147, 131(4/92)], R [89-26, 48(3/92)-49, 41(1/91)-62]; Guidebooks: Bechtel's *Lander Bouldering,* Piana's *The Legendary Wild Iris.*

Directions: From Lander go approximately 25 mi. southwest on Hwy. 28. At first high summit, turn north (right) on Limestone Mountain Rd. At approximately 1 3/10 mi., turn up first right. Follow cutbacks and park at road closure sign on left or near quarry. Wild Iris Wall is a twenty-minute walk and visible to north. Faces south. The Erratic is a boulder five minutes north of west end of Wild Iris Wall. Remuda Area (long south-facing wall) is ten minutes north of The Erratic. The OK Corral is east of road closure sign at parking area, a west-facing wall running north/south at quarry.

69 Cutoff Boulders (on Route 287) ☆

This climber's squirt stop when traveling from Lander to Rawlins has 35' sandstone bouldering walls for toproping or highballing. Just don't land in a cow patty. Spring–autumn. Private land.

Directions: From Lander burn 17 mi. south on Hwy. 287. Cutoff Boulders are obvious, short walls on ridgeline to right or left of road. Faces south.

70 Granite Mountains/Sweetwater Rocks ☆☆☆

Extensive granite rock piles, domes, and boulders make for a free-ranging climbing trip. McIntosh Peak (8,508') is highest dome. Nice beginner/intermediate 5.7–5.10 routes on Lankin Dome. Agate flats. Much private land with sportsman-access signs. Please maintain good relations with landowners, e.g., drive a Chevy truck and stay off private ranchland. Beware rattlesnakes and skeeters in summer. Also, high winds in a lonely land. Or, as one local explained, "Sure hard to find a girlfriend around here." Free camping. Spring–autumn. Private/BLM, (307) 332-8400.

Directions: Area north of Jeffrey City, extending 10 mi. west and 15 mi. east on Hwy. 287. Accessed via various dirt roads from Agate Flats Rd. 6 8/10 mi. east of Jeffrey City. BLM map recommended. Named Granite Mountains formations include: Moonstone Buttress, Lankin Dome, Point of Rocks, Point 6,467', and Great Stone Face. Majority of routes on south faces.

Classics: Lankin Dome: Sky Route 8, South Face Starjumper 10a; Point 6,467': Drifting 7, Arc of the Diver 8, Student of the Future 9, Driving 10+; Moonstone: Flake Route 5, Wind Walker II 7.

Ref: C 81(12/83)-4; Guidebooks: Collins's *Climber's Guide to Sweetwater Rocks,* Bonney's *Guide to the Wyoming Mountains and Wilderness Areas,* NOLS guide.

71 Lankin Dome ☆☆☆

Lankin Dome is obvious turtle-backed landmark visible to north of Hwy. 287. Eight pitch routes on this monstrous, 700', classic granite slab. Cragging and bouldering interspersed below south face of Lankin at Point of Rocks. More established climbs on Point 6,467' and Great Stone Face, granitic islands to south of Lankin Dome. Also on Moonstone Buttress to northeast of Lankin. Free camping. Spring/autumn. Private land/BLM, (307) 332-8400.

Classics: Lankin Dome: South Face 6, Sky Route 8, Star Jumper III 10a.

Ref: G. Collins; AAJ '84, C 81(12/83)-4, S (7/81, 8/77, 2/75); Guidebooks: Collins's *Climber's Guide to Sweetwater Rocks,* Bonney's *Guide to the Wyoming Mountains and Wilderness Areas,* NOLS topo sheet.

Directions: From Jeffrey City follow Hwy. 287 east. In the time it takes to guzzle down a cold one (approximately 7 mi.), turn northeast on Agate Flats Rd. (very muddy clay when wet). After 3 mi., cross Sweetwater River. In 2 more mi., turn right at 9A Ranch, following dirt roads through obvious gap, then across agate fields to north side of Lankin Dome et al. Drive to south face for mainstay of routes. Please leave all gates as you find them!

72 Split Rock ☆☆☆

This famed Oregon Trail landmark features giant, multi-pitched slab routes and cragging areas with views of rolling prairie and distant rock mountains. Many fine pitches of granite cracks and face, especially good in the 5.7–5.10 range. A teaching area for National Outdoor Leadership School (NOLS). Free camping. Spring/autumn. Private/BLM, (307) 332-8400.

Classics: Split Rock: Standard 6, Prometheus 9+, High Plains Saga; Easter Island Man 10c, Roof of All Evil 12+; Rubber Rose Buttress; new sport climbs?

Ref: G. Collins; Guidebooks: Collins's *Climber's Guide to Sweetwater Rocks,* Bonney's *Guide to the Wyoming Mountains and Wilderness Areas.*

Directions: From Jeffrey City go east 15 1/2 mi. to Cranner Rock Rest Area (aka Split Rock Overview). From rest area go 1 3/10 mi. east on Hwy. 287. Turn left onto dirt road. At 5 mi. (through ranch houses and over bridge), turn at first left past ranch. Park at hill overlooking east side of Split Rock. Faces south/east. Note: Partially private access.

73 Cranner Rock ☆☆☆

A hardman's "rest?" area. Several great granite crack routes in the middle of the great Wyoming "nowhere" make for an easy-access highway pump. Some good dispersed bouldering here as well. Greg Collin's classic Cranner's Roof 5.12d/13a has as many crack techniques as you'll ever find on an overhanging line. Spring–autumn. BLM, (307) 332-8400.

Classics: U238 11-, Geophysical 11, Heet 12-, Cranner's Roof 12d/13a.

Ref: G. Collins; C 102(6/87)-29; Guidebook: Collins's *Climber's Guide to Sweetwater Rocks.*

Directions: From Jeffrey City crank 15 1/2 mi. east on Hwy. 287. Park at BLM's Split Rock Historical rest area. Hike five minutes to front or backside of Cranner Rock. Routes on north, south, and west sides.

74 Alcova Boulders ☆

Alluring 40' sandstone boulder formations at first glance, but the abundance of loose rock leaves a taste in your mouth like flat beer. Still some challenging cups await. Pay camping available nearby or free at Fremont Canyon. Spring–autumn. Private land.

Directions: From Alcova, Alcova Boulders are approximately 1 mi. north on Hwy. 220. Obvious roadside boulderfield on south-facing hillsides.

75 Independence Rock and Sentinel Rocks ✪✪

Independence Rock is roadside 100′ granite dome. Sentinel Rocks are a granite exploratory area beyond. This 200′ dome and National Historic Landmark is known as "the Great Register of the Desert," with names of pioneers dating back more than one hundred years. Steep slab routes on north face are now fenced off, but the rock in the foothills beyond abundantly makes up for it. Spring– autumn. BLM, (307) 332–8400.

Ref: Guidebook: Bonney's *Guide to the Wyoming Mountains and Wilderness Areas.*

Directions: From Alcova shoot 25 mi. west on Hwy. 220. Signs point to Independence Rock. Sentinel Rocks off to south.

76 Fremont Canyon ✪✪✪✪

Fine granite canyon climbing developed over the years by Casper mainstay climbers Ilgner, Moore, Parmenter, and Petro. A crack climber's wet dream or nightmare, i.e., don't drop your gear! One hundred and forty routes. Spring/autumn. Camping at area. BLM, (307) 261–7600.

Classics: Casper Crusader 7, Pet Cemetery 8, B-25 9, Greystoke 10c, Wine and Roses 11a, Jesters in the Palace 11+, Gleaming the Cube 11d, Guilty as Charged 12, Psychodelic Psycho 12+, Fiddler on the Roof 13, many more!

Ref: S. Petro; AAJ '86-173, C [133(2/92)-31, 130, 122(10/90)-59, 114, 104(10/87)-26, 89, 79(8/83)-28, 67], R 21(9/87)-18, S 7/83; Guidebooks: Petro's *Climber's Guide to Fremont Canyon and Dome Rock*, Bonney's *Guide to the Wyoming Mountains and Wilderness Areas*, Parmenter, Ilgner, and Moore's *High Plain Climbs*, Harlin's *Rocky Mountain.*

Directions: From Alcova punch it 7 ½ mi. south on Alcova Dam Road. Bear right at fork for 3 mi. to Bridge Area of Fremont Canyon. Routes lie below in either direction from bridge. Rappel in for all routes. The Narrows Area is north of Bridge Area, and Power Tower Wall is north of Narrows on east side; both accessed from parking pullout at white rock north of third road pullout north of bridge. Or, continue farther west from bridge, taking various dirt roads to south from pavement to West Canyon (Wine and Roses, et al.) for rappel-in entries. Walls face all directions. Loveshack Area is 2 ¹/₁₀ mi. west of the Bridge to a pullout on the left. Hike across road north away from canyon to slot canyon and wall.

77 Pathfinder Dam Area ✪✪

Some nice, short granite crack routes and boulders. This is essentially a satellite area of Fremont Canyon, a getaway from the hardman's trench. Spring/autumn. BLM, (307) 261–7600.

Directions: From Alcova pop up 5 mi. west on Hwy. 220. Turn approximately 7 mi. south on Pathfinder Dam Rd. to obvious rocks west of road. Faces east.

78 The Chimneys (aka M-2) ✪✪✪

Austere, isolated 140′ granite crags. First climbs here as early as 1950s with Walt Bailey and the Wyoming Mountaineers of Casper College. At one time very popular, but now an obscure area west of Dome Rock. Murder One and Two are 200′ walls on north side. See Bonney's guide. Free camping. Spring–autumn. BLM, (307) 261–7600.

Classics: Raspberry Route 9-, Pathfinder 10.

Ref: S. Petro; Guidebook: Bonney's *Guide to the Wyoming Mountains and Wilderness Areas.*

Directions: From Alcova drive 7 ½ mi. south. Turn onto left fork for Dome Rock. At ½ mi. past cattle guard, go southwest on dirt on private land (Pedro Mountain Ranch). The Chimneys are approximately twenty minutes from car to obvious rock to south.

79 Dome Rock ✪✪✪

Casper climbers' solid 140′ granite dome playground. A plentitude of intermediate routes—wind. Free camping. Spring–autumn. BLM, (307) 261–7600.

Classics: Hidden Delight 9, Precambrian Squeeze 10-, Troll's Handshake 11-, Geeks and Gooiness 11, Shark Bait 12+.

Ref: C [104, 89, 79(8/83)-14], R, S 7/83; Guidebooks: Petro's *Climber's Guide to Fremont Canyon and Dome Rock*, Bonney's *Guide to the Wyoming Mountains and Wilderness Areas*, Parmenter, Ilgner, and Moore's *High Plain Climbs.*

Directions: From Alcova swerve 7 ½ mi. south. Take left fork 15 mi. to Dome Rock on left. When parallel to rock, turn east onto dirt road. Main area is on west side.

80 Ferris Mountains ✪✪

Unexplored, vertical south-facing flanks of limestone several hundred feet high. These white fins are striking when sunlit from Hwy. 287 at dusk—great views on Ferris Mountain. Free camping. Spring–autumn. BLM, (307) 328–4200.

Ref: Guidebook: Bonney's *Guide to the Wyoming Mountains and Wilderness Areas.*

Directions: From Lamont trend approximately 1 mi. north on Hwy. 287. Turn east on Ferris Mountain Rd. (soft-sand driving—beware of getting stuck) to Ferris Mountains' cliffs. Access is via private lands; then hike to rock. Other approaches from north also possible. Check BLM maps.

81 Seminoe Reservoir Dam ✪✪

Scenic, hidden canyons with small, scattered 80′ granitic rock piles. Watch for rattlers in summer. Free camping. Spring–autumn. BLM, (307) 328–4200.

Directions: From Sinclair go 35 mi. north on paved road to Seminoe Reservoir Dam.

82 Casper Mountain/Casper Area ✪✪

Casper Mountain is good . . . if you're there. The 100′ sandstone crags make nice, quick-hit practice area for time-

locked Casper climbers. Or, there's always Casper's Industrial Crags around town for those who like to dodge the police (see Steve Bechtel's fun[k] guide, Taboo, for details). Spring- autumn. Government land.
Classics: The Trainer 11+.
Ref: S. Petro, P. Parmenter; Guidebooks: Parmenter, Ilgner, and Moore's *High Plain Climbs*, Bechtel's *Taboo*.
Directions: Casper Mountain: From Casper go approximately 2 ½ mi. south on Hwy. 251 to Red Rocks. Park. From the first big viewpoint above town, hike west approximately five minutes. Faces north. Privately owned access. Casper: One can find urban climbing in Casper in case your truck or Rolls breaks down.

83 Ayres Park and Natural Bridge (closed) ✰

Difficult bouldering at this 150'-long and 60'-high limestone/sandstone formation (one of few natural bridges in the world with water flowing under it) is off-limits to climbing. Entry hours posted (8:00 A.M. to 8:00 P.M. from April 1 to October 31), don't get locked in. Pay camping at park. Spring–autumn. County park.
Ref: T. Henry.
Directions: From Douglas go approximately 10 mi. west on Hwy. 25 to Ayres Park and Natural Bridge exit 151 (signs). Then go south 4 mi. to Ayres Park. Limestone bridge and sandstone cliffs are off-limits to climbers.

84 Esterbrook Areas ✰✰✰

Several areas here contain a plentitude of 100' granite rocks. Access sometimes difficult because of broken private and government land parcels. Nearby Laramie Peak, at 10,272', is highest peak in the Laramie Mountains and is visible for 100 mi. to the east. Free camping on Forest Service lands. Spring–autumn. Private land/ USFS–Medicine Bow NF, (307) 745–2300.
Ref: B. Scarpelli.
Directions: Climbing areas surrounding Esterbrook include: Point of Rocks, Little Point of Rocks, The Limestone, and Gray Rocks.

85 Duck Creek ✰✰✰

Outback 140' granite cragging. Check access for trespass! Rattlers! Summer. Private/government land.
Classics: Duck's Breath 12- (bolts), What the Big Boys Eat 12.
Ref: B. Scarpelli.
Directions: From Wheatland go on I–25 south. Take Hwy. 34 southwest. Turn right on Tunnel Rd. Duck Creek is on right at Game and Fish Winter Range Sign.

86 Chugwater Bluffs ●

This area would have unique and unlimited climbing if the rock stayed in one piece. These 100' conglomerate cliffs are crumblier than the crackers put in the locally made, world-

famous Chugwater Chili. It may be wiser to stop for the Chugwater Chili than for the climbing. Private/government land.
Classics: Chili Cook-off in June.
Directions: From Chugwater a panorama of bluffs lies north off I–25.

87 Boar's Tusk (Red Desert Spires) ✰✰

The black Boar's Tusk pinnacle (7,095') rises 200' above a 200' talus cone. This outback volcanic neck is barely visible to the northeast when driving north out of Rock Springs on Hwy. 191. One of the first technical ascents was made by Ken Driese on one sane, fairly solid route. As for the rest of the rock quality, take your chances. If you combine this with a trip to Sinks Canyon and climb on all three rock types (sandstone, limestone, and granite) there, you can say you climbed on four different types of rock in one day, a feat not easily accomplished in the United States. Bad sand fleas in June. Surrounded by chaste, white-beach sand dunes—believe it or not. Free camping. Spring/autumn. BLM, (307) 352–0256.
Classics: Route between South and West Towers 5.
Ref: C. Rollins; Guidebook: Bonney's *Guide to the Wyoming Mountains and Wilderness Areas*.
Directions: From Rock Springs furrow 12 mi. north on Hwy. 191 (to Chilton's Cutoff). Turn approximately 4 mi. northeast. Continue 14 mi. north on CR 17. Turn east for 2 mi. north (rough). Turn north to east of Boar's Tusk. See BLM maps. Roads may be impassable during bad weather. Coming south from Farson/Eden on Hwy. 191, just south of milepost 33, turn east onto main dirt road heading east/southeast for roughly 11 mi. to junction with minor dirt roads that lead east to Boar's Tusk.

88 Superior Canyon (The Corrals) ✰

Canyon full of volcanic boulders and short 40' rhyolite crag climbs. Spring/autumn. Private land.
Ref: J. Wendt.
Directions: From Rock Springs go east on I–80 to exit 122 for Hwy. 371 north. Follow Hwy. 371 to Superior. Area is across from plant. Hike into canyon to walls. Ask a local, or put 'er on automatic pilot.

89 Baggot Rocks ✰✰

Lots of small, coarse granite formations well suited for the boulderer and short wall toprope enthusiast. On-site camping. Spring–autumn. BLM, (307) 352–0256.
Classics: Peace Rocks, Right Arm 5.10, The North Wall 5.10/11, Bat Ass Boulder.
Directions: From Saratoga bust-a-move south on Hwy. 130, then continue on Hwy. 230 to mm 33 (still north of the town of Riverside). Baggot Rocks are obvious roadside boulder mounds on east side of road.

90 Snowy Range (Lake Marie) ★★★

Multiple east-facing, 1,200′ quartzitic faces offering fun, staircased, alpine routes rise above Lake Marie in the scenic Medicine Bow Range. Long history since after World War II from classic fourth-class solos to 5.9 face/crack routes as exemplified by Nessle and Hull's Diamond Direct 5.7 A2 in July 1959. As the Bonneys note in their 1960 *Guide to the Wyoming Mountains*, "The absence of pitons on a route you put up is no proof it's a 'first'; the last guy there may not have scared so easy." Descent by gullies between buttresses. Beware detached blocks on solid faces and blindside thunderstorms from the west. Free/pay USFS camping. August–September. USFS– Medicine Bow NF, (307) 745–2300.

Classics: Formations include Schoolhouse Rock, 300′ southmost; The Diamond, fourth buttress from left; Old Main, 1,200′ northmost; Gill Problem B1-.

Ref: S 1/62; Ament's *Master of Rock;* Guidebooks: Bonney's *Guide to the Wyoming Mountains and Wilderness Areas,* Jacquot and Huff's *A Climber's Guide to the Snowy Range of Wyoming,* Fryxell's *The Medicine Bow Mountains of Wyoming.*

Directions: From Centennial wind up switchbacks 14 1/10 mi. west on Hwy. 130 into the Snowy Range with rock walls above Lake Marie. Interesting, old rock mountaineering routes on the Diamond (and to the right) include: Diamond Ledges, Braack Ridge, Third Gully, and Dark Ridge. These are multipitched slab routes. Old John Gill (white arrow) bouldering problem 200 yd. north of Lake Marie near streambed, approached via Mirror Lake Picnic Ground.

91 Roger's Canyon/DMZ Wall/Ragged Top ★★★

Roger's Canyon holds 35′ toprope problems with fingery cranks on sharp limestone rock: fun, terse, and challenging. Historic granite formations up road blend the old with the new. Free camping. Spring–autumn. Government land.

Classics: Roger's Canyon: The Bulge 12-.

Ref: S. Blunk; Guidebooks: Blunk topo, Halfpenny's *Climbing Guide to Southeast Wyoming.*

Directions: From Laramie go 10 mi. north up Ninth St. to obvious roadside toprope bands in Roger's Canyon mostly on left. For the DMZ (Demilitarized Zone) Wall, take first dirt road south (left) for 1 1/2 mi. to 50′ sport climbs. Faces south. Farther up Roger's Canyon road, a granite area known as Ragged Top (amongst the earliest of Laramie climbing areas) holds many pinnacled formations on private ranch land (permission required), which include: Narrow Sphinx, Osmium Crystal, Thumb, Pontiac's Head, Mitten, Altar Boy, and Storm Point. All fifth-class scrambles or short technical (less than 5.7) sections.

92 University of Wyoming ★★★

Campus limestone buildering for bored or crazed students, poor huddled masses, or party athletes. Best season: during class. State land.

Ref: *Laramie Boomerang* newspaper carrier, T. Skinner.

Directions: At University of Wyoming on Grand Ave. Buildering at the Dining Hall, Classroom Building, and for the best check out the North Face of the Student Union.

93 Vedauwoo ★★★★

A crack climber's paradise renowned for scintillating, flared 140′ hand cracks and offwidths through coarse granite. The "bleeding" ground for the University of Wyoming hardmen and hardwomen. Bring tape and/or suture. High elevation at 8,000′—often cold and windy. Blair is an extension of Vedauwoo to the west. Pay camping. Summer. USFS–Medicine Bow NF, (307) 745–2300.

Classics: Main Area: 5.7 Cracks 8, MRC Direct 9, Currey's Diagonal 10, Friday the 13th 10, left Torpedo Tube 10d, Horn's Mother 11, Trip Master Monkey 12, Hypertension 12b, Remote Control 12c; Blair: Spectreman 11; Reynold's Hill: I'd Rather Be In Philadelphia 12, Silver Salute 13-.

Ref: C [171-62, 162-48, 155 (10/95)-74, 122(10/90)-56, 89, 75, 74, 72(5/82)-24, 71, 69], R [91-96, 89-92, 61, 44], OTE 28, Ament's *Master of Rock;* Guidebooks: Kopischka's *Vedauwoo Rock,* Harper and Kelman's *Heel and Toe: The Climbs of Vedauwoo,* Kopischka's *Cracks Unlimited,* Harlin's *Rocky Mountain,* Kopischka's *Crack Country Revisited,* Scarpelli's *The Cracksmen,* Bonney's *Guide to the Wyoming Mountains and Wilderness Areas,* Sublette, Garson, and Zimmerman's *Vedauwoo Climbs,* Garson, Kopischka, and Pousch's *Crack Country,* Halfpenny's *Climbing Guide to Southeast Wyoming,* Halfpenny and Mathiesen's *Vedauwoo Climbing.*

Directions: From Laramie blow 19 mi. east on I-80 (exit 329). Turn 1 mi. north on dirt road. Several Vedauwoo formations around picnic and campground areas include: Poland Hill (first formation passed en route to campground), Nautilus, Holdout, Walt's Wall, Old Easy, Turtle Rock, and Reynold's Hill. Blair Area is to the west. Entrance fee.

94 Ames Monument ★★

This 60′ pyramidal railroad monument was erected in honor of the Ames brothers, the driving force behind the construction of the first transcontinental railroad. Fun climbing on the sides of quarried granite blocks. Airy views of Vedauwoo to the north and Snowy Range to the west. Summer. Private land.

Classics: 5.6 on granite blocks to top (rappel anchor).

Ref: Guidebook: Bonney's *Guide to the Wyoming Mountains and Wilderness Areas.*

Directions: From Laramie take I-80 east to exit 329. Go 2 mi. south on dirt road. Ames Monument is a novelty climb on pleasing, staircased quarried blocks.

95 Sitting Camel (aka Chimney Rock or Camel Rock) ★★

Any camel jockey worth his saddle will find sanctity in this crumbly, 100′ red-rock sandstone formation with cairns on top. Looks distinctly like a camel from an east or west profile. First ascent in 1937 via iron spiked ladder by Jack Sickles. Less than 50′ of technical climbing on Head and Hump summits. Nearby historical Indian animal traps from blowing winds (West Animal Trap), ½ mi. south from top of west ledges. (See Bonney guide.) Spring–autumn. No camping. Possibly private land.

Classics: West Face 5, ESE Face 5 A2, Northeast Face 9.

Ref: S 7/83; Guidebooks: Bonney's *Guide to the Wyoming Mountains and Wilderness Areas*, Halfpenny's *Climbing Guide to Southeast Wyoming*, Ormes's *Guide to the Colorado Mountains*.

Directions: From Tie Siding (19 mi.), head approximately 1 mi. north on Hwy. 287. Turn approximately 13 (?) mi. west on dirt road #316 (Sportsmans Lake Rd.) to crossroads with dirt road #34 (Sand Creek Rd.). Turn south on #34 (dirt, fainter road) for approximately 6 mi. At Colorado-Wyoming border. From gate, trail goes west to top ledges of Camel Rock. Good luck! (Can also be accessed from Laramie via Hwy. 287, then left on Rd. #34.)

96 Wall Rock Creek ☆☆☆

Wall Rock is blessed with beautiful 200′ Wyoming mountain dolomite. Rick Aune and Ric Miller from Cody found the area along with John Warning and Tricia Stetson of Lander, Wyoming. Over the summer of 1998, some twenty-four routes were established. Pay camping nearby. Summer. USFS–Bighorn NF, (307) 674–2600.

Classics: Parent's Day Out 10c, Making America Beautiful 11c, Caress Me Down 12b, V-force 12c, Don't Eat Too Much Candy 12d.

Ref: J. Rowan.

Directions: Fr. Lovell drive east on Hwy. 14A toward the Bighorns and Burgess junction. Ascend the mountain pass, driving for about fifty minutes. About ten minutes past Bald Mt. Campground, there will be a dirt road on the right, FR 10 (Hunt Mountain Rd.). Turn right here and follow it up for 3 mi. until there is a large clearing. There should be a corral on the right side of the road; park across from it. From the parking area walk east and south toward the trees (more east than south). After descending the hill, walk east across the meadow and look for cairns. Follow these through the trees to the top of the cliff. From here the trail is quite clear. Once at the base of the cliff, follow the trail west, and after a minute the first formation comes into sight. This is the 75′ Onion Cave. More walls and routes are farther to the west.

N

0 Kilometers 100

0 Miles 100

Alberta

Alberta

Like a drop of water falls from the summit, that's the line I shall take. —E. Comici

Alberta holds magic in its mountain ranges. Along the Northern Rockies, rock climbers will want to acquaint themselves with the areas at Banff, Canmore, Bow Valley, Kananaskis Valley, and Yamnuska. Then, in your next life, enjoy the alpineering along the incredible length of the Columbia Icefields.

1 Columbia Icefield/Jasper National Park (Mt. Edith Cavell and Mt. Alberta) ✫✫✫✫✫

An area abounding in wild peaks for mountaineers experienced in ice and snow work. Mt. Edith Cavell, one of the more famed peaks of the Canadian Rockies, has good quartzite on its north face. Mt. Alberta is known for shoddy rock. Mt. Columbia is the highest point in Alberta at 12,293'. The Columbia Icefields contain the largest amount of ice in the Canadian Rockies. Though not as high as other Rocky Mountain peaks, these peaks can be more unforgiving due to latitude. Dougherty's *Selected Alpine Climbs in the Canadian Rockies* is a good introductory guidebook for newcomers. Summer. Government park.

Classics: Mt. Edith Cavell: North Face IV 7; Mt. Alberta: Japanese Route IV 6, Mt. Cromwell, Diadem Peak, North Twin, Mt. Woolley, Mt. Brussels III 7, Mt. Geikie, Bastion Peak, Oubliquette Mountain, Mt. Athabasca, Mt. Andromeda, Mt. Kitchener, Little Snow Dome, Mt. Bryce, Mt. Columbia, Roche Miette, CR2, Mt. Colin.

Ref: AAJ ['92-99/146, 87-185, 86-73, 82 to 79], *Canadian Alpine Journal* (CAJ), C [187-82, 166(2/97)-15, 129, 117(12/89)-76, 100, 94, 72, 70], M 98, OB [8/80, 3/80, 12/78], R 88-88, S [5/86, 10/64]; Jones's *Climbing in North America;* Guidebooks: Whipple et al.'s *Columbia Mountains of Canada: Central,* Dougherty's *Selected Alpine Climbs in the Canadian Rockies,* Toft's *Banff Rock Climbs,* Steck and Roper's *Fifty Classic Climbs,* Putnam et al.'s *RMC-North,* Kelsey's *Climber's and Hiker's Guide to the World's Mountains,* Sole's *Waterfall Ice,* Burpee's *Among the Canadian Alps,* Horne's *Route Cards.*

Directions: The Columbia Icefields describe an area extending northwest to southeast from Banff to Jasper. Access points along Hwy. 93A and Hwy. 93. For Mt. Edith Cavell: From Jasper drift south on Hwy. 93 to Hwy. 93A to Cavell Lake. Ascent of western ridge east of lake is most common.

2 Icefields Parkway ✫✫✫✫✫

For alpinists seeking mixed rock and ice climbing, here is an area of amazing scenery with abundant wild peaks. Some peaks of interest: Mt. Hector, Mt. Patterson, Howse Peak, Mt. Chephren, White Pyramid, and Mt. Forbes. All majestic beauties between 3,200 m and 3,700 m. For more pure rock climbing, try the limestone at Mt. Wilson's walls, Weeping Wall, and the Big Bend Cliffs at base of Sunwapta Pass. Also, in poor weather, unlimited crags can be found east of the Saskatchewan River Crossing on the north side of David Thompson Hwy. Summer. Government park.

Classics: Mt. Hector, Mt. Patterson, Howse Peak, Mt. Chephren, White Pyramid, Mt. Forbes.

Ref: C 102, *Canadian Alpine Journal;* Guidebooks: Whipple et al.'s *Columbia Mountains of Canada: Central,* Dougherty's *Selected Alpine Climbs in the Canadian Rockies,* Putnam et al.'s *RMC-North,* Kelsey's *Climber's and Hiker's Guide to the World's Mountains.*

Directions: An area extending northwest to southeast between Lake Louise and Sunwapta Pass on the Icefields Pkwy. (Banff/Jasper Hwy.). Access points along Hwy. 93. An area as fantastic to drive as it is to climb.

3 Back of the Lake (aka Lake Louise) ✫✫✫✫✫

From June to September this is the finest rock-climbing crag in Alberta and one of the best and most scenic sport-climbing areas in western Canada—yes, Christmas comes more than once a year. High-quality, 165' blocky quartzite crags in a touristy area. Pay camping in park. Summer. Government National Park.

Classics: Pub Night 6, Imaginary Grace 8, Standing Ovation 10a, Wicked Gravity 11a, Rubber Lover 11c (The Triple Strike: Liquid Sky 11c, Air Voyage 11+, Scared Peaches 11+), Elbow Venom 12a, Scared Peaches 12a, Female Hands 12b, Jason Lives 12d/13a.

Ref: *Canadian Alpine Journal;* C [169-121, 132 (topos), 117(12/89)-76, 110, 106, 98, 93], R [96-42, 36(3/90)-88, 14(5/86)]; Guidebooks: Martin and Jones's *Sport Climbs in the Canadian Rockies,* Dougherty's *Selected Alpine Climbs in the Canadian Rockies,* Howatt and Zacharias's *The Back of the Lake.*

Directions: At Lake Louise on Trans Canada Hwy. #1 (one hour from Banff and two and a half hours from Calgary). Park at Chateau Lake Louise. Hike trail (approximately twenty minutes) on western shore (on right) of Lake Louise to Southside Crags or eastern shore of lake to Goblin Wall, Kaleidoscope Pinnacle, and Fraggle Rock. Bouldering below Liquid Sky and near pond at south-facing cliff end.

4 Lake Louise Alpine Routes/Saddleback
★★★★

As backcountry alpinistic endeavors, these peaks offer classic alpine climbs: Haddo Peak, Mt. Aberdeen, The Mitre, Mt. Lefroy, Mt. Victoria, Popes Peak, and Mt. Whyte. Saddleback offers intermediate four-pitch routes on quality rock. Pay camping in national park.

Classics: Mt. Aberdeen: East Slope; The Mitre: Normal Route II 5.

Ref: Guidebook: Dougherty's *Selected Alpine Climbs in the Canadian Rockies*.

Directions: At Lake Louise on Trans Canada Hwy. #1 (one hour from Banff and two and a half hours from Calgary). Park at Chateau Lake Louise. For Saddleback: Hike one hour on Saddleback Trail from Lake Louise Parking Lot toward the Saddleback. When one to two switchbacks from saddle, contour grassy east slopes to east shoulder below cliff.

5 Bf★-(Banff Area) Valley of the Ten Peaks (Mt. Temple) ★★★★

An incredible arena for sedimentary alpinistic endeavors. Mt. Temple is known as the "Eiger of the Rockies." Colgan Hut via either Perren Route or Scheisser Ledges offers shelter. Summer. Government park.

Classics: Mt. Temple: East Ridge IV 7, Greenwood/Locke IV 8 A2, Grand Sentinel II 8, Tower of Babel III 7.

Ref: AAJ ['86-185, 77-204, 71, 70, 68, 67], C 117, *Canadian Alpine Journal*, M 98, OB 8/80, S [3/70, 4/67]; *Heroic Climbs*, Jones's *Climbing in North America*; Guidebooks: Kane's *Scrambles in the Canadian Rockies*, Whipple et al.'s *Columbia Mountains of Canada: Central*, Dougherty's *Selected Alpine Climbs in the Canadian Rockies*, Steck and Roper's *Fifty Classic Climbs*, Toft's *Banff Rock Climbs*, Putnam et al.'s *RMC-North*, Wheeler's *Climbs at Banff and Vicinity*.

Directions: From Banff go west on Trans Canada Hwy. Alpine routes are on the following: Mt. Fay, Mt. Temple, Mt. Little, Mt. Babel, Mt. Quadra, Mt. Little, Mt. Bowlen, Peak 4, Mt. Perren, Mt. Allen, Mt. Tuzo, Mt. Deltaform, Grand Sentinel. More pure rock climbing on the Tower of Babel above Moraine Lake parking lot and the Grand Sentinel on the north side of Pinnacle Mountain.

6 Bf–Banff Rockaneering (Mt. Louis) ★★★

Numerous summit-oriented, alpine limestone rock routes close to Banff. Mt. Louis is the most famous technically rock climbed summit with many good routes. Expect long approaches and long days. Southwest buttress of Mt. Cory has quality rock. Summer. Government park.

Classics: Mt. Cory, 9,194'; The Finger, 8,380'; Mt. Louis, 8,800': Kain Route III 6, Greenwood/Mackay III 7, Homage to the Spider III 8; Mt. Edith, 8,380'; Mt. Norquay, 8,276'; Castle Mountain, 9,076'.

Ref: S 5/86; Guidebooks: Dougherty's *Selected Alpine Climbs in the Canadian Rockies*, Toft's *Banff Rock Climbs*, Putnam et al.'s *RMC-North*.

Directions: Banff vicinity. Mt. Edith, Mt. Louis, The Finger, Castle Mountain, Storm Mountain, Stanley Peak. See guidebooks for exact map/directions for this complex area.

7 Bf–Carrot Creek ★★★

Steep (aka overhanging) 120' limestone with big sloping holds. Excellent sport area for 5.11s and 12s. Government land.

Classics: Abracadabra 11+, The Wizard 12a, The Lizard 12b.

Ref: C [132 (topos), 113, 110, 107]; Guidebook: Martin and Jones's *Sport Climbs in the Canadian Rockies*.

Directions: From Banff National Park go 1 mi. west of entrance on Trans Canada Hwy. Turn off for Carrot Creek hiking trail. Hike thirty minutes.

8 Bf–Guides Rock ★★★

Mt. Cory was once called "an island of beautiful solid rock in a sea of rubble." Corner and roof lines on good 400' limestone crag. Cory's Southwest Buttress has many fine routes. Pay campgrounds around Banff.

Classics: Paper Chase 11a, Street Life 11a.

Ref: C 117-59; Guidebook: Toft's *Banff Rock Climbs*.

Directions: From Banff go west to junction of Trans Canada Hwy. and Hwy. 1A. Take Hwy. 1A 2 mi. west to Johnston's Canyon. Hike twenty minutes to Guides Rock.

9 Bf–Rundle Rock and Mt. Rundle North Ridge ★★★

Spot-from-your-car bouldering. Beginner one- to two-pitch routes are often used for teaching. Various pay campgrounds around Banff. Government land.

Classics: Sugarloaf Boulder.

Ref: C 93, R 67-83; Guidebooks: Perry et al.'s *Bow Valley Update*, Perry et al.'s *Bow Valley Rock*, Toft's *Banff Rock Climbs*, Putnam et al.'s *RMC-North*.

Directions: From the Banff Springs Hotel at Bow Falls (west of Canmore), take golf course road ½ mi. to Rundle Rock.

10 Bf–Spray Slabs ★★

Topropes on solid rock but 10' of loose rubble on top of 75' crag. Intermediate routes. Gets sun in afternoon. Site of quarry for Banff Springs Hotel. Pay campgrounds around Banff.

Classics: Heavy Metal 10c.

Ref: Guidebook: Toft's *Banff Rock Climbs*.

Directions: From first hole on Banff Springs Golf Course,

follow horse trail up east bank of river for twenty minutes to Spray Slabs.

11 Bf–Sundance Canyon Picnic Area

Leads or topropes. Intermediate crag features crack climbing. Pay campgrounds around Banff.

Classics: Tourist Attraction 10.

Ref: C 107; Guidebook: Toft's *Banff Rock Climbs*.

Directions: From Banff take Cave Ave. to the Old Cave and Basin Pool. Continue on to Sundance Canyon Picnic Area.

12 Bf–Sunshine Slabs

Bumper belay topropes on 70′ exfoliation slabs. Pay campgrounds around Banff.

Ref: Guidebook: Toft's *Banff Rock Climbs*.

Directions: From Banff go west on Trans Canada Hwy. Turn left (south) on Sunshine Ski Resort Rd. for ⁴/10 mi. Sunshine Slabs are on left (east) side of road.

13 Bf–Tunnel Mountain ★★★

Quick and easy access from Banff. South Face has one- to two-pitch routes. East Face has seven-pitch limestone rockaneering routes. Some aid pitches. Pay campgrounds around Banff. Spring–autumn.

Classics: Gonda Roof 11a.

Ref: Guidebook: Toft's *Banff Rock Climbs*.

Directions: East of Banff on Tunnel Mountain Dr. Descend Hoodoos Trail to cliff.

14 C★–(Canmore Areas) Cougar Canyon ★★★

Limestone face routes on both sides of the valley. Excellent 150′ sport area for new leaders. Crown and Anchor Pub in Canmore recommended. Spring–autumn. Government land.

Classics: Surface Tension 10c, Poolside Pleasure 10c, Wilt 11c, Stygian Arye 12d.

Ref: *Canadian Alpine Journal*; C [117-41, 110]; Guidebook: Spohr's *Selected Climbs to the Canmore Area*.

Directions: From Canmore travel north of town 1 mi. Hike 1 mi. (twenty minutes) up Cougar Canyon.

15 C–Stoneworks ★★★

Limestone 60′ sport climbs. Government/private land.

Ref: Locals.

Directions: From Canmore go west of town. Next drainage west of Cougar Creek. A forty-five-minute approach to Stoneworks. Ask local climbers for directions at Coffee Mine Coffee Shop.

16 C–EEOR/Numbered Buttresses (Mt. Rundle) ★★★

Mt. Rundle is a series of long 1,000′ limestone buttresses extending from Canmore to Banff. EEOR (500 m) stands for East End of Rundle and is the most popular of these buttresses. It is defined by its three large, right-slanting corners. The other buttresses are referred to by number and are comparatively little used because of long approaches and mostly poor rock. Nice, long multipitched routes. Reprobate on EEOR is a highly recommended climb for its grade. Government land.

Classics: The Guides Route III 6, Eeyore's Tail 8, Reprobate IV 7A1 or 9, Drop Out IV 9, True Grit 10a.

Ref: C 138, R 67-89 (topo); Guidebook: Toft's *Banff Rock Climbs*.

Directions: From Canmore go south on Spray Lakes Rd. to north end of Whiteman Pond at Whiteman Gap. EEOR and Chinaman's Peak share same parking. Head north from gap. Walk short way from dam south on road, then up open valley and scree slopes. Descent is to the south from the top of cliff over scree and meadows to ridge with trees.

17 C–Whiteman Crag (Mt. Rundle) ★★★

Ease of access has made poor rock routes on this crag more enjoyable. Three-pitch beginner and intermediate limestone routes. Summer. Government land.

Classics: South Corner 7, Die Young, Stay Pretty 10a.

Ref: C 85(8/84)-42; Guidebooks: Perry et al.'s *Bow Valley Update*, Perry et al.'s *Bow Valley Rock*.

Directions: From Canmore head south on Spray Lakes Rd. to Whiteman Pond. Whiteman Crag is located at south end of Whiteman Pond. Five-minute approach.

18 C–Kanga Crag (Mt. Rundle) ★★★

Steep, featureless, 380′ limestone cliff with one- to three-pitch routes. Government land.

Classics: California Dreaming 10b.

Ref: C 85(8/84)-42; Guidebooks: Perry et al.'s *Bow Valley Update*, Perry et al.'s *Bow Valley Rock*.

Directions: From Canmore drive south on Spray Lakes Rd. south to Whiteman Pond Dam. From dam walk a short distance south along the road and then follow an open valley leading directly to Kanga Crag.

19 C–Grassi Lakes (Mt. Rundle) ★★

Grassi Lakes has a number of small 75′ limestone crags located nearby. Few routes. Scenic, but grassy rock. Summer. Government land.

Classics: Gardener's Question Time 10a, Fiberglass Undies 10c, Graceland 11a.

Ref: C 110, R 96-80; Guidebooks: Martin and Jones's *Sport Climbs in the Canadian Rockies*, Perry et al.'s *Bow Valley Update*, Perry et al.'s *Bow Valley Rock*.

Directions: From Canmore head south on Spray Lakes Rd. to Whiteman Pond, at top of hill overlooking Canmore.

Approach from Grassi Lakes Hiking Trail or from above, starting at Whiteman Pond.

20 C–Chinaman's Peak ✩✩✩✩

This summertime climbing area is the impressive landmark to the south of Canmore. Climbable 1,000′ limestone walls usually good from mid-June to mid-August. Expect routes up to fifteen pitches. Summer. Government land.

Classics: Northeast Face IV 7, Quick Release/Finishing Touch 9/10a, Premature Ejaculation IV 10b.

Ref: C [138, 85(8/84)-42], R 67-88; Guidebooks: Perry et al.'s *Bow Valley Update,* Perry et al.'s *Bow Valley Rock.*

Directions: From Canmore go south on Spray Lakes Rd. to north end of lake at Whiteman Gap. Hike across earth dam to trail leaving west, following around reservoir to a clearing. Then up through trees to trail at west face of Chinaman's Peak.

21 B✩–(Bow Valley) Overview and Three Sisters Area ✩✩✩✩

Bow Valley is a mountain valley loaded with giant 1,300′ limestone walls. All of the following climbs (except Kananaskis Areas) are located essentially in Bow Valley, i.e., Bow River Drainage. Three Sisters: Only the First and Second Sister offer rock-climbing routes (easy adventure rockaneering genre). One of the oldest climbs in Bow Valley was Lawrence Grassi's 1925 ascent of First Sister. Ship's Prow 5.8 A2 is a very prominent, sharp buttress between The Three Sisters and Chinaman's Peak. Can-more Wall is a 350′ flat face midway between Ship's Prow and Chinaman's Peak consisting of poor rock. Camping is preferable at Canmore, Seebe, Bow Valley Park, Lac des Arcs, Dead Man Flat, and Bow River Cross-ing. In good years, weather allows climbing from April to October. Camping at parking area, Alpine Club of Canada clubhouse in Canmore, or Banff Youth Hostel. Government land.

Classics: Bow Valley (Mt. Rundle): Reprobate 9; Goat Wall: Goat Buttress 10d; Yamnuska: CMC Wall 11a, Wind Tower 10a; Chinaman's Peak: Premature Ejaculation 10b, Iron Butterfly VI 11A4, Venus 10a, Sticky Fingers 10c, Existence Mundane 14b.

Ref: C 173-25, R [80-96, 67-83], *Canadian Alpine Journal;* Guidebooks: Perry et al.'s *Bow Valley Update,* Perry et al.'s *Bow Valley Rock,* Putnam et al.'s *RMC-South,* Spohr's *Selected Climbs in the Canmore Area.*

Directions: From Calgary go approximately 60 mi. (approximately one hour) west on Hwy. 1 (Trans Canada Hwy.) to the start of Bow Valley between Canmore and Exshaw. Three Sisters approach: From Canmore head east on Hwy. 1 to just west of Deadman Flat. Access by hiking south up Three Sisters Creek. See an area topo map for specifics.

22 B–Wind Valley (Wind Tower) ✩✩✩✩

Wind Tower is a magnificent wall of rock that overwhelms Bow Valley with its 450 m north face. This twelve-pitch Northeast Face is some of the better climbing in Bow Valley. Rim tower is another equally sizeable formation northwest of Windtower. Camping at Westwind Pass. Summer. Government land.

Classics: Northeast Ridge IV 5, Northeast face IV 10a, Iron Butterfly VI 11a A4 (described as screamin' freaking scary and possibly only done once).

Ref: C [138, 110, 107], R 67-90 (topo); Guidebooks: Perry et al.'s *Bow Valley Update,* Perry et al.'s *Bow Valley Rock.*

Directions: From Canmore, for the short approach: South on Spray Lakes Rd. to trailhead 4.8 km past Spray District office at Three Sisters Dam. Hike up west bank of dry streambed west of Spurling Creek. Walk up dry streambed (one-hour hike to West Wind Pass, which offers both approach and descent route). Long approach: East on Hwy. 1 (Trans Canada Hwy.) to Deadman Flat in Bow River Valley. Hike south up West Wind Creek (approximately four-hour approach). Wind Tower is 6 km south of Trans Canada Hwy. at head of West Wind Creek.

23 B–Grotto Mountain (Grotto Corner/ Crag X) ✩✩✩

These two areas on Grotto Mountain only have a few good routes on 450′ of limestone. Summer. Government land.

Classics: Grotto Corner: Grotto Crack 8; Crag X: Sideline 9.

Ref: C [132 (topos), 117(12/89)-58, 113, 110, (10/86)-23, 107, 93]; Guidebooks: Martin and Jones's *Sport Climbs in the Canadian Rockies,* Perry et al.'s *Bow Valley Update,* Perry et al.'s *Bow Valley Rock.*

Directions: Grotto Mountain lies east of Canmore. Go east on Hwy. 1A. Two climbing areas are on Grotto Mountain: Grotto Corner and Crag X. Grotto Corner approach: on south slopes of mountain before Crag X below. One-hour approach via streambed just west of prominent S-shaped corner. Crag X approach: on southeast slope of Grotto Mountain at mouth of Grotto Creek. Fifteen-minute hike approached from Hwy. 1A. Park at Gap Lake picnic area. Walk through trees at east end of Rockwool Plant and follow an open ridge above a smaller cliff to top of descent gully at south end of main crag. Grassy platform is staging area for climbs.

24 B–Grotto Canyon ✩✩✩✩

This beautiful canyon is composed of several limestone crags on both sides of the valley. Grotto is mainly a sport crag, the first one in this region and the focal point of hard routes in the Canmore Area. Roughly 150 climbs. Bring hexes/nuts as well as friends to protect irregular Bow Valley cracks. Good on hot summer days. Summer. Government land.

Classics: Pensioner's Outing 8, Falling from Heaven 9, Pitrun 10b, Tabernaquered 10c, Trading Places 10c, Farewell to Arms 10d, Grey Matter 10d, Submission 11c, Walk on Wild Side 11c, Mr. Olympia 12a, Importance of Being Earnest 12a/b, Cracked Rhythm 12+, Tin Tin and Snowy Get Psyched 12+, Tropicana 12+. Also a chipped, overhanging wall offering a 13b, 13a, 13b, and a 12d/13a.

Ref: C [125, 117(12/89)-58, 103, 100(10/86)-23];
Guidebooks: Perry et al.'s *Bow Valley Update,* Perry et al.'s
Bow Valley Rock.

Directions: From Canmore (this area lies northeast of
town), go east on Hwy. 1A past Grotto Mountain. Turn
left to parking area at small lake/picnic area 2.4 km east
of Gap Lake. Hike into valley. Several Grotto Canyon
developed buttresses include: Water Wall, Hemingway
Wall, Three Tier Buttress, Paintings Wall, The Right
Wing, The Headwall, The Balcony, The Alley, Lower
Narrows, Illusion Rock, Delusion Rock, Upper Narrows,
Upper Tier, Whiskey Wall, Garden Rock, Armadillo
Buttress, and Grotto Slab.

25 B-Steve Canyon ★★★

Extremely short limestone climbs ranging from 5.9 to 5.11-.
Not visited by many locals. Summer. Government land.

Classics: Moist 'n' Easy 10+.

Ref: C [107, 103-28]; Guidebooks: Perry et al.'s *Bow Valley
Update,* Perry et al.'s *Bow Valley Rock.*

Directions: This area lies northeast of Canmore. Go east on
Hwy. 1A past Grotto Mountain. Park at Grotto Pond
Picnic Area, 2.4 km east of Gap Lake. Hike up Grotto
Canyon trail briefly to watercourse leading uphill fifteen
minutes to cliffs. Below waterfall are the Bathtub Crags.
Above is the Main Crag. (Steve Canyon is just east of
Grotto Canyon.)

26 B-Mt. Fable ★★★

Major 1,000' limestone peak with impressive routes visible
above Hwy. 1A. Very lightly developed area. Summer. Government land.

Classics: South Ridge II 4; South: East Ridge II 5, South
Face The Boulevard IV 10a (has one, maybe two ascents).

Ref: C [138, 110], R 67-83; Guidebook: Dougherty's *Selected
Alpine Climbs in the Canadian Rockies.*

Directions: From Canmore go east on Hwy. 1A to Exshaw.
Walk up Exshaw Creek into secondary valley to south
face of Mt. Fable.

27 B-Exshaw Slabs ★

A small 100' limestone slab for locals. Only a few routes.
Summer. Government land.

Classics: Strictly for Bolten 10a.

Ref: Guidebooks: Perry et al.'s *Bow Valley Update,* Perry et
al.'s *Bow Valley Rock.*

Directions: From Canmore head east on Hwy. 1A to
Exshaw. Exshaw Slab lies 5 km northwest of Exshaw near
Mt. Fable. Turn left up Exshaw Creek on east side
through residential area to parking near footbridge. Hike
across creek, going north up valley beside wire fence, then
abandoned road, then trail. In an hour's time, take a left
at fork in valley. Hike fifteen minutes more to large cairn
on right, 100 m past treed slab. Still not visible, Exshaw
Slab is five minutes uphill to the right (east of the cairn).
Routes are on the far right end.

28 B-Bataan (Exshaw Area) ★★★★

This area is composed of 45–50 m walls of very overhanging
pocketed limestone and comprises some of the finest sport
climbing in all of western Canada. Summer. Government
land.

Directions: Access from Canmore on the 1A highway
toward Exshaw. Park in pullout located about ½ mi.
from the Alpine Clubhouse turnoff. Bataan is on the
north side of Hwy. 1A. Hike up via trail and flagging,
about one and a half hours.

29 B-Pigeon Buttresses (Pigeon Mountain) ★★

Easy adventure climbs on two prominent 500' limestone
buttresses on north side of mountain. Only a couple climbs
since 1988. Summer. Government land.

Classics: TV Buttress 7.

Ref: Guidebooks: Perry et al.'s *Bow Valley Update,* Perry et
al.'s *Bow Valley Rock.*

Directions: From Canmore head east on Hwy. 1 past West
Wind Creek Rd. Pigeon Mountain is south of Trans
Canada Hwy. to west of Mt. McGillivray. Parking area on
Trans Canada Highway. Hike up through forest; uncer-
tain if there are trails.

30 B-McGillivray Slabs ★★

Long, 600' north-facing limestone slab has a handful of
seven-pitch routes. Mostly easy routes up to 5.8. Summer.
Government land.

Classics: Pythagoras 7, Kahl Crack 8.

Ref: Guidebooks: Perry et al.'s *Bow Valley Update,* Perry et
al.'s *Bow Valley Rock.*

Directions: From Canmore head east on Hwy. 1 to south
side of Lac Des Arc. Long line of cliffs with several buttresses on the north side of Mt. McGillivray. Routes are
on formations closest to road. Parking area on Trans
Canada Hwy. Two different approaches and descents.
East End approach: Via fourth-class gully with snowmelt
waterfall in a large cirque. Other approach: Walk up a
road slanting up and right to a tunnel at base of slabs.

31 B-Heart Creek Canyon ★★★★

Features 100' limestone sport climbs and headwalls of 400'.
Two-pitch slab climbs. Multipitch climbs can be found on
the sunny, popular Heart Slab on the lower slopes of Heart
Mountain.

Classics: First Buttress: Sticky Fingers 10c; Jupiter Rock:
Venus 10a; Heart Slab: Rough Mix 9; Upper Heart Crag:
Fear of Flying 10d.

Ref: C [107, 103, 100]; Guidebooks: Perry et al.'s *Bow Valley
Update,* Perry et al.'s *Bow Valley Rock.*

Directions: From Canmore head east on Hwy. 1 to southeast side of Lac Des Arc. There is a parking area for this
creek (well marked). Hike along highway for 700 m to
creek then south into drainage. Several formations
greet climbers: First Rock, Jupiter Rock, Patriot's Groove,

Lower Heart Crag, and Blackheart. Heart Slab is east of waterfall.

32 B–Acephale (east of Heart Creek) ✩✩✩✩

The sport crag wall is composed of very steep streaked limestone consisting of sinker pockets and edges, approximately 20–30 m in height. The area is under development, with ample projects/more than fifty routes ranging from 12- to 13+. This, along with Prairie Creek, is the place to climb for its high-quality stone and its north-facing location. Summer. Government land.

Ref: Local; Guidebook: Martin and Jones's *Sport Climbs in the Canadian Rockies*.
Directions: Located ³/₄ mi. east of Heart Creek. Access is a trail to the east of the dry (sometimes wet) creekbed, then follow the creek to a waterfall, go to the left, and regain the creek to the base of the Acephale wall. A thirty- to forty-five-minute hike.

33 B–McConnell Ridge ✩✩

This 800' limestone face is high cliff on north face of McConnell Ridge. One seldom-visited route called the Diamond Cross Face 5.8 A0. Loose rock. Summer. Government land.
Ref: Guidebooks: Perry et al.'s *Bow Valley Update*, Perry et al.'s *Bow Valley Rock*.
Directions: From Canmore head east on Hwy. 1 past Lac Des Arc to Yamnuska Centre. (Directly across Bow Valley from Yamnuska to the south.) Diamond Cross Face is high cliff on north face of McConnell Ridge.

34 Y✩–(Yamnuska Area) Yamnuska Wall ✩✩✩✩✩

The most well-known cliff in the Canadian Rockies and the foundation of modern climbing in the Northern Rockies. One giant (1,000'), south-facing wall. Most routes are traditional, multipitched, limestone climbs. A traditional climber's dream. Climbs of intrigue and variety. Suicide Wall (Astro Yam) features the most serious routes. Austrian guides Hans Gmoser and Leo Grillmair pioneered the first route here in 1952. Beware rockfall on easier routes. A small sandstone practice cliff exists at the base. Summer area. Free camping in parking lot. Or, camp in Banff (and Youth Hostel), Canmore, or Seebe. Spring to autumn. Government land.
Classics: Easy Street 5, Red Shirt III 7, Directissima III 5.8, Forbidden Corner III 8, Pangolin III 9, Kahl Wall IV 10a, Excalibur IV 10+, CMC Wall IV 11a, Yellow Edge 11b, Moondance III 11b, Astro Yam IV 11c.
Ref: AAJ '89-161, *Canadian Alpine Journal*, C [171-25, 160-88, 138, 117 (12/89)-61, 113, 110, 107, 103, 100, 98, 93, 85(8/84)-35], R 67-86; Guidebooks: Martin and Jones's *Sport Climbs in the Canadian Rockies*, Perry et al.'s *Bow Valley Update*, Perry et al.'s *Bow Valley Rock*, Kalleen's *Climber's Guide to Yamnuska*, Greenwood and Kalleen's *Climber's Guide to Yamnuska*.
Directions: From Calgary go approximately 60 mi. (one

The incredible wall of Yamnuska.

TIM TOULA

hour) west on Hwy. 1A. Turn right into parking area (2.5 km before intersection with Hwy. 1X). Hike past gate through quarry to switchbacked trail to Yamnuska Wall.

35 Y–Mount Doom ☆
Broad ridge surrounded by limestone cliffs. Only a few routes. Autumn. Government land.

Ref: Guidebooks: Perry et al.'s *Bow Valley Update,* Perry et al.'s *Bow Valley Rock.*

Directions: From Calgary go approximately 60 mi. (one hour) west on Hwy. 1A. Turn right into parking (this is 2.5 km before intersection with Hwy. 1X). Hike past gate through quarry to switchbacked trail to wall. Mt. Doom lies just north of Yamnuska.

36 Y–CMC Valley ☆☆☆
Beautiful and secluded, CMC Valley provides climbers a backcountry climbing experience on Yamnuska-like cliffs, albeit smaller. Multipitched 1,000' limestone routes. The Maker is most popular route in CMC Valley. Free camping or Simpson hut (free) exists for shelter. Summer. Government land.

Classics: Weed 6, Double Direct 7, Chingle 8, Hurricane Holocaust 9, Dirty Dago 9, The Maker IV 10b.

Ref: C [138, 117-61, 93], R 67-83; Guidebooks: Perry et al.'s *Bow Valley Update,* Perry et al.'s *Bow Valley Rock.*

Directions: From Calgary go approximately 60 mi. (one hour) west on Hwy. 1A. Turn right into parking as for Yamnuska (This is 2.5 km before intersection with Hwy. 1X). Hike past gate through quarry to switchbacked trail to wall. CMC Valley is north of (behind) Yamnuska. Seventy-five-minute hike beyond east shoulder of Yamnuska Wall on horse trail. Fork right just above quarry. Several buttresses beckon climbers: Wakonda Buttress, Ripple Wall, Kiln Buttress, Frodo Buttress, The Runes, and Bilbo Buttress. Ephel Duath is another buttress to the west.

37 Y–Ghost Valley (aka Ghost River) ☆☆☆☆☆
Literally 40 mi. of good limestone. Lots of potential; this area has seen new development, and sport routes have made their way here. Routes up to 5.12, 60'–1,000' in length. One climber writes, "This valley contains the future of rock-climbing in Alberta. The limestone is of the best quality. Some of it compares to the best in France. The potential here is untapped with over 200 km of cliff line. Most prominent formations include North and South Phantom Crags, Wully Wall, and Sentinel Crag. The rock varies from technical slab to very steep overhanging bulges with potential for new climbs from 5.10 to 5.14." Spring to autumn. Government land.

Classics: Bonanza 7, Thor 9, Hoods in the Woods 10a; Bonanza 8, The Wraith 9+, Thor 10b, Creamed Cheese 11a, Alberta Jam 11b/c, Dreams of Verdon 11c.

Ref: C [167-56, 113, 110, 103, 102, 93]; Guidebooks: Perry's

Ghost River Rock Climbs, Martin and Jones's *Sport Climbs in the Canadian Rockies,* Sole's *Waterfall Ice.*

Directions: From Cochrane follow Hwy. 1A west. Turn right on the forestry trunk road and follow this road for 30 km. Turn off to the Ghost River Recreation access road (through a private ranch—close gate, please). Follow ever-worsening gravel road for 16 km to the top of the big hill. The cliffs are a two-hour walk from here but can be accessed with a four-wheel-drive vehicle. Alternate Yamnuska: Excellent access via Barcee Ranch to upper and lower Ghost River (see *Waterfall Ice* by Sole for description).

38 Y–Goat Mountain ☆☆☆☆
Kid Goat and Nanny Goat both have good rock limestone routes up to three pitches. Goat Slabs have several multi-pitch slab routes. The 1,200' Goat Buttress (eleven pitches) on Goat Wall is the showcase climb of the area. Summer. Government land.

Classics: Twilight Zone 6, Keelhaul Wall 6, Skywalk 9, New Hope . . . 9, Smoking Mirror 10a, Feeding Frenzy 10b, Predator 10c, Max Headroom 10d, Goat Buttress IV 10d.

Ref: C [138, 110, 107, 103], R 67-83; Guidebooks: Perry et al.'s *Bow Valley Update,* Perry et al.'s *Bow Valley Rock.*

Directions: West of Yamnuska. Goat Mountain is accessed from a paved pullout (across from dump) on south side of Hwy. 1A, east of Exshaw and west of Hwy. 1X. Several formations lie on the east side of Goat Mountain. From the parking area these are: Kid Wall, Nanny Wall, Goat Slabs, and Goat Wall.

39 K☆–(Kananaskis Valley) Barrier Lake Buttress ☆☆☆
Only a couple routes on east-facing limestone wall. Scenic valley. Spring to autumn. Government land.

Classics: Friends 9.

Ref: C [113, 100, 86-28]; Guidebooks: Martin and Jones's *Sport Climbs in the Canadian Rockies,* Martin's *Kananaskis Rock.*

Directions: From Kananaskis go south on Hwy. 40. On west shore of Barrier Lake approximately 4 km along power line road from Barrier Dam parking lot. Cliff is a rounded buttress due west of Barrier Mountain.

40 K–Barrier Bluffs (on Barrier Mountain) ☆☆☆
Since 1986, the technical climbing center of Kananaskis Rock. Contains 250' limestone cliffs with approximately one hundred traditional and sport climbs. Generally good vertical rock. Steep climbing on South Wing. Best potential of all the Kananaskis cliffs. Spring to autumn. Government land.

Classics: Lockin' or Hookin' 7, Lumpy Corner 8, Shadow Play 9, Rainbow Bridge 10b, Unknown Pleasures 10c, Iron in the Soul 11a, Winnebago Warrior 11b, In Us Under Us 11b, Koyaanisqatsi 11b, Ideal for Living 11b,

Sisyphus Goes to Hollywood 11c, Naked Teenage Girls 12a, Regatta de Blank 12b.

Ref: C [110, 107, 86-28]; Guidebooks: Martin's *Kananaskis Rock,* Tobey's *Barrier Bluffs: The Guide.*

Directions: From Kananaskis (approximately one hour from Calgary), go south on Hwy. 40. On left across from Barrier Lake. Pick up access trail at Hwy. 40 near road sign 150 m east of big hill crest northwest of mountain. Hike uphill twenty minutes. Three popular cliffs compose Barrier Bluffs: Lumpy Corner, Escape Wall, and Yellow Wall.

41 K–Prospector's Canyon ☆☆☆

Steep, pocketed limestone, but limited scope for development. Government land.

Classics: Vugs for Jugs 10b, Pumping for Jill 11b.

Ref: Guidebook: Martin's *Kananaskis Rock.*

Directions: From Kananaskis go south on Hwy. 40 to southwest side of Barrier Mountain, 2.7 km south of Barrier Mountain approach trail. Just 300 or 400 m south of a roadside attraction called O'Shaughnessy Falls. Hike forty-five minutes up watercourse to Prospector's Canyon.

42 K–Lorette Slab/Mt. Lorette ☆

Lorette Slab is a tilted 80′ limestone bedding plane on south side of Mt. Lorette. Mt. Lorette's South Ridge II 5.6 is an alpine classic. Government land.

Classics: South Ridge II 5.6, Park Place 10b, Nineveh 10d.

Ref: C 100-29; Guidebooks: Dougherty's *Selected Alpine Climbs in the Canadian Rockies,* Martin's *Kananaskis Rock.*

Directions: From Kananaskis go south on Hwy. 40 to Ribbon Creek. Mountain bike north, then east on power line access road (closed to vehicles) as far as a cleft at foot of Mt. Lorette. Turn left and follow gully up via faint trail until faint trail comes into view on east side. Detour intervening slabs on uphill left side. Going back down, it's easier to traverse south from base of Lorette Slab via scree descent.

43 K–Porcupine Creek ☆☆

Small limestone woodland outcrops. Government land.

Classics: The Hedgehog: Reclining Porcupine 10-, Spiny Norman 10b.

Ref: C 100; Guidebook: Martin's *Kananaskis Rock.*

Directions: From Kananaskis go south on Hwy. 40 past Barrier Bluffs to Porcupine Creek (before Wasootch Creek Parking Area). Hike east from parking on shoulder of road. Areas include: Hyperion, Blind Man's Bluff, and the Hedgehog.

44 K–Wasootch Slabs ☆☆

The army first began climbing here in the 1950s. One 150′ limestone vertical wall, the rest are slabs. Good beginner's area. Crowded on weekends. Spring to autumn. Government land.

Classics: The Funnel 8, Cracked Slab 9, Third Corner 9, Silver Bullet 10a, Nasty Habits 10a, Absolutely Unethical 10b, Aristocrat 10d.

Ref: C 107; Guidebooks: Martin and Jones's *Sport Climbs in the Canadian Rockies,* Martin's *Kananaskis Rock,* Gadd's *Climbing at Wasootch Slabs.*

Directions: From Kananaskis go south on Hwy. 40 past Barrier Bluffs to Wasootch Creek Parking Area for Wasootch Slabs.

45 K–Kilowatt Crag ☆☆☆

A small, 300′ south-facing limestone slabbing area of one-pitch climbs. Spring to autumn. Government land.

Ref: Guidebook: Martin's *Kananaskis Rock.*

Directions: From Kananaskis go south on Hwy. 40 to 1.4 km southwest of Wasootch Creek to open area. Hike uphill to gravel road near microwave tower. Turn left on road a short distance, then go directly up to the Kilowatt Crag. A fifteen-minute approach.

46 K–McDougall Slabs ☆☆☆

Steep friction fiesta. Good 80′ limestone sport climbing. Runout. Government land.

Classics: Flypaper 10b, Groover 10d, Pellucidar 11a.

Ref: C [107, 100]; Guidebooks: Martin and Jones's *Sport Climbs in the Canadian Rockies,* Martin's *Kananaskis Rock.*

Directions: From Kananaskis go south on Hwy. 40. ten minutes south of Barrier. Park at Mt. Allen overlook. Hike across road twenty-five minutes uphill (steep!). The first slabs reached are Little McDougall and Big McDougall Slabs.

47 K–Ribbon Slab ☆☆

Generally good limestone rock, but broken 300′ slabs on the west side of Mt. McDougall's northernmost peak. Minimal development on this triangular slab. Spring to autumn. Government land.

Ref: Guidebook: Martin's *Kananaskis Rock.*

Directions: From Kananaskis go south on Hwy. 40. One-hour hike to Ribbon Slab. Start midway between Mt. Allan (Nakiska) pullout and the Ribbon Creek intersection.

48 K–Kidd Falls Area ☆☆

An impressive 300′ limestone formation with 5.7/5.8 fifteen-pitch climbs. Much potential. Spring to autumn. Government land.

Ref: Guidebook: Martin's *Kananaskis Rock.*

Directions: From Kananaskis go south on Hwy. 40 past Ribbon Creek to Galatea Creek trailhead. Hike one hour on trail past Kananaskis River and Galatea Creek bridges. Then up brief hill and up open slopes to base of Kidd Falls Area.

49 K–Burstall Slabs ★★★★

Beautiful 650′ tilted slabs in an alpine setting on the Continental Divide. Alberta's premiere friction slabbing area. Rock is sixty- to sixty-five-degree prickly limestone—don't whip! Brilliant and bold slab climbing—be prepared for runouts. Because of its alpine nature on Mt. Sir Donald, Burstall has shortest climbing season of all Kananaskis cliffs. Lunatic Fringe 5.11b is an old two-pitch friction testpiece. Fixed and natural pro. Rack recommended. Summer.

Classics: Moonraker 9, Dark Side of the Moon 9, The Cobra 3p 10c, Moon Shadow 10c, Moon Dancing 11a, Scary Monsters 11a, Lunatic Fringe 11b.

Ref: C [117(12/89)-58, 110, 107-58]; Guidebooks: Martin and Jones's *Sport Climbs in the Canadian Rockies,* Martin's *Kananaskis Rock.*

Directions: From Canmore go south on Spray Trail to Mud Lake. Two-hour hike. Follow the Burstall Pass Trail almost to pass before contouring to Burstall Slabs.

50 K–King Canyon ★★★

Minimally developed 300′ limestone and quartzite cliffs. Spring–autumn. Government land.

Ref: Guidebook: Martin's *Kananaskis Rock.*

Directions: From Kananaskis go south on Hwy. 40. On right across from turnoff to the Kananaskis Lakes. Park in lot. Hike east to King Canyon.

51 K–Gibraltar Mountain ★★★

This 1,800′ alpine limestone wall became a prominent climbing area in the 1970s with the installation of the Davidson/White north face route. 5.8 A3. Rainbow Warrior is sixteen pitches. Government land.

Classics: East Face III 7, Davidson/White Route VI 8 A3, Rainbow Warrior IV 10b.

Ref: *Canadian Alpine Journal* 72, C 85(8/84)-35; Guidebook: Martin's *Kananaskis Rock.*

Directions: From Turner Valley follow secondary road 546 to its end. Hike 6 km up Sheep River Trail to this 500 m north face of Gibraltar Mountain.

52 K–Cowbell Crag ★★

Good beginner/intermediate area. Conglomerate cliff is split with many 170′ crack climbs. Spring to autumn. Government land.

Classics: Secret Agent 9, Vanishing Crack 9, Semi-Honed 10a, Isis 10b, Eclipse 10b, Shibalba 10c.

Ref: C 107; Guidebook: Martin's *Kananaskis Rock.*

Directions: From Kananaskis go south on Hwy. 40. Now go 5 km north of Highwood House and 9.6 km north of Highwood junction. Cowbell Crag is on east side of highway. Hwy. 40 closed December–June; use a bicycle.

53 K–Half Moon Crag ★★★

Generally good, vertical 300′ limestone crack climbing area. Bring a rack. Spring to autumn. Government land.

Classics: Moonstruck 10a, Hunter's Moon 10c, Eclipse 10d.

Ref: Guidebook: Martin's *Kananaskis Rock.*

Directions: From Kananaskis go south on Hwy. 40. Turn east on Hwy. 541. Half Moon Crag is on left, 4.4 km east of Highwood junction. Follow a good game trail on east bank of creek for approximately twenty minutes, then cross over to west side. Look for a cliff up on slope to the left approximately twenty minutes away.

54 Crater Rock and Split Rock ★★

A 15′ glacial erratic with a reportedly good bouldering traverse. Private land, but no access problems as yet—please respect this privilege. Watch out for the dog crap and broken glass (hmm, good route name?). Why don't people ever clean up? Great for kids and beginners, plus some neat overhang problems to keep the wizards from getting bored. Go climb it before they blow it up to make room for development. Spring/autumn. Private land.

Ref: B. May; locals.

Directions: Calgary. Encroaching development from the city has changed access. For Crater Rock, drive north of the Deerfoot Trail (Hwy. #2) to Country Hills Blvd. Turn west. Follow boulevard approximately 2 mi. around to Centre St. North. Crater Rock is on the northeast of this intersection, in a farmer's field (for now). Unless the field has been recently plowed, the rock is hard to see (only the top meter or so is visible). To get to Split Rock, go north on the Deerfoot, turn west on Beddington Blvd., turn north on Centre St. Immediately past the underpass (you'll have to turn left to go north, so watch the signs) to the east in the ravine is Split Rock.

55 Okotoks Rock ★★★

Two 40′, granite, house-size glacial erratic boulders that look like they fell from the sky. Offers beginner and expert topropes and boulder problems, to B1+. Superb. Good for poor-weather days in the mountains. Spring/autumn. Private land.

Ref: Locals.

Directions: From Okotoks go west on Hwy. 7 for approximately 4 mi. Okotoks Rock is at roadside on right.

British Columbia

British Columbia

When you have reached the mountaintop, then you shall begin to climb. —Kahlil Gibran

Where does rock climbing begin in British Columbia? The first word is Squamish. Sitting in an incredible setting under Mt. Garibaldi, Squamish is Canadian for Yosemite. From big walls to bouldering and everything in between, Squamish granite will charm any climber. Be sure to bring a raincoat.

Smaller crags are continually being discovered. Charmers like Skaha, Nordic Rock, and Green Bastion Buttress will enchant any traveling climber.

Mountaineering and British Columbia are actually the same words, just spelled differently. Look to the Bugaboos for long alpine faces, albeit ephemeral weather conditions. Then, look beyond to the Selkirks, the Monashees, and the Caribou Range for more of the Bugaboos. Look even farther to Mt. Robson, Mt. Waddington, and into the St. Elias Range for expeditionary events.

Now, look into your wallet and chuckle.

1 Mt. Fairweather (15,299') (St. Elias Range) ☆☆☆☆☆

Mt. Fairweather is the highest point in British Columbia. The dramatic St. Elias Range is one of the stormiest places on Earth. Carpé Ridge first ascended in 1931 by Carpé and Moore. This is a snow/ice ordeal but included because of its grandness. Winter weather seems to be better for successful ascents. A couple weeks' worth of supplies and lots of warm weather gear is all it takes . . . and a lot of mountain savvy.

Classics: Mt. Fairweather: Carpé Ridge (South Face).

Ref: AAJ ['97>95, '90-163, 87-184, '85-183], C [197-124, 105], See *Canadian Alpine Journal* (CAJ), *B.C. Mountaineer* (BCM), *Avalanche Echoes* (AE), *Island Bushwacker* (IB); *Climbing in North America;* Guidebooks: Roper and Steck's *Fifty Classic Climbs,* Kelsey's *Mountains of the World.*

Directions: From Yakutat or Haines take a plane ride to Cape Fairweather on the coast of the Gulf of Alaska. The journey starts here with a 15-mi. hike up Fairweather Glacier to base camp for south face routes of Mt. Fairweather.

2 Devil's Thumb ☆☆☆☆☆

This remote, prominent alpine pinnacle along the British Columbia/Alaska border offers wild rock climbing with ice/snow technicalities. The Cat's Ear Spire rests next door

to Devil's Thumb on a spectacular granite ridge. This formation could be found on any serious alpinist's life checklist. Government land.

Classics: Devil's Thumb: East Ridge IV 6.

Ref: AAJ ['97, '92-80, 74-34, 46-268], CAJ '73, 71, 47, C 50(10/78)-8, M 59(1/78)-32, R 2(5/84); Beckey's *The Mountains of North America,* Jones's *Climbing in North America;* Guidebook: Roper and Steck's *Fifty Classic Climbs.*

Directions: From Petersburg, Alaska, Devil's Thumb is accessed by helicopter or plane to the northeast. Other formations in the area include Cat's Ears and Witches Tits.

3 Mt. Robson Provincial Park (Mt. Robson) ☆☆☆☆☆

Mt. Robson holds the distinction of being the highest peak in the Canadian Rockies at 12,972'. Capped with snow and surrounded by multiple glaciers, the summit is grasped by the eye of mountaineers around the world. Emperor Face is the classic big face of the Canadian Rockies. Kain Face is one of the most sought-after routes. Though limestone is the main rock around, this is a snow and ice climb. Sharpen the ice axe and crampons. Ralph Forster Hut on SSW Ridge. Weather is the deciding factor for critical climbs. Nearest supplies in Jasper, Alberta. Government park.

Classics: Mt. Robson: Kain Face IV, Emperor Ridge V 6, North Face IV.

Ref: AAJ ['96, '83, 79, 75-147], CAJ, C [172-48, 114, 111, 70, 52(1/79)], M 98, S [3/85, 8/74, 12/72, 5/66, 3/62]; Jones's *Climbing in North America;* Guidebooks: Kane's *Scrambles in the Canadian Rockies,* Whipple et al.'s *Columbia Mountains of Canada: West and South, Selected Alpine Routes,* Horne's *Selected Climbing Routes of Mt. Robson,* Horne's *Mt. Robson Climbing Route Card,* Roper and Steck's *Fifty Classic Climbs,* Harmon's *Columbia Icefield.*

Directions: From Jasper, Alberta, go west to Mt. Robson town. Now go north to trailhead. A two- to three-day trek is the average ascent time for Mt. Robson.

4 Mt. Waddington (Coast Range) ☆☆☆☆☆

Rising above fiordlike surroundings, Mt. Waddington, at 13,104', is the alpine monarch of the rugged and remote

Coast Range as well as British Columbia. Its north face rises 6,000′ from the floor of Tiedemann Glacier. The first-ascent honors go to Fritz Wiessner and William House for their 1936 South Face Route. Routes reach the summit from all sides by at least seventeen different attacks. An extremely remote and difficult-to-access glacial area with all the challenges of bad weather, intricate glacial travel and rock climbing, and weather complexities. Autumn. Government land.

Classics: Mt. Waddington: South Face V 7.

Ref: A '69, AAJ ['98, '96, '90-179, 88-146, 87-185, 86-168, 82, 76-473, 74-166, 70], C [185-58 routes descriptions, 183-102, 176-32, 162-100, 157-138, 117(12/89)-76, 111, 88], S [1/88, 1/82, 8/78, 7/67, 6/66], *Canadian Alpine Journal*; Jones's *Climbing in North America*, P&K Munday's *The Unknown Mountain*; Guidebooks: Roper and Steck's *Fifty Classic Climbs*, Culbert's *Alpine Guide to Southwestern British Columbia*.

Directions: From Vancouver it's 175 air miles. Mt. Waddington Southern approach: From south via Knight Inlet (Queen of Charlotte Straight) three days from inlet to base camp at Dais Glacier. Then climb via south face (ten-day overall time frame). Northern approach: Via Williams Lake to Tatla Lake to Bluff Lake to Tiedemann Glacier. A planned expedition for which some parties use helicopter assists.

5 Yoho National Park (Lake O'Hara) ☆☆☆

Superb alpine peaks. For cragging try the small quartzite crags at east end of Lake O'Hara. Government park.

Classics: Wiwaxy Peak: Grassi Ridge II 7.

Ref: CAJ, AAJ, R 71-94; Guidebooks: Whipple et al.'s *Columbia Mountains of Canada: West and South*, Dougherty's *Selected Alpine Climbs*, Roper and Steck's *Fifty Classic Climbs*, Putnam's *RMC-South*.

Directions: From Jasper, Alberta, go west to Mt. Robson town. Now go north to trailhead. A two- to three-day trek is the average ascent time for Mt. Robson. In Yoho National Park at Lake O'Hara are these alpine summits with routes: Wiwaxy Peak, Mt. Hungabee, Mt. Biddle, Mt. Schaffer, Odaray Mountain, Watch Tower, Mt. Huber, Goodsirs, Mt. Stephen, The President, and Vice President.

6 Mt. Assiniboine Provincial Park (Mt. Assiniboine) ☆☆☆☆☆

Mt. Assiniboine is a top-notch Canadian Rockies climb known as the Matterhorn of the Rockies. Sunburst is also an attraction for mountaineers. R.C. Hind Hut at base of north face. Government park.

Classics: North Ridge III 7.

Ref: AAJ '91-182, CAJ, M 98; Guidebooks: Whipple et al.'s *Columbia Mountains of Canada: West and South*, Dougherty's *Selected Alpine Climbs*, Horne's *Selected Climbing Routes of Assiniboine*, Toft's *Banff Rock Climbs*, Putnam's *RMC-South*, Kelsey's *Climber's and Hiker's Guide to the World's Mountains*.

Directions: From Canmore go southwest to Spray Reservoir. For Mt. Assiniboine: Hike into Marvel Lake, then Magog Lake. The standard route ascends to the hut, then north ridge of Assiniboine. Other access from Banff into British Columbia.

7 Mt. Sir Douglas (11,174′) ☆☆☆☆

Classic lines and relatively short approaches make Mt. Sir Douglas, highest member of the British Military Group, a most popular peak for climbers. Government park.

Classics: East Ridge III 6, Southeast Face 6/7; Mt. Birdwood Southeast Ridge II 7.

Ref: CAJ; Guidebooks: Dougherty's *Selected Alpine Climbs*, Whipple et al.'s *Columbia Mountains of Canada*, Roper and Steck's *Fifty Classic Climbs*.

Directions: From Canmore, Alberta, head south on Spray Lakes Rd. For approach from Spray Lakes Rd. to Burstall Pass (see local maps), use Burstall Creek to Robertson Glacier, then up to Burstall Pass to access Mt. Sir Douglas and other peaks. Recommended bivi at pass.

8 Bugaboo Glacier Provincial Park (in Purcell Mountains) ☆☆☆☆☆

Spectacular, high-altitude rock with 2,000′ granite faces and ice climbs. Among the finest sheer granite spires in the world. History of many chivalrous climbers, most notably Beckey, Cooper, Chouinard, Kor, and Croft. The onset of afternoon lightning storms can be delayed by prompt predawn starts. Short season: mid-June to September, if you're lucky. The comfortable Conrad Kain Hut has running water, propane stoves, and lamps for a daily fee. Government land.

Classics: Pigeon Spire: West Ridge II 4, East Face 10; Snowpatch Spire: Southeast Corner IV 6, Sunshine 10+, Power of Lard 13c; South Howser Tower: Beckey/Chouinard V 10-, Igor Unchained; North Howser Tower: all along the Watchtower West Face VI 12; Bugaboo Spire: Northeast Ridge IV 7.

Ref: AAJ ['98, '97, '96, '95, '92-145, 91-183, 88-148, 82, 80, 79, 76-74, 72, 71, 69-66], CAJ, C [190-24, 172-22, 171-25, 168-68, 164-24, 162-74, 153-68, 117(12/89)-76, 112, 111, 107(4/88)-64, 105, 100, 54], R [96-36, 95-24, 88-91, 76-24], S [3/89, 5/73]; *Bugaboos: An Alpine History, Climbing in North America*; Guidebooks: Green and Benson's *Bugaboo Rock*, Steck and Roper's *Fifty Classic Climbs*, Kruszyna and Putnam's *Rocky Mountains of Canada North*.

Directions: From Brisco (north of Invermere and a few miles north of Radium Hot Springs), turn left, following signs for 28 mi. Good gravel road open from late spring to early fall. Two-hour uphill hike to reach Kain Hut in the heart of the Bugaboos.

9 Lillooet Edge ☆☆☆

This 300′ granite crag overlooks Lillooet Lake. Good potential. Summer/autumn. Government park.

Classics: Wonder Dog 10b.

Ref: R 50(7/92); Guidebooks: McLane's *The Rockclimber's Guide to Squamish*, Fairley's *A Guide to Climbing and Hiking in British Columbia*.

Mt. Assiniboine.

JAMES GARRETT

Directions: From Whistler go north on Hwy. 99 beyond Whistler for 39 km. Lillooet Edge is visible when driving into Joffre Lakes Alpine Recreation Area.

10 Green River Bastion ☆☆☆

Multipitch 650′ granite crag offers adventure routes. Lots of unclimbed rock. Hot in summer. Warmer than Squamish in spring and fall.

Classics: Fine Time 9, Memory Lane 10c, Shining City 6p 11c.

Ref: R 50(7/92); Guidebook: McLane's *The Rockclimber's Guide to Squamish.*

Directions: From Squamish go 60 km (28 mi.) north on Hwy. 99 to the ski resort of Whistler. Then go 29 km north of Whistler on Hwy. 99. Park in gravel pit off highway. Hike north approximately 100 m, then go left up faint trail to base of Green River Bastion.

11 Nordic Rock (aka Whistler) ☆☆☆

Nordic Rock's 70′ granite walls sport bolted routes of excellent quality on tiny finger edges. Also multipitch adventure routes at Green River Bastion to the north. Lots of potential. Summer/autumn.

Classics: Mary Chain 9, You Snooze You Lose 10d, Quicksilver 11c, Minutes from Home 12-, Fits of Rage 12b, Winking Ninja 13b.

Ref: C 147, R [63, 50(7/92)]; Guidebooks: *The Whistler Handbook,* McLane's *The Rockclimber's Guide to Squamish.*

Directions: From Squamish, Nordic Rock is 60 km (28 mi.) north on Hwy. 99 at the ski resort of Whistler. Just south of the village above the east side of Hwy. 99 near Nordic Estates. Turn right into Garibaldi Way, then left into small housing development. Please park respectfully of private property. Whistler 500, 5.12b, is 10 km south of Whistler Village on west side of highway. More great climbing just south at Cheakamus Canyon. A popular sport-climbing area.

12 SQ☆-(Squamish Chief Area) Overview and The Chief ☆☆☆☆☆

The Yosemite of British Columbia. An area of numerous granite crags and walls up to 1,800′ with varied climbing and spectacular scenery. The Chief is composed of The Grand Wall North and South, Tantalus Wall, and The Apron, which are all major eye-openers. The Apron sees the most continuous use with airy friction climbs. Long routes on the Squaw, the Zodiac Wall, the mighty Freewall, and new climbs on the Backside of the Chief at the Solarium and Above and Beyond. Petrifying Wall is a popular sport crag. Malamute and Smoke Bluffs are other fun short crags. The Cacodemon Boulders, below the Grand Wall, now hold the hardest free climbs in Squamish. Free camping at south end of the Chief in front of Bulletheads. Many other camp-

---

British Columbia Road Thoughts

Ray Garner and some others were going up to Canada to climb a peak there named Brussels Peak and decided they might use an expansion bolt.

They wanted to test the bolt to see if it would hold, so they tried it in the boulder behind the concession building. They hooked it onto the front bumper of his car with a carabiner, backed up, and pulled off the bumper of his car.

He said, "I think it will hold."

—As told by pioneer Teton guide Glenn Exum

---

ing areas exist. Cliffside pub. Quinn's Espresso Cafe on Second for food/route information. For general tourist info call (800) 667-3306. July–September. Private/ government land.

Classics: Apron: Unfinished Symphony 11b, Dream On 12a; Western Dihedrals: Freeway 11c; Grand Wall: Merci Me 8, Exasperator 10c, Cruel Shoes 10d, Grand Wall 11a, University Wall 12a, Left Side 12a, Genius Loci 12b; Bulletheads: Eurasian Eyes 13a,The Shadow V 13b; Backside: Sunblessed 10b; Cacodemon Boulders: Archives 12d, Permanent Waves 13c, Bravado 13d.

Ref: AAJ '68-180, CAJ, C [198-30, 181-27, 178-80, 166(2/97)-19, 162-70, 160-74, 159-40, 133(2/92)-32, 117(12/89)-76, 113, 109(8/88)-72, 96, 89], M [104, 64-25], R [87-106, 50(7/92), 16(10/86)-71], S [9/70, 6/70, 5/66, 3/66]; Guidebooks: Bourdon and Tasaka's *Squamish Select,* Michaux's *Squamish Boulder Problems,* McLane's *The Rockclimber's Guide to Squamish,* Failey's *Guide to Hiking and Climbing in Southwestern British Columbia,* Campbell's *Rock Climbs of Little Smoke Bluffs,* Harlin's *West,* Ourom's *Climber's Guide to Squamish Chief,* Smaill's *Squamish Chief Guide,* Woodsworth's *A Climber's Guide to Squamish Chief.*

Directions: From Vancouver go approximately 60 km north on Hwy. 99 at the town of Squamish. The Squamish Area has many formations, including Bulletheads, Tantalus Wall, Western Dihedrals, Grand Wall, The Apron, South Gully, North Walls, Squaw, and The Backside (East Face) of the Chief.

13 SQ–Little Smoke Bluffs ✦✦✦

This societal collection of small 150′ granite cliffs on a hill overlooking downtown Squamish is a good stopping place for the first-time Squamish visitor. About 250 climbs; noteworthy for its thin cracks and beginner's teething area. Some cliffs on private land.

Classics: Penny Lane: Penny Lane 9, Crime of the Century 11; Neat and Cool: Cat Crack 6, Neat and Cool 10a, Flying Circus 10a.

Ref: R 50(7/92); Guidebooks: McLane's *The Rockclimber's Guide to Squamish,* Campbell's *Rock Climbs of Little Smoke Bluffs.*

Directions: At Squamish. North Bluffs at McDonald's near downtown. Take Loggers Lane east to end of Blind

Channel. Park roadside. South Bluffs behind Cliffside Pub, end of Plateau Dr., Hospital Hill, or end of Blind Channel. Trails lead in varied directions from these parking areas to the rocks. Courtesy is requested for parking in local residential areas. Summer/autumn. Government/ private land.

14 SQ–Malamute ✦✦✦

Many beautiful 150′ granite cracks and corners make this a must-visit crag. Summer/autumn. Government land.

Classics: Caboose 10b, Clean Crack 11b, Strawline 11c.

Ref: R 50(7/92); Guidebook: McLane's *The Rockclimber's Guide to Squamish.*

Directions: At Squamish. Malamute is along the BC Rail tracks along the Howe Sound in front (west) of the Chief.

15 SQ–Murrin Provincial Park (Petrifying Wall) ✦✦✦

Excellent 165′ granite "Neapolitan" climbing with about 150 single-pitch rock climbs. Beginner/intermediate routes at Sugarloaf. Beautiful crack climbing at Nightmare Rock. Sport routes at Above-the-Lake and Petrifying Wall. Petrifying Wall contains mostly face climbs on small edges. Summer/autumn. Government park.

Classics: Petrifying Wall: Even Steven 10c, No Name Road 11b, Dead on Arrival 11c, The Flingus Cling 12b, Rocket 12d; Brunser Overhang 10d; Milkman's Wall: Mr. O'Clock 11a, El Ivan 11b, El Indio 11c, Horrors of Ivan 11c; Nightmare Rock: Big Daddy Overhang 12b.

Ref: C 113, R 50(7/92); Guidebook: McLane's *The Rockclimber's Guide to Squamish.*

Directions: From Squamish Chief go approximately 7 km south of the Chief and 2 km north of Britannia Beach. A central parking lot along the highway provides access to all the crags. Prominent formations in Murrin Provincial Park include Petrifying Wall, Nightmare Wall, and Sugarloaf.

16 SQ–Shannon Falls Provincial Park ✦✦✦

Many granite cracks and corners make for a must-visit. Summer/autumn. Government land.

Classics: Papoose: Centrefold 10b; Shannon Falls: Klahanie Crack 7, Local Boys Do Good 10d, Hungry Wolf 11b, Magic Carpet Ride 11c, Hunter's Moon 11d.

Ref: C 89, R 50(7/92); Guidebook: McLane's *The Rockclimber's Guide to Squamish.*

Directions: At Squamish. Shannon Falls Provincial Park is along the BC Rail tracks in front of the Chief.

17 Shannon Valley (Mt. Habrich) ✦✦✦

Mt. Habrich (5,600′) is a summertime area offering six- to eight-pitch, flaring crack climbs. Good 1,000′ granite area for intermediate-grade climbers. Sky Pilot (6,645′) is highest point back in Shannon Valley. Summer/autumn. Government land.

Classics: Mt. Habrich: Solar System 10b.
Ref: C 96, R 50(7/92); Guidebooks: McLane's *The Rockclimber's Guide to Squamish,* Fairley's *A Guide to Climbing and Hiking in British Columbia.*
Directions: Valley southeast of Squamish. Approach via four-wheel-drive logging roads in Shannon Valley behind the Chief or three- to four-hour walk. Formations in Shannon Valley include Mt. Habrich, Sky Pilot, Ledge, Ledgling, and Nai.

18 Comic Rocks ★★★
Laugh and tell jokes while climbing on thirty fun routes on sunny 150' granite crags. Bouldering, too. Summer/autumn.
Classics: Garfield 7, Peanuts 10c, Vargas Girl 12b.
Ref: Guidebook: McLane's *The Rockclimber's Guide to Squamish.*
Directions: From Vancouver go north on Hwy. 99 to Horseshoe Bay. About 30 km north of Horseshoe Bay and 12 km south of Squamish. Park at a wide pullout. Comic Rocks cliff lies 100 km to the east. Descents off the west.

19 Lighthouse Park ★★
Mostly short 40–70' granite routes characterized by juggy and sunny sea-cliff climbing. Toprope anchors and bouldering. Twelve routes. Summer/autumn. Free/pay camping.
Classics: Dolphin 8, Double Overhang 10b, Orca 12a.
Ref: Guidebook: McLane's *The Rockclimber's Guide to Squamish.*
Directions: West Vancouver. At Juniper Point in Lighthouse Park. From Upper Levels Frwy., take exit 43 from Horseshoe Bay. North of the shopping mall, turn left on Caulfield Dr. Descend 0.7 km onto Willow Creek Rd. for 0.5 km to Keith Rd. Turn left for 0.5 km to Marine Dr. Turn west and proceed for 1.7 km to the crest of a hill (park sign). Cut left down Beacon Lane and parking lot. Hike beyond "Fire Road" gate.

20 Capilano Canyon ★★
Four-pitch granite routes. Summer/autumn. Free/pay camping. Government park.
Classics: Capilano Classic 11a.
Ref: Guidebook: McLane's *The Rockclimber's Guide to Squamish.*
Directions: From Vancouver take Upper Levels Frwy. to exit 14. Go 1.7 km up Capilano Rd., then left onto Fish Hatchery Rd. In 200 m, park on left. Hike south into forest to Capilano Canyon rim. Hike north to drop to river, then back south to climb. It is actually illegal to climb in the Capilano Canyon, and if climbers are caught, they will be warned or fined. One four-pitch route of note in this thickly foliated canyon is a difficult but sweet climb. Possibly loose rock.

21 Penticton (aka Skaha) ★★★★
Since 1987, Skaha has had ever-increasing popularity as a sport-climbing area. Developed, one-pitch, "gneiss" crags with jug-hauling and great overhanging climbing. Skaha Bluffs will not much longer be a side trip on a much bigger adventure. With 500 routes, it is quickly becoming a main destination for climbers of all calibers. The semiarid climate of the Okanagan Valley adds length to the usually short Canadian climbing season: March–November. Pay camping in Okanagan Falls. Government land.
Classics: Little Peach 7, Double Exposure 8, Spring Fingers 8, The Plum Line 10a, Throw Zog Throw 10a, Primal Dream 10b, Doctor Crow 10c, Gang Bang 10c, Wings of Desire 11b, Mortal Combat 11b, Test of the Ironman 11c, Doctor Megatrip 11d, Isis 11d, Acid Test 12a.
Ref: James Briar 5/98; C 163-106, R [79-28, 74-28, 73-90, 56]; Guidebooks: Richardson's *Skaha Rockclimbs,* McClane's *Skaha: New Climbs 1994,* McClane's *The Climber's Guide to Skaha.*
Directions: From Penticton just east/southeast of town rocks are visible from highway. Two parking areas. North (reported closed to climbers): From South Main St. go east on Pineview Rd. to Cedar Rd. to gate at end of Juniper Rd. Hike south to Cave Hill/Morning Glory Wall et al. South (pay fee/most pleasant): From South Main St. go east on Crescent Hill Rd. to south on Valleyview Rd. leading to Braesyde Crags. The Skaha Loop Trail takes one around to various crags. Intricate areas—get a guidebook or, better yet, a warm-blooded local.

22 Purcell Mountains ★★★★★
Backcountry alpine rockaneering holds a lifetime of 2,000' alpine granite walls. Mt. Findlay, 10,374'; Mt. Farnham, 11,340'. See Bugaboo listing. Summer. Government land.
Ref: AAJ '98, CAJ, S [18(5/72)-1, 6/72]; Guidebooks: Roper and Steck's *Fifty Classic Climbs,* Kruszyna and Putnam's *Rocky Mountains of Canada—South,* Edward's *Exploring the Purcell Wilderness.*
Directions: The Purcell Mountains extend from southwest of Golden, British Columbia, south into northwest Montana. The Bugaboo Group, in the Northern Purcells, is the most famous rock climbing area of this couple-hundred-mile range.

23 Chehalis Range (Mt. Grainger) ★★★★
Supreme alpine granite climbing and splendor. Fred Beckey has called Mt. Grainger some of the finest rock he has ever seen. Summer. Free/pay camping. Government land.
Classics: Mt. Grainger: South Face III 10a, Mt. Ratney North Ridge.
Ref: AAJ '86-168, CAJ 1980(11), C 95; Guidebook: Fairley's *A Guide to Climbing and Hiking in British Columbia.*
Directions: Near Harrison Hot Springs, west/southwest of Harrison Lake. Major formations in the Chehalis Range include Grainger Peak, Mt. Ratney, Mt. Clarke, and Viennese Peak.

24 Mt. Slesse (7,850') (in the Chiliwack Group) ✩✩✩✩

Mt. Slesse is the savage alpine rock fang of the North Cascades. The most impressive and massive of Slesse's granite sides is the 3,000' Northeast Buttress, totaling thirty to thirty-four pitches. Summer. Government land.

Classics: Slesse Mountain: Southwest Face II 5.6, Northeast Buttress V 9 A2; Mt. Rexford: East Ridge III 8; Nesakwatch Spire: Southwest Ridge III 8.

Ref: AAJ ['95, '79], C [152-126, 151-40, 96], CAJ, OB 45(6/79), S 1/64; *Climbing in North America;* on-line guide www.ac.wwu.edu/~berdind; Guidebooks: Fairley's *A Guide to Climbing and Hiking in British Columbia,* Nelson and Potterfield's *Selected Climbs in the Cascades,* Beckey's *Cascade Alpine Guide,* Roper and Steck's *Fifty Classic Climbs.*

Directions: Chiliwack. Mt. Slesse is located in the Chiliwack Group, 2 ½ mi. north of International Border. Approach from Chiliwack River Rd. (off Trans Canada Hwy. 1 at Chiliwack exit). About 17 mi. up Chiliwack River Rd., turn right onto Nesakwatch Creek logging road to end. Hike Nesakwatch Creek to Northeast Buttress. Slesse is accompanied by other attractive sentinels near the Canadian border: Mt. Rexford, Illusion Peaks, Canadian Border Peak, American Border Peak, Guardian Peak, Mt. Lindeman, and South Peak.

25 Cheam Range ✩✩✩

An unusual range due to its east-west alignment. The Cheam Range spans 8 mi. between Fraser and Chiliwack Rivers. Poor alpine volcanic rock quality is interspersed with many outstanding glaciers. Four eastern peaks (Foley, Welch, Stewart, Baby Munday) are known as the "Lucky Four Group." Summer. Free/pay camping. Government land.

Classics: Lucky Four Group.

Ref: Guidebooks: Fairley's *A Guide to Climbing and Hiking in British Columbia,* Beckey's *Cascade Alpine Guide,* Roper and Steck's *Fifty Classic Climbs.*

Directions: South of Chiliwack. East of Abbotsford. Prominent rock peaks in the Cheam Range include Cheam Peak, Lady Peak, Knight Peak, Baby Munday, Stewart Peak, Welch Peak, and Foley Peak.

26 Cathedral Provincial Park ✩✩✩

Granitic, glacially carved, alpine peaks. Summer. Government park.

Ref: CAJ; *Climbing in North America;* Guidebooks: Fairley's *A Guide to Climbing and Hiking in British Columbia,* Beckey's *Cascade Alpine Guide.*

Directions: From town of Keremeos head southwest off Hwy. 3 to Cathedral Provincial Park. Many glaciated features in Cathedral Provincial Park include formations: Quiniscoe Mountain, Pyramid Mountain, Grimface, and Haystack Mountain.

27 Vancouver Island ✩✩✩✩

Mountaineering challenges can be found from the south part of the island to the north. Mt. Arrowsmith near Port Alberni has had a long history of mountaineering. Cragging cliffs also—see number 30, Crest Creek Crag.

Ref: CAJ, OB 43(31); Guidebook: Fairley's *A Guide to Climbing and Hiking in British Columbia.*

Directions: Vancouver Island offers varied mountaineering challenges with mixed rock and ice climbing. Road conditions to the outback areas change frequently, and one is wise to get good forest maps. Mountaineering challenges include: South: Mt. Arrowsmith, Cats Ears Peak, The MacKenzie Range (Witch Hat, Flat Top, MacKenzie Peak, Redwall); Central: Elkhorn Mountain, Golden Hinde, Rambler Peak, Colonel Foster; North: Victoria Peak and Mt. Alava.

28 Selkirk Range ✩✩✩✩✩

The Adamant Range is an alpine granite backcountry similar to the better-known Bugaboo Group of the Purcell Mountains: large 2,000' alpine walls, ice couloirs, glaciers, pristine meadows, as well as long stays of bad weather and bugs. Fairy Meadow Hut near Swan Creek or Great Cairn Hut below Mt. Sir Sanford (11,590') offers accommodations. Check with Alpine Club of Canada. For the enormous amount of climbing in the Selkirk Range, one should consult the guidebooks *Columbia Mountains of Canada: Central and West and South* as well as *A Climber's Guide to the Interior Ranges of British Columbia.* Summer. Free/pay camping in government park.

Classics: Northern: Mt. Sentinel: South Ridge III 8; Mt. Quadrant: West Face III 7; Mt. Adamant: III 7; Mt. Austerity: Northeast Buttress IV 7 A1; Central: Mt. Sir Donald (Northwest Arête): III 2.

Ref: AAJ ['90-176, 77-74, 72, 70, 68, 67], C [142, 117(12/89)-76, 88, 65], OB 50(4/80)-18, S [5/69,1/63]; Guidebooks: Whipple et al.'s *Columbia Mountain Guidebooks,* Roper and Steck's *Fifty Classic Climbs,* Putnam's *Peaks and Routes of the North Selkirks,* Putnam and Kruszyna's *A Climber's Guide to the Interior Ranges of British Columbia,* Wheeler's *The Selkirk Range,* CMC's *Climbing in the Selkirks,* Green's *Among the Selkirk Glaciers.*

Directions: The popular Selkirk Range extends for hundreds of miles from the "big bend" of the Columbia River and south into northern Idaho. The Northern Selkirks ("big bend" of the Columbia River south to the Trans Canada Hwy.) are renowned for the Adamant and Gothic Groups (both alpine clusters of impressive rock walls). These can be accessed via helicopter northwest from Golden or long trail hikes (e.g., Swan Creek). The Central Selkirks are exemplified in peaks like Mt. Sir Donald in Glacier National Park (2 mi. south of Roger's Pass). The Southern Selkirks are cut by Hwy. 3, west of Creston, British Columbia, and are well known for Chimney Rock in northern Idaho.

29 Kelowna Crags ☆☆☆

A fun, gneissic climbing area with 300, mostly one-pitch, routes. Many classics in the area. The majority are face routes 5.11a–5.11c. See Dean Urness's guidebook for all the fine details. Federal land.

Classics: Chain Lightning 5.9, Express Way 5.9, Natural Gas 5.10+, DDT 5.11a, See the Light 5.11b, Trads Gone Mad 5.11b, The 9 Minute Holiday 5.11d, Bewildered 5.12, and many more.

Ref: Guidebooks: Urness's *Rockclimbs: Kelowna and Area,* Smith's *Central British Columbia Rock.*

Directions: From Vancouver follow Trans Canada Hwy. east and take the turnoff onto Hwy. 5. After two hours, a turnoff onto Hwy. 97C will take you straight into Kelowna. From Kelowna eight cragging areas (Lonely Crags, Kelowna, Mt. Boucherie, Boulderfield, Idabel Lake, Beaver Lake, Paul's Tomb, and Yak Peak's long slab routes) exist in every direction fifteen minutes to one hour from town off Hwy. 97. For the main Kelowna Crag, go south of town on Pandosy St. to Lakeshore Rd. to Chute Lake Rd. From where Chute Lake Rd. turns to dirt, continue (staying right and passing cattle guard) for 2.9 km to parking pullout on right. Walk ten minutes on four-wheel-drive road past creek to crags.

30 Crest Creek Crag (Vancouver Island) ☆☆☆

Good mix of face and crack climbing; very fingery stuff at this 25' intermediate basalt crag. One hundred and twenty routes. Summer. Pay camping. Government park.

Classics: Red Earth 5.9–5.10a, big streak down the middle of the climb easier on either side; Collaboration 5.10b, fun stuff on main crag; Raptor 5.11c?, a 50 m bad boy that you need a boat or a precarious belay station at the bottom of the climb to do. You can see this climb across the lake.

Ref: James Perry 5/98.

Directions: From Nanaimo or Victoria go north until you reach the town of Campbell River. Head east on Hwy. 28 for approximately 50 km until you see main crag on the right-hand side of the road. One hundred meters ahead is pull-in that has facilities and a map of the crags and trails.

31 Cheakamus Canyon ☆☆☆

Popular metamorphic sport climbing area developed since 1992. March–October. Camp at Squamish Bulletheads area.

Classics: Chek: Savage Beagle 10-, Kigijushi 10+, Wayward Bovine 12-, Gom Jabbar 13, Division Bell 13+, Pulse 14a; Rogues' Gallery: Gravity Can't Dance 10, Pockets Full of Kryptonite 11.

Ref: C [186-118, 181-27, 173-25, 159-42, 155-44], R [69-20, 67-77]; Guidebook: Chayer's *Cheakamus Canyon Guide.*

Directions: North of Squamish. South of Whistler. From Squamish go 25 km north to Chek Area and 4 km beyond to west-facing Rogue's Gallery. Nordic Rock (mentioned here previously) is another 30 km north.

Todd Guy looking strong on the first ascent of Bewildered, 5.12c, at the Boulderfield, Kelowna.

DEAN URNESS

32 Horne Lake ☆☆☆☆

Vancouver Island's premiere limestone sport-climbing area. Fifty routes up to four pitches in 1999—more to come. Jim Sandford's Driven 5.14b is the testpiece. No local camping. Nearest camping/supplies at town of Qualicum. Logging-company land.

Classics: The Body 10b/11b, The Waterspout 11c, Code of Honor 12, Save the Pushers 13a, Globetrotters 13d, Driven 14b.

Ref: C [190-23, 189-58 (topos), 180-109, 172-18]; Guidebook: Boyd's *Climber's Guide to Horne Lake.*

Directions: From Vancouver take the ferry ($45 one-way) to Nanaimo. Drive one hour from Nanaimo via Inland Hwy. 30 mi. to a left onto Horne Lake Rd. Turn right on Horne Lake Caves Rd. for 5 mi. to Adventure Camp to ask for parking information. Steep fifteen-minute hike.

Areas Noted but Not Described

33 Mt. Pope, 34 Prince George, 35 Bella Coola, 36 Williams Lake, 37 Marble Canyon, 38 Kamloops, 39 Yak Peak, 40 Vernon, and 41 Revelstoke.

Ref: Guidebook: Knight's *Central British Columbia Rock.*

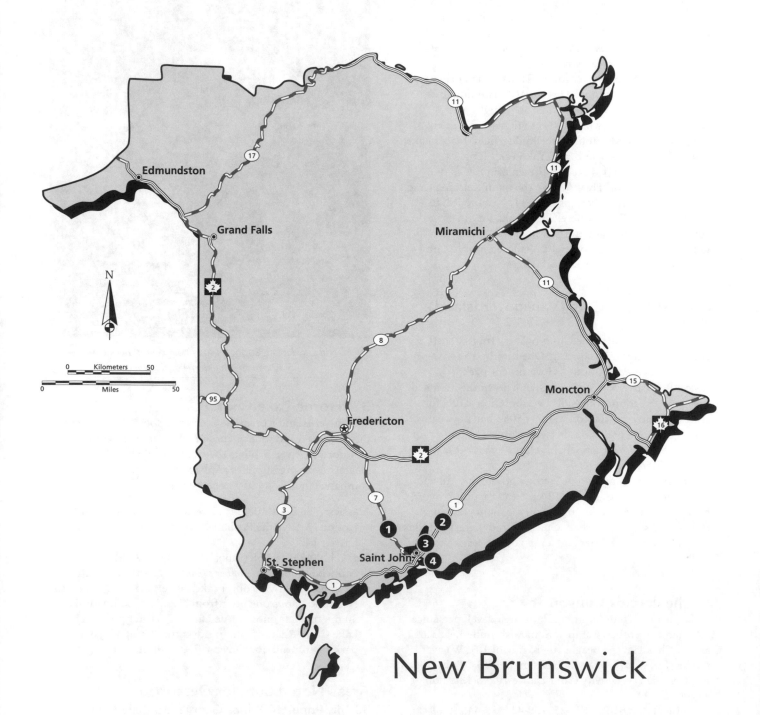

New Brunswick

New Brunswick

I much preferred to make my own hunt for knowledge, even if I found it raw and unpalatable as often I would do. —Marco Polo

In our for-what-it's-worth department, here's some rock climbing news from New Brunswick and Nova Scotia . . . in case you decide to hop a bus to Halifax.

1 Welsford Cliffs (Cochrane Lane) ✪✪✪

Forested rural 300' west-facing granite crags with varying rock quality. Two hundred traditional routes established in the 1970s by Colin Bell and later by Steve Adamson and Ghislain Losier. Summer. A reader writes that the area is located on land owned by the Canadian Armed Forces. At present it is still accessible and will probably remain that way as long as visiting climbers are as low impact as possible and respect the military requests for voluntary closures if needed. It is also reported that the Canadian Federal government has made a suggestion that the area be blasted for rock to build a new highway. Also in Welsford, park at the school, hike behind school toward sand pit, enter woods and hike for twenty-five minutes. Great view of Bald's Peak awaits any hiker or climber.

Classics: Reindeer Land 5, Cheekbone Corner 6, Snakepeel 7, Waterfall Layback 8+, Warm and Sultry Evening 9, Rock Star 9, Strata Factor 10, Joint Venture 10a, Telefunken U-47 10a, Farewell to Arms 11b, Granite Planet-11c, Perfect 5.12b, Icon 13?

Ref: Locals; *Canadian Alpine Journal* (CAJ); R 92-93; Guidebooks: Baker, Graham, Dixon, and Dixon's *A Climber's Guide To Welsford, New Brunswick;* Bell's *New Brunswick Rock and Ice,* Adamson's *Climber's Guide to New Brunswick.*

Directions: Situated in Welsford. Take the Cochrane Lane, passing on a covered bridge, and drive till you arrive at the farm. A sign indicates the boundaries for parking. Hike up the farmer's field, staying mainly left on a faint trail. Then you'll enter the forest and continue for fifteen-minute hike to the climber's box.

New Brunswick Road Thoughts

Where the hell is New Brunswick?

---

2 Hampton ✪✪

Fifty-foot gneiss crags. As of 1998, four bolted routes (from 5.9 to 5.10 and two 5.12 topropes). There is a lot of excellent potential for desperate sport routes. Autumn. Private land.

Directions: From Saint John take Highway 1, heading east. Drive for fifteen minutes until you come to Hampton. Take exit into Hampton. You will come to a set of lights; turn left here, heading toward the Kennebecasis River. You will cross a bridge and come to a store on the left side of the road. Take the road right after the store on the left. This road follows the river back toward Saint John; stay on this for about 2 mi. You will then come to a fork. Stay on the road, hugging the river (it's a dirt road). The cliffs are right on the road. Faces south.

3 Ministers Face ✪✪

With beautiful views of the river, this 250' conglomerate crag is said to be a fantastic area to climb. No camping. County land.

Directions: From the city of Saint John, head east to the town of Rothesay. Go to the beaches. The huge cliffs are across the river on an island. The only way out is to swim a mile or paddle and belay out of your boat. The cliffs are highly visible from Rothesay. During the winter, walk across the ice to great ice climbs.

4 Saint John Airport Crag ✪✪✪

Fifty-foot metamorphic sport crag. There are two bolted routes graded 5.10+. There are a few easy trad routes along with some topropes at 5.8 (yet to be bolted). There are also some boulder problems. No camping. City land.

Directions: The cliff is located on the right-hand side of the highway just before the airport. "Lisa" is painted on the cliff and is visible from the road.

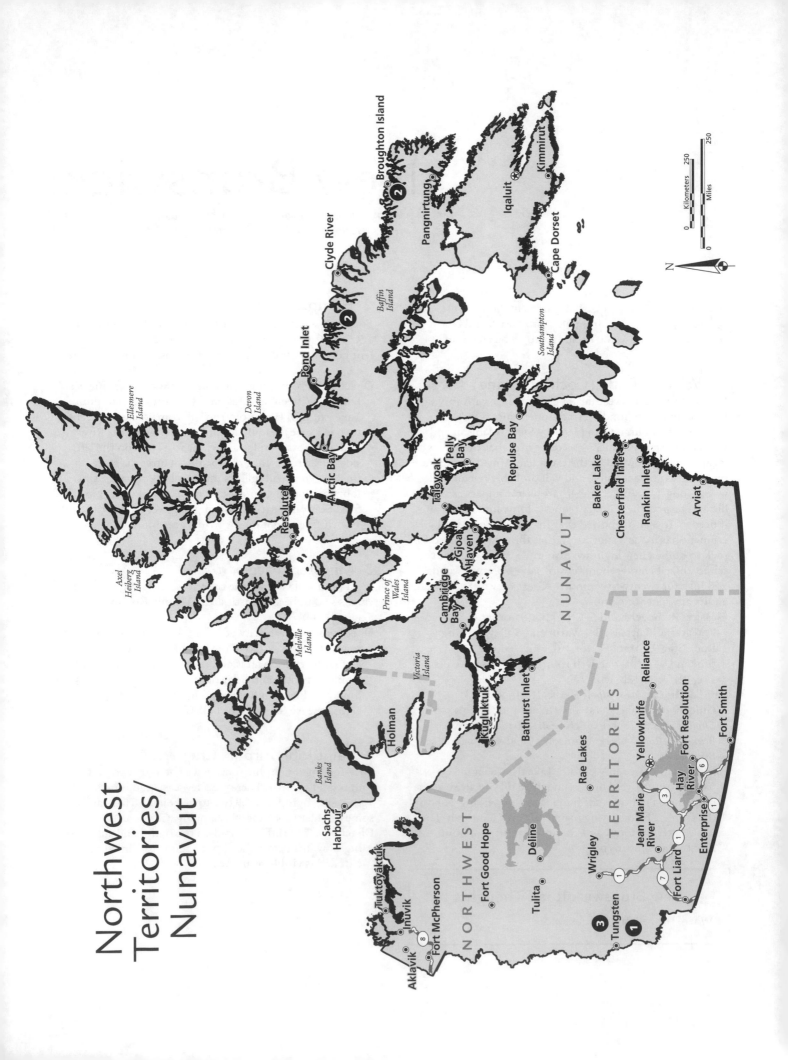

Northwest Territories/Nunavut

NORTHWEST TERRITORIES

NUNAVUT

Ellesmere Island

Devon Island

Axel Heiberg Island

Melville Island

Banks Island

Baffin Island

Southampton Island

Prince of Wales Island

Victoria Island

Broughton Island

Pangnirtung

Iqaluit

Kimmirut

Cape Dorset

Clyde River

Pond Inlet

Arctic Bay

Repulse Bay

Pelly Bay

Taloyoak

Gjoa Haven

Baker Lake

Chesterfield Inlet

Rankin Inlet

Arviat

Resolute

Holman

Sachs Harbour

Cambridge Bay

Kugluktuk

Bathurst Inlet

Rae Lakes

Reliance

Yellowknife

Fort Resolution

Fort Smith

Hay River

Enterprise

Jean Marie River

Fort Liard

Tungsten

Wrigley

Déline

Tulita

Fort Good Hope

Tuktoyaktuk

Inuvik

Aklavik

Fort McPherson

N

0   Kilometers   250

0   Miles   250

Northwest Territories, Nunavut, and the Yukon

The only truly predictable aspect of arctic weather is its unpredictability. —Kevin O'Connel

Amid the farthest reaches of most climbers' minds lie these areas in the farthest reaches of northern Canada. All are gigantic, glaciated rock buttresses or alpine summits accessed only by airplane transport and expeditionary approaches. Though the stakes are high to get there, the rewards and drama are usually higher. Among the top three in this vast region of faraway mountains are Baffin Island, Cirque of the Unclimbables, and the St. Elias Mountains.

Northwest Territories and Nunavut

1 Cirque of the Unclimbables ☆☆☆☆☆

Parlez vous expedition? A panoply of alpine monoliths in no doubt one of the wildest rock palaces on Earth. The 2,000′ plumbline crack on Lotus Flower Tower has been revered for years. Records go back to 1955 with an ascent of Mt. Sir James MacBrien. In 1968, the first ascent of the Lotus Flower Tower's famed Southeast Face (V5.8 A2) by McCarthy, Frost, and Bill. In 1977, freed at 5.10 by Levin, Robinson, and Stewart. In 1992, Skinner, Piana, and Rowell put up The Great Canadian Knife VI 5.13b on Mt. Proboscis, followed by another free route 5.12c in 1994 by Smith, Jackson, and Cosgrove. The cleanest walls have at least partial southern exposure, while north-facing rock equals grunge. Thus, most walls with southern exposure have routes on them. Long summer days mean eighteen to twenty hours of sunlight. Requires self-sufficient expeditions. Government land.

Classics: Lotus Flower Tower Southeast Face 10; Mt. Proboscis: Great Canadian Knife VI 13, Bustle Tower.
Ref: AAJ ['98, '97, '95, 93-66, 91-186, 78-545, 77-201, 76-465, 74-37, 72, 69], C [157-70, 153-118, 136, 131(4/92), 65], R [76-28, 57]; Kor's *Beyond the Vertical*, Piana's *Big Walls;* Guidebook: Roper/Steck's *Fifty Classic Climbs.*
Directions: The Cirque of the Unclimbables is in the remote and expansive Logan Mountains. From Watson

Lake (it's 1,500 mi. from Seattle, Washington to Watson Lake, which is just off the Alaskan Hwy.), charter a plane for a 150-mile flight to Glacier Lake (aka Brintnell Lake). Hike 1–2 mi. west up Brintnell Creek, then up steep hillside to north (long day hike to Fairy Meadow). Or, an outdated way: 180-mile gravel-road drive Cantung (or Tungsten), where helicopter can sometimes be chartered for flight to Fairy Meadow. From Fairy Meadow go north a few mi., then west into Cirque of the Unclimbables.

2 Baffin Island (Mt. Thor and Mt. Asgard) ☆☆☆☆☆

Many unbelievable and extreme big-wall challenges in one of North America's farthest reaches. Famed features include Mt. Asgard, Mt. Thor in Auyuttuq National Park, and The Chinese Wall, Kiguti, Great Cross Pillar, Walker Citadel, and Broad Peak to name but a few in the Sam Ford Fjord to the north of Auyuttuq. Mt. Asgard (7,071′) with its twin summits, lies just above the Arctic Circle. Its 3,500′ alpine granite face was first done in 1972 by a Doug Scott expedition, and then later, as an amazing grade VI solo in 1975 by Charlie Porter. Logistically and financially challenging, these expedition climbs are for highly skilled climbers of the highest dedication and commitment (see Climbing 10/94). Polar bears—bring a gun . . . a big one . . . and don't forget to load it. Light twenty-four hours a day from April to September. Ice cap travel requires strategic planning. July–September are main access seasons, but the only predictable aspect of arctic weather is its unpredict-ability. Park service.

Classics: Mt. Thor: Direct West Face, The Diagonal Buttress (West Face) VI 9 A4.
Ref: *Canadian Alpine Journal* (CAJ), AAJ ['98>95], C [198-32, 197-116, 182-27, 181-31, 174-56, 169-84, 166(2/97)-81, 164-23, 158-94], M 109, R [89-20, 87-26, 76-24, 70-26], S [5/86, 4/79, 6/78, 1/78, 5/75, 3/74]; on-line guide www.qullikkut-guides.com; Guidebook: Kelsey's *Mountains of the World.*
Directions: Air access from Montreal or Ottawa by First Air. Then from Clyde by Qullikkut Outfitters via snow-

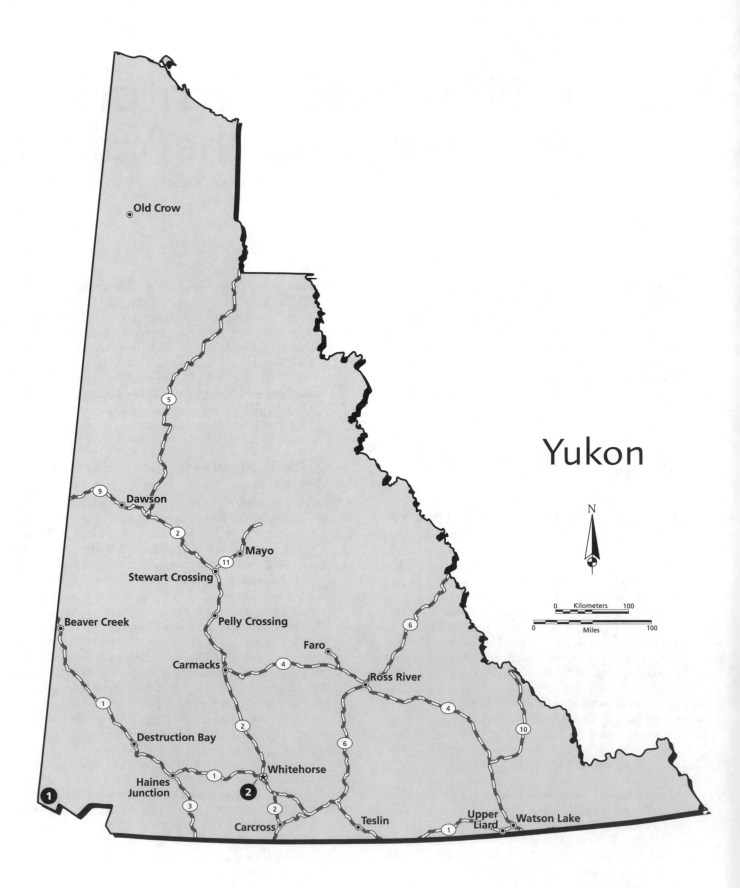

Yukon

Old Crow

⑤

⑨ Dawson

②

⑪ Mayo

Stewart Crossing

Beaver Creek

Pelly Crossing

Faro

⑥

Carmacks ④ Ross River

① ④

Destruction Bay ② ⑩

⑥

① Whitehorse

Haines
Junction ②

③ ②

Carcross Teslin Upper Watson Lake
Liard

①

N

0 Kilometers 100

0 Miles 100

❶

❷

mobiles and Komotik sleds. Or from Pangnirtung, via fjords by boat and cross-country travel via snowmobile to Summit Lake in Auyuttuq National Park. Attention must be given to ice break-up for evacuation.

3 Vampire Spires

These 2,000' granite formations are named The Phoenix, Golden Wing Buttress, Vampire, Canine, and The Fortress. Expedition climbing. July–August.

Ref: C [192-30, 187-95].

Directions: Just 15 mi. north of the Cirque of the Unclimbables in the Logan Mountains. Accessed via Kluane Airways (250–860–4187 or www.inconnu.com). The Phoenix and Golden Wing Buttress are at drop-off point. Vampire Spires are a one-and-a-half-hour hike northwest.

Yukon

1 St. Elias Mountains (Mt. Logan, 19,520', and Mt. St. Elias, 18,008')

This alpine range was named on St. Elias Day in 1742 by European explorers. Isolation, serious weather, and climbs of expedition-style Himalayan magnitude color this coastal range. Mt. St. Elias first climbed in 1987 by Duke of Abruzzi et al. Mt. Logan first climbed in 1932 and is now famed for the incredible Hummingbird Ridge (an 8-mile corniced arête), climbed in 1965 by Allen Steck et al.; also the site of the fatal Cheesmond/Freer accident. At 19,520', Mt. Logan is the second-highest mountain in North America. Included here for its prominence in elevation. Hundreds of unclimbed summits. Long waits (possibly ten days) for bad weather is the norm. Avalanche knowledge a must. In Kluane National Park.

Classics: Mt. Logan: Hummingbird Ridge, East Ridge; Mt. St. Elias: Abruzzi Ridge.

Ref: AAJ ['95-93, 91-96/176, 90-177, 88-76/138, 85-181/213, 80-78, 77-196, 75-140, 74, 72, 71, 69-65], *Canadian Alpine Journal*, C [Mar 98-63, 163-66, 123-61, 117, 61], M [65-37, 56], R [72-36, 8], S [1/79, 10/78, 2/75, 9/70, 11/66], *Climbing in North America*, Guidebook: Steck and Roper's *Fifty Classic Climbs*.

Directions: For Mt. Logan fly west into base of Hummingbird Ridge at glacier. Commercial air services available at Whitehorse or Haines Junction, Yukon Territories. Also here is registration with Kluane National Park rangers. Mt. St. Elias: From Yakutat, Alaska, charter aircraft southeast to northeast corner of Oily Lake. From here it's a few weeks' time to complete the climb of Mt. St. Elias via Agassiz and Newton Glaciers. Various approaches for other reaches of the park.

2 Rock Gardens ★★★

A nice 60' granite crag with bouldering to stop at while driving through Whitehorse. See Keitels and Pohl's guidebook for nine other worthwhile rock-climbing areas in the Whitehorse area.

Classics: Crucifix Direct.

Ref: R. Yadon 5/98; Guidebooks: Keitels and Pohl's *A Guide to Single Pitch Climbs of The Yukon*, Dallaire's *The Rock Gardens: A Climbing Guide and Journal*.

Directions: Located on Alaska Hwy. across from the south access of Whitehorse. From Alaska Hwy., turn onto Lobird Rd. for about 1 mile. Turn right to parking and trail to rocks.

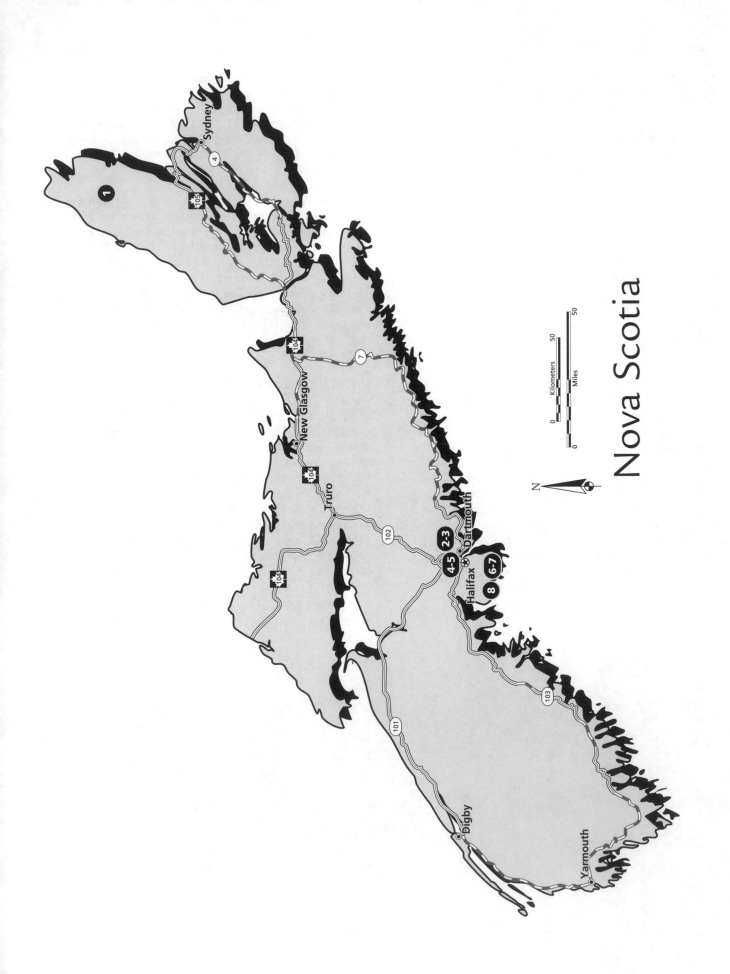

Nova Scotia

Nova Scotia

1 Cape Breton Highlands National Park

The guidebook *Climb Cape Breton* lists roadside crags northwest of Sydney. August and September are two best months for a climbing visit to Nova Scotia. Much potential but no specifics.

Ref: Guidebook: Read and Kronstedt's *Climb Cape Breton*.

Directions: Northwest of Sminuteney. Visible roadside granite crags in Cape Breton Highlands National Park.

2 Railway Crag

Seldom visited 90′ crag. Good bouldering in valley below.

Classics: Sickle 12.

Ref: Guidebook: Willett's *Climb Nova Scotia*.

Directions: From Halifax go east on Hwy. 7. Turn west on Hwy. 357 and go for 1 km. Cross Musquodoboit River on bridge to right and follow road to end at gravel pit near small lake. Ten-minute hike to Railway Crag along railroad tracks.

3 Paces Lake (First Face and Main Face)

Possibly the best cliff in the Halifax area. Steep quartzite sport climbs and gear routes. Nova Scotia's most popular climbing area among beginners and veterans. Because this is private land, owners request all climbers register or be a member of Climb Nova Scotia.

Classics: First Face: Black Diamond 9, Snakeskin 10a, Pyramid 10d, Sins and Transgressions 11d, Mea Culpa 12a; Main Face: Popcorn 6, Point of View 7, Scratch and Sniffle 9, Priceless 10a, E-Gads 10, Eyrie Arête 10b, AIDS 11a, Enervator 12b; Neverland: Lost Boys 12c.

Ref: Guidebook: Willett's *Climb Nova Scotia*.

Directions: From Halifax. First Face: East on Hwy. 7. Turn west on Hwy. 357 and go for 6.1 km from Musquodoboit Harbor Junction. Turn left for 1 km to boat dock. Hike south a few minutes from boat dock to Paces Lake cliff (dozen routes). Main Face: Access via boat at Innis Cove or drive 4 $^8/_{10}$ mi. from Musquodoboit Harbor Junction. Park. Hike trail (taped) twenty minutes to top of cliff. Rappel or hike gully down to base of cliff. Neverland is another area just south of Main Face $^1/_2$ mi. to large boulder and then up streambed to rock.

4 Eagle's Nest

Popular quartzite crag with twenty good beginner routes. Summer/autumn City park.

Classics: Evening Wall 9.

Ref: Guidebook: Willett's *Climb Nova Scotia*.

Directions: Halifax. Eagle's Nest has three areas: 1) Main Crag, 2) Buck Slabs, and 3) Schoolroom.

5 Dalhousie University

Small 25′ artificial climbing wall since 1992 at Dalhousie University built as a memorial to local climber Ben Adams, who died of heart failure.

Ref: Guidebook: Willett's *Climb Nova Scotia*.

Directions: Downtown Halifax.

6 Chebucto Head

Rocky granite headland with lighthouse. Excellent bouldering.

Ref: Guidebook: Willett's *Climb Nova Scotia*.

Directions: From Halifax follow Hwy. 379 south to Chebucto Head. Park by lighthouse and walk toward water.

7 Terence Bay

Granite rocks arising from sea and also best cliff set back from shore.

References: Guidebook: Willett's *Climb Nova Scotia*.

Directions: From Halifax twenty minutes south to Terence Bay.

8 Peggy's Cove

Clean, white granite bouldering along the sweeping Atlantic headlands.

Ref: Guidebook: Willett's *Climb Nova Scotia*.

Directions: From Halifax trend south on Hwy. 333, following signs to Peggy's Cove. Park at restaurant/lighthouse. Bouldering at lighthouse and northeast along shore.

Ontario

Fort Severn

Attawapiskat
Kashechewan
Moosonee

Pickle Lake

Red Lake

Sioux Lookout
Savant Lake
Silver Dollar
Dryden
Kenora
Fort Frances

Armstrong
Nakina
Geraldton
Hearst
Kapuskasing

Atikokan
Thunder Bay
Marathon
Wawa
Timmins
Chapleau

Elliot Lake
Sault Ste. Marie

Kirkland Lake
Sudbury
North Bay
Pembroke
Ottawa
Cornwall
Kingston

Parry Sound
Barrie
Toronto
Niagara Falls
Kitchener
London
Sarnia
Windsor

1 **2** **3-6** **8-14** **15** **7** **16** **17**
18-26 **27-30** **31-43** **44** **45** **46** **47** **48**
49 **50-57** **58** **59**

599 105 516 642 599 72 71 11 17 527 11 16
101 144 129 101 17 17 11 69 17 17 60 62 7
416 417 401 401 12 11 400 10 21 40 401

Kilometers 0 200
Miles 0 200

N

Ontario

A day without sunshine is like night. —Unknown

While Quebec is gifted with granite, its neighboring province to the west, Ontario, is loaded with limestone. The main focus of Ontario climbing is on the abundant limestone of the Niagara Escarpment. Natural beauty and top-quality limestone cragging walk hand in hand from Niagara Falls to Lion's Head. Most of these crags seem to coincide with the Bruce Trail, making a hiking guide to the Bruce Trail an auxiliary friend. The copious potential for new routes and bizarre names the climbers are so fond of here should keep visitors coming back for years.

But keep an open mind. Limestone is just the beginning. Fine climbing adventures on granite to diabase can be found in other areas of the province, such as at Bancroft, Bon Echo, Gananoque, and Thunder Bay.

The pure natural beauty of Ontario is yet another reason to take a tour of the region. Bon chance!

1 TB☆–(Thunder Bay Area) Kopka Wall ☆☆

Short 150′ diabase cliffs offer scenic face and crack cragging. The first all-encompassing on-line guide is available at www.norlink.net/~mtjoseph/rocguide.html. Enjoy. Three hundred routes. Note that this does not include the Kopka Wall. Good kayaking and canoeing at base of cliff. Spring– autumn. Better in fall as summer is buggy. Free camping. Federal land.
Classics: GoJo 7, This Is Indian Land 7, Flying Circus 10b, Nasty Girls 11a, Flying Dutchmen 12a, (2p) Silver Harbour Dream Line 12?
Ref: A. Joseph 7/99, S. Parent; *Canadian Alpine Journal* (CAJ); Guidebooks: Parent's *A Guide to Climbing Routes at the Scenic Bluffs of Thunder Bay,* Spencer and Aitchinson's *Rock Climbs in the Manitoba and Ontario Border Region,* Mark's *Rock Climbing In Ontario.*
Directions: From Thunder Bay crack 100 km west on Hwy. 527 to Kopka River for the Kopka Wall. (Seven hours east of Winnipeg, seven hours north of Minneapolis, fifteen hours northwest of Toronto.) Faces southwest.

2 TB–Orient Bay ☆☆☆☆

The Bay features a 180′ diabase crag. Also, extremely excellent ice-climbing area. Home of the annual North of Superior Orient Bay Ice Festival. Shaun Parent is knowledgeable local rock and ice expert. Cascade Falls. Free camping. Spring–autumn. Federal land.
Ref: S. Parent; Guidebook: Parent's *A Guide to Climbing Routes at the Scenic Bluffs of Thunder Bay.*
Directions: From Nipigon travel 40 km north on Hwy. 11 to Orient Bay.

3 TB–Claghorn Bluffs (on Black Sturgeon Rd.) ☆☆

An 180′ diabase crag. Icefalls up to 100′ in winter. Lots of bugs in summer. Spring–autumn. Free camping. Government land.
Classics: Fairdinken 5, Bridge of Sign 9.
Ref: S. Parent; Guidebook: Parent's *A Guide to Climbing Routes at the Scenic Bluffs of Thunder Bay.*
Directions: From Thunder Bay fishtail 80 km east on Hwy. 11/17, then 20 km north on Black Sturgeon Rd. to Claghorn Bluffs. Faces north.

4 TB–Chipmunk Rock ☆☆☆

Great 80′ gneiss crag for intermediate climbers. Great swimming and fishing, too. Spring–autumn. Free camping. Federal land.
Classics: Highway Pancake 10.
Ref: S. Parent; C 93; Guidebook: Parent's *A Guide to Climbing Routes at the Scenic Bluffs of Thunder Bay.*
Directions: From Nipigon chip off 3.5 km north on Hwy. 11. Chipmunk Rock is right on highway. Faces southwest.

5 TB–Kama Point ☆☆

This 180′ diabase crag offers great views of Lake Superior Islands. Nice intermediate/expert routes. Icefalls in winter. Spring–autumn. Free camping. Federal land.
Ref: S. Parent; C 93; Guidebook: Parent's *A Guide to Climbing Routes at the Scenic Bluffs of Thunder Bay.*
Directions: From Nipigon go 2.6 km south on Hwy. 17 to Kama Point. Faces southwest.

6 TB–Mt. Helen ☆☆☆

A 160′ gneiss crag with great swimmin', fishin', and blueberry pickin'. Spring–autumn. Free camping. Federal land.

Classics: Neutron Dance 8.

Ref: S. Parent; C 93; Guidebook: Parent's *A Guide to Climbing Routes at the Scenic Bluffs of Thunder Bay.*

Directions: From Nipigon shoot 2.5 km north on Hwy. 11 to Mt. Helen. Faces southwest.

7 TB–Atikokan ☆☆☆☆

Great finger and face climbing on this 200' andesite crag. Old open pit mine. Salmon farm at Marmion Lake. Spring–autumn. Free camping. County land.

Classics: Bolts are for Deadheads 11.

Ref: S. Parent; Guidebook: Parent's *A Guide to Climbing Routes at the Scenic Bluffs of Thunder Bay.*

Directions: From Atikokan go east 10 km to Rayland mine site. Faces north/west.

8 TB–Dorion Towers ☆☆☆☆

Highly recommended 75' diabase pinnacle. Spring–autumn. Free camping. Federal land.

Classics: Standard Route 7.

Ref: S. Parent; C 93; Guidebook: Parent's *A Guide to Climbing Routes at the Scenic Bluffs of Thunder Bay.*

Directions: From Dorion float south on Hwy. 11/17. Take Quimet Canyon Rd. for 2.7 km. Then take first right. Go 1.6 km to first road on left. Go to gate. Follow trail to Dorion Towers.

9 TB–Pearl Roadcut ☆☆☆

This 40' granite slab makes for an easy roadside stop and blueberry pickin'. Spring–autumn. Free camping. Federal land.

Classics: Honk if You Love Climbers 8.

Ref: S. Parent; C 93; Guidebook: Parent's *A Guide to Climbing Routes at the Scenic Bluffs of Thunder Bay.*

Directions: From Pearl shine 5 km east on Hwy. 11/17 to Pearl Roadcut. It's 50 km northeast of Thunder Bay. Faces south/east.

10 TB–Silver Harbour ☆☆☆

Lots of variety at this 50' diabase crag. Close to lake—good fishin'. Spring–autumn. Free camping. Private land/county park.

Classics: Mashed Potatoes 5, Alpha A1 5.11.

Ref: S. Parent; Guidebook: Parent's *A Guide to Climbing Routes at the Scenic Bluffs of Thunder Bay.*

Directions: From Thunder Bay, Silver Harbour is 14 km outside of town. Go east on Lakeshore Blvd. Faces east.

11 TB–Pass Lake ☆☆

Look out for loose blocky flakes anytime, anyplace on this 70' sandstone crag. Bouldering, too. Great desserts, food, sodas across street. Spring–autumn. Pay camping. Federal land.

Classics: Go Joe 7, Dogs Life 10a.

Ref: S. Parent; Guidebook: Wrajez and Barbeau's *Pass Lake: The Next Generation.*

Directions: From Thunder Bay go 45 km east. Turn south on Hwy. 587 for 8 km to Pass Lake. Faces south.

12 TB–Sleeping Giant Provincial Park ☆☆☆☆☆

Highest, longest cliff in Ontario. Good long rock and ice climbs on this 450' diabase cliff. It's a 7-km hike to Chimney area of Giant. Good view of Isle Royale and Lake Superior. Spring–autumn. Free camping. Government park.

Classics: Discovery 350' 5.7–5.10.

Ref: S. Parent; C 117(12/89)-76; Guidebook: Parent's *A Guide to Climbing Routes at the Scenic Bluffs of Thunder Bay.*

Directions: From Thunder Bay saunter 45 km east. Turn south on Hwy. 587 for 30 km to Sleeping Giant Provincial Park. Faces southeast.

13 TB–Scenic Bluffs ☆☆☆☆

This 45' diabase sport crag offers easy access and is great for training. More than 200 routes. Bouldering, too. Spring–autumn. Pay camping. City park.

Classics: Split Beaver 5, Assgripper 8, Galaxian 10.

Ref: S. Parent; Guidebook: Parent's *A Guide to Climbing Routes at the Scenic Bluffs of Thunder Bay.*

Directions: In Thunder Bay. Scenic Bluffs are near Boulevard Lake. Faces east.

14 TB–Climber's Cliffs ☆☆☆

A 150' diabase crag with icefalls up to 150' in winter. Summer. Free camping. Private land.

Classics: Five Finger Discount 7, Uncle Frank's Supper Club 5 10, A3.

Ref: S. Parent; Guidebook: Parent's *A Guide to Climbing Routes at the Scenic Bluffs of Thunder Bay.*

Directions: From Thunder Bay, Climber's Cliffs are just west of town on Hwy. 61. Contact landowner first. Faces north.

15 TB–Squaw Bay and Milky Way Wall ☆☆☆

These 260' diabase walls have great views of Lake Superior Island. Mountain biking to climbs. Historical landmark and navigation aid "The Peeping Squaw Pillar." Spring–autumn. Free camping. Land owned by local Indian council.

Classics: Spiral Galaxy 7, American Demon A4.

Ref: S. Parent; Guidebook: Parent's *A Guide to Climbing Routes at the Scenic Bluffs of Thunder Bay.*

Directions: From Thunder Bay tread 10 km west of town, on Mt. McKay/Squaw Bay Rd. Then trend 5 km along gravel road along lake for Squaw Bay and Milky Way Wall. Faces east.

16 TB–Coldwell ✩✩

A 150′ volcanic crag. Spring–autumn. Free camping.
Federal land.

Ref: Guidebook: Parent's *A Guide to Climbing Routes at the Scenic Bluffs of Thunder Bay.*

Directions: From Coldwell (just west of Marathon on Hwy. 17), go 1 km west of town on Hwy. 17. Easy access. Faces south.

17 Kilarney Park (Lake George)

Granite crag. Fault splits lake. Camping at government park.

Ref: Guidebooks: Smart's *Ontario's Finest Rock Climbs,* Filion and Chisnall's *Rock Climber's Guide to Killarney Provincial Park: George Lake (EC).*

Directions: From Sudbury drive south on Hwy. 69 past Estaire. Turn right on Hwy. 637 to Kilarney Park. At Lake George.

18 BP✩–(Bruce Peninsula Area) Cave Point and Shelf Beach ✩✩✩

Good routes and great rock at this 90′ limestone crag. Scenic bouldering and swimming. Terminal Beach at Cave Point is a beautiful crack line. The Bruce Peninsula is a climber's dreamscape of dream climbs. Summer/autumn. Pay camping. Government land.

Classics: Shelf Beach: The Valve 9, Serenade 10+, Eurosport 11-; Cave Point: Terminal Beach 12+.

Ref: *Canadian Alpine Journal (CAJ);* C [117(12/89)-76, 110], R 45; Guidebooks: Barnes and Oates's *A Sport Climber's Guide to Ontario Limestone 1997,* Bracken, Barnes, and Oates's *The Escarpment,* Smart's *Ontario Limestone.*

Directions: From Miller Lake take Hwy. 6N. Turn east on Emmett Lake Rd. Turn left at fork. Park at area with Georgian Bay access sign. Follow road to Bruce Trail. When you see a happy face, go 50′ right and you've reached the top of Shelf Beach's Serenade route. Cave Point is just slightly farther north. Faces north.

19 BP–Cabot Head and South Bluff ✩✩✩

Beginner and intermediate 150′ limestone crag. The continued use of this cliff requires minimum-impact use by climbers. Please refrain from trespassing. Summer/autumn. Pay camping. Government land.

Classics: Pinnacle of Deception 10-, Frequent Flyer 10.

Ref: Guidebooks: Bracken, Barnes, and Oates's *The Escarpment,* Smart's *Ontario Limestone.*

Directions: From Wiarton take Hwy. 6N. Turn east to Dyer Bay to Cabot's Head lighthouse. Park. Hike north one hour, following beach around a cove to a cairn marking a faint path to the cliff on private land. Cabot's Head is farther north than South Bluff.

20 BP–White Bluffs ✩✩✩✩

How do picturesque blue waters, white bluffs, and gentle lake breezes sound? This 130′ limestone crag rings with that as well as the stunning Monument Roof, a 40′ 5.12c roof crack. Spring–autumn. Pay camping. Government land.

Classics: Tic In the Toc 10a, Bed without Sheets 10, Thing That Only Eats Hippies 12c, The Monument 12+.

Ref: C [105, 103, 101, 100]; Guidebooks: Bracken, Barnes, and Oates's *The Escarpment,* Smart's *Ontario Limestone.*

Directions: From Lion's Head take Bruce Co. Rd. 9N. Turn east on Whippoorwill Lane. Park on Hwy. 9 (at green P.O. box) but not on private land. Hike north on Bruce Trail 2 km. Faces south. Rappel in to White Bluffs. Wander and boggle.

21 BP–Lion's Head Cliff ✩✩✩✩

Simply the best area on the Bruce Peninsula. White 150′ limestone cliffs and blue waters. More than one hundred routes and counting; most require 5.10 spark plugs or better. Home to Sonnie Trotter's The Titan 5.14a. Great swimming. Few bugs. Summer–autumn. Pay camping. Now a Provincial Nature Preserve—please be environmentally aware.

Classics: Queue de Leon 8, Maneline 10a, Lost at Sea 10c, Thunderball 10d, Nemesis 11, Lord of the Flies 11c, Rum, I Wonder Where the Lions Are? 12a, Sodomy and the Lash 12, Laputa 12c, The Titan 14a.

Ref: C [198-35, 117(12/89)-76, 105, 103, 100], R [97-92, 45]; Guidebooks: Bracken, Barnes, and Oates's *The Escarpment,* Smart's *Ontario's Finest Rock Climbs,* Smart's *Ontario Limestone.*

Directions: From Lion's Head go east on Moore Rd. At second zigzag, head right on jeep trail. Park. Hike northeast on Bruce Trail to Lion's Head Cliff edge. Faces north.

22 BP–TV Tower Crag ✩✩✩

Kill your TV and come cragging at this 50′ limestone crag! The good routes here are cracks mainly 5.9 and 5.11. Also, a most excellent poison-ivy patch. Summer/autumn. Private land, no-o-o camping—that means you, eh?

Classics: Heart of Stone 9, Sluggo 10, Mirror Crack'd 11, Excalibur 11b, Desperado 11c.

Ref: C [110, 105]; Guidebooks: Bracken, Barnes, and Oates's *The Escarpment,* Smart's *Ontario Limestone.*

Directions: From Lion's Head go south on Hwy. 9. Turn east on Rush Cove Rd. Turn left on Grieg's Scenic Caves Rd. Park at ruined house. Hike down path to TV Tower Crag on right. Faces east.

23 BP–Disneyland ✩✩

Spectacular 80′ limestone caves. Summer/autumn. No camping. Government land.

Classics: Conan, What's Good in Life 10-, Hear the Lamentations of the Women 10+.

Ref: C 110; Guidebooks: Bracken, Barnes, and Oates's *The Escarpment*, Smart's *Ontario Limestone*.

Directions: From Lion's Head, off Hwy. 9S, turn east on Rushcove Rd. Turn right on Grieg's Scenic Caves Rd. Park at end. Hike south on Bruce Trail to Disneyland. Faces south.

24 BP-Cape Croker and Indian Ladder ☆☆

These 100′ limestone crags have many excellent 5.11 routes, with lettering system at base of routes. Poison ivy. Summer/autumn. Pleasant pay-camping facilities. Owned by Chippewa Indians. Access sensitive—do not climb on any other cliffs on the reservation.

Classics: No Rest for the Wicked 10c, Quest for Fires 11-, Swept Away 11b, Isolated Beauty 11b, Helen 12+.

Ref: C [110, 101]; Guidebooks: Bracken, Barnes, and Oates's *The Escarpment*, Smart's *Ontario Limestone*.

Directions: From Wiarton go north briefly and use Hwy. 9 turnoff to Cape Croker Park. Climbing on nature path. Faces south.

25 BP-Malcom Bluff ☆☆☆

One-hundred-foot limestone crag. Summer/autumn. Government land.

Ref: Guidebooks: Bracken, Barnes, and Oates's *The Escarpment*, Smart's *Ontario's Finest Rock Climbs*, Smart's *Ontario Limestone*.

Directions: From Wiarton take Hwy. 6N. Turn onto Hwy. 9E to Malcom Bluff. Faces southeast.

26 BP-Bruce Caves ☆☆☆☆

This 100′ limestone cave is accentuated by one route—a 100′ roof crack. Gigantic caves exist. Summer/autumn. Government land.

Classics: Black Hole 11b.

Ref: C 103; Guidebooks: Bracken, Barnes, and Oates's *The Escarpment*, Smart's *Ontario Limestone*.

Directions: From Wiarton from south of town, go east 5 km to BRUCE CAVES sign with road on right. Drive to end and walk path briefly. Faces north.

27 OS☆-(Owen Sound Area) Popcorn Rock ☆☆

A 60′ limestone crag with three good intermediate routes. Summer/autumn. Free camping. Government land. All climbing is banned on land owned by the Grey Sauble Conservation Authority.

Classics: Black Book 8, Lost in Pittsburgh 9, Farmer's Almanac 10.

Ref: *Canadian Alpine Journal* (CAJ); M 101; Guidebooks: Bracken, Barnes, and Oates's *The Escarpment*, Smart's *Ontario Limestone*.

Directions: From Owen Sound go north on Hwy. 70. Turn south—Downtown Line. Park at 1 km west of drive-in theater. Hike south on Bruce Trail to Popcorn Rock. Faces east.

28 OS-Owen Sound Bluffs ☆☆

If you climb 5.9, you'll think you died and went to heaven . . . or Ontario. A 40′ limestone crag with a baker's dozen of routes with some excellent clean hand cracks. Summer/autumn. Free camping. Government land.

Classics: Regensburg 9, Closet of Anxieties 9, Lady in Red 10+.

Ref: C 101; Guidebooks: Bracken, Barnes, and Oates's *The Escarpment*, Smart's *Ontario Limestone*.

Directions: In Owen Sound, follow walkway across from the house at 201 Sixth Ave. West. Or, access is possible from the top of Catalan Quarry; follow Bruce Trail south for twenty minutes, following the edge of the cliff until its end. Faces south.

29 OS-Catalan Quarry ☆

Varied quality of a dozen routes on quarried 45′ limestone cracks. Spring-autumn. Free camping. Government land.

Classics: Happy Face 8, Pioneer Cemetery 10-, Knifed in the Head 11+.

Ref: C 103; Guidebooks: Bracken, Barnes, and Oates's *The Escarpment*, Smart's *Ontario Limestone*.

Directions: In Owen Sound, follow Hwy. 6/21 through town to second left at top of hill. Go left and then turn at first right. Park at front of West Hill Secondary School. Take path across from school up to Catalan Quarry.

30 OS-Harrison Park ☆☆

Just a few 60′ limestone routes, but they're good. Redneck "Lycra" Bars. Summer/autumn. Free camping. Government land.

Classics: Puppet on a Fine Line 10+, Yukon Buddy 12.

Ref: C [105, 103]; Guidebooks: Bracken, Barnes, and Oates's *The Escarpment*, Smart's *Ontario Limestone*.

Directions: In Owen Sound. Harrison Park North Area: On Seventh Ave. east at its end. Hike five minutes west on trail. South Area: On Hwy. 10, just south of town at Storybrook Park Rd. where a hydro cut is visible. Rap in from ledges. Faces west.

31 E☆-(Eugenia Area) Duncan Rock ☆

Ref: C 110; *Canadian Alpine Journal* (CAJ); Guidebook: Bracken, Barnes, and Oates's *The Escarpment*.

Directions: Near Kimberly. Go west of Pinnacle Rock to Duncan Rock.

32 E-Pinnacle Rock ☆☆

An 80′ limestone crag with over a dozen routes—good potential. Sunny in the morning. Summer. Free camping. Government park.

Classics: White Wall: Cailin 11+; Drought Wall: 98.6 10d.

Ref: Guidebooks: Bracken, Barnes, and Oates's *The Escarpment,* Smart's *Ontario Limestone.*
Directions: From Singhampton follow Hwy. 4 to Grey Rd. 2. Turn north on Hwy. 19 to end. Go right on concession road and turn left at Collingwood TWP side road 9-10. Go past DUNCAN CAVES sign for 1/4 mi. to brown-bricked Duncan Union Church. Turn left for approximately 1 mi. when Bruce Trail-Pinnacle Rock Trail sign is on left. Hike Bruce Trail to Pinnacle Rock and then use blue side trail to yellow-blazed trail to base. Two walls of note: White Wall to left and Drought Wall to right. Faces east.

33 E–Metcalfe Rock ★★★★

Good 100' limestone crag climbing with more than fifty routes. Attention: For people who like to read rules: Camping and campfires banned on public land within 1 km of Metcalfe Rock. This area has been designated a Provincial ANSI (Area of Natural and Scientific Interest). Further bans on parking or a total ban on climbing may result if camping/fire ban not respected. Drinking water should be treated, especially after heavy rainfall. No toilet facilities available; bring portable toilet or plastic bag. "Waterfalls" is on public land, but with no public access. Do not trespass on University of Toronto Outing Club property. Had enough? Onto the next area . . . . Spring–autumn. No camping. Government land.
Classics: White of Spring 9, Agitez Bien 10a, Dynamic Duo 11a, Grace Under Pressure 11b, Looking Pretty Swell, White Hand 12b, Big Ascent Dynamite 12.
Ref: B. Parkes 5/98; C [117(12/89)-76, 110, 105, 103, 101]; Guidebooks: Bracken, Barnes, and Oates's *The Escarpment,* Smart's *Ontario's Finest Rock Climbs.*
Directions: From Singhampton go south on Hwy. 24. Turn west on Grey Co. Rd. 4. Turn north on Grey Co. Rd. 2, following it to Hwy. 19, then going west until it ends. Turn left and find crag on left. Park at pullout across from Outer's Hut club. Please don't block gate. Take Bruce Trail across field to Metcalfe Rock. Faces west.

34 E–Young's Crag ★★★

Small 100' metamorphic crag outcrop of a dozen routes up to 5.11. Summer/autumn. Free camping. Private land.
Classics: Ziplock 8, Into the Light 8+, Sabre 11, Jeunesse Oblige 11b.
Ref: Guidebook: Bracken, Barnes, and Oates's *The Escarpment.*
Directions: From Kimberley take right on first dirt road north out of town (steep road!). Go right. Park in parking area. Hike on Bruce Trail north 100', going left into grass gully to Young's Crag base. Faces south.

35 E–Old Baldy/Black Forest ★★★★

Excellent climbing on more than eighty good intermediate and expert routes. Old Baldy is bolted face climbing, Black Forest is natural geared lines. The route Crystalline (aka "The Skinner Filter" 11c) is a challenging sandbag.

Spring–autumn. Free camping. Private land.
Classics: Resplendence 10a, Pins and Needles 10-, Split Leggins 10, Shot Across the Bow 12-, Christina's World 12+.
Ref: C [117(12/89)-76, 110, 105, 101], R 74-28; Guidebooks: Bracken, Barnes, and Oates's *The Escarpment,* Smart's *Ontario's Finest Rock Climbs.*
Directions: From Kimberley take right on first dirt road north out of town (steep road!). Go right. Park in parking area. Hike on Bruce Trail to Old Baldy, going left. Faces west.

36 E–Bowles Bluff ★★

More than a dozen good routes on this 40' limestone crag. Be easy to landowners, i.e., stay off their land on cliff top. Summer/autumn. Free camping. Government land.
Classics: Elvis in America 10, Diedre a Dada 11+.
Ref: Guidebooks: Bracken, Barnes, and Oates's *The Escarpment,* Smart's *Ontario Limestone.*
Directions: From Eugenia go north on Hwy. 13. Turn left on Grey Co. Rd. 30. Take first right. Park at Talisman sign for Bowles Bluff. Faces east.

37 E–Cliff Barnes ★★★

A small 80' limestone crag with some good challenges on approximately twenty routes. Summer/autumn. Please respect private land!
Classics: Ihor 7, Dryhedral 10a, Mister Rogers Enema Party 11-, Rebel Yell 12+.
Ref: C [105, 103, 101]; Guidebooks: Bracken, Barnes, and Oates's *The Escarpment,* Smart's *Ontario Limestone.*
Directions: From Eugenia go north on Hwy. 13 until 1 1/2 mi. south of Kimberley. Park on left across from a white-chimneyed house. Please do not block driveway! Hike west (by cornfield) into woods to Cliff Barnes. Walk south to access base. Faces west.

38 E–Lost Dog ★

A handful of routes 5.8 to 5.10 on this difficult-to-find 70' limestone crag. Summer/autumn. Free/pay camping. Government land.
Classics: Stray Bullet 9.
Ref: Guidebooks: Bracken, Barnes, and Oates's *The Escarpment,* Smart's *Ontario Limestone.*
Directions: From Kimberley go just south of town (when across from Grey Co. Rd. 30), then turn east on first road going up the hill to end. Hike Bruce Trail to sharp left turn on old road. Turn sharply right across field to south. Upon reaching fence line turn right, going downhill until even with hillcrest on your left. Enter woods shortly, coming to a half dozen routes on Lost Dog in a wide gully. Faces west.

39 E–Eugenia Falls ✯✯

Eighty-foot limestone crag. Forty routes. Closed to climbing due to its status as a conservation area. Attractive natural crack lines in a scenic gorge. Summer/autumn. No camping. Government park.

Classics: Book of Hours 7, Wide Open Beaver 8, Dr. Tongue's 9, Endless Warrior 11a, Trance and Transformation 11d.

Ref: C 101; Guidebooks: Bracken, Barnes, and Oates's *The Escarpment,* Smart's *Ontario Limestone.*

Directions: In Eugenia, park at Conservation Area west of Main on small side street for Eugenia Falls. Faces west/south.

40 S✯–(Singhampton Area) Berlin Wall (aka Molson Rock) ✯✯✯✯

Almost twenty routes on this short 40′ limestone workout wall will suit those who like to lap up a pump. Can be wet. Camp at Metcalfe. Summer.

Classics: John Be Careful 10, Under the Volcano 11+, Winning at Badminton 12a.

Ref: *Canadian Alpine Journal* (CAJ), C [117(86), 110]; Guidebooks: Bracken, Barnes, and Oates's *The Escarpment,* Smart's *Ontario Limestone.*

Directions: From Singhampton go west on Hwy. 4. Turn north on Hwy. 2. Turn 5 km east on Hwy. 19. Turn south on dirt road. Park on left at small outcrop. A quick dash left into gully will get you to the Berlin Wall. Faces west.

41 S–Osprey Bluffs ✯✯✯

If you're looking for just a few good routes, try this 50′ limestone crag. Could be wet. Summer. Government land.

Classics: Nailbomb Song 10, The Sickness Unto Death 11+.

Ref: C 110; Guidebooks: Bracken, Barnes, and Oates's *The Escarpment,* Smart's *Ontario Limestone.*

Directions: From Singhampton journey due north on Hwy. 24. Park at 90M-0 west turn. Hike on Bruce Trail down to Osprey Bluffs.

42 S–Groundhog's Graveyard ✯✯✯

A handbasket of continuous 60′ limestone face routes. Spring–autumn. No camping. Government land.

Classics: Dead Hockey Moms 11b, Stench on the Deadbird 12-, Hog Heaven 12b, Psychetech 12c.

Ref: C 101; Guidebooks: Bracken, Barnes, and Oates's *The Escarpment,* Smart's *Ontario Limestone.*

Directions: From Singhampton go east on Osprey St. Turn right. Go left along Mad River. Park at old lime kiln. Hike south/southeast to Groundhog's Graveyard. Faces west.

43 S–Devil's Glen ✯✯✯

Wealth of classic intermediate 90′ limestone routes. Vampiric black flies in spring. Nutcracker is one of the best 5.8 cracks in Ontario. Summer/autumn. No camping. Government park.

Classics: Looney Tunes 7, Nutcracker 8, Plunging Necklines 11 (fingers), Slippery People 11c, Il Migrior Fabbro 13.

Ref: C 105; Guidebooks: Bracken, Barnes, and Oates's *The Escarpment,* Smart's *Ontario's Finest Rock Climbs,* Smart's *Ontario Limestone.*

Directions: From Singhampton go east on Osprey St. Turn right at 90M-0. Park at bridge. Hike ten minutes east along an old road on north shore of river. Yellow blazes lead left to Devil's Glen crag. Faces south.

44 Diamond Lake

Granite crag.

Ref: Guidebook: Smart's *Ontario's Finest Rock Climbs.*

Directions: From Combermere go south on Hwy. 514 to Diamond Lake. Canoe across lake.

45 Bancroft ✯✯

Two-hundred-foot granite crag. Icefalls in winter; nice town. Summer. Free camping. Government land.

Classics: Overhanging 165′ Finger Crack 11c.

Ref: Guidebook: Smart's *Ontario's Finest Rock Climbs.*

Directions: In Bancroft. Park at school. Faces northeast.

46 Bon Echo Provincial Park ✯✯✯✯✯

Boat belays and multipitch adventure climbing on this 300′ granite crag. Possibly loose rock. Camping at Alpine Club Hut. Summer/autumn. Pay camping. Government park.

Classics: Sweet Dreams 8, The Joke 9, Compulsion 10, Fool's End 11a, Spiderman 12+.

Ref: Guidebooks: Adcock's *A Guide to Rock Climbs at Bon Echo 1990,* Mark's *Climbing In Southern Ontario.*

Directions: From Cloyne go north on Hwy. 41 into Bon Echo Provincial Park. Cliff accessed by boat. Obtain craft at boat rental. Faces southwest.

47 Gananoque (closed?)

Great climbing for a small 80′ granite cragging area. Twenty routes. St. Peter's 5.8 would be a classic anywhere in the world. Private land. *Area closed by landowner until further notice.*

Classics: Sit-down Climb 6, St. Peter's 8, A-Okay 10, Presto Digit Eater 11a, Strawberry Jam 12a.

Ref: Guidebooks: Smart's *Ontario's Finest Rock Climbs,* Chisnall's *Climber's Guide to the Gananoque Area (EC).*

Directions: At Gananoque.

48 Kingston Mills

Small 35′ granite bouldering area, but a lot of variety and a lot of routes (fifty). Generally short, bouldery power problems. Some serious aid problems as well. Kingston's nightlife has people coming up from as far south as Syracuse on a regular basis. Spring–autumn. Free camping. Government land.

Classics: Free: Kiddies Corner 1, Odeum Direct 6, Fred's

Folly 9, Deliverance 10, Camisole Cusp 12, Kamasutra Surprise 13?. Aid: Dangling Delight A3, 5 RURPS A3 (with high funk factor).

Ref: Guidebooks: Smart's *Ontario's Finest Rock Climbs,* Smart's *Ontario's Limestone,* Chisnall's *Climber's Guide to Kingston Mills (EC).*

Directions: From Hwy. 401 exit at Hwy. 15 at Kingston. North to Kingston Mills Road, then minutes to Kingston Mills. Walk south beside locks to crags.

49 Elora Gorge ●

Throw a rope down and start toproping on this 75′ limestone crag. Loose rock. Summer/autumn. Government land.

Classics: Leap of Faith 11.

Ref: Guidebook: Smart's *Ontario Limestone.*

Directions: In Elora. Follow Elora Rd. over Elora Gorge. Turn right on David St. crossing older bridge, and take first right. Shortly, on the right a park offers easy parking where stairs lead into gorge.

50 M☆-(Milton Area) Cow Crag ☆☆☆

This 60′ limestone cragging area is closed as of 1992. The Dickens Pub recommended instead . . . argh! Site of Ontario's first sport climb, Moby Fly. Summer/autumn. Pay camping. Government land.

Classics: Fearless Warrior 10+, Moby Fly 11.

Ref: C [117(12/89)-76, 105, 103]; Guidebooks: Bracken, Barnes, and Oates's *The Escarpment,* Smart's *Ontario's Finest Rock Climbs,* Smart's *Ontario Limestone,* Marsh's *Climbing in Southern Ontario.*

Directions: From Milton head west on Derry Rd. Turn north on Hwy. 25. Turn west on Hwy. 9. Turn north on Halton Hills. Park at road's end. Hike uphill ten minutes to Cow Crag. Faces southeast.

51 M-Sunset Rock ☆☆☆

A well-liked bouldering area sports classic 25′ "multi-pitched" limestone bouldering. Look for orange triangles denoting routes. Autumn. Pay camping. Government land.

Ref: Guidebooks: Bracken, Barnes, and Oates's *The Escarpment,* Smart's *Ontario Limestone,* Marsh's *Climbing In Southern Ontario.*

Directions: From Milton go west on Derry Rd. Turn north on Twiss (1 mi.). Sunset Rock is on roadside at right, in front of your face. Faces west.

52 M-Punk Rock ☆

Sixty-foot limestone crag. Private land.

Ref: Guidebook: Smart's *Ontario Limestone.*

Directions: From Milton go west on Derry Rd. Turn north on Gwelf Line. Park at turnout. Hike to Punk Rock. Faces east.

53 M-Rattlesnake Point and Buffalo Crag ☆☆☆

Rattlesnake Point, nicknamed "The Beach," is Ontario's most popular limestone crag (80′) with more than 140 routes. This teaching area sports well-polished holds. Day-use entrance fee. Buffalo Crag (one hundred routes) is Ontario's second most-popular cliff. Both areas have been climbed out. The Bottle Glass Cliff lies between the two areas. Pay camping. Autumn. Government park.

Classics: Rattlesnake: Final Finale 5/6, Holy Cow 8, Crepidation 10b, Funky Fingers 10+, Jeopardy 10d; Buffalo: Orange Wall 9, Rainy Day Woman 9, Sad Eyed Lady 10d.

Ref: 101; Guidebooks: Bracken, Barnes, and Oates's *The Escarpment,* Smart's *Ontario's Finest Rock Climbs,* Smart's *Ontario Limestone,* Marsh's *Climbing In Southern Ontario.*

Directions: From Milton go west on Derry Rd. Turn north on Hwy. 25. Turn west on Steeles Ave. Turn south on Appleby Line. Park at park for Rattlesnake Point and Buffalo Crag.

54 M-Kelso and Milton Heights ☆☆☆

Kelso's 90′ limestone crag has more than forty routes, natural gear, swimming. Good beginner's lead area. Milton Heights is owned by a quarry and closed to climbing.

Classics: Kelso: Jolly Rodger 5, Alan's Layback 7, Shimmy 8, Our Man In Space 10b; Milton Heights: Fearless Freep 11a.

Ref: C 110; Guidebooks: Bracken, Barnes, and Oates's *The Escarpment,* Smart's *Ontario Limestone,* Marsh's *Climbing In Southern Ontario.*

Directions: Kelso: From Milton go west on Derry. Turn north on Hwy. 25. Just before reaching Hwy. 401, turn west on Steeles Ave. Turn right on First, following signs to Kelso Conservation Area. Park. Walk road under bridge, then up and right to east part of cliff. Milton Heights (closed): From Milton go west on Derry. Turn north on Hwy. 25. Turn west on Steeles Ave. Turn north on Tremaine. Faces north.

55 M-Mt. Nemo (North) ☆☆☆

The high-octane area of Nemo. Some have called this 100′ limestone crag vegetated hiking, but Nemo North is the most extensive and developed (more than 200 routes) climbing area near Toronto. The abandoned Mt. Nemo Quarry (take a right before the lookout) also has some good climbing. Summer/autumn. Pay camping. Government park.

Classics: Camel 7, Ground Zero 8, Cat's Tail 9, Dehydrated Yuppie Brains 10b, Dick's Direct 10c, The Long Wait 10d, Train in Vain 12-, Fear and Loathing 12-, Psycho Lust for Yuppy Chicks 12-.

Ref: C [110, 105, 103, 101]; Guidebooks: Bracken, Barnes, and Oates's *The Escarpment,* Smart's *Ontario's Finest Rock Climbs,* Smart's *Ontario Limestone,* Marsh's *Climbing In Southern Ontario.*

Directions: From Milton go west on Derry Rd. Turn south on Guelph Line. Park at pullout on left (Colling Rd.) for Mt. Nemo. Faces north.

56 M–Mt. Nemo (South) ★★

Low-octane 90′ limestone crag with approximately fifty routes from 5.7 to 5.11. Summer/autumn. Pay camping. Government park.

Classics: Fly Away Dreams 9, Strike One 10a.

Ref: Guidebooks: Bracken, Barnes, and Oates's *The Escarpment,* Smart's *Ontario's Finest Rock Climbs,* Smart's *Ontario Limestone,* Marsh's *Climbing In Southern Ontario.*

Directions: From Milton go west on Derry. Turn south on Guelph Line. Same as Nemo North, but continue 2 km farther south for Mt. Nemo (South). Faces south.

57 Dundas Rock ★

This 30′ limestone beginner and intermediate crag lies in the Spencer Gorge. Summer/autumn. Pay camping.

Classics: Making Flippy Floppy 11.

Ref: C. Oates, J. Barnes; Guidebook: Bracken, Barnes, and Oates's *The Escarpment.*

Directions: From Dundas go north on Hwy. 8. Park at Dundas railroad station. Follow path from east side of parking lot for ten minutes to obvious left uphill and placing one below Dundas Rock.

58 Niagara Glen Park ★★★

Buffalo's Boulderama. Huge number (more than 200 and rising) of 35′ sandstone bouldering routes can be found at Niagara Glen. Currently undergoing large amounts of development. Check with locals at climbing gyms nearby for access details and new route information. Climbing on the main headwall is currently banned, but bouldering in the actual "Glen" is still okay. Sandstone bouldering (less than B1) at river. Bring toprope (poor landings) and partner. In February 1997 Darrel Porter wrote: "The Glen has seen huge amounts of development in the past six months. The bouldering is outstanding and many of the landings have been cleaned. Problems range from V0- to V8. Locals are waiting for V10 and over to go up . . . they're there for the picking. An updated guide will be out by March 1997. Check with the local gyms in Ontario and western NY." April–October. No camping. Government land.

Classics: Several fine areas. Bizzaro World: Lichen It V1; Wonderland: Walking Spanish Down the Glen V0; Central: Cal's Problem 5.11b/c, O'Flake 5.10b, Electric French Fries V0+, No U-Turn V1, Crimp-de-la-Crimp V5, Contact V7; The Neighborhood: Gillronamoe V3; Romper Room: Spiderman V0, Mamma Mia V4, The Great Wall of China V5; Land of OZ: God Must Be a Climber V3, Thunder and Lightening V6; Waterworld: Monday Monday V2; River Wall: Monkey Hang 9; All Mod Cons V7.

Ref: Millard 3/97; R [94-116, 75-26]; Niagara Glen on-line guide www.vantek-corp.com/glen; Guidebooks: Bracken, Barnes, and Oates's *The Escarpment, The Glen,* Smart's *Ontario Limestone.*

Directions: From Niagara Falls, Canada, head 5 km north on Niagara Pkwy. to Niagara Glen Park. Stroll across picnic area and down stairs to headwall and boulders flung about. Faces south. From Buffalo, New York, go north on I-90. Proceed west across Niagara River on Hwy. 405. Once in Canada, turn south onto Niagara Pkwy. for 3 mi. Park on left. Take metal staircase down, turn left, and start circuit.

59 Lake Temiscaming (Devil Rock) ★★★

The longest multipitch (150 m) granite routes in Ontario surround Lake Temiscaming.

Classics: Bombay Sapphire III 11b.

Ref: Guidebook: Johnston and Smart's *Devil Rock: The Anti Guide 1997.*

Directions: South out of New Liskeard.

Quebec

A smile comes often from a souvenir. —French expression

What abounds in the province of Quebec besides the French tongue, scenic forests, white-water streams, black flies, cold, and rain? Granite crags, ne c'est pas? Ahway! A virtual profusion of granite awaits any climber heading du nord—it's a mere forty-four-hour drive from Hueco Tanks, Texas.

In brief, Quebec hosts fine rock at these area hubs: Val David (the most developed area in Quebec), Sherbrooke, Quebec City, St.-Urbain, and Chicoutimi. Val David pens a number of crags in the most developed area in Quebec. The Sherbrooke area shines with areas such as Mt. Orford. A climber can find excellent climbing near Quebec, and a trip up the east bank of the St. Lawrence River to Rimouski will set one's sights on the limestone crags of the future.

As for the locals, there are quite a few climbers around Montreal and Sherbrooke. There are very few climbing locals in the city of Quebec and farther east. Hence, there are very few routes being opened in the area every year; almost all the routes being opened are by the same few active climbers.

Like everywhere else in the world, the tendency in the last few years has been toward short and easily accessible cliffs. The presence of many of these short and generally very steep gritstone cliffs around Quebec City has permitted the standards to rise to a pretty high level. These "high standards" have been applied to a few cliffs farther east as well.

Traveling north from Quebec, the remoteness of wild crags in the Malbaie River Gorge and the Chicoutimi area should tend to make any climber do a double take. Stunning plates of granite arise from the Saguenay River, enticing multipitched climbers to chew china.

It's not all glitter, though. Perhaps this excerpt from *Mountain Magazine* describes what the weather in Quebec equals: "The temperature, for instance is either too cold or too warm, never just right; and if by chance it was right, the swarms of black flies and mosquitoes would ensure that nobody climbed. And if the wind blew the flies away, you would still be faced with the uninviting prospect of having to bushwhack for hours, having to cross large rivers, arriving at the cliff only to find out that the crack system you were planning to climb was hopelessly filled with lichen and mud, and that you lacked the time and patience to clean your way up."

In other words, check May or August/September on your calendar as the time to tick a climbing trip to Quebec.

Otherwise contend with buckets of cold, wet weather and spoonfuls of ferocious insects. The wild, quiet rock of the northwoods sits like an unguarded ice-cold beer and a bowl of hot, buttered popcorn on a quiet barroom table.

1 Le Face de Singe (aka Monkey Face) ☆☆☆

Face climbing on this 60' granite crag.

Ref: S. Lapierre; *Canadian Alpine Journal* (CAJ).

Directions: Near a small town called Chibougamau, 500 km north of Quebec City. Follow a well-marked path fifteen minutes to Le Face de Singe.

2 Cap Chat (Chic-Chocs Provincial Reservoir) ☆☆☆

Climbing right out of the water on a 60' sedimentary sport crag and on a spire called "Cape Cat." Classic 5.12s. Expect an entrance fee at the small park.

Ref: S. Lapierre.

Directions: At Cap Chat. On Hwy. 132 on the Gaspe Peninsula. Faces north.

3 Ile de Bonaventure ☆

Novel 100' spire with a hole in it. Summer. Government park.

Ref: Maurice.

Directions: From Perce, on Hwy. 132 on the Gaspe Peninsula, just off the coast in the Gulf of St. Lawrence on the Ile de Bonaventure.

4 St. Fabien Sur Mer (at Bic Provincial Park) Bas Du Fleuve

A 140' limestone sport crag with good pockets everywhere. Lots of new route potential. First-class boulder on beach. Fantastic views on the St. Lawrence River. Spring/autumn.

Classics: L'aiguille 7, Bobinette 11b, Blade Runner 12a, Entre Meret ciel Direct 12d.

Ref: S. Lapierre; C 117(12/89)-76.

Directions: Rimouski. At Bic Provincial Park. Hike twenty minutes up a steep scree slope for St. Fabien Sur Mer. Sketchy access. Faces northwest.

Quebec

5 Croix de St.-Anne

One-hundred-foot granite crag.

Ref: Guidebooks: Garneau's copy in Universite de Chicoutimi, Levesque and Sylvain's *Parois, D'Escalade au Quebec.*

Directions: In northwest Chicoutimi, on north side of Saguenay River, is Croix de St.-Anne.

6 Cap St. François

One-hundred-foot granite crag.

Ref: Guidebooks: Garneau's copy in Universite de Chicoutimi, Levesque and Sylvain's *Parois, D'Escalade au Quebec.*

Directions: In northwest Chicoutimi, on north side of Saguenay River, is Cap St. Francois.

7 Valin

A 175′ granite crag.

Ref: Guidebook: Levesque and Sylvain's *Parois, D'Escalade au Quebec.*

Directions: In Valin, twenty minutes northeast of Chicoutimi.

8 Cran Carré

Four-hundred-foot granite beginner crag.

Ref: Guidebook: Levesque and Sylvain's *Parois, D'Escalade au Quebec.*

Directions: From Ste. Rose-du-Nord west 2 km, Cran Carré is riverside cliff on Saguenay River. Faces south.

9 Mont Francis

Granite crag.

Ref: Guidebook: Levesque and Sylvain's *Parois, D'Escalade au Quebec.*

Directions: From St. Basile de Tableau, Mont Francis is approximately 10 km east downstream from town. Faces southwest.

10 Cap Saguenay

Granite crag.

Ref: Guidebook: Levesque and Sylvain's *Parois, D'Escalade au Quebec.*

Directions: From St. Basile de Tableau, go approximately 15 km east downstream from town to Cap Saguenay. Faces southwest.

11 Le Petit Dome (near Jonquière)

Beginner/intermediate 75′ granite crag.

Ref: Guidebook: Garneau's *Parois d'escalade de Chicoutimi et Jonquiéres.*

Directions: Le Petit Dome is in Jonquiére.

12 Tableau ★★★

Steep-walled 500′ granite plate with north-facing cracks. This cliff falls straight into the Saguenay River. One very beautiful free route (5.11c) and couple A1 routes. One hundred and twenty-five meters. Summer. Free camping.

Ref: S. Lapierre; Guidebook: Levesque and Sylvain's *Parois, D'Escalade au Quebec.*

Directions: Accessed from Ste. Rose-du-Nord, where you can rent a boat. Tableau sits on south shore of Saguenay River to the southeast of town. Faces north.

13 Cap Trinité ★★

Big, big granite wall arising from the Saguenay Fiord: 1,000′ high and remote; perhaps the most impressive in Quebec. Many small cliffs with lots of potential around Cap Trinité. First route established in 1966. Now approximately fifteen routes to top, one free line. Whale watching. Autumn. Free camping at base. Government park, (418) 544–7388.

Classics: Les Joyeaux Lurons IV 11+, Vire du Curé Dallaire IV 12, Les Grand Galais 5.12c A3.

Ref: S. Lapierre; C [159-62, 117(12/89)-76], M 59(1/78)-36, R 97-26; Guidebooks: Harlin's *East*, Levesque and Sylvain's *Parois, D'Escalade au Quebec.*

Directions: From Rivièrre-Eternité (northeast of Quebec— last good supply point), drive north to Saguenay River, looking for signs for Parc du Saguenay on road's east side. In 5 mi. come to road's end at Bay Eternité sans information center. March one and a half hours to the statue at Saguenay River. Then continue down river, following flags to Cap Trinité for thirty minutes. Or, access to Cap Trinité via boat with Compagnie de la Baie Tadoussac (418–235–4548). Faces north.

14 Cap Eternité ★★★

Eight-hundred-foot beginner granite crag.

Ref: Guidebook: Levesque and Sylvain's *Parois, D'Escalade au Quebec.*

Directions: From Rivièrre-Eternité, go northeast to Saguenay River for Cap Eternité. Another granite tableau like Cap Trinité. Faces north.

15 Mont Cardinal

Granite crag.

Ref: Guidebook: Levesque and Sylvain's *Parois, D'Escalade au Quebec.*

Directions: From Petit Saguenay, Mont Cardinal is approximately 10 km south of town.

16 Les Palissades ★★★★

The rock du jour of the province. One of the best places to climb in Quebec if you want hard routes. Four-km-long cliff: 3 km vertical to overhanging, 1 km low angle, 1,000′

slabs. Le Pilier is super-mega classique. Adventure and a variety of climbing routes. Nice hut at base. Short approach. Immense, untapped potential for excellent new routes. At least 110 routes, up to 5.13b (may be hardest in province). Beware: Poison ivy at north end of cliff! Spring/autumn. Pay camping. Government park.

Classics: L'Arête 6, L'Envers de la Detaché 10, Le Pilier 11c, La Forteresse de la Solitude 13b.

Ref: S. Lapierre; C [159-62, 78(4/83)-32], M 78; Guidebooks: Heinault's *Les Parois Des Charlevoix Rock Climbs: Palissades St. Simeon*, Harlin's *East*.

Directions: From St.-Simeon go north 7 mi. on Hwy. 170. Les Palissades is on right. Hike five to twenty minutes on easy-to-follow paths.

17 Malbaie Valley ✯✯✯

The most beautiful valley and largest cliffs in the province. High-quality 1,000′ granite rock, but often dirty (bring a big scrub brush); heavy bushwhacking/exploration and adventure climbing. Access can sometimes be difficult. Incredible 1,000′ ice-climbing routes. Offers hiking with fantastic views. Autumn. Nice camping near the river at the entrance of the park. No services except water.

Ref: S. Lapierre; C 78(4/83), M 59(1/78)-36.

Directions: From St. Aime-des-Lacs, go northwest along Malbaie River Canyon. Ten cliffs of 1,000′ high. Comprises the following areas: La Muraille, l' Equerre, l'Ecluse, Le Gran des Erables, and Isaie/Jérémie.

18 La Muraille

On the left of the cliff are long corners and beautiful 900′ granite walls. Right side is rotten. Four routes between 5.9 and 5.10 A2. Summer. Pay camping.

Classics: Poussiére d'étoile 5.8 A2.

Ref: S. Lapierre; Guidebook: Levesque and Sylvain's *Parois, D'Escalade au Quebec*.

Directions: From St. Aime-des-Lacs, go approximately 40 km north up Malbaie River to La Muraille. Horrible approach: three hours of scree slope.

19 Isaie and Jérémie

Huge 1,100′ granite slab faces in forest.

Ref: S. Lapierre; Guidebook: Levesque and Sylvain's *Parois, D'Escalade au Quebec*.

Directions: From St. Aime-des-Lacs, go approximately 35 km north up Malbaie River from town. Isaie and Jérémie are 5 km east of river.

20 L'Equerre

Huge 1,100′ granite walls, mostly rotten rock. In winter, hosts "La Pomme d'or," the best ice route in Eastern America. Pay camping.

Ref: S. Lapierre; Guidebook: Levesque and Sylvain's *Parois, D'Escalade au Quebec*.

Directions: From St. Aime-des-Lacs, go approximately 35 km north up Malbaie River from town to L'Equerre. Take a canoe to cross the Malbaie River.

21 L'Ecluse

This 900′ granite crag offers fantastic views of the valley. Four routes, 5.7 to 5.10c. Monarque, a 5.10 corner on the left of the cliff, is said to be the best route in the valley. From the summit a nice path takes one down the mountain. Pay camping.

Classics: Monarque 10.

Ref: S. Lapierre; Guidebook: Levesque and Sylvain's *Parois, D'Escalade au Quebec*.

Directions: From St. Aime-des-Lacs, go approximately 32 km north up Malbaie River from town. L'Ecluse approach: two hours of slalom on dirty slabs.

22 Gran des Erables ✯

Huge overhangs and corners compose this 900′ granite crag. The left part is a beautiful orange wall with nice long cracks, very clean. Three km long. Eleven routes: 5.6 to 5.10d and a few aid routes. Autumn. Pay camping.

Classics: Le Grande Allee 8, Les Courants d'air 9.

Ref: S. Lapierre; Guidebook: Levesque and Sylvain's *Parois, D'Escalade au Quebec*.

Directions: From St. Aime-des-Lacs, go approximately 30 km north up Malbaie River from town to Gran des Erables. One- to two-hour bushwhack. Faces south.

23 La Mi Dalle

Ninety-foot granite crag. Mostly easy slabs with a lot of lichen.

Ref: S. Lapierre; Guidebook: Levesque and Sylvain's *Parois, D'Escalade au Quebec*.

Directions: From Riviere du-Loup go south on Hwy. 132 approximately 20 km. The La Mi Dalle crag lies approximately 2 km northeast of Andreville.

24 Le Mur (St. André-de-Kamouraska– Andreville Cliff) ✯✯✯✯

This 140′ sandstone sport crag with more than one hundred bolted routes is the sport-climbing magnet of the country. Enjoyable rock with overhanging face. Prend Ton Trou, aka 2 Holes, is reportedly one of the finest routes in Eastern North America, north of New River Gorge. Topos of cliff at Le Cormoran grocery store. Free camping next to St. Lawrence River. Spring/summer. Private land.

Classics: Prend Ton Trou (aka 2 Holes) Route 12d/13a.

Ref: S. Lapierre; Guidebook: Levesque and Sylvain's *Parois, D'Escalade au Quebec*.

Directions: Le Mur is near Andreville (between St. Germain and Riviere du-Loup). Short hike through a field. Faces west.

25 PDGJ☆–Parc des Grand Jardins– Le Dôme ☆☆☆

The main face of this 600′ granite crag (200 m, twenty-five routes) has long slabs with holes like bubbles, easy cracks, and small overhangs. Far right has big overhangs with lots of hard routes (25 m—fourteen routes 5.9 and up). Autumn. Camping at hut. The camping area for Parc des Grands Jardins. Government wildlife area.

Classics: L'Initiation 4, Tache Blanche 10, Hayahaka (aka Two Slings Route) 11c, Raz de Marée 12b.

Ref: S. Lapierre; C 78(4/83); Guidebooks: Lapierre's *Topos de Palissades, des Grands-Jardins et D'ailleurs*, Harlin's *East*, Levesque and Sylvain's *Parois, D'Escalade au Quebec*.

Directions: From St.-Urbain go north on Hwy. 381. Le Dôme is on right. Easy approach.

26 PDGJ–Mont de l'Ours ☆

Long slabs on this 400′ granite crag. Parc des Grands Jardins is a provincial park and offers free access unlike national parks that charge entrance fees. Pay camping. Autumn–spring. Government park.

Classics: La Directe 6.

Ref: S. Lapierre; Guidebooks: Harlin's *East*, Levesque and Sylvain's *Parois, D'Escalade au Quebec*.

Directions: From St.-Urbain go north on Hwy. 175. Mont de l'Ours is on right before Le Dôme. Faces east.

27 PDGJ–Mont du Gros Bas ☆☆

Corners and big overhangs on 700′ granite adventure climbs. Cracks often wet. Approximately twenty routes. Lots of shaky flakes since the big fire of summer 1991. Autumn–spring. Pay camping. Government park.

Classics: Campanule 7, Harmonie Interieure 9, Li-Do 10+, Pour Enfants sans Reserve 11d.

Ref: S. Lapierre; Guidebooks: Harlin's *East*, Levesque and Sylvain's *Parois, D'Escalade au Quebec*.

Directions: From St.-Urbain go north on Hwy. 381. On left. Hike on steep path for twenty minutes to Mont du Gros Bas.

28 Mont Carignan

Granite crag.

Ref: Guidebook: Levesque and Sylvain's *Parois, D'Escalade au Quebec*.

Directions: From Carignan, Mont Carignan is approximately 1 km south on Hwy. 155, on northwest bank of St. Maurice River.

29 Dalles des Rats

Granite crag.

Ref: Guidebook: Levesque and Sylvain's *Parois, D'Escalade au Quebec*.

Directions: From Rivière au Rat drive 5 km south of town. Dalles des Rats is on St. Maurice River.

30 Luskville Area

This is a collaboration of granite cliffs east of Luskville. Climbing areas mentioned in *Parois, D'Escalade au Quebec* (the all-inclusive book of crags for Quebec) have not necessarily received use by climbers. Summer. No camping. Park.

Classics: Sausages 10c (Down Under).

Ref: Guidebook: Levesque and Sylvain's *Parois, D'Escalade au Quebec*.

Directions: From Hull (west edge of Ottawa), go approximately 10 km west on Hwy. 148 (2 km past Heyworth); many crags to east of road (crags due north of Heyworth). Many granite cliffs in the Luskville area mentioned in *Parois, D'Escalade au Quebec* include: Home Cliff, Gallery Cliff, Farm Rock, Bald Face, Big Overhang, The Chin, Throne Rock, Cirque, Castel Wall, Froggy Crack, Balcony Step, Hidden Face, and Cardinal Rock. Faces south.

31 Miguick (in Portneuf Provincial Park)

Three-hundred-foot granite beginner crag. Government park.

Ref: Guidebook: Levesque and Sylvain's *Parois, D'Escalade au Quebec*.

Directions: From Rivière-à-Pierre go north of town; approximately 2 km south of Miguick.

32 Des Aulnes (Portneuf Provincial Park)

Granite crag. Government park.

Ref: Guidebook: Levesque and Sylvain's *Parois, D'Escalade au Quebec*.

Directions: From Rivière-à-Pierre, Des Aulnes is approximately 20 km north of town and approximately 3 km southeast of Miguick in Portneuf Provincial Park.

33 Bellevue (Portneuf Provincial Park)

Four-hundred-foot granite beginner crag just beside a lake. Pay camping at the base. Government park.

Ref: S. Lapierre; Guidebook: Levesque and Sylvain's *Parois, D'Escalade au Quebec*.

Directions: Bellevue is approximately 20 km north of Rivière-à-Pierre, approximately 4 km south of Miguick on northwest shore of lake.

34 La Cachée (Portneuf Provincial Park)

One-hundred-foot granite beginner crag. Government park.

Directions: From Rivière-à-Pierre go approximately 20 km north of town and approximately 5 km southeast of

Miguick. La Cachée is a lakeside cliff at east shore.
Ref: Guidebook: Levesque and Sylvain's *Parois, D'Escalade au Quebec.*

35 Gros Bonnet

Eight-hundred-foot granite beginner slabs. Expect fees to enter this hunting reserve. No camping. Private land.
Ref: S. Lapierre; Guidebook: Levesque and Sylvain's *Parois, D'Escalade au Quebec.*
Directions: From St. Raymond (west of Quebec), Gros Bonnet is approximately 25 km north of town. Faces east.

36 Le Cyriac (in Jacques Cartier Provincial Park)

One-hundred-foot granite beginner crag. Once a teaching place, now all but forgotten. Government park.
Ref: Guidebook: Levesque and Sylvain's *Parois, D'Escalade au Quebec.*
Directions: Le Cyriac is approximately 18 km northwest of Stoneham.

37 Le Promontoire (in Jacques Cartier Provincial Park)

Hardly worth mentioning for rock climbing: The rock is very poor, and no natural line exists on these 500'–1,000' high granite cliffs. But, the Jacques Cartier Valley is worth it for ice climbing. Government park.
Ref: Guidebook: Levesque and Sylvain's *Parois, D'Escalade au Quebec.*
Directions: From Barrière-de-Stoneham go approximately 20 km north of town. Le Promontoire Cliffs named the Grand Cime, Engolevent, La Glissade, and Lambert.

38 Stoneham Cliffs (aka Vieux Stoneham) ✫✫

Three-hundred-foot granite boulders and crag. Excellent lead and topropes. Twelve routes. Was becoming a sport-climbing area in the 1990s. Easy corners and a few steep faces. Twelve routes to 5.12b. Autumn–spring. Free camping.
Classics: Cul de Sac 4, La Niche 11d.
Ref: S. Lapierre, Malchelosse; Guidebook: Harlin's *East.*
Directions: From Stoneham drive on First Ave. for a few miles. Park on the right side of the avenue, near boulder on the left. Please do not block the dirt road. From the parking the Stoneham Cliffs are visible. Hike steep slope fifteen to twenty minutes. Bouldering at the beginning of the path. Faces southeast.

39 Stoneham Cliffs #2 (aka Nouveau Stoneham) ✫✫

Steep 60' granite face, cracks, and chimneys. Twenty routes up to 5.12b. Boulderfield with interesting potential near cliff. Autumn–spring.

Classics: Damier 7, Ti-Poil 10b, Orange Crush 12a.
Ref: S. Lapierre, Malchelosse; Guidebook: Harlin's *East.*
Directions: From Stoneham (22 mi. from Quebec City), drive 1 mile past "Petro Canada" station on Hwy. 175. Stoneham Cliffs #2 visible above treetops from Petro sign. From the station take the second street to the right, on the Chemin de la Montagne. After the street, turn to the left. Park at the end. Hike fifteen to twenty minutes on obvious, steep path through forest. Faces south.

40 Val Belair (closed?) ✫✫✫

Steep 100' granite face and cracks. Twenty routes to 5.12c. Spring/autumn. Private land.
Ref: S. Lapierre.
Directions: Quebec City. Hike five minutes on a nice path to Val Belair. Faces north. Ask locals.

41 Le Champlain and Le Pylone ✫✫✫

Two areas with difficult gritstone bouldering and topropes; aka School Rock. Le Champlain, 30' high by 200' long, is an experts' area with thirty overhanging routes of 5.11 or better. Le Pylone is the beginner area, with mostly 5.8 routes. Great climbing in a less-than-attractive setting. Total of approximately sixty-five routes. Autumn. No camping.
Classics: Le Diedre 4, Il Faut Qu'y En Ait Un Qui le Fasse 11, Ep 13a.
Ref: S. Lapierre, Malchelosse; C 117(12/89)-76; Guide-books: Malchelosse's *Grimper à Quebec,* Harlin's *East.*
Directions: In Quebec City. On Blvd. Champlain, first exit north of bridge. Park. Areas lie to west of Blvd. Henry IV. Twenty-second approach from car. Five-minute walk from Le Champlain to Le Pylone.

42 Dalle Blanche

Three-hundred-foot beginner granite crag.
Ref: Guidebook: Levesque and Sylvain's *Parois, D'Escalade au Quebec.*
Directions: From St. Georges, Dalle Blanche is approximately 15 km north on Hwy. 155, 4 km past (north of) Grand Piles.

43 Mont des Piles

Beginner-intermediate 250' granite crag.
Ref: Guidebook: Levesque and Sylvain's *Parois, D'Escalade au Quebec.*
Directions: From St. Georges, Mont des Piles is approximately 11 km north on Hwy. 155, 1 km past (north of) Grand Piles.

44 Vache Noire

Beginner-intermediate 500' granite crag.
Ref: Guidebook: Levesque and Sylvain's *Parois, D'Escalade au Quebec.*

Directions: From St. Faustin, Vache Noire is approximately 25 km north on east side of Rivièrre du Diable.

45 Mont Nixon ✩✩✩
Fine 200′ granite bouldering and very steep crag. Autumn. Good potential.
Classics: 2+1 6, L'Illusion 10+, XYB 11.
Ref: Guidebooks: Harlin's *East,* Levesque and Sylvain's *Parois, D'Escalade au Quebec.*
Directions: From St. Faustin, Mont Nixon is due north 11 mi. On right, two hours from Montreal.

46 La Diable
Granite crag.
Ref: Guidebook: Levesque and Sylvain's *Parois, D'Escalade au Quebec.*
Directions: From St. Faustin go west on Hwy. 117. Then go northwest as Hwy. 117 makes sharp turn south. La Diable is on east side of Rivièrre du Diable.

47 Montagne Noire
Two-hundred-foot granite crags.
Ref: Guidebook: Levesque and Sylvain's *Parois, D'Escalade au Quebec.*
Directions: From Ste. Agathe-des-Monts, drive approximately 17 km north on Hwy. 329. Montagne Noire Cliffs are just southwest of the town of Chemin Guay.

48 Catherine
Two-hundred-foot granite crag.
Ref: Guidebook: Levesque and Sylvain's *Parois, D'Escalade au Quebec.*
Directions: From Ste. Agathe-des-Monts, go approximately 2 km northeast of town to Catherine.

49 VD✩-(Val David Area) Condor ✩✩✩
Good 100′ granite rock, toproping area. Usually most crowded Val David area. Forty routes from 5.1 to 5.13. First visited in 1928 by Swiss climber John Brett. Today it is still the most frequented climbing area of Quebec. Spire jump across from top. Free camping at base of Mt. King. Autumn.
Classics: Face Quest 8, Midnight Express 10.
Ref: C [117(12/89)-76, 78(4/83)-32], M 59-36; Guidebooks: Harlin's *East,* Levesque and Sylvain's *Parois, D'Escalade au Quebec.*
Directions: Val David. Southeast of town on La Sapiniere. Condor can be seen from town of Val David. Faces south.

50 VD-Dame de Coeur ✩✩✩
New 120′ granite sport cliff. Bolted routes. Climbing is varied, from slabs to slightly overhanging. The main wall is slightly overhanging with reversed holds (underclings and side pulls). The main wall has all bolted routes; other areas are mixed trad/sport protection. New site just uphill of main wall overlooking the valley ("Pain de Sucre"), with about twenty routes in 1994. Autumn. Pay camping/free. BIA.
Ref: Jean-Francois Dumont 10/98; C 117(12/89)-76.
Directions: Val David. Turn right 200′ after the beginning of the trail for Mt. King. Dame de Coeur is a fifteen-minute walk. Faces north. For possible new trail access, contact Federation Quebecois de la Montagne et de l'Escalade (FQME) at (514) 252-3004.

51 VD-La Bleue ✩✩✩
Good 100′ granite sport routes, uncrowded; 5.10 or harder routes. Worthy cracks. About fifty routes. Anorthosite rock. Summer/autumn. Free camping.
Ref: C 117(12/89)-76; Guidebooks: Levesque and Sylvain's *Parois, D'Escalade au Quebec.*
Directions: Val David. La Bleue is west of Les Fesses on branch trail. Faces southwest.

52 VD-Les Fesses ●
One-hundred-foot granite crag. Summer/autumn.
Ref: C 117(12/89)-76; Guidebook: Levesque and Sylvain's *Parois, D'Escalade au Quebec.*
Directions: Val David. Les Fesses is just north of Mt. King on branch trail. Slabbiest of Val David areas. Faces southwest.

53 VD-Mont Cesaire ✩✩✩✩
Very popular 100′ granite beginner's crag; 5.8 or easier climbing. High quality. Spring-autumn. Free/pay camping. Private land.
Ref: C 117(12/89)-76; Guidebook: Levesque and Sylvain's *Parois, D'Escalade au Quebec.*
Directions: Mont Cesaire is at Val David. Faces north.

54 VD-Mont King ✩✩✩✩
Fine bouldering and 170′ granite cragging. The largest and highest cliff of Val David. One- and two-pitch routes. Most developed and best for leading lots of overhangs. Approximately one hundred routes. François Roy made all the moves on the five huge overhangs of Zebra in 1988, rating it 5.13c/A0. Spring-autumn. Private land. Free camping.
Classics: Sorcerer 9, Zebra A1 (5.14? if freed), Le Toit de Ben (Ben's Roof) 12c.
Ref: S. Lapierre; C 117(12/89)-76; Guidebooks: Harlin's *East,* Levesque and Sylvain's *Parois, D'Escalade au Quebec.*
Directions: Val David. Park at the end of road. The approach to Mont King is the same as Condor, only follow trail uphill through the woods approximately 400 yd. Faces west.

55 Les Palissades
Granite crag.

Ref: Guidebook: Levesque and Sylvain's *Parois, D'Escalade au Quebec.*

Directions: From Ste. Adele, Les Palissades is 3 km north on Hwy. 370, then west of golf course. North of Lac Gascon.

56 Mont Baldy
Three-hundred-foot granite crag.

Ref: Guidebook: Levesque and Sylvain's *Parois, D'Escalade au Quebec.*

Directions: From Ste. Adele, Mont Baldy is 2 km north on Hwy. 370. To west of road 0.5 km before river crossing. Mont Baldy lies southeast of Les Palissades.

57 Mont Weir Cliff ☆☆☆
A 350' gneiss crag with up to four pitches of good rock mixed with loose rock. Future potential. New sport climbs right of Black and White. No camping. Spring–autumn.

Classics: Adagio 8, Black and White 3p 10+, Clochard Celeste 5.11+, Bicentenaire 12.

Ref: C 169-124; Guidebooks: Harlin's *East,* Levesque and Sylvain's *Parois, D'Escalade au Quebec.*

Directions: Mont Weir Cliff is at Weir. Go east on Hwy. 364. Go left to Teleglobe. Park. Faces west.

58 Mont Molson
Beginner granite crag.

Ref: Guidebook: Levesque and Sylvain's *Parois, D'Escalade au Quebec.*

Directions: From Mont-Belvedere, Mont Molson is 1 km northwest of town to west of Hwy. 15.

59 Wizard (Piedmont)
Beginner 100' granite crag.

Ref: Guidebook: Levesque and Sylvain's *Parois, D'Escalade au Quebec.*

Directions: From Piedmont, Wizard is 2 km north of town.

60 Ste. Hippolyte
Beginner 150' granite crag.

Ref: Guidebook: Levesque and Sylvain's *Parois, D'Escalade au Quebec.*

Directions: From St. Jerome, Ste. Hippolyte is 20 km north of town on south side of Lac de l'Achigan.

61 Mont de l'Achigan
Beginner 180' granite crag.

Ref: Guidebook: Levesque and Sylvain's *Parois, D'Escalade au Quebec.*

Directions: From St. Jerome, Mont de l'Achigan is 20 km north of town. On east side of Lac de l'Achigan.

62 Shawbridge
One-hundred-foot granite crag.

Ref: Guidebook: Levesque and Sylvain's *Parois, D'Escalade au Quebec.*

Directions: From Piedmont go 2 km east of town to Shawbridge.

63 Mont Beaupre
Three-hundred-foot granite crag.

Directions: From Val-des-Bois (junction of Hwy. 307 and Hwy. 309), go 5 km north on Hwy. 309. Mont Beaupre Cliff is to right (east).

64 Le Dôme (at Val-des-Bois)
Granite crag.

Ref: C 78(4/83); Guidebook: Levesque and Sylvain's *Parois, D'Escalade au Quebec.*

Directions: From Val-des-Bois (junction of Hwy. 307 and Hwy. 309), drive 2 km north on Hwy. 309. Le Dôme is on right (east).

65 Grenville Cliff
Beginner 100' granite crag.

Ref: Guidebook: Levesque and Sylvain's *Parois, D'Escalade au Quebec.*

Directions: From Grenville go 2 km northeast of town to Grenville Cliff.

66 Rigaud ☆
Seventy-foot crag. Spring–autumn. Private land.

Ref: Guidebooks: Poisson's *Escalades: Guide Des Parois Region de Montreal,* Alpine Club of Canada.

Directions: Rigaud is 30 mi. west of Montreal. Access by the old ski station. Faces north.

67 Montreal University Sport Center
A 42' by 60' artificial wall. These universities sport several climbing walls: Montreal Universite, 25' high by 30' long; Chicoutimi Universite (the best one in Quebec); Quebec Universite, 38' by 30'; Sherbrooke Universite. Expect fees or fake . . . uh, take student ID.

Directions: Montreal. At Montreal University Sport Center.

68 Ile Ste. Helene
Sandstone bouldering. Most popular bouldering in Montreal. Most of the climbers in Quebec reside in Montreal and Sherbrooke. Few can be found in the city of Quebec and farther east. Prime time for any climbing excursion to Montreal area is May, August, September, and October. Montreal was the site of 1967 Expo.

Directions: Montreal. At Ile Ste. Helene.

69 Mont St. Hilaire ✩✩✩

The steep 200′ granite north face is a popular after-work/weekend destination. An 80 m small edging traditional and sport routes. Access problem—falcon nesting closures. Owned by university. Views of Montreal's skyscrapers and Olympic stadium. Summer. Private land.
Ref: C 100; Guidebooks: Deuz's *Line Guide du Mont St.-Hilaire*, Levesque and Sylvain's *Parois, D'Escalade au Quebec.*
Directions: From Montreal, Mont St. Hilaire is approximately 20 mi. east on Hwy. 116. Twenty-minute talus approach.

70 Mont St. Gregoire ✩

Seventy-foot granite crag. Spring/autumn. Private land.
Directions: From Montreal, Mont St. Gregoire is 30 mi. southeast of town. Faces south.

71 Lac Larouche ✩✩✩

Small 75′ granite crag now (1999) owned by a climbing school named Adrenaline. Fee to enter. Crowded learning/toprope teaching area. Hard (right) routes can be very scary leads. Toprope routes are swell. Beautiful low traverse. Summer/autumn. No camping. Private land.
Classics: Liberte 10, Mur de Freud 11c.
Ref: J. Roussel 1/99; Guidebooks: Cote's *Escalades Dans Les Cantons de L'est*, Harlin's *East*, Levesque and Sylvain's *Parois, D'Escalade au Quebec.*
Directions: From Sherbrooke, Lac Larouche is 9 mi. west on Hwy. 222 (east of St.-Denis-de-Brompton). Northwest of Lac Brompton.

72 Mont Orford Provincial Park ✩✩✩

Great climbing on this 160′ gneiss sport crag. One can climb on white wall when raining. Topropes on top right section of cliff. Very overhanging, sustained routes in center. Autumn/spring. Provincial park.
Classics: Souverainete 11c, BMW 12a.
Ref: S 5/70; Guidebook: Jide's *D'escalade Au Mont Orford Guide Des Voies et Blocs.*
Directions: From Sherbrooke go 30 mi. west on I-10 to Mont Orford Provincial Park. The cliff can be seen from Hwy. 10 by Mont Orford Provincial Park near the trailhead on Hwy. 112. A twenty-five-minute walk. Faces south.

73 Mont Pinnacle ✩✩✩

Mostly excellent, 350′ granite slab climbing (possibly an oxymoron), though cracks and roofs exist from 5.4 to 5.12. Traditional lead climbing area. Good routes for the intermediate climber. Check with local shop in Sherbrooke. Mont Pinnacle and Lac Larrouche compose Les Cantons de L'Est, the second most-developed area in Quebec. Superb granite with easy access. Summer. Free camping. Private land.
Classics: Directissima 5, Paradissiaque 11.
Ref: Guidebooks: Cote's *Escalades Dans Les Cantons de L'est*, Harlin's *East*, Levesque and Sylvain's *Parois, D'Escalade au Quebec.*
Directions: From Barnston go south of Hwy. 141. Mont Pinnacle is situated on the shores of the lovely and serene Lac Lyster. Faces west.

74 Grand Morne

This 450′ crag has big bulges and corners made of pillow lavas, the kind of rock that very rarely forms cliffs. Sixty routes up to 5.10. A topo of existing routes was placed at the base of the cliff to promote climbing. Pay camping at the house just in front of the cliff.
Classics: La Voie du King 4, Le Grand Dietre 6, Les Voies de La Vire 9.
Ref: S. Lapierre; Guidebook: Nicholas and Rodrigue's *Guide D'escalade Du Grand Morne.*
Directions: Grand Morne is between Quebec City and Sherbrooke, near the town of Broughton-station. Hike fifteen minutes from parking. Faces east.

75 24 Heures

Seventy-five-foot granite crag. Summer. No camping. City land.
Ref: Locals 11/97.
Directions: Chicoutimi. At your left at the end of Dubuc bridge from town. You can climb twenty-four hours a day—it has a street spotlight. Faces east.

76 Mont des Trois Lacs

Granite crag. Routes range from 5.5 to 5.12. Summer. No camping. Private land.
Ref: J. Roussel 1/99.
Directions: Sherbrooke. Faces north.

77 Pointe-au-Pic

Seaside overhanging 75′ sport crag with more than twenty routes, 5.8–5.13.
Directions: At Pointe-au-Pic.

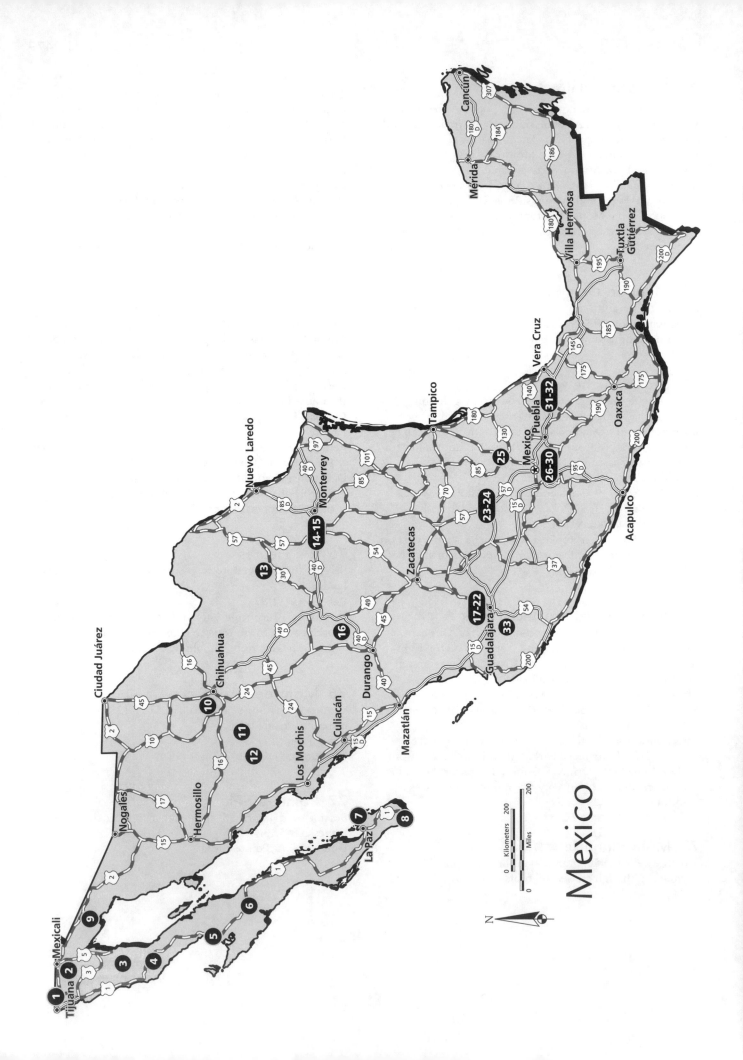

Mexico

Mexico

Si la montaña no viene a mi, yo iré a la montaña. If the mountain will not come to me, then I will go to the mountain. —Old Mexican proverb

Does the future of winter rock climbing lie in Mexico? With an untapped supply of unique and unlimited rock formations, mild winter temperatures, and chile peppers and tamales, it would appear to be the hot spot.

Here we mention a few of the areas worth visiting: El Gran Trono Blanco, Cabo San Lucas, Copper Canyon Area, La Huesteca Canyon, and Mexico City Basalt. What is shown here is just a taste, a starting point from which to begin a Mexican climbing tour.

Percentage wise, there are few Mexican climbers in proportion to the amount of rock. Literature or guides on climbing are scanty, all adding up to a first-rate adventure.

To get a tourist card, be sure to have your passport or birth certificate. Your U.S. auto insurance will not cover you in Mexico. To obtain Mexican auto insurance, you must have full coverage on your rig in the United States. Supplemental insurance is available at U.S. and Mexican border towns.

In most big cities and border towns, people are happy to take your U.S. currency, but they may give your change back in pesos.

Try the guidebook: *Mexico: A Travel Survival Kit.* Warning for traveling in Mexico: Watch the attendants to be sure they reset the pumps before a fill-up, or you'll find your gas bill higher than expected. Whenever possible, keep the gas tank full; an all-night 7-Eleven is probably not around the next corner. Avoid driving at night. No matter how big your habit, try to stay drug free. A drug bust in Mexico could make for an unwanted pump. Stay clean!

Drink the beer and margaritas, not the water. Beware thieves, pickpockets, and the police. Go placidly in life, remembering what peace there may be in silence.

P.S. They speak Spanish south of the border.

1 Baja Peninsula–Valle Azteca

An afternoon Mexican sport crag with quality routes. Bring ten quicks.
Ref: R 92; Guidebook: Vogel's *Climber's Guide to Valle Azteca.*
Classics: TP for Cornholio 10c/d, Virgin Sacrifice 10d, Montezuma 12a.
Directions: From Tijuana (Baja Toll Rd. 1), exit at La Mision (mm 42). Cross bridge and go east on dirt road through town, finally bending right with a steep road and junction. Park at rock barrier. Hike uphill via trail to crag.

2 Sierra Juarez Range (El Gran Trono Blanco) ☆☆☆☆☆

Muy grande crags and colossal 1,600' granite big walls injected with intricate dikes. El Trono, Mexico's "El Capitan," first climbed in 1972 by K. Karlstrom, S. Baxter, and Lee Dexter. The fourteen-pitch Pan Am Route freed in 1993 by Piana and Badaracco at 5.12 via controversial bolts (pitch four). More than 300 routes (in 1990) up to 300' high at Canon Tajo. Canon Tajo is the largest of all canyons in the Sierra Juarez Range, cutting through its eastern escarpment. Palm and pine trees inhabit the same vicinity. Tecate brewery tours make for a relaxed drive in. Autumn. Free camping. Travel self-sufficient and self-contained.
Classics: El Trono Blanco: East Face: Pan Am V 12 (or 9A3), South Face IV 10c, El Paseo Blanco IV 5.11, La Joya IV 5.11+, Giraffe VI 10 C3.
Ref: P. Piana; AAJ ['98, '94, '91-189, 78-555, 77-208, 76-476, 75-154, 72-157], C [189-108, 173-96, 142, 107(4/88)-82, 81(12/83)-4], R [92-70, 60, 10(10/85)], S [4/76, 9/72, 7/68, 5/66, 3/66, 12/63]; Guidebook: Robinson's *Camping and Climbing in Baja.*
Directions: Northwest Baja Peninsula. From Mexicali festina lente (make haste slowly) west on Hwy. 2 to Rumerosa. At Rumerosa, turn south on main dirt road for approximately 24 mi. (watch odometer). At approximately 15 mi. from Rumerosa, pass Rancho La Ponderosa. Continue until a left turn (domes to the southeast) takes one past barbed wire fence remains on right and just beyond to a stone house on right. Veer right ¹/₁₀ mi. past house for a curvy 5 mi. more, complete with riverbed crossings to scattered campsites. From here you're approximately 1 mi. on back side (west) of the 1,600' wall of El Gran Trono Blanco in Canon del Tajo. Hike southeast to gap and domes. Good Mexican road map necessary for all travels in the Baja Peninsula. Daylight driving recommended for first-time travelers.

3 Sierra San Pedro Martir (near Ensenada) ☆☆☆☆

Vast granite boulders, crags, and 1,500′ granite walls. Cerro de la Encantada (aka Picacho del Diablo) is highest peak in Baja at 10,100′ (3,098 m) with superb granite. Travel self-sufficient and self-contained. Summer/autumn. Government land.

Ref: Kelsey; AAJ '95; Guidebook: Underground guide.

Directions: Northwest Baja Peninsula. East approach: From San Felipe drive due west on dirt roads to Santa Clara; drive northwest to Diabilito Canyon or others in the Sierra San Pedro Martir. It's approximately 6 mi. northwest from Santa Clara. West approach: From Encantada drive south on Hwy. 1, turn west on road to Observatorio Astronomico Nacional. Good Mexican road map recommended.

4 Catavina ☆☆☆

Vast, 35′ granite boulders and sport crags among the giant Cardon cactus and boojum trees. Camp at place called La Virgin pullout. Travel self-sufficient and self-contained. Autumn–spring. Free camping. Government land.

Ref: B. Hatcher; C 154-88, R 92-74.

Directions: Northwest Baja Peninsula (seven hours south of American border). From Catavina go north 1 mi. from town on Trans Peninsular Hwy. #1. Drive through boulders.

5 Man Thing Canyon

El supreme roadside bouldering on igneous conglomerate stone.

Ref: R 92.

Directions: From Santa Rosalilitta go just ¼ mi. on Hwy. 1 south of town.

6 Sierra San Francisco

Beautiful basalt crags and boulders.

Directions: From the village of Vizcaino, drive south on Hwy. 1 for 25 km. Turn east for a rough ride for about 40 km to the town of San Francisco de la Sierra. One km before town, a water tank marks the place to park and follow trail to the Arroyo San Pablo boulders. Cliffs can be reached by going through town to Rancho Guadalupe for 2 km where a guide will take one on a thirty-minute hike to crags.

7 La Paz Bouldering ☆☆☆

Unique, 20′ black volcanic conglomerate rock along the blue Gulf of California shores. Winter. Free beach camping on romantic, white sands. Government land.

Ref: B. Hatcher; R 60.

Directions: From La Paz head out to peninsula east of town. La Paz Bouldering is along northern shore of peninsula.

8 Cabo San Lucas ☆☆☆

Muy pequeno bouldering and 40′ topropes/routes on the beaches. Stately granite pinnacles, e.g., Key Rock, arise from water at seashore. Decomposing granite. Camping on some beaches. Be on the qui vive for prowlers. Dave Northup writes, "Last time I was there, there was a large billboard lying against the rocks near 'Lovers Beach' stating that 'No climbing allowed.' Is this only around the tourist beach? No one knew, although water taxi drivers said they knew of no government closure. Remember no dogs through Hotel Solmar and the water taxi drivers will drive you if you give them a rope to climb for a while." Winter. Free camping. Government land.

Classics: Lover's Beach B1 traverse, 40′ "Climb and Dive" pinnacle.

Ref: D. Northup 2/99; C [142, 55(7/79)-8], R [60, 17(1/87)-58].

Directions: At Cabo San Lucas shoreline, southern tip of Baja California. Walk through the Sol Mar Hotel to access rocks. Bouldering at Sol Mar Beach—easiest access. Western Beach (west of town and north of the Sol Mar) is ½ mi. north of Finisterra Hotel along beach. Good, deserted 30′ boulders on the Pacific side.

9 Elegante Crater (in El Pinacate National Park) ☆☆

In a surreal spaghetti-western setting, several volcanic craters measure up to a mile across and 600′ deep. Limited amounts of 30′ high, outlandish bouldering blocks in a uniquely beautiful crater 1/4 mi. in diameter. The bad news: For the expert boulderer who is not afraid of rattlesnakes, there are dangerous landings and rattlers the size of railroad ties. The good news: You won't die a slow, lingering death. Very dry area; it rains once every eight years here. Recommended visit: December–January. Four-wheel-drive or high-clearance vehicles recommended. Spring/autumn. Free camping. Government land.

Ref: J. Sherman; R 89, S 9/64.

Directions: From Sonoita go 31 mi. southwest to Espinoza Jct. Take road north out of Espinoza junction. Turn northwest slightly before Agua Dulce to Elegante Crater. Bouldering in the bottom of the crater. Other craters in region.

10 Las Muelas ☆☆☆

One-hundred-foot volcanic crags. Fifteen routes in 1997. No camping. Private land.

Classics: La Ciruela 4p 9+, Kryptonite 9+, 10+, 11a, Pale Face 11, Diablito 11+, Sotol Sunrise 12b.

Ref: A. Elias 11/97 (aelias@infosel.net.mx).

Directions: From Chihuahua City go 31 km north on the highway to Juarez (El Paso, Texas) from El Paso, Texas, about 290 km (180 mi.) on same highway. Turn *west* on dirt road besides "El Perico" roadside store, pass Nuevo Majalca (very small town, thirty homes, many pigs and cows), and turn left (south). After about 2 km at sign TO

MUELAS, go 300 yd. and park. Walk south, cross fence, and 75 more yd. on creek (by now you're in the middle of it). Established routes are up to the left (east). Faces north. Contact Andres Elias for information about access to the private property and establishing new routes (most are welcomed). Potential abounds.

11 El Gigante

The El Cap of Mexico! This 2,700' andesite big wall features the twenty-five-pitch Simuchi 5.11b A4, the proud work of first ascenders Carlos Garcia Ayala and Cecilia Buil. Yawira Batu twenty-pitch 5.10 A4+ is another big line.
Ref: R [94-36, 89-22].
Directions: West of Chihuahua by 350 km and a full two-day hike.

12 Barranca Del Cobre (aka Copper Canyon) ☆☆☆☆

Larger than the Grand Canyon of Arizona. One can behold miles of 200' volcanic pinnacles and welded tuff cragging in Copper Canyon wonder country. Supplies available in Creel. This is home of the Tarahumara Indians, amazing long-distance runners. Wet season: June–September. Summer/autumn. Free camping. Government land.
Classics: Toro Toro Taxi 12c, Pocketful of Pesos 12, Bo Da Thon 13b.
Ref: C 103(8/89)-32, R 18(3/87)-30, S [5/89, 11/88, 4/72, 12/64]; Guidebook: Fayhee's *Mexico's Copper Canyon Country.*
Directions: Southwest of Chihuahua (approximately 300 mi. south of El Paso). One can drive or take the train that goes to Creel for the same reason that birds fly south in winter: It's easier than walking. Abundant rock climbing at Creel and 6 mi. southeast at Sisoguichi in the Barranca Del Cobre.

13 Cuatrocienegas

This bouldering area lies in an area of unique thermal springs.
Ref: C 189-92; Guidebook: Jackson's *Mexico Rock: A Climber's Guide.*
Directions: Cuatrocienegas (northwest of Monterrey).

14 El Potrero Chico (aka A Little Corral) ☆☆☆☆☆

Possibly one of the best areas in Mexico. Certainly one of the major ones. Abundant walls of overhanging, 2,000' pocketed limestone with more than 500 routes in 1999. Pared de Toro (Bull Wall) looms up 800 m. Outrage Wall is dry when raining. U.S. climbers should not camp in park. There are now two options for camping: La Quinta Santa Graciela is the original climbers' hovel, with kitchen, showers, and a sense of security ($3.00 per person per night in 1999). The other option is Kurt Smith's operation, Rancho

Cerro Gordo private campsites, showers, and covered cooking/common area ($3.00 per person per night). Both are ten minutes from cliffs. Is it possible to have too much rock in one area? This may be the place. Es mas bastante. Autumn–spring. Pay camping. Government park.
Classics: Jungle Mountaineering 9+, Spaceboys 10+ (11p), Argos 10b, Jungleman 10d, Sancho Panchez 11a, Steel Pulse 11a, Don Quixote 11c, Mexico in Flames 12b, Fit for Life 12, Cyclops 12d, Palm Sunday 13-, Sendero Luminoso 12+; Jungle Wall: Spaceboys 10+(11p), El Toro 18 pitch 10.
Ref: 10/97; Zowie 1/99; AAJ ['97, '95], C [187-31/105, 174-116, 172-56, 169-27, 161-41,156-44, 142, 128-36], R [99-56, 93-24, 88-93, 82-38, 74-17, 73-28], SC 12/92; Guidebooks: Jackson's *Mexico Rock: A Climber's Guide,* Texas Mountain Guides's *El Potrero Chico: A Pocket Guide.*
Directions: Three hours from Laredo, Texas. Bring passport or notarized birth certificate, car title, and credit card in car owner's name for border crossing. Take Mex. Hwy. 85 from Laredo—where Hwy. 85 splits into free and toll roads, take the cuota (toll road—approximately $12 U.S. [varies due to peso fluctuations]). Just before Monterrey, take right toward Saltillo, then right at Mex 53 toward Monclova. When you get to Hidalgo, follow signs to Parque Recreativo. Several walls of bolted sport climbs on west side of road include: Las Agujas (spires), La Infamia (Steel Pulse 11-), and La Resaca (west of tin pavillion); La Selva and El Escrutador; La Virgen (Don Quixote 11) and Las Planchas just south of swimming pools; Central Pillar; and Plutonia (bouldering). On east side of road: Fin de Semana across from swimming pools, then Las Estrellas to south, followed by Los Lios, Ola, and El Sentido Religioso.

15 La Huasteca Canyon ☆☆☆☆☆

Miles and miles of grand Buoux-like 2,000' limestone walls. Opportunities for sport and multipitch routes. Unlimited potential. Camping may be dangerous (theft). Burglarproof your rig. Camping/hotels at El Potrero may be safer. Need passport, birth certificate, or voter registration card. Full-coverage American insurance necessary. Mexican insurance a wise idea—obtain at border. Winter– spring. Free camping. Government park.
Classics: Independencia A1.
Ref: C 128(10/91)-36, R 7(3/85), SC 3/91; Guidebook: Jackson's *Mexico Rock: A Climber's Guide.*
Directions: From Monterrey, La Huasteca Canyon is northwest to suburb of Santa Catarina (no specifics). Three hours from Laredo, Texas.

16 Sierra Blanca (aka Sierra Urbanus Range) ☆☆☆☆

Grand, 1,500' granitic walls that were possibly first ascended in 1983. Motes, Ward, and Bjornstad's Route V 5.9+ installed in 1985. Expect a true Mexican backcountry experience. Winter. Free camping.

Classics: Cerro Blanco III 9.
Ref: AAJ '88-155, C 90(6/85)-12, R 7(3/85).
Directions: At Penon Blanco (700 mi. south of El Paso). Sierra Blanca can be seen from town. Faces south.

17 El Escalone (aka La Nueva Zona/The New Zone) ★★★★

This Mexican Devil's Tower offers columnar 200' rhyolite cragging with mucho cracklines. So, bring the trad gear. New routes may require cleaning. A circuit of the Guadalajaran areas to rest fingers from the pain of edges is recommended. Climbing shop in Guadalajara is Verti Mania. Guadalajara's weather makes climbing possible year-round with May being the driest month. Bring water. Free camping at all crags or Hostel or Hotel Country Plaza in Guadalajara. Government land.
Classics: Falling Rocks 10b, Los Ansancasas De Don Juan 10c, Dados de Acaro 11d, Huevos de Acaro 12a.
Ref: I. Vigil; C [12/98, 181-95].
Directions: From Guadalajara (approximately 40 mi.), go north to San Cristobal de la Barranca. When rock spire (El Mono 5.9) becomes visible on left, turn left (izquierda) on dirt road to base of basalt columns. Hike twenty minutes to La Nueva Zona rock. Faces east.

18 El Cuajo ★★★

Imperceptible sequences on up to 40-m climbs on unique flowstone.
Ref: C [12/98, 181-95]; Guidebook: Jackson's *Mexico Rock: A Climber's Guide.*
Directions: From Guadalajara suburb of Zapopan, go northwest on road to Tesistan. Turn right on road to San Cristobal de la Barranca (passing HUAXTLA sign). Turn right at sign for San Lorenzo. Turn right at first intersection. Go uphill along stone wall, staying left at Y. Follow road to wall, walking when road gets too rough for your car.

19 El Canon de Huaxtla ★★★★

Upstream from El Cuajo, this committing rappel-in, multi-pitch area features climbing on diamond-hard, steep incuts.
Ref: Guidebook: Jackson's *Mexico Rock: A Climber's Guide.*
Directions: From Guadalajara suburb of Zapopan, go northwest on road to Tesistan. Turn right on road to San Cristobol de la Barranca for fifteen minutes. Turn right at HUAXTLA sign on cobble/asphalt road. Shortly thereafter, turn at first left, then right at next intersection.

Park at top of hill. Hike wash down to canyon rim, then up and right to chains on Luna de Octubre 5.11b climb. Rappel in 70 m.

20 El Diente (aka The Tooth) ★★★

Mix of 100' granite face climbing and powerful bouldering. All sport routes feature short friction, overhangs, edges, and small pockets. Lots of potential bouldering. Minimal entrance fee. Camping at El Diente is highly recommended for all Guadalajara climbing areas. Private land.
Classics: Universal Cero 11c, El Vuelo de Icaro 12a, Sorti Lagios 12d, Massacre Digital 13b.
Ref: I. Vigil; C [12/98, 181-95]; Guidebooks: Jackson's *Mexico Rock, A Climber's Guide,* Magallon's guidebook (o.o.p.).
Directions: From Guadalajara go north on the Loop. Turn right on road to San Isidro. Turn right on highway for La Hidro. Take left turn on first dirt road and continue going through Rio Blanco Puebla. Bear right at Y, passing soccer field on left to gate on right. Pay at gate (honk if no attendant). Drive on to boulders. Contigo, pan y cebolla!

21 Cola De Caballo (aka Horsetail Canyon) ★★★

Six-hundred-foot limestone face routes for experts. Rappel in and climb. Lots of potential—expect to clean routes. Camp at El Diente. Winter. Government land.
Ref: I. Vigil.
Directions: From Guadalajara go through San Isidro, then turn left to Saltillo for a few minutes. Turn right into Dr. Atl Park. Pay admission. Walk to left side of observation deck. Two rappels in to Pilotos del Resplandor Morado 5.12.

22 La Hidro (aka Paredes De La Hydroelectrica) ★★★

Pull down on 65' pocketed volcanic tuff routes. Easy on the fingers.
Classics: Combata dal Nopal 11b, Guerra Vazatal 12a, Solijut 7 11b, Paris Da Mis Suanos 13a.
Ref: I. Vigil; C [12/98, 181-95].
Directions: From Guadalajara suburb of Zapopan, go northwest on road to Tesistan. In a few miles, turn right onto San Isidro exit. Go to security gate for gated community, get pass from guard for passing through, and give pass to next gate attendant. Continue on to highway. Turn right to hydroelectric plant on left. Make U-turn. Park at pullout. Hike down to crag.

23 Pena de Barnal ★★★

This big 700' volcanic rock dome is mostly undeveloped (fifteen multipitched routes in 1999) with lots of potential. Characterized by multipitched, pocketed routes. Autumn/spring. Free camping. Private land.

Classics: Bernalina, Grapas, Tres de Mayo, Noroccidental, Suroeste, El Lado Oscuro de la Luna, Horizonte de Estrellas, etc.
Ref: Rodulfo Araujo 5/98; I. Vigil.
Directions: From Bernal, Pena de Barnal rocks visible to southwest (no specifics). Two hours northwest of Mexico City on Camino de Cuota.

24 Aculco Canyon National Park ★★★★
Very attractive 80' basalt crag climbing, especially for the 5.10 climber. Protections from the routes have been stolen, there are few left, so there is only climbing in the cracks, but it is still great. Autumn–spring. Free camping. Government park.
References: I. Vigil, L. Arturo 11/97.
Directions: From Mexico City go approximately 80 km northwest to Aculco Canyon National Park. To go to Aculco, take the road Mexico-Queretaro, and about km 117 to 120 you must take the detour to the town of Aculco, then drive on a federal road, pass one town, then pass the town of Aculco. Go straight until you reach a canyon, which is the Canyon of Aculco. Camp on the side that is near to the road.

25 Pachuca Hidalgo (aka Parc De National Las Ventanas) ★★★★
A very beautiful, mountainous (approximately 10,000') area with up to five-pitch, 600' conglomerate spires in a pine-tree forest. These are adventure routes with possible long run-outs! Velaquez's *Guia Del Escalador Mexicano,* published in 1955, is the charming patriarch of Mexican climbing guidebooks. It's very difficult to find—try UC Boulder. Summer/autumn. Free camping or inexpensive hostel. Supplies obtainable in El Chico or Pachuca. Government park.
Ref: I. Vigil; Guidebook: Velasquez's *Guia Del Escalador Mexicano.*
Directions: From Mexico City go approximately 50 km northeast to the town of Pachuca. Continue north toward Mineral El Chico. Rock towers and walls en route. Several areas.

26 Chiquihuite ★★★
Two-hundred-foot columnar basalt crags. Columnar cracks. Winter.
Ref: I. Vigil; Guidebook: Velasquez's *Guia Del Escalador Mexicano.*
Directions: From Mexico City, Chiquihuite is approximately 10 mi. north, near Basilica de La Virgen de Guadalupe. Depart from Ticoman Bridge.

27 Condominios (aka Copilco) ★★★
Sixty-foot volcanic bouldering and crags of pocketed black rock. Mostly now for bouldering. Use Metro Subway. Autumn/spring. No camping. Climbing shop in Mexico

The basalt columns near Pachuca.
GLEN RINK

City. In Copilco there have been problems with the people that live there: They refuse to let climbers use the Zone, and that makes it impossible to climb there sometimes. Many bolts have been smashed or stolen, so there are few routes to climb. Many climbers still use it to boulder. No camping.
Ref: I. Vigil, L. Arturo 11/97.
Directions: In Mexico City. Take Metro Subway to Condominios (no specifics).

28 University Bouldering Areas ★★★
Six bouldering areas near university.
Ref: I. Vigil.
Directions: In Mexico City, bouldering areas near university (no specifics).

29 La Acoconetla ★★★
Two-hundred-foot columnar basalt crags offers good climbing at 9,000' elevation. Winter.
Ref: I. Vigil.
Directions: From Mexico City, La Acoconetla is 10 mi. southwest (no specifics).

30 Popocatepetl (17,781') and Ixtaccihuatl (17,343') (Mexican Volcanoes) ★★★★
The second and third highest volcanoes in Mexico are renowned as alpine volcanic slogs. Along with Orizaiba, these are the mountaineering focus for any Mexico-bound climber. Popocatepetl (Popo), at 5,452 m, is more well known and higher than Ixtaccihuatl (aka Ixty or Sleeping Lady) (5,286 m) to the immediate north. Both visible from Mexico City on a clear day. Lung-building giant snow and ice slogs. Minimum technical equipment needed: ice axe/crampons (rentable). Sleeping huts scattered on the moun-

---

Summit of Ixta.

JAMES GARRETT

tains. Bring water/supplies. Bus travel recommended. Buy water across from bus station. Dry season: December–April. Christmas very popular. Popo, Ixty, and Orizaiba are the only three peaks in Mexico with permanent snowfields. Popo has been active and closed since fall of 2000. Government land.

Classics: Popocatepetl, 17,781': Las Cruces Route (safest, most popular), Ventillo Route (possibly better route); Ixtaccihuatl, 17,343'.

Ref: C [163-42,152-28, 96], OB 47(10/79)-31, R [103-60, 88-92, 66-18], S [10/79, 2/78, 10/75, 10/73, 3/73, 10/71, 11/66, 9/61]; Mountain Gazette 11/77; Guidebooks: Secor's *Mexico's Volcanoes: A Climbing Guide,* Kelsey's *Climber's and Hiker's Guide to the World's Mountains,* Velasquez's *Guia Del Escalador Mexicano.*

Directions: Thirty mi. east of Mexico City. Both peaks lie just east of the town of Amecameca. For Popocatepetl (Popo) go east of Amecameca to Paso de Cortez by bus. The Paso de Cortez is a common departure point for both Popo and Ixta. For Popo head south to Tlamacas where the comfortable Guerrero climber's hut exists. For Ixtaccihuatl (Ixty) go north from Paso de Cortez.

31 Cofre de Perote (14,050') (Mexican Volcano) ✫✫✫

A volcanic cone in Mexico's "earthquake zone of fire." The summit is a 140' coffin-shaped, volcanic rock (may have good climbing) on a 3,000' volcano summit. The summit rock is covered with radio antennas. Cofre de Perote is named for pueblo at its base. Autumn–spring. Free/pay camping. Government land.

Ref: S [1/78, 6/70]; Guidebooks: Secor's *Mexico's Volcanoes: A Climbing Guide,* Kelsey's *Climber's and Hiker's Guide to the World's Mountains.*

Directions: This is 60 mi. east of Mexico City, just southeast of Perote. Cofre de Perote dominates the skyline. North of Pico de Orizaba. An all-day hike on four-wheel-drive roads.

32 El Pico de Orizaba (18,851') (Mexican Volcano) ✫✫✫✫✫

The primary objective summit for the Mexico-bound alpinist is El Pico de Orizaba; at 18,851' (5,760 m), it's the highest point in Mexico and third highest in North America. Breathless, giant snow and ice slogs, though some rock can be climbed. Dry season: December–April. Good testing ground to see how one's body functions at altitude. Alpine start (2:00 A.M.) from Piedra Grande is advisable to avoid whiteouts. Great during full moons. This is one of the Big Tres Montagnes in Mexico. The three highest Mexican peaks are Pico de Orizaba, 18,851'; Popocatepetl, 17,781'; and Ixtaccihuatl, 17,343'. Senor Reyes in Tlachichuca recommended for accommodations and four-wheel-drive taxi (011–52–5–595–1203). December–March. Government land.

Guide Services

United States

Alaska

Alaska Mountain Guides, P.O. Box 1081, Haines 99827; (800) 766-3396; http://kcd.com/ams/

Alaska Mountaineering School, P.O. Box 13, Talkeetna 99676; (907) 733-1016; www.climbalaska.org, climbing@alaska.net

Alaska-Denali Guiding Inc, P.O. Box 566, Talkeetna 99676; (907) 733-2649; www.denaliexpeditions.com, adg@alaska.net

K2 Aviation, P.O. Box 545, Talkeetna 99676; (800) 764-2291; www.flyk2.com

McKinley Air Service, P.O. Box 544, Talkeetna 99676; (800) 564-1765; www.alaska.net/mckair, mckair@alaska.net

Mountain Trip Denali Climbs, P.O. Box 111809, Anchorage 99511; (907) 345-6499; www.mountaintrip.com, mttrip@aol.com

Patagonia Mountain Agency, P.O. Box 210516, Auke Bay 99821; (907) 789-1960; www.mountainagency.com, ptgmtnag@alaska.net

Talkeetna Air Taxi, P.O. Box 73, Talkeetna 99676; (800) 533-2219; www.gorp.com/flytat

Arizona

Flagstaff Mountain Guides, P.O. Box 2383, Flagstaff 86003; (520) 635-0145; nazclimb@aol.com

Wilderness Adventures, 4211 East Elwood St. #1, Phoenix 85040; (602) 438-1800; www.wildernessadventures.com

Venture Up Expeditions, 2415 East Indian School Rd., Phoenix 85016; (602) 955-9100; www.ventureup.com

California

Cosley and Houston Alpine Guides, 1627 Dunbar Lane, Bishop 93514; (760) 872-3811

Joshua Tree Rock Climbing School, HCR Box 3034, Joshua Tree 92252; (800) 890-4745; www.rockclimbing school.com

Mammoth Mountaineering School, www.California Rock.com

Mountain Adventure Seminars, 148 Bear Valley Rd., Bear Valley 95223; (209) 753-2249; www.mtadventure.com/

Natural High Adventures, P.O. Box 1338, Burbank 91507; (818) 415-3816; www.naturalhighadventures.com

Peak Adventures, 6000 J St., Sacramento 95819; (916) 278-6321; www.csus.edu/asi/peak

The Sierra Mountain Center, P.O. Box 95, Bishop 93515; (760) 873-8526; www.sierramountaincenter.com, info@sierramountaincenter.com

Sierra Mountain Guides, www.climbnet.com/smg/

Sierra Outdoor Guides, www.sierraguides.com

Shasta Mountain Guides, 1938 Hill Rd., Mount Shasta 96067; (530) 926-3117; www.shastaguides.com

Sonora Pass Mountaineering School, P.O. Box 1294, Pinecrest 95364; (877) 586-0901; www.climbit.com

Southern Yosemite Mountain Guides, P.O. Box 301, Bass Lake 93604; (559) 877-8735

Ultimate Ascents, 2002 Huntington Dr., #49, Chico 95928; (530) 897-0100; www.ultimateascents.com, info@ultimateascents.com

Vertical Adventures, P.O. Box 7548, Newport Beach 92658; (800) 514-8785; www.vertical-adventures.com, BGvertical@aol.com

Yosemite Mountaineering School, Yosemite National Park, 95389; (209) 372-8344; www.yosemite mountaineering.com/

Colorado

Adventures to the Edge Ltd., Box 91, Crested Butte 81224; (800) 349-5219; www.atedge.com, atedge@crestedbutte.net

Aspen Climbing Guides, P.O. Box 1991, Aspen 81612; (970) 920-4553; www.aspenclimbingguides.com

Boulder Rock School, 2829 Mapleton Ave., Boulder 80301; (303) 447-2804; www.boulderrock.com

Colorado Mountain School, P.O. Box 1846, Estes Park 80517; (970) 586-5758; www.cmschool.com, cmschool@cmschool.com

Fantasy Ridge, P.O. Box 1679, Telluride 81435; (970) 728-3546

Gold Camp Resort, 40579 North Hwy. 24, Buena Vista 81211; (719) 395-3234

Outward Bound, http://obn.scd.net

Rocky Mountaineering Guides, 11 Grey Fox Lane, Dillon 80435; (970) 468-8049

San Juan Mountain Guides, P.O. Box 895, Ouray 81427; (970) 325-4925; www.ourayclimbing.com
Savelli Elite Training Alpinism Corps, P.O. Box 670, Ophir 81426; (970) 728-3705; www.savellialpinist.com, savelli@mri.net
South West Adventures, P.O. Box 3242, Durango 81302; (800) 642-5389; www.mtnguide.net, climb@mtnguide.net
Tower Guides, 450 Main, P.O. Box 1073R, Ouray 81427; (888) 345-9061; www.towerguides.com, info@towerguides.com
Vertical Horizons, P.O. Box 9031, Grand Junction 81501; (970) 245-8513; www.desertcrags.com, crags@wic.net

Connecticut

Connecticut Mountain Recreation, East Hartford; (860) 569-3113
EMS, West Hartford; (860) 561-4302

Georgia

Granite Arches, 265 Oak Grove Rd., Athens 30607; (706) 552-1619; www.granitearches.com

Illinois

Vertical Heartland Guides, 5050 Lick Creek Rd., Buncombe 62912; (618) 995-1427; www.verticalheartland.com

Maine

Acadia Mountain Guides, P.O. Box 121, Orono 04473; (888) 232-9559; www.acadiamountainguides.com, climb@acadiamountainguides.com
Atlantic Climbing School, 36 Main Street, Orono 04473; (207) 866-7562; www.acsclimb.com

Maryland

Earth Treks Climbing Center, 7125-C Columbia Gateway Dr., Columbia 21046; (800) CLIMB-UP; www.earth treksclimbing.com

Michigan

Vertical Ventures, (517) 485-7681

Nevada

Sky's The Limit, HCR 33 Box 1, Calico Basin, Red Rock 89124; (800) 733-7597; www.skysthelimit.com, climb@skysthelimit.com

New Hampshire

Accents North East Climbing School, North Woodstock; (603) 745-2867

Chauvin Guides International, P.O. Box 2151, North Conway 03860; (603) 356-8919; www.chauvinguides.com, marc@chauvinguides.com
Eastern Mountain Sports, (800) 310-4504, www.emsclimb.com
Jay Phillbrick (Independent), P.O. Box 2151, North Conway 03860; (603) 356-8919
Mountain Guide Alliance, P.O. Box 266, North Conway 03860; (603) 356-5310, www.mountainguidesalliance.com

New Jersey

Mountain Sports Adventure School, 107 Sidney Rd. (Route 617), Annandale 08801; (908) 735-6244; www.gorockclimbing.com

New York

Adirondack Rock and River Guides, P.O. Box 219, Keene 12942; (518) 576-2041; www.rockandriver.com, ed@rockandriver.com
Alpine Adventures, P.O. Box 179, Keene 12942; (518) 576-9881; www.alpineadven.com, mail@alpineadven.com
Diamond Sports Inc., 3 Crispell Lane, New Paltz 12561; (800) 776-2577
High Angle Adventures, 178 Hardenburgh Rd., Ulster Park 12487; www.highangle.com
High Peaks Mountain Adventures, 331 Main St., Lake Placid 12946; (518) 523-3764; www.highpeakscyclery.com
Mountain Adventure Guide Service, P.O. Box 539, Margaretville 12455; (914) 586-3919; www.mountainadventures.com, mtnman@catskill.net

North Carolina

Appalachian Mountain Guides, 126 Roaring Rock Rd., Vilas 28692; (828) 963-9528; www.ncrock.simplenet.com, moomaw@skybest.com
Black Dome Mountain Guides, www.blackdome.com/guides.htm
High South Mountain Guides, P.O. Box 254, Linville 28646; (828) 963-7579

Oregon

First Ascent Climbing Services, 1136 Southwest Deschutes, Redmond 97756; (800) 325-5462; www.goclimbing.com
Timberline Mountain Guides, Inc., P.O. Box 1167, Bend 97709; (541) 312-9242; www.timberlinemtguides.com, info@timberlinemtguides.com

South Dakota

Sylvan Rocks, Box 600, Hill City 57745; (605) 574-2425; www.sylvanrocks.com/

Tennessee

Desiderata Institute (Warrior's Way Course), 315 Oakwood
Cove, La Vergne 37086; (615) 793-3630

Texas

Arun Treks and Expeditions, 301 East Thirty-third St.,
Suite 3, Austin 78705; (888) 495-8735;
aruntrek@onr.com

Aspire Adventures, P.O. Box 10998, Austin 78766; (512)
335-9529; www.climbtexas.com

Hangdog Mountaineering, www.flash.net/~hangdog

Texas Mountain Guides, P.O. Box 49894, Austin 78765;
(512) 482-9208

Utah

Exum Utah Mountain Adventures, 2070 E. 3900 South,
#B, Salt Lake City 84124; (801) 555-3986; www.exum.
ofutah.com

Moab Cliffs and Canyons, 5 Center St., Moab 84532; (435)
259-9786

Moab Desert Adventures, 801 E. Oak St., Moab 84532;
(877) ROK-MOAB; www.moabdesertadventures.com

Washington

Alpine Ascents International, 121 Mercer St., Seattle 98109;
(206) 378-1927; www.alpineascents.com

American Alpine Institute, Ltd., 1515 Twelfth St.,
Bellingham 98225; (360) 671-1505; www.aai.cc

Cascade Alpine Guides, www.cascadealpine.com

International Mountain Guides, 6216 Seventh Ave.
Northwest, Seattle, 98107; (206) 784-1425;
www.mountainguides.com

Mountain Madness, 4218 Southwest Alaska, Suite 206,
Seattle 98116; (800) 328-5925; www.mountain
madness.com

Mt. Rainier Alpine Guides, LLC, www.climbnet.com/
rainier/index.html

Northwest Mountain Guides, 17612 Southeast Twenty-
second Way, Vancouver 98683; (360) 882-0604;
www.rmiguides.com/

Northwest Mountain School, P.O. Box 329, Leavenworth
98826; (509) 548-5823; www.mountainschool.net,
jr@mountainschool.net

Rainier Mountaineering Inc, 535 Dock St., Tacoma 98402;
(206) 627-6242; www.rmiguides.com/

West Virginia

Seneca Rocks Climbing School, Box 223, Seneca Rocks,
26844; (800) 451-5108; www.senecarocks.com,
Climbing@Senecarocks.com

Wisconsin

Dairyland Expeditions LLC, 719 West Frances St., Appleton
54914; (920) 734-0321; www.athenet.net/~vertical

Wyoming

Aventuras Patagonicas, P.O. Box 11389, Jackson 83002;
(888) 203-9354; www.patagonicas.com,
climb@patagonicas.com

Exum Mountain Guides, P.O. Box 56, Moose 83012; (307)
733-2297; www.exumguides.com

Jackson Hole Mountain Guides, Box 7477R, Jackson
83001; (307) 733-4979; www.jhmg.com

Jim Williams, P.O. Box 4166, Jackson 83001; (307)
733-8812

National Outdoor Leadership School, 288 Main St., Lander
82520; (307) 332-5300

Trails Wilderness School, P.O. Box 123, Jackson 83001;
(800) 869-8228; www.trailsws.com

Canada

Alberta

M&W Guides, Box 8020, Canmore T1W 2T8; (403)
678-2642; www.mwguides.com

British Columbia

Alliance of Professional Mountain Guides,
www.ascentguides.com

Bear Mountaineering School, Box 4222, Smithers V0J 2N0;
(250) 847-2854; www.bearmountaineering.bc.ca,
bearent@bulkley.net

Revelstoke Alpine Adventure County, Box 3315, Revelstoke
V0E 2S0; (888) 837-5417, www.raamountainguides.com

Ruedi Beglinger Mountaineering SME, P.O. Box 2998,
Revelstoke V0E 2S0; (250) 837-2381;
www.selkirkexperience.com, selkirk@junction.net

Squamish Rock Guides, P.O. Box 1786, Squamish V0N
3G0; (604) 898-1750

Mexico

Ivan Vigil, 523-633-24-72

Juan Pablo Acosta Martinez, 523-633-22-18; jpclimb@
hotmail.com

Organizations

United States

Alaska
Alaska Alpine Club, www.uaf.edu/aac/

Arizona
Arizona Mountaineering Club, P.O. Box 1695, Phoenix
85001-1695; www.azmountaineeringclub.org/
Central Arizona Mountain Rescue Association, P.O. Box
4004, Phoenix 85030
5.10 Climbing Club, Tempe;
http://five.ten.tripod.com/

California
California Hiking and Outdoor Society,
http://emf.net/~chaos/
Rim of the World Climbing Club, Running Springs; (909)
867-3089; www.rowcc.8m.com/
Rock RendezVous, San Francisco; www.rockclimb.org/rr/
Sierra Club-Loma Prieta Chapter, http://lomaprieta.sierra-
club.org
Southern California Mountaineers' Association, www.rock
climbing.org

Colorado
The American Alpine Club, Golden;
www.americanalpineclub.org/
Colorado Mountain Club, www.cmc.org
American Mountain Guides Association, P.O. Box 2128,
Estes Park 80517; (303) 586-0571
James P. Beckwourth Mountain Club, 2444 Washington
St., Denver 80205; (303) 831-0564; jbcenter@ix.
netcom.com
The Access Fund, P.O. Box 17010, Boulder 80308; (303)
938-6870

Connecticut
Ragged Mountain Foundation, P.O. Box 948, Southington
06489; www.raggedmtn.org

Idaho
Boise State University Climbing Club, Boise, www.idbsu.edu/
Idaho Alpine Club, www.idahoalpineclub.org

Iowa
ISU Mountaineering Club (Iowa State University climbers),
www.stuorg.iastate.edu/mcc/

Kansas
KSU Rock Climbing Club, www.ksu.edu/ksurock/

Kentucky
Red River Gorge Climbers' Coalition, www.rrgcc.org

Maine
Maine Outing Club, University of Maine, Rock Climbing
Committee, Orono

Massachusetts
The MIT Outing Club,
www.mit.edu:8001/activities/mitoc/home.html

Michigan
MTU Ridge Roamers, Michigan Technological University,
www.sos.mtu.edu/climb/

Missouri
University of Missouri Climbing Club, Rolla (meets at
Capen Park Tuesday at 5:00 P.M.), http://climb.mu.org,
climb@mu.org

New Hampshire
New England Rock Club,
http://clubs.yahoo.com/clubs/nerockclub

New Mexico

Los Alamos Mountaineers,
www.losalamos.org/climb/zLAMC.html

New York

Adirondack Mountain Club, 814 Goggins Rd., Lake George
12845; (800) 395-8080; adkinfo@adk.org
American Sport Climbing Federation, 125 West Ninety-
sixth St., New York 10025; (212) 865-4383

Ohio

Eden Park Rock Climbers Association, Cincinnati
Ohio Climber's Organization
Outdoor Pursuits, Columbus; www.outdoor-pursuits.com

Oklahoma

Wichita Mountains Climbers Coalition (WMCC), P.O. Box
721567, Norman 73070; (405) 364-9390; wmcc@wichita
mountains.org

Oregon

Columbia River Climbing Association, 9405 Southwest
Second, Portland 97219; (503) 452-1594
The Mazamas, 909 Northwest Nineteenth Ave., Portland
97209

Tennessee

West Tennessee Climber's Association, P.O. Box 11124,
Memphis 38111; (901) 324-1832

Texas

Alamo City Climbing Club, San Antonio; (check the local
gear shops for information)
Austin Aspire Climbing Club, Austin;
www.climbtexas.com/club.html
Central Texas Mountaineers, Austin; www.texas
mountaineers.org (meets first Thursday of every month
at 7:30 P.M. Check with local climbing gym).

Utah

Wasatch Mountain Club, www.xmission.com/~wmc

Virginia

Blue Ridge Mountaineering Association, Roanoke;
www.geocities.com/roanokeclimber

Washington

Intermountain Alpine Club, 9104 West Pooler, Pasco 99301
Spokane Mountaineers, www.spokanemountaineers.org

Wisconsin

Hoofer Mountaineering Club; www.hoofers.org/
mountaineering/
Wisconsin Outdoor Access (WOA); WOA-action@
climbingcentral.com

Canada

Alberta

Alpine Club of Canada, Box 1026, Banff; (403) 762-3664;
www.alpineclubofcanada.ca

Ontario

Alpine Club of Canada, Saskatchewan Section; www.
alpineclubofcanada.ca
Alpine Club of Canada, Thunder Bay Section; www.
norlink.net/~alpinecc/
Alpine Club of Canada, Toronto Section; www.climbers.org

Mexico

Socorro Mountain Rescue Team, Tlamacus (Popocatepetl)

Guidebooks

Alaska

Alaska Mountain Guide, Vincent J. Hoeman, ca. 1971

Alaska: A Climbing Guide, Michael Woods and Colby Coombs, 2001

Blue Ice and Black Gold [Valdez], Andy Embick, 1989

Denali Climbing Guide, R. J. Secor, 1998

Denali's West Buttress: A Climber's Guide, Colby Coombs, 1997

Fairbanks Area Climbing Guide (third ed.), Stan Justice, 2000 [1994]

First Steps: A Climber's Guide to the Archangel Valley, Roger Pollard and David Whitelaw, 1988

High Alaska: A Guide to Denali, Foraker, & Hunter, Jonathan Waterman, 1992

McKinley Climber's Handbook, Glenn Randall, 1992 [1984]

Mount McKinley Climber's Guide, Alaska Alpine Club, 1976

Mount McKinley: Icy Crown of North America, Fred Beckey, 1993

Mount Prindle Area Climbing Guide (second ed.), Stan Justice, 2001 [1997]

The Scar: South Central Alaska Rock Climbing, Kristian Sieling, 2000

Thin White Line: A Climber's Guide to the Seward Highway, P. Denkewalter and D. Whitelaw, 1990

Tourist Guide to Mount McKinley, Bradford Washburn, 1984

Alabama

A Climber's Guide to the Mid-South, Jim Detterline, 1982

Climber's Guide to North America (East), John Harlin III, 1986

Dixie Cragger's Atlas, Chris Watford, 1999

Southern Rock, A Climber's Guide, Chris Hall, 1981

The Deep South Climber's Companion, Rob Robinson and Chris Watford, 1993

Yellow Creek Plus, Rob Robinson, 1990

Arizona

A Beanfesters Guide to the West Stronghold, Off White, 1985

A Better Way to Die: Rock Climber's Guide to Sedona and Oak Creek Canyon, Tim Toula, 1995

A Bouldering Thing—Caveat Emptor (East Cochise Stronghold), Paul Davidson, 1984

A Cheap Way to Die: Climber's Guide to Sedona & Oak Creek Canyon, Tim Toula, 1989

A Cheap Way to Fly: Free Climbing Guide to Northern Arizona, Tim Toula, 1991 [1986]

A Climber's Guide to Lower Devils Canyon [topo map], Marty Karabin, 1993

A Climber's Guide to the Granite Dells of Prescott, AZ, Rick Dennison and Alessandro Malfatto, 1989

A Climber's Guide to Central Arizona Crags, Jim Waugh, L. Treiber, and B. Grubbs, 1989

A Climber's Guide to the Paradise Forks, Mike Lawson, 1986

A Sport Climber's Guide to Atlantis (Queen Creek Canyon), Marty Karabin, 1991

A Supplement to Climber's Guide to Sabino Canyon and Mt. Lemmon Highway, Eric Fazio-Rhicard, 1989

A Topo Guide to Granite Mountain, Jim Waugh, 1982

A Topo Guide to Le Petit Verdon, James Symans, 1989

An Anarchist's Guide to Climbing Routes on the Mid-Mountain, Mt. Lemmon, Scott Ayers, ca. 1990

Arizona Rock Climbing Areas Map, J. J. Kurtz, 1988

Arizona's Mountains: A Hiking and Climbing Guide, Bob Martin and Dotty Martin, 1991

Backcountry Climbing in Southern Arizona (second ed.), Bob Kerry, 1997 [1992]

Beanfest Fall 88 Southwest Stronghold, Scott Ayers, 1988

Beardsley Boulder Pile, Marty Karabin, 1994

Big Fat Funky Booty: Secret Canyon Topo Map [Flagstaff], David Bloom, 1993 [1990]

Bouldering beyond Campbell, Bob Murray, 1982

Buffalo Park Bouldering & Climbing Guide, Cloud Walker Publications, 1996

Camelback Mountain Climbing Guide, Marty Karabin and Scott Hynes, 1992

Castles in the Sand [Sedona], David Bloom, 2002

Climber's Guide to Sabino Canyon and Mt. Lemmon Highway, John Steiger, 1985

Climbing Guide to the Pit, Robert Miller, 1995

Fifty Classics of Southern Arizona, Karl Rickson, ca. 1990

Flagstaff Bouldering Guide, Bob Murray, 1982

Grand Canyon Loop Hikes I, George Steck, 1989

Grand Canyon Loop Hikes II, George Steck, 1993

Grand Canyon Treks, Harvey Butchart, 1998

Granite Mountain Topo, Rand Black, 1990 [1988]

Granite Mountain: Rock Climbing in Granite Basin, David Lovejoy, 1973

Groom Creek, Marty Karabin, 1994

Hiking and Climbing Guide to Lookout Mtn [Phoenix Mountain Preserve], Marty Karabin, 1993
Hiking the Grand Canyon, John Annerino, 1986
Hiking the Southwest, Dave Ganci, 1983
Hiking the Southwest's Canyon Country, Sandra Hinchman, 1990
Ice Castles, Marty Karabin, 1993
Jacks Canyon Sport Climbing, Jim Steagall and Deirdre Burton, 2001 [1997]
McDowell Mountains, Marty Karabin, 1996
Mount Lemmon & East Windy Point Climber's Guide, Marty Karabin, 1991
Mount Lemmon (East Windy Point) Topo Map, Marty Karabin, 1994
Oak Flats Bouldering Area, Phoenix Bouldering Contest, 1990
Paradise Forks, David Bloom, 1995
Phoenix Rock (second ed.), Greg Opland, 1996
Phoenix Rock: A Guide to Central Arizona Crags, Jim Waugh, 1989
Pinnacle Peak Topo Map, Marty Karabin, 1993
Prescott Bouldering Guide, Bill Cramer, 1998
Prescott Bouldering, Quentin Lauradunn, 1993
Queen Creek Canyon, Scott Hynes and Marty Karabin 1991
Rock Climbing Arizona, Stewart Green, 1999
Rock Jock's Guide to Queen Creek Canyon, Superior, Arizona, Marty Karabin, 1996
Rockclimbing Routes in Granite Basin, "Lizard Head," no author, 1972
Rockclimbing Routes in Granite Dells, Rusty Baillie and David Lovejoy, 1971
Seneca Falls Rock Climbing, Jim Steagall and Deirdre Burton, 1994
Southern Arizona Climber's Guide, Michael Jimmerson and Bob Smolinsky, 1983
Sport Climbing at the Pit, John McMullen, 1990
Squeezing the Lemmon: A Rock Climber's Guide to the Mt. Lemmon Highway, Eric Fazio-Richard, 1991
Street Map to Phoenix Climbing Areas, no author, ca. 1990
Superstition Select: Climber's Guide to Multi-pitch Routes of the Superstition Mountains, Greg Opland, 1998
Supes Climbs: Supplement Climbing Guide to the Superstition Mountains, Rick Percival, 1991
The Arm Pit, Damian Suess, ca. 1993
The Dells, J. Mezra, 1976
The Hiker's Guide to Arizona, Stewart Aitchison and Bruce Grubbs, 1991 [1987]
The Promised Land / Sullivan Canyon, Rusty Baillie and Nate Murray, 1995
Thumb Butte Climbing Guide, Rusty Baillie, 1991
Thumb Butte, A Climber's Guide, Charles Rugeley, 1988
Topo Guide to Carefree Rocks/Camelback Mountain, Larry Treiber and Bruce Grubbs, 1977
Tucson Area Climber's Guide, Dave Baker, 1980-present
Upper Devils Canyon [topo map], Marty Karabin, 1993
Vegas Rocks: Rock Climbs, Dan McQuade, 2000
Welcome to Las Vegas Limestone, Roxanna Brock McCray, 2000
Windy Point First Ascents (and Possible 1st Ascents), Scott Ayers, 1988

Arkansas

A Climber's Guide to Lake Lincoln, Cliff Robertson, 1998
A Climber's Guide to the Mid-South, Jim Detterline, 1982
Climber's Guide to the Midwest's Metamorphic Forms, Marcus Floyd, 1998
Mt. Magazine—A Rock Climber's Guide, Kerry Allen, 1996
Rock Climber's Guide to Mount Magazine, S. Bearden, G. Hollis, and T. Morris, 1992
Sam's Throne: Classic Rock Climbs, Clay Frisbee, 1997
The Natural: Climber's Guide to Sam's Throne, Clay Frisbee, 1990

California

A Climber's Guide to East Tahoe Region, Ron Anderson, 1991
A Climber's Guide to Glacier Point Apron, Bruce Morris, 1981
A Climber's Guide to Local Rock Climbing: Cragmont Rock, Richard M. Leonard, 1939
A Climber's Guide to Local Rock Climbing: Indian Rock, Richard M. Leonard, 1939
A Climber's Guide to Local Rock Climbing: Pinnacle Rock, Richard M. Leonard, 1939
A Climber's Guide to Local Rock-Climbing: Pinnacles National Monument, David Hammack, 1955
A Climber's Guide to Lover's Leap, Gene Drake, 1973
A Climber's Guide to Mission Gorge, Eric Beck, 1964
A Climber's Guide to Mount Rubidoux, Steve Mackay, 1984
A Climber's Guide to Mount Rubidoux. Steve Mackay and Randy Vogel, 1988
A Climber's Guide to Sonora Pass Highway, B. Young, H. Wolfe, and J. Lundeen, 2001
A Climber's Guide to Table Mountain, Grant Hiskes, 1993
A Climber's Guide to Tahquitz Rock, William Shand, Jr., 1943
A Climber's Guide to the High Sierra: Preliminary Edition, David Brower, 1949
A Climber's Guide to the High Sierra: The Evolution Region and the Black Divide, Alan Hedden and David Brower, 1942
A Climber's Guide to the High Sierra: The Ritter Range, Walter A. Starr, 1938
A Climber's Guide to the High Sierra: The Sawtooth Ridge, Richard M. Leonard, 1937
A Climber's Guide to the High Sierra: The Whitney Region, John and Ruth Mendenhall et al., 1941
A Climbing Guide to Bastille Buttress, Craig Peer, 1983
A Guide to Miraloma Rocks, Edward Kostinen, 1974
A Guide to the Tuolomne Domes, Alan Nelson, 1982 [1981]
A Photo Guide to Climbs in Mission Gorge, Gerberding, D., 1983
A Rock Climber's Guide to Local Rock-Climbing: Pinnacles National Monument, David Brower, 1939
A Rock Climber's Guide to Pinnacles National Monument, Paul G. Gagner, 1983
A Sport Climber's Guide to the Castle Rock Area, David Caunt and Bruce Morris, 1993
Anza-Borrego Desert Region, Lowell Lindsay and Diana Lindsay, 1988
Bald Rock Dome, no author, 1984
Bay Area Rock, Jim Thornburg, ca. 1990
Big Rock, Mike Wise, 1965

Big Rock, Pat Merrill, 1963

Bishop and Mammoth Areas, California Classic Rock Climbs, Randy Vogel, 1997

Bishop Area Rock Climbs, John Moynier and Marty Lewis, 1996

Book Rock, Greg Vernon, 1986

Bouldering at Stanford University, no author, 1986

Bouldering, Buildering, and Climbing in the San Francisco Bay Area (third ed.), Marc Jensen, 1988 [1983]

Bouldering Guide to Rexrodes, Eric Gomper and Peter Gomper, 1986

California County Summits, Gary Suttle, 1994

California's Fourteeners: A Hiking and Climbing Guide, Stephen F. Porcella and Cameron Burns, 1995 [1991]

Camp 4 Bouldering Guide, Don Reid, 1992

Camping and Climbing in Baja, John W. Robinson, 1967

Castle Crags Wilderness, John F. Bald, 1991

Climber's Guide for Moonstone and Luffenholtz Beach, Douglas W. LaFarge, 1992 [1991]

Climber's Guide Pinnacles National Monument, Dave Rubine, 1991

Climber's Guide Tahoe Rock, Mike Carville, 1994

Climber's Guide to Devil's Gate, Southern California RCS, ca. 1937

Climber's Guide to Eagle Rock, Southern California RCS, ca. 1937

Climber's Guide to Lake Tahoe, Mike Carville, 1991

Climber's Guide to Lake Tahoe and Donner Summit, Eric Beck, 1973

Climber's Guide to Mission Gorge, Werner Lantry, 1973

Climber's Guide to Owen's Ridge, no author, 1974 ca.

Climber's Guide to Pinnacles National Monument (third ed.), Steve Roper, 1974 [1966]

Climber's Guide to Santa Susanna, Southern California RCS, ca. 1937

Climber's Guide to Santee Boulders, Schaffer, G. and Walker, T., 1982

Climber's Guide to Southern California, Paul Hellweg and Nathan Warstler, 1988

Climber's Guide to Tahquitz Rock, Jim Smith,1937

Climber's Guide to the High Sierra, Hervey H. Voge, 1965 [1954]

Climber's Guide to the High Sierra, Sierra Club, 1949

Climber's Guide to the High Sierra, Steve Roper, 1976 [1967]

Climber's Guide to the High Sierra: The Palisades, Hervey H. Voge and David Brower, 1954

Climber's Guide to the Lake Tahoe Region, G. Dexter, R. Sumner, J. Taylor, and B. Todd, 1976

Climber's Guide to the Lake Tahoe Region, Rick Sumner, 1980

Climber's Guide to the Needles, Patrick Paul, 1986

Climber's Guide to the Riverside Quarry, Richard Jensen and Mark Smith, 1982

Climber's Guide to Tollhouse Rock, Fresno Big Wall Society, 1973

Climber's Guide to Tollhouse Rock and Vicinity, Mark Haymond, ca 1980

Climber's Guide to Tollhouse Rock and Vicinity, The Unknown Climber, 1988

Climber's Guide to Yosemite Valley, Steve Roper, 1987 [1964]

Climbing Guide to Crest, San Diego, CA, David Goode, 1993

Climbing Guide to Joshua Tree National Monument, John Wolfe, 1970

Climbing Guide to Joshua Tree National Monument, John Wolfe and Bob Dominick, 1979 [1976]

Climbing Guide to Mount Woodson, Michael Paul, 1987

Climbing in Santa Barbara and Ventura Counties, Stephen Tucker, 1981

Climbing Mt. Whitney, Walt Wheelock and Tom Condon, 1978 [1960]

Climbing Routes on Yosemite's Walls, Paul Harmon, 1972

Climbing Routes of Southern California's Big Bear Valley, W. Scott Hoffman, 1994

Climbing Santa Barbara, Ventura, San Luis Obispo, Stephen Tucker and Kevin Steele, 1993

Climbs in Cascade Mountains, Oregon and California, Thomas J. Samuel and Charles B. Hardin, 1939

Completely Off the Wall: A Climber's Guide to Bishop Peak (third ed.), Peter H. Gulyash, 1990 [1982]

Corte Madera, no author, ca 1990

Courtright Reservoir, Greg Vernon, 1986

Crags and Boulders of San Diego County, Douglas White (ed.), 1978

Crest, San Diego, CA: A Climber's Guide to the Singing Hills, David Goode, 1994

Database of Rock Climbs in California, Chambers, 1996

Day Climber's Guide to the Santa Clara Valley, Bill Craig, 1974

Deerhorn Valley Topos, Ray Olson, 1985 [1984]

Desert Peaks Guide I, Walt Wheelock, 1971 [1964]

Desert Peaks Guide II, Walt Wheelock, 1975

Desert Summits: A Climbing and Hiking Guide to California and Southern Nevada, Andy Zdon, 2000

Devil's Punchbowl, David Tidwell, 1992

Devil's Punchbowl Climber's Guide, S. Bouclin, D. Kovach, and S. Kovach, 1976

Dome Rock Climber's Guide, Dick Leversee, 1981

Domelands: Southern Sierra Rock Climbing, Sally Moser and Greg Vernon, 1992

Donner Summit, Gene Drake, 1986 [1982]

Eagles Peak [Lake Dixon], Andy Redding, 1939

El Capitan Climbing Poster Guide, Clay Wadman, 1996

Feather River Rock, Robert Stahl, ca. 1980

Fossil Falls, Bob Lindgren, 1988 [1985]

Free Climbs at Mission Gorge, Ron Amick, 1980

Getting High In L.A., David Katz, 1992 [1990]

Goat Rock, Joe Nickerson, 1985

Granite Crags of California, C. F. G. Cumming, 1884

Guide to Big Rock Climbing Area, G. Cobb, 1981

Guide to Joshua Tree 1982, Randy Vogel, 1982

Guide to Lover's Leap, Gene Drake, n.d.

Guide to Mt. Shasta, Allen Steck, n.d.

Guide to the Hinterlands (Tollhouse Rock et al.), Royal Robbins, ca. 1975

Guidebook to the San Bernadino Mountains of California, Russ Leadabrand, 1964

Guidebook to the Sunset Ranges of Southern California, Russ Leadabrand, 1965

High Sierra Guide, R. J. Secor, 1992

Hiking The Great Northwest, Ira Spring and Harvey Manning, 1991

Hunk Guide to Orange County, Randy Vogel, 1982

Iris Slab Mini Guide, Matt Artz, 1997

Joshua Tree Bouldering, Mari Gingery, 1993

Joshua Tree Rock Climbing Guide, Randy Vogel, 1986

Joshua Tree Rock Climbing Guide (second ed.), Randy Vogel, 1992

Joshua Tree Select, Randy Vogel, 1990

Joshua Tree Sport Climbing Guide, Randy Vogel, 1992

Joshua Tree Supplement, Randy Vogel and Alan Bartlett, 1989

Lassen County Climbs, F. T. Neff, ca. 1980

Lover's Leap, Bob Grow, 1982

Mammoth Area Rock Climbs, Marty Lewis, 1996

Mammoth Area Sport Climbs, Marty Lewis and John Moynier, 1993

McCain Valley Bouldering, Chris Hubbard, 1996

Mount Whitney Guide, Paul Hellweg and Scott McDonald, 1990

Mount Woodson Bouldering, Keith Brueckner, D. White, G. Kirkwood, and F. Noble, 1978

Mountaineer's Guide to the High Sierra, Hervey H. Voge and Andrew J. Smatko, 1972

Mountaineering, Freedom of the Quad, Stanford Alpine Club, 1971

Mr. Bobo's Guide to Mt. Diablo Rock, Patrick J. Ciminera, 1987

Mt. Woodson Boulder Maps, Ron Amick, 1987

Mt. Woodson—Feb. '87, Ron Amick, 1987

Needles: Southern Sierra Rock Climbing, S. Moser, G. Vernon, and P. Paul, 1992

Northwest Trails, Ira Spring and Harvey Manning, 1982 [1974]

Of Rocks, Fog, and Poison Oak: A Pseudo-Climbing Guide to Bay Area Crags, John Phelan, 1983

Off The Wall: A Climber's Guide to Bishop Peak, Dwight Kroll, 1979

Owens River Gorge Rock Climbs, Marty Lewis, 2000 [1990]

Pinnacles Guide, Elvin R. Johnson and Richard P. Cordone, 1984

Pinnacles National Monument Topographical Maps, Jonathan Richards, 1989

Quickdraw Guide to Northern California Sport Climbing Areas, Jim Thornburg, 1991

Rock Climber's Guide to Skyline Boulevard (third ed.), Bruce Morris, 2000

Rock Climbing Guide to Donner Summit, Max Jones, 1978

Rock Climbing Guide to Lassen Volcanic National Park, John F. Bald, 1991 [1987]

Rock Climbing Santa Barbara and Ventura, Steve Edwards, 2000

Rock Climbing Yosemite's Select Climbs, Don Reid, 1998

Rock Climbs at Big Bear Lake, Alan Bartlett, 1995

Rock Climbs of Central Joshua Tree (Joshua Tree National Monument), Alan Bartlett, 1992

Rock Climbs of Consumnes River, William H. Cottrell, 1997

Rock Climbs of Hidden Valley (Joshua Tree N.M.), Alan Bartlett, 1992

Rock Climbs of Indian Cove (Joshua Tree National Monument), Alan Bartlett, 1991

Rock Climbs of Lost Horse Valley (Joshua Tree National Monument), Alan Bartlett, 1991

Rock Climbs of Lost Horse Valley/Indian Cove, Allan Bard, ca. 1990

Rock Climbs of Tahquitz and Suicide Rocks, Randy Vogel, 1985 [1980]

Rock Climbs of Tahquitz and Suicide Rocks, Tim Messick, 1985

Rock Climbs of Tuolomne Meadows, Don Reid, 1992

Rock Climbs of Tuolumne Meadows (third ed.), Don Reid and Chris Falkenstein, 1992 [1983]

Rock-Climbs in Yosemite: Topo Drawings of Selected Routes, Dave Nicol (ed.), P. Livesey, and K. Nannery, 1975

San Bernadino Mountain Trails, John W. Robinson, 1975 [1972]

Scumbag Digest (Mission Gorge), Doug White and Bob Van Belle, 1976

Selected Bouldering: Yosemite Valley, Don Reid, 1996

Selected New Routes at Joshua Tree, Randy Vogel, 1980 [1979]

Sequoia-Kings Canyon Courtright Climber's Guide, Greg Vernon, 1993

Sequoia/Kings Canyon: Southern Sierra Rock Climbing S. Moser, G. Vernon, and D. Hickey, 1993

Shooting Star Guides: Cathedral Peak Southeast Face, Allan Bard, 1991

Shooting Star Guides: Matterhorn Peak Northeast Buttress, Allan Bard, 1991

Shooting Star Guides: Mt. Sill Swiss Arete, Allan Bard, 1991

Shooting Star Guides: Mt. Whitney East Buttress, Allan Bard, 1991

Shooting Star Guides: Mt. Whitney East Face, Allan Bard, 1991

Sierra Classics: 100 Best Climbs in the High Sierra, John Moynier, 1993

Sierra Classics: 100 Best Climbs in the High Sierra, John Moynier and Claude Fiddler, 1993

Sierra Classics: Best Routes in the Sierra Backcountry, Stephen F. Porcella and Cameron Burns, 1993

Sierra East Side, Alan Bartlett and Errett Allen, 1988

Sierra South 100 Backcountry Trips, (fourth ed.), Thomas Winnett & Jason Winnett, 1986 [1968]

SoCal Select, Randy Vogel, 1993

Southern California Bouldering Guide, Craig Fry, 1990

Southern California Bouldering (second ed.), Craig Fry, 1995

Southern California Peaks, Walt Wheelock, 1973

Southern California Sport Climbing: The Guide, Troy Mayr and Anthony Sweeney, 1995

Southern Yosemite Rock Climbs, Mark and Shirley Spencer, 1988

Sport Climber's Guide to Skyline Boulevard, Bruce Morris, 1995

Sport Climbing Guide to Southern California, Troy Mayr, 1992

Sport Climbing in Southern California's High Desert, Richard Yamin and Shelli Yamin, ca. 1990

Sport Climbing in the Santa Monicas, Louie Anderson, 1998

Stinson Beach Area, North Face, 1987

Stonemasher Guide to Kern River Canyon and Environs (Needles), E. C. Joe and Dick Leversee, 1983

Stonemasher Guide to Kern Slabs, E. C. Joe, 1982

Stoney Point Guide, Paul Hellweg and Don Fisher, 1982

Strawberry Peak—North Wall (Tahquitz), John D. Mendenhall, 1943

Tahoe Rock Climbing, Christine Jenkewitz-Meytras, 1988

Tahoe Rock Climbs, Christine Jenkewitz-Meytras, 1986

Tahquitz and Suicide Rock Climbs, Randy Vogel and Bob Gaines, 1993
Tahquitz and Suicide Rocks, Chuck Wilts (ed.) et al., 1979 [1962]
Temple Rock, Steve Mackay, 1973
The Best of Mother Rock, Matt Artz (ed.), 1997
The El Cap Route Map, Rand Black, 1992
The Mt. Shasta Book, A Guide to Hiking, Climbing, Skiing, and Exploring, A. Selters and M. Zanger, 1989
Timberline Country: The Sierra High Route, Steve Roper, 1982
Tuolomne Sport Climbs, Steve Schneider, ca. 1990
Tuolomne Topropes, Rob Floyd, 2000
Turtle Rock Bouldering Guide, Mike Artz, 1997
Urban Rock: Stoney Point Toprope Guide, Chris Owen, 1994
Wawona Rock, Mark Spencer, 1984
Williamson Rock, Troy Mayr and Anthony Sweeney, 1997
Yosemite Big Walls Supertopos, Chris McNamara, 2000
Yosemite Bouldering, Don Reid, 1999
Yosemite Climbs, George Meyers and Don Reid, 1987 [1982]
Yosemite Climbs: Big Walls, Don Reid, 1993
Yosemite Climbs: Free Climbs, Don Reid, 1993
Yosemite Climbs: Topo Drawings of the Best Rockclimbing Routes in Yosemite Valley, George Meyers, 1976
Yosemite Select, Don Reid, 1991
Yosemite Topropes, Rob Floyd, 1999
Yosemite Valley Sport Climbs, Chris Falkenstein, 1996 [1992]

Colorado
100 Select Classic Boulder Climbs, Fred Knapp and Mike Stevens, 1995
100 Select Classic Rocky Mountain National Park Climbs, Fred Knapp, 1994
200 Classic Shelf Road Climbs, Fred Knapp, 1996
200 Select Classic Shelf Road Climbs, Fred Knapp, 1994
5.10: A Rock Climber's Guide to Boulder, CO, Pat Ament and Jim Erickson, 1972
50 Select Classic Desert Climbs, Fred Knapp, 1994
A Backpacking Guide to the Weminuche Wilderness, Dennis Gebhardt, 1976
A Climbers Guide to Colorado's Fourteeners, Walter R. Borneman and Lyndon J. Lampert, 1978
A Climber's Guide To Creedmore Crag & Cinco De Mayo, Jim Brink, 1980
A Climber's Guide to Rocky Mountain National Park Area, Walter W. Fricke, Jr., 1972 [1971]
A Climber's Guide to The High Colorado Peaks, Elinor Eppich Kingery, 1931
A Climber's Playground: A Guide to the Boulders of Flagstaff Mountain, Pat Ament, 1980
A Pictorial Guide to Boulder Climbs, Richard Rossiter, 1986 [1981]
A Rock Climber's Guide to Castlewood Canyon State Park, Colorado, Thomas Hanson, 1996
Aspen Rock Climbing, Greg Davis, ca. 1981
Aspen Rockclimbing: Selected Routes, Greg Davis, 1979
Best of Boulder Bouldering, Bob Horan, 2000
Best of Boulder Climbs, Richard Rossiter, 1996 [1991]
Bite the Bullet: Rifle Mountain Park Climbing Guide, Dave Pegg, 1997

Boulder Climbs North (second ed.), Richard Rossiter, 1996 [1990]
Boulder Climbs South (second ed.), Richard Rossiter, 1996 [1989]
Boulder Rock Climbs, John D. McCrumm and Carleton C. Long, 1934
Boulder Sport Climber's Guide 1996, Mark Rolofson, 1996 [1993]
Boulder Top Ropes: Boulder's Best Top Roping Areas, Fred Knapp, 1996
Bouldering Guide to Marmot Rocks, National Park Service, 1986
Bouldering in the G Spot (Gunnison, Colorado), Jonathan Houck, 1997
Clear Creek Classic Rock Climbs, Peter Hubbell, 1998
Climber's Guide to Castlewood Canyon, Alan Mosiman, 1987
Climber's Guide to Eleven Mile Canyon, Dave Bamberger and Bob Glaze, 1979
Climber's Guide to Estes Park Area, Bob Bradley and Steve Hickman, 1962
Climber's Guide To North Rock [Glen Haven], Bill Todd, n.d.
Climber's Guide to Rifle Mountain Park, Media West, 1997
Climber's Guide to Rifle, Hassan Saab, 1995
Climber's Guide to Shelf Road, Mark Van Horn, 1990
Climbing Reports in Black Canyon National Monument [NPS office book], n.d.
Colorado Bouldering, Phillip Benningfield, 1999
Colorado Fourteeners, Gerry Roach, 1996 [1992]
Colorado Fourteens: A Condensed Guide, S. Richards, 1978
Colorado Ice Climber's Guide, Cameron Burns, 1997
Colorado Ice, Jack Roberts, 1998
Colorado Thirteeners, Gerry Roach and Jennifer Roach, 2000
Colorado's High Thirteens: A Climbing and Hiking Guide, Mike Garratt and Bob Martin, 1984
Colorado's Indian Peaks: Classic Hikes & Climbs, Gerry Roach, 1998 [1989]
Colorado's Other Mountains, Walter R. Bornemann, 1984
Crested Butte Guide, Douglas D. Scott, 1991
Dawson's Guide to Colorado's Fourteeners: Volume 1, The Northern Peaks, Louis W. Dawson II, 1995
Dawson's Guide to Colorado's Fourteeners: Volume 2, The Southern Peaks, Louis W. Dawson II 1995
Devil Made Me Do It: Climber's Guide to Devil's Head, Colorado, Tod Anderson, 1998
Diamond of Longs Peak Climbing Poster Guide, Clay Wadman, 1995
Diamond of Longs Peak, Colorado Classic Rock Climbs, Richard Rossiter, 1996
Durango Area, Tom Norton, n.d.
Durango Sandstone: A Topo Guide to X-Rock and East Animas, Tim Kuss, 1988
Durango Sandstone: Guide to X-Rock and Other Legendary Areas, Tim Kuss, 1994
El Dorado CD-ROM, no author, 1997
Eldorado: A Rock Climber's Route Guide, Pat Ament, 1980 [1975]
Eleven Mile Canyon, Mark Rolofson, 1984
Flatiron Classics: Easy Climbs and Trails, Gerry Roach, 1990 [1987]

For Turkeys Only: Climber's Guide to Turkey Rock, Steve Cheyney and Bob Couchman, 1989 [1984]

Front Range Bouldering Vol. 1: Fort Collins Area, Bob Horan, 1995

Front Range Bouldering Vol. 2: Boulder Area, Bob Horan, 1995

Front Range Bouldering Vol. 3: Southern Areas, Bob Horan, 1995

Front Range Bouldering, Bob Horan, 1989

Front Range Crags, Peter Hubbel, 1993

Front Range Top Ropes, Fred Knapp, 1997

Golden Cliffs Rock Climbs, Peter Hubbel, 1998

Grand Junction Rock: Rock Climbs of Unaweep Canyon, K. C. Baum, 1997 [1992]

Guide to the Colorado Mountains (ninth ed.), Robert M. Ormes, 1997 [1952]

Heinous Cling: A Climber's Guide to Independence Pass, Aspen, Colorado, Andre Wille, 1996 [1994]

High Country Crags: A Rock and Ice Climbing Guide to Summit County, Scott Astaldi and Mike Gruber, 1993

High Country Stone: Gunnison and Crested Butte Rock, Douglas Scott, 1993

High Over Boulder, Pat Ament and Cleveland M. McCarty, 1967-1985

High Over Boulder: A Historical Guide to Rock Climbing near Boulder, Colorado, Pat Ament and Cleveland M. McCarty, 1995

Hiking Colorado's Summits, John Drew Mitchler and Dave Covill, 1999

Hiking Colorado's Weminuche Wilderness, Donna Ikenberry, 1999

Hiking the Southwest's Canyon Country, Sandra Hinchman, 1990

Hiking Trails of Southwestern Colorado, Paul Pixler, 1981

Independence Pass West Climbing Guide, Perkins, 1997

Longs Peak Free-climber [topo map], Scott Kimball, 1984

Longs Peak: Its Story and a Climbing Guide, Paul W. Nesbit, 1972 [1946]

Lumpy Ridge (Estes Park Rock Climbs), Scott Kimball, 1985

Lyons Area Classic Rock Climbs, Peter Hubbell, 1998

Master of Rock, Pat Ament, 1992 [1976]

Monitor Rock Select, Aspen Climbing Guides, 1999

Mountaineering in Colorado: The Peaks about Estes Park, Frederick H. Chapin, 1889 [1987]

Mountaineering in the Gore Range: A Record, Joseph D. Kramarsic, 1989

Mountaineering in the Rocky Mountain National Park, Roger Toll and Robert Sterling, 1921

Mountaineers Weekend (Garden of the Gods), Colorado Mountain Club, 1962

Mueller State Park and Eleven Mile Canyon: Classic Rock Climbs, Bob D'Antonio, 1996

Naturita and Paradox Valley Rock Climbs (second ed.), Charlie Fowler, 1991

Not Won: Climbing Colorado's Highpoints in a Day, Jack Bennett, 1999

Notes on Mountaineering in the Elk Mountains, Colorado, 1908–10, Colorado Mountain Club, 1956

Ophir Wall Bums, no author, 1986

Photographs Guide, Gerald Clarke, ca.1930

Pikes Peak and Garden of the Gods Classic Rock Climbs, Bob D'Antonio, 1996

Rock and Ice Climbing Rocky Mountain National Park: The High Peaks, Richard Rossiter, 1997

Rock Climber's Guide to Aspen, Larry Bruce and Molly Higgins Bruce, 1989 [1985]

Rock Climber's Guide to Greyrock, Craig Luebben, 1991

Rock Climber's Guide to the Garden of the Gods, Jim McCristal, 1976 [1975]

Rock Climbing Boulder Canyon, Richard Rossiter, 1998

Rock Climbing Colorado, Stewart Green, 1996

Rock Climbing Guide to The Boulder, Colorado, Area, David Dornan, 1961

Rock Climbing in Lake County, Wes Peterson, Lance Hadfield, and Doug Ranck, ca. 1990

Rock Climbing in Ten Mile Canyon, (Dillon, Colorado), Dave Hurst, 1984

Rock Climbing Rocky Mountain National Park: The Crag Areas, Richard Rossiter, 1996

Rock Climbing the Flatirons, Richard Rossiter, 1999

Rocky Heights: A Guide to Boulder Free Climbs, Jim Erickson, 1985 [1980]

Rocky Mountain National Park: A Climber's Guide, Bernard Gillet, 1993

Rocky Mountain National Park: Classic Hikes and Climbs, Gerry Roach, 1988

Rocky Mountain National Park: The Crag Areas, Richard Rossiter, 1996

Rocky Mountain National Park: The High Peaks, Richard Rossiter, 1996

Roof of the Rockies: A History of Mountaineering in Colorado, William M. Bueler, 1974

San Juan Ice Climbs, Charlie Fowler, 1996

San Juan Mountaineers' Climber's Guide to Southwest Colorado, D. G. Lavender, C. C. Long, and T. M. Griffiths, 1932

San Juan Mountains: Climbing and Hiking Guide, no author, n.d.

San Luis Valley: Penitente Canyon Climbs, Bob D'Antonio, 1994

Scenic Solitude: Castlewood Canyon State Park Climber's Guide, Drysdale and Crooks, 1988

Select Rock Climbs of the Boulder Area, Richard Rossiter, 1990

Selected Climbs in Rocky Mountain National Park, Richard Dumais, 1980

Shelf Road Rock Guide, Mark Van Horn, 1998 [1995]

Soft Touch [Garden of the Gods], Mark Rolofson, 1983 [1979]

Soft Touch 3: Climber's Guide to Garden of the Gods, Mark Rolofson, 1997

Solitary Summits, Scott Kimball, 1982

South Platte and Garden of the Gods, Peter Hubbel and Mark Rolofson, 1988

South Platte Rock Selected Climbs, Ken Trout, 1997

South Platte: The Rock Climber's Guide, Peter Hubbel, 1997

Southwest Rock, David Kozak, 1985

Sport Climbs in Castlewood Canyon, Ken Werl, ca. 1990

Technical Rock Climber's Guide to East Face of Long's Peak, Peter Robinson, 1966

Telluride Hot Rock (Ophir Wall, Crack Cyn, Ames Wall), Antoine Savelli, 1986

Telluride Rock: A Climber's Guide, Vol. 1, Charlie Fowler, 1990

Telluride Rock: An Interim Guide, Bill Kees, 1978

Telluride Rocks, Andrew Sawyer and Charlie Fowler, 1997
Thath-Aa-Ai-Atah (Lumpy Ridge Guide), Chip Salaun and Scott Kimball, 1980
The Brown Book of Lies [South Platte], Peter Hubbel, 1983
The Climber's Guide to the Mountains of Middle Park, Wesley A. Brown, 1975
The Fourteener's: Colorado's Great Mountains, Perry Eberhart and Philip Schmuck, 1970
The Hard Stuff (Turkey Rock & South Platte), Mark Rolofson, 1984
The High Peaks [Rocky Mountain National Park], Richard Dumais, 1987 [1981]
The Monastery [Estes Park], Ned Gillett, 1997
The Pocket Book, Bob D'Antonio, 1991
The San Juan Mtns: A Climbing and Hiking Guide, Robert F. Rosebrough, 1988 [1986]
The Valley Climbs, Boulders (San Luis Valley), no author, n.d.
Upper Dream Canyon Classic Rock Climbs, Richard Rossiter, 1998
Vertigo Games, Glenn Randall, 1983

Connecticut
A Climbing Guide to Wolf Rock and Pothole, Ron Matous, ca. 1970
A Guide to the Main Cliffs and Small Cliffs at Ragged Mountain, John Reppy and Sam Streibert, 1964
Climber's Guide to Ragged Mountain, Marvin Johnson, Alan Long, and Simon Whitney, 1973
Climbing Guide to Ragged Mountain (supplement), Sam Streibert, 1966
Connecticut Rock Climbs: Traprock, Ken Nichols, ca. 1980
Hooked on Ragged: Rock Climbing on Ragged Mountain, Ken Nichols, 1997
Hooked on Traprock: Rock Climbing in Central Connecticut, Ken Nichols, 1995
Killingworth Cliffs, Tom Saunders and Joel Anderson, 1978
Ragged Mountain 1974, Ken Nichols, 1974
Rock Climbing Connecticut, David Fasulo, 2002
Rock Climbing New England, Stewart Green, 2002
Sleeping Giant, Dave Harrah, 1952
The Mountains of Eph, Williams Outing Club, 1927
Traprock: Rockclimbing in Central Connecticut, Ken Nichols, 1982
Woodbury Cliffs, Ken Nichols, 1984
Woodbury Rock Climber's Guide, Bill Ivanhoff and Ken Nichols, 1988

Georgia
Carolinas Climber's Guide, Buddy Price, 1977
Dixie Cragger's Atlas, Chris Watford, 1999
Southern Rock, A Climber's Guide, Chris Hall, 1981
The Deep South Climber's Companion, Rob Robinson and Chris Watford, 1993

Idaho
50 Eastern Idaho Hiking Trails, Ron Mitchell, 1979
Adventure in Idaho's Sawtooth Country, Lynne Stone, 1990
Basalt Climbs in Southcentral Idaho (second ed.), Mark Weber, 1995 [1992]
Black Cliffs Route Finder, no author, 1991
Boise Climbs, Sandy Epeldi, 1998
City of Rocks Select, Mike Forkash, 1997
City of Rocks Topo Overview, Jay Goodwin, ca. 1986
City of Rocks, Idaho, Classic Rock Climbs: One Hundred Fifty Best Routes, Laird Davis, 1997
City of Rocks, Idaho: A Climber's Guide, Dave Bingham, 2000 [1995]
Dierke's Lake Crag Topo, no author, ca. 1990
Exploring Idaho's Mountains: Guide for Climber's and Hikers, Tom Lopez, 1990
Hiking The Great Northwest, Ira Spring and Harvey Manning, 1991
Idaho Rock: Selkirk Crest and Sandpoint Areas, Randall Green, 1987
Idaho: A Climbing Guide, Tom Lopez, 2000
More Boise Climbs, Sandy Epeldi, 1998
Northwest Trails, Ira Spring and Harvey Manning, 1982 [1974]
Rock Climbing Idaho's City of Rocks, Tony Calderone, 1998
Trails of Western Idaho, Margaret Fisher, 1982

Illinois
50 Short Climbs in the Midwest, Alan Bagg, 1978
A Climber's Guide to the Mid-South, Jim Detterline, 1982
Climber's Guide to Kankakee River State Park, Matthew Nicodemus and Andrew Nicodemus, 1979
Climber's Guide to the Midwest's Metamorphic Forms, Marcus Floyd, 1998
Guide to Mississippi Palisades, Demetri Kolokotronis, 1967 [1965]
Jackson Falls, Michael Simpson, 1995 [1990]
River Rock: A Climber's Guide to Mississippi Palisades State Park (third ed.), Gary Taylor and William Collett, 1991 [1983]
S.I.C. Routes of Illinois, Jim Thurmond 1990
The Gritstone Mountaineer, Adam Grosowsky, 1976
Vertical Heartland: A Rock Climber's Guide to Southern Illinois, Eric Ulner, 1996 [1993]

Indiana
Portland Arch Guide, Pete Zvengrowski, n.d.
Rock in Indiana, Kevin Fay, 1996

Iowa
50 Short Climbs in the Midwest, Alan Bagg, 1978
Rock: The Climber's Guide to Palisades-Kepler State Park, John B. Ferguson, 1978

Kansas

Climber's Guide to the Midwest's Metamorphic Forms, Marcus
  Floyd, 1998

Kentucky

A Climber's Guide to the Mid-South, Jim Detterline, 1982
Climber's Guide to Pilot Rock, Geoffrey L. Irons, 1979
Climber's Guide to the Red River Gorge, Ed Pearsall, 1980
Red River Gorge Bouldering, Chris Redmond, 2000
Red River Gorge Climbs, John H. Bronaugh, 2000 [1993]
Red River Gorge: A Climbing Guide, Frank Becker and Diane
  Blazy, 1974
Rock Climbs in Southcentral Kentucky, Jack Dickey, 1981
Selected Climbs of Red River Gorge, Porter Jarrard and Chris
  Snyder, 1997
Selected Climbs of Red River Gorge, Porter Jarrard, 1992
Stones of the Years III, Martin Grant, 1993
Stones of the Years: Climber's Guide to Red River Gorge, Martin
  Hackworth, 1984

Maine

AMC Guide to Maine, Appalachian Mountain Club, 1988
AMC Guide to Mount Desert Island and Acadia NP, Appalachian
  Mountain Club, 1988
AMC Guide to New Hampshire and Adjacent Parts of Maine,
  Appalachian Mountain Club, 1987
AMC Maine Mountain Guide, Appalachian Mountain Club,
  n.d.
AMC Mount Desert Island and Acadia National Park, Elfring,
  1993
Clifton Rock Climbs [central Maine], Les Ellison, 1974
Climber's Guide to Mt. Desert Island, Geoffrey Childs, 1981.
Climbing Areas in Southwestern Maine, Appalachian Mountain
  Club, 1965
Greater Portland Rock Peter Beal, 1985 [1984]
Mountain Climbing Guide in Maine, no author, 1959
*Obscure Crags Guide, A Guide to Cliffs in New Hampshire, Maine,
  and Vermont*, Dwight Bradley and Tad Pfeffer, n.d.
Osgood's White Mountains, James R. Osgood, 1876
Rock and Ice Climbs in the Camden Hills, Ben Townsend, 1995
Rock Climber's Guide to Clifton Crags, Jon Tierney, 2000
Rock Climbing in Acadia National Park (third ed.), Pete Warner,
  1998
Shades of Blue: A Guide to Ice Climbing in New England, Peter
  Cole and Rick Wilcox, 1976

Maryland

184 Miles of Adventure: Hiker's Guide to the C&O Canal,
  Mason-Dixon Council, Boy Scouts of America, 1983
A Climber's Guide to Great Falls Park, Nelson and Grossman,
  1975
*Carderock Big Wall: The Ultimate Guide to Rock Climbing at
  Carderock*, Robert J. Borotkanics and Dan Feer, 2001
Carderock: Past and Present, PATC [Selma Hanel], 1990
Climber's Guide to Carderock, John Forrest Gregory, 1980

Climber's Guide to Great Falls of the Potomac, James A. Eakin,
  1985
Map D, Potomac Gorge Climber's Edition, Potomac
  Appalachian Trail Club, 1971
Nearby Climbing Areas, Ron and Kathy Canter, 1980

Massachusetts

A Climber's Guide to Quincy Quarries, William R. Crowther
  and Anthony W. Thompson, 1976 [1964]
A Guide to Crow Hill, Bob Hall, 1967
AMC Guide to Massachusetts and Rhode Island, Appalachian
  Mountain Club, 1988
Blasted Rock: Quarry Climbs, John Strand, 1987
Blasted Rock Two: Quincy Quarries, John Strand, 1990
Boston Rocks, Larry La Forge, n.d.
Boston Rolls, Larry La Forge, 1987
Bouldering around Boston, John Hollerback, n.d.
Bouldering Boston by Bus, Harvard Mountaineering Club,
  1981 [1980]
Central Massachusetts Climbing Areas, Al Rubin, n.d.
Climber's Guide to Chapel Ledges, Richard Wilcox, Jr., 1970
Climbing in Eastern Massachusetts, Steve Hendrick and Sam
  Striebert, 1976 [1975]
Crow Hill: Leominster State Park on Rt 31, Bill Phillips, 1966
Guide to Black Rock, Berkshire School, n.d.
Guide to Westford Quarries, Paul Duval, n.d.
MIT Boulderer's Guide, John Hollerback and Skip King, n.d.
Monson, no author, n.d.
Rock Climbs North of Boston, Appalachian Mountain Club,
  1966
Rose Ledge Rock Climbs, Al Rubin, 2000
The Crow Hill Guidebook, Ed Webster, 1973
WOC Climbing Guide, Williams College Outing Club, 1986
  [1978]

Michigan

50 Short Climbs in the Midwest, Alan Bagg, 1978
A Climber's Guide to Grand Ledge, Bruce K. Bright and J. Van
  Laar, 1972 [1969]
Michigan Ice, Bill Thompson, 1998

Minnesota

50 Short Climbs in the Midwest, Alan Bagg, 1978
A Rock Climbing Guidebook to Blue Mounds State Park, Scott
  Wudinger, 1989
Ice Climbs of Lake Superior Region: A Compendium, Don Hynek
  (ed.), 2000
Minnesota Rock: Selected Climbs (third ed.), Mike Farris, 1998
  [1995]
Prairie Walls: Climber's Guide to Blue Mounds State Park, Don
  Hynek and Eric Landmann, 1989
Rock Climbing Minnesota and Wisconsin, Mike Farris, 2000
Superior Climbs: A Climber's Guide to the North Shore, David
  Pagel, 1991 [1984]

The Barnyard Boogie: Guide to Barn Bluff, Red Wing, Minnesota, Nate Postma, 1990
The Climber's Guide to Taylor Falls, Swenson, 1972

Mississippi
A Climber's Guide to Midwest, Jim Detterline, 1982
Tishomingo: A Climber's Guide to Mississippi Rock, Jim Detterline, 1998

Missouri
A Climber's Guide to Devil's Elbow, Garet Denise, 1987
A Climber's Guide to Henley Forgotten Wall, Norm Reed, 1989
A Climber's Guide to the Mid-South, Jim Detterline, 1982
Boone County Climbs, Charly Oliver and Chris Taylor, 1981
Climber's Guide to the Midwest's Metamorphic Forms, Marcus Floyd, 1998
Johnson Shut-ins State Park, B. Hagen, 1989
Missouri Limestone, Sean Burns, 1996
WVOC A: Climber's Guide to St Louis, Jim Thurmond, 1995

Montana
A Climber's Guide to Butte, Dwight Bishop, 1990
A Climber's Guide to Glacier National Park (fourth ed.), J. Gordon Edwards, 1995 [1961]
A Rock Climber's Guide to the Bitterroot Valley, Rick Torre, 1990
Alpine Ice and Rock Guide to Southwest Central Montana, Ron Brunckhorst, 2000
Bitterroot Bouldering Guide, Rick Torre, 1996
Bitterroot Climber's Guide Book: Rock Climbs (second ed.), Rick Torre, 1996
Bitterroot Guidebook, Rick Torre, 1993
Bozeman Rock Climbs (second ed.), Bill Dockins, 1995 [1987]
Climber's Guide to Montana, Pat Caffrey, 1986
Climbing Granite Peak: Beartooths, Donald Jacobs, 1992
Hiker's Guide to Glacier National Park, Dick Nelson and Sharon Nelson, 1978
Hiking Glacier and Waterton Lakes National Parks, Erik Molvar, 1999
Hiking Montana, Bill Schneider and Russ Schneider, 1999
Hiking the Beartooths, Bill Schneider, 1996
Hiking the Great Northwest, Ira Spring and Harvey Manning, 1991
Montana Mountain Ranges, Rick Reese, 1981
Montana Rock Climbs in the Mission Range, no author, n.d.
More Climbs in Butte, Kurt Krueger and Keith Calhoun, 1993
Northwest Trails, Ira Spring and Harvey Manning, 1982 [1974]
Rimrock Beach [Billings], no author, 1989
Rock Climbing Montana, Randall Green, 1995
Stone Hill: Rock Climbs of Lake Koocanusa, Greg Stenger, 1989
The Climber's Guide to Lolo Pass, Brad Hutcheson, 1992

Nevada
Desert Summits: A Climbing and Hiking Guide to California and Southern Nevada, Andy Zdon, 2000
Guide to Nevada's Rocky and East Humboldt Mountains, Carmie R. Dafoe, Jr., 1971
Hiking and Climbing in Great Basin National Park, Michael R. Kelsey, 1990 [1988]
Hiking Great Basin National Park, Bruce Grubbs, 1998
Hiking the Great Basin, John Hart, 1992 [1981]
Keyhole Canyon Guide, no author, ca. 1990
Red Rocks, Randy Faulk, 1991
Red Rocks of Southern Nevada, Joanne Urioste, 1984
Red Rocks Select (second ed.), Todd Swain, 1995 [1992]
Vegas Rocks: Rock Climbs, Dan McQuade, 2000
Welcome to Las Vegas Limestone, Roxanna Brock McCray, 2000

New Hampshire
A Climber's Guide to Mt. Washington Valley, Joseph Cote, 1972
A Climber's Guide to Pawtuckaway State Park and Southeastern New Hampshire, Todd Swain, 1980
A Rock Climbing Guide to Cathedral and White Horse Ledges, Joseph Cote and Karen Cote, 1969
AMC Guide to Mt. Washington and Presidential Range, Appalachian Mountain Club, 1988 [1976]
AMC Guide to New Hampshire and Adjacent Parts of Maine, Appalachian Mountain Club, 1987
AMC Guide to White Mountains, Appalachian Mountain Club, 1952
AMC White Mountain Guide, no author, n.d.
Cannon, Cathedral, Humphrey's, and Whitehorse: A Rock Climber's Guide, Paul Ross and Chris Ellms, 1982 [1978]
Cannon: A Climber's Guide, Howard Peterson, 1975
Climber's Guide to Cannon Cliff, Howard Peterson and John Porter, ca. 1972
Climber's Guide to Mt. Washington Valley (supplement), Henry Barber, 1973
Climber's Guide to Rock Rimmon, Mark Hudon, 1975
Climbing Routes on Cannon Cliff, Earle Whipple, 1965
Guide to Bouldering at Round Pond [Pawtuckaway], no author, n.d.
Guide to Crawford Notch, Mike Dickerman with Steven D. Smith, 1997
High Peaks of the Northeast, Scofield, 1994
Manchester Rock: Rock Climbs in the Greater Manchester, New Hampshire Area, P. Boissonneault, D. Saball, and M. Saball, 1996
Monadnock Guide, Henry I. Baldwin, 1970
Obscure Crags Guide, A Guide to Cliffs in New Hampshire, Maine, and Vermont, Bradley Pfeffer and Tad Pfeffer, n.d.
Osgood's White Mountains, James R. Osgood, 1876
Pawtuckaway Rock Climbs (second ed.), P. Boissonneault, D. Saball, and M. Saball, 1996
Revised Guide to Cannon Cliff, Bob Hall, 1968
Rock Climbing Guide to Cathedral and Whitehorse Ledges, Jerry Handren, 1996
Rock Climbing Guide to Rumney, Ward Smith, 1996
Rock Climbs in the White Mountains of NH (third ed.), Ed Webster, 1996 [1982]
Rumney, Ward Smith, 1999
Schist Another Hangover: Rumney Rock Notes, Den Danna, 1992

Secrets of the Notch: A Guide to the Rock and Ice Climbing of Cannon Cliff and the Crags of Franconia Notch, Jon Sykes, 2001

Shades of Blue: A Guide to Ice Climbing in New England, Peter Cole and Rick Wilcox, 1976

The Conn Course, Earle Whipple, 1965

Trails and Summits of the White Mountains, Walter Collins O'Kane, 1926

New Jersey

Climber's Guide to the Delaware Water Gap, Mike Steele, 1989 [1987]

New Jersey Classic Rock Climbs, Paul Nick and Neil Sloan, 1996

Quick and Dirty Guide to Cradle Rock, Paul Nick, 1993

Rock and Ice in the Gap, Hugh Dougher, 1978

New Mexico

50 Hikes in New Mexico, Harry Evans, 1984

A Climbing Guide to Palomas Peak, Berard Moret, 2000

Climber's Guide to Box Canyon, Erick Hufnagel and Betrand Gramont, ca. 1986

Climber's Guide to the Lower Sandia Mountains, Barry and Rita Loucks, 1989

Fifty Classic Climbs of North America (second ed.), Steve Roper and Allen Steck, 1996 [1979]

Guide to New Mexico Mountains, Herbert E. Ungnade, 1988 [1965]

Guide to the Sandia Mountains, Bob Kyrlach, 1970

Hikers and Climbers Guide to the Sandias, Mike Hill, 1993 [1983]

Hiking the Southwest, Dave Ganci, 1983

Hiking the Southwest's Canyon Country, Sandra Hinchman, 1990

Rock Climbing New Mexico and Texas, Dennis R. Jackson, 1996

Sandia Select, Mick Schein, 1999

Sport Climbing in New Mexico: Cochiti Mesa, White Rock, Las Conchas, Randall Jett and Matt Samet, 1991

Sport Climbing in New Mexico: Socorro, Datil, New Canyon, Big Block Wall, Randall Jett and Matt Samet, 1991

Taos Rock III, Ed Jaramillo and Cayce Weber, 1991 [1981]

New York

Adirondack Rock and Ice Climbs, Thomas R. Rosencrans, 1976

Bouldering in the Shawangunks, Ivan Greene and Marc Russo, 1997

Climber's Guide to the Adirondacks: Rock and Slide Climbs in the High Peaks, Trudy Healy, 1972 [1967]

Climber's Guide to the Shawangunks, Arthur Gran, 1964

Climbing in the Adirondacks (third ed.), Don Mellor, 1995 [1983]

Climbs in the Adirondacks, James A. Goodwin, 1938

Gunks Guide (third ed.), Todd Swain, 1995 [1986]

Gunks Select, Richard C. Williams, 1996

High Peaks of the Northeast, Scofield, 1994

Little Falls: A Rock Climber's Guide, R. L. Stolz and Christopher Davis, 1985

New Gunks Guide, Todd Swain, 1990

Rock and Routes of the North Country, Bradford B. Vandiver, 1978

Shawangunk Climbs List, W. Crother, 1964

Shawangunk Grit, Ivan Rezucha, 1984 [1981]

Shawangunk Rock Climbs, Richard DuMais, 1985

Shawangunk Rock Climbs (third ed.), Richard C. Williams, 1991 [1972]

Shawangunk Rock Climbs, Vol. 1 (Trapps), Richard C. Williams, 1990

Shawangunk Rock Climbs, Vol.2 (Near Trapps), Richard C. Williams, 1990

Shawangunk Rock Climbs, Vol.3 (Skytop), Richard C. Williams, 1990

North Carolina

A Climber's Guide to the Carolinas, Arthur Williams, 1973

Blowing Rock Boulders Topo, Joe Henson, 1991

Carolina Crags, Art Holden, n.d.

Carolinas Climber's Guide, Buddy Price, 1977

Dixie Crystals: A Climber's Guide to Stone Mountain, Roid Waddle, 1983

Guide to the Carolinas, George Dewolf and Hugh Owens, 1967

Southern Rock, A Climber's Guide, Chris Hall, 1981

The Climber's Guide to North Carolina (third ed.), Thomas Kelley, 1995 [1987]

The Knob Boulders Topo, Joe Henson, 1991

Ohio

50 Short Climbs in the Midwest, Alan Bagg, 1978

A Climber's Guide to Clifton Gorge, Jack DeGuiseppi, 1978

Oklahoma

Climber's Guide to the Midwest's Metamorphic Forms, Marcus Floyd, 1998

Oklahoma on the Rocks, Jack Wurster and Jon Frank, 1986

Oklahoma on the Rocks II, Jon Frank, Jack Wurster, and D. Raleigh, 1989

Southern Exposure: A Climber's Guide to Oklahoma, Duane Raleigh and Bill Thomas, 1980

The Oklahoma's Climber's Guide, Chuck Lohn, 1999

Tulsa Rock '90, Bo Mosel, ca. 1990

Oregon

A Climber's Guide to Columbia River Gorge, Nenburger, 1958

A Climber's Guide to Mt. Hood, Mazama, 1956

A Climbing Guide to Oregon, Nicholas A. Dodge, 1976 [1968]

Basalt and Boulders [Smith Rock], Chuck Buzzard, ca. 1984

Climber's Guide to Smith Rock, Alan Watts, 1992

Climbs in Cascade Mountains, Oregon and California, Thomas J. Samuel and Charles B. Hardin, 1939

Columbia River Gorge: A Complete Guide, Phillip N. Jones, 1992

Exploring Oregon's Wild Areas, William L. Sullivan, 1988

Hiking Oregon's Central Cascades, Bruce Grubbs, 1998

Hiking Oregon's Eagle Cap Wilderness, Fred Barstad, 1997
Hiking Oregon's Mt. Hood and Badger Creek Wilderness, Fred Barstad, 1998
Hiking Oregon's Three Sisters Country, Bruce Grubbs, 1998
Hiking the Columbia River Gorge, Russ Schneider, 1997
Hiking the Great Northwest, Ira Spring and Harvey Manning, 1991
Mount Hood: A Complete History, Jack Grauer, 1975
Northwest Trails, Ira Spring and Harvey Manning, 1982 [1974]
Oregon Coast Hikes, Paul M. Williams, 1985
Oregon High: A Climbing Guide, Jeff Thomas, 1991
Oregon Rock, Jeff Thomas, 1983
Portland Rock Climbs: A Climber's Guide to Northwest Oregon, Tim Olson, 1993
Red Point: Smith Rock 1989 Topo Guide, Hubert Staub and Dan Carlson, 1989
Rocky Butte Quarry: A Climber's Guide to Urban Rock, M. Pajunas, 1989
Rocky Butte Quarry: A Climber's Guide to Urban Rock, R. McGown and M. Pajunas, 1987 [1980]

Pennsylvania

A Climber's Guide to Boileau Rocks: Ralph Stover State Park, Pete Kolman and Kirby Ellis, 1975 [1974]
A Climber's Guide to Tohickon Gorge: High Rocks, Doug Reilley, 1992
A Guide to Climbs at Chickies, Sue E. Holland, 1988
AK Handbook, Ivan L. Jirak, 1977 [1975]
Bellefonte Climbing Guide (third ed.), Jim Bowers, 1991 [1987]
Climb Pennsylvania (second ed.), Curt Harler, ed., 1994 [1985]
Climber's Guide to the Delaware Water Gap (second ed.), Mike Steele, 1989 [1987]
Climbing at St. Peters, Jim Detterline, 1978
Gritstone Climbs, Bill Webster, 1978
Guide to White Rocks, Explorer's Club, 1965
Local Climber's Guide, Ivan L. Jirak, 1966
McConnell's Mill State Park Classic Rock Climbs, Pennsylvania, Bob Value, 1998
Nearby Climbing Areas, Ron and Kathy Canter, 1980
Pittsburgh Area Climber's Guide, Ivan L. Jirak, 1975 [1971]
Ralph Stover State Park, Pennsylvania: Classic Rock Climbs, Paul Nick, 1997
Red Rock: A Climber's Guide to High Rocks, Thomas N. Stryker, 1985
Stoneyridge: A Crag Climber's Guide, Richard Pleiss, 1982
Stover Park Rock Climbs, Bob Chambers, 1957
Susquehanna River Rock, Eric J. Horst, 1993

Rhode Island

AMC Guide to Massachusetts and Rhode Island, Appalachian Mountain Club, 1964
Diamond Hill, R. Rocha and A. Li, 1980
Rock Climbs of Snake Den State Park, Ed Sewall, 1991

South Carolina

Carolinas Climber's Guide, Buddy Price, 1977
Southern Rock: A Climber's Guide, Chris Hall, 1981

South Dakota

A Climber's Guide to the Needles, Bob Kamps, 1971
Climber's Guide to Mt. Rushmore, Mike Lewis, 1989
Custer State Park/Needles Climbing Guide, R. Dickerson and J. Whittle, 1995
Devils Tower Wyoming and Black Hills, South Dakota Classic Rock Climbs, John Harlin, 1996
Hiking South Dakota's Black Hills Country, Gildart, 1996
Mt. Rushmore National Memorial Climber's Guide, Vernon R. Phinney, 1995
Needles of Custer State Park, in the Black Hills of South Dakota, John Page, 1995
Poor Person's Guide to the Black Hill's Needles (sixth ed.), Dingus McGee and The Last Pioneer Woman, 1996 [1981]
Recommended Needles Climbs, John Page, 1994
Rock Climbs in the Needles, Herb Conn, ca. 1957
Rushmore Needles Climbing Guide, Mountain Mania, 1994
Rushmore Needles, Paul Piana, 1991
Selected Free Climbs: Black Hills, Dennis Horning and Hollis Marriot, 1995 [1994]
Touch the Sky [the Needles], Paul Piana, 1983

Tennessee

A Climber's Guide to the Mid-South, Jim Detterline, 1982
An Underground Guide to Above Ground Memphis, M. C. and H. C., ca. 1980
Black Mountain Underground Guide, East Tennessee Climbers Association, ca. 1991
Buzzard Point Route Log, Glenn Ritter, 1992
Cherokee Bluff Guide, East Tennessee Climbers Association, ca. 1991
Dixie Cragger's Atlas, Chris Watford, 1999
Heart of Stone: A Guide to Climbing on the Cumberland Plateau, Eddie Whittemore, 1990 [1988]
Searching for Stone: A Climber's Guide to Clarksville Cliffs, "The Rain Man" [Terry Porter], 1992
Shades of Gray: Ice Climbers Guide to Dixie, Jim Detterline, 1998 [1990]
South Cumberland and Falls Creek Falls: A Hiker's Guide, Russ Manning and Sondra Jamieson, 1990
Southern Rock: A Climber's Guide, Chris Hall, 1981
Southern Sandstone: A Climber's Guide to Chattanooga, Rob Robinson, 1985
Southern Sandstone: Chattanooga Area, Rob Robinson, 1989
The Deep South Climber's Companion, Rob Robinson and Chris Watford, 1993
The Illustrated Underground Guide to the Tennessee Wall, Rob Robinson, 1989

Texas

A Poor Climber's Guide to Hueco Tanks SP, Tim Toula, 1990

Central Texas Limestone: A Climber's Guide, J. Jackson and K. Gallagher, 1992

Climber's Guide to Point of Rocks and Environs, Ft. Davis, Carrick M. Eggleston and Bill Davey, 1982

Climbing at Enchanted Rock, Jim Walker and Tom Richards, 1976

Dome Driver's Manual, J. Crump, R. Price, and S. Harris, 1990

Great Rock Hits of Hueco Tanks, Paul Piana, 1992

Guide to Penitentiary Hollow [Lake Mineral Wells SP], Texas Climber's Coalition, ca. 1990

Hiking and Backpacking Trails of Texas, Mildred J. Little, 1981

Hiking Big Bend National Park, Laurence Parent, 1990

Hiking Carlsbad Caverns and Guadalupe Mountains National Parks, Bill Schneider, 1990

Hiking the Southwest, Dave Ganci, 1983

Hueco Tanks State Park Classic Rock Climbs, John Sherman, 1997

Hueco Tanks Guide, J. Sherman, M. Head, J. Crump, and D. Head, 1990

Hueco Tanks Guide (second ed.), John Sherman, 1995

Indian Heights: A Climber's Guide to Hueco Tanks, James Crump, David Head, and Mike Head, 1985

Rock Climbing New Mexico and Texas, Dennis R. Jackson, 1996

Selected Climbs at the Academy [Austin], Alex Catlin, 1990

Stranger than Friction: Climber's Guide to Enchanted Rock, Dale Bergeron and James Crump, 1985 [1984]

Texas Limestone II: A Climber's Guide (second ed.), Jeff Jackson, 1995

Utah

200 Select Classics Indian Creek Climbs, Fred Knapp, 1994

A Bouldering Guide to Joe's Valley (second ed.), Jeff Baldwin, 2000 [1998]

A Climber's Guide to Rock Canyon, Adams and Mickelson, 1995

A Guide to Climbing in Snow Canyon, M. Kindred, T. Goss, and Duck, 1994

A Rockclimbing Guide to the Uintas, Jeff Baldwin, 2001

Arch Bagger: A Scrambler's Guide to Arches National Park, Gerry Roach, 1982

Canyon Country Climbs, Kate Cassidy and Earl Wiggins, 1989

Canyon Country Hiking & Natural History, F. A. Barnes, 1981

Canyon Hiking Guide to the Colorado Plateau, Michael R. Kelsey, 1991

Canyoneering: San Rafael Swell Guidebook, Steve Allen, 1991

Central Utah Climbing, Jason Stevens, 1995

Climber's Guide to American Fork and Rock Canyons, Bret Ruckman and Stuart Ruckman, 1995

Climbing Reports in Zion National Park, Zion Rock Climbing Pioneers, 1930–1993

Climbs of the Northern Wasatch: A Supplement, Tony Calderone, 1995

Climbs to Nowhere: Guide to Wall Street/Long Canyon, Kyle Copeland, 1990

Desert Rock I: Rock Climbs in the National Parks, Eric Bjornstad, 1996

Desert Rock II: Wall Street to the San Rafael Swell, Eric Bjornstad, 1997

Desert Rock III: Moab to Colorado National Monument, Eric Bjornstad, 1998

Desperate Grace, A Book of Climbs, R. Green and T. Turville, 1975

High Country Climbing: A Guide to the Climbing in the Uinta Mountains, Jim Stone, 1999

Hiking and Exploring Utah's Henry Mountains and Robber's Roost, Michael R. Kelsey, 1983

Hiking the Southwest's Canyon Country, Sandra Hinchman, 1990

Hiking Utah, David Hall, 1991 [1982]

Hiking Utah's Summits, Tom Wharton and Paula Huff, 1998

Hiking Zion and Bryce National Parks, Erik Molvar and Tamara Martin, 1997

Ibex and Selected Climbs of Utah's West Desert, James Garrett, 2001

Ice Climbing Utah, David S. Black, 2000

Indian Creek Climbs, Marco Cornacchione, 1998

Indian Creek Climbs (An Interim Guide), no author, 2002

Logan Canyon Climbs (third ed.), Tim Monsell, 1998 [1992]

Maple Canyon Rock Climbing, Jason L. Stevens, 1999 [1997]

Ogden Rock Climbs, Brian Mecham, 1993

Rock Climbing Utah, Stewart Green, 1998

Rock Climbing Utah's Wasatch Range, Bret Ruckman, 1998

Rock Climbs of Southern Utah: A Guide to 35 Crags, Todd Goss, 1998

Select Classic Desert Climbs, Fred Knapp, 1996

Selected Climbs in the Desert Southwest, Cameron Burns, 1999

Snow Canyon Select (second ed.), Todd Goss, 1999 [1995]

The Sportsman's Guide to Wasatch Pickles, Bill Boyle, 1990

Too Much Rock, Not Enough Life: Sport Climbing Guide to St. George and Southwestern Utah, Todd Goss, 1995

Utah Mountaineering Guide and Best Canyon Hikes, Michael R. Kelsey, 1983

Wasatch Climbing—North, Bret and Stuart Ruckman, 1995 [1991]

Wasatch Climbing—South, Bret and Stuart Ruckman, 1991

Wasatch Granite, Dave Smith, 1977

Wasatch Quartzite, John W. Gottman, 1979

Wasatch Range Utah Classic Rock Climbs, Bret Ruckman, 1997

Wasatch Rock Climbs, Les Ellison and Brian Smoot, 1984

Zion Rock, Alex McAfee, 2001

Vermont

An Ice Climber's Guide to Northern New England, Rick Wilcox, 1992 [1982]

Local's Guide to Smuggler's Notch Ice, Patrik Viljanen, 1999

Obscure Crags Guide: A Guide to Cliffs in New Hampshire, Maine, and Vermont, Dwight Bradley and Tad Pfeffer, n.d.

Select Bouldering Problems in Smuggler's Notch, Vermont (seventh ed.), Duke of Jeffersonville, ca. 1990

Shades of Blue: A Guide to Ice Climbing in New England, Peter Cole and Rick Wilcox, 1976

Trails and Summits of the Green Mountains, Walter Collins O'Kane, 1925

Virginia

Climber's Guide to Great Falls of the Potomac, James A. Eakin, 1985

Complete Great Falls Climbing Guide, Marida Brinkworth, 1998

Guide to Skyline Drive and Shenandoah National Park, Henry Heatwole, 1985 [1978]

Hiking The Old Dominion: The Trails of Virginia, Allen De Hart, 1984

Hiking Virginia, Randy Johnson, 1992

Nearby Climbing Areas, Ron and Kathy Canter, 1980

Virginia Climber's Guide, Jeff Watson, 1998

Washington

A Climber's Guide to Washington Rock, Don Brooks and David Whitelaw, 1982

A Topo Guide to Icicle Canyon Rock Climbs, Viktor Kramar, 1989

Adventure Guide to Mt. Rainier: Hiking, Climbing, and Skiing in Mount Rainier National Park, Jeff Smoot, 1991

Bellingham Rock, Josh Henrie, 1997

Big Fact Book about Mount Rainier, Bette Filley, 1996

Cascade Alpine Guide I (Columbia River to Stevens Pass) (third ed.), Fred Beckey, 2000 [1973]

Cascade Alpine Guide II (Stevens Pass to Rainy Pass), Fred Beckey, 1989 [1977]

Cascade Alpine Guide III (Rainy Pass to Fraser River), Fred Beckey, 1995 [1981]

Climber's Guide to Lowland Rock in Skagit and Whatcom Counties, Dallas M. Kloke, 1971

Climber's Guide to the Cascade and Olympic Mountains of Washington, Fred Beckey, 1961 [1949]

Climber's Guide to the Northwest Volcanoes, Jeff Smoot, 1990

Climber's Guide to the Olympic Mountains, Olympic Mountain Rescue, 1988 [1972]

Climber's Guide to the Olympic Mountains, Seattle Mountaineers, 1972 [1979]

Climbing Guide to Darrington, Gunstoke, 2000

Climbing Guide to Mt Erie, Mountain Rescue, 1999

Climbing History and Routes of Mt. Rainier, Dee Molenaar, n.d.

Climbing the Cascade Volcanoes, Jeff Smoot, 1992

Darrington and Index, Rock Climbing Guide, Fred Beckey, 1976

Exit 32 [Little Si], Brian Burdo, 1992

Frenchman's Coulee, Jim Yoder and Marlene Ford, 1997

Guide to Leavenworth Rock Climbing Areas, Fred Beckey and Eric Bjornstad, 1965

Guide to Rock Climbing in the Spokane Area (third ed.), Loomis, 1990 [1983]

Hiking Olympic National Park, Erik Molvar, 1996

Index Town Wall Guide, Clint Cummins, 1993

Index Town Walls, Jeff Smoot and Darryl Cranner, 1985

Leavenworth Rock Climbs, Viktor Kramar, 1993

Leavenworth Rock, Viktor Kramar, 1996

Mt. Rainier Climbing Guide Number 1, no author, 1997

Mt. Rainier Climbing Guide Number 2, no author, 1997

Mt. Rainier Climbing Guide Number 3, no author, 1998

Mt. Rainier: A Record of Exploration, E. S. Meany, ca. 1960

Mt. Shasta Climber's Review, Summary of Climbing Routes, no author, ca. 1990

Northwest Mountaineering, Edward A. Rossit, 1965

Olympic Mountains Trail Guide, Robert L. Wood, 1984

Oregon Rock (Beacon Rock), Jeff Thomas, 1983

Private Dancer, David Whitelaw, 1985

Rock Climber's Guide to Fossil, Jim Yoder and Marlene Ford, 1996

Rock Climbing Leavenworth and Index, A Guide, Rich Carlstad and Don Brooks, 1976

Rock Climbing Washington, Jeff Smoot, 1999

Routes and Rocks in the Mt. Challenger Quadrangle, D. F. Crowder and R. W. Tabor, 1968

Selected Climbs in the Cascades, Jim Nelson and Peter Potterfield, 1993

Sky Valley Rock, Cramer, 2000 [1999]

Spire Rock, Washington [Seattle], J. Phillips and M. Webster, 1982

Spokane Rock Climbs, Jim Speaker, 1996

Swauk Pinnacles: A Climber's Guide, Dale Boyle, 2000 [1996]

The Royal Columns: A Rock Climber's Guide, Matt Christensen, 1988

The Washington Desert: A Rock and Ice Climber's Guide to Frenchman Coulee, J. Eminger and J. Kittel, 1991

Tieton River Rock, Matt and Holly Bell Christensen, 1989

Traveler's Guide Puget Sound, Western Mountain Alliance, 1999

Vantage Rock: A Climber's Guide to Frenchman's Coulee, Matt Stanley, 1995

Washington Rock Climbs, Jeff Smoot, 1989

West Virginia

A Climber's Guide to Seneca Rocks, F. R. Robinson, ed., 1971

Best Sport Climbs of the New River Gorge, Featuring the Cirque, R. Brock, 1997

Climbing Guide to Cooper's Rocks, A. Clark, n.d.

Cooper's Rock, West Virginia, Classic Rock Climbs, Rick Thompson, 1998

Gritstone Climbs, Bill Webster, 1978

Kaymoor Guide, Doug Cosby, 1991

Nearby Climbing Areas, Ron Canter and Kathy Canter, 1980

New River Gorge: Rock Climbers' Handbook, Steve Cater, 1995

New River Gorge: Select Rock Climbs, Steve Cater, 1997

New River Rock (third ed.), Rick Thompson, 1997 [1987]

Seneca Rocks Guide, Tony Barnes, 1995

Seneca Rocks Route Sketches, Ivan L. Jirak, 1965

Seneca Rocks, West Virginia: A Climber's Guide, Bill Webster, 1980

Seneca, John Bercaw, Herb Laeger, and John Stannard, 1976

Seneca: The Climber's Guide, Tony Barnes, 1995

Take Me to the River: Rock Climbers' Guide to New River Gorge, West Virginia, S. Cater and H. Saab, 1992

Wisconsin

50 Short Climbs in the Midwest, Alan Bagg, 1978

A Climber's Guide to Devil's Lake, Errol Morris, 1969

Chicago Mountaineering Club Guidebook to Local Practice Areas, William Primak, 1965

Climber's and Hiker's Guide to Devil's Lake, David Smith and Roger Zimmerman, 1970

Climber's and Fisherman's Guide to Gibraltar Rock, Roger Weigand, J. Stewart, and Ed Wright, 1982

Climber's Guide to Devil's Lake, William Widule and Sven Olaf Swartling, 1979

Climber's Guide to Devil's Lake, Wisconsin, Sven Olaf Swartling, 1995

Climber's Guide to Gibraltar Rock, Eric Landmann and Don Hynek, 1993 [1987]

Close to the Edge, Down by the River [Interstate Park], Pete Von Grossman and Peter Scott, 1989

Devil's Lake: East Bluff, Pete Gardiner, 1967

Extremist's Guide to Devil's Lake, Leo Hemacinski, 1985

Rock Climbing Minnesota and Wisconsin, Mike Farris, 2000

The First Sport Climbing Guidebook and Coloring Book to Gibraltar, Eric Zschiesche, 1992

Wyoming

A Climber's Guide to Devils Tower, Terry Rypkema and Curt Haire, 1977

A Climber's Guide to the Snowy Range of Wyoming, R. G. Jacquot and R. O. Huff, 1970

A Climber's Guide to the Teton Range (third ed.), L. Ortenburger and R. Jackson, 1997

Beyond the Tetons, Ralph Maughan, 1981

Bighorns East, Alex Catlin, 1989

Blacktail Butte Topo, Teton Mountaineering, 1989

Bonney's Guide to Jackson's Hole and Grand Teton National Park, Orrin H. and Lorraine G. Bonney, 1961

Climber's Guide to Fremont Canyon and Dome Rock, Steve Petro, 1992 [1988]

Climber's Guide to the Teton Range (third ed.), L. Ortenburger and R. Jackson, 1996

Climbing and Hiking in the Wind River Mountains, Joe Kelsey, 1994

Climbing and Hiking in the Wind Rivers, Joe Kelsey, 1980

Climbing Gannett Peak: Wind Rivers, Donald Jacobs, 1990

Climbing Guide to Southeastern Wyoming, Jim Halfpenny, 1972 [1971]

Cloud Peak Primitive Area, M. Melius, 1984

Crack Country Revisted, Layne Kopischka, 1982

Cracks Country: A Climbing Guide to Vedauwoo, J. Garson, L. Kopischka, and G. Pousch, 1977

Cracks Unlimited: A Climbing Guide to Vedauwoo, Layne Kopischka, 1987

Cube Point (East Ridge) Baxter Pinnacle (South Ridge) [Alpenglow Teton Route Guides], Alpenglow Photography, 1980

Devil's Tower, New Mexico: A Climber's Guide, Steve Gardiner and Dick Guilmette, 1986

Devil's Tower, Wyoming and Black Hills, South Dakota Classic Rock Climbs, John Harlin, 1996

Devil's Tower National Monument Climbing Handbook, Dan Guillmette, 1995

Disappointment Peak (East Couloir/Lake Ledges/East and Southwest Ridge) [Alpenglow Teton Route Guides], Alpenglow Photography, 1980

Disappointment Peak (Irenes Arete/Caves Arete) [Alpenglow Teton Route Guides], Alpenglow Photography, 1980

Disappointment Peak (Southwest Ridge/West Side Story/Southwest Couloir) [Alpenglow Teton Route Guides], Alpenglow Photography, 1980

Field Book Teton Range and Gros Ventre Range, Orrin H. Bonney and Lorraine G. Bonney, 1963

Field Book: Bighorn Range, Orrin H. Bonney and Lorraine G. Bonney, ca. 1970

Field Book: Wind River Range, Orrin H. Bonney and Lorraine G. Bonney, 1968 [1962]

Field Book: Yellowstone and Absaroka Range, Orrin H. Bonney and Lorraine G. Bonney, 1963

Free Climbs of Devil's Tower (fifteenth ed.), Dingus McGee and Last Pioneer Woman, 2000 [1979]

Fremont Canyon and Dome Rock, Central Wyoming Classic Rock Climbs, Steve Petro, 1997

Full Circle: Jackson Hole Sport Climbing Guide, Maxwell Yanoff, 1991

Grand Teton (Owen-Spalding) [Alpenglow Teton Route Guides], Alpenglow Photography, 1980

Grand Teton East Ridge (Hossach-MacGowan Route) [Alpenglow Teton Route Guides], Alpenglow Photography, 1980

Grand Teton North Face [Alpenglow Teton Route Guides], Alpenglow Photography, 1980

Grand Teton North Ridge (Montopoli-Baldwin) [Alpenglow Teton Route Guides], Alpenglow Photography, 1980

Guide to Jenny Lake Boulders, John Gill and Yvon Chouinard, 1958

Guide to Jenny Lake Boulders, John Gill, 1987

Guide to the Wyoming Mountains and Wilderness Areas, Orrin H. Bonney and Lorraine G. Bonney, 1977 [1960]

Heel and Toe: The Climbs of Vedauwoo, Skip Harper and Robert Kelman, 1994

High Plains Climbs, P. Parmenter, K. Moore, and A. U. Ilgner, 1983

Hiking Grand Teton National Park, Bill Schneider, 1999

Hiking the Great Northwest, Ira Spring and Harvey Manning, 1991

Hiking Wyoming's Cloud Peak Wilderness, Erik Molvar, 1999

Hoback Shield Topo, Teton Mountaineering, 1989

Jackson Hole Area Sport Climbing, Forest Dramis and Mark Daubin, 2000

Jackson Hole Sport Climbing Guide, Joe Sottile, 1992

Lander Bouldering, Steve Bechtel, 1999

Middle Teton (Southwest Couloir) [Alpenglow Teton Route Guides], Alpenglow Photography, 1980

Mount Owen (East Ridge/Koven Route), Alpenglow Photography, 1980

Mountain Climbing Guide to the Grand Tetons, Henry Coulter and Merrill F. McLane, 1947

Mountaineering in Tetons: The Pioneer Period 1898-1940, Fritiof Fryxel, 1978

Northwest Trails, Ira Spring and Harvey Manning, 1982 [1974]

Rock Climber's Map to Sinks Canyon, Tim Toula, 1991

Shoshone Topographics, Kirt D. Cozzens, 1983

Sinks Canyon Climbs, Tom Axthelm, 1981

Sinks Canyon—Sandstone and Limestone, Greg Collins, 1994 [1989]

South Teton (Northwest Couloir/West Ridge)/Middle Teton (Variation) [Alpenglow Teton Route Guides], Alpenglow Photography, 1980

Split Rock Topos, NOLS, ca. 1988

Sport Climbs of Sinks Canyon, Paul Piana, 1999

Storm Point (Southwest Ridge/Guides Wall) [Alpenglow Teton Route Guides], Alpenglow Photography, 1980

Symmetry Spire (Southwest Couloir/Durrance Ridge) [Alpenglow Teton Route Guides], Alpenglow Photography, 1980

Taboo: A Climber's Guide to Casper's Industrial Crags, Structural Spider, 1989

Teewinot (East Face/Southwest Couloirs) [Alpenglow Teton Route Guides], Alpenglow Photography, 1980

Teton Classics: 50 Selected Climbs in Grand Teton National Park (second ed.), Richard Rossiter, 1995

Teton Range Climber's Guide, L. Ortenburger and R. Jackson, 1990

Teton Skiing: A History and Guide, Tom Turiano, 1995

The Cracksmen (Vedauwoo Area), Bob Scarpelli, ca. 1980

The Legendary Wild Iris (third ed.), Paul Piana, 1996

The Medicine Bow Mountains of Wyoming, Fritiof N. Fryxell, 1926

The Teton Controversy: Who First Climbed the Grand, William M. Bueler, 1980

Vedauwoo Climbing, Jim Halfpenny and Jan Mathiesen, 1966

Vedauwoo Climbs, J. Sublette, J. Garson, and R. Zimmerman, 1972

Vedauwoo Rock, Layne Kopischka, 1997

Vedauwoo Rock: A Climbing Guide to Vedauwoo, Layne Kopischka, 1992

Whiterock Bouldering Guide, Tim Toula, 1988

Wind River Trails, Finis Mitchell, 1975

Wyoming Hiking Trails, Tom and Sanse Sudduth, 1978

Alberta

95 Hikes in the Canadian Rockies (Banff, Kootenay, Assiniboine Parks), Vicky Spring, 1982

Among the Canadian Alps: Canadian Alpine Journal, Lawrence J. Burpee, 1914

Banff Rock Climbs, Murrray Toft, 1985

Barrier Bluffs: The Guide, Kelly Tobey, 1987

Bow Valley Rock, Chris Perry and Joe Josephson, 2000

Bow Valley Rock, Alberta, C. Perry, J. Martin, and S. Dougherty, 1988

Bow Valley Rock, Alberta Supplement, C. Perry, J. Martin, and S. Dougherty, 1990

Climber's Guide to Yamnuska, Brian Greenwood and Urs Kalleen, 1970

Climber's Guide to Yamnuska, Urs Kalleen, 1977

Climbing at Wasootch Slabs, Ben Gadd, 1980

Climbs and Explorations in the Canadian Rockies, Hugh E. M. Stutfield and J. Norman Collie, 1903

Climbs at Banff & Vicinity, Arthur O. Wheeler, 1930

Ghost River Rock Climbs, Chris Perry, 1997 [1980]

Hiking The Great Northwest, Ira Spring and Harvey Manning, 1991

Kananaskis Rock: A Climber's Guide, John Martin, 1989

Mixed Climbs in the Canadian Rockies, Sean Isaac, ca. 1990

Mt. Andromeda Climbing Route Card, Gregory Horne, 1989

Mt. Athabasca Climbing Route Card, Gregory Horne, 1989

Mt. Edith Cavell Climbing Route Card, Gregory Horne, 1989

Mt. Temple Climbing Route Card, Gregory Horne, 1989

Mt. Victoria Climbing Route Card, Gregory Horne, 1989

Northwest Trails, Ira Spring and Harvey Manning, 1982 [1974]

Selected Alpine Climbs in the Canadian Rockies, Sean Dougherty, 1991

Selected Climbing Routes of Athabasca, Gregory Horne, 1989

Selected Climbing Routes of Edith Cavell, Gregory Horne, 1989

Selected Climbs in the Canmore Area, Gregory Spohr, 1976

Sloping Climbs, John Martin, 1985

Sport Climbs in the Canadian Rockies, Jon Martin and Jon Jones, 2000 [1996]

The Back of the Lake (Lake Louise), Bruce Howatt and Colin Zacharias, 1987 [1984]

The Canadian Rockies: New and Old Trails, A. Coleman, 1911

The Glacier Trail, Jack W. Brewster, 1931

The Rocky Mountains of Canada North, W. Putnam, C. Jones, and R. Kruszyna, 1974

The Rocky Mountains of Canada South, W. Putnam, C. Jones, and R. Kruszyna, 1979 [1973]

Waterfall Ice [Canadian Rockies], Albi Sole, 1988 [1980]

British Columbia

103 Hikes in Southwest British Columbia, Mary Macaree and David Macaree, 1980

93 Hikes in the Canadian Rockies, Dee Urbick, 1983

A Climber's Guide to Squamish Chief and Surrounding Area, Glenn Woodsworth, 1967

A Climber's Guide to the Interior Ranges of British Columbia, North, J. Monroe Thorington, 1975

A Climber's Guide to the Interior Ranges of British Columbia—South, William L. Putnam and Robert Kruszyna, 1979 [1974]

A Climber's Guide to the Rocky Mountains of Canada, Howard Palmer and J. Monroe Thorington, 1966 [1921]

A Guide to Climbing and Hiking in Southwestern British Columbia, Bruce Fairley, 1991

Alpine Guide to Southwestern British Columbia, Dick Culbert, 1974

Alpine Select, Kevin McLane, 2001

Among the Selkirk Glaciers, William Spotswood Green, 1890

Away to the Canadian Rockies and British Columbia, Gordon Brinley, 1938

Bugaboo Rock: A Climber's Guide, Randall Green and Joe Bensen, 1990

Central BC Rock, Lyle Smith, 1996

Cheakamus Canyon Guide, Roger Chayer, ca. 1990

Climber's Guide to the Rocky Mountains of Canada—North, W. Putnam, C. Jones, and R. Kruszyna, 1974

Climber's Guide to the Rocky Mountains of Canada—South, G. Boles, R. Kruszyna, and W. Putnam, 1979

Climber's Guide to Chehalis River Gorge, Mike Capo et al., 2001

Climber's Guide to Squamish Chief, Anders Ourum, 1980

Climbers Guide to the Coastal Ranges of British Columbia, Dick Culbert, 1969 [1965]
Climbing at Wasootch Slabs, Ben Gadd, 1981
Climbing in the Selkirks, Chicago Mountaineering Club, 1961
Climbs in the Canadian Rockies, Frank S. Smythe, 1950
Cloud Walkers: Six Climbs on Major Canadian Peaks, Paddy Sherman, 1965
Columbia Icefield: A Solitude of Ice, Don Harmon, 1981
Columbia Mountains of Canada Central: The American Alpine Club Climber's Guide, William Putnam et al., ed., 1992
Columbia Mountains of Canada, West and South: The American Alpine Club Climber's Guide, Earl R. Whipple et al., ed., 1992
Exploring Manning Park, Andrew Harcombe and Robert Cyca, 1979
Exploring the Purcell Wilderness, Anne Edwards, 1979
Ghost River Ice Climbs, Frank Campbell, 1987
Hiking the Great Northwest, Ira Spring and Harvey Manning, 1991
In the Heart of the Canadian Rockies, James Outram, 1905
Mt. Assiniboine Climbing Route Card, Gregory Horne, 1989
Mt. Garibaldi Park: Vancouver's Park, Randy Morse, 1922
Mt. Robson Climbing Route Card, Gregory Horne, 1989
Northern Cordillera, British Columbia Mountain Club, 1913
Northwest Trails, Ira Spring and Harvey Manning, 1982 [1974]
On the Roof of the Rockies: Great Columbia Icefield, Lewis A. Freeman, 1925
Peaks and Routes of the North Selkirks, Putnam, 1956 [1954]
Place Names of the Canadian Alps, William L. Putnam, Glen W. Boles, and Roger W. Laurilla, 1990
Rock Climbs of the Little Smoke Bluffs, Jim Campbell, 1984
Rockclimbs: Kelowna and Area, Dean Urness, 1999
Scrambles in the Canadian Rockies, Alan Kane, 1992
Selected Alpine Climbs in the Canadian Rockies, Sean Dougherty, 1991
Selected Climbing Routes of Andromeda, Gregory Horne, 1989
Selected Climbing Routes of Assiniboine, Gregory Horne, 1989
Selected Climbing Routes of Mt. Robson, Gregory Horne, 1989
Skaha Rockclimbs, Howie Richardson, 1997 [1996]
Squamish Boulder Problems, Peter Michaux, 1999
Squamish Chief Guide, Gordon Smaill, 1975
Squamish Rock Climbs (seventh ed.), Jim Campbell, 1989 [1985]
Squamish Select, Mark Bourdon and Scott Tasaka, 2000
Squamish: The New Free Climbs, Kevin McLane, 1984
Strathcona Park: Selected Rock and Ice Climbs [Vancouver Island], Phillip Stone, 1996
The Bugaboos: An Alpine History, John F. Garden, 1987
The Call of the Mountains, Le Roy Jeffers, 1923
The Canadian Alps, Robert W. Sandford, 1990
The Canadian Rockies: Alpina Americana, Charles E. Fay, 1911
The Climber's Guide to Powell River, Chris Armstrong, 2002
The Climber's Guide to Skaha, Kevin McLane, 1993
The Climber's Guide to West Coast Ice, Don Serl and Bruce Kay, 1993
The Mountains of Canada, Randy Morse, 1978
The Purcell Range of British Columbia, J. Monroe Thorington, 1946

The Rockclimber's Guide to Squamish, Kevin McLane, 1992
The Selkirk Mountains: A Guide for Mountain Climbers and Pilgrims, Arthur O. Wheeler, 1912
The Selkirk Range, Arthur O. Wheeler, 1905
The Whistler Handbook, no author, ca. 1990
Trails to Timberline in West Central British Columbia, Charles E. Fay, 1911
Whistler Rock Climbs, Kevin McLane, 2000

New Brunswick
Climber's Guide to New Brunswick, Stephen Adamson, 1987
New Brunswick Rock and Ice, Colin Bell, 1985 [1978]

Nova Scotia
Climb Cape Breton, John Read and Don Kronstedt, 1978
Climb Nova Scotia, Sean Willett, 1994

Ontario
A Guide to Climbing Routes at the Scenic Bluffs of Thunder Bay, Shaun Parent, 1990
A Guide to Rock Climbs at Bon Echo, Adcock, 1990
A Sport Climber's Guide to Ontario Limestone 1997, M. Bracken and C. Oates, 1998
Climber's Guide to Kingston Mills, Robert Chisnall, 1985
Climber's Guide to the Gananoque Area, Robert Chisnall, 1985
Climber's Guide to the Ice of Orient Bay, Shaun Parent, 1987
Climbing Guide to Thunder Bay Area, Shaun Parent, 1984 [1983]
Climbing in Southern Ontario, James Marsh, 1980
Climbing on the Niagara Escarpment, David Smart, 1985 [1984]
Devil Rock: The Anti Guide (second ed.), Carl Johnston and David Smart, 1997
Manitoba and Northwest Ontario Rock Climbing Guide, no author, 1986
North of Superior Climbing Route Cards (Canine, Mt. Helen, Pearl Roadcut, Chipmunk Rock), Shaun Parent, 1990
Ontario Limestone, David Smart, 1988
Ontario's Finest Rock Climbs, David Smart, 1997
Pass Lake: The Next Generation, Chris Wrazej and Marc Barbeau, 1989
Rock Climber's Guide to Killarney Provincial Park: George Lake, Shaun Mark Filion and Robert Chisnall, 1982
Rock Climbing in Ontario, James Mark, 1974
Rock Climbs in the Manitoba/Ontario Border Region, Hugh Spencer and Peter Aitchinson, 1977
The Escarpment: A Climber's Guide, M. Bracken, J. Barnes, and C. Oates, 1991
The Glen [Niagara Glen], Terry Fox, ca. 1990

Quebec
D'Escalade au Mont Orford: Guide des Voies et Blocs, JiDe et al., 2000
Escalades dans les Cantons de l'Est, Bernard Mailhot and Charles Lauberte, 1990

Escalades dans les Cantons de l'Est, Bertrand Cote, 1979

Escalades: Guide des Parois Region de Montreal, Bernard Poisson, 1971

Grimper Quebec, Sylvain Malchelosse, 1987

Guide d'Escalade du Grand Morne, Nicolas Rodrigue and Bernard Gagnon, 2000

Les Parois des Charlevoix Rock Climbs: Palissades St. Simeon, Alain Heinault, 1988

Line Guide du Mont St-Hilaire, Julien Deuz, 1987

Mountaineering around Montreal, Alpine Club of Canada, 1964

Parois d'Escalade au Quebec, Eugenie Levesque and John Sylvain, 1978

Parois d'Escalade de Chicoutimie Jonquieres, Francois-Xavier Garneau, 1988

Topos de Palissades des Grands-Jardinset D'ailleurs, Stephan Lapierre, 1989

Val-David: Guide des Parois d'Escalade, Paul Laperriere, 1994

Yukon

A Guide to Single Pitch Climbs of the Yukon, Greg Keitel and Alan Pohl, 1997

The Rock Gardens: A Climbing Guide and Journal, Alain Dallaire, ca. 1990

Mexico

Backpacking in Mexico and Central America, H. Bradt and Rachowiecki, ca. 1970

Camping and Climbing in Baja, John W. Robinson, 1967

El Diente (AKA The Tooth) Guidebook, Hector Magallon, n.d.

El Potrero Chico: A Pocket Guide, Texas Mountain Guides, 1994

Guia del Escalador Mexicano, Thomas Velaquez, 1955

Mexico Rock: A Climber's Guide, Jeff Jackson, 1999

Mexico's Copper Canyon Country, John Fayhee, 1989

Mexico's Volcanoes: A Climbing Guide, R.J. Secor, 1993

Pico de Orizaba or Citlaltepetl: Geology, Archaeology, History, Natural History and Mountaineering Routes, John Fayhee, 1989

Valle Azteca (Baja), Randy Vogel, 1995

Regional and North America in General

50 Short Climbs in the Midwest, Alan Bagg, 1978

A Climber's Guide to the Mid-South, Jim Detterline, 1982

A Souvenir of Western Summits, Francis Peloubet Farquhar, 1947

Beyond the Vertical, Layton Kor, 1983

Bibliography of American Mountain Ascents, Joel E. Fisher, 1946

Climber's and Hiker's Guide to the World's Mountains, Michael Kelsey, 1990 [1981]

Climbing In North America, Chris Jones, 1979

Fifty Classic Climbs of North America (second ed.), Steve Roper and Allen Steck, 1996 [1979]

Fifty States Summits: Guide with Maps to State High Points (second ed.), Paul L. Zumwalt, 1998 [1988]

First Ascents of the United States 1642-1900, Francis Peloubet Farquhar, 1948

Glaciers of North America: A Field Guide, Ferguson, 1992

Great American Rock Climbs, Dick Dumais, 1995

Heroic Climbs, Chris Bonnington (ed.), 1994

Highpoints of the States, F. Ashley, 1970

Highpoints of the United States, Don Holmes, 1990

Mountaineering and its Literature, W. R. Neate, 1980 [1978]

Mountaineering Literature, Jill Neate, 1986 [1978]

Mountains of North America, Fred Beckey, 1982

Rock Games: Escalades Aux USA, Patrick Edlinger and Gerard Kosicki, 1986

Shades of Blue: A Guide to Ice Climbing in New England, Peter Cole and Rick Wilcox, 1976

Southern Rock: A Climber's Guide, Chris Hall, 1981

Sport Climbs of the East, Steve Cater, 1994

Stone Crusade, John Sherman, 1994

The Climber's Guide to North America (East), John Harlin III, 1986

The Climber's Guide to North America (Rockies), John Harlin III, 1985

The Climber's Guide to North America (West), John Harlin III, 1987

The Climbing Guidebooks of the United States, Randy Vogel, 1993

Twenty American Peaks and Crags, Thomas Morrisey, 1978

Climbing Area Index

ACCESS: It's every climber's concern

The Access Fund, a national, non-profit climbers organization, works to keep climbing areas open and to conserve the climbing environment. Need help with closures? land acquisition? legal or land management issues? funding for trails and other projects? starting a local climbers' group? CALL US! Climbers can help preserve access by being committed to Leave No Trace (minimum-impact) practices. Here are some simple guidelines:

• **ASPIRE TO "LEAVE NO TRACE"** especially in environmentally sensitive areas like caves. Chalk can be a significant impact on dark and porous rock—don't use it around historic rock art. Pick up litter, and leave trees and plants intact.

• **DISPOSE OF HUMAN WASTE PROPERLY** Use toilets whenever possible. If toilets are not available, dig a "cat hole" at least six inches deep and 200 feet from any water, trails, campsites, or the base of climbs. *Always pack out toilet paper.* On big wall routes, use a "poop tube" and carry waste up and off with you (the old "bag toss" is now illegal in many areas).

• **USE EXISTING TRAILS** Cutting switchbacks causes erosion. When walking off-trail, tread lightly, especially in the desert where cryptogamic soils (usually a dark crust) take thousands of years to form and are easily damaged. Be aware that "rim ecologies" (the clifftop) are often highly sensitive to disturbance.

• **BE DISCRETE WITH FIXED ANCHORS** *Bolts are controversial and are not a convenience*—don't place 'em unless they are *really* necessary. Camouflage all anchors. Remove unsightly slings from rappel stations (better to use steel chain or welded cold shuts). Bolts sometimes can be used proactively to protect fragile resources—consult with your local land manager.

• **RESPECT THE RULES** and speak up when other climbers don't. Expect restrictions in designated wilderness areas, rock art sites, caves, and to protect wildlife, especially nesting birds of prey. *Power drills are illegal in wilderness and all national parks.*

• **PARK AND CAMP IN DESIGNATED AREAS** Some climbing areas require a permit for overnight camping.

• **MAINTAIN A LOW PROFILE** Leave the boom box and day-glo clothing at home—the less climbers are heard and seen, the better.

• **RESPECT PRIVATE PROPERTY** Be courteous to land owners. Don't climb where you're not wanted.

• **JOIN THE ACCESS FUND** To become a member, make a tax-deductible donation of $35.

The Access Fund
Preserving America's Diverse Climbing Resources
P.O. Box 17010
Boulder, CO 80308
303.545.6772 • www.accessfund.org